A Companion to
Latin American Literature and Culture

# Blackwell Companions to Literature and Culture

This series offers comprehensive, newly written surveys of key periods and movements and certain major authors, in English literary culture and history. Extensive volumes provide new perspectives and positions on contexts and on canonical and post-canonical texts, orientating the beginning student in new fields of study and providing the experienced undergraduate and new graduate with current and new directions, as pioneered and developed by leading scholars in the field.

## Published Recently

A COMPANION TO

# LATIN AMERICAN LITERATURE AND CULTURE

EDITED BY

**SARA CASTRO-KLAREN**

A John Wiley & Sons, Ltd., Publication

*Library of Congress Cataloging-in-Publication Data*

A companion to Latin American literature and culture / edited by Sara Castro-Klaren.
         p. cm.
    Includes bibliographical references and index.
    ISBN 978-1-4051-2806-3 (cloth) – ISBN 978-1-118-49214-7(pbk.)   1. Latin American
literature—History and criticism.   2. Latin America—Intellectual life.   3. Latin America—Social
life and customs.   I. Castro-Klaren, Sara.
    PQ7081.A1C555 2007
    860.9′98—dc22
                                        2007043481

A catalogue record for this book is available from the British Library.

Cover image: David Alfaro Siqueiros, *Geographic Architecture*, 1959. Private Collection/Photo
              © Christie's Images/The Bridgeman Art Library © DACS 2007.
Cover design by Richard Boxall Design Associates

Set in 11/13 pt Garamond 3 by Toppan Best-set Premedia Limited
Printed in Malaysia by Ho Printing (M) Sdn Bhd

1   2013

To the delightful company of Peter, Ali, and David

# Contents

# Notes on Contributors

**Adriana J. Bergero** (University of California at Los Angeles) has published *El Debate político: Modernidad, poder y disidencia en* Yo el Supremo *de Augusto Roa Bastos* (1994); *Haciendo camino: Pactos de la escritura en la obra de Jorge Luis Borges* (1999); *Memoria colectiva y políticas de olvido: Argentina y Uruguay* (1997, with Fernando Reati); *(1970–1990) Estudios literarios/Estudios culturales* (2005, with Jorge Ruffinelli). She has published on cultural studies with a focus on the Southern Cone, urban and sensuous geography, gender studies, and postcolonial studies. Her *Intersecting Tango: Cultural Geographies of Buenos Aires, 1900–1930* is forthcoming.

**John Beverley** is Professor of Spanish and Latin American Literature at the University of Pittsburgh and an advisory editor of *boundary 2*. His publications include *Del Lazarillo al Sandinismo* (1987); *Literature and Politics in Central American Revolutions* (1990, with Marc Zimmerman); *The Postmodernism Debate in Latin America* (1995, coedited with Michael Aronna and José Oviedo); and *Subalternity and Representation: Arguments in Cultural Theory* (1999).

The late **Álvaro Félix Bolaños** was Professor of Spanish and Latin American literature at the University of Florida. His publications include *Barbarie y canibalismo en la retórica colonial: Los indios Pijaos de Fray Pedro Simón* (1994) and *Colonialism Past and Present: Reading and Writing about Colonial Latin America Today* (2002, with Gustavo Verdesio).

**Adriana Michèle Campos Johnson** is an Assistant Professor in Comparative Literature at UC-Irvine. She is currently finishing a manuscript on the subalternization of Canudos. Her recent publications include "Everydayness and Subalternity," *South Atlantic Quarterly*, 106:1 (2006); "Two Proposals for an Aesthetic Intervention in Politics: A Review of Nelly Richard, *Masculine/Feminine* and *The Insubordination of Signs* and Doris Sommer, *Bilingual Aesthetics*," *New Centennial Review*, 5:3 (2005); and a translation of Ticio Escobar, *The Curse of Nemur: On the Art, Myth and Rituals of the Ishir Peoples of the Paraguayan Great Chaco* (2007).

**Sara Castro-Klaren** is Professor of Latin American Culture and Literature at Johns Hopkins University. She has been the recipient of several teaching awards. Most recently the Foreign Service Institute conferred upon her the title of "Distinguished Visiting Lecturer" (1993). She was appointed to the Fulbright Board of Directors by President Clinton in 1999. Her publications include *El Mundo mágico de Jose Maria Arguedas* (1973); *Understanding Mario Vargas Llosa* (1990); *Escritura, sujeto y transgresion en la literatura latinoamericana* (1989); and *Latin American Women Writers* (1991, coedited with Sylvia Molloy and Beatriz Sarlo).

**Rocío Cortés** is an Assistant Professor of Colonial Latin American Literature in the Department of Foreign Languages and Literatures at the University of Wisconsin-Oshkosh. Her research interests focus on the relationship between Mesoamerican cultural indigenous heterogeneity and colonial transculturation in indigenous chronicles of the sixteenth and seventeenth centuries. She has published articles on the subject in *Modern Language Notes* and *Colonial Latin American Review*. She is working on a book on the life and works of Don Hernando de Alvarado Tezozomoc.

**Lucía Helena Costigan** teaches Luso-Brazilian and Spanish American literatures and cultures at the Ohio State University. She has published articles and books on colonial and postcolonial Brazil and Latin America. Many of her publications focus on comparative analyses between Brazil and other Latin American countries. Some of her recent publications include *Diálogos da conversão: Missionários, índios, negros e judeus no contexto ibero-americano do período barroco* (2005), and with Russell G. Hamilton, "Lusophone African and Afro-Brazilian Literatures," *Research in African Literatures* (Spring 2007). Her forthcoming *Literature and the Inquisition in the New World* elaborates on migratory movements from Europe to the Americas during the sixteenth and seventeenth centuries and on the institutionalization of religious violence and censorship in the New World.

**Fernando Degiovanni** is Assistant Professor of Romance Languages and Literatures at Wesleyan University. He is the author of *Los textos de la patria: Nacionalismo, políticas culturales y canon en Argentina* (2007). His work has been published in *Revista Iberoamericana*, *Journal of Latin American Cultural Studies*, and *Revista de Crítica Literaria Latinoamericana*, as well as in several edited volumes. He specializes in issues of cultural politics and canon formation in the Latin American *fin de siècle*. He is currently working on a book-length project that examines the emergence of Latin American literature as a field of study.

**Lisa DeLeonardis** is lecturer and curator of Art of the Ancient Americas at the Johns Hopkins University. She has conducted decades-long research in Peru and is completing a manuscript on Paracas. Her work has appeared in the Blackwell series Andean Archaeology and several essays on the Andean Baroque are forthcoming in the *Guide to Documentary Sources for Andean Studies, 1530–1900* (2008). She has recently begun a pilot project on eighteenth-century Jesuit haciendas.

**Peter Elmore** (Ph.D., University of Texas-Austin, 1991) is Professor of Latin American Literature at the University of Colorado-Boulder. He is the author of three novels and three scholarly books, and has published numerous articles on Spanish-American historical fiction and Andean literature. He has written several plays in collaboration with Yuyachkani, Peru's premier theatre group.

**Sibylle Fischer** (Ph.D. Columbia) is Associate Professor of Spanish and Portuguese, Comparative Literature, and Africana Studies at New York University (NYU). Before joining NYU, she taught in the Literature Program and Department of Romance Studies at Duke University. Her *Modernity Disavowed: Haiti and the Cultures of Slavery in the Age of Revolution* (2004) received the Frantz Fanon Award (Caribbean Philosophical Association), the Singer Kovacs Award (Modern Language Association), and the Bryce Wood Award (Latin American Studies Association), and in 2007 was the co-winner of the Sybil and Gordon Lewis Award (Caribbean Studies Association). She is the editor of a new translation of Cirilo Villaverde's *Cecilia Valdés* (2005), and is currently working on a project about political subjectivity and violence.

**Todd S. Garth** is Associate Professor of Spanish at the US Naval Academy in Annapolis, MD. He is the author of *The Self of the City: Macedonio Fernández, the Argentine Avant-Garde, and Modernity in Buenos Aires* (2005), along with articles on Borges, Horacio Quiroga, and Machado de Assis. He is currently writing a study of seven interwar authors in the Río de la Plata region and their interrelated quests for pioneering, autochthonous ethical discourses. His ongoing research on Machado de Assis similarly examines that author's efforts toward a transformation in Brazilian ethical thought.

**Edouard Glissant** has been a Visiting Professor of French Literature at the City University of New York (CUNY) since 1995. His publications include *Le discours antillais* (1981); *The Ripening* (1985); *Mahagony: Roman* (1987); *Faulkner, Mississippi* (1999); and *Une Nouvelle région du monde* (2006).

**Leila Gómez** is Assistant Professor and Associate Chair for Undergraduate Studies in the Department of Spanish and Portuguese at the University of Colorado-Boulder. She specializes in travel literature in South America. She has edited *La piedra del escándalo: Darwin en Argentina* (2007), a collection of essays on Darwin and the theory of evolution in Argentina in the nineteenth century. Professor Gómez has published a number of articles on travel literature, indigenism, photography, and cinema in Latin America. She is also the director of *The Colorado Review of Hispanic Studies*.

**Stephen M. Hart** (PhD, Cambridge, UK, 1985) is Professor of Latin American Film and Latin American literature at University College London. He is Director of the Centre of César Vallejo Studies at UCL. He has published a number of books, including *A Companion to Spanish American Literature* (1999) and *A Companion to Latin American Film* (2004). He holds an honorary doctorate from the Universidad Nacional Mayor of San Marcos in Lima and the Orden al Mérito from the Peruvian Government for his research on César Vallejo.

**Hermann Herlinghaus** is Professor of Latin American Literature and Cultural Studies at the University of Pittsburgh. His *Violence Without Guilt: Ethical Narratives from the Globalized South* will be published in 2008. Among his recent publications are *Renarración y descentramiento: Mapas alternativos de la modernidad en América Latina* (2004); *Narraciones anacrónicas de la modernidad: melodrama e intermedialidad en América Latina* (2002); and *Modernidad heterogénea: Descentramientos hermenéuticos desde la comunicación en América Latina* (2000). He has edited a variety of volumes on the history of concepts, and on contemporary literary and cultural debates.

**Franklin W. Knight** is Leonard and Helen R. Stulman Professor of History at the Johns Hopkins University, Baltimore. He has published extensively on Latin America and the Caribbean, including *Slave Society in Cuba during the Nineteenth Century* (1970) and *The Caribbean: Genesis of a Fragmented Nationalism* (1990). He served as president of the Latin American Studies Association as well as of the Historical Society.

**Silvia G. Kurlat Ares** has recently completed her postdoctoral fellowship at the Johns Hopkins University, where she also taught courses in Latin American literature and culture. She has published articles on the literature of the transition to democracy in the Southern Cone, on the crossroads between literature and other forms of cultural productions, and on Argentine science fiction. Her book, *Para una intelectualidad sin episteme* (2006), traces the collapse of the aesthetic and ideological paradigms of Argentinean cultural field during the 1970s and 1980s and the emergence of new narrative forms during the early 1990s. Her forthcoming book, *Futuro imperfecto: Ciencia ficción en Argentina*, analyzes science fiction as an experimental way *to read*, not only canonical literature, but also sociopolitical and ideological agendas in times of political turmoil.

**Horacio Legras** teaches Latin American literature and culture at the University of California-Irvine. He has published articles on the Mexican Revolution, Andean literature, and nineteenth-century Argentine culture. His forthcoming book, *Literature and Subjection,* explores the historical role of the literary form in the incorporation of marginal subjectivities to representation in Latin America.

**Carlos M. López** is a professor and researcher in the Department of Modern Languages at Marshall University, Huntington, West Virginia. His specialization is in the study of the Popol Wuj and the production of texts under conditions of colonization. Among his publications is *Los Popol Wuj y sus Epistemologías: Las diferencias, el conocimiento y los ciclos del infinito* (1999). He is the academic director of the online edition of the manuscript of the *Popol Wuj* in the collaborative project developed by Ohio State University Libraries and the Newberry Library (http://library.osu.edu/sites/popolwuj) and also the academic director of the online site *The Popol Wuj and Mayan Culture Archives* (http://sppo.osu.edu/latinAmerica/archives/PopolWujLibrary/) hosted by the Department of Spanish and Portuguese and the Center for Latin American Studies at Ohio State University.

**Elizabeth A. Marchant** is Associate Professor of Spanish and Portuguese and Women's Studies at UCLA, where she won the Distinguished Teaching Award in 2005. Among her publications are *Critical Acts: Latin American Women and Cultural Criticism* (1999); "National Space as Minor Space: Afro-Brazilian Culture and the Pelourinho," in *Minor Transnationalisms* (2005); and "Naturalism, Race, and Nationalism in Aluísio Azevedo's *O mulato*," in *Hispania*, 83:3 (2000). She is currently editing an anthology on conflict and community in Afro-Latin American culture and completing a book on contemporary cultural production, development, and citizenship in Brazil.

**Gerald Martin** is Andrew W. Mellon Professor Emeritus at the University of Pittsburgh. He is the author of a critical edition of Miguel Angel Asturias's *Hombres de maíz* (1981), *Journeys through the Labyrinth: Latin American Fiction in the Twentieth Century* (1989), and is currently completing a major biography of Gabriel García Marquez.

**Kathryn Joy McKnight** is Associate Professor of Spanish at the University of New Mexico, where she teaches Latin American colonial literatures and discourses. Her areas of research include nuns' writings and narratives by Afro-Latinos recorded in archival documents. Her book *The Mystic of Tunja: The Writings of Madre Castillo, 1671–1742* (1997) received the MLA's Katherine Singer Kovaks Prize in 1998. Her articles have appeared in the *Colonial Latin American Review*, the *Colonial Latin American Historical Review*, *Revista de Estudios Hispánicos*, and the *Journal of Colonialism and Colonial History*. She is currently coediting an anthology of Afro-Latino narratives from the Early Modern Iberian World.

**Walter D. Mignolo** is William H. Wannamaker Professor and Director of the Center for Global Studies and the Humanities at Duke University and Associated Researcher at the Universidad Andina Simón Bolivar in Quito, Ecuador. His inquiries have focused lately on the analytic of modernity/coloniality and the prospective of decolonial thinking. Among his publications are *The Darker Side of the Renaissance: Literacy, Territoriality and Colonization* (1995; which received the Katherine Singer Kovas Prize in 1996) and *Local Histories/Global Designs: Coloniality, Subaltern Knowledges and Border Thinking* (2000). The third volume of the trilogy, *Global Figures, Decolonial Option(s)*, is forthcoming. In the meantime, he published *The Idea of Latin America* (2005) and received the Frantz Fanon Award in 2006. Recently he edited a special issue of *Cultural Studies* (21:2/3; with Arturo Escobar), devoted to *Globalization and the De-Colonial Option*. He coedited a special issue of *South Atlantic Quarterly*, 105:3 (2006; with Madina Tlostanova) on *Double Critique: Scholars and Knowledges at Risk in the Postsocialist World* and *The Black Legend: Discourse of Religion and Race in the European Renaissance* (with Margaret Greer and Maureen Quilligan, 2007).

**Elizabeth Monasterios P.** is Associate Professor of Andean Studies and Latin American Poetry, and currently Chair of the Department of Hispanic Languages and Literatures at the University of Pittsburgh. In 2006 she founded a new series of Latin American cultural theory: *Entretejiendo crítica y teoría cultural latinoamericana* (La Paz–Pittsburgh). She serves on the Pittsburgh Comité de Publicaciones for *Revista Iberoamericana*, is a Contributing Editor for the *Handbook of Latin American Studies* (Library of Congress), and has served as contributor and section coordinator for the *Literary Cultures of Latin America: A Comparative History* (edited by Mario J. Valdes, 2004) and for *A Historical Companion to Postcolonial Literatures in Continental Europe and its Empires* (edited by Prem Poddar, Rajeev Patke, and Lars Jensen, forthcoming). She has written *Dilemas de la poesía latinoamericana de fin de siglo: Jaime Saenz y José Emilio Pacheco* (2001), and a series of edited books and essays published in Bolivia, Canada, and the United States. She is currently working on a book on the Andean avant-garde.

**Francisco A. Ortega** is the Director of the Center for Social Studies (CES) at the National University of Colombia, Bogotá. He is also an associate professor in the Department of History and teaches in the Cultural Studies graduate program of the same university. Dr. Ortega did his undergraduate studies at the University of Massachusetts-Boston and went on to obtain his MA and PhD from the University of Chicago (2000), where he specialized in colonial Latin American studies and critical theory. From 1995 to 1999 he was a visiting scholar at Harvard University and from 2000 to 2004 he was an assistant professor at the University of Wisconsin-Madison. In 2003 he was awarded a Fulbright scholarship to teach and research in Bogotá, Colombia. Professor Ortega edited a Spanish-language anthology of Michel de Certeau's works and wrote the introduction. He has also published extensively on colonial Latin American intellectual history.

**Juan Poblete** is Associate Professor of Latin American Literature and Cultural Studies at the University of California, Santa Cruz. He is the author of *Literatura chilena del siglo XIX: Entre públicos lectores y figuras autoriales* and the editor of *Critical Latin American and Latino Studies* (both 2003.) He is currently at work on a project on forms of mediation between culture and the market in the context of the neoliberal transformation of Chilean culture. He recently edited interdisciplinary Special Dossiers on the Globalization of Latin/o American Populations and Studies for the journals

*Iberoamericana* (Germany), *LASA Forum*, and *Latino Studies Journal*. He is coediting two forthcoming volumes: *Andres Bello* (with Beatriz Gonzalez-Stephan) and *Redrawing The Nation: Latin American Comics and The Graphic Construction of Cultural Identities* (with Héctor Fernández-L'Hoeste).

**José Rabasa** teaches in the Department of Spanish and Portuguese at UC Berkeley. His publications include *Inventing America: Spanish Historiography and the Formation of Eurocentrism* (1993) and *Writing Violence on the Northern Frontier: The Historiography of New Mexico and Florida and The Legacy of Conquest* (2000). He is in the process of collecting together into one volume his numerous articles on postcolonial theory and subaltern studies, and is completing a study of the intersection of pictography, orality, and alphabetical writing in Nahuatl colonial texts.

**Ileana Rodríguez** is Humanities Distinguished Professor of Spanish at Ohio State University. Her areas and fields of specialization are Latin American literature and culture, postcolonial theory, and feminist and subaltern studies with an emphasis on Central American and Caribbean literatures. Her books include *Transatlantic Topographies: Island, Highlands, Jungle Women* (2005); *Guerrillas, and Love: Understanding War in Central America* (1996); *House/Garden/Nation: Space, Gender, and Ethnicity in Post-Colonial Latin American Literatures by Women* (1994); *Registradas en la historia: Diez años del quehacer feminista en Nicaragua* (1990); and *Primer inventario del invasor* (1984). She has edited *Marxism and New Left Ideology* (with William L. Rowe, 1977); *Nicaragua in Revolution: The Poets Speak. Nicaragua en Revolución: Los poetas hablan* (2nd ed. 1981, with Bridget Aldaraca, Edward Baker, and Marc Zimmerman); *The Process of Unity in Caribbean Society: Ideologies and Literature* (1983, with Marc Zimmerman); *Convergencia de tiempos: Estudios subalternos/contextos latinoamericanos – estado, cultura, subalternidad* (2001); *The Latin American Subaltern Studies Reader* (2001); and *Cánones literarios masculinos y relecturas transculturales: Lo trans- femenino/masculino/queer* (2001). Her current research is on violence and criminality in Caribbean and Central American cultural texts.

**Fernando J. Rosenberg** (Ph.D. Johns Hopkins University, 2001) is an Associate Professor of Romance and Comparative Literature at Brandeis University. Previously he taught at SUNY-Binghamton and Yale. He is the author of *Avant-Garde and Geopolitics in Latin America* (2006) and of numerous articles on modernism, the avant-gardes, and modernity in Latin America. He coedited (with Jill Lane) the issue of of *e-misferica* (online journal of the *Hemispheric Institute of Performance and Politics*, 3.1) entitled *Performance and the Law*. His current research focuses on issues of justice in contemporary Latin American artistic production.

**Javier Sanjinés C.** is Associate Professor of Latin American Literature and Cultural Studies at the University of Michigan-Ann Arbor. He has also been a visiting professor at Duke University and at Universidad Andina Simón Bolívar, in Quito, Ecuador.

Sanjinés has published three books. His most recent is *Mestizaje Upside-Down* (2004). He has just finished a manuscript on the crisis of historical time in the Andean region.

**Freya Schiwy** is Assistant Professor of Latin American Media and Cultural Studies at the University of California, Riverside. She is coeditor of *Indisciplinar las ciencias sociales* (2001) and has published in journals and collected volumes in Latin America, Europe, and the United States. Her book manuscript on Indigenous Media and Decolonization is currently under review. Currently she is coediting a special issue of *Social Identities* that focuses on digital technology and speculative capitalism from a transnational perspective.

**Nicolas Shumway** is the Tomás Rivera Regents Professor of Spanish Language and Literature at the University of Texas at Austin. His book *The Invention of Argentina* (1991) was selected by *The New York Times* as a "Notable Book of the Year" and appeared in a revised version in Spanish in 2005. He has also published numerous articles on the literature and cultural history of Spanish America, Brazil, and Spain, and been a visiting professor at the Universidade de São Paulo as well as at the Universidad Torcuato Di Tella and the Universidad San Andrés in Buenos Aires.

**Doris Sommer** is Ira Jewell Williams, Jr. Professor of Romance Languages and Literatures and Director of the Cultural Agents Initiative at Harvard University. Professor Sommer's research interests have developed from the nineteenth-century novels that helped to consolidate new republics in Latin America through the particular aesthetics of minoritarian literature, including bilingual virtuosity, to her current more general pursuit of the constructive work in rights and resources that the arts and the humanities contribute to developing societies. She is the author of *Foundational Fictions: The National Romances of Latin America* (1991); *Proceed with Caution, When Engaged by Minority Writing in the Americas* (1999); and *Bilingual Aesthetics: A New Sentimental Education* (2004), and editor of *Bilingual Games: Some Literary Investigations* (2004) and *Cultural Agency in the Americas* (2006). Professor Sommer has enjoyed and is dedicated to developing good public school education; she has a BA from New Jersey's Douglass College for Women, an MA from the Hebrew University of Jerusalem; and her Ph.D. is from Rutgers State University.

**Abril Trigo** is Distinguished Humanities Professor of Latin American Cultures at the Ohio State University. He is the author of *Caudillo, estado, nación: Literatura, historia e ideología en el Uruguay* (1990), *¿Cultura uruguaya o culturas linyeras? (Para una cartografía de la neomodernidad posuruguaya)* (1997), *Memorias migrantes: Testimonios y ensayos sobre la diáspora uruguaya* (2003) and *The Latin American Cultural Studies Reader*, coauthored with Ana Del Sarto and Alicia Ríos (2004). Currently, he is working on *Muerte y transfiguración de los estudios culturales latinoamericanos*, a book-length essay on the effects of globalization on Latin American cultures, and *Crítica de la economía* *politico-libidinal*, a theoretical inquiry on the political economy of contemporary culture.

**Gustavo Verdesio** is Associate Professor in the Department of Romance Languages and Literatures and the Program in American Culture at University of Michigan. He teaches courses on colonial Latin America, indigenous societies, and popular culture. A revised English version of his book *La Invención del Uruguay* (1996) has been published as *Forgotten Conquests* (2001). He is the coeditor (with Alvaro F. Bolaños) of the collection *Colonialism Past and Present* (2002). He has also edited an issue of the journal *Dispositio/n* (52, 2005) dedicated to the assessment of the legacy or the Latin American Subaltern Studies group. His articles have appeared in *Trabajos de Arqueologia del Paisaje*, *Arqueología Suramericana*, *Bulletin of Hispanic Studies*, *Revista de Estudios Hispánicos*, and *Revista Iberoamericana*, among other journals.

# Editor's Acknowledgments

In any project there are always more and less visible collaborators and individuals without whose generosity the project could have never taken place. In the case of this *Companion* the contributors gave this project more than their expertise; they freely gave of their spirit for the texts included here stand for the vast revamping of the study of Latin America that has taken place in the last forty years. Mario Valdes is absent from the table of contents, but the breath of his work and the force of his desire to see Latin America writ large in the world map is present in many ways here. There are also the other colleagues who, in one way or another, have been supportive of this enterprise, even though their commitment to other projects did not allow sufficient time for them to write here. Among them I want to thank Vicky Unruh, Beatriz Sarlo, Mabel Moraña, and Julio Ortega. Most especially I appreciate the dialogue that I have been fortunate to have with my graduate students at Johns Hopkins and Georgetown University. Nothing moves without financial support, and I am grateful for the conference support of Dean Adam Falk at Johns Hopkins. Peter Klaren, my indefatigable companion, also plays a large role in the making of Latin American scholars and scholarships. And last but not least, I thank Martin Carrión without whose energy, organization, and electronic and social skills this volume would have simply not been possible. From the beginning to the end he managed and kept alive the myriad communications about large and small things, so that the making of the volume kept on chugging along, until, like the little engine that could, the *Companion* claimed the hill and was able to breathe the clean and fresh air at the top of the mountain.

# Acknowledgments to Sources

The editor and publisher gratefully acknowledge the permission granted to reproduce the copyright material in this book:

Chapter 31: Extract from *Caribbean Discourse* by Edouard Glissant, pp. 120–50. Copyright © 1989 University of Virginia Press.

Chapter 33: "*Testimonio*, Subalternity, and Narrative Authority," by John Beverley in *Strategies of Qualitative Inquiry*, edited by Norman K. Denzin and Yvonna S. Lincoln, pp. 319–35. Copyright © 2008 by Sage Publications. Reprinted by permission of Sage Publications Inc.

Every effort has been made to trace copyright holders and to obtain their permission for the use of copyright material. The publisher apologizes for any errors or omissions in the above list and would be grateful if notified of any corrections that should be incorporated in future reprints or editions of this book.

# Introduction

*Sara Castro-Klaren*

The idea of Latin American literature as a cultural system, anchored in time and space by texts of epoch-making writers who are, in turn, gathered together by contextualizing concepts of period and cultural movement, gave rise, in the 1940s, to the first attempt to produce a global view of the avatars of writing in Spanish America since the Spanish Conquest introduced the alphabet, print, and the culture of the book. The historians and essayists who interpreted the nation in the nineteenth century had spent a great deal of energy and no less talent in producing national literatures that, as powerful cultural constructs, would be capable of providing a rich and flexible, albeit contradictory, imaginary for the integration of the past into the future projection of the nascent republics.

Pedro Henríquez Ureña (1884–1946), a diasporic Dominican intellectual who lived most of his life in Cuba, Mexico, Argentina, and the United States, and who is probably one of the first Spanish Americans to obtain a PhD in literature (University of Minnesota, 1918), published, in 1945, the influential *Literary Currents in Spanish America* as a result of having been invited to Harvard University to give the Norton Lectures. These lectures, conceived to address a public on the whole ignorant of anything Latin American, had already been tried out in his much earlier *Seis ensayos en busca de nuestra expresión* (1928). Both the titles and the contents of the two works signal the bifurcated path that all future anthologies, histories, and even companions, such as the present one, ultimately face in thinking Latin America as a whole.

The historian and critic is, on the one hand, struck by a keen sense of basic facts, assumptions, recurrences, evolutions, reiterations and transformations, similarities, simultaneities, and epochal changes; that is to say, patterns. On the other hand, one also quickly discovers that all patterns and visions of unity are woven into a fabric that highlights vast and uneven heterogeneities, contradictions as well as endless dissemination. Mario Valdés, inspired perhaps by the felicitous findings of Antonio Cornejo Polar regarding the non-dialectical, heterogeneous condition of history and culture in the Andes (1994), has recently written that he conceives of this globalizing endeavor as the writing of the cultural history of heterogeneity. As such, it demands a comparative method in which literature is analyzed and understood as one type of discourse engaged in dialogue with other forms of signification.[1] This contextualization of literature in relation to artistic, religious, political, philosophical, and oral discourses does not imply a cause-and-effect relationship between material "context" and literature. The perspective that combines deep cultural contextualization with a comparative method avoids the commonplace fallacy of situating authors next to one another as if they dangled from a string which holds them above the magma of the cultural matrix where they are formed. An approach that intertwines deep historical cuts with extensive cultural views of the space connoted by and inscribed in the great canonical works not only configures their emergence, but in fact submerges them into the historiography of their making and interpretation essayed through the ages. The idea of differences in dialogue, the notion of dialectic contextualization, the view that cultural texts of all kinds intersect constantly in contestatory spaces, has gained dominance over the previous historiography informed by notions of influences, cause, and effect arranged in a singular chronology still tied to the constructs of nineteenth-century European periodization. To a large extent the essays written for this volume take deep contextualization as the necessary norm for the understanding of literature and culture.

In Latin America thus far, one of the chief structures for understanding the cultural imaginary, that is to say the collective symbolic expressions of communities that create significations of identity, has been the national literary and cultural histories and genre anthologies. Rarely have literary critics, rooted in the cultural institutions of a given country, attempted histories or anthologies that aspired to account, in a systematic manner, for the whole of Latin America. Even in the case of the great cultural theorists of the nineteenth and early twentieth century, José Enrique Rodó (1871–1917), Jose Martí (1853–95), and José Carlos Mariátegui (1884–1930), if they spoke of Latin America, they did so as an extension of the cultural problematic that they knew best; the region where they had been born, the geopolitical place from where they mounted their struggle and which they had thus learned to analyze with searing weapons. The great exception to this general situation is perhaps Ricardo Rojas (1882–1957), the Argentine intellectual and educator born in the northern province of Tucumán, who wrote with eloquence of the common threads that underline the uniqueness of the Americas. Both his *Blasón de plata* (1912) and his *Eurendia* (1924) exhibit some of the most lasting, inspiring, irritating, provoking, and also wrongheaded ideas that have informed the constructions of national literatures and the idea of Latin America's cultures as essentially *mestizo* conjunctions.

This reticence to engage "Latin America" in a larger geohistorical frame in part has been due to the fact that the republics in the nineteenth century and even throughout the twentieth century have had a curriculum that teaches history and literature either as a set of artistic and intellectual events defined and understood as part of a "national" history or a "universal" culture and literature. In the latter case literary studies mainly devolve around the Eurocentric canon, not infrequently portrayed in a normative light. Only in the last 40 years, and perhaps owing to the "boom" of Latin American literature, have the universities in Latin America seen professorships dedicated to the study of the cultural history of the region as a whole.

Another reason for the lesser number of books dedicated in Latin America to "Latin America" as a whole has been the fact that, from colonial times, Spanish American and Brazilian artists and cultural agents have not traveled much to neighboring colonial countries, with the exception of Rubén Dario and other *modernistas*. Just four years ago, when the Universidad de San Martin in Buenos Aires held a symposium on the state of Latin American Studies as it inaugurated its new center for Latin American Studies, one of the invited scholars from Mexico informed the audience, which included me, that in Mexico there is not much interest in Latin America because Mexico considers itself to be the result of an exceptional history rather than part of a general Latin American history. In general, Latin American and Caribbean men and women of letters looked instead to Europe, if not as their interlocutor, at least as a desired place of learning and thinking. The fact that Brazil and Spanish America are generally regarded as parallel and different rather than similar or integrated literary and cultural systems also accounts for the absence of histories, anthologies, or collections of texts that attempt to encompass "Latin America" as a whole, imagined and conceived by intellectuals working in the region. There are, of course, notable exceptions, such as Darcy Ribeiro (1922–) who, in his *As Américas e a Civilizaçao* (1970), does develop some comparative perspectives for his study of the formative colonial period.

The larger or greater view of the region has been the project of diasporic intellectuals like Henríquez Ureña, Emir Rodriguez Monegal and, most recently, Roberto González Echeverría, Enrique Pupo-Walker, and Mario Valdés, all of whom eventually came to occupy influential positions in the US or Canadian academy. In several generational waves, many intellectuals left their motherland and went into exile to another Latin American country. I am thinking, for example, of Henríquez Ureña, Ángel Rama, and Nelson Osorio who, by virtue of their lengthy stay in Mexico, or Venezuela, in a way discovered the Latin America that the national agenda had occluded. Another example of diasporic intellectuals is provided by the academic trajectory of Roberto González Echeverría and Mario Valdés, who studied in the United States. And yet another by Walter Mignolo and Silvia Molloy, who spent many significant years in France before they migrated to the academy in the United States. The view from the North is, of course, not just the work of diasporic intellectuals from the South. English-speaking scholars such as John Englekirk and John Crow published some of the earliest anthologies and histories of Latin American literature destined for the classroom. These successful publications were followed by several others, as perspectives and criteria for inclusion changed with the impact of feminism, gay studies, testimonio, and the recognition of previously ignored cultural agents. Jean Franco's *An Introduction to Spanish American Literature* (1969) circulated widely and David Foster's anthology of Spanish American literature (1994), which has the picture of a young Indian woman in the cover, is often adopted for course assignments. In a way, the *Blackwell Companion to Latin American Literature and Culture* is one of the first examples of North–South collaboration.

Of the group who migrated to the United States, the work of the Argentine Enrique Anderson Imbert (1910–98?) stands out because of the impact it had in canon formation. In the literary history and anthology that he authored in the 1950s, during his years at Harvard, Anderson Imbert expanded the Latin American literary archive tenfold. Because its objective was to be exhaustive of all genres, his history had a lasting impact in the dynamics of the canon. The sheer volume of literary production in Spanish America alone evidenced in Anderson Imbert's history is enough to deter anyone from tackling any project dealing with a portrayal of the entirety of Spanish American lettered representation, let alone the history of orality or nonalphabetic representations. Such an endeavor would call for nothing less than the Borgean "Funes el memorioso" and the well-known descent into chaos that the Borgean conceit involves.

Himself a disciple of Henríquez Ureña, with whom he studied in his native Argentina, and probably in open breach with Ricardo Rojas, Anderson Imbert seemed not to be satisfied with the idea of literary and cultural patterns that cut across the boundaries of the newly created national literatures and regional histories which, by definition, left out the works that did not fit the patterns. In *Historia de la literatura hispanoamericana* (1954) he tried to compile a literary history, but the sheer volume of what his research uncovered spelled out instead a chronology closer to the style of an inventory. The aim was to exhaust the published records of an ample if diffusely defined literary production. While Anderson Imbert's generational and regional organization of the magma that emerged from his search left much to be desired in terms of a critical and historiographical approach, the immense body of the corpus that his history unearthed gave rise to a very large number of monographic studies that, in turn, produced a distinct sense of the profound heterogeneity of the corpus of Latin American literary production and the subsequent demand for scholarly specialization by literary categories of scholarly research: author (s), period, region, genre, movement, and nation. Major writers such as Jorge Luis Borges, the Inca Garcilaso de la Vega, Sor Juana Inés de la Cruz, César Vallejo, Alejo Carpentier, José María Arguedas, and Rubén Dario were the objects of entire books. The regional novel, the Mexican baroque, *indigenismo*, Spanish-American *modernismo*, and colonial satirical poetry also began to appear as clearly defined objects of critical inquiry. Minor writers from smaller countries also began receiving attention in monographs fully dedicated to them, and these studies came to enlarge and complicate both the views held on national literatures as well as the weight and expanse of literary production in Latin America from the very first day that Columbus began his diary, to the intervention of the many colonial subjects who, while not belonging to the lettered city, sought nevertheless to be heard in both public spaces, such as courts, churches, the stage, rituals, and bars/cafés, and domestic arenas such as salons and parties of all kinds. To a great extent, the corpus of Spanish-American letters was becoming unmanageable in its very richness and multiplicity.

But if the very multiplicity of the corpus threatened the discovery and sustainability of the idea of common patterns, developments, and identities, the emergence of the assumptions and critical methods of New Criticism served to check the potential dispersion and leveling of hierarchies implicit in the new thickness and heterogeneity of the corpus. New Criticism offered carefully crafted arguments and methods that enabled students of literature to establish aesthetic distinctions of value between literary objects in order to identify those texts so finely crafted as to have inscribed within themselves the codes necessary to their interpretation. The finely crafted and self-contained piece of art could then be contemplated in exemplary isolation, for it represented the culmination of the possibilities of genre and genius. The dialogic relations of literature to other circulating discourses were comfortably eschewed by the notion that each literary gem contained within itself all the means for its interpretation. Literature, in extreme cases of the New Criticism approach, existed in a realm of its own, as this strict textual practice would reject the biographical and emotional fallacies which had previously informed literary appreciations and which had led to the confusion of the author's ascribed life with the meaning of the text. It would take the creation of a whole new hermeneutics to reintroduce psychological and biographical problematics into the practice of textual analysis and appreciation of highly crafted literary artifacts. As the highest point in a vertical line of ascendancy, the idea of the well-wrought urn permitted the classification of a corpus that grew retrospectively in time and also reached deeply below the surface in each specific zone. A shapeless but definitely hierarchical order of artistic achievement informed by norms still quite tied to European models began to emerge. In this order *indigenista* novels were less accomplished than some of the "great" *novelas de la tierra*, and Alejo Carpentier ranked higher than José María Arguedas in complexity and understanding of his own baroque aesthetics.

Despite this tendentious use of New Criticism, the rigor of the method in some ways prepared the way to read the testimonio texts that were soon to appear, as New Criticism claimed a method of textual analysis of universal application. But in other ways, the idea of the well-wrought urn blocked the aesthetic and historical appreciation of many texts whose "literary" status would be ranked very low, as some of these texts were not intended to be "literary" or did not conform to the reading expectations of "literary critics." This was, for instance, the case with many texts authored during the long centuries of colonial life, or some texts authored by women and other subaltern subjects whose plan of action was not so much to comply with the models offered, but rather to interrupt the flow of the colonial power–knowledge complex, and inscribe their memory or position. Despite Borges's essays on the preeminence of the reader in the hermeneutic circle, reader-response theory had not yet made its appearance. It had not yet injected its corrective energy into the hermeneutics of text-based criticism. Notwithstanding its often ahistorical approach, the legacy of New Criticism in conjunction with an explosion in the field of Latin American literary studies owing to the relentless appearance of captivating writers, the recovery of the past and the boom of the Latin American novel was positive. The apogee of New Criticism coincided with the opening of hundreds of positions for academic critics in both the United States and Latin America. This aperture in the American academy was, in part, owing to the impact of the Cuban Revolution and the institution of regional studies partially funded by the US government. This affluence of activity contributed to the creation of a professional, scholarly class of critics, who, for a number of different reasons, were poised to revamp the received understanding of Latin America's cultural development, its variegated history, and above all its place in the world.

The Cold War brought about the inception of Regional Studies in the United States, and the growth of specialists on Latin America coincided with a multifaceted export and political exile of Latin American intellectuals to both the United States and Europe. The boom of Latin American writers in the international market and the self-identification of the major authors of the boom with a broad Latin American identity that spelled out a brotherhood beyond the countries where they had been born contributed greatly to advance the idea, both at home and overseas, of a shared and indeed cohesive, if uneven, Latin American culture and literature. The Cuban Revolution, with the romantic figure of the Argentine Che Guevara, underlined further the idea of a common Latin American identity capable of overarching differing histories and distinct regional traditions cast in contrasting colors, and even the language diversity that constitutes the different histories of the Amerindian linguistic legacies.

However, at the scholarly foundries of knowledge, the problematic, multiple, and heterogeneous immensity of the Latin American canon and processes of cultural formation grew more evident every day. Not one single individual, not one lifetime, could attempt at this juncture what Anderson Imbert had tried and in fact failed to do in the 1950s. As philology and positivist historiography came under intense critique, it became clear that his *Historia* was not really a history. It did not account for either change as part of internal processes in Latin America itself, nor did it provide for the multiple plays of differences that construct the heterogeneous dynamic of Latin American culture, a space where literary works did play a huge, even disproportionate role in political and cultural life. Above all, Anderson Imbert's general organization of breaking up the magna of literary production into generations of authors neither confronted nor resolved the problem of periodization, inherited from the colonial perspective, which had failed to understand that periodization based on European models only distorts the picture and bars the way to understanding.

The need for a major work that could critically account for the uneven development of the forms and contents of Latin American literature was indeed pressing. Readers of the boom the world over needed, just as a sick man needs a doctor's prescription, an overarching account of Latin American literature. It was painfully insufficient to simply offer a discussion based on the perceived similarities and differences with other "great writers" of the European canon. Something other, something else had to account for the flaming brilliance and consuming stories of *Cien años de soledad* (1967; *One Hundred Years of Solitude*, 1970), or *Rayuela* (1963; *Hopscotch*, 1969). The intricate connection between the Mexican Revolution and *La Muerte de Artemio Cruz* (1962;

*The Death of Artemio Cruz*, 1964), the driving force of the historical events of Canudos between 1874 and 1897 in Brazil over *La Guerra del fin del mundo* (1981; *The War of the End of the World*, 1984) had to be established so that journalists at the *New York Times*, not unlike Egyptian or Chinese readers, did not assume that these novels had mushroomed out of nothing but out of the imagination and the pen of genial writers, some of whom, like Mario Vargas Llosa and even Carlos Fuentes, went about creating the idea that before their narrative nothing important had been written in Latin America.

Roberto González Echeverría and Enrique Pupo-Walker were the first to understand that, at this juncture, any comprehensive account of that massive and unbelievably rich literary legacy would have to be the collaborative work of a good number of scholars. Early in the 1980s they began work on editing the three-volume *Cambridge History of Latin American Literature* (1996), a huge endeavor that brought together critics from both the South and the North.

Almost ten years later, and from a very different perspective, the field saw the appearance of the three-volume *Literary Cultures of Latin America: A Comparative History* (2004), edited by Mario Valdés and Djelal Kadir. While very different in their separate conceptions of literature and culture, both these collections spell out highly sophisticated understandings of literature, the circulation of culture, and its institutional instances. Above all they present clearly discernible plans that express the differences between a history of literature constructed through a set of periodic histories of the major genres: lyric, theater, chronicle, journalism, narrative sub-genres, as is the case with the *Cambridge History*; and the totally new departure in the study of Latin America, as represented by the *Literary Cultures of Latin America*. The latter three volumes include some 240 scholars contributing on questions that range from "Geographic Factors and the Formation of Cultural Terrain for Literary Production" to "Demography, Language Diversity, and Cultural Centers." Its interdisciplinary approach moves easily between sociology, geography, history, literature, and even the visual arts. For instance, it considers sociological topics such as the historical relationship of poverty to literary cultures, right next to the more strictly literary "The Rhetoric of Latin American Nationalism from the Colonial Period to Independence." One of the outstanding features of these ambitious and highly complex histories is that for the first time Brazil is included in a systematic way, adding without a doubt to the problematic of representing the variegation of Latin American literature and culture.

As *The Cambridge History* was being written and edited to correspond to the highest standards of historiography and literary criticism of the moment, a theoretical revolution was taking place in the halls of the North American academy, one that would challenge the very definition of "literature" as a fine art and replace it with the idea of "culture" as transported from anthropology and developed in cultural criticism theory. Literature, as an object bound by the history of certain genres to which high degrees of aesthetic value were ascribed, lost its central place in the humanities as a result of the theoretical changes that both postmodern theory and cultural studies were to bring about in the last 30 years of the twentieth century. Literary analysis informed by semiotics, hermeneutics, Michael's Foucault discourse theory, and dissemination theory could now focus on any written text and yield surprisingly interesting and obviously neglected layers of sophisticated meaning. While the novelists of the boom still commanded most of the discussion in the classroom, in journals, books, and newspapers, the force of testimonio and the disaster and diasporas of the dirty wars brought other, insurgent voices and agencies into the corpus of literature, forcing the reconsideration of the making of the canon and all its attendant institutions.

Feminism and women authors interpolated the established canon and its cultural institutions, such as anthologies and genre histories, with devastating force. As Adriana Bergero and Elizabeth Marchant argue in this companion, women like Rosario Castellanos, Elena Poniatowska, Diamela Eltit, and Alfonsina Storni listened and responded to an inner polemic as they sought to recode women's social spaces and symbolic formations. Women questioned universality by embarking on a new quest for gender-sexual identity. What is more, the study of the colonial period, inspired by Edmundo O'Gorman's inquiry into the philosophy of history; the appearance of Guamán Poma; and the forceful entry of French theory, especially Michael Foucault and his concept of genealogy in which local knowledges and memory intersect with erudite knowledges; were to transform our sense of culture and literature and the nature of the colonial legacy. As colonial studies set out to problematize the received understanding of the meaning of "colonial" in relation to the European conquest of the Americas as an epistemological deployment of violence and domination, a radical reconfiguration of the "colonial" emerged.

The theoretical force of this reconfiguration of what the "colonial" encompassed and meant as a formative period for Latin America extended the duration of the period into the present, so that scholars began to conceptualize the study of Latin American cultures and literatures within a broad sense of a continuous aesthetic and epistemological struggle for decolonization embedded in the very disciplines that had given us the prevailing concepts of "literature" and "culture" as Eurocentric categories of self-description and mechanisms of "othering." This revision of critical assumptions and parameters set the stage for a transformative questioning of "literature" as a whole and of the chronological line that used periods as a main principle of organization. Although not grounded on the colonial reflection in a strict sense and rather inspired by the problematic of testimonio, itself an interpellation of the not so hidden and lasting work of colonization, John Beverley's *Against Literature* (1993) advanced, in a polemical essay, the view that the ideology of the literary as a universal had exerted an exclusionary hegemony over nonliterary forms of cultural practices and that the displacement of such hegemony could take place with the introduction of cultural studies. The result of the multiple and variegated changes taking place in the field, one that had never been critically integrated, yielded an object of study understood or rather strategically visualized in ways radically different from the many national histories of literature, and also from the patterns and corpus of the earliest attempts to see Latin American literature in some kind of global shape. To a large extent *The*

*Literary Cultures of Latin America* captures these radical changes in our understanding of culture and the repositioning of literature within the whole of the socius.

*The Blackwell Companion to Latin American Literature and Culture*, informed by the voluminous scholarship that filled library shelves in the second half of the twentieth century and, keenly aware of the fact that there has been a paradigm shift in the ways in which we conceive of Latin America, intends, by means of 38 strategically chosen essays, to put the reader in touch with the key issues involved in this great shift. In many of these essays, the reader will find a critical perspective grounded in the necessity to decolonize the assumptions with which we read in order to take proper account of both the locus of enunciation inscribed in the text and the position that the critic self assigns to him or herself. The great shift operated by the theoretical revamping implicit in the recovery of the colonial past and present, the feminine, the local, the non-"literary," has implied as much the introduction of innovative problematics as it has meant a systematic delearning of the inertia that sustained the legacy of philology. Such a challenge is met in essays that posit an understanding of the avant-garde as a geopolitical project in which the old, colonial relationships to European learned elites is completely revamped. Nothing less underlines the essay on Gauchesca literature. The essay on *El carnero* shows that once the veil of "literature" is lifted from the surface of the text, it is the deep contradictions and fractures of a vicious colonial semiosis that both form and inform the meaning of this disheveled but pivotal text.

In *The Darker Side of the Renaissance* (1995), perhaps the most influential book in the reframing and redefining of the study of literature and culture of Latin America, Walter Mignolo deploys the notion of colonial semiosis. He shows how deep historicizing of the past and, by extension, the present, is indispensable in order to gain an understanding that addresses the possibility of engaging the totality of signs in their ceaseless exchange and negotiation in a given moment. One of the virtues found in the concept of colonial semiosis is that it places on the same footing any number of signifying practices at a given historical moment and frees us from having to search for patterns and continuities over territories and timelines that are obviously discontinuous and fragmented. And, while in this case it emerges and responds to the colonial history of Latin America, colonial semiosis is a concept that can travel in space and time. Colonial semiosis, then, can speak not only of the process that ensues when radically different cultures come in contact and conflict, as with the European conquest of the Amerindian societies, but its emphasis on the circulation and negotiation of signs, forms of communication, and knowledge allows us to avoid the often restrictive image conveyed by a narrow reading of transculturation (from one to the other) and especially the "happy" notion of syncretism. Because it does not depend on Europe's idea of a single universal historical time and, in fact, challenges it, colonial semiosis has allowed, to some extent, the dismantling of the European-based arrangement of cultural production by periods with clearly defined beginnings and endings, a conceit that often classified Latin American cultural phenomena as either behind or, as it is often does now with both postcolonial and postmodern theory, ahead. This multidirectional extension of the plane of operations as a space of asymmetric semiotic struggles constitutes an open invitation to the configuration of many kinds of different and new objects of study, such as, for instance, a history of the formative years of the cathedral in Cuzco as a complex mixture of architecture, engineering, Catholic ritual, painting, music, methods of evangelization, and the mutual transformation of the subjects involved in the enterprise. The idea of an ongoing colonial semiosis also offers a way of skirting the artificial divide that some critics originally read in the modern/postmodern relation, and it refines the function of historical time in relation to the cultural formation at hand. Conceiving of the world's situation, at least since the drastic changes introduced since 1492, as an ongoing flux of memories, discursive formations – visual, lettered, pictographic, oral, musical, notational, and architectural – as a universe engaged in an unending network of negotiations, allows for a far-reaching redrawing of the geological features of the maps that constitute Latin America. Like Borges's notion of the inter-text as an endless and deceivingly permanent space of aesthetic and hermeneutic action, the notion of a colonial semiosis can easily be extended, and in fact has been extended, to the study of any temporality as redesigned by criteria emerging from the very constitution of the object in question.

More recently, Mignolo has developed the concept of the "coloniality of power," a concept originally advanced by the Peruvian sociologist Anibal Quijano (1992). The "coloniality of power," no doubt inspired by the work of Michael Foucault on the inextricable links between knowledges and power and world-systems theory coming from the social sciences, advances the idea that modernity and coloniality constitute a single system of power and knowledge. They are simply the two faces of the same coin and not, as it has been believed and managed for the last 500 years, an opposition between subject and other, or civilization and barbarism, or democracy and despotism, or wealthy and poor societies. Mignolo has put this concept to work in many of his recent interventions. In his essay here he pushes the idea of the coloniality of power to challenge the concept of modernity as the inevitability of history, a history that is Europe's exclusive province. Mignolo argues that if one accepts the idea of the coloniality of power, a historical thesis in which modernity cannot have occurred without the advent of the colonization of the world by Europe, then one can no longer posit "alternative modernities," subaltern modernities, or singular and exceptional modernities as categories that enable us to understand Latin America as a difference, that is, as a relational term. Positioned in this manner, the coloniality of power constitutes a challenge not only to the humanities but also to the social sciences, for what we have is "worlding" or "mundialization" of what was once thought as a regional peculiarity.

In as much as the concept of the coloniality of power embraces not only economic relations, but especially addresses epistemic spaces, it can be said that the essays in *The Blackwell Companion to Latin American Literature and Culture* in part take in the spirit of the leveling power of the concept of the coloniality of power. In these essays the reader will find a recognition of a struggle for self-affirmation and creativity, for the invention of maneuvers that allow for conquering of discursive spaces denied by the power of colonization of the mind that emphasizes that most of the texts and problems chosen for discussion in this companion are part of the beginning of a three-way conversation between author, reader, and critic.

The *Blackwell Companion to Latin American Literature and Culture* embraces the idea that Latin America represents a number of uneven developments over space and time. Thus patterns and periods that convey the idea of uniformity and often keep the critic's gaze on the surface have been replaced by a focus on clusters and cuts that allow the critic and historian to descend and touch bottom at the most secret and intimate point of the hidden pleats that constitute a nodal point of understanding. Nevertheless, the organization of the companion recognizes key and long epochal flows as points of both emergence and exhaustion of important cultural formations such as the formation of national literatures, the long tradition of poetic expression, the spread of radio in the hinterlands and its effect on the revival of Amerindian languages, or the invasion of the lettered city by cinema and the telenovela. The tone and modulation of this companion are intended to resonate with scholarship across the disciplines, especially anthropology and the humanities in general.

The idea of the *Blackwell Companion* is not to present an exhaustive or comprehensive view of Latin America's immense cultural production. Instead, what the reader will find is a set of essays which, like a traveling companion, offer the opportunity for a learned and stimulating discussion of the most important and heated issues of the moment in the study of Latin America's and, for that matter, the world's cultural history. At every point, the essays that comprise the *Blackwell Companion*, whether centered on a single author like Joaquim Maria Machado de Assis (1839–1908) or Jorge Luis Borges (1899–1986), for instance, or on a cluster of writers, or on a given problematic such as women's writing, or the writing violence of the chroniclers, the authors take up their thinking at the cusp of the discussion of the key issues informing their essays, so that the reader will find both a sense of the received understanding on the topic and a strong and stimulating point of departure for future reflection. Perhaps this consistent invitation to further thought and informed reflection is to be regarded as the high point and the essential spirit of this book. The spirit of critical reason that permeates this companion will stimulate and enhance any previous and most future reading of any of the cultural agents and issues here discussed as Latin America, with its uneven and multiple histories, is repositioned on the world's map.

## NOTE

1   Mario Valdés, "Introduction," in *Literary Cultures of Latin America: A Comparative History*, vol. I (Oxford University Press, 2004), p. xvii.

# Preamble: The Historical Foundation of Modernity/Coloniality and the Emergence of Decolonial Thinking

*Walter D. Mignolo*

## I

Readers familiar with current intellectual debates in Latin America, as well as among Latin Americanists and Latino and Latina scholars in the United States, are also familiar with the concept of "modernity/coloniality." Readers in other disciplines, especially those in Europe, may not be so familiar with these concepts. With this in mind, I will start by spelling out what is at stake here; and why it matters to the understanding of the spirit of this collection, as Sara Castro-Klaren explains in her Introduction.

In the many books and essays on "modernity" published since the late 1970s in Europe and in the United States, the word "coloniality" never appears. Modernity seems to be a totality ("what you see is what it is"), with its good and bad aspects, which is at the same time the inevitability of the unfolding of history. Confronted with the illusion of such a totality, scholars and intellectuals trying to find their way have coined terms such as "peripheral modernities," "subaltern modernities," "alternative modernities," "postcolonial modernities," and so forth. Fredric Jameson responded to this diversified scenario with a clear-cut "singular modernity" (Jameson, 2002). If we have a singular modernity, those who dwell in the periphery (intellectually and linguistically, not just physically), who do not belong to the Euro-American singular modernity, have to fight for the rights of people and events that have been forgotten, silenced, ignored, and neglected, to argue that, for example, Zara Yacob (a seventeenth-century Ethiopian philosopher) has to be legitimized as a philosopher of modernity (Teodros Kiros, 2005). One could argue (as did Fischer, 2004 and Chapter 15 in this volume) that the Haitian Revolution was disavowed as modernity. Such disavowal had enormous historical, ethical, political, and epistemic (or gnoseological, or whatever word one would like to use to keep to the fore the principles of knowledge that are always implied in any and every conception of the world) consequences.

Historically, the Haitian Revolution was not accorded the same importance as the bourgeois French Revolution, the white American revolution in the British colonies, or even the wars of independence fomented by Creoles of Spanish and Portuguese descent in South America after the Haitian Revolution. The disavowal is, in my argument, a direct consequence of the logic of coloniality: by 1804 blacks were not considered to have the same level of humanity by which they could have claimed and gained *freedom* by themselves. Slavery was unjust, many progressive European intellectuals claimed, and slaves were not "allowed" (by the white intelligentsia) to have their own freedom. That is why whites were ready to give them *liberty*, but not the freedom that a French citizen enjoyed. The Tupac Amaru uprising in Peru "failed," but for the Haitian revolutionary it was one episode in a genealogy of decolonization in the Americas. Perhaps, today, the elections in Bolivia should be read, on the one hand, as the continuation of Tupac Amaru (and previous uprisings in the Andes), and on the other, of the Haitian Revolution in the Caribbean. National and imperial histories do not invite us to think in terms of genealogies of freedom takers, blacks and Indians. They are, for imperial discourses, different "races." From a decolonial perspective, however, Indians and blacks were the first to suffer the consequences of imperial expansion and the formation of Eurocentrism (e.g., the superiority of Christians, and then of the whites).

These are some of the reasons why I will argue that "modernity" is a concept inextricably connected with the geopolitics and body-politics of the knowledge of white European and North Atlantic males. "Modernity," in other words, is not the natural unfolding of world history, but the regional narrative of the Eurocentric worldview. Once the narrative was put in place, and it flew all around the world as an integral part of imperial designs, the rest of the non-Euro-American world had to deal with the concept. Thus, we can understand why there is a proliferation of "alternative modernities" as well as Jameson's call to order to a "singular" modernity.

From the early 1990s the darker side of modernity started to emerge. Peruvian sociologist Aníbal Quijano made a statement in the very title of an article that marked a turning point in the politics and ethics of scholarship: "Coloniality and Modernity/ Rationality." A simple semiotic analysis reveals that "coloniality" is missing the equivalent of "rationality" that accompanies "modernity" and, secondly, that "coloniality" is something different from "modernity/rationality" (Quijano, 1991, 1992, 2000).

The concept opened up new vistas in relation to two dominant paradigms up to that point. One was represented by the Uruguayan and Peruvian critics, Ángel Rama and Antonio Cornejo Polar, who focused on the "lettered city" (Rama, 1982) and "cultural heterogeneity" (Cornejo Polar, 1994). The first placed the emphasis – inflecting his experiences of living on the South Atlantic coast of Latin America – on the political power of alphabetic writing, not just in literature but in the affairs of the state. The second brought forward his experiences of living in the Andes, where the presence of indigenous people shaped the histories of these mountains, as we witnessed in the presidential election of Evo Morales in Bolivia. Rama – in Uruguay, closer to France than to the Andes – took the lead in conceptualizing the "lettered city" from Michel Foucault's *Archeology of Knowledge* and *The Order of Things*. Cornejo Polar, in Peru (between Arequipa and Lima), and closer to the profound memories of Tawantinsuyu and the Spanish conquest, took his lead from another Peruvian thinker, José Carlos Mariátegui (in the 1920s), who was very aware and critical of Spanish colonial legacies as well as the US need for imperial domination in South America. And Cornejo Polar also took his lead from the exceptional Peruvian writer, José María Arguedas who, born into a Creole family, crossed the colonial divide and found himself growing up, literally, in the kitchen, where he found his cultural Indian mother and his cultural Indian brother. By "cultural" here I mean that it was through living with the Indian servants of his Creole "genetical" parents that Arguedas learned to love what he was taught to despise.

During the same years that Quijano published his article, Argentinean literary and cultural critic Néstor García Canclini published his ground-breaking book whose theme was the bringing together of hybridity and modernity (García-Canclini, 1989). García-Canclini and Jesús Martín Barbero (a Spaniard living in Colombia; Martín Barbero, 1987) introduced the cultural studies turn in Latin America. The "lettered city" was complemented by the prominence that new technology, television, and the media in general had in the research and works of Martín Barbero and García Canclini himself. Beatriz Sarlo (1988) in Argentina and Renato Ortiz (1985) in Brazil became associated with the former names. Sarlo moved from literature to popular culture; and divided her energy between scholarship and politics. Ortiz focused on globalization (as also did Canclini later on). What all these authors share is a concern with modernity in Latin America, its formation and transformation, its pros and cons.

"Coloniality of power" reactivated a spatial epistemic shift that had had its moments since the sixteenth century (Guamán Poma de Ayala, the Taky Onkoy; see Burga, 1988, Castro-Klaren, 1993 – indigenous uprisings during the colonial era, slave maroons, etc.) but that for several reasons had never been articulated in confrontation with the generalized idea that there is only one game in town, modernity; and that it could be peripheral or central, "real" or alternative; hegemonic or subaltern, and so on. Colonial history, imperial domination, and racism became cornerstones in describing the colonial matrix of power (e.g., coloniality of power). The shift was to bring to the fore, as another perspective, the interpretation of the Americas and of modern/colonial history.

Peruvian dissident José Carlos Mariátegui was one of Quijano's genealogical sources. The other was dependency theory. While dependency theory made the slavery between a "person" master and a "non-person" slave into a metaphor for the slavery between a master-country and a slave country, decolonial thinking extended the analysis to the sphere of knowledge (or, to make an analogy, to political epistemology) and subjectivity. If, beyond this analysis, dependency theory presupposed independence (or the sovereignty of the dependent country), the critical analysis of the colonial matrix of power leads to decolonial thinking: no longer independence within the same system of knowledge in which political theory and political economy are founded, but decoloniality starting from a questioning of the reasons and the interests that motivate the existing imperial rationality. Although the initial concept of coloniality of power was further developed by Quijano himself and others, the basic conceptual structure shared by all participants in the project consists of four interrelated sociohistorical domains glued together by the historical foundation of the modern concept of "racism." Let's take one step at a time. The four sociohistorical domains in which the logic of coloniality or the colonial matrix of power operate are the following:

1   *control of the economy* based on appropriations of land (and subsequently natural resources) and control of labor; financial control of indebted countries;

2   *control of authority*, based on the creation of imperial institutions during the foundation of the colonies or, more recently, by the use of military strength, forced destitution of presidents of countries to be controlled, the use of technology to spy on civil society, etc.

3   *control of gender and sexuality*, having the Christian and bourgeois secular family as a model and standard of human sexual heterosexual relations; and heterosexuality as the universal model established by God (sixteenth to eighteenth centuries), first, and then by Nature (from the nineteenth century to the present);

4   *control of knowledge and subjectivity* by assuming the theological foundation of knowledge, after the Renaissance, and the egological foundation of knowledge, after the Enlightenment; and by forming a concept of the modern and Western subject first dependent on the Christian God, and then on its own sovereigns, reason and individuality.

While dependency theorists made the economy (and its links with the state) the central and only focus, coloniality of power reoriented and enlarged the analytic dimension, and did not touch the imperial complicity between knowledge, racism, and patriarchy, the colonial matrix of power giving the subjective dimension a crucial role both in the formation and transformation of the colonial matrix of power as well as in the location of decolonial struggles – decoloniality of knowledge became the site of the struggle without which there can be no decolonization of the state nor of the economy. Domination is not just economic, but it operates at all levels of interrelation between the different domains of the colonial matrix or power. Why was the invention of racism (and the implied patriarchy) crucial to hold together and implement the colonial matrix of power? Race, according to North Atlantic scholarship (in France, England, and the United States) is a post-Enlightenment invention (Eze, 1997). For others, "race" and "racism," although anachronistic in the meaning they acquired in the nineteenth century, had already been conceived in the sixteenth century in the hierarchical classification of people as human beings. From the perspective of the colonial matrix of power, whether "race" or "caste" were the terms in which the chain of human beings was conceived is a moot point. There are, of course, historical differences in the theological vocabulary of the sixteenth century and the egological vocabulary of the late eighteenth and nineteenth centuries. The point is not "what is race?" Nor is it whether race exists, is a social construct, or is different from caste. The point is that Spanish men of letters and officers of the state established the historical foundation of a classification of human beings according to their religion or lack thereof. Thus, while Muslims and Jews had religions with firm historical bases, Indians and blacks in America had none. If in Spain blood was the sign that divided some people from others in the Spanish colonies, color became the signpost which distinguished white Christians from Indians and from blacks. In other words, in Spain blood connected human beings with religion and in the New World, blood connected human beings with skin color, barbarian mores, and human underdevelopment (e.g., Indians were on a par with women and children). *Mestizos*, mulattos, and Zambos were the result of the mixing of the three prime human stocks, Europeans, Africans, and Indians from Tawantinsuyu to Anahuac. What matters, then, is not whether these three stocks were caste or race. What matters is that "racism" was established as a classificatory system in which (a) the classification itself was determined by Christian and European men; (b) they defined themselves as superior in relation to the other groups classified (by religion, by blood, and by color); (d) since other human groups were denied their possibility of classification, only Christian European men could determine that they were the point of arrival of the human race.

If, then, the classificatory system that ranks human beings was established by white European Christians, they were men and, therefore, women also were left out of the locus of enunciation that classified non-European and Christian human beings. Women and children became the point of reference to describe the inferiority of non-Europeans. Patriarchy, Christianity, and white blood established the epistemic foundation of modernity and the colonial matrix of power: the justification to convert, appropriate, and exploit, and justified the expendability of human lives that were not needed or that refused to be integrated to the system; a system known today as Western modernity and capitalism grounded in Western Christianity (Catholic and Protestant, but not Eastern Orthodox Christians). Because each domain in which control was to be performed responds to the same purpose or global and imperial designs, each level is interrelated with the other three. Just devote a few minutes to focusing on one level and ask yourself how each related to the other. I assure you that you won't need instructions to find those connections! Last but not least, the imposition of the colonial matrix of power in each of its levels, in their interconnection, implies that societal forms of life and economy which the juggernaut of the colonial matrix of power confronts are pushed aside or erased – but not completely eradicated. And we are witnessing today, particularly among indigenous movements in South America and the Islamic world, that human subjectivities (which is not one and universal) die hard. Muslims and Indians have been relegated to the shelf of "traditions" in the rhetoric of modernity, in order to justify their repression or suppression. But today – surprise! – Indians are alive and well, and so are Muslims. Evo Morales was elected by an overwhelming majority, and so was Hamas. Democracy can no longer be managed by liberal political principles. Nor can socialism be managed by Marxist political principles.

Aspects of Spanish colonial literature and culture were fully-fledged instruments of colonization: they contributed to the control of subjectivity and the control of knowledge – some more than others. Sepúlveda clearly justified violence to control economy and authority. De Vitoria was a Christian "liberal" (in terms that will emerge from the secular revolution) who worked hard on theological principles of international law. Las Casas was a defender of social justice but, like his contenders, he pushed aside subjectivity and did not take into account the input of the indigenous population. Guamán Poma de Ayala was one, and today the best-known case of decolonial thinking. He stood up and proposed to Philip III the need for a new chronicle in order to organize new forms of government that he labeled *"buen gobierno."*

By this I mean that modernity/coloniality is an imperial package that, of necessity, generates decolonial thinking and action. But actions by themselves cannot be decolonial if they are not conceptualized as such. And decolonial conceptualization means to denounce the colonial matrix of power and to work toward forms of social organization that reinscribe the economy, political organization, gender and sexual relations, and subjectivity and knowledge of those who are being denied, who are declared racially inferior, and whose concept of social organization is considered lacking and, later on, as traditional.

The colonial matrix of power (or coloniality of power) – contrary to the alphabetic paradigm of the lettered city or the technological and communicative paradigm of cultural studies, mentioned above – may seem detached from the question of literature and culture. My argument is that if that is the case, it is just an illusion owing to the change of terrain that the coloniality of matrix is proposing. This change of terrain is a particular kind of decolonial critique. To simplify matters, I would propose the following. While Ángel Rama on the one hand, and Nestor García-Canclini, Beatriz Sarlo, and Jesús Martín Barbero on the other practiced a certain version of what we could call "critical theory" (in the case of Martín Barbero, directly connected to the Frankfurt School; García-Canclini draws from Pierre Bourdieu and Beatriz Sarlo, cultural studies in Birmingham and particularly from Raymond Williams), for Ángel Rama it was Michel Foucault who offered him the tools to conceive the archeology of knowledge in South America linked to the "lettered city" (parallel to what Said was doing at the same time in the United States).

At this juncture, Cornejo Polar's concept of "cultural heterogeneity" and Quijano's "coloniality of power" parted and opened up another paradigm. Cornejo Polar, like Quijano, found the seed of their feeling and thinking in Mariátegui and the long history of Indian, Spanish, and Creole tensions in the Andes. While Cornejo Polar has José María Arguedas as his second source of inspiration (which is not alien to Quijano's intellectual trajectory), Quijano continues the legacy of dependency theory, which he reformulates and expands in the colonial matrix of power. Cornejo Polar and Quijano departed from the genealogy of thought that nourished the lettered city as well as cultural studies; and indirectly departed also from postcolonialism. While cultural studies, in Latin America, found their genealogical source of inspiration in European thinkers, Cornejo Polar and Quijano grounded theirs in the intellectual and political history of Latin American thinkers. In this regard, both shared the drive that nourished indigenous and Afro-Caribbean intellectuals who found the source of their critical decolonial thinking first, in their own history of oppression, and secondly, in the history of slavery.

Coloniality of power as an *analytic concept* builds on a critical genealogy of thought that, in Latin America, emerged as a decolonial impulse with variegated faces. As I have already mentioned, this includes Mariátegui and dependency theory, but also the theology and philosophy of liberation that emerged in the late 1960s, and the strong presence of Frantz Fanon (1961). Fanon contributed to the familiarity of the concept of "decolonization." While "decolonization" during the Cold War and in Asia and Africa described the struggle for independence in the British and French colonies, Colombian sociologist Orlando Fals Borda (1988) proposed the decolonization of the social sciences. Paradoxically enough, Fals Borda was proposing to decolonize the social sciences at the very moment in which the social sciences (as a disciplinary and institutional formation) were being propelled into Latin America from the United States and embraced, by local "scientists" in Argentina, Chile, Mexico, Brazil, and Colombia as a sign of "development and modernization." The face of modernization and modernity was shown in the program of industrialization from the 1950s to the end of the 1960s, and the social sciences were part of the package: the pretense or illusion that, like in the First World, the Third World will have industrialization and a modern society needing the social sciences for their analysis and management!! Fals Borda thought that the introduction of the social sciences was, indeed, a particular sector of the colonial matrix of power that Quijano describes as "the coloniality of knowledge" (Quijano, 1992a) Thus, implicit in the *analytical concept* of the colonial matrix of power (or coloniality of power) is the *programmatic concept* of decoloniality. From Fals Borda on we are no longer talking about decolonization in the sense of the takeover of the state by the local elite (Creole, as in South America, or native, as in Asia and Africa), but of decolonization of knowledge and of being; which imply a decolonial subject that shifts political theory and political economy in another direction, non-capitalist and non-communist. From the perspective of decolonial thinking and projects, liberal capitalism and communist/statism are two coins of the same Western and post-Enlightenment currency. Two coins of Western imperial expansion: Western European and US imperialisms on the one hand, and Soviet Union imperialisms on the other. Decolonization of knowledge, however, does not mean that the state is no longer in question, but that the state, as controller of authority, depends on the enactment of the conception of knowledge (political theory). In Bolivia today we are witnessing, first and foremost, a radical decolonial epistemic shift and its effects on the organization of the state and the handling of the economy. Let us look at two examples of how decolonization of knowledge and decolonization of being are of crucial importance to the decolonization of the control of economy and of authority.

For liberal capitalism, land is private property and the individual (or the corporation) the sovereign proprietor. For the Marxist version of communism (by which I mean without the sense of community we find among the indigenous peoples around the world or in the Islamic concept of subjectivity and community), land cannot be private property (owned by individuals or corporations) but it is property of the state given to the community. For indigenous people land cannot be property at all, neither private nor of the state. This is one of the central principles in Evo Morales's negotiation of natural gas and coca leaves, products of the land but not the land in itself. For liberal or Marxist political theory, the structure of the state is the same. The emphases are in the relationships between the state and the economy and in the function of the state in one or the other regime, democratic or socialist. For Morales, the state is neither. It is an empty structure that has to be filled with agents whose relationships with civil and political society are not that of the state functionary that "represents" sectors who are detached from their social and life experience (except when those represented are the economic elite to whom the "representers" belong, who have vested interests). This model of liberal political theory that, in the Soviet Union, was translated into clientelism and party membership reached its critical point in Bolivia; and Morales is restructuring the state precisely in that direction: that is why he will have as Minister of Foreign Relations a lawyer and activist in human rights; and as Minister of Education and Culture an Aymara intellectual and activist who wrote a book on the communal system as an alternative to the (neo-)liberal system (Patzi Paco, 2004). Community here is not a borrowing from Marxism/communism (and even less so from communitarian liberalism), but a recasting of the communitarian model of indigenous histories in the Andes. How are we to interpret Latin American literatures and cultures with this turn of events?

The notion of "modernity/coloniality" is an antidote to all previous debates. It de-links from the one-sided rhetoric of modernity (like the bright side of the moon that leaves its other side hidden) by introducing "coloniality" as its constitutive but hidden side. The hegemonic idea of one-sided modernity generates parallel alternatives: peripheral modernity, subaltern modernity, alternative modernities, and so on. All of them leave untouched the very imperial logic sustaining the idea of modernity. Coloniality, instead, reveals its darker side and opens up decolonial avenues for thinking, living, and acting – that there is a *singular modernity* (that singularity is not just modernity but *modernity/coloniality*), a singular modernity formed by a variegated histories of imperial/colonial relations. Therefore it is not necessary to invent alternative modernities, or peripherals, or posts, or subalterns, because that is what modernity/coloniality is: the triumphal rhetoric of salvation (by conversation, civilization, development, and market democracy) that needs inevitably to unfold (and to hide) the logic of coloniality. Interestingly enough for this *Companion*, modernity/coloniality is the vocabulary of a narrative that, contrary to the single narrative of modernity, has its historical foundation in the Atlantic world of the sixteenth and seventeenth centuries (Western Europe, Western Africa, and the emergence of the Americas), instead of the European Renaissance and Enlightenment alone. This Eurocentered narrative, of course, has its right to exist, since it corresponds with the experience of Euro-American histories, but it does not have the right to be the narrative for the rest of the world, except in its imperial/colonial dimension. "Modernity" is a word that, just like "democracy" and many others, has a global scope owing to imperial expansion over five centuries. What then can be done?

Instead of conceiving alternative or peripheral modernities, what are needed are alternatives *to* modernity; that is, to the single narrative of modernity by a subject that is not universal and disincorporated but that has been and continued to be geo-historically and biographically dwelling in the history of Euro-America. If the narrative of a single modernity or of modernity at large anchors its locus of enunciation in Christian theological and secular egopolitics of knowledge (e.g., the hegemony of theology in the European Renaissance and of egology in the European enlightenment), the narrative of modernity/coloniality shifts the geography of reason and anchors its locus of enunciation in the decolonial politics of knowledge. Such politics needs to de-link from the imperial dominance of theological and egological categories of thought in which all structures of knowledge (from the European Renaissance to the Enlightenment and beyond) have theology and Cartesian egology as their basis. Decolonial knowledge shifts the reason and rationality that sustain and motivate knowledge.

For example, Jamaican scholar and intellectual Sylvia Wynter analyzes Frantz Fanon's concept of "sociogenesis." Sociogenesis is a way of de-linking from the onto-logical scientific limits of phylogenesis and ontogenesis. It brings another dimension to our understanding of what it means to be "human." "Scientific" discourse assumes that imperial definitions of "humanity" are what "we know" humanity is. What we understand by human and humanity are constructions of the European Renaissance and Enlightenment, based on the paradigmatic model of the European heterosexual male, which Leonardo da Vinci's Vitrubian Man[1] exemplified perfectly. What scien-tific phylogenetic and ontogenic analysis provide are just material information of a preconceived notion of Man and Human. Sociogenesis shows the imperial and Euro-centered assumptions of this notion, and opens up toward "the Human, after Man," as Wynter has it. For Chicana scholar and intellectual Chela Sandoval, epistemic de-linking is located in the limits of the modern and postmodern notion of the "subject" – the crisis of the modern subject announced by David Laing, Michel Foucault, and Fredric Jameson comes as a surprise to someone like Sandoval, who dwells in the experiences and legacies of "fractured colonial subjects" that are totally unnoticed by internal and regional European postmodern speculations. For Maori anthropologist, intellectual, and activist Linda T. Smith, the moment of de-linking is located in the "method." In tandem with Sandoval's "methodology of the oppressed," Smith focuses on "decolonizing methodology." Decolonizing methodology implies a de-linking from anthropological agendas which have been formed by the interest of anthropology as a discipline and anthropologists as academic scholars, to agendas that emerge from the decolonial needs of indigenous communities. albeit independent of each other.[2]

And allow me to repeat, out loud this time, a statement I have made several times but which has not yet been heeded: indigenous intellectuals do not represent all the indigenous people in the same way that white intellectuals do not represent all whites and women intellectuals do not represent all women, as queer intellectuals do not represent all queers. The statement is not heard because the concept of "representa-tion" is on the way. What I am saying is simply that Wynter's, Sandoval's, and Smith's arguments and claims are anchored in local histories of slavery, Aboriginals in New Zealand and Australia and Chicanos and Chicanos, in ways similar to which Foucault's, Arendt's, or Jameson's arguments and claims do not represent all homosexuals in France, Jews in Germany, or Marxists in the United States.

After Wynter, Sandoval, and Smith we can say that decolonial thinking based on the analytic "modernity/coloniality" is an alternative *to* modernity (as Arturo Escobar puts it) because the locus of enunciation has shifted to inhabit other bodies and other geo-histories (the colonial ones); not because "colonial modernities" are a different version of a paradigmatic and zero-sum of a neutral modernity. This is a radical and needed shift in the geography of reason. Without it (a shift that is a de-linking) we will remain locked in the battle between the universals and the particular, the center and the periphery, modernity and alternative modernities, etc., allowing some of us to believe that we inhabit a house of knowledge independent from the particular national-imperial language in which we think and write; independent of material inscriptions of history in our bodies and, finally, that we – as objective thinkers – have to be vigilant and denounce the fact that indigenous intellectuals do not represent all the Indians (and that Derrida does not represent all Algerians)!

The variety of alternative modernities is to the geopolitical epistemic spectrum what the hyphen is to the body-politics of knowledge. Let's read Lewis Gordon's observations on the social sphere of blackness:

> Why, we may ask, is being black treated as antipathetic to being an American? This leads to the notion of irreconcilable doubleness, whereby being black does not equal being an American . . . the mainstream (i.e., White) American self-image is one of supposedly being an original site from which blacks play only the role of imitation. To be an imitation is to stand as secondary to another standard – namely the original or the prototype. We see this view of blacks in popular music, where the adjective "black" is added to things white to suggest imitation: black Jesus, black Mozart, Ms. Black America, and so on. (Gordon, 2006: 8).

The analogy is obvious: any "alternative" is derivative from the standard model of modernity, just as blackness (or any other hyphenated American) is derivative in relation to the standard idea of America. Even "Latin" America is derivative in relation to America. Gordon has put the finger on the body-politics of knowledge: aren't black philosophers just white philosophers who bring the naturalization of the hyphen to the level of coloniality of knowledge and coloniality of being?

Thus the variegated proposal for alternative modernities goes hand in hand with the hyphenated categorization of people along ethnic (and racialized) lines. Both the global distribution of alternative modernities in relation to the standard model and the global distribution of hyphenated people who do not quite fit the national and racial standard of a given country, as well as the global distribution of people by continents (e.g., Africa identified with blacks, Asia with "yellows," and the Americas and the Caribbean with indigenous people, and the population of European descent and sub-Saharan African descent) are caught in the web of modernity/coloniality and

in the racial matrix of imperial/colonial power. In other words, the question of whether
there is one or several modernities brings to the fore the geopolitics of knowledge,
while the question of people of color and continental divide (recently mobilized by
massive migrations from poor to richer countries) put forward the bio-graphic (body)-
politics of knowledge. This brings sensing into epistemology and, therefore, aesthetics
– aiesthesis, before the eighteenth century, refers to the senses and not to a particular
sensibility related to what, in a given culture, is considered beautiful. Literature and
culture are woven into the matrix and "Latin America" (or any other region) is
not only an economic and political demarcation, but a subjective construction (of
particular agents) as well as a source of subjective formations (of particular
subjects).

Modernity/coloniality (Quijano, 1992; Mignolo, 2006) has been proposed as a
departure and a de-linking from the illusion that there is *only one* totality that shall
be seen either as a single modernity or as a standard modernity and its alternatives.
The thesis here is that *there is no modernity without coloniality; coloniality is constitutive of
modernity and not derivative.* There is a single modernity/coloniality that is the consequence of the geopolitical differential distribution of epistemic, political, economic,
and aesthetic (e.g., sensing, subjectivity) power. Thus, modernity/coloniality is held
together by the *colonial differences*: colonial differences, epistemic and ontological, are
constructed in the rhetoric of modernity – inferior beings (colonial ontological difference), racially or sexually, are beings not well suited for knowledge and understanding (colonial epistemic difference).[3] Modernity/coloniality, in other words, is what
unites, *like conjoined twins in a differential power relation*, Spain and the New World,
England and India, the United States and Iraq; what unites whites and blacks, whites
and Indians, whites and Muslims, white and yellow races. Would it then be possible
to think of another type of relations between the New World, India, and Iraq and
between blacks, Indians, Muslims, and the yellow race that does not depend on imperial whiteness? This is one move proposed by decolonial thinking as a programmatic
of which the very concept of modernity/coloniality and the colonial matrix of power
is its analytic counterpart. Which means that the very concept of coloniality of power
is already a decolonial move that, subsequently, opens up the gates for imagining
possible futures rather than just resting on the celebratory moment of critical explanation of what the social world really is like.

History seen in this way, when we ask whether there is a single or multiple (and
alternative) modernity, is a moot question. Thus, is "modernity" a concept of a self-
serving narrative constructed on the experience, desires, and expectations of a regional
group of people identified with the European Renaissance and European Enlightenment, or an objective historical period independent of the narrative that describes and
explains it? Because the emphasis of all narratives (either celebratory or critical) of
modernity privileges the enunciated over the enunciation, modernity became an historical agent itself, an entity, a thing, a cloud that, like the fog of Chernobyl, moves
with the winds of imperial expansion. When modernity as a historical agent or as the
codified moment of the historical modern self (the momentum that brings salvation,
happiness, civilization, progress and development, and democracy) is pinched in its

incantatory effects and the invisible hands moving the puppets become visible, we realize that what is left is, once again, a very geopolitical- and body-political-anchored locus of enunciation that celebrates the universality of the enunciated.


## II


A companion to "Latin American literature and culture" demands – today – that we revisit several assumptions I mapped out and critiqued in Section I. We will revisit these first assumptions because the very idea of the colonial period and of modern Latin America (that is, the period of nation-building in the nineteenth century) are mixed up with some views and conceptions of modernity, as is the single movement of world history. What, then, can "coloniality" do for us? How can this concept help us in organizing this "companion"?

Let us begin by exploring how our perception of "Latin American literature and culture" may change with regard to a the presumption that there is one single modernity and that some modernities may be peripheral, alternative, or subaltern; and that there is an America that is "Latin" in relation to a totality, America, which is not "Latin" – somehow similar to the logic that Lewis Gordon unveiled for the hyphenated Afro-America or black Mozart. Although "Latin" America is a concept introduced in the second half of the nineteenth century, we shall start from this concept because the present companion is of "Latin" American literature and culture. Thus, the standard perception could be described and summarized as both an homogeneous "culture" opposed to the Anglo component of the Americas, as Samuel Huntington recast it after Hegel's canonical distinction between the two Americas; or as the homogeneous "culture" that defines the identity of the people that identified themselves as "Latin" Americans and of which its literature is a fundamental manifestation of the imaginary of sub-continental identification.

How would things look from the perspective of the colonial matrix of power? The canonical "colonial period" (ca. 1492–1810) or "de la colonia a la independencia," as Mariano Picón Salas canonized it, was first dominated by the Spaniards and Portuguese and then by the Creole elites of Iberian descent. Until recently (perhaps since Murra and Adorno's edition of Guamán Poma de Ayala's *Nueva Corónica y Buen Gobierno*, 1982, as well as the Franklin Pease edition in *Biblioteca Ayucucho*, vol. 75, 1980), indigenous "literary" and cultural production were hardly taken into account. If they were, a couple of texts like *The Popol Wuj* appeared in a short section of literary and cultural histories, as *pre-Columbian* literature. *Popol Wuj* is a text composed in alphabetic writing around 1550 and only discovered at the beginning of the eighteenth century (see Chapter 3 in this volume). Histories of Latin American literatures and cultures have been written, since the nineteenth to almost the end of the twentieth century, by Creoles of Spanish or Portuguese descent for whom the history of "Latin" America began with the discovery of the region, and whatever was there before.

What do these examples tell us? First, and in general, they are particular cases of the control of knowledge and subjectivity (and, of course, gender and sexuality). Think about Sepúlveda's argument in favor of the just war; a clear case of control of authority, denying the enemy even the possibility of argument. Just war opens up the space for the creation of administrative institutions, pushing aside existing forms of social organization because dominant narratives declared them to be barbarians or weak people easily persuaded by the Devil. Think of Francisco de Vitoria. He was working toward a system of international law that would allow Spaniards to own land without affecting the rights of the Indians. John Locke, in the next century, would express the same concern for the interest of the emerging British Empire. Indians' relation to the land, and the fact that landownership was alien to them, did not cross the minds of either Vitoria or Locke. Las Casas was concerned with excessive violence and also with morals. The *pecado nefando* (sodomy) in which Indians indulged was Las Casas's nightmare. And of course, Spaniards never understood the complementarity of gender (the sun and the moon) in Indian cosmology. Christian cosmology was blinded by original sin and the virginity of Mary as principles to control subjectivities of Christians and non-Christians alike. Las Casas's contributions to the formation of the colonial matrix of power was in the area of gender and sexuality, and knowledge and subjectivity. Sepúlveda and Vitoria contributed instead to the institutionalization of control and authority; and Vitoria to the control of economy and authority though international law. The three of them pushed aside the statements, beliefs, ideas, principles of knowledge, social and political organization, subjective formations, and so on, of indigenous intellectuals like themselves, and indigenous people in general, at all levels. Ethical and political questions remained within the colonial matrix of power itself and the debates, among imperial agents, of how to cause least harm to the Indians, respecting as much as possible their rights to property, but not to the point to which Spaniards would be deprived of what they thought they deserved. Guamán Poma de Ayala was in confrontation with the colonial matrix of power, and his chronicle, political treatise, and model of a new government remains the foundation of decolonial thinking. Guamán Poma de-linked from the rules of the game that Sepúlveda, Las Casas, and Vitoria were playing and proposed new rules for good government. His proposal was a decolonial project articulated in border thinking. The Spanish would not listen to him. The situation does not prove that Guamán Poma was wrong, rather it proves that the Spanish were deaf and blind to the possibility of an Indian having anything of interest to propose; or to the possibility that Indians had rights to make any claim (see Chapters 5 and 6 in this volume).

Apart from a few Aztec and Mayan codices, nothing was written by indigenous people that was not "colonial." Most of the extant codices were produced under Spanish rules. Indigenous production coexisted and was mixed up with the cultural production (texts, architecture, music, painting, etc.) of the Spanish and Portuguese invaders. However, the same logic that made "modernity" visible (and modernity meant European history in all its manifestations) at the same time also made non-European histories and ways of thinking invisible. Placing the *Popol Wuj* as a pre-Hispanic or pre-Columbian text was one such move. From the beginning of the 1980s, the situation started to change and art historians, anthropologists, ethno-historians, and literary and cultural critics contested previous history. In their contestations, they helped make visible one of the consequences of coloniality of knowledge and of being – to relegate, silence, and dismiss the knowledge and subjective formations of indigenous people throughout the Americas. The situation is similar with people of African descent, and today – although on a different scale – with Latinos and Latinas in the United States.

Parallel to the historical work of European scholars and intellectuals, indigenous people began to assert themselves as human beings, intellectuals, activists, and political leaders, taking their destiny in their own hands. Their self-affirmation did not come so much in "literature" (as was the case for Creoles, *mestizos/as*, and immigrants of European descent who flocked to the continent from the second half of the nineteenth century) but in intellectual and political terms – first they requested land rights, then linguistic and cultural rights and, finally, epistemic rights. Indigenous video-makers, like CEFREC in Bolivia and the *Amawtay Wasi* (House of Wisdom, also called Universidad Intercultural de los Pueblos y Naciones Indígenas del Ecuador), are two outstanding achievements of epistemological dimension (Amawtay Wasi, 2004). The first, because video makers are claiming the right to knowledge by bypassing the lettered city and alphabetic writing that served well both colonial administrators and officers of the colonial nation-states (i.e., when the logic of coloniality was rearticulated through the nation-states controlled by Creoles of European descent). The second, because it is a claim that, taking away the monopoly of the colonial viceroyalties and, later, that of the colonial nation-states, higher education can be controlled through theology and egology; that is, the epistemic authority of God and of secular reason. Sor Juana was caught at the critical period of that transition, as a woman (see Chapter 10). But this is not all, because the indigenous impact on the literary domain emerged as a complement to video makers and the planning of *Amawtay Wasi* (see Chapter 32). Today, the indigenous social movements in the Andes and the presidency of Evo Morales in Bolivia, the reestablishment of the Zapatistas in Southern Mexico, the undeniable presence of indigenous ways of life, of thinking, of doing, of acting, are repressed beneath the rhetoric of modernity. Modernity/coloniality is a coin with two faces, the same in the center as the periphery. In other words, center and periphery are so because modernity/coloniality became the rhetoric of salvation and the logic of oppression that managed the world order in the past 500 years. In this regard, the indigenous contributions to global history made and being made by indigenous people in South (Latin?) America goes hand in hand with the revival of indigenous struggles in North America, and parallels the indigenous struggle in New Zealand and Australia. The authors of "el boom de la literatura latinoamericana," progressive writers and intellectuals of the 1960s and 1970s, are disoriented. Mario Vargas Llosa lost his balance after his defeat by Fujimori and seems to understand less and less of what Hugo Chávez and Evo Morales stand for, whether one is for or against their politics. Writing in favor of Nación Camba, in Bolivia, and disparaging the figure of Morales, Vargas Llosa epitomizes the radical bent toward the right of the Creole/*blancoide* intelligentsia of Latin America. A recent article by Carlos Fuentes, not as extreme as Vargas Llosa's, reveals that "Latin American" [*blancoide*] writers have a hard time dealing with the emergence of the indigenous population (at all levels of social life). In compensation for the history of the "boom" and its ideology residing in the past, we are witnessing the reemergence of indigenous intellectuals who are rewriting their own history, rewriting the analysis of society, and reviving forgotten indigenous intellectuals. The fact is that Indians are not exactly Latin. These writers have not yet pay attention to the black "menace." But it is coming.

When Mariano Picón Salas entitled his book *De la conquista a la independencia* (From conquest to independence) in a way that became the frame of 300 years of history in Spanish and Portuguese America, continental and insular, he did not include the Haitian Revolution (1804) in his scheme. The problem was that Haiti was inhabited mainly by blacks of African descent. And in the mainstream mentality, blacks (like Indians) are not exactly Latin, and certainly not Spanish or Portuguese-Americans either. It was a black colony that became an independent country. The language was French/Creole, while "Latin" America was forged upon the image of two defeated empires and their respective languages, Spain and Spanish, and Portugal and Portuguese. Martinique, Guadeloupe, and Haiti were left out of the loop and, for that reason, Aimé Césaire and Frantz Fanon were not included in the "Latin" American canon. For the same reason, writers such as Afro-Colombian Manuel Zapata Olivella and Afro-Costa-Rican Quincey Duncan were left out of the picture and are only recently receiving the attention they deserve. The US State Department is more attentive to the emergence of Afro-Latinity than scholars, intellectuals, and journalists in "Latin" America.[4]

For historical reasons that one can guess at but which have not been explored in detail, the French and British Caribbean have a very visible and strong intellectual tradition that Padget Henry recently summarized as "Afro-Caribbean philosophy" (Henry, 2003). Afro-Caribbean philosophy is different from European continental philosophy. While in Europe philosophy has its academic and disciplinary rules, Caribbean philosophy comes in all forms: literature, oral tradition, Bob Marley, voodoo, and Rastafarianism; political essays by Fanon and Césaire; historical narratives like C. L. R. James's *The Black Jacobins* (1938). All this potent intellectual, literary, and cultural production is constantly left out of the "Latin" literary and cultural mentality, that is, of Spanish and Portuguese stock in languages and memories. In that regard, do not ask what "Latin" American literature and culture *are*. Ask and look for what they *do*. And what they do is to enact a politics of inclusion and exclusion.

# III

What is the job, then, of a companion to Latin American literature and culture? The answer is not inscribed in some transcendental place, of course, but comes from the needs in the field and the decision of the editors and contributors as to how to fulfill them.

It could be helpful to compare the recent *Blackwell Companion to African-American Studies* with *The Blackwell Companion to Latin American Literature and Culture*. The first has a disciplinary orientation marked by the word "studies," while the second emphasizes the contour of a fuzzy domain mapped by a set of practices, "literature and culture," in a geopolitical space (Latin America). However, as we have seen above, "Latin" in this context is the sphere of "white Latin" in South America and the Caribbean, in contradistinction to Indians and Afro. "Latinity," in other words, is the hegemonic literature and culture that affirmed its identity, repressing, on the one hand, "Indianity" and "Africanity" and, on the other, confronting "Anglicity." In between all of these, the emergence of Latino/as in the United States and Afro-Latinos forces a question mark on what are we considering at this point to be "Latin American literature and culture," and why.

The "why" is a question that is readily addressed in *The Blackwell Companion to African-American Studies*. In the introduction Gordon and Gordon pressed the question of method and scholarly rigor as they moved "from foci on social scientific approaches to explorations in the humanities and now, in some instances, to the life sciences, such as biology, medicine and epistemology" (2006: xxi). The authors observe that, after the civil rights movement, proponents of black power saw their task as economic, political, and pedagogical. They continue by noting that this orientation "took the form of black communities seeking control over their own and their children's education, which led to discussion not only of the *form* and *structure* of that education but also its *content*." And they conclude with a programmatic statement: "We would call this effort the goal of *decolonizing the minds of black people*" (Gordon and Gordon, 2006: xxi).

"Decolonizing the mind" is not a project alien to literature (and therefore, of culture). As such, it was articulated in the mid-1980s by African writer Ngugi wa Thiong'o (1986). Neither is it alien to "Latin American culture." "Decolonization of scholarship" was one of the fighting fronts – as I already mentioned – of Colombian sociologist Orlando Fals Borda and, in a parallel fashion, of Paolo Freyre's "methodology of the oppressed." And Quijano proposed "decolonization of knowledge" as a logical consequence of the analysis of the logic of coloniality and as epistemological reconstruction. He wrote:

> The critique of the European paradigm of rationality/modernity is indispensable, even urgent. But the critique will be doubtful if it only consists of a simple negation of all its categories . . . It is necessary to extricate oneself from the linkages between rationality/modernity and coloniality, first of all, and definitely from all power which is not constituted by free decisions made by free people. It is the instrumental use of reason to control power, of colonial power in the first place, which produced distorted paradigms of knowledge and spoiled the liberating promises of modernity. The alternative, then, is clear: the obliteration of the coloniality of world power. Epistemological decolonization is needed, first of all, to clear the way for new intercultural communication; for interchanging experiences and meaning as the basis of another rationality which may legitimately pretend to some universality. Noting is less rational, finally, than the pre-

tension that the specific cosmic vision of a particular ethnicity should be taken universal rationality. (Quijano, 1992: 19)

Could the *Blackwell Companion to Latin American Literature and Culture* be a decolonizing project? Not all its contributors will endorse such a project. Each author has her and his own answer. Whatever the individual responses are, the reader will have their own agenda in mind. Most likely, that agenda will be guided by some naturalized principles or ideas of what Latin America is and what its literature and culture should be. In this case, the reader may expect to know "more" about an existing entity called Latin America. I would like to close by inviting the reader to shift their presuppositions and, instead of thinking that there is an entity called Latin America whose literature and culture they will learn more about, to think instead that the literature and culture that this volume brings forward is part of the construction and survival of an artificial entity called Latin America. The epistemic shift I am suggesting is already underway. Once the colonial matrix of power is identified, its decolonization is a necessary consequence. The unveiling of the colonial matrix of power, in Quijano's ground-breaking work, is in itself a decolonial move. The colonial matrix of power could not have been revealed from the very epistemic imperial principles that produced it, even if those very principles were deployed to perform a critique of their results. Marx's brilliant unveiling of the logic of capital, for example, was an operation performed from the very principles of knowledge that brought capitalism into existence, and from the very perspective of European history. That is, Marx was conformed by the history of Europe and by the marks that that history left on his body – Marx's critical thought is, just ;like anybody else's, grounded in the historical marks left in his body by the position he occupied in his society. Quijano had a different grounding, both in his body and in the history of his society. He is not German and his first language (in the sense of *idioma*) is not German. His body and historical experience carry the mark of a particular imperial/colonial history, that of the Andes. And that means that Quijano experienced imperial capitalism in the history of the colonies, while Marx experienced capitalism in its very core. This is one example of decolonial epistemic shift in its geopolitical domain. I am inviting the reader to choose his or her seat when looking at the literature and cultures of "Latin" America. I will offer, in closing, a few more possibilities.

Let's think of Fanon's skin and Anzaldúa's borderland (Mignolo, 2005a; Milian, 2006). In both cases there is a decolonial shift in the body-politics and the geopolitics of knowledge. Anzaldúa's borderland (geopolitical shift) goes hand in hand with the "new *mestiza* consciousness" (body-political shift, which is simultaneously racial and sexual). If the borderland is the "colonial wound – 'una herida abierto' where the Third World grates against the first and bleeds" (Anzaldúa, 1987: 25), then the conjunction of borderland (geopolitics) and bio-graphy (gender–sexuality–ethnicity) is not a social phenomenon "to be studied" (by whom, from where, under which epistemic presuppositions?), but a locus of epistemic enunciation that now coexists in conflictive struggle with Cartesian overarching principles in which reason has no geohistorical location and is not incarnated in the gender, sexuality, and race (racism) in which the body is conformed. Similar observations could be made about Fanon. The border between black skin and white mask is the border of the colonial difference at all levels, but also at the epistemic level: knowledge and epistemology are located in the white-skinned body, not in the black. And that is why the black-skinned body has two kinds of options: to become white or, like Fanon, to unveil the colonial racial matrix and its epistemic consequences. That is the reason why Fanon began his argument addressing the question of language, in which epistemology and knowledge are located. Before Fanon, Afro-American W. E. B. Dubois conceptualized as "double consciousness" a phenomenon and an experience that, for Fanon, was the borderland and the new *mestiza*, and the space where the black skin grates with the white skin and bleeds. But also in Bolivia, between 1960 and 1975, Aymara intellectual Fausto Reinaga made a solitary although monumental effort to shift both the geopolitics and the body-politics of knowledge. Rejecting Christian and liberal modes of oppression also rejected Marxism as a mode of liberation. He reclaimed the negated and silenced perspective of indigenous people, as valid as the one of European people in their variety (Christians, liberals, and Marxists) as well as the clones of the European variety (e.g., the Creoles of European descent in Bolivia.) I could go on and on, bringing to the fore other examples from Native Americans in the United States, the Fourth Nation in Canada, or Aboriginals in New Zealand and Australia; from the past of black radical intellectuals in the Atlantic and in Africa. And I could also look at the genealogy of decolonial thinking in the Middle East, the Mahgreb, or India to show that the epistemic hegemony of Europe is ending its cycle and remains one epistemology among others. "Latin" American literature and culture can of course be looked at from *the traditional epistemology of modernity*; but there are other and more convenient games in town for people who would prefer to decolonize themselves and contribute to the decolonization of the world including, of course, as Fanon insisted, the imperial colonizer themselves; colonizer either from the left, the right, or the center.

In sum, while the European intellectual tradition had in St. Thomas Aquinas and René Descartes two monuments of the rules of knowing (and understanding) and knowledge (and the understood), rules that structured the hegemonic and imperial perspective on the world, in all of its domains (from political economy to political theory, from religious believers to Freud's unconscious), the decolonial tradition of which the genealogy of its thoughts is yet unknown but not at all nonexistent (just silenced by the monuments of European epistemic imperialism), is on the march. Latin America itself was conceived from the European perspective, even when the Creoles from European descent, in South America, acquiesced (Mignolo, 2005b). Now a shift is taking place, the decolonial shift, that put forward coexisting paradigms in which denied rationalities rearticulate themselves on the unintended consequences of Western epistemology. Aztec and Guamán Poma, Ottobah Cugoano, Frantz Fanon, Fausto Reinaga, Gloria Anzaldúa, and the Zapatistas are some of the signposts of the decolonial project.

Today it is obvious that "Latin" America was an ideological and political project of the elites, Creoles of Spanish descent, and mixed-blood, European-minded *mestizos* (Bautista, 2005). The "literature" that emerged from that project covers a wide spectrum, from internal colonialism to decolonial dissent. But Afro- and indigenous projects remained uninvited to the feast. Thus the spectrum had changed already. A variety of projects are on the table, many proposed by intellectuals of European descent in South America and the Caribbean, others by indigenous intellectuals and activists, and others by intellectuals of African descent in Brazil, the Andes, and the Caribbean (the Spanish, British, and French Caribbean). Concepts in the United States like "modernity" (Dussel, 2005), "interculturality" (Macas, 2004; Walsh, 2002), "coloniality of being" (Maldonado-Torres, 2007), "hubris of the zero point" (Castro-Gómez, 2005), and "Latinidad" (Grosfoguel, 2006; Mignolo, 2006) are already opening up the decolonial horizon and taking us beyond "Latin" America, toward a pluralist America where Latins and Anglos of European descent will coexist – economically and politically – with indigenous languages and cultures from southern Chile to Canada, and with those of African descent in Brazil, the Andes, the Caribbean, and North America. The Zapatistas' quiet but relentless work, currently invested in education (EZLN, 2007), are showing that coexistence is possible and how it could work. Evo Morales, in Bolivia, is moving in the same direction. Afro-Brazilians, in Bahía, already have a similar vision of the future. A companion to "Latin" American literature – at the beginning of the twenty-first century – should be also a companion to subaltern projects (non-managerial but dialogic) and concepts, with the aim of a democratic and truly just world.

## NOTES

1  (http://leonardodavinci.stanford.edu/submissions/clabaugh/history/leonardo.html).
2  Sylvia Wynter, "Toward the sociogenic principle: Fanon, identity, the puzzle of conscious experience, and what it is like to be 'black,'" in I. Durán-Cogan et al. (eds), *National Identities and Sociopolitical Changes in Latin America* (New York: Routledge, 2001), pp. 30–65; Chela Sandoval, *Methodology of the Oppressed* (Minneapolis: University of Minnesota Press, 2001); Linda T. Smith, *Decolonizing Methodologies: Research and Indigenous People* (London: Zed Books, 1999).
3  On colonial ontological and colonial epistemic difference, see Nelson Maldonado-Torres, "On the coloniality of Being: contributions to the development of a concept," *Cultural Studies*, 21:2/3 (2007): 240–70.
4  (http://usinfo.state.gov/wh/Archive/2005/Feb/28-95114.html).

## REFERENCES AND FURTHER READING

Amawtay Wasi (2004). *Sumak Yachapi, Alli Kawaypipash Yachakuna/Learning Wisdom and the Good Way of Life*. Quito: UNESCO.

Anzaldúa, Gloria (1987). *Borderland/La Frontera: The New Mestiza*. San Francisco: Aunt Lute Books.

Bautista, Juan José (2005). "¿Que significa pensar desde América Latina?," www.afyl.org/quesignificapensar.pdf

Burga, Manuel (1988). *Nacimiento de una utopía: Muerte y resurrección de los Incas.* Lima: Instituto de Apoyo Agrario.

Castro-Gómez, Santiago (2005). "La hybris del punto cero: ciencia, raza e ilustración en la Nueva Granada (1750–1816)." Bogotá: Editorial Pontificia Universidad Javeriana.

Castro-Klaren, Sara (1993). "Dancing and the sacred in the Andes: from the Taky Onkoy to Rasu-Ñiti," *New World Encounters,* special issue of *Representations,* 6: 159–76.

Cornejo Polar, Antonio (1994). *Escribir en el aire: Ensayo sobre la heterogeneidad socio-cultural en las literaturas andinas.* Lima: Editorial Horizonte.

Dussel, Enrique (2005). "Transmodernidad e interculturalidad (interpretación desde la filosofía de la liberación," www.afyl.org/transmodernidadeinterculturalidad.pdf

Eze, Emmanuel Chuckwudi (1997). "The color of reason: the idea of 'race' in Kant's anthropology." In *Postcolonial African Philosophy: A Critical Reader,* pp. 104–38. London: Blackwell.

EZLN (Ejército Zapatista de Liberación Nacional) (2007), www.prensadefrente.org/pdfb2/index.php/a/2007/12/31/p3413

Fals-Borda, Orlando (1987). *Ciencia propia y colonialismo intelectual: Los nuevos rumbos.* Bogotá: C. Valencia Editores.

Fanon, Frantz (1961). *Les damnés de la terre.* (Trans. Richard Philcox, New York: Grove Press, 2004).

Fischer, Sibylle (2004). *Modernity Disavowed: Haiti and the Culture of Slavery in the Age of Revolution.* Durham, NC: Duke University Press.

García-Canclini, Nestor (1989). *Culturas híbridas: Estrategias para entrar y salir de la modernidad.* Mexico City: Grijalbo and Consejo Nacional de las Literaturas y las Artes.

Gordon, Lewis (2006). "African-American philosophy, race, and the geography of reason." In Lewis R. Gordon and Jane Anna Gordon (eds), *Not Only the Master's Tools: African-American Studies in Theory and Practice,* pp. 3–50. Boulder, CO: Paradigm.

Gordon, Lewis R., and Gordon, Jane Anna (2006). *A Companion to African-American Studies.* London: Blackwell.

Grosfoguel, Ramón (2006). "Decolonizing political-economy and post-colonial studies: coloniality, transmodernity, and border thinking," www.afyl.org/descolonizingeconomy.pdf

Henry, Padget (2003). *Caliban's Reason: Introducing Afro-Caribbean Philosophy.* New York: Routledge.

Jameson, Fredric (2002). *A Singular Modernity: Essay on the Ontology of the Present.* London: Verso.

Kiros, Teodros (2005). *Zara Yacob: Rationality and the Human Heart.* Boston: Read Sea Press.

Macas, Luis (2004). "La interculturalidad es una estrategia del proceso organizativo," www.llacta.org/organiz/coms/com852.htm

Maldonado-Torres, Nelson (2007). "On the coloniality of being: contribution to the development of a concept," *Cultural Studies,* 21(2&3), 243–8. Special issue on *Globalization and the De-colonial Option,* ed. Walter Mignolo with Arturo Escobar.

Martín-Barbero, Jesús (1987). *De los medios a las mediaciones: Comunicación, cultura y hegemonía.* Mexico City: Ediciones G. Gili.

Mignolo, Walter D. (2003). "Un paradigma otro: colonialidad global, pensamiento fronterizo y cosmopolitanismo crítico." In *Historias locales/diseños globales: Colonialidad, conocimientos subalternos y pensamiento fronterizo.* Madrid: Editorial Akal.

— (2005a). "Anzaldúa's borderland and Fanon's skin: shifting the geopolitics of knowledge." Lecture delivered at the University of Michigan, October.

— (2005b). *The Idea of Latin America.* Oxford: Blackwell.

— (2006). "Huntington's fears: 'Latinidad' in the colonial horizon of the modern/colonial world." In R. Grosfoguel, N. Maldonado-Torres, and J. D. Salivar (eds), *Latino/as in the World-System: Decolonization Struggles in the 21st Century U.S. Empire.* Boulder: Paradigm Press, pp. 45–70.

Milian, Claudia (2006). "Open double consciousness and mulatinidad in Latin America." Lecture delivered at Duke University, February.

Ortiz, Renato (1985). *Cultura brasileira e identidade nacional.* São Paulo: Brasiliense.

Patzi-Paco, Félix (2004). *Sistema communal: Una propuesta alternativa al sistema liberal.* La Paz: Comunidad de Estudios Alternativos.

Quijano, Aníbal (1992). "Colonialidad y modernidad/racionalidad," *Perú Indígena*, 13(29): 11–20.

— (2000). "Colonialidad del poder y clasificación social," *Journal of World-System Research,* VI/2: 342–86.

Quijano, Aníbal, and Wallerstein, Immanuel (1992). "Americanity as a concept: or, the Americas in the modern world system," *International Social Science Journal*, 44: 549–57.

Rama, Ángel (1982). *La Ciudad letrada*. Dartmouth, NH: Ediciones del Norte.

Sarlo, Beatriz (1988). *Una Modernidad periférica: Buenos Aires 1920 y 1930*. Buenos Aires: Nueva Visión.

Thiong'o, Ngugi Wa (1986). *Decolonising the Mind: The Politics of Language in African Literature.* London: Heinemann.

Walsh, Catherine (2002). "(De) construir la interculturalidad: Consideraciones críticas desde la política, la colonialidad y los movimientos indígenas y negros en el Ecuador." In N. Fuller (ed.), *Interculturalidad y Política: Desafíos y posibilidades.* Lima: Red para el Desarollo de las Ciencias Sociales en el Perú, 115–42, www.cholonautas. edu.pe/modulo/upload/walsch.pdf

# PART I
# Coloniality

# 1

# Mapping the Pre-Columbian Americas: Indigenous Peoples of the Americas and Western Knowledge

*Gustavo Verdesio*

The power of the first chronicles to relate the stories of exploration and colonization of the Americas is still intact. They represent a land that appears to these authors as pristine and untouched by what the West has called civilization. If one were to believe this corpus of texts about lands that were at that time unknown to European subjects, those lands showed no evidence of significant traces of human labor. The predominance of this early perception of the Americas occurs in spite of both the existence of later chronicles and documents that describe, to a European audience, the wonders of human settlements as complex and sophisticated as Mexico-Tenochtitlán and Cuzco – just to mention the two most spectacular concentrations of people in the first half of the sixteenth century – and the constant presence of indigenous peoples in the daily social lives of most American nations.

In my courses about indigenous societies from the past I usually encounter the following situation: a vast majority (actually, almost the totality) of students who, when asked about the way in which they imagine the pre-contact land of what today is the territory of the United States of America, respond with a depiction of a landscape that contains idyllic images of woods, rivers, and prairies that seem to be, in their different versions, uninhabited. In other words, they often present answers that offer a portrayal of the Americas as a wild territory untouched by human hand. It is only after several questions that lead them to admit the obvious (that is, that the lands were populated by a wide variety of human societies and cultures) that they begin to realize how pervasive the initial views we inherited from the explorers of the European expansion era still are. Why is it, then, that the myth that represents the Americas as a blank page where European settlers are free to leave their imprint still survives in the collective unconscious of Western culture? Why this inertia of collective memory that privileges only one of the different images of the past?[1] There are, in my view, no simple answers to these questions. Maybe if we try to view this state of affairs as the result of a combination of factors we could understand it a little better.

I will address these factors briefly later on, but first, I will go back in time and try to deal with the issue of how the scholars and indigenous peoples believe the Americas were populated, and since when.

This is not a conflict-free matter. On the contrary, there are several contending versions from different camps. The main disagreement can be identified as the one that confronts, on the one hand, several Amerindian nations and, on the other, scholars who believe that Western disciplines can reveal the secrets of the distant past. In general, the latter can be found in the ranks of archaeologists and biological anthropologists. Many an indigenous group claims to know where they come from and when they came to the Americas. In their oral traditions, we learn about stories of origins that present us with peoples who believe that they have occupied the territory of the Americas since time immemorial – since the beginning of time (Zimmerman, 2002: 16). These versions of the origins of the different indigenous groups are contested by Western scholars who have a completely different perspective on this issue. In their opinion, and in spite of the differences among them that we will discuss later, Amerindians arrived in the Americas as immigrants from Asia.

It should be pointed out that although Western scholars have a tendency to view indigenous oral histories as nonscientific, the stories passed from generation to generation by Amerindians are a useful tool to reconstruct the past – even the very distant past. As Roger Echo-Hawk has shown, it is possible to use traditional tales together with geological, archaeological, and historical evidence to have a richer picture of the distant past, as long as "the historical content of the oral or written information should be compatible with the general context of human history derived from other types of evidence" (2000: 271). In other words, "the oral information must present a perspective on historical events that would be accepted by a reasonable observer" (ibid.). He makes a very convincing case about the time depth of some indigenous stories about their origins. He even goes as far as to say that some Arikara origin accounts can go as far back as describing the Arctic Circle and Beringia as the place where everything started for them (275–6).

The idea that indigenous peoples came from Asia, which now passes as the uncontested truth among Western scholars, despite many Amerindian groups' rejection of it, was (probably) first advanced in 1590 by a Jesuit priest, Father Joseph de Acosta, in a passage about the origins of the indigenous peoples of the Americas. In it, Acosta makes a huge intellectual effort to reconcile the teachings of the Bible about the origins of humankind (a part of which narrative is the Noah's Ark story), and the undeniable evidence of long and continued human occupation of the lands then known as the Indies (2002: 51). After a careful analysis of the possibility that Amerindians had arrived in the Indies by sea, he concludes:

> The argument that I have pursued leads me to a great conjecture, that the new world that we call the Indies is not completely divided and separated from the other world. And, to state my opinion, I came to the conclusion some time ago that one part of the earth and the other must join and continue, or at least that they come very close. To the

present day, at least, there is no certainty that things are otherwise, for toward the Arctic or North Pole the whole longitude of the earth has not been discovered and there are many who affirm that above Florida the land runs very far in northerly direction, which they say reaches the Scythian or German Sea. Others add that a ship has sailed there and state that the sailors had seen the coast of Newfoundland running almost to the ends of Europe. Above Cape Mendocino in the Southern Sea no one knows how far the land extends on the other side of the Strait of Magellan . . . Therefore there is no reason or experience to contradict my conjecture or opinion that the whole earth must join and connect somewhere or at least that the parts are very close. If this were true, as indeed it appears to me to be, there is an easy answer for the difficult problem that we propounded, how the first dwellers in the Indies crossed over to them, for then we would have to say that they crossed not by sailing on the sea but by walking on land. (63)

The idea of a migration of peoples from Asia has taken, with time, the form of a popular hypothesis: the crossing of what after 1728 was to be known as the Bering Strait. The template of said hypothesis goes like this: in the Wisconsin period (the latest glacier advance of the Ice Age) glaciers retained so much water that the level of the sea descended dramatically, transforming the Bering Strait into dry land that connected Siberia and Alaska. This land, called Beringia by scholars, allowed the passage of human beings from Asia (there is no agreement, however, about the exact region or regions of the continent they came from) to North America, from where they later moved south, thereby occupying the rest of the continent. This hypothesis has it that the migratory groups of human beings entered the continent through the ice-free corridors that opened during the short periods of de-icing. And of course, some elaborate conjectures have been advanced about the different possible routes that those human travelers followed.

In a more recent development of the crossing of the Bering Strait hypothesis several scholars (among them Thomas Dillehay, one of the major voices today on the issues pertaining to the peopling of the Americas) have advanced the idea that the migration may have taken place, among other ways, by sea – thus contradicting some of Acosta's conjectures. The new version of the story is based on recent geological investigations that point to different climate changes, on disagreement about dates of deglaciation, on newly discovered patterns of settlement in South America, and many other factors. In South America, for example, the archaeological record is clear about the survival of the megafauna of the Pleistocene well into the early Holocene – something than cannot be said about North America, where most of the megafauna had already disappeared by that time.[2] For this reason and many others – among them the once controversial site known as Monte Verde, located in the present-day Chile – a narrative considered as the true one in North American academic circles is much more difficult to defend for the South American case. I am referring to the "Clovis first" hypothesis that in its most traditional (and I dare say reactionary) versions includes the variation known as "overkill."

The first hypothesis maintains that the culture that produced the fluted point known in academic circles as Clovis was one organized as bands of hunter-gatherers who moved from one place to another in search of food. The food, so the story goes, was mostly taken from big animals such as mammoths and other giants known as part of the megafauna of the Pleistocene. In the "overkill" version of it, these bands were so greedy and so environmentally irresponsible – they would have refused to sign the Kyoto protocol, I guess – that they ended up depleting their hunting grounds. Therefore, the big animals that fed them for millennia vanished from the face of the earth. This culture would have been the one that populated the rest of the Americas.

There are many problems with the application of this narrative to the vast territory south of what today is the USA. One of them is, as we said, that those big beasts survived into the Holocene in South America. Another element to take into account is that the Ice Age did not end between 11,000 and 10,000 BF in South America, but sometime between 14,000 and 12,000 BP.[3] But another set of problems is raised by the study of the evidence found in Monte Verde, Chile. That site – like several others in the southern hemisphere – shows very clearly that not only were its inhabitants not hunting big mammals, but also that their way of life differed dramatically from the one described not only by the "overkill" version but also by the more comprehensive one: "Clovis first." Many a society in South America developed, at an early stage of human occupation of the Americas, complex and diverse cultural habits – those of foragers – that differ dramatically from the model that presents Amerindians of the ancient past as predators. This relatively new evidence puts into question the simplicity and most of all the appeal of the Clovis theory that, in its basic form, states that the hunters of megafauna were the first society in the Americas and that later they populated different parts of the continent for a relatively long period of time. As a consequence, the population of South America, according to this theory, must have been a much later development. Unfortunately for its proponents, archaeological evidence shows that some radiocarbon dates of South American archaeological sites are much older (12,500 BP, in the most conservative estimates) than the ones identified as Clovis, which are only 11,200 years old – and very short-lived, because the most recent dates for Clovis place the end of that culture at around 10, 800 BP.[4]

Of course, there is more than science behind this dispute about dates, ancestry, and genealogy. There is also politics: the "Clovis first" narrative is mostly supported – not surprisingly – by North America-based scholars. Some have even said that the Clovis fluted point is the first manifestation of American (understood as pertaining to the US) ingenuity, which also gave us Coca-Cola and baseball caps.[5] This situation, besides being a blatant case of academic imperialism – it took Dillehay years (many more than the usual period for any investigation) to be able to get his radiocarbon dates and stratigraphic analyses broadly accepted by the archaeological community – it is also a dispute that may help us rethink the way in which we represent the past. That is, it may help us realize how important are the narratives we produce in the present to create a past that suits our community's – whatever community one belongs to – needs in the present, and how those pasts one invents are going to determine the futures that will actually happen or take place in real life.

The way in which one represents the very different indigenous pasts is no small part of the reconstruction of the past Western society has been producing for several centuries now. In this sense, the Clovis case is a very pedagogical introduction to the contradictions present-day scholars incur when trying to write a past that favors the cause of their own culture. For example, it is clear that the image of the first Amerindians as predators who exterminated the megafauna, and as nomads who had no abode, are not the ones preferred in the West to represent civilization. On the contrary, the less complex the society, the more "savage" or "primitive" it appears to Western eyes. On the other hand, Clovis defenders seem to be interested in presenting a scenario where the inventors of the fluted point appear as the pioneers who led the migration from Asia. Therefore, one could even speculate further and say that they could be seen as leaders of a prehistoric expansion that foretells the conquest of the West undertaken thousands of years later by (North) American pioneers. It was they who populated all there is to populate in the Western hemisphere. In this way, US-based scholars make a nationalist claim in the name of science – or if you prefer, disguised as science – in order to appropriate, once again, the territories located south of the Rio Bravo (or Rio Grande, depending on your perspective and geopolitical situation of enunciation). So to sum this contradiction up, I would like to play a little with an extravagant and impossible experiment: to be able to enter the mind of an imaginary "Clovis first" supporter. If that were possible, I bet we could hear something along these lines: "Those Amerindians may have been kind of primitive, but they are ours and they led the peopling of the Americas."

The diversity of indigenous peoples in what today is Latin America only grew with time. In addition to the already complex and diverse panorama of ancient times we are starting to get glimpses of the wide array of peoples and cultures that flourished south of the territory of what today is the USA. The most sobering thing for those who yearn for evolutionist narratives is that there is no visible line that shows any "progress" or "development" in the life and history of indigenous societies throughout the Americas. If an ideal observer could travel through time and space at will she would see hunter-gatherers coexisting with settlements of early agriculturalists, or fishers and hunters living side by side with state-like organized societies. There is, then, no single line of "progress" that societies followed. That is to say, there is nothing in the archaeological and ethnographic evidence available to us today that points in the direction of the existence of a rule or set of rules that determine the "evolution" of societies. Let us now take a look at just a handful of societies that existed in the past, and some that exist in the present, to get an idea of the enormous diversity and the wealth of human variety existent in the Americas.

Let us start with the most vilified ones: ancient hunter-gatherers. These indigenous peoples are the ones who get the worst press: they are represented as simple, primitive, and as not very careful with the environment. The representation has it that those nomads of the past were constantly struggling against the elements, defending themselves from a hostile environment that did not offer them enough resources in the way of food and shelter to have a decent, less difficult life. It follows from this model that these peoples spent most of their time trying to get food and shelter, which is tantamount to saying that they were too busy to dedicate time and energy to undertake activities unrelated to the production and reproduction of life – that is, activities without relation to subsistence patterns. From this academic perspective, it is with the practice of agriculture that certain activities not related to subsistence get better chances to take place.

However, several years ago, the work by scholars like Jon Gibson and Joe Saunders, who focused on the archaic mounds of the US Southeast, started to change this way of viewing things. These scholars came to the conclusion that the earthworks known as Indian mounds (human-made earthen elevations) located in the US Southeast (Louisiana, Arkansas, Mississippi, Florida, and other locations) were the work of peoples without agriculture. These mounds were built, in some cases, 5,400 years ago (Watson Brake, extensively studied by Saunders, is a case in point), and they were the product of societies without agriculture. This was something unexpected, to say the least, because archaeologists had trouble picturing nonagricultural societies staying at a place for long periods of time and with free time to construct massive works that required, without a doubt, a significant organization of the community as a whole – the building of the mounds requires great quantities of earth and, therefore, a high number of human labor hours.

Thus, a new model started to emerge: it was possible to view these societies (the mound builders of the archaic period) as capable of producing monumental collective works without having developed agriculture first. It is societies like the one known as Poverty Point that prompted some scholars to review the old evolutionary model. This complex is a very big site located in northeastern Louisiana, which contains a number of mounds and embankments. The historical period and culture that bear its name cover the years 3,730 to 3,350 BP and it extends over a large area of the lower Mississippi valley from a point near the conjunction of the Mississippi and Arkansas rivers to the coast of the Gulf of Mexico. The artifacts that characterize this culture are made of rocks not available locally, which means their makers must have had to import them. Trade, then, must have been very important for the people who built the earthworks.

The series of questions that places like Poverty Point posed were very difficult to understand for people working on the old paradigm. Those questions include, according to Jon Gibson:

> How did the conditions for large-scale construction appear at Poverty Point while everyone else in America north of Mexico was still following a simpler way of life? Was Poverty Point one of the first communities to rise above its contemporaries to start the long journey toward becoming a truly complex society? If Poverty Point did represent the awakening of complex society in the United States, how and why did it develop? Was it created by immigrants bearing maize and a new religion from somewhere in Mexico? Was it developed by local peoples who had been stimulated by ideas from Mexico? Did it arise by itself without any foreign influences? Did it come about without agriculture? Could hunting and gathering have sustained the society and its impressive works? (1999: 1–2)

The responses to those questions, implicit or explicit, show us an academic community that believed, 40–50 years ago, that such a large site like Poverty Point must have been the abode of a large, permanently settled, and therefore complex society. As I mentioned earlier, the prevailing idea at that time was that complex societies developed thanks to agriculture. However, no plant remains have ever been found at the site. The prejudice in favor of agriculture as a trigger of social complexity is such that even Gibson is very cautious when he talks about the food production and consumption at the site:

> it was impossible to tell if Poverty Point people had farmed, or if they had made a living some other way, such as by intensively gathering native wild plants or by hunting and gathering along the especially bountiful narrow environmental seams where uplands joined the Mississippi floodplain. We still do not have much information about foods eaten by Poverty Point peoples, but we have enough to be sure about one thing. Poverty Point peoples were not corn farmers. They were hunter-gatherers. We are only beginning to find out what they ate. We have more information about meat than plants, because bones are more resistant to decay through time and are more easily recovered by standard excavation methods. (1999: 12–13)

This attitude is understandable for at least two reasons: first, because Gibson himself had the same prejudices archaeologists had, in general, vis-à-vis so-called "primitive" societies and cultural complexity, and second, because it is always extremely difficult to go against commonly accepted knowledge – that is, it was hard to go against the dominant paradigm in the discipline. If we look at the questions posed by Gibson himself, we will see, between the lines, some of the anxieties that haunt archaeologists even today. One of them is the relationship of agriculture to social complexity, as we have already seen. Yet an even more important one is present throughout the whole series of questions: the one that has complexity itself, as a concept, at its center. That is, I believe, one of the more serious problems faced today by those of us concerned with the past of indigenous peoples.

If one looks at the questions carefully, there is a constant tension between the pair of concepts "simple/complex," which is always resolved, at least value-wise, in favor of the latter. In this context (that of the disciplines produced by Western knowledge apparatuses and institutions), complex is better or more desirable than simple. Complex, according to the above-mentioned questions, are those communities that "rise above" (to quote Gibson literally) their contemporaries. Now we see another dichotomy enter the scene: above/below. "Complex" and "above" go together, while their opposites are "simple" and "below." The axiology these oppositions propose is based on a series of Western concepts and prejudices that philosopher Jacques Derrida called logocentrism: the division of the world into conceptual pairs, one of which is considered to be better than, or above, the other. In this context, some scholars who try to vindicate indigenous cultures from the past or the present are caught in the trap of trying to prove that Amerindians are not as simple as portrayed by Western scholarship and popular beliefs while at the same time are reaffirming the very same structures that postulate the inferiority of indigenous peoples in comparison with Western culture.

For example, if one wants to study aboriginal societies in a place that is at the other end of the world from Poverty Point, say, in Uruguay, it is important to attack the popularly held prejudices that present Amerindians as backward, simple people. For this reason, one of the first things that a young team of archaeologists did in 1986 was to show the academic community, first, and the Uruguayan general public, later, that there was a culture or a series of cultures never mentioned by history textbooks that were much more socially complex than they ever imagined. The excavations conducted mostly by José López Mazz and Roberto Bracco and the papers written and ideas expressed by Leonel Cabrera Pérez began the careful construction of a new way of understanding indigenous peoples from the distant past in Uruguay. That new way included ideas similar to those advanced by Gibson, owing to a series of factors, of which I will only mention two: first, the fact that the cultures studied occupied the Uruguayan territory during, among other epochs, the archaic period (some are said to go as far back as 5,000 BP); second, because the archaeological evidence they encountered presented characteristics similar to those of hunter-gatherer societies that built mounds. Their work, then, presented the Uruguayan public opinion with a picture that was completely different from the predominant one. And yet this was done within the framework provided by the logocentric pairs that tell us that complex is better than simple.

However, where this defense of complexity gets even worse is in the work produced about regions populated by the most prestigious Amerindian societies: those located in the Andes and Mesoamerica. And beyond academic production, the masses, whether they know it or not, are also under the spell of a cluster of notions associated to complexity. It is not a secret to anyone that sites such as Machu Picchu, Tikal, and others constitute not only a source of revenue for the states of Mexico, Peru, and Guatemala, but also pilgrimage destinations for believers and new-agers of all kinds. The people who comprise this public are almost exclusively interested in the societies that constructed the structures that are now, for the most part, in ruins. These structures are, more often than not, monumental in nature, so monumental that they do not cease to astound the visitors who look at them in amazement for long periods of time – sometimes for many hours or even days. Anybody who has visited any of those sites knows that the image of astounded tourists is part of the landscape. Western amazement before monumentality from the past is twofold. On the one hand, there is a genuine wonder caused by the sheer spectacularity of some of the buildings constructed by indigenous peoples of the past. On the other, there is an assumption that the cultures that built those structures must have been very complex and, therefore, very civilized.

A word about the concept "civilization" when applied to an indigenous culture: it is another form of saying that said culture resembles Western civilization in some way or another. That is, it refers to cultures that are, in the occidental eyes of the observer, comparable to ours. To our eyes, then, those societies who were civilized were capable, like ours, of building monumental structures and vice versa: they were able to build those structures *because* they were civilized. Monumentality, then, is a standard against which Western subjects measure the degree of civilization of the culture that produced it. And monuments built 500 years ago or earlier are, in general and very likely, in ruins. This leads me to another related issue: the fascination of our culture with ruins. Some prefer them clean and tidy, others (like Christopher Woodward) like them invaded by nature – that is, covered by vegetation – but both segments of the public love ruins, period. What does this penchant for decaying structures tell us about our culture and our relationship to indigenous societies of the past?

To begin with, it tells us that we prefer to see Amerindians as people from the past whose buildings are there as a testament to their past greatness. This means that they are not here, with us, anymore, which would explain why there is nobody to take care of, or to use the ruins in the ways they were intended to be used at the time of their construction. It also means that we can take care of those ruins without much of a feeling of guilt: if the original dwellers are not here anymore, why not honor their memory by taking care of them? Again, as in the case of the Clovis theory, this is a way people from the present appropriate the work and objects produced by indigenous peoples from the past.

This appropriation has several negative consequences for the way we envision Amerindian pasts. One of them is that in the regions where the Inca, the Mexican, or the Maya cultures flourished, other cultures from the past do not get the same kind of attention. Although for academics who specialize in the America's past the existence of other cultures that preceded, and coexisted with, those major cultures is a well-known fact, this is not so clear to public opinion. For most people in the world, the Amerindians who thrived in the Andes are the Incas; the ones who dominated Mesoamerica are the Maya and the Mexica (or Aztecs, the most popular name applied to them). And even if one looks at the body of scholarly work, one will see that the enormous majority of research produced about those areas has been devoted, until very recently, to the aforementioned cultures. It is only in the last few decades that work like that produced by Steve Stern on Huamanga, or Karen Spalding on the Huarochirí (for the Andes), and that produced by James Lockhart (for Mesoamerica), just to offer some of the most prominent examples of this kind of scholarship, started to become a well-established trend. Thanks to people like them and others, the cultures under Inca or Mexica rule started to get more attention. Those peoples were, sometimes, very different from, and sometimes very similar to, their rulers. A book like Michael Malpass's (1993), that shows the different way in which the Incas dealt with those under their aegis, suggests that the differences between those subjected peoples were big enough to warrant a differential treatment from Cuzco, the Inca center from which power radiated.

And yet, even now, after the production of a wonderful growing corpus of scholarship about peoples subjected to, or in conflict with the Incas or the Mexicas, we still need to see more work on cultures that preceded those encountered by the European explorers at the time of contact. Although it is true that ancient cultures that preceded the Inca, such as the Moche, Chavin, and Chimu (in the Andean region) have been getting much more attention in the last decades, it is also true that the amount of research produced about those cultures pales in comparison to that devoted to the Inca. And this is even truer of the cultures of the pre-ceramic horizon: only when it comes to the early horizon, to which Chavín the Huántar belongs, does one begin to see a significant corpus of scholarship coming from different disciplines.[6] But early hunters from the Puna (8,000 BP) and early coastal populations do not get the attention of many scholars. This means that the great diversity of cultures that thrived, in ancient times, in what is called (incorrectly, in my opinion) the Andean region, who adapted in very different ways to a series of very diverse and complex environments, get very little attention and, therefore, little justice is given to the almost miraculous ways in which different groups of humans dealt with some of the toughest environmental conditions imaginable.[7] The Inca civilization and all those that preceded it developed a mastery over extreme environmental conditions. In Michael Moseley's words: "If thriving civilizations had matured atop the Himalayas while simultaneously accommodating a Sahara desert, a coastal fishery richer than the Bering Sea, and a jungle larger than the Congo, then Tahuantinsuyu [the name given by the Inca to their world] might seem less alien" (2001: 25). This amazing adaptability took, with time, the form of a simultaneous adaptation to all those ecological niches by a single population – a phenomenon that had no precedents in the history of humankind until it happened in the Andean region.

A similar scholarly situation presents itself to the observer in the case of Mesoamerica as well: there are thousands of articles on the Maya Classic and Post-Classic periods, but very little, in comparison, about the early hunters who populated the area of Los Tapiales 10,700 years ago. Even serious books for college survey courses written by major scholars like Michael D. Coe dedicate an insignificant number of pages (15 out of a total of 256) to those he calls the "earliest Maya" in his book *The Maya* (2001). The situation is a little better in the case of Mexico, where significant research is available about the Early Pre-Classic and Archaic periods. However, it is also the case that the majority of the research produced about Mexico covers a period that begins, roughly, with the Middle Pre-Classic, of which the most representative culture is the one known as Olmec, and that ends with the arrival of the Spaniards to the region.[8]

As I suggested above, the lack of monumentality among those early peoples from different parts of the Americas might as well be one of the reasons we do not pay much attention to them. But there are also other important factors that come into play. One of them is their social organization. This is why hunter-gatherers or early agriculturalists are not very interesting to the masses and even to scholars: their social organization differs too much from that which constitutes our ideal. It is the states or the societies that showed more complexity (at least understood as we understand it in our culture) that get most of the attention from both the general public and the experts. It seems that those peoples who did not have a state or a similar institution for social and political organization do not deserve much of our interest.

This is part of a general tendency in Western societies, which consists of perceiving indigenous cultures from our culture-specific perspective. As a consequence,

occidental subjects compare the aboriginal peoples and their cultural and social institutions and habits against the background of the known, therefore failing to assess or
understand Amerindians in their own terms, as Alvin M. Josephy, among others,
pointed out many years ago (1969: 4). For this reason, a high number of sites and
cultures are not as present in our social imaginary as are, say, Machu Picchu or Chichen
Itzá. Places like Cahokia (located in Collinsville, Illinois), for example, which seem
to exhibit all the traits that characterize a highly "civilized" indigenous group according to occidental standards, are relatively little known today – after having attracted,
not surprisingly, the attention of the colonizers for many years, until the nineteenth
century, when the general public and the academic community began to lose interest
in mounds in general – even in the United States.[9]

Cahokia is a huge site, with several mound complexes, and with a central mound
(known as Monk Mound) that was the second tallest construction in the Americas
before the arrival of the European explorers – it is even taller than the monuments of
Tikal – and which is aligned with other mounds and the cardinal points – which
reflects a significant astronomical knowledge as well as a sophisticated landscape
layout. And yet, people are not interested in it or do not even know that it exists.
The reasons for the current situation are many, for sure, but I would like to focus on
at least one: the materials used for the construction of the large, monumental structures at the site. Clay is not as prestigious as stone, apparently, in spite of the durabil-
ity proved by the longevity of the many mounds that comprise the Cahokia complex.
Maybe this is why for a while the predominant view on this site has been that it was
not a state but a chiefdom. That is, scholars maintained (and still maintain) that the
social complexity and the power exerted by the society that built and inhabited
Cahokia were not enough for it to reach the status of a state.[10] They also refuse to call
the platform mounds pyramids and the concentration of mound complexes known as
Cahokia a city, but as Timothy Pauketat states in his most recent book: "if Cahokia,
Cahokians, and Cahokia's mounds had been in ancient Mesopotamia, China, or Africa,
archaeologists might not hesitate to identify pyramids in a city at the center of an
early state" (2004: 3). This is probably why Pauketat, a long-time proponent of the
chiefdom hypothesis, has admitted that the limits between certain concepts and categories such as state and chiefdom are not very clear in some cases: "we have to admit
that no two archaeologists in any part of the world completely agree on how to identify
a city, a chiefdom, or an early state" (4). For this reason, he is now more open than
before to the possibility that Cahokia could have been a state or something that
resembled it very closely.

As a summary of this chapter we could say that indigenous peoples of the Americas
offer a rich spectrum of human diversity but that the very same expression with
which we refer to them fosters the production of a view that homogenizes them.
The misnomer "Indians" given by Columbus to the inhabitants of the lands he
encountered, because he thought he was in Asia or the Indies, is a term that presents
aboriginal peoples as a single entity. And we know that this is not true: indigenous
peoples of the Americas are very different from each other: they organize their soci-

eties in many different forms, they have very diverse beliefs, and so on. Moreover, the groups we put together in the same category ("Indians") did not think of themselves as part of the same polity – there is plenty of evidence to support this view. Only after they realized that by considering themselves part of an oppressed kind of people – regardless of ethnic differences – and that collective claims and actions under the rubric "Indians" were useful on some occasions, did indigenous peoples began to call themselves Indians. Therefore, to call them Indians is an intellectual operation similar to those that characterize what Edward Said called Orientalism: it is a discourse we create to talk about our others because we can do so thanks to a differential of power. In some cases (very few), we have a relatively good idea about how a certain indigenous society from the past was, but in most cases we have a very spotty, fragmentary knowledge of indigenous cultures before the time of contact and the little that we know is tainted by the prejudices that pervade our gaze and our episteme. It will take the work of generations of scholars and educators to change this state of affairs and to create the ground from where a more respectful image of the diversity and cultural wealth of indigenous peoples of the Americas could emerge.

## NOTES

1   Said inertia is blatantly patent in another diehard myth from the times of "discovery" and "conquest," to judge from a recent study conducted at the Institute for Social Research at University of Michigan. In it, experts state that 85 percent of Americans describe Columbus in a positive light and claim that he "discovered" America. Only 2 percent of the individuals surveyed said that Columbus could not have discovered a land that was already inhabited and, therefore, already discovered. Only 4 percent of the individuals surveyed present Columbus as the man who brought diseases, death, and a grim future to indigenous peoples.

2   For a detailed discussion of these issues see Dillehay (2000: xiii, passim).

3   BP means "before the present." It is a way of measuring time without having to resort to Western religious markers such as the birth of Jesus Christ.

4   For a comprehensive discussion of the radiocarbon dates and the Clovis theory in general, see the first chapter of Dillehay (2000).

5   Interestingly, one of the most vocal supporters of Clovis first, Tim Flannery, lives outside the USA. However, he includes himself in the "Monte Verde skeptics" camp: "Although lacking a convincing explanation for the site, I am one of the Monte Verde (and thus pre-Clovis) skeptics, and from here on will write as if reports of a pre-Clovis occupation of the Americas result from dating or other interpretive error" (2001: 178). This is typical of the incredibly, unabashedly biased view – which includes very few arguments but very strong prejudices and preconceived ideas, as can be appreciated in the fragment quoted above – of the majority of (if not all) the Clovis-first supporters.

He is one of the scholars who propose the Clovis fluted point as the first American innovation (182) and who suggests a parallel between said invention and other American cultural artifacts: "From Guatemala to the Dakotas, and from the Pacific to the Atlantic coast, the method of manufacture of Clovis points and other artifacts was uniform. Unless we count our own time, with its ubiquitous Coca-Cola cans and baseball caps, such cultural homogeneity has never been seen since in North America" (183).

6   For an overview of the wide array of Andean cultures, see Lumbreras (1989) and Moseley (2001). For research on Chavin de Huantar, see Burger (1995).

7   For a description of the difficult environmental conditions that peoples from the Puna, the Altiplano, the Coast, and the Amazon basin had to deal with, see Moseley (2001).

8   For an overview of the different stages (that is, arbitrary divisions proposed by archaeologists) in the history of human occupation of Mexico, see Coe (1994).

9   And even in St. Louis, a city located 7 or 8 miles from the main site of the cultures known as Mississippian, as I was able to confirm in the summer of 2005, when only one person – among forty or so – I asked about the Amerindian place knew what I was talking about.

10  See Emerson (1997) and Pauketat and Emerson (1997), where the hypothesis that presents Cahokia as a paramount chiefdom is the point of departure of most of the analyses contained in those two volumes.

## REFERENCES AND FURTHER READING

Acosta, José de (2002). *Natural and Moral History of the Indies*. Trans. Frances López-Morillas, ed. Jane E. Mangan, intro. and commentary by Walter D. Mignolo. Durham, NC: Duke University Press.

Bracco, Roberto (1990). "Dataciones 14C en sitios con elevación," *Revista Antropología*, 1(1): 11–17.

— (1992). "Desarrollo cultural y evolución ambiental en la región Este del Uruguay." In Renzo Pi Hugarte et al. (eds), *Ediciones del Quinto Centenario: Vol. I*, pp. 43–73. Montevideo: Universidad de la República.

Burger, Richard L. (1995). *Chavin and the Origins of Andean Civilization*. London: Thames & Hudson.

Byrd, Kathleen (1991). *The Poverty Point Culture, Local Manifestations, Subsistence Practices, and Trade Networks*. Geoscience and Man, Vol. 29. Baton Rouge: Louisiana State University Press.

Cabrera Pérez, Leonel (1989). "El pasado que negamos . . .," *Anales del VIo encuentro nacional y IVo regional de historia*, 1(1): 115–17.

Coe, Michael D. (1994). *Mexico: From the Olmecs to the Aztecs*. 4th edn. London: Thames & Hudson.

— (2001). *The Maya*. 6th edn. London: Thames & Hudson.

"Columbus is still widely admired, U-M study shows" (2005). *News Service*. October 4, University of Michigan, *http://www.umich.edu/news/index.html?Releases/2005/Oct05/r100305*

Dillehay, Thomas D. (2000). *The Settlement of the Americas: A New Prehistory*. New York: Basic Books.

Echo-Hawk, Roger C. (2000). "Ancient history in the New World: integrating oral traditions and the archaeological record in deep time," *American Antiquity*, 65(2): 267–90.

Emerson, Thomas E. (1997). *Cahokia and the Archaeology of Power*. Tuscaloosa: University of Alabama Press.

Flannery, Tim (2001). *The Eternal Frontier: An Ecological History of North America and Its Peoples*. New York: Atlantic Monthly Press.

Gibson, Jon (1999). *Poverty Point: A Terminal Archaic Culture of the Lower Mississippi Valley*. 2nd edn. Baton Rouge: Department of Culture, Recreation and Tourism: Louisiana Archaeological Survey and Antiquities Commission.

Gibson, Jon L., and Carr, Philip J. (2004). *Signs of Power: The Rise of Cultural Complexity in the Southeast*. Tuscaloosa: University of Alabama Press.

Josephy, Alvin M., Jr. (1969). *The Indian Heritage of America*. New York: Bantam Books.

Lockhart, James (1992). *The Nahuas after the Conquest: A Social and Cultural History of the Indians of Central Mexico, Sixteenth through Eighteenth Centuries*. Stanford, CA: Stanford University Press.

López Mazz, José María (1992). "Aproximación a la génesis y desarrollo de los cerritos de la zona de San Miguel (Departamento de Rocha)." In Renzo Pi Hugarte et al. (eds), *Ediciones del Quinto Centenario: Vol. I*, pp. 76–96. Montevideo: Universidad de la República.

— (1995a). "Aproximación al territorio de los 'constructores de cerritos.'" In Mario Consens, José María López Mazz, and María del Carmen Curbelo (eds), *Arqueología en el Uruguay: VII*

*Congreso Nacional de Arqueología Uruguaya*, pp. 65–78. Montevideo: Universidad de la República.

— (1995b). "El fósil que no guía y la formación de los sitios costeros." In Mario Consens, José María López Mazz, and María del Carmen Curbelo (eds), *Arqueología en el Uruguay: VIII Congreso Nacional de Arqueología Uruguaya*, pp. 92–105. Montevideo: Universidad de la República.

Lumbreras, Luis G. (1989). *The Peoples and Cultures of Ancient Peru*. Trans. Betty Meggers. Washington, DC: Smithsonian Institution Press.

Malpass, Michael (1993). *Provincial Inca: Archaeological and Ethnohistorical Assessment of the Impact of the Inca State*. Iowa City: University of Iowa Press.

Moseley, Michael (2001). *The Incas and Their Ancestors: The Archaeology of Peru*. Revised edn. London: Thames & Hudson.

Pauketat, Timothy R. (2004). *Ancient Cahokia and the Mississippians*. London: Cambridge University Press.

Pauketat, Timothy R., and Emerson, Thomas E., eds (1997). *Cahokia: Domination and Ideology in the Mississippian World*. Lincoln: University of Nebraska Press.

Saunders, Joe (2004). "Are we fixing to make the same mistake again?" In J. L. Gibson and P. J. Carr (eds), *Signs of Power: The Rise of Cultural Complexity in the Southeast*, pp. 146–61. Tuscaloosa and London: University of Alabama Press.

Saunders, Joe, and Thurman Allen, E. (1998). "The Archaic Period," *Louisiana Archaeology*, 22: 1–30.

— (2003) "Jaketown revisited," *Southeastern Archaeology*, 22: 155–64.

Saunders, Joe W., Mandel, Rolfe D., Saucier, Roger T., Thurman Allen, E., Hallmark, C. T., Johnson, Jay K., Jackson, Edwin H., Allen, Charles M., Stringer, Gary L., Frink, Douglas S., Feathers, James K., Williams, Stephen, Gremillion, Kristen J., Vidrine, Malcolm F., and Jones, Reca (1997). "A mound complex in Louisiana at 5400–5000 years B.P.," *Science*, 277(5333): 1796–9.

Spalding, Karen (1984). *Huarochirí: An Andean Society under Inca and Spanish Rule*. Stanford, CA: Stanford University Press.

Stern, Steve (1982). *Peru's Indian Peoples and the Challenge of Spanish Conquest: Huamanga to 1640*. Madison: University of Wisconsin Press.

Woodward, Christopher (2001). *In Ruins: A Journey through History, Art, and Literature*. New York: Vintage.

Zimmerman, Larry J. (2002) *Indios norteamericanos: Creencias y ritos visionarios, santos y embusteros, espíritus terrestres y celestes*. Cologne: Taschen.

# 2
# Writing Violence
## *José Rabasa*

The concept of writing violence points to the ways in which violence is written about and the ways writing itself exerts violence in colonial and postcolonial texts. The notion of the colonial/postcolonial divide bears less on a historical break traditionally marked by the wars of independence in Latin America than with the interrogation of the logic of colonialism. As such, the "postcolonial" dates back to the very earliest moments in the Spanish invasion of the Americas; it is coterminous with colonialism and the undoing of its civilizing claims. Colonialism and the justification of wars of conquest depend on the articulation of moral, religious, and epistemological grounds. If religion and morality are quite apparent in the denunciation of idolatry, sacrifice, and cannibalism, these conceptualizations of indigenous life entail epistemic violence. Epistemic violence reduces indigenous life to superstition, magic, and irrationality.[1]

In its most benign form, the consequences of writing violence institute developmentalist tropes that place Christianity and its institutions as historical necessities within spiritual and material teleology. In its most destructive form, writing violence sets the moral and political scenario for wars of extermination. This would be instances of writing that exert violence, but they are often intertwined with writing about violence as in telling the stories of wars against Indians, in describing massacres, or in characterizing indigenous life as inherently violent. Having said this, I would add that Spaniards, Indians, and *mestizos* were particularly lucid in exposing the violence of writing in the colonial period. With the exception of Christopher Columbus's *Diario*, the journal of his first voyage to America, which remains exemplary of writing that discovers, my examples will be drawn mainly from sixteenth- and seventeenth-century Mexican sources, but similar examples could be drawn from the eighteenth century and the Republican period, up to the present time. The current uprising of the Zapatistas in Chiapas should be conceived, at least partially, as an epistemic struggle.

To compensate, though also to complement the concept of writing violence, I will briefly outline the parameters for an echography of voice.[2] Literacy is most often opposed to orality as distinct realms that exclude each other. Thus writing would exert violence to the extent that it brings about the destruction of oral cultures. Beyond alphabetization and the transformations of speech brought about by the homogenization of culture through a written grammar, one often finds arguments concerning the ways in which written representation of oral discourse destroys the spontaneity and creativity of orality. Speech, like the gestures that accompany it, pertains to the ephemeral. They disappear in the flow of time. But in the same ways that one speaks of photography as capturing the real, one may speak of writing as the recording of voice, both internal and external. It fixes speech in time. It leaves the trace of what once was. The concept of echography would seek to explore ways of talking about the traces in alphabetical texts of voices that once were. If the photographic image can be manipulated, doctored, altered, one can also speak of the real that remains in spite of the changes. Recorded speech bears a similarity in that minimally it conveys an internal voice of someone who thinks that his or her representation of speech approximates what speakers would have sounded like. Alphabetically recorded speech also partakes of ghosts that are brought to life in the act of reading.

Rather than assuming that writing by its nature stands in opposition to speech, one would have much to gain to observe the multiple definitions of writing practices. The ephemeral pertains to all mimetic technologies, whether they are alphabetical writing or live video recording. They mark the end of time in unbridgeable distance. There are, of course, ideologies that seek to domesticate speech or that pretend that only alphabetical writing is worth considered such. Schooling brings about processes of homogenization by implanting correct forms of address and grammatical regimentation of thought. The tyranny of the alphabet presumes that only writing can preserve memory and history. That pictography is deficient. But these absolute definitions and reductions of writing to ideology and prejudice must be complemented with an awareness that the processes of education and adoption of alphabetical writing form part of a two-way street, in which the subjects that practice alphabetical writing might very well have things in mind that the rectors of correctness and western hubris might not have anticipated. That is why writing violence must be complemented with an echography of voice if we are to avoid oppressive absolutes and theoretical dead ends. Otherwise, we run the risk of perpetuating claims to superiority and power. We should devise reading (as well as writing) strategies that would recognize as well as enable acts of resistance and transculturation.

At this point I would like to raise the paradox implicit in the call to invent forms of writing, reading, or teaching (against) violence. The parenthetical "against" points to the agonistic dimension implicit in making manifest the ways violence operates in texts. Texts clearly carry material implications insofar as they may unchain terror, persecution, and torture (acts of war generally), but also consider the benevolent discourse that denounces all violence while constituting one exclusive form of thought, what in Spanish is referred to as "el pensamiento único," which in English would translate as "the only valid thought." If "democracy" and neoliberal economic policies reign today, Catholic universality constituted a most lucid antecedent. Indians in the sixteenth century could not afford to refuse the acts of love by missionaries and bureaucrats.

## Writing that Discovers

Those involved in the exploration and conquest of the Americas were expected to write about their findings and significant events, and provide exhaustive descriptions of the lands and peoples they invaded. I prefer the term invasion to that of encounter in that the later often diminishes the violent nature of the exchanges, tending to suggest a peaceful gathering of cultures that examine each other in symmetrical power relations. This might seem a truism, but it must be emphasized that the explorers and conquistadores of the sixteenth century approached the native cultures they came in contact with the intent of subjecting them politically, if not by military means. This conceptualization necessarily entails asymmetrical power relations insofar as the indigenous cultures were oblivious to the conquering aspirations of the Europeans. In order to carry out this political objective, Europeans counted on firearms, horses, and the ability to draft armies consisting of thousands of Indian allies. But writing constitutes a technology that enabled Europeans to record information regarding natural and cultural phenomena, but also to create a memory of the expeditions. Over the course of the sixteenth century the Spanish crown devised a series of laws and ordinances, *ordenanzas*, which were intended to rationalize expeditions as well as to structure the communities that settled in appropriated territories. These laws were intended to systematize the acquisition of knowledge and to regulate the behavior of those participating in the discovering enterprises. Note that discovery is bound to appropriation to Spanish rule and that Columbus, in his contract with the Spanish crown, was granted the titles of Admiral of the Ocean Sea, as well as that of governor and viceroy of all the lands he would discover. Discovery also uncovers, makes manifest what had not been visible before, hence the insistence on mapping and description. Discovery in its most elemental mode amounts to the act of having seen first, in fact, of having reconnoitered the territory for the first time without actually visiting the lands and even less established settlements. Claims will be bitterly disputed by other European nations, who challenged Spain's possession with arguments that only territories with permanent settlements could be considered legitimate possessions. Needless to say, for indigenous peoples discovery is a fraught concept, but we need to account for the ways Indians return the gaze of the intruders by which they circumscribe them to their worlds.

For Columbus the act of discovering is inseparable from taking possession. Writing in this regard does not just constitute an ideological justification of territorial claims and the eventual wars of conquest, it also constitutes devices for the appropriation of peoples and natural resources. Laws and the definition of religious motivations can obviously be unmasked as offering ideological alibis, but the question of ideology can also be pursued in the examination of the categories used in recording information. As early as Columbus's first voyage, his *Diario* produces a textual place in which the new lands would be mapped out; indeed, he speaks of creating a new map of the world and of a detailed inventory of natural resources. His systematic recording of data and descriptions of the lands under survey continues to surprise us today:

> Also my Lord Princes, besides writing down each night whatever I experience during the day and each day what I sail during the night, I intend to make a new sailing chart. In it I will locate all of the sea and lands of the Ocean Sea in their proper places under their compass bearings and, moreover, compose a book and similarly record all of the same in a drawing, by latitude from the equinoctial line and by longitude from the west. (Columbus, 1989: 21)

Writing the discovery entails a systematic ordering of the world on a blank page. It is a textual production that intends to locate the new lands within a new picture of the world. Writing has as its objective "to compose a book," but also a visual representation that would "record all the same in a drawing." The location of places in their "proper places" (*propios lugares*) carries the sense that the proper location gives place to appropriation, to making the lands one's own by means of knowledge (Rabasa, 1993).

Too much has been said on how mistaken Columbus was when he spoke of having arrived at Asia. There is clearly a blind spot in his descriptions of the new lands, but blindness and the violence that it introduces continue to haunt us all even today. In denouncing violence we must remain vigilant of treading blindly. That is, unless we want to claim that our generation has finally overcome all blind spots. If it is the case that Columbus died with the conviction that he had arrived at what medieval maps had charted at the farthest regions of the East, we still need to observe that he always imagines himself in the vicinity of Cathay (China) and Cipango (Japan), never fully there, and that along with the intent of reaching China and Japan, his voyage was circumscribed by the project of incorporating into the Spanish crown all the islands and mainland he would discover. When not identified with Asia, these new lands, which Columbus imagined on the borderlands of those thriving mercantile centers that Marco Polo had described in his *Il Milione,* were imagined in terms that connected them to the conquest of the Canary Islands.

In Columbus's writing the description of idyllic lands that he often associates with Terrestrial Paradise (a centerpiece for claiming their newness and ideologically binding his journey and persona to a prophetic tradition) morphs into a systematic inventory of natural resources and a projection of mines, sawmills, and harbors. Here I should remind the reader that the *Diario* as it has come down to us is a summary by Bartolomé de Las Casas, with the exception of passages in which he quotes, or at least creates the semblance of giving us Columbus's voice. The passages I will cite from the entry corresponding to Sunday, November 25, 1492 are in the summary version of Las Casas, hence in the third person. I will lay out four moments in the process of exploring and discovering (as in uncovering).

First, Columbus situates the beginning of the day: "Before sunrise he got into the launch and went to see a cape . . . because it seemed to him that some good river should be there." I have cut out the indications of orientation and the number of leagues. I am mainly interested in calling your attention to the effect of exploration in which description resembles a cinematographic camera that brings particulars into resolution: "he saw coming toward him a great stream of very pretty water that descended the mountain and made great noise." We have to be cautious with the adjective "pretty" – given that in *linda agua* (pretty water) lurks the practical, the eventual projection of tree trunks descending to a sawmill – but let's go on more slowly. The second moment consists of the identification of "stones with gold-covered spots on them, and he remembered that in the Tagus River, in the lower part, near the sea, gold is found; and it seemed certain to him that this one should have gold." The prettiness of the stream has been further determined as rich in gold, and as he points out later on in the entry, along the beach he found "other stones the color of iron and others that some said were from silver mines." In the third moment, the ship's boys shouted "that they saw pine groves. He looked up toward the mountain and saw them, so large and admirable that he could not praise them [sufficiently] their height and straightness, like spindles, thick and thin, where he recognized that ships could be made, and vast quantities of planking and masts for the greatest ships of Spain." Las Casas, even if citing in indirect speech, wants us to feel the excitement of the ship's boys' cries. The beautiful trees turn into planks and masts in the process of describing them, of discovering, that is, of uncovering a location rich in natural resources. The fourth moment closes this process of transformation by inventorying "a good river and material to make a water-powered sawmills." Columbus assures Isabel and Ferdinand that the climate is most temperate and that there is "an opening at the foot of the cape . . . which was very deep and large, and in which there would be room for a hundred ships without cables and anchors" (Columbus, 1989: 171–3).

Native Americans undergo an analogous textual transformation when the initial connection of the term "cannibal" with those under the rule of the Great Khan of Cathay turn into dog-faced monsters and eventually to a group of people, the Caribs, who purportedly practiced cannibalism and terrorized the "peaceful" Arawacs, who have subjected themselves willingly to the Spanish crown (Hulme, 1986). Columbus constitutes the Carib's future within the new colonial order as slaves, in the best of scenarios, and as subject to extermination, in the worst: "The Admiral told him by signs that the sovereigns of Castile would order the Caribs destroyed, and they would order all of them to be brought with hands tied" (Columbus, 1989: 287). The history of the Americas will reiterate this bad vs. good Indian narrative for the next 500 years. On Columbus's return to the Island of Hispaniola (the Dominican Republic and Haiti) during his second voyage, he learns that the 36 Europeans he had left behind had been killed – the initial mapping of friendly/unfriendly Indians turns murky. Columbus sent 500 enslaved Arawacs back to Spain, to the horror of Queen Isabel, who demanded that he abstain from enslaving her new subjects; nevertheless, he set the grounds for the systematic subjection of natives under *encomiendas* (a system of tribute in kind and labor) and the enslaving of resistant Indians. According to the consuetudinary laws governing the rights of victors in war, the defeated could be enslaved. The practice of enslaving resistant Indians remained within the colonial order until the wars of independence. But if Miguel Hidalgo y Costilla and Simón Bolívar eventually called for the dissolution of slavery, not only of Indians but also of blacks, debt peonage has remained a reality up to the present time.

## Writing that Conquers

In 1511, Fray Antonio de Montesinos delivered a sermon in Santo Domingo in which he exposed the atrocities and condemned those responsible as living under mortal sin. This denunciation led to an ideological crisis that led to the drafting of the Laws of Burgos. In essence, these laws sought to establish criteria for determining when Indians could be subjected to war and, as a consequence, enslaved. The Laws of Burgos gained further solidity when the jurist Juan López Palacios Rubio wrote a legal instrument known as the *Requerimiento*. The *Requerimiento*, perhaps, constitutes the purest expression of writing that conquers (Rabasa, 2000: 67–72, 88–94, and passim). After narrating the history of the world from the creation of the earth to the universal rule granted to St. Peter, the first pope, the *Requerimiento* goes on to explain that a most recent pope had granted sovereignty of the New World to the Spanish crown, and that Indians had the choice of either recognizing Spanish sovereignty over their territories or being subjected to war and slavery. It also points out that those who have accepted Spanish rule live happy and prosperous lives. This document became a standard in the establishment of first contact after 1514 when Pedrarias Davila first read it in the Castilla del Oro. From the start the *Requerimiento* was cast as a cynical attempt to justify violence; the impossibility of conveying its meaning to a people whose language was unknown was one of the concerns, but also the absurd situation in which it was reputedly read several miles off the coast to people who, for practical purposes, could not have heard it, let alone understood its implications if they did not welcome the invading Spaniards.

The *Requerimiento* plays a fundamental role in Hernán Cortés's *Second Letter* to Charles V. Having committed mutiny by refusing to follow the instructions of the Governor of Cuba Diego Velasquez, Cortés constantly draws from the *Requerimiento* to establish the legality of his conquering expedition into the hinterland of Mexico to subdue Motecuzoma in Tenochtitlan:

> And, trusting in God's greatness and in the might of your Highness's Royal name, I decided to go and see him wherever he might be. Indeed, I remember that, with respect to the quest of this lord, I undertook more than I was able, for I assured Your Highness that I would take him alive in chains or make him subject to Your Majesty's Royal Crown. (Cortés, 1986: 50)

Cortés prefaces every contact with people on the way to the basin of Mexico with variations of the *Requerimiento*. In some instances, he responds with acts of war to negative responses to the demand to recognize Spain' claims to sovereignty; in other instances Cortés chooses to ignore the negative reply: "So as not to offend him and for fear that some calamity might befall my endeavor and my journey, I dissembled as best as I could and told him that very soon I would have Mutezuma order him to give the gold and all that he owned" (ibid.: 56). This astuteness in following the consequences of resistance already presages his manipulation of Motecuzoma's response to Cortés in which the call to recognize the sovereignty of Spain plays into a narrative that identifies Charles V with the return of Quetzalcoatl, the god-man who, according to native narratives, had abandoned those who had settled in the basin of Mexico and had promised to return. Cortés offers one variation of this story in his representation of Motecuzoma's welcoming speech. Observe his circumspection: "I replied to all he said as I thought most fitting, especially in making him believe that Your Majesty was he whom they were expecting" (Cortés, 1986: 86–7). Much has been written and debated over the supposed identification of Cortes and his cohorts as "gods." I do not pretend to settle the disputes here but merely raise a few questions that should complicate whatever response you may want to give to this issue.

First, it is important to note that the term *teutl* or *teotl* used to speak of the Spaniards as gods carries an ambivalence in that, according to the Franciscan Fray Bernardino de Sahagún, one of the greatest scholars of Nahuatl in the sixteenth century, it meant "cosa estremada en bien o en mal" (thing consummate in good or in evil). Sahagún lists as examples "teuhpiltzintli, niño muj lindo: teuhpiltontli, muchacho muy traujeso, o malo" (*teopiltzintli*, a very handsome boy; *teopiltontli*, a very mischievous or bad boy; Sahagún, 1950–82: 1, 87). While *tzintli* marks a reverential, the diminutive *tontli* denotes contempt; however, both share the term *teo-tl*.

Second, observe that Quetzalcoatl is a god-man and that, accordingly, he participated in both the natural and the supernatural from within a spiritual economy in which these two discrete realms lacked the separation commonly attributed to them in post-Enlightenment Western discourse. I stress the notion of *after* the Enlightenment, because for the Spaniards of the sixteenth century God, the Virgin, or St. James were agents of history. Cortés's silence could only be temporary because from within the spiritual economy of Catholicism Quetzalcoatl must be reduced to the status of devil, hardly a pagan deity that Cortés and his cohorts could identify with for long. This does not mean, of course, that Cortés would deny the centrality of Quetzalcoatl in the indigenous conceptualization of the invaders. In fact, Cortés knows that as long as Quetzalcoatl exists independently of the Spaniard's reduction to expressions of the devil, the Nahuas retain their own world and thereby remain epistemologically inaccessible.

Third, in Nahuatl history and cosmology, regions of the world have different temporalities. As much as the voice of Motecuzoma might be distorted in Cortés's representation in the language of chivalry novels, one can trace the voice of a Nahua. That is, this Nahua story carries an ontology and epistemology that will remain inaccessible to the ethnographic reductions of the missionaries. Thus we find in Chapter XXVII of Diego Durán's *History of the Indies of New Spain* [*Historia de las Indias de la Nueva España e islas de Tierra Firme*] an account of when the first Motecuzoma sent wizards, witches, and enchanters to Aztlan to learn about the land of the ancestors and to find out if Coatlicue, the mother of Huitzilopochtli, the main Mexican deity, was still alive (Durán, 1994: 212–22). When the wizards and enchanters arrive at the seven caves from where the Nahua ancestors had first departed, they invoke the "devil" and rub their skin with ointments that enable them to assume the forms of birds, wild cats, and other fierce animals so that they can travel through the wilderness that leads to the place were their ancestors originated. Once they cross the lands filled with dangers, they transform back into humans at the foothills of the caves of Culhuacan. The people from Aztlan approach them and are surprised to learn that the ancestors who led the Nahuas in their migration have died. The narrative goes on to reproduce the conversations they had, but let this brief account suffice as an example of multiple temporalities in Nahua geography. In short, there is nothing in Nahua cosmography that impedes the notion that Quetzalcoatl could still be alive and that the Spaniards could have issued from a place not unlike the Aztlan described in Duran's *Historia*.

Fourth, one of the most compelling forms of epistemic violence resides precisely in undoing the belief in the power of enchanters, witches, and wizards. Thus, the Tlatelolca version of the conquest collected in Book 12 of the Florentine Codex emphasizes the fact that the wizards Motecuzoma sent to enchant the Spaniards failed. Note, however, that the informants continue to tell stories that implicate both the Nahuas and Spaniards in magical realms. If the inquiry requested that informants "tell the story of how they were conquered," they respond with a story in which magic fails but continues to be integral to the narrative. As it were, it is a magical story of how magic failed. Wouldn't the Spaniards be seen as extremely powerful *teotl* precisely because the power of native wizards, forms of *teotl* (which would include by definition anyone extremely good or bad, including Motecuzoma himself), did not affect them? In this process, wouldn't St. James, the Virgin, and the rest of the Christian spirits, and for that matter "*el diablo*," be variations of *teotl*? Wouldn't the Nahua retain their epistemology and life forms to the extent that they continued to conceptualize the conquest in "magical" terms? Wouldn't the ultimate conquest achieve its end when the Nahua would no longer tell stories of conquering *teotl*, but simply provide a narrative based on military superiority or the decimation of the population by epidemics? In answering these questions, shouldn't we remain vigilant of the writing violence we may impose by insisting on the "rationality" of the Nahuas, who couldn't have believed that the Spaniards were "gods"?

## Writing that Converts

In itself the notion of converting someone to the Christian religion entails violence in that earlier beliefs must be discarded to give way to the new universal creed. It is not merely abandoning one creed for another, but reducing the other creed to falsity. There is a whole literature in indigenous languages that was devised to uproot and denigrate native spirituality. I choose spirituality to avoid the more specialized notion of religion. Spirituality does not necessarily entail a separate realm that one might define as secular. In the West, in the culture of the sixteenth-century missionaries, religion (and the discipline of theology) exists side by side with philosophy, art, literature, and science. For the missionaries of the sixteenth century, there is only one true religion: revealed Christianity in its Roman Catholic form. In addressing native spirituality, the first task was to define all native beliefs as superstitious, as induced by the trickeries of the devil, as idolatrous. It is only for scholars of post-Enlightenment religious studies that Mesoamerican life forms are understood as religion. In central Mexico, Franciscan missionaries wrote a most extensive ethnographic literature for conversion purposes. One could argue that the origins of religious studies should be traced back to conceptualization of another culture's beliefs as an object study. And one should wonder if the supposedly value-free disciplines of religious studies has not carried a colonialist frame of reference in spite of their scientific intentions. It is not a symptom that one does theology when exploring one's beliefs, but religious studies when studying religious phenomena that are not one's own? Has not religious studies, much like anthropology, been linked to various form of imperialism and their civilizing missions? I can only raise these questions here.

The genres devised for converting Indians in the sixteenth century included treatises on demonology, exaltations to abandon their false gods, confessionals, catechisms, and spiritual exercises. In what follows I will limit myself to some generalities concerning Alonso de Molina's *Confesionario mayor en lengua mexicana y castellana (1569)* and the group of texts by Bernardino de Sahagún commonly known as his "enciclopedia doctrina," a doctrinal encyclopedia. I will argue, however, that the *Exercicio quotidiano*, which was found among the papers of the Chalcan historian Domingo Chimalpahin, suggests that it was written under the supervision of Dominican friars.

Molina's *Confesionario* establishes the need that Indians become conscious of being sinners, it implants a new memory for the examination of one's self. In one place it specifies that all humans sin at least seven times a day, but goes on to emphasize that these sin are, for the most part, venial rather than mortal. Indigenous subjects are under the obligation of learning to examine their conscience to discover sins. The confessional presents itself as a guide in which the Ten Commandments, the five senses, and the theological and cardinal virtues guide the penitent through an exhaustive account of his sins. It concludes with discussion of absolution and the required contrition for the restitution of grace.

We should note here that Sahagún's *Historia general de las cosas de la Nueva España*, or the Florentine Codex, conceives itself as a linguistic project in which the accumulation of examples of proper Nahuatl, which would also document idolatries, superstitions, auguries, and omens, among other things, would aid missionaries in writing sermons in Nahuatl and confessing Indians:

To preach against these matters, and even to know if they exist, it is needful to know how they practice them in the times of their idolatry, for, through [our] lack of knowledge of this, they perform many idolatrous things in our presence without our understanding it. And, making excuses for them, some say they are foolishness or childishness, not knowing the source whence they spring (which is pure idolatry). And the confessors neither ask about them, nor think that such a thing exists, nor understand the language to enquire about it, nor would even understand them, even though they told them of it. (Sahagún, 1950–82: 1, 45–6)

Beyond the *Historia general* and its pedagogical end of training preachers and confessors in the art of Nahuatl, Sahagún wrote a series of doctrinal texts that address Nahuas. The so-called *enciclopedia doctrina* would include the appendix to Book 1 of the *Historia general*, "Las veintiseis adiciones a la postilla" and "el apendice a la postilla o las siete colaciones." This last text is a fragment. In his Spanish and Nahuatl edition of these texts Arthur Anderson also includes the *Exercicio quotidiano*, a text that was found among Chimalpahin's papers. The *Exercicio quotidiano* includes the following note at the end: "I found this exercise among the Indians. I do not know who produced it, nor who gave it to them. It had many errors and incongruities. But in truth it may be said that it was done anew rather than that it was corrected. In this year of 1574. Fray Bernardino de Sahagún" (Anderson and Schroeder, 1997: 2, 183). Note that the handwriting is Chimalpahin's. We must remember that at least part of Chimalpahin's intellectual formation was under the Dominican friars in Amaquemecan.

An echography of internal voices would attend to the different forms of devotion and conversion implicit in evangelical writings. As Edmundo O'Gorman has correctly pointed out in writing about Las Casas's *De unico vocationis modo*, the Dominican and Franciscan orders differed in the emphasis they placed on the will and the understanding in their evangelical practices (O'Gorman, 1942: 31–60). Neither is the will an exclusive domain of the first nor is the understanding of the latter. Both reason in addressing Indians and both presuppose on the part of Indians a desire to accept the articles of the faith. However, the *habitus* they pursue differs (Rabasa, 1998). Observe that the *Exercicio quotidiano* emphasizes the formation of an intellectual habit, which to my mind seems indicative that it was written under Dominican supervision.

Sahagún's doctrinal writings have two modalities. In the first, Sahagún exposes the falsehood and cruelty of the pagan gods. One can trace instances of these modalities in the appendix of Book 1 and the *Apéndice de la postilla*. In the appendix of Book 1 he limits himself to making declarative statements: your gods are false, hence you must abandon them. That's how it is, period. In the second, Sahagún works on declarative sentences that establish the tenets of the faith that all Christians must accept and are under the obligation of believing. Again, there is no reasoning; rather he works on the transformation of desire and the will. Sahagún seeks an affective transformation of the subject. The source of knowledge is the truth of the Gospel, of those who know how to interpret the divine word. The objective is to infuse in the Indian subject "the desire of the desire that will take him to love by the love of God"

(Sahagún, 1993: 33). Truth is transparent; it is only a matter of developing the will to desire living according to Christian principles. But the realization of this "will to desire" would be further complicated by the fact that faith entails a participation in grace. In this regard it foments a *habitus* of the will that prepares the subject for recognizing and receiving the gift of faith. A glance at the *Apéndice de la postilla* will find the repetition of the terms "desire" (*nequilia*), "your obligation" (*monauatil*), and "it is necessary" (*monequi*). Needless to say, one finds descriptions of Heaven and Hell that should motivate the new life of the neophyte. Among these fully converted Christians, whose desires are in perfect harmony with the teachings of the church, one would find the Tenochca elite, to which the Nahua historian Fernando de Alvarado Tezozómoc belonged and celebrates in his *Crónica mexicáyotl*: "With this, here ends the account of the ancient ones who were the first Christians, the noblemen who were the first neophytes" (Anderson and Schroeder, 1997: 1, 62). Tezozómoc's internal voice is consistent with what Sahagún seeks to implant. He defines himself as a Christian and constitutes himself as the inheritor of the ancient histories of the Mexican: "But these accounts of the ancient ones, this book of their accounts in Mexico, we have inherited. These accounts certainly are in our keeping. Therefore we too, but especially our sons, our grandchildren, our offspring, those who will issue from us, they too will also guard them. We leave them for them when we die (Anderson and Schroeder, 1997: 1, 60–2).

Let us now examine the language of learning and knowledge in the *Exercicio quotidiano*. The refrain now consists of "it is necessary that you should know [as in the Spanish *saber*]" (*ticmiximachiliz*), and "it is necessary that you should know [as in the Spanish *conocer*]" (*ticmatiz*). If the language of care opens the discussion of the nature of love, "it is necessary that you care for the love with which God is loved and the love by which your neighbors are loved," the meditation for Saturday ends by placing the emphasis on knowledge: "Clearly this is the knowledge (*iximachoca*) by which the only Deity, God, is known, and the love with which he is loved, and the knowledge (*iximachoca*) by which your neighbors are known, and the love by which they are loved, and the nature of good love. Take [all these admonitions] very much to heart" (ibid.: 169). The *Exercicio quotidiano* emphasizes the creation of a *habitus* that will lead to the understanding of the Deity. It certainly also entails a transformation of affect, but it no longer resides in desire and the will, rather on the intellectual preparation of the soul for the reception of grace and the knowledge it imparts. Once the *Exercicio quotidiano* establishes the need to live by the Ten Commandments and the obligation to confess all sins, it goes on to compare the soul to a *milpa*, a cornfield: "This is esteemed to be like seeding and planting. For your soul is a spiritual field, and you are to take care of the spiritual green corn stalk that is aforementioned keeping of the divine commandments and living in accordance with the virtues" (131–3). This recommendation is systematized when it insists on the development of an intellectual *habitus*:

> To this work is necessary that you apply yourself if you wish to be saved. And it is necessary that you importune God each day and each night, so that he will strengthen you

and you will perform your obligations well. For later, when you become a follower of what is good and righteous, you will be much comforted. You will live as if in a fresh, green field. (133).

The *Exercicio quotidiano* juxtaposes explanations of the nature of God to discourses that constitute a first person that the reader will assume to direct himself or herself to God. This is a text to be read silently and internalized by the reader. It records voices directed to the reader, and also reproduces voices that the reader will use to address God. This is the terrain in which the Nahua historians Tezozómoc and Chimalpahin were intellectually formed. To what extent were their internal voices, which critically reflect on the task of collecting the accounts of the elders and establishing the criteria for the identification of more credible versions, formed by this kind of training in self-examination? But also, to what extent did this critical *habitus* also lead to the interrogation of the colonial institutions that surrounded them? Indeed, these questions should not make us exclude what, for lack of a better term, we may define as an autochthonous critical thought. The accounts that Chimalpahin and Tezozómoc collect document the genres of speech acts that supplemented the pictographic histories. Beyond the alphabetical texts, pictography provides leads for an inquiry into native critical thought.

## Writing Pictograms

In its most elemental form alphabetical writing exerts violence on the pictographic by denying the status of writing to the latter. This is what Walter Mignolo has defined as the "tyranny of the alphabet." This "tyranny' does not merely refer to those places in colonial writing by Spaniards, *mestizos*, and Indians that reduce pictography to limited form of documenting information and specify that only alphabetical writing can be historical. As Mignolo has argued, the reproduction of phonetic sound has defined the criteria for tracing the evolution of forms of inscriptions from pictography to alphabetical writing; only alphabetical writing constitutes true writing (Mignolo, 1989, 1995). On a second level, alphabetical writing exerts violence by means of glosses that are written on the margin of precolonial and colonial pictographic texts. Beyond the dismissals of pictographic writing by historians, one finds that colonial authorities most often recognize the knowledge inscribed using pictographs. We find the use of pictographic documents in Indian and Spanish courts throughout the colonial order. If on an ideological level alphabetical writing represents a more evolved stage for some indigenous and Spanish members of the colonial elite, in the courts pictography often carried more weight. As Barbara Mundy has shown, we can observe the force of pictography in land-grant or *mercedes* maps drawn by native painters who were commissioned to establish the boundaries of wastelands that could be claimed and appropriated by people not associated with the indigenous communities (Mundy, 1996: 181–211; also see Gruzinski, 1993). There is a rhetorical weight to pictography that, in this instance, authenticates the legality of land claims. Disputes between indigenous communities would also be settled by means of pictographic documents. I have also argued that the production of the Codex Mendoza (Berdan and Anawalt, 1992) in the years corresponding to the implementation of the New Laws of 1542 makes the documentation of precolonial tributary patterns all too appropriate for legitimizing the *encomienda* as a system that continues precolonial patterns of tributaries (Rabasa, 1996).

In the Codex Mendoza and the Codex Telleriano-Remensis (Quiñones Keber, 1995), the Spanish religious and secular authorities ordered the production of these pictographic texts with the intent of not just creating a record of information regarding indigenous social patterns, religious beliefs, and history, but also to document systems of writing. There are ample alphabetical documents in Spanish and in indigenous languages that record detailed information about Indian life – we have spoken of Sahagún's projects – a fact that should make suspect the production of pictographic texts if it were only for the purpose of recording information. The Spaniards charged with supervising these projects knew well that pictography contained information that alphabetical writing could not record. This makes the relationship between pictography and alphabetical writing more complex. We may mention, in passing, that *khipus* in the Andean region were used throughout the colonial period, and continue to be used even today in indigenous communities. This leads to another modality of writing violence that is implemented not by the denial of the pictography as a form of writing, but by the glosses that were written in codices like the Mendoza and Telleriano-Remensis in spaces the *tlacuilos* left blank for this purpose. The glosses were often written by different hands that included Spaniards and indigenous as well as *mestizo* scribes. In the case of the Telleriano-Remensis one can actually draw a difference between those glosses written by native scribes with a handwriting that approximated the typography of print and those written by missionaries in which scribbles and scratches destroy the aesthetic if not the epistemological integrity of the pictorial text.

Let me briefly call attention to fol. 46r of the Codex Telleriano-Remensis (Plate 2.1) that offers a complex and troubling view of the colonial order. My contention is that supervising missionaries faced a disconcerting representation of their institutions and evangelical practices that led the missionaries to take over the production of the manuscript. In soliciting the *tlacuilos* to "tell the story of how they were conquered," the missionaries found themselves in the position of being observed by the observed. This page poses a dramatic instance of the observer-observed in that the *tlacuilo* managed to represent a most vulnerable aspect of the Christian theological edifice, one that perhaps was commonly accepted as a long tradition of debate between the different orders and philosophical traditions but that brought about a crisis when articulated by an Indian painter. The depiction of a Dominican friar imparting baptism on a willing Indian leaning over the baptismal font makes manifest the centrality of the proper indoctrination of Indians before baptism favored by the Dominican order and in particular by Bartolomé de Las Casas. We have already spoken of the

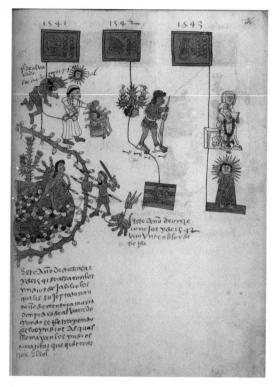

*Plate 2.1*    Codex Telleriano-Remensis, fol. 46r (Courtesy of the Bibliothèque nationale de France)

preference of the Dominicans for an evangelical practice that emphasized the under-standing and the formation of an intellectual *habitus* in the process of exposing Indians to Christian truths. Now, observe that on the right-hand section of this folio we find a Franciscan holding a doctrine, perhaps a confessional manual, that would have laid down the articles of the faith that Indians were required to accept as true simply on the grounds that they were informed that these tenets of the church were true because they were revealed by God. The Franciscans preferred multitudinal baptisms that would then be followed by the implantation of the doctrine and confession. In prac-tice, once baptized one had the obligation to accept the Christian dogma. So, the whole process of conversion comes down to the practice of leading neophytes to will and desire to live according to the Catholic dogma.

Earlier on we read passages from Sahagún that illustrated this position among Franciscans. Declarative sentences call for a willing Indian subject. Confessional manuals were thus designed to lead the subject through the Ten Commandments, the theological and cardinal virtues, and, once examined, the subject would express repentance and contrition. The *tlacuilo* lucidly depicts these two attitudes that, on a deeper philosophical level, imply incompatible philosophical traditions. Universality on these grounds is a desired end rather than an established fact. It is a horizon in which the different traditions debate but also know that it is futile to pursue an agreement when the backgrounds, that is, the absolute presupposition from which and against which philosophical doctrines makes sense of the world, are radically heterogeneous. They presuppose different understandings of the self and culture that lead to different ethnographic practices. Elsewhere, I have discussed these differences in more detail (Rabasa, 1998). The *tlacuilo* of the Codex Telleriano-Remensis manifests a particularly critical acumen in depicting the dominant evangelicals and their philosophical traditions from and against a background that remains unintelligible to missionaries.

## Epilogue: Ignorantiam Invincibilem

In the introduction to this chapter I mentioned that in the sixteenth century one finds most lucid critiques of empire among Spanish, *mestizo*, and Indian intellectuals. The *tlacuilo* of Telleriano-Remensis made manifest with exceptional acuity the limits of empire when he responded to the request, "tell me the story of how I conquered you" by providing a "snapshot" of the observer. This snapshot reminded the missionary that he had been observed all along in ways that eluded and continued to elude his gaze. The *tlacuilo* exposed a blind spot that further deepened the crisis missionaries faced when they realized that the truths of Indian life would remain inaccessible regardless of how willing informants might be to convey the secrets of their cultures: the missionary would have to assume the background from which and against which an indigenous subject would not only make sense of their own world but of that of the missionaries. This dwelling in multiple worlds would entail a perspectival distance that underscored the truth that Indian worlds were articulated in their specific languages and backgrounds. Minimally, this crossing over would force the missionary to reflect in and on Nahautl terms. Is this what the project of the nahuatlization of Christianity entailed? Only by learning to debate and feel the world would the evangelical mission of converting Indians by appealing to the understanding or by working on the transformation of affect ever begin to leave a mark. If willing to entertain the necessity of a two-way street, the missionaries would have come to the realization that their understanding and affect also would be transformed in the process.

In closing I would like to briefly mention Alonso de la Vera Cruz's treatise on just war and dominion, *Relection de dominio infidelium & justo bello* (A discussion on the dominion of unbelievers and just war) – a series of lectures he delivered at the University of Mexico in the academic year of 1553–4.[3] In these lectures Vera Cruz analyzes the basis for arguing whether the supreme pontiff had supreme power, whether the emperor was lord of the world, whether the indigenous leaders were their own master, and whether Spaniards had the right to deprive them of their dominion. But Vera Cruz also raises questions pertaining to the payment of tribute, when to make restitution when abuse has been committed, and the examination of whether the recognition of Spanish sovereignty and the appropriation of lands were attained without extortion and violence. These are just a few questions and doubts the treatise examines. Now, these lectures were delivered with the intent of training future confessors of Spaniards. Confessors would be charged with leading Spaniards into a thorough examination of motives, practices, and awareness of ways in which they might have abused Indians. It is in the context of these questions that Vera Cruz addresses the need to consider the possibility of excusing Spaniards from restitution or from being evicted from lands in their possession. It is a treatise clearly more concerned with the effects of colonization and the pursuit of remedies than with the legality of the Spanish invasion. With regard to this point he is clearly on the side of those who condemn the conquest:

> I beg you, good reader, to put aside prejudice and reflect on what law, by what right did the Spaniard who came to these regions, and armed to the teeth, attack these people subduing them as though they were enemies and occupying lands not their own, seeking arbitrarily with force and violence all their valuable possessions and robbing the people? I do not see by what law or right; perhaps I am just beating the air. (Vera Cruz, 1968: 2, 163)

The last lines read in the Latin as "Ego non video; fortassis in medio sole decutio!" (I cannot see; perhaps I am melting in the midst of the sun!).

The humility of Vera Cruz leads him to question his own certainty. Moreover, the question of "ignoratiam invincibilem" would retain the possibility that some Spaniards, or, for that matter, Indian rulers and caciques, might have broken a law or, even more precisely, acted in bad faith. Vera Cruz demands that the will of the people be taken into account in assessing the justice of transactions, even if it is in the nature of government for those who rule to interpret the will of the people. There remains the semblance of caciques who "are not lords but rather like wretched slaves do they help in exacting tribute for the Spaniards themselves"; however, note that he is not blaming the caciques here but underscoring the abuse by the Spaniards that leads them to act on their behalf: "they are insulted, they are flung into prison, they 'bear the day's burden and heat', a condition proper not to lords but rather to servants" (ibid.: 2, 201). Vera Cruz also mentions caciques that have been bought with wine, European clothing, a horse, and what not. The examination of conscience would find its limit in "ignoratiam invincibilem"; this state, however, would in some instances absolve Spaniards from the obligation to restitute goods illegally obtained or the losses incurred owing to violence. But there are other occasions in which ignorance does not exclude fault and restitution demanded. We would only wish that our leaders today who have made war on Afghanistan and Iraq would be subjected to the thorough examination of conscience that Vera Cruz recommended for his contemporaries. But also consider the blind spots we carry, the "ignoratiam invincibilem" of the violence we inflict, when exposing the writing violence of yesterday but also of today.

## Notes

1 This chapter builds on the concept of "epistemic violence" as developed by Gayatri Chakravorti Spivak in her essay "Can the Subaltern Speak?" (1988). I have developed these ideas on writing violence in *Inventing America* (Rabasa, 1993) and *Writing Violence on the Northern Frontier* (Rabasa, 2000).

2 I derive the concept of "echography" from Jacques Derrida and Bernard Stiegler, *Echographies of Television* (2002). This book is the full and literal transcript of a recorded conversation filmed by Jean Joseph Rosé under the auspices of the Institut National de l'Audiovisuel, on December 22, 1993. This conversation reflects on the nature of television as a medium that captures and transmits live events. The transmission of the live event is never as direct nor as unmediated as the concept would suggest, but the effect, the capacity to reproduce the immediacy of an event suggests a most accomplished technology for producing mimetic artifacts. The reproduction of reality, however, is implicit to the inscription and reception of images. As Roland Barthes has argued, it is particular to the analog image of photography to have first made possible the preservation of reality as "this was" (1981), but as Derrida and Stiegler argue, the pursuit of the effect of the real antedates the invention of photography. Within the West, written letters have a privileged place in the history of recording the real, which would be followed by analog and, more recently, by digital reproducibility. I further elaborate the concept of echography in "Ecografías de la voz en la historiografía nahua" (Rabasa, forthcoming).

3 The title of Vera Cruz's lectures was *Relectio edita per Reverendum Patrem Alfonsum a Vera Cruce, Sacrae theologiae magistratum, Augustinianae familiae priorem, et cathedra primariae eiusdem facultatis in Academia Mexicam regentem* (A discussion by the Reverend Father Alonso de la Vera Cruz, master of Sacred theology, prior of the Augustinian order, and head professor of the same subject in the University of Mexico). He referred to this treatise as *Relectio de dominio infidelium & justo bello* (A discussion on the dominion of unbelievers and just war) in the first edition of his *Speculum coniugiorum* (Mirror of the married, 1556) (Vera Cruz, 1968: 53).

## References and Further Reading

### References

Anderson, Arthur J. O., and Schroeder, Susan (1997). *Codex Chimalpahin. Society and Politics in Mexico Tenochtitlan, Tlatelolco, Texcoco, Culhuacan, and Other Nahua Altepetl in Central Mexico. The Nahuatl and Spanish annals and accounts collected and recorded by don Domingo de San Antón Muñón Chimalpahin Quauhtlehuanitzin.* 2 vols. Trans. Arthur J. O. Anderson and Susan Schroeder. Norman: University of Oklahoma Press. (Original manuscripts ca.1593–mid-1620s.) (This book contains transcriptions of a selection of Chimalpahin's Nahuatl and Spanish texts with an English translation; it also includes a transcription and translation of Fernando Alvarado Tezozómoc's *Crónica Mexicayotl*.)

Barthes, Roland (1981). *Camera Lucida: Reflections on Photography*. Trans. Richard Howard. New York: Hill & Wang. (This text offers a theory for understanding the experience of photography.)

Berdan, Francis F., and Anawalt, Patricia Rieff (1992). *The Codex Mendoza*. 4 vols. Facsimile edition. Berkeley: University of California Press. (This facsimile of the Codex Mendoza is accompanied by studies of the pictorial forms, contents, and materiality of the manuscript.)

Columbus, Christopher (1989). *The Diario of Christopher Columbus's First Voyage to America 1492–1493. Abstracted by Fray Bartolomé de Las Casas.* Trans. Oliver Dunn and James E. Kelley,

Jr. Norman: University of Oklahoma Press. (Original manuscript ca. 1530.) (This edition offers a rigorous transcription and translation of Columbus's journal of his first voyage to America.)

Cortés, Hernán (1986). *Letters from Mexico.* Trans. Anthony Pagden. New Haven, CT: Yale University Press. (Original manuscripts 1519–26.) (Pagden's is arguably the best translation of Cortés's five letters to Charles V.)

Derrida, Jacques, and Stiegler, Bernard (2002). *Echographies of Television: Filmed Interviews.* Trans. Jennifer Bajorek. Cambridge: Polity Press. (In their conversation, Derrida and Stiegler reflect on television as a most accomplished form of reproducing the real.)

Durán, Diego (1994). *The History of the Indies of New Spain.* Trans. Doris Hayden. Norman: University of Oklahoma Press. (Original manuscript ca. 1580). (This offers a complete translation of Diego Durán's historical section of the *Historia de las Indias de Nueva España e islas de Tierra Firme.*)

Gruzinski, Serge (1993). *The Conquest of Mexico: The Incorporation of Indian Societies into the Western World, 16th–18th Centuries.* Trans. Eileen Corrigan. Cambridge: Polity Press. (This book, which was first published in French in 1988 with the title *La Colonisation de l'imaginaire,* traces in indigenous pictorial texts colonizing processes in which Indians were, to borrow Gruzinski's term, "occidentalized.")

Hulme, Peter (1986). "Columbus and the cannibals." In *Colonial Encounters,* pp. 14–43. London: Methuen. (This chapter examines the ideological determinants in the discursive production of the cannibal in Columbus's journal of his first voyage to America.)

Mignolo, Walter (1989). "Literacy and colonization: The New World experience." In René Jara and Nicholas Spadaccini (eds), *1492–1992: Rediscovering Colonial Writing,* pp. 51–96. Hispanic Studies 4. Minneapolis: Prisma Institute. (This chapter examines the ways literacy constituted a form of conquest.)

— (1995). *The Darker Side of the Renaissance: Literacy, Territoriality, and Colonization.* Ann Arbor: University of Michigan Press. (Mignolo draws an exhaustive inventory of the ways the Western book, literacy, and mapping colonized the world in the sixteenth century.)

Molina, Alonso (1984). *Confesionario mayor en lengua mexicana y castellana (1569)* [Major confessionary in the Mexican and Castilian language]. Mexico City: Universidad Nacional Autónoma de México. (Roberto Moreno provides a facsimile edition of Molina's manual for confession.)

Mundy, Barbara (1996). *The Mapping of New Spain: Indigenous Cartography and the Maps of the Relaciones Geográficas.* Chicago: University of Chicago Press. (This book examines the methods, questionnaires, and failings of the imperial project of mapping the totality of Spain's possessions.)

O'Gorman, Edmundo (1942). *Fundamentos de la historia de América* [Foundations of the history of America]. Mexico City: Imprenta Universitaria. (O'Gorman lays out the ground for reflecting on the philosophical conquest of America.)

Quiñones Keber, Eloise (1995). *Codex Telleriano-Remensis: Ritual Divination, and History in a Pictorial Aztec Manuscript.* Austin: University of Texas Press. (In this facsimile edition, Quiñones Keber offers an exhaustive study of the contents, style, and history of this major pictorial colonial codex.)

Rabasa, José (1993). *Inventing America: Spanish Historiography and the Formation of Eurocentrism.* Norman: University of Oklahoma Press. (This book traces four moments in the semiotic invention of America.)

— (1996). "Pre-Columbian pasts and Indian presents in Mexican history," *Dispositio/n* 46: 245–70. (This essay examines the Codex Mendoza and Carlos de Sigüenza y Góngora's *Alboroto y motín de los indios de México* [Uprising and riot of the Indians of Mexico] as two modalities of constituting Indians as subalterns.)

— (1998). "Franciscans and Dominicans under the gaze of a *tlacuilo*: plural-world dwelling in an Indian Pictorial Codex," *Morrison Library Inaugural Lecture Series 14.* Berkeley: Doe Library, University of California. (A page from the Codex Telleriano-Remensis provides an entry point for reflecting on native critical thought.)

— (2000). *Writing Violence on the Northern Frontier: The Historiography of Sixteenth-Century New Mexico and Florida and the Legacy of Conquest.* Durham, NC: Duke University Press. (This book analyzes forms of writing violence in aesthetic, legal, descriptive, and historical colonial texts.)

Sahagún, Bernardino de (1950–82). *Florentine Codex: General History of the Things of New Spain.* 13 parts. Trans. Arthur J. O. Anderson and Charles Dibble. Santa Fe, NM: School of American Research and University of Utah. (Original manuscript ca. 1579). (This is a bilingual edition of the Nahuatl versions of Sahagún's monumental *Historia general de las cosas de la Nueva España*; it also includes a bilingual volume that contains prefaces, additions, and appendixes written in Spanish.)

— (1993). *Adiciones, Apéndice a la apostilla y Ejercicio cotidiano* [Additions, appendices to the apostilla and daily exercise]. Nahuatl text and Spanish translation, ed. and trans. Arthur J. O. Anderson. Mexico City: Universidad Nacional Autónoma de México. (Original manuscripts ca. 1574.) (In this transcription of Nahuatl texts with Spanish translations, Anderson collects what is known as Sahagún's doctrinal encyclopedia.)

Spivak, Gayatri Chakravorti (1988). "Can the subaltern speak?" In Cary Nelson and Lawrence Grossberg (eds), *Marxism and the Interpretation of Cultures*, pp. 280–316. Urbana: University of Illinois Press. (This chapter provides a complex argument concerning the discursive constraints that constitute the impossibility of subaltern speech.)

Vera Cruz, Alonso de la (1968). *Relection de dominio infidelium & justo bello* (A discussion on the dominion of unbelievers and just war). In *The Writings of Alonso de la Vera Cruz*. Vol. 2. Trans. Ernest J. Burrus, SJ. Rome: Jesuit Historical Institute. (Original manuscript 1553–4). (Burrus offers a bilingual Latin and English edition of the lectures Alonso de la Vera Cruz delivered at the University of Mexico on the dominion of unbelievers and just war; volume 3 contains a photographic reproduction of *De domino*.)

## Further Reading

Rabasa, José (2006). "Ecografías de la voz en la historiografía nahua" [Echographies of voice in Nahua historiography], *Historia y Grafía*, 25: 105–51. (This article defines echography as a method for examining voice in Nahua historical writings.)

Wood, Stephanie (2003). *Transcending Conquest: Nahua Views of Spanish Colonial Mexico*. Norman: University of Oklahoma Press. (As the title implies, this book examines the ways the Nahuas viewed the Spanish invasion with the intent of transcending conquest, that is, victimization.)

# 3
# The *Popol Wuj*: The Repositioning and Survival of Mayan Culture

## Carlos M. López

The history of the *Popol Wuj* as both a collection of texts recorded among the indigenous peoples of Guatemala and also written down in the manner of the western canon is a history of successive repressions, recoveries, and appropriations. In the *Popol Wuj* we can see the distortions introduced in the texts as a result of their conservation within systems of registers and epistemological frameworks differing from the original, thus becoming tainted by Western culture paradigms. For this reason, the Mayan text can be seen as one of the most visible and illustrative cases of what occurred with many other belief systems existing in the Amerindian continent during the European colonization.

Currently the title *Popol Wuj* refers to a collection of *tzijs* – truths, stories, narratives, wisdom, and traditions – originating from the highlands of present-day Guatemala, dating from before the Spanish invasion lead by Pedro de Alvarado in 1524. Father Ximénez's manuscript, containing the oldest available version today (ca. 1701), is housed in the Newberry Library, Chicago, Illinois, USA, as one of the documents bound in the volume cataloged as the *Ayer MS 1515*. It is important to read the *Popol Wuj* for two major reasons. First, because it is the most complete and intelligible surviving cultural record of pre-Columbian Mesoamerican societies. Secondly, because part of the epistemologies, cosmogonies, philosophical trends, and values contained in some of its *tzijs* could become the seeds of new thought if they enter in contact with our contemporary worldviews. A great deal of the contents of the *Popol Wuj* could offer alternative points of view for revisiting most of the ominous challenges arising from the current relationship between humans and nature. This Maya-*K'iche'* text is not a book of solutions or revealed truths that will save us, but it offers different approaches to the way we think and feel. It is perhaps for this reason that Mayan cosmogonies might allow us to enrich our own epistemological perspectives.

The reading of such texts implies a significant risk. Given their profound discrepancies with our Western epistemology, we cannot avoid the tendency to invade, distort, overlay, or absorb their "non-Western" views. Because the Maya have been subjugated by Western powers for over 500 years, the reading of their texts is not a simple literary exercise. In this case there is contact with a cultural artifact bound by a long-standing system of oppression. Thus, a reading from the Western-dominant perspective implies an inevitable invasion of native discourses which becomes a new form of scholarly colonization. An alternative reading should seek to avoid this risk. In this chapter I will discuss the repercussions of the inherent dilemmas arising from readings of historically colonized texts.

The texts of the *Popol Wuj* – which originate from many diverse sources – are arranged in three main sections. The first part comprises the *tzijs*, which recount the origin of life, of plants, animals, and human beings. The creation of humans is the centerpiece of these *tzijs*, and is presented in four successive stages: the creation of animals, the creation of the Earthen Man, the Wooden Man, and finally the Maize Man. This process of creation is headed by the principal *kab'awils* (deities) of the Mayan cosmogony: *Uk'ux kaj, Juraqan, Ch'ipi Kaqulja, Raxa Kaqulja, Tepew, Q'ukumatz, Alom, K'ajolom, Xpiyakok, Xmukane, Tz'aqol,* and *B'itol* (the orthography of the names are from Sam Colop); which are translated into English as: the Heart of Sky, Hurricane, Newborn Thunderbolt, Raw Thunderbolt, Sovereign, Plumed Serpent, Bearer, Begetter, Grand Mother, Grand Father, Maker, and Modeler (Tedlock's translation). These *kab'awils* join together to create a being capable of knowledge, but they did not preconceive the forms and characteristics of such a being. Through trial and error they tried different materials and forms that allowed the production of a creature capable of knowledge. The choice of materials and craftsmanship was tested by the capacity of the new creature to speak meaningfully. To determine the traits of these creatures, the deities used new combinations of materials (mud, wood, and maize) and random chance by casting together red beans and yellow corn kernels. Then, they interpreted the resulting patterns. The first three attempts failed, but each one of them signified a step forward toward greater complexity and perfection. On the fourth attempt, once the proper material – maize – was obtained, they produced the sought-after being: a creature capable of knowledge, and therefore capable of thanking the *kab'awils* for their existence. The names of the first four men were *B'alam Kitze', B'alam Aq'ab', Majukutaj,* and *Ik'i Balam* (Jaguar Quitze, Jaguar Night, Mahucutah, and True Jaguar); the first four women were *Kaja Paluda, Chomi Ja, Tz'ununi Ja,* and *Kaq'ixa Ja* (Celebrated Seahouse, Prawn House, Hummingbird House, and Macaw House).

The second group of *tzijs* is more diverse and complex. It includes the stories of different beings, whose nature was not strictly divine, human, legendary (in the Western sense), nor symbolic-metaphoric; instead they embodied some characteristics of all of these. These *tzijs* are subdivided into two large sections. On the one hand are the tales of *Wuqub' Kak'ix* (Seven Macaw) and his sons *Sipakna* and *Kab'raqan*, and on the other, the struggles between *Jun Junajpu* and *Wuqub' Junajpu*, and later between their sons *Junajpu* and *Xb'alanke* and the Lords of *Xib'alb'a*.

*Wuqub' Kak'ix* and his sons are characterized by their arrogance and are defeated by the tricks played on them by the Twins *Junajpu* and *Xb'alanke*. The other series of *tzijs* tells how the Lords of the Underworld (*Xib'alb'a*, a place of suffering and trials) defeat *Jun Junajpu* and *Wuqub' Junajpu*. However, the daughter of *Kuchumakik'*, one of the Lords of *Xib'alb'a*, disobeys her father's prohibition and goes to the *Jícaro* (gourd tree) where the decapitated head of *Jun Junajpu* is hanging. The skull spits on the maiden *Xkik*'s hand, and she conceives the tiwns *Junajpu* and *Xb'alanke*. She is then condemned to death for her disobedience and subsequent pregnancy, but she manages to escape and is received and protected by the elder *Xmukane*, the mother of *Jun Junajpu*. When *Junajpu* and *Xb'alanke* were born, they were harassed by their step-brothers *Jun B'atz'* and *Jun Chowen*, who made them submit to all kinds of abuse. As time passed the Twins grew up and took revenge on their older brothers. Using their wisdom, they tricked *Jun B'atz'* and *Jun Chowen* and transformed them into monkeys, freeing themselves of their hostility. After this first deed, they descended to *Xib'alb'a*, to avenge the death of their parents. At the entrance to the Underworld, there were four different-colored rivers: blue, red, black, and yellow. They followed the black river, which led them to the House of Suffering, but thanks to the collaboration of the ants and the mosquitoes, they managed to overcome and destroy the Lords of *Xib'alb'a*. Their triumph ends in an apotheosis: one transforms into the sun and the other into the moon.

Finally, the last section of the *Popol Wuj* contains the *tzijs* that refer to the peregrination of the first four forefathers (*B'alam Kitze'*, *B'alam Aq'ab'*, *Majukutaj*, and *Ik'i Balam*), accompanied by the group of peoples who later will form the *K'iche'* federation in their migration from Tulan. This journey begins in the dark, as they await the rising of the sun (*Q'ij*), the Moon (*ik'*), and Venus (*Ik'oq'ij*), at which time they go into the highlands. These forefathers bring the symbols of power from the Tulan (Toltecs), introducing the *kab'awils Tojil*, *Awilix*, and *Jakawitz*. This excursion of warriors defeats and subjugates the populations that did not want to accept the *kab'awil Tojil*, and installs the three Houses and their respective dynasties: the *Ajaw K'iche'*, the *Nija'ib'ab*, and the *Kaweq*. Basically, these *tzijs* describe the formation of the *K'iche'* reign, and end with a catalog of the lineage of Toltec origin of those living in the capital *Kumarcaaj* (or *Gumarcaj*, which means "place of old reeds"), also known as *Utatlán*.

As we can see, the names have a certain significance, but not in a direct way. The *K'iche'* language is founded on a system of metaphoric meanings or polysemantic symbols. For example, the word *Q'ij* means sun, but it also means day, and is the name of a day in the *K'iche'* calendar. The word *tzij* means truths, stories, narratives, wisdom, and traditions. The word *pop* means mat (*petate*), stories, time, events, facts, and, through extension of *petate*, it means also council and community. In the same way, the whole structure of K'iche' language and discourse has the same properties and characteristics. Likewise, polysemantic expressions, or the aggregation of meanings through chains of transferences, are a trait of Mayan epistemology, which obviously differs from that of the West. From the moment that these texts were captured and set down within the framework of colonization, they were subjected to the interferences and appropriations from the outside, which is to say, from Western paradigms and colonizing pressures. This process started in social as well as in cultural spheres from the very first moment of invasion by the imperial army of Spain.

During Lent in the year 1524, K'umarcaaj was conquered and destroyed, causing the downfall of one of the most powerful groups and sociopolitical organizations in Mescamerica, perhaps second only in importance to Tenochtitlán. With the destruction of this military and ceremonial center, a very rapid breakdown of the cultural and social fabric of the *K'iche'* nation ensued. Its military and religious leaders were executed and the general populace was subjected to a regime of servitude or slavery, which together with forced migration, resettlement, and European diseases, left them with very few chances to organize a resistance. It was in this context that the *tzij*, rooted in the past "before the arrival of Christianity" (fo. 1r, lines 24–5), acquired a very important status: they formed the center of resistance for surviving invasion and destruction.

Possibly around 1555, the friars charged with indoctrination of the Christian faith realized the importance of the "stories" from "pagan" antiquity. Presumably, young *K'iche'* nobles recorded in their language, but using Latin characters, *tzijs* heard as children in their homes or ceremonial centers and recalled from memory, perhaps with the help of some sort of visual aids – *wujs*, ceramics, pictures, or stone inscriptions carved into stelae, murals, temples, and buildings, and in the notable case of a stone housed at the Chichichastenango Museum. Ruud van Akkeren emphasizes the oral nature of these *tzijs* and maintains that "the *Popol Wuj* seems an amalgamation of dance-dramas and oral history," adding that "it only received its detailed, written form, as we know it today, when it was composed by a group of Maya scribes in the middle of the 1550s" (2000: 3). It is probable that this record was solicited by the indoctrinating friars, who in order to convert the indigenous people had closer contact with them than most colonizers. If indeed it occurred in this manner, the circumstances gave rise to one of the peculiarities of the *Popol Wuj*: with each recovery, it survived, but at the same time it suffered adulterations.

When the *tzijs* were recorded in a European fashion (using Latin lettering and phonetic systems, and employing paper and ink) they acquired a further characteristic feature: fossilization in the written form. This format, now set as a block, almost certainly never existed in this form before the arrival of Alvarado. Very likely the *tzijs* were a part of a more or less disperse *corpus* (Sam Colop, 1999: 13), and were repeated or read in different circumstances and within a framework completely different from that which it began to inhabit after 1524. In a departure from existing Mayan *tzijs*, during the period of the formation of the K'iche kingdom, the intent of the *tzijs* was to justify and impose the legitimacy of the invaders' hegemony over ancient Mayan settlements. During the conquest of the Maya, the new Toltec-created *tzijs* recorded the clashes between the various houses or bloodlines (the *Ajaw K'iche'*, the *Kaweq*, and the *Nija'ib'ab'*). A testimony of the conflicts between the *K'iche'* of K'umarcaaj and those of Rabinal or the Cakchiqueles was recorded in the *Rabinal Achi* and the *Memorial de Solola.* This means that the texts narrating those events were in constant interaction with other texts and within the collection of social, political, and religious realities in a process of transformations originating from within the culture itself. As of 1555, all of this was wiped out owing to a sudden interruption of that historic dynamic when both the society and its cultural texts were subjected to colonial rule.

Setting down the *tzijs* as a single piece during transcription into Western writing not only eliminated the dynamics and differences within the core of the corpus, but also determined and imposed the impossibility of its evolution. It became fixed as a document, which is to say a text that informs about the past but will not be able to change in accordance with new realities. It enters, literally, the shelves of the monastery, the administration, or overseas powers. Thus it is transformed into an informant, an object of scrutiny, a tool of power. This transmutation is of course much more complex, but we can say that the aforementioned impacts comprise the most important repercussions of the entry of the Maya-*K'iche' tzij* into the "lettered city" of the Spanish colony and those which followed.

## The Evangelizing Period

The friar Bartolomé de Las Casas (1484–1566) recorded, early on, the existence of *tzijs* referring to *Xb'alanke*, *Jun B'atz'*, and *Jun Chowen*. In his *Apologética Historia Sumaria* (1559) he claims to have had knowledge of the belief in these "gods" in the region of *K'iche'* (chs. CXXIV, CCXXXV). The friars knew that many oral "stories" circulated about and also knew of the existence of "books" which the natives had hidden. They were also cognizant of the large number of rituals practiced by the *K'iche'*. However, neither in Las Casas nor in later chronicles that refer to the *K'iche'* region can one find more information about these *tzijs* or *kab'awils*. It is puzzling that Las Casas, a Dominican friar and bishop of Chiapas in Mexico who assiduously kept abreast of the news from the recently invaded territories, did not have more precise information about the *tzijs* which we now know under the name *Popol Wuj*. Likewise notable is his lack of mention of this first document written in Latin characters, of which there were probably copies existing in Santa Cruz del Quiché or in other areas such as Chichicastenango, Rabinal, Momostenango, or Quetzaltenango (Gavarrete, 1872: 3).

According to Friar Francisco Ximénez in his *Historia de la Provincia de San Vicente de Chiapas y Guatemala*, apparently the Augustinian friar Jerónimo Román was the first chronicler to meticulously collect some of the *tzijs* and traditions included in the *Popol Wuj*. Father Román incorporated into his text parts of the work of Bartolomé de Las Casas and added other details about the *K'iche'* that the Dominican friar had omitted. This leads one think that Las Casas must have had further concrete information. Why did he not record it in writing? We do not know, but one thing is certain: his work formed a part of a large debate among mainland Spanish intellectuals, in particular Juan Ginés de Sepúlveda (1494–1573), during the *Controversia de Valladolid* in 1550. Because Las Casas was himself a part of the colonial system but also a defender of the indigenous people, perhaps he preferred not to record in writing information that might be used to justify greater abuses. This silencing of the contents of the *Popol Wuj* was henceforth one of its dominant characteristics: previously the *tzijs* were alive in the communities as oral tradition that was invisible to the eyes of the colonizers, and when they surfaced they were considered by colonial powers to be dangerous and damaging and therefore were (and continue to be) targeted for eradication, suppression, or appropriation. In this way, from the sixteenth century on, the *tzijs* of the *Popol Wuj* have been mired in the tension between conversion and resistance.

Of the chronicles of the first years of Spanish domination, only Father Francisco Ximénez includes the stories preceding colonization. The other chroniclers, although they probably had knowledge of them, left them out and concentrated on the record referring to administrative branches and control of power in the occupied territories. This approach could not erase the underlying theological–linguistic struggles that appeared in documents such as *artes*, *vocabularios*, and *confesionarios*. In the Ximénez transcription these confrontations are also present, reflecting the manipulation to which the text was subjected. For example, from the earliest days of evangelization, the Franciscan and Dominican orders were divided over whether or not *cavoil* or *cabovil* were equivalent to the Castilian word *Dios* (God). The Franciscans maintained that they were not, and therefore in translating indigenous texts they substituted the word *cabovil* with *Dios* in order to avoid the perpetuation of "pagan" vocabulary. On the other hand, the Dominicans held that the native word should be kept intact (Suárez Roca, 1992: 276–87). In the *Popol Wuj* manuscript archived at the Newberry Library (Ayer MS 1515), Ximénez, in 29 of the pages in which the word *cabauil* appears, translated it as *ídolo* (idol) and not as *Dios*, and only on one page (fo. 40r) does he render it into Castilian as *cabauil*. Ximénez was to a certain extent an exception among the various chroniclers, but he did not escape the contradictions resulting from his membership in the colonizing system.

In his "Prologue" two things are evident. First, at the end of the seventeenth century there were many versions of what had been the precolonial *tzij*, and in the opinion of the friar, they differed quite a bit from each other. Second, approaching this *corpus* of *tzijs* involved a two-sided attitude on his part as a colonizer: on the one hand he sees the stories as somewhat worthy, but at the same time replete with errors, so he feels obliged to eliminate them from the native culture – an attitude linked with the strategy of indoctrination. The task of this exegesis was to find as many similarities between the *tzij* and biblical texts as possible, in order to later attack those specific elements that the Catholic Church considered heretical. In this way the aboriginal narratives were legitimized, but at the same time they were destroyed at their religious, philosophical, and epistemological core. The intent was for an indigenous person to feel that upon baptism only a few parts of his beliefs had been changed – those parts the Christians considered dogmas of the faith. Through these modifications alone, the missionaries changed the meanings of what remained of the native *tzijs*. In the case of the *Popol Wuj* coinciding elements were highlighted, such as the Creation, the Flood, the virgin conception of princess *Xkik'* (for which *Junajpu* came to be the heretical replica of Jesus Christ), or the resurrection of *Xb'alanké*. They are presented as the "same" tales from the Bible, but distorted by Satan. The friars also looked enthusiastically for a connection between the natives and one of the ancient tribes from the Old Testament that had been lost after the Flood, or for an unknown visit from one of the Apostles whose preachings were twisted by Satan. This was one of the explanations for the cross of the four corners of the universe found by preachers in some Mayan temples.

This evangelistic strategy requires a close understanding of the beliefs and narratives of the indigenous people. In his efforts to absorb them, a genuine admiration awoke in the scholarly colonizer, and even a respect for the texts and beliefs. But it is also true that as he recorded this admiration, Ximénez also had the intention of "correcting" theological–doctrinal errors. The coexistence of these two stances in the same person – or group, as was the case with the Dominican order – seems paradoxical, but it is the inevitable result of the purpose of the mission with which the friar was charged by the colonial apparatus.

The collection of *tzijs* we now know as *Popol Wuj*, organized in the form they were recorded and distributed, is the result of choices made by one – or more likely – various scribes in 1555. Later, if Ximénez or another copyist made further changes, we do not know. Given the extremely high level of overall coincidence between these *tzijs* and the narratives that have persisted to this day in oral form in *K'iche'* communities, we can conclude that no significant changes have been made, effectively "fossilizing" them. Accepting how these characteristics and influences served to set down and make immutable the *Popol Wuj* manuscript that we find today does not in any way detract from or destroy its cultural legitimacy. But the facts show that the version we have available today is one that gained its fixed character from colonial interference. On the other hand, the manuscript archived at the Newberry Library is the product of a desire to preserve the *tzijs*, but in addition it is the result of a series of fortuitous coincidences. Among these indeterminate factors, it can be noted, for example, that the *tzijs* that the first scribes recorded – and those that they forgot or omitted – owed much to chance, or to some unknown agenda. Others occurred with those they recorded and the form in which they were written. A further problem is the lack of accuracy with which the manuscripts were transcribed by successive copyists, among them Father Ximénez, the degree of arbitrariness in the phonetization of the *K'iche'* language in adjusting it to the Castilian ear, and lastly how Ximénez at the very least read the orthography and calligraphy of the document he found in the church in Chichicastenango. In neither of these cases was there any rigor or bias.

This tumultuous process resulted in the manuscript that we now know as the *Popol Wuj*, which before colonization did not exist as a text limited to a certain set of *tzijs* recorded in an untouchable and immutable form.


## Modernity and "Ladinization"

The events that shook Europe and North America at the end of the eighteenth century impacted upon the *K'iche'* as well as the colonies of the Spanish, Portuguese, English,

French, and Dutch empires. In the first thirty years of the nineteenth century, a process of breaking from the colonizing powers arose, promoting a Creole independence and the formation of modern nation-states. The founding of these states was inspired by the political, judicial, and doctrinal organizations of the bourgeois states of Europe – especially France – and of the United States. Nevertheless, for the *K'iche'*, as for almost all indigenous peoples, these happenings did not have the positive consequences that they did for creoles or *ladinos* (mixed-blood, Spanish-speaking inhabitants).

Modernization did not in fact bring positive changes for the vast majority of the population. In particular the cases of indigenous Guatemalans such as the *K'iche'*, *Kaqchi'*, *Tz'utujiil*, *Kaqchiquel*, *Q'eqchi'*, *Poqomchi"*, *Q'anjob'al*, and *Mam*, among others, these political changes meant finding themselves in worse conditions than those of colonial times. In the new struggle for power and economic control, indigenous peoples were evicted from the little land they had left and their almost slave-like manual labor was of great benefit to modernizing companies. The political plan of the elite was clearly Western and monocultural. In fact, this policy meant that the natives were not considered citizens of the new states, especially in economic matters (landownership and the cost of manual labor) and in language use. With modernity an accelerated process of "ladinization" began for the natives that further fractured what still remained of the pre-Columbian cultures.

These changes – external and internal – had repercussions that were linked with the manuscript and *tzijs* of the *Popol Wuj*. In the new modern industrial states, religious epistemology was supplanted by science. This change meant that the cultures of the colonized territories lost interest in evangelization and the arena of taxonomical observation emerged to bring data to the idea of evolution, not just of natural species, but also of societies and history. Following Hegel's premises for the explanation of universal world history, they tried to corroborate that Western Christian civilization was the most "evolved."

In 1854 the Austrian traveler, explorer, and diplomat Karl Scherzer visited Guatemala as a member of a scientific committee. He had embarked on a global voyage in search of information and data that could be of interest to European scientists. It was a very similar journey to those undertaken years earlier (1799–1804) by Alexander von Humboldt. On this voyage Scherzer became aware of Father Ximénez's manuscripts, archived at the library of the San Carlos University. They had been taken there from the convent of Santo Domingo in 1830 when General Morazán expropriated the holdings of the Catholic Church. Three years after his visit, Scherzer published *Las Historias del origen de los indios de esta Provincia de Guatemala* in Vienna; he included only Ximénez's Castilian translation, not the *K'iche'* text.

Shortly thereafter, in 1855, the French traveler and antiquarian Charles Brasseur de Bourbourg arrived in Guatemala. The abbé was scouring Central America in search of old documents he judged to be of interest to scientific circles in his country. In Guatemala he found the part of Ximénez's manuscript containing the transcription and translation of the *K'iche' tzijs*. Somehow he took possession of the document, and later published it in Paris in 1861 under the title *Popol Vuh, Le Livre Sacré et les mythes de l'antiquité américaine.* Thus it was the Frenchman who gave it the name we are familiar with and who traced in his title some of the new lines of interpretation which have been very important to this day.

With the expansionist thrust of the start of the nineteenth century and the repositioning of imperial powers it became necessary to take into account the disputing territories and of all they held: material and cultural assets. Cataloging them, classifying them, researching them – all were ways of taking possession. The knowledge belonged to the West, and the objects became peripheral, generally seen as distant and exotic. What caught the attention of the overseas territories undergoing reconquest were the past and the "antique" world. The realities of the indigenous communities where the *tzijs* of the *Popol Wuj* still thrived were ignored by Scherzer and Brasseur.

Brasseur introduced important changes in the manner of reading the *K'iche'* text that contrast with the Spanish colonial approach. Starting with the title, he calls the *Popol Wuj* "Sacred Book." Giving it a sacred nature implies two things. First, it indicates recognition of the validity of a religion outside of Christianity, which traditionally had been denied. This shows a secularization of the study of cultures and peoples, a fact that implies a fundamental change in scholarship. Second, bestowing a sacred classification tied to a concept of history suggests an immutable nature that belongs to an absolute past. In any case, in the abbé's analysis the first idea predominates.

A second contribution is his translation of the *K'iche'* words *Popol Wuj* as *Livre national* (national book) (viii). This interpretation places the Mayan texts within the "national" plan; that is, the agenda of the Creole and mixed-blood elite who had created the Central American republics in the European mold. Brasseur follows the model put forward, among others, by Ernest Renán in France, indicating the need to create a history that would justify the new political entity. Reaffirming the cultural centralism of the West, he thinks that the first written version of the "odd book" was the means that saved the text from complete destruction (viii). In other words, he only sees the aspect of its conservation through writing, but was not aware that the original *tzijs*, those produced from within the Maya culture, had been taken to the brink of extermination by European invasion and colonization.

Brasseur brought two more elements to his work. One was the assertion that the explanation of the origin of the American populations should be made in accordance with the data gathered by the new, "natural" disciplines, using empirical and factual evidence instead of biblical theological references. The resituation of the texts of the *Popol Wuj* within an ethnic and historic framework originating in migrations from Asia, as held by Alexander von Humboldt, eliminates many of the problems encountered by the exegetes of the colony in attempting to determine whether the natives were descendants of a lost tribe of Israel. The other significant element was that he put aside the linking of the *tzijs* of the *Popol Wuj* with those of the Bible. In any case, it is a big change from the interpretations made by Spanish missionaries. Furthermore, Brasseur uses comparative exegesis with other Mesoamerican texts. In this way, Brasseur was a pioneer in the discovery of the existence of a pan-Mesoamerican culture.

This precolonial macro-culture had as its main characteristic a continuity of deep interconnections and mutual influences, despite variations observed in each region.

These observations do not imply a judgment of the personal attitudes of Scherzer or Brasseur, who undoubtedly admired and respected the indigenous text. They describe how biases in interpretation entered the picture in the nineteenth century and they help to see how many of these viewpoints and interpretations have at times been perpetuated with few variations. The preceding observations also show how the two voyagers of the nineteenth century were trapped in a situation analogous to that of Francisco Ximénez. On one hand they experienced a great seduction and admiration for the *tzijs* of the *Popol Wuj*, but on the other, as a part of the Western system of domination and of academia, they had to relegate them in relation to their European cultures. The difference between the voyagers of modernity and the doctrinal monk lies in that the latter proposed erasing those beliefs from the minds of the *K'iche'*, while Scherzer and Brasseur unburdened themselves of the problem, leaving the validity of the stories to antiquity. With this approach, for them the matter was settled.

Concurrent with these intellectual and political movements, within Guatemala a repositioning also occurred in the wake of the end of 300 years of Spanish colonization. When General Carrera created the Republic of Guatemala in 1847, Juan Gavarrete transcribed *Historia de la Provincia de San Vicente y Chiapas y Guatemala*, by Ximénez. Son of the wealthy notary Juan Francisco Gavarrete y Narváez, this Creole antiquarian and historian inserted himself into the political aims of modernity. Interested in recovering a past that would serve to justify the present new aim, Gavarrete dedicated himself to compiling unknown colonial texts. His main concern was to save them, then conserve them, and if possible distribute them. This was a fundamental part of the rewriting of the foundational discourse.

In 1872, in the "Foreword" for a general history to be edited under the auspices of the Economic Society of the Republic of Guatemala, Gavarrete makes an exposition about the necessity of writing the first history of the country, just as had been done by "civilized countries" and other republics that had become independent (1). The agenda of the new historical discourse should open with "recollections recorded by natives who learned to write after the conquest," which is to say, the *Popol Wuj* (2). The precolonial past is mentioned as the Quiché Kingdom, which qualifies it as a nation. Its "myths and historical memories" are presented as the "NATIONAL BOOK, SACRED BOOK or COMMUNITY BOOK, meaning the *POPOL-BUJ*" (3). With this approach, the Mayan past receives important recognition, but at the same time it is lumped into the national agenda hegemonized by Creoles. It is not an assimilation that respects the integrity of the values of the native culture, but rather it absorbs them, stripping them of their philosophical and religious cores. This approach assimilates *K'iche'*-Mayan epistemology within the Christian one, which constitutes a strategy of making the former disappear, given that the validating reference is Western, not native. This recognition is gained only to the degree to which it resembles the paradigm brought by colonizers and perpetuated by the Creole-*ladino* elite, not by its own distinct values.

In Guatemala, in 1927, J. Antonio Villacorta and Flavio Rodas published *Manuscrito de Chichicastenango (Popol-Buj)*. Villacorta was a historian, anthropologist, linguist, and paleographer, who also had a turn in the administration of the state as Minister of Culture during the government of General Jorge Ubico (1913–44). Flavio Rodas, native of Chichicastenango, was familiar with *K'iche'* vocabulary, but in Edmonson's judgment had serious grammatical limitations (1971: x). This was the second bilingual edition of the *Popol Wuj*, and in it the authors used a new orthography, rephoneticizing the text to adapt it to modern Castilian prosody. Nevertheless, the element of this version that had the most impact was the theme of the native speaker as competent authority to handle the language of the Ximénez manuscript. From here onward, the legitimate voice is to be that of the native. But it was the open debate over this edition that started the concern over fidelity to the original *K'iche'* text.

This bilingual edition marks the start of the *indigenist* phase of *Popol Wuj* studies, which coincides with *indigenism* as a movement that opened the way in the intellectual climate of Central America during the 1920s and 1930s. This movement sought a national inheritance for Guatemala, and the *Popol Wuj* fit this ambition very well because it recovered a "soul" that had sunk deep into the past. The *Prehistoria e historia antigua de Guatemala* that Antonio Villacorta published in 1938 is along these lines. But at the same time, this interest in a "glorious" indigenous past became disconnected from the reality of the natives of the twentieth century. For Villacorta, and in general Guatemalan *indigenism*, the indigenous reality belonged to a pre-Columbian past and did not have any projection into contemporary history. Therefore, the *Popol Wuj* was read as a "classical text" – that is, something of interest and competence to intellectuals.

Adrián Recinos, another of the founding members of the Sociedad de Geografía e Historia de Guatemala, published for the first time in 1947 what has been the most widely distributed translation within the Spanish language. He had been working on it for many years, obtaining the highest fidelity with the meaning of the manuscript. Recinos, knowing that in 1928 Walther Lehmann had rediscovered the bilingual manuscript of Father Ximénez (Schultze Jena, 1944: iv), visited the Newberry Library. There he worked with the Ximénez original and put aside the Brasseur version, avoiding following in the footsteps of Noah Eliécer Pohorilles (1913), Georges Raynaud (1925), and Villacorta y Rodas (1927).

This translation, indigenist in philosophy and documented academically in his implementation, was very important because it allowed a wide distribution of the text among the intellectual community and middle-class Creoles and *ladinos*, who in general were strongly racist in Guatemala. The elegant prose of Recinos gave access to the *Popol Wuj* locally in the same way that the translation into French (Brasseur, 1861; Raynaud, 1925) and German (Pohorilles, 1913; Schultze Jena, 1944) had done in Europe. It must also be noted that the wide impact that this work had both within and outside of Guatemala is due also to the important work of distribution undertaken by the Fondo de Cultura Económica de México. This publisher incorporated the text, which was previously virtually unknown to the entire continent, in a deliberate effort to promote a sense of national, regional, and Latin American cultural identity.

However, even in this era of modernity, marked by scientific discourse and indigenism, many of the contradictions and ambiguities that had arisen during Spanish colonialism persisted.

## Globalization versus Mayan Resurgence

"Globalization" spans from the height of the Cold War to the present. Among the *K'iche'* this period of history has continued to be very turbulent and tragic time. There was a departure from the historical, sociological, and judicial discussion that characterized the governing periods of Juan José Arévalo (1944–50) and Jacobo Arbenz Guzmán (1951–4), who had been active participants in the implementation of fairer policies with the indigenous people, and the region slipped directly into civil war. The dictatorship of Coronel Castillo Armas launched a strategy of isolation and repression of the natives, using as excuses the paradoxical outcome of the *indigenist* policies of the Arévalo and Arbenez governments and the simplistic arguments of Cold War doctrines imported directly from the army and ultraconservative sectors. Between 1960 and 1980 these elites also developed a policy of appropriating land and exploiting indigenous workers that progressively transformed itself into a campaign of extermination perpetrated by the elite and the army, both predominately *ladino*.

The failure to recognize native rights generated responses from indigenous communities by diverse political groups, generally leftist, various churches (some postconciliar sectors of the Catholic Church and some liberal Protestant churches), and some activist groups with indigenous roots. From this movement guerrilla groups arose – never very numerous – *Grupos de Base* (a Catholic-inspired organization, with much influence from liberation theology), social movements and unions (mostly on plantations and farms), and groups for the recovery of language and traditions.

The repression led by the army against this widespread movement was called a "civil war" despite the fact that the vast majority of those killed or missing were unarmed civilians. In fact it was an ethnic war against natives, especially the *K'iche'* (83 percent of the victims from 1962–96 were Mayans, and of those almost 50 percent were *K'iche'*, according to a report from Proyecto Recuperación de la Memoria Histórica). The worst period was under the dictatorship of General Efraín Ríos Montt, from 1982–3, with genocide that continued almost until the end of the decade. The *K'iche'*s refer to those years as "the time of violence."

In the midst of these collapses and the repositioning of hegemonies at world and regional levels, reinterpretations of the *Popol Wuj* continued. One of the topics of debate was how to resolve the issue of the translations; the other was about the influences and eventual appropriations to which the text might be subjected, whether from political, religious, cultural (endo- or exo-ethnic), or other types of organizations or institutions.

Continuing in pursuit of a faithful recuperation of the *K'iche'* text, in 1955 Dora M. de Burgess and Patricio Xec published a new *K'iche'* version in Quetzaltenango, Guatemala, with the backing of the evangelical church. According to Paulo Burgess, a missionary at the church, the goal was to return to the natives the right to read "their sacred book" in their own language and not in the Castilian of Recinos (1955: iii). The missionary believed that the publication could illuminate some of the aspects missed by the "savants," owing to the fact that Patricio Xec Cuc had gone over the vocabulary with young students at the Instituto Bíblico Quiché from all over the *K'iche'* region (ibid.).

In 1962 Antonio Villacorta wrote a second edition of the manuscript, this time translated word-for-word in a hyper-textualist approach, seeking complete semantic "purism." He calls it "Crestomatía Quiché" – that is, a collection of writings chosen with educational aims, which seems to suggest the importance he gave to the dissemination of the text amongst the newer generations of Guatemalans.

After having worked from 1945 on the rephoneticization of Mayan writing and having created special characters to represent the phonemes of the language, in 1977 Adrián Inés Chávez published a new version of the *Pop-Wuj (Libro de Acontecimientos,* or *Book of Events)*. In 1997 he reedited it under the title *Pop Wuj. Libro del Tiempo (Book of Time)*. It is a translation in four columns: a literal transcription, a phoneticized transcription, a literal translation in Castilian, and a Castilian version employing syntactical rules comprehensible to contemporary readers.

The idea of this project was to recover precolonial phonetics and to decolonize the native language contaminated by Castilian sounds. He adds that the negative impact of Latin orthography on the *K'iche'* language resulted in transmitting "feelings and ideas which are of a completely different nature than the *Mayan cultural essence*" (Matul Morales, 1997: xii; emphasis added). Antonio Pop Caal also maintains that those who wrote about natives while ignoring the basic characteristics of their culture represented them in a completely mistaken way (1988).

Daniel Matul Morales did not limit the task of recovering the *Popol Wuj* to speculative activity. For him, as for many other Mayan activists, this intellectual work is a part of a plan to construct a "Multilingual and multicultural nation in its fundamental structures" (1997: xiv). It is a new political plan constructed during the insurgency against exploitation and segregation, in resisting genocide, and in building a process to achieve peace in the face of difficulties that persist until today. Matul Morales trusts that, with the "secrets" contained in the contents of the *Popol Wuj tzijs*, "the Maya are contributing to the construction of a new society wherein our philosophers, in a context revindicated after four hundred and seventy-three years of struggle, will continue in search of the latest truths" (ibid.).

Perhaps today it might be said that the concrete results of Chávez's translation are not its greatest contribution. The originality of this *K'iche'* was to revindicate the value and dignity of the Mayan population and its culture, recovering the language and the text of the *Popol Wuj* in its precolonial integrity as living cultural artifact – a language and text that belongs to a community that is not primitive, and of course not backward. As Guzmán Böckler states, they belong to a community that despite the "multisecular aggression which it has been a victim of, has known how to maintain its vitality and historical continuity" (1997: xx). From Chávez's reading, this is the contribution which has survived, despite the fact that his Catholic credo notoriously interfered with the terms in which the translation was rendered.

In 1971 Munro Edmonson published *The Book of Counsel: The Popol Vuh of the Quiche Maya of Guatemala*. This translation, the second into English (in 1950 Delia Goetz and Sylvanus Morley had translated the Recinos version), made some changes in the reading of the *Popol Wuj*. Situated in academia and with an ethnographic, rather than a linguistic, religious, philosophical, or literary focus (xi), he abandons the traditional form of translation into prose and instead presents paired verses. His idea was that "The Popol Vuh is in poetry and cannot be accurately understood in prose" (xi). And he insists that "Words matter, and formal discourse matters even more" (xii). Because of this Edmondson proposed capturing the essence of the text through the nature and "style" of language.

With the assistance of a spiritual guide (*daykeeper* and seer) Andrés Xiloj, in 1986 Dennis Tedlock published his translation entitled *Popol Vuh. The Definitive Edition of the Mayan Book of the Dawn of Life and the Glories of Gods and Kings*. On the cover it also says: "commentary based on the ancient knowledge of the Modern Quiché Maya." Tedlock's focus was to read the original from a perspective of the "divinatory art" of seers and spiritual guides: "Diviners are, by profession, interpreters of difficult texts" (15). Tedlock states that when Andrés Xiloj began to read the *Popol Wuj* almost without difficulty, he understood that something special was occurring. Tedlock told Xiloj the meanings of archaic terms, and in turn the reader rendered an interpretation full of meaning (15). Tedlock concludes that his work is the result of a three-way dialogue between the wisdom of Xiloj's profession, the manuscript, and his academic knowledge (16). The central theme is religious spirituality. Because of this the format of his translation alternates paragraphs in prose with others having the structure and tone of prayer – which is something he perceived as evident in the original text – in order to restore its ritual content.

Tedlock's translation was an inspired reading, based in mysticism and religion that interpreted the text from an astronomical and calendaric perspective (15). This is the way the translator found to link the text written in 1555 with the tumultuous present of the *K'iche'*. In this sense it is a subversive mysticism because it opposes the doctrine of the majority of the dominant Western religions in Guatemala. It subverts the inspiration in the biblical creed and in a God in Heaven, and centers its religiosity in the Earth – where it is assumed that life sprang, according to the *Popol Wuj*. This reading by Tedlock and Xiloj links the precolonial past with the present, erasing the gap opened by European civilization. Nevertheless, it admits that the two timelines will have to run in parallel in the future (13).

Recently, Allen Christenson published his new translation of the *Popol Wuj* (2003–4). Taking up Edmonson's point of view, Christenson saw the text as a "sublime work of literature" and he placed it on the same plane as classical works such as the epic poems of cultures having prestige in the West (42). The conceptual emphasis of this interpretation is to recover a word whose nature was to have always been written, and that as writing it suffered the trauma of the Spanish conquest and Catholic missionaries. Christenson focuses on the destructive effect of colonization exclusively in this historic period and on the modality particular to these forms of colonialism. The *K'iche'* text is meant as a relic that in itself encompasses a sacred truth (17). Thus the task of the reading is to give it life by way of being faithful to the old Word, which later becomes wisdom through the ritual of uttering the Word. The accurate reproduction of the perfection of antiquity is the ultimate goal of the reading, and its authority is established by adhering to a text that was set down in writing during distant times. Therefore the work of the translator is to recover the desire to set down the story in writing; that is, through a system similar to that of the West but that had already existed for many centuries before the arrival of the Spanish. In this way the meaning of the text comes from linking poetic and literary value with archaic forms.

Finally, the last version we will mention is that by Enrique Sam Colop, published in 1999 under the title *Popol Wuj. Versión Poética K'iche'*. Sam Colop, of *K'iche'* origin, emphasizes the "multiple authorship" of the text, and indicates that the Ximénez version gathered elements from different systems of register and transmission of the text, just as it did differences in dialects, all of which originate before colonization (13). He also notes that owing to the astronomical correlation of many of the passages, the narrative of the *Popol Wuj* is distinct from that of other cultures, both in its nature and in its form of articulation (13).

But the core of his reading lies in "attempting an interpretation of the text in the original language in which it was written" (14). In this recovery recognizing the differences in the style of the *K'iche'* language plays an important role, but most importantly the tradition and language before the burst of Spanish invasion. This value does not lie in that, to us, the language seems archaic, but rather it was the form of expression and feeling of the people of these pre-Columbian communities, and it is through the recovery of its forms that the original meaning can be accessed. Just as for the majority of present-day Maya, one of the concerns of Sam Colop is education and literacy. His presentation of the *Popol Wuj* intends, without separating itself too much from Ximénez manuscript, to be within reach of contemporary *K'iche'* (19).

In addition to previous readings of the *Popol Wuj* in translation, other summaries of critical interpretations could be presented. Because it is beyond the scope of this chapter, we will simply say that in this area there is also a large variety of tendencies, intentions, critical frameworks, and projects. We find readings ranging from para-biblical exegeses to the esoteric; from the most orthodox philology to ethnohistory and ethnolinguistics; from cultural anthropology to structuralism, poststructuralism, psychoanalytical, Marxist theories; and also those derived from cosmo-archeology.

Translations as well as critical studies have always had theoretical frameworks and ideologies strongly tied to very diverse political, epistemological, and religious projects. If this can occur with any text, in the particular case of the *Popol Wuj* these perspectives have been sharpened by the sociopolitical–cultural contexts of the Maya communities to which the *tzijs* are actively linked. This can also be seen in what happened to Ms. Rigoberta Menchú Tum. The debates, acceptances, and rejections toward her person, career, activities, and decisions are an example of the close relationships between the conditions of internal colonization with which the *K'iche'* live, the plans and agendas far removed from them, and the conflicts within the hearts of the collective native community. The overall view of these stances serves to illustrate to what extent evaluating the conditions of the survival of the Maya culture and the texts that they gave rise to is problematic and controversial.

The synopsis – which has not been complete – shows, among other things, how persistent attempts to appropriate, manipulate, divert, or simply exterminate Mayan cultural discourses have been. These actions have been part-plans that have completed their cycles and have left their imprints, as much on the indigenous nation as on the text of the *Popol Wuj*. In recent times the most tragic point of these extermination plans was the genocide during the 1970s and 1980s. But military campaigns have had their parallels or counterparts in other activities. Cultural asphyxiation – erasing the presence of Mayan cosmogony, philosophy, ethic, language, and religion – was given a boost through some of the campaigns for religious expansion that are carried out in Latin America, and in particular Guatemala.

The new missionaries, in the same way as the Spanish of another era, have sought to erase the weakened remnants of native traditions and beliefs. The categorization used has been the same as that of the Spanish: they are pagan beliefs. The difference is that the contemporary missionaries have been more radical than the Catholics, because they, to a certain degree, tolerated spaces for ritual negotiation and for beliefs. It is not by chance that the institutional labor of some churches, like the evangelical Pentecostal – closely connected with Ríos Montt and Jorge Serrano, among others – has had a strong penetration into the Maya region.

But it has not been the only church that has laid out a campaign of aggressive expansion. According to a November 2005 report by the US Department of State, the religious composition of Guatemala is 40 percent Protestant, the majority of which are recognized as evangelical, but there is also a strong presence of other churches, such as the Jehovah's Witnesses and the Church of Latter-day Saints (Mormons).

Added to this are political agendas, those which during the Cold War were closely linked with the political blocs and ideologies of that time. But once this confrontation ended the penetration of the "global" system began, with its culture of hyperconsumption in the central countries, with technological development and the productivity that often do not respect the environment nor native cultures, and that transforms the collection of peripheral societies to a rhythm of needs and parameters far removed from local conditions. Taking into account this enormous complexity, one can ascertain that the conditions under colonialism during the sixteenth, seventeenth, and eighteenth centuries have not vanished, although they have changed and operate through different agents.

As readers today prepare to read the *Popol Wuj*, a legitimate question arises: Why read it? All readings are a form of recovery and re-creation of the text. The idea is to decide from which point we direct our work: From the perspective of the colonizer or the colonized? From the culture that fights to survive and carry on into the future, or from an academic position? From a respect for life in all its forms from all corners of the planet, or from the immediate and increasingly out-of-control urgencies? From the notion that there are privileged cultures and epistemologies, or from the perspective of the existence of cultural pluralism? And perhaps many other questions. What is certain is that the *Popol Wuj*, just as other native texts of the continent, has been silenced, either by ignoring it or by relegating it to an archaic space. Nevertheless, its resurgence is a fact of contemporary reality.

Its existence and survival have been linked with the fate of the community and culture to which it pertained and continues to pertain. Its survival also has been the result of innumerable repositioning of the subjects and agents that have been tied to these *tzijs*. This chapter is also subject to the same phenomenon.

## References and Further Reading

### References

Akkeren, Ruud van (2000). *Place of the Lord's Daughter: Rab'inal, its History, its Dance-Drama*. Leiden, The Netherlands: CNWS Research School.

Anonymous (1935). *Isagoge Historica Apologética de las Indias Occidentales y especial de la Provincia de San Vicente de Chiapa y Guatemala*. Guatemala: Biblioteca "Goathemala" de la Sociedad de Geografía e Historia, Vol. XIII.

Brasseur de Bourbourg, C. E. (1861). "Avant-propos" (i–vi), "Notice Bibliographique sur Le Livre Sacré" (vii–xv), and "Dissertation sur le Mythes de l'Antiquité Américaine, sur la probabilité des communications existant anciennement d'un continent a l'autre, et sur les Migrations des peuples Indigènes de l'Amérique, etc." (xvii–cclxxix). In *Popol Vuh, Le Livre Sacré et les mythes de l'antiquité américaine*. Paris: Arthus-Bertrand.

Burgess, P. (1955). "Introducción." In *Popol Wuj: Texto de R.P.F. Ximénez*. Trans. Dora M. de Burgess and Patricio Xec. Quetzaltenango, Guatemala: El Noticiero Evangélico.

Carmack, R. (1981). *The Quiché Mayas of Utatlán: The Evolution of a Highland Guatemala Kingdom*. Norman: University of Oklahoma Press.

Christenson, A. (2003). "Translator's Preface" and "Introduction" (14–56). In *Popol Vuh: The Sacred Book of the Maya. The Great Classic of Central American Spirituality, Translated from the Original Maya Text*. Vol. I. Winchester, UK and New York: O Books.

Cojtí Cuxil, D. (n.d.). "Problemas de la identidad nacional guatemalteca," *Revista Cultural de Guatemala*, 5(1): 17–21.

de Las Casas, Fray B. (1967). *Apologética Historia Sumaria*. Vols. I and II. Mexico City: Universidad Nacional Autónoma de México, Instituto de Investigaciones Históricas.

Edmonson, M. (1971). "Introduction." In *The Book of Counsel: The Popol Vuh of the Quiche Maya of Guatemala*, pp. vii–xvi. New Orleans, MS: Middle American Research Institute, Tulane University.

Gavarrete, J. (1872). *El Popol-Buj*. "Advertencia" [Foreword]. Typed version of archive at the Academia de Geografía e Historia de Guatemala. June 20.

Guzmán Böckler, C. (1997). "20 años después: recuerdos de la primera edición del 'Pop Wuj'" (xv–xvi) and "Prólogo" (xvii–xxiv). In the *Pop – Wuj: Poema Mito-histórico Kí-chè*. Trans. Adrián

Inés Chávez. Quetzaltenango, Guatemala: TIMACH.

Matul Morales, D. (1997). "Don Adrián Chávez, mensaje de maíz y de poesía." In *Pop – Wuj: Poema Mito-histórico Kí-chè*, pp. xi–xiv. Trans. Adrián Inés Chávez. Quetzaltenango, Guatemala: TIMACH.

Pohorilles, N. E. (1913). *Das Popol Wuh die mythische Geschichte des Kičé-Volkes von Guatemala*. Leipzig: J. C. Hinrich'sche Buchhandlung.

Pop Caal, A. (1988). "Réplica del indio a una disertación ladina." In Guillermo Bonfill (ed.), *Utopía y revolución: El pensamiento político contemporáneo de los indios de América Latina*, pp. 145–8. Mexico City: Editorial Nueva Imagen.

Raynaud, G. (1975 [1925]). *Les Dieux, les héroes et les hommes de l'ancien Guatémala d'après le Livre du Conseil*. Paris: Librairie D'Amerique et D'Orient.

Recinos, A., ed. (1957). *Crónicas indígenas de Guatemala*. Guatemala City: Editorial Universitaria.

Sam Colop, E. (1999). "Introducción." In *Popol Wuj: Versión Poética K'iche*, pp. 13–19. Guatemala City: CHOLSAMAJ.

Scherzer, C. (1857). "Introducción." In *Las Historias del origen de los indios de esta Provincia de Guatemala*, pp. iii–xvi. Vienna: Casa de Carlos Gerold e Hijo.

Schultze Jena, L. (1944). "Vorwort" [Preface]. In *Popol Vuh: Das Heilige Buch der Quiché-Indianer von Guatemala*, pp. iii–v. Stuttgart and Berlin: Kohlhammer.

Suárez Roca, J. L. (1992). *Lingüística misionera española*. Oviedo, Spain: Pentalfa Ediciones.

Tedlock, D. (1986). "Preface." In *Popol Vuh: The Definitive Edition of the Mayan Book of the Dawn of Life and the Glories of Gods and Kings*, pp. 13–21. New York: Simon & Schuster.

US Department of State (2005). http://www.state.gov/g/drl/rls/irf/2005/51641.htm International Religious Freedom Report Home Page. Released on November 8.

Villacorta Calderón, J. A. (1929). "Prólogo." In Fray Francisco Ximénez, *Historia de la Provincia de San Vicente de Chiapas y Guatemala*. Guatemala City: Biblioteca "Goathemala" de la Sociedad de Geografía e Historia, Vol. I.

— (1938). *Prehistoria e historia antigua de Guatemala*. Guatemala City: Tipografía Nacional.

Ximénez, F. (1973). *Empiezan las Historias del origen de los indios de esta Provinçia de Guatemala tradvzido de la lengua qviche em la castellana para mas comodidad de los ministros de el S<sup>to</sup> Evangelio por el R.P.F. Francisco Ximénez cvra doctrinero por el Real Patronato del pvueblo de S<sup>to</sup> Thomas Chvíla. (Popol Vuh)*. Verbatim transcription by Carlos M. López, published in the online edition of the *Popol Wuj*, http://library.osu.edu/sites/popolwuj/

## Further Reading

Carmack, R., and Morales Santos, F. (1983). *Nuevas perspectivas sobre el Popol Vuh*. Guatemala City: Editorial Piedra Santa.

Centro de Estudios Mayas, Timach (1999). *Memorias del segundo congreso internacional sobre el Pop Wuj*. Guatemala City: Timach.

López, C. (1999) *Los Popol Wujs y sus epistemologías: Las diferencias, el conocimiento y los ciclos del infinito*. Quito: Editorial Abya.

Online edition of the *Popol Wuj* manuscript, http://library.osu.edu/sites/popolwuj/

# 4

# The Colegio Imperial de Santa Cruz de Tlatelolco and Its Aftermath: Nahua Intellectuals and the Spiritual Conquest of Mexico

*Rocío Cortés*

One successful device in the colonization of New Spain was the appropriation of linguistic and cultural knowledge of and about the *vencidos* (defeated people). While monastic orders applied this knowledge toward their own evangelistic designs, the colonial administration also did not fail to recognize that such knowledge could be used to achieve more effective control of the conquered. The members of mendicant orders – Franciscans, Dominicans, and Augustinians – opened schools alongside their monasteries as soon as they arrived in New Spain. While the friars learned native languages and customs, the native youth acquired an education in Christian principles in those schools and, occasionally, literacy. Realizing the potential that these first schools had in teaching and providing knowledge about indigenous policies, the colonial administration gave their "blessing" for the Franciscans to establish the Colegio Imperial de Santa Cruz de Tlatelolco, an institution of higher education principally for noble indigenous[1] intellectuals. This project entailed expectations that generations of well-educated indigenous linguistic/cultural intermediaries would facilitate smoother evangelization and colonization. This extraordinary plan featured much experimentation on the part of the friars in the earlier stages, a time when the colonial design for New Spain was still being shaped by a variety of secular and religious factions that interpreted colonial methods differently. Only three years after the Colegio's inauguration, advanced native education would be seen as dangerous to social and religious order. Opponents to a higher education for indigenous students dreaded that knowledge would only encourage neophytes to question Christian dogma. Lack of funds owing to growing opposition to the project and a stricter royal administration, among other causes, would contribute to its decline by the 1580s.

Despite criticism about educating the indigenous people, and economic struggles, the Colegio became a center of linguistic and historical compilations, as well as of the translation of Christian doctrinal materials. Friars and students together designed

Nahuatl grammars and dictionaries, assembled a valuable corpus of pre-conquest customs, and translated doctrinal works into native languages with the intention of proselytizing the native masses. But literacy and knowledge of European systems of thought also opened up a space for new forms of subaltern negotiation on the part of the students. From the Colegio emerged an educated elite that would influence, directly and indirectly, other subaltern intellectuals in the uses of knowledge as a form of social and political agency. The Franciscans' legacy of the Colegio project would continue through the exchange of knowledge by members of other religious orders – such as the Jesuits – and by ethnically diverse intellectuals well into the seventeenth century. The narrative discourses of this ethnically and politically asymmetric group reveal a production of subjectivities through struggles of power in a "contact zone."

## The Colonial Enterprise of Conversion through Education

Intertwined with economic and expansionist motivations, the colonization of the Americas by the Spaniards was also driven by evangelization. With the *Reconquista* of the last Muslim kingdom in the Iberian Peninsula and the arrival of the Spaniards to the New World, Spain became a powerful nation. Supported by the papacy in a series of papal bulls, Spain would legitimize its presence in the new lands through a series of political theories based on the observation of indigenous peoples' lives and manners. Taking the European way of life and religious beliefs as the model of civilization, the colonizers developed unscientific images of the indigenous populations. Indigenous cultural practices and beliefs that differed from the European paradigm were perceived as barbaric. But Christian principles, for the Iberians, had derived from Roman law. Debates emerged on the legal and moral bases to justify the conquests and "civilization" of the indigenous people, who by natural law had the right to their own laws and practices. From different schools of thought emerged what B. Keen has called "anti-Indian" and "pro-Indian" policies (1990: 108). For some, such as the Spaniard Juan Ginés de Sepúlveda, who negatively portrayed the indigenous people as inferior to Spaniards because of their lack of civil laws and peaceful manners, a Spanish civil superiority gave them the right to "civilize" the indigenous populations, even if it had to be by force. On the other hand, proponents of an indigenous image based on the nature of human equality, represented in the ideas of the Dominican Friar Bartolomé de las Casas, proposed that, since the indigenous people were human beings with equal natural rights and capabilities to all men, their manners could be changed by merciful persuasion. For the religious orders, evangelization had to be achieved mainly by instructing the indigenous masses in Christian doctrine and conduct. The *encomienda* system, whose purposes were native labor and tribute as compensation for Christian education, and which adhered to anti-Indian policies, was proving to be inefficient in its pedagogical purposes. Instead, to the proponents of pro-Indian policies, it had become a vehicle for native exploitation and for economic gain. The friars' instruction in European value systems was based on experimentation; they implemented a variety of techniques, from theatrical representation to painting, to preaching, to alphabetization. Unlike secular priests accustomed to operating in European urban centers, friars were used to a more ascetic lifestyle, and proved to be a better choice to convert the indigenous masses. As early as 1503 the Franciscans inaugurated the first convent in Santo Domingo, and even before the proclamation of the Laws of Burgos (1512), which recognized the indigenous people as vessels of Spain and encouraged conversion through education, the Franciscans were already gathering in their convents noble indigenous children to convert them.

In 1523 – only three years after the conquest of Tenochtitlan – three Franciscans arrived and began the enterprise of evangelization-colonization, followed, a year later, by another twelve. The Franciscan Pedro de Gante founded the first school of New Spain, *San José de los Naturales*. This school proved the natives' ability to learn, in subjects ranging from manual labor and crafts to grammar and basic Latin. Although the Franciscans were the first order to arrive in New Spain, optimistic projects to evangelize through education were also designed by the Dominicans upon their arrival in 1526, and by the Augustinians when they later came on the scene in 1533. By the 1530s perhaps 600 natives had already begun to learn to write as a result of the friars' education projects (Gruzinski, 1993: 47). Learning in those first centers went both ways. The friars evangelized and alphabetized the natives, but they also acquired linguistic proficiency in native languages facilitating inquiry into indigenous polities. For the friars, the more linguistic and cultural knowledge they gained from the *vencidos*, the more effective would be the enterprise of conversion. This knowledge would also be beneficial to Spanish officials in designing economic and political policies for the new colony.

After the *Primera Audiencia* (1528–30; a court of law and administrative body) had failed to establish effective colonial government, research on types of tribute, political organization, and social institutions was encouraged by the president of the *Segunda Audiencia* (1530–5), Sebastián Ramírez de Fuenleal, to aid the governmental logistics of the new colony. To exploit these enquiries, Fuenleal petitioned the Franciscans Andrés de Olmos and Martín de Valencia to produce a book on the antiquities of the natives, with special regard to the major centers of Mexico, Texcoco, and Tlaxcala. European education, for the indigenous people, especially of noble status, would serve several purposes. On the one hand, well-educated indigenous people would aid research into native languages and polities; on the other, they could serve as intermediaries in religious and secular matters. Outnumbered by the natives, Spaniards believed they would benefit from trusted native participation in developing the logistics for a better colonization. The moral and intellectual benefits of a higher education were also needed to prepare future *caciques* (lords) to lead Christian communities. Thus higher education for the native elite was considered achievable as well as advantageous. The Viceroy Don Antonio de Mendoza and the Franciscan Bishop Juan de Zumárraga granted to the Franciscan order the privilege of opening an institution of higher education to natives.

## The Colegio's Students and Textual Productions

The Colegio Imperial de Tlatelolco opened on January 6, 1536, with 80 students from various geographical regions in central Mexico. Despite conflicts and controversies that would arise later against higher education for natives, the Colegio became a crucial center for research on indigenous languages and cultures. Following a curriculum modeled on European elite higher education, the students studied the *trivium* (grammar, rhetoric, and logic) and the *quadrivium* (arithmetic, geometry, astronomy, and music), which the friars adjusted according to the students' needs. The *gramáticos*[2] are recognized in several of the friars' writings for their translation of works from Latin, Nahuatl, and Spanish and for their help in the elaboration of dictionaries and grammars on indigenous languages. One of the most famous *gramáticos* was Don Antonio Valeriano of Atzcapozalco, who later served 20 years as the governor of Tenochtitlan, beginning in 1573. He helped with etymology and semantics in the development of the *Vocabulario en lengua castellana y mexicana* of Friar Alonso de Molina, a dictionary designed to help friars in learning Nahuatl. He also helped Friar Bernardino de Sahagún (1499–1590), one of the most active researchers on native history and culture, with the *Coloquios y Doctrina Cristiana*, a reconstruction of a debate that took place in 1524 between the twelve Franciscans, who had just arrived in New Spain, and a gathering of secular and religious native leaders. Valeriano also served as Sahagún's interpreter in the compilation of his *Historia general de las cosas de la Nueva España*, and wrote glosses to the *Sermonario* of Friar Juan Bautista.

Also well versed in Spanish, Latin, and Nahuatl was Pedro of San Buenaventura of Cuauhtitlan, who collaborated with Sahagún, writing the section on pre-conquest medicine and the animals of New Spain for the *Hymns of the Gods*. He also illustrated Sahagún's Mexican calendar. Hernando de Ribas from Texcoco translated the *Diálogos de paz y tranquilidad del alma* of Juan de Gaona and helped Friar Alonso de Molina with his *Vocabulario* in Nahuatl and Friar Juan Bautista with his *Vocabulario Eclesiástico*. Francisco Bautista de Contreras from Cuernavaca, before becoming governor of Xochimilco in 1605, worked with Friar Juan Bautista on the translation into Nahuatl of the *Imitación de Cristo*, known as the *Contemptus mundi*, and collaborated with Hernando de Ribas on the translation of *Vanidad del mundo*. Juan Badiano of Xochimilco collaborated on the translation from Nahua into Latin of the *Libellus de medicinalibus Indorum Herbis*, known as the *Códice Badiano*, attributed to the Xochimilcan Martín de la Cruz. This codex contains information about plants and medicines used in pre-conquest times. Esteban Bravo from Tezcoco helped in the writing of a lost *Sermonario* of Friar Alonso de Trujillo. Pedro de Gante, named after the Franciscan friar who inaugurated *San José de los Naturales*, assisted Friar Juan Bautista in the Colegio and wrote about the lives of saints. Although none of Gante's texts have been discovered, Friar Bautista relates that he always consulted his abilities and talents (Garibay, 1954: 2: 225). Agustin de la Fuente from Tlatelolco served as copyist and editor for Sahagún and Bautista.

In the *Florentine Codex* Sahagún also recognizes the help of the ancient *titicih* or indigenous physicians (León-Portilla, 1990: 54). Diego Adriano of Tlatelolco and Agustín the la Fuente collaborated in painting the *Codex*. Martín Jacobita of Tlatelolco, who from 1561 to 1565 was rector of the Colegio, Antonio Vegeriano of Cuauhtitlán, and Andrés Leonardo of Tlatelolco helped Sahagún in the rewriting of the *Coloquios* and *Códices Matritenses* (León-Portilla, 1990: 48). That the Franciscans documented the names of the most brilliant students was to show evidence of the Colegio's success, emphasizing the students' abilities and their willingness to cooperate in the enterprise of evangelization. However, the *gramáticos'* textual production would later play an important role in the development of a native historiography.

For the Colegio's translations and transcriptions the friars and *gramáticos* standardized regional differences in Nahuatl into a prescriptive refined model known today as Classical Nahuatl, contrasting with the "Colonial Nahuatl" used by notaries for mundane purposes (Karttunen, 1982: 400–1). Friars looked for synonyms and parallel concepts between Spanish and Nahuatl to develop a Nahuatl rhetoric based upon Christian models (Buckhart, 1989: 10–11). For some scholars the prescription of Classical Nahuatl was another form of colonization. It was a means to aid the process of acculturation by educating the indigenous elite; to replace the authority of native priests; and, among other aims, to assist the imposition of a unifying canon that would de-legitimate local Nahuatl dialects (Klor de Alva, 1989).

The introduction of the alphabetic system altered Nahua methods of recording history, which had been previously achieved by oral performance and pictographic or ideographic representations. Historical indigenous systems of recalling the past were based on unique coordinates of time and space. The use of colors and other elements gave coherence to the natives' way of life, a coherence which they began to explain to the friars by adopting European pictorial techniques. By the end of the sixteenth century, pictorial representation remained in use primarily in practical and mundane documents – legal accounts, land records, tributes, and histories and genealogies (Hill-Boone, 1998: 164).[3]

Even if Sahagún and like-minded friars believed in the equality of human souls and had a thirst for legitimate cultural and linguistic knowledge of the indigenous cultures, Christian intolerance also justified the study of pagan things for purposes of facilitating their eradication (Buckhart, 1989: 3). Sahagún, in his prologue to his *Historia*, compares the friars' enterprise of conversion to that of the physician who needs knowledge to cure the sick. So, for Sahagún, knowledge about native culture provided the "medicine" to extract the disease of paganism. Translation at the Colegio involved the "purification" of pagan resonances, and Christian notions served as models for the adjustments of traditional ideas.

But translations require more than simply supplanting native codes with Christian ones. A coherent understanding of the cosmos organizing native religious beliefs was required to adjust the alien European systems of thought and representation. The task of the *gramáticos* was monumental. On the one hand they provided a written corpus to serve the friars' understanding of native practices against Christian ethical and moral principles, which provided the reasons for the Spanish presence in their territories; on the other hand their translations were also intended to persuade other natives to embrace a foreign system of thought, refuting traditional beliefs. Christianity, whether by true conviction or not, provided the space for cultural negotiation. By declaring their affiliation to Christianity, the *gramáticos*, and other indigenous writers, conveyed traditional beliefs and practices. This enunciative space not only allowed them to escape possible charges of apostasy but enabled them to maintain the echoes of their ancient traditions.

The ambivalence of transcribing ancient beliefs for the purposes of conversion is revealed in the translation of the *Coloquios y Doctrina Christiana*. This text is in the dialogue genre, with friars engaging the *Tlamatinimeh* (Nahua wise men) to convey Franciscan arguments for the superior truths of Christianity. But in the course of this dialogue the *Tlamatinimeh* elaborate on the coherence of the ancient way of life, and in the end refuse to repudiate it even in the face of the best persuasions of the friars. Because the *Coloquios* are transcriptions of oral exchanges, traditional Nahua techniques could be used by the *gramáticos*. In contrast to the indirect style, at times used in annals, where everything is told in the third person, it is through quoting the words uttered by the characters where Nahuas express emotion. This technique, known also as direct style, gives immediacy to speech that reflects the collision of the indigenous system of beliefs with the European ones. In their role as linguistic authorities, the *gramáticos* were able to preserve the sacred beliefs Christianity was erasing, even if the intent of the texts was the opposite. The highly emotive re-creation of the words of the elders – which indigenous people would consider sacred – would in some cases reinforce these beliefs. Refusal to "forget" the teachings of the elders was a main reason given for difficulties in "eliminating idolatries" in the *Manual de ministros para el conocimiento de sus idolatrías y extirpación de ellas* of priest Jacinto de la Serna in 1636 (León-Portilla, 1990: 63). The preservation of the word of the elders, so emotively re-created by the *gramáticos*, would continue as a practice of resistance in future textual creation by native intellectuals in the late sixteenth and seventeenth centuries.

Just as transcription of ideas from the pre-conquest past opened a space for indigenous preservation of old practices and beliefs, adjustments to the coherence of that past were necessary to explain their colonial present. The *gramáticos* tried to give coherence to a reality in which the indigenous people were losing so much of their territories and traditions by searching for answers in their own past and implementing what they learned from European knowledge. The transcription into Nahuatl of Book XII of Sahagún's *Historia general* (also known as the *Florentine Codex*) at the Colegio is a good example of creative interpretation of initial Nahua reaction to the Spanish encounter and rationalization of their defeat. Accounts passed through several hands when transcribed at the Colegio, including those of friars who might have collaborated in the *gramáticos'* interpretations. For example, the section on the omens – which certainly was added *a posteriori* – may be highly influenced by European Christian and pagan myths (Rozat Dupeyron, 2002: *passim*), and a spreading belief that don Hernando Cortés was mistaken for Quetzalcoatl has been questioned by some scholars (Elliot, 2002: 105–8; Rozat Dupeyron, 2002; Lockhart, 1992). However, being a compilation of many sources, Book XII gives us a good idea of how the indigenous people perceived Spanish phenomena.

Book XII also illustrates the *gramáticos* preserving their ethnic identities, founded in the collective memory of their own *altepetl* (ethnic community established in a specific territory). It also reveals that each *altepetl* had its own views on the ancient past which, at times, competed against each other. The conquest in the *Florentine Codex* is written from the point of view of the Tlatelolcans (inhabitants of Tlatelolco), relatives of the Mexicas (inhabitants of Tenochtitlan) but from separate communities. This account of the conquest clearly sympathizes with the Tlatelolcans at the expense of the Mexicas, who had conquered them in 1473. The writing of local histories not only preserved tradition, but would also have a pragmatic use during the sixteenth and seventeenth centuries as a means to restore previous positions of high status and to appeal for privileges and territory restitution.

The Colegios' half-century trajectory reflects the struggles that the different secular and religious factions had in their purposes and methods of colonization. For the first 20 years, the Colegio operated under a general atmosphere of optimism. The *Nuevas Leyes* (1542–3) favored the protection of the indigenous people against the exploitation of the *encomienda* system, and debates suggesting natives as potentially "perfect" Christians gave friars motivation to advocate for their education-conversion projects. Later, however, in the face of the Counter-Reformation and emerging social pressures in an established colony, colonial policies would turn to favor further the economic goals of colonization by Hispanicizing the natives.

## The Struggles of the Colegio Imperial de Santa Cruz de Tlatelolco

Some scholars believe that one of the goals the Franciscans had for the Colegio was the ordination of native priests (Ricard, 1996: 342). Perhaps Franciscan optimism and desire to build a new Christian society (Baudot, 1995: *passim*), further fed by the success of the first indigenous students, was what gave birth to the belief that the Colegio would produce the first generation of indigenous priests. The Colegio's intent to ordain natives was assailed almost immediately, however. Some critics doubted the capabilities of neophytes to interpret Christian dogma, and feared errors would lead to heresy. To friars such as the Dominican Domingo de Betanzos, indigenous education must be limited to tutelage because the natives lacked the authority and understanding for preaching (Cuevas, 1946: 440). Indeed, only three years after the Colegio's inception, ex-student Don Carlos Ometochzin, lord of Texcoco, was condemned for apostasy. There is little doubt that this development raised questions about the effectiveness of native education (Ricard, 1966: 343–97; Cuevas, 1946: 439). Perhaps these pressures from the opposition (along with rejection of celibacy vows by many students) contributed to Friar Juan de Zumárraga's disappointment in 1540 (Cuevas, 1946: 441). In a letter written to *visitador* Juan de Ovando in 1570 the Franciscans recognized that the initial goal of teaching theology had to be abandoned, stating that the students proved to be better in grammar (*Documentos para la historia de México*, 1941: 63).

The decline of the Colegio by the late 1580s had much to do with power conflicts among different factions in an increasingly established colonial structure. In the first years of evangelization of New Spain the religious orders were granted by papal bulls the authority to convert the indigenous peoples. Members of the religious orders even served as bishops and archbishops, positions held usually by the secular clergy. The Franciscan order, the first group to come upon the scene in the first quarter of the sixteenth century, had many schools and monasteries in the central Nahua-speaking areas. Whether or not they had utopian projects to begin a new Christian society, they did clearly acquire an early monopoly on indigenous matters. They were accepted by the indigenous people, knew the native tongues, and controlled many monasteries.

By 1555 opposition to native higher education and literacy had swelled and was formally addressed by the formal Provincial Council. The policies that emerged prohibited the natives' access to catechisms and sermons, their study of native languages, and even their right to paint without supervision by an ecclesiastical authority (Romano, 2004: 269; Gruzinski, 1993: 56). "The composite of contradictory administrative directives and policies coming out of this council illustrates how ecclesiastical or secular assumptions about reading and writing, race and authorship, had begun to diverge from those of the Franciscans who had been developing policy via practice since the 1530s" (Romano, 2004: 268). These drastic policies were enacted not only in response to the spread of literacy among the indigenous people, but also to the existence of clandestine circles reproducing texts independently of the church (Gruzinski, 1993: 56).

The decline in support of native higher education was also precipitated by a shift away from pro-Indian policies. The era of debate about the natural right of natives, promoted by Bartolomé de Las Casas in 1552, was closely followed by an era of anti-Indian crown policies, with a series of royal orders mandating the confiscation of all works concerning indigenous antiquities. In Peru these policies spurred Viceroy Francisco de Toledo to campaign to discredit the Inca rulers and Las Casas's doctrines (Keen, 1990: 108). Las Casas's pro-Indian policies were also muffled by the Council of Trent (1563). Ultimately, Spain became a model for the Counter-Reformation, in which Christian orthodoxy was carefully controlled by the Tribunal of the Inquisition (1571), and economic motivations would favor colonizers' rights to continue indigenous exploitation (Keen, 1990: 108).

The native population declined in numbers during the 1570s as a result of devastating epidemics of disease, while growing populations of *criollos* (Spanish born in America), *mestizos* (offspring of Spaniard and natives), and other ethnically diverse individuals additionally reduced their profile in society. Hispanicization, first advocated at the first Provincial Council, gained increasing support from religious and secular factions. They feared that continued study of indigenous affairs without controlled official supervision might only encourage resistance to acculturation. This view is reflected in a royal decree in 1577 in which Sahagún was ordered to submit to the crown his *Historia general de las cosas de la Nueva España* and suspend all research on indigenous affairs. Economical support for the Colegio decreased, contributing to its decline as a higher education institution.

## Evangelization and Its Consequences: A "Spiritual Conquest"?

The Franciscans' disappointments went beyond the struggles of the Colegio project. They had started education to convert the majority of the indigenous population. The successes of the first schools had proven the indigenous capacity for learning, but the friars had erred in thinking that Nahuatl culture was inert clay to mold as they pleased. However, views of the conversion achievements by the monastic orders were varied. Behavior in compliance with Christian doctrine was enough for some friars, even if it was not based upon understanding on the metaphysical and philosophical levels (Buckhart, 1989: 184). Even by the late sixteenth and early seventeenth centuries some missionaries such as the Franciscans Geronimo de Mendieta (1526–1604) and Juan de Torquemada (1550–1625) overstated the successes of evangelization, perhaps contributing to an assumption of a "spiritual conquest" (Ricard, 1966; Kobayashi, 1996).

Other missionaries viewed the failure of conversion not in the understanding that indigenous agency was an inherent element in the dynamics of cultural negotiation, but as an example of the indigenous people's negative behavior. This view perceived an indigenous tendency to deceive and a stubbornness to accept what was good for them. Sahagún's disappointments are explicit in his Prologue to Book IV of the *Historia general*. He recognizes that the first friars did not perceive that indigenous conversion was not sincere, and so maintains the church in New Spain was established on a false foundation (León-Portilla, 1990: 61). That Sahagún did not publish the *Coloquios,* the dialogues between the wise men and the Franciscans, in which introduction he describes the successful efforts of conversion by the first missionaries, even when granted permission, might be an indication of his disappointments (Klor de Alva, 1988: 83–92). The Dominican Diego Durán at the end of the sixteenth century recognized that indigenous "Christian" festivals disguised ancient rites, and in the seventeenth century Hernando Ruíz de Alarcón and Jacinto de la Serna would see superstitions, vices, and barbarism (Rabasa, 1993: 85). Enough research on Nahua testimonies and other sources have contributed to a reevaluation of the degrees of conversion during the sixteenth and seventeenth centuries so as to question a "spiritual conquest" as held by Robert Ricard in his *Spiritual Conquest of Mexico* (León Portilla, 1990; Klor de Alva, 1982; Buckhart, 1989; Gruzinski, 1993: 152).

## The Diffusion of Writing and the Written outside the Colegio Letters of Appeal

The advantages of learning European negotiation techniques were quickly perceived by the conquered lords. In pre-conquest times, alliances between city-states were pragmatic means to further economic and political interests; for example, Texcoco and Tlacopan sided with the more powerful Tenochtitlan, forming the so-called "Triple Alliance." After the conquest, the indigenous elite developed alliances with the Spaniards to negotiate their place in the new society and to preserve their privileges. In addition, the imposition of Spanish law introduced the natives to the rights of private property, legitimacy, and inheritance, which could be disputed, defended, or appealed (Borah, 1982: 272). A corpus of letters offers evidence that even before the Colegio was founded former *tlatoque* (dynastic rulers of city-states) and the indigenous elite were already acquainted with Spanish legal procedures and were using them to their own benefit.

Letters written by the native elite and intellectuals after the three Provincial Councils held between 1554 and 1562 suggest they were aware that colonial policy changes were increasingly affecting their social status and political participation. The letters also show that the native elite were in close contact with the friars, since they continued to advocate in favor of indigenous welfare. A letter signed in 1554 by educated nobles of central Mexico shows that their services to the king had been recognized only by the Franciscans; in another letter written in 1556 the same nobles petitioned the king for Bartolomé de Las Casas to serve as their protector (*La nobleza indígena del Centro de México*, 2000: 191–4).

Some *gramáticos* wrote letters that display a sophisticated use of knowledge, the very thing so criticized by many colonizers. Letters by two of the *gramáticos,* Pablo Nazareo, rector, teacher, and translator, and by Antonio Valeriano, also a translator and teacher and later governor of Tenochtitlan, were written in Latin and present clear evidence of the well-versed knowledge of the art of rhetoric. The use of Latin over Spanish or Nahuatl not only allows these subjects to display their great capabilities for commanding the language but also to share a common ground with the European educated elite. As trained rhetoricians these *gramáticos* construct persuasive arguments tracing their genealogical and territorial rights to pre-conquest times through the collective memory of their own ethnic groups. The pragmatic use of the collective memory is astutely combined with European discursive practices. These letters also reveal that if the *gramáticos* had helped the friars, they were also actively using their knowledge to help their communities and themselves.

## The Emergence of an Intellectual Circle on Indigenous Matters

Between 1540 and 1570, mainly under the efforts of the Franciscans, there is an emergence of works whose authorship was recognized as that of some former students of the Colegio or linked in some other ways to the highly educated elite. Among them, Tadeo de Niza wrote a history of the conquest of Tlaxcala that unfortunately has been lost (1548–54); Don Pedro Ponce de León, ruler of Tlaxcala, authored *Breve relación de los dioses y ritos de la gentilidad*; Francisco Acaxitli, ruler of Tlalmanalco, wrote about the mission of viceroy Mendoza to fight the Chichimecs; Don Alfonso Izhuezcatocatzin Axayacatzin, governor of Texoco, wrote in Spanish and Nahuatl the history of his ancestors; and Don Antonio Pimentel Ixtlilxochitl authored *Memorias históricas del Reino Acolhua* (Garibay, 1954: 1: 227–30). However, following a pre-conquest tradition, some historical compilation continued to be anonymous, such as the *Codex Aubin* (1576), the *Annals of Cuauhtitlan* (1560–70), *Legend of the Suns* (1558), the *Annals of Tlatelolco*,[4] and the *Historia Tolteca Chichimeca* (1544), to name just a few.

From the 1560s to well into the seventeenth century research on indigenous cultures and languages continued in spite of harsh colonial policies. The prohibitions of 1577 seemed to have developed to control future investigations. On the one hand the ban on native research would bring to an end the Franciscan monopoly on indigenous matters; on the other hand perhaps the prohibitions were a way to discourage the development of professional research on native matters by the indigenous students. By the 1570s there were Spanish and *mestizo* individuals already fluent in native languages who perhaps were perceived to be more objective and less dangerous for such research. In addition, the Jesuit order had arrived in New Spain in 1572. Their projects of conversion followed different methods than those of the Franciscans. Jesuits opened schools not only for indigenous students but also for Spanish and *mestizos*. For the teaching of native languages to novices, they benefited from individuals who were fluent in indigenous tongues, were connected to the secular church, and had access to materials on indigenous matters. Be that as it may, parallel to the time of Sahagún's *Historia general,* a branch of research on indigenous matters was ordered by Viceroy Don Martín Enríquez Almanza (1568–80) to be carried out by individuals other than the Franciscans.

The topics of some of the works Enriquez Almanza requested suggest that he was interested in information regarding indigenous economic production and social situation in the colonial present, as well as information on the pre-conquest past. The *mestizo* Diego Muñoz Camargo collaborated on this project with his *Relación particular de la grana cochinilla que ofrecía a S.M.D. Felipe N. Señor.* This focuses on the cultivation of the *cochinilla* (cochineal insect), on the quality of its red pigment known as *grana*, and on the rules to recognize its falsification (Carrera Stampa, 1945: 93–142). As a result of Almanza's commission to a Juan Bautista, an indigenous official, to collect tribute from indigenous vagabonds, a *diario* by several indigenous writers, however attributed to Juan Bautista, gives economic information on indigenous tribute (Reyes, 2001: 19). Recently edited, this *diario* is referred as the *Anales de Juan Bautista*. Although this narrative, written in Nahuatl in the annals format, includes dates that range from 1519 to 1582, it focuses primarily on the everyday life of *tlahcuiloque* – native codex painters – and *amanteca* – hand-labor artisans – from 1566 to 1574. In addition to being an excellent source on *tlahcuiloque* and indigenous artisan circles, it also provides important information on the conflictive reaction to the new regulations on tribute, on the repercussions of the imposition of paid work, the introduction of private property of land, and the use money had in the political and social system of the native population during those years (Reyes, 2001: 13).

The research on the indigenous polities of Tenonchtitlan, Texcoco, and Tula corresponded to the Jesuit Juan de Tovar (ca. 1541–1626). A relative of the Spanish Dominican historian Diego Durán, Tovar was born in Texcoco and was well versed in the indigenous languages Nahuatl, Otomí, and Mazahua. He was first a secular priest and later joined the Jesuits in 1573. Tovar became one of the key individuals in bringing together much of the corpus already produced on native languages and history by Franciscans and other intellectuals.

By the 1580s other narratives were produced that reveal to have benefited from exchanging information with the Franciscans. For his *Relación de la Nueva España* (1585) the *oidor* of the *Audiencia Real,* Alonso de Zorita, acknowledges writings by Sahagún, by the Franciscan Toribio de Benavente, known as Motolinía, and, among others, by the indigenous Pablo Nazareo, one of the *gramáticos*. In the introduction to his *Relación*, Zorita includes a substantial bibliography of New World historians and gives us evidence of an active exchange of sources among them. By the end of the 1550s or beginning of the 1560s, parallel to Sahagún's research, the Spanish Dominican Diego Durán (1537–88), who visited the Colegio, began to gather information for his *Historia de las Indias de Nueva España* (1570–81). His works would also serve as a source for his relative Juan de Tovar's writings and would also be included in Book VII of the *Historia natural y moral de las Indias* of the Jesuit José Acosta (1540–1600).

At the beginning of the seventeenth century, evidence of an active circle of intellectual exchange on native and colonial historiography is noticeable in the *Monarquía Indiana* by the Franciscan Juan de Torquemada (1564–1624). Torquemada, the Guardian of the Convent of Tlatelolco at the Colegio's decline, was named Chronicler of the Order of San Francisco of New Spain. He was charged with writing a history that would include Franciscan missionary labors and the most notable native traditions. His *Monarquía Indiana*, in three volumes, includes, among many issues, affairs related to the colonial administration, native traditions, and the history of the evangelization in New Spain. Torquemada benefits from the narratives of the Franciscans Andrés de Olmos, Motolinía, and Gerónimo de Mendieta. He also acknowledges his familiarity with works by the Dominican Diego Durán and the Jesuits Juan de Tovar and José de Acosta. His native sources from *Tlaxcala* have much in common with the *Descripción de la ciudad y provincia de Tlaxcala* by the *mestizo* Diego Muñoz Camargo, and those, from the *Texcoco* region, share similarities with narratives by the *castizo* Fernando de Alva Ixtlilxóchitl, by the *mestizo* Juan del Pomar, and by the indigenous writer Don Antonio Pimentel Ixtlilxóchitl.

## Native and *Mestizo* Intellectuals: The End of Sixteenth Century and the First Half of the Seventeenth Century

A dialogue opened up between the friars and the indigenous people, even if politically and socially asymmetrical, rendered not only an exceptional documentation of inter-cultural contact, but also made possible the production of a large corpus on native cultures. It also put in motion an active exchange among intellectuals of different ethnic backgrounds and affiliations.

A post-Colegio generation of indigenous writers and of ethnically mixed intellectuals emerged at the end of the sixteenth century and well into the seventeenth century who were connected to the intellectual Franciscan–Jesuit circle on native research. Most of the writers belonged to the noble elite from Central Mexico and went to great efforts to show their Christianity while glorifying the pre-conquest past of their own *altepetl*. These individuals included genealogical accounts in their histories to authenticate their nobility, on the one hand as a hallmark of an authority to write the local history of the ethnic group; on the other as a vehicle to claim economic and social privileges in the colony. Two of the most famous indigenous writers of this generation were the noblemen Don Hernando de Alvarado Tezozomoc, commonly known as Tezozomoc, and Don Domingo Francisco de San Antón Muñón Chimalpahin Quauhtle-huanitzin, or Chimalpahin for short. Although Tezozomoc was not mentioned in any source as a student of the Colegio, he belonged to the educated Nahua elite. He was the brother-in-law of the famous student Antonio Valeriano and a document known as *Tlalamatl Huauhquilpan* recognizes him as a *nahuatlato*, or Nahuatl interpreter.

He wrote two historical narratives on his *altepetl* Mexico-Tenochtitlan. The so called *Crónica mexicayotl* (1609) is attributed to him since he appears as the narrator in the introduction. Written in Nahuatl, the *Crónica mexicayotl* is a compilation of oral, pic-tographic, and written accounts. The *Crónica mexicayotl* follows the pre-conquest style of the annals and addresses directly the *Mexica-Tenochca,* instructing them in the importance of remembering their past and taking pride in their heritage. That he wrote his *Crónica mexicana* (ca. 1598) in Spanish in the form of a European chronicle is a possible indication that the intended audience were colonial officials. Perhaps the production of this chronicle had some connections with the Tovar circle of research. Tovar finished his history, ordered by Enríquez Almanza, in 1578, but nine years later, after the original was lost, he rewrote it from memory and with the help of the *Historia de las Indias de Nueva España* of his relative, Diego Durán (Garibay, 1954: 2: 275). Today we have two manuscripts of Tovar's rewritten history: the *Códice Ramírez* and the *Códice Tovar.* Duran's and Tovar's historical narratives on the Mexicas' past are closely related to Tezozomoc's *Crónica mexicana* for which Robert Barlow suggested the possibility of a primary text he called *Crónica X.* We know that Durán's *Historia* was a source for Tovar's and, later, for Acosta's. Although there is a relationship between Durán's work and Tezozomoc's *Crónica mexicana*, there is no information on the particulars of such a correlation. Unlike Chimalpahin, who expresses that he knew

Tovar when he (Tovar) was a member of the cathedral chapter under Chimalpahin's patron Don Sancho (Schroeder, 1991: 15), Tezozomoc's chronicles are very limited in information about his sources and acquaintances. However, his relation to individuals connected to the Colegio, his noble status, and the production of his two chronicles suggest that Tezozomoc moved with ease in this educated circle.

Chimalpahin's education was independent of the Colegio, but he was acquainted with a Nahua intellectual circle (Anderson and Schroeder, 1997: 6), as he mentions them in his works. In his dual role of author and copyist he wrote in Nahuatl eight *Relaciones*, a *Diario*, the *Anales Tepanecas*, a *Crónica mexicana*, and other works. He also copied the *Crónica mexicayotl*, and wrote in Spanish a *Historia mexicana* and a *Conquista de México*. This last narrative is Chimalpahin's version of the second part of Francisco López de Gómara's *Historia de las Indias*, known as *La crónica de la Nueva España* (1552) (Schroeder, 1991: 21). His contribution to the ethnohistory of pre-conquest and colonial Mexico has been recognized to be just second to that of Sahagún's. But unlike Sahagún's works, his histories furnish a firsthand, personal perspective of the indigenous world (Schroeder, 1991: xv). His *Relaciones* seem to have been the result of compilations ordered by the viceroy Antonio de Mendoza to one of his relatives. However, it was not until 1620 that an uncle asked him to finish the work (Schroeder, 1991; 9). Unlike Tezozomoc, Chimalpahin was of a lesser social status but he did the best he could to present himself as a reliable writer. The circumstances of his life as a copyist are not known, but he wrote the largest and most distinguished corpus of annalistic history known to have been produced by a Nahua of any time period (Lockhart, 1992, 387).

A connection between Tezozomoc and Chimalpahin is revealed in the *Crónica mexicayotl*. Since the earliest manuscript is in Chimalpahin's handwriting, it is believed that he was the copyist but he also included some parts of his own (Anderson and Schroeder, 1997: 8). History for Tezozomoc and Chimalpahin is viewed as the work of a collective effort from different genres and modes. Tezozomoc's role in this *Crónica* seems to be that of the main authority who, by his prestige and nobility, has the recognition to authenticate all the sources and testimonies he presents. That some were still orally transmitted or pictographically represented is revealed in the constant use of sensory verbs such as "hear" and "see." However, in the *Crónica mexicayotl* Chimalpahin intervenes. Since local histories focus on the unique qualities of the individual's *altepetl*, for Chimalpahin the Mexica's account needed to be edited. An ancient rivalry and resentment toward the Mexicas by the Chalcas is revealed in his "correcting" the Mexicas' story with that of his own *altepetl* Chalco-Amaquemecan, which he constantly exalts in his histories (47–9). When it came to defend one's *altepetl*, as was the case of the Tlatelolcans in Book XII, Chimalpahin's interaction in this text is another example of local histories competing against each other.

A sense of urgency to keep to tradition while securing vestigial positions of high status within the colonial system is perceived in the indigenous written histories (Anderson and Schroeder, 1997: 6). By the end of the sixteenth century and the beginning of the seventeenth century, when Tezozomoc and Chimalpahin wrote, colonial society was becoming more complex. The European presence was strengthening and mixed ethnic groups were growing while indigenous people were declining in great numbers owing to epidemics. Noble indigenous people were losing their status through the infiltrations of *macehuales* (non-noble indigenous people) who were becoming *señores principales* (Gruzinski, 1993: 64–5).

Social and demographic changes would also open the domain of local native histories to secondary-status nobles – such as Chimalpahin – or to non-noble indigenous people and *mestizos*. The writer Cristóbal Del Castillo, whom Jesuit Horacio Carochi (1579–1662) identifies as a *mestizo*, might fall into these categories. If indeed he was a *mestizo*, unlike other *mestizos*, who wrote in Spanish, he writes both *Historia de la venida de los mexicanos y de otros pueblos* and *Historia de la conquista* in Nahuatl, and there is not enough information about this writer to know to what social class he belonged (Navarrete Linares, 2001: 76). He neither identifies himself as belonging to a particular *altepetl*, nor traces his genealogy as a source of authority as other indigenous and *mestizo* writers do. Although he writes about the Mexicas, he does not provide information to conclude that he belonged to that *altepetl* (Navarrete Linares, 2001: 76–7). Unlike Tezozomoc or Chimalpahin, whose role is to authenticate the ancient word, Del Castillo's *Historia* seems to be the interpretation of an outsider who had access to the oral, pictographic, and written corpus of the Mexicas' collective memory. Because his *Historia* shares some dates and events with that of Sahagún's Book XII of the *Florentine Codex*, and because there is evidence in his text that he knew the *Coloquios*, it is probable that he was in close contact with the Franciscans, and most likely, he received his education in one of their institutions (Navarrete Linares, 2001: 64–7). However, that he is mentioned by the Jesuit Carochi is an indication that his *Historia* became part of the manuscripts collected by the Jesuits' circle initiated by Tovar.

From the middle of the seventeenth century (ca. 1662) to 1692, the noble Nahua Tlaxcalan – from the Tizatlan region – Don Juan Buenaventura Zapata y Mendoza (1600?–89?) wrote his *Historia cronológica de la noble ciudad de Tlaxcala*. Written in Nahuatl and mainly in the annals format, this narrative is yet another case of historiographic production on local histories by a noble Nahua author. Zapata y Mendoza, who held several administrative positions, including that of governor, delivers a chronological account on Tlaxcala's pre-Hispanic past (ca. 1310) as well as firsthand accounts on colonial Tlaxcala to 1689 (Lockhart, 1992: 391). In his *Historia cronológica* Zapata y Mendoza mentions important intellectual Tlaxcalans such as Tadeo de Niza and Diego Muñoz Camargo. Although we have no evidence that Zapata y Mendoza's *Historia* was produced within the Franciscan or Jesuit circles, the amendments and interventions by another Nahua author, who had been a cacique and was later a secular priest, Don Manuel de los Santos y Salazar (?–1715), certainly puts the *Historia* within an intellectual ecclesiastical circle by an ordained Nahua. An acquaintance of Zapata y Mendoza, Santos y Salazar was from Quiahuiztlan, also a region in Tlaxacala. An intellectual himself, Santos y Salazar had already written *Cómputo cronológico de los indios mexicanos*, a history of early Tlaxcalans based on printed works. Santos y Salazar was also involved in the production of the drama *La invención de la Santa Cruz por Santa Elena* and collected the materials for the making of a traditional calendar wheel, later used by *criollo* intellectuals during the eighteenth century (*Historia cronológica*, 1995: 20). He was, with other of his contemporaries from the Jesuit circle, a precursor of native historiographic tradition which later flourished during the eighteenth and nineteenth centuries. The *Historia cronológica de la noble ciudad de Tlaxcala*, a valuable text, needs specialized study. The name of Zapata y Mendoza will then be as well known as Chimalpahin's and Tezozomoc's (Lockhart, 1992: 392).

Within the group of the post-Colegio generation who wrote pre-conquest local histories are bi-cultural individuals, almost all of them *mestizos*, who were descendants of the indigenous nobility of the most powerful city-states. They also focus on the local history of their indigenous side, emphasizing a pre-conquest prestige. But their historical narratives follow Western historiographical conventions in which they show a more profound command of European and indigenous systems than their indigenous counterparts. These go-betweens appropriate their maternal local histories, "creating a new locus of enunciation where different ways of knowing and of individual and collective expressions meet" (Mignolo, 2001: 13).

From Texcoco were the *castizo* (offspring of a *mestizo* and a Spaniard) Don Fernando de Alva Ixtlilxochitl and the *mestizo* Juan Bautista de Pomar. The latter, a descendant of Texcocan nobles, wrote the *Relación de Texcoco* in 1582 as an extension of a 1577 Texcocan *Relación geográfica*. His *Relación* is an extensive document that includes Aztec deities and aspects of pre-conquest culture. Alva Ixtlilxochitl, also a Texcocan noble, wrote extensively about this *altepetl*. He was probably a student of the Colegio de Tlatelolco during the last years of the institution (Garibay, 1954: 2: 228). Even though Ixtlilxochitl writes in Spanish, mainly for the European reader, he was actively involved with the Texcocan indigenous intellectuals. He mentions prominent indigenous nobles as some of his sources (ibid.). Similar to the Peruvian *mestizo* Inca Garcilaso de la Vega, Ixtlilxochitl presents Texcoco as a pre-Christian civilized *altepetl* using equivalences taken from Christian and European history to understand Texcoco's past. Ixtlilxochitl "punctuate[s], on the one hand, the plurilingual and multicultural character of colonial situations and, on the other, illustrate[s] how such written practices collided with the Renaissance philology of language and writing held by missionaries and men of letters" (Mignolo, 2001: 204). Alva Ixtlilxochitl and his family would be active compilers of indigenous research in the Tovar–Jesuit circle.

If in Ixtlilxochitl his indigenous background serves as a locus of enunciation, for the *mestizo* Don Diego Muñoz Camargo, it serves as his identification with his Spanish side. His *Descripción de la ciudad y provincia de Tlaxcala*, which originated in a *relación geográfica* on the Tlaxcala *altepetl*, is written from the point of view of an outsider. It becomes a sort of "ethnographic discourse" in which pre-conquest Tlaxcalans with their "idolatry" are compared to Jews (Velazco, 2003: 127). However, his *Descripción* also reveals a political purpose for his contemporary Tlaxcalans. The services of the Tlaxcalan nobility to the crown plus the prestige of never having been conquered by the Aztec empire are underlined in this history.

Knowledge of alphabetic writing, if not with the sophistication of the *gramáticos* and the intellectual elite, had been spreading to the indigenous population since the early sixteenth century. Classical Nahuatl as developed by friars and educated Nahuas was limited to the special education for natives, which declined during the seventeenth century. However, Colonial Nahuatl, which includes various dialects with spelling variations, coexisted with Classical Nahuatl and survived. The mundane documents produced by Colonial Nahuatl have been an extremely useful source to delve into the realities of indigenous life in colonial times. They present the dynamism and creativity of the preservation of local indigenous collective memory in wills and land tenure titles called *Títulos primordiales* and *Códice Techialoyan*. They are mentioned here because *Títulos,* purporting to authenticate the right to *altepetl*'s territory and belonging to popular culture, incorporate indigenous genres – songs, *huehuetlatolli*, annals – in the production of local history. From the middle of the seventeenth to the eighteenth centuries, *Títulos* continued the memory of the indigenous nobles and writers and what they perceived of importance for their *altepetl* by developing quite a different approach and relationship to the past (Gruzinski, 1993: 130).

## The Legacy of the Colegio and the Jesuit Circle

There is still much research to be done on the facts surrounding the relationships that some of the native intellectuals such as Tezozomoc and others had with the Franciscan–Jesuit circle at the beginning of the seventeenth century. We have more information about the connections with a Franciscan-Jesuit circle that Don Fernando de Alva Ixtlilxochitl and several members of his family had. One of his relatives, Don Bartolomé de Alva Ixtlilxochitl (1600–70), was a secular priest who had helped some of the Jesuits with the study of Nahuatl. Bartolomé de Alva had not only written a *Confesionario mayor y menor en lengua mexicana*, he also translated several Golden Age playwrights (Schwaller, 1994: 393). That a friendship had developed between Bartolomé de Alva and the Jesuits is revealed in his prefatory comments to the *Arte de la lengua mexicana* (1645) of Jesuit Horacio Carochi (1579–1662), a grammar that illustrates innovative techniques in the use of diacritics to mark the phonological uniqueness of Nahuatl. Bartolomé de Alva not only approves the publication of Carochi's *Arte*, but also praises the Jesuit's command of Nahuatl (Schwaller, 1994: 393) and, later, dedicates to Carochi the translation of Lope de Vega's *La Madre de la mejor* (ibid.).

A compilation of the works produced by natives, *mestizos*, Europeans, and *criollos*, from the Franciscan initial projects to the Tovar–Jesuit circle, included some of the most important writings by Tezozomoc, Chimalpahin, and Alva Ixtlilxochitl. The ancient books and manuscripts in the Alva Ixtlilxochitl family and Jesuit collections were also accessible to the *criollo* intellectuals Sor Juana Inés de la Cruz and Don Carlos de Sigüenza y Góngora. Sometime between 1680 and 1690 the Alva Ixtlilxochitl archive was donated to Sigüenza y Góngora (Schwaller, 1994: 397). This collection, which ended up in the Jesuit convent of San Pedro y San Pablo on Sigüenza's death, was cataloged in the mid-eighteenth century by the Italian Lorenzo Boturini Benaducci. This archive continued to be studied by Jesuits and *criollo* seculars during the eighteenth and nineteenth centuries, and has been associated with the emergence of a Mexican historiography and national identity.[5]

The last years of the seventeenth century close an era of historiography written by educated natives. Educated indigenous people pragmatically used the alphabetic and legalistic Spanish system to their advantage but not without consequences. Some scholars have seen that in Peru and in New Spain, the reliance on a juridical system arbitrated by the colonial power created a dependency that weakened the natives' capacity for self-determining confrontation, limiting resistance to lack of cooperation (Stern, 1982: 311; Borah, 1982: 284). Writing local histories at the end of the sixteenth and beginning of the seventeenth centuries provided temporary solutions for continuing tradition and securing positions of high status, as was the case for Tezozomoc, Ixtlilxóchitl, and others. But once the generation of educated natives declined, the steady use of local histories as sources to appeal privileges or to authenticate territorial rights – as indigenous communities do in the *Títulos* or *Códices Techialoyan* – continued to feed ethnic fragmentation and struggles among the natives. Conceivably, ethnic divisions weakened the possibilities of native communities' unification for radical resistance.

The narratives produced by ethnically diverse individuals in the Colegio and after its decline are important sources for critical investigations in different areas of research, from linguistic perspectives, to those of the social sciences, cultural studies, and postcolonial theories. Written after the shock of the conquest under an alien political and ideological hegemony, these narratives provide inquiry in the processes of meaning-making and representation. Since neither the colonizers nor the colonized were two antagonistic and monolithic factions, the multiple interactions and relations among these groups have to be taken into consideration when enquiring about processes and productions of identities in these narratives. The diffusion of writing and written materials was one of the most powerful tools of colonization in Indo-America, but was also the vehicle for different types of negotiations and creativity. Perhaps textual productions from the in-between spaces produced by colonization provide the "location and energy of new modes of thinking whose strength lies in the transformation and critique of the 'authenticities' of both Western and Amerindian legacies" (Mignolo, 2001: xv). These narratives are also testimonies that remind us that Latin American histories have the modalities of an aggressive concert started 500 years ago in which the hierarchy of "harmony" is constantly interrupted by counterpoint and dissonance.

## NOTES

1   I use the terms indigenous people and natives interchangeably for individuals not mixed biologically with Spanish or Africans.

2   I borrow this term from Susana Romano. The term was originally used for European students of grammar and rhetoric. But in the Colegio it

came to mean a "trilingual proficiency in Latin, Spanish, and at least one vernacular such as Nahuatl, and which later would qualify the educated Tlatelolco *indio* for coauthor ship of bi-and [*sic*] trilingual catechetical texts" (Romano, 2004: 262).

3  In December 2003 a mural depicting life around Texcoco Lake was discovered underneath what it used to be the convent of Santiago de Tlatelolco. The paintings were on the walls of a cistern that supplied water to the Colegio. Elements such as aquatic plants and animals, fishing gear, figures of fishermen, and pre-Hispanic symbolic animals such as a jaguar, an eagle, and a heron have been identified, in colors of red, ocher, blue, and black. However, Christian figures, such as angels, have also been depicted. So far only about 13 ft (4 m) of about 52 ft (16 m) have been excavated. This archeological jewel, painted a few years before or around the Colegio's inauguration (1536), will provide valuable information on pictographic techniques and scene depiction of early New Spain. The information about the discovery was published by the archeologist Salvador Guilliem, in "Noticias," *Arqueología Mexicana*, 11:64 (2003): 10–12. I would like to thank Mr. Guilliem for allowing me access to the archeological site and for his valuable explanations about the mural's composition.

4  Although some scholars have dated the *Annals of Tlatelolco* to 1528, by studying some linguistic aspects of Nahuatl, for James Lockhart, the texts could not have been written before the 1540s (1993: 3).

5  There is still much research to be done on the circle of intellectuals linked to the Jesuits during the seventeenth century. In the second volume of the *Codex Chimalpahin* (4), fn 6, Susan Schroeder states that a study on the topic will appear in the forthcoming sixth volume of *Codex Chimalpahin*.

## References and Further Reading

Anderson, A., and Schroeder, S. (1997). "Introduction." In *Codex Chimalpahin*. Vol. 1. Norman and London: University of Oklahoma Press.

Baudot, G. (1995). *Utopia and History in Mexico: The First Chronicles of Mexican Civilization (1520–1569)*. Trans. B. R. Ortiz de Montellano and T. Ortiz de Montellano. Boulder: University Press of Colorado.

Borah, W. (1982). "The Spanish and Indian law: New Spain." In G. A. Collier et al., *The Inca and Aztec States 1400–1800*, pp. 265–88. New York and London: Academic Press.

Buckhart, L. (1989). *The Slippery Earth*. Tucson: University of Arizona Press.

Carrera Stampa, M. (1945). "Algunos aspectos de la *Historia de Tlaxcala* de Diego Muñoz Camargo." In H. Díaz-Thomé et al. (eds), *Estudios de historiografía de la Nueva España*, pp. 93–142. Mexico City: Colegio de México.

Cuevas, M. (1946). *Historia de la Iglesia en México*. Vol. 1. Mexico City: Patria.

*Documentos para la historia de México: Códice Franciscano del siglo XVI* (1941). Ed. Joaquín García Icazbalceta. Mexico City: Chavez Hayhoe.

Elliot, J. H. (2002). "Cortés and Montezuma." In G. M. Joseph and T. J. Henderson (eds), *The Mexico Reader: History, Culture, Politics*, pp. 105–9. Durham, NC and London: Duke University Press.

Garibay, M. A. (1954). *Historia de la literatura Nahuatl*. 2 vols. Mexico City: Porrúa.

Gruzinski, S. (1993). *The Conquest of Mexico*. Cambridge: Polity Press.

Hill-Boone, E. (1998). "Pictorial documents and visual thinking in postconquest Mexico." In E. Hill-Boone and T. Cummins (eds), *Native Traditions in the Postconquest World*, pp. 149–99. Washington, DC: Dumbarton Oaks Research Library and Collection.

*Historia cronológica de la Noble Ciudad de Tlaxcala* (1995). Ed., transcribed, and trans. Luis Reyes García and Andrea Martínez Baracs. Tlaxcala, Mexico: Universidad Autónoma de Tlaxcala.

Karttunen, F. (1982). "Nahuatl literacy." In G. A. Collier et al. (eds), *The Inca and Aztec States 1400–1800*, pp. 395–417. New York and London: Academic Press.

Keen, B. (1990). "The European vision of the Indian in the sixteenth and seventeenth centuries: a sociological approach." In *La Imagen del indio en la Europa moderna*, pp. 101–16. Seville: Publicaciones de la Escuela de Estudios Hispano-Americanos.

Klor de Alva, J. (1982). "Spiritual conflict and accommodation in New Spain: toward a typology of Aztec responses to Christianity." In G. A. Collier et al. (eds), *The Inca and Aztec States 1400–1800*, pp. 345–66. New York and London: Academic Press.

— (1988). "Sahagún and the *Colloquios* project." In J. Klor de Alva, H. B. Nicholson, and E. Quiñones Keber (eds), *The Work of Bernardino de Sahagún: Pioneer Ethnographer of Sixteenth-Century Aztec Mexico*, pp. 83–92. Studies on Culture and Society, Vol. 2. Austin: University of Texas Press.

— (1989). "Languages, politics, and translation: colonial discourse and Classic Nahuatl in New Spain." In R. Warren (ed.), *The Art of Translation*, pp. 143–62. Boston: Northeastern University Press.

Kobayashi, J. M. (1996 [1974]). *La Educación como conquista*. 3rd edn. Mexico City: Colegio de México.

León-Portilla, M. (1964). *Aztec Thought and Culture: A Study of the Ancient Nahuatl Mind*. Norman: University of Oklahoma Press.

— (1990). *Endangered Cultures*. Dallas, TX: Southern Methodist University Press.

— (1999). *Fray Bernardino de Sahagún en Tlatelolco*. Mexico City: Secretaría de Relaciones Exteriores.

— (2003). *Literaturas indígenas de México*. Mexico City: Fondo de Cultura Económica.

Lockhart, J. (1992). *The Nahuas after the Conquest*. Stanford, CA: Stanford University Press.

— (1993). *We People Here [Florentine Codex]*. Berkeley, Los Angeles, and London: University of California Press.

López-Austin, A. (1997). *Tamoachan and Tlalocan: Places of Mist*. Boulder: University Press of Colorado.

Mignolo, W. (2001). *The Darker Side of the Renaissance*. Ann Arbor: University of Michigan Press.

Navarrete Linares, F., ed. (2001). "Introduction." In *Historia de la venida de los mexicanos y de otros pueblos e historia de la conquista* de Cristóbal del Castillo. Mexico City: Consejo Nacional para la Cultura y las Artes.

*La Nobleza indígena del centro de México* (2000). Ed. Emma Pérez-Rocha and Rafael Tena. Mexico City: Instituto Nacional de Antropología e Historia.

Rabasa, J. (1993). "Writing and evangelization in sixteenth-century Mexico." In J. M. William and R. E. Lewis (eds), *Early Images of the Americas*, pp. 65–91. Tucson and London: University of Arizona Press.

Reyes, L. (ed.) (2001). *¿Cómo te confundes? ¿Acaso no somos conquistados? Anales de Juan Bautista*. Mexico City: CIESAS, Biblioteca Lorenzo Boturini, Insigne and Nacional Basílica de Guadalupe.

Ricard, R. (1966). *The Spiritual Conquest of Mexico*. Berkeley: University of California Press.

Romano, S. (2004). "Tlatelolco: the grammatical-rhetorical *Indios* of colonial Mexico," *College English*, 66(3): 257–77.

Rozat Dupeyron, G. (2002). *Indios imaginarios e indios reales en los relatos de la conquista de México*. Xalapa: Universidad Veracruzana.

Schroeder, S. (1991). *Chimalpahin and the Kingdoms of Chalco*. Tucson: University of Arizona Press.

Schwaller, J. F. (1994). "Nahuatl studies and the 'circle' of Horacio Carochi," *Estudios de Cultura Nahuatl*, 24: 387–98.

Stern, S. (1982). "The social significance of judicial institutions in an exploitative society: Huamanga, Peru, 1570–1640." In G. A. Collier et al. (eds), *The Inca and Aztec States 1400–1800*, pp. 289–320. New York and London: Academic Press.

Velazco, S. (2003). *Visiones de Anáhuac. Reconstrucciones historiográficas y etnicidades emergentes en el México colonial: Fernando de Alva Ixtlilxóchitl, Diego Muñoz Camargo y Hernando de Alvarado Tezozomoc*. Guadalajara: Universidad de Guadalajara.

5

# Memory and "Writing"
# in the Andes
*Sara Castro-Klaren*

How the past is understood marks indelibly our sense of the present and its possibilities. The idea of discussing memory and "writing" in the Andes during the first century after the Amerindians came into contact with Europeans allows for an all too necessary inclusion of semiotic systems that engage memory but do not engage "writing" in the restrictive sense in which the term has been used in European history. While "writing" sets the introduction of European alphabetic writing as the point of departure for the examination of historiography and all literacy in the Andes, memory opens up the possibility of considering other modes of encoding knowledge and memory, such as the khipu, *keros* (drinking vessels), the ceque system (Zuidema, 1990), dance, ritual, and even architecture. In *The Shape of Inca History: Narrative and Architecture in an Andean Empire* (1999), for instance, Susan Niles argues that "in royal architecture, no less than in their narratives, the Incas shaped historical events, giving material form to claims based on victories in battle, encounters with gods, and deeds carried out by their kings" (xvii). In fact it is the numeracy of the khipu and the relation of architecture to narrative poetics (2–84) that has recently made Inca history visible. It has been brought forth from the burial that the ideology of alphabetic writing had performed on it.

This chapter attempts to deal with a long century in which some of the major forces that shaped the discursive history of Latin America appeared and blossomed: the right of the Spanish crown, and by extension other European nations, to conquer other peoples, and the place in the power–knowledge grid of modernity, assigned to Amerindians and their cultures in the world that empire inaugurated. This century also saw the response and resistance that such discourse elicited in the Andes. Although long silenced by the standing historiography of the New World, the voice of the *panacas* – patrilineal descent groups in charge of preserving specific noble Inca houses – is now being repositioned in the "writing" of the Andes. Thus the encoding of information of the khipu system merits a full discussion along with chronicles and letters written by the *letrados*, the Spanish men of letters who wrote or gave shape to the events of the conquest and its aftermath.

The timeline that accounts for the events that characterize human activity in the territory that we call the Andes today has often been moved back and forth as modern historians and archeologists try to come to grips with the phenomenon of continuous human habitation and creation in the Andes. Recent archeological findings stretch the timeline for urban life back into the second or third millennia (2400 BCE) *before* the birth of Christ, making the Andean invention of irrigation, social organization, and urban life contemporary with the pharaohs of Egypt. The remains of various urban centers offer abundant evidence of large populations and complex social and religious life in the valley of Caral situated about 200 kilometers north of Lima.

This push into the ancient past not only underscores the antiquity and originality of Andean civilizations, but also makes the fabled Incas our very recent contemporaries. And yet there is no question that both modern and postmodern citizens of the world consider the distance between them and the Inca empire to be great, if not insurmountable, owing to the *difference* that marks the spread of European modernity and them. Much of this sense of difference is, of course, owed to the Spanish chroniclers, those soldiers, priests, and crown officials who first related the Spanish encounter with Inca civilization, for all that was written then was told from the intellectual and aesthetic conditions of possibility of warriors and sackers furiously engaged in the conquest of the unimaginably wealthy Inca empire. As the conquest of America constituted the inaugural act in the play of modernity, the ideological and epistemological legacy of these texts remained unchallenged for the better part of 500 years. It is only since the mid-twentieth century that scholars have begun to study, understand, and dismantle the epistemic complexity involved in the construction of the hierarchical difference (colonial difference) that is itself the result and the companion of conquest.

Perhaps the most important *difference* believed to have existed between Amerindian civilizations and Europe was what the Spanish reported and understood as the absence of writing. Among other things, this absence implied a diminished sense of self-consciousness, a questionable memory of the past and poor conditions for the development and accumulation of knowledge. Despite the fact that the Maya priests of Yucatan showed the Friar Diego de Landa (1524–79) how the Yucatec phonetic syllabarian glyph system worked, he not only went on to burn every Maya book that he came across, but he also denied that the glyph system was "writing." The Aztec books were quickly characterized as pictures only, and the khipu, the knotted cords used in the Andes, were found not to have the slightest similarity to writing, for they did not even resemble books or paper in their physical appearance.

Lately, however, great strides have been made in reversing this Eurocentric mistaken appreciation of the modes and techniques of memory and knowledge accumulation and transmission in Amerindian cultures. Semeioticians, anthropologists, linguists, literary theorists, and philosophers have shown that alphabetic writing is neither the only mode of developing and conserving knowledge nor is it the best, most accurate, or all-encompassing. A consensus has developed about the need for a more broadly based concept of "writing," one that can go beyond the alphabet-bound phonetic sense of writing and can thus encompass other systems of visuality as well as tactile systems of recording information. The problem, as Elizabeth Hill Boone has pointed out, is how to speak about writing without tying it to language (1994: 6). In the introduction to *Writing without Words: Alternative Literacies in Mesoamerica and the Andes* (1994), Boone grapples with the key problems embedded in the longstanding, narrow definition of writing that thinks of writing as a graphic system that captures and makes speech visible. Boone opens the way for a more ample definition of writing, one capable of housing Aztec iconographic representations and Maya glyphs. Part of this discussion is supported by the fact that the final decoding of the Maya glyph system came about as scholars were able to overcome inherited ideas about the location of the invention of writing (only in the "Old World") as well as convictions about the alphabetic necessity of any writing system.

The new thinking about the multiple invention of writing forced scholars to set aside the idea that "natives" did not understand their own cultural systems. Maya scholars first returned to the instructions given by the Maya priest to Landa in the sixteenth century (Coe, 1992: 145–66), and later to contemporary Maya speakers, for linguistic and ethnographic data and interpretation in order to finally decipher the Maya code. The riveting story of all the misconceptions and racist attitudes that impeded the recognition of the Maya glyphs as writing and the recent interdisciplinary findings that led to its deciphering have given scholars a new impetus for deciphering the codes in Aztec and Mixtec iconography, as well as the khipu.

Boone (1994) points out that the assumption that writing is visible speech has been fundamental to the construction of European ideas about writing. This assumption establishes an inextricable link between writing and the voice. It is further assumed that writing was invented only once in the course of human history, and that such an invention is constitutive to the singular position of Europe as the place where original cognitive events of the highest order take place. These assumptions normalize and universalize our received ideas about writing and, in doing so, they get in the way of conceiving of writing as other modalities of recording and communicating information (1994: 3). This notion informs, for instance, the Spanish claim that Atahualpa threw the Bible on the floor because he expected to hear the book speak. The Spanish friar who "reported" the event intended to convey the idea that the Inca was not sophisticated enough to know that writing enables one to *see* rather than *hear* speech. His reader, imbued with the same idea of writing, would of course come to the same conclusion without regard for any cultural and epistemological differences in play at the scene in Cajamarca. Contrary to the friar's account of the scene with the Bible, Boone states that for Indigenous American cultures "visible speech" was not always the goal. In Mexico, for instance, what we call "art" and writing were one and the same thing. Aztecs used one single graphic system (3) which does not necessarily record language (5). This system conveys meaning without expressing language (6). In this sense, the Aztec system is not unlike music, mathematics, or visual ideas; systems which express meaning without falling back into language. Boone observes that in the West, the "notational systems of math and science were developed precisely because ordinary language could not express the full import of scientific relations" (9). In fact, structure is generally effectively depicted visually (diagrams), for the eye can take in at once a greater sense of relations that the serial linguistic form allows.

Thus Boone goes on to propose a new definition of writing: "the communication of relatively specific ideas in a conventional manner by means of permanent, visible marks" (15). Under this definition, the glottographic system of Maya writing, the Mixteca-Aztec semasiographic system (picture writing), finds a place as an effective means of communication and accumulation of knowledge. This definition also allows for the khipu to enter the hall of "writing," for despite the fact that it has no phonetic counterpart, the khipu holds and conveys information, separate from language (20), in a system that has been lately compared to the way computerized programming works. Khipus, too, function semasiographically, for the elements – color, size, location, texture, complication of the knot, number – are conventional rather than iconographic.

Khipus, like other systems of recording memory and knowledge, indeed like "writing" itself, can be understood as a system of human semiotic interaction inasmuch as khipus are produced in "a community and within a body of knowledge in which: a) a person produces a visible sign with the purpose of conveying a message to somebody other than himself; b) a person perceives the visible sign and interprets it as a sign produced for the purposes of conveying a message; and c) the person attributes a meaning to the visible sign" (Mignolo, 1994). In this definition of writing or conception of the khipu as a semiotic system, there is no need to necessarily institute the representation of speech.

Lately scholars have made great strides in decoding the khipu system. The question under consideration is whether the khipu was a simply a mnemonic device that offered "cues" to the khipukamayuc, as the Spanish chroniclers claimed, or whether the system can be considered "writing." New incursions have been characterized by a mathematical approach to the tactile–visual system of cords, knots, colors, and textures. Marcia and Robert Ascher in *Code of the Quipu: A Study of Media, Mathematics and Culture* (1997) have led the way. Scholars have also been keenly interested in the idea that khipus did not only encode mathematical knowledges, but were also capable of encoding narrative. Gary Urton, in *Signs of the Inka Khipu: Binary Coding in the Andean Knotted-String Records* (2003), characterizes the khipu as a "powerful system of coding information that was at home in pre-Columbian South America, and which, like the coding system used in present-day computer language, was structured primarily as a binary code" (1). Urton has examined the largest number of archeological and colonial khipu thus far included in any study. His historical and theoretical study leads him to think that the khipu – the system of knotted strings – was used for recording both statistical and narrative information. With this claim, Urton's understanding of the khipu moves beyond mathematical studies and explores the earlier claims made by the *mestizo* intellectuals like Garcilaso de Vega, Inca (1539–1616), and Blas Valera (1545–97) regarding the khipu's capacity to encode and store narrative information. Urton thinks that the khipu were constructed with "conventionalized units of information that could be read by khipu masters throughout the empire" (3). So it seems that the type of information stored in the khipu was at least of two kinds: statistical and narrative. Thus the khipu allowed for accounting and recounting or telling.

Like other modern scholars, Urton draws on the system of conceptualization and organization that is peculiar to the Andes. In an effort to bring to bear the Andean modes of thinking Urton introduces a new analytical idea: binary coding. This enables him to propose a "separation between the recording code and the script, or the 'readable' message, in the khipu" (162). He can thus conclude that the binary coding of the khipu "constituted a means of encoding paired elements that were in relationships of binary opposition to each other, and that, at a semantic level, these relations were of a character known in the literature as markedness relations" (162). Urton states that he has "sketched out a theory of interpreting the hierarchical and asymmetrical signs" of non-decimal khipu as the "architecture for canonical literatures [e.g., poetry, historical narrative] whose essential components would have been noted by the khipukamayuc and used as the framework . . . for constructing narrative recitations" (164).

The guiding idea here is that binary coding was one of the principal mechanisms and strategies for thinking in the Andes. Thus Urton looks for features of cords that apparently mimic Andean logical structures rather than depart from the Indo-Arabic arithmetic as an a priori assumption. Urton privileges binarism because it is widely recognized as the primary category of Andean thought and social organization. He argues that fiber working requires binarism from the very initial stages of spinning to cord and textile making. In this sense, cord-making mimetizes the logical operations that generate Andean order. For Urton the sign that a cord contains is not the cord, but rather the aggregate of binary combinations (left/right, cotton/wool, single/double, colored/neutral) that construct the cord and function as bits of information. Urton's theory is not wedded to a mathematical model and as such leaves open the possibility that the khipu cord could encode segments of speech, words, or even syllables. In this way the khipu would be capable of registering "writing" in the usual sense of visible signs that correspond to segments of speech.

One of the most important aspects of Urton's research is that his method and arguments might finally put to rest the notion originally put forth by José de Acosta (1540–1600) and Bernabé Cobo (1580–1657) in 1653, and repeated throughout the centuries with respect to the khipu. Both argued that the khipus were simply a mnemonic device – not a system – that was used as a memory aid by the khipukamayuc. Thus, the intellectual capacity of the khipu depended entirely on the interpreter's own abilities. This notion may have been developed in view of the fact that the Inca empire was multilingual, and neither Cobo nor Acosta could imagine how a khipu knotted in one part of the empire could be "read" in another if the languages spoken were not the same. The conception of "writing" as visible speech impeded the cognitive imagination of both scholars. Despite the fact that neither Cobo nor Acosta managed to explain how the khipu was "read" across the many languages spoken in the Inca empire, a problem that would have called for positing the existence of a system rather than simple "cues," nor how the khipu served as the primordial tool in the governance of a huge and efficient state, their ideas remained unchallenged through the centuries. In fact they served to manufacture and cement the epistemological violence that characterized the colonization of the Amerindian cultures by Europe.

While *Signs of the Inka Khipu* has been widely regarded as a major breakthrough in Andean studies, Galen Brokaw writes that, despite the fact that Urton presents compelling archeological evidence for the conventionality of the khipu system, he nevertheless does not present enough ethnographic evidence to support the argument about the conventionality of the binary features, nor about the computer-style binary code (Brokaw, 2005: 574). Further, Brokaw argues that Urton "conflates the referential and the poetics" or the structure of cultural interactions (577). For Brokaw it does not follow that "Andean Cultures organize the world into binary categories . . . a homologous structure characterized the operation of reference itself" (578). This scholar also finds it hard to imagine how the khipu could support two readings, one numeric and one binary. Brokaw believes that the numeracy direction, as pursued by the Aschers, will eventually result in a better understanding of the khipu than the binary-code model proposed by Urton (2003: 586–7). However, in "The Poetics of *Khipu* Historiography" (2003), Brokaw also attempts to make the case for the khipu as a system capable of storing narrative information. By comparing two colonial documents that certifiably claim khipus as their immediate source and khipukamayuc as their "readers" in the Quechua oral rendition of the contents, Brokaw is able to establish that there existed a khipu biographical narrative genre (112).

One of the documents Brokaw examines is the *Primer nueva corónica y buen gobierno* (1615) by Guamán Poma de Ayala (–1516). Contrary to almost all of the interpreters of Guamán Poma who have detected and commented on the European models operating in his work, Brokaw makes the case for a khipu-based historiographic genre as the guiding model in the first part of Guamán Poma's extensive letter to the king (908 pages). Brokaw goes as far as hypothesizing that "much of the information about indigenous Andean history that appears in the *Nueva corónica* was collected either directly or indirectly from khipus" (116). In his study of khipu poetics Brokaw concludes that "undeniably the khipu employed a set of highly complex conventions capable of encoding semasiographic or even phonographic information that included highly stable genres of discourse" (141). He thus agrees, if not on the same grounds or with the same methodology, with the claims that Garcilaso de la Vega, Inca, in his *Comentarios reales* of 1606, made for the khipu. This revalidation of Garcilaso as a reliable informant is important because the ethnohistorian María Rostworowski (1983) found some of her findings at variance with the Incas, and concluded from there that Garcilaso's work was not to be trusted, especially when it came to cognitive and narrative claims for the khipu.

Frank Salomon, in his *Cord Keepers* (2005), tackles anew the question of the colonial and the ethnographic khipus. His book is the most comprehensive study of both

archeological and ethnographic khipu to date. Salomon points out that the archeological or pre-Hispanic khipus that have thus far been examined with radiocarbon dating
show that by 600 CE Andean peoples were making highly complex khipus (11). Thus
the art of khipu-making is not only Pan-Andean, but also indicates a deeply rooted
continuous use and development of an art that precedes the Incas by a millennium
(11). In Inca times, Salomon asserts, the khipukamayuc or royal khipu masters used
the cords for imperial censuses, the calendar, inventories of all kinds (food, clothing,
tribute, arms, soldiers, gamekeeping,), *chansons de geste*, royal chronicles, sacrifices,
genealogies, successions, postal messages, and even criminal trials (11). The khipu
was thus not only versatile, but also demotic, as the information managed by the
khipukamayuc originated in very small or even remote localities such as the household, the herder, the soldier, or the chasqui. Salomon writes that the khipu developed
among peoples who spoke a multitude of languages and that the art of putting information on a string may be a branching tree of inventions (13). In view of the fact
that we do not have a graphogenesis for the khipu as we do for writing and its origins,
Salomon thinks that it makes better sense not to think of the khipu as a single code
(13). Khipus may have been, at the state level, very conventional and capable of registering maximally comparable accounts proceeding from different parts of society.
But at the local level, khipus may have been more actor-centered (17) and encoded
with greater iconical dimensions.

Salomon is mainly interested in showing, based on his ethnographic work, that the
"khipu's double capability for simulating and documenting social action" works as
the "hinge for the articulation between kinship organization and political organization" (7). He argues that his reconstruction is compatible with the structure of ancient
khipu specimens (7). Salomon also shows that the supposed political demise of the
cord in the early colony constitutes a misreading of the colonial life of the art of the
cord. In the province of Huarochiri, for instance, the khipu was used alongside the
lettered culture (21) that entered the Andes with the introduction of Spanish imperial
linguistic policies. Finally, he argues that his ethnographic study of the Tupicocha
khipu practices demonstrates a root relationship between inscription and Andean
social complexity (7).

Salomon, Urton, and Brokaw are not the only scholars to approach the khipu from
an Andean perspective. Thomas Abercrombie (1998) argues that the Andean ideal of
knowledge is itself centered on the metaphor of pathways. The past was imagined as
"chronotopography." In this regard John Rowe had suggested earlier that the ceque
system resembled a khipu spread out in the shape of a circle. For Abercrombie, khipu
cords are paths guiding the hands, eyes, and mind to the trans-temporal, genealogical
line of the sources of things. In this sense it is the spatial and not the verbal faculty
that organizes recall (Salomon, 2005: 19).

In his *Royal Commentaries*, Garcilaso de la Vega Inca writes that the khipu also
registered poems and narrative (Book 2, chapter 27). Scholars are still searching for
the understanding that would allow cord structures to be matched to narrative structures. Gordon Brotherston, in *Book of the Fourth World: Reading the Native Americans*

*through Their Literature* (1992), argues that khipus could record and "therefore transcribe not just mathematics, but also discourse" (78), and he cites as an example the hymn that Garcilaso published in his *Royal Commentaries.* However, Brotherston's best examples and support for his argument are drawn from the postcolonial Quechua alphabetic literary corpus that arises in the Andes after 1532. Brotherston speculates that the presence of khipus in burials suggests that they could tell the biographies of persons (78–9). The study of the chronicles by Martín de Murúa (1590) and Guamán Poma also lead Brotherston to think that the khipu recorded not only annals capable of reaching deep into the past, like the Mesoamerican *teomoxtli* (78), but also ceremonial cycles, calendars, hymns of worship, and kinship dramas (79). From this perspective, Guamán Poma's *corónica* can be seen as "a complete account of empire based on native-script records and submitted to the Spanish authorities" (80) by the last of the khipukamayuc (Mendizábal Losack, 1961) who drew directly on the taxonomy and the ideology of the khipu (decimal system, reciprocity, oppositional duality, hanan/hurin, chronotopography).

Brotherston's detailed study of the play *Apu Ollantay* and its inescapable inscription into both Inca literary pastoralism and kinship drama shows convincingly how the story of the forbidden love between the princess Cusi Coyllor and the heroic commoner Ollantay is part of a khipu literary corpus performed in Cuzco by courtiers on public holidays (204). Much work is yet to be done on the considerable corpus of postcolonial Quechua drama, which ranges from the overtly pagan, as *Apu Ollantay*, to the Christian, manifesting deep roots in both the artistic legacy of the Inca and the Spanish secular and religious theater.

But if postcolonial Quechua language texts found conditions of possibility in both secular and religious drama as well as the lyric, alphabetic Quechua did not find its way in almost any other genre, be it precolonial or postcolonial. Scholars who lament the absence of court documents, letters, annals, or even personal life-stories in Quechua are equally astonished by the abundant production of visual representation in art and architecture. In the new space of violence, engagement, resistance, and negotiation that the conquest inaugurated for Andean peoples, the life of written Quechua or Aymara registers a puzzling silence. It is difficult to ascertain the shape and dynamics of the arts of communication and thought in the post-conquest Andes if one's vision remains circumscribed to alphabetic scripted Amerindian languages. One must look beyond the alphabet to other means, modes, and conceptions of communication. A more ample sense of colonial semeiosis would allow for the idea of including iconographic signs into a system of communications in which the sign is not always linked to speech. By definition, this colonial cultural space also implies alternative and conflicting literacies and concepts of knowledge, as we have seen above in the case of the khipu.

Why did Andeans not engage writing in Quechua in order to memorialize the past or offer witness to their present? It is true that there were many prohibitions and obstacles, but despite these there appeared in the Andes a significant theater production. In tension with Spanish literary canons, Quechua lyrical traditions persisted through colonial times and reached up to the present. This absence of written texts appears in stark contrast with the wealth of images on paper, canvas, and other aesthetic or valuable objects such as *keros*, textiles, and *aquillas* (large silver bowls) that Andeans produced, exchanged, and used during and after the first hundred years after the fall of Cajamarca.

Inquiring into the issue of native Andean visual traditions, the art historian Tom Cummins in "Let Me See! Reading is for Them: Colonial Andean Images and Objects" (1998) advances the notion that alphabetic writing was a technology and mode of memorializing life too distant from Andean visual and tactile modes of communication (95). Cummins interprets the scene at Cajamarca as an example of the fact that Andean culture relates orality (speech acts) to objects (the book) in an entirely different way in which Europe conceives of writing and thus books as printed speech (142). Cummins thinks that the Spanish explanation of why Atahualpa rejected the book (the book did not speak when Atahualpa put it to his ear) is completely bogus. The Spanish interpretation of the scene at Cajamarca relies on the Talmudic tradition of close textual reading that scrutinizes the text in search of an interpretation that can reveal the meaning of history. In the Western textual tradition all relationships between the object and a sense of the past are ruptured (142). In contrast, objects in the Andean world had a greater place as sites of memory and knowledge. Textiles and *keros* functioned not only as testimony of the past but provided also a living link to history. They helped to keep the memory of the past alive and viable. These objects constituted a form of inalienable wealth, a material site for the continuation of history, and as such they were venerated and brought out into public view at the time of the performance of the highest rituals when communication with the Apukuna was in order (143).

The will to persist prompted native Andeans to engage with and contest colonial rule in a number of negotiations and exchanges. It is clear from the *Huarochiri* (1598?) manuscript and the documentation on the campaign to extirpate native Andean religion that the will to continue religious practices and social conduct led Andeans in search of representational spaces in which they could find room for their modes of perceiving and understanding the world. Cummins believes that the tactile and visual modes of representation in relation to oral discourse remained for Andeans the mode through which they preferred to "inscribe" their existence (95). While there appears to be a meeting ground of European and Andean symbolic representation, it is neither the province of "syncretism" nor the deployment documents and other sites of writing. The mutual entanglement that defines colonial situations can be ascertained in the Andes in the maintenance and circulation of costumes, images, and objects of tradition (140). The images found in *keros*, *aquillas*, and portraits do not appeal to the written word (134).

This space of entanglement presupposes the fragmentation of Inca iconography with a subsequent redeployment in a colonial space ruled by European visual and iconographic understandings. It is best illustrated by the frontispiece that Guamán Poma chooses for his *El Primer nueva corónica y buen gobierno* (1615). In this image

Guamán Poma redeploys a number of iconographic signs in order to fabricate his "coat of arms." He breaks up his name into a heraldic syntax in which the symbols of his "house" are the eagle (*guamán*) and the mountain cat (*puma*). These mark the two fields of his "coat of arms." In a descending hierarchical line he places an image of himself below that of the Spanish king, and the two, in turn, under the pope. Dividing the two fields of the frontispiece, he lines up the three coats of arms with the pope's at the top and his at the bottom, thus producing an integration, exchange, and circulation of meanings that speak of a single, if ambivalent, space of signification. In this intellectual feat Guamán Poma has unmoored a number of signs. He redeployed them, creating a space for the inscription of significations that could be decoded by both Europeans and Andeans. The insertion of the *tiana* – the traditional Andean seat of authority for *kurakas* – under the *guamán* on the left-hand side of his coat of arms underscores the Andean effort to resignify European spaces of representation with Andean objects and codes (101).

The study of objects and images produced around the first seventy years after the fall of Cajamarca shows a strong continuation of native Andean representational practices. Images and symbols taken from a fragmented Inca iconographic canon appear now conjoined to European images and symbols in a representational space now rendered bivalent by their very presence and articulation. The new representational space flows as the images, despite their radical differences, "speak" to one another. This mutual entanglement of Andean images and symbols with European values, signs, and spaces enables the Andean objects and images to express meaning within both sides of colonial society (94). This tactic for producing bivalent spaces and values of representation would remain in place throughout the colonial period and extends into the present.

## REFERENCES AND FURTHER READING

Abercrombie, A. Thomas (1998). *Pathways of Memory and Power: Ethnography and History among an Andean People*. Madison: University of Wisconsin Press.

Boone, H. Elizabeth (1994). "Introduction: writing and recording knowledge." In E. Boone and W. Mignolo, *Writing without Words: Alternative Literacies in Mesoamerica and the Andes*, pp. 3–26. Durham, NC: Duke University Press.

Brokaw, Galen (2003). "The poetics of *Khipu* historiography: Felipe Guamán Poma de Ayala's *Nueva Corónica* and the *Relación de los quipucamayoc*," *Latin American Research Review*, 38(3): 111–47.

— (2005). "Toward deciphering the Khipu," *Journal of Interdisciplinary History*, 35(4): 571–89.

Brotherston, Gordon (1992). *Book of the Fourth World: Reading the Native Americans Through Their Literature*. Cambridge: Cambridge University Press.

Coe, Michael D. (1992). *Breaking the Maya Code*. London: Thames & Hudson.

Cummins, Tom (1998). "Let me see! Reading is for them: colonial Andean images and objects 'Como es costumbre tener los caciques Señores.'" In H. Boone and T. Cummins (eds), *Native Traditions in the Postconquest World*, pp. 91–148. Washington, DC: Dumbarton Oaks Research Library and Collection.

Mendizábal Losack, Emilio (1961). "Don Felipe Guamán Poma de Ayala, señor y príncipe, último quellcakamayoc," *Journal of Latin American Lore*, 5: 83–116.

Mignolo, Walter (1994). "Signs and their transmission: the question of the book in the New World." In E. Boone and W. Mignolo (eds), *Writing Without Words: Alternative Literacies in Mesoamerica and the Andes*, pp. 220–70. Durham, NC: Duke University Press.

Niles, A. Susan (1999). *The Shape of Inca History: Narrative and Architecture in an Andean Empire*. Iowa City: University of Iowa Press.

Rostoworowski, María (1983). *Estructuras andinas del poder: Ideología religiosa y política*. Lima: Instituto de Estudios Peruanos.

Salomon, Frank (2005). *The Cord Keepers: Khipus and the Cultural Life of a Peruvian Village*. Durham, NC: Duke University Press.

Urton, Gary (2003). *Signs of the Inka Khipu: Binary Coding in the Andean Knotted-String Records*. Austin: University of Texas Press.

Zuidema, Tom R. (1990). *Inca Civilization in Cuzco*. Trans. Jean Jacques Decostes. Austin: University of Texas Press.

# 6

# Writing the Andes

## *Sara Castro-Klaren*

From the perspective of the Amerindians, 1492 marks the inauguration of major, violent, and irreversible changes in their histories, ways of life, and situation in the world. That year inscribes the establishment of a potent and permanent machinery of war supported by devastating weapons (horses, gods, steel swords), fueled by a providential concept of history and the power of alphabetic writing. The conquest moved along the path of destruction created by ravaging epidemic diseases for which the Amerindians had no defenses. In less than thirty years the peoples of the Caribbean were nearly extinct, while Mexico and Central America began to experience the ravages of the destruction of their entire cultures by the military, the bureaucracy, and the evangelizing clergy. As the Spaniards moved South of El Darien (Panama) in search of El Dorado (a kingdom made of gold), smallpox, colds, measles and pneumonia preceded them. The death of Huayna Capac, the last Inca, the father of Huascar and Atahualpa, is attributed to one of these plagues. Much of this "glorious" march west and south is reported during the early stages of the conquest to His Majesty and crown officials in diaries, letters, chronicles, and reports (*relaciones*) and later, in local and general histories, as the Spanish *letrados* traveled side by side with the soldiers and priests in search of treasure and free labor.

In examining this palimpsestic corpus of materials, often written in the immediate aftermath of battle in America or in the midst of the endless struggle over the Spanish rights of possession and authority over the new lands and the Indians, it is clear that the polemic over the humanity of the Indians, and the issue of just war, permeated every page. Had the extinction of the Indian populations not become part of the generalized understanding of the conquest, this debate might not have reached the dominant tone that it acquired at the time and the force with which it thunders through the ages. The writing of the memory of the Spanish invasion, conquest, and colonization of America as available in the texts written by Christopher Columbus (ca. 1451–1506), Gonzalo Fernández de Oviedo (1478–1557), Francisco López de Gómora (1511–66), Hernán Cortes (1484–1547), Bernal Diaz del Castillo (1495–

1584), Bartolomé de Las Casas (1474–1566), Pedro Cieza de León (1520–54), Juan de Betanzos (–1576), José de Acosta (1540–1600), Garcilaso de la Vega, Inca (1539–1616), and Guamán Poma de Ayala (–1615?), among many others, may vary a great deal in the practice of history that animates them, the kinds of rhetoric that they deploy, and their possible philosophical sources in Spain, but they all drip with blood, and to that extent the idea of reading them as an extended practice of writing violence, as José Rabasa has recently done (see Chapter 2 in this volume), does indeed go to the core of these texts. For reasons that cannot be taken up here, this heterogeneous corpus constitutes what Latin American literary critics and historians refer to as *letras coloniales*, or "colonial literature." Despite the fact that the great majority of these texts were not intended by their authors as literature, nor were they read by their contemporaries as such (a good number of them were not published until the nineteenth century), critics have studied them under the lenses of literary analysis and have produced more complex interpretations than the first readings accorded to them by social scientists in search of "facts."

However, as the distinction between literary and nonliterary texts has become less theoretically sustainable, and the interpretative power of this distinction has waned under the more general idea of "text," these "letras coloniales" are often now accorded an interdisciplinary approach. Conceived as a cultural object, a text is a highly priced verbal act that plays a significant role in the organization of a given culture. Although most literary corpuses are articulated within the confines of a single language, in the case of the colonial corpus, it is the referent – America – that confers upon them a certain "unity," despite the fact that some of these texts were written in Latin and even in Quechua. Walter Mignolo (1982) has classified this corpus into three major components: (1) *cartas relatorias*, or letters that tell of some event in some detail often provided by the eyewitness; (2) *relaciones*, or reports generally, but not always, requested by the crown in order to obtain extensive and detailed information not intended for publication or book form; (3) *crónicas*, or chronicles that generally narrate a series of events. However, the *cronistas de Indias* generally did not write *crónicas* in the medieval tradition of annals. Inasmuch as they tried to recover the past in texts that exhibit certain literary or historiographic characteristics and emphasized discursive organization, the *cronistas* wrote *historia* (Mignolo, 1982: 59). These histories are centered on heroic and even exemplary lives (76). *Cronistas* such as Las Casas and Garcilaso de la Vega, Inca were much influenced by Roman historians, Cicero above all.

The consensus of the time held that the writing of history should be in the hands of the lettered (*letrados*) class and not in the hands of soldiers like Bernal Diaz del Castillo or Indians such as Guamán Poma. History writing was itself divided into several kinds: divine, human, natural, moral, and general (Mignolo, 1982: 78). History writing during the period of the conquest was practiced by men who were both soldiers and *letrados*. Fernández de Oviedo, who had spent some time in Italy before coming to America and was thus acquainted with Italian humanism, is the first to attempt one of these new histories with his long *Historia general y natural de las Indias*

(1535). Oviedo wrote also as an official crown historian. He wanted to be remembered as the Pliny of the Indies. His idea of *historia natural* was to pull away from the medieval bestiaries and offer instead descriptions and interpretations based on eyewitness observations made in the new lands. The conqueror-historian thought that history should deal with big and important subjects. Like other *cronistas*, Oviedo was also trying to follow Cicero when he fashioned his *historia moral* in a temporal frame that organized the reporting of worthwhile events from various sources. The influence of Pliny in the arrangement of nature would determine a hierarchical model with which to view America. Thus from the start, the idea of an *historia natural* allowed for the classification, not just of plants and animals, but also of peoples and civilizations in an ascending ladder in which Europe would figure at the top and the Amerindians somewhere at the bottom. This classification would blend the natural with the moral and infuse all reports, letters, histories, and polemics about the new world from Oviedo to Ginés de Sepúlveda (1490–1573), to Las Casas and Acosta in *Historia natural y moral de las Indias* (1590).

The conquest of this continent brought about a profusion of texts beyond those identified above. Tracts, learned treatises, and even poems found an avid audience in both Europe and the colonial administrative centers. It gave rise to fierce debates about the nature of the Indians, colonial policy, and the right to wage war on civilian populations. Lawyers, jurists, academic intellectuals, crown officials, evangelizing and colonizing priests, official historians, and even Charles V himself participated. The early, prelapsarian image of the Indians created by the Italian humanists, who either worked in Spain or for the Spanish crown, soon came under attack by Spanish warriors and colonists in the Caribbean who painted their enemies as fierce, anthropophagic societies (Hulme, 1986).

The implicit critique of the conquest imbedded in the characterization of Indian societies as fresh versions of Ovid's world by the Italians (Peter Martyr d'Anghera, Amerigo Vespucci) was not lost on the Spanish *letrados* or the crown. Despite the fact that by 1530 the demographic catastrophe was universally acknowledged, and despite the evidence that the Indians were exhausted by famine, slave labor conditions, and disease, Oviedo and Sepúlveda wrote stinging attacks on Indian societies. For these two members of the imperial school of *cronistas*, the Indians were lazy, vicious, lying, traitorous, half-witted beings given to melancholy, anthropophagy, and sodomy, among other things. The list of phobias remained expandable, as can be seen in Acosta's rehearsal of the Indian portrait in 1590 and especially in his *De procurandam indorum salute* (1557), a manual for the evangelization of the Indians printed in Lima and quickly disseminated throughout the rest of the empire. Both Garcilaso and Guamán Poma would spend considerable ink and paper in responding to Acosta (Castro-Klaren, 2001).

Oviedo began making his cunning views public in various polemics and short publications. He arrived for the first time in the New World in 1514 as a notary public, and soon after participated in the bloody conquest of El Darien (Panama) in 1517. There he proudly took his booty in human flesh and himself branded the Indians to be enslaved. In 1532, after having gone to Spain to publish his *Sumario de la natural historia de la Indias* (1524) and to ask for royal favors, he returned to the New World. He then accepted the lifelong appointment as constable of the royal fortress of Santo Domingo and royal chronicler of the Indies (Brading, 1991: 33). Oviedo is regarded as one of the principal advocates of Spain's imperial power. His arguments were fundamental to the cynical deployment of the idea of providential history in which Spain figures as the nation chosen by God to be universally triumphant. Along with the Spanish Neoplatonist theologians, Oviedo believed that the Emperor Charles V was indeed the new sun.

Subscribing to the same doctrine of providential history, Las Casas, a colonist and also slaveowner, suffered in 1514 a crisis of conscience. This crisis was due in part to his daily witnessing of the Caribbean holocaust, and in part to the preaching of Franciscan monks in Cuba who realized that the conquest ran contrary to almost every Christian principle. In 1531 Las Casas wrote a memorial to the Council of the Indies. There he warned Spain of eternal damnation if it did not stop the slaughter of the Indians. For years he had been intervening on behalf of the Indians as well as preparing a massive treatise in their defense and conservation.

Las Casas came from a family of *conversos* (Jewish people who had converted to Christianity). As an adventurous lad of 18, he arrived in Hispaniola in 1502 eager to make his fortune as a colonist. His father and uncle had accompanied Columbus on his second voyage. They brought him and an (enslaved) Indian boy as a souvenir from the islands. Between 1502 and 1514 Las Casas fought as a soldier in the conquest of Cuba. In 1510 the Dominicans arrived in Hispaniola and began denouncing the Spaniards' treatment of the Indians. They also noted the demographic collapse. Friar Antonio de Montesinos gave an impassioned sermon in 1512 in which he articulated the questions and critique that Las Casas and his followers were to repeat throughout the centuries: "Are they [the Indians] not human? Do they not have rational souls? Are you not obliged to love them as yourselves?" (Brading, 1991: 59). The response was the official wrath of the crown and the church. More atrocities followed.

After his conversion, with the support of the Dominicans, he returned to Spain to campaign on behalf of the Indians and to build alliances, most especially with the bishop of Burgos (Castro, 2007: 63–102). Las Casas's strategy, not unlike the advice Guamán Poma offered the Spanish king almost a century later, was to make the church and the crown realize that it was in their benefit to keep the Indians in good condition. His proposals were always reform. He wanted to improve the conditions under which the Indians were integrated, albeit more slowly and peacefully, into the strictly hierarchical colonial world that was emerging. The very title of one of his best known tracts, *Memorial de remedios* (1516), indicates that Las Casas's project, heroic as it was in demanding that the power system in place recognize the humanity of the Indias, could not advocate a radical turn away from the policies of conquest and colonization. As one of his most recent analysts has put it: "What differentiates him from the rest is his willingness to reach out to offer temporary succor to those being victimized so that they could be benevolently converted, peacefully exploited, and successfully incorporated as members of the new subject-colony where existence depended on the dictates of the king in the imperial capital" (Castro, 2007: 8).

Nevertheless, Las Casas recommended the abolition of the *encomienda*, that is, the king's donation of immense tracts of land and thousands of Indians in perpetuity to individual Spaniards who had served in the armies that carried out the conquest. The *encomienda* system and its later modifications stayed firmly in place until the first half of the twentieth century as the coloniality of power, or rather the dependence of the modern world on its colonial underside, never really entirely waned (see Mignolo's Preamble in this volume). The Dominican friar hoped to persuade the king of the evils of the *encomienda* by citing the particular horrors and grief that accompanied the population collapse. In Hispaniola, he reported, out of the two million Indians in 1492, only 15,000 remained at the time he wrote the *Memorial*.

Las Casas, who had an *encomienda* in Cuba, described the forced labor conditions and wanton killings in wrenching detail. He had lost all confidence in the ability of his compatriots to treat the Indians in a Christian way. By way of remedies he suggested that Indians and Spaniards live in separate communities, a measure that to some extent was later put in place in Peru, not so much to protect the Indians as to better exploit their labor. The idea that the Indians should be left in communities of their own was predicated on the notion that they had demonstrable intelligence to rule themselves, even though they still needed the light of Christianity to fully achieve their divinely intended purpose on earth. Thus the Indian communities would be put under the care and tutelage of an evangelizing priest. This idea of separate communities was later embraced by Guamán Poma, who also wrote to the king in search of relief from the death toll of the conquest and Spanish rule. Guamán Poma, however, went beyond Las Casas in that he would also expel the priests about whose greed and unchristian practices he writes a scathing tract in his *El primer nueva corónica y buen gobierno* (1615).

The reforms spelled out in the *Memorial de remedios* constituted the seedbed for many of the later attempts by the evangelizing orders and even some crown officials to engage in what Las Casas envisioned as a peaceful conversation. His stance in defense of the Indians against the charges made by the school of Spanish imperial jurists, theologians, and historians (Brading, 1991: 2–75) has earned Las Casas the title of defender and protector of the Indians. He is also credited as the progenitor of the modern idea of human, that is, universal, rights.

As we shall see below, Las Casas went even further. After the killings of Moctezuma and Atahualpa, he argued that pagan civilizations had the right to keep their governments, and their members were entitled to restitution of the goods and life the conquerors had usurped. All of this swimming against the current earned him the hatred of many people in both the colonies and Spain. During his long life (1474–1566) he was feared, despised, and opposed by many who saw him as the enemy of Spain. Indeed, from the official point of view among Spanish historians, he was and is still regarded as the architect of what they called the Black Legend – the myriad facts and arguments that together question the legitimacy of Spain's right to conquer and govern Amerindian societies, together with the unmitigated and unavoidable condemnation of the destruction of the Amerindians. The polemic that Las Casas's criticism of conquest fueled with his *Memorial* dominated the whole of the sixteenth century, and nowhere was it heard more loudly or did it play a stronger role than in the dynamics of memory and writing of the former Tahuantinsuyo.

Las Casas crossed the Atlantic several times as he sought to obtain changes in policy in Spain and see them implemented in the New World. What he saw in his many journeys to Venezuela, Mexico, and Nicaragua never ceased to astound and shock him. Peaceful conversation was not even an idea in the heads of most of the evangelizing priests. In his *Del único modo de atraer a todos los pueblos a la verdadera religión* (1530–40), he argued that all peoples of the world were endowed with the same human qualities and cognitive faculties and that God had predestined all souls for salvation. This universalist argument could, however, be interpreted in two opposing ways. On the one hand, it could support the idea of a God-given human universal condition of all peoples, but on the other, it made conversion only the more urgent. In order to stem the force of the second reading, Las Casas argued that the Gospel should be predicated slowly and peacefully, that evangelists should seek to persuade and engage the cognitive capacities of peoples who, like all men endowed with natural enlightenment, sought to know the true God. Preaching was thus coupled with persuasion, an appeal to knowledge and love (Brading, 1991: 64). The violence of the conquest had created impossible conditions for the proper preaching of the Gospel, and it should stop, he argued.

The news from the Americas was shocking and alarming to many Europeans and there developed a great deal of pressure for reform. The pope finally declared the Indians to have souls. Las Casas's most radical denunciation of Spain and proposals for change were published in his summary work *Brevísima relación de la destrucción de las Indias* (1542). In this text he draws stark differences. Resting on the idea that the discovery of America was an act of divine providence, an idea that Garcilaso de la Vega would later exploit also, Las Casas paints the Indians as gentle and humble human beings in virtual expectation of conversion. The Spaniards, in contrast, are nothing but thieves and tyrants. They burn, torture, murder, enslave, and rape at will, as most eyewitness accounts attest. His proposal for radical reform not only recommends the abolition of the *encomienda*, but also the idea that once the Indians are converted and Spain has accomplished its duty as provided by God, the Spanish should retreat from America, a suggestion not lost in Guamán Poma, who not only promises the king good Indians (Christian vassals) but also unimaginable tribute. The restoration of Andean order and wealth will only be possible if the Spanish retreat to the coastal cities and leave the Andeans to govern themselves.

In 1542 the Spanish crown came out with new legislation for governing the colonies. Known as the New Laws, and in part influenced by Las Casas's critique and recommendations for better government, the New Laws were rejected by the colonists. Civil war broke out in Peru and more Andeans were compelled to fight and die in the opposing armies of the Pizarros, Almagros, and other sundry *caudillos*. Las Casas, deeply influenced by Augustine's *City of God* and the difference in the social orders created by the love of God as against the love of self, continued to question the entire legitimacy of the Spanish empire (Brading, 1991: 78). Derived from Augustine's *On the Predestination and the Gift of Perseverance*, the idea of the providential discovery of America provides Las Casas with an explanation for the failure of the Spanish to establish the city of God in America. Carried away by the self-love that rules in the earthly city, the Spanish acted as if inspired by the devil (Brading, 1991: 76). The paramount role that providence plays in the polemics and policies of conquest and relations with other civilizations is only comparable to the extended functions invested in the Devil (Cervantes, 1994: 5–75) as the chief presider over the construction of Amerindian "otherness," or colonial difference.

In response to the barrage of questions brought about by the vociferous interventions of Las Casas, Charles V called for a "junta" or meeting of jurists and theologians. The chief questions to be put to rest in Valladolid in 1550–1 were the human status of the Indians and the problematic behavior of the conquerors, never Spain's right to dominion over the earth. The jury was composed of Dominican theologians and the two debaters were to be Las Casas, the friar, and Juan Ginés de Sepúlveda (1490–1573), the lawyer, known as a defender of the imperial rights of the Spanish crown. The chief debaters never saw each other over the long year in which the debate took place. When Las Casas's turn came he took five days to read his *Apologetica historia* to the judges.

In the debate at Valladolid Las Casas had to contend not only with Sepúlveda, but also with another, absent adversary. Juan López de Palacios Rubios (1450–1524) had been one of the first Spanish jurists to come to the defense of Spanish lawful right to empire. He based his arguments on scholastic theology and medieval canon law rather than civil law. As far as he could reason and, basing himself on Aristotle, the Indians were "slaves by nature" in need of tutelage and correction before they could be fit for self-rule. This argument, like several of Las Casas's arguments, would also reverberate through the centuries and can even be found today when "modern" democracies demand to be regarded and adopted as the universal model.

Palacios Rubios also worked very cleverly in finding an imperial genealogy for the pope's political authority over the world. He argued that the world had seen four previous, universal "monarchies" – Assyrians, Medes, Greeks, and Romans – before Christ had inaugurated the fifth and last monarchy of the world. Thus the pope, as the vicar of Christ, exercised both spiritual and temporal power over the entire world and could indeed, delegate such authority on Spain (Brading, 1991: 80–1). So Palacios Rubios devised the *Requerimiento* (Seed, 1995), a document to be read to the Indians upon their first encounter with the Spaniards that would inform them of the hegemony of the pope and the king over the entire world. It followed that any Indian who did not accept the authority of the pope was subject to legitimate acts of war and conquest. The *Requerimiento* was used for the first time in the conquest of El Darien in 1517, a campaign in which Oviedo participated. This document made Oviedo's taking and branding of slaves and the atrocities denounced by Las Casas "legal." The stakes in the Valladolid debate could not have been higher.

Another absent interlocutor in Valladolid was the Dominican and professor of theology and philosophy at Salamanca, Francisco de Vitoria (1486–1546). Like Palacios Rubios, Vitoria had never been to America. He did not have the benefit or the authority of the ocular observer. He worked from reports and from his rich library. In 1534, he, like many others, was shocked to hear of the unlawful execution (regicide) in Cajamarca of the Inca Atahualpa and he wrote on the problem of Spain and the Amerindians without being solicited by the crown to do so (Pagden, 1982: 64–80). Vitoria was one of the leaders of the Thomist revival in Spain. He followed Thomas Aquinas's reasoning regarding the difference between pagans and Christians. The theory of natural law was the discursive frame within which the theologians at Salamanca analyzed the critical question that Amerindians posed for European epistemology.

In 1537 Vitoria wrote *Relectio de Indis* (1557), a work that circulated widely in manuscript form and had a lasting imprint in all future discussion concerning the Indies. In *de Indis*, the theologian tries to find an answer to the unthinkable question: What if there is no just title to the conquest of America? As Anthony Pagden points out, with this question Vitoria takes the problem of "just title" out of the strict realm of the law and places it in the space of theology for the problem involved, settling the chief question regarding the nature of the Indian *qua* man (66–7). It was clear to Vitoria from the report received on Mexico and Peru that the Indians were not simple irrational beings, and thus any common-sense discussion could demonstrate that the Indians were not monkeys, but human beings. Relying on Aristotle, Vitoria reasoned that the Indians clearly had the use of reason, in their own way. They had order in their affairs, they had properly organized cities, recognizable forms of marriage, magistrates, rulers, laws, industry, and commerce. They also had religion. For Vitoria, as it had been for Aristotle, the city stood for the most perfect unit of society, the "only place where the practice of virtue and the pursuit of happiness" are at all possible. Man, for both Plato and Aristotle, can only realize himself as a citizen. Christianity transforms the secular, Greek city into a spiritual community (Pagden, 1982: 69). Indeed, St. Augustine could only conceive of the world, both celestial and earthly, as urban. People who built cities and lived in them could simply not be thought of as barbarians or natural slaves. By definition they were civilized. Vitoria found that the Indian societies also exhibited two other traits of civilization: they engaged in trade and hospitality and they had visibly organized religions.

However, in the second part of *de Indis*, the part that deals with just title to conquest, Vitoria starts to back-pedal and begins to offer the *contra* argument required in scholastic argument (Pagden, 1982: 80). There he speaks not of what Indian societies practiced but of what they did not, or rather how they did not resemble Europe, whose assumed normative character had underlined the entire discussion on natural and divine law. Vitoria argued that Indian law was insufficiently wise and unsatisfactory. He abandoned the urban model argument and focused instead on the reports of cannibalism, sodomy, and bestiality which he thought violated the natural order. The Indians' dietary and sexual practices showed that they were not only irrational but even mentally defective and thus incapable of governing themselves (Pagden, 1982: 85–7).

Vitoria's arguments exposed the insurmountable contradictions driving the discourses of the conquest-cum-evangelization. The contradictions embedded in the theory of natural law itself were brought to their critical limits, for they were being used to account for the simultaneous, but unthinkable, perception of *sameness* and *difference* that the European cognitive complex obtained from contact with the Amerindians. This conundrum, this limitation in European epistemology, has shadowed the history of Amerindian peoples to the present, for "if the natural slave is incapable of participating in a state of happiness, then he must also be incapable of achieving his proper end (*telos*) as a man. If nature never creates anything which is, of itself, incapable of accomplishing its ends – for such a thing would be useless – then the natural slave is not a man" (Pagden, 1982: 94).

Vitoria managed to cover over this blind spot in his discourse by appealing to the idea that God created man and that the essential characteristic of man is his rational mind. Thus the Indians' faults and deficiencies could eventually be rubbed out with proper education and discipline, a solution that was not that far away from Las Casas's idea of peaceful and slow conversion. Paradoxically this idea translated into the very harsh laws and bodily punishment that Toledo (1515–82) put in place in the Andes, in part supported by the denigrating ideas that Acosta put forth in the Third Council of Lima in (1579) and in the earlier *De Procuranda* (1557). From the clay that Vitoria's hands molded, the Indian came out not a slave, but a child. In this scheme the king of Spain was the tutor of the Indians. When the Indians no longer required tutoring, they would be left to enjoy their proper liberty. Vitoria managed to dismantle Palacios's argument on the universal authority of the pope and he even ended up reasoning that idolatry was not grounds for dispossession of the Indians. Upon hearing of this scandalous position, Charles V ordered Vitoria to stop interfering in the question of the Indies (Pagden, 1982: 106, Brading, 1991: 84).

Juan Ginés de Sepúlveda was partly educated in Bologna and Rome. He had been a tutor to Philip II, and by 1536 he was appointed imperial chronicler. He published a tract against Erasmus's pacifism in order to defend the European warrior code and social structure (Brading, 1991: 86). In 1544 he wrote a dialogue, *Democrates Secundus*, in order to defend the Spanish conquest and empire in the world. He drew his information and arguments in part from Oviedo and Gómora. For him the Indians were slaves by nature for they lacked prudence, intelligence, virtue, and even humanity, all the attributes that the Renaissance thought citizens ought to have. He also defined the Indians by what they were not, especially when it came to lacking "writing." From there he surmised that Indians also lacked history and laws, had no sense of self-consciousness, had no notion of private property and were, in general, ruled by tyrants. Sepúlveda's challenge caused Las Casas to rethink his materials in order to demonstrate that the Indians were *not* different and that they could be both savage and as civilized as the Europeans (Brading, 1991: 88–9). The Dominican had to begin moving toward a comparative ethnography with the ancient world, a move not lost on Garcilaso de la Vega, Inca. In the Valladolid debate, Las Casas's job was to prove that the Indians were neither natural slaves, nor "homunculus," as Sepulveda would have it, but rather normal human beings created by God, even if the Bible did not mention them. By and large he accomplished this task.

The arguments that Las Casas brandished in this fight were garnished from his *Historia de las Indias* (1542) and his later *Apologetica historia sumaria* (1551). Probably the best study to date of Las Casas's thought on the matter can be found in David Brading's *The First America* (1991). In order to frame a sense of cultural evolution Las Casas turned to Cicero and his idea of stages in the natural history of humanity. For Cicero, all men in all nations are essentially the same in their nature. For Las Casas, it was not hard to show that the Aztecs and the Incas resembled the Greeks and the Romans. For instance, of Aristotle's six requirements or marks of civilized life, all could be found in the Amerindian societies: agriculture, artisans and artists, a warrior class, rich men, organized religion, lawful government, and city life. Once again he deployed St. Augustine's argument on natural enlightenment and the desire of all men to seek and serve God (Brading, 1991: 90). Las Casas's approach to Amerindian religions required that he really stretch the comparative frame, and while the Greek and the Aztec pantheon could be safely compared, some of the rituals and practices of Amerindian religions simply had to be attributed to the Devil's ability to gain hold of pagans. He made a particular point of arguing that the Incas had been very close to monotheism.

Despite his comparative ethnology and defense of the Indian's humanity, Las Casas still had to devise a reason that would justify the Spanish empire, as he was an advocate of royal authority. He agreed with Vitoria's argument on the natural right to rule of the Indian monarchs. Idolatry alone did not justify deposing or killing them. He attacked Sepúlveda's argument on the natural slavery of the Indians by saying that it was blasphemy against God to say that He had created a brutish and inferior "race" (Brading, 1991: 95). Therefore, all wars of conquest against the Indians were unjust. At this point, caught in a dilemma, Las Casas had no choice but to follow Vitoria in defining papal authority as only spiritual, not political – a claim that left the king with no right to a universal empire. The Dominican friar pulled out of his blind spot, not unlike Vitoria, by claiming that very same spiritual authority obliged the pope and the king to see to it that the Indians were Christianized, that is to say, "educated" into being better men. With this argument he restored all political authority to the crown. Indeed, "the only way out," as he entitled one of his tracts, was peaceful conversion, which to the conquerors and colonists sounded like more of the same. It proved impossible to find a balance between the right to convert the peoples of the world and the right of the pagan rulers to preserve their independence. How to serve God in the midst of thieves? is the question that hounded Las Casas all his life, as he saw the New World fall off a precipice of evil and injustice.

It is in the horns of these irreconcilable claims, these epistemological and ethical dilemmas, that the intellectual and political project of all those who wrote about the Andes after the fall of Cajamarca in 1531 are inscribed. The polemic on the nature of the American Indian that took place, as a result of confusing the Bible with world history, reverberated through the centuries, causing all kinds of distortions and misconceptions, blocking the ability to produce new learning and even a more accurate approach to empirical realities. When Francisco Pizarro (1478–1541) decided to execute Atahualpa and march to Cuzco with his Huanca allies, the priest who accompanied him wrote a report, today considered bogus, to justify the regicide. According to the Spaniards, Atahualpa had committed blasphemy. The scene has the Spanish showing the Inca a book – the Bible – and telling him that that is the word of God, to which the Inca must submit. Atahualpa receives the book from the friar's hands, puts it to his ear, and upon hearing nothing, shakes it. He still hears nothing. Then, angered, he throws the book on the floor, saying that it cannot be God because it does not speak to him. Tom Cummins (1998) disputes the idea that the Inca would have expected an object to mimic the word because in the Andes, speech and writing were not associated with objects, as they were in Europe. It is clear also from the lack of adequate translators at the time that the Spaniards could not have conveyed the message they claim to have given Atahualpa about "the book–the–Word-divinity." What the fiction of Father Valderde speaks of is the power claims that the written word and the representative relation with the king of Spain allowed them to make in imperial territories. This is the brash and unreflecting power amalgam of ideas and military strength that Andeans, and even Spaniards, would have to address every time they took up the pen to tell the story of the conquest, reconstruct the history of the Incas, petition for favors or advancement, or contest the practices and justifications for the injuries wrought upon people by the colonial regime. Again, providential history was the umbrella that protected all, from those who praised the conquest and destruction of the Andean way of life, to those who, like Garcilaso de la Vega, Inca wrote to correct the Spanish imperial historians, or Guamán Poma, who hoped to tutor the Spanish king into understanding what good government really would be like.

The conquest of Peru is dominated by a fractious engagement of Spaniards and Andean peoples who saw in the arrival of the Spaniards an opportunity to rebel against Inca rule. Starting with Father Valverde, many Spaniards wrote the memory of their part in the conquest in various forms and addressed different publics. The *Crónica del Peru* (1553) by Pedro Cieza de Leon (1518–53), a soldier and *letrado*, is the closest thing to a narrative of the conquest. The second part of the *Royal Commentaries* (1609) by Garcilaso de Vega, Inca (1539–1616) remains the classical account of the conquest because of its ample view of events, the clear concept of history that articulates it, and the beautiful style in which it is written. The recent *Conquest of the Incas* (1970) by John Hemming draws fully on the corpus of reports, letters, memorials, *crónicas*, treatises, and narratives that the conquest of the Andes, the ensuing civil wars, and the campaign for the extirpation of idolatries produced during the sixteenth century.

He especially draws on Garcilaso and Cieza. The issues that dominated Las Casas's writings are replayed in the writing of the Andes: *encomienda*, just conquest, evangelization, the right to universal empire, providential history, the place of the Indians in the new scheme of things, rights to private property, rights of the Indians to self-rule, and the quality of their culture.

One way of making sense of the proliferation of writings from Peru is to look at the authors of these texts as part of the ongoing Sepúlveda–Las Casas polemic and separate them by the perspective that they had on the Inca empire. This is more helpful than a generational or referential classification (Porras Barrenechea, 1962). Although the edges of all groupings are always blurred, and *cronistas* like Juan de Betanzos (–1576) are hard to place neatly on one side or the other, the separation in terms of the particulars of the polemic allows for a better understanding of the discursive forces unleashed into modernity by the conquest as well as the problematics of positionality that accompanied writing in the Andes. In general terms we can speak of two oppositional groups: (1) the Toledo Circle, a number of *letrados* who pushed forward, with all the resources of the crown, the basic principles of a justificatory imperial history and (2) the various individuals who wrote outside of the circle and who, for reasons of their own, resisted and opposed the ideological thrust of imperial history. The Toledo Circle encompasses the chroniclers, jurists, translators, notaries public, priests, and other *letrados* and scholars engaged by the viceroy to continue the Spanish imperial school of history and provide the crown with the necessary information and arguments to denigrate and deauthorize Inca rule and culture. In this group one can easily place the *letrados* hired by the viceroy himself: Juan de Matienzo (1520–79), Pedro Sarmiento de Gamboa (1530?–92), Juan Polo de Ondegardo (–1575), and others who, like the Jesuit José de Acosta (1540–1600), had views of their own and were weary of the viceroy but did nevertheless confirm the normative and "superior" sense of European modes of cognition. They produced a harsh interpretation of Inca history, one in which they basically characterized the Incas as vicious rulers to whom Plato's definition of the tyrant – a man ruled by the desires of the lower organs of the body – applied fully (Castro-Klaren, 2001).

Although very different among themselves and writing at a good distance from one another, the men who contested, in different ways, the discourse of the imperial historians were the *mestizo* Jesuit Blas Valera (1545–97; Varner; 1968), the Indian Guamán Poma de Ayala and the *mestizo* humanist Garcilaso de la Vega, Inca, the latter writing from Spain. Cieza de Leon, although holding onto the view of providential history and the superiority of Spanish culture, cannot be aligned with either group as he wrote with great admiration of the Inca empire. Although considered "reliable chroniclers," their information needs to be corroborated with other sources. Cieza de Leon, for instance, is noted for his more or less objective descriptions of Andean culture and Inca rule. However, in this respect, his work cannot compare with Betanzos, who knew more Quechua and had direct access to the memory of one of the royal *panacas* (patrilineal descent groups in charge of preserving specific noble Inca houses).

Cieza de Leon never failed to subscribe to the notion that Inca religion was inspired by the Devil, a "fact" that he did not try to reconcile with his extensive reports on and admiration for the exemplary laws and wise statecraft with which the Incas governed the immense *Historia del Tahuantinsuyo* (Pease, 1978).

Although hired by viceroy Antonio de Mendoza and with probably only an elementary education, Betanzos wrote quite a reliable history of the Incas. He had the great benefit of having learned Quechua in the field. This gave him an unusually great power to understand what was being reported to him and to attempt feats of cultural translation. His marriage to Doña Evangelina, one of Huayna Capac's granddaughters, gave him unparalleled access to the Cuzco elite whose khipu and oral memory clearly informs both the contents and the shape of his narrative. In fact there are times when the *Summa y narración de los Incas* (1557) reads as if Betanzos were both transcribing and translating directly from the narrative of a Quechua speaker. It could be that one of his chief sources is Doña Evangelina herself, and certainly a good number of members of her family.

Gómez Suárez de Figueroa was born in Cuzco in 1539 and died in Spain in 1616. His mother was the Inca princess Chimpu Ocllo, later baptized as Isabel Suárez, and his father was the captain and nobleman Sebastian Garcilaso de la Vega. How Gómez Suárez de Figueroa became a canonical "author" in the Spanish language and better known as Garcilaso de la Vega, Inca, is a fascinating story of self-fashioning that involves the most amazing journey through personal and collective memory, the Renaissance, with its revival of Greco-Roman culture, and the will to recover the Inca past for posterity. Garcilaso has been fortunate with his critics. With the exception of a nineteenth-century Spanish critic who failed to appreciate Garcilaso's ethnographic presentation of the Inca empire, and the ethnohistorian María Rostworowski, most of his biographers and analysts have described and brought out the complexity, subtle maneuverings, and intelligence of the Inca's task with satisfied admiration.

His attempt, well into the sixteenth century, to write an account of the Inca empire that corrected and contradicted official Spanish historiography, was a monumental project for one man alone. *El Inca: Life and Times of Garcilaso de la Vega* by John Grier Varner (1968) still stands as the best biography and overall study of the political and intellectual milieu in which Garcilaso had to move in order to safeguard his person, arrange for conditions favorable to becoming an intellectual, and see to the possibility of writing and being published. He changed his name several times and each time the changes coincided with a new stage of consciousness and self-assurance. From the time of his birth the rights and the social and economic standing of *mestizos* had diminished rapidly. Officers of the crown considered them dangerous rivals, treacherous allies, and racially inferior (Mazzotti, 1996: 22–3). *Mestizos* did not fare any better with the Indians. In fact Guamán Poma, for a set of very complicated reasons that included wanting to stop the sexual practices that engendered *mestizos*, almost always illegally, recommended that the existing *mestizos* move to the Spanish towns. Garcilaso wrote to suture the split and the trauma that the conquest brought about. But he never rejected his father. Instead he sought to clear his name of accusations made about his conduct in one of the many battles of the civil war in which Spaniards changed sides easily.

For Garcilaso, *mestizaje* did not mean hybridity, as some recent commentators have wanted to label his efforts. Neither did it mean syncretism. Nor did it mean writing in between two worlds as if dangling from the edges that separated them. One of the purposes of his writing was to bring the two worlds together, in a dynamic of double valence, to create an epistemological and aesthetic space where double voicing was possible. The Inca in Spain practiced a doubled consciousness of wholeness rather than hybridity of dismemberment and paranoia (Castro-Klaren, 1999). From an Andean perspective, in love with the concept of duality, he sought complimentary and reciprocity. The binary of the duality of the khipu can also be seen to inspire the Inca's efforts to find a harmonious "new world." Each of the parts was to remain whole, with a logic of its own, and come together in a dance of complementarity. In a telling gesture of his Andean search for complementarity and reciprocity he translated from the Italian (1590) the *Dialoghi di Amore* by Leon Hebreo (1535), for in this piece from the "Old World" he found not so much inspiration as confirmation for the development of his capacities as a Andean writer and for his philosophical and aesthetic of complementarity.

As an illegitimate *mestizo* in Spain and despite his Jesuit connections, Garcilaso needed to authorize himself as a subject of knowledge in order to intervene in the ongoing discourse on the Indies. Any cursory reading of the *Royal Commentaries* yields an ample list of the many contemporary and ancient authors that Garcilaso read in order to prepare for his work. Further confirmation of his firm grasp of issues and debates came to light when in 1948 José Durand found the Inca's last will. It included a list of the books he owned, which was considerable, given the size of private libraries at the time (Durand, 1963). The Inca had clearly immersed himself in the Italian Renaissance, the Christian theological and philosophical tradition, the rediscovery of Greek and Roman culture, and the literature and political thought of his Spanish contemporaries. He had difficulties in assembling an equally rich bank of sources for his writing on the Incas. Garcilaso relied chiefly on his memory, the memory of friends in Peru who responded to his letters and answered his queries, the chronicle authored by Cieza de Leon, and the great book that the Jesuit Blas Valera was writing in Latin on Inca history. The Inca seems to have incorporated this massive treatise wholesale into his commentaries. Beyond the efforts to recover the memory of the Inca world, the chief move that Garcilaso made was to claim greater and better authority over all Spanish theologians and historians, based on his knowledge of Quechua, his free access to the *amautas* on his mother's side of the family, and his persistent demonstration of errors incurred by the Spaniards owing to their ignorance of Quechua and their misunderstanding of Andean concepts which only a thorough knowledge of the language could prevent. With one single move, Garcilaso authorized himself and deauthorized most of the detractors of the Indians, something that Las Casas would have dearly loved to do, but could not do because he never learned any Indian languages. Garcilaso slyly argued that not knowing Quechua and wanting to understand Andean culture was like not knowing Hebrew and wanting to understand the Bible.

Margarita Zamora (1988) has written at length on how Garcilaso deployed his savvy understanding of philology to institute Quechua as a language of knowledge comparable only to Latin or even Hebrew in the Christian tradition of exegesis. Antonio Mazzotti and other critics have pointed out that the majority of studies on the Inca concentrate on the humanist aspects that allow for the configuration of his works, an emphasis which does not allow for an analysis of the many features of both content and style that resist the European colored lenses. In *Coros Mestizos del Inca Garcilaso* (1996) he seeks to remedy the situation. He posits a reading of Garcilaso in which Quechua narrative modes and understanding of the past, concepts of time and subject, operate as a kind of subtext (28–9). Mazzotti brings out in Garcilaso the presence of the conventions of Quechua oral narrative and especially the discursive tradition of the Cuzco court and all the symbolism that such choral tradition implies (31–2). This kind of interdisciplinary study surpasses the more narrowly conceived literary and philological analysis. It brings to bear the information and methods made available by iconography, archeology, and ethnohistory in order to detect in the Inca's text more than sheer information conveyed by the Cuzco arts of memory. Studies of post-conquest textualization of Andean memory in alphabetic texts and iconographic structures show that Garcilaso's change of names owes as much to Spanish costumes of the time as to Andean practices of naming according to life stages. Christian Fernández (2004) analyses in detail Garcilaso's coat of arms and shows how Garcilaso redeploys the European conventions of fields and arrangement of totems in order to represent his filiations with the Andean Amaru (97–111), the symbol of his *panaca* (37).

Garcilaso wrote at the time when the erasure of Amerindian memory and knowledges was already advanced. He wanted to stem the wave of forgetting that the claims of alphabetic writing, as the only site of memory, had already spread over the Amerindians' sense of the meaning of their cultures. Drawing on the organizing principles of Roman historians, in chapter after chapter, peppered with seemingly arbitrary digressions, Garcilaso places the stones that together amount to the rebuilding of the Inca empire and way of life. He systematically moves from the location of the Andes in a world that is *one* and a human kind that is *one*, to the particulars of the Andean landscape, the agricultural system, social organization, war, legal, religious, and communications systems. Garcilaso stages his narrative rhetoric in order to assure his reader of the veracity of the facts and events presented and to distinguish his history from fables and fictions (Fernández, 2004: 32; Mignolo, 1982). Mignolo has pointed out that the Inca makes clear that he is in charge of writing history, that is to say, he organizes and gives meaning to the materials while his sources simply tell the story (*relato*) as best they remember (90).

The fact that he entitled his book "commentaries" and not history has always puzzled his readers. It has been said that he took Caesar's commentaries as his model (Fernández, 2004: 26–8). It has also been argued that the Inca had in mind the genre of the philological biblical commentary prevalent at the time (Durand, 1963: 322–32 in Fernández, 2004: 29). Fernández shows that the commentary genre was widely practiced during the Middle Ages, establishing a heterogeneous legacy (41) of which Garcilaso was well aware (41–7). It would seem that the Inca chose the tradition of the critical commentary as practiced by St. Jerome in his *Contra Rufino* because this practice allowed him to gloss, expand, clarify, criticize, correct, and dispute, in collaboration with the subtle reader. For Fernández, the reader in Garcilaso, as in St. Jerome, is the necessary counterpart who will bring to full fruition the half-sentences, digressions, allusions, and invitations to draw the appropriate conclusions sprinkled throughout the text (48–55). This thesis is quite persuasive, for it fits Garcilaso's rhetoric.

The richness and complexity of Garcilaso's endeavor – to take on the entire panoply of imperial history that denigrated the Inca and, by extension, other Amerindian civilizations – has not yet been properly assessed. Although the chief villain of his history, the viceroy Toledo, was dead by the time the *Commentaries* appeared, readers understood that this was not a chronicle, but a formidable rebuttal that showed the refined intelligence of the Incas and the creative capacity of Andean culture. The influence that the Inca's work had in shaping the European and American imaginary with respect to Inca society as sort of a utopia can never be underestimated. The *Royal Commentaries* rejoiced and influenced contemporary audiences in Peru and inspired many eighteenth-century encyclopedists and playwrights. It has been reprinted many times and its many and rapid translations into all the major European languages made it a bestseller. It accompanied Tupac Amaru II in dreaming of a more ordered and just world. Despite the fact that the circulation of the book was forbidden by the Spanish authorities, it was always to be found in Bolívar's tents and San Martín's luggage. Its readers recognized a monumental recovery of memory and epistemological potential essential to the maintenance of the community of mankind.

By the 1550s it was clear throughout the Spanish-American empire that the idea of evangelizing the Indians had failed rapidly. Between 1567 and 1582 the church held a council in Lima to discuss many matters, including the arrival of the new order: the Jesuits. Among other things it was decided to deny the Indians admission to holy orders and to forbid them from taking communion. The Indians were basically disenfranchised as Catholics. Toledo had put his ordinances in place and the whole Andean world was near collapse, with the demographic catastrophe in full swing. It is conservatively estimated that the population went down from 16 million to 3 million. Exhausted, resistance was no longer possible. Confusion and grief reigned everywhere. People fled their villages and abandoned their families in search of work in the Spanish towns. Guamán Poma seems to have paid very close attention to the proceedings of the Council as well as to all other matters in Peru.

In 1614, when he is about to hand his manuscript to the person who will take it to Spain and hand it either to Philip III or some trusted advisor, Guamán Poma claims to be 80 years old. Most of what we know about him is gleaned from his own autobiographical presentation as "author" of the *Primer Nueva corónica y buen gobierno* (1516). He claims to be from Lucanas, to be the son of a *curaca,* or "prince," as he translates the term into Spanish. He casts himself as servant of the king, a noble Andean Christian who has sought to serve the cause of the king and justice, as a defender of poor Indians in court, as translator and advocate of true Christian causes. For such dedication to the king's interests he has only received scorn and unjust treatment from the Spaniards, especially the priests, whose main interest is the spoliation of Indian labor and property, not to mention their compulsive desire for Indian women.

Guamán Poma, not unlike Garcilaso, knew Toledo's work very well. He was surely familiar with Toledo's *Ordenanzas* – the viceroy's legislation over every aspect of human life in the Andes (Castro-Klaren, 2001). In fact his familiarity with the events of the extirpation of idolatries as well as the format of the *informaciones* – the canvassing of the Andean territory for information useful to the crown – suggests that Guamán Poma may have been a translator for Spanish extirpators, magistrates, priests, and other *letrados*. His familiarity with Christian doctrine is firm and well grounded. There is no doubt that Guamán Poma was endowed with a powerful mind and an indefatigable thirst for knowledge, for he seems to have heard of every argument and piece of information animating the polemic of the American Indian and his political and intellectual right to rule the land of his ancestors.

His *Corónica* or extended letter to the king (of 908 pages) is surprisingly critical of the Incas. He would agree with the Toledo Circle in claiming that the Incas were only recent rulers who, through conquest and tyranny, expanded their original Cuzco holdings into the huge territory of the Tahuantinsuyo. Guamán Poma even denies that the Incas were originally from Cuzco. But in a crafty redeployment of Las Casas, Guamán Poma proposes that the land and government of Peru be given back – restituted–to the Indians, that is to say to the *curacas* or ethnic lords, like his family, not the descendants of the Incas. On this other matter he was squarely against the Toledo Circle, and that included Acosta.

Guamán Poma's account of universal time is even more surprising, as he not only tries to find the point to link Amerindian time to biblical unilinear time, but pushes back Andean time deeply into four pre-Inca epochs. New research into the differences that account for the passage of time in the Andes and the events concerning Inca rule and the making of the Tahuantinsuyo shows that some of the discrepancies among the cronistas are due to the fact that they interviewed different Inca *panacas* or came into contact with different ethnic accounts (Rostworowski, 1987). In this light it is clear that Guamán Poma offers an account of time and history that not only differs substantially, but is in fact at odds with the Cuzco accounts prominent in Garcilaso de Vega, Inca and Juan de Betanzos, for instance. The four ages that Guamán Poma figures preceded Inca times postulate about a million years after Adam (Brading, 1991: 150). He begins the history of the New World with the arrival of Noah sometime after the universal flood. The four ages tell of a human cultural development that precedes the arrival of Manco Capac – the first Inca and cultural hero – and accounts for most of Andean cultural developments: agriculture, cities, laws, and the building of fortresses. Brading notes that the evolutionary development in Guamán Poma is reminiscent of that advanced by Cicero and redeployed by Las Casas (1991: 150–1).

Guamán Poma's boldness never ceases to amaze his readers, given the climate of orthodoxy and censorship in both Spain and the colonies. Not content with having grafted Andean time onto biblical time by having found the common and universal phenomenon of the flood, the khipukamayuc advances the notion that Andean civilization is actually a forerunner of Christianity. This idea is also advanced by Garcilaso. Although it is not possible to know how Guamán Poma came to learn the details of the Spanish controversy on the American Indians (Adorno, 1986), it is clear in the text that he nimbly uses the natural law argument developed by Las Casas and Vitoria in order to argue that in pre-Hispanic society, people were organized and governed by the reason of natural law. Andean peoples led virtuous lives, as they followed their own laws and the Devil was not anywhere to be seen, except in the person and life of some of the *Collas*, or Inca queens. There is no doubt that even in this account of Andean pre-Christian virtue, which defies the consensus reached in Spain about the Indian's immaturity (as in Kant's immaturity also), Guamán Poma feels "safe." It may be that he is aware of the fact that his portrayal of the Incas as usurpers and tyrants coincides with the views sought and propounded by the circle of *letrados* serving the viceroy Toledo. He must have reasoned that his devastating critique of Spanish colonial rule, coming as it did from a doubly virtuous person, that is, Christian pre-Christian, or a natural intelligence taken to its true *telos* by the enlightenment of Christianity, would gain him an audience with the king.

If his account of universal history would have seemed outrageous to his contemporaries had they had a chance to read it – the manuscript got lost and was not read until 1911 – his daring to give advice to the king of Spain on how to govern so as to save his soul is as admirable as it is laughable. In one of his now famous drawings he imagines a scene in which he sits next to the king of Spain who, as his pupil, listens to the information and recommendations that Guamán Poma, the good governor, offers to His Majesty. Like Las Casas, Guamán Poma envisions the time when the Indians and Spanish will live in separate towns with the Indians having been given back their lands. In this utopian set-up all work would be paid, and the *mita*, and for that matter all daily life, should be modeled on Inca times and Inca ethics, for they, after all, had the best laws and really knew how to govern. Toledo instead is only creating havoc. His policy to move the Indians to towns, his exigencies of tribute and long periods of work in the mines, together with the neglect of the fields, is bringing the Andes to a catastrophic end, for the world is now upside down and the Indians are becoming extinct. In the end Guamán Poma's *Corónica* is saturated by the grief of seeing an orderly and healthy world come to end, as he says, "without remedy in sight." The pages written by the self-styled prince speak of the terrifying sense of holocaust, for an entire ancient civilization was about to disappear. The urgency of the demographic collapse is written on every page of text and picture that make up the 908 pages of his letter to the king.

How Guamán Poma was able to become conversant with the entire discursive complex of the conquest-cum-evangelization and redeploy it to critique the conquest and colonial rule, as well as offer a plan for good government, is a feat that remains unequaled in the history of colonial or modern letters. Compared with Garcilaso, his disadvantages were greater and his subalternity was extreme. He managed to learn doctrine by attending sermons, law by frequenting the courts, drawing by apprenticing himself to various churchmen and artists. Adorno also traces Guamán Poma's ecclesiastical rhetoric to written sources that he quotes in his letter. He seems to have been thoroughly familiar, for instance, with Fray Luis de Granada's sermon *Memorial de la vida cristiana* which was printed and widely circulated in the New World for evangelizing purposes (Adorno, 1986: 57). The new catechisms and *sermonarios* printed in Lima after the meeting of the Third Council of Lima allow Guamán Poma a firmer grasp of the problems that preaching Christianity to the Andean people entail. These texts help him sharpen his "pose as a preacher" (Adorno, 1986: 57). No less important are the confession manuals circulating in the Andes, for they offer a model to Guamán Poma for eliciting information and even for inventing the scene in which he instructs the king. Adorno writes that "Guamán Poma's defense of his race is a direct reaction to the biases expressed in [the] doctrinal texts" (66), texts circulating in the Andes at the time of the Third Council in which the intellectual potential of Andeans is denigrated by none other than Acosta.

There is no doubt that Guamán Poma was also keenly aware of Las Casas's position regarding the problematic justification for imperial rule and the natural intelligence and ethics of Indian societies. Like Garcilaso and Las Casas, he had no choice but to seek refuge under the umbrella of providential history and thus accept the king's legitimate authority to govern. This move left open the possibility of demanding good government.

In conclusion, if, as it has been argued by Mendizabal, Botherston, and Brokaw, Guamán Poma worked from the cognitive order of the khipu, from the Andean ontology of numbers and the art of rectification (Brokaw, 2002: 293), perhaps we could say – as with the Cuzco school of painting – that we are confronting something new – modern – in the history of the world inaugurated by the year 1492. Perhaps we could suggest that it is the Andean structure of knowledge that allows him to dismantle European discourses, locate the fragile seems that hold the parts together, break the fragments, and reassemble them into new series with new semiotic relations, as he does in the *Nueva corónica y buen gobierno*. Perhaps we could say that in a perverse way, the urgent need to respond to the destructuration of the self-world, the vital impulse to retreat from agony, allowed Garcilaso and Guamán Poma – from their respective subaltern subject positions – to hone the subject position and discursive perspective that would allow them to redefine the polemic for the postcolonial world.

## REFERENCES AND FURTHER READING

Adorno, Rolena (1986). *Guamán Poma: Writing and Resistance in Colonial Peru*. Austin: University of Texas Press.

Brading, David A. (1991). *The First America: The Spanish Monarchy, Creole Patriots, and the Liberal State 1492–1867*. Cambridge: Cambridge University Press.

Brokaw, Galen (2002). "Khipu numeracy and alphabetic literacy in the Andes: Felipe Guamán Poma de Ayala's *Nueva córonica y buen gobierno*," *Colonial Latin American Review*, 11(2): 275–303.

Castro, Daniel (2007). *Another Face of Empire: Bartolomé de Las Casas, Indigenous Rights, and Ecclesiastical Imperialism*. Durham, NC: Duke University Press.

Castro-Klaren, Sara (1999). "Mimicry revisited: Latin America, post-colonial theory and the location of knowledge." In Alfonso de Toro and Fernando de Toro (eds), *El debate de la postcolonialidad en Latinoamerica*, pp. 137–64. Madrid: Vervuert Iberoamericana.

— (2001). "Historiography on the ground: the Toledo Circle and Guamán Poma." In Ileana Rodríguez (ed.), *The Latin American Subaltern Studies Reader*, pp. 143–71. Durham, NC: Duke University Press.

Cervantes, Fernando (1994). *The Devil in the New World: The Impact of Diabolism in New Spain*. New Haven, CT: Yale University Press.

Cummins, Tom (1998). "Let me see! Reading is for them: colonial Andean images and objects 'Como es costumbre tener los caciques Señores.'" In H. Boone and T. Cummins (eds), *Native Traditions in the Postconquest World*, pp. 91–148. Washington, DC: Dumbarton Oaks Research Library and Collection.

Durand, José (1953). "La biblioteca del Inca," *Nueva Revista de Filología Hispánica*, 2: 239–64.

Fernández, Christian (2004). *Inca Garcilaso: Imaginación, memoria e identidad*. Lima: Universidad Nacional Mayor de San Marcos.

Hemming, John (1970). *The Conquest of the Incas*. New York: Harcourt, Brace, Jovanovich.

Hulme, Peter (1986). *Colonial Encounters: Europe and the Native Caribbean 1492–1797*. London: Routledge.

Mazzotti, José Antonio (1996). *Coros mestizos del Inca Garcilaso: Resonancias andinas*. Lima: Fondo de Cultura Económica.

Mignolo, Walter (1982). "Cartas, crónicas y relaciones del descubrimiento y la conquista." In Iñigo Madrigal (ed.), *Historia de la literatura hispanoamericana: Época colonial*, pp. 57–116. Madrid: Cátedra.

Pagden, Anthony (1982). *The Fall of Natural Man: The American Indian and the Origins of Comparative Ethnology*. Cambridge: Cambridge University Press.

Pease, Franklin (1978). *Del Tahuantinsuyo a la historia del Perú*. Lima: Instituto de Estudios Peruanos.

Porras Barrenechea, Raúl (1986). *Los cronistas del Perú (1528–1530)*. Lima: Ediciones Centenario/ Banco de Crédito.

Rostoworowski, María (1983). *Estructuras andinas del poder: Ideología religiosa y política*. Lima: Instituto de Estudios Peruanos.

Seed, Patricia (1995). *Ceremonies of Possessions in Europe's Conquest of The New World 1492–1640*. New York: Cambridge University Press.

Varner, John Grier (1968). *El Inca: Life and Times of Garcilaso de la Vega*. Austin: University of Texas Press.

Zamora, Margarita (1988). *Language, Authority, and Indigenous History in the Comentarios reales de los Incas*. Cambridge: Cambridge University Press.

7

# Court Culture, Ritual, Satire, and Music in Colonial Brazil and Spanish America

*Lúcia Helena Costigan*

Owing to the fact that, unlike the Spanish American colonies, such as New Spain, Peru, and New Granada, Brazil did not have viceroys, printing presses, and universities during its first centuries, court culture took a long time to flourish in the Portuguese America. However, despite the absence of a court culture during the sixteenth and seventeenth centuries, literary expressions related to Brazil emerged in Portugal right after Pedro Álvares Cabral accidentally landed in the newly "discovered" lands. *Carta do achamento do Brasil*, the letter written by Pero Vaz de Caminha (ca. 1450–1501) in 1500 and first published in 1817, is often considered the birth certificate of Brazilian letters. After this, most of the literature produced in Brazil during the sixteenth and seventeenth centuries was written by either European-born Jesuits or by a few Creole intellectuals with Jesuit education.

The Jesuit Order, also known as the Company of Jesus, appeared in Europe a few decades after Martin Luther (1483–1546) started a religious reform that caused a split in Western Christendom. Luther opposed the sale of indulgences by the Catholic Church and proposed a new theology that led to the appearance of Protestant denominations. The Jesuit Order was founded in 1540 by Ignatius of Loyola (1491–1556) and his followers, a group of students at the University of Paris. Wishing to defend the Spanish Counter-Reformation and moved by the spirit of the medieval crusades, they intended to march to the Holy Land to preach to the infidels. Soon after the Order was founded, the Jesuits started to become known in Europe and in European colonies throughout the world.

The Jesuits soon became known as excellent missionaries and educators owing to their superior education. Soon after the company was founded, Portugal granted the Jesuits the monopoly of the conversion of the infidels and gentiles in all of its Asian, African, and American colonies. The Portuguese King John III (1521–57) also directed the Jesuits to establish the educational system in Portugal and in the colonies. The University of Coimbra became one of the most important Jesuit educational centers.

In 1568 the Jesuits started the construction of a church in Rome. This Jesuit church, known as *Del Gesù*, is traditionally considered the first example of a new form of aesthetics. In the later part of the nineteenth century critics like Heinrich Wölfflin, who studied the artistic, literary, and musical production that emerged in Europe between the Renaissance and the Neoclassic periods, classified the new aesthetics as the *Baroque*. The Baroque emerged in Spain during the period of the Trent Concilium (1545–63).

## The Jesuits and Baroque Culture in Brazil

In 1549, almost half a century after the landing of Cabral in Brazil, the Jesuit Manuel da Nóbrega (1517–70) arrived in Portuguese America. He came as part of the expedition led by Tomé de Sousa (ca. 1503–79), the first governor of the colony. The Jesuits were the first missionaries charged with the catechization of the Brazilian natives. From the second half of the sixteenth century until the middle of the eighteenth century the Jesuits not only worked among the natives, but also helped to shape the educational and cultural development of the new society. As Luiz Francisco de Alencastro points out, the company also became one of the wealthiest institutions in Portuguese America owing to its careful administration and the management of businesses that linked Brazil and Africa, particularly the slave trade. Dauril Alden also explains that because the company was free from taxation and received many donations, it was able to accumulate a great deal of wealth. Its patrimony included land, sugar plantations in rural areas, and lavish buildings and schools in urban centers.

Manuel da Nóbrega (1517–70), José de Anchieta (1534–97), and Antonio Vieira (1608–97) are the most distinguished Jesuits of colonial Brazil. Like other Jesuits who were engaged in missionary work, these three members of the company saw themselves as direct successors of the first Christians who sought to convert Romans and barbarians alike. The first Jesuit to arrive in Brazil, Father Manuel da Nóbrega, landed in the colony in 1549 with the royal governor, Tomé de Sousa. On his arrival, Nóbrega started to work directly with the natives in their villages, or *aldeias*. His major contribution to colonial Brazil consisted of his missionary work among the Indians, in which he promoted literature. His interest in finding effective ways to teach the natives led him to encourage José de Anchieta to write and direct theatrical plays aimed at facilitating the catechization of the natives. Nóbrega also added his own contributions to the literary field. His *Diálogo sobre a conversão do gentio* (1556) presents arguments both for and against the conversion of the natives. In the text, Nóbrega considers the American Indians to be no better and no worse than any other people, and he had no illusions about their inherent innocence. According to Nóbrega, the salvation of the natives would not be accomplished by divine miracle, but only by hard work and sacrifice on the part of the missionaries. In addition to the *Diálogo*, Nóbrega wrote an extensive number of letters to his Jesuit colleagues overseas, most of which was not published until the twentieth century. Those letters relating to his missionary experience in Brazil seem to alternate between optimism and pessimism. Although at times they express a gentle affection for the Indians, at other times Nóbrega seems to despise them and see the need to treat them with violent authoritarianism.

José de Anchieta was the most distinguished literary and religious figure of sixteenth-century Brazil. Because of his work among the natives, he became known among them as the *Apóstolo do Brasil* (Brazilian apostle). His literary work consists of poetry and plays. Born in the Spanish Canary Islands and educated in Coimbra, Portugal, Anchieta arrived in Brazil in 1553, three years after Manuel da Nóbrega had started his missionary work among the Tupi Indians. Anchieta's writings were influenced by medieval and renaissance tradition, and he is best known for his theatrical production aimed at the evangelization of the natives. However, Anchieta is also famous for his two epic poems, *De Beata Virgine Dei Matre* and *De gestis Mendi de Saa*. Both poems link Anchieta to Medieval Marist epics and to the tradition of Virgil. *De Beata Virgine* was first written on beach sand during Anchieta's captivity by the *Tamoios* Indians in 1563. After his release he reconstructed the whole epic. *De gestis Mendi de Saa* was dedicated to Mem de Sá (ca. 1500–72), the third Portuguese governor sent to Brazil. Mem de Sá played an instrumental role in freeing Anchieta from captivity. Unlike his epic poems, which were written in Latin, Anchieta's lyric and verse plays were written in a combination of languages that included Tupi, Portuguese, and Spanish. They were primarily designed for presentation in Indian *aldeias*.

Anchieta's plays were simple and straightforward. Since there were no formal theaters in the colony, his *autos* were performed in churchyards or in the central areas of small towns and Indian villages. The tropical forest was very often used as a backdrop, and the casts were always all-male and made up of local residents and natives who lived in the missions. Severino João Albuquerque, a literary critic of Brazilian and Latin American drama, has observed that although Anchieta's theatre was introduced in Brazil as an instrument of indoctrination, "it had undeniable dramatic qualities" (107). Anchieta's theatrical production consisted of tragedies written in Latin and *autos* based on Gil Vicente's didactic t heater. The *auto da pregação universal*, written around 1567 and first published in 1672, is considered to be the first dramatic text written in Brazil. Written in a combination of Portuguese and Tupi, the *auto* was intended to appeal to natives and settlers alike. The *auto* was could also be performed in different places of the Portuguese America by changing the names of individuals and references to local events and geography. Due to the fact that early theatrical production was aimed at conversion and not publication, only a few of Anchieta's works have survived. Of his surviving *autos, Auto representado na festa de São Lourenço*, written about 1583, reveals Anchieta's talents as a playwright. According to Severino Albuquerque, Anchieta's *autos* "reveal a remarkable feeling for spectacle, calling for the use of body paint, native costumes, song and dance, fights, torches, and processions" (106).

Toward the end of the sixteenth century, Bento Teixeira (1561–1600) wrote the first epic poem written in Portuguese in Brazil. Teixeira was a "New Christian," or a descendant of converted Jews, who immigrated to Brazil as a young child and studied with the Jesuits. His epic, *Prosopopéia*, was written in the last years of the sixteenth century, at a time when Teixeira was being scrutinized by the Inquisition for suspicion of secretly practicing Judaism. The poem was published in Portugal in 1601, shortly after the writer had died in the jails of the Portuguese inquisition. The publication of his epic poem indicates that Bento Teixeira had connections with influential people, as the Inquisition generally prohibited the publication of texts by those persecuted as heretics. The poem was dedicated to Jerônimo de Albuquerque Coelho (1548–1618), a relative of Duarte Coelho (ca. 1485–1554), who was prestigious and influential both in Pernambuco and in Portugal. Teixeira lived in Pernambuco prior to his imprisonment by the Holy Office in Lisbon. It is possible that Teixeira dedicated the poem to Albuquerque in an attempt to gain his protection. It is also possible that Jerônimo de Albuquerque had something to do with the publication of the poem in Portugal.

Using Camões as his model, Teixeira describes the beauty, wealth, and safety that new immigrants would find in Pernambuco. He also praised the bravery of noble Portuguese men such as Albuquerque Coelho, who fought the French and the Indians in Brazil. Because *Prosopopéia* was modeled on Camões's *Os Lusíadas*, some critics tend to see Bento Teixeira as an insignificant and mediocre poet. However, if one pays attention to the poem's content, it is possible to detect Teixeira's hidden message of resistance. He was persecuted because his ethnic and religious background did not fit mainstream European society. In terms of style, Bento Teixeira's *Prosopopéia* can be situated at the crossroads of the renaissance and of the baroque.

In the seventeenth century, the best representative of the Baroque rhetoric among the Jesuits was Antonio Vieira. Vieira was born in Lisbon in 1608 and at the age of 6 moved with his family to Bahia. At 15 he ran away from home to live with the Jesuits. At the age of 17 he was sent to study with the Jesuits in Olinda, Pernambuco, to teach rhetoric. Vieira is considered to be one of the great preachers, writers, and missionaries of the seventeenth century. He was also "a key actor in European and Ibero-American politics of the period," as the historian Thomas M. Cohen has shown in his book *António Vieira and the Missionary Church in Brazil and Portugal*. Vieira's work differs from that produced by Nóbrega and Anchieta in quantity and style. His writings consist primarily of sermons to be given in churches in Brazil and Europe. His sermons are typical examples of Spanish baroque culture, both in content and in form. Some address questions related to the political situation that he experienced in Brazil when Portugal and its colonies were part of the Spanish Empire. In 1640, Portugal once again became independent from Spain, but there was still conflict in Brazil, this time with the Dutch. His sermons after this date deal with political questions and express a sense of what he considers Portugal's fall from divine grace. These themes are particularly obvious in his *Sermão pelo bom sucesso das armas de Portugal contra as de Holanda* (1640), in which he questions God for having deserted his chosen people (the Portuguese) in favor of Protestant Dutchmen.

In 1641 Vieira was sent to Lisbon as part of a delegation of Brazilians to the court of King João IV, the new monarch who had been chosen to rule the independent

Lusitanian Empire. Vieira became João IV's adviser and one of the most powerful men in Portugal. In 1652, he gave up his role as a diplomat and advisor to the King in order to return to Brazil and work among the natives in the northern region of Maranhão. Vieira and other Jesuits strongly opposed the exploitation of the natives by Portuguese settlers and colonizers. The subsequent conflicts between Jesuits and the Portuguese colonizers resulted in the expulsion of Vieira and his fellow Jesuit missionaries from Maranhão in 1661. Marked by the contradictions of the Baroque era, many of Vieira's sermons reveal a crisis of faith and a kind of subversive disregard for religious and social orthodoxy. His open defense of subaltern groups such as the Indians of Brazil, the poor of Portugal, New Christians and Jews brought him to the attention of the Inquisition. Prohibited from preaching, he returned to Bahia in 1681 and remained there until his death in 1697.

Other writers who produced Baroque texts are the Portuguese New Christian Ambrósio Fernandes Brandão (1555–ca. 1634) and the Creoles Frei Vicente do Salvador (1564–1636?), Sebastião da Rocha Pita (1660–1739), Gregório de Matos Guerra (1636–96) and Manuel Botelho de Oliveira (1636–1711).

Brandão's *Diálogos das grandezas do Brasil* (1618) seems to have been written with the purpose of attracting European immigrants to Portuguese America. The book consists of six sets of dialogues that celebrate the greatness of Brazil. Brandão establishes a dialogue between Brandonio, a long-time resident of Brazil and Alviano, a skeptical newcomer from Portugal. Gonsalves de Mello considers Brandão's text a significant work of Brazilian literature and one of the foundational documents in the history of the Brazilian Northeast. The discussion between Brandonio and Alviano typifies the conflict that extended over several centuries between those Europeans who saw the New World as a land of innocence or promise and those who considered it savage, dangerous, and degenerate. This controversy gave rise to a vast literature on both sides of the issue, as Frederick Holden Hall observes in the introduction to the English translation of Brandão's *Dialogos das grandezas do Brasil*. The book also speculates about the possible Hebrew origin of the Indians, and describes the different social groups and customs of the region. It also suggests that the immigrants who come to Brazil should not seek fast profits and return to Portugal. Instead, Brandonio argues, they should stay in Brazil and work for the benefit of the new society. An incomplete version of the *Diálogos* was published in Rio de Janeiro in 1930, and a complete and definitive edition was not published until 1966. This later edition also contains a detailed analysis of all theories of authorship, an account of the known facts of Brandão's life, and a history of the various editions by the Brazilian critic José Antonio Gonsalves de Mello.

Gregório de Matos Guerra, a major baroque poet and a contemporary of Antonio Vieira, was born in Bahia into a wealthy family of sugar planters. As a member of the colonial elite, Gregório was sent to Portugal to pursue higher education. He studied at the University of Coimbra, and upon completing his education in 1661 he married a local woman and became a judge in Portugal. As a result of personal and political problems, Gregório lost his position as judge and returned to Brazil 1682. The cultural and material changes he experienced during his lifetime make him one of the best representatives of the Brazilian baroque poets. His models included the Spanish poets Quevedo, Calderón, and Góngora. In contrast to Vieira's elegant sermons defending the interests of the Jesuit order, the satirical verses attributed to Gregório de Matos depict the economic and social upheavals that he experienced in Portugal and in Brazil.

Gregório de Matos wrote religious and lyrical poetry, but he is best known for his satirical poetry. These satirical verses describe the contradictions of colonial Brazilian society. Gregório focuses on what he saw in Bahia upon his return from Portugal and portrays the colony as an upside-down world. Like Quevedo, Gregório de Matos sought to correct the excess of liberty that he believed was the cause of the decadence of society through satire. Many of his aggressive and pornographic verses were directed towards the governor of Bahia, Luis Alves da Câmara Coutinho, and led to Gregório's exile in Angola. Later on, he returned to Brazil on the conditions that he give up writing satirical verses and no longer live in Bahia. He died in Recife in 1696, a year before the death of Antonio Vieira in 1697. In the last four decades, particularly with the neo-baroque and tropicalist movement, Gregório's poems have been recycled by poets like Harold de Campos, and also by the popular singer-songwriter Caetano Veloso. João Adolfo Hansen's book, *A sátira e o engenho*, is one of the best critical studies of the satirical poetry attributed to Gregório de Matos. James Amado's edition of *Obras completas de Gregório de Matos* (1969) is the most complete collection of the poetry attributed to the most important baroque satirist of Brazil.

Botelho de Oliveira was a contemporary of Gregório de Matos and Antonio Vieira. Although critics such as Varnhagen and Antonio Candido feel that Botelho's baroque production does not compare in quality to the writings of Vieira and Matos, Botelho de Oliveira's *Música do Parnaso* has the merit of being the first volume of poetry published in Portugal by a native-born Brazilian poet. One of the most celebrated poems found in the collection is entitled "Ilha da Maré." The poem is a good example of the *ufanista* spirit that characterized writings such as the *Carta* by Caminha and the *Prosopopéia* by Bento Teixeira that glorified the Brazilian land and all its resources. *Música do Parnaso* praises the natural beauty and delicious foods found in Bahia, the poet's homeland.

In the fields of history and historiography, some names stand out in colonial Brazil. Pero de Magalhães Gândavo, a Portuguese historian who lived in Brazil around 1570, is thought to be the author of *História da privíncia de Santa Cruz a que vulgarmente chamamos Brasil and Tratado da terra do Brasil*. Gabriel Soares de Sousa, a plantation owner who lived in Bahia at about the same time, is believed to have written *Tratado descritivo do Brasil*, published in Rio in 1851. The work of these early historians can also be considered exemplary of *ufanismo*. They portray Brazil as a land of beauty and wealth.

Not all historians were so positive in tone. Frei Vicente do Salvador's (1564–1636) *Historia do Brasil* details the political and military crisis that he observed in Brazil during the period that Portugal and its possessions were part of the Spanish Empire.

Rocha Pita's baroque *História da América Portuguesa*, published in Portugal in 1730, comprises ten volumes. The first two volumes describe the geography and the inhabitants of Brazil. The remaining volumes describe the political and administrative aspects of Brazilian colonial society.

The Baroque style did not end with Gregório de Matos, Antonio Vieira, and the other writers of the period, but rather extended far beyond the chronological frontiers of the seventeenth century. The Baroque influence remained strong not only in literature but also in architecture and art. In the first part of the eighteenth century, the town of Vila Rica de Ouro Preto became the center of the baroque architecture, sculpture, and other forms of visual arts that characterized the Portuguese Empire at that time.

## Neoclassicism, Arcadianism, and the Arcadias

In the second half of the eighteenth century, particularly under the patronage of the Marquis de Pombal, the literature that emerged in Brazil shows the predominance of neoclassicism, the style favored by the Marquis. In his recent book *Mecenato Pombalino e Poesia Neoclássica*, the Brazilian scholar Ivan Teixeira makes extensive use of archival sources to study Pombal's relationship with the Portuguese and Brazilian writers and artists of his time. Following in the footsteps of their counterparts in Portugal, many Brazilian intellectuals who wanted the patronage of the powerful Marquis of Pombal wrote encomiastic poems praising his enlightened ideas and his neoclassic style. José Basílio da Gama (1741–95), educated by the Jesuits as a student, wrote laudatory verses to Pombal's daughter and also produced the epic poem *O Uraguai*. Basílio's epic, which was written a few years after Pombal expelled the Jesuits from the Portuguese territories in 1759, conformed to Pombal's policies and saved the Brazilian neoclassic poet from being persecuted as a Jesuit.

José de Santa Rita Durão was an Augustinian priest who, although born in Brazil, lived in Portugal, where he had problems with the Portuguese elite. Perhaps to gain the sympathy of the members of the court, Durão wrote a wordy and pedestrian epic entitled *Caramuru* (1781). Durão's epic poem praises the Portuguese people for bringing civilization to the Indians of Brazil. The hero of his epic was not a figure like Anchieta, who spent his life teaching the Indians, but a Portuguese sailor named Diogo Álvares Correia, who was saved by Indians after a shipwreck on the coast of Brazil around 1510. Diogo Alvares is transformed into a hero and portrayed as the one responsible for transforming the natives into civilized people.

Arcadianism appeared in Europe as a result of the Enlightenment and the formation of the first academies. The two movements arrived in Brazil almost simultaneously. Abandoning the baroque tradition, the followers of Arcadianism preached a return to the peaceful joys of nature and the purity and simplicity of thought and diction associated with Greek and Roman verse. Although marginalized in a colony such as Brazil, where printing presses were still prohibited, the first gatherings of intellectuals in Brazil occurred during the second decade of the eighteenth century. In 1724, the short-lived Brazilian Academy of the Neglected was founded in Bahia. Other groups of isolated intellectuals gathered sporadically to study and discuss such subjects as literature, history, botany, and zoology. Some of them re-created the Brazilian Academy of the Neglected and the Academy of the Happy Men.

The term Arcadias refers to the neoclassical cultural and philosophical groups that surfaced in colonial Brazil in the last half of the eighteenth century. The adverse intellectual environment in which these intellectuals lived without a press and dissociated from contemporary developments in Europe and from their homeland killed off the first Brazilian academies. It was not until the last decades of the eighteenth century that the Arcadian movement gained strength in Brazil. Following the model of the philosophers of the French enlightenment and the foundation of the *Arcádia Lusitana* in Lisbon in 1756 under the patronage of King José I (ruled 1750–77), a group of Brazilian intellectuals, including clergymen, lawyers, doctors, and scientists, frequently gathered to share ideas. These intellectuals were known as *arcades mineiros* owing to the fact that most of them lived in Minas Gerais.

The members of this movement included writers such as Tomás Antonio Gonzaga (1744–1810), Inácio José de Alvarenga Peixoto (1744–93), Cláudio Manuel da Costa (1729–89), and Manuel Inácio da Silva Alvarenga (1749–1814). Many of them had been supported by the Marquis of Pombal. They adopted Arcadian pseudonyms and wrote poetry that associated them with Greek and Roman idyllic poets. However, Pombal fell from power around 1777, as a result of King José's death and the beginning of the reign of Queen Maria I (ruled 1777–96). The members of the Mineiran Arcadia suddenly found themselves disenfranchised and without a patron. Their poetry became less an emotional escape from reality, and more a catalyst for protest. The dissatisfaction of these intellectuals during the reign of Queen Maria I led them to start a movement to free Brazil from Portugal. This movement, known in Brazil as *Inconfidência Mineira*, was discovered and harshly quashed by the Portuguese crown. One of the leaders of the groups, Joaquim José da Silva Xavier (1746–92), known as *Tiradentes*, was killed, and Cláudio Manuel da Costa died in jail while awaiting trial. The other participants were sent into exile in Africa.

Cláudio Manuel da Costa is generally considered the best poet of the group. His poetry incorporates aspects of both the Baroque and the Neoclassic. His poems were published in *Obras* (1768) and later in *Obras Poéticas* (1903), organized by João Ribeiro and published in Rio. Tomás Antonio Gonzaga is considered by Antonio Candido and Aderaldo Castello as a typical representative of neoclassic poets. Like Basílio da Gama, Gonzaga used love as a pretext to affirm himself as a poet. In addition to his poetry, Gonzaga is known as the author of the satirical poem *Cartas Chilenas*, written around 1787. It is a severe criticism of the corruption and abuses of power of Luis da Cunha Meneses, governor of Minas Gerais from 1783 until 1788. Due to his involvement in the *Inconfidência Mineira*, Gonzaga was exiled to Mozambique in 1792. In Mozambique he married into an important family of Portuguese colonizers and became a prosperous man. Alvarenga Peixoto and Silva Alvarenga were also exiled to

Africa. Alvarenga Peixoto perished, but Silva Alvarenga survived the exile and in 1797 he was granted a pardon from the queen and returned to Brazil. When the royal family arrived in Brazil in 1808, Silva Alvarenga was working for the journal *O Patriota*, one of the first magazines published in Brazil. Like the other members of the Mineiran Arcadia, Silva Alvarenga is mostly known for his lyrical poetry. Critics such as Antonio Candido and José Aderaldo Castello consider Silva Alvarenga a pre-romantic poet for his poem *Glaura* (1799) and for his modern ideas. Silva Alvarenga's poetic work was published by Joaquim Norberto Sousa e Silva in 1864. The literature written in Brazil during the period that extends from 1792, the year when the *Inconfidencia Mineira* became public, until 1822, the year of independence, is usually considered inferior, in both content and form, in comparison with the vibrant work produced by the Jesuits and by the baroque and neoclassic writers. Finally, it was with the arrival of the Portuguese imperial family in 1808 that music, literature, and other expressions of European court society were implanted and flourished in Brazil in a way never seen in other parts of nineteenth-century Latin America.

## REFERENCES AND FURTHER READING

Albuquerque, Severino J. (1996). "The Brazilian theater up to 1900," in R. Gonzalez Echeverría and E. Pupo Walker (eds), *The Cambridge History of Latin American Literature, Vol. 3: Brazilian Literature, Bibliographies*, pp. 105–26. Cambridge: Cambridge University Press.

Alencastro, Luiz Felipe de (2000). *O Trato dos viventes: Formação do Brasil no Atlântico Sul*. São Paulo: Companhia das letras.

Alden, Dauril (1996). *The Making of an Enterprise: The Society of Jesus in Portugal, Its Empire, and Beyond, 1540–1750*. Stanford, CA: Stanford University Press.

Brandão, Ambrósio Fernandes (1987). *Dialogues of the Great Things of Brazil*. Trans. and annotated by F. A. Holden Hall, W. F. Harrison, and D. Winters Welker. Albuquerque: University of New Mexico Press.

Candido, Antonio e Castello, José Aderaldo (1974). *Presença da literature brasileira: I. Das origens ao Romantismo*, 6th ed. São Paulo: Difusão Européia do Livro.

Hansen, João Adolfo (1989). *A sátira e o engenho: Gregório de Matos e a Bahia do século XVII*. São Paulo: Companhia das Letras/Secretaria de Estado da Cultura.

Mello, José Antonio Gonsalves de, ed. (1966). *Diálogos das grandezas do Brasil*. 2nd ed. Recife: Imprensa Universitaria.

Teixeira, Ivan (1999). *Mecenato Pombalino e poesia neoclássica*. São Paulo: Editora da Universidade de São Paulo.

# 8

# Violence in the Land of the *Muisca*: Juan Rodríguez Freile's *El carnero*
### Álvaro Félix Bolaños

### *El carnero* as a Book of Brazen Tales

Juan Rodríguez Freile is perhaps, and definitely for the wrong reasons, the most famous colonial writer to emerge from northwestern South America. He is credited with having written a book filled with impudent – if not outright pornographic – stories related to the Spaniards and *criollos* residing in the main urban centers of the New Kingdom of Granada (today's Colombia). However, *El carnero* – as the book has been popularly known for over 350 years – seriously intends to give an accurate report of the first century of Spanish conquest and settlement in the region. It was written between 1636 and 1638, probably during the idle moments provided by Rodríguez Freile's not-too-demanding schedule as an employee for the local municipal bureaucracy.

A unique and interesting detail about *El carnero* is that it is the work of an old man who had little at stake in his job as a chronicler and amateur historian. Rodríguez Freile started writing the book when he was 70 years old and without the pressure of an official request. This may explain the pleasure he seems to convey in his writing – the relaxed style of his prose, the casual commentaries, the use of humor, sarcasm, and the frequent moral admonitions he displayed while reporting on both the transcendental and trivial historical events of the New Kingdom of Granada's first century. This work circulated for 200 years in several different manuscript copies, until the Colombian *criollo* novelist and cultural promoter Felipe Pérez published it for the first time in Bogotá in 1859. Since then it has been republished over twenty times and has become an important part of the canon of Latin American literature, despite the fact that it was deliberately written as a work of history with no literary pretensions. There is even an English translation by William C. Atkinson, *The Conquest of New Granada* (1961); however, its scholarly benefit is limited by its severe abridgment.

Rodríguez Freile's historical sources are similar to those used by most historians of the conquest and colonization working in the New World (Gonzalo Fernández de

Oviedo, Pedro Cieza de León, Juan de Castellanos, Fray Pedro Simón, etc.). They include testimonies by at least one indigenous informant, the author's own observations of events, legal documents from the local *cabildo*, and the available histories of the region, either published or in manuscript form, such as those from Juan de Castellanos's *Elegéas de varones ilustres de Indias* and Fray Pedro Simón's *Noticias historiales de las conquistas de Tierra Firme en las Indias Occidentales*.

Although its reputation as a treatise concerning solely (or mainly) fictionalized stories about European and Euro-American people's moral transgressions is an exaggeration, the fact remains that *El carnero* delves into a few scandalous stories (some of which are simply colorful vignettes), and it is on these, quite understandably, that most readers tend to focus. Sexual transgression has thus become a metonymy for the whole book; by combining themes of sex, greed, violence, lust, betrayal, and political manipulation with the stories of shameful celebrities (the O. J. Simpsons and Scott Petersons of colonial Spanish America), a small number of narrative units have allowed most commentators to consider it a text packed with imaginary, brazen stories. Infidelity is their most visible theme, and a few examples are in order.

Among the vignette-like stories is the case of *don* García de Vargas, a resident of the city of Tocaima (founded in 1544 in Panche Indian territory), who kills his wife in a jealous rage after an absurd misunderstanding. García de Vargas had bumped into a retarded *mestizo* man (who clumsily communicated with guttural sounds and sign language), and asked him where he was coming from. This colorful fellow, who had just witnessed the slaughter of an enormous steer destined for the marketplace, responded to *don* García de Vargas's question with excitement by "putting both hands on his head in the shape of bull horns" (Chapter 16). *Don* García de Vargas misinterpreted this sign as a scornful reference to his wife's infidelity, and the aforementioned tragedy ensued.

Among the more elaborate stories is the case of *licenciado* Gaspar de Peralta. In a male gathering Peralta is amused by a young man (F. de Ontanera) boasting about his wild escapades with a married woman, during one of which the baluster of her bed collapsed. Three days later *don* Gaspar de Peralta's wife says: "Dear, call a carpenter to fix one of our bed's balusters which has been broken" (Chapter 15). After a calculated plot with the help of one of his servants (a Pijao Indian, to be precise), Gaspar de Peralta murders his wife and her lover. There is also the case of Inés de Hinojosa, "a beautiful rich woman," a sort of black widow, who has several of her husbands murdered by her own lovers before finally being brought to trial and executed: "She was hung from a tree, which still remains today, albeit dried out, more than 70 years later" (Chapter 10). This story has fascinated readers for centuries and has been the subject of two novels (*Los tres Pedros en la red de Inés de Hinojosa*, 1864, by Temístocles Avella Mendoza; and *Los pecados de Inés de Hinojosa*, 1986, by Próspero Morales Pradilla), as well as a very popular Colombian soap opera of the late 1980s.

Nevertheless, the most famous and complex case, which, as a paradigmatic narrative, has found its way into both Latin American short-story collections and US graduate students' reading lists, is that of Juana Garcéa. A freed African slave settled in Santafé (today's Bogotá), García sets up a profitable business advising women from the white elite on matters of secret love (witchcraft was among her alleged skills). In doing so, she amasses a considerable fortune and soon becomes interested in local political intrigues, furtively posting commentaries about local male politicians in the main plaza. Among her clients is a beautiful young woman who, during her husband's long absences, "wanted to get pleasure from her beauty as to not let it go to waste" (Chapter 9), and whose unexpected pregnancy requires Juana Garcéa's intervention. Through witchcraft she reveals to the young lady not only that her husband is going to be away long enough for her to give birth and pass the child off as an adopted orphan, but also that her husband is having an affair with another woman. Upon the husband's return, and owing to the young wife's audacious jealousy of his affair, her dealings with Juana García (as well as the great extent of Garcia's clientele) are exposed. The black woman is denounced as a witch and eventually as the author of the clandestine posters. She is finally put on trial by the Inquisition and deported back to the Caribbean. None of her numerous white clients, however, is ever brought to trial.

On account of these stories, Juan Rodríguez Freile has been identified as a writer who is obsessed with female beauty and the pitfalls of women's illicit love, and *El carnero* has been identified as a book about the moral weaknesses of the human flesh. However fascinating these outrageous cases might be, the fact remains that they are but a handful among a long series of narrated events that comprise the history of a century of conquest, settlement, and governmental organization of the New Kingdom of Granada (1538–1638).

There are 21 chapters in *El carnero*, and although the first one focuses on the origin and identity of the earliest Spanish conquistadors, Chapters 2 through 7 are a careful (albeit highly prejudicial) illustration of the indigenous culture of the area (the *Muisca*), including the civil war that crippled their resistance to the invading Spaniards. This chapter's title is a good example of this focus on the indigenous: "Which tells who chiefs Guatavita and Bogotá were, who the ruler of this Kingdom and the Kingdom of Tunja were, as well as his entourage. It tells how they named chiefs and kings, and explains the origin of the misleading name El Dorado" (Chapter 2).

The following 14 chapters are structured in chronological order, and include comprehensive reports on a variety of vicissitudes of every civil and ecclesiastical administration throughout those hundred years. These contain details about the official terms and the personal lives of each president, judge (*oidor*), royal auditor (*visitador*), every bishop and priest of some distinction, as well as the most resonant civil, economic, criminal, and problems of public order (Rodríguez Freile called them "cases") that these crown officials had to contend with during their respective administrations. This structure of the text follows the gradual establishment and recurring crisis of Spanish rule in the region, allowing an explanation not only of a few spectacularly criminal or shameful events and different clashes and conspiracies among powerful local men, women, and political figures, but also of the petty everyday cases of a culturally and racially diverse population. Even though the most shocking cases took place in the main cities of this Spanish kingdom (particularly Santafé), the book is not concerned solely with urban events but also with those taking place in the countryside and on the frontier. In this sense, *El carnero* follows the general pattern of most Spanish chronicles or histories of America in the sixteenth and seventeenth centuries.

The title of Chapter 8 illustrates the structure and general theme of *El carnero*, that is, the intricacies of Spanish colonial imperial management: "Which tells of the arrival of *don* Luis de Lugo as Governor of this Kingdom; of the arrival of *licenciado* Miguel Díez de Armendáriz, the first auditor and judge, as well as of the events that took place until the foundation of the *Real Audiencia*." A reiteration of this rigid structure is made in two final additional sections, entitled not "chapters" but "catalogues." The first one is devoted to civil and military leaders: "A catalogue of governors, presidents, judges, and Royal auditors that this kingdom has had since 1538, the year of its conquest, until this present year of 1638, a hundred years after this Kingdom was conquered." The last catalogue, in the same fashion, deals with ecclesiastical authorities "since the year 1569 when the holy church was given metropolitan status." These final two summaries of sorts reiterate the plan of the book, which celebrate the colony's consolidation during the first century of the Spanish presence in the region.

All of these stories (from the impudent to the serious) are nonfictional, well-researched and well-documented reports. However, like most writers of his time, Rodríguez Freile relies on literary strategies in the exposition of his stories and displays ample knowledge of the popular humanist literature available in Spain and the New Kingdom of Granada. Some of these literary techniques include the author's effort to make the readers participants in the unfolding of the story by having direct contact with them. He fictionalizes himself as a busy narrator inside the text, appeals to his readers' attention, and manipulates their interpretation. He creates suspense, by advancing or withholding pieces of information throughout several chapters, and by skillfully using dialogues. However, these literary strategies do not obscure the fact that the author explicitly states in his prologue, as well as throughout his work, that his purpose is to write a history of real events, based on existing documentation and available testimonies. Rodríguez Freile reminds us, for instance, that historians like himself "are compelled to tell the truth lest their conscience be compromised" (Chapter 11). He also frequently alludes to the historical documents consulted, "which can be found in the *cabildo* of this city of Santafé" (Chapter 8).

Rodríguez Freile's frequent focus on the moral and civil corruption of Spanish and Spanish-American subjects has promoted, particularly among literary critics, a utopian interpretation of *El carnero* in which the text is seen as a glaring critique of the colonial status quo and the author as a candid social reformer. Such focus has also frequently encouraged (particularly among Colombian historians, sociologists, and literary commentators) an indictment of sorts of an alleged essential flaw in the region's governmental fitness. These scholars tend to attribute Colombia's persistent social and political crisis to the pervasive sleaziness of the same social and political classes targeted by Rodríguez Freile, while still having faith in the sound Iberian political and economic institutions that – according to them – were thwarted in the New World by the contingency of unreliable imperial administrators.

However, and as is apparent to anyone familiar with historiography on the Spanish conquest and colonization, venality and corruptibility of conquistadors and civil and religious authorities were not only widespread in the Americas but also inevitable in an Iberian migration program based on conquest (that is, the violence toward and plundering of the indigenous communities), and the notion of "getting rich over-night" in the imperial administration by whatever means necessary. In this sense, Rodríguez Freile's focus on dishonesty is not unique, nor can this malady be identified with a single Euro-American society during early modernity. The three centuries of effective Spanish domination in America were the product of a rigid structure of control over its colonies. Not only did the Spanish crown establish a highly stratified social system that kept *peninsulares* at the top of the social hierarchy, followed by *criollos*, *mestizos*, indigenous, and Africans at the bottom – and which canceled upward social mobility and solidified the status quo – but also managed to permanently foster political, jurisdictional, and even personal divisions among the region's authorities and powers in order to assert its uncontested domination.

These strategies encouraged both the total submission to royal authority and the immediate reward for corrupted officials who did whatever was necessary to protect the status quo during their presence on American soil. It was an official system designed to fracture potentially independent or rebellious American constituencies by sponsoring complacency, espionage, duplicity, and betrayal. Such a system of distrust and mixed signals created the climate for rampant fraud, embezzlement, and kick-backs (sometimes even assassinations) among the civil government and clergy. Examples of this situation are found not only in a text like *El carnero* (which happens to add a few cheeky twists to its illustration), but also "in the accounts of travelers, in the reports of bishops and viceroys, in edicts of the Inquisition, and in royal decrees and papal bulls," as historian C. H. Haring reminds us.

## Juan Rodríguez Freile: A Proud *Cristiano Viejo* in a Spanish Colony

Concomitant with the utopian readings of *El carnero*, Rodríguez Freile has been portrayed as a straightforward critic of the Spanish colonial system under which he lived, and as a man whose profession as a farmer offered an alternative spirit of government. This view is based on the author's proud identification with a *labrador* (farmer) who carefully works on "the best plots of land with his well-primed tools that burst the plot's veins" (Chapter 21). Literary critics have glamorized Rodríguez Freile's self-ascribed profession, considering his depiction of a decent, morally superior inhabitant of a pristine countryside a metaphor serving to criticize the corruption of urban power centers like Santafé de Bogotá. A look at his biography, however, complicates such a utopian view.

The little that is known of Juan Rodríguez Freile's life comes from the scattered information in his own book and the legal documentation he left regarding a lawsuit leveled against him in 1621. He was born in Santafé de Bogotá on April 25, 1566. According to his own proud assertion, his parents came to *Las Indias* in 1553 in total compliance with the Spanish crown's immigration policy. That policy demanded that permits were given only to *cristianos viejos*, or "old Christian" Spaniards (as opposed to persons of Jewish or Moorish ancestry); it also limited those permits to married persons emigrating together with their spouses (which discouraged miscegenation with the natives). Rodríguez Freile grew up surrounded by conquistadors. He was well acquainted with Gonzalo Jiménez de Quesada (the conqueror of the region and founder of Santafé), and his own father participated in a military campaign against the Tairona Indians under the command of Pedro de Ursúa. Years later Rodríguez Freile himself participated in a similar repressive campaign, this time against the Pijao Indians, under the command of Diego de Bocanegra (probably around 1583). As a young man in 1585 he followed his tutor (*oidor* Alonso Pérez de Salazar) to Spain, where he stayed for six years – an experience that strengthened his pride of and allegiance to Spanish culture and nationalism, as seen in *El carnero*, when he narrates how he hurried to the defense of the port of Cadiz from Francis Drake's attack: "I was not among the latecomers because I quickly boarded one of the first ships, which belonged to a friend of mine, and we were among the first ones to arrive in San Lúcar" (Chapter 16).

As a teenager, a shortage of priests to carry out the evangelization of the indigenous encouraged him to enter the priesthood, which allowed him to study grammar and possibly an indigenous language. "In this school they started teaching the language of the natives, which was the general one because it was studied by all the students" (Chapter 11). He eventually abandoned this religious school and became first a soldier fighting rebellious indigenous groups in the frontier, then a gold prospector (which in that region meant taking it from the indigenous), and lastly, a farmer.

There is no evidence that any authority or important figure commissioned his work, but he dedicates his book to the King of Spain, Philip IV. As a resident of Santafé de Bogotá, and a writer and reader acquainted with the historical and literary production of his time, he probably had contact with other important writers who lived in this same city or surrounding areas at the end of the sixteenth and the beginning of the seventeenth century, such as Pedro de Vargas Machuca, Juan de Castellanos, Fray Pedro Simón, and Juan Flórez de Ocáriz. It is believed Freile died in 1642 at the age of 76 in Santafé, or perhaps in one of the nearby cities where his business frequently led him, such as Guasca, Guatavita, or Guachetá.

Rodríguez Freile's autobiographical details in *El carnero* show us a man who defined his identity through his allegiance to Christianity, the urban lettered culture in the Castilian language as well as in its powerful social elites, and the Spanish crown together with its imperial program. Such definition is based on his categorical differentiation from the indigenous, African, and *mestizo* subjectivities. After lamenting, for instance, the relaxation of official immigration control to the New Kingdom of

Granada by people different from the Spaniards, he further explains that his parents were *cristianos viejos* brought from Spain by Bishop Juan de los Barrios. Amid the theme of the indigenous from Bogotá, he rushes to clarify that his godparents were the Spanish captain and *encomienda* holder Alonso de Olalla and his daughter Juana de Herrera, and in Chapter 7, again dealing with pre-Hispanic history, he emphasizes his family's close ties with Gonzalo Jiménez de Quesada: "whom I knew well, because he was my sister's godfather, and my parents' friend." This deliberate association with the secular and clerical white, powerful elites governing the region is striking considering that he lived in a culturally diverse society.

As a resident of an area in which the great majority of the population was indigenous and reduced to servitude, Rodríguez Freile ensured for himself a comfortable living for most of his life, that is, until his differences with his former business partner (Francisco Gutiérrez de Montemayor) resulted in the lawsuit against him. The *estancia* (farm) that he lost had previously provided him with a handsome income. According to existing documents of the lawsuit, Rodríguez Freile also lost 120 cows that were able to produce eight packages of cheese daily. The property was worth "more than 800 gold *pesos*," and the annual profits from it amounted to "300 gold *pesos*." By his own account, he also cultivated the land. According to calculations made by today's Colombian farmers, a dairy farm of this capacity would have been at least 580 acres, with a workforce of approximately 6 to 12 individuals (who, very probably, were indigenous).

As to his supplemental income as a gold prospector of sorts, he tells a story that sheds light on the extractive gold economy imposed by the Spanish in the region. While talking about sacred *Muisca* lagoons, he tells us about what he calls a *pecado* (sin), that is, about having persuaded an old shaman of the Teusacá lagoon into helping him extract gold, which, reputedly, had been thrown into the lagoon as part of native religious rituals. The shaman fell on the ground once they reached the lagoon, and as Rodríguez Freile continues, "I was never able to get him up or get another word out of him. I left him there and came back empty-handed with the loss of my investment" (Chapter 5). Did the shaman fall on the ground because he suddenly died? If this is the case, then the sin confessed is not only his greed but also his anti-Christian treatment of a dead man. Or, since he was a shaman previously in charge of that sacred site, did he simply drop to his knees to pray? If this is the case, then it would be a clear instance of indigenous resistance against the domination and plunder of the Europeans and Euro-Americans.

What is clear in this story is the author's participation in the exploitation of the natives' wealth and resources, as well as his contempt for the old shaman's fate. *El carnero* is, therefore, written in a sociopolitical structure defined by the crown of Castile's expansionist power and its concomitant encouragement of Spanish immigration; it is the Castilian textual site in which a formal education and access to libraries was limited to the white minority (Spanish and *criollo*) who controlled the land, its native people, its resources, and the administrative bureaucracy. By its insertion into this sociopolitical and cultural structure, *El carnero* was written for an elite readership that was generally hostile toward non-European subjectivities and as involved in the ideology of empire as Rodríguez Freile himself was.

## The Violent Land of *El carnero*

A great tension between the indigenous population and Spanish colonialism seeps through the lines of *El carnero*. The region in which the author lived and wrote was the highland area of today's provinces of Cundinamarca and Boyacá in central Colombia, which was inhabited by the *Muisca*, also known as the *Chibcha*. The descendants of these people correspond today to the majority of the population in these same areas, and some of them (indigenous or *mestizo*) have embarked upon a process of recuperation of their indigenous culture and territories, as well as in the construction of political agency.

At the beginning of the sixteenth century, the *Muisca* occupied a territory of about 10,000 square miles. As a rule, the Spanish were attracted to this kind of densely populated area because their main economic enterprise was based on the acquisition of local labor for the extraction of the precious metals accumulated by the natives or present in the mines. The abundant gold in the *Muisca*, however, was the product of trade, since there were no gold mines in their region. The *encomienda* (an institution of extraction of riches in which a Spanish *encomendero* received tributes and a labor force from an indigenous community and their land in exchange for Christianization) was the first economic system used for the extraction of these minerals; it also provided the native labor for the agricultural production needed to feed the Spanish and *criollos*, as well as the construction of the urban infrastructure needed for the comfort of this invading population. Most studies of *El carnero* pay no heed to the link between this infrastructure, the wealth accumulated by Spanish and Euro-Americans, including Rodríguez Freile himself, or the massive amount of indigenous forced labor needed to make this accumulation possible.

Different estimates of the *Muisca* population at the time of the Spanish conquest go from 300,000 to as high as 2 million, although most scholars agree that a figure somewhere between the two was most likely, as historians Frank Safford and Marco Palacios point out. A century later, and as a result of the pressure of the Spanish and *criollo* mistreatment and demands for labor and resources, as well as European diseases, 90 percent of this population had perished, a fact that Rodríguez Freile acknowledged: "of all of them, only a few remain in this jurisdiction and that of Tunja, and even these ones, *we'd better say no more about this*" (Chapter 7). In spite of desperate military resistance by the *Muisca* (such as that of chief Tundama or Duitama), the Spaniards quickly prevailed on the account of the natives' less advanced military technology and ongoing civil wars.

The *encomienda* flourished until the end of the sixteenth century. By 1570 (when Rodríguez Freile was about 14 years old) a contemporary Spanish historian, López de Velasco, found in Santafé de Bogotá about 600 male Spaniards who lived off the labor and resources of approximately 40,000 indigenous tribute-payers. In Tunja, a city close to Santafé, there were 200 male Spaniards who had in their service 50,000 indigenous tributaries. At the beginning of the seventeenth century, this region (as was the case with most of the eastern highlands) lost its importance as a producer of gold, even though, as Rodríguez Freile himself complains, there was still much of this precious metal buried but little indigenous labor to extract it. The rich farmland of the region was, before and after the conquest, a great breadbasket that benefited adjacent regions. After the conquest, the Spaniards produced a good deal of grains, woven textiles, and some luxury products such as cheese for export. Agricultural crops and cheese were produced on Rodríguez Freile's farm, as stated in his lawsuit documentation, and procured him generous returns.

The significance of the elaborate *casos* of civil and moral transgressions of the powerful white elite lies not only in the fact that in them Rodríguez Freile masterfully narrates private, scandalous stories by making use of numerous literary strategies, but more importantly in the fact that these stories demonstrate the violence that plagues the New Kingdom of Granada. However, while this horizontal violence (among powerful white equals) has gained much attention from literary critics as illustrating the origins of Latin American literature, the existence of a more prevailing and enduring vertical violence is ignored: that against the dominated indigenous peoples.

An anonymous 1560 report on a *visita* (inspection by a crown official) to the New Kingdom of Granada when Rodríguez Freile was about 4 years old illustrates well the daily violence of the Spanish and *criollo* as well as their predatory reliance on the natives' labor and resources. According to this report (transcribed by historian Hermes Tovar) there were in Santafé at this time 55 *encomienda* holders, 57 tribes, and 36,550 indigenous, whose meticulous taxation on behalf of the Spanish seigneurial comfort yielded the following products:

> By what can be seen in this tally, the gold quantity amounts to 9,241 *pesos* of good gold, and the blankets to 9,772; the yield of all the wheat, barley, corn, and bean seeds planted for each *encomendero* amounts, according to the record, to 1,548 bushels; these crops are planted, taken care of, harvested, and stored in their respective *encomendero* house by the Indians; besides all this shown in this tally, they hand over many trifles of the land such as salt, deer, fiber thread, chickens, eggs, fish, and coca leaves which they got from their plots, and grass and firewood for the sustenance of their houses [obviously the *encomenderos'* residence].

Furthermore, this violence was not limited to public spaces but was present also in the silent enslavement and mistreatment of native women as maids in private residences. There is also judicial violence. Rodríguez Freile celebrates the Spanish authorities' draconian treatment of indigenous people, which, according to him, "kept the land in peace" (Chapter 15). A case in point is that of the government of his admired tutor, *licenciado* Alonso Pérez de Salazar (who took him to Spain when he was a young man), and whose application of judicial power over the uprooted, displaced, terrorized, and overworked natives are, for Rodríguez Freile, proof of the able construction of a colonial order. The following description leaves room for the author's pride and plea-sure in the public humiliation and punishment suffered by the indigenous:

> Pérez de Salazar would bring a bunch of Indians out on foot, beating them in the middle
> of the streets, some of them with chickens hanging from their necks, others with ears
> of corn, others with playing cards, spatulas or balls on the account of their vagrancy,
> that is, each with the standard of his/her crime. (Chapter 15)

Rodríguez Freile's distaste for the issue of protecting the native population from abuse, as well as that of our contemporary commentators, who think of seventeenth-century society as peaceful, are good examples of the naturalization of everyday vio-lence in both the New Kingdom of Granada during that time and in today's opinions about colonial cultural history. Either through systematic military repression (the case of the rebellious Pijao) or gradual and persistent exploitation, the violence exercised over the indigenous population in the society in which *El carnero* was written was ubiquitous to the point of appearing natural for those subjects not affected by it.

Juan Rodríguez Freile grew up in what historian Germán Colmenares called a "gold economy" which, in the sixteenth and seventeenth centuries' transatlantic mercantile capitalism, through a complex web of commercial exchanges, connected the Spanish metropolis with many corners of the American territory. This trade network deter-mined both the nature and quantity of the goods produced in America as well as the excruciatingly exhausting work demanded from the indigenous and African peoples. Large landowners (at first primarily *encomenderos*), with an economy based on tributes from the indigenous, coexisted with extensive mining operations, which frequently depended on local indigenous technology. The dominance of the *encomenderos* was derived from the first shares of the conquest loot, including the indigenous lands and labor force. However, by the end of the sixteenth century, and when Rodríguez Freile was a grown man, the *encomendero* economy was showing signs of exhaustion. The growing non-*encomendero* Spanish and *criollo* population competed fiercely for the increasingly scarce indigenous labor force monopolized by the *encomenderos*, and the progressively more regulatory presence of the Spanish state put great pressure on the *encomienda* system, which, by the mid-seventeenth century (when Rodríguez Freile was an old man), had become practically obsolete in the area. The demise of this system meant greater economical opportunities for the average Euro-American like Rodríguez Freile.

As a cattle and dairy-farm owner who supplemented his income with the occasional extraction of gold, Rodríguez Freile fit into a gold economy that was beginning to depend less on agricultural goods provided by the native communities and more on those produced by small, nonindigenous farmers. These small farmers depended upon native labor, the hiring of which (with a nominal wage) was now permitted by the crown. Hence, two kinds of economic activities took place in the central region of the New Kingdom of Granada which directly involved Rodríguez Freile: diminishing gold production and increasing agriculture and commerce.

In the written history of the New Kingdom of Granada, the most apparent social force is that of *encomenderos*, merchants, miners, the state and its bureaucracy, and of course, the church. These kinds of Spanish and *criollo* characters and their vicissitudes profusely occupy, as we saw, Rodríguez Freile's attention as well as most of the literary criticism that *El carnero* has received. The principal position of other social forces is less apparent in this society and its written history. This is the case of the indigenous people whose voice was seldom expressed in *El carnero* in any ideological formulation that resulted in an appreciation of their culture or political agency. The violent revolts during and after the conquest (such as those of the Pijao and Carare Indians – see Chapter 19) were marginalized in a portrayal of perfidious expressions of savagery; or in the case of the early conflicts with the indigenous under the *encomienda* system, which tended to be conceptualized inside the dominant scholastic ideology, their representation amounted (according to the Spaniards) to an improper understanding of the natives' place in their segregated *república de indios* (Indian republic). A clear example is that of the *cacique* of Turmequé, *don* Diego de Torres (and his struggle against the mistreatment of his people), whom Rodríguez Freile represented as a marginal chief unduly and ineptly involved in Spanish politics (Chapters 13–14).

## Rodríguez Freile's Opportunity as A Farmer

When the indigenous communities were first subjected to the *encomienda* system in the region (ca. 1538) and provided the agricultural goods needed by the Spanish population, they still lived and farmed in their ancestral lands, which at the time were largely untouched by Spanish confiscations. However, by the end of the sixteenth century, and with the demographic collapse of the indigenous population, the state aggressively encouraged the relocation and confinement of the remaining population into *poblamientos* (towns) and *resguardos* (reservations of sorts). The move was intended to break the *encomenderos'* monopoly over the indigenous labor force as well as more easily control the indigenous people for religious proselytism and the Spaniards' and *criollos'* own labor demands. This move also freed more indigenous land for the colonizers' confiscations. *El carnero* illustrates this situation when dealing with president Andrés Venero de Leiva's term in office. According to Rodríguez Freile, he "ardently encouraged the natives' conversion by making them live close together in their towns and by supporting their churches" (Chapter 10).

The increase in the Spanish and *criollo* urban population and the native's demographic collapse broke the original balance between the needs of colonizers and the indigenous economy to satisfy them, which supported the *encomienda* system. The result was the emergence of the first *estancias* (farms juridically different from the *encomienda*) around the land of the *encomenderos*, one of which was acquired by Rodríguez Freile. In other words, the author of *El carnero* found his economical opportunity with the breakup of the *encomendero* power. And since by then the indigenous were not able to make a living by solely cultivating the small land of their *resguardos*, they were compelled to work in the Spaniards' and *criollos'* farms. This was very probably Rodríguez Freile's source of labor for his own *estancia*. These farms, once Spanish legislation made it easier to secure an indigenous labor force, were able to create a type of agricultural unit capable of supplying the cities and mining centers in and outside the Santafé de Bogotá area with cereals, dairy products, and root vegetables.

These intricacies of the social inequalities among Spaniards, *criollos*, poor *mestizos*, and the indigenous are totally erased in Rodríguez Freile's self-portrait as an *estanciero*, an erasure that has been preserved by most nineteenth- and twentieth-century readings of *El carnero*. This is evident when Rodríguez Freile, paraphrasing the Latin poet Horace and resorting to a literary trope known as *beatus ille* (praising the charms and simplicity of country life), proudly proclaims:

> Fortunate is the man who, far away from business, and with modest assets, quietly and peacefully retires; he whose nourishment is assured by the fruits of the land that he cultivates, because, as virtuous as mother nature is, it produces them; fortunate is the one who does not expect his reward from the hands of greedy and tyrannical men. (Chapter 21)

## *El carnero*, Its Commentators and the Indigenous Subject

The scholarly attention given to this text has stemmed in two opposite directions. On the one hand, historians such as Juan Friede, David Brading, Germán Colmenares, Julián Vargas Lesmes, and Martha Herrera Ángel – among others – have great confidence in *El carnero*'s referential value. This is evident in the frequent consultations they make of it in order to illustrate historical characters as well as colonial society, politics, and culture involving both Iberian newcomers and native subjectivities. Literary critics, on the other hand, tend to dismiss or downplay *El carnero*'s referentiality and have popularized the text's current reputation as a work of fictional, impudent narratives comprising part of the Latin American literary canon. They are also the only ones who have studied the text as a whole. Most literary studies, however, have been overly concerned with *El carnero*'s typological nature and with elucidating its place in that discursive formation called (European) literature. Conversely they have paid less attention to the cultural milieu in which the author lived and wrote his text, a propensity which has allowed them to overlook, for instance, the significance of the indigenous population among which the author lived and its impact in the composition and assessment of his work.

Even though scholarly approaches to colonial texts during the last quarter of a century have been altered, often with interesting results, by postmodern cultural theories (particularly cultural studies, postcolonial studies, feminism, queer theory, and subaltern studies), most studies of *El carnero* have not been affected by these changes. They have been faithful to the parameters of literary appreciation and have overlooked the "colonial situation" in which the text was produced, that is, the condition under which an invading European and Christian minority controlled and profited from a non-European, non-Christian majority (as Walter Mignolo explains in the Preamble to this volume). With this prevailing literary approach, the presence of the indigenous people and the author's relation to them are missed; also missed is the regimen of colonial servitude to which the former were subjected.

Despite the visibility of the indigenous in Rodríguez Freile's daily life and society, he managed to define *El carnero* exclusively as a history of Europeans and Euro-Americans: "I wanted, as best as I could, to inform others about the conquest of this New Kingdom, about what happened between the time when its first Conquistadors settled it until the present time of writing, the year 1636" (Chapter 1); he then marginalized the indigenous subjectivity by means of a controlled and denigrating representation of it: "I have wanted to say all of this so that it would be understood that the Indians are capable of committing any evil act, that they kill men to rob them . . . I say all of this lest you let your guard down with them" (Chapter 16).

*El carnero* makes frequent references to the indigenous as servants throughout the text, or as a precious commodity (workforce), whose demographic decline threatens the material well-being of Spaniards and *criollos*. From the start, Rodríguez Freile laments the fact that there are still huge quantities of precious metals to be unearthed and taken to Spain, but there are not enough Indians to do it: "Many more and greater treasures could have been taken, as was necessary, had it not been for the lack of natives" ("Prologue to the reader"). Rodríguez Freile also gives the indigenous ample narrative space on five occasions. However, in all of them they are presented as either a flawed culture that needs to live under Spanish rule, as a people unworthy of good treatment by Spaniards or *criollos*, as individuals who hold riches they do not need or deserve, or as a threat to the security and development of colonial society.

Those first two (of five) instances are: (1) his account of the pre-Hispanic *Muisca* culture and civil wars (Chapters 2 through 7), in which the indigenous are represented as incapable of self-government and unable to manage their accumulated resources, including the fertile land they occupied; and (2) the resistance of the Pijao groups (a "perverse pestilence," as the author calls them) and the military campaign against them led by Juan de Borja with the purpose of securing the commercial routes between the New Kingdom of Granada and Peru (Chapter 19). The theme of the plunder and theft of gold allows Rodríguez Freile to elaborate two main stories. In the first one (3) a defiant shaman, who persists in his native religious rituals, is tricked, and his golden idols are taken by a Catholic priest who specializes in stealing the natives' riches on the pretext of evangelization. He "took from him 4,000 pesos in gold which the shaman had as offering in an altar" (Chapter 5). In the second story (4), a "thieving Indian" already integrated into colonial society as a servant of a priest named Reales (who treats him well by allowing him to dress in silk and carry a blade) takes advantage of his master's trust and snatches gold from the royal offices, among many other thefts. After being caught, "he confessed his crimes and was condemned to being burned alive, a sentence that was carried out in the central plaza" (Chapter 16).

The final story (5) deals with the threat of indigenous subversion. *Don* Diego de Torres, *cacique* (chief) of Turmequé, is falsely accused of sedition against the Spanish rule in the context of conflicts between rival Spanish political factions; however, the white population take the accusation seriously and react in panic, demonstrating with such reaction not only the presence of a large indigenous population among the Spanish and *criollos* but also the ever-present fear of their rebellion against subjugation. All five of these instances take place during 1536 and 1605, a significant detail because it underscores Rodríguez Freile's view of the indigenous as an essentially wretched representation of humanity that plagues his kingdom for at least an entire century.

Histories of Latin American literature often isolate *El carnero* as a privileged, unique, and wonderfully ambivalent instance of a referential narrative gone astray due to what is perceived as a lack of historical rigor that results in an outburst of literary imagination. Such discursive deterioration, according to these critics, accounts for the seemingly indecisive position of *El carnero* inside a recognizable literary genre, which becomes a sign of its historical objectivity compromised by a supposedly negligent historian. According to this widely held belief, colonial literary narratives are not only the deliberate product of fiction writers, but also the unforeseen end result of history irresponsibly written. Such frivolity, as assigned to the historian from Santafé de Bogotá, is embraced as a fortunate mistake that brings about the modern, prestigious Latin American literary narratives. Guiseppe Bellini's history of Latin America literature, one of the most widely available, states that Rodríguez Freile started with the sincere intention of being a historical chronicler but soon got carried away with fiction: "*El carnero* is precisely the product of the author's defiance of his original plans." Or, as literary historians Eduardo Camacho Guizado and José Miguel Oviedo have respectively put it, this is the case of "a book full of literary possibilities, of novelistic virtuosities, which does not go beyond historiography" and a "disintegration of history into tales."

All of these efforts to place *El carnero* inside the realm of a discursive literary formation have, of course, more to do with the epistemological and ideological framework that informs late twentieth- and early twenty-first-century literary critics than with the ones that informed Rodríguez Freile. As Walter Mignolo clarified as early as 1982, such framework has allowed literary critics and literary historians to retrieve from the past those texts which show, from the perspective of their *reception*, certain properties deemed today as literary, even though such properties were not present in the *production* of those discourses. Literary critics' choice to consider a historical text of the past as literary today is, certainly, a legitimate decision, especially if their interest is improving the quantity and complexity of the Latin American literary canon. However, such choice, by virtue of its exclusive attention to a literary discursive formation (that in turn requires an exclusive competence in European literacy), has called excessive attention to the Spanish or Euro-American perspective and has left aside the standpoint of other subjectivities (such as the native Americans, poor *mestizos*, and people of African descent).

The still-dominant tendency in the study of *El carnero* has been to embrace the notion of the unquestionable ascendancy of Castilian language and culture in a territory that, still today, shows the cultural, social, and political clashes brewed in the colonial period. *El carnero*, as a text that intends to memorialize the first hundred years of the Spanish and *criollo* presence in the *Muisca* territory, and which was written in a language that only the Spanish and Euro-American elite was able to read and enjoy, it is a cultural artifact whose production was only possible within the "colonial situation" that benefited Rodríguez Freile and his ethnicity, yet caused great detriment for his "Others." Understanding such a text today, when the land of the *Muisca* in which Rodríguez Freile lived and wrote is still inhabited by many *Muisca* descendants who deplore and resist the postmodern version of that "colonial situation," demands an reading of *El carnero* not limited to its insertion into the vicissitudes of European-based literary typologies. Also very relevant to its understanding is the social and political life of its author, his cultural and material context, and his conflictive relationship with the *Muisca* – the very subjects that surrounded him with services and tributes during the writing of his history.

### REFERENCES AND FURTHER READING

González Echeverría, Roberto (1990). *Myth and Archive: A Theory of Latin American Narrative.* Cambridge: Cambridge University Press.

Rodríguez Freile, Juan (1961). *The Conquest of New Granada.* Trans. William C. Atkinson. London: Folio Society.

Safford, Frank, and Palacios, Marco (2002). *Colombia: Fragmented Land, Divided Society.* Oxford: Oxford University Press.

# 9
# The Splendor of Baroque Visual Arts
*Lisa DeLeonardis*

## Introduction

Baroque describes visual arts traditions that developed during the seventeenth century throughout the viceroyalties of New Spain, Peru, and Brazil: the region that today encompasses Central and South America. It arose with the advent of urbanism amid ethnically diverse societies grounded in Catholicism and the Counter-Reformation. Religion, the church, and all its pageantry served both as inspiration for images and building construction, and the market in which artists participated and flourished.

In the realm of visual arts, the construct "Baroque" has not been without debate (see Armstrong and Zamudio-Taylor, 2000; Sullivan, 2001). One contentious issue concerns a scholarly emphasis which, in the past, has placed European influence over local innovation. There is a general consensus that the transmission of ideas and images (via books, prints, imported paintings, and emigrant artists) and their interpretation was not smooth and consistent in all regions of Latin America in either a temporal or philosophical sense. Some facets of the European Baroque, such as the use and manipulation of space in church architecture, were never elaborated upon in Latin America as in Europe. Conversely, the form and style of the exterior façades and portals of Latin American churches finds no comparison in Baroque Europe. An equally important and related issue concerns agency and innovation. The diverse body of architects, sculptors, and painters of seventeenth-century Latin America accepted and rejected ideas, methods, and solutions on the basis of their own sensibilities, not from lack of expertise or skill. Ideas and art forms were interpreted and translated with intent, resulting in novel images and structures, distinct from their European counterparts. Lastly, a blanket term such as Baroque misses the regional, ethnic, and individual variability of styles. For architecture alone, a brief survey of the literature gives us the Jesuit baroque, altiplano baroque, Querétaro baroque, Mexican baroque, and others, each an attempt to give identity to regional styles. A Cuzco- or Potosí-style painting of seventeenth-century Viceregal Peru is difficult to reconcile stylistically with the work of Villalpando in New Spain of the same period. Nor is there necessarily a consistency of style within religious orders. The Jesuit churches of La Compañía in Cuzco and Arequipa underscore this variability. Yet we can speak of a Latin American Baroque, bound precisely by these tensions, diverseness of form, and myriad styles.

Counter-Reformation church doctrine lies in part at the art-historical roots of the Baroque both in Europe and Latin America. Works of art were visible, tangible manifestations that sought to inspire and directly engage their audience with the promise of heaven and divine order. Baroque marks a transition from the visual and intellectual to the sensual and theatrical in ecclesiastical art and architecture. It was designed to evoke both emotion and contemplation. The tortured Christ and ecstatic saint, dramatically juxtaposed in the sanctuary, were meant to be viewed and *felt* amid the brilliant gilt ornamentation, the fragrance and smoke of incense, the flicker of scores of candles, and the sounds of music and prayer. Baroque art emphasized the very tenets rejected by the Protestant Reformation: opulent churches over austere meeting houses, the veneration of Marian and saintly images, pageantry, performance, and display.

In this chapter, I present a broad overview of the trends in architecture, sculpture, and painting that characterize Latin American Baroque visual arts. In synthesizing a vast literature I have necessarily omitted some geographical regions, themes, and artists deserving of attention. Greater detail on specific artists, their works, and documentary sources relative to their study appear in the reference and further reading sections. Issues such as the extirpation of idolatry, Jesuit influences, Guamán Poma's work, and literary parallels to the Baroque are discussed in greater detail elsewhere in this volume.


## Baroque Visual Arts in Their Sociopolitical Context

Viceregal Baroque visual arts emerged in a cosmopolitan milieu drastically removed from the social, economic, and political conditions of its historical past. Centers of artistic production flourished in the newly configured metropolises of Mexico City, Antigua, Bogotá, Quito, Cuzco, Lima, Vila Rica, and Potosí. An enlarged base of wealthy arts patrons, both citizens and church authorities, enabled mass building campaigns that included churches and cathedrals, sumptuous private residences, and municipal parks. Bishop Manuel de Mollinedo y Angulo's reign in Cuzco (1673–99) is notable. Mollinedo, following his predecessor's initiative, was responsible for the construction and completion of over fifty churches, many of which he financed himself. The building campaign of Bishop Juan de Palafox y Mendoza (1640–9) in New Spain is comparable. Former rural areas such as the Andean altiplano and the Brazilian sertão were transformed into prosperous colonial towns. Potosí is a case in point. Once home to scattered Inca settlements, by 1630 it held the largest population in the Americas, 160,000, and produced more than half the silver in the world. By the eighteenth century, Vila Rica was the principal gold-producing center of Brazil and one of the country's largest cities.

Throughout Latin America but especially in cities such as Antigua, Bogotá, Quito, Lima, Cuzco, Arequipa, and Santiago de Chile, the Baroque is closely linked to the building construction and artistic production that occurred in the wake of major earthquakes (ca. 1650–1785). Such destruction provided the momentum for introductions of the Baroque style in art and architecture and was accommodated by the ideas, resources, and skill of artisans to carry out the work. Earthquakes gave rise to new icons such as the Cristo de Temblores (Christ of the Earthquakes) in Lima and Cuzco.

Reconstruction efforts in post-earthquake times were made possible by a larger body of professional artists organized by workshops, guilds, and confraternities. Led by master architects, sculptors, and painters, guilds united artisans from various occupations and sub-specialties: architecture (carpenters, masons, joiners, quarrymen), painting (painters, gilders), sculpture (sculptors, retablists, engravers), metalwork (platers in silver and gold), and others. Guild membership could be restricted by accreditation examinations, familial ties, ethnicity, gender, or social class. Notable family guilds at this time were the Porres architects of Santiago de Guatemala (1635–1835) and the Figueroa painters of Bogotá (1615–1738). Some guilds comprised exclusively native artists while others were grouped by Spanish-born, Creole, and native artists. The Cuzco School was represented by such a grouping until 1684, when a split occurred over academy rules and natives left to work independently. Confraternities (*cofradía*), as religious associations, were directly linked to the church, specific religious objects, and events such as processions, feast days, altars, and triumphal arches. Membership was relative to the parish church or to the discretion of the confraternity's leader (*mayordomo*). Like the guild, membership criteria were based on social class, ethnicity, and gender. Brazil's counterpart to the confraternity (*confraría*) included brotherhoods (*irmandades*) and third orders (*ordens terceiras*).

Arts organizations were one of the few social institutions that permitted those of lower social status (natives, blacks, and mulattos) to rise through the professional ranks (apprentice to master). Within the rigid social hierarchy of Baroque Latin American society, there was otherwise little vertical movement. Hence, artists who might never have been eligible for guild membership or art commissions rose to the top of their field. Of note are Diego Quispe Tito (painting, Peru), Manuel Chili (sculpture, Quito), Juan Correa (painting, Mexico), Juan Tomás Tuyru Tupac Inca (architecture and sculpture, Peru), and Bernardo Legarda (sculpture, Quito). José de Porres, an illiterate architect of mixed heritage, rose to become the first great master (*maestro mayor*) of architecture in Santiago de Guatemala. During the course of his apprenticeship he learned to read and was exposed to the writings of Serlio and Vignolo. He and his descendants became the most celebrated architects in Central America for almost two centuries. Recognition did not assure wealth, however. Many well-known artists bartered their works for basic living expenses. It is also important to note that there are fewer named artists for the Baroque than in subsequent epochs, and this may have less to do with guild recognition than with the practice of not signing works.

Art commissions were contracted primarily for churches and cathedrals – the principal galleries in which artists displayed their work and competed. Tridentine policy advocated artworks that were visually provocative and awe-inspiring, but also required a clarity and correctness in their rendering. These directives were interpreted and translated in different ways. Church-sanctioned images could be copied from missals, Bibles, prints, and engravings in circulation, or from imported paintings, sculpture, and the work of emigrant artists. Artists thus had access to images favored by the church: the Holy Trinity, Christ (from infant to crucifixion), the Virgin Mary, the saints, angels, and martyrs. Variation in form, content, and theme was closely tied to the tenet that sanctuaries and icons be pious, engaging reminders of the divine order. That a relationship be established between the devotee (audience) and object of veneration (icon) permitted a wider range of interpretation on the part of the artist. For example, the church's light-skinned, bearded, Judaic Christ took on the ethnicity of the local congregation. Dark-skinned Christs, Virgins, and saints' images from Mexico City to Pernambuco invoked pre-Columbian memory and reflected the ethnic diversity of contemporary society. In New Spain, the Virgin of Guadalupe was wholeheartedly embraced as a native. In the Andes, images of the Christ Child were attired in garments of the royal Inca. The Virgin's body also took the shape of Cerro Rico, the core of Potosí's silver vein. Calamarca painters conceived of and portrayed angels as military agents, complete with uniforms and harquebuses. Unorthodox images were also tolerated. A tri-facial Christ was a recurring theme that portrayed the Holy Trinity in the form of a single Christ figure with three faces. Another form of this trinity was the portrayal of three figures of the adult, bearded Christ. Mujica Pinilla (2004: 37–9) notes that in conceiving the Trinity, Andean artists may have been referencing the Inca hierarchical triad of Inka Pachacutec and his two sons, Tupac Inka Yupanqui and Amaru Tupac Inka, who are shown as three identical figures grouped together. Figural sculpture that adorned the church's altars and was carried onto the streets during religious processions itself became the subject of paintings. These fixed, static representations were characteristic of the Cuzco and Potosí genres.

## Cathedral and *Parroquia*

Imposing and ornate, Baroque churches punctuated the landscape of urban and rural Latin America. Their interiors were designed to envelop the devotee in the sacred realm and shut out the banalities of the secular world. The church edifice was the defining feature in every central square and, during the early phases of town planning, was the building in relation to which all other important civic and ecclesiastic buildings were positioned. Since many towns were founded on the turf of pre-Columbian empires, church structures were imposed upon the sacred sites, palaces, and administrative buildings of the former occupants. The Dominican church and monastery built on the Inca foundation of the sun temple, or Korikancha, in Cuzco is one of the most visible examples of this practice. Others include the Cathedral of Mexico City atop Tenochtitlán, with its enormous *zócalo* reminiscent of the Aztec plaza. The Franciscans appropriated one of five Maya pyramids at Tiho, Mérida as the building foundation for their convent.

With the advent of the Baroque style emerged the cathedral, the great, visible symbol of church power and wealth and the *axis mundi* of the urban center. Cathedrals were the work of, and home to the bishop, a lasting testament to his authority and influence in a particular city or region. Although they served large congregations for mass, ceremonies, and major processions, as the diocesan seat, their function was not parochial. Cathedral architecture was characteristically rectangular, with three aisles corresponding to the same number of entrances on the façade. Each aisle was separated by pillars or columns that supported a vaulted ceiling. Constructions were primarily of stone, although the vaults might be of brick masonry, wood, or quincha (cane and adobe). The lavish façades were flanked by towers that often served as belfries.

Parish churches, or *parroquia*, were present in nearly every village and town in Latin America. They directly served a local congregation and all that it entailed, administering the sacraments and celebrating feast days, ceremonies, and processions. Confraternities were closely tied to *parroquia* activities. Although generally smaller in size, *parroquia* were no less attentive to exterior embellishment or interior opulence. Unlike the decades-long building period entailed by cathedral construction, the single-nave churches were constructed more quickly. The materials for church construction were variable: local stone, plaster, quincha, and wood.

Baroque-style cathedrals and churches shared a number of characteristics. Unlike the emphasis placed on curvilinear space and movement noted in European Baroque churches, those of Latin America followed a rectilinear plan. Ornamentation was elaborate, however, and focused on façades, particularly around the portal. Portal embellishments included the use of twisted, Solomonic columns and their arrangement in a retablo format. Interiors had as their focus the apse, which held the main altar or retablo. Side chapels (*capillas*) each held devotional altars and were enhanced according to the preferences of a particular congregation. Confraternities were often responsible for the *capillas* – raising funds for art commissions, and maintenance of its images and accoutrements. Walls and ceilings were carved and gilded or polychromed. Some retained the interlaced wooden *mudéjar* ceilings (*artesonado* or *alfarje*), an Andalusian influence more prevalent in the Viceroyalty of Peru than New Spain or Brazil. Choir lofts and pulpits, each the work of specialists, could be carved from wood, polychromed, gilded, or crafted from pure silver. Gold and silver liturgical objects (chalices, monstrances), candelabras and other altar pieces completed the saturated effect of luminous color and texture.

Toward the end of the seventeenth century, the ornamentation of church interiors and exteriors reached an exaggerated or ultra-Baroque expression. In New Spain, but especially Mexico, the Baroque was interwoven with the Churrigueresque in the form of *estípite* columns and polychromed ornamentation. *Estípite*, an inverted pyramidal

*Plate 9.1*   Cloister, La Compañía. Arequipa, Peru (Department of Image Collections, National Gallery of Art Library, Washington, DC; Wethey Collection)

column, found its greatest expression on the façade of the Sagrario in Mexico City. Polychromed plasterwork or *yesería* relief on interior ceilings and walls is best represented in the Puebla region at churches such as the Rosary Chapel at Santo Domingo. In the highland regions of the Viceroyalty of Peru, the ultra-Baroque was manifest in the intricately carved stone portal façades, or planiform designs of churches from Quito to Potosí (see Plate 9.1).

### *La Compañía, Cuzco (1651–68)*

The Jesuit presence in Latin America (1568–1767) is practically synonymous with the Baroque. The urban churches, colleges, and rural missions of the Jesuit legacy attest to a rigorous emphasis on art and education. Notable examples of Jesuit churches are La Compañía de Jesús in Quito, with its grand, spiraling solomonic columns, and the white-textured façade of the church at Arequipa (see Plate 9.2).

Widely considered one of the finest and most unified examples of the Latin American Baroque is the church of La Compañía in Cuzco (Plate 9.3). The Order had initially

*Plate 9.2*    La Compañía. Arequipa, Peru (Department of Image Collections, National Gallery of Art Library, Washington, DC; Wethey Collection)

purchased land for the church from Hernando Pizarro in the sixteenth century and established its foundation atop the Inca Palace of the Serpents (Amarucancha), adjacent to Cuzco's cathedral. Its position on the Plaza de Armas, the city's central square, within view of the cathedral, enhanced the Society's visibility in Cuzco and must have created a charged political dynamic with the bishop's seat.

The initial construction, which was destroyed in the earthquake of 1650, held important works by Jesuit Bernardo Bitti (1548–1610), a highly influential master artist. Bitti and fellow Jesuit Pedro de Vargas had also collaborated on the principal retablo. A new church (1651–68), featuring a Latin-cross ground plan and dome over the transept, formed part of a building complex that included the Penitents' Chapel (also known as the Chapel of St. Ignatius), the Indians' chapel (or Chapel of the Virgin of Loreto), and college. Jesuit Juan Bautista Egidiano is often credited with the construction plan of the new church edifice and portal, although by and large Diego Martínez de Oviedo is considered the architect of the façade. Martínez de Oviedo was also involved in the construction of the façade and portal of the college under the architect Francisco Domínguez Chávez de Arellano.

*Plate 9.3* La Compañía. Cuzco, Peru (photograph by Humberto Rodríguez-Camilloni; used with permission)

La Compañía is distinguished for its architectural features and its wood reliefs, wall murals, paintings, and carved altars. Earlier, Kubler and Soria (1959: 92) had called attention to the façade and its innovative tri-lobed entablature as well as its vertical twin towers that give rise to octagonal domes. Samanez Argumedo (2004: 158–64) has continued in this vein to detail the façade of the school and to document construction dates for various parts of the complex. The Society's founder, Ignatius Loyola, is commemorated in a series of in-situ paintings, *The Life of Saint Ignatius* (ca. 1762), by native painter Marcos Zapata with Cipriano Toledo y Gutiérrez. Zapata was also responsible for one of two paintings beneath the choir that depict marriages associated with the descendants of Loyola and Francis Borja. Zapata's painting, *Matrimonio de Don Beltrán García de Loyola y de Doña Teresa de Idiaquez y, de Don Juan Idiaquez con Doña Magdalena de Loyola*, painted in the late seventeenth century, is a group portrait emphasizing the prestigious links between these families. A second painting, *Matrimonio de Don Martín de Loyola con Doña Beatriz Ñusta*, is thought to have been painted slightly earlier by an anonymous, indigenous artist. It also depicts a wedding scene but links the Loyola and Borja families to Inca nobility. Details of the painting and its copies are outlined in García Saíz (2004: 206–7) and Dean (1999: 112–13).

By all accounts, the Society's presence in Cuzco was linked to its indigenous constituency in the realm of the arts. Its confraternity of the Infant Jesus comprised wholly natives. Cummins (2004: 12–13) and Dean (1999: 87) have noted that the image of the infant Jesus was the responsibility of this confraternity. The statue was attired with the insignia of the royal Inca for public processions, including the red fringe or *mascaipacha* worn on the forehead. Such appearances of the "Inca Christ Child" are recorded for the 1610 celebration honoring the beatification of Ignatius Loyola and the 1668 centennial of the Jesuits' arrival in Peru. Dean (1999: 87) points out that the Christ Child appears without this native attire in the much-celebrated *Corpus of Santa Ana* paintings (ca. 1680) that document the annual Corpus Christi procession in Cuzco and the confraternity's participation. This would have corresponded to Bishop Mollinedo's reign in the city. The bishop had expressed his distaste for the practice and could well have been influential in having the Inca clothing removed from the statue for solemn, public occasions (see Cummins 2004: 35). Although his successors also complained, the practice continued well into the eighteenth century.

## San Lorenzo de los Carangas, Potosí (1728–44)

Towards the end of the seventeenth century, a new style of planiform carving emerged on church exteriors in the Andean altiplano from Arequipa to Lake Titicaca and across the Bolivian highlands. This late Baroque or ultra-Baroque style did not correspond to architectural modification of the church plan but rather attention to stone portal façades that were carved with exquisite detail and ornamentation.

Planiform carving was the work of mostly anonymous stone carvers who fused geometric patterns with indigenous figural motifs, flora, and fauna to create an almost filigree textural effect. There was no attempt at chiaroscuro but one of shadows resulting from designs in bas-relief. Planiform has been compared to a similar trend in Puebla, Mexico where artists employed stucco as their preferred medium.

Although the planiform style was uniform as a convention, the work of individuals and their techniques are evident from city to city. The earliest forms are found in Arequipa, where carvings of the local white tufa adorn the city's buildings (see Plates 9.1 and 9.2). The portal of La Compañía (1698), designed by Agustín de Costa and sculpted by Agustín de Adrián, is considered a masterpiece of the genre. The design features a distinct Andean iconography that includes cantuta flowers (*flor del Inka*) and maize (see Plate 9.2). Adrián added a beveled edge to the work and included background in the design. At Collao, rose-colored stone was employed in the lateral porch of Santiago at Pomata (ca. 1726). Here, a shadowy, embroidered effect was achieved through the use of diagonal cuts in low relief. An expanse of flora and fauna, including viscacha and vicuña, are interspersed with the heads of puma and sun disks, perennial references to an Incan past.

San Lorenzo de Carangas is widely considered the ultimate in planiform design. Initially known as Asunción, the parish church was built in the mid-sixteenth century by an unknown architect. Upon the visit of Viceroy Toledo in 1572, the name of the church was changed. The early church was a single nave structure constructed of adobe; major reconstruction in the eighteenth century included a cruciform plan with a dome over the transept and two towers. The portal and planiform façade are below the central pediment, framed by a deep, brick arch.

The portal is framed by a stone entablature that has been completely carved in bas-relief with filigree precision. The design is composed of geometrical motifs, scrolls, faces, and figures arranged in a balanced symmetrical composition. Solomonic columns set on pedestals on either side of the door support figures in foliated skirts (*mujere follaje*) which, in turn, support Corinthian capitals. An image of St. Michael is set above the door in a smaller entablature. Above the arch which encloses the image, St. Lawrence and St. Vincent mark the uppermost limits of the carved façade. To the right and left of St. Michael are sirens playing the *charango*, an Andean five-stringed instrument. The sirens are surrounded by the sun, moon, and stars.

The designer and stone carver of the façade are unknown, but the work is clearly that of a master sculptor who employed diagonal cuts akin to wood carving. The façade is dated (1728–44).

## The Baroque Retablo

At once awe-inspiring and visually spectacular, the retablo commanded a presence in all churches in Latin America, whether humble or majestic. These floor-to-ceiling architectonic forms were designed with columns and niches to display images and paintings of Christ, the Virgin, and saints. A tabernacle could also be incorporated into the design. Retablos were placed in the apse behind the main altar and also occupy the side chapels of some churches (see Plate 9.4).

Design and construction of the retablo were major undertakings, analogous to church construction. A confraternity might issue a commission for an altarpiece but the work was directed by a church authority (parish priest) who guided decisions in selecting works of art to be displayed. Retablos were created in workshops, directed by a master painter or sculptor. They employed the expertise of *ensambladores*, responsible for structural sculpture and joinery, *doradores*, who applied gold leaf, and *estofadores*, painters of structural elements and statues. The work of Berlin and colleagues (1958: 63–73) on the retablo of Huejotzingo, a Franciscan convent, provides details of the procedures and artists involved in the construction and finishing process. Three notary documents in the Tlaxcala archive indicate that master painter Simon Pereyns would direct the work. The dimensions and arrangement of the structure are listed and the artists preferred for the paintings (Pereyns and Andrés de Concha) are specified. Under the supervision of Pereyns, three Indian carpenters from Huejotzingo were to cut boards and carve columns and friezes. Pereyns would receive a payment of 6,000 pesos for the work as well as a tabernacle valued at 1,000 pesos. Also specified was the delivery date for the retablo (1586), which was honored by Pereyns. A second

*Plate 9.4*    Lateral retablo, La Compañía. Cuzco, Peru (Department of Image Collections, National Gallery of
Art Library, Washington, DC; Wethey Collection)

document records the commissioning of 15 images from Pedro de Requena, a local
sculptor. The dimensions of the saints are listed as well as the preferred saints for the
retablo. A sum of 1,095 pesos is mentioned as payment. A third document names the
retablo gilder, Indian Marcos de San Pedro.

These historical documents attest to the collaborative efforts involved in the design
and execution of a retablo, the number of artists, their level of expertise, salaries, and
the number of years taken to execute the work. They also underscore the degree of
participation by local artists in the process. This case contrasts with the retablo history
of the cathedral of Mexico City. For example, the decision over the design and commission of the retablo of the Chapel of the Kings (1718–37) alone took 40 years.
Ultimately the commission was awarded to Jerónimo de Balbás, a Spanish architect
who is widely recognized for introducing the *estípite* column to the Mexican retablo
repertoire. Balbás's other work at the cathedral demonstrates that he met with resistance from native and Creole artists. Some of his commissions were carried out overseas. Retablos were also imported. Juan Martínez Montañés, a prominent Sevillian
sculptor, sent altars to Chile and Peru such as that at the Convent of La Concepción
in Lima.

Retablos were carved mostly from wood but could also be made of stone or metal (particularly silver). Carved wood retablos exhibit the most variable appearance as they could be polychromed, gilt, or left unpainted. Unique to Cuzco, the retablo of Santa Clara (1660) is covered almost entirely with small mirrors.

The church of San Francisco in Santa Fe de Bogotá (1630) is notable for its carved panel retablo. This radiant structure in gold leaf encompasses the entire apse walls in the manner of a gilt cave. The creation of the retablo marked a turning point in Bogotá's history as the new center of Baroque art previously ascribed to Tunja. The work was directed by Ignacio García de Asucha, an Asturian. García de Asucha established an atelier, comprised of Creoles and black slaves, in the district of Las Nieves. His premature death (1629) left the work to a Franciscan lay brother and his assistants. Another Spaniard, Lorenzo Hernández de la Camara, was contracted to complete the polychrome. The retablo is divided into three sections: the retablo proper behind the main altar with niches for images of the saints, and the sides of the apse which are carved panels in high and low relief. Each panel is separated by paired columns carved in diagonal twists in the manner of solomonic movement. A lower row of panels is carved with biblical scenes. The lives of women saints, rarely depicted in groups such as these, occupy the center row. The upper register, completed after García de Asucha's death, portrays the lives of the apostles. Interspersed throughout these renderings are flora and fauna of a tropical paradise. Grape vines and avocados, monkeys and macaws, an elephant and a lion, represent a mix of the local and exotic.

A more somber, academic design is evident in the retablo of La Compañía in Cuzco (1670), considered the largest in the city and the finest example of the Baroque. The work is attributed to Diego Martínez de Oviedo, who was also responsible for other retablos in the city. The gilded wood ensemble follows a plan similar to the church's tri-lobed façade. Its spatial elements and lofty proportions accommodate arched niches, images, and paintings. At its base, spiraling solomonic columns accentuate the tabernacle and are paired at the sides. Corinthian columns on the second level bracket monumental paintings of military angels and a central image of the Virgin. Curved niches in the upper portions enclose a painting of Christ, and an image of St. Ignatius. The entire structure is capped by images of angels that appear to float and swirl around the central image of God. The effect is one of unified proportions, brilliance, depth, and movement.

## The *Imagineros* of Quito

Sculpted images of the sacred – visual representations of Christ, the Virgin, saints, and angels, served as tangible objects of worship and invariable reminders of church doctrine. In Latin American Baroque style, life-size personifications of holy persons and angels were rendered with realism, movement, agony, and grace. As objects of display and veneration they were handled, arranged in groups, and enhanced with a crown, or seated on a throne. Many images became associated with healing powers, apparitions, and other miraculous acts (the Virgen de Quinche, the Virgen de Copacabana, the Señor de Milagros) and the subject of intense cult worship. Certain images and themes proliferated in the Americas: the cherubic Christ Child (*Niño Jesús*), the tortured suffering Christ of the passion and crucifixion, the Virgin of the Apocalypse, and the newly beatified saints – Ignatius and Rosa.

Images were created for church altars, processions, nativity (*nacimiento*) and passion scenes, and for personal use in private chapels, as relics and ex-votos. Large-scale images were created for churches, religious scenes, and processions. Mexican processional sculpture was so admired by Spain for its realism and light weight that it was regularly imported.

Images were produced from a range of media (wood, stone, bone, ceramic, shell) and by varied finishing techniques. Wood was the preferred medium, particularly cedar and walnut. Balsa, a lightweight wood native to Ecuador, was used for processional figures and some statuary. Its Mexican equivalent, a spongy, cork-like wood (*tzompantli*), was employed in New Spain. For Pátzcuaro sculptors, the lightness required for processional figures was achieved through compositions of organic material. Paper and cornstalk armatures swathed in cotton or agave cloth were coated with a vegetable paste and oil, then modeled and polychromed. *Tagua*, a nut native to Ecuador, was substituted for ivory in small objects. Its soft texture dried to a hard consistency suitable for carving. Maguey and other cacti also formed the carvers' "block," as did pastes of corn, rice, and maguey. Stone was usually reserved for façade images, although marble and alabaster (*tecali, piedra de Huamanga*) were used for statuary.

Sculpted figures were the work of image makers (*imagineros*), painters, and gilders. Once an object had been carved, polychrome was applied. For sculpture, this took the form of flesh coloring (*encarnación*) and cloth-texturing or quilting (*estofado*), each the work of specialists. Gilt details were achieved through *estofado* – applying tempura paint to a gilded surface, then removing it carefully to create a design on clothing. In some cases cloth was affixed to the statue to create folds and drapes before it was starched and polychromed. Details such as wigs and eyelashes of human hair and glass eyes imbued figures with lifelike qualities. Tears were formed from crystal or resin. Drops of blood were created from painted resin or paint alone. Gold and silver crowns, haloes, sandals, wings, and staves completed the accoutrements.

Statues were carved completely in the round or consisted of an armature on which carved head, hands, and feet were attached. These images were dressed in ceremonial clothing, largely the work of confraternities. Marionettes or statues with mobile hands and arms were also fashioned.

In the context of seventeenth- and eighteenth-century Baroque sculptural images Quito is distinguished for its tradition of polychrome wood statues and the glossy verism of *encarnación*. By the mid-eighteenth century, Quito was the major export center for religious images. The city's sculptural works had a sixteenth-century precedent in the College of San Andrés and the work of Diego Robles. Robles is best known for his image the *Virgin of Quinche*, which achieved cult status in its time. Father Carlos, another renowned Quiteño, is recognized for figures of the saints and his dramatic processional figures of Christ. His student, José Olmos, or Pampite, continued the Quito tradition of portraying the poignant suffering of Christ in his work. *Mestizo* artist Bernardo Legarda (d. 1773) is thought to have worked with Pampite. Legarda's professional talents were many. In addition to sculpting, he was also a painter, gilder, gunsmith, and miniaturist. His atelier is reported to have been large. Legarda is best known for his images of the Virgin, particularly the *Virgin of Quito* (1734). His works are considered elegant and emotionally serene compared to those of his predecessors. The Virgin is often depicted in gentle motion, with swirling garments and wings.

Inspired by a painting of Miguel de Santiago, the winged *Virgin of Quito* was one of the most reproduced images of Legarda. Her iconography is a fusion of the Virgin of the Apocalypse and the Immaculate Conception. She is always shown standing on a crescent moon, as if in the process of alighting. Her right hand is raised upward and her left hand crosses her chest. She is embellished with wings and a crown or halo. Her blue garments drape over a white dress and seem to be flowing and moving. Her head tilts slightly to the left and her gaze is directed toward her foot, where she crushes a serpent's or dragon's head (although the serpent is not always shown). In some examples, her upraised right hand holds a weapon.

Manuel Chili, or Caspicara, a native, furthered the Quito tradition, embracing the naturalism of Pampite but reducing the size of his figures. He enlarged his repertoire to include group arrangements, including an emotive *Pietà*. His *Virgin of the Assumption*, with outstretched hands and upward gaze, was produced singly or in groups with kneeling and standing devotees. *Santa Rosa of Lima* became a popular theme for Quito sculptors and Caspicara portrayed the saint as serene and devout, cradling the baby Jesus against her gently flowing habit. The posture, gesture, and gaze of his saints and angels convey piety and sorrow. Few of Caspicara's works can be firmly dated.

## The Pictorial Baroque

Painted works proliferated during the seventeenth century, paralleling the pace of cathedral and church construction. Artists' workshops, "circles" of painters, and informal "schools" of painting flourished in every major city, and painting dynasties (e.g., the Juárez and Rodríguez Juárez families) emerged in New Spain. Monumental canvases were produced for the lofty halls of the church and cathedral as well as smaller paintings for private chapels. Mural painting embellished the domes and portals of churches and monasteries. By the late seventeenth century, portraits of public figures would occupy civic buildings and private residences.

Paintings were executed mostly on canvas (*lienzo*). Portable objects such as the *quero* (beaker) and *biombo* (screen) were also the subject of narrative pictorials. Themes of Baroque painting included the life of Christ, the Holy Family, martyrs, allegorical visions of Hell, Santa Rosa, and the Virgin of Guadalupe. By the early eighteenth century, a greater number of secular themes were executed, including portraits of viceroys, upper-class patrons, pre-Columbian heroes, and conquest-period battles. *Casta* painting, a genre that featured group portraits of racial types, became a popular export after 1720, especially in New Spain and Peru.

Latin American painters made use of prints and engravings as models for their work, particularly as a means of insuring iconographic accuracy in line with Tridentine policy. However, most masters reworked their paintings into singular forms. Wierix and Sadeler prints were widely circulated in New Spain and Peru, as were engravings by Schelte à Bolswert. In the Andean highland regions of Postosí and Cuzco a large number of original sixteenth-century Flemish paintings were consulted. Both the paintings and engravings of Martin de Vos (1532–1603) and Peter Paul Rubens (1577–1640) were influential in painting compositions and coloring.

## Visual narratives

Latin American Baroque painting encompassed a range of painterly techniques, thematic approaches, and artist's perspectives – both academic and independent – that resulted in a wide spectrum of visual interpretation of church and society. Artists of New Spain such as Sebastián López de Arteaga (1610–52) used dramatic lighting inspired from tenebrism to create graphic realism and emotion in such monumental works as the *Incredulity of Thomas* (ca. 1645). The prolific works of Cristóbal de Villalpando (c. 1645–1714) emphasized light and color over accuracy of form. His masterful compositions in Puebla Cathedral (*Heavenly Glory, Apotheosis of the Eucharist*) embody the brilliance and illusion of heaven through his expressive figures and sensual color. A triumphal arch dedicated to the Conde de la Monclova, Melchor Portocarrero, and Lasso de la Vega (1686) is also attributed to Villalpando. A distinct approach characterizes Villalpando's contemporary, Juan Correa (ca. 1646–1716), whose paintings employed deep, rich colors and ordered compositions of the Virgin and angels. His iconic *Virgin of Guadalupe* (e.g., 1667, 1704) exemplifies his style of coloring, perspective, and anatomic distortions. Correa's repertoire also included secular works such as his *biombo* painting *Meeting between Cortés and Moctezuma* (late seventeenth century).

Hieratic figures, a flatness of perspective and the red and gold coloring of *brocateado* (gold leaf) characterize the highland paintings of the Cuzco and Potosí circles. Far fewer artists of these circles signed their paintings, although many are named in historical documents. Diego Quispe Tito (1611–81), a painter of noble Inca heritage and the foremost proponent of the Cuzco School, is best known for his *Signs of the Zodiac* (1681) in Cuzco Cathedral. The series narrates the life of Christ and incorporates Quispe Tito's signature landscapes, complete with castles, birds, and red accents. Quispe Tito's rival Basilio de Santa Cruz Pumacallao (active 1650–99) also features imagined landscapes in *Virgin of Belén* (ca. 1690). The painting was commissioned by his patron Bishop Manuel de Mollinedo of Cuzco and features the bishop in the foreground, praying before the image. Santa Cruz Pumacallao's circle is thought to be responsible for the *Corpus of Santa Ana* (1674–80), a group of 16 unsigned paintings that detail Cuzco's Corpus Christi procession and Mollinedo's presence in the much-celebrated pageant. Dean's (1999) seminal work on the paintings details the social dynamics of Cuzco, arts patronage, and the participation of confraternities in the construction of triumphal arches and images.

The pageantry of procession is also the subject of a single monumental canvas by Cochabamba master painter Melchor Pérez de Holguín (ca. 1665–ca. 1724), who temporarily shifted his focus from sacred themes. *Archbishop Morcillo de Auñon's Entrance into Potosí* (1718) documents the city's reception of their esteemed native son upon his appointment as acting Viceroy of Peru. Across the sweeping landscape of the altiplano, a squadron of 300 men precedes the archbishop as he makes his way through a grand triumphal arch into the city. He is accompanied by judges and municipal authorities and by the silver-platers' guild, clad in red attire. Pérez de Holguín includes himself in the center of the painting, dressed in black, holding a paintbrush and palette. Two smaller insets show the bishop's reception: by church representatives of the indigenous *parroquia* of San Martín, and by the miners' masquerade. Like the bishop's presence at the Corpus Christi celebrations, a viceroy's tour was a much anticipated and honorable event for the host city. The historical events portrayed in this work are corroborated by the chronicler Bartolomé Arzáns de Orsúa y Vela, but the dynamics between the archbishop, the city, and the guilds before and after the visit were far more complex than the painting suggests.

## The Art of Pilgrimage

Veneration of Christ and the Virgin took on heightened dimensions in the rural sanctuaries of Latin America, distant from urban life with its proscribed pageants, processions, and decorum. Baroque pilgrimage centers were no less formal or opulent than the urban cathedral or *parroquia*, but their constituency was intermittent and international. Pilgrimage sanctuaries were home to Christian cults that developed to honor miracles by Christ or the Virgin. The Basilica of the Virgin of Guadalupe (1695–1709) at the foot of Tepeyac is the best known. Apparitions of the Virgin immortalized in Juan Correa's *Virgen de Guadalupe* (1667) became firmly embedded in Baroque consciousness. A century later, the Chapel of the Well, El Pocito (1779–91), was built at the site of a healing spring where the Virgin had appeared to Juan Diego.

The tradition of cult worship and the pilgrimage center had pre-Columbian precedent in Latin America, as evidenced by sites such as Chavín de Huantar, Cahuachi, Tiwanaku, and Teotihuacan. Viewed as pagan symbols, many were eradicated during seventeenth-century campaigns to extirpate idolatry. But Christian shrines often arose at or near remote pre-Columbian sacred sites and were largely attributed to miracles experienced or witnessed by indigenous peoples. Establishment of the church sanctuary usually involved political interplay between indigenous devotees and the bishop, who was responsible for verifying the miracle and supporting the construction of the church.

## The work of enchantment: Esquipulas and the Black Christ

In 1847, American traveler John Lloyd Stephens descended the high sierra of Honduras to behold the pilgrimage sanctuary of Esquipulas, Guatemala. Likening it to the "church of the Holy Sepulcher in Jerusalem, and the Caaba in Mecca," Stephens was awed by the white sanctuary and its bucolic setting: "the church, rising in solitary grandeur in a region of wilderness and desolation, seemed almost the work of enchantment" (Stephens 1841: 130–3).

Esquipulas has long been considered "the most impressive building of the [Baroque] period in Guatemala" (Kubler and Soria 1959: 84). The red-tiled interior houses, in its sanctuary, the cult image of the Black Christ (1594). The sculpture was commissioned by Cristóbal Morales, General Vicar of the New Bishopric of Eastern Guatemala, carved by Quirio Cataño (fl. 1594–1617), and completed in 1594. A year later, a small chapel was built as its sanctuary. Church records contain testimonials to the miraculous curative powers of the image. Legend has it that Archbishop Pedro Pardo de Figueroa recognized such power when he was cured of a contagious illness, and ordered that a fitting sanctuary be built.

The massive edifice has as its plan four corner towers. The apse projects beneath the half-dome, a unique feature for Central America. *Mudéjar* influence is apparent in the multifoil arches above the portal and the finial at each level of the towers. Its squat, heavy dimensions have led Pál Kelemen (1951: 122) to term the architecture for the period "earthquake Baroque," referring to the need for it to withstand the powerful tremors that destroyed most of Guatemala's churches between 1600 and 1773. The church was built between 1735 and 1785 with the support of the archbishop and his successor. Felipe de Porres supervised the work after 1740. There are indications that his father, Diego de Porres, designed the plan, inspired by the cathedral at Valladolid and influenced by the Spanish edition of Serlio.

The Black Christ, a processional Crucifixion figure, was carved from orangewood and acquired its blackened state from constant exposure to the pilgrims' incense and candle smoke. Esquipulas is located in close geographical proximity to the ancient Mayan cities of Copán and Quirigua. The area is surrounded by a number of sulfur springs, which were used in ancient times by the Maya and by pilgrims en route to the sanctuary. The Black Christ may have linked its Mayan constituency to, or kindled a revival of their black gods, who were both malevolent and paternal. By the end of the eighteenth century over forty cities in Central America had established branches of the cult.

## The sanctuary of Bom Jesus de Matosinhos, Congonhas do Campo

The curing powers of Christ were also commemorated at the sanctuary of Bom Jesus, widely recognized as one of the most exquisite monuments of the Baroque in Brazil. The sanctuary complex design integrated the undulating landscape to create a harmonious panorama of the church and its sculpted figures from a terraced ascent (Plate

*Plate 9.5*    Sanctuary of Bom Jesus de Matosinhos, Congonhas do Campo, Brazil (photograph by A. J. Russell-
Wood; used with permission)

9.5). The church replaced a simple, niched cross erected by Portuguese emigrant
Feliciano Mendes, who devoted his life to Christ after recovering from an illness. The
church plan was designed by Antônio Gonçalves da Rosa and Antônio Rodrigues
Falcate, who worked on the building with stonemasons, carpenters, and sculptors
until 1776. Antônio Francisco Lisboa, an accomplished architect and sculptor, was
commissioned to complete the façade and to contribute 12 statues of the prophets
and life-sized group figures for a series of passion scenes (see Plates 9.6 and 9.7). Lisboa
was long known for his work in Minas Gerais, his birthplace and a prosperous commercial region linked to the fortunes of its gold and diamond mines. He was appren-
ticed primarily to his father Manoel Francisco, a renowned architect, and draftsman
João Gomes Batista. Recognition for his work was gained early in his career for his
contributions to the Franciscan churches of São João d'El-Rei and Ouro Prêto and the
Carmelite churches of Ouro Prêto and Sabará. At São Francisco de Assis da Penitência
(1766–94), he introduced an original rococo curvilinear style that came to revolution-
ize Brazilian church architecture. He was affected by a debilitating condition, perhaps
leprosy, at midlife which earned him the name O Aleijadinho (little cripple). There
is some debate as to his condition when he arrived at Congonhas do Campo to begin
work with his apprentices in 1796, but his commission there was completed.

*Plate 9.6*     Antônio Francisco Lisboa, the Prophet Jeremiah, Sanctuary of Bom Jesus de Matosinhos, Congonhas
do Campo, Brazil (photograph by A. J. Russell-Wood; used with permission)

Lisboa first began work on 64 life-size figures in polychrome cedar wood. These figures were arranged in chapels corresponding to the Last Supper, the Agony in the Garden, the Betrayal, the Flagellation, the Crowning with Thorns, the Road to Calvary, and the Crucifixion. The chapels were positioned at ascending levels of a steep incline leading to the church. Lisboa's signature style is evident in the facial details of Christ: an elongated, angular face, arched brows, and mustache emanating from the nose. Lisboa imbued each of the Christ figures with deeply emotional expressions: sorrow, forgiveness, introspection, inspiration. The lowered eyes of the flagellated Christ, his gaunt appearance, and ashen complexion speak of exhaustion and despair.

High above the chapels, at the church's terraced atrium, Lisboa sculpted 12 soapstone figures of the Old Testament prophets: Isaiah, Jeremiah (Plate 9.6), Baruch, Ezekiel, Daniel, Hosea, Joel, Amos, Obadiah, Jonah (Plate 9.7), Nahum, and Habbakkuk. Lisboa's aim was to integrate his sculpture with the landscape and sanctuary rather than subordinate it to the architecture. The figures and their arrangement on the terraces provided movement to the combined group.

The prophet group (1800–5) reflects Lisboa's interpretations of biblical descriptions and, like the chapel group, the figures are unique and expressive in their bearing.

*Plate 9.7*   Antônio Francisco Lisboa, the Prophet Jonah, Sanctuary of Bom Jesus de Matosinhos, Congonhas do Campo, Brazil (photograph by A. J. Russell-Wood, used with permission)

The torsos are somewhat foreshortened in order to be seen from a distance, and do not correspond in the attention given to the heads. Hands are large and gnarled and may reflect the sculptor's own agony as his health deteriorated.

## REFERENCES AND FURTHER READING

### References

Armstrong, E., and V. Zamudio-Taylor (eds). (2000). *Ultra Baroque: Aspects of Post Latin American Art*. San Diego, CA: Museum of Contemporary Art.

Berlin, H., de Carvajal, P., and Gutiérrez, C. (1958). "The high altar of Huejotzingo," *The Americas*, 15: 63–73.

Cummins, T. (2004). "Silver threads and golden needles: the Inca, the Spanish, and the sacred world of humanity." In E. Phipps, J. Hecht, and C. Esteras Martin (eds), *The Colonial Andes: Tapestries and Silverwork 1530–1830*, pp. 2–15. New York: Metropolitan Museum of Art.

Dean, C. (1999). *Inka Bodies and the Body of Christ: Corpus Christi in Colonial Cuzco, Peru*. Durham, NC and London: Duke University Press.

García Saíz, M. C. (2004). "Una contribución andina al barroco Americano." In R. Mujica Pinilla (ed.), *El Barroco peruano*, Vol. I, pp. 200–

17. Lima: Banco de Crédito Colección Arte y Tesoros del Peru.

Kelemen, P. (1951). *Baroque and Rococo in Latin America*. New York: Macmillan.

Kubler, G., and Soria, M. (1959). *Art and Architecture in Spain and Portugal and their American Dominions, 1500 to 1800*. Baltimore, MD: Penguin.

Mujica Pinilla, R. (2004). "Arte e identidad: las raíces culturales del barroco peruano." In R. Mujica Pinilla (ed.), *El Barroco peruano*, Vol. I, pp. 1–57. Lima: Banco de Crédito Colección Arte y Tesoros del Peru.

Samanez Argumedo, R. (2004). "Las portadas retablo en el barroco cusqueño." In R. Mujica Pinilla (ed.), *El Barroco peruano*, Vol. I, pp. 144–99. Lima: Banco de Crédito Colección Arte y Tesoros del Peru.

Stephens, J. L. (1841 [1949]). *Incidents of Travel in Central America, Chiapas, and Yucatan*, Vol. I. New Brunswick: Rutgers University Press.

Sullivan, E. J. (2001). "Brazil: body and soul." In E. J. Sullivan (ed.), *Brazil: Body and Soul*, pp. 2–33. New York: Solomon R. Guggenheim Foundation.

## Further Reading

Bayón, D., and Marx, M., eds (1992). *History of South American Colonial Art and Architecture*. New York: Rizzoli.

Carrera, M. M. (2003). *Imagining Identity in New Spain: Race, Lineage, and the Colonial Body in Portraiture and Casta Paintings*. Austin: University of Texas Press.

Gasparini, G., ed. (1997). *Arquitectura colonial iberoamericana*. Caracas, Venezuela: Armitano Editores.

Gutiérrez, R., ed. (1995). *Pintura, escultura y artes útiles en Iberoamérica, 1500–1825*. Madrid: Ediciones Cátedra.

Mesa, J., and Gisbert, T. (1982). *Historia de la pintura cuzqueña, vols. I–II*. Lima: Fundación Augusto N. Wiese.

Mujica Pinilla, R., ed. (2002). *El Barroco peruano, vols. I–II*. Lima: Banco de Crédito Colección Arte y Tesoros del Peru.

Pillsbury, J., ed. (2008). *Guide to Documentary Sources for Andean Studies, 1530–1900*. Norman: University of Oklahoma Press.

Querejazu, P., ed. (1997). *Potosí: Colonial Treasures and the Bolivian City of Silver*. New York: Americas Society Art Gallery.

Rishel, J. J., and Stratton-Pruitt, S., eds (2006). *The Arts in Latin America 1492–1820*. Philadelphia, PA: Philadelphia Museum of Art.

Sebastián, S. (1990). *El Barroco iberoamericano: Mensaje iconográfico*. Madrid: Ediciones Encuentro.

Sociedad Estatal para la Conmemoración de los Centenarios de Felipe II y Carlos V (1999). *Los Siglos de oro en los virreinatos de América: 1550–1700*. Madrid: Sociedad Estatal para la Conmemoración de los Centenarios de Felipe II y Carlos V.

Sullivan, E. J., ed. (2001). *Brazil: Body and Soul*. New York: Solomon R. Guggenheim Foundation.

Toussaint, M. (1965). *Arte colonial en México, Colonial Art in Mexico*. Trans. E. W. Weismann. Austin and London: University of Texas Press.

União Latino, Petit Palais, Museé des Beaux-Arts de la Ville de Paris (1999–2000). *Brasil barroco: Entre céu e terra*. Paris: União Latino, Petit Palais, Museé des Beaux-Arts de la Ville de Paris.

# 10

# History of a Phantom

*Francisco A. Ortega*

> Allegory is to language what ruins are to things.
> *Walter Benjamin*

## Preamble

During a 1975 lecture in Caracas, Alejo Carpentier asked rhetorically: "Why is Latin America the chosen territory of the baroque?" (1995: 89–108). His response, anticipated in his 1949 prologue to *The Kingdom of this World*, was that America was baroque because "all symbiosis, all *mestizaje*, engenders the baroque" (100). The baroque, he argued, is a "*spirit* and not a *historical style*" (93); it realizes its potential "with the self-awareness of the American man . . . , the awareness of being Other, of being new, of being symbiotic" (100). Carpentier's categorical response has been exceptionally influential partly because it was implicated in another fundamental debate during the 1940s: the question of national origins and sensibilities.

I would like to take up Carpentier's rhetorical question in order to draw a different cartography. Instead of charting secured and unified national origins, I will examine this imagined affinity between the "spirit of the baroque" and "America" as the starting point to question the status of colonial studies and the political uses of the distant past.

Colonial studies – defined as the professional academic apparatus in charge of producing and administering the viceregal past – emerged as a systemic enterprise in the late 1940s. It was then that several important publications that included detailed discussions of the colonial period in a hemispheric context appeared – Mariano Picón-Salas, *De la Conquista a la Independencia* (1944), Germán Arciniegas, *Biografía del Caribe* (1945), Luis Alberto Sánchez, *¿Existe América Latina?* (1945), and Pedro Henríquez Ureña's *Historia de la cultura en la América hispánica* (1947) and *Las Corrientes literarias en la América hispánica* (1949). Placed in this context, the questions are: If Latin

America is the chosen territory of the baroque, then what is the precise nature of this spirit? Is the colonial period a foundational and thus privileged moment in the history of the Spirit, or just another return of its multiple manifestations? Furthermore, is there anything in the enterprise called "colonial studies" that needs or calls for the idea of the baroque and, conversely, is there anything in the baroque that illuminates the colonial enterprise? And, finally, now that the baroque has become a privileged concept for accessing the actuality of our own era, what do we learn by historically and critically engaging American colonial culture?

## Returns

Let us start with an apparent paradox. Prior to Pedro Henríquez Ureña's 1936 article "La América española y su originalidad," remarkably little had been written about the baroque in the Americas. Since then, a very significant body of criticism has appeared examining both the American baroque – or *Barroco de Indias* – and America-as-Baroque. It is as if the concept suddenly reached a degree of usefulness previously unavailable. One could say something similar for the European baroque, a relatively new term in the history of cultural criticism. As it is well known, the baroque emerged in the eighteenth century to designate the perceived excesses of past artists, and it only became the name of an artistic style (characterized by the proliferation of chiaroscuros, adornments, curves, and multiple perspectives) with Heinrich Wölfflin's *Renaissance and Baroque* (*Renaissance und Barock*, 1888). In Wölfflin's characterization, the baroque opposed the classic and worked in contrastive tandem, operating diachronically (recurring throughout history) and synchronically (typifying racial and national feelings) (9). At the beginning of the twentieth century, baroque designates other cultural manifestations – architecture, music, theater, and literature – under the assumption that the period shared an aesthetic regime. More recently, the term has been extended to cover other aspects of social life during the seventeenth century, such as government, religion, economy, and even a certain mode of criticism. Thus, Severo Sarduy (1999) spoke of the *retombée* of certain scientific models (Galileo's circle vis-à-vis Kepler's ellipse) within non-scientific symbolic production. Since the figure of the retombée challenges notions of causality and influence, the two archetypes – classical and baroque– represent fundamental operational modes of engaging symbolic production within power-laden contexts. It is as if the malleability of the baroque served a nominalistic impulse that has become urgent in our own late modernity.

I am not interested in censuring or rehabilitating the concept of the baroque as a style or as a period. Nor do I undertake an analysis of structures and concepts that can give us a more punctilious sense of the baroque. Rather, I am concerned with the ways in which a certain provocation – in the sense that Marshall Brown (1997 discusses the vitality of Wölfflin's writings – a paradoxical quality, and even an alterity have been constitutive of all discussions about the baroque, particularly of the colonial baroque. Thus, this "sudden usefulness" means several things at once, many of which I will not be able to address here, but its valiance is largely dependent on a rather spectral capacity to intimate a tight relationship between powerful and contemporary themes and a pre-Enlightenment and colonial epistemic moment. I say spectral because of the recurring and impertinent return of the past. Jacques Lacan's argument that the logic of the phantasm binds the subject with the Other, who in turn motivates the subject's unconscious desire, is quite pertinent here (1977: 293–325). Thus, the recurring returns of the baroque respond to the field's negative presence of the Other, before whom the self seeks to respond to the enigmatic *che vuoi?* In that sense the returns of the baroque are of greater importance because of their analytic value than because of their aesthetic doctrine or the political program they impart.

In order to probe the nature of such connections, in what follows I will sketch the dense and contradictory history manifested by the baroque's recurring returns. The returns I will briefly examine are (1) historical arguments about the *Barroco de Indias*; (2) America-as-Baroque; (3) the idea of a baroque reason in the field of contemporary critical theory; (4) the Neo-baroque of the 1970s and 1980s; and (5) the 1990s return of the baroque as a critical category for cultural historiography, cultural studies, and (anti)culturalist criticism. To be sure, one should start with the reception of Góngora by the Spanish generation of poets of 1927 and the discovery of the Hispanic Golden Age by German philologists. In both cases the appraisal of seventeenth-century poetry was connected to avant-garde views of language as opaque.

One of the most significant returns takes place under the guise of the American baroque, also known as the *Barroco de Indias*, the Baroque of the Indies. However, if the baroque is a dubious concept, the notion of an American baroque is even more perplexing. The concept was first used by Mariano Picón-Salas in a 1944 essay on the emergence of modern independent Latin American nations (121). With the concept Picón-Salas – and those who followed in his tracks – simultaneously designated three phenomena. First, the period from roughly 1580 to 1770, that is, from the moment of the colonial regime's consolidation and the Jesuits' arrival to the colonies to the various fiscal, political, and administrative reforms undertaken by the Iberian governments (including the expulsion of Jesuits in 1767) in order to modernize the bureaucratic apparatus and maximize colonial profits.

Secondly, the Barroco de Indias opened new vistas on the American past. Up to the late 1930s, colonial culture was the object of scant consideration on the part of local historians or critics. The seventeenth century was considered the dark ages of the Americas, the period wherein nothing worthwhile happened and the Inquisition and despotism reigned quite freely. If Latin Americans lagged behind, critics would say, it was because during this long century – the age of science and progress elsewhere – nothing worthwhile happened here. Picón-Salas overturned this grim view by thinking of colonial society in a state of flux. Colonial practices and material culture – such as churches and palaces, the reworking of native spiritual traditions into Catholic pictorial codes, and the staging of elaborate public ceremonials incorporating native and African performative traditions – were seen as evidence of the foundational moment in which disparate colonial elements began to congeal into harmonious national formations.

Thirdly, the Barroco de Indias also designated an aesthetic of conflict whereby peripheral or non-European cultural practices and forms were ultimately incorporated into mainstream collective sensibilities in the processes of forging "authentic" communal identities. It was a process of decolonization that announced the true identity of the nation. That is to say, cathedrals, paintings, and ceremonies, in addition to evincing conflicting sociocultural processes, also circulated modes of representation that suggested the eventual resolution of the conflict in a new national mode of being. The American baroque identified the very *dispositif* that Werner Weisbach had named as responsible for the art of the Counter-Reformation; in this case, however, it works against empire, as an art of counter-conquest, in Lezama Lima's felicitous formulation (1993: 80).

In this remarkable tripartite formulation – as a historical period, as national origins, and as the embodiment of a decolonizing thrust – the Barroco de Indias inaugurates the modern field of colonial studies in the continent. Since then, the colonial period is no longer the memory of that which must be extirpated, but that which persists against all odds and rebelliously announces the emergence of the new nation, the repository of genuine historical memory, the living impetus of a free people. As Carpentier wrote, "El barroquismo está siempre proyectado hacia adelante y suele presentarse precisamente en expansión . . . cuando va a nacer un orden nuevo en la sociedad" (123). The baroque constituted a useful framework for appropriating the collective past as it provided a grammar that reformulated patriotic nineteenth-century Creole ideologies into the founding myths of the popular nation-state. This occurred in the context of an unevenly modernized globalization after World War II (Chiampi, 1998: 4–22). The founding script inscribed colonial practices and products as necessary steps in the progressive chain of national integration and consolidation. From that moment on, the dominant question in Latin American colonial studies became whether certain cultural products mimic the European canon or are genuine cultural responses to empire and colonial antagonism. In other words, are they *Barroco* or *Barroco de Indias*? The implicit identitarian promise in such a formulation necessarily renders the baroque complicit with the chain of nationalist appropriations that silence or repress the cultural specificity of the seventeenth century to manufacture models of national identity and create a patriotic culturalist repertoire.

Towards the end of the 1940s, a host of Latin American literary figures, art historians, and critics – such as Alejo Carpentier, José Lezama Lima, Octavio Paz, Arturo Uslar Pietri, Martín Adan, and Oswald de Andrade – drew on the experience of the historical avant-garde and on Eugenio D'Ors's work to designate a mode of being appropriate to certain peripheral regions – Minas Gerais, Havana, or Mexico – that contrasted with the supposed rationality, pragmatism, transparency, and simplicity typical of the centers of modernity. This mode of being exhibited a patent opacity and excess, which – these critics claimed – are nonetheless the source of authentic realization – or revelation – of a Latin American identity. America-as-

Baroque practitioners staged the nation's diversity into new universal and cosmopolitan wholes. That is to say, America-as-Baroque – a formalist expression – satisfied the historicist and culturalist promises of the Barroco de Indias by actualizing those latent, age-old differences that had remained radically outside the modern nation into a register legible for contemporary cosmopolitan readers. As Cesar Salgado writes: "New World baroque theorists achieved this redefinition by focusing on the hybrid refigurations that European baroque paradigms have undergone when transplanted into the colonial arena" (1999: 317). By serving as a bridge between the appropriation of the past carried out by the Barroco de Indias and the populist nationalist ideologies that emerge in the 1940s, America-as-Baroque tantalizes us with culturalist promises.

It goes without saying that not all practitioners offer the same identitarian promise. Lezama Lima, for instance, seeks to liberate the baroque from the "fatalism" of morphology and referentiality by positing an interpreting self who actively metamorphoses data into a "historical vision" (1993: 49). Thus colonial baroque culture is the result of a poetic vision and represents the first flowering of an American "imaginary era" (1993: 79–106). And yet, for Lezama, just as for Carpentier and Andrade, the baroque is a foundational moment because its "originating fire shatters and unifies the fragments again" (1993: 80). Like its contemporary, "Magical Realism," America-as-Baroque is "a technical device within a larger and more encompassing apparatus of transculturating representation" (Moreiras, 2001: 185).

The third return, which I will only mention briefly, establishes an epistemic break with the previous two. It takes place in the field of contemporary theory and it is not directly related to the field of colonial studies. However, it makes new approaches to and imaginings of the colonial past possible. Whereas the American baroque and the notion of America-as-Baroque rest on a romantic and nationalist notion of expressive representation, philosophers and artists in the late twentieth century have extended the baroque beyond its historical limits by formalizing the concept and finding its operational specificity (Deleuze 1993: 33–4). Though historically informed, this intervention finds morphological analogies between seventeenth-century cultural practices and contemporary ones. The return of the baroque – as strategic and supplementary practice of disruption – is, therefore, linked to the enervation of master narratives (among which political liberalism figures prominently), the crisis of the social sciences, and the collapse of modern utopia. Thus, the baroque resurfaces in the critical vocabulary of Jacques Lacan and Jean Baudrillard to identify the emergence of a new order of the subject; in Roland Barthes and Michel de Certeau as the grounds for a critical heterology; in Gilles Deleuze, Mario Perniola, and Mieke Bal as a fundamental metaphor for critical thinking; and in Christine Buci-Glucksmann and Omar Calabrese as the appropriate semiotic frame for a post-utopian political cultural practice. Clearly, not all of them use the concept of the baroque, but their approach has defined the nature of this retombée (as Sarduy 1999 defines it). Their work operates in the polemic field that has helped establish the baroque as a legitimate question for post-utopian skeptic audiences.

It is impossible to explore the complexity of these philosophical projects in such a brief space. Suffice it to say that the return of the baroque invokes a certain theoretical and political actuality in as much as the seventeenth century simultaneously functions as the grounds for modern hegemony and as that which had to be excluded and rejected in order to accomplish such a desired sense of modernity. That simultaneous condition of inclusion and exclusion – constitutive of all relations with the baroque in our times – defines the operational mode of the phantasm, a category that allows us to understand its various returns. That is to say, the spectral dimension of the baroque founds the conditions for imagining new grounds for developing critique.

It is with the return of the baroque in the field of contemporary philosophy that a Neo-baroque emerges in Latin America during the late 1970s. Its practitioners – Severo Sarduy, Haroldo de Campos, Rodolfo Hinestroza, and Nestor Perlongher, among others – no longer appeal to collective identities; rather, they seek to disturb traditional social narratives and coherent moral universes to generate new spatial configurations and possibilities for social agency (see Echevarren Welker, 1992; Armstrong and Zamudio, 2000). As a mode of disenchantment, the Neo-baroque parodies and perturbs, irrupts and defies, advancing an aesthetic of the excluded, the abject, the fragment, the ruin: the Neo-baroque is heroic and melancholic at once. Its performances address the crisis that takes place with the collapse of romantic notions about art and populist utopias. Haroldo de Campos's reading of Gregorio de Matos exemplifies a particular appropriation of colonial culture as irreverent, impertinent, teeming with mockery and willful transgressions.

A fifth return, this time in the field of colonial cultural history, cultural studies and (anti-) culturalist critiques, takes place during the last decade. If the Neo-baroque places a greater emphasis on formalistic configuration, authors such as Bolívar Echeverría, Serge Gruzinski, Mabel Moraña, Janice Theodoro, and Fernando Rodríguez de la Flor, among others, draw on the theoretical language and insights of poststructuralism and seek to work within the historical specificity of the seventeenth century. They follow José Maravall's view of the baroque as a decisively modern accommodation by ecclesiastic and monarchic powers of the crisis that gripped the European-influenced world during the seventeenth century (1986: 19–55). However, in their conversations, the cultural logic of the baroque inaugurates a "beyond the principle of power" (Rodríguez de la Flor, 2002: 36); locates a historical precedent and eventual alternative to eighteenth-century capitalist modernity (Echeverría, 1998: 32–56); names the reified semiotic frame that permitted a *mestizo* language within the colonizer's cultural forms (Sallman); and explores a plausible source for contemporary political utopianism (Sousa Santos).

Recent debates between John Beverley and Alberto Moreiras, among others, exemplify new approaches to questions of domination and resistance. If colonial Hispanism is considered a site of epistemic appropriation, what, then, are the irruptive possibilities of thinking within university discourse? Is there an exteriority to this discourse that might anchor thought in a new horizon of possibilities? If Beverley sees the baroque as a form of imperial domination, a mediating structure that is always already compromised with its origins (1997: 9), Moreiras views in the baroque a possible delocalizing effect, an exodus or "abandonment of positions [that] unconceals the disciplining condition of the political and can thus claim a repolitization" (2005: 202–3).

# Modernity, Coloniality, Globality

In spite of its frequent usage (what I call its many returns), critics and historians agree on the problematic nature of the concept. They charge that the notion of the baroque is an anachronism tainted by a pejorative meaning, imprecise nature, idealizing thrust, and even ideological complicity with populist state formations. For these critics, the concept of the baroque is irrelevant or, in the worst of cases, vitiated by a long chain of nationalistic appropriations.

However, the baroque refuses to go away; it returns again and again and signifies – from its abjection – as a remainder, one might even say in a baroque manner. In fact, since the end of the twentieth century we have witnessed a significant number of publications that purport to explain the nature of the baroque, colonial or not. One must understand this recurrence as a result of an evocative – and not denotative – power. Indeed, debates about the colonial baroque and America-as-Baroque inevitably prompt four themes that are of fundamental importance for our age and locality: the question of modernity, of coloniality, of globality, and of the failure of modern colonial globality. In other words, the baroque preserves its recurring naming capacity in Latin America not because of what it positively signifies, but because in its many misnomers it marks a field of struggle over the meaning and legacies of our modernity, and frees up important symbolic resources to meet the challenges that result from its failure in the region. The complexities of these misnomers constitute what is truly difficult – in Lezama's sense.

## *Modernity*

A distinctive trait of the sixteenth and seventeenth century was the appearance of new modes of self-fashioning. Indeed, the early modern period witnessed the paradoxical proliferation of technologies of the self – that is, of specific practices by which individuals could monitor and constitute themselves as virtuous subjects – and of institutions that scrutinized and punished those who deviated from orthodoxy. The confluence of technologies of the self and institutionalized mechanisms of control and surveillance produced new modes of experiencing, of relating to, and of being in the world. These practices gave individuals a greater sense of self-control and constituted a fundamental break with previous modes of governance.

One might find partial confirmation of novel modes of self-fashioning in Ignatius of Loyola's *Spiritual Exercises* (1541). The aim of the exercises is to methodically instruct believers in "examining one's conscience, . . . meditating, . . . contemplating, . . . praying vocally and mentally, and . . . performing other spiritual actions," all with the goal of "conquering oneself" (Loyola, 1914: 12). Sensorial, imaginative (*anima secunda*) and intellectual (*anima prima*) resources are mobilized in order to "equip the subject with a structure that contains a mechanism for self-conquest" (Valle 2002: 142).

This account of the self starts out from the premise that "the power of forming up a good judgement – and of distinguishing the true from the false, which is properly speaking what is called good sense or reason, is by nature equal in all men" (Descartes, 1931: 81). In both Ignatius's and Descartes's formulations the method serves "little by little [to be] delivered from many errors which might have obscured our natural vision and rendered us less capable of listening to Reason" (Descartes, 1931: 87). Similarly, they both depart from the principle that helping others arrive at the truth entails employing persuasive – as opposed to repressive – means to convince those who had erroneous conceptions. As persuasion rests on the calculated usage of signs, rhetoric becomes the procedure through which members of society negotiate its demands.

To be virtuous was to be able to reduce desire to reason, aesthetics to communicative ethics, in favor of a patriarchal and imperial administrative logic. And yet, non-European and female desires resisted administration, caused complications – *turbaciones*, as Mother Jerónima, a Neogranadine nun, calls them – and brought out the monstrous within the modern – "Y ser yo un monstruo y aborto de la naturaleza," claimed another American mystic, Francisca Josefa del Castillo y Guevara (1968: I: 164). Begun at the behest of their confessors, mystic writing – with its powerful array of visions and dreams – constituted a highly controlled scenario in which the rich spiritual life of women in the Americas staged an amorous language of affirmation: "estando herida del deseo de entregarme totalmente . . . y que Su Majestad se entregase y me aprisionase para sí" (Robledo 1994: 154). A language that relentlessly threatens to explode the confines of the self – "nunca tuve por dichoso estado / amar bienes posibles," says Amarilis in her Epistle to Belardo (vs. 25–8) – it is always already a paradoxical inscription of desire, permitted to exist only in disavowal, that evinces the pervasive opacity of masculine desire. In a daring move, Sor Juana chides men "en promesa e instancia / juntaís diablo, carne y mundo" (Cruz, 1992: 288). And yet, a further paradox: this language of affirmation in disavowal had an earthly correspondence as these women's spiritual economy developed powerful political and financial webs throughout colonial societies (Burn, 1999; Toquica, 2005).

Not surprisingly, the baroque simultaneously evokes a number of interpellatory practices we associate with modern subjectivity, and behaviors, ideas, and cultural products we imagine as deviant or impervious to those modern ideals. Such an agonic mediation presents the baroque as embodying both the modern and its negation, or better yet, the reticent presence that through self-negation (a double monstrosity) makes the modern possible elsewhere. Hence, its phantasmatic nature.

## Coloniality

Modern colonialism yearns to retain a persuasive formula. Drawing on Francisco de Vitoria, Bartolomé de Las Casas argued that "para el todo el mundo y para todos los tiempos, [the] único modo de enseñarles a los hombres la verdadera religión [is through] la persuasión del entendimiento por medio de razones y la invitación y suave moción de la voluntad" (65). Las Casas's impossible formulation meant the paradoxical recognition of the desires of the Other, the others as rightly desiring beings, in a political environment of violent conquest and evangelical zealotry that thoroughly denied their right to desire.

If modernity bears the contradictory management of the self, monstrosity calls for its own technology of control. And mostly everything was monstrous in the Americas, "ni del todo Gentiles ni enteramente Christianos" (Bertonio 1612: 4). In such context, the claims that the road from savagery is one of systematically applying a method for self-instruction (Descartes, 1934: 83) and that evangelical zeal could only be effective with the other's consent were quickly withdrawn.

Indeed, colonial technologies of control departed from two improvements on modernity. On the one hand, the idea that the faculty of reason, which was "the most equally distributed" thing in the world (Descartes, 1931: 81), was substantially diminished in Native Americans, blacks, women, and others. On the other, the notion that Indigenous people's abilities to discern right from wrong abated due to their being deeply mired in what Christians regarded idolatrous practices. Jesuit Ludovico Bertonio writes in the preface to his *Vocabulario de la lengua Aymará* (1612) that "Toda esta nación de indios esta bien lastimada y herida en el *entendimiento* con su poca capacidad, y en la *voluntad* con la muchedumbre de malos habitos, y mucho estrago de vicios, con poca esperança de su mejoría (1612: A3, emphasis added).

Ill-desiring (will) and unfit to carry out judicious self-fashioning (reason), Native Americans must be subjected before they might become subjects; persuasion – the work of culture – must be supplemented with violence (Acosta, 1952: 85–9). This way of thinking was officially incorporated into the Third Provincial Council in Lima (1582) and surfaced most dramatically in catechisms, manuals for extirpation campaigns, and dictionaries of Indian languages. By the end of the sixteenth century, the evangelical task – and thus, indigenous subordination – was thought unfinishable.

Legitimation was still necessary, which might explain why aggressive subjugation called for a representation of the Natives as willingly and gratefully submitting: "[que] los indios llevan bien el castigo que es justo, y que si no se les castigan no hacen caso de solas palabras" (Acosta, 1952: 406). Conversely, denial of local native agency (in the form of feeble intellect and perverse will) calls for the vigorous reinscription of European and imperial agency, and allows missionaries to attain their own salvation:

Pero esta miseria y extrema necesidad de estas almas, antes no ha de mover a compasión para ayudarlas, que no a tibieza, o covardia para desmpararlas; y si con todas nuestras

diligencias no pudieremos curar sus llagas, ni librarlas del peligro de su eterna conde-
nación en que se hallan, no por esso perderemos el premio del cuydado que de nuestra
parte pusieremos para libarlas. (Bertonio, 1612: A3)

This ghastly exchange institutes the "colonial difference," as Walter Mignolo calls
the operation regulating social relations in colonial America. The colonial difference
justified and normalized the incorporation of the new territories and their inhabitants
into European administrative and juridical units and provided a rationalization for
the exploitative division of labor (Mignolo, 2002). Violence merely inscribed the
colonial difference on Native bodies.

Thus, the return of the baroque is, once again, the return of the abject, the *berrueco*,
the excluded. As with every return it urges us to consider the present as only one
among many possibilities. That is to say, in its multiple distortions, the baroque
preserves the historical memory of that which could have been but still has not been
resolved.

## Achieved globality

The returns of the baroque point to the moment when modern totality became
thinkable and the frame within which a particular understanding of such globality
was first ascertained. Immanuel Wallerstein argues that the global present has its
roots in the violences that ripped the world apart and stitched it back together into
a colonial globality in the seventeenth century (1974: 229). Such achieved globality
organized the radical heterogeneity of the world into a systemic whole which set in
motion the early capitalist world system; it constituted the colonial as the obverse
of the modern and the modern at the expense of humanity in the colonial (Wallerstein, 1974).

And yet the moral imaginings of the global were not exhausted by capitalism; even
within its logic there survived the longing for a globality that was not driven by
greed. In fact, one might add that the idea of the baroque evokes the first moment
of a promise regarding the pluri-national globality in which divergent social logics
coexist under a unified ethical criterion and under a coherent and reciprocal system
of representations. Examples of staged conviviality abound during the seventeenth
century, from allegorical paintings to atlases, and plays, like Sor Juana's "Sarao de
cuatro naciones," the final piece in *Festejo de los empeños de una casa*. Francis Bacon juxtaposed Bensalem's merchants exploring the Mediterranean and engaging in fair-trade
practices with actual European military and commercial fleets sailing the ocean and
coming onto American shores. With a keen moral vision (not far removed from the
Jesuits' *Theatrum sacrum*), Gottfried Leibniz wrote: "since this substance [God] is sufficient reason for all this diversity, which is utterly interconnected, *there is only one
God, and this God is sufficient*" (Leibniz, 1989: 218). "This city of God," he remarked
later, "this truly universal monarchy, is a moral world within the natural world"
(Leibniz, 1989: 224).

As mentioned, European-inflicted modernity incorporates American subjects as "simiente maldita, destituida del divino auxilio y destinada a la perdición" (Acosta, 1952: 58). Their destitution goes so far that they have no word for God in Mexican and Peruvian languages, "de donde se ve cuan corta y flaca noticia tenían de Dios, pues aun nombrarle no saben sino por nuestros vocablos" (Acosta, 1952: 3: 303). As a result, European-achieved globality completes and supplements God's work.

However, the promises of a new globality are not solely affirmed by those Europeans who sail the oceans and discuss the meaning of *Imperium*. The Andean *mestizo* Garcilaso de la Vega (who insisted Andeans had a word for God) opens his *Royal Commentaries of the Incas* (1609) pondering whether there are many worlds or just one ("Si hay muchos mundos") and replies categorically that there is just one: "Y a los que todavía imaginaran que hay muchos mundos no hay para qué responderles, sino que se estén en sus heréticas imaginaciones hasta que en el infierno se desengañen sus almas" (I:1, 9). It is he who reminds Europeans that there is no longer a world divided in many.

The meaning of such globality is in the best of cases uncertain, and in the worst, dominated by the violence and greed of the conquest and subjugation. In "Des Coches," Montaigne captures the conflictive uncertainty that defines such globality when he stages the encounter of a native Mexican and a Conquistador. In his rendering, the Spaniard asks the Mexican to give him all the gold and to become a vassal of the Spanish king. The Mexican informs the Spaniard that they do not have any usage for the gold and do not have any desire to change religion or king. Once again, such irony is not exclusively European. In fact, Garcilaso qualifies his previous assertion, writing that "Y aunque llamamos 'mundo viejo' y 'mundo nuevo' es por haberse descubierto aquel nuevamente *para nosotros* y no porque sean dos, sino todo uno" (ibid.; emphasis added). The well-known difficulty in locating this elusive narrator along the Andean–European divide makes this textual opening an enthralling moment: For, *who* was discovered again? By *whom* and for *whom*? Were Americans or Europeans discovered by and for *us*?

The return of the baroque signifies not just the discovery and invention of new worlds by Europeans, but the decentering principle by which totality is not exhausted by the center. Indeed, Garcilaso's language game makes evident the impossibility in locating the return of imperial reason outside of the colonial frame. The native at once became and ceased to be autochthonous upon the inaugural moment of colonial globality. And yet, though these *mestizo* logics are not dominant, they certainly inhabit and rehash imperial logic. In the periphery, cultural logics are already necessarily contaminated: they are *mestizo*, or ironic and indeterminate.

## Mestizo

Finally, if the baroque brings to mind the onset of the modern global colonial world, it also recalls its deep-seated failures. As we have already seen, the onset of modern colonialism brought with it technologies that were tremendously productive. However, the machinery of colonialism developed technologies of failure as well. Evidently the subaltern knows modernity's failures all too well, as the colonial condition means living through the consequences of a globalization not devoted to satisfying the ideological principles that sustain it. I call "technologies of failure" those strategies negotiated by colonial institutions *and* colonized subjects to render social life constrained by ideological stalemate inhabitable and minimally meaningful. I shall briefly mention three fronts on which these technologies of failure were enacted.

First, the subjugation and management of the Crown possessions' vast social diversity constituted an impossible political program, an impossibility best measured in the gradual shift from the ardent impetus of early militant missionaries and humanist ideologues (exemplified by Jerónimo de Mendieta and Vasco de Quiroga) to the more pragmatic attitude officially adopted by the colonial church during the second half of the sixteenth century. From this perspective – and only from this perspective – early modern colonialism comprised a set of practices that, though brutally effective, were not particularly efficient, at least with regard to its stated evangelical and humanist goals.

Second, the ample and brutal context of colonial violence undermined meaning-producing systems and resulted in impotence, uncertainty, and faithlessness; in such a precarious social order, forms substituted substance, and tactics replaced strategies as the privilege forms of advancing political claims (Gruzinski, 1999: 80–1).

Third, the imperial design was deformed in the very process of integrating and subordinating Indians, blacks and whites. In this process, imperial reason ceased to be entirely instrumental since it also constituted the colonized's habitus. In fact, the latter's speech returns imperial reason slightly modified, inevitably ironized. Let us recall Peruvian indigenous chronicler Guamán Poma de Ayala's map of the world in his extraordinary *Letter to the King* (1615). The *Letter* is meant to inform the king of the deplorable situation in the kingdom of Peru and to instruct him on how to remedy the ills caused by the colonial government. The map, drawn within European logic but certainly not by it, produces an ex-centric effect whereby the familiar becomes new. As González Echevarría writes: "the baroque issues from an impasse in the doctrine of imitation, it leads to the enthronement of 'ingenio,' of 'wit,' which is . . . the self-conscious shuffling of models" (1993: 164–5). It is a disorienting map.

Aware of the impossibility of total mastering, these technologies of failure controlled the unraveling of social domination by imposing a provisional, though unresolved arrangement. The return of the baroque, therefore, signals the presence of a persistent will that marked a critical distance from the self-affirmation of capital and empire as the only possible presents (González Echevarría, 1994: 13–36). Such critical distance, however, did not result in the imagining of possible futures or the setting up of enduring political alternatives. Furthermore, the ensuing radical skepticism coincided with other modes of disenchantment in the metropolis, perhaps best summarized by Francisco de Quevedo's musing over the inconsequentiality of life, "Ayer se fue; mañana no ha llegado." And yet, the opening of such a futureless present invites us to trace alternative genealogies, that is to say, to think the baroque as the question of a possibly different present.

# The Baroque: That Which Remains to be Thought

To argue over how adequate the label of the baroque is suggests we have forgotten its spectral nature. A critical reading of the baroque pays attention to that which does not find a satisfactory mode of expression and which returns once and again. Its recurrence must be analyzed – and can only be apprehended – as a structure of desire which is indicative of a foundational violence, since it maps out and responds to the promises and exclusions that structure the relation of the *communal* present with *its* past.

The so-called colonial period is a foundational and privileged moment in the history of the baroque because it fruitfully triangulates the historical promises contained with the onset of modernity with the violent legacies of colonialism and a contemporary need to recompose political imagination. In such a spirit one might argue, with Deleuze, that the baroque is not a concept but an "operative function" that conjoins space and time within a dynamic system (1993: 13). It is historicity built into the logic of the fold, a particularly contemporary mode of recurrence that actualizes the continent's colonial memory for contemporary audiences.

Ultimately, the place of the baroque is that of theory, or better, a theoretical insufficiency that is intimately linked to the impasse faced by philosophy and politics. Only in that sense is it possible to find in the returns of the baroque – and therefore in our field of colonial studies – the announcement of something which cannot be reduced to identity.

Furthermore, the logic of the phantom ties the question of the baroque to the enigmatic place of the Other, a formula already coined by Carpentier when he proposed that the baroque realizes its potential with the awareness of being Other. Thus, its returns must be seen as a recurring heterology, a copious – if anxious – discourse on the Other (Certeau, 2005: 3), which threatens to irrupt the language of mastering. Understood as *phantasie*, the returns of the baroque reinscribe the past's unfulfilled promises; it posits colonial material and symbolic culture as the repository of historical memory, both in the sense that its remnants are the vehicles of social violence and in the sense that they constitute the horizon that houses the possible. Consequently, these remnants might be the proper grounds for rethinking utopia, in as far as the baroque-as-specter allows us to reimagine what is possible, and to claim what is legitimate in our historical present. It is thus a discourse that stages the presence of an active ruin that might allow us to exercise a ruinous thinking, "or a thinking of the ruins of thinking" (Moreiras, 2001: 13), such as it is now possible.

## References and Further Reading

Acosta, José de (1952). *De procuranda indorum salute (Predicación del Evangelio en las Indias)*. Trans. Francisco Mateo. Madrid: I. G. Magerit.

— (2003 [1590]). *Historia natural y moral de las Indias*. Ed. José Alcina Franch. Madrid: Destin. (Originally published Seville: Juan de León.)

Armstrong, Elizabeth, and Zamudio, Víctor, eds (2000). *Ultra Baroque: Aspects of Post-Latin American Art*. San Diego, CA: Museum of Contemporary Art.

Bertonio, Ludovico (1612). *Vocabulario de la lengua Aymara: Primera parte, donde por abecedario se ponen en primer lugar los Vocablos de la lengua Española para buscar los que le corresponden en la lengua Aymará*. Juli, Provincia de Chucuitos: Casa de la Compañía de Jesus.

Beverley, John (1997). *Una Modernidad obsoleta: Estudios sobre el barroco*. Los Teques, Venezuela: Fondo Editorial ALEM.

Brown, Marshall (1997). "The classic is the baroque: on the principles of Wölfflin's art history." In *Turning Points. Essays in the History of Cultural Expressions*, pp. 88–113. Stanford, CA: Stanford University Press.

Burn, Kathryn (1999). *Colonial Habit: Convents and the Spiritual Economy of Cuzco, Peru*. Durham, NC: Duke University Press.

Campos, Haroldo de (1989). *O Sequestro do barroco na formação da literatura brasileira: O caso de Gregório de Matos*. 2nd ed. Bahia: Fundação Casa de Jorge Amado.

Carpentier, Alejo (1981). *La novela latinoamericana en vísperas de un nuevo siglo y otros ensayos*. Mexico City: Siglo XXI.

— (1995). "The baroque and the marvelous real." In Lois Parkinson Zamora and Wendy B. Faris (eds), *Magical Realism: Theory, History, Community*, pp. 89–108. Durham, NC: Duke University Press.

Castillo y Guevara, Francisca Josefa de la Concepción de (1968). *Su vida*. Ed. Darío Achury Valenzuela. 2 vols. Bogotá: Banco de la República.

Chiampi, Irlemar (1998). *Barroco e modernidade*. São Paulo: Editora Perspectiva.

Cruz, Sor Juana Inés de la (1992). *Obras completas*. México: Porrúa.

De Certeau, Michel (1988). *The Writing of History*. Trans. Tom Conley. New York: Columbia University Press.

— (2005). *La Possession de Loudun*. Rev. ed. Paris: Gallimard.

De Las Casas, Bartolomé (1975). *Del único modo de atraer a todos los pueblos a la verdadera religión: De unico vocationis modo c. 1536*. Trans. Atenógenes Santamaría, ed. Agustín Millares Carlo. Mexico City: Fondo de Cultura Económica.

Deleuze, Gilles (1993). *The Fold: Leibniz and the Baroque*. Trans. Tom Conley. Minneapolis: University of Minnesota Press.

Descartes, René (1931). *The Philosophical Works*. Trans. Elizabeth S. Haldane and G. R. T. Ross. Vol. I. London: Cambridge University Press.

— (1934). *The Philosophical Works*. Trans. Elizabeth S. Haldane and G. R. T. Ross. Vol. II. London: Cambridge University Press.

Echavarren Welker, Roberto (1992). "Barroco y neobarroco: los nuevos poetas." In Horacio Costa (ed.), *A Palabra poética na América Latin: Avaliação de uma generação*, pp. 143–57. São Paulo: Memorial-Fundação de América Latina.

Echeverría, Bolívar (1998). *Modernidad de lo barroco*. Mexico City: Ediciones Era.

Echeverría, Bolívar, ed. (1994). *Modernidad, mestizaje cultural: Ethos Barroco*. Mexico City: UNAM.

González Echevarría, Roberto (1993). *Celestina's Brood: Continuities of the Baroque in Spanish and Latin American Literature*. Durham, NC: Duke University Press.

Gruzinski, Serge (1999). *La Pensée métisse*. Paris: Fayard.

Hanse, João (1989). *A Sátira e o engenho: Gregório de Matos e a Bahia do século XVII*. São Paulo: Companhia das Letras.

Lacan, Jacques (1977). *Écrits: A Selection*. Trans. Alan Sheridan. New York: W. W. Norton.

Leibniz, Gottfried Wilhelm (1989). *Philosophical Essays*. Ed. Roger Ariew and Daniel Garber. Indianapolis: Hackett.

Lezama Lima, José (1993 [1933]). *La Expresión americana*. Ed. Irlemar Chiampi. Mexico City: Fondo de Cultura Académica.

Loyola, Ignatius of (1914 [1548]). *Spiritual Exercises*. Trans. Elder Mullan. New York: Kennedy & Sons. (Originally published as *Exercitia spiritualia*. Rome: IHS.)

Maravall, José Antonio (1986). *Culture of the Baroque: Analysis of a Historical Structure*. Trans. Jerry Cochran. Theory and History of Literature, Vol. 25. Minneapolis: University of Minnesota Press.

Mignolo, Walter (2002). "Geopolitics of knowledge and the colonial difference." *South Atlantic Quarterly*, 101(1): 57–96.

Moreiras, Alberto (2001). *The Exhaustion of Difference: The Politics of Latin American Cultural Studies*. Post-Contemporary Interventions, ed.

Stanley Fish and Frederic Jameson. Durham, NC: Duke University Press.

— (2005). "Mules and snakes: on the Neo-Baroque principle of de-localization." In Mabel Moraña (ed.), *Ideologies of Hispanism*, pp. 201–29. Nashville, TN: Vanderbilt University Press.

Picón-Salas, Mariano (1944). *De la Conquista a la Independencia*. Mexico City: FCE.

Robledo, Ángela, ed. (1994). *Jerónima Nava y Saavedra (1669–1727): Autobiografía de una monja venerable*. Cali: Universidad del Valle.

Rodríguez de la Flor, Fernando (2002). *Barroco: Representación e ideología en el mundo hispánico (1560–1680)*. Madrid: Cátedra.

Salgado, Cesar Augusto (1999). "Hybridity in New World baroque theory," *Journal of the American Folklore Society*, 112(445): 316–32.

Sarduy, Severo (1999). "Barroco." In *Obras completas*. Ed. Gustavo Guerrero and François Wahl.

Vol. II, pp. 1197–261. Madrid, Paris, and Mexico City: ALLCA XX, FCE.

Toquica, Constanza (2005). "El barroco neogranadino: De las redes de poder a la colonización del alma." In Ana María Bidegain (ed.), *Historia del cristianismo en Colombia: Corrientes y diversidad*, pp. 83–144. Bogotá: Taurus Historia.

Valle, Ivonne del (2002). "Jesuit Baroque," *Journal of Spanish Cultural Studies*, 3(2): 141–63.

Vega, Inca Garcilaso de la (1991 [1609]). *Comentarios reales de los Incas*. Ed. Carlos Aranibar. Lima: Fondo de Cultura Económica.

Wallerstein, Immanuel (1974). *The Modern World-System: Capitalist Agriculture and the Origins of the European World-Economy in the Sixteenth Century*. New York: Academic Press.

Wölfflin, Heinrich (1950 [1915]). *Principles of Art History: The Problem of the Development of Style in Later Art*. Trans. M. D. Hottinger. New York: Dover.

# 11

# Colonial Religiosity:
# Nuns, Heretics, and Witches
*Kathryn Joy McKnight*

Religiosity, or the observance of religious norms and practices, molded the ways in which all three of the major continental cultures that met in the Americas understood the natural world and human society. Religious traditions, institutions, and specialists played fundamental roles in structuring and controlling societies in Europe, Africa, and the indigenous Americas. Differing spiritual beliefs and practices lay at the heart of many of the cultural and social interactions of the colonies, including conflicts over the unequal access to power and resources imposed by colonization. Members of all these groups interacted with each other, borrowing selectively, bowing in varying degrees to colonially imposed practices, and reshaping their religiosity into richly varied phenomena that defy any neat description and categorization.

This chapter provides an entry point to colonial religiosity through three types of colonial religious subjects and their spheres of activity: nuns, heretics, and witches. Each term paradoxically defined both the center and the extremes of colonial religiosity, the limits of good and evil. These were apparently eccentric subjects, who expressed beliefs, concerns, and practices shared by large populations within colonial society. Though European meanings value the term "nun" as positive, and "heretic" and "witch" as negative, all three terms impose a single view of the world on a diverse population; the heretics and witches of colonial times would, today, be considered skeptics, freethinkers, and members of minority religions. Nuns, heretics, and witches struggled for power with representatives of the colonial state and church who defined and held them up as examples of good or evil to encourage or discourage emulation and to exercise social control. They participated in their own production as exemplars and actively resisted the constraints of church and state. Some who challenged Catholic orthodoxy acted to preserve or re-create cultural practices that predated colonization or enslavement. Others affirmed their singularity of talent, spirit, or intellect, supported themselves economically, or resisted the political and social effects of colonialism, racism, and enslavement.

Nuns, witches, and heretics allow exploration of how these apparent extremes of religious being did not inhabit marginal spheres, separate from the whole of colonial religiosity, but rather lived and practiced their beliefs in a web of relationships. Only a fine line separated the mystic from the heretic. Spanish Catholics of good standing sought out the help of Amerindian and Afro-Hispanic ritual specialists – "sorcerers" and "witches" – while other Spaniards adopted Amerindian and African religious practices and identities. Blacks, mulattos, and *mestizos* appeared in the imaginary of Spanish nuns as devils, and Brazilian and Peruvian nuns of African descent wrote down their transculturated visions.

## Nuns and other Religious Women and their Communities

Male clerics and members of religious orders arrived in the New World with the first European expeditions, but nuns awaited the foundation of convents in established colonial cities where they would serve spiritual, symbolic, and social ends. The first female convents were founded in the mid-sixteenth century: La Concepción in México around 1550 (Lavrín, 1986: 166), La Encarnación in Lima in 1561 (ibid.), and Santa Clara la Real in Tunja, Nuevo Reino de Granada, in 1572 (McKnight, 1997: 83). The majority of colonial convents, however, were not founded until the seventeenth century, including those in Brazil, where the Convento de Santa Clara do Destêrro was the first, in 1677 (Soeiro, 1974: 210).

The Mexican Creole intellectual Carlos de Sigüenza y Góngora expressed the symbolic meaning that female convents held for colonial societies when, in the dedication of his *Parayso occidental*, he described the Royal Convent of Jesus María as increasing Eden's magnificence through the divine grace, primitive virtues, and innumerable virgins inflamed with the love of Christ contained therein (n.p.). Wealthy founders and donors saw convents as providing good examples for the populace, expressing the material and spiritual wealth of a city, and offering a refuge for women who lacked the economic means to obtain an appropriate marriage, and an opportunity for the Christian education of girls (Lavrín, 1986: 168).

Nuns elevated their communities to their symbolic social role partially through passive obedience. They prayed the divine office, read the lives of saints and biographies of other exemplary Christians, confessed to and followed the guidance of their spiritual directors, fasted and mortified their flesh with hair shirts and whips, and burned with mystic love for their divine spouse. In sum, they fulfilled their vows of poverty, obedience, chastity, and enclosure as virgins dead to the world. But, as Stephanie Kirk has demonstrated, this patriarchal image of the "community of collective solitude" tells the story of the ideal, which colonial realities often disrupted, as women molded their lives into communities of choice (2007: 37, 50). Real convent communities often engaged in conflict with the male ecclesiastics charged with their control in order to determine for themselves the structure of their lives and relationships (2007: 81–126).

Real convents were microcosms of the racial diversity and social tensions of the external world (Lavrín, 1986: 175). Some enclosed hundreds of women, only a small portion of whom wore the black veil that marked the elite status and power of those who could dedicate themselves fully to spiritual activity. Others wore the white veil of the poorer, working lay nuns, or no veil at all, as was the case of servants, slaves, and children raised by their cloistered relatives. Generally, only the black-veiled nuns took the vow of enclosure (McKnight, 1997: 84), and so multitudes of non-enclosed women engaged in constant physical communication with the outside world, threatening the purity on which the nuns' spiritual symbolism depended. Black-veiled nuns, too, participated in the contentious political battles that often governed the convent's business in the world, because convents served as colonial banking institutions.

Convents also provided women a space in which to study and express their creativity and singularity in writing. Many did so, knowing that if they wrote carefully, and successfully negotiated their relationships with male clergy, a broad Catholic public might consume the verbal self-portraits they drew as filtered through the exemplary biographies their confessors wrote. Thus through an act of writing that challenged the religious ideal of feminine passivity, some nuns created a public image for themselves. In a variety of ways, nuns lived out the tension between the extreme ideal of holy femininity and the realities of a community in which women shared the daily religious struggles and secular dealings of the non-cloistered colonial society.

Nun writers caught the attention of individual historians and literary scholars both in their own lifetimes and in later centuries, though a rich and complex body of criticism has only emerged since the late 1980s. The works of the great Mexican intellectual Sor Juana Inés de la Cruz and scholarship on her female European predecessors – most importantly Santa Teresa de Jesus – first drew colonial historians and literary critics to convents as spaces of female intellectual pursuit. In 1989, Electa Arenal and Stacey Schlau's *Untold Sisters* provided a critical model for examining the writings of Hispanic nuns within a matrix of power, knowledge, body, and tongue, and a rich bibliography that nourished the blossoming field of convent scholarship. Since then historians have examined the gendered social, economic, and racial dynamics of convent communities, as well as the histories of individual convents (e.g., Burns, 1999; Lavrín, 1986; Soeiro, 1974). Throughout the 1990s, literary scholars explored the writings of individual Spanish American and Brazilian nuns, creating a body of work that Kristine Ibsen (1999) and McKnight (1997) drew on to characterize the gendered genres of spiritual autobiographical writings.

Convent critics increasingly have engaged methods of cultural studies and broadened the scope of the discourses they examine. Kathleen Ann Myers (2003), for example, has studied the production of religious women as holy, and not-so-holy, subjects within the confessional relationship between religious women and male clerics, the biographies their confessors wrote, and the institutional processes of canonization and the Inquisition. Stephanie Kirk (2007) has furthered the study of religious women's voices by showing how nuns expressed and realized communal solidarity against assaults by the upholders of the orthodox ideal of female passivity and solitude.

The colonial American characteristics of religious women's writings are not always as evident as their gendered qualities, but scholars have identified differences between the writings of Ibero-American religious women and their European sisters. Male clerics' writings that molded nuns and convents into exemplars of European spiritual conquest and Creole spiritual wealth equal to the best of European civilization may provide a more explicit and positive discourse of Americanness. New World realities frequently appeared in religious women's writing as an impediment to spiritual perfection. Nun writers often belonged to the black-veiled elite, who exercised the political power to determine how the convent's wealth would be loaned to agricultural enterprises, thus engaging in politicking that emerged in their writing as temptation and sin (see McKnight, 1997: 141–8).

The racial categories that colonizers constructed to justify their domination also infused nuns' writings as they expressed fear and exteriorized temptation in the form of the black, mulatto, Indian, and *mestizo* devils who populated their visions. In unusual instances when the writers themselves were Indian or Afro-Hispanic, they challenged the values given to blackness and Indianness by colonizers, either explicitly or implicitly, and created transculturated texts that incorporated non-European values and practices (Mott, 1993; Van Deusen, 2004; Arenal and Schlau, 1989: 355–60).

What follows is the briefest of discussions of the writings of a few representative nuns and lay religious women to illustrate how they conformed to and defied the ideal of passive obedience and how they expressed both the extreme ideal of holy femininity and the struggle with the temptations of sin, thus providing models of thought and behavior for colonial lay people.

Rosa de Lima (Peru, 1586–1617) gave the Dominicans, Lima, and the Americas their first canonized saint (Myers, 2003: 23–5). Not constrained by convent walls, the *beata* or lay Franciscan lived a life of ascetic mysticism, wrote letters and collages of mystical theology, and proved "America's parity with the Old World" (29). Inspiring subsequent American religious women with her perfection, she nonetheless passed under the Inquisition's wary gaze, and encouraged female followers who were punished as *alumbradas* (illuminists) in a 1625 auto-de-fé (27, 34).

By far the most acclaimed of intellectual nuns who succeeded Santa Rosa in the Iberian colonies was the Mexican poet, playwright, and essayist Sor Juana Inés de la Cruz (New Spain, 1648–95). A vast critical bibliography examines her life and writings, emphasizing her difference as the American nun writer who explicitly – though with the winking eye of baroque ambiguity – broke into male spheres of intellectual activity (see Paz, 1982; Merrim, 1999). If the traditional mythification of Sor Juana focuses her difference as the eccentric and the freakish, recent scholars uncover the ways in which she mastered the rules in order to transgress them (Glantz, 1995), how she wrote within a female tradition, as for example in the *Respuesta* she engaged the *querelle des femmes* (Merrim, 1999), and how – contrary to her usual portrayal as lonely victim – she also participated with pleasure in female intellectual community (Kirk, 2007: 127–75).

María de San José (New Spain, 1656–1719) and Francisca Josefa de Castillo (New Granada, 1671–1742) exemplify the more characteristic writing of American nuns, which lays out the tormented purgative path to spiritual intimacy with Christ. The first sections of María de San José's *vida* go beyond the pervasive trope of the "old child" that anticipates the protagonist's path of torment, as she develops a lengthy narrative on female life in rural New Spain. Myers detects a Creole identity in María's self-portrait, in which she expresses her failure to live up to European models because of her isolated life on the colonial hacienda, where she is in close contact with an Indian servant. Myers also finds Creole characteristics in the narration itself, which blends "colloquial and literary styles and . . . New World realities with Old World conventions" (1993: 29).

Writing a few years later in New Granada, Madre Castillo develops the common feminine religious trope of the sinful but paradoxically redemptive body. More than a personal deviance, her body expresses the sins of colonial society. While a cancer of the mouth symbolizes her engagement in convent politicking, a redemptive vision situates her body face-to-face with Christ on the cross. She interprets their shared pain as internalizing the discord between local priests and prelates (McKnight, 1997: 156–61). Like most nun writers of the period, Madre Castillo portrays the act of writing itself as a torment, since any assumption of authority by a daughter of the fallen Eve was suspect (35–8). Yet, as was usual among nun writers, Madre Castillo also finds visionary affirmation of her writing, as when she spiritualizes elements of colonial material wealth, seeing a balm of brilliant pearls and gold drip from her writing hand (43).

If relatively few European colonial women knew how to write, almost none of African and Amerindian descent did. There were, however, a few who left a written record of their view of the world. At least two enslaved women in the early colonial Americas left texts and inspired biographical writings that permit a glimpse into the strategies they used to refashion themselves against the negative images of people of African descent forged by colonial racism. Ursula de Jesús (1604–66) was born in Peru and entered the convent of Santa Clara in Lima as a *donada*, a servant who took religious vows, after working as a slave in the household of the controversial upper-class mystic Luisa de Melgarejo. In her spiritual diary, Ursula de Jesús, who developed a popular following, implicitly criticized racism by portraying herself as an intercessor for the souls of purgatory. She reinterpreted the negative symbolism of blackness more explicitly in some of her visions, as when she described a deceased slave as a good Christian and saw the blackness of her face as resplendent. Her visionary conversation with the slave confirmed that there was a place for black women in heaven (Van Deusen, 2004: 80).

The African-born Brazilian Rosa Egipciaca (ca. 1719–ca. 1765) also produced a transculturated text. In her public persona, she lived as both pious mystic and diabolical sorcerer (Mott, 1993: 85–6, 451–88). Born on the West African Mina Coast, she was enslaved and brought to Minas Gerais as a girl, and there engaged in prostitution. Repentant of her life of ill repute, she met a priest who specialized in exorcisms and who became her spiritual guide and champion. Rosa experienced both holy visions and diabolical possession, in which Luiz Roberto de Barros Mott sees African forms (66–8; 85–99; 463–6). She also founded a *recolhimento*, or home for "worldly women" (255–92). On one occasion she appeared in the choir loft on her knees, singing the liturgical hymn *Ave Maris Stella* (Hail, thou Star of Ocean), a symbol popular in the transculturated religious practices of West African Brazilians (Mott, 1993: 88). She danced in front of the altar until she fell to the floor, then arose and distributed to four lay sisters slips of paper, each containing the name of one of the four evangelists. She then charged them with writing down everything that happened in the *recolhimento*. Rosa either wrote or dictated her visions in a text she referred to as *Sagrada Teologia do Amor de Deus Luz Brilhante das Almas Peregrinas*, a few pages of which survive (247–50). Living the extremes defined by Catholic discourse as holy and diabolical, it is not surprising that in 1763, Rosa was sent to Lisbon to be prosecuted by the Portuguese Inquisition (625–721).

## Heretics: Enemies of the Faith or of the Colonial Political Project?

The line between sanctity and heresy was not always clear. Rosa de Lima, Luisa de Melgarejo, and Rosa Egipciaca were among many religious women examined by the Inquisition to ascertain whether their visions were God-sent or diabolical. Threat of such examination motivated much of the fear women expressed about the act of writing. Some religious women, nuns included, were convicted as *ilusas*, or falsely religious, but their prosecution often had to do with the colonial authorities perceiving them as a threat to the social order rather than as a threat to Christian practices alone. Lower-class, urban women were especially susceptible to the charge (Schlau, 2001: 30). Teresa Romero Zapata, arrested in New Spain in 1649, and Bárbara Echegaray, accused in 1797, both engaged in spiritual lives not dissimilar in form to those of mystic nuns. They communed with the saints through prayer, expressed passionate feelings for Christ, experienced lengthy trances, and used Christian tropes to describe their visions (27–53). If Romero charged money for her public demonstrations, these actions were not entirely different from those of cloistered nuns who prayed in exchange for their room and board. Both Romero and Echegaray, however, also engaged in sexual activities outside the sanctity of marriage. Stacey Schlau concludes that their primary crime in the eyes of the male ecclesiastical establishment, more than an attack on the faith, was their boldness as women in seeking too much subjectivity and too much power (33, 49). In prosecuting them, the Inquisition used charges of heresy to control an unruly and sexualized public female presence in colonial society.

The Spanish Inquisition set up tribunals in Lima (1570), Mexico City (1571), and Cartagena (1610). Brazil never had a tribunal of its own, though the Portuguese

Inquisition made six visits to the American colony, five of which fell within the period that Portugal spent under the rule of the Spanish crown (1580–1640). Ecclesiastical authorities in Brazil could also send suspects to Lisbon for prosecution. Over the course of its American history, the Inquisition prosecuted as heretics Jews, Muslims, Protestants, illuminists, witches, sorcerers, bigamists, blasphemers, clerics who solicited women, and people who made declarations that contradicted Catholic doctrine. Different heresies were more intensely prosecuted at different times and in different places, a fact linked to the reality that the Inquisition operated as an arm of a state that defended the supremacy of a racial and cultural minority against a vast populace of "others" it had created. Thus the Inquisition operated as much to achieve political and social ends as it did to protect the purity of the faith. The prosecutions of Jews in Brazil (1591) and New Spain (1642–9) and those of slaves in early-seventeenth-century New Spain for blasphemy are paradigmatic of this intertwining of faith and politics. They also show that what the church defined as beyond the limits of orthodoxy often represented the norm within the colonial religiosity of large communities of colonial subjects.

The prosecution of Jews in Brazil and New Spain played out the political tensions between Portugal and Spain during the period of annexation. Jews recently converted to Christianity also played a fundamental role in the sparring among Spain, Portugal, and the Netherlands to dominate Atlantic commerce. The annexation of Portugal to Spain in 1580 provoked the exile of thousands of Portuguese New Christians to Amsterdam, Portuguese Africa, and the Americas. Thus in the first visit of the Portuguese Inquisition to Brazil, a large percentage of the heretics it identified were Jews, many of them wealthy merchants whom Catholic colonials saw as competitors. One of the prosecuted émigrés was Bento Teixeira (1561–1600), the author of the encomiastic poem *Prosopopéia*, which initiated the Brazilian baroque. Lúcia Helena Costigan detects in Teixeira's poem not only crypto-Judaism, but also criticism of Felipe II's anti-Semitic exclusionary politics (2003: 38–9).

The Portuguese-Jewish link also emerged in the early seventeenth-century prosecutions by the Inquisitions of Lima, Cartagena, and Mexico. The Mexican Inquisition tried more than two hundred Jews between 1620 and 1650. In examining these trials, J. I. Israel finds that almost half of the accused were born in Portugal, and many others were thought to be of Portuguese ancestry (1975: 125). Many of those prosecuted belonged to the merchant class of the Jewish elite and, for non-Jews of Spanish origin, represented a religious, political, and economic enemy. Israel proposes that the intensity of the violent feelings expressed toward the Portuguese Jews arose from the perception of crypto-Jews as the unseen enemy who had managed to "pass" within mainstream Spanish society. The persecution culminated on April 11, 1649 in what Israel calls the "most memorable *Auto* ever to be held outside the Iberian peninsula": the Inquisitors punished 40 Jews, 13 of whom they burned at the stake (246).

In the prosecution of both Portuguese Jews and slaves of African descent, the Inquisition acted as what Irene Silverblatt calls "a significant arbiter in race thinking designs" (2004: 7). Between 1590 and 1620, the Mexican Inquisition examined over one hundred blasphemy cases involving slaves (McKnight, 1999: 229). In most cases, the enslaved men or women renounced God or the saints as a protest against physical abuse and cultural domination at the moment of being whipped as punishment for having escaped. Not coincidentally, during this same period, blacks in New Spain far outnumbered whites, and they rebelled or plotted revolts four times, drawing strength and numbers from among those who had run away from their masters (235). The Inquisition, in turn, used the public floggings and humiliation of the autos-da-fé to terrorize and inhibit further resistance from the colonial others it both needed and feared.

## Witches: Ritual Specialists and their Engagement of Natural and Supernatural Powers

The three religious types named in this chapter's title express a European colonial point of view, but of the three, it is the word "witch" and its related terms that most profoundly hide the cultural realities to which they claim to refer. To Europeans, witchcraft implied a relationship with the devil and often named the antagonism between Catholic colonizers and those Amerindians and Africans who practiced non-Catholic religions. Colonizers did not apply these terms in an entirely arbitrary fashion, as Spaniards brought with them the pagan–Catholic practices of European witchcraft, and soon specialists of all social groups engaged with each other, producing complexly transculturated phenomena. Authorities applied the terms of European witchcraft to practices that brought Europeans, Amerindians, and Africans together, and bore similarities to practices the Inquisition had prosecuted in Europe. Modern scholars are complicit in the colonizers' act of "othering" when we adopt the terms "witch" and "witchcraft" uncritically. We often further homogenize the phenomena in question when we fail to recognize the broader range of actors among which the Inquisitors did distinguish: *bruja/o, hechicera/o, yerbatera/o, herbolaria/o, and curandera/o* (Ceballos Gómez, 1994: 87). These terms might be translated – albeit problematically – as witch, sorceress, herbal-healer, herbalist, and healer.

Religious specialists in Amerindian and African cultures saw their rituals as a way of understanding and controlling the surrounding world, and of communicating with the supernatural in order to diagnose and heal individual and social ills. In many African practices, specialists communicated with the spirits through possession of the individual or of a fetish by a natural or ancestral spirit. With this communication, the specialists could restore harmony to the community, heal the individual, or harm others by controlling their will. Their practices and the belief systems on which they were based did not share with Christianity a dualist concept of good and evil that opposed God and the Devil as archenemies, but rather saw forces of both good and evil working in and through their various gods and ritual practices. This difference led many non-Spaniards to understand the Spanish devil as a potential ally (Lewis, 2003: 133), rather than as a wholly malevolent and principal enemy of a singular God.

If Thomist theology led Spaniards such as Bartolomé de las Casas to read Amerindian religion as a step toward the knowledge of God, Nominalists saw devil worship in indigenous religions and those of African slaves (Cervantes, 1994), and thus they carried out extirpation campaigns against Amerindians and prosecuted *mestizo*, mulatto, and black "witches" and "sorcerers." Conversely, some scholars argue that Africans first came to understand the European concept of witchcraft as purely evil through the experience of the slave trade, believing that slavers must have used powerful witchcraft against them. They feared that Europeans baptized them in preparation to eat them, and made oil, wine, gunpowder, and cheese from their bodies (Sweet, 2003: 197, 162–3).

Spaniards used all the institutional and social resources in their power to combat pagan religions and evangelize Amerindians and Africans. Nevertheless, these groups sustained their beliefs and practices, creatively restored them, or transformed them through transculturation, and often saw these practices as vital means to survive the hardships of domination (Sweet 2003: 187). Africans, for example, brought to Brazil from the Guinea and Mina coasts *bolsas mandingas*, a type of amulet that invoked supernatural protection for the wearer (179). Brazilian slaves used African potions to defend themselves from physical abuse, and even to poison their masters (165). A female spiritual-military leader of a Central–West African and Creole-dominated maroon community in Cartagena de Indias fortified her community's leaders and their resolve against Spanish military attacks through ritual violence infused with Angolan symbolic meanings (McKnight, 2004).

Colonial authorities drew a sharp distinction between *hechiceros/feticeiros* and *brujos*, seeing the former as practicing a less threatening sorcery, with a more individualized impact, while they imagined *brujos* as witches engaged in collective devil worship, and used the term to stigmatize entire groups. An even less threatening category was that of *curanderos* or traditional healers, who often escaped colonial persecution. But at certain historical moments, Spaniards manifested their fear of the collective religious activities of their cultural and colonized others in witch crazes, often converting into witchcraft practices they saw at other times as sorcery. Cartagena de Indias, for example, experienced several witch crazes at the end of the sixteenth and the beginning of the seventeenth centuries, likely motivated by the rapid numerical growth of African-descent populations and by the multiplication of *palenques*, clandestine communities of escaped slaves.

A typical case is that of Guiomar *negra*, an herbalist from the black community in Getsemanía on the outskirts of Cartagena. The Inquisition trial transformed her from *yerbatera* into *bruja* as witnesses drew on images from the archetypal European witches' coven to interpret her herbal healing as devil worship, attributing to her and other herbalists acts of infanticide and African practices of transformation into animal forms (Ceballos-Gómez, 1994: 131–51). If this nightmarish European imagery so divorced from the practices of an herbalist stigmatized the behavior of a group that threatened colonial order, the marginalized and mostly enslaved community of African descent learned to use these same images to foment fear among the slave owners and thus they, too, exercised a measure of oppositional power.

The witch scare in Peru in the late 1620s responded to the cultural unruliness of colonialism in which not only did the colonized persist in their unorthodox religious practices, but members of the colonizer race and culture adopted these practices as their own. In fact, what the Inquisition saw as sorcery, witchcraft, and pacts with the devil comprised an area of lively cultural interaction and transculturation between the magical practices that Spaniards and Portuguese brought to the New World, the religious practices of enslaved Africans and those of colonized Amerindians. In Cartagena, African and Amerindian medicine attracted a white clientele as it proved more effective than European, humor-based medicine (Ceballos Gómez, 1994: 77), while in Peru in the early 1600s, Indian lore was "considered the most dangerous and the most deadly of all" (Silverblatt, 2004: 173). By the mid-seventeenth century, non-Indian women in Peru were adopting coca as the central element in their group rituals, and sang songs in which not only Catholic saints, but also Inca nobility appeared (174). Some non-Indian practitioners believed that it was precisely the never-baptized Inca's pagan status that imbued the invocation with power (177).

In the Iberian colonies, the indigenous and African religious beliefs and practices that the colonizers treated as sorcery and witchcraft became both a potent phenomenon of coloniality and a powerful means of resistance. Authorities used discourses of witchcraft to condemn, ostracize, and strike fear into colonized and enslaved groups through exemplary punishment in the Inquisition. As both Irene Silverblatt and Laura A. Lewis persuasively demonstrate, official discourses on the practices of witches and sorcerers played key roles in the construction and deployment of racial categories that reinforced colonial domination. At the same time, the deployment of indigenous and African supernatural powers and their transculturated practices "helped free people from their sanctioned places in the colonial social hierarchy while bringing others under their control" (Lewis, 2003: 109). Lewis sees witchcraft and sorcery as an exercise of unsanctioned power by marginalized groups that mirrors and opposes the sanctioned power exercised by Spaniards (107).

While Sigüenza y Góngora and priest biographers held up the lives of nuns and convents as models to emulate, other intellectuals wove sorcery and witchcraft into their analysis of colonial social ills. Arzáns de Ursúa y Vela's early eighteenth-century concerns exemplify those of the Inquisition when he condemns the adoption of Indian religious practices by Spanish women:

> Great good would follow were [coca] to be extirpated from this realm: the devil would be bereft of the great harvest of souls he reaps . . . Let us choose one among innumerable examples, that of a woman who by taking this infernal herb caused all manner of evil in this city . . .
> This woman was born in one of the cities of Tucumán. Her parents were Spaniards, her name was Doña Claudia, and her aspect was pleasing both in face and body. So great a witch was she in this realm of Peru that Erinto, Circe, and Medea were not her equal.

Among the Indians, pagans as well as believers, in a number of Indian villages where she went in Tucumán, Tarija, and Chichas she froze the clouds whenever she wished, covering the face of the sun with them, and on other occasions she made the most stormy sky serene; she brought men from faraway lands and formed beautiful gardens with beautiful women in them, with which she drove men mad by making them love those visions. (trans. Frances M. López-Morillas, 1975: 120)

This adoption of powerful Indian witchcraft by Spanish colonials deeply worried officials and elites of European descent. Women like Claudia manifested the disturbing reality of colonial society: that people of all origins, races, and cultures engaged in a daily exchange of beliefs and practices that dangerously exceeded the limits of acceptable religiosity.

## Connections and Conclusions

Nuns, heretics, and witches populated the pages of colonial literature, as they did the imaginations of Spanish and Creole colonizers. Colonial clerics and governors, religious women of all races and classes, Jews, enslaved people, and members of indigenous and African-descent religious communities thought and dreamed about each other, wrote themselves and each other into their own stories, confronted each other, and took on aspects of each others' religiosities. Little physical distance separated them, and historical circumstance, racial identity, economic conflicts, or political connections often mattered as much as Catholic doctrine in attempts to maintain divisions that the church called religious. Colonial religiosity cannot be separated from any other aspect of colonial life. As Irene Silverblatt states, "Much more than a set of beliefs, religion was a worldview, a model for living in the world – reinforced in daily practice that both specified the boundaries of community and one's place within it" (2004: 21).

References and Further Reading

Arenal, E., and Schlau, S. (1989). *Untold Sisters: Hispanic Nuns in Their Own Works*. Trans. Amanda Powell. Albuquerque: University of New Mexico Press. (A seminal bilingual anthology of Spanish and Spanish-American nuns, with extensive critical introductions.)

Arzáns de Orsúa y Vela, B. (1975 [1705–36]). *Tales of Potosí*. Ed. R. C. Padden, trans. F. M. López-Morillas. Providence, RI: Brown University Press. (Eighteenth-century chronicles from the richest colonial silver-mining center in the Spanish colonies.)

Burns, K. (1999). *Colonial Habits: Convents and the Spiritual Economy of Cuzco, Peru*. Durham, NC: Duke University Press. (An analysis of cuzqueña nuns' central role in producing colonial social order, including racial, economic, and spiritual interests.)

Ceballos Gómez, D. L. (1994). *Hechicería, brujería e Inquisición en el Nuevo Reino de Granada: Un duelo de imaginarios* [Sorcery, witchcraft and Inquisition in the New Kingdom of Granada: a duel of imaginaries]. Medellín: Universidad Nacional. (A detailed examination of the

Inquisition's prosecution of sorcery and witch-craft in colonial New Granada [Colombia] as a means of social and ideological control.)

Cervantes, F. (1994). *The Devil in the New World: The Impact of Diabolism in New Spain.* New Haven, CT and London: Yale University Press. (A seminal study of the interwoven elite and popular conceptions of the devil among the diverse racial groups of New Spain.)

Costigan, L. H. (2003). "Empreendimento e resisência do cristão-novo face à política de Filipe II: O processo inquisitorial de Bento Teixeira" [The New Christian's enterprise and resistance in the face of Philip II's politics: the Inquisition trial of Bento Teixeira], *Colonial Latin American Review*, 12(1): 37–61. (An analysis of Jewish themes and resistance to Spanish antisemitism in Bento Teixeira's baroque epic *Prosopopéia*.)

Glantz, M. (1995). *Sor Juana Inés de la Cruz: ¿Hagiografía o autobiografía?* [Sor Juana Inés de la Cruz: hagiography or autobiography?] Mexico City: Grijalbo and Universidad Nacional Autónoma de México. (An examination of the relationship between Sor Juana's life and writings, her understanding and transgression of colonial social norms by a prominent sorjuanista.)

Ibsen, K. (1999). *Women's Spiritual Autobiography in Colonial Spanish America*. Gainesville: University Press of Florida. (A comprehensive study of and bibliographical resources on the genre of spiritual autobiography in colonial Spanish America.)

Israel, J. I. (1975). *Race, Class and Politics in Colonial Mexico, 1610–1670*. Oxford: Oxford University Press. (A classic historical study of the politics of race in seventeenth-century New Spain.)

Kirk, S. L. (2007). *Convent Life in Colonial Mexico: A Tale of Two Communities*. Gainesville: University Press of Florida. (A complex argument, based on original archival research, demonstrating female solidarity in New Spanish convents.)

Lavrín, A. (1986). "Female religious." In L. S. Hoberman and S. M. Socolow (eds), *Cities and Society in Colonial Latin America*, pp. 165–95. Albuquerque: University of New Mexico Press. (An overview of social, economic, and cultural aspects of female convent life.)

Lewis, L. (2003). *Hall of Mirrors: Power, Witchcraft, and Caste in Colonial Mexico*. Durham, NC: Duke University Press. (An ethnohistorical approach to witchcraft and its prosecution by the Inquisition as producing the colonial meanings and relationships of caste.)

McKnight, K. J. (1999). "Blasphemy as resistance: an Afro-Mexican slave woman before the Mexican Inquisition." In Mary Giles (ed.), *Women in the Inquisition: Spain and the New World*, pp. 229–53. Baltimore, MD: Johns Hopkins University Press. (A reading of cultural meanings and strategies of resistance in the Inquisition testimony of female African-born slave in 1609.)

— (1997). *The Mystic of Tunja: The Writings of Madre Castillo, 1671–1742*. Amherst: University of Massachusetts Press. (An interdisciplinary examination of spiritual autobiographical writings as a conflicted expression of the realities of female colonial life.)

— (2004). "Confronted rituals: Spanish colonial and Angolan 'maroon' executions in Cartagena de Indias (1634)," *Journal of Colonialism and Colonial History*, 5(3). (An analysis of symbolic violence between Spanish officials and clandestine community of escaped slaves, based on archival testimonies.)

Merrim, S. (1999). *Early Modern Women's Writing and Sor Juana Inés de la Cruz*. Nashville, TN: Vanderbilt University Press. (A cross-cultural study of seventeenth-century female literary production in New Spain, England, and France, by a prominent sorjuanista.)

Mott, L. R. de B. (1993). *Rosa Egipcíaca: Uma santa africana no Brasil* [Rosa Egipciaca: an African saint in Brazil]. Rio de Janeiro: Bertrand. (A study of the life and writings of the first and most well-known Afro-Brazilian female writer.)

Myers, K. A. (1993). *Word from New Spain: The Spiritual Autobiography of Madre María de San José (1656–1719)*. Liverpool: Liverpool University Press. (A critical edition of a prolific Creole nun writer, with an extensive scholarly introduction.)

— (2003). *Neither Saints Nor Sinners: Writing the Lives of Women in Spanish America*. Oxford: Oxford University Press. (A cultural studies approach to the production of women's lives through autobiography, biography, and institutional politics.)

Paz, O. (1988 [1982]). *Sor Juana or the Traps of Faith*. Trans. M. S. Peden. Cambridge, MA: Belknap Press. (An exhaustive intellectual biography of Mexico's foremost colonial writer, by a preeminent Mexican intellectual.)

Schlau, S. (2001). *Spanish American Women's Use of the Word: Colonial through Contemporary Narratives*. Tucson: University of Arizona Press. (An argument focusing on the political and social aspects of women's participation in creating Spanish America's literary legacy.)

Sigüenza y Góngora, C. de (1995 [1684]). *Parayso occidental* [Western paradise]. Mexico City: Facultad de Filosofía y Letras, UNAM, Centro de Estudios de Historia de México Condumex. ( A Creole baroque history of the founding of one of New Spain's first female convents.)

Silverblatt, I. (2004). *Modern Inquisitions: Peru and the Colonial Origins of the Civilized World*. Durham, NC: Duke University Press. (An argument based on archival research regarding the Peruvian Inquisition as a modern bureaucratic instrument of state creation.)

Soeiro, S. A. (1974). "The social and economic role of the convent: women and nuns in colonial Bahia, 1677–1800," *Hispanic American Historical Review*, 54(2): 209–32. (A brief and useful overview of the topic.)

Sweet, J. H. (2003). *Recreating Africa: Culture, Kinships, and Religion in the African-Portuguese World, 1441–1770*. Chapel Hill: University of North Carolina Press. (A history of the cultural lives of African slaves in Portugal and Brazil.)

Van Deusen, N. E., ed. (2004). *The Souls of Purgatory: The Spiritual Diary of a Seventeenth-Century Afro-Peruvian Mystic, Ursula de Jesús*. Albuquerque: University of New Mexico Press. (A critical edition and extensive introduction to a unique and important text, including full translation and excerpts from the Spanish original.)

# PART II
# Transformations

# 12

# The Tupac Amaru Rebellion: Anticolonialism and Protonationalism in Late Colonial Peru

*Peter Elmore*

The Tupac Amaru II rebellion of 1780–2 was the most serious challenge to Spanish colonialism in the Andes since the Conquistadors had captured and killed the Inca emperor, Atahualpa, in 1533, thus paving the way to both the destruction of the Inca state and the establishment of European rule over the indigenous population of Peru. The very foundations of the viceroyalties of Peru and Rio de la Plata were shaken by a social, cultural, and political upheaval so powerful and widespread that, at more than one juncture, victory appeared to be within the grasp of the rebels. An official report issued shortly after the end of the rebellion quoted a death toll of 100,000 Indians and 10,000 Spaniards, a startlingly high – and perhaps somewhat exaggerated – figure for a territory whose entire population was 1,800,000. The Great Rebellion – which encompassed several movements, the largest and most powerful being the one led by Tupac Amaru – dramatically exposed and deepened the ethnic, social, and political fault lines cleaving Colonial Peru and Upper Peru.[1] It also brought to the forefront a complex array of visions and agendas ranging from the reform-minded to the radically separatist.

José Gabriel Condorcanqui Thupa Amaro, as he was known long before he took up arms and led a massive anticolonial uprising, was an influential *curaca* and wealthy muleteer who proudly traced his lineage back to Tupac Amaru I, the ruler of the neo-Inca state of Vilcabamba, whose execution in 1572 marked the end of open resistance to the foreign invasion and conquest of the Andes.[2] The relatives of the defeated Inca had not faded into obscurity, for the Spanish crown recognized them as bona fide members of a small but prestigious group in Peruvian colonial society – the Indian nobility. Often, descendants of the Inca royal family joined the colonial state apparatus as *curacas*, or local chieftains, who in exchange for tax exemptions and other privileges acted as intermediaries between Spanish authorities and tribute-paying Indian communities.[3] Doubtless the most renowned of the *curacas* – or *caciques*, as they were also called – in late eighteenth-century Peru was Tupac Amaru, who in 1776 inherited the office of cacique of three peasant communities – Tungasuca, Pampamarca, and Surimana, all in the Cuzco province of Tinta or Canas-Canchis. A few years later, large numbers of Quechua- and Aymara-speaking peasants in the Peruvian southern Andes and Upper Peru – the latter having been incorporated in 1776 to the newly created viceroyalty of Rio de la Plata – rose up against colonial institutions and regarded Tupac Amaru II as a messianic restorer of indigenous rule. Tupac Amaru II himself espoused an elite version of such a restoration – one that envisioned a multiethnic state ruled by an Inca emperor – even though he initially portrayed himself as a reformer and loyal subject of Charles III, the Spanish king. Rather paradoxically, Tupac Amaru II claimed to be carrying out orders given by the Spanish king when he ignited the general revolt of the 1780s by having the *corregidor* Antonio de Arriaga executed in the main square of Tungasuca.

The year 1780 was marked by unrest and open rebellion in the South American dominions of the Spanish crown. Tupac Amaru II and his followers were certainly not alone as they took on the colonial status quo. Furthermore, the 1700s – particularly during the second half of the century – were punctuated by numerous outbreaks of violent protest against corrupt local officials and their exactions. Peruvian scholar Scarlett O'Phelan documented 26 local uprisings for the period 1730–60 in what is now Peru, and similar actions took place in modern Bolivia, Ecuador, northern Argentina, and northern Chile.[4] Moreover, an increasingly contentious climate pervaded the two decades prior to the Tupac Amaru rebellion, as evinced by a more than threefold increase in the number of peasant revolts (Golte, 1980: 140). Certainly, Arriaga was neither the first nor the only Spanish official in Cuzco to draw the wrath of the people within his jurisdiction – as a matter of fact, there were nine attempts on the life of provincial governors – or *corregidores* – in the 1770s (Flores Galindo, 1980: 129).

Clear signs of unrest among a wide spectrum of the colonial population, rural and urban alike, were disturbingly evident for the Spanish authorities in the months preceding the great rebellion. José Antonio de Areche, the *visitador-general* whom King Charles III had appointed in 1776, entertained no illusions as to the gravity of the situation. In a letter addressed to a close friend in Mexico, he wrote:

> The lack of righteous judges, the mita of the Indians, and provincial commerce had made a corpse of this America. Corregidores are interested only in themselves . . . How near everything is to ruin, if these terrible abuses are not corrected, for they have been going on a long time. The Indians are very near their tragic end unless a remedy is taken. (quoted by Fisher, 1966: 20)

Ironically, Areche was soon to be directly involved in a merciless military campaign against the rebels. Actually, on May 18, 1781, he would personally supervise and stage the gruesome execution of Tupac Amaru II and members of his family. Humanitarian protestations aside, Areche's original mission was to significantly increase the tax yield for the Spanish crown by streamlining the tax-collection system, expanding the number of tribute-payers, setting up new customs houses, and raising rates on such taxes as the *alcabala* (sales tax). On January 14, 1780, the urban poor of Arequipa, an important city on the south Andean trade route, rioted and destroyed the recently built customs house. In March, Indians and *mestizos* – people of mixed blood – rioted in La Paz, angry over taxes imposed on muleteers and traders (O'Phelan Godoy, 1985: 170). Even in the city of Cuzco, which during the Great Rebellion proved to be a royalist stronghold, a conspiracy plotted mostly by Creoles and *mestizos* – the majority of them being silversmiths and landowners – was defused after a priest betrayed a secret entrusted him in the confessional by one of the rebels. As the tax net was cast considerably wider, swelling numbers of people from different class and ethnic backgrounds found themselves among the catch. Since grievances afforded a common ground, the prospect of a multiethnic alliance against the perceived injustices of the colonial system did not look unfeasible by the end of the 1770s. Tupac Amaru II, who mourned the fate of the silversmith plotters, bemoaned the fact that Indians in the city of Cuzco and neighboring communities had not come to the aid of the rebels (Stavig, 1999: 225).

Stringent and unwelcome as they were, the tax reforms implemented by Areche were not the only trigger for the Great Rebellion of 1780–2. Areche's measures had basically the effect of both heightening preexisting tensions and increasing long-standing burdens. The *reparto* system – a form of compulsory distribution of goods to tributaries by *corregidores* – and the *mita* – a labor draft system Viceroy Toledo adapted in the 1570s from an institution predating the Conquest – were actually the principal means of extracting wealth and labor from the Indian population. The sweat and toil of indigenous workers kept the mines, landed estates, and textiles workshops – called *obrajes* – running. Rather than invest in capital goods, Creole and Spanish landowners, miners, and textile manufacturers relied on chronically indebted Indian workers (Golte, 1980: 15). The highest official in each province was the *corregidor*, who was in charge of collecting tribute for the Crown, administering justice, enforcing the *mita*, carrying out the *reparto*, and allocating labor. The *corregimiento* had been established in the 1560s to rein in the *encomenderos*, who as beneficiaries of huge land grants, posed the risk of developing into a feudal class at odds with the Crown. Since *corregidores* purchased their five-year appointments from the Crown for substantial sums of money, sources of income other than salaries were of the essence. Legalized by the Spanish crown in 1756, the *reparto* had been one such source since at least the late seventeenth century, when officials eager to cash in on their tenures started to compulsorily sell imports and locally manufactured goods to the Indians living within their jurisdictions. Not coincidentally, the arc of discontent that reached its apex in 1780 began in the 1760s, shortly after the *reparto* received legal sanction and joined the tribute as yet another obligation Indians were forced to meet. Although Indians bore the brunt of the system, individuals from other colonial castes and strata also felt its impact. For instance, *mestizo* muleteers had no other way of buying mules than through the virtual monopoly imposed by *corregidores*, and the enforced sale of such imported goods as Spanish cloth – which, though called *ropa de Castilla*, mostly came from Catalonia – did not spare Creoles (O'Phelan Godoy, 1985: 107).

Being charged with the collection of both *reparto* debts and tributes for the Crown, it is not surprising that *corregidores* proved to be far more successful in collecting the former, thus arousing the suspicion of the Royal Exchequer. Indeed, in just over a quarter of a century the yield of the *reparto* dwarfed the combined output of indigenous tributes and the mining *mita*. As Jürgen Golte put it:

> The volume of repartimientos tripled from 1754 till 1780, increasing from 1,224,108 pesos to 3,672,324 pesos. The latter figure roughly amounts to wages for 14,689,296 workdays. Within the same time period, Indian tributes equaled 4,619,160 workdays, and *mita* work in the mines of Potosí and Huancavelica amounted to 611,904 workdays. (1980: 16)

The transition from a Hapsburg to a Bourbon dynasty in Spain was belatedly felt in the Americas, as it was during the reign of the third Bourbon king – Charles III – that major reforms were undertaken in the Indies. From the vantage point of Madrid, the revenue stream from the colonies was not flowing adequately to the metropolis – the *repartimiento* being a major diversion of resources due to the Crown. It was certainly a perception borne out by political and economic realities. In the overhauled colonial administration envisioned by the Bourbon reformers, the office of the *corregidor* would be scrapped and replaced by French-style intendants who, being dependent on salaries as their only source of income, would focus on raising revenue for the Crown. Being a prominent Bourbon reformer, *visitador general* José de Areche regarded *corregidores* as both a hindrance and a liability – even though he acted as the chief enforcer of the status quo during the rebellion. Ironically, the abolition of the *corregimiento* and the *reparto* did feature prominently, albeit for sharply different reasons, both among the demands of the rebels and in the agenda of the Bourbon administrative elite. Having come under attack from opposite quarters, the days of the *reparto* were numbered – and, in fact, Viceroy Jáuregui decreed it out of existence in December 1780, when the Tupac Amaru II Rebellion was still in its early stages.

An inventory of *reparto* items is bound to invite disbelief, particularly as one takes the targeted consumers' needs and habits into consideration. With utter disregard for their traditions and requirements, Indian peasants were sometimes forced to buy such unlikely products as razors, silk stockings, and mirrors. On occasion, books were also among the articles for distribution: "Shortly before the Indian revolt, Baltazar de Arandia, corregidor of Chicas, found in the storehouse of his predecessor, Francisco García de Prado, some surprising items for sale to people supposed to be illiterate. Among them were eleven volumes of *The Christian Year*, six books of the Dominicans, two of *Spiritual Discoveries*, and two of the *Economic Dictionary*" (Fisher, 1966: 12). The most common and profitable *reparto* items, however, were mules, cloth – be it locally manufactured or imported from Spain – coca leaves, iron, and tools (Golte, 1980: 100). Given the compulsory nature of the system, *corregidores* were prone to abuse their prerogatives – shoddy quality of the products was the norm, as was price-gouging:

*Reparto* prices were, nonetheless, often double or triple the market. For instance, Castilian cloth that had a market price of five pesos had a list (*arancel*) price of seven pesos four reals and a *reparto* price of sixteen pesos. A basket of coca went respectively – market, list, *reparto* – for four pesos, eight pesos four reals, and twelve pesos, while mules had a market price of eleven pesos and a list and *reparto* price of thirty five pesos. (Stavig 1999: 216)

Thus, market prices served as a reliable standard whereby exactions committed by local officials could be gauged – hence, proximity to fairs and involvement in trade were circumstances likely to highlight both the *reparto*'s fundamentally unfair nature and the local *corregidor*'s cupidity. Significantly, the epicenter of the Tupac Amaru rebellion was Canas-Canchis and Quispicanchis, provinces strategically situated on a major trade route connecting Cuzco to Potosí. The changing fortunes of the local *corregidor*, Antonio de Arriaga, tell a tale of lost legitimacy and squandered authority – blatant corruption undermined the *corregidor* to such a degree that a once feared enforcer of colonial laws wound up being put to death as a common criminal.

Both tributes and *reparto* debt had the intended effect of forcing Indian peasants out of a self-subsistence economy and into a private sector largely run by Spaniards and Creoles. By the mid-eighteenth century, as the mining sector started to climb out of a steady decline and a new cycle of expansion began, there was a renewed demand for Indian labor (O'Phelan Godoy, 1985: 99). Although colonial Peru was overwhelmingly rural and most of its inhabitants tilled the land, mining was by far the most profitable activity and, as such, it was the engine that drove interregional markets and transatlantic trade. The *reparto* proved to be more efficient in ensuring a constant labor supply than the *mita,* which since 1720 was no longer an obligation all Indian communities had to meet. Among all of the provinces of Cuzco, only two were singled out as purveyors of *mita* workers – the aforementioned Canas-Canchis and Quispicanchis. The *mitayos* from these provinces trekked three months each way to reach their destination, the silver mines of Potosí. Indians who lived in upper Peru had to cover shorter distances, but working conditions were equally harsh and dangerous for them.[5]

*Mita* service was demanded exclusively from Indians who lived and worked in their natal communities. Access to land and recognition of one's status as a member of a community were fully dependent on complying with labor drafts – which, indeed, meant that one's livelihood and cultural identity were at stake. And yet, forced labor in the mines was so harrowing that a sizable number of Indians fled their communities, relinquishing their status as *originarios*. Having left their ancestral homes, they became landless workers who survived by either toiling in Spanish society or renting land in indigenous communities other than their own – *forastero*, meaning "outsider," was the term used in colonial society to describe this segment of the Indian population. Not all *forasteros* fared worse than *originarios* – artisans and other skilled workers having more of a chance to make a living and even prosper – but it is undeniable that most *forasteros* stood on the lower rungs of colonial society. In 1754, a census commissioned by Viceroy Superunda showed that 40 percent of Indian adult males were *forasteros,* and similar results were reported in a census carried out twenty years later. In La Paz and Chuquisaca, which were among the main areas engulfed by the rebellion, as many as 60 percent of adult Indians were *forasteros* (Cornblitt, 1976: 156) Although attempts made in the 1750s to impose *mita service* upon them had met with strong resistance and proved short-lived, *forasteros* were not entirely free from tribute obligations – since the 1720s, they had been forced to pay tribute, usually at half the rate of *originarios* (Stavig, 1999: 144). *Forastero* Indians were not necessarily an itinerant, transient population – in fact, there is evidence that many of them relocated as close to their natal communities as they could. Nevertheless, the very fact of migration either loosened or altogether severed the bonds formerly tying them to their *curacas.* Interestingly, *forasteros* flocked to the Tupac Amaru II camp when the rebellion broke out in November 1780. Uprisings caught on like wildfire in areas with large concentrations of landless Indians, such as upper Peru and the region around Lake Titicaca, while loyalist forces managed to douse the fires of rebellion easily in regions lacking a substantial *forastero* population (Cornblitt, 1976: 177). The prospect of Inca restoration under the charismatic leadership of Thupa Amaro greatly appealed to them, since it held out a promise of social and cultural redemption. As Cornblitt intimates, supporting Tupac Amaru II "meant for *forasteros* inclusion in a movement endowed with great power" (1976: 176).

The *mita* was also known as the *séptima* – on account of a regulation limiting the quota a community had to meet in a given year to one-seventh of able-bodied Indian males. Being responsible for community tribute, *curacas* were the ones charged with sending tributaries to the Potosí *mita* José Gabriel Condorcanqui Thupa Amaru was loath to perform such a task, which ran counter to his deeply held conviction that all forms of forced Indian labor should be abolished. In 1777, while in Lima, he actively sought exemption from the *mita* for his constituents and for other communities in his home province. The mission, although unsuccessful, did much to enhance the *curaca's* authority and prestige in the eyes of the Indians (Szeminski,1993: 243).

The execution of *corregidor* Antonio de Arriaga must be set against the backdrop of broad and mounting opposition to both the Bourbon tax reforms and such institutions as the *repartimiento* and *mita.* The Tupac Amaru rebellion, however, differs significantly on several counts from the numerous local revolts that erupted throughout the Andes from the 1750s and gained in both intensity and frequency after 1776. Local revolts were spontaneous, unplanned affairs that sometimes took place during holidays, when alcohol consumption was high – Indian tribute and other taxes being customarily collected on St. John's Day, June 24, December 25, and on festivities honoring patron saints. A combination of relaxed norms and unpleasant deadlines could prove explosive, to the chagrin of many a functionary. The solemn execution of Arriaga stands in stark contrast to such outbursts. Indeed, the event that ushered in the rebellion more than hints at the kind of ethnic and class coalition Tupac Amaru II hoped to forge, while also highlighting his charisma and leadership style:

Having determined that corregidor Antonio de Arriaga should be hanged, José Gabriel Thupa Amaro called on Antonio López de Sosa, a trusted old friend and the *criollo* priest of Pampamarca, to inform the corregidor of his fate. Handing Arriaga a picture of Christ, the priest conveyed the sentence of death. On 10 November 1780, Arriaga, dressed in a penitential habit, was led to the gallows in Tungasuca. The corregidor asked Thupa Amaro's pardon for once having called him "a fraudulent Indian". Then Antonio Oblitas, a shoemaker and former slave of the corregidor who had been selected to be the executioner, carried out the Inca's order and hanged Arriaga. (Stavig, 1999: 207)

Thus, the execution can be construed as a spectacle of retribution and reparation featuring, at opposing ends, a disgraced Spanish official and an exalted Indian leader. A Creole priest and a mulatto artisan played secondary yet active roles in the proceedings. Three rows of armed men surrounded the plaza, cordoning off the stage where a drama of great political and cultural significance played out before the eyes of a predominantly Indian audience. Tupac Amaru II's sense of stagecraft had been honed by a passion for the theater – his favorite play, *Ollantay*, was often shown in Tungasuca – and it proved to be a most valuable skill as he embarked on recruiting a large rebel army made up of mostly illiterate Quechua-speaking Indians.[6] Significantly, the rebellion he led drew extensively on iconography, dance, dress, and ritual (Castro-Klaren, 2003: 164). Spectacle, rather than written text, was the medium most favored by the rebel leader. Immediately after Arriaga's execution, Tupac Amaru II addressed the hushed crowd in Quechua. His bearing and attire were pointedly regal, as befitted an act he regarded as both legal and legitimate: "Mounted on a fiery charger and dressed in the princely costume of his ancestors, he carried a banner bearing his coat of arms" (Fisher, 1966: 50). In what was the opening salvo of the insurgency, Tupac Amaru II was careful to portray himself as a legitimate ruler – indeed, his stated goal was not breaking the law, but restoring order. It might seem as if the Inca leader advocated reforms within a colonial polity he did not mean to overthrow, a view apparently borne out by many of the edicts and proclamations Tupac Amaru wrote in Spanish. In fact, they are more than merely deferential to the Spanish king, who is even credited with having ordered the execution of *corregidores* and the abolition of the *reparto* (O'Phelan Godoy, 1985: 239). John Fisher is one noted scholar who regards Tupac Amaru's intent as being that of a reformer who did not envision an independent, postcolonial state: "Seen in the light of 1780, the rebellion gives credence to the view that it was a failed attempt to ensure legal redress of past injustices, followed by a sudden, violent social explosion. Independence from Spain was not a conscious goal" (1976: 118). And yet, it is worth restating the obvious – José Gabriel Condorcanqui Thopa Amaro entered the stage of Andean history as Tupac Amaru II. Thus, an Inca – a member of a proud but subordinate elite – played the role of the Inca. Two centuries after its demise, the Inca state was not thought of as an erstwhile ethnic kingdom which, in the mid-fifteenth century, under the rule of Pachacutec Inca, had begun to expand from Cuzco through military and political means until it became a major empire ruling over myriad Andean ethnic groups. After the European conquest, the former rulers and the peoples over whom they ruled were lumped together as members of one and the same caste. Under colonial law, two separate collective bodies coexisted in society – the "Republic of Spaniards" and the "Republic of Indians." Ethnic allegiances and identities were rich and varied among Indians, but as direct experience of Inca imperial policies receded into the past it became increasingly common to equate the Inca with a sovereign, autonomous Andean order. In the 1560s, the nativist *Taqui Onqoy* movement aimed to expel the Spaniards but it did not advocate a return to Inca rule – the Inca having bloodily conquered less than a century earlier the region where the movement broke out.[7] What the *Taqui Onqoy* leaders seem to have envisioned was a Pan-Andean alliance of native peoples, each of them represented by their local *huacas*, or sacred sites. Two great ceremonial centers – Titicaca, in the Aymara high plateau, and Pachacamac, near Lima, on the coast – were to symbolize unity and guarantee parity among all Indian groups. The movement aborted, even though the support it garnered was not negligible: Spaniards detected 8,000 *Taqui Onqoy* devotees in the Huamanga area, located in the south central Andes (Flores Galindo, 1980: 51). Inca restoration and Indian revival would become almost interchangeable – or rather, the former will be encoded as the signifier of the latter – only after the neo-Inca state of Vilcabamba ceased to exist and its last ruler, Tupac Amaru I, met his tragic end in the imperial city of Cuzco. The millenarian belief of Inkarri – the term itself a conflation of Inca and *rey*, Spanish for king – later recast historical events in the idiom of myth, turning a defeat into a story of death and resurrection: the Inca would return, bringing order and justice to a world the Spaniards had turned upside down. Millenarian ideas brought by Spanish priests in early colonial times welded with the native notion of *Pachacuti* – a social and natural cataclysm ushering a new era. Belief in the Inkarri myth was widespread in the late colonial period, though it would be wrong to assume all Indians shared it. Furthermore, the existence of the Inkarri myth did not suffice to turn believers into rebels, though it helped to spur them into action (Campbell, 1987: 113).

Seen in this light, a messianic aura emanates from Tupac Amaru II's avowed goal of restoring order to the land. Cultural redemption lay at the very core of the rebellion – the leader's appeal to their followers stemming in considerable part from his charismatic persona and the heritage he claimed. Nevertheless, the rebel's platform articulated economic and social demands previously expressed through spontaneous local revolts against the *reparto* and recent tax increases. The platform spelled out by the Inca called for the abolition of the *reparto*, the Potosí *mita*, forced labor in textile workshops, and the sales tax, while also advocating the destruction of customs houses, and, most notably, the end of the *corregimiento* (Golte, 1980: 188). Both the grievances listed and the proffered solutions to them clearly indicate Tupac Amaru II's desire to create a wide coalition cutting across ethnic lines – Indians, *mestizos*, and Creoles were burdened, albeit to different degrees and in various ways, by the practices and institutions the rebel leader set out to abolish.

It is interesting to note, however, that Canas-Canchis — the cradle and hotbed of the insurgency – was neither a poor province nor was it subjected to the highest *reparto* rate (O'Phelan Godoy, 1985: 104). Admittedly, a low legal *reparto* rate may have been meaningless whenever a corrupt official was in charge of collecting revenue: "According to José Gabriel, Arriaga collected 300,000 pesos when the book of rates for five years showed 112, 000 as the legal amount allowed" (Fisher, 1966: 39). At any rate, other indicators – e.g., the small number of *mita* workers going to Potosí in 1780 and preceding years – suggest that so-called "objective" factors, while carrying weight, may be misleading, if overstated (Morner and Efraín, 1985: 9). In 1780, what had been undermined and compromised in the colonial Andes was the uneven exchange regulating people–State relations – a crisis of legitimacy ensued as corrupt local officials and Bourbon tax reforms alienated Indian tributaries as well as people from other castes and strata.

Tupac Amaru II proved enormously successful as a recruiter of Indian combatants. His charisma and prestige extended well beyond the immediate radius of the rebellion, reaching as far as upper Peru – and, indeed, reaching well beyond the grave, for the second and most violent phase of the insurrection unfolded after his execution in May 1781. The messianic motif of resurrection strikingly shaped Indian views of Tupac Amaru II, attesting to the supernatural and mythical qualities attributed to the Inca by popular lore. The Spanish visitador-general, Areche, had the Inca's corpse beheaded to dispel belief in his immortality, a belief he knew was widespread among his followers (Robins, 2002: 143, Szeminski, 1993: 224). It was also reported that fallen combatants would rise from the dead three days after Tupac Amaru II's coronation in Cusco (Campbell, 1987: 126). Tupac Amaru was even said to have informed his troops that only those who refrained from invoking the name of Jesus would be resurrected after three days (Stavig, 1999: 244). Tupac Amaru II himself always professed to be a devout Roman Catholic and, given his background as a noble Indian educated by the Jesuits in the city of Cuzco, it is unlikely that he shared the syncretic views of rank-and-file combatants. At any rate, Andean myths and popular religion underpinned many a rebel's commitment to the cause. Popular eschatology held the promise of a new order where death would be literally conquered: "In 1780 the time had come: the era of the Spaniard was about to end, and the Inca was due to return. The resurrection of the flesh and the return of the vanquished loomed closer. Prophecies had intensified in 1777: the year of three sevens . . . Perfect numbers: end of a cycle, beginning of a new one" (Flores Galindo 1987: 153).

Couched in language heavily laden with terms borrowed from Christian millenarianism and native beliefs, Inca restoration as conceived by Quechua- and Aymara-speaking peasants was hardly acceptable to Creoles, urban *mestizos*, and members of the Indian nobility. In addressing different constituencies, Tupac Amaru II was keenly aware of class, ethnic, racial, and cultural differences. Sharp social distinctions prevailed in colonial society, although throughout the eighteenth century there was increasing and significant interaction between people from different strata. Few individuals could navigate through the complex, diverse ethnic mosaic of colonial Peru as confidently as José Gabriel Condorcanqui. His formal education was advanced, even by the standards held for Inca descendants, although it is probably untrue that – as a contemporary observer wrote – he "was a doctor in both laws" (cited by Fisher, 1966: 26). As Clements Markham wrote: "He read Latin readily, spoke Spanish correctly, and his native language, Quechua, with peculiar grace" (1892: 194). Literate and proficient in several languages, Tupac Amaru II was able and willing to reach out to Creole merchants, soldiers, and clergymen in ways the Aymara leader and *forastero* Indian Tupac Catari could not – and would not – emulate. As a muleteer, José Gabriel Tupac Amaru traveled extensively and frequently along the most important trade route of the Andes, developing in the process a vast network of contacts stretching from the port of Arica in the south to the province of Tucumán in northern Argentina. Far from being an isolated backwater, Tinta was actively linked through trade to Lima, Cuzco, Arequipa, Potosí, and Buenos Aires. One of the largest market fairs in the South Andean region was held every September in Tungasuca, one of the towns over which Tupac Amaru was *curaca*. Trade generated mobility, spread information, expanded horizons – understandably, a vision transcending local boundaries did not baffle those who made their living on the road. Thus, it does not come as a surprise that eight Creole and *mestizo* muleteers were among Tupac Amaru II's closest collaborators. Nevertheless, Tupac Amaru's attempts to broaden the ethnic and class makeup of the rebellion met with only mixed success. The rebellion's high command was indeed staffed with people from diverse backgrounds: "Of the forty-two persons holding the most important military titles, sixteen were *españoles*, a social classification including both Spaniards and Creoles; seventeen were *mestizos*; and nine were considered Indians" (Stavig, 1999: 226). And yet, even though the rebellion's command was indeed multiethnic – as a matter of fact, to the point of having Indians underrepresented – the overwhelming majority of Creoles failed to rally behind Tupac Amaru II. Creoles who joined the upper echelons of the rebellion were persuaded by the Inca leader himself – face-to-face interactions proving crucial. On the other hand, edicts and proclamations addressed to Creoles failed to win them over – ironically, future historians based their assessment of the movement's goals and ideology on such texts. As John Rowe wryly put it:

> A reader who pores over the edicts of the Inca leaders may be under the impression that the rebels' program was limited to calling for the abolition of a few taxes which were more prejudicial to Creoles and *mestizos* than they were to Indians. Had whites in 1780 taken rebel propaganda as seriously as whites do nowadays, the fate of the insurgency might have been a different one. (Rowe, 1976: 51)

Tupac Amaru II's vision was of a realm in which all native-born subjects – Creoles, *mestizos*, Indians, and *zambos* – would "live together like brothers and congregated in a single body, destroying the Europeans" (cited in Lewin, 1957: 402). Tupac Amaru explicitly states his will to rid the land of foreigners – a point stressed by calling Spaniards "*europeos*." The native-born/foreign dichotomy seems to take precedence over ethnic identities: the bond of national brotherhood would tie all those who were born on American soil and had suffered under the rule of Peninsular Spaniards. Under

Bourbon administrative reforms, high government posts were reserved for Spaniards born in the Peninsula; therefore, expelling or "destroying" them meant – claims of loyalty to King Charles III notwithstanding – the destruction of the colonial state apparatus. Interestingly, foreign-born priests were not to be disturbed and the Catholic Church would maintain all of its privileges – e.g., parishioners would continue paying tithes and first fruits to local priests (Thomson, 2002: 170).

In Peruvian colonial society, Peninsular Spaniards were a despised and resented minority, as terms of derision attest – Creoles and *mestizos* called them *"chapetones,"* making fun of their rosy complexion, while Quechua-speaking Indians referred to them as *"puka kunka,"* which literally translates as "red necks." A broad anti-European coalition did not materialize, however, as most Creoles rallied behind the Crown and Indian rebels increasingly took to targeting all whites – Peninsular and Creole alike – as the enemy.

As envisioned by Tupac Amaru II and members of his inner circle, Inca restoration was a nationalist project, rather than a nativist one. Unlike modern nationalism, such as the one espoused by the generation of South American Creoles who four decades later were to wrest political independence away from the Spanish Empire, it was neither inspired nor influenced by the French Enlightenment.[8] Members of the Indian elite like Tupac Amaru avidly read – and interpreted in a variety of ways – a book written by one of their own almost two centuries earlier: Garcilaso de la Vega Inca's *Royal Commentaries* (1609). In a seminal monograph, John Rowe traced the inception of the Inca revival of the eighteenth century back to, among other things, a 1723 edition of *Comentarios reales*, which before that year had had little impact on indigenous nobles (Rowe, 1976: 27–32; Lewin, 1957: 290–3). For literate Indians who owed their standing in colonial society to their Inca heritage, Garcilaso de la Vega's book was both a source of collective pride and a powerful identity-fashioning tool – though, to be sure, noble *curacas* did not act as a unified force in the political arena. As depicted by Garcilaso de la Vega, Inca emperors had been benevolent rulers who bestowed the gift of civilization upon their subjects. During the rebellion, Tupac Amaru II and his wife, Micaela Bastidas, sat for a portrait dressed as an Inca royal couple (Stavig, 1999: 237). Iconography mattered, but it was in Garcilaso's prose that Tupac Amaru II believed he had found the substance of his role:

> *Comentarios reales*, that book of Renaissance history, came to be read much as a pamphlet by figures such as Tupac Amaru, who took as emphatic denunciation the comparison of the Incas and the Romans, the criticisms of Viceroy Toledo, the veiled suggestion that a just and equitable empire ought to be reconstructed. Garcilaso turned the Inca era, Tawantinsuyo, into a golden age. (Flores Galindo, 1987: 194)

Read through a subversive lens, *Royal Commentaries* was construed by Tupac Amaru II as the utopian blueprint of a native monarchy and a national society.[9] The radical potential of such a reading was belatedly acknowledged by his foes. In 1781, the bishop of Cuzco, Juan Manuel de Moscoso y Peralta, "directly attributed the force and restorative clarity of the rebellion to the reading of the book" (Castro-Klaren, 2003: 176). Moscoso has been credited with – or, depending on one's view, accused of – prompting Tupac Amaru II to dispose of *corregidor* Arriaga, who at the time of his death was entangled in a bitter feud with the bishop (Fisher, 1966: 48–9; Stavig, 1999: 240–1). Fearful of being perceived as disloyal to the Crown, Moscoso came strongly against the rebellion and was instrumental in securing support for the royalist camp from the clergy and members of the Indian nobility (Lewin, 1957: 399). Biased as it was, the bishop's testimony is not to be discounted – Moscoso was certainly quite close to the most powerful *curacas* in Cuzco and, prior to the rebellion, had kept in touch with Tupac Amaru II. In a letter dated April 13, 1781, Moscoso told Areche that Tupac Amaru II would not have dared to embark on a rebellion had he not been inspired by Garcilaso de la Vega's work (Golte, 1980: 184; Szeminski, 1993: 230; Castro-Klaren, 2003: 176) Areche later banned the book (Lewin, 1957: 291). In 1782, the Spanish Council of the Indies ordered that copies of the *Royal Commentaries* "be gathered up even if it requires secretly purchasing the issues through third persons" (cited by Robins, 2002: 141).

Important as elite Inca nationalism was in shaping the views of Tupac Amaru II and members of his inner circle, it must be stressed that Inca nobles and *curacas* did not join the rebellion in large numbers outside Canas-Canchis and Quispicanchis. Out of 2,073 *curacas* in Peru and Upper Peru (Golte, 1980: 153), only a small number fought on Tupac Amaru II's side. Most significantly, *curacas* who were descendants of Inca emperors did not cast their lot with Tupac Amaru II and remained actively loyal to the Crown. In Cuzco, the Twenty-four Electors – i.e., the patriarchs of the wealthiest and most aristocratic Indian families – rejected to a man the rebel's plea to restore Inca rule under his leadership (Cahill, 2002: 156). The electors dressed as Inca emperors during the festivities of Corpus Christi (82) and, as local patrons of the arts, they commissioned portraits honoring their royal ancestors or had themselves portrayed in Inca garb (Rowe, 1976: 22; Stastny, 1993: 140). In 1781, Spanish authorities banned such paintings and had the portraits of Inca kings removed from the walls of the Colegio of San Francisco de Borja, the Indian nobility's alma mater. Enforcement of culturally repressive policies was intense in the aftermath of the rebellion, but it started to wane and waver by the end of the 1780s. It is important to note that even though the *curaca* system was weakened in the wake of the rebellion, descendants of Inca emperors did not lose their clout – e.g., Mateo Pumacahua, Tupac Inca Yupanqui's direct descendant and Tupac Amaru II's nemesis in 1781, remained a powerful figure, leading a large but ultimately failed Creole-Indian uprising in1810.

Tupac Amaru II's movement mobilized large Indian and *mestizo* masses in colonial Peru's most densely populated areas, but in a context of general crisis key constituencies – Creoles and Indian nobles – remained on the royalist side. Thus, the multiethnic, counter-hegemonic strain of Inca nationalism Tupac Amaru II heralded did not take root among native-born elites. Discontent over Bourbon tax reform and Inca revival did not ultimately sway them to the rebel camp as the Inca leader hoped – it may very well be that the January 1781 siege of Cuzco, when 40,000 rebel troops encircled the city, came to naught because Tupac Amaru II waited in vain for a revolt to break out within the ranks of the besieged (Flores Galindo, 1987: 146). The retreat from Cuzco marked a turning point, since early military successes were followed by a string of defeats at the hands of colonial forces. Among Indian peasants, the project of Inca restoration increasingly meant waging war against all whites – annihilation of non-Indians and destruction of their property becoming a precondition for the fulfillment of messianic expectations. On April 6, the insurgency's high command was dealt a devastating blow as mulatto soldiers sent from Lima captured the rebel leader, who was then jailed and tried in Cuzco. A month later, on May 18, 1781, Tupac Amaru II was put to death in the same city where two centuries earlier Tupac Amaru I met his end. Spanish colonial authorities staged the execution of Tupac Amaru II, his wife, eldest son, and captains as a chilling, gruesome display of state power. The rebels were not brought back to heel, though, as the theater of operations shifted southward to upper Peru and a radically nativist ideology epitomized by Tupac Catari permeated the movement – combatants fought in Tupac Amaru's name, but his view of a multiethnic national monarchy had by then been discarded. By August 1782, Spanish colonial authorities announced the total pacification of the realm. Almost four decades later, in 1821, as the Argentine general José de San Martín declared Peru's political independence from Spain, he invoked the name of Tupac Amaru II in calling on the Indian population to support the new Creole-led republic. The Indian masses in both Peru and upper Peru were conspicuously absent from the 1821–4 war of independence. Patriotic rhetoric claimed Tupac Amaru II as a forerunner of Peru's political independence, even though the movement he led – Andean-based and Indian-supported – greatly differed in both political ideology and ethnic makeup from the Great Colombian and Argentine armies which were ultimately successful in driving the Spaniards away from their South American dominions.

## Notes

1   For a detailed narrative account of revolts and rebellions in Peru and upper Peru during the 1780–2 period, see Lewin (1957).

2   On José Gabriel Condorcanqui Thupa Amaro's background, see Lewin (1957: 384–97) and Fisher (1966: 22–6).

3   On *curacas* in Colonial Peru, see Golte (1980).

4   See "A general table of revolts and rebellions during the eighteenth century," in O'Phelan Godoy (1985: 284–98).

5   For an excellent description of the Potosí mita and its effect on indigenous populations, see Stavig (1999: 162–206).

6   For a record of versions and manuscripts of *Ollantay*, a colonial three-act play based on a Inca story, see Meneses (1983: 261–79).

7   On *Taqui Onqoy*, see Millones (1990).

8   A passing reference in Benedict Anderson's *Imagined Communities* rates the Tupac Amaru II rebellion as a "great jacquerie"(Anderson, 1983: 51). As Anderson points out, unsettling memories of the rebellion were still fresh when Creoles pushed for independence in the 1810s and 1820s.

9   Commenting on Flores Galindo's *Buscando un Inca*, Eric Hobsbawm praises Flores Galindo's "excellent treatment of the Indian movements and their supporters," (1992: 67) but fails to remark on elite views of Inca restoration as a form of proto-nationalism. On popular proto-nationalism see Hobsbawm (1992: 46–79).

## References and Further Reading

Anderson, Benedict (1983). *Imagined Communities: Reflections on the Origin and Spread of Nationalism.* London: Verso.

Bendezú, Edmundo, ed. (2002). *Literatura quechua.* Caracas: Biblioteca Ayacucho.

Cahill, David (2002). *From Rebellion to Independence in the Andes: Soundings from Southern Peru, 1750–1830.* Amsterdam: CEDLA.

Campbell, Leon (1987). "Ideology and factionalism during the Great Rebellion, 1780–1782." In Steve Stern (ed.), *Resistance, Rebellion, and Consciousness in the Andean Peasant World, Eighteenth to Twentieth Centuries,* pp. 110–39. Madison: University of Wisconsin Press.

Castro-Klaren, Sara (2003). "The nation in ruins: archaeology and the rise of the nation." In Sara Castro-Klaren and John Charles Chasteen (eds), *Beyond Imagined Communities. Reading and Writing the Nation in Nineteenth-Century Latin America,* pp. 161–95. Baltimore, MD and Washington, DC: Johns Hopkins University Press and Woodrow Wilson University Press.

Cornblitt, Oscar (1976). "Levantamientos de masas en el Perú y Bolivia durante el siglo XVIII." In Alberto Flores Galindo (ed.), *Tupac Amaru II-1780,* pp. 129–98. Lima: Retablo de papel.

Estenssoro, Juan Carlos (1993). "La Plástica colonial y sus relaciones con la Gran Rebelión." In Henrique Urbano (ed.), *Mito y simbolismo en los Andes,* pp. 157–82. Cuzco: Centro de Estudios Bartolomé de Las Casas.

Fisher, John (1976). "La Rebelión de Tupac Amaru y el programa imperial de Carlos III." In Alberto Flores Galindo (ed.), *Tupac Amaru II-1780,* pp. 107–28. Lima: Retablo de papel.

Fisher, Lillian Estelle (1966). *The Last Inca Revolt, 1780–1783.* Norman: University of Oklahoma Press.

Flores Galindo, Alberto (1976)." Túpac Amaru y la sublevación de 1780." In *Tupac Amaru II-1780,* pp. 269–323. Lima: Retablo de papel.

— (1980) *Buscando un inca: Identidad y utopía en los Andes.* Mexico City: Grijalbo-CNAA, 1988.

— (1987). "In search of an Inca." In Steve Stern (ed.), *Resistance, Rebellion, and Consciousness in the Andean Peasant World: Eighteenth to Twentieth*

Centuries, pp. 193–210. Madison: University of Wisconsin Press.

Flores Galindo, Alberto, ed. (1976). *Tupac Amaru II-1780: Sociedad colonial y sublevaciones populares.* Lima: Retablo de papel.

Golte, Jürgen (1980). *Repartos y rebeliones: Tupac Amaru y las contradicciones de la economía colonial.* Lima: IEP.

Hobsbawm, Eric (1992). *Nations and Nationalism since 1780: Programme, Myth, Reality.* 2nd ed. Cambridge: Cambridge University Press.

Lewin, Boleslao (1957). *La rebelión de Túpac Amaru y los orígenes de la emancipación americana.* Buenos Aires: Hachette.

Markham, Clements R. (1892). *A History of Peru.* Chicago: C. H. Sergel & Co.

Meneses, Teodoro, ed. (1983). *Teatro quechua colonial: Antología.* Lima: Edubanco.

Millones, Luis, ed. (1990). *El Retorno de las huacas: Estudios y documentos del siglo XVI.* Lima: IEP.

Morner, Magnus and Trelles, Efraín (1985). *Dos ensayos analíticos sobre la rebelión de Túpac Amaru en el Cuzco.* Stockholm: LAIS.

O'Phelan Godoy, Scarlett (1985). *Rebellions and Revolts in Eighteenth-Century Peru and Upper Peru.* Cologne and Vienna: Bohlau.

Robins, Nicholas (2002). *Genocide and Millennialism in Upper Peru: The Great Rebellion of 1780–1782.* Westport, CT: Praeger.

Rowe, John (1976). "El movimiento nacional inca del siglo XVIII." In Alberto Flores-Galindo (ed.), *Tupac Amaru II-1780,* pp. 11–53. Lima: Retablo de papel.

Stastny, Francisco (1993). "El Arte de la nobleza inca y la identidad andina." In Henrique Urbano (ed.), *Mito y simbolismo en los Andes,* pp. 137–56. Cuzco: Centro de Estudios Bartolomé de Las Casas.

Stavig, Ward (1999). *The World of Túpac Amaru: Conflict, Community, and Identity in Colonial Peru.* Lincoln and London: University of Nebraska Press.

Stern, Steve (1987) *Resistance, Rebellion, and Consciousness in the Andean Peasant World: Eighteenth to Twentieth Centuries.* Madison: University of Wisconsin Press.

Szeminski, Jan (1993). *La Utopia tupamarista*. 2nd ed. Lima: Pontificia Universidad Católica del Perú.

Thomson, Sinclair (2002). *We Alone Will Rule: Native Andean Politics in the Age of Insurgency*. Madison: University of Wisconsin Press.

Urbano, Henrique, ed. (1993). *Mito y simbolismo en los Andes: La figura y la palabra* [Myth and symbolism in the Andes: the face and the word]. Cuzco: Centro de Estudios Bartolomé de Las Casas.

# 13

# The Caribbean in the Age of Enlightenment, 1788–1848

*Franklin W. Knight*

> The work of the eighteenth century is sound and good. The Encyclopaedists, Diderot
> at their head, the physiocratists, Turgot at their head, the philosophers, Voltaire at their
> head, the Utopists, Rousseau at their head: these are four sacred legions. To them the
> immense advance of humanity towards the light is due.
>
> *Victor Hugo, Les Misérables, VII, iii*

The eighteenth century represented the immense high-water mark of the Enlightenment; a period of profound changes that ushered in the great Industrial Revolution
of the nineteenth century and in many regards may be seen as the beginning of the
period of modern history. The Enlightenment, although still shrouded in controversy
surrounding its exact periodization and what exactly represented its most significant
achievements, provided the broad context for a series of fundamental transformations
(Pocock and Emerson, 2002: 26–8) A new rationalizing spirit of inquiry presented a
series of revolutionizing new discoveries and a proliferating series of writers articulated
new visions of their contemporary world. An internationally minded group of writers
mainly from France, Germany, Great Britain, and the United States produced a series
of critical essays dealing with history and society that greatly influenced policy makers
on both sides of the Atlantic. Their works generated a new attitude about society,
history, and the world as they saw it. They included Edward Gibbon (1737–94),
David Hume (1711–76), Adam Smith (1713–90), Jeremy Bentham (1784–1832),
and Edmund Burke (1727–97) in England and Scotland; Jean Jacques Rousseau
(1712–78), François Marie Arouet de Voltaire (1694–1778), Denis Diderot (1713–
84), Charles Montesquieu (1689–1755), and Abbé Guillaume-Thomas-François
Raynal (1713–96) in France; Gotthold Lessing (1729–81), Moses Dessau Mendelsohn
(1729–86), Johann Gottfried von Herder (1744–1803), and Alexander von Humboldt
(1769–1859) in Germany; and Benjamin Franklin (1706–90), Thomas Paine (1737–
1809), and Thomas Jefferson (1743–1826) in the United States. They were all part

of a succession of thinkers whose ideas significantly shaped the modern world. The significance of this new attitude was the conviction that the world needed to be altered and that alteration was possible through human intervention. William Woodruff expressed this elegantly: "Under the 'enlightened' revolutions of the eighteenth and nineteenth centuries, right became what the individual conscience determined; truth what the individual reason recognized" (1967: 6).

The age of the Enlightenment coincided with the rise of the biological sciences, notable advances in chemistry and physics, as well as altered conventional mentalities. Between 1770 and 1840 a plethora of new inventions in steam technology, telegraphic communications, and mechanical engineering laid the foundation for what has sometimes been called the age of revolution (Davis, 1975). Steam technology revolutionized textile manufacturing and railroad transportation, telescoping time and distance and integrating previously distant markets (Blainey, 1966). Eli Whitney's cotton gin contributed enormously to the expansion of cotton culture, especially in the southern United States. Railroads eclipsed canals and steamships quickly outpaced sailing vessels (Woodruff, 1967; Ransom, 1984; Headrick, 1988). The Atlantic world community achieved remarkable coherence and viability with an increasingly symbiotic connection between Europe, Africa, and the Americas – and maritime tentacles spreading outward across the Pacific and Indian Oceans to Asia. European commerce and manufacturing achieved a sort of dominance in many parts of the world (Coclanis, 2005). In military strategy, armaments, shipbuilding and navigation, the production of books, and long-distance administration, the Europeans were discernibly more advanced than the rest of the world. In a few other areas, especially textile and porcelain production, at the beginning of the nineteenth century they lagged behind parts of India and China.

## Changes at the Macro Level

The later eighteenth century ushered in the age of political revolutions and witnessed the first movement toward an industrial revolution with major developments in iron manufacture, steam technology, and labor-saving inventions such as the previously mentioned Eli Whitney cotton gin. Between 1776 and 1848 vast political, social, and economic changes occurred throughout the Caribbean in particular and the Americas in general. These changes, some introduced from outside and other developed by local residents, clearly illustrate the ways in which Caribbean residents were also seriously engaged in thinking about their local societies, economies, and cultures.

The American Revolution of 1776–83 shattered the nominal cohesiveness of the British North American Empire, established the precedence for artificial state engineering, and published a constitution that became widely imitated throughout the Western hemisphere in the decades that followed. In many ways the constitution of the United States of America is highly representative of Enlightenment thinking.

The French Revolution of 1788–1815 redrew the political map of Europe and seriously undermined the public appeal of dynastic government. Above all the French Revolution unleashed nationalism as a potent centripetal force across the European continent, changing the philosophy and nature of politics. The Haitian Revolution – an outgrowth of the metropolitan French Revolution – created the second independent state in the Americas and the first entirely free society in any area where slavery and slaveholding societies had taken root. As the letter of Jean-François and Georges Biassou indicates, and as the constitution dictated later by Toussaint Louverture in 1801 powerfully demonstrates, residents in the colonies had strong views about their local situations (Dubois and Garrigus, 2006: 99–102, 167–70). Unlike the revolutionaries in the United States and France, the colonists in Saint-Domingue were not reluctant to examine the practice of slavery and its implication for state formation and nation building. They wanted an entirely free society within the colonial system in which slavery and distinctions based on color and race would have no place. Never before in history had such a society ever been contemplated.

With the declaration of a free state of Haiti in 1804, the centuries-old institution of American slavery began to disintegrate. It was not a rapid demise but it was an inexorable disintegration conditioned by place, time, and prevailing circumstances. Abolition followed two sequential phases, with the overall transatlantic trade terminated before the slaves in the Americas were set free. The British abolished their portion of the transatlantic slave trade in 1807 and thereafter initiated the systematic, but largely unsuccessful, persecution of those who continued to traffic in human cargoes across the Atlantic. Transatlantic slave trading persisted until the 1870s, although the demand fell drastically after 1850 (Eltis et al., 1999). The institution of slavery was abolished in piecemeal fashion across the Americas between 1792 and 1888. The Spanish Caribbean, where the institution first re-created itself in the hemisphere, abolished slavery in Cuba in 1886, the next to last state to abolish slavery in the Americas.

All these political, social, and economic changes of the era constituted an integral part of what Eric Hobsbawm called "the age of revolution." It was an era of dramatically profound changes across Europe and the Americas. Spain lost its vast continental American empire mainly owing to irrepressible local aspirations of political independence. The Portuguese royal family fled to Brazil to escape the expansive tendencies of Napoleon Bonaparte and later acquiesced to the independence of Brazil. Cultivation, commerce, and culture underwent drastic modification everywhere throughout the Americas between 1770 and 1840.

The profound changes that engulfed Europe and the United States had resounding repercussions across the Caribbean region. The progressive breakup of the English and Spanish-American mainland empires accentuated the impetus for state formation and nation building across the American hemisphere. A free United States of America became a new catalyst for international trade and played an increasingly inordinate role in Caribbean commerce (Carrington, 1988, 2002). France, having failed to suppress the slave revolution in its most important colony – the highly productive Saint

Domingue – sold its Louisiana territory to the United States in 1803 and greatly reduced its interest in an American empire for the next few decades. The mainland Spanish colonies won their independence through prolonged warfare and in 1819 Spain sold Florida to the United States, giving the latter total control of the area below the Great Lakes and east of the Mississippi River. This economic territorial consolidation would provide the basis for a later irrepressible spirit of "Manifest Destiny" that eventually culminated in the 48 contiguous states that stretched across the continent from the Atlantic Ocean to the Pacific. By 1848 Cuba and Puerto Rico were the only remaining remnants of the once far-flung Spanish-American Empire. Both would emerge as major Caribbean sugar-producing territories during the nineteenth century, with Cuba achieving singular attainment in gross production and mechanical innovation.

The transformation of the Caribbean world between roughly 1776 – the beginning of the outbreak of the North American Revolution – and 1848 – the beginning of the industrial revolution in the Caribbean – took place at several interrelated levels: political, social, intellectual, and commercial. It is obvious that individuals and groups in the Caribbean were just as deeply concerned about their world and the changes taking place as were the Europeans. It is also obvious that the ideas associated with the Enlightenment in Europe would also be at work across the region.

## Caribbean Political Changes

For the Caribbean the establishment of the free state of Haiti in 1804 represented the most significant political event of the period. Haiti was not the accidental consequence of an uncontrollable political explosion but rather the calculated construction by warriors who had no option but to establish a state to secure their collective freedom and implement their uniquely democratic ideas. But other significant political changes were also taking place. In Jamaica large proprietors of land and slaves like Edward Long (1734–1813) and Bryan Edwards (1743–1800), heavily influenced by the philosophical ideas of John Locke (1632–1704) and Charles-Louis de Secondat, the Baron de Montesquieu (1689–1755), were thinking about their colonial societies in radically different ways, as their histories illustrate (Goveia, 1956; Lewis, 1983; Braithwaite, 1971). Although born in England, their on-the-ground experience in Jamaica and intimate participation in the social, economic, and political affairs of the island gave legitimacy to their observations that made them influential participants in the political debates within British society on the issues of slavery and colonialism.

The British Caribbean colonies had, through their local assemblies, passed a series of resolutions in the early 1770s that declared themselves to be loyal to the British crown while sympathizing with the position of the North American colonies on the issue of stamp duties. The Jamaican petition that declared the white people in Jamaica (or more properly, the members of the assembly) to be "colonists, Englishmen, and Britons" did not prevent their making claims for some sort of political autonomy. It was precisely what Louverture had written into the first colonial constitution for French Saint-Domingue in 1801.

The political and economic importance of Cuba within the reduced Spanish-American empire at the beginning of the nineteenth century coincided with the first agricultural revolution already taking place on the island. (This constituted an expansion of the sugar revolutions in the Caribbean that had started in Barbados in the middle of the seventeenth century; Higman, 2000). This belated manifestation of the sugar revolution simultaneously took place in Puerto Rico, Trinidad, and British Guiana. In the British Caribbean a sort of rivalry developed between the older settled colonies such as Barbados, St. Kitts, Nevis, and Antigua, as well as Jamaica – captured from the Spanish in 1655 – and the newer colonies – Grenada, Dominica, as well as St. Vincent – acquired after the Seven Years' War (1756–63) and during the wars of the French Revolution – St. Lucia, Trinidad, Demerara, and Berbice. The administrative structure of the British colonies was far from uniform. "The British West Indies in the middle of the nineteenth century," wrote John Parry and Philip Sherlock, "formed a rich and varied museum of antiquated constitutional and administrative devices" (Parry and Sherlock, 1971: 205). The first two sets of colonies (Barbados, St. Kitts, Nevis, Antigua, and Jamaica) pretended that they were microcosms of English society and that their representative assemblies reflected the political position of the British parliament. Nothing could be farther from reality since by 1800 the Caribbean colonies were not representative of English societies but of slave plantation communities. Although after 1797 the British crown directly administered the newly acquired Caribbean colonies, these were allowed to continue with most of the laws and administrative forms of the Dutch in the case of Essequibo, Berbice, and Demerara and the Spanish in the case of Trinidad. After 1830 the July Monarchy in France, following the practice of the Haitians after 1804, introduced the concept of equality before the law, and that applied to its overseas colonies. In 1834 the French Antilles (Martinique and Guadeloupe) initiated a period of locally elected councils on a restricted franchise – more generous than in the British Antilles – that prefaced the direct election of French Caribbean representatives to the National Assembly in 1848.

At the level of local politics across the Caribbean a relatively small, propertied class exerted inordinate influence over local administration and local legislation. In the Spanish and Dutch Caribbean free property-owning non-whites were largely denied political power, although their legal status as free citizens was recognized. The local municipal councils, the *cabildos*, constituted the principal loci of political power and reflected the views of the landed and commercial elite notorious for its interlocking longevity and narrow, self-interested control. The situation was similar in Jamaica, as Edward Long noted: "Most of the old Creole families are allied, by the inter-marriages among their ancestors before the island was populously settled. The same remark may be made on many other communities in the world, which have sprung from a few families; for example, the Welsh and the Scotch [*sic*]" (Long, 1774, II: 266).

While no Caribbean colony opted to join the liberation movements of the mainland, Cuba, Puerto Rico, Bermuda, and the Bahamas actively supported the British

North Americans in their War of Independence between 1776 and 1783. By the early nineteenth century a new spirit of self-consciousness began to develop in several Caribbean territories and locals began to articulate ideas about themselves and how they saw their world.

In the British Antilles the politically enfranchised represented a miniscule minority of the male adult population, although before 1833 the franchise had gradually expanded to include property-holding non-whites as well. In 1823 Grenada granted full franchise to all adult colored males with property. A British government Order in Council of 1828 granted full legal equality to adult males in its Crown Colony territories by abolishing all civil and military distinctions based on race and color. The Jamaica Assembly followed suit in 1830 and Barbados did so in the following year. By 1834 all propertied adult males, including Jews, could vote in all territories with elected legislatures across the English-speaking Caribbean. Despite the official announcement of these changes in the metropolis, the motivation most probably came from the colonies since in some ways these all-inclusive laws were far ahead of similar laws applicable for Great Britain.

The long-term significance of this emerging political pluralism was enormously important. By opening the franchise to all property-owning adult males, regardless of color, before the abolition of slavery, the British inadvertently established the principle of equality before the law and removed that aspect of civil rights from the list of grievances that required attention in the years after full emancipation in 1838. The British West Indies then joined Haiti in upholding the juridical principle of equality before the law – more than a hundred years before the same was true for the United States of America. This did not mean that the issue of civil rights lost its contentiousness but merely that it lost urgent primacy. The principles of upward mobility and political plurality became established in the British Caribbean.

Political access did not immediately follow the broadening of the electoral franchise, however, in the British Caribbean. Property remained the difficult hurdle. The vast majority of adult males were non-white and poor and remained excluded from active political participation until the establishment of universal adult suffrage beginning in 1944. The legal situation – as opposed to the de facto reality – contributed to a different type of political evolution in the British Caribbean in the later nineteenth century and during the early twentieth century. Political contestation in the British Antilles, the French Antilles, and Puerto Rico took legalistic and constitutional forms rather than bellicose confrontations as occurred in Cuba. Nevertheless, the Caribbean, as elsewhere in Latin America, did not experience the conflictive and harshly segregationist racial policies that took place in the United States throughout the nineteenth century and even well into the twentieth century.

Haiti, of course, represented the most startlingly revolutionary political change anywhere in the world at that time. But the Haitian Revolution had its origins in the spirit of change produced by the Enlightenment. Seizing the initiative after the calling of the Estates General in 1788, the free colonists of French Saint-Domingue – white as well as non-white – assumed that they shared the political identity of their metropolitan peers and immediately collected their *cahiers de doléances* and enthusiastically elected competing delegates from among the white and free colored populations in the colonies (Shapiro and Markoff, 1998). The immediate consequence was an explosive colonial political situation that quickly developed a life of its own within the rapidly changing scene of the emerging domestic French revolution. Suddenly, defining Frenchness assumed conflictive proportions. By 1794 the 80 percent of the non-free population in the colonies of Saint-Domingue, along with those in Martinique and Guadeloupe had, thanks to the massive slave revolts, won legal freedom – albeit only temporarily – from the French National Assembly. Napoleon did not like the idea when he assumed power. Nevertheless, reversing legal emancipation by military means proved impossible in Saint-Domingue and in 1804 Jean-Jacques Dessalines declared the independence of Haiti.

Before that took place, the colonists themselves had reacted to the new constitution declared in France in 1800 by Napoleon with a surprising constitution of their own. Louverture gathered at Le Cap a group of mostly white planters who wrote an enlightened and farsighted constitution that named Louverture governor for life, abolished slavery forever, and established the absolute equality of all citizens before the law. Such a society had never existed anywhere before, as the following three articles illustrate:

> Article 3. There can be no slaves in this territory: Servitude is abolished within it forever. All men who are born here live and die free and French.
> Article 4. All men, whatever their color, are eligible for all positions.
> Article 5. There exists no distinctions other than those based on virtues and talents, and no superiority other than that granted by the law to the exercise of a public function.
> The Law is the same for all, whether it punishes or protects.

While a colonial constitution ran counter to the plans of Bonaparte, the momentum toward independence could not be reversed in French Saint-Domingue. Haitian independence in 1804 represented a monumental achievement. The new constitution published in 1805 was even more radical than before. It declared all persons to be equally free and all citizens of the new republic to be black – a declaration that had profound political and social impact all along the Atlantic coast from Bangor, Maine to Buenos Aires, Argentina. The Haitian Revolution was the most thorough revolution in history. The declaration of political independence in the United States of America as well as later in Spanish and Portuguese America had merely transferred local political power from the metropolis and its representatives to the former colonies, while investing that power in the propertied classes and their male representatives (Rodriguez, 2000; Langley, 1996). There was no social revolution and no challenge to the elites from the non-elites as happened in Haiti. When the newly penned North American Declaration of Independence in 1776 referred to the equality of all men it assumed narrowly that "men" could only be property holders and equality referred only to the elites. In short, political independence in the United States of America and the newly emerged states of the Spanish and Portuguese empires did not result in truly democratic societies. That was precisely the significant achievement in Haiti. The independence of Haiti invested political power immediately in everyone in the state irrespective of gender, education, race, color, wealth, or occupation. It was a major political and social revolution rolled into one and it was not an accidental occurrence. The elimination of social privileges as well as the permanent abolition of slavery represented the fearsome prospect to all slaveholders throughout the Americas, but it was the only way the new state would have survived. To Haitians liberty, equality, and fraternity were not just convenient political slogans. Haitian leaders took the ideas of the Enlightenment seriously indeed and wanted to rationally engineer their society.

## Changes in Society

The Caribbean represented a vast kaleidoscope of changing social situations during the period between 1788 and 1848. The common experience with slavery and the plantation society tended to mask the highly significant variations across the region in social structure – largely influenced by the development of the slave plantation society and by demographic composition. To some extent the political changes mirrored the changing social situation and the social situation resulted from the fortuitous combination of geographical size, topography, population, and colonial relationship.

Cuba, Puerto Rico, and the Dominican Republic still reflected, to varying degrees, the basic social structure of Spain at the end of the eighteenth century. John McNeill's description of Cuban society around the middle of the eighteenth century was no longer true by the 1790s, as the population and the social scene had changed rapidly:

> Cuban society reflected Spanish society a good deal more than did most parts of Spanish America. Of the social classes present in Spain, Cuba lacked only a powerful landed nobility . . . A landed aristocracy of sorts decorated Cuban society, ranch owners and sugar mill owners for the most part; but few of these owned large tracts, and few lived handsomely off their holdings. (McNeill, 1985)

By 1790 Cuba boasted a titled nobility of 20 persons, a fourfold increase over the number in 1760. The titled nobility ranked at the top of the social elites as well as the commercial and administrative elites. They used their wealth and influence to purchase supernumerary captaincies and colonelcies both in the regular army and the colonial militia. Cubans held a majority of positions in the local garrison by 1800 as well as a majority of positions in the municipal government. Gonzalo O'Farrill (1754–1831), born in Havana, rose to be lieutenant-general of the Spanish army and minister of war. Cuban-born Joaquín Beltrán de Santa Cruz y Cárdenas spent seven years at the Spanish court and returned with the title of Conde de Santa Cruz de Mopós, as well as the ranks of brigadier in the regular army, and sub-inspector-general for the army in Cuba. Both achievements were singularly distinguished. Service at the metropolitan center did not appear to diminish the sense of *cubanidad* that both were prominent members of the Creole Sociedad de Amigos del País, founded in Havana in the 1790s to foster the economic development of the colony.

To a greater extent than elsewhere in the Caribbean, Cuba's diversified white population included peasants and landless laborers; artisans, construction workers, shopkeepers, import and export merchants, prostitutes, butchers, salters, stevedores, ditch diggers, tailors; a bureaucratic class serving city, colony, and empire; a professional class of officers in the army and navy, lawyers, doctors, chemists, priests, scribes, ships' captains and university professors (Johnson, 2001; Kuethe, 1991; Knight, 2005). The social and occupational complexity in Cuba reflected the fact that it was a longstanding settler society of great strategic importance in the Spanish imperial system. It served as the most important Caribbean fortified harbor, the permanent location of thousands of troops, and, after 1763, the locus for experimental imperial administrative reforms introduced by Charles III. Cuba also had a population that, more than elsewhere in the region, exploded between 1774 and 1841. In 1774 the island had 171,620 inhabitants, of which slaves comprised a modest 22.8 percent. By 1840, however, the population exceeded a million inhabitants and the slave sector had grown to 43.3 percent of the total population (Knight, 2005: 22). The introduction of the sugar revolution had radically transformed Cuban economy and society.

By the end of the eighteenth century the city of Havana grew physically and almost doubled the population it had at mid-century. By 1790 the city and its immediate hinterland had a population approaching 100,000, the third largest urban density in the Americas and far exceeding that of any of its Caribbean rivals – at that time, Kingston counted a mere 23,508 inhabitants; Cap Français around 15,000, Port-au-Prince a little more than 6,200; and Basse-Terre and Point à-Pitre 9,000 and 13,000, respectively. Havana established a university in 1728 and by 1840 it enjoyed a rich and varied urban cultural life that was not quite matched by its neighboring Caribbean cities and towns.

Urban populations were as mixed as they were mobile. Slaves represented a significant proportion of these urban populations, since they constituted much of the labor force. The occupational ranges of most Caribbean towns matched the complexity given above for Cuba. Obviously the sizes would have been less and Havana had many more of the large planter families living there at the beginning of the nineteenth century than would the other smaller Caribbean port towns like Kingston, Port-au-Prince, Point-à-Pitre, or Port-of-Spain. In small islands like Antigua, Nevis, St. Kitts, and Barbados the towns were easily accessible to the rural great houses of the planter classes.

Anomalies certainly arose among Caribbean urban populations. Although figures are not precise for most towns and the figures fluctuated depending on the time of the year, some observations are in order. Havana probably had a larger number of ecclesiastical and military-cum-naval persons than the other towns. It was, after all, a garrison city as well as a major depository for commodities awaiting the convoys to Spain. Sherry Johnson claims that in the 1770s "between one in two and one in three of the adult males walking Havana's streets was a peninsular soldier" (2001: 56). French and English Caribbean towns did not have the permanent military garrisons that were a prominent feature of Havana. On the other hand, they had far more non-whites proportionally than did Havana. Part of this resulted from the function of the various towns; some, like Havana, being the principal bureaucratic center and others not.

Whatever the city, mixing across lines of race and occupation seemed to be commonplace throughout the Caribbean. Each urban center served a changing population that comprised whites, free coloreds, free blacks, females of all colors, African- born and Creole slaves, as well as foreigners in transit. After the Haitian Revolution the presence of foreigners, especially non-white foreigners, attracted much attention. As B. W. Higman (2000) shows for Jamaica, the Kingston Common Council was always trying in the early nineteenth century to ascertain and expel foreigners deemed undesirable. This was not an easy task, as some foreigners owned property and many performed services of great value to the community.

Despite the legally rigid segmentation based on race and occupation, Caribbean societies could not afford the luxury of an operationally rigid or inflexible caste structure. Social necessities excluded that. Even the Caribbean society that best exemplified the European settler model – that of Cuba – could not provide the sort of occupational differentiation within the white sector that satisfied the growing needs of a dynamic community. Occupations and skills were of necessity randomly distributed. No group was sufficient unto itself. Mutual needs forced a sort of crude integration in the cities that extended from patterns of living to the effective distribution of services. But this integration also meant that the intellectual elite could not think of their societies as monolithic and the problems introduced by the presence of African slaves were unavoidable. Caribbean thinkers probably placed more urgency on the social questions than their counterparts on the mainland or in Europe. The pattern that Anne Pérotin-Dumon (2000) described for Guadeloupe around the end of the eighteenth century was probably fairly characteristic of much of the rest of the population across the region. In Guadeloupe she found the captain of a black privateer ship, many black sailors, black ships' carpenters, hairdressers, dressmakers, schoolteachers, and small shopkeepers, but no non-whites among the goldsmiths, apothecaries, and large shopkeepers. Spanish law excluded non-whites from the professions or service in the upper layers of the imperial bureaucracy.

## Caribbean Intellectual Life

The great intellectual ferment in ideas that possessed European societies throughout the eighteenth and early nineteenth centuries had its Caribbean counterpart. Never-

theless, most Caribbean societies were less interested in the larger moral and philosophical ideas that agitated the Abbé Raynal (1713–96) or Adam Smith (1723–90)
than in the immediate complex realities of their local communities. These realities
varied considerably. As Philip Curtin wrote in his remarkably insightful study, *Two
Jamaicas*:

> The fact that a given society is colonial opens special problems in its intellectual history
> – problems that would have little meaning in a metropolitan society. Such problems,
> emerging from a study of nineteenth-century Jamaica, concern the origin and transfer
> of ideas. The ruling Jamaicans were European in culture and education; therefore they
> might be expected to turn to England for a solution to their problems. At the same
> time, Jamaican society was very different from British society, and British ideas could
> hardly be applicable to Jamaican conditions. Mother country and colony differed in
> respect to climate, geography, social structure, and the cultural background of the
> majority of the people. (1955: iii)

By the eighteenth century Caribbean societies had developed along two clearly
distinct paths. The histories of Jamaica and Cuba illustrated this divergence. Jamaica,
after its capture by the British in 1655, rapidly developed as a plantation slave society,
in which the primary operational imperatives revolved around the efficient production
of sugar and other export commodities for an overseas market. Over time an organic
community outside the sugar business inevitably developed, and although sugar continued to provide the official barometer for the overall economic health of the island,
a viable secondary economy had developed based on the emergence of a free non-white
sector of predominantly peasant producers. The problem, as Curtin hinted above, was
that the political, social, and administrative structure of the island continued to reflect
the formalities of earlier settler societies such as that of Barbados, St. Kitts, Montser-
rat, Antigua, and Nevis before they underwent sugar revolutions. Then they represented overseas microcosms of English society and their social and political forms were
less incongruous than during the later years after the sugar revolutions. By contrast,
Cuba remained a quintessential settler society between its occupation by the Spanish
in 1511 and its transformation into a plantation society after 1760. The belated
transformation did not obscure the solid traditions of the majority of European settlers
and military who had contributed to the material success of the colony. In short, Cuba,
with its university, seminaries, and its strong, cohesive elites, could foment and
articulate an especially vigorous self-consciousness or *conciencia de sí* that was rare
elsewhere in the Americas.

This is not to say, however, that intellectual activity was absent in the British
Caribbean. After the 1770s, with the publication of Edward Long's *History of Jamaica*
(1774), a steady steam of writings – mainly political tracts but also some solid works
of political and natural history – appeared about several islands, the majority dealing
with Barbados and Jamaica. Most of the publications were by white writers who had
some longstanding interest in the Caribbean and were representative of the planter
classes. However hard they tried – as in the case of the two famous Anglo-Jamaicans

Edward Long (1734–1813) and Bryan Edwards (1743–1800) – to present a local perspective, their ethnocentricity and self-interest overwhelmed their objectivity. Nevertheless, their "reflections" – the term is taken from Long – convey invaluable insights into Jamaican society at the end of the eighteenth century.

Long and Edwards were both born in England. They were contemporaries, good friends, and had personal experience as property owners and public figures in Jamaica. Long, a lawyer trained at Gray's Inn, arrived in Jamaica in 1757 following the death of his father to assume proprietorship of estates that had been in the family since his ancestors acquired them as rewards for participating in the Oliver Cromwell expedition that captured the island from the Spanish in 1655. In 1758 Long married Mary Ballard Beckford, one of the wealthiest and best-connected widows on the island. He served as a member of the local assembly, private secretary to the governor of the island, Sir Henry Moore, and a judge in the Vice-Admiralty Court. Poor health forced Long to return to England in 1769, where he continued to direct the affairs of his Jamaican estates and write his famous history published in 1774.

Bryan Edwards lost his father in 1756 and shortly thereafter was sent to live with his maternal uncle, Zachary Bayly, one of Jamaica's leading merchants, who gave him an outstanding private education. Edwards arrived in 1759 and by the early 1770s had not only inherited his uncle's mercantile operations as well as a large sugar estate but also had become a prominent member of the local assembly. He returned to England in 1782, where he sought unsuccessfully to become a member of parliament. He spent the years from 1787 to 1792 in Jamaica but returned to England, where he finally entered parliament in 1796. Like Long, Edwards was a vigorous defender of the slave trade and of Jamaican autonomy while being staunchly loyal to England and its monarch. As Edward Braithwaite points out, "They were Englishmen, as well as Jamaicans, at a time when it was becoming increasingly difficult to be both" (1971: 76). Their positions, however, were not identical.

While Long and Edwards were profoundly influenced by the Enlightenment and their social views coincided, their attitude to politics and the state varied. Long, writing before the outbreak of the American War of Independence, shared with the leaders of the North American colonies a strong distrust of monarchical tyranny. Edwards, writing some twenty years later, focused his distrust on parliament, and indeed dedicates his book to the King. Edwards is far more sympathetic to the local instruments of administration than Long, and indeed posits that the British West Indian Assemblies were coequal to the British parliament. If politically Edwards was more radical than Long, on social issues they were closer in their thinking. Both disliked the institution of slavery but found it indispensable for the prosperity of the colonies and opposed metropolitan intervention. For Edwards, who had personally witnessed the slave revolution in Saint-Domingue, tampering with slavery was tantamount to inviting anarchy. The Haitian Revolution he described as "a spirit of subversion." Neither Long nor Edwards was enlightened enough to consider Africans potential subjects of the king, as equal as any other subject.

If the Enlightenment produced a stronger reaction in Cuba than elsewhere in the Caribbean, the reason was clear. Unlike the Spanish, the English government did not pay much attention to the general education of its colonial subjects before the nineteenth century. By the beginning of the nineteenth century they had two shortsighted reasons for neglecting popular education in their Caribbean colonies. The first was that the sugar industry, their prime indicator for economic well-being, was in crisis. The second was that the numerically small local elites sent their offspring abroad for education in England (or in some cases in the United States), and their control of politics allowed them to set the priorities for islands. To make matters worse, many of these leading local families were absentee landowners with mostly an economic interest in their overseas territories. Bryan Edwards was a member of the British parliament. Edward Long's concept of a free society, like that of Thomas Jefferson, did not include women and slaves. Neither could articulate a democratic worldview of Jamaican society, despite having pronounced Creole sympathies. Not surprisingly, Kingston, despite having a number of elegant houses, a magnificent harbor, and gorgeous mountain backdrops, never impressed nineteenth-century travelers as a vibrant or beautiful city. In the 1830s the planter, Mathew Lewis, described Kingston as resembling "booths at a race course" and the writer Richard Madden found it "so desolate and so decayed."

If Jamaicans were not thinking or otherwise engaged in other intellectual pursuits, they certainly were busy planting and diversifying the flora of the island. Douglas Hall notes the healthy curiosity in introducing new plants that expanded the botanical variety of the islands as well as the variety and availability of foodstuffs. In the last decades of the eighteenth century Jamaican planters imported and propagated a number of ornamental, fruit, and hardwood trees, and vines and herbs including mango, breadfruit, watermelon, Madeira peach, litchi, horse chestnut, amaryllis, wallflower, amaranthus, oaks, cypress, walnut, and mulberry. Jamaica, however, did not possess the sort of intellectual dynamism that characterized Havana society at the end of the eighteenth century. One reason probably derived from the composition of the local elites. Jamaican and other British Caribbean elites had an outward-looking, transient sort of mentality. Cuban elites thought of their island as their permanent home.

The Cuban elites were predominantly local residents. So too was the situation in Puerto Rico and Santo Domingo, although San Juan, Ponce, and Santo Domingo city were much smaller than Havana. More important, the Spanish Caribbean presented a relatively cohesive elite in terms of values and views. That, perhaps, made it possible to defend their interests more coherently than elsewhere in the Caribbean. By the end of the eighteenth century Havana was a city in lively intellectual ferment. The *Sociedad Económica de Amigos del País* brought together a number of the leading citizens whose views reflected the encompassing range of Enlightenment sensibility. Chartered in 1791 with an initial membership of 27 leading Creole landholders, the group later expanded into a body with a membership approximating 200 persons. Of the 126 members registered in 1793, 113 resided in the capital. Only a few members attended the meetings regularly. In every respect the *Sociedad* constituted an exclusive club whose members aggressively pursued economic power and political influence both locally and in Madrid. The program of activities encompassed science and the arts, commerce and industry, beautification, agriculture, and education. Most activities were pragmatic rather than theoretical, such as advocating a system of paved roads, the introduction of steam and railroads, the elimination of the forest reserves in the interest of agricultural expansion, and the modification of the structure of landholding in Cuba, thereby creating a lucrative real-estate market that accelerated the formation of new towns.

One of the significant achievements of the *Sociedad*, under the leadership of Bishop Juan José Díaz de Espada y Fernández de Landa (1756–1832), was the promotion of a more rigorously scientific curriculum in Cuba than in Spain, the founding of free local schools throughout the island, and the placing of education under the control of local political authorities. Education became less centralized and leading local institutions – the Real y Pontificia Universidad de San Gerónimo de la Habana, the San Carlos and San Ambrosio Seminary (the former Jesuit Seminary of Colegio San José) in Havana, the San Basilio Seminary in Santiago de Cuba, as well as the Colegio San Cristóbal (founded by the Spanish immigrant Antonio Casas) – produced two generations of ardently nationalist educational leaders such as Félix Varela Morales (1788–1853), José de la Luz y Caballero (1800–62), José Antonio Saco (1797–1879), José María de Heredia y Heredia (1803–39), Domingo del Monte (1804–53), José Agustín Caballero de la Torre (1771–1835), Nicolás Calvo Puerta y O'Farrill (d. 1802), Francisco Arango y Parreño (1765–1837), Juan Francisco Manzano (1797–1854), and Gabriel de la Concepción Valdés, the poet Plácido (1809–44). Formal education introduced many of these scholars to the ideas of the European Enlightenment.

## The Commercial Revolution

The sugar revolutions in the Caribbean encompassed a series of changes affecting demography, cultivation, and commerce. The tempo of the revolutions could be measured in slaves imported, sugar produced, land under cultivation, and increases in shipping. In 1680 Barbados was probably the most valuable tropical colony in the world, and it received the largest number of African slaves shipped across the Atlantic and sold in the Caribbean. As predominantly monocultural plantation exporters, the Caribbean colonies assumed a commercial importance that transcended their merely bartering slaves and foodstuffs for their plantation commodities of sugar, tobacco, indigo, hides, coffee, and cotton. The region was also a market for all sorts of diversified products that eventually made the conventional mercantilist principles of trade obsolete. The Caribbean comprised the hub of a multifaceted trading system that brought olive oil, brandy, gin, beer, wine, butter, cheese, potatoes, garlic, onions, soap, medicines, candles, perfumes, glass, horses, cattle, fish, firearms, flour, salted meat, barrel staves, nails, lumber, tools, slaves, machinery, cloth, furniture, utensils, paper, and a range of luxury products to supply the economic, dietary, and production needs of the various plantation societies. Meeting the local demand for these products conflicted with the imperial notions of monopoly and mercantilism. Free ports represented a rational solution to the problem of supply and demand.

By 1778 the Spanish crown expanded the number of Cuban ports accessible to Spanish shipping in accordance with the privileges prevailing in Havana since 1764. By the end of the century Santiago de Cuba, Trinidad, Batabanó, Nuevitas, Matanzas, and Remedios were all serving along with Havana as international free ports. Havana remained the dominant port, with about 450 annual sailings at the end of the century. Linda Salvucci shows that the Cuban trade was important not only within the Spanish empire but also for the United States of America:

> The Caribbean as a whole, accounted for nearly one-half of all departures and two-fifths of all tonnage declared for foreign ports at Philadelphia. When the islands are classified by parent state, the Spanish possessions – primarily Cuba but also Santo Domingo and Puerto Rico – easily outrank the others as Philadelphia's preferred trading partners. This pattern appears to have stabilized over time. Moreover, when individual Caribbean ports are ranked by tonnage at five-year intervals, Havana usually occupies either first or second place while Santiago frequently ranks within the top five as well. Furthermore, in 1800 and 1805, Havana led all foreign clearances from Philadelphia, including those to Europe and the Far East. (1991: 44)

As John Stewart wrote in the 1820s:

> The Commerce of Jamaica may be classified under the following heads: The trade with the mother country – which is far the more considerable than the other branches together; the trade with British North America; and the trade with the island of Cuba and the Spanish islands, the Spanish Main or Tierra Firma [*sic*], and territories on the American continent formerly belonging to Spain. (1823: 117)

Jamaica's complex trading relations were common for the rest of the Caribbean. Cuban ports traded, legally and illegally, with Spain, the United States, England, Germany, France, Mexico, Venezuela, and Jamaica. Puerto Rico in the early nineteenth century exported its products in English, Spanish, Danish, American, Hanseatic, and Dutch ships not only to the distant European and mainland American markets but also to neighboring Caribbean islands.

The growth of cities and towns, along with the general population increase, provided the catalyst for the internal economy. As Havana grew so did its immediate hinterland, producing the fruits, vegetables, and meat required by the expanding urban population. All across the Caribbean this domestic market flourished during the nineteenth century, supplementing plantation food production and sometimes contributing to the export trade.

More important, the increased internal trade contributed substantially to the economic resources that enabled the recently freed slaves and their already free counterparts to move into landholding in a major way. The development of free villages throughout the British West Indies after emancipation in 1838 represents one of the heroic chapters of Caribbean history. Freedom provided the impetus for land purchase, massive home building, and extensive small-scale cultivation. In Jamaica, freeholders increased from 1,204 in 1838 to more than 50,000 at the middle of the century. In Barbados the number of freeholders with less than five acres of land increased from 110 in 1844 to 3,537 in 1859. In St. Vincent the black population built 8,209 houses between 1837 and 1857 and bought and subdivided more than 12,000 acres of land. The case of British Guiana was the most dramatic of all. By 1842, 1,000 black families had purchased some 7,000 acres of prime Guyanese coastal land worth more than £100,000. By 1848 Guyanese peasant families had built more than 10,000 new houses and owned land valued at more than £1 million. This was the sort of impressive industry that slavery and the slave system retarded and nullified. A free society efficaciously brought out the creativity in the population that had been advocated by Long and Edwards in the eighteenth century for the white population.

## Final Observations

Although this is a short general overview of the Caribbean during the later years of the Enlightenment, it is possible to make some observations that help explain the Caribbean variation in the broader hemispheric experience of the plantation and slave societies in the Americas.

The Enlightenment, however demarcated and defined, had a far-reaching impact on Caribbean societies affecting all areas of politics, economy, and society. It contributed to the expansion of commerce, the rationalization of the administrative structure in some colonies, as well as the independence of Haiti. The unfortunate state of Haiti created a model of a truly democratic society, albeit one that was anathema to the United States of America and the other newly independent states of the Americas as well as those continuing areas of colonialism in the Caribbean. But the Enlightenment also produced an intellectual ferment throughout the Caribbean region, resulting in education reforms in Cuba, as well a spirit of scientific inquiry and curiosity that would contribute to major developments in sugar manufacturing as well as crop diversification. The expansion of botanical gardens throughout the region also reflected this new rational curiosity. Bolstered by the ideas of the Enlightenment, Caribbean Creoles could turn their attention to their own societies and even discus the nature of politics.

Caribbean societies developed systadially, not synchronically, and that affected the timing and eventual nature of their societies. They all experienced the common stages of settlement, sugar revolutions, and "the ordeals of free labor" in the post-slavery societies. They did not all, however, go through those experiences at the same time. Timing, along with other extraneous factors, explained why neighboring islands or islands within a single imperial system could, and did, have a different history. This is an extremely important consideration when looking at the history of sugar and slavery in the Caribbean.

The importance of the Haitian Revolution looms large in the history of the Caribbean, of the Americas, the Atlantic World, or even in general world history. That revolution set in motion a series of changes that reached as far as China. It accelerated the disintegration of the transatlantic slave trade and the American slave systems. It boosted immigration and widened the scope of the sending societies from Madeira to China. It hastened the dissemination of sugar culture to Cuba, Puerto Rico, Trinidad, Surinam, and Guyana.

The Haitian Revolution and the abolition of slavery provided a major fillip for the expansion of the Caribbean peasantry. Peasants helped cushion the economic effects of the collapse of the sugar industry in some places such as Jamaica, Barbados, Antigua, and Guiana. More important, peasants boosted overall economic activity and helped diversify exports. In Puerto Rico, St. Lucia, Dominica, and some of the other small islands peasants constituted the largest number of landholders, and peasants remained the mainstay of the local economy.

Sugar was the most important Caribbean export, but it was not the only important export, and its domination of the regional economy should not be allowed to obscure the dynamic diversification that took place across the region beginning toward the end of the eighteenth century. Small farmers were largely responsible for the local markets in foodstuffs as well as a number of export products such as cocoa, coffee, beeswax, indigo, cotton, coconuts, honey, and timber.

Caribbean societies were quite dynamic, with various opportunities for economic and social mobility, even during the period of slavery. The slave systems, for various reasons, could never generate and maintain the mutually reinforcing social cleavages that were the hallmark of the United States. Instead, Caribbean societies represented societies with significant crosscutting social cleavages and that facilitated a less contentious post-slavery social development.

The progressive inclusion of non-whites in the local political operation of the British West Indian colonies before the abolition of slavery contributed to the democratizing of those societies. Extending the vote to non-whites, including Jews, helped remove that political dimension of human rights and the electoral franchise from the disputatious adjustments required after the emancipation of the slaves. But it also helped emphasize the importance of political control in the quest for equality and justice in Caribbean societies. That quest for political participation was not easy, but the exploration of that theme lies outside the scope of this chapter.

## REFERENCES AND FURTHER READING

Blainey, Geoffrey (1966). *The Tyranny of Distance: How Distance Shaped Australia's History.* Melbourne: Sun Books.

Braithwaite, Edward (1971). *The Development of Creole Society in Jamaica, 1770–1820.* Oxford: Clarendon Press.

Carrington, Selwyn H. H. (1988). *The British West Indies during the American Revolution*. Leiden: Fortis Publications.

— (2002). *The Sugar Industry and the Abolition of the Slave Trade, 1775–1810*. Gainesville: University of Florida Press

Coclanis, Peter, ed. (2005). *The Atlantic Economy during the Seventeenth and Eighteenth Centuries: Organization, Operation, Practice and Personnel*. Columbia: University of South Carolina Press.

Curtin, Philip D. (1955). *Two Jamaicas: The Role of Ideas in a Tropical Colony, 1830–1865*. Cambridge, MA: Harvard University Press.

Davis, David Brion (1975). *The Problem of Slavery in the Age of Revolution, 1770–1823*. Ithaca, NY: Cornell University Press.

Dubois, Laurent, and Garrigus, John (2006). *Slave Revolution in the Caribbean, 1789–1804: A Brief History with Documents*. New York: Bedford/St. Martin's Press.

Eltis, David, Behrendt, Stephen D., Richardson, David, and Klein, Herbert, eds (1999). *The Transatlantic Slave Trade: A Database on CD-ROM*. Cambridge: Cambridge University Press.

Gaspar, David B., and Geggus, David P. (1997). *A Turbulent Time: The French Revolution and the Greater Caribbean*. Bloomington: Indiana University Press.

Goveia, Elsa V. (1956). *A Study on the Historiography of the British West Indies to the End of the Eighteenth Century*. Mexico: Instituto Panamericano de Geografía e Historia.

Headrick, D. R. (1988). *The Tentacles of Progress: Technology Transfer in the Age of Imperialism, 1850–1940*. New York: Oxford University Press.

Higman, B. W. (2000). "The sugar revolution," *Economic History Review*, n.s., 53(2): 213–36.

Jensen, Larry R. (1988). *Children of Colonial Despotism: Press, Politics and Culture in Cuba, 1790–1840*. Tampa: University of South Florida Press.

Johnson, Sherry (2001). *The Social Transformation of Eighteenth Century Cuba*. Gainesville: University Press of Florida.

Knight, Franklin W. (2005). "The Haitian Revolution and human rights," *Journal of the Historical Society*, 5(3): 391–416.

Kuethe, Allan J. (1991). "Havana in the eighteenth century." In Franklin W. Knight and Peggy K. Liss (eds), *Atlantic Port Cities: Economy, Culture and Society in the Atlantic World, 1650–1850*, pp. 13–39. Knoxville: University of Tennessee Press.

Langley, Lester (1996). *The Americas in the Age of Revolution 1750–1850*. New Haven, CT: Yale University Press.

Lewis, Gordon K. (1983). *Main Currents in Caribbean Thought: The Historical Evolution of Caribbean Society in its Ideological Aspects, 1492–1900*. Baltimore, MD: Johns Hopkins University Press.

Liss, Peggy K. (1983) *Atlantic Empires: The Network of Trade and Revolution, 1713–1826*. Baltimore, MD: Johns Hopkins University Press.

Long, E. (1774). *The History of Jamaica*, 33 vols. London.

McNeill, John R. (1985). *Atlantic Empires of France and Spain: Louisbourg and Havana, 1700–1763*. Chapel Hill: University of North Carolina Press.

Moore, Brian, Higman, B. W., Campbell, Carl, and Bryan, Patrick (2001). *Slavery, Freedom and Gender: The Dynamics of Caribbean Society*. Kingston: University of the West Indies Press.

Parry, J. H., and Sherlock, P. (1971) *A Short History of the West Indies*. London: Macmillan.

Pérotin-Dumon, Anne (2000). *La Ville aux isles. La Ville dans l'île: Basse-Terre et Point-a-Pitre, Guadeloupe, 1650–1820*. Paris: Karthala.

Pocock, J. G. A., and Emerson, Roger (2002). Letters in *Historically Speaking*, 3(5): 26–8.

Ransom, P. J. G. (1984). *The Archaeology of the Transport Revolution 1750–1850*. Tadworth, UK: World's Work (Windmill Press).

Rodríguez, Jaime (2000). "The emancipation of America," *American Historical Review*, 105(1): 131–52.

Salvucci, Linda (1991). "Supply, demand, and the making of a market: Philadelphia and Havana at the beginning of the nineteenth century." In Franklin W. Knight and Peggy K. Liss (eds), *Atlantic Port Cities: Economy, Culture and Society in the Atlantic World, 1650–1850*, pp. 40–57. Knoxville: University of Tennessee Press.

Shapiro, Gilbert, and Markoff, John (1998). *Revolutionary Demands: A Content Analysis of the*

*Cahiers de Doléances of 1789.* Stanford, CA: Stanford University Press.

Stewart, John (1823). *A view of the past and present state of the island of Jamaica; with remarks on the moral and physical condition of the slaves, and on the abolition of slavery in the colonies.* Edinburgh: Oliver & Boyd, Tweeddale-House.

Williams, Eric (1970). *From Columbus to Castro: The History of the Caribbean 1492–1969.* New York: Harper & Row.

Woodruff, William (1967). *The Impact of Western Man: A Study of Europe's Role in the World Economy, 1750–1960.* New York: St. Martin's Press.

# 14

# The Philosopher-Traveler: The Secularization of Knowledge in Spanish America and Brazil

*Leila Gómez*

## Introduction

With the fall of the Spanish imperial monopoly, wars of independence, and commercial and technological development in the Age of Reason, the eighteenth and nineteenth centuries became an era of scientific travel and discoveries in Latin America. It is impossible to distinguish exploratory and scientific travels from the most modern discursive practices of the empire. Travelers, naturalists, geologists, geographers, astronomers, traders, draftsmen, and cartographers served as the main mediators between the New World Otherness and the metropolitan literate public. The task of building an imperial imagination followed the logic of cultural evolutionism, forged in the Enlightenment and propagated and intensified by the Positivism and Social Darwinism of the nineteenth century. These discourses placed the geographical and cultural center of Empire in the most advanced evolutionary stage in human history.

In the building of a "planetary consciousness" (Pratt, 1992) it was necessary to specify not only the spatial but also the temporal parameters of the New World Otherness. The explorers and travelers of the period focused on measuring and classifying what they deemed pristine territory in order to form a more complete image of the planet. To establish the temporality of their findings, it is useful to distinguish between two types of scientific travelers: the naturalist-traveler and the archeologist-traveler, or antiquarian. These travelers assigned different temporalities to the phenomena of the New World. While natural history emphasized the unmodified or prehistoric aspect of the continent, -archaeology focused on the traces of civilization in cultures considered more or less "developed" in the Western evolutionist pattern. These cultures were named "archaic" and, although not "savage," were regarded as fossilized, lacking evolutionary strength. The naturalist and the archaeologist travelers represent two different methodologies of research, and the results of their discoveries influenced imperial identities in different ways (Leask, 2002: 1–14).

Today it is clear that with the discourse of the scientific travelers, empire employed its most sophisticated strategies of colonial domination. Enlightened science developed ideological discourses that validated its actions as being free from economic and political interests. Enlightenment values of objectivity, progress, and liberation were professed by many travelers of the period. While they saw their task from a variety of perspectives, they shared a self-image as martyrs in the name of science. Their heroic discourse employed the rhetoric of deprivation and extreme danger (including the specific menaces of shipwreck and cannibalism), and in so doing the traveler as martyr cemented the pivotal role of science in the emerging modern culture. These travelers were the "*nomothètes*" (Bourdieu, 1966: 61) – that is, the "founding heroes" of science. Whereas religion had once served as a primary justification for travel, science now was assuming that role. Unchanged was the use of progress to provide cover for the economic interests which conveniently benefited from this noble intent.

For the local travelers who followed and subverted the steps of early European visitors, this heroism became associated with the rise of a Creole consciousness. As the colonial era yielded to the republican, such travelers promoted an independence discourse that challenged "enlightened" yet pejorative images of the New World (e.g., Buffon's theory of the inferiority and underdevelopment of New World Nature with respect to the Old World). During the final years of the Spanish empire in Mexico, travelers such as Guillermo Dupaix followed the tradition of Sigüenza and Clavijero in exalting the grandeur of autochthonous cultures through descriptions of Mayan and Aztecan archeological sites (Bernal, 1980: 93–8). As late as the mid-nineteenth century, naturalists such as Florentino Ameghino published for the first time in Spanish studies of New World fossils using the discursive parameters of scientific modernity. The science of local travelers was the vehicle to global modernity for Latin American nations. In Ricardo Rojas's words, while the new republics had only known the glory of clerics and armies ("the resonant forms of martial glory"), local scientific travelers became "heroes of peace" (1922: 218). The Creole identity incorporated those travelers into its national pantheon as archetypal figures of the transition from barbarism to civilization. Thus, Creole science negotiated the reconciliation of the foreign and the local within the discourse of the nation.

## Science and Imperial Power: Relative Autonomy

The production, distribution, and consumption of both imperial travel and its narrative adhere to economic parameters. The key to understanding this economy lies in retracing the traveler's steps, exposing the cultural standards that tie him to his epistemological point of departure, what Bruno Latour has called the "center of calculation" (1987: 215). In what he describes as "cycles of accumulation of Science," imperial travelers selected, edited, and prioritized the cultural commodities they encountered in their travels. Using these cultural commodities, the specialized institutions of "the center of calculation" (e.g., libraries, museums, universities, and publishing houses) promoted and diffused a disciplined knowledge for specialists, as well as material for general consumption (1987: 215–39).

With regard to Lapérouse's travel narrative of the Pacific, Latour comments on the benefits of the former's exchange with the Chinese merchants of Sakhalin. These merchants revealed the existence of a strait that connects Kamchatka with the rest of Asia; they even drew Lapérouse a map of the region. But how was this Chinese geographical knowledge transformed once it entered the French "center of calculation"? How did this local knowledge and these "savage" beliefs become "universal" and "precise" cartographic knowledge? According to Latour, the answer lies in considering the observer's process of packaging his cultural commodities for their long journey home.

> How to act a distance on unfamiliar events, places and people? Answer: by *somehow* bringing home these events, places and people. How can this be achieved, since they are distant? By inventing means that (a) render them *mobile* so that they can be brought back; (b) keep them *stable* so that they can be moved back and forth without additional distortion, corruption or decay; and (c) are *combinable* so that, whatever stuff they are made of, they can be cumulated, aggregated, or shuffled like a pack of cards. (1987: 223)

Cartographic representations, collections, measurements, and engravings became the scientific means of collecting and constructing "mobile and stable" commodities. Upon their safe arrival at the "center of calculation" such commodities defined the success of these scientific expeditions. For example, although the Lapérouse expedition never returned to France, it was nevertheless considered successful, as the traveler managed to send his maps and accounts to the metropolis. Through such commodities a traveler could confirm the connection between Sakhalin and Asia, determine the depth of the strait that connects them, measure the speed of the winds, and relate information about the natives' habits and resources. By November of 1797, for example, when the English ship *Neptune* made a second expedition to Sakhalin, metropolitan knowledge (originally weaker than that of the natives) was bolstered by its possession of maps of the region, instructions for navigation, and accounts of the natives' habits. This pattern defined the metropolitan cycles of knowledge accumulation, with a scientific methodology that enabled the conversion of knowledge into mobile products which could be transported to the center of calculation.

In the same period, Alexander von Humboldt made his own distinctive contribution to the cycle of accumulation. In one letter to Fourcroy from Cunama dated October 16, 1800, Humboldt emphasized the quantity and quality of his collection, as well as the efficacy of his methods of transferring it to the center of calculation. His methodology included desiccation, detailed descriptions, drawings, and dissection of corpses to observe the internal parts of organisms.

> In the six months that we have been traveling over this vast region between the coast, the Orinoco, the Rio Negro and the Amazon, the citizen Bompland has dried more than

six thousand plants. With him, I have described in the field two hundred species, most of which seem to be of a different genre than those described by Aublet, Jacquin, Mutis and Dombey. We have collected insects, *conchillas*, dark wood; we have desiccated crocodiles, lamentis, monkeys, gymnotus electricus (whose fluid is absolutely galvanic, not electric) and have destroyed many serpents, lizards, and fish. I have drawn many of them. After all, I dare to say that I am proud that my ignorance is not caused by my laziness. (Humboldt, 1908, 54; my translation)

In 1804, after five years in the Spanish colonies and America, Humboldt returned to Europe with 35 boxes full of botanic, astronomic, and geologic treasures. His account of his travels filled 32 volumes, entitled *Voyage of Humboldt and Bompland*. This *Voyage* includes six parts and comprehensively treats the botany, zoology, geology, astronomy, meteorology, public affairs, economy, and geography of Mexico, Cuba, Venezuela, Colombia, Ecuador, and Peru. It is a monumental work that took over thirty years to complete, and became a standard reference for travelers who followed him. More so than his collection of "mobile and stable" objects, it was Humboldt's written work that succeeded in advancing the accumulation of metropolitan knowledge.

The logic of scientific accumulation can be properly understood only in relation to the dialectic between the supposed autonomy of the scientific field and its relation to imperial power. Science constituted a powerful economic, as well as symbolic, weapon of imperial power. Institutions at the center of calculation, such as the *Jardin du Roi* directed by George Louis Leclerc, Conde de Buffon (founded in 1635 by Louis XVIII as a medicinal garden and renamed the Musée National d'Histoire Naturelle in 1793), suddenly became imperial projects. The garden counted an immense classified collection of vegetables and minerals sent to France by travelers from around the world. Two similar enterprises were undertaken in Portugal by the Marques de Pombal: the Museu Nacional de Historia, and the Jardim Botanico of the University of Coimbra.

Indeed, rivalries between imperial powers were played out to a remarkable degree in scientific expeditions. Pratt remarks on this aspect of La Condomine's expedition to the Equator to demonstrate the shape of the earth. Arguments over whether the earth was a sphere (a hypothesis held by French Cartesian cartography), or that if it was spheroid and flat on the poles (as held by the Newtonian theory) had become a matter of contention between France and England. As part of this debate, a group of geographers and other scientists under the leadership of Maupertius was sent to Laponia to measure the longitudinal grade of the meridian, while the La Condomine expedition was sent to Quito to measure the equator (Pratt, 1992: 16).

It was an age of cartographic precision, and contemporary travelers undertook the task of correcting former Spanish travelers, who had previously enjoyed a monopoly in the production of knowledge in the colonies. Such corrections were interpreted as evidence of the enlightened "superiority" of the new empires over the old conquerors. The credibility previously granted to the text as the testimony of *in situ* witnesses was challenged. It now became more important to value inner textual coherence and absence of contradictions over external characteristics or the social and moral merits of the witness (Cañizares-Esguerra, 1998: 338).

A prime example of this new credibility are La Condomine's efforts to provide an accurate name for the river we know as the Amazon. His nomenclature clarified the confusing geographic accounts of Spanish and Portuguese conquerors, which resulted in the following.

*Several names for the Amazon River*

Some have called it the Orellana River, but before Orellana, it was called the Marañón, originating from the name of another Spanish Captain. The geographers who have made two different rivers of the Amazon and the Marañón, deceived, as was Laet, by the authority of Garcilaso and Herrera, undoubtedly ignored not only that the most ancient Spanish authors had called this river "Marañón" since 1513, but also that Orellana himself recounts that he had found the Amazon Jungle after descending the Marañón, which has not been contradicted; in effect, it has always kept this name, without interruption until now, for over two centuries . . . However, the Portuguese who settled after 1616 in Pará, a village with a bishop located towards the eastern mouth of the river, do not know the river with any other name than the Amazon, and in the upper section by the name of Solimões, and they have transferred the name Marañón to a village near Pará. I will use the names of Amazon and Marañón interchangeably. (1941: 14; my translation)

In these cycles of scientific accumulation, science was interwoven with political and economic interests. At the same time and paradoxically, with the Enlightenment came the ideology of scientific disinterest and the universal progress of humanity under the guiding light of reason. Reconciling these materialistic and idealistic motives was the task of the philosopher-traveler.

## America in the Spatial and Temporal Maps of the Enlightenment

Enlightenment-era travelers contributed to the formation of a "planetary consciousness" that situated Europe at the center. Reason granted a new "ontological certainty" (Giddens, 1984: 375) to the enlightened world. Previously, this role had been filled by the church, whose worldview guided man's life according to a fixed and unified plan. In *History of Curiosity*, Justin Stagl analyzes the different conceptions of travel in frontispieces of two different epochs. One of the frontispieces corresponded to a Baroque traveler (*Welt-Beschauung* of 1653 by Georg Christoph von Neitzschitz) and the other to a travel book written during the Enlightenment (*Der reisende Deutsche* of 1745 by Martin Schmeitzels). According to Stagl, the seventeenth century viewed travel as an allegorical version of pilgrimage, the passage of suffering and temptations to reach the eternal afterlife. The ontological certainty of the Baroque subject rested

on the conception of a closed universe with the promise of an eternal life that transcends and gives meaning to the Baroque universe. During the Enlightenment, on
the other hand, the universe was conceived of as an open panorama that humans could
objectify, study, and explain using new, modern tools (Stagl, 1995: 157–66). The
work of the philosopher-travelers represents this transition away from the spiritualiza-
tion of the cosmos to its conceptualization as a scientific system.

In his travels to the Equinoctial regions, Humboldt emphasized this transition in
famous passages, one being his beautiful description of the Southern Cross viewed at
sea. Here, Humboldt quotes Dante's lines about the constellation and compares his
experience as a modern man with that of the conquerors centuries before. Yet while
Humboldt is aware of the allegorical significance of this constellation, he immediately
goes on to describe it with the precision of a cartographer:

> A star in the loneliness of the sea is greeted as a friend from whom you had been long
> separated. The Portuguese and Spanish seem to add to this interest other particular
> motives: they link a religious feeling to the constellation whose form reminds them of
> that symbol of faith established by their ancestors in the deserts of the New World.
>
> The two large stars that mark the head and foot of the cross having more or less the
> same straight line, it turns out that the constellation is nearly perpendicular at the
> moment they pass the meridian. All the villages beyond the tropics or in the Austral
> hemisphere are familiar with this circumstance. It has been observed that for part of the
> night, during the different seasons, the Southern Cross is straight or inclined to the
> right. It is a clock that moves forward very regularly around four minutes per day, and
> no other group of stars offers such an easy observation of the time to the naked eye.
> (Humboldt, 1956: 206–7; my translation)

It was Humboldt's poetic vision of nature that allowed him to bridge the gap
between the allegorical conception of the constellation and the scientific precision of
his examination. Carl Becker points out that Enlightenment thinkers were charged
with making the transition from the old religious beliefs to the new faith in Reason
and its capacity to decipher natural laws (1932: 56–7). Such laws did not proceed
from the Bible, but from direct observation, comparison, and experimentation. As in
the enlightened traveler's frontispiece analyzed by Stagl, the universe was neither
closed nor fixed in a transcendental totality. The universe was open to the human eye
and mind.

The metaphor of the "universal machine" was frequently used to describe Nature
as a mathematical system divinely created and administered. In his *Dialogue Concerning
Natural Religion*, Hume writes:

> Look around the world; contemplate the whole and every part of it. You will find it to
> be nothing but one great machine, subdivided into an infinite number of lesser machines,
> which again admit of subdivisions, to a degree beyond what human senses and faculty
> can trace and explain. All these various machines, and even their most minute parts, are
> adjusted to each other with an accuracy, which ravishes into admiration all men, who

have ever contemplated them. The curious adapting of means to ends throughout all nature resembles exactly, though it much exceeds, the productions of human . . . intelligence. Since therefore the effects resemble each other, we are led to infer . . . that causes also resemble; and that the Author of Nature is somewhat similar to the mind of man; though possessed of much larger faculties, proportioned to the grandeur of the work, which he has executed. (quoted in Becker, 1932: 55–6)

Hume upholds the direct observation of nature as the way to discover the laws governing this "perfect machine." In the building of this planetary consciousness, science developed sophisticated means of classifying the natural phenomena of the colonial world; the most important of these systems of visibility was developed by Carl Linné (1707–78). The objective language of his *Sistema Naturae* (1758) served to elaborate a method for classifying plants, animals, and minerals. It attempted to overcome vernacular and symbolic conceptions of the natural world, differentiating species based on the quantity, quality, and disposition of morphological characteristics. The relation between parameters allowed for comparative measurement, which in turn helped establish a system of equivalencies. The clarity of taxonomies made them very attractive to travelers of the period as it provided standardized rules of collection. Taxonomy provides visibility, for it permits the transfer of samples as commodities from their original habitat to the center of calculation, where they can enlarge and improve already existent taxonomies. They also enabled their conversion of samples into Latour's "mobile and stable objects."

Enlightenment-era travelers to Brazil provide a good example of this. Ana Maria de Moraes Belluzzo mentions the use of Linné by Brazilian travelers educated in Lisbon, such as Alexandre Rodrigues Ferreira, the Humboldt of Brazil. The first Brazilian in charge of an expedition to the country's interior, Rodrigues Ferreira traveled in the company of two draftsmen, Joaquim José Codina and José Joaquim Freire, visiting the *capitanias* of Grão-Pará, Rio Negro, Mato Grosso, and Cuiba between 1783 and 1793. During this period, Portugal promoted scientific travel to Brazil, thanks to the efforts of Domenico Vandelli at the University of Coimbra. Vandelli spread the Linnean system throughout the Portuguese-speaking world and was the inspiration behind Rodrigues Ferreira's travels. Rodrigues Ferreira observed and collected many samples from the visited *capitanias* and sent them to the Museu da Ajuda in Lisbon; he also compiled political, economic, and ethnographic comments. As part of the enlightened reforms undertaken by Portugal, these expeditions emphasized taxonomies and attempted to develop applied science in order to obtain medicinal and agricultural profit (Moraes Belluzo, 1994: 60).

In his *Viagem Filosófica,* Rodrigues Ferreira offers a detailed description and classification of the flora and fauna of Brazil. This naturalist traveler also paid attention to the economic uses of his accounts. Talking about the turtles of Brazil, for example, Rodrigues Ferreira described all the encountered species (Matamatá, Iurará-pitiú, Iurará-uirapequé, Jabutim-tinga, Uruaná, etc.), but as demonstrated in the following passage, he frequently went beyond merely anatomic taxonomy:

Iurará-uaçu or reté means great or true turtle. This name is given in the countryside of
the State of Pará, for in the surroundings of the city it is called true turtle, the one used
for making combs out of its shell . . . They can be caught all year around, nevertheless
the best time to catch them is when the rivers are low, from September to December,
when they come to the river banks to lay eggs . . . In the months the rivers are full,
from April to July, they are harder to catch, but then is when they are full grown and
tastier.

    There are five ways to catch them:

1.   with an arrow.
2.   with nets.
3.   with hook.
4.   with harpoon.
5.   in their nests. (1972: 25; trans. Luciano Picanço)

The Linnean method, however, did not explain change in nature: it assumed that
species repeat themselves constantly and mechanically. Yet modern science studied
the hidden order of nature not only to classify and organize based on shape and proportion, but also to explain its internal logic, the internal functioning of organisms,
and their mutual relations and interdependence – in other words, to explain the
change and transformation of the total organism. The notion of the organism was
elaborated and developed first by French thinkers (e.g., Maupertius, Diderot, Buffon)
but reached a watershed with the inclusion of fossils in taxonomies (Moraes Belluzo,
1994: 20).

    Fossils undermined the immutable atemporal order established by Linné, causing
a rupture in Enlightenment epistemology. The obsession of imperial knowledge then
turned to establishing what was the "time" of the New World. History was, as Foucault puts it, "the mother of all human sciences" (Pagden, 1997: 382), as it provided
them with a matrix from which to explain and into which to insert their findings. As
Anthony Pagden points out, humanity only became a meaningful category with a
general theory of historical progress. After Kant, Man was not only a rational being
but also a temporal being. Pagden explains that in this historic consciousness, "[t]o
understand him (Man) therefore, one had to unravel the process of construction"
(227).

    Natural history and archaeology began to base their explanations on this linear,
progressive model of historical development, advanced during the Enlightenment and
unquestioned by nineteenth-century positivism. Proto-historic naturalistic representations of New World Nature and Man formed the basis of what would become
twentieth-century anthropology. Archaeologists, on the contrary, studied "archaic
culture and antique civilizations or the Antique Lands," focusing on the "Oriental"
tradition of the eighteenth and nineteenth centuries as studied by Edward Said in
*Orientalism* (1978). "Antique World" and "Primitive World" thus fell into two different categories of evolutionist classification.

    These disciplines were charged with providing examples of primitive and fossilized
societies to support this philosophy of history. At the same time, they also legitimized

the superiority of empire over its colonies, for in an evolutionist framework, New World Man was at the beginning of a series, with the hegemonic culture at the most advanced stage. Any of the different cultures coexisting on earth could be ordered according to its level of development on this scale. As a result, the contemporary Tasmanian or pre-Columbian "primitive" would be located near the beginning of a centuries-long process.

This incipient cultural evolutionism, the precursor of Social Darwinism, relied on the principle of progressive, slow, natural, and unavoidable cultural change. For Buffon, anatomic and cultural differences among men were caused by (a) climate, which explained skin color; (b) nutrition; and (c) habits, which were responsible for such physical characteristics as the shape of one's nose, and size of one's lips. Along with migration and generational change, Buffon believed these three above-mentioned factors to be responsible for the contemporary variety of humanity. Additional factors cited by Buffon include epidemics and the mixing of different populations (Bittloch, 2002). Although still recognizing the essential unity of humanity, this theory was profoundly ethnocentric in its assumption that all cultures – past and contemporary – can be plotted on a single timeline of evolutionary development in which Western culture occupies the most advanced position. The principle of stagnation held that many cultures developed to a certain point along the Western trajectory, but then stopped progressing and fossilized. Only European culture, according to this model, was capable of progressing from the simplest to the most sophisticated point, that is, from the primitive stage to civilization.

It was not only the natural sciences that adopted this evolutionary model of historic matrix, but philology as well, in its classification of primitive versus civilized languages (i.e., those of Indo-European origin, as well as Arabic and Chinese). The supposed infantilism of species in primitive regions was also perceived in languages of those regions. Thus, as the New World puma was smaller than the Old World lion, New World languages evidenced an analogous infantilism which rendered them incapable of expressing abstract or universal concepts. Walter Mignolo and others have pointed out that European colonizers based their idea of superiority not only on their capacity for abstract conceptualization, but also on their possession of an alphabetic writing system which employed a sophisticated technology and was not iconic (Mignolo, 2002: 125–69; Pagden, 1993: 129).

If it is true that natural history was the preferred discipline of hegemony among Enlightenment-era travelers, archaeology was also slowly opening new paths and finding new "stages" of temporality among people in the New World. Orientalist archaeology viewed "archaic" cultures not as proto-historic or primitive but rather as analogous to later stages in the Western historic trajectory, often classical or medieval (Leask, 2002: 49).

During the eighteenth century, archaeological travelers to South America took an interest in archaeological artifacts and ruins with the characteristic viewpoint of the romantic period. Such was the case of the French traveler Joseph Dombey, who went to South America with botanists Ruiz and Pavón to study plants in Peru. Dombey, who exhibited an unprecedented archaeological curiosity, visited Pachacamac, the huacas of Torres Blanca in Chancay, and the caverns of Tarma, and he took back to Louis XVI's court 400 huacos (pieces of antique indigenous ceramic) and some weavings from Pachacamac. These pieces later passed to such museums as the Louvre and Trocadéro (Porras Barrenecheas, 1954: 57).

Moved by a similar impulse, the nineteenth-century *Incidents of Travels to Yucatan* (1843) of John Lloyd Stephens and Frederick Catherwood emerged as the first study of archaeological ruins by scientific travelers; it soon became the obligatory reference for later travelers. Thanks to Stephens's book, American ruins (specifically Mayan) started to gain visibility in the North American and metropolitan imagination. An editorial success, *Incidents* was translated into several different languages. It contains 120 engravings by Catherwood (with corresponding descriptions by Stephens) along with accounts of their travels in Copan, Quirigua, Quetzaltenango, Las Cuevas, Palenque, Uxmal, Mayapan, and Chichen Itza, among other places.

*Incidents* is the account of two separate journeys between October 1839 and October 1841. Both Stephens and Catherwood had been informed by Orientalist discourses on ruins during their previous trips to Eastern Europe and the Middle East. Moreover, Stephens had previously achieved recognition for his editorial success with *Incidents of travel in Egypt, Arabia Petrae, and the Holy Land* (1837).

Influenced by his previous travel experience and by Orientalist discourse, Stephens interpreted Mayan culture according to the contemporary view on ruins. Thus, in many parts of his narration we find comparative descriptions with Egyptians ruins such as the following:

> in the adjoining apartment were the remains of paintings, the most interesting, except those near the village of Xul, that we had met with in the country, and, like those, in position and general effect reminding me of processions in Egyptian tombs. The color of the flesh was red, as was always the case with the Egyptians in representing their own people. Unfortunately, they were so much mutilated to be drawn, and seemed surviving the general wreck only to show that these aboriginal builders had possessed more skills in the least enduring branch of the graphic art. (122)

By comparing Mayan to Egyptian drawings, Stephens posited a connection between two archaic cultures. Both Oriental and American ruins were similarly used by enlightenment science to support the perceived superiority of the conquerors' culture. This ideology associated victorious colonial power with cultural "vitalism," which saw Western civilization in a state of constant evolution and progress, as opposed to fossilized and ruined cultures.

The organicist and evolutionist models of natural science became the dominant approach to historic and aesthetic analysis as well. In the case of Humboldt, Cuvier's scientific distinction between extinct and vital species provided the Prussian traveler with a convenient and seemingly convincing system for classifying cultures as either vital – (e.g., Hellenic and Western), or fossilized (e.g., Egyptian and Mayan) Oriental cultures (Leask, 2002: 51). The influence of natural science on cultural theories grew stronger as the nineteenth century progressed, with the popular application of Darwin's findings and the propagation of Social Darwinism.

Creole travelers elaborated alternate ways of representing New World space and time as a result of their "double consciousness" (Mignolo, 2002: 473), which was in constant dialogue and negotiation with the center of calculation. Mignolo points out that this Creole "double consciousness" is characteristic of subjects operating in a colonial situation, at the margins of hegemonic thought. While this double consciousness has the potential to be disruptive, in the hands of the Creole elite it had quite the opposite effect. They elaborated discourses of national identity in a triangular relationship with the autochthonous population and the imperial center, together forming "three corners of a triangular foreign–local nexus" (Stern, 1998: 56). Local travelers fashioned their accounts in terms of this triangular relationship, trying to integrate the indigenous past of archaeological monuments and prehistoric fossils into the modernity of Western science. In this context, the primitive and the archaic enabled a dialogue between local knowledge and metropolitan disciplines.

In the case of Mexican independence, the proto-nationalist work of Jesuits after their expulsion from the New World deserves special attention. Against the passivity and inferiority of New World Man argued by Buffon and de Pauw, Jesuits such as Clavigero embarked on the task of constructing a local history that upheld its inherent "national greatness." Bernal points out that with his *Storica Antica del Messico* and other writings, Clavigero inaugurated a nationalist-archaeologist spirit in Mexico that inspired later travelers (1980: 69).

As part of this impulse, and under the patronage of King Charles IV of Spain, Guillermo Dupaix made three trips to the Oxaca Valley to study local archaeological monuments. His main objective was to determine the state of cultural progress among these pre-Columbian populations (that is, in comparison to the Egyptians, Persians, Chinese, or Indians). New World greatness would thus be proven by its antiquity and its location on the trajectory of Western history (Bernal, 1980: 100).

In the mid-nineteenth century, local scientific travelers to Rio de la Plata retraced the routes of their predecessors. Given the absence of archaeological ruins, these travelers were naturalists (proto-anthropologists, paleontologists, and geologists). Again following the tendency of the epoch, the predominant question was that of the temporality of New World Man. Building on the work of Lamarck and Darwin (whom he complemented with the application of his mathematical laws), Florentino Ameghino supported for many years the mistaken theory of the Patagonian origin of humanity. He based this theory on fossil evidence collected during his travels in the Pampas and Patagonia. The importance of this land without culture lay precisely in its alleged role as the cradle of humanity. Human migrations that populated the planet were seen as having departed from the south of the American continent on bridges no longer in existence. (Among Ameghino's prolific work, see *El hombre fósil argentino* (1877), *La Antigüedad del hombre en el Plata and Los Mamíferos fósiles en la América Meridional* (1878), *Un Recuerdo a la memoria de Darwin: El transformismo como ciencia exacta* (1882), *Paleontología Argentina: Relaciones filogenéticas y geográficas* (1904), and *Mi Credo* (1906)).

## Conclusion: The *Nomothètes* of Science

As explained above, the activity of both metropolitan and local travelers is closely associated with a cycle of scientific accumulation that generates systems of classifying and organizing Otherness, systems that follow the ethnocentric logic of European travelers and institutions. There exists, however, another constitutive characteristic of the philosopher-traveler, which is perhaps the only one of which the traveler himself is fully aware: the conceptualization of his task as that of a science *nomothète*.

In the transition from a religious vision of the world to one of the universe as a mechanical system, it is important to note that the scientific traveler based his work on new allegories such as that of the "martyr of science," the *nomothète,* the pioneer of a new ideology of knowledge who sought above all else the progress of humanity through science. In the case of travelers such as Humboldt, the rhetoric of the romantic hero and the martyr of science were emphasized as guaranteeing of objectivity and authority. This rhetoric also supported, and indeed demanded new and more radical forms of experimentation. Becker points out that the philosopher-traveler consciously adopted a messianic role in the task of emancipation through reason, embracing these ideals with conviction, devotion, and quasi-religious enthusiasm.

> We can watch this enthusiasm, this passion for liberty and justice, for truth and humanity, rise and rise through the [eighteenth] century until it becomes a delirium, until it culminates, in some symbolical sense, in that half admirable, half pathetic spectacle of June 9, 1794, when Citizen Robespierre, with a bouquet in one hand and a torch in the other, inaugurated the new religion of humanity by lighting the conflagration that was to purge the world of ignorance, vice, and folly. (1932: 43)

The languages of religion and science were melded; indeed, some philosophers merely replaced the word God with such terms as Supreme Being, Author of the Universe, Great Contriver, Primer Mover, and First Cause (Becker, 1932: 50). Nature and its laws now provided an ontological security previously lost with the cosmogonist world of the Sacred Book. Newton's discoveries made nature accessible, enabling humanity to control it to an unprecedented degree. Alexander Pope's epitaph, "Nature and Nature's laws lay hid in night; / God says, 'Let Newton be!' and all was Light" (Audi, 1999: 530) epitomizes the epoch's blurring of science and religion.

In this context, the rhetoric of ritual and sacrifice transformed the figure of the traveler into a martyr of science. The shipwreck as literary motif (cf. Robinson Crusoe, for example) became *de rigeur* for travelers' accounts because of its appeal to a repressed desire for adventure and the experience of primal instincts that urbane society accepted only in literature. However, the motif of shipwreck, with its threats of cannibalism, illness, extreme hunger, and the loss of mental health, can also be interpreted as a vestige of a rhetoric of pilgrimage and martyrdom for transcendental goodness. The best-known examples of this quasi-spiritual suffering are John Cook and his death in a cannibal ritual in the Pacific; the demise of dozens of men in La Condomine's expedition to Ecuador; and of course the corporal experimentation of Humboldt's scientific method, which Leask portrays as bordering on the sadomasochistic (2002: 249):

> What a pleasure, my noble friend, it is to live in the middle of the richness of a majestic and powerful nature! I have accomplished my most ardent and longed for desire, in this thick forest of the Rio Negro, surrounded by tigers and ferocious crocodiles, with my body martyrized by the bites of formidable mosquitoes and ants, and without having eaten other food than water, bananas, fish and yucca; among the indigenous Otomacs that eat sand and at the *rivera* of Casiquiare, (under the equator) where for one hundred thirty leagues around it is not possible to see a human soul; in the most risky moments, I never regret my projects. The suffering is great but short lived. (Humboldt, 1908: 54; my translation)

Such discourse betrays an underlying ambivalence with scientific autonomy, which called for an aloofness from extraneous interests. On the one hand, it was important to validate geographical, astronomical, and mineralogical findings to the imperial patrons; on the other, it was also important to satisfy the avid bourgeois reader of adventure and provide validations of masculinity (Nouzeilles, 2002: 166–8).

However, the main goal of this rhetoric of shipwreck seemed to be establishing the scientific traveler as the new hero of progress, cultivating and affirming a new global order in which science played the special role that religion had previously held. Mindful of these high stakes, Humboldt not only exhausted his entire fortune in underwriting his own travels, but after five years in the new continent, he decided to return not home but rather to the Parisian scientific community, his real interlocutors. Spain and Germany, despite being his sponsors, were disregarded; thus, a new autonomy for the scientific field was defined. The philosopher-traveler as the "martyr of science" represents a new stage in the scientific urge to be free of direct or indirect pressures from temporal powers. Such an ideology also served to alleviate the guilty consciousness of imperial modernity.

In the case of local or Creole travelers, the emergence of the scientific ethos is directly related to the configuration of a national epic. These travelers negotiated the entrance of the new national states into Western "civilization" by means of their trailblazing science; as such they were, in the words of Ricardo Rojas, "heroes of peace." Francisco P. Moreno, an Argentinean traveler in the unexplored Patagonia, was charged with demarcating the borders between Argentina and Chile along the Andes between 1897 and 1902. In his *Reminiscencias*, the *Perito* Moreno reflected on what he conceived of as a civilizing and patriotic mission:

> Material pleasure has made us forget, unfortunately more than once, our duties to our fatherland. We are now absorbed by cosmopolitanism, alongside which we should

uphold . . . the fugitive memory of past glories . . . I would divulge, as much as I can, the composition of the soil of my fatherland, and difficulties will not stop me. I wish to pursue the same ideals of the men who had faced circumstances a thousand times more difficult without complaint. (1999: 23–4); my translation)

Science also became a discourse where Latin American intellectuals negotiated a definition of the "We" (Latin Americans) as modern and distinct from the inner "Barbaric Otherness." Nevertheless, Latin American intellectuals continue to think and imagine themselves as "other" with respect to metropolitan knowledge (Jáuregui and Dabove, 2003: 7–35). This tension would seem to be traced back to Latin American travelers of the Enlightenment.

## REFERENCES AND FURTHER READING

Audi, Robert, ed. (1999). *The Cambridge Dictionary of Philosophy*. New York: Cambridge University Press.

Becker, Carl (1932). *The Heavenly City of the Eighteenth-Century Philosophers*. New Haven, CT: Yale University Press.

Bernal, Ignacio (1980). *A History of Mexican Archaeology: The Vanished Civilizations of Middle America*. London: Thames & Hudson.

Bittloch, Eduardo (2002). "Ciencia, raza y racismo en el siglo XVIII," *Ciencia Hoy*, 6(33), http://www.ciencia-hoy.retina.ar/hoy33/raza01.htm

Bourdieu, Pierre (1966). *The Rules of Art*. Stanford, CA: Stanford University Press.

Cañizares-Esguerra, Jorge (1998). "Spanish America in eighteenth-century European travel compilations: a new 'art of reading' and the transition to modernity," *Journal of Early Modern History*, 2(4): 329–49.

Giddens, Anthony (1984). *The Constitution of Society: Outline of a Theory of Structuration*. Berkeley: University of California Press.

Humboldt, Alexander von (1908). *Cartas americanas*. Trans. Marta Traba. Caracas: Biblioteca Ayacucho.

— (1956). *Viaje a las regiones equinocciales del Nuevo Continente*. Vol. 1. Caracas: Ediciones del Ministerio de Educación.

Jáuregui, Carlos A., and Dabove, Juan Pablo (2003). "Mapas heterotópicos de América Latina," in C. A. Jáuregui and J. P. Dabove (eds), *Heterotopías: Narrativas de identidad y alteridad latinoamericana*, pp. 7–35. Pittsburgh: IILI.

La Condamine, Charles Marie de (1941). *Relación abreviada de un viaje hecho por el interior de la América Meridional*. Madrid: Espasa-Calpe.

Latour, Bruno (1987). *Science in Action: How to Follow Scientists and Engineers through Society*. Cambridge, MA: Harvard University Press, 1987.

Leask, Nigel (2002). *Curiosity and Aesthetic of Travel Writing: 1770–1840*. New York: Oxford University Press.

Mignolo, Walter (1955). *The Dark Side of the Renaissance*. Ann Arbor: University of Michigan Press.

— (2002). "Commentary" to José de Acosta, *Natural and Moral History of the Indies (Chronicles of the New World Encounter)*, pp. 451–523. Durham, NC: Duke University Press.

Moraes Belluzzo, Ana Maria de (1994). *Un Lugar no universo: O Brasil dos viajantes*. Vol. II. São Paulo: Odebrecht.

Moreno, Francisco (1999). *Reminiscencias del Perito Moreno*. Buenos Aires: El elefante blanco.

Nouzeilles, Gabriela (2002). "El retorno de lo primitivo. Aventura y masculinidad." In G. Nouzeilles (ed.), *La Naturaleza en disputa: Retóricas del cuerpo y el paisaje en América Latina*, pp. 163–86. Buenos Aires: Paidós.

Pagden, Anthony (1993). *European Encounters with the New World: From Renaissance to Romanticism*. New Haven, CT and London: Yale University Press.

— (1997). "Eighteenth-century anthropology and the 'history of mankind.'" In Donald Kelley (ed.), *History and the Disciplines: The Reclassification of Knowledge in Early Modern Europe*, pp. 223–5. New York: University of Rochester Press.

Porras Barrenecheas, Raúl (1954). *Fuentes históricas peruanas: Apuntes para un curso universitario.* Lima: J. Mejía Baca.

Pratt, Mary Louise (1992). *Imperial Eyes: Travel Writing and Transculturation.* New York: Routledge.

Rodrigues Ferreira, Alexandre (1972). *Viagem filosófica.* Vol. 6. Rio de Janeiro: Conselho Federal de Cultura.

Rojas, Ricardo (1922). *Los arquetipos. Seis oraciones: Belgrano, Güemes, Sarmiento, Pellegrini, Ameghino,* Guido Spano. Buenos Aires: Librería "La Facultad."

Said, Edward (1978). *Orientalism.* New York: Pantheon Books.

Stagl, Justin (1995). *A History of Curiosity: The Theory of Travel 1550–1800.* Chur, Switzerland: Harwood Academic.

Stern, Steve (1998). "Paradoxes of foreign–local encounter." In M. Joseph, C. C. Legrand, and R. D. Salvatore (eds), *Close Encounters of Empire: Writing the Cultural History of U.S.–Latin American Relations*, pp. 47–68. Durham, NC: Duke University Press.

# 15

# The Haitian Revolution

*Sibylle Fischer*

## I

Between 1791 and 1804 a series of events unfolded in the French colony of Saint Domingue that changed the political and cultural landscape of the Atlantic forever. Saint Domingue, the "Pearl of the Antilles," had been the most profitable slave colony in the Americas. At the onset of the French Revolution, nearly half the sugar and coffee consumed in Europe and the New World was produced in Saint Domingue. With 500,000 slaves, 40,000 whites, and 30,000 free people of color, it also represented by far the greatest concentration of slaves in the Caribbean. In the five years before the onset of the insurrection, more than 30,000 Africans were brought to Saint Domingue each year. When the revolution began, more than half of the slaves were African-born.

In August 1791 a massive slave uprising on the northern plain broke out which involved some 30,000 slaves and soon spread to the other parts of Saint Domingue. Having brutally suppressed the efforts of free people of color to gain political rights at an earlier stage, France responded to the unrest by finally granting full citizenship to all free people in 1792. For a brief period Saint Domingue was ruled by an alliance of white republicans and free people of color. In 1793 war broke out between revolutionary France, Spain, and Britain, and the last two tried to seize France's prize colony. Although general emancipation was by no means the goal of the imperial powers, all sides tried to gain the support of the black masses, and the insurgents successfully played the powers against each other. When France finally declared the slavery abolished in 1794, it was merely underwriting a *fait accompli*. But abolition did not bring peace to the colony. Several more years of warfare ensued, in the course of which Toussaint Louverture, a former slave, established himself in a position of unrivaled authority in Saint Domingue. France was left with no choice but to recognize him as the governor of the colony.

In 1801, Toussaint issued a constitution for Saint Domingue which unequivocally banned slavery and made him governor for life, but stopped short of declaring independence. Napoleon, enraged by the insubordination of what he contemptuously called the "gilded Africans," sent troops to reestablish metropolitan control and bring back the slave regime. The French invasion of 1802 soon turned into a genocidal war against the black population. But the attempt to subdue the colony failed. When France finally evacuated from Saint Domingue, over 50,000 French soldiers and sailors had lost their lives. On January 1, 1804 Jean-Jacques Dessalines, who had taken over the military leadership after Toussaint's abduction and death in a French dungeon in 1803, declared independence.

The Haitian Revolution was an enormously complex event. It was a revolution that involved three continents and two interdependent revolutionary chronologies – the French and the Haitian. Moreover, the events in Saint Domingue in themselves were in a sense already three revolutions in one: that of the slaves who demanded liberty, that of the free people of color who demanded political equality, and that of the French settlers, who aspired to greater autonomy from the metropolis. But complexity is not the only challenge. The slaves, who were after all the real protagonists of the events, could in their vast majority not read or write and left behind no written testimony. While white eyewitnesses of the revolutionary events, pro-slavery agitators, and reformist abolitionists of the cultural elites produced a considerable archive, radical antislavery in the colonies always was a subaltern project. It relied on rumors rather than newspapers, songs rather than novels, drawings rather than manifestoes. The Haitian Revolution was not an event in what Ángel Rama called "the lettered city," and this in itself becomes a challenge for anyone who wants to give an account of the cultural and political significance of the events that does not merely reproduce the vision of those who had access to writing.

The most compelling rendition of the events continues to be C. L. R. James's *The Black Jacobins* (1938), which the Trinidadian scholar and activist conceived in response to the Abyssinian crisis of the mid-1930s, anticipating thereby anticolonial struggles that had not yet begun. (For an updated narrative account of the Haitian Revolution, see Dubois, 2004; for a survey of scholarly debates and disputes, see Geggus, 2002). Though this is not the place to enter into a discussion of the growing historiography of the Haitian Revolution, it is important to signal some of those issues that have proven to be significant from a broadly political and ideological perspective.

There is, first of all, the question of the relationship between the events in the colony and in France. Can we – should we – consider the colonial events in separation from the French Revolution, as Aimé Césaire argued in *Toussaint L'Ouverture: La Révolution française et le problème coloniale* (1962), or are they part of the transatlantic revolutionary currents between 1789 and 1848? After all, James gave his influential study of the revolution the title "Black Jacobins," despite his considerable interest in the local aspects of the insurrection and his insistence that the Haitian Revolution was by no means a sideshow of the French Revolution. Many Haitian historians, by contrast, have suggested a genealogy that in fact plays down the revolution itself by linking it to maroon societies and making it part of patterns of resistance among slaves that long predate the revolutionary age. In this story the key ideological force is not Jacobinism, but long-standing local cultural and social practices. And finally there is the issue of African practices and beliefs. Although it seems highly likely that the style of guerrilla warfare that proved so successful in Saint Domingue, the well-documented royalism of some of the insurgent slaves, and some other aspects of the insurgency originated in Africa, this remains the least understood aspect of the Haitian Revolution. Whatever the reasons may have been – an institutionally consecrated Eurocentrism of much mainstream historical study, the nationalist tendencies in Haitian scholarship, the essentialist and antimodern ideology of *noirisme* of the Duvalierist regime – few people have been prepared to recognize that in the Haitian Revolution practices of African origins and a modern universalism of liberty and equality had become inseparable.

As the first post-slavery state in the hemisphere and the second independent nation in the Americas, Haiti was decidedly not welcome among its neighbors (Jordan, 1968; Trouillot, 1995, Fischer, 2004). From the early days of the revolution, the colony had been subjected to a *cordon sanitaire* that would, it was hoped, curtail the flow of people and information and thus prevent the "cancer of revolution" (Jordan, 1968: 375) from spreading to other territories. Diplomatic correspondence between the colonial administrators and the metropolises in the years after 1791 is replete with calls for vigilance and admonitions to maintain controls "in order to prevent the entrance . . . of any reports about what is happening in the French Islands and Empire" (Franco, 1954: 64). As other sugar producers stepped into the space opened up by the demise of Saint Domingue, the end of slavery in Haiti meant, in fact, an increase in the numbers of slaves elsewhere. This is particularly true for Cuba, which eventually became the main sugar producer in the Caribbean. With the increase in slaves, fears of slave uprisings grew as well, and with that the sense that isolating the insurgent colony was of utmost importance.

The impact of the events in Haiti on the developing local cultures in the region, and particularly on the way in which Creole elites established their hegemony, was thus enormous. Neither Bolívar's fear of "pardocracia," nor the racial fantasy that underwrites Dominican right-wing nationalism, nor Cuba's delayed independence process can be understood in separation from the events in Haiti.

None of the great powers in the region recognized Haitian independence in 1804. In order to gain French recognition in 1825, the Haitian government had to agree to pay a large indemnity for the losses France had incurred (a fact that came to haunt France in recent times, when Haitian president Jean-Bertrand Aristide demanded repayment of the contemporary equivalent of that sum, with interest, from France, thereby creating a diplomatic *éclat* that may well have contributed to his loss of international support and eventually to his downfall in 2004). The Vatican did not recognize Haiti until the Concordat of 1860, a fact that had a significant impact on the Haitian system of popular education as well as on its relations with Latin America. Recognition of Haiti by the United States did not come until 1862.

And yet, the abolition of the institution of racial slavery in the Atlantic did not dramatically change the way in which Haiti's revolutionary origins were perceived. Haiti's history of authoritarianism, political upheaval, and economic disaster after independence has continued to cast a long shadow over most stories of the Haitian Revolution. Scholarly work on Haitian history and culture tends to be careful nowadays to weigh the relative importance of international ostracism, the persistence of social and economic structures from the colonial era, and the effects of the revolution itself, particularly the emergence of a new elite among the insurgents. But writing of a more popular sort tends to draw a rather more simple picture. The media reports in the United States about the commemorations of the Bicentennial of the Haitian Revolution in 2004 are a case in point. As the commemorative events were from the beginning overshadowed by the increasingly violent rebellion against President Aristide, the events of 1791–1804 were typically presented as ominous prefigurations of future catastrophe. "200 Years after Napoleon, Haiti Finds Little to Celebrate," the *New York Times* headline proclaimed on January 2, ending caustically with a quote from "a young man from Gonaïve": "Don't come to the celebration tomorrow. There will be blood." As the *National Review* on March 1, 2004 bluntly put it, "Haiti has been a failed state for 200 years": the Haitian Revolution becomes part of a negative teleology according to which the troubles of post-independence Haiti are the necessary outcome of its bloody origins in a slave revolution. Haiti's history is always already part of a story of peripheral underdevelopment and Third-World authoritarianism.

It does not come as a surprise, then, that most mainstream accounts of the revolutionary age ignore the events in the French colony and continue to focus on France and the United States. If Haiti is mentioned at all, it is usually considered a minor sideshow of the revolution in France. A similarly glaring absence can be found in Western political theory. While the texts surrounding the foundation of the United States of America are taken to be canonical by most political theorists, Haiti and its founding ideology of revolutionary antislavery has yet to be noticed, despite the fact that at least from a typological and ideological perspective the only revolution that put issues of racial equality at the center of the agenda would seem to be of considerable interest.

Clearly, the absence of the Haitian Revolution from our accounts of the revolutionary age has far-reaching consequences. It was in the revolutionary age that the ideological and political landscape of the West took shape. It was a time when the meaning and scope of "liberty" and "equality" were contested in parliamentary debates and the subject of endless pamphleteering. Revolutionary antislavery in the Caribbean was at least in part a struggle over what was meant by "liberty" and "equality" and how to revise a universalism that, up to that point, had always found means for allowing the continuation of racial subordination and racial slavery. Slave liberation started in the Caribbean, with the actions of slaves and their free allies – black, mulatto, and white; it did not begin in the Assembly in Paris. When Haiti is written out of the picture, we lose sight of this internal contestation within modern political discourse. Western modernity becomes a phenomenon of European, metropolitan origin. Political agency of slaves remains a non-thought and racial equality and racial liberation are removed from what are conventionally understood as "political" issues.

In light of this history, it is not surprising that much scholarship in recent years has focused on what Trouillot called the "silencing" of the Haitian Revolution. But it is equally important to recognize that the silence that accompanied the events was never complete and never meant that events were truly not known. The press in Europe in fact reported on them at some length (Jenson, 2008; Schüller, 2001; Buck-Morss, 2000), and within the African diaspora the Haitian Revolution has always been an event of great significance. In the United States, Haiti was a key reference point for nineteenth-century black abolitionists, and later for black nationalists like Martin Delany (Nwankwo, 2005). It was in the plantation zone that the greatest efforts were made to contain the news, but it is now clear that there, too, reports were circulating among slaves and free people of color. Rumor is promiscuous in nature and would have reached people of color as much as white slaveholders. Newspapers can be read aloud to those who cannot read themselves, and many people of color could in fact read. In the dominant sector of nineteenth-century societies, finally, knowledge and silence coexisted in a paradoxical symbiosis, where the same colonial authorities who claimed the events were insignificant kept meticulous records of them. Knowledge and silence, recognition and denial did not exist in separate realms, but were always part of the same story.

Records relating to slave conspiracies on the Spanish American mainland suggest that the insurgents tended to use the term "la libertad de los franceses" (the liberty of the French) to distinguish the goal of general emancipation from what Creole elites meant by the term liberty. Songs from northern Brazil contain references to the leaders of the Haitian Revolution. One of the best-documented examples relates to the trial against José Antonio Aponte, the supposed leader of a far-flung antislavery conspiracy in Cuba in 1812. A key concern of the tribunal in charge of the investigation was any connection of the conspiracy to Haiti, and while no actual participation of Haitians could be shown, it became obvious that the example of Haiti had been an important source of inspiration for the conspirators. The trial records indicate that portraits of the leaders of the Haitian Revolution had been circulating among the people of color, and that there had been some expectations that Haiti might lend support once the insurgence was underway. The mere names of the Haitians appear to have acquired a quasi-mythical status: it seems, for instance, that Jean François, one of the generals in the revolution's earlier stages, and invoked repeatedly in the Aponte trial as "Juan Francisco," had become shorthand for slave revolution and that new "Juan Franciscos" continued to appear in distant areas of the Spanish Caribbean long after Jean François's demise (Childs, 2001).

It almost seems that the odd coincidence of tight-lipped silence and passionate debate, informational blockade and archival chatter, knowledge of detail and denial of transcendence, public ignorance and private recognition, is the historical condition in which the Haitian Revolution has existed ever since it began in 1791. Some recent historical and cultural work has therefore suggested that the most challenging issue may be how to understand this puzzling coexistence of silence and knowledge. Rather than thinking about the Haitian Revolution simply as silenced or unthinkable history, it may be more promising to focus on the contradictory nature of the responses and their profound social and geographical heterogeneity (Ferrer, 2008; Fischer, 2004, Dubois, 2006). We need to ask ourselves what colonial authorities were doing when they both denied the events and meticulously recorded them; or what European philosophers were thinking when they used the term "slaves" as a metaphor for people oppressed by a despotic ruler, but failed to include real slaves under the term "slaves." The situation seems be a form of disavowal, a term that in its everyday sense just means a "refusal to acknowledge" or "repudiation," but which Sigmund Freud occasionally used to describe epistemologically unstable or contradictory responses to traumatic perceptions. Acts of disavowal are, in Freud's account, "half-measures," "incomplete attempts at detachment from reality": "disavowal is always supplemented by an acknowledgement" (1953–74: 23: 204).

Thinking about Haiti through the concept of disavowal would allow us to see that Haiti (and all it came to represent) is in some sense present in European and Eurocentric thought, even where its name is carefully avoided. It allows us to see that people who we know knew nevertheless would not acknowledge their knowledge. It is a strategy (although not necessarily one voluntarily chosen) that in itself can turn productive and bring forth further stories and fantasies that hide from view what must not be seen: a colonial modernity that organizes and interprets the core principles of enlightenment discourse in a way that challenges white supremacy and European dominance.

We could illustrate this with the writings of European thinkers and philosophers. But it is equally instructive to take a brief look at the reaction to Haiti in the nationalist imaginary in the Dominican Republic (San Miguel, 1997). Many scholars and critics have pointed out to what extent Dominican nationalism is driven by virulent anti-Haitian sentiment, an ideology that came to a head in 1937, when at least 20,000 Haitians living in the Dominican Republic were massacred during the Trujillo dictatorship. But ultimately Dominican anti-Haitianism cannot be understood without reference to the Haitian Revolution and the effects it had on the adjacent territory.

In the course of the nineteenth century, Dominican nationalism developed along two apparently contradictory lines: indigenism and Hispanism. With indigenism representing a noble savage ideology and Hispanism a conservative colonialist catholicism, this can only strike us as an odd mixture indeed, unless we add a third term: Haitian modernity. The formation of this ideology is a complex story that cannot fully be explored here. Key to it are obviously the various invasions of the Spanish territory by armies of former slaves, beginning with Toussaint Louverture's occupation in 1801, followed by Dessalines's occupation in 1805, and then Haitian president Boyer's negotiated occupation after the first Dominican declaration of independence from Spain in 1822 – an occupation that lasted until 1844. Each invasion entailed an abolition of slavery, and eyewitness accounts often report them as an intrusion of a modern secularism and egalitarianism in traditional Dominican society. Under the

Haitian President Boyer, Dominican legal codes were rewritten in the spirit of the Code Napoléon, the church lost many of its holdings and privileges, and property titles were regularized – in short, the Spanish territory was submitted to a process of forced modernization. Resistance to Haitian rule crystallized around these policies, which did not agree with traditional Dominican practices. Yet very few Dominican scholars and intellectuals remembered this in later years. Dominican nationalism developed by rewriting the Haitian occupier as a barbarian force opposed to the civilizatory force of a Spanish colonization intent on converting the indigenous population and creating a new Garden of Eden. It was easier, it seems, to reconcile indigenism and Hispanism, than Haiti and modernity.

Thinking about the Haitian Revolution through the concept of disavowal, then, allows us to think about Haiti in relation to modernity without denying its particularities. Clearly, there were constitutive influences that cannot be reduced to a Western enlightenment in the colonies. But that becomes a problem only if we want to claim primacy for modernity's European and supposedly more homogeneous face. If we read modernity from the perspective of the Caribbean colonies, we see that heterogeneity was a congenital condition of modernity. It may well be best to think of conventional accounts of Western modernity as having been distilled out of the hybrid hemispheric phenomenon – distilled by ideological operations, forgetfulness, and active suppression of "impure," "hybrid" elements. Familiar claims about the "unfinished project of modernity" would, from this perspective, just be one of the strategies of "purification," since they transform into a utopian promise claims that have in fact been articulated in the past and whose suppression became essential to the "pure" discourse.

## II

The founding documents of the new state of Haiti clearly reflect the new elite's distinctively modern political ideology. They also show how the whole map that surrounds the core values of liberty and equality of the revolutionary age begins to shift once the issues of racial equality is placed at the center: liberty takes on the shape of equality, "social" and "political" rights start to look indistinguishable, and the notion of citizenship becomes internationalized and racialized. But by the same token they reflect the aporias that underlie the foundation of a state based on revolutionary antislavery at a time when slavery continued to be a profitable labor arrangement in the Atlantic. The impasse Haiti was facing goes beyond the familiar troubles of postcolonial foundations and points to the limitations and blind spots of modern political theory and of a practice of politics that could not respond to the reality of racial slavery as a hemispheric business.

Having rejected an earlier draft for a Proclamation of Independence which contained lengthy discussions of the motives for secession as well as lists of rights and principles of justice, Dessalines turned to a young officer by the name of Louis

Boisrond Tonnerre. Boisrond Tonnerre, a French-educated mulatto, had expressed his more radical vision of Haitian independence in these terms: "To prepare the independence act, we need the skin of a white man for parchment, his skull for a writing-case, his blood for ink, and a bayonet for a pen" (Madiou, 1985: 3: 145). In light of the massacre of the remaining French people ordered by Dessalines after independence, despite his earlier promises that their lives would be protected, this may be seen as an ominous sign of things to come. But it can also be read as a prescient hint at the difficulties Haiti was facing after independence and an uncanny prefiguration of Caliban/cannibal as an emblem of the postcolonial predicament in the Caribbean. In a situation where even the revolutionary leaders could barely sign their names (Toussaint Louverture, who is said to have been able to read French, is the exception, though even he needed to rely on secretaries for his correspondence) and French was a foreign language to practically all insurgents, Boisrond Tonnerre evidently sensed that there was something incongruous about producing a formal declaration of independence in writing and, moreover, in French. The act of revenge, which is at the heart of his notorious statement, is thus mediated through what we might call a cannibalization of writing. Before Haiti can come into being, before there can be a subject that could write its own name, writing needs to be reconstituted on new grounds. Haiti's name needs to be both written with the master's hand, as it were, and written in a completely new script, a different form of writing.

But like most texts written at the time of the founding of the new state, this one too has a double valence. On the one hand, it is a reflection on the difficulties of postcolonial foundations. On the other, it is a response to an international realm where the Haitian Revolution was routinely disavowed. The savage imagery of the statement self-consciously appropriates a discourse of barbarism that had been commonplace in the reports of observers of the revolution who could conceive of the slave insurrection only in terms of body counts, rape, material destruction, and infinite bloodshed. To the eyewitnesses who left behind written testimony (a first-person narrative of the events by a person of African descent has yet to be found), it was unspeakable violence, outside the realm of civilization, outside politics, and beyond human language: not a struggle for liberty, equality, and sovereignty, but the "catastrophic" result of a "primeval" societal situation, as the Dominican ideologue of the Trujillato Manuel Arturo Peña Batlle once put it.

The brief Declaration of Independence on January 1, 1804 was accompanied by an Address to the Nation, also written by Boisrond Tonnerre and read out aloud as part of the official ceremony (Madiou, 1985: 3: 146–50). Predictably enough, it calls for a complete break with France. "We have dared to be free, let us now dare to be free by ourselves and for ourselves." But things are not quite as simple as one might have hoped. "The French name still grieves [*lugubre*] our lands. Everything here bears the memory of the cruelty of these barbarous people: our laws, our customs, our towns, everything still carries the French imprint." French will speak the truth only if it is forced to do so: the adjective *lugubre* [lugubrious] is twisted into a verb that French did not have, *lugubrer*.

But the problems of Haiti's postcolonial foundations are not just of a linguistic or cultural order. If we read "the French name" that "grieves our land" to refer not to the former French master, but to the name that France gave to its slave colony, we see that what is at stake here is not just a melancholy reflection on the postcolonial conundrum, but the problematic interpellation of a new citizenry. The people who defeated the French had been brought into existence as "the slaves of Saint Domingue." It was antislavery that provided them with an identification and constituted them as a subject. How can that interpellation be turned into something that would serve as a foundation for a new state? The former name lingers, and continues to "grieve the land."

The interpellative nature of the text also shows itself in the forms of address employed. It starts out with the customary revolutionary appellation "citizens," which invokes a formal legal category, and then moves to ever more substantive forms of address, from "citizens, my compatriots," to "indigenous citizens," to "indigenes of Haiti." What constitutes the Haitians? Merely saying that they are not French does not seem to be enough, but the alternatives are not entirely compelling either. After proleptically invoking the nation, the final address returns to the negative identification: "you, a people ill-fated for too long," in other words, the slaves of Saint Domingue.

This final turn to the history of slavery signals a very important aspect regarding the constitution of Haiti as a nation. Haiti was the only state in the hemisphere to have emerged in a revolutionary struggle against racial slavery. But radical antislavery, like the slave trade itself, was an international phenomenon and transcended the boundaries of nations and empires. The foundational texts of Haiti are testimony to the fact that revolutionary antislavery had generated political goals that could not simply be contained in the borders of the new state: one may well fight against colonialism at home, and not object to the colonial regime next door; but one cannot fight against slavery on account of racial equality, and remain indifferent to slavery elsewhere. Already in the Address of 1804, we find a trace of this problem, when the audience is admonished to make sure "that the spirit of proselytism does not destroy our work": "let us allow our neighbors to breathe in peace; that they shall live peaceably under the laws that they have given themselves" (Madiou, 1985: 3: 148). There is little evidence that post-revolutionary Haiti ever tried to support insurrections elsewhere (unless we count the support Pétion gave to Bolívar for his Venezuelan expedition in 1816), but the imperial powers nevertheless demanded guarantees. All early Haitian Constitutions thus contain provisions according to which Haiti would abstain from "engaging in any wars of conquest," and "disturbing the peace and internal regime of foreign islands" (Art. 2, Constitution of 1806). But they also find a way of allowing for a liberal asylum practice for all people escaping slavery or genocide, without raising the specter of "Haitian ships" and "Haitian soldiers" intent upon liberating slaves in adjacent territories. The earliest constitutions do so by remaining silent on general rules for Haitian citizenship, while placing detailed restrictions on whites and their entitlements in Haiti. Rather than reading this as an exclusionary or even racist strand in Haiti's foundational ideology, as some commentators have done, it should be seen as the trace of an attempt to hide an internationalism Haiti inherited from its origins in revolutionary antislavery that had become dangerous to its survival in the slaveholding Atlantic. This is why, I think, an explicit clause regulating the status of non-whites cannot be found until the Republican constitution of 1816, and why, when it does appear, it takes on a decidedly inclusive approach to what constitutes Haitian nationality: "Art. 44 – All Africans and Indians, and those of their blood, born in the colonies or in foreign countries, who come to reside in the Republic will be recognized as Haitians, but will not enjoy the right of citizenship until after one year of residence." This provision, predictably, was objected to by some on the grounds that it violated the noninterference clause and thus posed a danger to the survival of the state.

The provisions regulating residency and citizenship in Haiti thus must be seen as directly linked to those that regulate Haiti's relation to neighboring countries or colonies. It would seem that the difficulty of interpellating the "former slaves of Saint Domingue" into a nation is not the result of a mere "lack" – the absence of a constitutive ideology, or a misunderstanding of core concepts like "liberty," as some scholars have claimed. Rather, it is testimony to the constraints that the modern world system imposed on the politics of revolutionary antislavery. The core demand of the slave revolution – racial liberation – could become constitutive for the new state only if, and to the extent that, Haiti inscribed in its own constitution the strictures of the colonial world order and the slaveholding Atlantic.

It is in this context that the reference to Haitians as "indigenous" in the 1804 Address to the Nation, as well as the inclusion of Amero-Indians among those who become Haitians the moment they take up residency, takes on special significance. In fact, the shifts in the concept of "indigenism" will allow us to trace some of the major ideological changes in Haitian culture and literature from independence to the twentieth century.

Obviously, people of African origin are no more native to Hispaniola than Europeans. But in 1802 Dessalines had begun to use epithets denoting native status for his insurgent army. For a brief period, "Army of the Incas" and even "Sons of the Sun" was used. Eventually the term "indigenous" became the preferred term. It is in this context also that we need to consider the choice of "Haiti" – a name of Taino origin – as the name for the territory (Geggus, 2002: 207–20).

The indigenous symbolism was probably part of an effort to overcome the heterogeneity of an army composed of Africans of different ethnic origins as well as Creoles and to produce a Haitian interpellation that would transcend "the French name." In this respect, the early "indigenism" could be considered as equivalent to the much-quoted Article 14 of Dessalines's Constitution of 1805 which abolishes all distinctions of color among Haitians and stipulates that "Haitians will henceforth be known by the generic denomination of blacks," with the at first sight surprising implication that certain Poles and Germans who had been given citizenship rights in the article immediately preceding Article 14 would count as black as well. While in the course of the nineteenth century dominant ideologies in the Atlantic world increasingly treated differences of color and ethnicity as a matter of "science" and "biology," revolutionary ideology in Haiti took the opposite direction and interpreted them as political categories.

Article 14 of the first Haitian Constitution disappeared in later constitutions, but indigenism continued to play an important role in post-independence Haiti. There is, for instance, a historical essay by the romantic writer Emile Nau, entitled *Histoire des Caciques d'Haïti* (1855; History of the chieftains of Haiti), incidentally centered around the same events as the better-known novel *Enriquillo* (1882) by Manuel Galván, which represents the rather different Dominican variant of indigenism. Nau's *Histoire* is a vindication of a transgenerational and transcultural link between the Amero-Indians and African slaves. The Haitian Revolution avenged the failed rebellion of the indigenous people in the early years of the conquest: "The African and the Indian join their hands in chains" (vol. 1: 12).

Interestingly, the term *indigène* was appropriated again a century later by a cultural-nationalist movement that developed in response to the US occupation of Haiti (1915–34). It is striking, however, that the term, with its evident roots in the anti-slavery revolution, is now employed in a very different sense. Here is what the Haitian anthropologist, founding figure of the twentieth-century indigenist movement, and precursor of the *négritude* movement, Jean Price-Mars, has to say about the revolution: "despite the successive upheavals which led to the ruin of the old regime and the advent of the new nation, one is astonished to find that the change has been more apparent than real." Even though power passed on into the hands of people of mixed or African ancestry, the structures of domination remained intact. "As radical as this change appeared to be, it was only accomplished through a monopoly of public authority by an audacious and energetic minority" (1983: 104–5) While in Boisrond Tonnerre's revolutionary rhetoric *indigène* was proposed as an equivalent of "citizen" and "compatriot" and was meant to interpellate all the inhabitants of the territory into the new nation, Price-Mars identifies *indigène* with those whose de facto access to citizenship rights was severely curtailed: the peasant. "Indigenism" has shifted from representing the claims of the revolutionary leaders against colonial oppressors and slaveholders to signify the claims of those oppressed by elites that emerged as a result of the revolution. At the same time, indigenism also loses its symbolic links to a transnational politics of resistance and liberation and thereby becomes available for appropriation by the ultranationalist and antimodern *noirist* ideology of the Duvalier regime (1957–71). If the term *indigène* originally signaled a political subject constituted by a revolutionary alliance of ethnically diverse groups against the genocidal politics of colonialism and slavery, in the twentieth century it becomes the basis of an obscurantist and extremely authoritarian ideology.

The radical changes regarding the notion of "indigenism" illustrate what makes giving an account of the significance of the Haitian Revolution within a larger cultural context an extremely difficult task. The issues may be further illuminated by the analysis Michel-Rolph Trouillot (1990) offers of the impasses created by the Haitian

Revolution. According to Trouillot, the antislavery revolution and the subsequent foundation of the Haitian state brought about a profound disconnect between the goals of the state and the goals of the populace. For the state, liberty meant independence from France; for the former slaves, freedom from the grueling work on the plantation. For the state, survival depended on a return to the plantation economy; for the former slaves, survival meant a subsistence economy built on the garden plot and Sunday markets. This pitted the state – and of course the elites that had emerged as a result of the revolution and that subsequently appropriated the state – against the vast majority of the population and explains why from the beginning the state took on a decisively authoritarian character.

The result of this is that an invocation of the revolution can mean vastly different things for different social groups and cannot be properly understood in purely thematic terms, without careful consideration of the historical, social, cultural, and institutional contexts that bestow a particular valence on the invocation (or avoidance) of the revolutionary thematic. There is a very strong presence of revolutionary themes and symbols in Haitian visual arts, especially in the nonacademic, "naïve" tradition of painting. The religious practices associated with vodou, particularly the so-called Petro rites which include Dessalines among the *lwa* (spirits), are imbued with references to the revolution and cannot be properly understood without taking that into account (Dayan, 1995: 16–73). And finally there is the state itself which lays claim to the revolutionary heritage through national holidays, monuments, street names, and similar references of high visibility and ritualistic performativity. Given that vodou was a banned and much denigrated religion for most of the 200 years of Haiti's existence, it may serve here as an illustration of the complexities of the issue that both the state and the subalternized religion should lay claim to the revolution's heritage.

From the perspective of literature, matters are further complicated by the fact that the Haitian Revolution occupies quite a different place inside Haiti and outside. There are of course important twentieth-century Haitian authors who wrote about the revolution (e.g., Marie Chauvet and René Philoctète). It is striking, however, that the literary works that have received most international recognition and have achieved emblematic status regarding the theme of the Haitian Revolution are not those written by Haitian authors, but by writers like Aimé Césaire and Edouard Glissant (both from Martinique), Alejo Carpentier (Cuba), and Derek Walcott (Trinidad).

This is not to say that there is not a substantial literary tradition in Haiti about the revolution. Despite the fact that the intellectual elite remained minuscule throughout the nineteenth century, that writing was done almost exclusively in French, i.e., a foreign language to most Haitians, and that literacy rates barely changed until well into the twentieth century (estimated at two percent for the end of the nineteenth-century), nineteenth-century Haiti produced a surprisingly large amount of literature, including a significant body of texts about the events that led to the foundation of the country (for a survey of Haitian history see Nicholls 1996; on Haitian literary history, see Dash, 1981; Hoffmann, 1995 and articles by Arnold, Breslin, and Jonassaint in Garraway, 2008). For the most part, these texts were not novels, but poems and plays in the neoclassical or romantic vein, whose overall impact on Haitian culture was clearly limited by the institutional weakness of literature and the ideological limitations of a form of cultural production that mostly seemed to serve the purpose of legitimizing elite rule.

This may explain in part why some prominent twentieth-century Haitian authors such as Jacques Roumain, Jacques-Stéphen Alexis, or René Depestre seem to have avoided full-length treatments of the revolution. After the renewal of Haitian literature that took shape as a reaction against the US occupation of Haiti and led to a sharpened awareness of the linkages between the cultural and literary preferences of the Haitian elites and the elites' patent inability to put up effective resistance against the American occupiers, it may have seemed that what Haitian literature needed most was a break away from those themes and emblematic references that had been used to legitimize and solidify elite rule.

It is only in the last few years that a new generation of Haitian writers that includes Evelyne Trouillot, Jean-Claude Fignolé, and Fabienne Pasquet has returned to the revolution. No doubt, this needs to be understood in part as a response to the increased public interest prior to the Bicentennial of the Revolution in 2004 (see, e.g., Casimir, 2001, 2004). It may also signify a rethinking of the foundations of the Haitian state and the status of the writer and intellectual in Haiti in light of the crisis of the second Aristide presidency.

It could be said, skeptically, then, that all of this simply shows that we should not hope to find any specific normative or political meaning in the Haitian Revolution, and that it is best understood as a symbolic reference that can be appropriated for ever-changing purposes. But considering the tremendous challenges in creating a state based on the principles of antislavery and anticolonialism, as discussed above, one could also say that the antislavery revolution produced a legacy that exceeded the political ideas, practices, and institutions that entrenched themselves in the Age of Revolution, and that it is this excess that explains why the Haitian Revolution, unlike the contemporaneous French or American Revolutions, seems to be a matter as much of the present as of the past.

## References and Further Reading

### *References*

Buck-Morss, Susan (2000). "Hegel and Haiti," *Critical Inquiry*, 26: 821–63.

Casimir, Jean (2001). *La Culture opprimée*. Delmas, Haïti: Impr. Lakay.

— (2004). "Pa bliye 1804 – Souviens-toi de 1804." Haiti : Jean Casimir.

Césaire, Aimé (1962). *Toussaint L'Ouverture: La Révolution française et le problème coloniale*. Paris: Présence africaine.

Childs, Matt (2001). "A black French general arrived to conquer the island': images of the Haitian Revolution in Cuba's 1812 Aponte

Rebellion." In David Patrick Geggus (ed.), *The Impact of the Haitian Revolution in the Atlantic World*, pp. 135–56. Columbia: University of South Carolina Press.

Dash, Michael (1981). *Literature and Ideology in Haiti, 1915–1961*. Totowa, NJ: Barnes & Noble.

Dayan, Joan (1995). *Haiti, History, and the Gods*. Berkeley and Los Angeles: University of California Press.

Dubois, Laurent (2004). *The Avengers of the New World: The Story of the Haitian Revolution*. Cambridge, MA: Belknap Press of Harvard University Press.

— (2006). "An enslaved enlightenment: rethinking the intellectual history of the French Atlantic," *Social History*, 31(1):1–14.

Ferrer, Ada (2008). "The archive and the Atlantic's Haitian Revolution." In Doris Garraway (ed.), *Tree of Liberty: Cultural Legacies of the Haitian Revolution in the Atlantic World*. Charlottesville: University of Virginia Press.

Fischer, Sibylle (2004). *Modernity Disavowed: Haiti and the Cultures of Slavery in the Age of Revolution*. Durham, NC: Duke University Press.

Franco, José Luciano (1954). *Documentos para la historia de Haití*. Havana: Publicaciones del Archivo Nacional de Cuba.

Freud, Sigmund (1953–74). *The Standard Edition of the Complete Psychological Works*. Trans. James Strachey. London: Hogarth Press.

Garraway, Doris, ed. (2008). *Tree of Liberty: Cultural Legacies of the Haitian Revolution in the Atlantic World*. Charlottesville: University of Virginia Press.

Geggus, David Patrick (2002). *Haitian Revolutionary Studies*. Bloomington and Indianapolis: Indiana University Press.

Hoffmann, Léon-François (1995). *Littérature d'Haïti*. Vanves: EDICEF.

James, C. L. R. (1989). *The Black Jacobins: Toussaint L'Ouverture and the San Domingo Revolution*. New York: Vintage.

Janvier, Louis Joseph (1886). *Les Constitutions d'Haïti (1801–1885)*. 2 vols. Paris: Flammarion.

Jenson, Deborah (2008). "Toussaint Louverture, spin doctor? Launching the Haitian Revolution in the French media." In Doris Garraway (ed.), *Tree of Liberty: Cultural Legacies of the Haitian Revolution in the Atlantic World*. Charlottesville: University of Virginia Press.

Jordan, Winthrop D. (1968). *White over Black: American Attitudes toward the Negro 1550–1812*. Chapel Hill: University of North Carolina Press.

Madiou, Thomas (1985). *Histoire d'Haïti: Vol. 3 (1803–1807)*. Port-au-Prince: Editions Henri Deschamps.

Nau, Emile (1963). *Histoire des Caciques d'Haïti*. 2 vols. Port-au-Prince: Panorama.

Nicholls, David (1996). *From Dessalines to Duvalier: Race, Colour and National Independence in Haiti*. New Brunswick, NJ: Rutgers University Press.

Nwankwo, Ifeoma Kiddoe (2005). *Black Cosmopolitanism: Racial Consciousness and Transnational Identity in the Nineteenth-Century Americas*. Philadelphia: University of Pennsylvania Press.

Price-Mars, Jean (1983). *So Spoke the Uncle [Ainsi parla l'oncle]*. Trans. and intro. Magdaline W. Shannon. Washington, DC: Three Continents Press.

San Miguel, Pedro Luis (1997). *La Isla imaginada: Historia, identidad y utopía en La Española*. San Juan and Santo Domingo: Isla Negra and La Trinitaria.

Schüller, Karin (2001) "From liberalism to racism: German historians, journalists, and the Haitian Revolution from the late eighteenth to the early twentieth centuries." In David Patrick Geggus (ed.), *The Impact of the Haitian Revolution in the Atlantic World*, pp. 23–43. Columbia: University of South Carolina Press.

Trouillot, Michel-Rolph (1990). *Haiti: State Against Nation. The Origins and Legacy of Duvalierism*. New York: Monthly Review Press.

— (1995). *Silencing the Past: Power and the Production of History*. Boston: Beacon Press.

*Further Reading*

A selection of literary and cultural journals with special issues devoted to the 2004 Bicentennial of the Haitian Revolution

*Casa de las Americas* (spring 2004)
*Research in African Literatures* (35:2, 2004)

*Small Axe* (9:2, 2005)
*Yale French Studies* (107, 2005)

## Selected literary texts about the Haitian Revolution

Bell, Madison Smartt (2000). *All Soul's Rising* (novel).
— (2000). *Master of the Crossroads* (novel).
— (2004). *The Stone that the Builder Refused* (novel).
Buenaventura, Enrique (1963). *La Tragedia de Henri Christophe* [The tragedy of Henri Christophe] (play).
Carpentier, Alejo (1949). *El Reino de este mundo* [The kingdom of this world] (novel).
— (1962). *El Siglo de las luces* [*Explosion in the Cathedral*] (novel).
Césaire, Aimé (1963). *La Tragédie du Roi Christophe* [The tragedy of King Christophe] (play).
Chauvet, Marie (1957). *Danse sur le volcan* [Dance on the volcano] (novel).
Fignolé, Jean-Claude (2004). *Moi, Toussaint Louverture . . . avec la plume complice de l'auteur* [I, Toussaint Louverture . . . with the complicitous pen of the author] (novel).
Glissant, Edouard (1963). *Monsieur Toussaint* (play).
Hugo, Victor (1826). *Bug-Jargal* (novel).
Kleist, Heinrich von (1812). *Verlobung in Santo Domingo* [Betrothal in Santo Domingo] (novella).

Lamartine, Alphonse de (1850). *Toussaint Louverture* (dramatic poem).
Lechat de Coëtnempren de Kersaint, Claire-Louise (1824). *Ourika* (novella).
Métellus, Jean (1991). *Le Pont Rouge* (play).
— (2003). *Toussaint Louverture ou Les Racines de la liberté: théâtre.* [Toussaint Louverture or the roots of liberty: theater] (play).
Pasquet, Fabienne (2001). *La Deuxième mort de Toussaint-Louverture* [The second death of Toussaint Louverture] (novel).
Philoctète, René (1975). *Monsieur de Vastey* (play).
Placoly, Vincent (1983). *Dessalines, ou la passion de l'indépéndance* [Dessalines, or the passion for independence] (play).
Trouillot, Evelyne (2003). *Rosalie l'infâme* [Rosalie, the infamous one] (novel).
Trouillot, Hénock (1967). *Dessalines; ou le sang de Pont-Rouge* [Dessalines, or the blood of Pont-Rouge] (play).
Walcott, Derek (1948, 1958, 1984). *The Haitian Trilogy* (*Henri Christophe*; *Drums and Colors*; *The Haitian Earth*) (plays).
Wordsworth, William (1803). "To Toussaint Louverture" (poem).

# PART III
## The Emergence of National Communities in New Imperial Coordinates

# 16
# The Gaucho and the Gauchesca
## *Abril Trigo*

### Gauchos and Caudillos

The gaucho was the ethnic product of very specific ecological, economic, social, and geopolitical circumstances that coalesced in the prairies of what is today Argentina and Uruguay from middle seventeenth century to the end of the nineteenth century. The word "gaucho" – whose etymology, still uncertain, has inspired innumerable interpretations – originally designated the socially marginal but economically exploited semi-nomadic horseman who roamed through the uninhabited and unpoliced, though politically contested and belatedly colonized by the Spanish and Portuguese (later Brazilian) empires, cattle-abundant pampas. Although ethnically and culturally a *mestizo* – a miscellany of Spanish and Portuguese deserters, runaway African slaves, stranded French sailors and English pirates, and indigenous peoples, most prominently the Guaraní – the gaucho was the social byproduct of a proto-capitalist economy fully integrated at the margins of the colonial mercantile world-system, and the cultural byproduct of a dangerous and unruly geopolitical and utopian borderland. The abundance of herds of wild cattle (*ganado cimarrón*), wild horses, and bountiful plains loosely controlled by colonial authorities enabled the formation of an extremely individualistic, anarchic, and semi-nomadic society of small gangs of men who recognized no other authority than that of the caudillo, a form of authority – whose archetype is the Cid Campeador – established along the eight centuries of warfare between Muslims and Christians in medieval Spain and duly legislated by King Alfonso "El Sabio" (1829). The caudillo embodied an embryonic form of organization in a marginal, uncertain, and liminal society at the militarized, mobile, and disputed borderland between civilizations. Either exploited as *changador* in the *vaquerías* (cattle-hunting expeditions for extracting the cowhides exported to Europe) or persecuted as the predatory, vagrant, and idle *gauderio*, the gaucho was the protagonist of a matriarchal society of dysfunctional families and solitary men "without God, without King, without Law." This motto captures the values of absolute negative freedom and indomitable pride that materialized into arrogance and violence, contempt toward death and praise of individual courage, and a stubborn disdain for private property (with the exception of his horses, knife, and woman, in that order) in a colonial system in which the prohibition to possess land galvanized his imaginary as an outlaw and his existence as a contrabandist. A materialist and practical religiosity and a complete disregard for women, family, and offspring were balanced with a cordial sense of hospitality and community bonding which allowed him to enjoy an anarchic sense of personal freedom while living in appalling poverty.

But this anthropological profile does not exhaust the gaucho's many existences. Actually, this prehistoric social existence as the anonymous agent of an original, though later aborted, proto-ethnicity, as Darcy Ribeiro (1992) has put it, would become a mere pretext for his entrance in history – either as hero or as villain, as solitary *matrero* or as faithful soldier – by converting him into a veritable military machine during the wars of independence and the protracted period of civil wars. It also would be a pretext for his interpellation as a political subject and his transformation in a literary subject by the gauchesca poetry; his enshrinement in the national literary canon; and his ultimate consecration as the mythical foundation of the national imaginary. In other words, his obscure social existence gave way and was given away by a heroic military existence, a manipulated political existence, a reified literary existence, and a mystified imaginary existence upon which the modern nation-state would be built. All these existences together add up to his ultimate phantasmal existence, which explains why the gaucho – a symptom of the modern nation, that is, a traumatic, pathological signifier which resists interpretation and keeps returning as a source of enjoyment – still haunts the utopian fantasies, the social frustrations, and the historical guilt of both Argentineans and Uruguayans.

## The Leathern Age

Until the installation of the first meat-salting houses in the second half of the eighteenth century, which made possible the profitable processing of jerk-beef, *cimarrón* cattle and horses multiplied by the millions in the large plains which, lacking any additional economic value other than the extraction of cowhide and tallow, had remained uncolonized and almost neglected by colonial authorities. Leather was not only the main economic product; doors and windows, beds and chests, rafts and fences, ropes and garments were also made out of cowhide.

Two main economic activities characterized this Leathern Age: the *vaquerías*, either in the form of large hunting expeditions organized by rich merchants who obtained the required permits with the sole purpose of extracting the animals' only exportable products; or the massive rodeos carried out by the Jesuit Missions or the Portuguese *bandeirantes*, which were in fact military enterprises and contraband expeditions on a grand scale. And contraband, not only with Brazil and the Missions, but also with the English and the French, was the other main economic activity, which instilled among patricians the passion for free trade.

Meanwhile, immense tracts of land had been granted to Spanish merchants living in Buenos Aires and Montevideo in order to monopolize the seasonal slaughtering of thousands of cattle. *Vaquerías* and the *estancia cimarrona*, an immense latifundium without borders, laid the foundations for an extractive, single-product export economy based upon the extensive exploitation of land, and a society split between a small class of absentee landowners, merchants, shipping owners, and bureaucrats entrenched in the city-ports, and the rural masses of gauchos, Indians, African slaves, and (very few) small farmers. Two dissimilar societies, in fact, and two opposing cultures coexisted side by side, cemented only by the colonial regime and their mutual hostility and indifference: the colonial society, economically, politically, and symbolically subordinated to the Spanish monarchy, the Catholic oikoumene and the European mercantile world-system, and the gaucho's barbarian society, excluded but integrated to the colonial system. Although relentlessly chastised and persecuted for vagrancy and contraband, the gaucho provided the necessary labor force, as a seasonal peon, for the exploitation of the *estancia cimarrona* that activated the entire cycle of colonial trade. He was a peon, not a peasant, who was kept at the margins of society and denied access to the land; he was a contrabandist because the *estancia cimarrona* did not call for a permanent labor force. He was thus the byproduct of the lack of available land and the excess of beef that a land-extensive system could not absorb. The abundance of leftovers was the source of his misery; the lack of employment the basis for his freedom; and the modesty of his needs the source of his arrogance. He was, in that sense, more a pariah than a master of the plains, a social detritus of the inefficient and unequal colonial socioeconomic system.

## The Era of the *Patriadas*

With the introduction of meat-salting houses and the production of jerk-beef for the slave markets of Cuba and Brazil, beef acquired, for the first time, economic value. This new industry required a constant supply of smaller herds, rendering unprofitable the wasteful techniques of the traditional *vaquerías*, in which thousands of animals were corralled at the confluence of two rivers and slaughtered in just a few days, leaving the carcasses to rot in the fields. For the first time, it was necessary to brand the animals, thus expanding the realm of private property and excluding even further the gauchos from the benefits of progress. The plains were still open to wander but the beef was no longer free. From then on, whoever slaughtered a cow for a *churrasco*, or beefsteak, would be either persecuted and drafted into the army, or forced to carry a job-identity card and settle in a permanent position, or be taken in chains for forced labor, depending on the political circumstances and the military needs.

Therefore, when the revolution against Spanish rule started in 1810, the gauchos were ready for revolt. They became, by their own will or by persuasion, the main military component in the armies led, for their most part, by patrician creoles. The gaucho, a consummate horseman, naturally trained in hand-to-hand combat and accustomed to the harsh daily subsistence on the run, became a formidable war machine. The knife he inherited from the Spaniard, the bolas he took from the Indian, and the long lance made out of the hamstringing knife he used to wield in the *vaquerías*, made him the master of the *montonera*, a hand-to-hand combat tactic which terrorized the academic formation of European armies. The convoluted wars of independence, which would last in the region until 1830, were complexly intertwined to local uprisings; regional conflicts (between the port-city capitals and the interior provinces, between Buenos Aires and Montevideo, between Rio de Janeiro and Buenos Aires); civil wars (particularly those between federalists and unitarians, which reached their climax during the rule of Juan Manuel de Rosas from 1935 to 1952 and the nine-year siege of Montevideo); and European interventions (both England and France, in several instances, plus the bands of adventurers, mercenaries, and corsairs, which included Irish nationalists and the Italian hero Giuseppe Garibaldi). This intricate geopolitical scenario ended up with the Balkanization of the region and the genocidal war of Paraguay (1865–71), which set the stage for the neocolonial integration of the national economies to the global sphere of English capital. The gauchos were, in every single war and all along this tortuous history, both cannon fodder and objects of extermination. Ironically, they had contributed with their own flesh to the building of the very modern nations that made them expendable.

However, this military role of undeniable epic proportions – and for the same reason so easily transposed into mythology – largely obscured the equally important function that gauchos played in the socioeconomic construction of modern society. The nineteenth-century political and military instability had intimate connections to the successive economic modernizations and social readjustments required by the global needs of English imperialism. Consequently, in the same way the extractive economy based on the *estancia cimarrona* and the exportation of cowhides were partly replaced by the end of the colonial period by the jerk-beef semi-industrial economy, by the middle of the nineteenth century two dramatic innovations would finally decide the fate of the gauchos: the introduction of sheep for the production of wool and the development of the meat-packing industry made possible by the invention of refrigerator ships.

Shepherding already required large sums of capital investment and a more intensive mode of production; the meticulous daily care of small herds of purebred imported animals in fenced grazing fields transformed the gaucho from a horseman into a shepherd. The English and Irish entrepreneurs who introduced the new industry would compete and eventually mix with the patrician sectors, outmoding the traditional extensive exploitation of land and contributing to shape a modern, progressive, truly capitalist oligarchy. But the arrival in 1870 of the steamship *Le Frigorifique* revolutionized forever the socioeconomic landscape. At last it was technologically feasible to export the abundant beef that had been "wasted" until then to the most sophisticated European markets. Major investments were made in order to cultivate the prairies, crossbreed the herds, and fence the pasture grounds, all measures necessary to improve the quantity and quality of beef produced by each animal. Meanwhile, very few peons were needed to exploit the modern estancia, which therefore expelled all unnecessary personnel along with their families to what became known as the "rat villages" surrounding the estancias. Efficiency then became the call for progress, making the gaucho, his culture, and his lifestyle not only irrelevant but also an obstacle to modernity. The modernization of the countryside – which not only involved the implementation of the latest technologies, including telegraphic lines and railroads, but also the military defeat or political cooptation of the local caudillos and the policing of the population in order to eradicate the *patriadas* and other forms of popular rebellion and guarantee safe commerce and private property – would finish the cycle of physical extermination, social subordination, and cultural annihilation of caudillos and gauchos. Once transformed into a manageable labor force, they could be appropriated as the soul of the modern nation, culminating a process of historical exploit, ethnic cleansing, and cultural genocide which pieced together military exploitation, political manipulation, social transformation, literary sublimation, and ideological appropriation.

## The Gauchesca Poetry

Despite colonial antecedents of satirical poetry or parodic *sainetes* (short theatrical pieces) mimicking the gaucho's dialect and mocking his lifestyle, gauchesca poetry properly originated under very specific circumstances: the need to incorporate the gauchos first into the revolutionary armies, and later on into the competing factions and political parties during the long series of civil wars. It involved, in that sense, the literary and political appropriation of the gaucho's language and culture in order to exploit his flesh as a military machine and labor force. As Josefina Ludmer's elegant formula explains: "the genre defines in the voice of the gaucho the word 'gaucho': voice (of the) 'gaucho'" (1988: 31). The gauchesca, however, is much more than the political manipulation of gauchos or the textual representation of the fatherland through a literary genre: it is a system of social communication and a cultural mode of production, circulation, and consumption that articulates two opposite ethno-cultural worlds at a historical crossroads; a truly original mass medium whose most remarkable feat is to create distinct publics according to the contingency of its political needs. It is, in a word, a cultural field of struggle for the hegemony between contending national projects in a fractured and colonial society traversed by multiple antagonisms; a peculiar mode of transculturation whose political success would end up determining its ultimate ethical failure: the modern nations would be built over the remains of a defeated ethno-culture.

Nevertheless, most of the literary critics have studied the gauchesca as a literary genre or, in the best cases, as a discursive formation; likewise, most of the anthropological, sociological, and historical studies on the gauchos have paid little attention

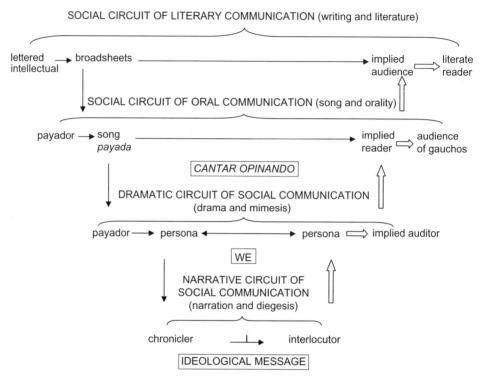

SOCIAL CIRCUIT OF LITERARY COMMUNICATION (writing and literature)

lettered → broadsheets ——————————————————→ implied ⇒ literate
intellectual                                                     audience      reader

SOCIAL CIRCUIT OF ORAL COMMUNICATION (song and orality)

payador → song ——————————————————→ implied ⇒ audience
            *payada*                                                  reader         of gauchos

CANTAR OPINANDO

DRAMATIC CIRCUIT OF SOCIAL COMMUNICATION
(drama and mimesis)

payador → persona ←————————→ persona ⇒ implied auditor

WE

NARRATIVE CIRCUIT OF
SOCIAL COMMUNICATION
(narration and diegesis)

chronicler ——→ interlocutor

IDEOLOGICAL MESSAGE

*Figure 16.1*   Gauchesca Poetry: System of Communication and Mode of Production

to the formidable documentary corpus provided by the gauchesca. It is imperative to overcome these narrow and amputated approaches in order to read the gauchesca against the grain: to hear the voices garbled by the mimic: to recover the silences and the silencing from the cumulative layers of literary and historical plotting: to unveil the historical crimes and the lost opportunities in the weave of the national fabric. Accordingly, the gauchesca should be read as a social system of cultural production, circulation, and consumption already found in a nutshell in the *cielitos* and patriotic dialogues of the founder, Bartolomé Hidalgo. As shown in Figure 16.1, gauchesco texts work simultaneously on four overlapping planes of communication, two regarding their actual production, reproduction, and consumption in the social sphere, and two fictionalizing the social communication within the text, thus reinforcing the ideological message. These planes unfold from song to drama, from drama to narration, from narration to oratory, configuring a system best captured by Martín Fierro's famous formula, "cantar opinando."

Gauchesca literature starts with a lettered intellectual writing a poem (or other piece of literature), imitating the gaucho dialect and portraying gaucho characters, for an illiterate gaucho audience. Necessarily, this incongruous piece participates at once in two dissimilar means and circuits of communication. The literary poem, published in the form of broadsides, is also sung at campfires and social gatherings, where the social circuit of oral communication is finally brought to completion. Only later, with the literary development of the "genre" by Hilario Ascasubi, Estanislao del Campo, and Antonio Lussich, until its culmination in José Hernández, would the social circuit of literary communication be fulfilled by a literate reader. This splitting of the communication of the text in the social sphere is due to the fact that the gauchesca involves two different media (the written broadsides and the oral *payadas*) but, more importantly, it articulates two heterogeneous social and cultural milieus. The social, political, and ethnic heterogeneity is thus reproduced – and negotiated – through a series of simulacra in which a Europeanized intellectual, organically linked to the patrician elite and bearer of its civilizing project, poses as a *payador* who sings for a gaucho audience (social circuit of literary communication), the story of a *payador* who narrates for a gaucho audience (social circuit of oral communication), and the encounter between two gauchos (dramatic circuit of social communication), in which one of them recounts recent historical events spiced with political commentaries (narrative circuit of social communication). The fact that the implied reader-spectator-interlocutor is elliptically indicated points up the highly contextual grounding of a text that is only realized on its performance. This layered structure not only helps to conceal the writer's ultimate authority, but effects yet another simulacrum: the espousal of contemporary ideologies and aesthetic movements (from the Enlightenment to positivism; from neoclassicism to romanticism and realism) was wrapped in traditional aesthetic forms (like the octosyllabic *redondilla*; the use of proverbs, metaphors, and tropes; or the recycling of old Spanish popular genres characterized by rigidity and conventionality, such as *cielitos*, *diálogos*, and *romances*).

## The Gauchesca Cycle

Gauchesca was born with the revolutionary wars of independence against Spanish rule. There were some antecedents of neoclassical poetry and parodic *sainetes* written in the gauchos' dialect (the romance "Canta un guaso en estilo campestre los triunfos del Excelentísimo Señor Don Pedro de Ceballos," 1777, by Juan Baltasar Maziel, and the anonymous sainete "El amor de la estanciera," between 1780 and 1795) are among the oldest texts recorded), but they were produced for their sole consumption by the elites, and in this sense, the gaucho was just a colorful pretext. Bartolomé Hidalgo (1788–1822) represents the inaugural moment of patriotic gauchesca, shaped by revolutionary politics and enlightened ideology, in coincidence with the radical national project of the first great federalist caudillo, José Artigas, and its popular and democratic republican federalism. During the short years in which Artigas dominated the regional scene (1811–15), he was able to materialize within his political agenda the amorphous magma of cultural desires, life experiences, and social needs of a community in embryo. He gave institutional form and political consistency to the bundle of psycho-social traits of a scant, scattered, isolated frontier population, and amalgamated in the process their skills for survival as the cultural *gestũs* of an emergent society. Accordingly, the gaucho's courageous individualism, arrogant sense of freedom, stubborn pride in rags, and quasi-medieval sense of honor had taken the shape of a social and political system, which would endure in the popular cultural memory for years to come.

Hidalgo's texts, technically agitprop literature, summarize the genre: its structures and models, its language and idioms, its topics and types, its metaphors and tropes became conventions. His *cielitos* established the lyrical and epic tone of the gauchesca; his *diálogos patrióticos* consolidated its dramatic nucleus and performative substratum; his *relaciones* introduced the oratorical convection of ideological messages, supported by a collective subject. Following the fate of Artigas's Federal League, which after being the most powerful political entity in the region was crushed by the conspiratorial stratagems of Buenos Aires's Unitarian party and Rio de Janeiro's imperial aspirations, patriotic gauchesca would go from the exultant optimism and insolent arrogance of the victorious, to the somber melancholy and bitter disillusionment of the defeated.

The following decades, affected by interminable civil wars, always entangled with social unrest, regional conflicts, and European interventions, witnessed the emergence of *gauchipolítica*, or factional gauchesca. *Gauchipolítica* reached its climax as a populist and pedagogic propaganda machine during the times of Juan Manuel de Rosas – the federalist caudillo who realized the de facto unification of the Argentine provinces under the aegis of Buenos Aires – from his ascendancy to the governorship of Buenos Aires in 1929 to his final defeat in 1852. This period of internationalized civil wars marks a geopolitical turning point, consummating the Balkanization of the region, the triumph of the free-trade, and open-market liberal policies espoused by England, and the beginning of a period of national reorganization that would establish the logistical infrastructure, the political institutions, the demographic cleansing, the educational apparatus, and the cultural imaginary necessary for the modernization of Argentina and Uruguay as neocolonial partners of British capitalism. In this warlike atmosphere, in the process of which the original dissensions between federalists and unitarians became increasingly blurred (federalism was actually defeated by the consummation of two separate national states centrally organized), a formidable generation – aesthetically romantic, politically liberal, and socially conservative – emerged amid the intellectual circles gathered in Montevideo and Santiago. This "first romantic generation," which includes Domingo F. Sarmiento (1811–88), Esteban Echeverría (1805–51) and Juan Bautista Alberdi (1810–84), would shape political, institutional, and cultural modern nations.

*Gauchipolítica*, characterized by fierce partisanship, romantic excess, and grotesque verbal violence, resorted to overt emotional manipulation instead of rational persuasion, contrary to the enlightened principles behind patriotic gauchesca. However, in the long run, this strategy had a dual paradoxical effect: while its scope of ideological interpellation shrunk from the nation to the faction, thus losing part of the original illiterate public, the romantic literary self-awareness would upgrade its aesthetic aspirations, which resulted in the attraction of new reading publics. Some of the best gauchipolíticos, like Hilario Ascasubi (1807–75), although still restrained by the gauchesca's inferior literary status, in time became aware of the strictly literary possibilities of the genre. By the 1860s, when gauchesca was no longer needed as a propaganda machine directed toward gauchos, Ascasubi collected his scattered publications in three volumes and finished *Santos Vega o Los mellizos de La Flor*, a gauchesco-inspired but literarily-minded long poem, entirely intended for a sophisticated cosmopolitan readership.

The literary conversion of the genre would be accomplished by Estanislao del Campo (1834–80), whose *Fausto* – a gaucho's interpretation of Charles Gounod's opera – is a double-mirrored satire of both the gaucho's ignorance and the elite's snobbery. *Fausto* (1966), in fact, liquidates the gauchesca, insofar as it illustrates the needlessness to address a gaucho audience no longer politically or militarily necessary, and consummates the final appropriation of the gaucho's voice by the lettered writer. This split of the original alliance between *letrados* and gauchos is much more than an apparent depoliticization of an intrinsically political genre; it actually amounts to an aestheticization of politics which reversed the original politicization of aesthetics that in fact defined the genre.

A few years after the publication of *Fausto*, José Hernández (1834–86) published *El gaucho Martín Fierro* (1872), which became an instant bestseller, inspiring a sequel released in 1879, *La vuelta de Martín Fierro*. Unanimously considered the genre's canonical masterpiece, *Martín Fierro* responds to the devastating social consequences of the intensive modernization of the economic, political, demographic, and social structures carried out by the liberal oligarchies in the last quarter of the century. The process resulted in the elimination of the last caudillos, who had been the constant foci of social unrest; the devastation of Paraguay and its experiment of autonomous development; and the subjugation, or outright extermination, of the Patagonian peoples, thus extending the central government's control of the territory. The gauchos continued to be the cannon fodder in the expansion of the national frontier, as *Martín Fierro* denounces, but there was no need to persuade them to enlist: they were enlisted, sent and kept there by force. The Campaign of the Desert accomplished the physical extermination of gauchos and Indians, who exterminated each other for the worthy cause of civilization.

*Martín Fierro* denounces, in the first part, the military and social extermination of gauchos from a paternalistic and conservative point of view, while in the second part he calls for their assimilation into the modern national body, insofar as they abandon their premodern lifestyle. In a complete reversal of the gauchesca system of communication, the book addresses the civilized citizenry assuming the representation of the vanishing gauchos; but it also moralizes the *paisanos*, descendants of gauchos, urging them to become good Catholics and reliable workers in a modern, progressive nation. In that sense the book is a pedagogic manual, an elegy and a eulogy that captures the knowledge, lifestyle, values, and language of the gauchos, which were fading away.

But perhaps more importantly, it sets the foundations for a xenophobic national identity built on the relics of gauchos and the exclusion of his attributed others – Indians, blacks, foreigners, women – who do not qualify as heirs of what is already no more than a ghost. Reversing the popular and democratic alliance of patriotic gauchesca, *Martín Fierro* ultimately establishes the ideological basis for the legitimacy of the modern – racist, sexist, and chauvinistic – nation.

## Fading Out in the City

Since its beginnings with Hidalgo, the recurrent plot of the gaucho who tells another gaucho his adventures, or rather misadventures, in the alien city, anticipated the gradual but inevitable dissolution of the gauchesca in the modern forms of literature and mass culture. At the turn of the century, some peculiar derivations occurred, such as the popular poetry which originated through the encounter in the slums of the displaced gauchos and the newly arrived immigrants. This *poesía orillera* would be related first to the emergence of an urban popular culture which materialized in tango, and its almost immediate highbrow appropriation by the intellectuals of the Florida group led by Jorge Luis Borges (1899–1986), in the form of avant-garde *criollismo*. By mid-century, fostered by populist politics, gauchesca inspired a folk-music renaissance which, intersecting politics and mass media, would acquire, in the "cantar opinando" of popular poets – from Atahualpa Yupanqui's *Coplas del payador perseguido* to Alfredo Zitarrosa's *Guitarra negra* – a central role in the contemporary development of both the Argentinean and Uruguayan popular imaginaries.

However, at the turn of the century, it was in the adaptation of circus-staged gauchesco drama – a rowdy form of total theater extremely popular among the heterogeneous audience of the outskirts, which included horses, dances, *payadas*, and knife-duels – to the physical, aesthetic, and cultural conventions of modern realist rural drama where the actual taming of gauchesca ultimately occurred. The heroes of gauchesco dramas, paradigmatically exemplified by José Podestá's adaptation of Eduardo Gutiérrez's serial novel, *Juan Moreira* (1884), were outlaws driven into criminal life by the economic, social, and political forces of modernization, thus exerting an intense identification from the public, which interacted with the play and carried it over into the barrio's life. This, of course, made gauchesco drama morally and politically unsuitable to a modern, cosmopolitan, and Europeanized society, determining, as a result, a process of domestication which began by folklorizing it and ended up dissolving the epic melodrama staged in the arena into the psychological drama performed in the Italian frontal stage. A continuous process of ideological domestication is expressed in the parallel urbanization of the gaucho and the theater: from the pampas to the estancias, farms, suburbs, tenement houses, and middle-class living rooms, both are shrunk from the arena to the frontal stage, from the mural to the fragment, from the panorama to the close-up, from spectacle to literature, from the social arena to the national imaginary.

## The Gaucho in the National Imaginary

Simultaneously, by the turn of the century, history and literature had become the privileged fields from which to construct, a posteriori, the historical memory of the modern national imaginaries: the capitalist, rationalist, and civilizing *ethos* of the nation-state – always driven by a progressive *telos* – was legitimized in a precapitalist, mythical, and barbarous proto-historical *pathos*. Amid an intense debate held in the 1880s regarding the historical reevaluation of Artigas, Carlos María Ramírez (1848–1898) cleared the way for the manufacturing of a new historical memory, stating that "*gauchos*, who used to be a beautiful manifestation of our primitive civilization, are being replaced by a more advanced civilization. *Caudillos*, a necessary means for the *gaucho* masses to adapt to the rule of law and political freedom, have extinguished themselves . . . This organic evolution, which eliminated the *caudillo* as a political factor, has cleared its historical examination" (1953: 394).

Upon the disappearance of *gauchos* and *caudillos* from the sociopolitical arena, their elegy could be sung; once the enemies of order and civilization had been reduced to anachronistic remains, they were ripe for their symbolic appropriation. It was the definitive triumph of the lettered city over its territory, of the oligarchic circles over the dispossessed, of the modern state over the anarchy of the borderland. As a result, Artigas, the most barbarous Argentinean *caudillo*, according to Sarmiento, was enshrined as the foundation of the national imaginary of the modern Uruguayan state. It should be an imaginary capable of producing an identity malleable enough to assimilate future generations of immigrants and to distinguish them from Argentines, whose pedagogic history, ideologically inspired by oligarchic liberalism, would continue to vilify the *caudillos*, and particularly Artigas and Rosas, with disproportionate rancor.

Coinciding with the splendors of a blooming economy, the ebullience of a fast growing mass society and the demands of an ethnically heterogeneous cultural market, the Argentine national imaginary would be forged upon the literary appropriation of the gaucho rather than on the historical reconstruction of the caudillo. The 1910 celebrations of the Independence Centennial provided a magnificent backdrop for the consecration of a national literature and the canonization of *Martín Fierro* as the foundational national epic poem, by Ricardo Rojas (1882–1957), among others. In his famed conferences of 1913, published later as *El payador*, Leopoldo Lugones (1874–1938) asserted: "It will be easy to find in the *gaucho* the prototype of contemporary Argentina . . . We are not *gauchos*, of course, but that product of the environment contained in latency the Argentinean of today, so different under the confusion produced by current crossbreeding" (1979: 50). Heir to the true national character embodied by the eponymous hero, the Argentinean Creole oligarchy could preserve, in a strictly imaginary way, its political and cultural hegemony, contested by "The ultramarine plebeians who, like ungrateful beggars, [are] making trouble in our doorway" (1979: 15). This nationalistic notion of the national identity had been advanced by "nativism," a traditionalist literary, cultural, and social movement responsible for the urban domestication of late gauchesco poetry and theater. The *chiripá* of the gaucho became the loincloth of an ideology, used by the Creole patriciate to preserve its economic privileges as well as its cultural and political hegemony. Lugones built his argument through a chain of syllogisms, according to which Hernández's poem encapsulated the primeval national character represented in the language, the race and the epic embodied in the gaucho, a character nowadays substantiated in the modern nation-state and the gaucho's natural heir, the Creole oligarchy: "We are this being: the formidable synthesis of generations" (Lugones, 1979: 196). Argentine identity thus came into being by excluding Martin Fierro's others: Indians, blacks, gringos, and women; a racist and xenophobic identity mined by fear and violence for years to come. Perhaps due to this predominantly literary and essentialist manufacture, the Argentine nationalist imaginary reveals its mythopoetic genesis more explicitly than the Uruguayan does.

But in order to proceed to this fabrication, the patrician establishment had to relegate caudillos and gauchos to another prehistoric, mythical temporality. It was necessary to embalm gauchos and caudillos in some sort of proto-history, a primitive time, a limbo of containment where they could be fossilized as objects of study, or evoked as legendary heroes. Through this device of ideological containment they were deprived of social agency, ceased to be historical subjects and became mythical phantoms. The military, social, and political elimination of caudillos and gauchos in the historical present made feasible their consignment to a mythical past; if historical coexistence was absolutely unacceptable, their imaginary preexistence was embraced like a blessing. By distancing and confining *caudillos* and *gauchos* into a mythical time, the patriciate could finally identify the modern nation-state with their vanquished others.

## References and Further Reading

Alberdi, Juan Bautista (1981). *Bases y puntos de partida para la organización política de la República Argentina*. Buenos Aires: Plus Ultra.

Alfonso X, el Sabio (1829). *Las Siete partidas del Sabio Rey Don Alonso el IX, glosadas por el Lic. Gregorio Lopez, el Consejo Real de Indias de S.M. Tomo I, Partida 2, Título XXIII, Ley XI*. Madrid: En la Oficina de D. Leon Amarita.

Altamirano, Carlos, and Sarlo, Beatriz (1980). "La Argentina del Centenario: campo intelectual, vida literaria y temas ideológicos," *Hispamérica*, 25/26: 33–59.

Anderson, Benedict (1983). *Imagined Communities*. London: Verso.

Anderson, Perry (1984). "Modernity and revolution," *New Left Review*, 144: 96–113.

Assunçao, Fernando O. (1963). *El Gaucho*. Montevideo: Instituto Histórico y Geográfico del Uruguay.

Becco, Horacio Jorge (1972). *Antología de la poesía gauchesca*. Madrid: Aguilar.

— (1977). *Félix Weinberg, Rodolfo Borello, Adolfo Prieto: Trayectoria de la poesía gauchesca*. Buenos Aires: Plus Ultra.

Berman, Marshall (1988). *All That is Solid Melts Into Air: The Experience of Modernity*. New York: Penguin.

Bhabha, Homi, ed. (1990). *Nation and Narration.* London: Routledge.

Borges, Jorge Luis (1979). *El "Martín Fierro."* Buenos Aires: Emecé.

Castagnino, Raúl H. (1953). *El Circo criollo: Datos y documentos para su historia, 1757–1924.* Buenos Aires: Lajouane.

— (1969). *Teatro argentino premoreirista (1600–1884).* Buenos Aires: Plus Ultra.

— (1980). *Circo, teatro gauchesco y tango.* Buenos Aires: Instituto Nacional de Estudios de Teatro.

Castoriadis, Cornelius (1997). "The social imaginary and the institution." In *The Castoriadis Reader.* Oxford, MA: Blackwell.

Castro, Julio César (1972). *Don Verídico.* Montevideo: Arca.

— (1975). *Don Verídico se la cuenta.* Buenos Aires: De la Flor.

Coni, Emilio A. (1969). *El gaucho: Argentina – Brasil – Uruguay.* Buenos Aires: Solar/Hachette.

Deleuze, Gilles, and Guattari, Félix (1987). *A Thousand Plateaus: Capitalism and Schizophrenia.* Minneapolis: University of Minnesota Press.

Ghiano, Juan Carlos (1957). *Teatro gauchesco primitivo.* Buenos Aires: Losange.

Gutiérrez, Eduardo (1961). *Juan Moreira.* Buenos Aires: Eudeba.

Leumann, Carlos Alberto (1953). *La Literatura gauchesca y la poesía gaucha.* Buenos Aires: Raigal.

Ludmer, Josefina (1988). *El Género gauchesco: Un tratado sobre la patria.* Buenos Aires: Sudamericana.

— (1999). *El cuerpo del delito: Un manual.* Buenos Aires: Perfil Libros.

Lugones, Leopoldo (1979). *El payador y antología de poesía y prosa.* Caracas: Ayacucho.

Martínez Estrada, Ezequiel (1948). *Muerte y transfiguración de Martín Fierro.* Mexico City: Fondo de Cultura Económica.

Podestá, José J. (1930). *Medio siglo de farándula: Memorias.* Río de la Plata: s/e.

Pomer, León (1971). *El Gaucho.* Buenos Aires: CEDAL.

Ponce, Livio (1971). *El Circo criollo.* Buenos Aires: CEDAL.

Prieto, Adolfo (1988). *El Discurso criollista en la formación de la Argentina moderna.* Buenos Aires: Sudamericana.

Rama, Ángel (1976). *Los Gauchipolíticos rioplatenses: Literatura y sociedad.* Buenos Aires: Calicanto.

— (1977). "El sistema literario de la poesía gauchesca." In *Poesía gauchesca.* Caracas: Ayacucho.

Rama, Ángel, and Rivera, Jorge (1977). *Poesía gauchesca.* Caracas: Ayacucho.

Ramírez, Carlos María (1953). *Artigas.* Montevideo, Biblioteca Artigas.

Ramos, Julio (1989). *Desencuentros de la modernidad en América Latina: Literatura y política en el siglo XIX.* Mexico City: Fondo de Cultura Económica.

Real de Azúa, Carlos (1969). *Legitimidad, apoyo y poder político: Ensayo de tipología.* Montevideo: Fundación de Cultura Universitaria.

Ribeiro, Darcy (1992). *Las Américas y la civilización: Proceso de formación y causas del desarrollo desigual de los pueblos americanos.* Caracas: Ayacucho.

Rivera, Jorge B. (1968). *La Primitiva literatura gauchesca.* Buenos Aires: Jorge Alvarez.

— (1968). *El Folletín y la novela popular.* Buenos Aires: CEDAL.

Rodríguez Molas, Ricardo E. (1968). *Historia social del gaucho.* Buenos Aires: Ediciones Maru.

Rojas, Ricardo (1946). *Blasón de Plata.* Buenos Aires: Losada.

— (1957). *Historia de la literatura argentina: Los gauchescos.* Buenos Aires: Kraft.

Romero, José Luis (1965). *El Desarrollo de las ideas en la Argentina del siglo XX.* Mexico City: Fondo de Cultura Económica.

Sarlo, Beatriz (1982). "Vanguardia y criollismo: la aventura de *Martín Fierro*," *Revista de Crítica Literaria Latinoamericana,* 15–16): 56.

Schneider, Samuel (1962). *Proyección histórica del gaucho.* Buenos Aires: Ediciones Procyon.

Schvartzman, Julio (2003). *La Lucha de los lenguajes.* Vol. 2 of *Historia crítica de la literatura argentina.* Buenos Aires: Emecé.

Seibel, Beatriz (1985). *Los Artistas trashumantes: Testimonios de circo criollo y radioteatro.* Buenos Aires: Ediciones de la pluma.

Trigo, Abril (1990). *Caudillo, estado, nación: Literatura, historia e ideología en el Uruguay.* Gaithersburg, MA: Hispamérica.

— (1992). "El teatro gauchesco primitivo y los límites de la gauchesca," *Latin American Theatre Review,* 26(1): 55–67.

— (1995). "Fundación imaginaria de la nación-estado uruguaya," *Cuadernos de Marcha*, 109: 3–9.

— (1997). "Fronteras de la epistemología: Epistemologías de la frontera," *Papeles de Montevideo,* 1: 71–89.

— (2003). *Memorias migrantes: Testimonios y ensayos sobre la diáspora uruguaya*. Rosario and Montevideo: Beatriz Viterbo and Trilce.

Vidart, Daniel (1968). *El Gaucho*. Enciclopedia Uruguaya 7. Montevideo: Editores Reunidos/Arca.

Viñas, David (1964). *Literatura argentina y realidad política*. Buenos Aires: Jorge Alvarez.

— (1996). *Literatura argentina y política: De Lugones a Walsh*. Buenos Aires: Sudamericana.

— (1998). *De Sarmiento a Dios: Viajeros argentinos a USA*. Buenos Aires: Sudamericana.

Williams, Raymond (1976). *Keywords: A Vocabulary of Culture and Society*. New York: Oxford Univerity Press.

Yupanqui, Atahualpa (1972). *Coplas del payador perseguido* (disc).

Zitarrosa, Alfredo (1980). *Guitarra negra* (disc).

# 17

# Andrés Bello, Domingo Faustino Sarmiento, Manuel González Prada, and Teresa de la Parra: Four Writers and Four Concepts of Nationhood

*Nicolas Shumway*

This chapter considers how four widely different thinkers understood and helped invent national and regional identities in Latin America. The first, Andrés Bello, was born in Venezuela in 1781, but spent many years in England and is most associated with the cultural development of Chile, where he lived from 1829 until his death in 1865. The second is Domingo Faustino Sarmiento, who was born in 1811 in San Juan, Argentina, just over the border from Chile, and died in Buenos Aires in 1888. The third is Manuel González Prada, an acerbic critic of Peruvian culture, who lived from 1844 to 1918. The final person we study is Teresa de la Parra, a Venezuelan writer who lived from 1890 to 1936. Together, these four intellectuals span nearly 150 years, from Bello's birth in 1781 to the death of de la Parra in 1936. Despite many differences, they share a common concern with the origins, substance, and meaning of collective identity in Latin America.

## Andrés Bello (1781–1865)

Born in 1781 in Caracas, Venezuela, Andrés Bello had extraordinary influence on all of Latin America, particularly in the fields of jurisprudence, literature, and Spanish grammar. He is also a man of paradox, a modernizer anxious to preserve tradition, a reformer seeking inspiration in the Roman roots of Hispanic culture, and a gradualist attentive to the most radical ideas of his time.

Bello's astonishing intellectual abilities caught the eye of teachers and local leaders early in his life. At 19, he already had an excellent command of Latin and an extensive background in classical literature and philosophy. In 1810, he accompanied Simón Bolívar to England hoping to secure support for the Venezuelan independence movement. Not given to military life, he remained in England until 1829, providing diplomatic services for several Latin American independence movements and hosting prominent liberals like Francisco de Miranda of Venezuela, José María Blanco White of Spain, and Bernardino Rivadavia of Argentina. In 1829, the Chilean government invited Bello to give intellectual assistance to Chile's emerging national project. As noted by Iván Jaksíc, Bello's best biographer, it was under "Bello's influence that [Chile's] liberalization proceeded by institutional means" (2001: 123), thus helping the country avoid the civil wars that decimated much of nineteenth-century Spanish America.

Bello's contributions to Chile and to all the Spanish-speaking world seem almost superhuman, the work of several men and not just one. Today, Bello's ideas might seem so familiar that we forget how revolutionary they were at the time, particularly as they emerged on the periphery of Western civilization in Chile, the Latin American country most distant from the cultural capitals of Europe and North America. Always interested in education, Bello began giving private classes shortly after arriving in Chile and soon thereafter took a position at the Colegio de Santiago, a secondary school for the children of the Chilean elite. In 1836, he published an important essay, "On the Aims of Education and Means to Promote It," in which he argues that a representative republic must have an educated populace (Bello, 1997: 110–11). He further maintains that the state, not the church, should assume primary responsibility for educating its citizens, but without abandoning the moral guide of "our Catholic religion" which, "by putting the brake of morality on the heart's wild impulses, enables us to perform our duties to God, to men, and to ourselves" (113). In 1841, the Chilean government asked Bello to head a commission to prepare a Bill that would establish the University of Chile. Two years later Bello was named the first rector of the new university.

Bello's inaugural address as rector figures among his most significant writings. In it, he reiterates the importance of an educated populace and a modern education system in the life of a republic. But unlike more radical elements in both Chile and other parts of Latin America, he defines the mission of the new university as an extension of rather than a break with the past. He thus includes as one of his five "faculties" (what today's universities would call colleges, schools, or departments) a faculty of theology that could train clerics as well as offer courses to students from other disciplines. Bello's refusal to embrace anticlerical sentiment, which at the time almost seemed a defining characteristic of liberal thought, is striking and bold. With great eloquence, he argues that "all truths touch one another, and I extend this statement to religious dogma, to theological truth. Those who imagine that there can be a secret antipathy between religious and letters slander either one or the other, I do not know which" (126).

Even more remarkable, Bello sees the University of Chile as an institution descended from Chile's colonial past. Anti-Spanish bias was strong among Chileans and Spanish Americans anxious to embrace "modernity." For example, Joaquín Victorino Lastarria, a young Chilean intellectual with whom Bello had several public debates, once famously remarked that progress and "de-Spanishization" were synonymous. Bello would have none of it. In his description of how law should be taught at the University of Chile, he defends the Roman roots of Spanish jurisprudence and insists that Chile should not lose sight of that heritage (131–2). Similarly, he argues that the faculty of philosophy and humanities should recognize the richness of Spanish letters and not be excessively anxious to seek cultural models elsewhere. These attitudes underline a singular aspect of Bello's thought. He is both a traditionalist and a modernizer. He distrusts violent revolutions of all sorts, preferring a gradualist approach that can incorporate the new without abandoning the old.

Bello's gradualism is also apparent in his most lasting contribution to Spanish letters: his *Grammar of the Castilian Language* of 1847, a project sustained by Bello's belief that only through good use of language can one think clearly. How can a grammar be gradualist? First, Bello's grammar never loses sight of the Latin roots of the Spanish language. Bello is intensely aware of the linguistic evolution by which Latin became Spanish, and in his discussions of morphology, syntax, and the Spanish verb system, he repeatedly finds meaning in the historical roots of modern Spanish. What distinguishes Bello's grammar, however, is his incorporation of traditional notions of correctness with an astute perception of what modern usage entails, using as examples innumerable quotations from largely Spanish writers. In brief, he not only *prescribes* what is correct; he also *describes* with great acuity what speakers and writers of Spanish actually do. It is as a describer of the modern language that Bello joins modern linguists.

Bello also seeks to combine past and present in his juridical writings. The Chilean republic emerged when legal thought was in great flux. On the one hand, the Napoleonic Code, inaugurated in 1804, was much in vogue. On the other, Bello was familiar with the Common Law tradition of Great Britain and the United States that is based on case law and precedent rather than on a comprehensive legal code. While Bello found much to admire in both traditions, true to form, he sought a middle path. In 1843, he published *Instituciones de Derecho Romano*, in which he praises the clarity, rationalism, and practicality of Roman law regarding matrimony, transfer of property, and the rights of children. Further, he found that same clarity in Spanish jurisprudence, particularly the thirteenth-century set of laws known as the *Siete partidas*. In 1834, the Chilean congress appointed a committee to write Chile's first civil code. The code went through many revisions and was not approved until 1857. Bello is the undisputed author of most of the code as it was finally adopted. The code, true to Bello's desire to combine the best of the old with the best of the new, draws from the Napoleonic Code while also incorporating elements from Roman law, Catholic canon law, the Spanish legal tradition, and even British utilitarianism. The result is an astonishing achievement that still underlies modern Chilean law, and contributed to the civil codes of other Latin American countries, including Brazil.

Bello was also an exceptional poet and literary critic. While it is written in a neo-classical style, filled with ornate language and classical allusions that often escape today's readers, his poetry also invokes the need for the American nations to establish their own destiny – an idea particularly apparent in his much anthologized poem,

"Silva a la agricultura de la zona tórrida" (Ode to the agriculture of the tropical region), one in which he counsels future generations of Americans never to lose contact with their native soil. Yet, although a thoroughgoing Americanist, Bello found in the great works of Spanish literature an enduring foundation with which American cultures should not lose contact.

The vision that emerges of Andrés Bello in all this is a man of paradox, a modernizer who reveres tradition, a liberal who remained a devout Catholic all his life, and a forger of new identities who recognized that identity must inevitably draw from the past. Although his name is most associated with Chile, he was indeed a teacher of all the Americas whose accomplishments still mesmerize and provide ample proof that this was a truly great man.

## Domingo Faustino Sarmiento (1811–88)

The Argentine Domingo Faustino Sarmiento often said, "Las cosas, hay que hacerlas; salgan bien o salgan mal, hay que hacerlas" (Things have to be done; whether done well or done badly, they have to be done). This dictum summarizes well his impassioned, driving, and energetic desire to hammer Argentina into a modern nation. It also signals how different he was from the gradualist Bello.

Born in the foothills of the Andes in the small town of San Juan, Sarmiento took advantage of the meager educational resources of his home province and then launched a lifelong process of self-schooling. With Benjamin Franklin as a model, Sarmiento made educating himself and educating others a driving passion of his entire life. While still in his teens, he began offering classes to younger sanjuaninos, marking the beginning of his most enduring legacy to Argentina: a public education system that gave Argentina what remains the highest national literacy rate in Latin America. Sarmiento had an intense career in public service, crowned by serving as president of Argentina from 1868 to 1874. Yet, despite these accomplishments, he also found time to write. His *Obras completas* fill 52 volumes.

Sarmiento's most important work, *Civilization and Barbarism: The Life of Juan Facundo Quiroga,* began as a biography of Sarmiento's old nemesis, Juan Facundo Quiroga, the *caudillo* of San Juan who prompted Sarmiento's first exile in Chile. But in 1844, just as Sarmiento was putting the final touches to the biography, Juan Manuel de Rosas, governor of the Province of Buenos Aires and virtual dictator of the entire country, filed a formal protest to the Chilean government regarding Sarmiento's repeated criticism of Rosas in the Chilean press. Wanting to avoid conflict with Argentina, the Chilean president Manuel Bulnes Prieto asked Sarmiento to tone things down. Toning down not being his style, Sarmiento reacted by converting the Quiroga biography into a full-scale attack on Rosas's Argentina. The "biography" thus morphed into a book that defies easy categorization. A mixture of biography, history, anthropology, cultural analysis, and political platform, the book is ultimately a sustained attack on the Argentina that produced Rosas and Rosismo, followed by policy recommendations that would ultimately constitute many of Sarmiento's goals for Argentina. To understand the book, some historical background is in order.

Argentina's road to nationhood started well but then foundered badly as a split developed between a "Unitarian" vision for the country that would centralize power in Buenos Aires and a "Federalist" vision that sought greater autonomy for the provinces. Things came to a head in 1829 when Buenos Aires Unitarians launched a coup against the Federalist government of Manuel Dorrego and had him executed. The ensuing disorder made the Province of Buenos Aires ripe for "saving." A savior was found in the person of Juan Manuel de Rosas, a wealthy rancher who also had a small private militia. Invited by the provincial legislature, Rosas quickly restored order, ruled the province for three years, and then returned to his ranch in 1832. The province and its capital city again slipped toward chaos, so much so that in 1835, the provincial legislature again invited Rosas back as governor. Rosas made it clear that he would accept only if given all public authority – *la suma del poder público.* The legislature accepted, and Rosas came to power as a virtual dictator – not through force but by the vote of a duly constituted legislature.

Between 1835 and 1852, Rosas governed as a petty potentate, charming the masses with populist paternalism while showing disdain for civil liberties and liberal institutions. Sarmiento, however, did not see Rosas merely as a tyrant whose removal would put Argentina back on a proper course; rather, he considered Rosas a symptom of much deeper problems in Argentine culture and the incarnation of personalist government that yields power to a charismatic leader, the *caudillo,* and thereby fails to develop the rule of law and institutions. Sarmiento's task, then, was not just to attack Rosas, but to explain the failure of a culture capable of producing and empowering such a man. To this end, the *Facundo.*

Sarmiento opens the book by invoking the ghost of Facundo to "explain the hidden life and the inner convulsions that tear at the bowels of a noble people!" (2003: 31). But almost immediately he assures the reader that Facundo is not really dead, that he lives on in popular traditions, in Argentine politics and revolutions, in Rosas, his heir, his complement; his soul has moved into that new mold, one more perfect and finished, and what in him was only instinct, impulse, and a tendency, in Rosas became a system, means, and end. Rural nature, colonial and barbarous, was changed through this metamorphosis into art, into a system, and into regular policy, able to present itself to the world as the way of being of a people, incarnated in one man who has aspired to take on the airs of genius dominating events, men, and things (*Facundo*: 31). Thus, the book is ultimately about Rosas, with Quiroga being his forerunner. Throughout the book, Sarmiento refers repeatedly to the horrors of the Rosas dictatorship – its repression, its backwardness, its violence. But his real goal is to identify the causes of the failure Rosas represents.

For Sarmiento, the first cause of Argentina's failure is "the Spanish tradition and the iniquitous, plebeian national consciousness that the Inquisition and Hispanic absolutism have left," along with a "supine lack of political and industrial ability" (33). Unlike Bello, but like most of his Spanish American contemporaries, Sarmiento finds little to admire in the Spanish tradition. Spain for Sarmiento is medieval and unenlightened, forever linked to the authoritarianism of Philip II and the Counter-Reformation, of which Rosas is merely the most recent incarnation.

A second cause of Argentina's failure as explained by Sarmiento is the land itself. "The disease from which the Argentine Republic suffers is its own expanse," he tells us, and with considerable flourish he compares the Argentine pampas to the plains of North Africa and Mongolia (47). Sarmiento argues that the mixed-breed, semi-nomadic gauchos of the Argentine pampas developed a culture much akin to that of Genghis Khan and his hordes, making them unpropitious material for a modern nation (49).

The third cause of Argentina's failure, according to Sarmiento, is race. Used in its nineteenth-century sense, the term "race" for Sarmiento includes notions that today we would divide into categories of nationality, ethnicity, and biological ancestry. In Sarmiento's description, the "races" that made Argentina are Spanish, Amerindian, and African. But following the prejudices of his time, he argues that

> the fusion of these three families has resulted in a homogenous whole, distinguished by its love for idleness and incapacity for industry, except when education and the exigencies of social position put the spurs to it and pull it out of its customary pace. The incorporation of indigenous races caused by colonization has contributed much to produce this unfortunate result. The American races live in idleness, and demonstrate an incapacity, even when forced, to apply themselves to hard, uninterrupted work. This prompted the idea of bringing blacks to America, which has produced such fatal results. But the Spanish race has not shown itself to be any more given to action when, in the American deserts, it has been left to its own instincts. (51)

Sarmiento's negative views on race and racial mixing jar modern readers, but they are largely consistent with the European racism of his time, as found in intellectuals like Gustave Le Bon and Joseph Arthur Gobineau.

Yet an underlying ambivalence mitigates Sarmiento's negative views of the mixed-blood gauchos. On the one hand, he sees gaucho culture as too backward to provide the foundations "for any sort of political organization," much less "the triumph of European civilization, its institutions, and the wealth and liberty that come from it" (59). On the other, he finds in gaucho life extraordinary skills and intelligence as well as "an underlying poetry, born of the natural features of the country and the unique customs it engenders" (60). He further notes that the gauchos' "customs and tastes . . . someday will embellish our national drama and novel and give them an original hue" (64).

Of course, Sarmiento's real goal is to offer solutions – solutions that might also serve Sarmiento's own political ambitions. At the top of Sarmiento's proposed solutions is immigration from Europe. He argues that immigration "alone would be enough to cure in ten years, at most, all the homeland's wounds made by the bandits, from Facundo to Rosas" (248), as well as whiten the country's inhabitants. Sarmiento and his generation promoted various schemes to attract Europeans to Argentine shores, giving Argentina the highest percentage of immigrants of any American country prior to World War I. Sarmiento's second solution for Argentine ills is education. And in effect, no one anywhere in the Americas did more for public education than him.

History treats Sarmiento ambivalently. He was clearly racist and condescending toward people of color. Moreover, these attitudes, which were widely shared by other men of his time, translated into policies of displacement, if not outright annihilation, of Argentine indigenous peoples. Yet despite these flaws, Sarmiento worked tirelessly for the betterment of society as he understood it. As a writer, he left an enduring legacy in Spanish-American thought, couched in a stylistic virtuosity, clarity, and command of language that astonish the most demanding readers. Moreover, his subjects – personalist government, the psychology of *caudillos* and their followers, the effect of land on national character, the relationship between America and its colonial forebears – anticipate enduring debates in Spanish American letters as well as a necessary point of departure for virtually every discussion that Argentines have about themselves and their country.

## Manuel González Prada, 1844–1918

Although the object of numerous studies, including a highly readable novel based on his life – Luis Alberto Sánchez's *Don Manuel* – Manuel González Prada remains an elusive figure. An acerbic critic of his native Peru, he was born into a conservative society that gave a restless spirit like his plenty to rebel against. Of all Spanish-American republics, Peru generated the weakest independence movement, so much so that without the intervention of outsiders like Venezuela's Simón Bolívar and Argentina's José de San Martín, Peru might have remained a Spanish colony for decades. The third son of a conservative politician, young Manuel studied alongside other upper-class Peruvians. Following his father's death, when Manuel was only 19, he considered studying engineering in Europe, but, yielding to his mother's opposition, he remained in Peru, where he increasingly involved himself in the country's literary scene, publishing his first poem in 1867. In 1873, he helped found a Club Literario where he interacted amicably with the best literati of Lima.

The peaceable world of the Club Literario was soon interrupted by political events that would alter González Prada's life and thought forever. After years of squabbling about their borders, war broke out in 1879 involving Bolivia, Chile, and Peru in what is now called the War of the Pacific. Peruvian forces, despite support from the United States, could not match the Chileans, and in 1880 Chile occupied Lima. Reportedly, González Prada remained secluded in his Lima home for three years to avoid any possible contact with any Chileans. In 1883, Peru and Chile signed the treaty of Ancón by which Peru surrendered the nitrate-rich province of Tarapacá to its southern neighbor. Despite the cessation of hostilities, Chile continued to occupy the provinces of Tacna and Arica until ten years after González Prada's death.

González Prada emerged from these humiliating events a much changed man. In 1886, he helped found a new literary group called the Círculo Literario, which, along with the Club Literario, provided him a forum for several of his most famous speeches and essays, all of which show a growing radicalization alongside deepening pessimism about the viability of Peruvian society. In an untitled speech that he gave at the Politeama Theater in 1888, González Prada signals themes that will dominate much of his writing for the rest of his life: the failures of Peruvian leadership, whether conservative or liberal; the inadequacy of the "degenerate, spendthrift legacy" (2003: 48) left by three hundred years of Spanish colonial rule; the ongoing sabotage of true modernization wrought by the baneful influence of Catholicism; and the inability of Peru's leaders to forge an inclusive national identity that would incorporate the indigenous populations into an overarching national project. González Prada thus sees Peru's ignominious defeat in the War of the Pacific as all but predestined by Peru's internal failure, by its "ignorance and spirit of servility" (47). Peru, he argues, had no sense of common identity sufficient to fight a focused, coordinated war since real union was rendered impossible by "selfishness, imbecility, or disillusionment" (48), producing a country fragmented by class, education, region, and ethnicity. He is particularly harsh on the country's leaders for failing to give the indigenous population (more than eighty percent of the total population in 1888) a sense of state identity to "galvanize a race fallen asleep under the tyranny of the justice of the peace, the governor, and the priest, that unholy trinity responsible for brutalizing the Indian" (49). His conclusion holds that Peru was incapable of victory, as he summarizes in the statement, "We didn't win and we couldn't win" (48). The future lies with the young who, to realize themselves and their country's promise, must discard "the men of the past: those decrepit, worm-eaten trunks [who have] already produced their flowers of unwholesome aroma and bitter fruit. It is time for new trees to proffer new blossoms, new fruits. Old men to the grave, and young men to the task at hand" (50). And those young men must never forget the shame of Chile's victory. "True," he writes, "we can do nothing today, we're impotent, but let's nurse our rancor and wallow in our indignation like a wild beast in thorns" (51).

Also in 1888, González Prada published an essay titled "Propaganda and Attack" in which he combines his interest in both politics and literature. The essay begins with a broadside against contemporary Peruvian writers to whom he refers as journalists (tantamount to calling them hacks) "who talk like Sancho Panza, with idiotic nonsense, crude sayings, and ill-suited refrains" and "archaizing jargon for nostalgic *criollos*" (93–4). While González Prada does not name names, he is clearly targeting Ricardo Palma, the genial author of countless historical sketches known as "Tradiciones" that do indeed romanticize Peru's colonial past (93–4). The conflict between Palma and González Prada typified two very different visions of Peru. Palma was much more akin to the spirit of Andrés Bello, seeking innovation while not abandoning the past. In contrast, González Prada despised traditional Peru and hoped for nothing less than an entirely new "positivist" republic, based on modern science.

He reserved his best barbs, however, for Catholicism, both the Peruvian sort and the Ultramontane variety typified by the reactionary pope, Pio Nono, whose long papacy coincided almost exactly with González Prada's first thirty years. Pio Nono's legendary *Syllabus of Errors* of 1864 told González Prada exactly what he wanted to think about Catholicism: that it was reactionary, antiliberal, antiscientific, and anti-modern. His 1892 essay, "Catholic Education," begins with "Let's get a map of Lima and mark in red the buildings occupied by religious orders, the way doctors mark on the world map the places infected by an epidemic" (73). Catholicism for González Prada is a "theological virus we inherited from the Spaniards" (94), and nowhere is its retrograde influence more pervasive than in an educational system dominated by religious orders that, in González Prada's view, are singularly ill prepared for teaching the positive sciences, mathematics, engineering, and liberal principles of government, all of which he deems essential for a modern nation. Worse yet, he sees no chance of Catholic education improving itself, for it is undermined from the outset by an unnatural, dehumanized clergy:

> There is something rigid, marmoreal, and unappealing about a person who lives segregated from his fellow men and passes through the world with his gaze fixed on some unknown goal and his hopes fixed on something that never comes. His emptiness of heart without the love of a woman and his bitterness at not being a father or having to be one secretly turn the bad priest into an angry soul, the good priest into a bottomless well of melancholy. There's nothing quite so unbearable as the hysterical geniality or the mewling sweetness of priests, who have all the defects of old maids and none of the good qualities of women. A species of androgynes or hermaphrodites, they combine the vices of both sexes. (80)

Unfortunately, González Prada reveals himself as a man of his times; he cannot put down priests without also putting down women.

González Prada's overarching goal, however, is social justice and an improvement in the material circumstances of poor Peruvians, particularly the indigenous. In a strikingly modern turn, he sees poverty itself as a form of violence, arguing that "Social spoils are born of violence, are based on violence dissembled one way or another." If poverty is violence, he argues, the poor have the right to respond in kind: "To fight such violence is to exercise the right to respond to force with force" (96). Thus González Prada is seen by many as a forerunner of armed revolutionary struggle. With words like these, González Prada provided ample reason for some of his intellectual descendants – from the twentieth-century *apristas* to the Shining-Path guerrillas – to consider him a forerunner of armed revolutionary struggle.

In 1891, González Prada embarked for Europe and spent the next seven years in France and Spain. There he encountered for the first time French anarchists such as P. J. Proudhon and, through them, the Russian anarchists Mikhail Bakunin and Peter Kropotkin. No sooner had he returned to Peru than he gave one of his most blistering speeches, the justly famous "The Parties and the National Union," which he later converted into an essay that establishes once and for all his sympathies with European anarchism. Here he argues for the first time for a radical individualism in which all authority is concentrated in the moral individual who can in turn join hands with other individuals in resisting oppression. Moreover, like his European counterparts, he argues that traditional political labels do little but mask the quest for power of the oppressor. "This is why the world is divided today not between republicans and monarchists, or liberals and conservatives, but between two large segments: the haves and the have-nots, the exploiters and the exploited" (158). He further advocates violent revolution, but only by workers aware of their rights who can voluntarily enter agreements of mutual respect and cooperation with similar individuals – what Proudhon called *mutualism*. The task of anarchism is "to educate men capable of bringing about such revolutions" and thereby be free of "ignorant priests, self-serving politicians, and hack journalists" in order to destroy "the edifice raised during four centuries of iniquity," that is, the Peruvian nation and its Spanish forebears (248). He advises the workers to distrust all politicians, "especially those clowns who cloak themselves in the rags of liberalism and shake the rattles of electoral reform, universal suffrage, civil rights, and federalism" (249). But he is no less harsh on the socialists who, despite their advocacy of workers' rights, would still build hierarchies based on centralized authority. "Anarchists should remember that socialism, in any of its multiple forms, is oppressive and rule-bound, quite unlike anarchy, which is utterly free and rejects all rules of any subjection of the individual to the laws of the majority" (249). Of course, like his European counterparts, González Prada remains forever unclear regarding the structures that will educate workers to that sublime moment when revolution can create a utopian, cooperative society free of centralized authority and voluntarily respectful of individual rights.

Where González Prada most shines, however, is in his defense of the Peruvian indigenous. As noted in the preceding section on Sarmiento, the nineteenth century was a century of racism. Widely admired thinkers like Gustave Le Bon, Joseph-Arthur Gobineau, Herbert Spencer, and Sir Francis Galton all preached a "scientific racism" that considered darker people inferior to lighter people and saw mixed bloods as heirs to the worst qualities of their forebears. In his seminal essay, "Our Indians," González Prada denounces every racist as "blind and a fool" (282). He then notes the barbarism of the Spanish and the *mestizo* toward the Indians and asks us to consider on which side the barbarism was more apparent. He is just as quick, however, to condemn the patronizers and the romanticizers as "being political gunrunners cloaked in a philanthropic banner, . . . sentimentality" and "a cheap display of patriotism" (187). Nor does he think the condition of the indigenous has improved since independence, for the Peruvian republic still maintains "the Indian in a state of ignorance and servitude." The state for him is "a monstrous lie" that keeps the Indians "outside the protection of the law" and therefore does not "deserve to be called a democratic republic" (189). What Peru needs is a genuine incorporation of the Indian: "either the heart of the oppressors must be moved to recognize the rights of the oppressed, or the spirit of the oppressed must acquire sufficient virility to punish the oppressors" (193). The Peruvian Indian thus became for González Prada what the workers were for the

European anarchists, Proudhon and Bakunin. González Prada finishes his short essay with this ringing declaration: "We should not be preaching humility and resignation to the Indian, but pride and rebellion . . . the Indian will be saved through his own efforts, not by the humanization of his oppressors (194).

Manuel González Prada has run a strange course in Peruvian intellectual history. Despite his spirited defense of the Peruvian masses, modern sensibilities are repelled by some of his attitudes, particularly his tendency to mention women only as a point of comparison for men he disliked. Yet, despite such objections, González Prada remains a man of extraordinary clarity in his criticisms of the Peruvian ruling class and his uncanny ability to see through the ideological cant of Peru's rulers to the power struggle that pitted one ambitious group against another while always managing to leave out the Indian. Moreover, his blunt rejection of the scientific racism of his time makes him a true precursor of current thinking in human rights. While his vision for Peru was no doubt muddled by a naïve, anarchist faith in the moral individual, his criticisms of the power structures and injustice of his time still ring true today.

## Teresa de la Parra (1890–1936)

Cultured, cosmopolitan, attractive, financially comfortable, socially prominent, vivacious, and unabashedly female, the Venezuelan writer Teresa de la Parra could hardly be more different from the three men discussed above. Her life coincided with some of the most distressing events of the early twentieth century, including the harsh yet effective rule of the Venezuelan dictator General Juan Vicente Gómez which lasted from 1908 to 1935, World War I, and the events leading to the Spanish Civil War, which began in the year of her death. Yet despite this violent and tumultuous backdrop, Parra seemed oddly disinterested in her own time. Unlike the men we have looked at, she showed no interest in promoting grand modernization projects, in correcting Latin American "backwardness" or, for that matter, building new and modern nations. Indeed, her subjects are primarily the lives of women, both of her own time and of Latin America's colonial, Spanish, and Catholic past. In portraying women's lives, she seeks to evoke durable values of Latin American society – values she views as ultimately more constant than "masculine" concerns like the ever-changing world of commerce, politics, and war.

The daughter of a diplomat, she was born in Paris in 1889. Two years later, her parents, along with her two older brothers, returned to Venezuela and spent several idyllic years at Tazón, the family sugar plantation, where four more children were born, including three sisters who would throughout her life remain among Teresa's closest friends and confidantes. After the death of Teresa's father in 1898, her strong-willed and very Catholic mother, Doña Isabel, moved the family to Valencia, Spain to be near their grandmother and aunt. After completing her education at an all-girl convent school under the careful tutelage of Spanish nuns, Teresa spent two years in

Paris and returned to Venezuela in 1909. There, she became fast friends with an older woman, Emilia Ibarra de Barrios Parejo, who encouraged Teresa's writing and read early versions of her first novel. Emilia died childless in 1924, but left the income from her property to Teresa, thus providing her lifelong financial security. While Teresa did not lack for male suitors, she apparently preferred the company of women, and never married.

Her literary production is relatively small, consisting primarily of two novels, several short stories and essays, sets of diaries (including a fictionalized diary based on the travels of her sister María), and many remarkable letters. Only her novels have been translated into English (consequently, all quotations below that come from works other than the novels are in my translation). With a prose style that manages to be urbane yet informal, elegant yet chatty, she contributed frequently to Venezuelan and other Spanish-language newspapers, occasionally under the self-effacing pseudonym "Frufru." In 1915, she published her first short stories, which appeared almost simultaneously in Caracas and Paris. In 1924 she published her first novel, *Iphigenia: The Diary of a Young Lady who Wrote Because she was Bored*, which appeared two years later in French translation. Between 1928 and 1929, she published her second novel, *Mama Blanca's Memoirs*, first in French and later in Spanish. Both novels won her widespread recognition in both Spanish America and Europe, bringing her invitations to speak in Cuba and Colombia, where she was hailed as one of the finest new writers in the Spanish language. In Cuba, she began an enduring friendship with the Cuban poet, Lydia Cabrera. Then, tragically, in 1931 she showed early symptoms of tuberculosis. She spent the next five years in Europe going from one sanatorium to another, seeking a cure. During this period, she wrote several important letters and kept a diary almost until her dying day. Lydia Cabrera lived with her in Madrid during her final months, serving as both friend and nurse. In the spring of 1936, at the age of 46, Teresa succumbed to the disease. Her body was transported to Venezuela for burial in 1947.

To date, only her two novels have been translated into English. While these are important and captivating texts, they speak – inevitably – through the characters themselves and do not allow an unambiguous view of Parra's own opinions. What they do show, however, is Parra's remarkable ability to imagine convincing characters, mostly women, in circumstances that are distinctly Latin American. *Iphigenia* consists entirely of the diaries of María Eugenia Alonso, a young upper-class woman torn between lovers. The man she loves, Gabriel, is eloquent, sensitive, passionate, and handsome. He is also trapped in an unhappy marriage, therefore making him unavailable to María Eugenia unless both violate strong societal taboos against adultery and divorce. The other man, to whom she is engaged, is the dutiful but dull, attentive but condescending Leal (which translates as "loyal"). Marriage to Leal will inevitably lead to a life of quiet desperation – which is exactly what society expects of women of María Eugenia's station. Despite the diary frame of the narration, María Eugenia includes transcriptions of letters and lengthy reconstructions of conversations with other characters, most significantly with her black maid, Gregoria, whose relative amorous freedom as a poor black woman provides a fascinating counterpoint to the restricted, rule-bound life expected of a wealthy white girl like María Eugenia.

Critics have never quite known what to do with *Iphigenia*. The lengthy passages on the moral quandary of choosing between love and duty, personal freedom and societal expectations have been called didactic, reductive, and simplistic. They have also offended readers who might like a more decisive, assertive character, or at least someone who portrays with less ambiguity the societal confines that delimited women's lives. Some critics have also found racial and gender stereotyping in the implied sexual freedom of the black servant Gregoria as well as in the cruel portrayal of Clara, Iphigenia's joyless maiden aunt whose only solace is religion. The novel was, however, an immediate *succès de scandale*, partly because of the enraged reaction of conservatives who preferred tales of exemplary Catholic women to the confused confessions of a young woman who fantasizes about adultery, hopes that her beloved Gabriel will divorce, and fears matrimony as legalized servitude. Parra herself defended the novel as an exposé of the "submission and passivity imposed by force" on Spanish American women that can only "embitter the souls that in their peaceful appearance . . . end up becoming whitened sepulchers" (1992: 474; my translation). Yet, notwithstanding Parra's disclaimers, *Iphigenia* is not merely a thesis novel about women's suffering. Indeed, what makes the novel excellent literature is its convincing portrayal of a young woman made believable precisely because of her contradictions and her apparent inability to understand fully her own feelings, much less the societal strictures that bind her.

Parra's second novel, *Mama Blanca's Memoirs*, also tells a story of women, but with greater gentleness and less psychological depth. Framed as the memories of a septuagenarian woman told to a 12-year-old girl who wants to be a writer, the novel recalls life on a plantation reminiscent of Tazón, where Teresa spent a very happy childhood. This second novel is populated by a huge cast of characters, none developed to any great degree. Of Parra's two novels, *Iphigenia* is usually considered the better.

Due to the success of her novels, Parra received invitations to lecture in both Colombia and Cuba. These lectures, regrettably not available in English, signal an important new current in Parra's work: her wish to reclaim and describe the role women played in the formation of Latin American culture. The three lectures given in Colombia are titled "The Influence of Women in the Formation of the American Soul." The first lecture begins with an odd disclaimer in which Parra declares that her "feminism is moderate" (Parra 1992: 19) and that she has no wish to follow the example of Gabriela Mistral, who "crisscrosses the world, suffering and struggling in her work as apostle, socialist, Catholic, defender of liberty and of the noble spirit of our race" (21). Rather, Parra says, "I plan to look for my self-sacrificing women" who created the American soul (21). The real goal of the lectures, then, is to establish a genealogy for women in Spanish-American history, or as Parra puts it, "the humble lives" of women "filled with suffering and love, that do not get told" (23). Accordingly, she dedicates each essay respectively to three different groups: "the [women] of the conquest: the sorrowful women, crucified in the clash of races. The women of

colonial times: the mystics and the dreamers. The women of the independence movement: the inspirers and the doers" (25).

Parra chooses two women to characterize the conquest: doña Marina, Cortez's Aztec
interpreter, and doña Isabel, mother of the Peruvian chronicler, Inca Garcilaso de la
Vega. What most astonishes in Parra's narrative is the richness of the text despite the
paucity of available documentation. Aside from brief references to doña Marina in
Bernal Díaz del Castillo's famous chronicle, almost nothing is known about her.
Cortez, in his letters to Charles V, never mentions her by name, nor does she appear
in any other document of the time. Little more is known about Inca Garcilaso's
mother, except that she was of noble Incan birth and provided contact for the young
Garcilaso with his Incan forebears – as he tells in his nostalgic memoirs written in
Spain well after the fact. Parra, however, does not hesitate to imagine the details, or,
as she puts it, "Through what little is said, one determines the great deal that is not
said" (25). Moreover, she feels fully justified in imagining the history of women since
"it is almost a duty to proclaim the moral superiority of these kinds of stories . . . the
other history, the official version, ends up being a kind of banquet for men only . . . If
you leave out women, you cut one of the channels of life" (30).

So imagine she does. In her retelling of the life of doña Marina, we learn that this
Aztec woman not only served as Cortez's interpreter, gave birth to one of his children,
and later became the wife of another Spanish soldier; she also gave him "accurate
advice" and once saved his life (25). Indeed, without her, Parra tells us, Cortez could
well have failed – all of which may be true, despite the paucity of evidence. In her
reconstruction of the story of Inca Garcilaso's mother, Parra again fills in details about
doña Isabel's life that her son most surely does not tell. But again, Parra's story is not
implausible and perhaps it is true that "beneath the transparency" of Garcilaso's prose,
"we hear the sound of tears, a lament from beyond the grave . . . the echo of a mother's
voice" (35).

The second essay begins with a beautiful invocation to Spanish America's colonial
past and particularly to the nuns who "went to the convent because they were lovers
of silence – eternally thirsty for the inner life and, although it might seem contradictory, precursors of the modern feminist ideal" (40). Parra finds in convent life a
freedom from the constraints of patriarchal society, whose primary expression is the
submission of wives to husbands. In the convent, women live with women and submit
their immediate existence to serving other women, all of which Parra summarizes in
the paradoxical statement "Voluntary slavery of the free women in this fashion set the
slave free" (41). Parra describes the life of several exemplary nuns drawn from the fif-
teenth through the eighteenth century, one being the Spanish mystic Santa Teresa de
Ávila, famous reformer of the Order of the Discalced Carmelites, and another being
the Mexican nun Sor Juana Inés de la Cruz, arguably the best Spanish-language poet
of her time. The world Parra imagines in the convents is one of good humor and
freedom, all framed by women serving other women. She also suggests that such
devotion was affectionate as well as holy and cites as an example Sor Juana's love for
Queen Laura, wife of the Mexican Viceroy. Parra further suggests the devotion of nuns
serving nuns characterized women throughout society:

Undecided mystics, with vocation for neither the convent nor marriage, ambitious or disillusioned by their first love, they remained on the margin of life. Sowing affection and self-denial in the family, they grew old as single women. More maternal than their actual mothers, they were in large measure the aging maiden aunts who created our characteristic Creole sentimentalism, that always loves with pain, and exalts itself even to the point of tragedy in cases of absence, illness or death. (48)

The third essay/lecture is devoted almost entirely to the women who nurtured and protected Simón Bolívar, the liberator of northern South America. Again, given the paucity of documentary evidence, Parra largely imagines what these women might have been like, seeing them through a glass darkly as necessary elements in the life of the great man. Thus, she tells of Bolívar's great love for his young Spanish bride, María Teresa, who died tragically when Bolívar was barely 19 years old (68–9). She later gives careful attention to Manuelita, Bolívar's mistress and his constant support during the last years of his life when he was beset by illness and surrounded by political enemies. For modern scholars, Parra's reconstruction of these women's lives does point toward some of the available evidence. But what most enlivens these excellent essays is her imagination and her insistence on the often overlooked but obvious fact that women played a huge role in Latin America's past. Although Parra often goes beyond what the documentary record might justify, she tells a compelling, plausible, and necessary story.

Of course, the real question that confronts us for the purposes of this note is "Should Teresa de la Parra be studied as a nation-builder?" This question begs another more basic one: "Where does the national project reside?" In Bello, Sarmiento, and González Prada, the nation emerges as an enterprise forged (or betrayed) in its institutions. In contrast, Teresa de la Parra suggests that Latin American society, despite its political fractures, has a special kind of continuity that both undergirds and transcends politics, economics, and state institutions, that continuity being the personal, the intimate, and the communal – values she finds most visible in the lives of women.

## REFERENCES AND FURTHER READING

Bello, Andrés (1997). *Selected Writings of Andrés Bello*. Trans. Frances M. López-Morillas, ed. Iván Jaksic. New York: Oxford University Press.

Bunkley, Allison (1952). *The Life of Sarmiento*. Princeton, NJ: Princeton University Press.

Caldera, Rafael (1977). *Andres Bello: Philosopher, Poet, Philologist, Educator, Legislator, Statesman*. Trans. John Street. London : George Allen & Unwin.

Castro-Klaren, Sara, and Chasteen, John Charles, eds (2003). *Beyond Imagined Communities: Reading and Writing the Nation in Nineteenth-Century Latin America*. Baltimore, MD: Johns Hopkins University Press.

De la Parra, Teresa (1992). *Obra escogida*. 2 vols. Ed. María Fernanda Palacios. Mexico City: Fondo de Cultura Económica.

— (1993). *Iphigenia (The diary of a young lady who wrote because she was bored)*. Trans. Bertie Acker, ed. Naomi Lindstrom. Austin: University of Texas Press.

— (1993). *Mama Blanca's Memoirs*. Trans. Harriet de Onís and Frederick H. Fornoff. Pittsburgh: University of Pittsburgh Press.

González Prada, Manuel (2003). *Free Pages and Other Essays: Anarchist Musings.* Trans. Frederick H. Fornoff, ed. David Sobrevilla. Oxford: Oxford University Press.

Halperín Donghi, Tulio et al., eds. (1994). *Sarmiento: Author of a Nation.* Berkeley: University of California Press.

Jaksic, Iván (1989). *Academic Rebels in Chile: The Role of Philosophy in Higher Education and Politics.* Albany: State University of New York Press.

— (2001). *Andres Bello: Scholarship and Nation-Building in Nineteenth-Century Latin America.* New York: Cambridge University Press.

Rodriguez, Ileana (1994). *House/Garden/Nation: Space, Gender, and Ethnicity in Post-Colonial Latin American Literatures by Women.* Trans. Robert Carr and Ileana Rodriguez. Durham, NC: Duke University Press.

Sarmiento, D. F. (2003). *Facundo: Civilization and Barbarism.* Trans. Kathleen Ross. Berkeley: University of California Press.

— (2005). *Recollections of a Provincial Past.* Trans. Elizabeth Garrels and Aza Zatz. New York: Oxford University Press.

Shumway, Nicolas (1992). *The Invention of Argentina.* Berkeley: University of California Press.

# 18
# Reading National Subjects
*Juan Poblete*

As recently as 2004 Felipe Lindoso asked, in the title of a book, *O Brasil pode ser um pais de leitores? Politica para a cultura. Politica para o livro* (Can Brazil be a country of readers? Cultural policies. Book policies). The question is symptomatic and historical. It is symptomatic because it reveals the always unfinished nature of both the nation as cultural project and reading as a national practice. The nation and reading are both active forms of imagining ourselves and our connections to others and as we will see below, there have been influential attempts to establish a constitutive link between them. Moreover, what Lindoso's question highlights in 2004 is not only the connection itself but also three related aspects: that this trajectory of the nation and reading has a long and unfinished history in the continent; secondly, that the nation-state may have a stake in turning its citizens into readers; and finally, that the book itself, as a form and a discursive vehicle, continues to occupy an important position when it comes to positing the links between culture, citizens, and the nation. In the last few decades, there has been a relative delinking of literary markets and national markets due first to the contemporary transnational restructuring of book publishing and, secondly, due to the proliferation of forms of communication and discourses reaching the nation but originating beyond its borders (cable TV, Internet, videos, etc.). Faced with this relative non-coincidence of the space of the book (and more generally the field of discourse-production) and the space of the nation, the state has had at least two vested interests in reacting to the process. Both are connected to publishing as an important cultural industry. Printed discourses continue to be central to the forms of socialization of citizens the state privileges in its educational policies and, secondly, they constitute a potentially valuable and strategic sector in both economic and geo-political terms. Thus in providing an overview of some of the problems involved in the terms of the title of this chapter, we can distinguish for the Latin American nineteenth century at least two print-producing and consuming spheres and two sets of practices which attempt to create, expand, and administer said spheres and their markets. The two very broad spaces are what we could call civic and state spheres.

The civic sphere is constituted by the set of practices that take place in the many strata and classes conforming civil society in its broadest sense (that is to say, encompassing at least elite and popular versions of civil society and elite and popular versions of public spheres.) By state sphere on the other hand, I mean the many efforts the state will enact to develop cultural policies concerning publishing and reading. They range from the educational efforts to extend schooling and textbook production to the funds devoted to the creation of public libraries and official newspapers. As we will explore below, when viewed historically, the connection between the nation and reading consists of the relations (collaborations and contradictions, points of intersections and divergence) between those two spheres and the forms of territorialization and subjectification they promote or make possible. Furthermore, those two spaces are the two sides of a paradoxical relation between publicness and the state, on the one hand, and the many components of civil society, on the other. Publicness from which we derive both publication and publicity, publics and republics, functions as the end result of the efforts developed by the state to, on the one hand, create its own social initiatives and, on the other, control, direct, or influence the efforts produced in this same area and within the territory of the nation by its multiple social actors. A national public sphere is thus a contradictory and complex array of discourses constituted and circulated by multiple actors through a vast network of mass mediations. In the nineteenth century, those actors are centrally the state, the Catholic Church and the different publics produced by the emergence of a modern market space. The mediation was provided by newspapers and novels, but also by broadsides, private and public letters, pamphlets, albums, and magazines, among the printed forms and by multiple urban oral and visual practices (both elite and popular) among the nonprinted. All these mediated discourses and the practices of the actors that made them possible became crucial for the active imaginative production of the national as a sociocultural and political link.

## The Argument

The main contention of this chapter is that discourses (written and oral, published or private) and the reading practices they engendered were central to the formation of certain forms of subjects (citizens), certain forms of community (nations), and certain discursive spaces (national public spheres, themselves the result of the interactions between civic and state spheres in the formation of national markets) under particular political and institutional arrangements (nation-states). My claim is not that these discursive practices and spaces are the only means connecting the nation and the heterogeneous populations of the national territory. A long trajectory of state-sponsored physical and symbolic violence and the multiple forms of physical and symbolic resistance thus engendered in oppressed populations, especially indigenous and other racialized people, are of course a constitutive part of the history of the national in Latin America. However, my focus here is more narrow. My argument is that written discourses, reading practices, and the forms of oral discursive interactions they made possible, though clearly not the only factors, crucially provided practical and theoretical means through which subjects conceptualized themselves in/and their interactions with others in nations undergoing a transition from traditional to modern cultural configurations. In that process the subjects used conceptual/practical frameworks that gave meaning to their actions, thoughts, and feelings. These frameworks included a series of discursive formats such as newspapers, novels (published as books and serialized in periodicals), letters, albums, and salon-based *tertulias* (regular social and cultural gatherings.) All of them shared at least one important characteristic: they functioned as discursive spaces where mediating forms of a new, nationalized, modern cultural literacy developed. These mediating forms connected social spaces theretofore separated by deep cultural binaries such as private/public, masculine/feminine, legitimate/illegitimate, elite/popular, and local-regional/national levels. Therefore, reading and writing practices became crucial to the imagination of the nation to the extent that they allowed its subjects to find connecting, intermediating discursive spaces constituted by the amalgam of symbolic and material practices in the sociability of daily life (Rama, 1996; González-Stephan, 2004; Cornejo Polar, 1995; Anderson, 1991; Castro-Klaren and Chasteen, 2003).

Up until their declarations of independence, most Latin American countries showed at the urban social and cultural levels, if not always at the political one, a traditional economy of the circulation of texts dominated by the type of semiotic practices produced by 300 years of imperial and Catholic colonization. While this colonization elicited active resistance and reactions from the colonized (Gruzinski, 1991), the fact remains that the church and the priests practically controlled many of the types of texts and the types of readings and commentary that could circulate socially. The priest was in charge of providing the semiotic clues to most discourses and had a strong say in the ways in which the male elite, but especially women and subaltern publics, related to the production of meaning in everyday urban life (from the texts read to the religious and social festivities.) This cultural configuration, which would persist until mid-nineteenth century, was nevertheless modified by the type of national polities created by the declarations of independence. If, in practice, all countries in the region continued to be culturally Catholic after independence; in theory, the state needed to produce new nationalized forms of cultural and social legitimation for its newly constituted national populations. Thus postcolonial states and their elite leaders, having often used the subversive potential of letters and the press to champion the independence cause, attempted to reposition the production of discourses (including literature) within the national discursive formation. This was developed gradually and through a somewhat contradictory process. While the entry and access of the people to these discourses were initially limited, eventually there was, on the one hand, a relative explosion of printed discourses (made possible by liberal and conservative contributions) and, on the other, a secular attack led by the liberals on the ideological perspective inspiring the ecclesiastical and conservative censure of this thriving publishing market. In this way, in the second part of the century a new national public sphere came into being. It emerged in the midst of a prolonged discussion on the nature of cultural change and at the intersection of the efforts developed – sometimes jointly and, as time went by, increasingly separately – by the State and the Catholic church to control the new configuration of proto-massive, market-based, modern reading publics.

In Latin America the state was constituted as a result of a power vacuum in an emergency situation produced by the Napoleonic occupation of Spain and Portugal. Radicalized shortly thereafter, the Latin American polities became self proclaimed nation-states. Thus the states saw themselves as having to meet the challenges of creating the social and cultural basis of the nation. This was a long process of centralization, culminating for most countries at the end of the nineteenth and the beginning of the twentieth century. Through this process, the state attempted to concentrate and truly nationalize political power by creating an institutional infrastructure that allowed a centralized administration of resources in the educational, socioeconomic, and political realms. The nation, on the other hand, in all its constitutive plurality – from locational diversity (rural–urban, local–regional), to class (elite, popular) and cultural heterogeneity (women, indigenous and *mestizo*, black) – produced multiple forms of national imagination. Some of those reacted against state efforts; some went along or were in fact sponsored or subsidized by the state. Crucial in both respects was the development of new forms of sociability.

Discursive exchanges (extended and intensive, public and private discussions, reading and writing practices) were important aspects of those forms of new sociability and will allow me here to establish connections between the multiplication of print and the emergence of new national reading subjects. That is to say, of all the different discursive practices of the nineteenth century in Latin America, including oral, visual, and written discourses, I will only deal with those written and read and, to a lesser degree, with those forms of oral discursive practice that were made possible by them. Before I do so, it seems important to at least give an indication of another side of the problem at hand. Along with the practices of writing and reading that grounded a relationship between the nation and representation in the process of emergence of national reading subjects, there are other practices such as political, economic, and social groups and associations where a form of citizenship and thus of national subjectivity was promoted and created. While I will refer to their many publications later, it seems crucial to indicate their importance as social practices beyond the elaboration of written discourses and reading forms.

## Nation and Representation I

The classic forms of public-constituting sociopolitical activities in the Western tradition are political and civic participation. In general, the standard view of the Latin American nineteenth century has emphasized the lack of active and free democratic participation at both levels. Thus, the supposed underdevelopment of both the political and civil arenas in the continent have been used to explain an alleged lack of democratic development. Whether this failure is attributed to the legacies of colonialism, the predominance of premodern forms of political legitimacy based on charismatic authority (*caudillismo*) or the absence of truly productive bourgeois classes and revolutions, the end result is always to note a lack of participation. In recent years, after the catastrophic dictatorships of the 1970s and 1980s, and inspired by a wave of contemporary democratizations, a series of studies have appeared reclaiming, against the political and civic deficit hypothesis, the need to understand historically, in all its specificity and without acritically using Eurocentric developmentalist paradigms, the actually existing forms of political and civic participation in nineteenth-century Latin America.

Summarizing some of these proposals, Hilda Sábato has stated:

> In the past, citizenship was not absent from the literature on the [Latin American] nineteenth century. But its history was understood almost exclusively in terms of the development of political rights, particularly the right to vote, and measured against an ideal modernizing course of gradual expansion of the franchise . . . The new historical literature has left behind this restricted and linear approach and defined a wider, multilayered view of political citizenship . . . At the same time, other previously unnoticed or neglected dimensions have acquired increasing visibility. Among them . . . the types and modes of sociability, the formation of public spheres and the construction of public opinion have become main topics of historical inquiry. (Sábato, 2001: para. 11)

At the level of political elections, for example, Antonio Annino and his collaborators have stressed the need to go beyond the concentration on the output of elections (their results and their weight in political disputes) to focus instead on the inputs (how did heterogeneous voters enter the homogenous space of modern political representation, how did actors, who differed socially and culturally, practice the categories of nation and representation?). Rather surprisingly, Annino suggests three new findings of this latter wave of historical research: elections were a constant and accepted fact in the legitimation of political power throughout the century; Latin Americans were extraordinarily precocious when it came to organizing political elections; finally, the territorial fragmentation affecting Latin American countries right after independence was both horizontal and vertical. It was horizontal in that, in many places such as Argentina, colonial unity gave way to multiple provincial states (while in others such as Brazil, the now independent country remained fully unified). But fragmentation was also vertical: both Brazil and Argentina shared the same destructuration of old territorial hierarchies (cities lost power vis-à-vis the countryside, power was ruralized; small provincial cities claimed relative degrees of autonomy from provincial capitals). More importantly, this vertical fragmentation included for the Hispanic American countries a *sui generis* mix of new and old forms of legitimating political representation. According to Annino, pre-independence redeveloped municipal powers after the Cádiz Spanish Constitution of 1812 and the new form of representative democracy advocated by the independent governments later on came

together to create the specificity of the nineteenth-century Latin American political
scenario:

> Our research suggest that in Latin America the early electoral experience, by legitimat-
> ing local autonomy, confronted the elites [not so much with the issue of expanding an
> already expanded access to voting and citizenship, but] with the problem of how to
> invert the tendency towards vertical fragmentation of territories to consolidate the new
> national spaces. (Annino, 1995: 13)

A number of additional and perhaps counterintuitive conclusions derive from this
analysis: political representation in nineteenth-century Latin America is a hybrid
between communitarian and individual-based citizenship, and the latter was often
used to control and subject the former. The space between the two was in constant
negotiation in a very active and recurrent political process. There is no uniform
gradual expansion of suffrage for most male voters (Sábato, 2001; Annino, 1995;
Murilo de Carvalho, 1999: 327–8).

At the level of civic participation there is a similarly robust and emerging literature
for the Latin American nineteenth century. One of the most ambitious recent efforts
is that of Carlos Forment. In *Democracy in Latin America 1760–1900* – in two volumes:
one for Mexico and Peru (published) and one for Cuba and Argentina (unpublished
at the time of writing) – Forment proposes a view of Latin America according to
which "civic democracy, understood in Tocquevillian terms as a daily practice and
form of life rooted in social equality, mutual recognition, and political liberty, was
by the mid-nineteenth century rooted in the region" (Forment, 2003: XI). This
actually existing democracy

> was distinctive in several ways. First it was radically disjointed . . . [citizens engaged
> with each other much more than they did with institutional structures]. Second, it was
> radically asymmetrical. Citizens practiced democracy more readily and intensely in civic
> society than in any other public terrains (economic society, political society, and the
> public sphere) . . . Third, it was radically fragmented . . . [along socio-ethnical fissures].
> Fourth, democratic life in Latin America was culturally hybrid. Catholicism was the
> language of public life in the region. Citizens used its narrative resources to create new
> democratic meanings from old religious terms, thereby fusing the two to create an
> alternative vocabulary – call it Civic Catholicism. (Forment, 2003: XI–XII)

While Forment's Civic Catholicism is a fairly abstract and imprecise concept, his
research on actual civic organizations is extraordinary in its scope and ambitions. It
combines quantitative with qualitative research to establish some basic data on civic
associations and, most importantly for my purposes here, on their abundant discursive
production (as manifested in organizing practices and all kinds of publications).
Forment also provides a useful classification to understand the many forms of public
life in nineteenth-century Latin America. There are, according to him, four terrains
of public life and each one is subdivided into fields and subfields as follows:

- Civil society: Cultural (literary-scientific, educational, professional); Societal (mutual aid, artisan, racial-ethnic, patriotic, Masonic, community development); Public service (charity-welfare, fire brigade); Religious (moral improvement, church); Recreational (hobby-leisure, social).
- Economic society: Financial organizations (banks and insurances companies, savings and loans); Credit networks (cooperatives); Business (family firms, joint stock companies).
- Political society: electoral clubs, municipal townships, mass movements.
- Public sphere: Literate (reading and writing practices, newspapers); Oral (rumor and gossip networks); Visual (theater, clothing). (Forment, 2003: 22)

Forment's data for the second half of the nineteenth century in Mexico, or Sergio Grez Toso's for Chile, speak of hundreds of such social, political, economic, and cultural organizations (Grez Toso, 1995: 614–15).

Florencia Mallon has also brought to relevance thick political and discursive networks present not only at the national but also the regional and, above all, communal local levels, in her work on the making of postcolonial Mexico and Peru. According to Mallon, "The contrast between these three regions [Morelos and Puebla in Mexico and Junín in Peru] demonstrate that national politics were constructed through a three-tiered, nested process of struggle and interaction among communal hegemonic processes, regional political cultures and emerging 'national' arenas" (Mallon, 1995: 315). As a result of her analysis, Mallon posits the existence and importance for national politics and nation-formation processes, of popular nationalisms articulated at the local and regional levels as alternatives to the hegemony of capital-city-centered versions of liberalism. An important part of the activities of all of these social, economic, political, and civic popular organizations was the production of what has been called a "plebeian literature" (Gutiérrez Sanín, 1999: 182).

This brief excursus through the social, economic, and political forms of organizations of public life in nineteenth-century Latin America was meant to highlight their perhaps surprising abundance and complexity. When the fact that many of these organizations developed writing and reading practices is considered, one is faced with a discursive landscape that goes well beyond the standard view of elite books, novels, and newspapers. This task of expanding a horizon based on the elite's discourses and projects and on a restricted and narrow concept of political citizenship remains to be fully undertaken.

## Nation and Representation II

There are a number of existing ways of conceptually positing the connection between nation and representation: imagined communities, civil society, and public sphere are among them. While these concepts partially overlap in their efforts to explain the connection between discourses and national subjectivities, it is useful to define them separately. I will return below to the concept of imagined communities. At this point it would be useful to distinguish civil society from public sphere. Civil society as developed by G. W. F. Hegel is that sphere of social life placed between the private realm of the family and the official sphere of the state. It refers to an array of voluntary civic associations such as political parties, trade unions, and cultural and educational organizations. They all share their public nature, which has to be distinguished both from the privacy of the family and the official publicness of the state. In those free associations individuals subject themselves and are subjected to the open, public exercise of their reason on matters of collective concern without government tutelage. As such, civil society has in Hegel a constitutive educational component. Not only is it the sphere where a functional education for labor takes place but it is also that sphere where the formation of socially educated subjectivities occur. We learn to live together by educating ourselves and each other, in the practice of freely associating and debating with others (Cohen and Arato, 1992). The concept of public sphere, on the other hand, has been developed by Jürgen Habermas in his classic book *The Structural Transformation of the Public Sphere*. In its most essential definition the public sphere is that domain of social life in which citizens come freely together and exercise their reason to constitute a form of publicness (public opinion) which is independent from the state's controls and can in fact function as balance and check of the state. It is a mediating sphere between society and the state, and in Habermas is constituted originally as an eighteenth-century European bourgeois phenomenon whereby the forms of associations and the formats developed in the sphere of letters (literature and other written discourses) acquire a political significance. Starting with letter writing, in which a certain form of privateness and self-reflection is oriented toward somebody else (the addressee), there develops a type of discourse, generally fiction and literature, where a strong form of intersubjectivity manifests itself. This intersubjectivity (functioning for both writer and readers) allows for the exploration of the individual's subjectivity, of its connection with other subjectivities, and of the actions of the state that impinge on social life (Habermas, 1989). Even in this cursory description of civil society and public sphere it is possible to perceive how both concepts attempt to connect, via discursive exchanges, the individual subject with others with whom she associates in daily life. Reading and writing discourses, as mediated by artifacts and forms of circulation such as newspapers, letters, pamphlets, and novels, become crucial practices of such a public-forming exchange. We see also how both concepts act as counterbalances to the power of the state over the administration and organization of social life. Referring to this latter work of the modern state, Michel Foucault proposed the category of governmentality (1991). Governmentality manifested in state and civil institutions and practices, and it controlled through calculations (political economy) the life of mass populations. As such governmentality combined the individualizing aspects of pastoral power (evident, for example, in the work of religion in the formation of subjects) with the centralizing rationality that characterizes the modern state. In so doing, governmentality both produced and controlled subjects who were then subject to and subjects of power. In modern societies this meant producing national subjects fully educated in the ways of the nation, subjects who could not but see themselves as belonging freely to the order of the nation-state. From this perspective, the organizations and practices of civil society and those of the public sphere can be described as always performing a dual form of educational labor on their citizens–members. On the one hand, Habermasianly, we can emphasize how crucial those practices and organizations are for the emergence and sustainability of a critical public. On the other, following Foucault, we can stress to what extent those practices and institutions are in consonance with state efforts to govern (both control and produce) fully nationalized subjects. Both perspectives share, from different viewpoints, the emphasis on the emergence of a moral political economy of populations. These efforts attempted to redirect the material, intellectual, moral, and physical energies of mass populations toward productive goals. Popular, elite, and government-driven initiatives sought to harness the social energies of mass populations via the moralization of sociability in the realms of work, economics, education, entertainment, and culture (Poblete, 2002).

Therefore, as an alternative to public sphere and civil society, in this chapter I will propose to use the concept of sociability. Sociability is perhaps one of the nodal points around which it is possible to organize the multiple discourses (social, political, educational, religious, cultural) of the Latin American nineteenth century. Sociability is, first, a concept widely used in nineteenth-century discourses, i.e., it is an analytical category actively operating in the conceptual and practical framing of social processes involving especially elite sectors but also popular ones at the time. Secondly, while referring to the forms of voluntary association which characterize analogous concepts such as civil society and public sphere in the European tradition, sociability alludes to forms that are not exclusively bourgeois (one can talk about popular sociability, for example), it allows a distinction between formal and informal sociabilities, and it has a particular semantic emphasis on its competence or performative component as developed in the practice of everyday life. One of the key forms of national sociability in the Latin American nineteenth century is the reading and writing of novels, newspapers, and a wide range of printed material. My claim is that a study of those forms of sociability connected to reading and writing involves a dual consideration of the practices as such and of the surfaces (texts) in which those practices are performed and inscribed. Both, practices and spaces of legibility, are socially produced and have complex and perhaps contradictory effects. They both help produce autonomous subjects and are crucial in the process of subjection of those subjects to the social logic of the nation. It is in those discourses and practices where it can be seen how subjectification is part of a process that includes subjection. Connecting both there is what can be called a practical national reason embodied in the daily lives of the national subjects. A reason connecting public spheres (discourses and issues of textual representation) with public spaces – which, along with books, pamphlets, and newspapers, include other social spaces such as the street, the city, cafés, and tertulias – also linking state practices such as mass and compulsory education with civil society's free associations and discussions. Thus, in the performance of national daily life forms of social action based on representation (centrally textual and visual) come together with forms of direct sociability (multiple social practices), the saying and the doing. What is done when we say and what is said when we do are connected. Sociability grounds discourses in the representation of society and in social practice, it is both public sphere–civil society and governmentality; a clear manifestation of the deepening of democratic life and an extension of the penetrating capacity of governmentality. It also highlights the mimetic and thus imitable and performative nature of social relations, going beyond some of the dichotomies separating social, material, and intellectual history. Again, this is not to deny the very crucial role violent conflicts of all types, from riots and racial uprisings to civil and external wars, have played in the formation of the nation. It is to simply focus on a different aspect of the formation of the national.

In order to empirically ground my claim around the concept of sociability, I will now describe in the next sections the types of sociability generated at the civil and state levels by different reading (and later on, writing) practices exercised on multiple objects in diverse social spaces by an array of cultural agents.

## The Civil Sphere I: Imagining the Nation in Newspapers and Books

More than twenty years ago, in his classic book, *Imagined Communities*, Benedict Anderson posited the crucial role the reading of newspapers and novels, as forms of imagining the social collective, had in the emergence of modern nationalisms. At least since then, both the concept of social imaginary and the attribution to written literature and its reading of a key function in the task of constructing – daily and within the subjectivities of the citizens – that form of belonging and mooring we call nationality, have had an important critical trajectory and a clear impact on the study of culture in Latin America and elsewhere. That significance is all the more obvious today when we face new forms of de/re/linking literature, written discourse, and the nation. The emergence of nascent transnational imaginaries – be them those of new social movements such as ecologism or global anti-globalization, or those embodied by new transnational and translocal networks of migrant circulation and displacements, to say nothing of new global capitalism itself – makes more evident than ever the specificity of the nineteenth-century ways of imagining the nation, while it also highlights the roles the novel and the newspapers as mass media played in that process.

Without fully revisiting Benedict Anderson's well-known argument, it is useful to highlight for our purposes here how, in Anderson's thesis, print-capitalism and its two main nineteenth-century forms, the novel and the newspaper, created an important part of the cultural basis on which a political entity such as the nation-state could be both defined and practiced by the active imagining of ordinary people. For the claim about these two forms of printed culture in Anderson is that they made possible what could be expressed as the emergence of the nation as a categorical form for the imagination of the social (as both a link and a space) and for its practice in everyday life. This meant an expansion of the space of politics as the nation was centrally, although not exclusively, imagined in the reading of printed material which capitalism was now able to produce in mass quantities for their consumption by thousands of citizens. It was a different type of politics based on the circulation of ideas and narratives, images and behaviors which allowed the active imagination of a common frame of reference in a cultural imaginary whose forms of legitimation and meaning were internal and not external. Contrary to the religious foundations of a sacred time reaching back to Genesis and moving forward with teleological certainty, the nation was characterized as history moving in a homogeneous, empty-time for which the here and now of the daily life of a self-identified community constituting the nation provided a central focus. In this respect, both newspapers and novels as cultural artifacts, and their actual reading by national publics, shared the capacity of allowing that community the cultural experience of this new form of modern temporality, connectivity and meaningfulness. Thus the reading of newspapers and novels became crucial for how the nation was represented, how its claims were legitimized, and how its history (origins and trajectory) were narrated (Eley and Suny, 1996: 24). They were also fundamental to the task, previously performed by religions, of giving meaning to individual existential contingency connecting it to a community and a social horizon of intelligibility. National citizens exist as anonymous agents who simultaneously imagine themselves as belonging to and pertinent in a community. The reading of newspapers and novels provides both an example of and an instrument for the development of such an imagination. Both are predicated on the idea of their relevance for an implied community of readers who share the cultural encyclopedia of references and the memory of common narratives and experiences alluded to in the texts.

At this point it becomes crucial to ask about literacy levels in the continent. While the historical record is far from definitive, certain figures seem indicative enough. Generalizing the available Hispanic American data, Carlos Newland comes to the following estimates: 10 percent or less literacy level for the first few decades of the nineteenth century, 15 percent around 1850, and 27 percent in 1900 (Newland, 1991: 357). These limited levels of literacy were nevertheless enhanced by multiple forms of actual cultural consumption of the newspapers going well beyond the individual, solitary reading we take for granted. From the collective readings at the Cuban cigar-making factories to the readings of all kinds of publication at street corners, including the reading aloud in the family's living room and the work of *pregoneros* and the numerous borrowings of any single copy, a number of reading practices multiplied the cultural effects of newspapers in nineteenth-century Latin America (Coudart, 2001; Tinajero, 2006; Poblete, 2004a).

Not only did reading contribute to create the kind of imagined bond that makes possible the experience of nationalism, it also, and more concretely, helped create the type of subjectivities that are central to the secularization and modernization of life and on which nationalism as a cultural experience became, later on, viable politically and institutionally. That is to say, reading written discourses and the series of connected practices those readings and the writings they were based on generated were not simply or not directly the glue holding together Colombians or Peruvians. Much more crucially, they were central to the formation of the culturally determined type of territories and subjectivities on which it was possible for the newly centralized state of the *fin de siècle* and the first third of the twentieth century to produce a culturally based nationalism, via the extension of the state-controlled educational process to the majority of the population now residing within the national territory. In macro terms, this means that the secularization of daily life in the process of modernization of Latin American polities in the long nineteenth century stretching to 1914 was instrumental in the creation of the nation insofar as it allowed a new power and labor distribution between different publics, the state, and the Catholic Church in the production of social meanings, forms of subjectification, and cultural spaces (González-Stephan, 2004; Ramos, 2001; Poblete, 2003).

That actual expansive and homogeneous quality of national cultures in the continent would be aided by the increase in literacy levels and the expansion of the educational systems that made those levels possible in the first part of the twentieth century. By the same token, this relatively late spread of literacy would mean that, in the same first half of the twentieth century, a number of other cultural media and practices were to have a decisive role in the formation of national-popular cultures in Latin America. Radio and film became crucial to the emergence of the national cultures of Argentina, Mexico, Brazil, Chile, Uruguay, Peru, etc. Argentines, Mexicans, and Brazilians would act, think, and feel like national citizens because they had been schooled simultaneously in the expanded formal educational systems of their countries and in the powerful media-based cultural industries. Those industries provided them with a visually and aurally based cultural literacy to add to their newly acquired alphabetic one (Monsivais, 1976; Martín Barbero, 1991).

### Reading newspapers and books

The standard division of the social space in four terrains – civil society, economic society, political society, and public sphere and their respective forms of operation as centered on mutual recognition (civil society), collective participation (political society), socioeconomic decentralization (economic society), and deliberation according to universal rules (public sphere) – presupposes that those four terrains remained somehow separate in the daily lives of nineteenth-century Latin Americans. Contrary to this presupposition, newspapers, for example, were always and perhaps have continued to be until today, hybrid discursive spaces. They did not simply refer to public life with the rational language of public discussion imagined by strict Habermasians, nor were they read in any single form such as private, individual, bourgeois reading. They did not simply concentrate on economic or political "facts," neither were they limited to like-minded citizens as they actually circulated in vast networks of oral reproduction, collective reading, and gossip. As cultural hybrids, Latin American newspapers provided discursive scenarios where the full complexity of life in the continent was performed. Micro-level and locally produced discourses such as letters to the editors, mixed with "cut-and-paste" news derived from foreign Spanish- and Portuguese-based newspapers, and hastily prepared translations of news originally produced in other languages (English and French mostly), were all part of a discursive space complemented by good doses of similarly obtained creative fiction and non-fiction, and the emergence of modern advertising and forms of visual culture (drawings, cartoons, woodcuts, eventually photography, etc.). The genre of newspapers was thus a hybrid at both the level of its formal and semantic characteristics. As such, newspapers function also as a window into other forms of discourse being produced at the time: from orality at both the popular and elite level to the performativity of daily life culture in the cities and towns of the nineteenth-century Latin American republics.

In this regard, the gradual reorientation of newspapers from their early exclusively upper-class, male readerships to their later hybrid combination of discourses appealing to different readers through multiple discursive formats and tones is, perhaps, one the great cultural transformations of life in the continent during that century and one of the foundational aspects of national imagined communities in the region.

During the nineteenth century, the expansion of literature within the domestic sphere, which reached not only the female elite but also the middle classes through the expansion of book and newspaper circulation, made the church understand that one of the most powerful forms of secularization by which liberal ideas threatened its survival in the former colonies was now precisely the proliferation of publications addressed not only to the masculine elite in the public sphere but to an ever-increasing circle of other readers (Poblete, 1999).

In this context, the reading of literature or, more broadly speaking, of socially circulating discourses, underwent a series of transformations determined by several new historical developments. Just as there was a growing tendency for the mass circulation of books and printed matter – obvious, at least, to the men of the time (Henriquez Ureña, 1961: 59–94; Fornet, 1994; Subercaseaux, 1993) – so was there a separation between church and state during the second part of nineteenth century. These institutions no longer had the degree of identification and complementarity that had distinguished them during the colonial period (Pike, 1964; Hamnett, 1987). The control of the production, circulation, and interpretation of printed matter proved much more complicated and hence ineffective as soon as the secular and religious agencies began to differ in opinion. Moreover, the rise in the circulation of books and in printed matter (especially newspapers and periodicals) meant that the object of control had to be redefined. This was the decisive factor. Of course, this proliferation went hand in glove with the relative but important diversification of the sectors that had direct access – that is, not mediated by the priests – to this reading material. In other words, those subject to control also had to be redefined. The Indians, which were the focus of semiotic control in colonial times, had now been replaced by women, first of the upper and then of the middle classes, and toward the last third of the nineteenth century by lower middle-class male artisans and traders. This amounted to a persistent shift from the scarce and elitist book to the easily accessible newspaper and relatively large amount of mass-printed matter. Anticipating Sarmiento's call for novels and other forms of popular reading as means of educating the people, two Bolivian articles of 1833 sung the praises of the newspaper as a democratizing cultural tool: "A book in folio can produce a scholar; but in order to have an impact on the customs, habits or behavior of [regular] men, we need pamphlets [*folletos*], daily publications and newspapers" The second article insisted: "In order for most of the citizens to know their true interests, books are not enough . . . It is undoubtedly the case that the most useful means of propagating the knowledge of useful truths are well edited newspapers" (quoted by Unzueta, 2000: 45).

Newspapers then became ubiquitous, if not always long-lasting, in many nineteenth-century Latin American cities (Forment, 2003; Prieto, 1988: 34–5; Legrás, 2006). What were the cultural consequences of such a transformation in the patterns of circulation of printed material? Although I have elsewhere tried to respond to this question (Poblete, 1999, 2003, 2004a), it seems useful to at least summarize them. Those new forms of reading sociability, that is, those new social practices elaborated around the production and consumption of written discourses, meant that the three historical agents involved in the process of semiotic production and control (publics, church, and state) had to adjust their respective strategies. While publics became diversified and extended (along gender and class lines), the church reacted with a two-pronged plan. Confirmed in 1870 by the First Vatican Council (Paiva, 2004; Dussel, 1992), the conservative turn emphasized both the need to control access to and types of texts available to members of the family (and thus created from this moment on, lists of texts and genres that were deemed immoral and subversive) and the need to promote primary, secondary, and alternative education to the whole spectrum of society (elites, middle classes, popular sectors, male and female.) A considerable number of cultural institutions were thus organized to provide faith-based guidance to those believers living in a modernizing world full of temptation and sinful ways. From the very active Catholic newspapers, to the production of a considerable number of Christian family-oriented novels, including the creation of Catholic Workers' Associations (mutual-aid, educational, cultural and leisure-oriented groups), they meant a strengthening of the role of the church in civil society precisely when the states were pushing for a more radical separation between church and state and for secularized national worldviews (Dussel, 1992: 106).

One of the central terrains of this struggle turned out to be the novel as a modern genre. Liberals such as Alberto Blest Gana in Chile, Ignacio M. Altamirano in Mexico, and Domingo Faustino Sarmiento in Chile and Argentina extolled the civilizational capacities of the novel. The novel, their argument went, was capable of engaging, at their level of cultural literacy, mass populations who otherwise would never read at all. Since reading was for them a prerequisite of national development, the fundamental importance of the novel in the sentimental and practical education of the citizens was beyond doubt (Cornejo Polar, 1995; Zanetti, 2002). For this purpose it mattered little whether the novels being read were Catholic or had been approved by a priest.

Summarizing this view, Sarmiento stated: "the most effective way of raising the intellectual level of a nation, disseminating education to every social class, is to encourage the habit of reading until it becomes a distinctive feature of character and practice, as it has in Germany and the United States" (Sarmiento, 1887–1900a: 396) At first, any reading that developed a sociability of reading ("a distinctive feature of character and practice") would suffice. Next came the problem of what to read: "In Paraguay and in Chile, everyone knows how to read, the one thing they lack in order not to be the most backward among us is actually something to read. There are no books, no objects [or motivations] for reading, even if they existed. With the arrival of novels and newspapers [these readers] are beginning to exercise that heretofore sterile acquisition" (Sarmiento, 1887–1900b: 161). Finally the reading of novels needed to be fully nationalized. That would be the goal Alberto Blest Gana in Chile and Ignacio M. Altamirano in Mexico set for themselves in their respective programs for the development of national novels (Poblete, 1999, 2004a; Unzueta, 2003). Both saw the national novel as an intermediate form half-way between the complexities of high culture and the supposed banalities of popular and frivolous literature. Endowed with density and a style, with a set of recognizable cultural, geographic, and human references within the reach of proto-massive national populations, the national novel could educate the imagination, ideas, and feelings of the citizens. Furthermore, this national novel would require the development of a national language and a nationalized subjectivity capable of "taking civilization to the least educated social classes, on account of the appeal of its scenes drawn form everyday life narrated in simple and easy language" (Blest Gana, 1977: 119).

Beyond the nineteenth century, of course, the novel has been also identified with nation-building. In addition to Benedict Anderson's theory about the cultural working of a realist narration moving in a particular spatiality/temporality axis (here and now) and referring to a common world that allows its readers to imagine their mutual connection, the romance and the realistic novel have been respectively credited with providing imaginary solutions to real contradictions in the social world (Jameson, 2001; Sommer, 1990), constituting a form of social control that produces educated subjectivities through literacy, discourse, and reading (Armstrong, 1987), allowing the national bourgeoisie a form of self-awareness (Watt, 1957) and the building block of "a system of cultural signification . . . [through] the representation of social life" (Bhabha, 1991: 1–2).

As important as novels in the imagination of a national community of readers were *crónicas*. *Crónicas* were short journalistic texts often dealing with events or aspects of daily life depicted in a discourse that was the right mix between literature and journalism, fictional and non-fictional techniques. Antonio Cornejo Polar has highlighted for Peru the close connection between a style (and perhaps a genre) such as the *costumbrista* text and journalistic demands: *costumbrismo*'s "basic formats: brevity, amenity and its reference to everyday and immediate life, follow very closely the requirements of periodical publications" (Cornejo Polar, 1995: 14). More generally the *crónica* was a space for multiple mediations: between local, national, and foreign levels; between

private affairs and issues of public relevance, between the interest of the state to communicate with its citizens (the oldest form of publicity), the taste of enlightened elites
(a late eighteenth-century phenomenon in Latin America still very evident in the first
two-thirds of the nineteenth century) and the reading interest of an expanding and
diversified public who manifested their preferences via market consumption (a newer
development). (Poblete, 2003) As such the crónica along with the journalistic version
of the novel, that is, the serialized *folletín*, may have been two of the most important
discursive devices through which nineteenth-century Latin American readers imagined themselves as belonging to one community of nationals.

## The Civil Sphere II: Imagining the Nation in
## Letters, Albums and Tertulias

Often in their self-conception and, surely, in the discourse of both liberal and conservative elites, women performed a mediating role between public and private spaces.
They were supposed to be the republican mothers on whose reproductive and educational capabilities the future of men, and thus of the nation, depended. Women
themselves were thus often caught in the intermediate space between an embrace of
this unique and privileged but gendered position and the claims for more universal
equality vis-à-vis their male counterparts. Along with women, a number of formats
of written discourse performed a similar intermediary role. The private but publicly
oriented letter, the album and the social and literary tertulias were all forms of mediation between public and private spaces, between political and social networks, and
between male and female circles.

Studying the correspondence of three famous women of the first half of the nineteenth century *criollo* elites (Manuela Saenz, Mariquita Sánchez, and Carmen Arriagada),
Sarah Chambers notes that "The majority of the letters penned by these three women
cannot be considered private in the strictest sense of the word," as they were meant
to circulate among friends and family. Then she concludes:

> the similarities among the three [women] are striking. None conformed to the increas-
> ingly narrow definition of the ideal woman as "republican mother," nor did they confine
> their writing to women's issues alone. They did not claim a right to play and active and
> direct role in the political sphere, but rather turned their exclusion from formal politics
> and their social connectedness into a rationale for their influence as mediators in the
> increasingly partisan conflicts that threatened national unity. (Chambers, 2003: 62)

According to Chambers, while all three women were avid newspapers readers, they
did not provide the discursive means of imagining the nation: "Rather it was their
social relationships with fellow countrymen and women, forged by preference through
face-to-face conversation but maintained through correspondence, that led to
their varying degrees of identification with a more abstract community of nation"
(Chambers, 2003: 71). Thus female-led direct sociability, as manifested in close social

tertulias and extended networks of distant correspondence, exemplified alternative ways of imagining politics and the national community (Zanetti, 2002; Vicuña, 2001).

When the focus is shifted to the second half of the nineteenth century, women showed a decisive and increased role in the production and consumption of written discourses circulating publicly. I have elsewhere studied the case of Chilean Rosario Orrego (1834–79), who used to great effect her maternal pseudonym ("a mother") in order to create an authorial space for herself in the midst of a patriarchal, lettered republic (Poblete, 2003). In contradistinction to Alberto Blest Gana's efforts to domesticate (nationalize) the English and French realist novels in Chile, Rosario Orrego created – through serialized novels, poems, journalistic texts, and magazine-based *crónicas* – a different type of domestication. In her writing, the latter meant an exploration, from the perspective of domestic mediation, of the old, new, and changing roles of women in Chilean national society. These explorations often involved negotiating an expanded role for women in the education and socialization of not only the males (sons and husband) but also the females (daughters and servants) under their care. Frequently, this meant engaging with the patriarchal regulations separating what was proper reading material for women, writing the type of texts needed for the education of girls and women, and claiming their right to organize *tertulias*, charities, and other localized forms of politics. Having secured a public space for herself, Orrego moved on to found and edit *La Revista de Valparaíso* and became a member of José Victorino Lastarria's Academia de Bellas Artes in 1873. Similar is the case of Clorinda Matto de Turner (1852–1909) in Peru. Passionately committed to social reform, Matto de Turner wrote a famous and controversial novel (*Birds Without a Nest*, 1889), biographies of two prominent Peruvian Indians, literature texts for the education of young women and hundreds of editorial pieces and essays published in multiple periodicals. In 1883 "she became the editor of *La Bolsa*, thus becoming the first woman in the Americas to head an important daily paper" and in 1889 she was named "editor and director of the most prestigious literary periodical of its day, the weekly *El Perú Ilustrado*" (Berg, 1995: 81–3). Cuban writer Gertrudis Gómez de Avellaneda (1814–73) was also a pioneering figure. In 1860, having written two radical novels (*Sab*, 1841 and *Two Women*, 1842) and considerable poetry, she founded *Album cubano de lo bueno y lo bello* (Cuban album of the good and the beautiful.) Nina M. Scott states: "The content of the *Album* was standard fare for female readers of the time: serialized fiction, poetry, some essays, music commentary, edifying pieces on moral deportment, social gossip, letters to the editors, and lengthy pieces on fashion. Another feature was the Galería de Mujeres Célebres (Portraits of Famous Women)" (Scott, 1995: 59). All these genres have in common the intermediality of women's writing and reading within the national cultural formation. Thus these writers, by placing themselves in the spaces of mediation between sociocultural and political issues, transformed the forms of authorship and the types of discourses available to women. They expanded the patriarchal and restrictive citizenship imaginaries of the nineteenth-century Latin American republics of letters (Pratt, 1995) and anticipated the forms of direct political representation and participation that women would acquire in the twentieth century.

Many other types of mediating spaces could be mentioned here, ranging from manuals of manners, to textbooks and visual exhibitions (González-Stephan, 2004; Ossenbach and Somoza, 2001). I would like to conclude this section by concentrating on two. One is textual (the album), the other social (the *tertulia*). Both are discursive spaces for the negotiation of the boundaries separating the cultural and social agency of men and women. Both straddle the distance between privacy and publicity, domestic and social spaces, subjectivity and national community. They do so by connecting the writing and reading roles of women and men.

Gomez de Avellaneda's *Album* owed its name to the extended nineteenth-century habit of upper middle-class women of having an album. Similarly to the notebooks I will refer to later, albums functioned for the young female bourgeois both as a space of expression in which a personal memory was archived and as a space of social control by which she made visible and administrable her interiority. In her album, the upper-class young woman kept the written voice of those from whom she requested a poem or an homage, as well as the voice of those who volunteered to leave a written record of their interest in the album's owner. Always in a constant process of elaboration, by way of the intervention and the narrative gaze of others, the *señorita*'s album was thus constructed as a register of the interaction and constitution of the feminine subject in society. It inscribed in its surface both the social gaze, manifested in the perception of the subject others provided, and the most intimate expression of her desire to be recognized and seen according to a framework the album itself represented.

In 1879 the Chilean Eduardo Pérez described in his article "Charlas literarias" (Literary gatherings) how, in these gatherings, men and women of high social standing offered each other their attention, allowing themselves to seduce and be seduced by "intellectual pleasures" which are "unrivalled pleasures" (Pérez, 1879: 270) Comparing literary salons with the albums, he added: "The clever thoughts characteristic of these gatherings are not unlike those written on an album. A gallantry, a witty comment, a spark." Like the albums, the salons and *tertulias* functioned as nexus and separation between a private interior and a public exterior. In fact, the old colonial house, with its vast patios and spaces for meetings between family, tradespeople, and visitors, was being replaced by the bourgeois separation between the family *sala* and the social and roomier *salon* which acted as a hinge between the private space of the family and their social connections (friends and acquaintances).

Salons were an important means for the self-education of women, as manifested in some famous pages of Alberto Blest Gana's *Martín Rivas*. They were to be distinguished from the purely entertaining *tertulias* of yesteryear in which games and pastimes predominated. In salons, women were moved to prepare themselves for the kinds of intellectual exchanges cultivated men could provide (Zanetti, 2002; Batticuore, 2005). To that extent, the sociability there developed in connection with writing and reading practices was an important complement to the limited education offered by girls' schools.

## The State Sphere and Governmentality

In the last third of the nineteenth and well into the twentieth century, the secularizing and increasingly centralizing governments of Latin America began to develop their national systems of education. These systems were centrally concerned with the production of national subjects educated in the language, history, and meaningfulness of the nation to their lives. This required a particular form of administration of semiotic production and consumption capable of reaching homogeneously mass populations of students of increasingly diversified types and social provenance. "Spanish American educational systems were created at the end of the nineteenth century with the purpose of founding public schools that would regenerate society and eradicate cultural diversity" (Newland, 1994: 454). This process meant a quantitative change, increasing significantly both enrollment in primary schools and literacy levels, and a qualitative one, whereby the State became directly involved in the funding of schools, their administration, and the determination of the contents of the curricula. The ethical substance of the nation was identified with the centralizing State and the latter became the Teaching State ("Estado Docente") in charge of teaching its citizens how to feel, think, and live national lives.

While there are multiple cultural practices that lent themselves to the formation of a national imaginary, from the creation of national celebrations and monuments to the organization of the army, the postal and railroad systems, etc., I would like to address one of them which seems here particularly pertinent. I am referring to the connections between language, literature, and national subjectivities in the educational system. In fact it was as a result of the positivist reforms of the educational systems and philosophies (and the later reactions to them) that the Latin American centralized systems of education emerged to both regenerate society and homogenize it culturally by nationalizing its ways of being. Essentially, this nationalizing effort meant, at this level, developing a new connection between the classroom, texts, and daily life of the students. Standardized national languages would allow for the expression of a national subjectivity manifested first in school compositions dealing with the everyday life of the nation and later on, with its emergent national literature. A national way of reading and writing both printed and non-printed material became thus essential for the full emergence of a national(ized) imaginary.

In the search for solutions to the moral and practical dilemmas posited by the elite's perception of the need for a new non-religious social cement in an age of increasingly unruly and bigger populations, the State would find a new space for the exercise of its governmentality (Gordon, 1991). The class on language and literature and eventually the promotion of a national literature and language would meet those needs in a long and convoluted process that takes many shapes in different countries.

I have elsewhere fully discussed three basic Latin American scenarios (Chile, Colombia, and Argentina) where the relationships between traditional and modern, nationalized humanisms are played out in the context of the influence of positivism on educational thought and planning (Poblete, 2004b). I will summarize here the Chilean case to show briefly how what was at stake in all of these cases was the State's interest on (re)directing the creation of a national culture and in particular, of a national sensibility grounded on nationalized forms of perception, reading, and writing. This in turn demanded attention to the school curriculum and more specifically to the language and literature class in it.

In order to consolidate its place in the regional context, the Chilean State, which had triumphed over its Peruvian and Bolivian counterparts in the Pacific War (1879–83), attempted in the last decade of the nineteenth century to modernize its educational base. Part of this effort was the implementation of the concentric method of organizing the curriculum and, along with it, the creation of a new curricular subject: *Castellano*. The latter's key professor was Rudolf Lenz, a German who was to become one of the essential figures in the resurgence of a cultural nationalism in Chile through his proposals and texts for the reform of Castellano (as part of the curriculum) and the creation and institutionalization of folk studies in Chile.

Castellano as a school subject was destined to consolidate in one class the remnants of older and classical-oriented disciplines such as Rhetoric, Literary History, Grammar, and Poetics, along with the insights provided by the new human or social sciences (psychology, scientific pedagogy, school administration, etc.). Its fundamental innovation was a switch from deduction and normativeness to induction and empiricism. Here practice was to replace root memorization, and repetition to give way to the natural expression of a subject firmly placed in a local and national reality. This was a stark contrast with the supposed universality of the subjectivity generated by the contact with the classics and their paradigmatic functioning.

Lenz's work gives us an insight into the role played by instruction on (national) language and literature in the creation of a nationalized subjectivity capable of framing, describing, and valorizing its *realidad nacional* (national reality) and in so doing, preparing the cultural space for the production and consumption of a national *criollista* literature.

The pedagogical and psychological challenge of this emerging nationalism was superbly expressed by Lenz's thoughts on the writing class: the problem was, on the one hand, how to tie the writing topic to the child and, on the other, how to tie the child to the topic (Lenz, 1924: 7), a disciplinary conjunction in both the educational and state senses. The challenge was to generate *in* the child, *within* the child, in her own subjectivity, the need to write and learn a national language.

Lenz was also transforming the traditional cultural hierarchy where the classic writer provided the universal and atemporal *model* which was then supposed to be respected and followed as closely as possible by the student-subject. This hierarchical mimetism was viable while the elites did not posses aspirations to a national singularity and did not pretend to fully govern through cultural hegemony but used instead simple domination or a mix of both. On the wake of the ever-expanding educational system and the increasing massification of society though, the need arose for a nationalized mimetism shared across the complete social spectrum. At the same time, from the point of view of the state's governmentality, the expansion of a common bond and thus the potential expansion of common entitlements or rights demanded specific and effective forms of social control.

At the level of the Castellano composition this meant a particular surface of controlled expression, to dominate the shift from obedient imitation and deduction from rules to induction and expression as the only norms. In his *Proyecto de programa de Castellano* (1919) Lenz found that surface in similar notebooks and texts evenly distributed among the students. He also emphasized the importance of uniformed and mandatory notebooks (Lenz, 1899: 20).

The notebook, then, worked as an external surface where personal subjectivity could manifest itself in many forms. It was, on the one hand, the space where the I of the student wrote itself out. On the other, it became a material re-presentation of that interiority. As such, the *cuaderno de composición* presented, from the point of view of state governmentality, the invaluable advantage of being simultaneously the location of the free expression of that subjectivity and the space where the latter became susceptible of control, study, and discipline.

In this Chilean modernizing context of increased schooling for a greater part of society and rapid urbanization, this transition – from grammar and universal models of (classics)-based courses on language and literature to induction and expression-dominated forms of nationalized discourse – was instrumental in creating the conditions at both the individual and collective levels that made possible the production and appreciation of a national literature. The shift facilitated the development of a new fully hegemonic form of relation between State, ruling elites, and popular culture that was to characterize the Latin American political scenario during the rest of the first half of the twentieth century. That cultural hegemony implied expanded forms of alphabetic, visual, and civic literacy for national(ized) mass populations (Martín Barbero, 1991).

## Conclusion: Reading, Subjectivity, and Power

This chapter has claimed that written discourses and the forms of production, consumption, and circulation they generated were an important part of the process of construction of the national imaginary in Latin American nineteenth century. Through the types of discursive imagination that novels, newspapers, serialized novels in newspapers, personal letters, albums, and broadsheets allowed in the practice of forms of sociability centered on reading and its commentary, the nation became part of the way of thinking, acting, and feeling of an increasing number of its citizens. Those citizens became consuming publics within a national printing and reading market whose administration and control was disputed by the church, the state, and profit-oriented business interests. In this regard the subjectivity of nationalized publics emerged then at the confluence of their discourse-associated practices and those multiple interests. Later on the production of textbooks, notebooks, and compositions within an expanding school system fully nationalized reading and writing. Offering national subjects the means of temporally and spatially imagining themselves as co-nationals, the means of self-constitution as modern, urban types and a written and/or socialized injunction to behave in particular ways, written discourses and reading practices incarnate the two-sided nature of the complex connections between national subjectivities and subjections processes in nineteenth-century Latin America.

## REFERENCES AND FURTHER READING

Anderson, Benedict (1991). *Imagined Communities: Reflections on the Origin and Spread of Nationalism.* London: Verso.

Annino, Antonio (1995). "Introducción." In *Historia de las elecciones en Iberoamérica, siglo XIX.* Buenos Aires: Fondo de Cultura Económica.

Armstrong, Nancy (1987). *Desire and Domestic Fiction: A Political History of the Novel.* New York: Oxford University Press.

Batticuore, Graciela (2005). *La Mujer romántica. Lectoras, autoras y escritores en la Argentina: 1830–1870.* Buenos Aires: Edhasa.

Berg, Mary G. (1995). "Writing for her life: the essays of Clorinda Matto de Turner." In Doris Meyer (ed.), *Reinterpreting the Spanish American Essay. Women Writers of the Nineteenth and Twentieth Centuries*, pp. 80–9. Austin: University of Texas Press.

Bhabha, Homi K. (1991). "Introduction." In Homi K. Bhabha (ed.), *Nation and Narration.* London: Routledge.

Blest Gana, Alberto (1977 [1861]). "Literatura chilena: Algunas consideraciones sobre ella." Discurso leído por Alberto Blest Gana en su incorporación a la Facultad de Humanidades de la Universidad de Chile, el 3 de enero, reprinted in José Promis, *Testimonios y documentos de la literatura chilena*, pp. 108–28. Santiago: Editorial Nascimento.

Castro-Klaren, Sara, and Chasteen, John Charles (eds) (2003). *Beyond Imagined Communities. Reading and Writing the Nation in Nineteenth-Century Latin America*, Washington, DC: Woodrow Wilson Center Press and Johns Hopkins University Press.

Chambers, Sara (2003). "Letters and salons: women reading and writing the nation." In Sara Castro-Klaren and John Charles Chasteen (eds), *Beyond Imagined Communities: Reading and Writing the Nation in Nineteenth-Century Latin America*, pp. 54–83. Washington, DC: Woodrow Wilson Center Press and Johns Hopkins University Press.

Cohen, Jean L., and Arato, Andrew (1992). *Civil Society and Political Theory.* Cambridge, MA: MIT Press.

Cornejo Polar, Antonio (1995). La Literatura hispanoamericana del siglo XIX: Continuidad y ruptura (hipótesis a partir del caso andino). In Beatriz González-Stephan et al. (eds), *Esplendores y miserias del siglo XIX: Cultura y sociedad en América Latina*, pp. 11–23. Caracas: Monte Avila Editores.

Coudart, Laurence (2001). "Difusión y lectura de la prensa: El ejemplo poblano (1820–1850)." In Laura Suárez de la Torre (ed.), *Empresa y cultura de tinta y papel (1800–1860)*, pp. 343–55. Mexico City: IIB-Instituto Mora.

Dussel, Enrique (1992). "The church and the emergent nation states (1830–80)." In *The Church in Latin America 1492–1992*, pp. 105–37. London: Burns & Oates and Orbis Books.

Eley, Geoff, and Suny, Ronald Grigor, eds (1996). "Introduction." In *Becoming National: A Reader*, pp. 3–37. New York: Oxford University Press.

Forment, Carlos (2003). *Democracy in Latin America 1760–1900: Volume 1, Civic Selfhood and Public Life in Mexico and Peru.* Chicago: University of Chicago Press.

Fornet, Ambrosio (1994). *El Libro en Cuba:Siglos XVIII y XIX.* Havana: Editorial Letras Cubanas.

Foucault, Michel (1991). "Governmentality." In Graham Burchell, Colin Gordon, and Peter Miller (eds), *The Foucault Effect: Studies in Governmentality*, pp. 87–104. Chicago: University of Chicago Press.

González-Stephan, Beatriz (2004). "On citizenship: the grammatology of the body-politic." In Abril Trigo, Alicia Ríos, and Ana del Sarto (eds), *The Latin American Cultural Studies Reader*, pp. 384–405. Durham, NC: Duke University Press.

Gordon, Colin (1991). "Governmental rationality: an introduction." In Graham Burchell, Colin Gordon, and Peter Miller (eds), *The Foucault Effect: Studies in Governmentality*, pp. 1–51. Hemel Hempstead: Harvester Wheatsheaf.

Grez Toso, Sergio (ed.) (1995). *La Cuestión social en Chile: Ideas y debates precursores*. Santiago: Dirección de Bibliotecas, Archivos y Museos.

Gruzinski, Serge (1991). *La Colonización de lo imaginario: Sociedades indígenas y occidentalización en el México español. Siglos XVI–XVIII*, Mexico City: Fondo de Cultura Económica.

Gutiérrez Sanín, Francisco (1999). "La Literatura plebeya y el debate alrededor de la propiedad ("Nueva Granada, 1849–1854)." In Hilda Sábato (ed.), *Ciudadanía política y formación de las naciones: Perspectivas históricas de América Latina*, pp. 181–202. Mexico City: Fondo de Cultura Económica.

Habermas, Jürgen (1989). *The Structural Transformation of the Public Sphere: An Inquiry into a Category of Bourgeois Life*. Cambridge: MIT Press.

Hamnett, Brian R. (1987). "La Regeneración: 1875–1900." In Manuel Lucena Samoral (ed.), *Historia de Iberoamérica. Tomo III: Historia contemporánea*.

Henríquez Ureña, Pedro (1961). *Historia de la cultura en la América Hispánica*. Mexico City: Fondo de Cultura Económica.

Jameson, Fredric (2001). *The Political Unconscious: Narrative as a Socially Symbolic Act*. Ithaca, NY: Cornell University Press.

Legrás, Horacio (2006). "Lectura y pasaje en el fin de siglo." In *Cambio cultural y lectura de peridicos en el siglo XIX en América Latina*, special issue of *Revista Iberoamericana* (ed. Juan Poblete), 214: 19–34.

Lenz, Rudolf (1899). *Proyecto de programa de Castellano*. Santiago, Imprenta Cervantes.

— (1924). *La Composición escolar en lengua patria*. Santiago: Ediciones de la Revista Cultura.

Lindoso, Felipe (2004). *O Brasil pode ser um pais de leitores? Politica para a cultura: politica para o livro*. São Paulo: Summus Editorial.

Mallon, Florencia E. (1995) *Peasant and Nation: The Making of Postcolonial Mexico and Peru*. Berkeley: University of California Press.

Martín Barbero, Jesús (1991) *Communication, Culture and Hegemony: From the Media to Mediations*. London: Sage.

Monsivais, Carlos (1976). "Notas sobre la cultura mexicana en el siglo XX." In *Historia General de Mexico*, Vol. 4, pp. 303–476. Mexico City: Colegio de Mexico.

Murilo de Carvalho, José (1999). "Dimensiones de la ciudadanía en el Brasil del siglo XIX." In Hilda Sábato (ed.), *Ciudadanía política y formación de las naciones: Perspectivas históricas de América Latina*, pp. 181–202. Mexico City: Fondo de Cultura Económica.

Newland, Carlos (1994). "The Estado Docente and its expansion: Spanish American elementary education, 1900–1950," *Journal of Latin American Studies*, 26: 449–67.

— (1991). "La Educación elemental en Hispanoamérica: Desde la Independencia hasta la centralización de los sistemas educativos nacionales." *Hispanic American Historical Review*, 71(2): 333–64.

Ossenbach, Gabriela, and Somoza, Miguel (eds.). (2001). *Los Manuales escolares como fuente para la historia de la educación en América*. Madrid: Universidad Nacional de Educación a Distancia.

Paiva, Aparecida (2004). "The struggle over the printed word: the Catholic Church in Brazil and social discourse." In Mario J. Valdés and Djelal Kadir (eds), *Latin American Literary Cultures: A Comparative History of Cultural Formations*, Vol. I, pp. 401–9. Oxford: Oxford University Press.

Pérez, Eduardo (1879). "Charlas literarias," *La Revista Literaria*, pp. 270–1, Santiago.

Pike, Frederick B. (ed.) (1964). *The Conflict between Church and State in Latin America*. New York: Knopf.

Poblete, Juan (ed.) (1997). "El Castellano: La nueva disciplina y el texto nacional en el fin de siglo chileno," *Revista de Crítica Cultural*, 15: 22–7.

— (1999). "La construcción social de la lectura y la novela nacional: El caso chileno," *Latin American Research Review*, 34(2): 75–108.

— (2002). "Governmentality and the social question." In Benigno Trigo (ed.), *Foucault and Latin America*, pp. 137–51. London and New York: Routledge.

— (2003). *Literatura chilena del siglo XIX: Entre públicos lectores y fuguras autoriales.* Santiago: Cuarto Propio.

— (2004a). "Reading as a historical practice in Latin America: the first colonial period and the nineteenth century." In Mario J. Valdés and Djelal Kadir (eds), *Latin American Literary Cultures: A Comparative History of Cultural Formations*, Vol. I, pp. 178–92. Oxford: Oxford University Press.

— (2004b). "Literary education and the making of state knowledge." In Mario J. Valdés and Djelal Kadir (eds), *Latin American Literary Cultures: A Comparative History of Cultural Formations*, Vol. III, pp. 300–9. Oxford: Oxford University Press.

Poblete, Juan, ed. (2006), *Cambio cultural y lectura de periódicos en el siglo XIX en América Latina*, special issue of *Revista Iberoamericana*, 214.

Pratt, Mary Louise (1995). "Género y ciudadanía: las mujeres en diálogo con la nación." In Beatriz González-Stephan et al. (eds), *Esplendores y miserias del siglo XIX: Cultura y sociedad en América Latina*, pp. 261–76. Caracas: Monte Avila Editores.

Prieto, Adolfo (1988). *El Discurso criollista en la formación de la Argentina moderna.* Buenos Aires: Editorial Sudamericana.

Rama, Ángel (1996). *The Lettered City.* Durham, NC: Duke University Press.

Ramos, Julio (2001). *Divergent Modernities: Culture and Politics in Nineteenth Century Latin America.* Durham, NC: Duke University Press.

Romero, José Luis (1976). *Latinoamérica: Las ciudades y las ideas.* Mexico City: Siglo XXI.

Sábato, Hilda (2001). "On political citizenship in nineteenth-century Latin America," *American Historical Review*, 106(4), http://www.historycooperative.org/journals/ahr/106.4/ah0401001290.html, accessed April 6, 2007.

Sarmiento, Domingo Faustino (1887–1900a). "Bibliotecas populares." In *Obras completas*, vol. 30. Buenos Aires: Moreno.

— (1887–1900b). "Las novelas." In *Obras completas*, vols. 45–6, Buenos Aires: Moreno.

Scott, Nina M. (1995). "Shoring up the 'weaker sex': Avellaneda and nineteenth-century gender ideology." In Doris Meyer (ed.), *Reinterpreting the Spanish American Essay: Women Writers of the 19th and 20th Centuries*, pp. 57–67. Austin: University of Texas Press.

Sommer, Doris (1990). "Irresistible romance: the foundational fictions of Latin America." In Homi K. Bhabha (ed.), *Nation and Narration*, pp. 71–98. London: Routledge.

Subercaseaux, Bernardo (1981). *Cultura y sociedad liberal en el siglo XIX: Lastarria, ideología y literatura.* Santiago: Editorial Aconcagua.

— (1988). *Fin de siglo: La época de Balmaceda: Modernización y cultura en Chile.* Santiago: Editorial Aconcagua.

— (1993). *Historia del libro en Chile (cuerpo y alma).* Santiago: Editorial Andrés Bello.

Tinajero, Araceli (2006). "*El Siglo, La Aurora* y la lectura en voz alta en Cuba 1865–1868." In *Cambio cultural y lectura de peridicos en el siglo XIX en América Latina*, special issue of *Revista Iberoamericana* (ed. Juan Poblete), 214: 171–84.

Unzueta, Fernando (2000). "Periódicos y formación nacional: Bolivia en sus primeros años," *Latin American Research Review*, 35(2): 35–72.

— (2003). "Scenes of reading: imagining nations/romancing history in Spanish America." In Sara Castro-Klaren and John Charles Chasteen (eds), *Beyond Imagined Communities: Reading and Writing the Nation in Nineteenth Century Latin America*, pp. 15–60. Washington, DC: Woodrow Wilson Center Press and Johns Hopkins University Press.

Vicuña, Manuel (2001). *La Belle Époque chilena.* Santiago: Editorial Sudamericana.

Watt, Ian (1957). *The Rise of the Novel: Studies in Defoe, Richardson and Fielding.* Berkeley: University of California Press.

Zanetti, Susana (2002). *La Dorada garra de la lectura: Lectoras y lectores de novela en América Latina.* Rosario: Beatriz Viterbo Editora.

# 19
# For Love and Money:
# Of Potboilers and Precautions
*Doris Sommer*

Intercourse means commerce, they told us in school. And we giggled at the explosive word that went off in more than one direction. But the confusion is more than simply a joke of mistaken referents, or of metaphoric allusions between intimate contact and interested exchange. It is a tangle of productive sex and enterprising business that reveals an adjacency of practices that add up to modernity. In a metaleptic circle of cause and effect, modern desire for family and for wealth seemed to drive those practices, and they helped to form the kind of modern subject who desires them. The circularity illustrates what Nietzsche said about the fiction of empirical moorings. They make themselves up to produce an illusion of stability. This is what happened at the beginnings of European modernity, as Mary Poovey shows in *A History of the Modern Fact* (1998): Truth grounded in empirical "facts" turns out to be a metaleptic effect of the seventeenth-century fiction of precise accounting, a rhetorical compensation for numbers that could not add up in the precarious conditions of mercantilism. But a century later, precise and transparent accounts were no longer performances that interpreted irregular data, but required proofs of economic and civic credibility.[1] In a very broad stroke, we can say that the foundational fiction that followed from honorable entrepreneurship is the dynamic law of desire for development as the natural drive of our particular and collective lives. Laissez-faire was the slogan.

Desire for love-marriages and for free enterprise was learned from novels, among other manuals of idealized behavior, and it became both the motor and the result of single-minded productivity. It is the unspoken assumption of modernizing projects that peaked when interpersonal desire toppled kings and established republics based on bonds of affect and interest. Sliding from sentimental to economically rational referents, the tangle of modern desire channels (constrains, deforms) practically all activities as if they and their agents were interchangeable. No wonder the drive has been a target for critics of capitalism as the breeding ground for the single-mindedness of fascism. Consider, for example, Deleuze and Guattari's influential *Anti-Oedipus* (1972). "Desiring-Production" is the first and all-encompassing issue at hand:

It is at work everywhere, functioning smoothly at times, at other times in fits and starts. It breathes, it heats, it eats. It shits and fucks. What a mistake to have ever said *the* id. Everywhere it is machines – real ones, not figurative ones: machines driving other machines, machines being driven by other machines, with all the necessary couplings and connections.[2]

The heat of the attack on capitalist culture, and the warmth of reader response – including Michel Foucault's 1977 preface, where he called it "a book of ethics" – are sure signs of a formidable and familiar foe. In fact, the slippery desire of and for modernity has been incalculably productive, producing, among other things, the modern subjects who can desire to be free of its constraints. Alongside them, we will consider some unevenly modernized, minority subjects who remind the zealots of desire to proceed with caution, lest their "interest" in otherness repeat the bourgeois tangle of love and gain.

But Latin American independentists in the early nineteenth century embraced the confusion between eros and economics. The double-barreled, single-minded machine needed full steam to free colonial societies from the artificial distinctions and monopolistic constraints of Iberian administrations. And though England and France may have pioneered the fantasy of free and unencumbered relationships as the basis for a productive and moral society, Old World habits still frustrated natural desire there, whereas the New World could give it free rein. (Hannah Arendt even speculated that North American practice anticipated and dictated Locke's liberal formulae.[3]

"The French say, *l'amour fait rage, et l'argent fait mariage.* But here, love makes both, *rage* and *mariage!*" This quip from a comic character in *Martín Rivas* (Chile, 1862) gets the moral of his and other mid-century stories surprisingly right.[4] The speaker has recently returned from a long stay in Paris and is scandalized to learn that his clever sister wants to marry a social inferior. Her lover is a provincial law student who manages the family's banking business admirably and efficiently. This is not what should happen, the brother protests, in a novel obviously modeled after Stendhal's tragic *The Red and the Black*. Other Latin Americans knew that too; and though they admired French and English models, they did not simply imitate them. Imported novel styles were adjusted to flatter local figures. So, the disoriented fop back home in Santiago has actually managed – with this *bon mot* – to theorize the main ideological difference between European and Latin American novels of the period. It was the same difference between development and dissolution that made José Martí warn readers against foreign fictions. There, love is destructive, a threat to harmony and to prosperity. Desire versus duty is the theme of much aristocratic, and then of anti-bourgeois narrative. But "here" in the New World, the unsettled brother protests, desire has become the single agent of all happiness.

His surprise at the neatness of the formula is understandable. What European conventions would have made him expect it? And some results of that formula hardly fit conventional expectations either. They are evenhanded treatment of men and women, and the regular assertiveness of heroines while heroes can be coy and even delicate. These are unanticipated and still exhilarating moves that come from purpose-fully confusing reason with rapture. Surprising, also, is the fact that the formula repeats from country to country. The very fact of an international genre that is driven by productive desire is news for literary historians. The national novels – ones that governments require in schools and that by now blend into patriotic histories – seem like local variations on one theme. This had been hard to notice, because the books, mostly written during the generation between 1850 and 1880 when Latin American states were consolidating, did not travel far at first. And then, with the 1960s "Boom" of experimental narrative, they seemed too simple for sophisticated tastes. So hardly anyone read them together or made general observations. But the overlaps are astounding. To begin with, all of these books are love stories.

Why should national, state-promoted novels all be about romantic love? An easy answer, of course, is that nineteenth-century novels were all love stories in Latin America; but it just begs the question of what love has to do with the requirements of civic education. The novels were not immediately taught in public schools, except perhaps in the Dominican Republic, where *Enriquillo* (1882) appeared rather late and where the small number of students probably meant that there were enough copies.[5] In other cases, serialized sentimental novels were at first hardly academic or even proper literature, to judge by their exclusion from the first national literary histories that hoped to consolidate a "progressive-conservative" tradition through poetry.[6] The histories omitted the most useful renderings of oxymoronic consolidations: the romances that celebrated or predicted an identification between the Nation and its State.[7] Required reading came generations later; precisely when and under which particular circumstances in each country are questions that merit a different study.[8] But in general, one can surmise that after renewed internal oppositions pulled the image of an ideal Nation away from the existing State, like a mask from a masquer-ader, after nationalism could be understood as a political movement against the State,[9] nineteenth-century novels offered a way for states to cover over the gap between power and desire. The books, so immediately seductive for elite readers whose private desires overlapped with public institutions, might reinscribe for each future citizen the (natural and irresistible) foundational desires for/of the government in power.

Erotics and politics come together – in school, no less – almost everywhere in Latin America. A particular novel may be celebrated in its national tradition as autochtho-nous, characteristic, and somehow inimitable; yet each romance shares much more than its institutional status with the others. The resemblances may be symptomatic of nationalism's general paradox; that is, cultural features that seem unique and worthy of patriotic (self)-celebration are often typical of other nations also and even patterned after foreign models.[10] Almost like sexual intimacy, that which seems most private turns out to be embarrassingly public knowledge.[11] A range of partisan pro-grams might seem to overload any common structure to the point of crushing it. Read individually, the foundational fictions are very different indeed, accepting racism here, advocating abolition there, sometimes defending free trade, other times arguing for protectionism. Here is a very brief overview:

In *Amalia* (José Mármol, 1851), White Civilization's opposition to Black Barbarism figures as an elite love affair between a Buenos Aires boy and his provincial girl, a winning alliance against the dark forces. Chile's *Martín Rivas* (Alberto Blest Gana, 1862) mitigates class as well as regional oppositions between northern miners and southern bankers. But mitigation depends on more radical change in tragic Cuban novels, written before independence and with hopes perhaps of raising multicolored armies to win it. Racially amalgamated *Sab* (Gertrudis Gómez de Avellaneda, 1841) is desperate for love and legitimacy from his Creole mistress, dazzled by a blond Englishman. By the time of *Cecilia Valdés* (Cirilo Villaverde, Cuba, 1882), frustration is endemic to a system of color coding which the lovers never unlearn. Race relations are tragic, also, in *Aves sin nido* (Clorinda Matto de Turner, 1889), this time between Peru's Indians and whites, while *El Zarco* (Manuel Altamirano, 1888) promises national regeneration through an Indian who learns to love his *mestiza* admirer during the same years that Mexicans were learning to admire their Indian president Benito Juárez. And though color never seems an issue in *María* (Jorge Isaacs, 1867), Latin America's most popular nineteenth-century novel, racial disturbance erupts in the Colombian planters' paradise through the trembling body of originally Jewish María, doubly damned for representing the incestuous plantocracy *and* inassimilable blacks. In Brazil's *O guaraní* (José de Alencar, 1857), black slaves are figured (out) by an amorous Indian whose mistress finally reciprocates, while in *Iracema* (1865) the Tupí maiden's passion for a Portuguese produces the first Brazilian, both Tupí and not Tupí. Santo Domingo's *Enriquillo* (Manuel de Jesús Galván, 1882) similarly replaces rebellious blacks for peace-loving and long extinct natives.

As a rhetorical solution to the crises in these novels/nations, miscegenation is often the figure for subsuming the "primitive" or "barbarous" sector in color-coded flirtations between Creole liberals and conservatives. Brazil's romances are examples, as are Ecuador's *Cumandá* (Juan León Mera, 1887), where the Indian heroine is revealed as the missionary's lost daughter, and Uruguay's *Tabaré* (Juan Zorrilla de San Martín, 1888), which kills off the heroic *mestizo* (possibly associated with imperializing Brazil) so that Hispanic civilization can prevail. With *Doña Bárbara* (Rómulo Gallegos, 1929), the authoritarian father who had stepped aside during nineteenth-century courtships takes center stage again. Venezuela seemed neither ready for conciliation nor desperate enough to defer sovereignty to an indigenous Enriquillo. Instead the anti-imperialist novel makes its hero an apprentice to the *mestiza* vamp whom he will replace once he marries her daughter.

Is there common ground for Chile's vertical integration, Cuba's racial integration, Argentina's color-coded campaigns, Colombia's retrograde idyll, Ecuador's Jesuitical paternalism, Venezuela's vamp-raiding? I have already let on that they share the loopy logic of love mediated and heightened through patriotism. Read together, the novels produce a palimpsest that cannot derive from their historical or political differences, but from their common project to reconcile national sectors cast as lovers destined to desire one another. Whether the plots end happily or not, the romances are invariably about love. Passionate, heterosexual romance is what moved the imaginary protagonists along with their flesh and blood readers in countries that claimed legitimacy through Nature and rebelled against Spain and Portugal. The new nations continued their internal fighting, often between the centralists and the federalists, throughout the mid-nineteenth century.

Meanwhile, long novels came out in newspaper installments over enough time to rehearse readers in the novel feelings of bonding and citizenship. They were written by nation-builders themselves (generals, future presidents, legislators), during lulls in the civil wars or once peace promised to repair some of the damage. The novels appealed to virtual citizens to stop fighting and to become real citizens by founding national families. Make love not war, was the sometimes explicit slogan of legislation as well as literature. The author of Argentina's 1853 constitution didn't stop at slogans. He glossed them with practical programs for increasing the population, not only through the immigration policies for which he is remembered but also through marriages between industrious Anglo-Saxons and Argentina's "army" of beautiful women, eminently equipped for the eugenics campaign to "improve" local and "inefficient" Spanish stock. During the twenty years of his matchmaking, luring the sword-wielding Joshuas of independence to reform their tools into Isaiah's plows, novelists were also reforming one thing into another: valor into sentimentalism; epic into romance, hero into husband. This helped to solve the problem of establishing the white man's legitimacy in the New World, now that the illegitimate conquerors had been ousted. Without a proper genealogy to root them in the Land, the Creoles had at least to establish conjugal and then paternity rights, making a generative rather than a genealogical claim. They had to win America's heart and body so that the fathers could found her and reproduce themselves as cultivated men. To be legitimate, their love had to be mutual; even if the fathers set the tone, the mothers had to reciprocate.[12] The novels were training manuals, I am saying, intentionally paced over long periods of time to wean the public away from fruitless passions gradually, and then to quicken the pulse of productive desire. A typical plot begins with an easy erotic hook for conventional readers. But then the narrative undoes aristocratic tousles to follow the thread of new and liberal passions, beyond the murderous differences of class, region, and race. A wholesome object of desire displaces a corrupt fantasy. For examples, the Indian hero of *El Zarco* suffers for a ruthless blonde before the *mestiza* heroine turns his head; *Amalia*'s elitist boyfriend learns some flexibility from a double agent in order to survive in Argentina; Cuban Carlota realizes too late that she wasted her passion on an Englishman when mulatto Sab was her ideal lover; and Chile's haughty heiress dismisses poor Martín Rivas so often that she almost loses him.

Her final capitulation, as we saw above, exasperated her brother. This made him funny, in both senses of witty and ridiculous. It should be clear now that taking offense at the simplicity and apparent vulgarity of homey courtships keeps him from becoming a hero. Heroes are neither surprised nor embarrassed by simplicity. The liberal elite, ideal readers, evidently appreciated the economy of reducing love and money to just the first, natural, force. All over Latin America, the "active citizenry" were coming to understand personal desire as the motor for both passionate and patriotic projects. It mobilized modernity, as the goad for capitalist accumulation *and* as the unaffected, natural name for love (between opposite sexes, and opposing national sectors). Desire is the intensely personal feeling that risks intimate unions among dissimilar citizens. There was no shame in celebrating that. Old-world conventions that distinguished between illicit passion and vulgar productivity were out of place in America, the hemisphere that Hegel thought of as the home for modernity.

Latin Americans who read Hegel may have felt flattered, or confirmed in their mission to promote modernity. Like him, they knew that love was the grounding for ethics, which begin in the family unit where members subordinate their own interests to other members through feelings of love.[13] But they would have noticed how quickly Hegel moved from lateral bonds to patriarchal hierarchy, where women willingly submit to their men. The novelists were more patient; they took time to play out the lateral tensions of mutual desire, even if they agreed that families should be mini-polities naturally headed by fathers, like hegemonies of active citizens and willing supporters. In fact, *Martín Rivas* ends happily when the strong-willed heroine marries Martín and becomes his "angel of submission." But this happens at the end of 500 pages that strain to get the lovers together. It is the gambit of reciprocal desire – developed between equally ideal and coy lovers during long pages and many months of newspaper installments – not the endgame of submission that was so promising for the patriots. What it promised was a remedy for the rifts of civil war. Without representing both established money and risky businesses as equally powerful opponents who need one another (the popular classes only support the entrepreneurial hero, it is true), Chile's national romance cannot work. Desire is the name of the energy that pulls the heroes towards one another, and then holds them together through contracts, including that of marriage. Desire is the dynamism supposed by *laissez-faire,* a slogan for making love and money. The long, passionate novels unite ideal heroes to equally ideal heroines, across racial, regional, and/or economic differences that were keeping their countries mired in premodern conflicts. Thanks to their ardor, the lovers strive to overcome the obstacles to modernity, and thereby, simultaneously, to consolidate their new country. Subjective personal feelings can bring objective national results, in the fantasies that fueled patriotic purpose. When citizens are allowed to do as they will, in liberal fiction and philosophy, they will combine in productive associations.

Evidently, liberalism in Latin America (and elsewhere) went deeper than economic reasoning, unless of course economy recovers its original sense of household relationships and management. Liberalism, as we know from John Locke, Adam Smith, and others, includes a dimension of gregariousness and sympathy. Latin American romantics took unorthodox liberties to stretch that dimension toward passionate love. The stretch did not concern them. Philosophical rigor was one nuisance they could simply wish away, unlike the material nuisances of war debts, wasted fields, and mines, all of which fanned regional and racial rage. The will to repair the damage was certainly reasonable, and agents of modernity could appreciate that. But the energy required seemed beyond reasonable hope, in countries where elites were used to demanding submission rather than winning it through hegemonic arrangements. Love was that energy, irrational and benevolent, like the rest of God's Nature.

## Imagined Sexualities and Historical Communities

I have already hinted at *why* eroticism and nationalism become figures for each other in modernizing fictions. Now, I would like to suggest *how* this works rhetorically. It is through a literary sleight-of-the-invisible-hand that legitimates heterosexual passion in patriotism, and reciprocally legitimates hegemonic states in sexual desire. I want to consider these forces, and merely to suggest the matter of reciprocal allegory, which I argue elsewhere.[14] Briefly, Eros and Polis take each other as the stable ground of their own narrative. One represents the other and fuels it. The unrequited passion of the love story produces a surplus of energy, just as Rousseau suggested it would,[15] a surplus that can hope to overcome the political interference between the lovers. And the enormity of social abuse invests the love story with an almost sublime sense of purpose. As the story progresses, the pitch of sentiment raises along with it a cry of commitment, until the din makes it ever more difficult to distinguish between our erotic and political fantasies.

What I find ingenious, brilliant, about this novel productivity is that one libidinal investment ups the ante for the other. And every obstacle that the lovers encounter heightens more than their mutual desire to (be a) couple, more than our voyeuristic but keenly felt passion; it also heightens their/our love for the possible nation in which the affair could be consummated. The two levels of desire are different, which allows us to remark on an allegorical structure; but they are not discrete.[16] Desire weaves between the individual and the public family in a way that shows the terms to be contiguous, coextensive as opposed to merely analogous. And the desire keeps weaving, or simply doubling itself at personal and political levels, because the obstacles it encounters threaten both levels of happiness.

From our historical distance, both romantic love and patriotism can seem natural, although we know them to be produced, perhaps, by the very novels that (re)present them. To acknowledge this possibility is also to ask whether what may have passed for effects of the greater culture in the novel (romantic love or conciliatory nationalism) may be causes of that culture. If heroes and heroines in Latin American novels were passionately desiring one another by trespassing traditional lines and desiring the new state that would join them, they were not repeating timeless or essential affections. Those passions would not have prospered earlier. In fact, modernizing lovers were learning how to dream their erotic fantasies by reading the frustrating European romances they hoped to improve.

The appropriateness of European fiction for Latin American founders may perhaps be read backward (in a reflex learned from Benedict Anderson, who sees European nations imitate the Americans[17]), meaning that the appropriateness suggests a cultural intersection that points both ways. Therefore, my rather local observations about a particular moment and genre in Latin America tempt me to hazard some conjectures about more general implications. Is it possible, for example, that outside of Latin America, political passion was being grounded in erotics? Had sexual desire as the shorthand for human association become "the explanation for everything," as Foucault said it had?[18] The claim is hardly hyperbolic or even original. By 1865 in England, John McLean's influential *Primitive Marriage* considered "sexual attraction the underlying principle of all social formations," thus agreeing with other early texts of cultural anthropology, including those by Herbert Spencer, who would be so popular among Latin American positivists.[19] Alternatively, if there were no erotic or sentimental investment in the state, if our identities as modern sexually defined subjects did not take the state to be a primary object and therefore the partner on whom our identity depends, what could explain our passion for *"la patria?"*[20] Is it also possible that the romances are themselves synecdoches of the marriage between Eros and Polis that was taking place under the broad canopy of Western culture? I hesitate to say bourgeois culture because it is as much the child as the maker of the match. Nancy Armstrong's reading of domestic fiction as constitutive of bourgeois society in England is suggestive[21] for Latin America where, along with constitutions and civil codes, novels helped to legislate modern mores. But unlike the English books that privileged feminine domesticity by "disentangling" it from masculine politics, Latin American novels took advantage of the tangle to produce a secure knot of sentimentalized men.

The broad possibilities I am suggesting for readings of these novels are not (merely) a suggestion that Latin Americans may have general lessons to teach. A coincidence between Michel Foucault's *The History of Sexuality* and in Benedict Anderson's *Imagined Communities* is worth noting. Normal heterosexuality and republican patriotism develop contemporaneously, though neither book seems concerned with the other's project.

Foucault is almost indifferent to the most obvious deployment of bourgeois sexuality, the legitimate conjugal variety without which there could be no perverse difference, as indifferent as he was to the bestselling genre of bourgeois discourse, the novels that did so much to construct the heterosexual hegemony in bourgeois culture.[22] He defends this silence by saying that heterosexuality was itself discreet and decorous.[23] Yet from the concern of mothers and doctors, we know that it was being scandalously exhibitionistic. In the nineteenth century everyone was reading the forbidden romances, which is one reason the Mexican Ignacio Altamirano, among many others, was using them for patriotic projects. "Novels are undoubtedly the genre that the public likes best," he wrote in 1868; "they are the artifice through which today's best thinkers are reaching the masses with doctrines and ideas that would otherwise be difficult to impart."[24]

The obvious and public discourse of "normal" conjugal love must have had an enormous appeal to have kept all the pathologizing discourses in business. What monumental body flaunted this kind of public sex? Only one was inclusive and insecure enough to require public displays of ardor: the tenuously constructed antimonarchical state that needed a self-legitimating discourse and found one in erotic desire. Sexual love was *the* trope for associative behavior, unfettered market relationships, and for Nature in general. Is it conceivable that the state derived some of its power from its positive attractions as the guarantor (or promisor) of rights, services, and national pride, and that, like some jealous lover, the state punished disloyal affections?

This is what Benedict Anderson considers. For him, nationalism is an affective bond, is not "aligned" to abstract ideologies, but mystically inflected from the religious cultural systems "out of which – as well as against which – it came into being."[25] The fullness and uncompromising visibility of modern states – which were at the same time particular and universally proliferated in the West – brings to mind a different kind of body being constructed simultaneously. While nations were being embodied, their borders meticulously drawn and their resources territorialized, so too were the sexual bodies that attract Foucault's attention. He understands his project to be a "history of bodies,"[26] much as Anderson's is a study of national bodies. As if they assumed that the other's discourse were their own stable grounding, Foucault charts sexual bodies as sites of national production and governmental surveillance, while Anderson wonders at the libidinal attachment we have to bodies politic. The eighteenth century is not only remembered for rationalizing sex,[27] but also for drawing maps as the logos (locus, too?) of desire. Yet Foucault does not wonder about how the nation is engendered, and Anderson does not mention that the definite contours of the new (national) bodies were making them the objects of possessive bourgeois desire.

He values the novel, like the newspaper, for its synchronicity, its *horizontal* and democratizing commonality of time, rather than for the desire that drives time forward. Print communities were being consolidated because everyone read the same news, but also because readers were either laughing or (usually) panting and crying over the same installment of the serialized novel. Had Anderson stayed with his own featured example of homogeneous time, the "Social Gathering" at the beginning of José Rizal's Filipino national novel, time would have shown its forward drive at the party. There, the bored protagonist becomes a dynamic hero once he leaves the circle of men and crosses over to the heroine:

> The sala is almost full of people, the men separated from the women as in the Catholic churches and in the synagogues . . .
> The young man found himself alone in the middle of the sala: the owner of the house had disappeared and he found no one to present him to the young ladies, many of whom were looking at him with interest. After hesitating for some seconds, he addressed them with a simple and natural grace. "Permit me," he said, "to overstep the strict rules of etiquette. For seven years I had been absent from my country, and on returning, I cannot refrain from greeting her most precious adornment, her women." (pp. 3, 14)

Of course the allegories will appeal to some legitimating principle. Being a justification for modern and anti-authoritarian projects, that principle is often Nature that has been conveniently redefined since the days of enlightened independence as interactive rather than hierarchical. If erotic desire seemed to be the natural and therefore eternal grounding for happy and productive marriages (including national families, by extension), it was thanks to these redefinitions. Nature was no longer the classical space of predictable law but the scene of flux where energy could meet obstacles and turn frustration into excess. It was a world that produced angels and monsters, not clockwork. The allegories will strain at points. For one thing the writing elite was loathe to give up its hierarchical privilege to conciliatory projects, and for another characters may exceed or somehow miss an ideally assigned meaning.

But the observation I am making is more fundamental than any demonstration of the allegory's partial failures. I am simply registering the incredible measure of its success. In many cases, the double-dealing romance actually helped to give a cognitive expression and an emotive mooring to the social and political formations it articulates. The historical romances became national novels in their respective countries, a term that refers not so much to their market popularity, although some of these novels were immediately popular, but to the fact that they became required reading by the first decades of the twentieth century. Perhaps their promise of a nationalizing embrace was particularly appealing after massive immigration in some countries seemed to threaten a cultural core, and after Latin American regimes decided on patriotic programs for economic and civic development as responses to the Depression and to competing "foreign" ideologies. These states, in other words, tacitly accepted the nineteenth-century potboilers as founding fictions that cooked up the desire for authoritative government from the apparently raw material of erotic love.

## Some Beg to Differ

*Foundational Fictions: The National Romances of Latin America* (1991) was my effort to formulate and to trace the allegories as they escalate in a spiral of erotics and politics.[28] To be an ideal reader of these romances is to slide into the stories as participant observer in the love affairs. Identification with the frustrated lovers whose union could produce the modern state was precisely the desired effect on the tenuous citizenry of newly consolidated countries. It was a mirror effect, from elite lovers to a range of readers, a denial of difference in every compulsory embrace of public education. My project, in other words, was to explore foundations their own ideal terms, with a theory that conjugated imagined communities with dreams of love.

But some books beg to differ from their readers, as I have become painfully aware. Particularist texts would signal the distortions of sliding and of mirror effects, if we learned to read those signals. This will take a paradigm shift, because modern readers are generally unprepared to recognize a literary rebuff. *Proceed with Caution, When Engaged by Minority Writing in the Americas* (1999) is my attempt at a training program through rereadings of basic books (by Whitman, Morrison, Menchú, Villaverde, Cortázar, Vargas Llosa, and others). Training will take time, because tropes of unavailability have evidently seemed unremarkable. In the vicious hermeneutic circle of familiarity and predictability, the unanticipated lessons these texts could teach are hard to read. How can the books teach reading effectively, if we have only learned to overcome their lessons? At our most circumspect we have been assuming, with the New Critics and then with deconstruction,[29] that ambiguity cannot be conquered. But an ethical distance from the object of desire? Legitimate ignorance? No-trespassing signs that demand cautious steps? We have yet to recognize those purposefully off-putting enticements.

My advice is to be careful of some books. They can sting readers who feel privileged to know everything as they approach a text, practically any text, with the conspiratorial intimacy of a potential partner. Readers bent on understanding may neglect a different engagement that would make respect a reading requirement. The slap of refused intimacy from uncooperative books can slow readers down, detain them at the boundary between contact and conquest, before they press particularist writing to surrender cultural difference for the sake of universal meaning. The very familiarity of universalism as measure of literary worth, while its codependent term particularism sounds strange to contemporary criticism,[30] shows how one-sided interpretation has been, even when we read "minority" texts. If learning makes the distance between writers and readers seem superficial or circumstantial, mere interference on the way to understanding, particularist writing puts circumstance to work, resurfacing the stretch with fresh stop-signs. Those signs go unnoticed and have no rhetorical names, because the study of rhetoric has generally assumed cultural continuity between orator and public, writer and reader.[31]

Naming some figures of discontinuity is one purpose of my book; it is to contribute toward a rhetoric of particularism that will appreciate artful maneuvers for marking cultural distances. Differently situated and consequently limited understanding is news only to those who mistake their particularity for universality. Well-meaning readers who hope to overcome limits through empathy and learning inadvertently do violence to difference by conquering it. Without limits, writer and reader are ultimately redundant. One will do. Today's literary criticism is hardly offended by the reduction as readers disappear authors. The reduction cheats those readers too. It robs them of the aesthetic particularity, the specific charm or bite, of some books. The formal experiments and aesthetic thrill of particularism's seductive and defensive tangle with universalism are lost on readers who don't get them because they don't expect them. But discontinuity opens the space between particular histories, like a slap that stops an embrace, in Morrison's analogy between music and the rhythm of her writing;[32] it syncopates communication and heightens the pleasure of the next embrace with the poignancy of its dependence on an autonomous Other. Reading lessons will need to include those stop-signs; otherwise we will continue to dream of symmetrical romances and to wish away misfits; that is, to miss opportunities both for literary pleasures and for extra-literary confrontations in a public sphere. Can necessarily difficult dialogues follow from an education that conflates conflictive histories into universal understanding? Learning to read for historically constituted difference is practically a civic obligation, as well as good advice for readers who are waking up from romance.

## Notes

1   Mary Poovey, *A History of the Modern Fact* (Chicago: University of Chicago Press, 1998):

    The formal precision of the [Italian sixteenth-century and English seventeenth-century accounting] books created an effect of accuracy. Even though the accuracy of the initial records could not be verified, the formal precision of the books made the records function *as if* they were not only precise but accurate as well. . . .
    Because he assumed that trade obeyed laws, it did not even matter to Mun that the numbers recorded in the customs records did not always support his theories. Indeed, the inadequacy of these numbers – which constituted one of the few points these three writers all agreed on – became the basis of Mun's claims about mercantile expertise. For him, mercantile expertise consisted of the ability to *interpret* numbers, not to gather data through personal experience . . .
    Eighteenth-century theorists of the market system, like Adam Smith and David Hume, ridiculed the group they called the mercantilists for privileging a concept whose exact numerical value they could never establish . . . for Thomas Mun, who wanted to authorize merchants and not the numbers themselves, the accuracy of the numbers was not the decisive issue; his primary goal was to develop an analytic model that demonstrated his thesis that encouraging trade was more important than fixing the rate of exchange and simultaneously used his demonstration to promote expert interpretation. (pp. 64, 83–4)

2   Gilles Deleuze and Félix Guattari, *Anti-Oedipus*, trans. Robert Hurley, Mark Seem, and Helen Lane, preface by Michel Foucault (New York: Viking, 1977), p. 1.

3   Hannah Arendt, *On Revolution* (New York: Viking, 1963):

    On the contrary, if Locke in a famous passage states, "That which begins and actually constitutes any political society is nothing but the consent of any number of freemen capable of majority, to unite and incorporate into such society," and then calls this act the "beginning to any lawful government in the world," it rather looks as though he was more influenced by the *facts and events in American*, and perhaps in a more decisive manner, than the founders were influenced by his *Treatises of Civil Government* . . . the way Locke construed this "original compact," in line with the current social-contract theory, as a surrender of rights and powers to either the government or the community, that is, not at all as a "mutual" contract but as an agreement in which an individual person resigns his power to some higher authority and consents to be ruled in exchange for a reasonable protection of his life and property. (p. 168)

4   Jaime Concha, *Cronología* (Caracas: Biblioteca Ayacucho, 1977), p. 249.

5   Franklin J. Franco tells us that *Enriquillo* was "elevated since the past century to the level of required reading in the public school system" (*Trujillismo: Génesis y rehabilitación*, Santo Domingo: Editora Cultural Dominicana, 1971, p. 67). But other national novels became required reading later, after governments had resources for massive publication of anything but textbooks (often of natural law, philosophy, literature, through selections of Latin classics, and later history). As in the United States, American literature did not have immediate academic legitimacy. The first documented "Programa de literatura española y de los estados hispano-americanos" in Argentina is the 1884 course by Professor Calixto Oyuela for the fourth year at the Colegio Nacional de la Capital (Buenos Aires: Imprenta Biedma, 1884). On page 16, *Amalia* figures along with *La Cautiva* and gauchesca poetry. But literature as part of patriotic education was still being argued for by Ricardo

Rojas in *La Restauración nacionalista* (Buenos Aires: Librería de la Facultad, 1922 [1909]). In Mexico the first university courses in literature were instituted in 1912, with the beginning of the (antipositivist) Revolution. See Alfonso Reyes, "Pasado inmediato" (1939), in *Obras completas* (Mexico City: Fondo de Cultura Económica, 1960), 12, p. 214. By 1933, required readings had for some time included Altamirano along with Fernández Lizardi, Payno, Sierra, and others. See *Programas detallados para las escuelas secundarias* (Mexico: Secretaría de Educación Pública, 1933), p. 54.

The example of Chile has a documented analog in teaching national history. It is the delayed cult of Arturo Prat, the 1879 hero of the War of the Pacific. Iván Jaksic speculated for me that *Martín Rivas* was probably required by the same nationalist leaders and educators who responded to civic demands during the Depression – and in the face of "alien" ideologies – by institutionalizing Prat's heroism, turning it into a model of hard work and national reconciliation. See William F. Sater, *The Heroic Image in Chile: Arturo Prat, Secular Saint* (Berkeley, Los Angeles, and London: University of California Press, 1973).

6  Written at the same mid-century moment as the novels and with largely the same legitimating impulse, their authors had comparable political credentials but more classical criteria than the novelists. Literary historians selected a kind of elite prehistory for the "progressive conservative" consolidations that were stabilizing the new states. See Beatriz González Stephan, *La Historiografía literaria del liberalismo hispanoamericano del siglo XIX* (Havana: Casa de las Américas, 1987), esp. pp. 193, 159. Most of the literary historians had rigorous religious training, and some studied to be priests. They borrowed aesthetic criteria from Aristotle, Boileau, and Luzán, and worked in party politics as lawyers, university professors, or deans; most were senators, deputies, ministers, and diplomats. Often the project was more a desideratum than a record, since new countries, so resistant to their colonial past, had little literature to report on, Brazil being an exception.

7  Also excluded from first literary histories were indigenous literatures, oral Hispanic literature, many chronicles, and various hybrid forms (González Stephan, *La Historiografía literaria*, pp. 191–2).

8  In anticipation of such a sociology of literature, one way to read the history of institutionalization is symptomatically, from the record of publications. I am grateful to Antonio Cornejo Polar for this suggestion, and to Ludwig Lauerhaus of the library at UCLA for assenting. That record is often thin until the 1920s or 1930s, when large editions would follow one another almost yearly. In the admittedly spotty entries of *The National Union Catalog Pre-1956 Imprints*, several editions of *Amalia* appear before the 1930s (more in Europe than in Buenos Aires, and two editions for American students, with notes and exercises). But from 1930, Sopena – first in Barcelona then in Buenos Aires – begins to repeat printings every two or three years, even in this incomplete list. Simultaneous publishers of *Amalia* are Espasa-Calpe in Madrid and Buenos Aires, and Estrada. Altamirano's *El Zarco* (another favorite of American Spanish teachers, as indeed were almost all of these national novels) appeared in 1901 and shows three printings in this list until 1940. In the following decade, Espasa-Calpe of Buenos Aires and Mexico reissued it four times, joined by Mexico's Editora Nacional in 1951. *Tabaré*, by Zorrilla de San Martín, to give just one last example from the *Catalog*, has had a remarkable number of printings and editions over time, especially since the 1920s (two full pages of the catalog for this one work). And Blest Gana's *Martín Rivas* seems to have been standard reading early (for Chileans as well as for American students through the D. C. Heath edition). Jorge Román-Lagunas's "Bibliografía anotada de y sobre Alberto Blest Gana," *Revista Iberoamericana*, 112–13 (July–December 1980: 605–47) informs us that during the last century the novel had five printings; in this one, by 1980, it has already had thirty.

9  This is John Breuilly's general definition in *Nationalism and the State* (Chicago: University of Chicago Press, 1985).

10 See ibid., p. 342. "The demand for a nation-state with many of the features of other nation-states seems hard to reconcile with the justification that a unique nation needs its own special form of independence."

11 Beatriz González-Stephan repeatedly notes (e.g., *La Historiografía literaria,* p. 184) that this was one of the contradictions faced by elite nation-builders in the nineteenth century. Because they were elite they imitated Europe; and because they were American nation-builders they celebrated their premodern surroundings.

12 The uncompromising and heroic militarism that expelled Spain from most of America was now a threat to her development. What America needed now were civilizers, founding fathers of commerce and industry, not fighters. Juan Bautista Alberdi, whose notes for Argentina's 1853 constitution became a standard of political philosophy throughout Latin America, wrote that "glory has ceded its place to utility and comfort, and military heroism is not the most competent medium for the *prosaic* needs of commerce and industry" (as if to say the prose of domestic fiction should now replace grandiloquent epic verse). See Juan Bautista Alberdi, "Las bases y puntos de partida para la organización política de la República Argentina" (1852). See also Tulio Halperín Donghi, *Proyecto y construcción de una nación (Argentina, 1846–1880)* (Caracas: Biblioteca Ayacucho, 1980), pp. 84–111; 92 (emphasis added). Alberdi and Domingo F. Sarmiento agreed, if on little else, on the need to fill up the desert, to make it disappear. What sense was there in heroically reducing warm bodies to dead ones, when Alberdi pronounced that in America, "to govern is to populate" (Alberdi, "Las bases y puntos," p. 107). Few slogans have caught on and held on so well as this one. Husband the land and father your countries, he was saying. They have already yielded and now they must be loved and worked. The spirit inspired Paraguayan Jesuits to rouse their married countrymen to procreate after the disastrous War of the Triple Alliance.

13 Love, however, is feeling, i.e. ethical life n the form of something natural . . . Love therefore, is the most tremendous contradiction; the Understanding cannot resolve it since there is nothing more stubborn than this point of self-consciousness which is negated and which nevertheless I ought to possess as affirmative. Love is at once the propounding and the resolving of this contradiction. As the resolving of it, love is unity of an ethical type. (G. W. F. Hegel, "Philosophy of right," trans. T. M. Knox, London: Oxford University Press, 1967, pp. 261–2)

14 "Allegory and dialectics: a match made in romance," *Boundary*, 2(18) (1991): 60–82.

15 I owe this provocative comment to Jean Bethke Elshtain.

16 Catherine Gallagher, *Industrial Transformations in the English Novel* (Chicago: University of Chicago Press, 1985) develops a similar double reading. I am grateful to Marshall Brown for pointing the book out to me.

17 Benedict Anderson, *Imagined Communities: Reflections on the Origin and Spread of Nationalism* (London: Verso, 1983).

18 Michel Foucault, *The History of Sexuality*, vol. 1: *An Introduction*, trans. Robert Hurley (New York: Vintage Books, 1980), p. 78.

19 See Anita Levy, "Blood, kinship, and gender," *Genders*, 5 (Summer 1989): 70–85; 75.

20 Patriotic passion evidently has a long history, which Ernst H. Kantorowicz masterfully traced as a progressive reconquest of classical patriotism in "*Pro patria mori* in medieval political thought," in *Selected Studies* (Locust Valley, New York: J. J. Augustin, 1965), pp. 308–24. Very schematically one can summarize the progression as follows: the early Middle Ages denied an earthly patria; then made it (France is his prime example) parallel to Jerusalem; shifted the mystical body of the Church to the corporate body of the State; understood corporation as the nation's body with the king at its head; and finally left the king behind. But in this return, the ancient *patria* (city, polis) is substituted by the idea of inclusive nation as it developed during the Middle Ages.

21 Nancy Armstrong, *Desire and Domestic Fiction: A Political History of the Novel* (New York: Oxford University Press, 1987), p. 9. "Rather than see the rise of the new middle class in terms of the economic changes that solidified

its hold over the culture," she "shows that the formation of the modern political state – in England at least – was accomplished largely through cultural hegemony," primarily through the domestic novel.

22 D. A. Miller notes that "perhaps the most notable reticence in Foucault's work concerns precisely the reading of literary texts and literary institutions," as if they could not amount to objects of analysis. See *The Novel and the Police* (Berkeley, Los Angeles, and London: University of California Press, 1988), p. viii, note 1.

23 Foucault, *History of Sexuality*, p. 38.

24 Ignacio M. Altamirano, "La Literatura nacional" (1868), in *La Literatura nacional*, ed. and prologue by José Luis Martínez, Mexico City: Edit. Porrúa (Col. de Escritores Mexicanos, 52), 1949), pp. 9–40; 17.

25 Anderson, *Imagined Communities*, p. 19.

26 Foucault, *History of Sexuality*, p. 152.

27 Ibid., pp. 23–4.

28 Doris Sommer, *Foundational Fictions: The National Romances of Latin America* (Berkeley: University of California Press, 1991).

29 Steven Mailloux, in *Rhetorical Power* (Ithaca, NY: Cornell University Press, 1989), p. 133

insists, for example, that criticism should move from Theory (with its presumptions of pattern and predictability) to a history of differential readings as soon as possible. His project of "Rhetorical hermeneutics" apparently derives from Gadamer, by stressing a continuous tradition of readerly variations, but it parts company over the possibility of hermeneutics as achieving understanding.

30 Particularism is a word I borrow from historians to name cultural embeddedness in experience and circumstance. It was also a favorite term for New Critics, but it meant inimitable originality available for universal appreciation. See Allen Tate, "The structure of the 'concrete universal' in literature," *Proceedings of the Modern Language Association*, 62 (March 1947): 262–80.

31 See, for example, Richard A. Lanham's useful *Handlist of Rhetorical Terms* (2nd edn, Berkeley: University of California Press, 1993).

32 Toni Morrison, "Unspeakable things unspoken." In Matthew J. Bruccoli and Richard Layman (eds), *Literary Masters: Toni Morrison* (Detroit: Gale Group, 2000).

# PART IV
# Uncertain Modernities

# 20
# Shifting Hegemonies:
# The Cultural Politics of Empire
*Fernando Degiovanni*

The turn of the century was a period of deep political and cultural transformations in Latin America. The expansionist policies of the United States – already at work with the annexation of Texas (1845), the acquisition of half of the Mexican territory as a result of the Mexican-American war (1846–8), and the filibustering interventions of William Walker in Central America (1853–60) – were consolidated in the 1880s when the US Secretary of State, James G. Blaine, called the first Pan-American conference (1889–90) to develop his plan to control the continent's political and economic future through a system of common arbitration and customs union. Although short and unsuccessful, the French invasion of Mexico (1861–5) added another player to the imperialist race in the region. By the end of the century, the declaration of the Spanish-American war (1898) – in which Spain lost its last possessions overseas by ceding Puerto Rico to the United States and renouncing all claim to Cuba – contributed to irreversibly change the history of colonialism in the continent.

The rise of the United States to the status of world power had a profound impact on the way the Spanish-speaking countries imagined their place and mission in the new imperial order. On one hand, the growing interest of the United States in its neighboring territories to the south compelled Latin American politicians and intellectuals to formulate a new discourse of continental identity. For Spain, on the other hand, the end of a long era of transatlantic influence fostered a complex debate about the nation's modernity and its role in international affairs. Furthermore, the consolidation of US imperialism dramatically transformed the manner in which Spain and its former colonies redefined their relationship after nearly one hundred years of strong political and cultural disagreements over the consequences of the conquest and colonization. For the first time since the movements of independence, the necessity of curbing the power of the United States led some institutions and writers on both sides of the Atlantic to develop a unifying view of the Hispanic world by reconciling their differences within alternative historical and cultural referents.

The idea of a common legacy whose primary manifestation was the Spanish language, emerged in this context as one of the most politically effective ways to refashion the connection between Spain and its former colonies. This transatlantic discourse of cultural negotiation was not, however, initially supported by both parts, nor did it presuppose an equal standing within the new political and symbolic alliance. Indeed, the language argument was originally and primarily used by the old metropolis to reposition itself as the hegemonic power in the struggles for constructing a Latin American identity in a new era of imperialism. Since its beginning at the turn of the century, this version of Hispanism was largely developed by Spain's official institutions (in particular the Real Academia Española [Royal Spanish Academy] and the Centro de Estudios Históricos [Center for Historical Studies]) with the cooperation of some intellectuals on both sides of the Atlantic, and sought to spread the idea that the Spanish-American civilization represented above all a prolongation of Spain's cultural heritage in an overseas space.

After an initial period of Spanish-American resistance at the end of the nineteenth century, Hispanism was progressively assimilated by institutions and intellectuals of the continent, to the extent that it became a primary component of the narratives of cultural identity in the first decades of the twentieth century. The development of a series of specific institutional policies to promote a transatlantic alliance (e.g., the incorporation of Spanish-American intellectuals to peninsular organizations, the publication of commemorative books, and the creation of academic centers to foster scholarly collaboration), as well as the use of some discourses of critical authority (especially those of rhetoric and philology), made possible not only the endorsement of a non-controversial vision of imperial Spain, but also the articulation of epistemological and ideological discourses aimed at constructing a new cultural representation of the region. Indeed, one of the most striking manifestations of the eventual success of this politics of symbolic unification was the emergence of "Spanish-American" literature as a disciplinary byproduct of Hispanism at the turn of the century. The early configuration of this new field of study by Marcelino Menéndez Pelayo in the 1890s and its further development by Pedro Henríquez Ureña in the 1920s and 1930s is a clear example of how the tenets of Hispanism deeply permeated the new attempts to define the continent in a new age of empire.

## French Latin Americanism and Spanish Academicism

The United States' first expansionist policies toward Mexico and Central America did not immediately lead to the formation of a cohesive and systematic discourse of collective identity in the Spanish-speaking world. Despite the growing presence of the United States in the area, the unionist meetings held in Lima between the 1840s and 1860s still considered Europe the chief menace on the continent. In fact, Spain's several military attempts to recover its former overseas territories, as well as France's intervention in Mexico, were the most crucial point of concern for Spanish-American diplomats and *letrados* of the time (Ardao, 1980: 102–10). Spain's outlook on the advance of the United States over its neighboring territories did not trigger a decisive reaction either: Madrid became more attentive to the development of new forms of colonialism in its former dominions as soon as France, not the United States, began to show a greater interest in the area by spreading an aggressive cultural discourse of transatlantic identity intended to displace Spain's central position in the continent's affairs.

Indeed, as early as 1836 Maurice Chevalier (1806–79), a political economist and future advisor to emperor Napoleon III, had promoted the creation of a "pan-Latin" foreign policy under France's tutelage in order to justify the country's imperialist intervention in the territories that once belonged to Spain and Portugal. Defending the idea that Europe was divided into three racial groups – the Anglo-Saxons, the Latins, and the Slavonics, led respectively by England, France, and Russia – Chevalier contended that the Latins had been overtaken by the Anglo-Saxons in the capitalist race for world markets, and therefore needed to create an alliance to boost their position in the globe. As the most developed and wealthy Latin nation, France was supposed to assume leadership over the project. "Los pueblos de cepa latina" – Chevalier wrote – "no deben . . . permanecer inactivos en lo que se prepara . . . Es una admirable ocasión que se les ofrece para reconquistar la posición que han perdido" (The people of Latin stock should not . . . remain inactive in the midst of these developments . . . They have been given the ideal opportunity to reclaim the position they have lost) (1980: 162); and he added: "Nosotros, los Franceses, somos, de toda la familia latina, los major colocados, los únicos bien colocados, para asimilarnos estos progresos . . . En cuanto a las naciones europeas de la familia latina, no supongo que quede duda a nadie sobre la supremacía que debemos ejercer a su respecto" (Of all the Latin people, we, the French, are the best situated, indeed the only ones well situated, to adapt ourselves to these changes . . . In this respect, I suppose that nobody has any doubts as to the supremacy we must exert over other European nations that belong to the Latin family) (166). The Latin alliance, however, was not supposed to be limited to the countries of continental Europe. According to Chevalier, the project of successfully counteracting "Anglo-Saxon" capitalism depended on the incorporation of those territories across the Atlantic that shared a common religious and linguistic background with France. It is in this context that the idea of a "Latin" America – rather than a "Spanish" America – would come to exist. In Chevalier's words:

> Nuestra civilización europea procede de un doble origen, de los romanos y de los pueblos germánicos. Haciendo . . . abstracción de Rusia . . . [la civilización europea] se subdivide en dos familias, de las cuales cada una se distingue por su semejanza especial con una de las dos naciones madres que han concurrido a engendrarlas . . . Esta es protestante, la otra católica. Una se sirve de idiomas en los que domina el latín, la otra habla lenguas germanas. Las dos ramas, latina y germana, se han reproducido en el Nuevo Mundo. América del Sur es, como la Europa meridional, católica y latina. La América del Norte pertenece a una población protestante y anglosajona.

(Our European civilization comes from a double origin – the Romans and the Germanic peoples. Leaving aside . . . the case of Russia . . . [the European civilization] is subdivided into two families: each of them distinguishes itself from the other due to its special similarity to the two mother nations that have come together to engender them . . . One is Protestant, the other Catholic. One speaks languages in which Latin predominates; the other speaks Germanic languages. Both branches, Latin and German, have reproduced themselves in the New World. South America is, like Southern Europe, Catholic and Latin. North America belongs to a protestant and Anglo-Saxon people.) (162)

Eventually, these geo-ideological arguments were decisive in defending the launching of Napoleon III's imperial venture in Mexico. But if France's intervention in the region proved to be short-lived and disastrous, Chevalier's cultural justification, however, had long-lasting consequences for the cultural representation of the continent. In fact, some time before the French intervention, Chevalier's ideas had already impacted the works of José María Torres Caicedo (1830–89), a Colombian *letrado* who is regarded to be the first intellectual to use "Latin America" as a proper noun at the end of 1850s, and regularly employed the name in his articles published in France and Spain, influencing other politicians and writers. During the French intervention in Mexico, Chevalier's Pan-Latinist ideals also started to gain popularity in Europe as they appeared repeatedly in journals, pamphlets, newspapers, and books published by the ideologues and publicists of Napoleon III. Furthermore, in the 1870s and 1880s, increasing numbers of Spanish-speaking intellectuals and officials in Europe and the Americas adopted the new characterization of the continent.

The growing tendency to employ the name Latin America – in opposition to Spanish America – to designate the former possessions of Spain did not pass unperceived to the peninsular political and intellectual elite. Spanish critic Juan Valera (1824–1905) expressed one of the earliest concerns on this matter. In one of his *Cartas Americanas* (American letters) (1889), he argued that when those of Spanish origin in America called themselves "Latin," "it is because of disdain for the blood that runs in their veins. The only common bond among the people of those lands cannot be found in what is Latin, but in what is Spanish" (Pike, 1971: 198). The Spanish counter-offensive came soon, particularly because the new way of portraying its former possessions coincided with Spain's defeat in its last military attempts to recover its South American territories after the movements of emancipation – the wars against Chile and Peru (1865–6). In this context, instead of altogether abandoning its efforts to regain hegemony over the continent, Spain decided to tackle the issue of imperial influence by concentrating primarily on the symbolic sphere.

In the 1860s, Madrid started to organize a series of cultural campaigns devoted to reconstituting its tutelary place in the postcolonial world. The first official institution to be involved in developing a new strategy to reposition Spain's old place in Spanish-American affairs was the Royal Spanish Academy. The Academy argued that Spain would be able to hold ground on its former possessions against competing ideologies as long as it was capable of preserving the purity and unity of the Spanish language, its most durable and decisive legacy in the region. Therefore, the opening of the Academy to intellectuals across the Atlantic who were loyal to its prescriptive principles appeared to be the institution's most strategic maneuver towards consolidating Spain's hegemonic position. The appointment of corresponding members in the former colonies since 1861, as well as the creation of various chapters of the institution throughout the continent from 1870 onward, was the first formal step in the articulation of a new version of Hispanism that moved beyond divisive historical issues.

But Spain's attempt to recuperate its hegemonic position did not go as expected. Despite its efforts to gain influence, the Academy was unable to engage important sectors of the Spanish-American elite in the development of its cultural project. Even some of the most enthusiastic sympathizers of peninsular cultural policies – notably the Peruvian writer Ricardo Palma (1833–1919) – started to express their skepticism toward the Academy's intentions after noticing both the institution's persistent reluctance to consider their lexical proposals to improve the dictionary and its erratic criteria for adopting linguistic recommendations submitted by overseas members (Rama, 1982: 140–4). Furthermore, some liberal intellectuals immediately recognized the conservative implications behind Spain's official initiative, and denounced the neocolonial connotations of the Academy's normative and restrictive ideals. In a confrontation that showed the lasting scars of the colonial legacy in the post-revolutionary period, the Argentine Juan M. Gutiérrez (1809–78), one of the most important literary scholars of the nineteenth century, rejected his appointment as a corresponding member in a 1876 letter to the director of the Academy that openly articulated a position shared by other *letrados* of the time:

> Creo, señor, peligroso para un sudamericano la aceptación de un título dispensado por la Academia Española. Esa aceptación liga y ata con el vínculo poderoso de la gratitud, e impone a la urbanidad, si no entero sometimiento a las opiniones reinantes en aquel cuerpo que . . . profesa creencias religiosas y políticas que afectan a la comunidad, al menos un disimulo secreto y tolerante por esas opiniones . . .

> (Sir, I believe it is dangerous for a South American to accept a title granted by the Spanish Academy. Such an acceptance forges a powerful link of gratitude, and imposes as a matter of courtesy – if not a complete submission to the opinions dominant in that body which . . . professes religious and political beliefs that impact the community – at least a secret and tolerant pretense of agreement with these opinions . . .)

## Pan-Americanism and Cultural Monumentalism

The approval of Spain's cultural policies in Spanish America did not show any substantial sign of change until the United States demonstrated renewed interest in the Caribbean as an area of imperial expansion and, for that purpose, launched the Pan-American movement. Under the influence of James G. Blaine, two-time Secretary of

State in the 1880s, the US government had been working to strengthen the political and economic implications of the Monroe Doctrine (1823) in order to give the country a greater role in hemispheric affairs. The Washington Conference of 1889–90, intended to set the basis for future inter-American cooperation treaties in military, financial, and juridical matters, provoked increasing concern in some countries in the region. The rising determination of the United States to control the last two imperial possessions of Spain – Cuba and Puerto Rico – was seen as a common threat by both the peninsular government and some Spanish-American countries. These political circumstances allowed for the emergence of a new era of cultural negotiations between Spain and its one-time dominions.

The language question was once again at the center of the politics of reconciliation in this new period of transatlantic alliances, but the Academy soon realized that the only way to avoid further confrontations with Spanish-American *letrados* in its attempts to set foot in the continent depended on the possibility of executing its projects in a less openly unilateral and arbitrary way. The celebration of the fourth centennial of the arrival of the Spaniards in America (1892) was seen in this context as the ideal occasion to readdress Spain's hegemonic cultural policy. Besides organizing a series of meetings in Madrid, attended by men of letters from all over Spanish America, the Academy also sought to reposition itself through the launching of a "monumento levantado a la gloria de nuestra lengua común" (monument erected to the glory of our common tongue) (14), the *Antología de los poetas hispano-americanos* (Anthology of Spanish-American poets) (1892–5), a four-volume compilation edited and with a prologue by Marcelino Menéndez Pelayo (1856–1912), the most prestigious and influential scholar in the Spanish-speaking world at the time.

The *Antología* intended to be an instrument used to gain the favor of Spain's former colonies by strategically exalting the "richness" of Spanish-American literature (14). However, this new attempt to "reanudar la fraternidad" (renew the brotherhood) (13) did not necessarily mean a more open and critical approach to colonial affairs. By affirming that the discovery was a "maravilloso y sobrehumano acontecimiento, merced al cual nuestra lengua llegó a resonar preponente desde las orillas del Bravo a la región del Fuego" (a marvelous and superhuman event, thanks to which our language came to resound powerfully from the banks of the Bravo to Tierra del Fuego) (13), Menéndez Pelayo's *Antología* claimed once again a privileged position for Spain as the guardian of its most perdurable legacy: the shared language and the literary production that emerged from it. In the prologue to the second edition of his work (1911), Menéndez Pelayo made no attempt to hide the political implications behind the project. Following the imperial ideals articulated in Antonio de Nebrija's first Spanish grammar, he stated:

> Fue privilegio de las languas que llamamos clásicas el extender su imperio por regiones muy distantes de aquellas donde tuvieron su cuna, y el sobrevivirse en cierto modo a sí mismas, persistiendo a través de los siglos en los labios de gentes y razas traídas a la civilización por el pueblo que primeramente articuló aquellas palabras y dio a la lengua su nombre.

(It was a privilege of the languages we call classical to extend their empire throughout regions very distant from those where they had their origin, and to somehow outlive themselves, by persisting throughout the centuries in the mouths of the peoples and races brought to civilization by those who first articulated those words and gave their name to the language.) (11)

At the center of Menéndez Pelayo's argument stood once again the idea of regaining cultural hegemony over a space that Spain considered to be its own. In a new age of empire articulated through competing colonial discourses, the Spanish language was seen as the most powerful weapon of cultural cooptation that Spain could use to reaffirm its central position in world affairs at a moment of political decadence. Menéndez Pelayo's linguistic claims had unprecedented consequences for the construction of Spanish-American identity. Through a clear division of the areas of power and influence in the post-colonial world, Menéndez Pelayo not only intended to wipe out France's "Latin" allegations from the cultural game, but also to restrict any "Anglo-Saxon" attempt to advance over the region:

> Son dos las lenguas de los pueblos colonizadores que nos presenta la historia del mundo moderno: representates la una de la civilización de la Europa septentrional . . . la otra del genio de la Europa meridional . . . América es o inglesa o española . . . Nosotros [los españoles] también debemos contar como timbre de grandeza propia y como algo cuyos esplendores reflejan sobre nuestra propia casa, y en parte nos consuelan de nuestro abatimiento político y del secundario puesto que hoy ocupamos en la dirección de los negocios del mundo, la consideración de los cincuenta millones de hombres que en uno y otro hemisferio hablan nuestra lengua, y cuya historia y cuya literatura no podemos menos de considerar como parte de la nuestra.

> (The history of the modern world presents to us two languages of the colonizing peoples: one represents the civilization of northern Europe . . . the other [represents] the genius of southern Europe . . . The Americas are either English or Spanish . . . We [the Spaniards] must also count as a glorious deed and as something whose splendors reflect on our own house – and in part comfort us in our political despondency and the secondary position that we have today in the direction of the world's business – the consideration of fifty million people who, in both hemispheres, speak our language and whose history and literature we cannot but consider part of ours.) (12–13)

Through this statement, Menéndez Pelayo also wanted to establish that, as a product of an extensive linguistic empire, the literature of Spanish America belonged to Spain's cultural patrimony. Opposing all arguments of literary autonomy developed in Spanish America since the time of independence, Menéndez Pelayo tried to fight any separatist statements by underlining the idea that through the *Antología* the Academy sought to grant "a la poesía castellana del otro lado de los mares . . . entrada oficial en el tesoro de la literatura española" (an official place in the patrimony of Spanish literature to the Castilian poetry from the other side of the ocean) (13). Indeed, confronting the criteria used to edit previous anthologies of Spanish-American literature – especially the most famous of them all, *América Poética* (Poetic America)

(1846) by Juan M. Gutiérrez – Menéndez Pelayo made strategic use of the idea of linguistic continuity to counteract what he called the "antiespañolismo furioso" (fervent anti-Spanishness) that lay behind these compilations (18).

In this regard, the most important purpose of the *Antología* was to dramatically transform the Spanish-American canon as it was known during the nineteenth century, focusing particularly on the place of "colonial" literature in the continent's literary history. Usually not deemed an integral part of the Spanish-American production, and consequently excluded from the nineteenth-century compilations, the pre-revolutionary literature was seen by Menéndez Pelayo as the first and most evident cultural link between the "old" and the "new" worlds – and therefore the decisive element to be negotiated in the process of reinventing the Hispanic tradition. This operation had profound consequences for the reconfiguration of Spain and Spanish America's literary history. In fact, in order to reinforce the idea of a Spanish-American literary canon whose point of departure would be colonial production, Menéndez Pelayo was willing to hand over an important number of patrimonial texts, long regarded as inextricable components of the peninsular Golden Age canon, to the Spanish-American tradition. Owing to Menéndez Pelayo's process of cultural negotiation, monumental texts like Alonso de Ercilla's *La Araucana* (1569) and Pedro de Oña's *El Arauco domado* (1596), for example, "officially" became central pieces of the Spanish-American patrimony from 1892, marking the beginning of a new way of looking disciplinarily and historically at the Hispanic past. Characterizing this bequeathing as "nueva prenda del espíritu de fraternidad hispano-americana" (a new token of the spirit of the Hispano-American brotherhood) (18), Menéndez Pelayo intended to set the basis for the articulation of Spanish-American literature as a byproduct of Hispanism.

Yet this ideological operation could only be fully successful and consistent if Menéndez Pelayo introduced a further critical strategy in his assessment of the region's literary production. Indeed, the idea of repositioning colonial texts in order to promote neo-imperial ideals consequently required that Menéndez Pelayo play down the importance of the Spanish-American poems of the revolutionary period as crucial texts in the continental canon. Full of animosity toward Spain, these poems represented an obstacle in the process of reestablishing transatlantic alliances, and consequently Menéndez Pelayo decided to marginalize them in his version of Spanish-American literary history. But in order to present this operation in a less politically interested way – and therefore avoid the negative reaction that the Academy had faced twenty years earlier from Spanish-American intellectuals – Menéndez Pelayo preferred to exclude these poems by drawing on rhetorical criteria, rather than justifying his rejection on the basis of their controversial statements against Spain. The most striking example of the use of perceptive criticism to cover up obvious neocolonial intentions was the censorship of highly anti-Spanish pieces from the times of emancipation – such as the "national anthems" – owing to their poor technical composition. In his comment on a central piece of the Argentine national canon of the nineteenth century, Vicente López y Planes's "Marcha patriótica" (Patriotic march), Menéndez Pelayo said that this text did not deserve the central and undisputed place that it had enjoyed until then in the continental canon because the poem was not a "obra maestra, ni mucho menos. Desde luego, empieza con un verso que no lo es, si se pronuncia como es debido . . . y hay otros varios también mal acentuados, cosa doblemente grave en una composición destinada al canto" (masterpiece, far from it. Certainly, it starts with a line that is faulty if pronounced as it should be . . . and there are several others which are also wrongly accented – a matter doubly serious in a composition that is meant to be sung) (334).

The Academy's process of cultural negotiation developed under the authority and prestige of Menéndez Pelayo at the end of the nineteenth century was able to achieve a wider level of recognition from Spanish-American intellectuals of the time, but the reactions to this new approach to Hispanism were far from unanimous. Indeed, Spain's official policy toward Spanish America was openly backed, for instance, by Rubén Darío (1867–1916), the most renowned literary figure to emerge from either side of the Atlantic at the turn of the century. In his numerous statements on the political and cultural situation of the time, Darío did not perceive a fundamental contradiction between affirming his sympathy for the cause of Cuban independence and lamenting Spain's imperial decadence. In "El triunfo de Calibán" (The triumph of Caliban) he stated: "Y yo que he sido partidario de Cuba libre, siquier fuese por acompañar en su sueño a tanto soñador y en su heroísmo a tanto mártir, soy amigo de España en el instante en que la miro agredida por un enemigo brutal" (I, who have been a supporter of free Cuba (even if it was only to accompany so many dreamers in their dream and so many martyrs in their heroism), am also a friend of Spain at the moment in which I see her attacked by a brutal enemy) (1998: 455).

Furthermore, along the lines of the linguistic ideology developed by the Academy and Menéndez Pelayo, Darío gave language a central role in the creation of a common cultural front. For him, the rhetoric of affiliation to the linguistic law of the "Madre Patria" was a central factor in the constitution of a new discourse of identity devoted to confront the aggression of another imperial language. Since his arrival in Spain in 1892 as the Nicaraguan representative for the celebration of the fourth Centennial, Darío made sure that the Spanish intellectuals knew where he stood in the disputes over language: "nadie ama con más entusiasmo que yo nuestra lengua y soy enemigo de los que corrompen el idioma" (nobody loves our language more enthusiastically than I do, and I am the enemy of those who corrupt the language) (Díaz Quiñones, 1994: 88). Moreover, in his poem "A Colón" (To Columbus), composed on occasion of the Centennial, he not only condemned the political disarray brought about by the period of independence, but also accused its intellectual supporters of degrading the language by saying: "y tras encanalladas revoluciones / la canalla escritora mancha la lengua / que escribieron Cervantes y Calderones" (and after debased revolutions / debased writers foul the language / of Cervanteses and Calderons) (1978: 309).

Spain's neocolonial cultural policies were not equally supported by José Martí (1853–95), who at the time was in New York organizing the Cuban war of independence. Since the beginning of the 1880s, Martí had entered the struggle to build a discourse of continental identity that was meant to challenge all colonial implications. By working on the idea of "our" America, Martí rejected the image of the continent as a "daughter" of a foreign figure of knowledge and power, and projected a self-referential genealogy in which the region appeared as the mother of their people. In "Madre América" (Mother America), a speech for the delegates at the first Pan-American Conference, Martí imagined a homecoming scene through which he proposed a new perspective on the region: "Cuando cada uno de ellos (los delegados) vuelva a las playas que acaso nunca volvamos a ver, podrá decir, contento de nuestro decoro, a la que es nuestra dueña, nuestra esperanza y nuestra guía: 'Madre América, allí encontramos hermanos! Madre América, allí tienes hijos!'" (When each one of them (the delegates), content with our decorum, returns to the shores that we may never see again, he will be able to say to her who is our mistress, our hope, and our guide: "Mother America, we found brothers there! Mother America, you have children there!") (1985: 26). Therefore, without renouncing the ideology of the family, Martí systematically denied any possible alliance with Spain as a way to confront the United States, preferring to remain equally distant from all political or symbolic forms of colonialism.

## The End of the Empire and the Rise of Spanish-American Literature as a Field of Study

The Spanish-American War allowed Hispanism to become an even stronger cultural discourse in the disputes over continental identity. The defeat of Spain and the intervention of Cuba and Puerto Rico by the United States helped to pave the way for the development of new strategies of symbolic negotiation across the Atlantic. Indeed, in opposition to the initiatives in effect until the end of the nineteenth century, post-1898 Hispanism tried to find a less tutelary approach to further spread its ideological tenets in Spanish America. The expansion of its institutional basis, as well as the adoption of a scientific – yet still openly political – perspective on language and literature, were crucial operations for guaranteeing the institutionalization and recognition of Hispanism across the Atlantic. The establishment of the Center for Historical Studies, the nationalist research institution created by the Spanish government in 1910 under the directorship of Ramón Menéndez Pidal (1869–1968), performed an important function in refashioning Hispanism as a less controversial and paternalistic discourse for Spanish-American intellectuals. Trained in modern philology, the members of the Center focused on the scholarly study of historical and literary documents of the Spanish past in order to provide a new ideological basis for the hegemonic development of a post-imperial nation; at the same time, they also engaged in an active campaign to spread their philosophical and methodological principles by actively traveling and working in academic positions abroad.

Of all the Spanish-American countries, Argentina played a decisive role in the epistemological and institutional repositioning of Hispanism. Argentina's unique situation in the context of the continent explains the increasing attention that the Spanish agencies gave to the country as a critical platform for its project. On the one hand, Argentina was an especially challenging place for the development of

Hispanism since the country had a Francophile elite (often seen as having a patronizing view of Spain) as well as a substantial majority of Italian immigrants (whose language was often regarded as the main source of corruption for the local Spanish). But on the other hand, Argentina could also be a key player in the new neocolonial alliance promoted by Spain since the country had been not only the strongest bastion of anti-Pan-Americanism in the continent, but also had a wealthy Spanish immigrant elite eager to establish transatlantic links. The country's rapid assimilation to Hispanism was made possible by the aggressive cultural campaigns developed by both peninsular and local organizations and individuals; as a matter of fact, almost ten years after the 1898 war, Argentina had become the preferred destination of Spanish intellectuals in lecture tours and academic visits to Spanish America.

A part of a new cultural offensive, the series of lectures given by Menéndez Pidal in his 1914 visit to Argentina was a fundamental step toward the final institutionalization of Hispanism as a scientific discourse outside of Spain. The presence of the Center for Historical Studies' director in Buenos Aires was also a strategic move to sponsor the development of Hispanophile academic and social centers overseas. The creation of an endowed Menéndez Pelayo Chair in Spanish Culture at the University of Buenos Aires by the Institución Cultural Española (Spanish Cultural Institution) was the first tangible result of this new policy; Menéndez Pidal and Ortega y Gasset, among others, offered lecture courses there. But even more important and strategic was the eventual foundation of the Institute of Philology at the University of Buenos Aires in 1923 by the initiative of Ricardo Rojas, an intellectual engaged in promoting Hispanism as a way of legitimating the political and cultural role of the old *criollo* elite in a country deeply populated by non-Spanish immigrants. By giving Menéndez Pidal the power to recommend the Institute's director, Rojas was eager to guarantee the long-lasting influence of philological Hispanism through a new, highly influential framework. A official letter of 1928 from Ricardo Rojas (by then Rector of the University of Buenos Aires) to Menéndez Pidal, in which he indicates the political inconvenience of creating a chapter of the Royal Spanish Academy in Argentina, clearly describes this process of refashioning the objectives of Hispanism though a new disciplinary and institutional structure. In this document, Rojas basically presents the creation of the Institute as an alibi intended to make Spain's cultural program more acceptable to the local public without fundamentally altering its ideological principles:

Si la Academia local es nombrada y reglamentada desde Madrid se ve en esto un acto de *imperio*, que la conciencia popular rechaza y que haría estéril todo esfuerzo . . . Fue la conciencia de este escollo lo que me movió a organizar nuestro Instituto de Filología de acuerdo con Ud., creyendo que por aquí lograríamos major fruto que por el viejo camino.

(If the local Academy is appointed and regulated from Madrid this will be seen as an *imperialistic* act that the common sentiment will reject, making all our efforts fruitless . . . It was the awareness of this obstacle that led me to organize our Institute of Philology with your agreement, believing that by taking this path we would reach better results than through the old one.) (original emphasis)

With the arrival of some of Menéndez Pidal's most recognized disciples in Buenos Aires – Américo Castro (the Institute's first director) and Amado Alonso (who led the Institute for almost twenty years) – Hispanism assured its hegemonic place in Spanish America through the training of several generations of researchers and teachers. But besides the Institute's deep influence on keeping a prescriptive vision on questions of language – whose most important document was Américo Castro's *La peculiaridad lingüística rioplatense y su sentido histórico* (The linguistic peculiarity of the River Plate and its historical meaning) (1941) – one of its crucial contributions was to provide an academic context for the development of the field of "Spanish-American" literature as a by-product of Hispanism in the continent. The incorporation of Pedro Henríquez Ureña (1888–1946) to the Institute was not a minor factor in the consolidation of this process. After his initial scholarly training in the United States (1916–18) and his later work at the Center for Historical Studies (1919–20), where he focused on peninsular texts, Henríquez Ureña's long stay in Argentina (1924–46) coincided with the emergence of the heavily philological view of Spanish-American literature that he formulated in the 1920s and 1930s. In this regard, if Henríquez Ureña's Spanish-Americanism can be explained as a consequence of his extended exile (Díaz Quiñones, 1994: 65–73), his methodological approach is no less a product of this same trajectory.

The publication in Buenos Aires of *Seis ensayos en busca de nuestra expresión* (Six essays in search of our expression) (1928), Henríquez Ureña's first book specifically devoted to the construction of Spanish-American literature as a field of study, shows the deep effect of the ideological and epistemological tenets of philological Hispanism in his work. This influence is particularly clear in one of the programmatic essays of the book, "El descontento y la promesa" (Discontent and promise), where Henríquez Ureña defended the unity of Spanish by reacting against the intellectuals who promoted the development of "national" autonomous tongues, and consequently argued in favor of a continental cultural production within the established confines of the language. By claiming as an undisputed fact the idea that "cada pueblo se ha expresado con plenitud de carácter dentro de la comunidad imperial" (in the imperial context, each community has been able to express itself with fullness of character), Henríquez Ureña supported a limited literary autonomy for Spanish-American literature since, he maintained, "El compartido idioma no nos obliga a perdernos en la masa de un coro cuya dirección no está en nuestras manos: sólo nos obliga a acendrar nuestra nota expresiva" (Our shared language does not oblige us to lose ourselves in the mass of a choir whose direction is not in our own hands: it only obliges us to purify our own expressive note) (250–1). In fact, following the linguistically driven epistemological paradigm developed by philology as the basis of his argument, Henríquez Ureña contended that the Spanish-American literary "expression" was just one of the possible extensions of peninsular speech. His focus on the literary problem as a linguistic problem allowed Henríquez Ureña to claim that the future potential of Spanish-American literature – its "expressive originality" – resided in the idea of continuing and perfecting (not rupturing and questioning) the Spanish tradition.

Furthermore, his program for writing the history of Spanish-American literature as presented in another chapter of *Seis ensayos*, "Caminos de nuestra historia literaria" (Directions of our literary history), was profoundly mediated by the notion of language as a central component of the literary tradition throughout time: for Henríquez Ureña, "nuestra historia literaria . . . deberá escribirse como la historia de los renovados intentos de expresión y, sobre todo, de las expresiones realizadas" (our literary history must be written as a history of repeated attempts at expression and, above all, of fully realized expressions) (256). In this regard, even though Henríquez Ureña predicted that in the future "habrá pasado a estas orillas del Atlántico el eje espiritual del mundo español" (the spiritual axis of the Spanish world will have moved to these Atlantic shores), this eventual cultural displacement from the imperial center would never be seen by him as a irremediable fracture; instead, Henríquez Ureña imagined this repositioning as a simpler change of space within the limits of a linear and derivative master narrative that did not attempt to convey any sort of radical linguistic transformation. In his view, the future development of the Spanish-American literary tradition would occur in such a way that "Trocaremos en arca de tesoros la modesta caja donde ahora guardamos nuestras escasas joyas, y no tendremos por qué temer al sello ajeno del idioma en que escribimos" (We will turn the modest strongbox that contains our scarce riches into a treasure chest, and we will have no reason to fear the foreign stamp on the language in which we write) (253).

This language-centered perspective supposed the historical construction of a canon that not only originated in the arrival of the Spaniards to the continent, but also excluded the cultural production of subaltern groups. For Henríquez Ureña, the indigenous languages were unviable instruments of modern literary expression; following the principles of a long-established lettered perspective, Henríquez Ureña's definition of continental literature was limited to the works written by a learned elite for an educated public within a professionalized cultural field. In this sense, he claimed: "¿Volver a las lenguas indígenas? El hombre de letras, generalmente, las ignora, y la dura tarea de estudiarlas y escribir en ellas lo llevaría a la consecuencia final de ser entendido entre muy pocos, a la reducción inmediata de su público" (Return to the indigenous languages? The lettered man generally ignores them, and the arduous task of writing in and studying them would lead to the consequence of being understood by very few people, of immediately reducing the audience) (245). By limiting the symbolic manifestations of the continent to an integrative model whose center was the "idioma recibido de España" (language received from Spain) (245), Henríquez Ureña aligned himself with those who supported the political use of Spanish as a hegemonic instrument for neutralizing and regulating alternative discourses of cultural identity.

Díaz Quiñones has pointed out that, in the footsteps of Menéndez Pelayo, one of his most admired scholars, Henríquez Ureña's project of developing long continuities was meant to preserve a coherent meta-discourse that rejected a cultural heterogeneity whose origins dated back to colonial times (1994: 77). Perhaps the most striking example of the way in which Henríquez Ureña follows Menéndez Pelayo's version of

Hispanism is his highly favorable view of the cultural institutions of the imperial period, as well as his decisively Hispano-centric approach to the pre-revolutionary production as the foundational period for the continent's cultural history. This viewpoint is clear not only in the numerous essays Henríquez Ureña devoted to colonial authors throughout his scholarly career, but also in his book, *La cultura y las letras coloniales en Santo Domingo* (Culture and letters in colonial Santo Domingo) (1936), where he affirmed that the battles for independence "hicieron olvidar y desdeñar durante cien años la existencia colonial, proclamándose una ruptura que sólo tuvo lugar en la intención . . . Hubo empeño en romper con la cultura de tres siglos . . . pero acabamos destruyendo hasta la porción útil de nuestra herencia" (for one hundred years made us forget and disdain the colonial experience by proclaiming a rupture that took place in intention only . . . There was a determined effort to break with three hundred years of culture . . . but we ended up destroying even the useful elements of our heritage) (335).

Furthermore, like Menéndez Pelayo, Henríquez Ureña developed an elitist version of Hispanism according to which the Spanish-speaking *criollos* were responsible for preserving the "civilization" from the social and ethnic "others." In Menéndez Pelayo's view, when in 1822 Santo Domingo "cayó bajo la feroz dominación de los negros de Haiti que . . . intentaron borrar todas las huellas de su pasado, hasta el punto de prohibir el uso oficial de la lengua castellana" (fell under the ferocious domination of the negroes of Haiti, who were trying to erase all evidence of the past even to the point of prohibiting the official use of the Castilian language) (304), the civilization was saved because "un puñado de gentes de sangre española . . . luchando, primero, con elementos exóticos de lengua, después con elementos refractarios a toda raza y civilización europea . . . han resistido a todas las pruebas, han seguido hablando en castellano, han llegado a constituir un pueblo" (a bunch of people of Spanish blood . . . fighting first against exotic language elements, and then against elements refractory to all European race and civilization . . . resisted all pressures, continued to speak Castilian, and eventually were able to constitute themselves as a people) (312). Henríquez Ureña's interpretation of the events worked along similar principles. Maintaining an ethnocentric version of Hispanism, he wrote that as a consequence of the Haitian invasion:

Se cerró definitivamente la universidad; palacios y conventos, abandonados, quedaron pronto en ruinas . . . Todo hacía pensar que la civilización española había muerto en la isla preferida del Descubridor. Pero no. Aquel pueblo no había muerto. Entre los que quedaron sobrevivió el espíritu tenaz de la familia hispánica. Los dominicanos jamás se mezclaron con los invasores. La desmedrada sociedad de lengua castellana se reunía, apartada y silenciosa, en aquel *cautiverio babilónico*.

(The university was closed permanently; the abandoned palaces and convents ended up reduced to ruins . . . Everything indicated that the Spanish civilization had died in the Discoverer's [Columbus's] favorite island. But no – those people have not died. Among those who remained, the tenacious spirit of the Hispanic family survived. The Dominicans never mixed with the invaders. The declining Castilian-speaking society resisted together, isolated and silent, in that *Babylonic captivity*.] (368; original emphasis)

The series of references and metaphors used by Henríquez Ureña in these texts shows to what extent his initial Spanish-Americanism closely followed the ideological and methodological arguments repeatedly upheld by supporters of Hispanism. His understanding of the Spanish-speaking world as an ethnic and cultural "family," his strong defense of the unity of the language before challenging political, social, and cultural positions, and his consistently favorable interpretation of the role of the colonial lettered institutions demonstrate how Henríquez Ureña's early books on Spanish-American literature represent the culmination of cultural initiatives originally devoted to reaffirming the hegemonic place of Spain in the symbolic constructions of the continent. A central manifestation of his critical project, the initial articulation of Spanish-American literature as a field of study, can also be regarded as the result of the use of politically interested disciplinary approaches to Spanish. In this sense, Henríquez Ureña's production of the 1920s and 1930s makes him one of the most influential supporters of the neocolonial perspectives on continental literature that circulated since the turn of the century, and also places his foundational critical texts at the crossroads of the cultural politics of empire.

## Challenging Institutionalized Philology

This view of the field, however, did not remain uncontested for long. The institutionalization of a Hispano-centric perspective on language and literature was rapidly questioned by two intellectuals who would later become central figures in the reassessment of the relationship between knowledge and power in the continent. As early as 1928, the Peruvian writer José Carlos Mariátegui (1894–1930) articulated a systematic critique of the ideological assumptions and academic underpinnings of the philological paradigm in his *Siete ensayos de interpretación de la realidad peruana* (Seven interpretive essays on Peruvian reality) (1928). Lamenting the failure of the student revolts for university reform promoted since 1919, Mariátegui stated that in a country where the viceroyal aristocracy had disguised itself as a republican bourgeoisie in order to retain power after the emancipation, the university represented one of the most enduring "lazos de unión entre la República y la Colonia" (links between Republic and Colony) (1998: 120). Furthermore, he specifically claimed that the Faculty of Letters constituted a bastion of cultural conservatism in Peru, since most of its professors still followed strict Spanish "criterios y preceptos" (criteria and precepts) for linguistic and literary study (124).

Particularly aware of the deep influence of Menéndez Pelayo's vision of Hispanism in the work of some Spanish-American *letrados* – and above all in the texts of José de la Riva Agüero (1885–1944), the prestigious scholar who "idealized" and "glorified" the viceroyal period as the foundational moment of the nation and organized the local chapter of the Royal Spanish Academy (1998: 250) – Mariátegui questioned the "colonialismo supérstite" (surviving colonialism) implicit in their intellectual projects and called for radical cultural reform. In his attempt to confront the lettered authority of the philological paradigm, Mariátegui relied on the incendiary speeches of the Peruvian writer Manuel González Prada (1848–1918), who affirmed that "en materia de lenguaje el pueblo es un excelente maestro. Los idiomas se vigorizan y retemplan en la fuente popular, más que en las reglas muertas de los gramáticos y en las exhumaciones prehistóricas de los eruditos" (the populace is an excellent language teacher. Languages are invigorated and refreshed in the fount of popular speech, much more than in the dead rules of the grammarians and the prehistoric exhumations of the scholars) (229). Therefore, in order to undermine "el nexo oculto pero no ignoro que hay entre conservatismo ideológico y academicismo literario" (the hidden yet not unknown link between ideological conservatism and literary academicism) (230), and promote a postcolonial approach to language and literature, it was necessary to favor the works of those writers who wanted to make art by adopting "el lenguaje de la calle" (the language of the street) (242): "Los pocos literatos vitales, en esta palúdica y clorótica teoría de cansinos y chafardos retores, son" – Mariátegui wrote – "los que de algún modo tradujeron al pueblo" (The few writers with vitality in this feeble procession of weary dignitaries of rhetoric are the ones who somehow translated the language of the people) (218).

From a different point of view, more than ten years later the Argentine writer Jorge L. Borges (1899–1986) insisted on challenging yet again the ideological implications of the philological paradigm institutionalized at the university by Hispanism's supporters on both sides of the Atlantic. In "Las alarmas del doctor Américo Castro" (Dr. Américo Castro is alarmed) (1941), Borges showed how *La peculiaridad lingüística rioplatense y su sentido histórico*, the work which Castro had published as the result of his research activities in Buenos Aires, explicitly revealed the political underpinnings of a supposedly neutral scientific discourse. In his review, Borges claimed that the book's main thesis – the corruption of the Spanish language in the River Plate area – presupposed an argument with obvious colonial connotations, since Castro himself had indicated that the "grave alteración" (grave disorder) of the region's language – particularly as it appeared in tangos and *sainetes* – was the consequence of "las conocidas circunstancias que hicieron de los países platenses zonas hasta donde el latido del imperio hispano llegaba ya sin brío" (the well-known circumstances that made the River Plate an area where the heartbeat of the Spanish Empire had lost much of its vigor) (31). After pointing out that Castro's conclusions were derived from the application of one of philology's most questionable methods – that of employing literary sources to analyze common language usage – Borges criticized the disciplinary knowledge that had been consolidated in the Academy for the last several decades: "No adolescemos de dialectos, aunque sí de institutos dialectológicos. Esas corporaciones viven de reprobar las sucesivas jerigonzas que inventan" (We do not suffer from dialects, although we do indeed suffer from dialectological institutes. These organizations thrive on condemning every successive slang they invent) (32).

Thus, despite focusing on different contexts and having distinct political goals, both Mariátegui and Borges recognized the ideological consequences that the institutionalization of normative approaches to language and literature could have on alternative forms of symbolic representation. By demonstrating the strategic alliance between the practices of political and academic legitimation, they also took the first steps toward an analysis of the role of scholarly discourses in the construction of cultural identities in the continent. In this sense, challenging the hegemonic configuration of the field from different angles, Mariátegui and Borges set the basis for the critique of disciplinary epistemologies that would develop in the second half of the twentieth century.

## REFERENCES AND FURTHER READING

### References

Ardao, A., ed. (1980). *Génesis de la idea y el nombre de América Latina* [Origin of the idea and name of Latin America]. Caracas: Centro de Estudios Latinoamericanos Rómulo Gallegos.

Borges, J. L. (1989). "Las alarmas del doctor Américo Castro" [Dr. Américo Castro is alarmed]. In *Obras completas II*, pp. 31–5. Buenos Aires: Emecé.

Chevalier, M. (1980). "Sobre el progreso y porvenir de la civilización" [On the progress and future of civilization]. In A. Ardao (ed.), *Génesis de la idea y el nombre de América Latina*, pp. 153–67. Caracas: Centro de Estudios Latinoamericanos Rómulo Gallegos.

Darío, R. (1978). "A Colón" [To Columbus]. In *Poesías*, pp. 308–9. Caracas: Biblioteca Ayacucho.

— (1998). "El triunfo de Calibán" [The triumph of Caliban], *Revista Iberoamericana*, 64: 451–5.

Díaz Quiñones, A. (1994). "Pedro Henríquez Ureña: Modernidad, diáspora y construcción de identidades" [Pedro Henríquez Ureña: modernity, diaspora and construction of identities]. In G. Giménez and R. Pozas (eds), *Modernización e identidades sociales* [Modernization and social identities], pp. 59–117). Mexico: UNAM.

Henríquez Ureña, P. (1960). *Obra crítica* [Critical work]. Mexico City: Fondo de Cultura Económica.

Mariátegui, J. C. (1998). *Siete ensayos de interpretación de la realidad peruana* [Seven interpretive essays on Peruvian reality]. Mexico City: Era.

Martí, J. (1985). "Madre América" [Mother America]. In *Nuestra América* [Our America], pp. 19–26. Caracas: Biblioteca Ayacucho.

Menéndez Pelayo, M. (1911). *Historia de la poesía hispano-americana* [History of Spanish-American poetry]. Madrid: Victoriano Suárez.

Pike, F. (1971). *Hispanismo, 1898–1936* [Hispanism, 1898–1936]. Notre Dame, IN: University of Notre Dame Press.

Rama, C. (1982). *Historia de las relaciones culturales entre España y América Latina* [History of the cultural relations between Spain and Latin America]. Mexico City: Fondo de Cultura Económica.

### Further Reading

Balfour, S. (1997). *The End of the Spanish Empire, 1898–1923*. New York: Oxford University Press.

Berneker, W. L., ed. (1998). *1898: Su significado para Centroamérica y el Caribe* [1898: Its meaning for Central America and the Caribbean]. Madrid: Iberoamericana.

Beverley, J. (1983). "Can Hispanism be a radical practice?" *Ideologies and Literature*, 16: 9–22.

Conn, R. (2002). *The Politics of Philology: Alfonso Reyes and the Latin American Literary Tradition*. London: Associated University Presses.

Degiovanni, F. (2004). "The invention of the classics: nationalism and cultural politics in Argentina," *Journal of Latin American Cultural Studies*, 13: 243–60.

González Stephan, B. et al., eds (1995). *Esplendores y miserias del siglo XIX: Cultura y sociedad en América Latina* [Splendors and miseries of the nineteenth century: culture and society in Latin America]. Caracas: Monte Ávila.

Halperin Dongui, T. (1998). "España e Hispanoamérica: Miradas a través del Atlántico" [Spain and Spanish America: views across the Atlantic]. In *El Espejo de la historia* [The mirror of history], pp. 65–110. Buenos Aires: Sudamericana.

Ludmer, J., ed. (1994). *Las Culturas de fin de siglo en América Latina* [Fin-de-siècle cultures in Latin America]. Rosario: Beatriz Viterbo.

Montaldo, G. (1994). *La sensibilidad amenazada: fin de siglo y Modernismo* [The threatened sensibility: fin-de-siècle and Modernism]. Rosario: Beatriz Viterbo.

— (1999). *Ficciones culturales y fábulas de identidad en América Latina* [Cultural fictions and fables of identity in Latin America]. Rosario: Beatriz Viterbo.

Moraña, M., ed. (2005). *Ideologies of Hispanism*. Nashville, TN: Vanderbilt University Press.

Rama, Á. (1996). *The Lettered City*. Durham, NC: Duke University Press. (Original work published 1984.)

Ramos, J. (2001). *Divergent Modernities: Culture and Politics in Nineteenth Century Latin America*. Durham, NC: Duke University Press. (Original work published 1989.)

— (2001). "Hemispheric domains: 1898," *Journal of Latin American Cultural Studies*, 10: 237–51.

# 21

# Machado de Assis:
# The Meaning of Sardonic
*Todd S. Garth*

In 1881 Joaquim Maria Machado de Assis published what has become his most noto-rious and most studied work: *Memórias Póstumas de Brás Cubas* (*The Posthumous Memoirs of Bras Cubas*, 1997). Much of the attention devoted to this extraordinary novel is owing to its evidently modern character, well in advance of literary modernism. *Bras Cubas*'s qualification as modern is based on those five or six aspects that indeed resonate clearly with modernist innovations. The first of these is Machado's invention of his characteristic first-person "unreliable narrator," an essentially modern device in its refusal to tell a story or to serve as vehicle of a representation. Bras Cubas's narration, incomplete, inconsistent, and unsustainable, makes claims to a philosophical world-view and a systematic basis for his acts and ideas, but ends up being evidence of the exact opposite – a voice with no grounding in ethics or objectivity.

The nonlinear style of this narration, its inherent incoherence, constitute another quality viewed as modern. And while critics acknowledge the source of this frag-mented discourse in such explicit precedents as Sterne's *Tristram Shandy* and Cer-vantes's *Don Quixote*, the heteroglossia implied in these appropriations of Western classics is seen as further evidence of Machado's modernism. These same observations also note Machado's reliance on specifically Brazilian antecedents such as the great romantic novelist José de Alencar or the author of high satire, Manuel Antonio Almeida (Schwarz, 1977: xiii).

The parody and skepticism integral to this style and voice are also regarded as evidence of a writer of modernity. While these are not strictly modern phenomena, the unrestrained, relentless nature of Machado's parody can be seen as approaching the nihilism so pertinent to the modernist impulse. Similarly, Machado's focus on psychology, particularly on the psychology of his narrators in his most ambitious works – *Dom Casmurro* (1899), *Quincas Borba* (1891), and others as well as *Bras Cubas* – leads critics to view him as modern. John Gledson points out that this focus is not ingenuous. Machado was well versed in the ideas of Schopenhauer, an important precursor to Freud (Schwarz, 1977: xxix).

Jorge Bracamonte (2004) points out that *Bras Cubas* responds to the conditions of modernity by being a consummately readerly text. As a consequence of the narrator's fragmented unreliability, a reader – an Iseresque, theoretical reader – must continue the production of a text that Machado has set in motion. This is characteristic, in varying degrees, of all of Machado's later novels. *Dom Casmurro* implies a reader who must weigh whether or not the narrator's wife is guilty of adultery. *Counselor Ayres' Memorial* (1906) evokes a reader who might regard Tristão, the young "hero," as devious and self-centered rather than gallant.

Perhaps the most obvious innovation of *Bras Cubas*, however, is not its style but its opening premise: that the story was conceived, written, and transmitted to its readers by a dead man. This conceit is also not strictly limited to *Bras Cubas*. Both *Ayres' Memorial* and its twin, *Esau and Jacob* (1904), derive from the writings of a dead man who, although living when he "wrote" these accounts, figures as a character in both novels in such a way as to make him seem like a narrator telling his story from the grave. *Esau and Jacob* especially confounds the principles of narration: Ayres is sometimes an omniscient narrator recounting his tale as if from the beyond, sometimes an opaque character that the narrator fails to fathom, and sometimes a strangely pre-scient voice combining both opacity and omniscience.

The critical appreciation of these apparently modern qualities in a mainly nine-teenth-century author was sparked primarily by the watershed commentary of Roberto Schwarz. Schwarz's *A Master on the Periphery of Capitalism* (1990), translated in 2001, focuses on the "displaced ideas" characteristic of nineteenth-century Brazilian hege-mony which espoused the principles of capitalism and the ideals of the Enlightenment while maintaining a brutal and backward slave society. Machado's genius, according to Schwarz, lies in two innovations. The first of these is the exploitation of the entire Western intellectual and aesthetic tradition in order to reveal its misapplication to Brazilian life. The second is the creation of a voice that reveals this phenomenon of displacement *from within*. The narrators of Machado's later works are scions of the patrician class whose words reflect the fatal weaknesses of their worldview. Bras Cubas is the consummate egotistical prattler, betraying no awareness of his inconsistencies or prejudices.

Roberto Schwarz also reveals that a principal effect of Machado's strategy is to make visible Brazil's vast class of "dependents," citizens who, while nominally free agents in a supposedly modernizing economy, relied for their survival on the caprice of the quasi-medieval landholding elite. It is the displaced discourse of modernity in an unmodern society, argues Schwarz, which is responsible for the invisibility of an immense portion of the nation's populace.

A consequence of Schwarz's work is an enduring debate in Machado studies, one that has taken on a life of its own. Many Machado scholars today fall into one of two groups. In the first group are those who regard Machado's novels as essentially mod-ernist works whose entirely satirical meaning can be discerned with a proper calibra-tion of signifiers to context. In the second group are those who offer the postmodern argument that Machado's texts refuse any stable meaning, its signifiers persistently dead-ending in ambiguity and subjectivity. There are problems with both perspectives.

The postmodern perspective, while provoking fruitful examinations of Machado's prose, implies intentions that are impossibly anachronistic. Even José Raimundo Maia Neto's analysis (1994), placing Machado in an ancient and unbroken tradition of skeptic philosophers, updates the parameters of skepticism to conform to this post-modern reliance on indeterminacy. Machado de Assis was a self-educated mulatto living in a nineteenth-century slave society, a product of the very dependent class so central to his writing. It is most unlikely that such a man would overcome the obstacles to writing and publishing marketable works for the sole purpose of erasing his own identity and replacing it with a perpetual indeterminacy. Literary history shows us that people in such conditions write for a reason and wish their meaning to be discerned, however tardily or indirectly, even when their identities remain in shadow.[1]

The modernist perspective, while less problematic overall, sometimes stumbles against an essential flaw. Critics such as Schwarz, John Gledson (1984), and Paul Dixon (1989), in their provocative analyses, emphasize Machado's satirical, sometimes cynical, response to his contemporary conditions. But these critics regard Machado's poetics as a wholesale parody and an uncompromising break from literary, intellectual, and social tradition. Such criticism interprets the codes in Machado de Assis's writings as *unambiguously* sardonic. Machado's playful fragmentation, his burlesque of popular tastes and beliefs, his inventiveness, his orientation in favor of negativity, defeat, and nothingness, all tend – according to the modernist perspective – toward an avant-garde nihilism. Even at his most concrete and productive, Machado still *negates* reigning values and *defies* tradition.

But Machado de Assis is not T. S. Eliot. While Machado himself acknowledged the shift between his two "phases" of writing, he never repudiated the more conventional works he wrote prior to 1880. Upon republishing *Helena* (1878), often regarded as the most retrograde of his novels, he made a point, in the author's preface, to uphold its value (1984: 3). More importantly, in order to extract consistently negativistic meaning from Machado's texts, critics of the modernist perspective attribute to him ideologies that are not entirely sustainable. The most noteworthy of these are atheism and feminism.

Machado's novels are replete with biblical references and often portray clergy or represent religious rituals and institutions. The conclusion drawn by contemporary critics is that these references are either in keeping with Machado's apodictic skepticism, and thus part of a refusal of any belief system, or else constitute a modernist parody – thus a pointed rejection – of Christianity. Neither of these implications is supported by Machado's biography or by a close reading of his novels.

Two novels in which Christian symbols, rituals, and characters figure most prominently are, from Machado's early stage, *Helena*, and from his mature stage, *Esau and Jacob*. Neither novel constitutes a rejection of Christianity per se. *Helena* is the story of an adolescent girl of uncertain origin who is recognized as the natural daughter of a wealthy landowner, Counselor Valle, in his will. Obeying the stipulation of the will, Helena becomes a member of the Valle family, but just as she gains their full acceptance, both her integrity and motives are thrown into doubt. It turns out that she is not the deceased Counselor's real daughter, though his parental affection for her was genuine enough, as was his desire to legitimize her status. Her real father, alive and destitute, has sworn her to accept the legacy in order to insure her security. Helena, as a consequence, is in an impossible bind. She cannot reveal the truth without dishonoring her real father, but she must abandon him in order to fulfill the requirements of her benefactor's will. The novel's plot is complicated by the unlikely twist that she and her supposed half-brother, Estácio, have fallen in love. She, along with the entire family, exhorts Estácio to marry Eugênia, the daughter of a family friend – a connection of social and financial benefit to both families, but a marriage essentially repugnant to Estácio, who sees Eugênia as a frivolous and self-centered product of her father's indulgences. By the time the web is unraveled, Helena lies dying, her heart broken by the loss of her father, the shame of her revelation, and the impossibility of realizing romantic love. This is, on numerous levels, a story of betrayal – principally the betrayal by fathers of their children, especially their daughters.

*Helena* contains salient biblical markers. The two most obvious are the reference to *"Cantagallo"* (loosely, "Cockcrow"), the name of a distant plantation to which Estácio, his fiancée Eugênia, and her family must suddenly repair at a crucial juncture in the plot. The other is the peculiarity that Dr. Camargo, Eugênia's father, who has manipulated Helena, Eugênia, and Estácio so as to ensure the engagement, kisses his daughter three times during the story, the third time in the novel's closing line. Both of these markers are unequivocal references to the betrayal of Christ.

Similarly to all of Machado's novels, the theme of betrayal in *Helena* can be read on multiple levels – the betrayal of a nation by its politicians, of the faithful by their clergy, of the dependent classes by their patrons and protectors. Part of Machado's genius lies in this integral approach to themes and their symbols: stories of politics and faith are simultaneously stories of love. Also characteristic of Machado is the fact that the biblical references in *Helena* do not signal an unmediated allegory. These symbols do not make for a consistent, one-to-one interpretation, but are slippery or hanging symbols that can provoke doubt as to how they are to be read. The betrayal of Eugênia by her father, for example, is not a simple recycling of Judas's betrayal of Christ, but a signal that Machado is portraying a new kind of betrayal, one specific to his time and place yet no less profound. Eugênia is a girl raised by her father to marry, to be utterly dependent on a husband, which itself would not be unnatural or unattractive in a child of Brazil's patrician class. But she is also raised primarily as a function of her father's ego:

> He contemplated her with the same pride as a goldsmith feels when he admires a jewel in its setting as it goes from beneath his hands. It was an egoist's tenderness: he loved himself in his own handiwork. Capricious, obstinate, and superficial, Eugênia never had the good fortune of seeing her defects corrected; rather, it was her upbringing that gave them to her. (95)

An analogous betrayal is true of the title character. Helena is, on the one hand, the quintessential sacrificial lamb – the innocent who is given the role of expiating the sins of Counselor Valle, her protector, and who dies fulfilling this impossible task. On the other hand, she is a new kind of sacrificial lamb specific to nineteenth-century Brazil. Helena is white, has received a privileged education, and possesses the skills and knowledge needed to make her acceptable to Brazilian ownership society. In short, Helena mirrors the feminine ideal of the nineteenth-century Brazilian patrician class, but she has no means of her own and no opportunity to acquire those means. A representative of the dependent class, she is entirely at the disposal of the same people who have shaped her character and her talents; she exists mainly to confirm their values. Having served that purpose, and being unavailable to perpetuate the patrician ideal through marriage, there is no exit for her save death.

As Sidney Chaloub points out (1999), Helena is also not the pure innocent. Throughout the novel, she attempts to protect herself and her honor by dissembling; but she also attempts to find meager opportunities for self-expression and growth by manipulation. Rather than asking her brother to accompany her horseback riding, for example, Helena feigns ignorance of the sport and persuades Estácio to teach her. Only once she has him irrevocably committed does she demonstrate her considerable riding skills. Her ploy a success, Helena airily asserts that she could not otherwise have been confident of Estácio's willing compliance. Chaloub cites this passage as evidence of Helena's wiliness and Estácio's ingenuousness. In fact, Helena has an ulterior motive, a *"causa secreta."* Her first horseback ride later appears to have been an exploratory mission to locate her true father's house, a mission she successfully covers with her playful distraction. Even in this conclusion Machado de Assis is not explicit, but instead allows for it as a logical interpretation. As Chaloub notes, such manipulation, often vague and self-contradictory, is characteristic of Machado's dependent characters, male and female alike. Even the angelic Helena is forced, because of the circumstances imposed on her, to resort to deceptions that are ultimately self-destructive. Significantly, those imposed circumstances are the consequence of an authoritative text – in Helena's case, a will – penned by a thoughtless and self-indulgent dead, white male.

In *Helena*, Machado de Assis gives us an inversion of Christian self-sacrifice. Instead of the crucifixion serving as a model of self-abnegation for the betterment of society, Christian symbols point to the heartless, abject sacrifice of an innocent as the result of patrician self-love (Nunes, 1983: 192). The fact that the most obvious symbols of the betrayal of Christ remain unresolved and incompletely allegorical suggests a critical – but hardly indeterminate – stance on Machado's part regarding Christianity. He seeks resolution for these detached and unresolved symbols in a new application of Christian liturgy – an application relevant to Brazilian political and social reality. In Machado de Assis's sardonic treatment of Christianity there is a search for new meaning.

It is significant, as critics have pointed out, that *Helena* is set in 1871, the year of Brazil's "Law of the Free Womb," in which all slaves born henceforth were to be free on their twenty-first birthday. Casual references to slaves working in the Valle household are abundant in the novel, and one particular slave, Helena's favorite, whose freedom she has already requested of her new brother, plays a key role in the plot. Vicente informs on his mistress regarding her secret liaisons. He does not speak up under duress; the Valle family priest, Father Melchior, in an understated turn of Christian forthrightness, rejects the option of questioning the slave (161). Vicente lies out of loyalty to Helena, hoping to save her reputation but unwittingly worsening her conundrum and forcing her to confess the truth. By filtering this episode through Father Melchior's intervention, Machado makes the problem of inquisition, informing, and confession a study of Christian honesty and "purity" (162). By making the agent of Helena's undoing a loyal slave and setting his novel in 1871, Machado de Assis indicates the centrality of slavery, slaves, and dependent classes in the question over how Christian ethics and morals are to be exercised in the interest of Brazil's future, and how Christian symbols are to be interpreted.

This search for new, relevant meaning extends to the most fundamental of Christian concepts, the resurrection and the celebration of Christ's apotheosis simultaneous with the mourning of his sacrifice. It is a virtual constant in Machado de Assis's novels, starting with *Helena*, that the trouble is caused by a dead man. Counselor Valle's decision to recognize Helena in his will and to require her to join the family is criticized by various characters, including Helena herself. But it is Helena's birth father, significantly named Salvador, who is most explicit about the evils of fatherly egotism and its link with the powers of the dead. Salvador blames Helena's crisis on his decision to "come back to life and lay claim to a title that I had stripped myself of" (181). By the time Salvador tries to reverse course and "sacrifice himself" for his daughter's future, Helena's filial piety has made resolution impossible. The cynical, unreflective, and unchristian iteration of this fatherly egotism is personified in Camargo, described as a "nonbeliever" (9). Camargo sacrifices his daughter Eugênia, the object of his worship, to an engagement doomed never to realize itself in marriage.

From a feminist perspective, all of Machado de Assis's women suffer a similar sacrifice. Women in nineteenth-century Brazil indeed could be regarded as constituting their own dependent class, for they had no legal standing and virtually no social or economic opportunities outside of marriage. Marcia Cavendish Wanderley (1996) compares Machado's female characters with their English contemporaries, such as Jane Eyre, and finds that while English heroines of the era manage to achieve a degree of self-realization and empowerment, their Machadian counterparts fail to do so. English economic and social structure did allow for some slender means of independence, as women could, if necessary, operate as free economic agents. Brazilian women had no such options. The unlovely Jane Eyre could assert her independence, albeit at immense cost, while the angelic Helena has no alternative to her dependence on the Valle family.[2] Maria Manuel Lisboa, in *Machado de Assis and Feminism*, takes these observations further, asserting that women in Machado de Assis's novels are uniformly condemned to entombment, either literal or figurative, and that marriage for Machado always equals death.

Machado de Assis would not recognize such extreme assessments of the condition of women, despite his obvious concern for the consequences of their unmitigated dependent status. Happy marriages are not absent from his works, nor is every marriage he portrays based on the manipulation and deception that his female protagonists so often turn to as the only means to accomplish their goals. In *Counselor Ayres's Memorial*, Dona Carmo de Aguiar, although childless, is the contented wife of a considerate husband. What Lisboa observes as frivolous and wasted pastimes equivalent to a living death (1996: 174–6) are, in fact, presented by Machado as charitable and productive activity. Ayres's sister, Rita, far from being buried alive in her widowhood, is the counterpoint to the young widow Fidélia, who is about to sacrifice herself to a questionable marriage. Rita is a practical, energetic, and extroverted woman who, in *Esau and Jacob*, serves as the one genuine refuge for an ailing heroine, the helpless Flora (213). Even the ruthless Dona Cláudia, who in *Esau and Jacob* goads her husband into a feckless political career, and Dona Cesária, inveterate gossip of the *Memorial*, are presented as clever women (appropriately named after Roman emperors), capable of using the resources at their disposal.[3]

What Machado disparages is their *objectives* in deploying their abilities. Cláudia's adeptness at argument and persuasion is directed entirely at gratifying her yearning for status and deference enjoyed by a governor's wife. Cesária's talents for communication – her sharp eye and shrewd tongue – are a source of personal power rather than a means of empowering others. And in both *Helena* and *Esau and Jacob*, the heroine is at fault for her misdirected and aborted use of two well-honed feminine skills: letter-writing and drawing. Helena's skillful drawing of the idyllic country lane where she and Estácio first rode together emerges as the indicator of her prevarication: it depicts her biological father's house, the scene of her furtive visits. In *Esau and Jacob*, Flora's drawing of the twin suitors she is obsessed with merely serves to reveal and inflame her confusion; her letters, including those "written to her heart," serve to exacerbate that confusion (158, 203, 213, 215–16). In a greater sense, Machado de Assis's living women are guilty of the same misapplication of letters, as are his deceased men. Like Elena's late benefactor, Counselor Valle, their words and arts, though well intentioned, wreak havoc.

Counselor Valle himself is to become a kind of archetype for Machado de Assis. For in all of his novels from this point onward, with the exception, arguably, of *Dom Casmurro*, either the book itself, as stipulated by the authorial voice, or the crisis the book relates is the product of a dead man. And in the cases where the plot, rather than the book, is authored by the deceased, the crisis is set in motion by means of a document written by the deceased. These "defunct authors," as Brás Cubas calls himself, are, moreover, consistent in their lack of conviction, commitment, moral perspective, or any kind of foundation on which to base their actions. They are also womanizers. Counselor Valle, for example, is described thus: "Occasionally he did have political opinions of a sort, gathered on the frontiers of liberalism and conservatism at the exact point where the two dominions merge. But, if no partisan regret cast a last spade of earth on him, there was many a matron who saw interred with him the best page of her youth" (*Helena*, 6).

This description of a man lacking in any real grounding except of money, convention, and self-indulgence finds its most exaggerated expression in Brás Cubas, who is author, narrator, and prime mover of the tale he tells. But Machado's most artful and subtle rendering of this ungrounded voice is his last: Counselor Ayres, the sometimes narrator, sometimes character of *Esau and Jacob*, and the supposed author of *Counselor Ayres' Memorial*. The appropriately named Ayres not only exemplifies Machado's transparent, ungrounded, and uncommitted writer, but also incarnates the fundamental irony of Machado's poetics: the man specifically charged with establishing a meaningful and constructive legacy, the man with the best resources to do so, by virtue of talent, position, and profession, is the same man who endeavors most energetically to empty his texts of meaning. This is most obviously and emphatically the case of Brás Cubas, whose entire discourse aims to avoid assuming or communicating responsibility for a life that can only be regarded as wasted. It is exaggeratedly true of Quincas Borba and his vacuous philosophy of "*humanitismo.*" But it is also true of *Helena*'s Valle, who, as the prerogative of his class allows, in his last will and testament gives no excuses for his conduct or explanation for his directive other than his desire that it should be so.

In the case of Ayres, we find a man not only incapable and unwilling to affect history and avert disaster, but also willfully ignorant of his capacity to do so. Both Ayres and Valles bear the nomenclature "Counselor" ironically. It is an honorific title conferred by the largess of a monarch, the badge of a dying era, and of an irrelevant regime. In *Esau and Jacob*, Ayres is the first to insist on the title's lack of meaning (118), denying counsel to the desperate heroine Flora, who eventually will die from the crisis brought on by unresolved affections and allegiances. *Counselor Ayres' Memorial*, on one level, consists entirely of the narrator's refusal to assume the role his title implies. While spinning out the tale of his own retirement and final years, persisting in narrating his own life and identity, Ayres aggressively denies any meaning to that life and its account. The elegiac aspects of this narrative are glaringly obvious, as Ayres blithely contorts one poetic elegiac convention after another in his memoir. Ayres empties his elegy of any meaning or reason. The consequences, at the end of the novel, are the unexpected betrayal of his dearest friends by their new son-in-law; a betrayal Ayres has actually abetted by means of his talent for communicating nothing (see Garth, 1995).

In *Esau and Jacob*, the consequences of Ayres's demurral are broader. The fairly simple tale in *Esau and Jacob* has long been recognized as an allegory. Pedro and Paulo, identical twin sons of wealth and privilege, have fought "*ab ovo,*" or since the womb, disagreeing at every possible opportunity, and seizing politics as their main source of discord. The principal casualty of their feud is Flora, who, unable to decide between the twins and failing to elicit a marriage proposal from either, dies delirious, imagining the twins' presence and merging their two identities into one. Like *Helena*, *Esau and Jacob* is set at a critical moment in Brazilian history: the fall of the monarchy and the declaration of a republic in 1889, followed by the coup of 1893 in which Brazil's first military government imposes itself. Since the novel, on one level, serves as an allegory for these political crises, Ayres's abnegation of his role as counselor, his refusal to either take sides or enforce a meaningful conciliation between the feuding twins, Pedro and Paulo, also represent a failure of the empowered classes even to attempt an engagement between liberal and conservative, republican and royalist sentiments in Brazil.

As with *Helena*, it is not accurate to assert that the biblical references in *Esau and Jacob* are the direct application of religious symbols and tales to contemporary events, demanding a one-for-one interpretation. The biblical Esau and Jacob, after all, are not indistinguishable equals as they are in this novel. Unlike Machado's characters, their conflict results in the triumph of one over the other and the concomitant shame, neither of which applies in this case. The biblical question of birthright, however, and the concept that the children of authority and power are to be held responsible for the consequences of their actions, has immediate resonance with the novel. Like *Helena*, *Esau and Jacob* begs a readjustment or reapplication of Christian symbols – and Christian ethics – so as to be useful and relevant to a Brazil in crisis.

It is not just Christian symbolism that Machado de Assis wishes to invest with new, relevant meaning, and it is not just these novels in which he issues his call for reinvented discourse. As Schwarz argues, all of Western thought is implicated as a discourse of "misplaced ideas." Machado was extraordinarily well-read, both in the classics and in European philosophy and letters regarded as modern thought. Dante, Shakespeare, Pascal, and scores of others are presented as formative of the ideas and perspectives of his equivocating and unreliable narrators, most notably Ayres. But as with biblical references, Machado, rather than elaborating a pure parody that empties these discourses of all meaning, gives us narrators and characters who respond to crises with empty platitudes and misplaced ideologies in such a way as to entreat a recon-sideration and a reevaluation of meaning.

This explains the "readerly" quality of the *Memorias Póstumas*. Machado's call for a reader response can be applied both to readers inferred from the text and those deduced from historical evidence. Rather than simply throwing open the windows of interpre-tation in a way characteristic of twentieth-century avant-garde artists, Machado's requirement that the reader complete his works is a strategy that responds directly to a historical and political – and not strictly aesthetic – crisis. And while the *Memorias Póstumas* is the most radical and openly transgressive of these novels, it is not unique nor does it fit into a pattern of steadily increasing radicalization. Machado's "first-phase" novels such as *Helena* – those prior to 1880 – do not, as Texiera argues, accept the fundamental ideologies of Brazilian hegemony (44–5); nor do his second-phase novels reject *all* ideology on which that society rested. To varying degrees, all of Machado's novels and short stories participate in a fundamental strategy of seeking a new relevance for traditional discourses.

## NOTES

1  In both African American and Afro-Brazilian literary studies, this assumption is so commonplace as to be largely taken for granted. For an explicit reference, see Werner (1990: 203–5).

2  A more parallel comparison would be with the heroines of Trollope, Hardy, or George Eliot, who are virtually imprisoned by their dependence on fathers, husbands, and uncles; even Emily Trevelyan, Tess Darbyfield, and Mary Garth, however, can at points turn to the support of sympathetic families or communities who recognize their need to be heard or acknowledge their identity as individuals.

3  Lisboa elsewhere (1997: 171–2) supports the observations made here: those of Machado's women who suffer displacement and death at the hands of men – and many do – are most accurately seen as martyrs to the cruel hypocrisy of Brazilian positivism.

## REFERENCES AND FURTHER READING

Bracamonte, Jorge (2004). "Machado de Assis: O cuando los lectores reinventan lo literario en América Latina." In Daniel Balderston (ed.), *Literatura y otras artes en América Latina*, pp. 267–75. Iowa City: University of Iowa Press.

Chaloub, Sidney (1999). "Dependents play chess: political dialogues in Machado de Assis." In Richard Grinham (ed.), *Machado de Assis: Reflections on a Brazilian Master Writer*, pp. 51–84. Austin: University of Texas Press.

Dixon, Paul (1989). *Retired Dreams: "Dom Casmurro," Myth and Modernity*. West Lafayette, IN: Purdue University Press.

Garth, Todd S. (1995). "The authority of the elegiac in Machado de Assis' *Counselor Ayres' Memorial*," *Cincinnati Romance Review*, 14: 138–43.

Gledson, John (1984). *The Deceptive Realism of Machado de Assis: A Dissenting Interpretation of "Dom Casmurro."* Liverpool: Francis Cairns.

Lisboa, Maria Manuel (1996). *Machado de Assis and Feminism: Rereading the Heart of the Companion*. Lewiston, NY: Edwin Mellen Press.

— (1997). "Machado de Assis and the beloved reader: squatters in the text." In Nicholas White and Naomi Segal (eds), *Scarlet Letters: Fictions of Adultery from Antiquity to the 1990s*, pp. 160–73. New York: St. Martin's Press.

Machado de Assis, Joaquim Maria (1972). *Counselor Ayres' Memorial*. Trans. Helen Caldwell. Berkeley: University of California Press.

— (1984). *Helena*. Trans. Helen Caldwell. Berkeley: University of California Press.

— (1997). *The Posthumous Memoirs of Bras Cubas*. Trans. Gregory Rabassa. Oxford: Oxford University Press.

— (1998). *Quincas Borba*. Trans. Gregory Rabassa. Oxford: Oxford University Press.

— (2000). *Esau and Jacob*. Trans. Elizabeth Lowe. Oxford: Oxford University Press.

Maia Neto, José Raimundo (1994). *Machado de Assis, the Brazilian Pyrrhonian*. West Lafayette, IN: Purdue University Press.

Nunes, Maria Luisa (1983). "An artist's identity versus the social role of the writer: the case for Joaquim Maria Machado de Assis," *College Language Association Journal*, 27(2): 187–96.

Schwarz, Roberto (1977). *Ao Vencedor as batatas: Forma literária e processo social nos inícios do romance brasileiro*. São Paulo: Duas Cidades.

— (2001). *A Master on the Periphery of Capitalism*. Trans. John Gledson. Durham: University of North Carolina Press.

Texeira, Ivan (1987). *Apresentação de Machado de Assis*. São Paulo: Livraria Martins Fontes Editora.

Wanderley, Márcia Cavendish (1996). *A Voz embargada: Imagen da mulher en romances ingleses y brasileiros do século XIX*. São Paulo: Editorial da Universidade de São Paulo.

Werner, Craig (1990). "On the ends of Afro-American 'Modernist' autobiography," *Black-American Literature Forum*, 24(2): 203–20.

## 22

# The Mexican Revolution and the Plastic Arts

*Horacio Legras*

### Introduction

The Mexican Revolution created modern Mexico. It created a society like none other in Latin America. It was a country shaped by constant negotiations between different actors in a process that involved, directly or indirectly, almost every strata of Mexican society instead of, as was so common in Latin America, the opinions and desires of a restricted circle of power holders. This deliberative process happened against the background of frantic historical transformations. In the realm of ideas, nothing had as wide an impact as the new cultural nationalism which helped cement the new post-revolutionary state. The muralist movement was an integral part of this cultural nationalism and perhaps its most successful achievement in the early years of revolutionary consolidation.[1]

Muralism was a result of a state initiative. In 1921, José Vasconcelos, minister of education of Alvaro Obregón, summoned the muralist to create a national art able to reflect the meaning and extent of the revolutionary changes. A national art is, by definition, one that strives to represent the people, because only the people (not as separate individuals or as an aggregate of heterogeneous groups, but as a single, sovereign will) is the subject of a nationalist discourse. The revolution had revealed massive movements, unsuspected agencies, but not a "people" properly speaking. Instead of portraying an already existing sense of peoplehood, the muralist had to search for it and, to certain extent, invent it.[2] Which of the representations of the popular available in society and sedimented in historical memory could function as the basis for this act of imagination? And moreover, on what grounds could such a choice be both legitimate and meaningful? Muralists were not the only artists or intellectuals to confront this problem. But they were the first ones able to solve it at a time when traditional forms of re-presentation in Mexico had broken down. This goal was accomplished, essentially, in the second and third decade of the twentieth century, and I restrict my analysis of the movement to that period.

## 1910–20: Origins

The idea of creating a muralist movement in Mexico goes back to the final years of Porfirio Díaz's government. In 1910, as Mexico approached the celebration of its one hundred years of independence, Gerardo Murillo, who had changed his name to Dr Atl (for water in Nahuatl), convinced the government to grant access to the walls of the Escuela Nacional Preparatoria to a group of enthusiastic painters. Atl's idea of revitalizing mural painting was in line with an increasing appreciation of Mexico's pre-Columbian cultures. The excavation of Nahua ruins was already a key element in the process of nation-building at the end of the nineteenth century. Pre- and post-Columbian Mesoamerican codices began to be revered as true works of art; and although Mexican intellectuals knew a good deal about them through the writings of priests such as Bernardino de Sahagún or Diego de Landa, they were now able for the first time to look at the original scrolls (or their reproductions) and marvel at their fine mixture of art and cultural information. Compounded with the "nationalization" of this heritage, we find a new fervor for popular productions. Muralism breathed in this atmosphere of a revalorization of popular creation and ingenuity. Breaking with a centuries-long tradition of despising popular art, the three "greats" of Mexican muralism claimed to be indebted to figures such as José Guadalupe Posada, an engraver who sustained himself by illustrating various leaflets famous for depicting current affairs in engravings in which the different protagonists of the moment were portrayed as skulls and skeletons. As the muralists further elaborated the theoretical and ideological bases of their project, their resemblance to Posada grew. Posada was as much an artist as he was a craftsman. He always took a political stance of clear opposition to the abuses of Díaz dictatorship and identified with the struggles of the Mexican people. Finally, he was able to produce a truly popular art that was also connected to persistent motifs in the history of Mexican cultural expression.

While Atl's ideological motives were rather vague (he ended his life supporting Mussolini in fascist Italy), his aesthetic teachings had an important influence upon a younger generation of Mexican painters. In his autobiography, Orozco recalls how Atl organized a series of night workshops in which he questioned "the colonial status" in which the Mexican painter has been held so far. For Atl, "[t]he Mexican had been a poor colonial servant, incapable of creating or thinking for himself" (*Jose Clemente Orozco*, 19) Atl's characterization of Mexican painting as colonized expression is pertinent in a number of ways. No aesthetic medium was subjected to as a ferocious colonial policing as the figurative arts. Such repression did not end with the installation of the republic. One example is the persistence of the idea of the "copy" in Mexican culture, to the point that when Manuel Gamio writes *Forjando patria* in 1916, he included the concept of the copy as a subdivision of art (under the rubric "Art work of *reaparición*") and he adds that this subdivision includes all the copies "made in our times of foreign masters" (20, my translation). Meanwhile, for Atl and his followers the confrontation with a culture of the copy implied above all an existential transformation of the artist. After the revolution, this project of a Mexicanization of art increasingly took on the additional dimension of reaching out to the popular and destitute portions of the Mexican people.

Despite his foundational role in the history of Muralism, Atl could not maintain his influence on Mexican painters for much longer. When Rivera and Siqueiros returned to Mexico, they quickly overshadow Atl's influence upon the rest of the Mexican painters.

## Bad Beginnings

In 1921, when first summoned to work for the revolutionary government at the Escuela Nacional Preparatoria (the same place where the muralist movement started ten years before) José Clemente Orozco was 36 years old; Diego Rivera was 34; Siqueiros was 24. Of the three great artists, only Diego Rivera was already a recognized figure. The other artists enrolled to work in the Preparatoria included Jean Charlot, Fernando Leal, Fermín Revueltas, Xavier Guerrero, and Amado de la Cueva. Some of them were experienced painters, like the French Jean Charlot; others were surprisingly young, like the 18-year-old Fermín Revueltas. Despite differences they all were possessed by a desire to break with the past. Speaking in 1947 at the Palace of Fine Arts in Mexico City, Siqueiros referred to pre-muralist artists as vulgar imitators of things European. These artists, possessed of a "typical colonial" mentality, only "had eyes for the art of Europe and particularly for the art of Paris. There was no sign of rebellion against the artistic capital, not even the faintest desire for the right to participate in the international cultural movement on a national basis." (Siqueiros, 1975: 11). Muralists were supposed to reverse that tide. However, in their first works at the Preparatoria, they discovered that there was an appreciable distance between convictions and practices and that sometimes their hands might have ideas of their own.

Almost the totality of these paintings were later destroyed or painted over with other murals. From the sketches, photographs, and reproductions available today, one can see that almost all of them testify to a dismaying conservatism. Antonio Rodríguez, one of the great historians of Mexican Muralism, writes:

> One cannot help wondering why painters who started the revolutionary movement in the Escuela Preparatoria, a school which was pre-eminently secular, should paint Virgins, religious festivals, theological virtues, Landings of the cross, proletarian women with wings, etc. The contradiction becomes even more obvious when we observe that, next to the woman with wings, Siqueiros painted an enormous sickle and hammer. (1969: 182).

For Rodríguez, Siqueiros is a case in point, because he was, among all artists, the one "with the greatest revolutionary experience and the greatest theoretical knowledge of socialist doctrine." However, Rodríguez concludes, he "was possessed by a kind of inertia" (186).

At the Preparatoria, Siqueiros painted a mural titled *The Elements*, a painting depicting a winged angel figure that for Rivera evoked the work "of a somewhat Syrio-Lebanese Michelangelo." (Rochfort, 1993: 35). As for Orozco, when he was finally called to work at the Preparatoria he produced a mural of which only the panel called *Maternity* remains. The section – spared by time and the axe that Orozco took up against his own work – shows an unmistakable Renaissance influence: Virgins, children, angels – and although Orozco insisted that the virgin was in fact a mundane mother, little of the everyday world emerges in the representation. As for Rivera, he painted the only mural that is fully conserved from that first period, *Creation*, an important composition painted on the walls of the Anfiteatro Bolívar. The mural covers a surface of 110 square meters. As always with murals, Rivera had to accommodate his design to the architectural possibilities and limitations of the building on which they were painted. The mural portrays two naked human figures, one male, one female, that stand for the native Mexican race. Over them hover allegorical figures of the arts and sciences such as Dance, Music, Song, Wisdom, Knowledge, Fable, Tradition, Tragedy, and Justice. While the subject and treatment of *Creation* were obviously in line with the aesthetic preferences of José Vasconcelos (who prided himself for directing Rivera in the design of the mural) it was quite removed from the paintings that Rivera would favor in coming years.

*Maternity*, *The Elements*, and *Creation* are beautiful murals in and of themselves, but they hold no relationship whatsoever with the aesthetic ideology that these painters so noisily professed. The muralists were acutely aware of the problem and they addressed it with astounding diligence. The task was not easy. They would have to unlearn the formation which had turned them into traditional *artists*. A certain (excessively Italian and somewhat baroque) ideal of beauty was the first casualty of their battle. As soon as Rivera, Orozco, and Siqueiros began transforming their own styles through a desperate act of self-criticism, viewers started asking not only if what they were doing was art, but also if it held any connection to beauty whatsoever. The hesitations and ruminations one reads in the reviews of the work in progress were just a prelude to other, more far-reaching interactions between the muralists and their urban critics. As long as they painted virgins and winged angels they did not attract much public hostility. But when they started to cover the walls with popular references, social satyrs, and political proclamations, a good deal of conservative Mexico City turned against them. Vasconcelos himself, as he left the SEP, regretted the fact that the muralist had fallen "into the abjection of covering the walls of Mexico with portraits of criminals" (Rochfort, 1993: 62).

Technical issues also plagued the beginnings of the muralist enterprise. It is one thing to paint a mural – already in itself a complex and daunting technical accomplishment that requires calculations, knowledge of geometry, and mastery over chemical reactions – and an altogether different thing to secure the permanence of the mural over time. Rivera painted *Creation* in encaustic, a complex and arduous technique that turns mural painting into an odyssey. The muralists could not, at the beginning, master the fresco technique. Frescos existed in Mexico in, for example, popular anonymous art exhibited in pulquerías and other commercial establishments. But this tradition seemed lost. As for the technical secrets of the Italian frescos, it was even more remote and unfathomable. The muralists owned an old copy of a manual for fresco production written by Cellino Cennini, but were never able to figure out the exact formula or even find the mentioned components in Mexico. At the end, it was the intervention of Xavier Guerrero (who, in a story permeated with national mysticism, is said to have retrieved an ancient Toltec technique of fresco painting), combined with Rivera's dexterity, that allowed the muralists to create a reliable fresco technique.

## Siqueiros and the Elaboration of a Muralist Avant-Garde

David Alfaro Siqueiros's role in the early phase of muralism was more ideological than artistic. All through the 1920s Siqueiros privileged union activism over artistic engagement. He was the secretary general of Mexico's Revolutionary Painters, Sculptors and Engravers Union (that he founded), and toward 1924, he was much more concerned with promoting the revolutionary pamphlet *El Machete* (which would later become the official organ of the Mexican Communist Party) than with producing muralist paintings. In 1924, he traveled to Guadalajara, where he worked with Amado de la Cueva on a project that entailed woodcarving and mural work at the church of Santo Tomás, which was now university property. But in 1926 he went back full time to union activity and he became secretary general of the Miners Union of Jalisco. This union activism was not welcomed and Siqueiros found himself in jail several times between 1926 and 1931. In 1931 he was sent into internal exile in the city of Taxco, where Alma Reed and Sergei Eisenstein, among others, helped to organize an exhibit of his work that later traveled to Mexico City. In 1932, the Mexican government expelled him from the country owing to his leftist activities. He moved to Los Angeles, California, where he sustained himself with some commissions from American patrons. In 1934, as the left-oriented Lázaro Cárdenas became President of México, he was allowed to return to the country. It was a short return, as Siqueiros enlisted as a volunteer in the international forces that fought against Franco in the Spanish Civil War. He stayed in Spain for almost the whole duration of the conflict until the defeat of Republican forces in 1939. The Siqueiros that won a name in the history of Latin American art, the Siqueiros of the murals at the Palacio de Bellas Artes or the Jorge Negrete Theater, was largely the Siqueiros of the second half of the twentieth century.

Although as an artist Siqueiros was too young and too unskilled to leave any important imprint on the initial phase of muralism, he was surprisingly mature when it came to establishing the ideological goals of the movement. He met Rivera in Paris, in 1919, and many guiding lines of muralism sprang from this encounter that

Siqueiros phrased as the meeting between "the new fervor and ideals of the young Mexican painters . . . who had joined the armed struggle," and "the representative of an important period of the formal revolution in the plastic arts" (1975: 13). From this contact two important documents for the story of muralism, drafted by Siqueiros in 1921 and 1922, follow.

The first one appeared in the only number of the journal *Vida Americana* (published in Barcelona), under the title "A New Direction for the New Generation of American Painters and Sculptors." The form, typical of *manifestos*, is composed of three parts. The first one contains a strong condemnation of old and decadent forms of art which Siqueiros opposed to a new, invigorating aesthetic revolution, synthesized in the names of Cézanne, the Cubists, and the Futurists. Siqueiros called – in a way reminiscent of the Baudelaire of "Le peintre de la vie moderne" – for a practice of art able to grasp the present moment as it stands in fruitful contact with the whole of Western tradition. The second part, which better reflects his intense exchange with Rivera, is a passionate defense of constructivism (exemplified in the manifesto by Cubism) against the mostly "decorative" tendency that Siqueiros sees as the dominant force in Mexican art. The essentials of Siqueiro's program were volume over color, the thick dimension of the figural over the *trompe l'oeil* of "artistic" pastime. The call against a decorative impulse in art signals, also, a turn in the aesthetic–ideological direction of Mexican art, since Dr. Atl had conceptualized the merely decorative as a counter-force to the bourgeois and capitalist representative appropriation of the world (in which, family portraits are favored over "anonymous" landscapes, for instance). The *manifesto* closes with a call to pay closer attention to "*Negro Art* and *Primitive Art*," which was quite in line with the Parisian revival of primitivism of the 1920s.

The second influential text penned by Siqueiros is the manifesto of the Union of Technical Workers, Painters, and Sculptors. It was an aesthetic and a political profession of faith. In it, the already constituted muralist movement called for artists to abandon easel painting and embrace a social form of art. The document was addressed to the "indigenous races humiliated over centuries; to the soldiers turned into executioners by their leaders; to the workers and peasants who are oppressed by the rich; and to the intellectuals who are not servile to the bourgeoisie."[3] Although the Sindicato was short-lived and largely ineffectual in defending its members, it left a clear mark on the development of Mexican art. It radicalized the muralist movement and contributed to a clear conscience of their task in that particular historical juncture. It was because of texts like this that Rivera will be able later to praise Mexican muralism for making the masses the hero of monumental art "For the first time in the history of Art" (quoted in Rochfort, 1993: 8).

## Rivera and the Representation of the People

Rivera's life was no calmer than the agitated existence of Siqueiros. All through the 1920s and 1930s he worked on the walls of various public buildings. From 1931 on,

Rivera began a series of trips to and works in the United States. The second part of the 1930s found Rivera at the apogee of his public persona: he requested and obtained asylum for Leon Trotsky (whom Siqueiros tried to assassinate); entered, left, reentered, and was expelled from the Communist Party; married, divorced, and remarried Frida Kahlo; and attracted the attention of prominent foreign visitors from André Breton to Sergei Eisenstein. By then he was already the visible figure that synthesized the muralist project as a whole.

After his experience at the Preparatoria, Rivera was entrusted with painting the two emblematic buildings of post-revolutionary Mexico: the Secretaría de Educación Pública (SEP – under the direction of José Vasconcelos) and the National Palace. When Rivera began his work at the SEP, he had grown increasingly dissatisfied with the too metaphysical style of *Creation*. A firs correction to this style comes with the incorporation of a minute, almost archaeological reconstruction of popular and indigenous lore. At the SEP, Rivera painted his famous Courtyard of Labor and Courtyard of Fiestas. In this group of murals, he represented traditional forms of work, farming, mining, and the customs of the Mexican people. In the early 1930s, Rivera moved to the National Palace where he painted his famous *History of Mexico*. The subject was no longer, as in the SEP, the folk forms of Mexican culture, but the development of historical time from the perspective of nation formation.

Rivera's mural at the SEP and the National Palace had been criticized for their didacticism, their often celebratory tone, and the absence of criticism of social injustices that predominates at certain points in the Courtyard of Labor. There is no doubt that nationalism and statism played an important role in these murals commissioned and painted on the most important walls of the post-revolutionary state. It is arguable that his passionate support for the revolutionary process made Rivera oblivious to the vast landscape of injustice in post-revolutionary Mexico. But the murals' complexity is not exhausted by this observation. The murals also performed an act of imagination, a positing of the people, whose breakthrough is magnified by the general impotence of other intellectuals before the revolutionary event.[4] In the following sections, I will try to isolate the formal and stylistic mechanisms that allowed Rivera to create a new iconography and a new artistic code that performed an act of imagination able to bridge the chasm between the popular nature of the revolt and the representational demands of culture.

### Christianity and enumeration

Those present at the inauguration of the murals that Rivera painted at the SEP were astonished by what they perceived as an odd mixture of social, Marxist critique (condemnation of private property, exploitation, and colonialism) and allusions to a Christian iconography. One panel, "Exit from the Mine," shows a worker being searched by the mine officials, standing with outstretched arms that unmistakably evoke crucifixion, while another climbs a stair toward the surface, wearing a hat that the stylistic disposition of the painting invites us to confuse with a halo. In these and similar panels Rivera draws on Mexican popular religiosity to bridge the chasm that separates his revolutionary art from the masses.

It may seem ironic that the muralists, some of whose members boasted of a militant atheism, borrowed a perceptual schema from the religious tradition in order to relate their paintings to the revolutionary event. There are of course disciplinary reasons that made painters more aware of the possibilities afforded by Christianity in relationship to emergent social movements. Christian religiosity pervades the history of painting in a way that is almost totally absent in the tradition of modern liberalism that was dominant among Mexican intellectuals. But in using a Christian imagery, muralists were not simply slavishly following a Western tradition with which they had already broken in so many violent and yet imperceptible ways. The Christian tradition gave muralism a dignified version of the popular classes, a version that considers the popular sector to be exemplary of the category of the human in general, elevating these groups to a universality thus far negated by the Mexican political establishment. Muralism, however, borrowed from Christianity not its iconographic tradition (in which a certain figures carries an already codified meaning) but rather a figuration. The elevation of the neglected people to prototypes of the universal did not detach them from their place and their time. It entailed, rather, a carnivalesque inversion of the religious imagery. Instead of these peasants and Indians becoming more "saintly" and ethereal," "saintliness" became more mundane and embodied.

Now, although it allows for the presentation of an injured political subjectivity under an irrecusable aesthetic framework, Christian humanism is not the real answer to the crisis of the schema. Religious universalism is abstract, metaphysical, and exemplary. It presupposes a pure and preexistent realm of ideas to be incarnated into the world and perpetuates a sense of history as a teleological process. None of these conditions was compatible with revolution in general or the Mexican Revolution in particular. The challenge for Rivera was, then, to imagine a way to represent a claim to the universal by the revolutionary people that was able to invert metaphysics, belie transcendental embodiment, and give the present its due, independent of its subsumption into any teleological project. He found that element in the populist trope *par excellence*: enumeration.

We are all familiar with the apparently endless string of human faces that cover Rivera's murals. In *The Courtyard of Fiestas*, no figure stands out as allegorizing or symbolizing the joys and sufferings of all. The landscape, so important in some paintings of *The Courtyard of Labor*, is minimized as Rivera frantically covers every last inch of the wall with popular figures. It is impossible, even in compositional terms, to arrange the multiplicity of figures according to a system of values. Paired with Christian imagery, enumeration seemed to offer the solution to the problem of a dignified, universalizable presentation of the revolutionary masses. Enumeration creates the semblance of standing for the totality. It entices us to think that everybody is counted and that everybody counts. As a trope, enumeration allowed Rivera to accommodate his own political radicalism under a form of aesthetic populism that was irrefutable insofar as it also constituted the "official" ideology of the revolution, at least in those moments when the revolution was thought to have an ideology.

As much as Rivera wanted to imagine the popular based on its autonomy and to question the role that the elites had played in the building of the country, it is doubtful that enumeration could provide the solution to these problems. Enumeration seeks to create the illusion of counting the totality, one by one. But the totality is uncountable for a number of reasons: it is always changing; there is no perspective that allows for a contemplation of the totality; even if it can be counted, it cannot be remembered; and so on. At this point we realize that Rivera's tropological choice was unable to avoid the predicament created by the revolution as a sort of political sublime that could only address the people in a rhetoric of the abject and the amorphous, that is, as non-people. Although his figurative strategy was an enormous step forward in the aesthetic presentation of popular agency, with his use of enumeration Rivera essentially substituted one sublime for another. After all, an endless and uniform series is the other form (Kant called it the mathematical sublime) that the feeling of the inapprehensible can take in the experience of cognition. Now, according to the author of the *Third Critique*, every experience of the sublime creates a demand for synthesis. Likewise, nations and their attendant ideas of "national cultures" also demand synthesis out of their experiences of the uncountable. So, a contradiction arises inside Rivera's project between its extensive, non-synthetic use of enumeration and the parallel need to grasp this extensive proliferation of figures under a common and unique denominator. This problematic was so present to Rivera that at the height of his muralist project, the composition of *The History of Mexico* at the National Palace, he placed, at the center of the composition – as its axis and principle of determination – a colored eagle, whose model is an Aztec sculpture known as the *Teocalli de la guerra sagrada* (Temple of sacred warfare). The symbol is so powerful that it sublates and interrupts all enumeration. Through this symbol, a form of the absolute asserts itself in the democratic dimension of the popular. And yet, we have to equally acknowledge that in the Mexico of the 1920s and 1930s, this symbol had a disquieting ambiguity that prevents us from reading it exclusively in terms of the pedagogical dimension of nation formation. Rivera placed the Aztec heritage at the symbolic center of the impossible totality called Mexico. But what value did this relationship to the Aztec past have in the overall project of the murals?

## Peoplehood and the Rise of National Ethnography

The centrality of the temple of sacred warfare in *The History of Mexico* would be enigmatic if we were not aware of the prominence of indigenous themes in Rivera's murals. Rivera's murals include minute descriptions of pre-Columbian architectural trades, everyday life, and geography that show "the remarkable range of [Rivera's] research into his country's archaeological past" (Brown, 1985: 144). Immediately following his return to Mexico, Rivera became involved in an impressive project of research and collection of Mexican pre-Columbian indigenous lore. He acquired an exceptionally deep knowledge of ancient Mexico, reading frantically, interviewing dozens of experts (Manuel Gamio and Alfonso Caso among them), and traveling to archeological sites. Rivera's passion for the Mexican past also showed in the impressive collection of indigenous artifacts that he amassed over decades – some sixty thousand objects by the time of his death – and which he housed in a three-story museum that he had built in Mexico City. Especially, Rivera drew much inspiration for his depiction of the ancient Indian world from his persistent study of ancient codices. Traits like enumeration can be said to have an antecedent in the scrolls. Likewise the organization of space in the murals also recalls the scroll by the use of means other than perspective to suggest spatial depth. Both the scrolls and Rivera's paintings group different themes or periods in codified clusters of meanings and use an additive system of representation to display different characters and symbols in an arrangement that admits different routes of reading. Even the idea that the murals were for reading (books for the illiterate) was, in a sense, deeply related to the codices as we come to know them.

However, some doubts have arisen regarding the relationship between Rivera's representation and the actual indigenous masses living in Mexico during his time. As many critics have observed, Rivera's main concern was not with the actually existing Indians of post-revolutionary Mexico but with the indigenous past as this past was reconstructed by the arising anthropological discourse. Rivera was perhaps the first intellectual to fully realize the key role played by ethnography in grounding cultural claims to social legitimacy. If popular Christianity allowed painters to universalize the figure of the suffering Indian, ethnography secularized the indigenous question strongly enough to relocate it in a realm beyond the field of prejudices that constituted early twentieth-century Mexican common sense. The most immediate effect of this secularization was to allow intellectuals to speak of the Indians in a language other than the discourse of moral relativism that had dominated the relationship to Mexican indigenous people since the nineteenth century.[5] These observations do not seek to minimize the importance of Rivera's work on the indigenous traditions of his country. Mexican intellectuals had largely eschewed the indigenous past as dead weight hindering the development of Mexican modernity. The recovery of an indigenous lore was already a breakthrough, at least by the standards of the consciousness of the Mexican elite. Indigenous images were scarcely part of the archive of national culture when Rivera began painting his murals, and Rivera has been praised for advancing a perceptual schema that dominates the imagination of the indigenous past even to this day.[6]

Rivera's appropriation of indigenous motifs and symbology had very precise limits, however, ones that, not surprisingly, were related to the subjectifying effects that the murals pursued. Although the everyday life of the ancient people was minutely depicted in many murals, Rivera carefully avoided open references to indigenous forms of religiosity that could be perceived as morbid. Likewise, the values that he discovered in the Aztecs (discipline, work, communal organization) had more to do with the pedagogical project of the revolution than with historical accuracy. At this point we find, again, the central role played by the Christian imaginary, which was used to impose a fiercely humanist grid on the ancient cultures of Mexico. The most obvious and striking example of the predominance of a humanist schema in the treatment of the Aztec iconographic tradition is the absence of the most idiosyncratic traits of indigenous art, which bypass a realist-impressionist representation of the human form as the general principle of perceptual and representational organization. In fairness to Rivera, one should say that, unlike Vasconcelos, he did not retreat in horror from the complex imaginary that fuses snakes, as well as severed heads and hands, into the single form of a deity; but neither did he offer a ready made transposition of these kinds of motifs into his murals. Carefully, Rivera distorted the image and placed it in different contexts (like the transposition of the statue of Coatlicue into the murals on industry painted in Detroit, as Betty Anne Brown and others have noted), suggesting a subterranean power of disruption even as he secured – via the image's territorialization through ethnographic science – its displacement from the ideological center of irradiation of the murals.

## An Overdetermined History

The most far-reaching innovation in Rivera's vocabulary that comes about in *The History of Mexico* is, precisely, the attempt to create a new dimension of historical experience. Before the eyes of the visitor the whole history of Mexico unfolds according to a chronology that, if not entirely linear, is dominated by the theme of Mexico as a colonized country. As viewers ascend the main stairway of the national palace, they are presented with an idealized depiction of life in pre-Columbian Mexico. They then pass the crucial political and cultural junctures in the country's history (conquest, the Wars of Independence, Maximilian and the French occupation, the rise of liberalism, Benito Juárez, Díaz, Madero, Zapata, the Revolution). Finally, when viewers reach the top of the staircase, they face a utopian section titled "The World of Today and Tomorrow" in which the figure of Marx crowns the history of Mexico as he points the way to the future. The conceptual richness of the mural is stunning. Rivera plays on a complex dialectic between Marxism and indigenousness (between Marx and Quetzatcoatl in the mural) to propose a highly idiosyncratic and novel conception of history.

For Desmond Rochfort, with this mural Rivera accomplished the as-yet unrealized goal of placing "the Mexican revolution within some kind of historical perspective" (1993: 84). I think that he did more than that: he made the Revolution the year zero of a national history; and in doing so he brought about also a deep reconfiguration of the sense of the historical in painting. In this sense, the singular most extraordinary feature that *The History of Mexico* exhibits is the precipitation of representation into the web of an already existing history. One need simply compare Rivera's first mural, *Creation*, to these later productions to weigh the vast refashioning of ideological and existential coordinates that the sense of facticity presiding over this painting brings into the scene. *Creation* offered an Adamic and voluntaristic version of the revolution. In these later murals, in contrast, the revolution makes its first important break with the past by renouncing the mirage of absolute self-foundation. The figures depicted in *Creation* lived outside time. The revolution was so pure that it ended up being nonexistent. In *The History of Mexico*, Rivera shows a thoroughly overdetermined total-ity that appears indistinguishably as cause and effect of the Revolution. And since this history is no longer abstract, but rather a history in which painter and viewer are now immersed, Rivera does not wait for the sanction of time to regulate the entrance into representation. Rivera paints his own face, in addition to the faces of his friends and lovers, as he covers the walls with a history that now has many beginnings and an open end.

## José Clemente Orozco

Unlike Rivera, who spent many years in Europe studying the classics of Western art and witnessed first hand the emergence of the avant-garde, José Clemente Orozco had an important background as cartoonist that gave his work not only an uncompromis-ing agility but also a "corrosive" satirical impulse. He joined the other muralists in 1923. A year later, when Vasconcelos departed from the SEP, most of the muralist movement came to a halt. Only Rivera was able to negotiate his permanence on the project in a successful way. Orozco found himself unemployed. He returned to the SEP in 1926 to produce a series of paintings that will be discussed in more detail shortly. In 1927 he emigrated to the USA, where he lived until 1934. In these years he painted his famous *Prometheus* at Pomona College, and then the murals at the New School for Social Research of New York, and at the Bake Library of the Dartmouth College in Hanover, New Hampshire. In 1936, already back in Mexico, Orozco started the most productive period of his artistic life in Guadalajara. He painted the hall walls of the University Campus, the staircase of the City Hall, and a series of frescos at the Hospicio Cabañas chapel. In these paintings, Orozco gave way to his anguished and violent version of Mexico's history as a perpetual marginalization of the poor, the incomprehensible horrors of history, and the tragedy of Mexican figures, portrayed as men on fire, shrouded in flames, consuming themselves in their own passion and impotence. These are the paintings that made Orozco famous and won him the title of the most powerful aesthetic force of Mexican muralism in the eyes of many critics (among them Sergei Eisenstein, who transposed several spatial schemas that he found in Orozco's paintings into the *mise en scène* of his film *Que Viva México!*).

At first sight, it may seem that Orozco's paintings do not bear too much resem-blance to those of Siqueiros and Rivera and that even in his political and personal passions, the painter from Guadalajara was quite removed from the urgent calls from history that seems to have obsessed both Rivera and Siqueiros. Some biographical elements tend to sustain this misguided perception. In his autobiography, Orozco famously wrote that "Artists do not have political convictions, and those who say to have them, are not artists" (Orozco, 2001: 18). Compounded with this ideological skepticism is the fact that Orozco's paintings rarely indulge in a celebration of the Revolution as a popular movement. The perception of Orozco's work as lying somewhat removed from revolutionary concerns is, however, superficial. In an important sense, no other muralist can be said to have entertained such a deep meditation on the secret nature of the revolution as Orozco did in his unsettling murals.

After Orozco destroyed most of the original compositions he painted at the Preparatoria, he replaced his previous "metaphysical" murals with a series of astounding paintings: *Destruction of the Old Order*, *Revolutionary Trinity*, *The Strike*, *The Trench*, and *The Rich Banquet while the Workers Fight*. These paintings show how Orozco's first efforts "were but the mumbling words of someone trying to formulate transcendental truths in a language he has not yet mastered" (Rodríguez, 1969: 188) After these first attempts, "Orozco passed without hesitation from the Michelangelesque Maddona to *The Trinity*, which is entirely his own" (188). Two lines that would come to dominate his painting in the near future were already present in the paintings at the Preparatoria: on the one hand his very personal interpretation of the revolution from the point of view of tragedy and suffering in a dramatic expressionist style; on the other hand a caricaturesque style that his critics found repulsive and his sympathizers only bearable at the best.[7]

Many critics have noticed that an eerie stillness prevails in Orozco's expressionist murals. This stillness does not represent a flight from the ever-changing nature of historical reality, but rather a deeper immersion in it insofar as it contributes to a sheer (or naked, as Rodríguez put it) presentation of the present. We have seen that one of Rivera's greatest accomplishments was his comprehension of the overdetermined nature of historical time. In the case of Orozco, the greatest accomplishment of these paintings lies in their capacity to keep the eyes of the spectator fixed onto the present, onto the most immediate data of reality. In these paintings the Revolution is not celebrated in the clear lines that characterizes Rivera's murals. Everything in Orozco is both more nuanced and ambiguous. Actions are colored not so much by heroism, but by the incomprehensible rules of a fatality beyond understanding. This effect comes above all from the subtraction of any transcendental ground in the represented figures. It is the utter unavailability of a historical redemption able to subsume the singular pain and distress of the revolutionary fighters that gives to Orozco's paintings their sense of nakedness. But simultaneously, by removing any transcendental reference, Orozco makes a desperate attempt at penetrating whatever, as essential trait or as residue, can be considered unique to the revolutionary moment. Orozco was in fact the artist most obsessed with naming the blind impulse, the secret energy that was shaping Mexico at that time. *The Trench* is a powerful illustration of these qualities. The painting shows three men, in strange, unstable poses. Their clothes are mundane – they are revolutionary fighters – but the composition clearly suggests a rupture between the sphere of human decisions and a beyond – let us call it history – in which these figures are taken in as in a nightmare. To make Orozco's peculiar rendition of the rupture between history and popular agency more glaring, Rodríguez invites us to compare Orozco's *The Trench* and Delacroix's *Barricade*. In Delacroix's painting, "men seem to be fighting with the hymn of liberty on their lips" (Rodríguez, 1969: 189). Nothing can be further removed from Orozco's murals in which the Mexican painter presents us "with the bare essence of war" (189).

The stillness of the figures, combined with the exodus of any transcendental dimension in the paintings (an absence that can be marked as presence: for example by heavy, meaningless Christian crosses), seems to leave the people in the paintings in a state of poetic orphanhood. Even opinion, perhaps the most shocking feature of Orozco's caricaturesque style, has no voice in paintings like *The Trench* or *Revolutionary Trinity*. These paintings are neither sad nor optimistic. Orozco could well be the painter of the standstill of the Revolution, not as a negative indecision on the face of reality, but as the codification of an afterlife of the revolution in the subterranean force of bodies tortured by the demands that history makes upon them.

After 1930, Orozco abandons his rhetoric of the event as ciphered in its undecidedness and, like Rivera, embraces a historical narrative as the central concern of his mural painting. But unlike Rivera, who was trusted with the most emblematic walls of Mexico, Orozco started painting his epic of American history on the walls of the Baker library at Dartmouth College. He divided the mural between pre-Columbian and post-Columbian times, the latter reaching up to the contemporary life of Latin and Anglo-Saxon America. Like Rivera's *History of Mexico*, Orozco's epic of the Americas is an exceptionally complex painting. It shows, in contrast to Rivera's mural, a more somber and pessimistic idea of history, which is properly speaking not moving forward, but going in circles with endless processes of struggle and victory corrupted by greed and treason.

Finally, in 1938, Orozco had the chance to continue this project in his own country as he started working at the Hospicio Cabañas in Guadalajara on a series of panels entitled *The Spanish Conquest of Mexico*. In contrast to the idealization that characterizes Rivera's view of the indigenous world, Orozco showed an image of pre-Columbian civilization that was as much glorious as it was tainted by barbarism and cruelty of the Aztec civilization. The Spanish conquest, also, was presented as a mixture of relentless violence and mindless destruction that ended with the total submission of the Indians and the obliteration of their world. Orozco goes back here to his opinionated style, avoiding taking sides, condemning relentlessly all the forms of violence and corruption that, in his view, come back as a curse to put obstacles in the illusory development of a history of progress.

Although Orozco's view of the history of Mexico was glaringly different from that of Rivera, his painting displays some of the common trends that were adding up to build the ideology of nationalist post-revolutionary Mexico. The concern with history itself as a subject is an enormous concession to the consolidation of post-revolutionary hegemony. Orozco seems to admit that whatever politics the painter can uphold, it will be a politics in the limits of revolutionary nationalism. Like Rivera, and later Siqueiros, he turned his gaze back to the colonial origins of the Mexican nation, understood not so much as a historical fatality but rather as a structural matrix that could ground whatever critical gestures could be carried out into the present constitution of Mexican society.

## Muralism and the Basic Question of Western Art

Muralism is largely ignored in metropolitan histories of art. When these histories attend to it, they focus on the anecdotal and heroic elements of the movement to the absolute detriment of its artistic meaning. For many critics the art of the muralist is naïve and unpretentious, mostly driven by immediate political goals. Even Desmond Rochefort, in spite of his enormous admiration for the muralist movement, admits that "The presence of Mexican muralism in the history of twentieth-century culture is in many ways an anachronism in relation to the tenets of modernist aesthetics, practice and theory" (1993: 6). I would like to linger for a while on the paradox entailed in these descriptions of the marginal status of muralism *vis-à-vis* the Western aesthetic tradition. First of all, from whence does the marginality of muralism come? Rochfort explains that the reason muralism is peripheral to modern art is because content and not form is the main concern of muralist painting. For modern art, the content of art is the artistic form itself, a form that needs to be perpetually overcome, replaced by new and more daunting representations. Muralism, on the other hand, seems to draw its "novelty" from the inclusion of particular events and characters in the sphere of representation. Although events were once the content of Western art, this is no longer so. Hence, Rochfort is basically right in his appreciation of muralism in terms of anachronism. The point now is: Can we think that this regression is not merely a divergence from the canon of Western art but rather a confrontation with some of its basic and constitutive problems?

The primacy of form in the history of aesthetics was first systematized by Immanuel Kant in the *Critique of Judgment*, in which the German philosopher argued that aesthetic judgment was only concerned with the form of the object to the active disregard of its ontological qualities. One likes a still life representing pears and apples not because one plans to eat them, but just because one enjoys their representation. Even actual pears and apples can be considered from two different perspectives: as possible objects of consumption – and then the judgment upon them is interested in the qualities of the fruits – or from the standpoint of their mere appearance, and in this case the judgment is completely disinterested. Artistic contemplation and judgment are disinterested activities. This disinterest that originally seemed only to concern the judgment upon the work of art ended up taking the very being of this work into the intangible region of the nonexistent. This disinterested character of art grounds its autonomy in the modern world. Before courts and censors the artist always upholds his/her right to speak since what he/she produces are representations that have been subtracted from the thickness of the world. In an illuminating article on the paradoxes of modern aesthetics, Martin Jay offers a gloss of this Kantian principle of disinterest that further illuminates the point I am trying to make here. Jay recalls that the word *disinterest* has a Latin root that makes an explicit reference to being, in the sense of actuality. When we judge in the disinterested way, Jay says, "We are no longer immersed in being – inter-esse ... but somewhat outside it" (2003: 9). This quality of art as standing outside being and actuality gives way to a perplexing ontology. This paradoxical ontology of the work of art tells us that these productions, which are sold and bought, cherished and stolen, are instrumental to the hegemonic organization of modernity while, simultaneously, and in a certain sense, they are removed from reality's most practical goals.

In *The Man without Contents*, Giorgio Agamben acknowledges the in-actuality that characterizes the work of art, but in his view art and artists have been doing nothing but fighting this destiny for the last two centuries. The history of modern art consists for Agamben in a desperate search for grounding art among beings, that is, in Martin Jay philological rendering, in a search for an interested art. Now, the muralists claimed nothing less than that: to produce an art that would be a being among beings and yet, they also wanted to claim the exception, the deep heterogeneity that defines the realm of artistic creation as transcendence regarding the regimes of truth and power. Being artists, after all, they necessarily failed in this project of restituting the majesty of the actual to art. No one can, simultaneously, claim the exception and make a wager for actuality. And yet, the idea of an interested art, a contradiction in terms, presided over the activity of these painters and is the real nucleus upon which any interpretation of the muralist movement should finally rest.

Modern art and muralism (or muralism as a strange offshoot of modern art) seeks the transcendence of art, the end of its exile in the realm of the in-actual. They follow, however, different strategies. Modern art strategy for self-transcendence relies in the constant thematization of its own character as art. However, the more power and creativity modern artists invested into the enterprise, the more the object-hood of art itself escaped through their fingers. The strategy not only failed, but it ended up producing the opposite effect: an almost complete anesthetization of existence in which Harley Davidsons and Ferraris can be shown in art museums not as industrial productions but as possessing that aura that Walter Benjamin opposed, precisely, to the sphere of reproducibility. The muralists, meanwhile, proceeded through a complex set of operations which were not designed, however, to overcome the division between art and reality by operating exclusively or even mainly in the formal sphere of artistic production. Or better yet, while their attempt obviously went through profound changes in the formal schema of representation, the direction of the movement was not related to a shared language (the language of Western art) that was overcome in their paintings, but through a contamination of elements through the nonhierarchical incorporation of a variety of sources (the interpretation of the artists of the political moment, the knowledge acquired about indigenous groups, the quotation and appropriation of popular motifs, the breaking down of the limits between art and caricature, art and ethnographical illustration, etc.). All this transformation of a basic cultural and aesthetic education is a remarkable accomplishment but bears also the sign of renunciation. The fatherland of a writer is his/her language, an old Spanish adage goes. Likewise, the fatherland of a painter is the languages of painting. At this point, is pertinent to recall that all muralists went through a forgoing of their initial artistic languages in a more or less dramatic fashion. In this sense, perhaps the axe that Orozco used against his murals bears more resemblance to an act of sacrifice of a basic artistic impulse than to an exercise in self-criticism. This was the muralist's particular way of incarnating the crux of the modern artist, forever divided between the exemption that makes their activity unique and the exile of their work in the undesirable realm of the inefficient.

It would be simplistic – and deep down one intuits that it would also be wrong – to claim that the muralists achieved a rupture with the history of art as disinterest. Perhaps art has its unique way of confronting this problem, or perhaps the end of art's exile in disinterest is a matter to be decided outside its sphere and independently of the laws of its constitution. However, the practice of the muralists dealt with these determinations and in doing so they confronted, willingly or unwillingly, the fundamental problem of aesthetics. For this reason all patronizing views of muralism as a merely pedagogical enterprise or as an artistic movement reduced to state propaganda or an attempt to communicate with a childlike universe of humble and ignorant people are both superfluous and, at bottom, naïve. On the contrary, this most "aesthetically conservative" "un-artistic" and "naïve" of productions struggled in its practice with the most fundamental problems of Western art and in doing so, they hit the center of the system from the periphery of their practice.

## NOTES

1   An accessible introduction to the history of the Mexican Revolution is Camín and Meyer (1989).

2   There were, of course, forms of organization and mobilization that emerged with the popular revolt. Those were genuinely popular productions in the spheres of politics and representation. But few members of the intelligentsia, if any, were interested in them. On this issue see Knight (1991).

3   First published in *El machete*, 7 (1924). The manifesto responded to the increasing activities of Mexican reactionaries, of which de la Huerta's attempted coup d'état is just one example.

4   On the issue of the difficulties of early revolutionary education for transposing the politics of the Revolution into the language of the school see the introduction to Vaughan (1997). In the terrain of literary studies, John Rutherford has noted that as far as literature was concerned, "the Revolution might never have happened" (Rutherford, 1971: 2). I have elaborated on this point in Legrás (2003).

5   Manuel Gamio, the Mexican disciple of Franz Boas, is a figure that cast a long shadow upon Mexican intellectuals and artists. Following in the footsteps of Boas, he refused to accept the nineteenth-century condemnation of *mestizaje* as fatally producing inferior cultures. Since 1916, Gamio had urged Mexican intellectuals to reeducate themselves in line with the revolutionary events. In 1922, he published *La Población del Valle de Teotihuacán*, following his archaeological work on that site. Gamio is closely linked to the history of Mexican painting not just because of the weight that his word had in the public arena but also because two of the most important plastic figures of early Mexico, Francisco Goitia and Best Maugard

– whose lectures on indigenous conceptions of beauty greatly influenced Rivera upon his return to Mexico – worked directly under Gamio, reproducing in drawings the archaeological findings of Gamio's excavations.

6  Francis V. O'Connor agrees with Bertrand Wolf (Rivera's biographer) in that "Rivera faced the enormous task of establishing a revolutionary iconography for Mexico from scratch" (1986: 219).

7  Salvador Novo, for instance, saw these paintings as "repulsive pictures, aiming to awaken in the spectator, instead of aesthetic emotions, an anarchist fury if he is penniless, or if he is wealthy, to make his knees buckle with fright" (quoted in Rochfort, 1993: 43).

## References and Further Reading

Agamben, Giorgio (1999). *The Man without Contents*. Trans. G. Albert. Stanford, CA: Stanford University Press.

Aguilar Camín, Héctor, and Meyer, Lorenzo (1989). *A la Sombra de la Revolución Mexicana*. Mexico City: Cal y Arena.

Brown, Betty Ann (1985). "The past idealized: Diego Rivera's use of pre-Columbian imagery." In C. N. Helms (ed.), *Diego Rivera: A Retrospective*. New York and London: W. W. Norton.

Gamio, Manuel (1916). *Forjando patria: Pronacionalismo*. Mexico City: Porrúa.

Jay, Martin (2003). "Drifting into dangerous waters: the separation of aesthetic experience from the work of art." In P. R. and D. M. W. Matthews (eds), *Aesthetic Subjects*. Minneapolis: Minnesota University Press.

Knight, Alan (1991). "Intellectuals in the Mexican Revolution." In Charles Adam Hale, Roderic Ai Camp, and Josefina Zoraida Vázquez (eds), *Los Intelectuales y el poder en México*. Mexico City: Colegio de México.

Legrás, Horacio (2003). "Martín Luis Guzmán, el viaje de la revolución," *Modern Language Notes*, 118(2): 23–37.

O'Connor, Francis V. (1986). "An iconographic interpretation of Diego Rivera's Detroit murals in terms of their orientation to the cardinal points of the compass." In L. Downs (ed.), *Diego Rivera: A Retrospective*, pp. 157–83. New York: W. W. Norton.

Orozco, José Clemente (2001). *José Clemente Orozco*. New York: Dover.

Rochfort, Desmond (1993). *Mexican Muralists: Orozco, Rivera, Siqueiros*. London: L. King.

Rodríguez, Antonio (1969). *A History of Mexican Mural Painting*. Trans. M. Corby. New York: G. P. Putnam's Sons.

Rutherford, John (1971). *Mexican Society during the Revolution: A Literary Approach*. Oxford: Clarendon Press.

Siqueiros, David Alfaro (1975). *Art and Revolution*. London: Lawrence & Wishart.

Vaughan, Mary Kay (1997). *Cultural Politics in Revolution: Teachers, Peasants, and Schools in Mexico, 1930–1940*. Tucson: University of Arizona Press.

# 23

# Anthropology, Pedagogy, and the Various Modulations of *Indigenismo*: *Amauta*, Tamayo, Arguedas, Sabogal, Bonfil Batalla

*Javier Sanjinés C.*

*Indigenismo* has been traditionally conceptualized as a broad current, which gained momentum during the 1920s and the 1930s in the wake of the Mexican Revolution, and which was manifested in the "rediscovery" and revaluation of native cultures and traditions, as well as in the use of the Indian themes in literature and the visual arts, which are often articulated in terms of social protest. Yet, as Miguel León-Portilla wrote in 1975, official praise for the Indian heritage did not translate itself into forms of action which would really make possible the development of the indigenous communities. Indeed, Indians in Latin America have remained the principal victims of an official rhetoric which sought to assimilate them into the modern nation.

In this chapter I trace the process by which both *indigenismo* and *mestizaje* became the dominant discourses elaborated by intellectuals from the beginning of the twentieth century. Whether by postponing the social and political aspirations of the Indian component of society, or by coopting its consciousness, men of letters such as the Bolivians Alcides Arguedas and Franz Tamayo began a process of nation-building, of modernization, which I study in the first two sections. If Arguedas, an upper-class *criollo* (person of Spanish descent), constructed *indigenismo* around the positivist-liberal discourse that emphasized the Indian's innate racial inferiority, Tamayo, a *mestizo* (of mixed Spanish-Indian ancestry, assimilated to *criollo* culture and to Western values) new power-holder, counteracted Arguedas's *indigenismo* with a *mestizo* point of view on the autochthonous which introduced an incipient nationalist discourse that helped relocate the indigenous race within the *mestizo-criollo* view of the nation. In section three, I place the "indigenous problem" within the more modern and intellectually sophisticated environment of Peruvian society. *Amauta*, a leading radical avant-garde review of the 1920s, and its creator, José Carlos Mariátegui, were fundamental in reinterpreting *indigenismo*, in looking for cultural wholeness – the integration of the spiritual and the material – through the regeneration of the indigenous communities and the revitalization of the Indian traditions. The last section follows the anti-colonialist trend of thought that Mariátegui inaugurated in Latin America, through the brief discussion of Guillermo Bonfil Batalla's anthropologic approach to Mexico's schism between an "imaginary" construction of the *mestizo* nation and the real situation of the rejected and postponed rural "México profundo."

## Arguedas and Positivist-Liberal Discourse

Andean societies underwent a momentous transformation in the first quarter of the twentieth century. Like other Latin American countries, they had to begin their modernizing process in an international setting where there were already fully-fledged and powerful economic competitors. Andean countries had to accumulate capital for investment, build an infrastructure, and acquire technology and expertise. This they could not do on their own; despite the presence of a nascent *mestizo-criollo* bourgeoisie, Andean nations were forced to depend on foreign sources to a very large degree.

A new elite of power holders, the liberal *mestizo-criollo* sector, replaced the nineteenth-century conservative traditionalism of a declining *criollo* oligarchy, avid to preserve the wealth and social influence of the Church, the special privileges of the clergy and the army, the separate "republic" of the Indians, the legal and social restrictions on the *castas* – in short, all the trappings of an impermeable and hierarchical society. In contrast to this traditionalism, cities like La Paz, the new seat of government of Bolivia, were a clear example of the modernizing impulse promoted by the liberal *mestizo-criollo* sector. With powerful motives for changing Sucre, the stronghold of Bolivian conservatism, to their city, this rising bourgeoisie made of La Paz the physical expression of the sharp about-face taken by the nation's collective psychology after three-quarters of a century under military rule. During that era, neither Bolivia nor indeed any of its fellow Andean republics to the north had been able to establish an authoritarian liberal government along the lines of those in Argentina, Chile, and Mexico. Afflicted by obscurantist *caudillo* rule, persistent regionalism, and deep ethnic disparities, the Andean nations remained backward in comparison with those important metropolitan Latin American centers. They lacked the powerful institutions that would make a nation-building program possible. For this reason, Andean learned intellectuals, or *letrados*, lacked the political influence enjoyed by an earlier generation of Latin American thinkers, such as Argentina's Domingo Faustino Sarmiento and Esteban Echeverría, or Chile's José Victorino Lastarria, whose writings exercised enormous sway over the spheres of power in those nations over the nineteenth century.

As Edwin Williamson aptly indicates (1992: 294), the Peruvian upper classes had remained attached to things Spanish. The *leyenda* and the *cuadro de costumbres* were no match for the more robust tradition of romanticism, under which Argentina's liberalism acquired a radical political thrust. In Peru, and thanks to the wealth derived from the *guano* bonanza, Lima was able in the mid-nineteenth century to recover the glimmer of the social brilliance she had enjoyed in her colonial days. Peruvian men of letters like Felipe Pardo, Manuel Ascensio Segura, and, above all, Ricardo Palma, took their colonialist nostalgia to infuse it with the sardonic wit of the *limeño* traditions. While Ricardo Palma's *tradiciones* may have laid the foundations of a Peruvian national literature, it is clear that neither he, nor any other Andean writer of the nineteenth century for that matter, had the ability to construct a project of "national culture" comparable with the works of Echeverría and Sarmiento, whose writings set out the principles of classical liberalism.

Despite their origins among the great landowning families and the formative commercial bourgeoisie, the Bolivian *letrados* of the earlier twentieth century sometimes expressed deep disillusionment and a profoundly critical attitude toward the society in which they happened to live. The self-sufficient attitudes they displayed in their predominately sociological essays allowed them to get to the root of the problem afflicting Bolivia; as a result, their writings, though ignored by politicians, played a significant role in forming the nation's social milieu. An understanding of their disagreements with that milieu, as expressed in their mordant critiques of the liberal establishment, is indispensable for analyzing the social obstacles that surrounded the writings of *letrados* such as Alcides Arguedas and Franz Tamayo.

The main obstacle for *letrado* consciousness was the so-called "indigenous problem." The Indian had been (and indeed still remains) a source of constant anxiety for the *criollo* caste ever since the violent indigenous rebellions of the eighteenth century (Stern, 1987). Olivia Harris (1995) points to the late nineteenth century as a key historical moment when caste distinctions were being transformed into a complicated set of class relations. In that era, the emergent positivist-liberal discourse had elaborated the negative image of the Indian, not only as uncultured and alien to Western civilization, but also as situated outside the market economy. By naturalizing the idea that the Indian was incapable of participating in the market initiatives that the *mestizo-criollo* sector practiced so assiduously, liberal politics used indigenous "backwardness" as a handy excuse for continuing to expand the great agricultural estates and for appropriating products once manufactured and marketed by indigenous communities. Nineteenth-century pacts between Indians and *criollos* for the collection of indigenous tribute were now broken, and the *letrados* of the early twentieth century had to find new ways to conceptualize the "indigenous problem." They did this by reinventing and updating the nation's racial and ethnic taxonomies, adapting them to the political, economic, and ideological climate created by liberalism.

Like most Latin American liberals, Andean intellectuals conceptualized their ideologies of race and nation by appropriating European theories, which they then combined with their understandings, based on empirical observations of local cultures. In this vein of thought, Alcides Arguedas (1879–1946), a prominent *criollo* from La Paz – best known for *Raza de bronce* (The bronze race, 1919), one of the early examples of the *indigenista* novel – published his essay *Pueblo enfermo* (A sick country, 1909) causing an enormous and not entirely favorable impact on the nation's elite. In his essay Arguedas assumed a mechanistic relation between man and environment, leading him

to postulate a basically fatalistic vision of Bolivian reality. Geography, seen as determining the constitution of human groups, and race, determining the collective psychology of peoples, were the two axes along which Arguedas developed his rather
prejudicial analysis of Bolivian society. To be Indian, from this point of view, was to
be stamped by fate, for the Indian's being had been determined by the purely mechanical and immutable action exerted on him by the high plateau of the Altiplano region.
"The pampa and the Indian are but a single entity," Arguedas wrote. "The physical
aspect of the plateau . . . has molded the Indian's spirit in strange ways. Note, in the
man of the Altiplano, the hardness of his character, the aridity of his feelings, his
absolute lack of aesthetic emotions" (1937: 180). This deterministic relation between
man and environment, which Arguedas extended to an explanation of the backwardness of the republic, based on its broken geography, of course ignored all the historical,
economic, and social factors that outweighed the geographic ones on which he fixated.
According to this vision, man had lost any ability to transform nature. Similarly,
Arguedas saw a profound imbalance between the nation's territory and the quality of
its population. Because of this, Bolivia lacked the stability and harmony required to
produce progress. If Europe was a vast, uniform plain, Bolivia was a wild, chaotic
landscape. Geography thus determined development negatively.

As for the weight that race had on the nation's historic composition and collective
psychology, Arguedas set it apart from class interests, economic forces, and demography. Arguedas, influenced by Gustave LeBon's psycho-sociology, regarded *mestizaje*
with repugnance. He saw the most negative aspects of the Iberian and Indian races
combining to give birth to the *mestizo*, a being capable of playing a unifying role for
the nation and whose most representative type was the *cholo*, a *mestizo* looked down
upon because of his cultural linkage with the subjugated indigenous pole. With the
differentiation between *mestizos* and *cholos*, the *mestizo* group consolidated the social
position they had won by repudiating the *cholos* and appropriating the social and
cultural values of the *criollos*, thus conforming the *mestizo-criollo* apex of the *sistema
de castas.*

Whether he became a politician, a soldier, a lawyer, or a priest, the *cholo*, the
degenerate *mestizo*, with his smallness of spirit, never stopped to wonder – according
to Arguedas – whether or not his acts were moral or in keeping with the general
welfare. The learned *cholo*, though freed from ignorance, remained prey to contradictory emotions, still childishly credulous or savagely skeptical. Bolivia had generally
evolved in the opposite direction from all other human groups, owing to the predominance of *mestizos*, who by displacing the Iberian racial core had made it lose its qualities
and instead inherit those of the defeated race. In this way the white man had become
*encholado*, "cholo-ized."

## Tamayo, Sabogal, and the Discourse on the Autochthonous

The liberal elite apparently agreed with Arguedas's diagnosis. The nation's endemic
ills should be treated with the regenerative cure of awakening its inner energy, which

should begin by remodeling the physique of the Bolivian populace. Thus, in order to "endow the pupil with a healthy, vigorous, and beautiful body; a sensitive, generous; an intelligence rich in practical ideas" (*La Mañana*, 1910: 2–3), the liberal rulers placed particular emphasis on physical education. It was not simply a matter of creating strong and physically healthy bodies. The aim, above all, was to forge a strong will through the acquisition of the moral virtues of more advanced Western societies. To achieve this goal, the ideal of education had to be understood as molding the body's physique so that it would in turn condition the individual's spiritual and psychic transformation.

Integral education, a foreign model that the liberals copied from the teachings of Herbert Spencer, influenced the thought of two prominent liberals, Daniel Sánchez Bustamante and Felipe Segundo Guzmán, who each traveled to Europe to study the most appropriate educational systems for regenerating the indigenous race. From 1905 to 1908, Sánchez Bustamante presided over a commission charged with creating a system of teacher training, which did not exist in Bolivia until the 1909 opening of the Advanced Normal School of the Republic under the directorship of Belgian educator Georges Rouma. As head of the commission, Sánchez Bustamante traveled to France and Germany to observe their pedagogic models in person; he paid close attention to physical education in the schools he observed, and he decided that the most appropriate model was the Swedish gymnasium or high school. The foreign solution that Sánchez Bustamante found in the Swedish gymnasium seemed to be the key to resolving the "indigenous problem" and regenerating the race, both physically and mentally.

Franz Tamayo (1879–1956), Bolivia's foremost *mestizo letrado,* responded to the liberal's proposal for regeneration in a series of 55 editorials that he wrote in the newspaper he edited, *El Diario.* Collected and republished in 1910 under the title *Creación de la pedagogía nacional* (The creation of national pedagogy), these articles sharply criticized the liberal impulse to imitate European pedagogical models indiscriminately.

Resembling the well-known pedagogical debate on what to do with the "backwardness" of the indigenous population, which took place in Peru at the turn of the twentieth century, between the liberal Manuel Vicente Villarán and the conservative Alejandro Deustua, Tamayo's *Creación de la pedagogía nacional* formed an open debate with Felipe Segundo Guzmán (1879–1946), whose *El Problema pedagógico en Bolivia* (Bolivia's pedagogical problem) was published the same year. In his counterarguments, Tamayo argued that the nation's educational problems should not be addressed by contemplating European models, but only by looking to the vital strengths of Bolivia itself. What needed to be studied were not foreign methods or models, but the soul of Bolivia's own race. Departing from the positivist concept of civilization, Tamayo proposed that local culture be more closely studied. If civilization is the stage one reaches through instruction, Tamayo argued, it should be subordinated to the exercise of the will. Education is not a matter of accumulating the baggage of facts in our brains, but rather what we can forge with our own wills. More than ideas and knowledge acquired through intelligence, the important thing is to learn our own customs. Thus Tamayo placed two orders of knowledge in opposition to one another: education and instruction. Instruction is objective, rational, but not transcendent, because it does not allow us to discover the nation's essence. In *Creación de la pedagogía nacional* Tamayo sought to discover this will, this national character. If this is our goal, Tamayo argued, we will not get far by sending pedagogical missions to Europe so that they can study alien models that will be of no help in discovering our own vitality. The conclusion that Tamayo reached in his comparison of instruction and education could not have been more paradoxical: rational instruction leads to mummification, whereas education in one's own vitality leads to the discovery of existence. It is not by thinking but by acting that we reach a true comprehension of existence. This disdain of reason led Tamayo to the irrational suspicion that intelligence, divorced from the vital strengths of existence, falsifies reality (Albarracín-Millán, 1981).

As Tamayo continued writing his articles, however, he began to put an interesting twist on his argument for the primacy of action over reason, and his text ends by giving first place to *mestizo* intelligence, which may be disorderly, infantile, incipient, yet a factor for progress. Tamayo's discourse thus began to accommodate the inner factor of culture to the external factors of Western progress that indigenous vitality would not consider. Hard as the environment he inhabited, the Indian withstood the slings and arrows of Western civilization as if that were his strange vocation. His resistance to change and to passive acceptance of the foreign elements in the civilization that defeated him was both a virtue and a defect in his racial character. The Indian was a body and a will that endured. His soul, withdrawn into itself, explained the Aymara's psychology. Deprived of intelligence, the Indian was pure will and character, untouched by aesthetic imagination or metaphysical thought. It was thus pointless to search in the Aymara race for the hint of a higher intelligence. That was a quality of the *mestizo*, who displayed quick understanding, intellectual liveliness, and an aptitude for understanding aesthetic forms. The *mestizo*, however, lacked the European will. Worker or artist, writer or architect, his acts had no personality. He therefore lived a life of volunteering and of imitating what is not his own. Good at copying, but lacking sufficient willpower to create anything truly his own, the *mestizo* was incapable of putting the imprint of his will on things.

The sharp differences between Indian and *mestizo* could be overcome, Tamayo argued, by applying different pedagogical roles to each race. The Indian's education called for a pedagogy of love and patience, the *mestizo's* instruction for a disciplined pedagogy that would develop his intellect. The two pedagogies would take different paths: the Indian's would work from his will and regal physique; the *mestizo's*, from his head and his intelligence. Tamayo's proposal fashioned an ideal image relating the Indian to the Westernized, *criollo*-ized mestizo, but at all costs avoiding the Indian's devolution into a *cholo*.

Tamayo's discourse on the autochthonous, which sought to recuperate the indigenous, at the same time re-created the social fractures of the colonial order, for it could not resolve the contradictions between the indigenous "interior," with its particular communitarian vision, and the *mestizo-criollo* "exterior," ruled by European models of observation. Tamayo's discourse reflected these contradictory impulses. By referring to the Indian's vital energy, Tamayo showcased his differences with European positivist models. However, when he advocated the development of the *mestizo's* intellect, he combined the indigenous difference with Western forms, which, though deriving from a European irrationalism – mainly the German irrational "vitalism" that he borrowed from Nietzsche and Schopenhauer – that contradicted positivism, nonetheless added up to yet another foreign gaze on the local culture to which Tamayo hoped to return its strength and originality.

A moderate metropolitan thinker, Tamayo can only be understood if we link his thoughts to Schopenhauer, Nietzsche, and Goethe. Foreign models of observing Bolivian reality were never really questioned at any point in the twentieth century. However, the originality of his thought must be emphasized. Tamayo published his book well before Spanish philosopher José Ortega y Gasset founded his *Revista de Occidente*, a journal that deeply influenced other Latin American thinkers who questioned rationalism. Rooted in the identity crisis that Spain suffered after its defeat at the hands of the United States and the final loss of its colonial empire in the war of 1898, the *Revista de Occidente* carried articles of the German idealists that left a deep imprint on Spanish-American writers. Tamayo's writings also predated those of Keyserling, the German philosopher who predicted the birth of a vigorous civilization in South America. Tamayo wrote on the autochthonous long before Ricardo Rojas created his nativist metaphor "Eurindia" in 1924 as a synthesis of Argentine culture; long before Mexican thinker José Vasconcelos wrote *La Raza cósmica* [The cosmic race] in 1926.

This exploration of Franz Tamayo's discourse on the autochthonous leads us to the relation between the *indigenista* essay and the visual arts. In this sense, throughout the first half of the twentieth century Tamayo's reflections on *indigenismo* and *mestizaje* remained intrinsic to the development of Bolivian discourse on the autochthonous as reflected in the plastic arts. A close look at the paintings of Cecilio Guzmán de Rojas (1899–1950), one of the most prominent Bolivian painters of the first half of the twentieth century, indicates that his stylized representations of the autochthonous, painted in accordance with upper-class "good taste," are the best pictorial expressions of the discourse on *mestizaje*. Indeed, Guzmán de Rojas's paintings provide excellent examples to explain the *mestizo-criollo* representation of the indigenous people with a disciplinary optic that does not allow the Indian to come to its own terms. Guzmán de Rojas, who started painting in 1919, influenced by the Spanish painter Romero de Torres, also painted stylized Indians, following the Peruvian José Sabogal's appeal to "Incaism."

Sabogal, whose most important painting is *The Indian Mayor of Chincheros: Varayoc* (1925), and who returned from Europe in 1919 with his new Fauvist-influenced *indigenista* style, dominated painting in Peru during the 1920s and 1930s. Sabogal influenced Guzmán de Rojas with his highly dignified and static *indigenista* figures. Bringing the past into the present, he painted the Indians as Incas – that is, he presented a past grandeur in the context of nations that needed to assert their unity. This was an art of academic formalism, which reproduced the hierarchical structure of society in an historical setting. Peruvian art critic Mirko Lauer (1967: 100) suggests that the final achievement of this formalism "was to make the undernourished muscular, the poor rich, the ragged luxurious, and to create in the public mind a division between the Andean people's past and their present."

Guzmán de Rojas followed Sabogal in order to construct a vision that would give the Bolivian elites a sublime, idealized representation of the country and of themselves. Like Sabogal, who dictated artistic taste in Peru as the director of that country's National School of Fine Arts, Guzmán de Rojas served as the arbiter of "good taste" for the elites of La Paz, giving back to them a gratifying view of themselves. One of Guzmán de Rojas's most revealing paintings, *Cristo Aymara* (Aymara Christ, 1939), is indicative of both his deification of *indigenismo* and his one-dimensional representation of reality. *Cristo Aymara* is perhaps the best visual representation of the autochthonous in Bolivian art. Indeed, Guzmán de Rojas shared Tamayo's disdain for "Bovaryism," the copying of foreign literary and artistic trends to the detriment of Bolivia's identity rooted in its indigenous vitality.

## Peruvian *Indigenismo* and the Avant-Gardes

The more conservative or Westernized state of Bolivian *indigenista* thought came in sharp contrast to the robustness of Peruvian *indigenismo* during the 1920s. The real divide was between those, like the Peruvian *indigenistas* we will see next, who wanted to create a unique, non-Western culture for Latin America and others, like the Bolivian *letrados*, who did not wish to depart from modern Western civilization.

Antenor Orrego, a Peruvian writer associated with *Amauta,* review edited by José Carlos Mariátegui, and an enthusiastic follower of Waldo Frank (Williamson, 1992: 521), spoke of the need to find a new "integral" culture in Latin America. A socialist and an *indigenista*, Orrego accepted that such an enterprise would entail a revaluation of the orthodox Marxist theory. Indeed, Peruvian *indigenistas* were quite prepared to rethink history. As Williamson (1992: 522) indicates, Orrego's fellow *indigenista*, Víctor Raúl Haya de la Torre, the founder of APRA, the party that conceived revolution as the only possible way to liberate "Indo-America," instanced imperialism, which European Marxists considered as the last stage of capitalism, but which, viewed from "Indo-America," was the first stage of capitalist development. But if the rethinking of the historical process was to create a new theoretical space for Latin America, the most creative mind, capable of rethinking Marxism, was that of the Peruvian *mestizo* thinker José Carlos Mariátegui (1895–1930).

Founder of *Amauta*, José Carlos Mariátegui, author of the seminal *Siete ensayos de interpretación de la realidad peruana* (Seven interpretative essays on Peruvian reality, 1928) took the Indian heritage as the source of cultural authenticity. In this sense, Mariátegui, like Antenor Orrego, looked for "cultural wholeness" as the "praxis" – the integration of the abstract and the concrete, of the spiritual and the material – through which the regeneration of the indigenous communities and the revitalization of Indian traditions would take place. Believing that the Inca state was a prototype of a socialist society, Mariátegui argued that the Indian peasantry rather than the industrial proletariat were the true revolutionary class in Latin America.

Mariátegui was also the key figure of Peru's literary vanguards. As Vicky Unruh has indicated in her study on Latin American vanguards (1994), Mariátegui coincided historically with the reformist and modernizing dictatorship of Augusto Leguía (1919–30), who initiated social and educational reforms in order to eradicate the dissent of labor movements and student radicals that had emerged in the first two decades of the 1900s. Though the Leguía dictatorship stifled open intellectual and political exchange, Mariátegui gathered provincial intellectuals in the Peruvian capital, Lima, where they had been attracted by student reform activists, and he published there his journal *Amauta* (1926–30) to combat Leguía's plans to incorporate Peru's Indian population into upper-class Peruvian culture. Other Andean societies had no literary journal comparable to *Amauta*, nor any lasting regional vanguardist magazine like the *Boletín Titikaka* (1926–30) of Peru's Puno province, which vigorously promoted the values of an autonomous indigenous culture (Unruh, 1994: 71–124).

*Amauta* was the consequence of the radical artistic movements that transformed the arts in Europe in the first decades of the twentieth century. Indeed, Fauvism, Expressionism, Cubism, Dadaism, Purism, and Constructivism entered Latin America as part of a vigorous current of renovation during the 1920s (Ades, 1989: 125). *Amauta*, a Quechua word meaning "wise man" or "teacher," expressed the adherence of Peruvian radical thought to the Indian race. A review which explicitly linked the artistic and literary avant-garde to revolutionary politics, *Amauta* was militant and polemic. It made no concessions to intellectual tolerance, and, open to all "vanguardistas, socialistas, revolucionarios," it was committed to change. Indicating that no aesthetic can reduce art to a question of technique, Mariátegui laid out his position clearly in "Art, Revolution and Decadence," published in the third issue of *Amauta*: "The revolutionary nature of contemporary schools or trends does not lie in the creation of new techniques. Nor does it lie in the destruction of an old technique. It lies in the rejection, dismissal and ridicule of the bourgeois absolute" (Mariátegui, 1926).

While Mariátegui expressed particular admiration for the French Surrealist leaders André Breton and Louis Aragon, *Amauta* did not adhere to any particular Surrealist school of thought. As Dawn Ades points out (1989: 130), *Amauta*, with its broad avant-garde and leftist inclination, was mainly eclectic. Its contributors included César Vallejo, José Vasconcelos (the Mexican essayist and Minister of Education of Álvaro Obregón who founded the mural program), the British playwright George Bernard Shaw, the painter José Sabogal, and, among other Andean *letrados*, Franz Tamayo and the radical middle-class intellectual Gustavo Navarro, a follower of Mariátegui who wrote in the 1920s under the assumed name of Tristán Marof. None of these Andean intellectuals did, however, show Mariátegui's vigor, intellectual ability, or depth of thought. No Andean radical thinker had the Peruvian essayist's ability to see the artist's relationship to the world as one of engaged autonomy. Because Mariátegui and his journal saw art as "eternally heterodox," they were able to decentralize it, positioning themselves far in advance of all forms of orthodoxy when they argued that even politically engaged artists had a duty to provoke debate and to question the beliefs to which they themselves were committed.

From a postcolonial perspective, there are also clear epistemological differences between Mariátegui's thought and the writings of *letrados* promoting the autochthonous. While both Tamayo and Mariátegui revealed intellectual interests for Western thought, and coincided in their enthusiasm for Nietzsche, they each appropriated the Western tradition in contrasting ways. While Tamayo worked within Schopenhauerian and Nietzschean global designs without truly seeking the limits in their application to Bolivian culture, Mariátegui, on the other hand, moved inversely, from local histories to global designs. As a "border thinker" (Mignolo, 2000: 140), not just a metropolitan thinker from the margin, Mariátegui encountered the limits of Marxism in the domain of Peruvian colonialism and racism.

One last commentary on Mariátegui and the Peruvian vanguards. Unruh has detailed their anti-academic tone during the 1920s. This anti-academicism recuperated the nineteenth-century Peruvian intellectual Manuel González Prada's antipathy for the Spanish-oriented, linguistically conservative spirit. Mariátegui lauded González Prada's revolutionary spirit in "El proceso de la literatura" (The process of literature), the essay in his *Siete ensayos de interpretación de la realidad peruana* in which he dissected Peruvian aesthetic colonialism. Mariátegui criticized the institutionalization of colonialist models and the verbal artifices that denied the properties of vernacular language, and he interpreted Peruvian reality through the expanded field of a complex literary process full of contradictions and antagonisms. In "El proceso de la literatura," Mariátegui gave us not a history of Peruvian literature but a new way of seeing the construction of the modern nation through indigenous eyes. Advocating linguistic colloquialism, he affirmed that popular languages provided a perpetual source of literary innovation. What he was suggesting was the construction of a new vanguard, capable of searching for modernity and cosmopolitanism from the vernacular, from the languages of the street (Unruh, 1994: 226).

## Bonfil Batalla's Anti-Colonialism

In this brief final section we will move from the Andes to the anthropologist Guillermo Bonfil Batalla's (1935–91) reflections on Mexican society. Just as Mariátegui had done in his analysis of Peruvian reality during the 1920s, we also perceive in Bonfil Batalla's essays the presence of *indigenismo* and *mestizaje* as nothing but an upperclass *letrado* discourse whose purpose is to justify the continued domination of the *mestizos* who, in the case of Mexico, assumed power after the Mexican Revolution of 1910, in the wake of the modernizing days of Porfirio Díaz, and in opposition to his group of intellectuals, the *científicos*. As a homogenized *mestizo* version of the nation, Bonfil Batalla saw that the ideological construction of *mestizaje* imposes modernity, regulates the social imaginary, and postpones the claims of subalternity, the claims of what he described as "el México profundo."

In Mexico, the creation of *mestizaje* owed a great deal to the archaeologist Manuel Gamio, who, like Tamayo, promoted the integral education of the contemporary Indian, and founded, in 1917, the Department of Anthropology in Mexico City. Like Gamio, the influential José Vasconcelos, minister of culture under Obregón (1921–4), sought to identify Mexican identity with *mestizaje*. Later on, the influential *pensador* Samuel Ramos extended the concept of *mestizaje* to include foreign influences, and observed that Mexican culture had to ultimately be conceived as "universal culture made ours" (Williamson, 1992: 524–5). But the tensions between the "universal" and the "local" could not be better analyzed than in Bonfil Batalla's perception that, as different as Gamio's or Vasconcelos's construction of *mestizaje* may have been from the nineteenth-century endeavors to build the nation by dividing Western "civilization" from Amerindian "barbarism," *mestizaje* remained under European disciplinary hegemony and implied a necessary temporal and spatial distinction between the West and the non-West. Bonfil Batalla counteracted this historicism by demonstrating that Gamio and Vasconcelos applied to Mexican *mestizaje* Western forms of interpretation and of representation, thus upholding the "first in Europe, then elsewhere" temporal structure of history (Chakrabarty, 2000: 7). This historicism, that Bonfil Batalla watched critically, is just a local version of the same narrative that replaces "Europe" with the *mestizo* as a locally constructed center. In *México profundo: Una civilización negada* (*Mexico Profundo: Reclaiming a Civilization*, 1987), Bonfil Batalla's critical view of *mestizaje* runs counter to the very notion that historical time is the measure of the cultural distance that is assumed to exist between the West and the non-West. Consequently, he established the need to go beyond an "imaginary Mexico" modeled after Western civilization. Bonfil Batalla opposed to this Westernized version of Mexico the "de-Indianized" rural indigenous communities. They, together with vast sectors of the poor urban population, constitute the "México profundo." Their lives and ways of understanding the world continue to be rooted in Mesoamerican civilization.

It is the long process of "internal colonialism" that induced the upper classes to build an "imaginary Mexico" apart from the real population. What, then, is de-Indianization? For Bonfil Batalla, it was the social mechanism which determined the construction of an alienating *mestizo* national culture that forced the indigenous population to lose its identity; it implied the loss of Mexico's pluralism. De-Indianization is attained when the population stops believing in its own roots, accepting in turn the imposed and imaginary construction of a unified *mestizo* culture.

The "de-Indianization" of the indigenous populations was a key consequence of *indigenismo* and *mestizaje*, responding to a Westernized point of view organized around the thought of *pensadores* such as Arguedas, Tamayo, Gamio, and Vasconcelos, among others. In contrast, it is clear that the limitations of *indigenismo* were detected in the critical writings of radical intellectuals such as Mariátegui and Bonfil Batalla. Through them we found out that indigenous experience is an "exterior" positioning, one that uses its *locus* to break with *mestizaje* and the discourse of power. Indigenous exteriority calls into question the dialectics and philosophies of history that the discourses of national construction lean on for support, as do the discourses of power. As Bonfil Batalla put it: "We must learn to see the West from Mexico, not Mexico from the West" (1987: 235).

## REFERENCES AND FURTHER READING

### References

Ades, Dawn (1989). *Art in Latin America*. New Haven, CT and London: Yale University Press.

Albarracín-Millán, Juan (1981). *El Pensamiento filosófico de Tamayo y el irracionalismo alemán* [Tamayo's philosophic thought and German irrationalism]. Vol. I. La Paz: Akapana.

Arguedas, Alcides (1937 [1909]). *Pueblo enfermo* [A sick country]. 3rd edn. Santiago: Ediciones Ercilla.

Bonfil-Batalla, Guillermo (1996 [1987]). *México Profundo: Reclaiming a Civilization*. Trans. Philip A. Dennis. Austin: University of Texas Press.

Chakrabarty, Dipesh (2000). *Provincializing Europe: Postcolonial Thought and Historical Difference*. Princeton, NJ: Princeton University Press.

Harris, Olivia (1995). "Ethnic identity and market relations: Indians and Mestizos in the Andes." In Brooke Larson, Olivia Harris, and Enrique Tandeter (eds), *Ethnicity, Markets, and Migrations in the Andes: At the Crossroads of History and Anthropology*, pp. 351–90. Durham, NC: Duke University Press.

Lauer, Mirko (1967). *Introducción a la pintura peruana del siglo 20* [Introduction to twentieth-century Peruvian painting]. Lima: Mosca Azul Editores.

León-Portilla, Miguel (1975). "Aztecs and Navajos: a reflection on the right of not being engulfed," occasional paper, Weatherland Foundation, New York, pp. 10–11.

Mariátegui, José Carlos (1926). "Arte, revolución y decadencia," *Amauta*, 3: 6–10.

— (1979 [1928]). *Siete ensayos de interpretación de la realidad peruana* [Seven interpretative essays on Peruvian reality]. Mexico City: Ediciones Era.

Mignolo, Walter (2000). *Local Histories/Global Designs: Coloniality, Subaltern Knowledge, and Border Thinking*. Princeton, NJ: Princeton University Press.

Stern, Steve, ed. (1987). *Resistance, Rebellion, and Consciousness in the Andean Peasant World: 18th to 20th Centuries*. Madison: University of Wisconsin Press.

Tamayo, Franz (1975 [1910]). *Creación de la pedagogía nacional* [The creation of national pedagogy]. 3rd edn. La Paz: Biblioteca del Sesquicentenario de la República.

Unruh, Vicky (1994). *Latin American Vanguards: The Art of Contentious Encounters*. Berkeley: University of California Press.

Williamson, Edwin (1992). *The Penguin History of Latin America*. London: Penguin.

### Further Reading

Irurozqui, Marta (2000). "The sound of Pututos: politicisation and indigenous rebellions in Bolivia, 1826–1921," *Journal of Latin American Studies*, 32: 85–114. (An interesting presentation of nineteenth- and early twentieth-century Bolivian indigenous movements from the perspective of subaltern studies.)

Lauer, Mirko (1997). *Andes imaginarios: Discursos del indigenismo 2* [Imaginary Andes: discourses on *indigenismo* 2]. Lima: Centro de Estudios Regionales Andinos "Bartolomé de Las Casas" – Cuzco/SUR Casa de Estudios del Socialismo. (An excellent study on the distinctions between political *indigenismo* and cultural *indigenismo*, which the author calls *indigenismo* 2.)

Quijano, Aníbal (1997). "Colonialidad del poder, cultura y conocimiento en América Latina" [Coloniality of power, culture, and knowledge in Latin America], *Anuario Mariateguiano*, 9: 113–21. (A revealing analysis of racism and colonialism in the Peruvian Andes.)

Sanjinés C., Javier (2004). *Mestizaje Upside-Down: Aesthetic Politics in Modern Bolivia*. Pittsburgh: University of Pittsburgh Press. (An analysis of the presentation of *mestizaje* in the sociohistori-cal, political, and aesthetic traditions of twentieth-century Bolivia.)

Zevallos-Aguilar, Juan Luis (2002). *Indigenismo y nación: Los retos a la representación de la subalternidad aymara y quechua en el "Boletín Titikaka," 1926–1930* [*Indigenismo* and nation: challenges to the representation of Aymara and Quechua subalternity in the *Boletín Titikaka*, 1926–1930]. Lima: Instituto Francés de Estudios Andinos. (A renewed interpretation of the *Indigenista* group "Orkopata," linked to the social movements of southern Peru during the first decades of the twentieth century.)

# 24
# Cultural Theory and the Avant-Gardes: Mariátegui, Mário de Andrade, Oswald de Andrade, Pagú, Tarsila do Amaral, César Vallejo

*Fernando J. Rosenberg*

The avant-gardes emerged in Latin America as a new instance of the intellectual investment in the project of modernity, which the variously affiliated *vanguardistas*, so self-described or not, advocated and wanted to see fulfilled. Linked by their upbringing or by their association to the educated middle class, these artists and intellectuals identified with the values of that group, increasingly dominant in the cultural and political arena. Mexican *estridentistas*, Brazilian *modernistas*, pan-Hispanic *creacionistas* and *ultraístas* all believed actively in the radical novelty of what they brought to the cultural scene: the preponderance of metaphor, a radical vision of artistic freedom, a renewal of literary references that incorporated icons of modernity, and an original set of provoking ideas regarding national or continental identity. The emergence of an art under the banner of the "new" and the "modern" paralleled the democratization of the political sphere with the increasing protagonism of new agents, the growth of industrial sectors, and a demographic shift toward the expanding cities.

The role of the intellectual as champion and agent of modernity, in no way a novelty, is rather only a continuation of a quite traditional, exclusionary position in an elitist project. But at this historical juncture, the affiliation with the purported universalism of the modern project revealed itself to be particularly problematic and paradoxical. The reinvestment in and reconsideration of the idea of the modern during this time, with its emphasis on novelty, revolution, and the acceleration of history, demanded a concomitant questioning of its assumptions. For many Latin American writers and artists, this process entailed an examination of the place assigned for their native cultures, or for their particular site of production and consumption of cultural objects, by the universalistic assumptions and the sense of historical direction that the idea of modernity generates. The avant-gardes in Latin America thus undertook an inquiry into their own place in a global dynamic – which is to say, into the global allocation of value instated by the colonial encounter, into the ways this dynamic informed cultural production, and into the ways in which this production circulated and perpetuated systems of subordination, or opened new avenues of contestation.

It is generally assumed that the movements, known in Latin America as *las vanguardias*, updated the cultural field and the discussions of national and continental identity by creatively incorporating European aesthetic innovations and mixing them with native cultural traditions. Artists and writers who, even when not directly self-defined as *vanguardistas*, identified with a vanguardistic ethos and partook of the cultural climate that the movements wrought, resorted to such recognized avant-garde techniques as multiperspectivism and collage-like open works and to the mythical and the irrational to expand the limits of artistic expression. This development coincided with and also fed into a discussion that permeated the cultural production of the period between the world wars, a discussion in which the narratives of identity (continental and national) started to favor ideas of *mestizaje*, hybridity, and transculturation intended to include, in these collages of identity, realities and voices left aside by European models of modernity and nationhood.

In this manner, the vanguards have been regarded as fostering and sometimes even initiating the possibility of creative mixes and fluid sites of mediation – often projected as explanations or recommendations for Latin American cultural production in general – between foreign and native, indigenous and European, modernity and tradition, rural and urban, thus interrogating the fixed positions of these terms assigned by nineteenth-century elaborations of national modernity. The most radical intellectual and artistic processes and objects of this period drew attention to the diffusionist premise that lies at the core of modernity's sense of historical direction. That is, the idea that the historical developments in Latin America, in this case the shift effected by the vanguards in the cultural productions of the period, always followed only afterward, ineluctably secondary to developments that occurred at the centers of modernity. In this foundational narrative, disarmed by certain avant-gardists in various ways, modernity is a consequence of a universal history springing from a European site that only secondarily is exported and adapted to peripheral soil.

It is my contention that Latin American vanguards attempted not just to compensate for their supposed historical belatedness by rapidly incorporating the new European products of avant-garde artistic achievements, as it has been argued repeatedly, but more interestingly, to undermine the diffusionist premise altogether. The sites of enunciation opened up by the vanguards often undermined what is arguably the principal dynamic of modernity – its projection of a hierarchy ordered by a single temporality that it sets up in order to define what is and what isn't *yet* modern, constructing a world in which progress and backwardness are distributed geographically and define each other comparatively.

Therefore, it can be argued that the Latin American avant-garde movements participated in a cultural turn, that is, in an atmosphere of heightened cultural relativism and historical openness that, after World War I, cut against the narrative of a single line of progress and the idea of a teleological development toward a universal civilization, ideas ingrained into the European sense of identity. Concepts of cultural production elaborated during the period of the avant-gardes (in manifestos and the like) emphasized a cosmopolitan freedom that had been already granted by the very promises of modernity, a freedom in the midst of which these artists and thinkers found themselves already living, and the concomitant capacity to draw from both European and native frames of reference, aesthetic traditions, and articulations of knowledge. Notions of flexible and creative incorporations, rather than of culture understood as an expression of an ontological base, were a necessary component of the formula, and in fact they constituted one of the most relevant sites of contestation that Latin American intellectuals were able to outline. These incorporations, proposed as inaugural to the transatlantic colonial encounter – paradigmatically, but not only, in the Brazilian *modernistas'* theory of a constitutive anthropophagy as the emblematic Latin American stance – or enacted by the vanguardists themselves when borrowing from European movements (Futurism, Expressionism, Cubism, etc.), offered a strategy to counterbalance the diffusionist premise through the projection of a modernity that was already experienced as simultaneous, albeit uneven. But for the first time, unevenness did not necessarily imply belatedness, but represented the very site of production and contestation. It was by imagining Latin America as a site of continuous creative reaccommodations of both native and European legacies that the vanguards secured a place for the native in modernity, in establishing peripheral modernities – rejecting subordination to a single paradigm of modernity and instead offering re-creation of modernity as an authentic indigenous alternative.

Thus, the emphasis on borrowing European sources and adapting their production more or less creatively, so paramount among avant-garde texts and later critical approaches to them, has lent to an obscuring of a key, heterogenous site of contestation that I want to highlight in my discussion. Vanguardists such as Guatemalan Miguel Ángel Asturias and Brazilian Mário de Andrade did more toward consolidating peripheral modern nationalities, alternative to European models, than bringing together (in their narrative works *Leyendas de Guatemala* [Guatemala legends, 1930] and *Macunaíma, o herói sem nenhum caráter* [*Macunaíma, the Hero with No Character*, 1928) surrealist emphases on the non-Western imagination and the legacy of the native mythical world, so often treated. There is a still more radical project in such vanguardist texts as these, an unsettling of the very concept of a modern nation, even in cases when the officially adopted imaginary was explicitly indigenous. This chapter attempts to move beyond limiting the vanguards to their theories of creative incorporation as a national resource, in order to highlight their simultaneous interrogation of a dynamic that creates centers and peripheries, consumers and producers, in the first place.

The new critical position sought by the vanguards dovetails with a shift in global hegemony that characterized the aftermath of World War I. With the implosion of the imperial crisis in Europe, the United States started to project itself as a global power, in a continuation of the ambitions piloted on its own continent with the championing of a Pan-Americanism that granted itself sole hegemony from at least the end of the nineteenth century. The cultural production of the vanguardistic era can be read as different ways to map the location of Latin American cultures at a particular historical crossroads characterized by the crises of the European models of civilization and high culture, a receptivity and openness to radical change exemplified by the Mexican and Soviet Revolutions, the rise of fascism in Europe, and the forceful realignment of the US hegemony in the region.

By depicting the avant-gardes as engaged in making explicit a position in the geohistory of modernity, I am not favoring only artistic enterprises with professed affiliation to the internationalist Left. In fact, the opposite has been held: In comparison with the European avant-gardes, the Latin American movements were not as socially radical, and their function resided more in the building of cultural and artistic institutions that the European movements strove to destroy. But their radicalism, I contend, resides elsewhere: not in the alliance with revolutionary politics (although many artists voiced their affiliation and explicitly inscribed their work in the political Left) or in the extreme subversion of artistic rules (although they also infringed those rules), but in the reconsideration of Latin America's position in the West, in their gauging the condition of possibility of their own enunciation in the midst of shifting geopolitical forces.

Latin American avant-gardes resorted to the non-Western mythological imagination, as Europeans also did, to question the foundational myths of modernity. But the politics of location of course differed between the Europeans and the Latin Americans, and an awareness of this difference should inform any reading of the nativist attempts of the Latin American avant-gardes. A provocative artistic primitivism consisted in unleashing and unveiling the instinctive substratum of human societies, and the Europeans selectively appropriated and mobilized non-Western repertoire to make this point – the rest of the world imagined as the threatened resource of unconscious potential. The Latin Americans, it has been argued repeatedly, recovered their native roots for the reconstitution of the national imagination on a different-than-Western ground, which might suggest at first a less ambitious project. But this intellectual trend resorted to the accumulated knowledge of the anthropological science – toward which Latin American avant-gardists started to develop an ambivalent stance – relying on its authoritative legitimation of difference while suspicious of its participation in Western structures of power-knowledge.

The intellectual trajectory of Miguel Ángel Asturias is exemplary, in this regard, of many contradictions and paradoxes. Influenced by Herbert Spencer's social Darwinism, he had argued in the thesis for his law degree ("El problema social del indio," 1922) that the Indian race was decayed. But Asturias's literary breakthrough, mainly with his *Leyendas de Guatemala*, was informed by the critique of social evolutionism in the intellectual climate of the aftermath of World War I, when Europe (the author was living in Paris) considered itself to be decadent. The writer resorted to the Popul Vuh of the Maya-Quiché civilization of his native Guatemala, texts to which he had access through the institutionalized apparatus of French anthropology.[1] A comparable trajectory is part of Mário de Andrade's *Macunaíma*, whose plot actively cancels every evolutionist ideal (social, ethnic, national) characteristic of the nineteenth-century liberal project by favoring the simultaneous concurrence and festive interplay of all components of the nation (natives, Portuguese, and immigrants; rain forest and city; mythology and commerce; etc.). Both authors undermined the mimetic paradigm that was prevalent in earlier *indigenismos* with the intention of questioning Western rationalist pretensions along the lines of international modernism, but more importantly, as an attempt to do justice to heterogeneous narrative structures akin to Amerindian thought.

These texts indeed undermine the hierarchical evolutionary ladder of earlier positivist ethnologies, and propose instead either an anthropological mosaic of cultural relativism or a melting pot of ethnic and cultural *mestizaje* and transculturation. But we need to recognize that the project of shaking up the philosophical underpinnings of Western superiority, a vanguardist agenda in its own right, might be mobilized in favor of both old and new national hegemonic projects of the elite. European vanguards exercised their own cultural cannibalism by appropriating native others for their own agendas, but the cannibalistic appropriation here aligned native knowledge with the structures of Creole power in the nation-state, feeding the archive of national literature with a new argument that ended up confirming cultural, economic, and epistemological subordination. However, this criticism of the nativist incorporations of the vanguards, although no doubt valid, was also counterbalanced by the ironic self-reflection that these narratives were directed toward their own strategies of appropriation, which are often turned inside out. That is, these texts not only incorporate, but often reflect upon the structures of power/knowledge by which orality and native languages are recuperated and inscribed into the national literary canon.

These two narratives actively engage the idea of convivial coexistence suggested within the framework of *mestizaje*, while at the same time exploring the frustrated, unrealized, and even undesirable aspects of what *mestizaje* promised to bring together, since it would entail the perpetuation of a colonial system of hierarchies, turned now into a discourse of national identity. In *Leyendas de Guatemala*, indigenous voices and perspectives live amid the reality of colonial institutions, sometimes clashing, sometimes mixing, sometimes just existing as parallel experiences at different levels of perception and sensitivity. There is no single law (not incorporation, or conviviality, or transculturation) that gives sense to the whole and that provides a direction to national history. That is why the title is misleading, since despite the nationalistic intention, Guatemala remains in the book the region where the colonial and the indigenous ultimately cannot produce a positive sense of identity, or a desirable direction of history. Moreover, the title's suggested unity is at the same time unwelcome, since the nation-state would subsume within its framework the indigenous reality that the *Leyendas* present as beyond rationalizing Western grasp. Likewise, *Macunaíma*'s festive mixing of everything Brazilian (geographical features and historical traces, legends and rituals of various origins, city life and wilderness) seems to suggest a utopian, even carnivalesque, conviviality. Although this trend is coherent with the anthropophagic teleology of Brazilian *modernismo* (with its diet of Western and native made into the original gesture of postcolonial appropriation), the narrative is dotted with indigestible remnants – historical elements that the narrative of national incorporation is unable to integrate and tragic victims of its never-ending struggle for conquest.

Placing in dialogue two essays – one by the Peruvian writer César Vallejo and the other by the Peruvian Marxist philosopher José Carlos Mariátegui – will help further to highlight what I understand to be the most novel of the vanguardistic attempts: the strategies for reconfiguring the locus of enunciation of Latin American artists by unlocking the entrapments of their own place in the geography of modernity and by interrupting the reproduction of global cultural hierarchies that legitimated different levels of subordination. The stance devised for this purpose was defined by different and contradictory demands: the acknowledgment of the largely irrecoverable status of native values and sense of community, the undesirability of notions of progress and civilization that reproduced the abjection of Latin America's own situation, and the embrace of modern values as vehicles/apparatuses for gaining agency and effecting social change. This critical stance mobilized and displayed both native and cosmopolitan affiliations.

César Vallejo's essay "Contra el secreto profesional" (Against the professional secret, 1927; in Schwartz, 1991: 513) endorses a negative view of what we now might call "postcolonial mimicking" – a view of the former colonies as engaged in the superficial imitation of the achievements of the metropolitan center, a facile approach to modernity that he accuses some of his fellow contemporary Latin Americans of practicing. The article makes an explicit call to American (meaning Latin American) poets to reflect on the current state of their aesthetics. The "professional secret" is the collection of learned vanguardistic tricks that Vallejo enumerates – from matters of technique such as altered punctuation and use of the space of the page to voice revolutionary and cosmopolitan affiliations – copied literary devices that leave the Latin American writer in a position of inauthenticity. *Vanguardia*, for Vallejo, is almost synonymous with mimicking European artistic gestures and embracing, always too late, the icons of modernity. Although he was arguably one of the most radical innovators in Latin American poetry of the vanguard generation and beyond, for Vallejo, the vanguardistic impetus of the young Latin American artists is nothing new, just a continuation of the dynamic of postcolonial alienation.

In Mariátegui's view, however, Vallejo's stark characterization of the Latin American movements would be challenged by Vallejo's own radical poetry, which he discusses in a seminal essay. For its contemporaneity and its historical breath, Mariátegui's "El proceso de la literatura" (The process of literature, 1928) stands as an inaugural text in the conceptualization of the vanguards. The philosopher situates the movements within a historical scheme that responds to the particular location both at the level of the nation and at the level of the postcolonial circumstances of Latin America.[2] He distinguishes, at the outset of his essay, three periods with different logics of production and different ways of processing location – the colonial, the cosmopolitan, and the national. The teleological assumption of this scheme, which intends to draw a typical trajectory from dependency and alienation, to absorption of the foreign, to the achievement of national self-consciousness, reveals itself to be problematic when Mariátegui applies it to the authors and movements under examination. At odds with his own scheme of dialectical overcoming, in Mariátegui's own description of the state of literature in Peru, the colonial, the cosmopolitan, and the national all appear to partake of a multilayered present.

The cultural formation that would bring the national form into its own is still pending for Mariátegui, who locates the colony as lingering in the present. What he characterizes as the "intellectual and sentimental prestige of the Viceroyalty" (325) constitutes what we can identify as a colonial structure of feelings. This is clearly a Peruvian historical situation (comparable only to the Mexican in terms of the sophistication of the colonial apparatus), but it is nevertheless of continental projection in terms of Mariátegui's emphasis on affective attachment to structures of colonial subordination, that is, on the formation of colonial subjectivity that outlives the institutions that can be properly called colonial. "The Colony ends right now" (324), he states, marking a moment in Mariátegui's description of overlapping *indigenismo* and increasing cosmopolitan, international influences, a contemporaneousness that promises finally to move the country away from colonial subordination and toward the realization of a national self. The claim is performative inasmuch as it, while voicing the demise of the colonial, also recognizes the ineluctable presence of what is never quite finished.

Among the artists affiliated to different extents with vanguard movements that Mariátegui surveys – Alberto Hidalgo, César Vallejo, Magda Portal – it is Vallejo who most decisively incarnates Mariátegui's ideal of a national literature that is able to acknowledge modern trends and preoccupations within a nativist frame of mind, a general way of being that can be related to Andean native cultures. For Mariátegui, Vallejo represents the new – a key concept with clear vanguardistic allure. But this "new" is in its turn defined anew as the possibility of arriving at an indigenous vision that is strictly Peruvian – of arriving at the moment in which the dichotomies that Mariátegui problematizes throughout the essay are superseded, particularly the alienation represented by the cosmopolitan affiliations of the artists of the postcolonial era, perhaps unraveling the impasse of which Vallejo speaks in his own essay. The national, thus, has for Mariátegui a twofold definition: It is what calls forth the indigenous, and by this movement, it also supersedes alienation into metropolitan aesthetic trends. If measured by European parameters, Vallejo might be a symbolist, a romantic, or a vanguardist, but none of the former categories strictly applies. National literature is thus reborn to a temporality that is heterogeneous, neither colonial nor cosmopolitan in the old sense.

A different way in which the metropolitan affiliation of the national formation was challenged was through the self-conscious performance of the familiar, colonially ascribed roles, now, however, recast as a radically simultaneous theater of global power and thus no longer necessarily participating in the reproduction of subordination. In

Oswald de Andrade's *Pau Brasil* manifesto (1924; in Schwartz, 1991: 137) its very title revaluates brazilwood, the first colonial commodity and the one from which the colonial domain received its name, as implying a strategic position vis-à-vis the international assignment of cultural value. The vanguard reconstructs national consciousness as a tongue-in-cheek, albeit defiant recognition of itself as a derivative factor of the global circulation of commodities. Brazil will have modernity its own way, by making Brazilian culture for export, by impersonating the good savage, and by fabricating primitivism for European consumption – an ironic performance of postcolonial mimicry, now valued as a strategy of peripheral modernities.

Oswald de Andrade's 1928 *Antropofágico* manifesto (in Schwartz, 1991: 143), for its part, contains the scandalous affirmation, which would imprint a strong watermark in Brazilian intellectual history, that the Amerindian's infamous cannibalization of the Portuguese bishop Sardinha is the constitutive event of a nationality that comes into its own by repeating this antropophagy of the foreigner and selectively incorporating what is worthy. The radical revaluation of transatlantic relations contained in these two influential texts upsets the problem of imitation that preoccupied both Vallejo and Mariátegui, who ran the risk of supposing the existence of first-rate and second-rate cultural phenomena and paradoxically placed Latin American avant-gardes as always behind.

The theater of global dynamics also implied a radical simultaneity: The universal history that the Brazilian manifestos projected was one in which Europe was not the self-contained source of historical evolution. Instead, it was itself involved in a much more dynamic temporality of simultaneous and interdependent processes of interlocal cross-definition and power struggle for the distribution and adscription of meaning. Only by highlighting these multiple processes can we make some sense of an intriguing statement in the *Antropofágico* manifesto: "Without us [Brazilians, Latin Americans] Europe wouldn't even have its poor declaration of human rights." The Enlightenment, that is, the moment in which Europe declared its historical maturity and presented the notion of universal rights as an achievement of Reason, setting itself apart from the rest of the world and by the same token defining the temporality of all others as belated, mobilized an ongoing comparison with the non-European, a comparison that defined who was at the center. By this comparative map, America had indeed a foundational position in the project of modernity. It was by discovering America that Europe defined itself and its dominance over the savage world, and it was thus that modern subjectivity came into being, mirroring this dominance within itself. Where the *Pau Brasil* manifesto displays an anxiety to "adjust the Imperial clock of national literature," the urgency, while signaling a lack of simultaneity requiring remedy, nevertheless makes evident a need to break with an empire that is still in some sense working its way into the nation, biding its time, displaying a resiliency that is itself the cause of retardation or perhaps the source of all measurement through which this retardation is diagnosed.

The production of the avant-gardes is tinted by a sense of proximity to an epochal shift or a revolution, as is apparent in Mariátegui's claims. This can be said to be common in the movements across the Atlantic, but in Latin America, owing to its particular historical situation and its peripheral position in the West, the urge and promise of the future adopted a particular character. In part, the openness of historical time intersected with the topic of European decadence with which continental philosophers had articulated their self-critique since the late nineteenth century. Although this intellectual trend often was complemented by the prophecy of the rise of another "civilization" to come (emblematically in the work of Oswald Spengler), Latin American avant-gardists voiced their suspicion of this view even when they themselves were forecast as the future subjects of world history. Vallejo, Mariátegui, Mário de Andrade, Jorge Luis Borges, and other writers associated with the vanguards all believed in the certain demise of the West, all of them looked in one way or another to a different future (at least during this initial decade, the 1920s), and all of them had some more or less developed taste for the particularity of America – either as a source of non-Western vision or as a frame that could be used to evaluate and distance themselves from the West – but none of them embraced the future as the growth of new civilization. The image of Latin America as the site of the future is so embedded with Eurocentric conceptions about the New World that the projection of this prophecy struck thinkers situated in this periphery as profoundly suspicious, dismissive of the diverse complexion of Latin America in favor of a organic unity, indifferent to historical patterns of transatlantic struggles that were disavowed with a vision of history as the self-contained development of cultural or civilizational blocks.

A diagnosis of the moment as one of profound change, of a worldwide historical situation that has arrived to an often indeterminate shifting point, is indeed a common denominator of many manifestos and other vanguard texts. The temporal mark of the "right now" in which the colony is (always) ending for Mariátegui is echoed in many instances, as for example when the *Proa* (Argentinian) magazine's initial manifesto, probably written by Borges, assures that World War I represented a liberation for the young Latin American nations from the "tutelary" European role, ensuring historical coordinates that facilitated, among other things, the student rebellion of 1918 (in Schwartz, 1991: 226). Different artistic trends seem to concur on the attempt to imagine the variables of a new world in the making, on the more or less vague feeling of a historical circumstance that would upset the cultural hierarchies imprinted since the foundation of the Western world and would dissuade Latin America's solicitous aspirants to it. Even when, for Vallejo, the avant-garde movements on both sides of the Atlantic represented only an appetite for novelty devoid of any social commitment, the "furious multiplication" of these movements was also a factor of capitalist forces on the verge of extinction (Schwartz, 1991: 433). The generalized perception of living in a time of profound cultural upheaval thus persisted throughout these different, apparently incompatible avant-garde trends.

A paradigmatic representation of these upheavals was the gesture of inverting the map of America and the accompanying slogan "Our North is the South" with which the Uruguayan painter Joaquín Torres García inaugurated the School of the South in the 1930s (which effectively became a foundational workshop for Latin

American artists in 1943; in Barnitz, 2001: 130–1). A landmark in Latin American art, the school is doubtlessly part of the performance of a paradigmatic shift that attempts to think from elsewhere. Torres García's resort to myriad icons from arcane cultural sources ordered within the geometrical abstraction of the grid is neither a return to the primitive nor a reliance on a preexisting universal, but an attempt at epistemological repositioning. From the Native American archive, Torres García used geometric patterns, distancing himself from a more mimetic *indigenismo* (of Peruvian José Sabogal, for example) and from the nationalistic, redemptive grand narratives of the Mexican *muralistas*. Torres García eschewed both the national and the colonial in order to engage the pre-Columbian as an alternative figuration, a pictorial thinking as the key to a vernacular, situated universalism.

It is possible in this way to understand the common ground that this very program-matic endeavor had with the much more individualistic visionary artistic project of the Argentinian Alejandro Xul Solar, despite the fact that the latter's flamboyant paintings differ greatly from Torres García's restrained compositions. Xul's taste for parallel realities and imaginary landscapes is punctuated by the presence of actual national flags and other signs of political geography as bearers of the utopias and their wreckage that would constitute the material vision of the Latin American artist. The abstract and the mythical, two of the touchstones by which the European avant-garde defined its universalist longings, turned in the hands of these two artists into inter-pretations of their geopolitical situations. In the context of Brazilian *modernismo*, Tarsila de Amaral depicted urban scenes, mythical aboriginal figures, and sheer non-figural abstractions with equally studied conceptualism and self-conscious naïveté, becoming emblematic of the plastic imagination of the movement. Her paintings are permeated with a sensuality that imbues Brazilian reality with a heterogeneous tem-porality, although modern icons (buildings, train stations) are sometimes present as signatures of multilayered contemporaneity. These features would be developed later by Brazilian painters who were affiliated with the vanguards at the outset of their careers, such as Cândido Portinari and Lasar Segall.

The affective charge of what represented novelty was no doubt a principal resource for the vanguardistic attempt to gauge the times of uncertainty and to imagine a historical direction. Several manifestos resorted to an avid desire for technological novelty, poised against what they saw as conservative, rigid forces of history. Pablo Neruda's "Sobre una poesía sin pureza" ("On a poetry without purity," 1935; in Schwartz, 1991: 485), along with some poems of his *Residencia en la tierra* (*Residence on Earth*, 1931), however, are remarkable in comparison, inasmuch as they stand up for discarded, resting, worn-out objects, for abject bodily functions, for outmoded artistic styles – for what had been dissociated from every sense of historical direction. This text is no doubt a reaction against the fetishism of the new and the commo-dification of life that is so often upheld cheerfully in vanguardistic texts from everywhere.

But the aspiration for novelty, which might be accused of favoring the opening of new capitalist markets on the periphery, merges in these vanguard movements with a completely different constellation of problems: the search for a Hispanic or Latin American way of being. The argument of a Hispanic, Latin, or national immanent "spirit" was also rehearsed, arguably in continuation with the state of the debate toward the turn of the century (i.e., the dichotomy of the materialist, bellicose North versus the spiritualist South in which the terms were initially defined after 1898). Also notable is the insistence on using the term "America," not "Hispanic America" or "Latin America," an indication not of the association with the North of the continent (whose imperialistic adventures and policies are often denounced in these texts), but of a colonial constellation that has defined America since the time of its "discovery" and that finds in the South the privileged scenario of a continuous reenactment. One of the most relevant contributions, therefore, inasmuch as it articulates the desire for novelty with the search for identity, is that offered by the *Pau Brasil* manifesto, which underscores three related points that are played out in other texts from the period: the reliance of novelty value on the logic of the commodity; the system of colonial assignation, appropriation, and reappropriation of cultural value mediated through the circulation of commodities; and the war of positions through which each participant defines his or her way of being, not understood as organic identities, but as sites of contestation that are opened up or carved out forcefully in the system.

The seminal anthology *Índice de la nueva poesía americana* (Index of the new American poetry, 1926) can be taken as a practical example of this set of problems. The editors of the volume, the Argentinian Jorge Luis Borges, the Peruvian Alberto Hidalgo, and the Chilean Vicente Huidobro, although they effectively selected poetry written in Spanish representing the "new," take issue with the whole idea of Hispanic Americanism. "I rush to declare that Hispanic Americanism repulses me. It is a false, utopian, mendacious thing, transformed (it couldn't be different) into a profession equal to any other," proclaims Hidalgo (5). Meanwhile, Borges relates Hispanic Americanism to the illusions of the Uruguayan José Enrique Rodó, caricaturized by Borges as a Bostonian scholar (15). The newness of the "new" that this 1926 anthology promotes in its title is located, for Borges, in a sensibility shaped by the concrete reality of some street in Mexico or Buenos Aires – far from the prophetic grandeur of transcendental ideals of identity or from any other more metropolitan location of far more celebrated prestige. Hidalgo conceives the effort to achieve independence not as an historical era of triumphal decolonization, but as a constant struggle now in the hands of "Russian, Italian, German immigrants" who are de-Hispanizing America and shaping its reality anew. Clearly these claims were attempts to construct a new cultural hegemony based on the partial experience of some educated major-city dwellers. But rather than arguing the obvious, I find it far more productive to reemphasize how two of the fundamental values for these movements, novelty and Americanism, were articulated and often mobilized as positions for challenging the reproduction of coloniality.

Needless to say, Pan-Americanism was also an instrumental ideology for fostering the new hegemonic alignment with the emerging world power represented by the United States. Many texts from the period adopted positions explicitly against this neo-imperialism (especially in the avant-garde texts of the Caribbean and Central America, owing to the insurmountable historical fact that the grip of the United

States had been always more tangible there than further south). Mariátegui most explicitly conceptualized what was at stake in the different strategies when he described Pan-Americanism as an ideology allied to "the bourgeois order" and Hispanic Americanism as a purely bureaucratic or academic platitude. The new order to which a different Hispanic Americanism should aspire was to be based on the historical reality of the multitudes (*muchedumbres*) working toward a "belligerent, active, multitudinous ideal" ("Does a Hispanic American thought exist?" in Schwartz, 1991: 503).

But the positions of the avant-gardes with respect to the United States cannot be summarized as a straightforward denunciation of US imperial policies. In fact, Europe figures more prominently in avant-garde texts as the provider of models, values, and ideals that are to be left behind. It might be argued with a certain degree of historical accuracy that the avant-garde movements rejected the salient features of nineteenth-century modernity – the positivism of the old regime of landowners affiliated with European interests – but remained blind to the new constellations of political subordination. In this intellectual climate, symbols of US culture and the internationalization of its cultural industry are often mentioned – sports, the foxtrot, jazz bands, the cinema, as well as its metropolis, Chicago or New York – as indicators of a renovated dynamic of culture that is ungraspable by the institutions of high culture and the conservative regimes, representing possibilities for emancipation. But this enthusiasm must also be understood differentially (from the perspective that, for lack of a better name, we are forced to call Latin American): not as a salute to modernity in its new capitalist universality, but as the opening up of a promise that identifies with the here and now as the site of contestation. A thinker trained in the orthodoxy of the Left such as Mariátegui, for example, at the same time that he denounces the industrialist-financial conglomerates in their effort to dominate the South, praises both the idealism of the North and its people and points to the fluctuations of the dollar as an accurate indicator of the direction of world history, more relevant than the pompous speculations of Hispanic philosophers à la mode ("Does a Hispanic American thought exist?" in Schwartz, 1991: 501).

The decline of the old order merges with the promise represented by US mass culture and the threat of its new form of imperialism in one of the most interesting novels of the period, the diptych *Los Siete locos – Los Lanzallamas* (*The Seven Madmen – The flamethrowers*, 1929–31), by the Argentinian Roberto Arlt. It features a revolutionary cell led by the intriguing Astrologer, who proposes different plans not only to take over the world, but also to conquer and subsume subjectivity, using a flexible strategy of simultaneous chemical attacks and mass-media-produced events. Although his fantastic lucubrations might be a sheer farce for personal gain, the fact remains that with an uncannily clear vision, the novel is able to identify a number of shifts occurring in culture and politics on a worldwide scale and to question the rules of engagement opened up by this new context. Argentinian economic ties with England are always suggested, constituting what the novel identifies as the current state of development in which the characters' everydayness unfolds. But the present is about to collapse. That is where the United States figures prominently, although never unambiguously, in the narrative. A US map hanging from the wall of the Astrologer's study shows where the Klu Klux Klan is active; the Mafia is mentioned several times, along with captains of industry and finance; Hollywood narratives are consumed, and the dream machine affects the imaginations and desires of the characters. These elements are indices of the current state of the world that needed to be reshuffled in the revolutionary moment and in the creation of a new order. Arlt's novel is remarkable in bringing together, from a multitude of perspectives, different political stances that characterized the vanguard movements, from the diagnosis of the fall of the bourgeois order and the incipient emergency of totalitarian projects, to the critique of colonial aspirations past and present, to the incorporation of mass media into the discussion of contemporary culture and politics, which cannot ignore its influence.

The Latin American vanguards were outspokenly antimimetic and antisentimental. Vicente Huidobro's 1914 "Non serviam" manifesto (in Schwartz, 1991: 71) might be the most emblematic expression of these tendencies, which were generally expressed as accusations leveled against realism and Hispanic-American *modernismo*. Sentimentalism and realism are mobilized by Arlt to be undermined, not as preferences of certain artistic circle, but as narratives with effects in historical reality, ways of authenticating the social order. The characters of the novel are consumers of pulp fiction, which figures as a critique of the mass-mediatic manipulation of their imaginations. But mass media have a prominent role in the possible liberation of their imaginations, as well, or at least in a break from the instituted order of everyday life. The novel is also antirealist, inasmuch as it inquires into the fictions by which reality is woven. It never constructs a solid ground of enunciation, and as readers, we are confronted with the uncomfortable feeling that reality eschews us, that the powerful fictions that formed it have taken on a life of their own.

What is also noticeable in Arlt's novel is that the nation is merely a subordinated factor in a much broader game. At no point of the narrative does the nation – Argentina in this case – offer an epistemological vantage point from which to assess the current situation that includes or excludes it, nor does it offer a strategic organization by which to navigate this situation toward a better end. This problem was of utmost importance in the avant-gardes, not only in the work of those authors who were influenced by leftist internationalism (such as Mariátegui, Vallejo, Arlt, Oswald de Andrade, Vicente Hudibro, etc., at different stages and with different levels of commitment), but also in the work of those more identified with the narratives of the nation and the national project that they attempted to articulate anew. Many of these authors (such as Nicolás Guillén, Mário de Andrade, and Miguel Ángel Asturias) have been criticized for the inescapable irony of rediscovering their native roots as the effect of a recuperation, always after some European vanguardist has praised them as primitive and therefore newly valuable in the international market of cultural signifiers. But this criticism falls prey to the assumption that the Latin American artistic movements belatedly mirrored the production of the Europeans and that the Latin American strategy mainly consisted of creative adaptation and consumption.

I have been arguing that it is no longer helpful to analyze the intellectual stance of these authors as a Creole co-optation of subaltern subjectivities for the project of national cohesion. The historical moment in which these renewals of the national projects were experienced as necessary was one in which the European model of civilization imploded and in which the US hegemony operated under a new sense of political superiority, if not yet cultural superiority in the traditionally artistic sense. The nation-state responded accordingly, upholding its sovereignty as a structure against old and new colonial arrangements, and native and subaltern cultures were often made official and monumentalized. The vanguards joined in many instances this reaccommodation, sometimes anticipating it (as happened in Brazil with Brazilian *modernismo*, whose populism was latter made into the official doctrine of president Getulio Vargas's "new state" organization), sometimes working from and for the state (as in post-revolutionary Mexico).

The reconstitution of the nation on renewed ground interrogated the nation's involvement in producing mechanisms of subjugation that, for large sectors of the population, only continued the structural inequalities first put into place by colonial power. But the changes in political regimes that occurred in many regions (triggered mostly by the local consequences of the crisis of capitalism in the 1930s) inaugurated in Latin America an era of authoritarian populism with a prominent presence of the military class, which become a main player in national politics by interrupting movements of democratization in order to preserve the emblems of the nation and its system of privileges. In this new historical context, many vanguardists who in the 1920s were identified with a dilettante spirit of artistic rebellion leaned toward the organized Left and the international antifascist, pro-Spanish Republican movement. This change is generally depicted as a break with past attempts to create a vanguard art and literature, and it was actually experienced as such by some who abdicated from the 1920s trends, which were now identified with a bourgeois self-serving spirit. It is more revealing, however, to note certain continuities. The inquiry inaugurated by the vanguards into the place of enunciation of Latin American cultural production imprinted a mark onto this internationalist spirit. To put it differently, this new cultural politics was opened up by the situated cosmopolitanism of the vanguards, sensitive to the pulse of a modernity that was historically defined from elsewhere, but also to the structural entrapments of the peripheries in the dynamic of this modernity.

The identification with the program of the Left led some writers to direct their efforts toward the depiction of social injustices brought about by modernization. The 1938 "Por un arte revolucionario independiente" (Toward a free revolutionary art) manifesto elaborated by Leon Trotsky, André Breton, and Diego Rivera (in Schwartz, 1991: 486) can be read as the highest point of this era, when internationalism and the avant-gardes attempted a common program of emancipation against new forms of subordination and imperial domination. Oswald de Andrade's and César Vallejo's productions, to mention just two prominent examples, acquired a new sense of urgency and favored a more outspoken social commitment with the proletarian revolution – a revolution of an indigenous character, in Vallejo's realist novel *El tungsteno* (*Tungsten: A novel*, 1931). Oswald de Andrade and Vallejo deserve special mention in this context because whenever they supported their political concerns with the positivist clarity of a realist style, they impoverished their critiques of modes of representation, making their textual apparatuses much more conservative.

This is not, however, the case with Patricia Galvão, alias Pagú, who had made her debut as the promising child of the Brazilian *modernista* group that, toward the end of the 1920s, was gearing up for a socially committed agenda. In her novel *Parque industrial* (*Industrial Park*, 1933), she draws on the fragmented style that Oswald de Andrade had used in the 1920s as a tongue-in-cheek parody of the high aspirations of the bourgeoisie, creating a satiric collage depicting power structures and forms of exploitation brought about by industrialization. But the editorial circumstances of the novel, published with a pseudonym to comply with the orders of the Communist Party, which had judged her affiliation suspicious of individualistic, anarchic tendencies, dramatizes one of the tensions in the internationalist activist culture of the 1930s, pulled between the mirroring regimes of Stalinism and Fascism.

The social system of Galvão's *Parque industrial* is defined not only by the proletariat in tension with the bourgeoisie. The system produces class struggle, but also marginality and criminality. Moreover, the industrialization denounced in her novel sits atop long-established racial and sexual inequalities that are not class-based, but respond to power structures that are reproduced under this new regime and that call for forms of struggle beyond the class front.

Patricia Galvão is a pioneer of the feminist movement, which the male-dominated avant-garde surely did not promote directly, but which the transformation of the cultural field that the avant-garde fostered made possible, opening up the aesthetic field to different forms of emancipation. But even certain feminist trends are shown in the novel as being mobilized as instruments of exclusion, as refined, self-serving intellectual tool of the powerful. Desire and sexuality are in the foreground of this novel – but far from the aristocratic decadence of the turn of the century and from the caricatures of the repressed bourgeoisie entertained by vanguardists such as Oswald de Andrade and the Argentinian Oliverio Girondo in the 1920s. Sexual desire is embedded in the social fabric, cutting across different strata, constituting the medium through which social aspirations, fears, and frustrations circulate. Moreover, the naturalized privacy of biological reproduction is shown as always inseparable from social reproduction. Despite the moments when the narrative indulges in pedagogic proselytizing, the novel is a remarkable collage of sketches of peripheral modernization and power struggles occurring at the most intimate and public levels.

## Notes

1 Asturias studied pre-Columbian religions with Georges Raynaud at the École de Hautes Études.

2 I will highlight aspects of the *Siete ensayos* that are particularly relevant for the historiography of the vanguards, aware that the problem of *indigenismo* is taken up by other section of the *Companion*.

## REFERENCES AND FURTHER READING

Barnitz, Jacqueline (2001). *Twentieth-Century Art of Latin America*. Austin: University of Texas Press.

Borges, Jorge Luis, Hidalgo, Alberto, and Huidobro, Vicente, eds (1926). *Indice de la nueva poesía americana*. Buenos Aires: Sociedad de Publicaciones El Inca.

Mariátegui, José Carlos (1969). "El proceso de la literatura." In *Siete ensayos de interpretación de la realidad peruana*. Havana: Casa de las Américas.

Rosenberg, Fernando J. (2006). *Avant-Garde and Geopolitics in Latin America*. Pittsburgh: University of Pittsburgh Press.

Schwartz, Jorge, ed. (1991). *Las Vanguardias latinoamericanas: Textos programáticos y críticos*. Madrid: Cátedra.

Unruh, Vicky (1994). *Latin American Vanguards: The Art of Contentious Encounters*. Berkeley, Los Angeles, and London: University of California Press.

# 25

# Latin American Poetry

## Stephen M. Hart

### The Twilight of the Idols

Very much an aristocratic activity in the Spanish and Portuguese colonies in the New World, literature turned, at least by the nineteenth century, into a middle-class affair and, by the beginning of the twentieth century discordant, proletarian, and other subaltern strains were beginning to emerge. By all accounts the nineteenth century was a century of crisis. Friedrich Nietzsche's *Götzen-Dämmerung* (The twilight of the idols, 1889) encapsulated the dilemma of the age, which was overwhelmed by doubt as to whether the hallowed concepts of the past, in particular classical civilization, could really be seen as relevant in the modern age. The rise of Positivism had caused metaphysical and religious absolutes to dissolve. Some artists reacted to this tide of doubt with a gesture of ideological retrenchment. The founder of *modernismo*, the Nicaraguan poet, Rubén Darío, for example, drowned his angst under a sheen of Greco-Roman nostalgia. In a poem dedicated "To the joyful poets," for example, Darío invoked cultural icons from Greece, Rome, Spain, and France, respectively (Anacreon, Ovid, Francisco de Quevedo, and Théodore de Banville), and proclaimed in a rhymed sonnet that "prefiero vuestra musa / risueña, vuestros versos perfumados de vino, / a los versos de sombra y la canción confusa / que opone el numen bárbaro al resplandor latino" (I prefer your sonorous laughter, your charming muse, your wine-perfumed verse, to the gloomy verses and the confused song that barbarian inspiration offers in contrast to Latin brilliance) (Caracciolo-Trejo, 1971: 303). Darío's faith in "Latin brilliance" found a complement in the Brazilian Olavo Bilac's advice to a young poet that he should seek inspiration in the simplicity of Greek forms, and write "de tal modo, que a imagem fique nua, / Rica mas sobria, como um templo grego" (in such a way that the image appear bare, rich but sober, like a Greek temple) (Caracciolo-Trejo, 1971: 58). In their idealization of a form of cultural capital derived from Europe's distant past, Darío and Bilac were echoing the imperial expansion of capitalism which characterized the relationship between Latin America and Europe at the turn of the century, the prototype being the export–import growth of Argentina's economy during the last two decades of the nineteenth century; they were the spokesmen of a "new elite that longed to be the equal of the European aristocracy" (Gallagher, 1973: 8).

But there were other energies coursing through the veins of the Latin American lyric, a rush of anti-classicist adrenalin, disrupting the chora of the classical and producing semiosis, repetition, even psychosis. Though written decades before either Darío's or Bilac's poems, J. A. Silva's beautifully dramatic poem, "Nocturno" (Nocturne), substituted the quotidian for the classical and a more flexible compositional scheme for the de rigueur rhymed sonnet, and provided an artistic premonition of what lay in store. Describing a mysterious meeting between his shadow and that of his deceased lover, Silva repeats phrases for sonorous effect: "Y mi sombra / Por los rayos de la luna proyectada, / Iba sola, / Iba sola, / Iba sola por la estepa solitaria" (And my shadow, projected by the moonbeams, passed on alone, passed on alone, passed on alone through the solitary plain) (Caracciolo-Trejo, 1971: 175). It was clear that Silva had jettisoned the rhyme scheme in favor of a more subtle and incremental linguistic strategy which was closer to everyday speech. Just as important, Silva's poem possessed not one single reference to Greek or Roman myth or literature. Darío's swan song, in retrospect, may even be seen as a falsetto, since while he was using – indeed over-using – classical as well as Symbolist ideals in his poems, a new sense of cultural urgency had emerged in the work of the Cuban intellectual, José Martí, who argued that the whole education system in the Americas needed revamping, such that the Incas and the Aztecs should be studied rather than the Romans and the Greeks. As he put it memorably in his essay *Nuestra América* (Our America, 1893): "La historia de América, de los incas a acá, ha de enseñarse al dedillo, aunque no se enseñe la de los arcontes de Grecia. Nuestra Grecia es preferible a la Grecia que no es nuestra" (The history of America, from the Incas to the present day, should be taught by rote, even if this means not teaching the history of Greece. Our Greece is preferable to the Greece which is not ours) (149). There is no escaping the fact that Darío's poems are beautiful, but there is also no denying that they were papering over the cracks of an oligarchy which was moribund, supported by a value system which was outmoded. It is true that Darío was the poet who brought the Spanish galleons back to Spain, in the sense that his poetry demonstrably influenced the work of two great Spanish poets such as Juan Ramón Jiménez and Antonio Machado (see Hart, 1990: 34–40), but it is more true that it was the avant-garde which finally supplied Latin American poets with the ammunition they needed to shoot dead the Old Guard.

## Modernism and the Avant-garde

The first decade of the twentieth century was characterized by a shock-cut which seemed to sweep to one side the customary ways of thinking about the world. In 1899 Freud published his revolutionary study of dreams, *Die Traumdeutung*, in 1905

Einstein published his revolutionary theories about the energy–mass equation, and in 1909 Marinetti published his Futurist manifesto which glorified the technology of the motorcar and called for the destruction of museums and libraries. During the Modern Art Week which took place between February 13 and 17, 1922 in São Paulo, the poet Menotti del Pichia gave a sense of what had changed:

> We want light, air, ventilators, airplanes, workers' demands, idealism, motors, factory smokestacks, blood, speed, dream, in our Art. And may the chugging of an automobile on the track of two lines of verses, frighten away from poetry the last Homeric God who went on sleeping and dreaming of the flutes of Arcadian shepherds and the divine breasts of Helen, an anachronism in the era of the jazz band and the movie. (Bishop and Brasil, 1972: xix)

The spell of Greco-Roman culture – and particularly its association with ruralism – had suddenly been broken. "Poética" (Poetics) by Pichia's compatriot, Manuel Bandeira, epitomizes this paradigm-shift:

> Estou farto do lirismo comedido
> Do lirismo bem comportado
> Do lirismo funcionário público com libro de ponto expediente protocolo e manifestações de aprêço ao sr. diretor.
>
> Estou farto do lirismo que pára e vai averiguar no diccionário o cuhno vernáculo de um vocábulo.
> Abaixo os puristas

> (I've had enough of discreet lyricism / well-mannered lyricism / public official lyricism with its clocking-in, protocol and expressions of appreciation to Mr. Director Sir. / I've had enough of the lyricism which stops and goes to the dictionary to check the implication of a word in the vernacular. / Down with purists) (Caracciolo-Trejo, 1971: 65)

One of the most influential poets of the time, the Chilean Vicente Huidobro (1893–1948), began writing in French, earned something of a reputation among French poets and artists in Paris, and when he subsequently began writing poems in Spanish, galvanized the poetry of the period. His poem "Apaga tu pipa" (Put out your pipe), set against World War I, is intended to shock the bourgeois reader:

> Los obuses estallan como rosas maduras
> Y las bombas agujerean los días
> Canciones cortadas
> tiemblan entre las ramas
> El viento contorsiona las calles
>
> COMO APAGAR LA ESTRELLA DEL
> ESTANQUE

(Shells burst like ripe roses
And bombs puncture the days
Cut-off songs
tremble among the branches
The wind twists the streets

HOW TO EXTINGUISH THE STAR IN THE
POOL) (Caracciolo-Trejo ,1971: 104–5)

The main aim of the poem is to demonstrate how the trauma of war has truncated man's experience of life, shearing him off from his cultural roots, and this disconnectedness is echoed concretely by the cutting-up of poetic lines, which leaves phrases hanging, as it were, in the air. Rhyme has disappeared, as if to suggest that war has knocked the harmony out of life. Reflectiveness has been replaced by a sense of visual and audial immediacy. The use of capital letters in the last line brings home the sense of the poet's distance from the safe answers of an earlier era, and thrusts his existential lostness (for the question, even if it is a question, is unanswerable) violently before the reader's eyes. One poet whose work has some of the dislocated defamiliarization we associate with the avant-garde is the Argentine poet Oliverio Girondo (1891–1967). In one poem Girondo takes the concept of sadness and crying, and by a process of repetition, empties it of meaning, making it absurd. The first stanza begins with a normal expression and gradually begins to tear it apart: "Llorar a lágrima viva. Llorar a chorros. Llorar la digestión. Llorar el sueño. Llorar ante las puertas y los puertos. Llorar de amabilidad y de amarillo" (To weep with lively tears. To weep in floods. To weep of digestion. To weep the dream. To weep before doors and ports. To weep of kindness and yellowness) (Caracciolo-Trejo, 1971: 23). The reader is tempted to surmise that some of the associations have been created by phonetic coincidence more than the logic of cause and effect (namely, "puertas/puertos" and "amabilidad/amarillo"). This absurdity is pursued until it leads to deliberately non-logical associations: "Asistir a los cursos de antropología, llorando. Festejar los cumpleaños familiares, llorando. Atravesar el África, llorando" (To attend courses in anthropology, crying. To celebrate family birthdays, crying. To cross Africa crying) (Caracciolo-Trejo, 1971: 23). Girondo's poetry, like Huidobro's, is intended as a bracing shock to the bourgeois system of the reader, forcing him out of his complacency, allowing him to see the world anew.

Perhaps the most original book of avant-garde poetry to have emerged from Latin America is *Trilce* (1922) by the Peruvian César Vallejo (1892–1938). Vallejo set out to deconstruct the imaginary of his poetic ancestors the Symbolists. He takes a line from one of Albert Samain's poems, and tears it to shreds: 'Samain diría el aire es quieto y de una contenida tristeza. / Vallejo dice hoy la Muerte está soldando cada lindero a cada hebra de cabello perdido . . . (Samain would say the air is calm and of a constrained sadness. / Vallejo says today Death is welding each limit to each strand of lost hair) (*Trilce* LX; Vallejo, 2005a: 134–5). The aim here is to rip the sheen off well-written, decent poetry, revealing the anguish caused by death which animates all things. Likewise when Vallejo bases the inspiration for his poem on an example of Greek art, such as the Venus de Milo, it is in order to deconstruct the set of assumptions which normally underpin such an allusion. In *Trilce* XXXVI, for example, the statue of Venus de Milo – whose beauty is acclaimed despite the fact that it is lacking an arm – is invoked not as an icon of classical beauty but rather as a paradigm of the imperfections of everyday life: "Tú manqueas apenas, pululando / entrañada en los brazos plenarios de la existencia, / de esta existencia que todavía / perenne imperfección" (You hardly feign you're a cripple, budding / deep within the capacious arms / of existence, of this existence that furthers a / perpetual imperfection) (Vallejo, 2005a: 94–5). Not only does Vallejo reject the classical ideal of sculpted beauty, he uses it as a launching point for the drafting of a new *ars poetica*, one which favors the "new unevenness" of free verse over and above the harmony of rhyme: "Rehusad, y vosotros, a posar las plantas / en la seguridad dulpa de la Armonía. / Rehusad la simetría a buen seguro" (Refuse, and you as well, to set your soles in Harmony's doubled safety. / Refuse symmetry unfalteringly" (Vallejo, 2005a: 94–5).

## Surrealism and Elementalism

Surrealism produced a new poetic language in Latin America, a composition-in-depth, allowing the hidden elementalism of life to surface within poets' discourse (Wilson, 2004). André Breton's *Manifeste du surréalisme* (1924) proclaimed the unconscious as the true creative force within man and saw art as the main means whereby that energy could be released. In his *Residencia en la tierra* (Residence on earth, 1933), written while he was on a diplomatic posting in Rangoon, the Chilean Pablo Neruda (1904–73) explores unconscious impulses such as eros and thanatos, and foregrounds them to such an extent in his poems that everyday life – the ritual of "walking around," everyday objects such as false teeth and clothes hung on a washing line – becomes defamiliarized; in this way everyday life looks strange, unusual, disorientating. Often in these poems the reader becomes involved in the hermeneutic process itself, as if reliving the poetic subject's desperate groping for the meaning of the world, because of the stop-start nature of the syntax and the imagery, as occurs in the opening lines of "Galope muerto" (Mad gallop): "Como cenizas, como mares poblándose, / en la sumergida lentitud, en lo informe, / o como se oyen desde el alto de los caminos / cruzar las campanadas en cruz" (Like ashes, like seas filling up, / in the submerged slowness, in the formless, / and as when one hears from the top of roads the bells tolling on a cross) (Neruda, 1976: 9). The poem appears to be guided by the phonetic connections between the words; indeed, Neruda "located the Dionysiac source of poetry in incantatory sound' (Wilson, 2000: 15). A similar notion surfaces in "Arte poética" (Poetic credo) where the poet's prophetic insight indicates an enhanced awareness of "un golpe de objetos que llaman sin ser respondidos / hay, y un movimiento sin tregua, y un nombre confuso" (a clash of objects which call without being answered / emerges, and a movement without reprieve, and a confused name) (Neruda, 1976: 40). The poet's awareness of a "confused name" is specifically related to his vision of the liquid drives which animate the human as well as the animal and plant kingdoms, Freud's thanatos ("Sólo la muerte"; Only death) and eros ("Agua sexual"; Sexual water). In "Ritual de mis piernas" (Ritual of my legs) the accoutrements of civilization (manufactured objects, and particularly shoes) cut the poetic subject off from direct contact with those terrestrial energies: "Siempre, / productos manufacturados, medias, zapatos, / o simplemente aire infinito. / Habrá entre mis pies y la tierra / extremando lo aislado y lo solitario de mi ser, / algo tenazmente supuesto entre mi vida y la tierra, / algo abiertamente invencible y enemigo" (Always, / manufactured products, tights, shoes, / or simply infinite air. / There must be something between my feet and the earth / increasing the isolation and loneliness of my being / something which is tenaciously set between my life and my earth / something openly invincible and hostile) (Neruda, 1976: 59).

The Mexican Octavio Paz (1914–98) is often characterized as Latin America's Pope of Surrealism, such was the close relationship he established with André Breton. In his poem "Esto y esto y esto" (This and this and this) Paz characterizes Surrealism as a destructive as well as purificatory force:

El surrealismo ha sido la manzana de fuego en el árbol de la sintaxis
El surrealismo ha sido la camelia de ceniza entre los pechos de la adolescente poseída
　　por el espectro de Orestes
El surrealismo ha sido el plato de lentejas que la mirada del hijo pródigo transforma en
　　festín humeante del rey caníbal

(Surrrealism has been the apple of fire on the tree of syntax
Surrealism has been the camellia of ash between the breasts of the girl possessed by the
　　ghost of Orestes
Surrealism has been the dish of lentils that the glance of the prodigal son transforms
　　into the smoking feast of the cannibal king) (Paz, 1988: 516–17)

In "Cuarteto" (Quartet) he alludes to how "Es frágil lo real y es inconstante / también, su ley el cambio, infatigable: / gira la rueda de las apariencias / sobre el eje del tiempo, su fijeza" (The real is fragile, and is inconstant: / its law is restless change: / the wheel of appearance turns and turns / over its fixed axis of time) (Paz, 1988: 494–5). Providing a counterpoint to the poet's search for the "fixed axis of time" beneath the sea of appearances is the sense that the center (an image at once of knowledge and fixity) is always elusive. Man's meaning comes from elsewhere, yet the key is not given. As we read in the poem "Hermandad": "Soy hombre: duro poco / y es enorme la noche. / Pero miro hacia arriba: / las estrellas escriben. / Sin entender comprendo: / también soy escritura / y en este mismo instante alguien me deletrea" (I am a man: little do I last / and the night is enormous. / But I look up: / the stars write. / Unknowing I understand: / I too am written, / and at this very moment / someone spells me out) (Paz, 1988: 508–9). Caught on the knife-edge between knowing and unknowing (as suggested by the oxymoron "Unknowing I understand"), Paz's poetry searches out and also records the dizzying moment when opposites collide, and the impossible springs into being. As we read in "Proema" (Proem): "A veces la poesía es el vértigo de los cuerpos y el vértigo de la dicha y el vértigo de la muerte: / el paseo con los ojos cerrados al borde del despeñadero y la verbena en los jardines submarinos" (At times poetry is the vertigo of bodies and the vertigo of speech and the vertigo of death; / the walk with eyes closed along the edge of the cliff, and the verbena in submarine gardens) (Paz, 1988: 482–3). In two lines Paz juxtaposes height and depth – echoing Breton's sense that Surrealism attempts to identify that point atn which height and depth are no longer contradictory terms – and this epiphany involves a coming-closer to the roots of language to a point at which phenomenal world and language become one: "los sustantivos óseos y llenos de raíces, plantados en las ondulaciones del lenguaje" (the nouns, bony and full of roots, planted on the waves of language) (Paz, 1988: 482–3). As so often in his work the poet is caught, transfixed as it were between time and eternity, yet focused on the return to the birth of consciousness: "nos bañamos en ríos de latidos, / volvemos al perpetuo recomienzo" (to bathe in rivers of heartbeats / and return to the perpetual beginning anew) (Paz, 1988: 608–9). It is at points like these that Paz allows an elemental, even Jungian, consciousness to surface within the language of his poetry.

The most significant female Latin American poet to have been influenced by Surrealism was the Argentine Alejandra Pizarnik (1936–72). Like the Surrealists, Pizarnik's poems deal in apparently disconnected sets of images which operate in terms of emotional and visual impact; they deliberately lack a clear narrative. Her poems are characterized by a cult of death; in "En un ejemplar de *Les Chants de Maldoror*" (In a copy of *Les Chants de Maldoror*), for example, she explores Lautréamont's imagery in order to produce the simile "hermosa como el suicidio" (lovely as suicide) (Crow, 1988: 48–9). Pointing in a similar direction, "Exilio" (Exile) describes the poet embracing "lo que fluye / como lava del infierno: / una logia callada, / fantasmas en dulce erección, / sacerdotes de espuma . . ." (what is fluid / as lava from hell: a silent lodge, ghosts sweetly erect, priests of foam . . .) (Crow, 1988: 52–3), which is redolent of Lautréamont's cult of evil visions. Yet one of the most disarming insights of Pizarnik's verse is the connection she provokes and elicits between poetic creativity and death. As many of her later poems suggest, it is only through death – whether expressed as emotional death, self-death, or suicide – that her poetic voice is able to flourish. Her poem, "Cantora nocturna" (Nocturnal singer), for instance, projects herself as already dead and singing; as the first sentence reads: "La que murió de su vestido azul está cantando" (She who has died of her blue dress sings) (Crow, 1988: 54–5). The color blue appears here, as elsewhere in the later poetic works, to signify death, in contradistinction to the *modernistas* for whom blue stood for the ideal.

## Art and Politics

Stendhal once famously remarked that introducing politics into art is like letting a pistol shot off in the theater. Nobody, of course, stays around for the second act. It is clear, however, that many of Latin American's finest poetic moments are built around just such a pistol shot. César Vallejo's *Poemas humanos* (Human poems, 1939), for example, include some of the finest political poems written in the Spanish language. Yet they are able to retain an aesthetic value precisely because they never descend into the ranting of a pamphleteer, and are written from a personal perspective, thereby avoiding the trap of being merely "poèmes de circonstances." "Parado en una piedra . . ." (Standing on a stone . . .), for example, clearly focuses on one of the salient problems of Europe in the 1920s (unemployment), but it does so in such a way that the reader is drawn into the consciousness of the man who is described in the poem as "Parado en una piedra, / desocupado, / astroso, espeluznante" (Standing on a stone, / unemployed, / loathsome, dreadful) (Vallejo, 2005b: 138–9). Vallejo uses words which are double-edged; "parado" is a South-Americanism which means "standing up" but it also suggests "unemployment" ("en paro"). He gives the man's predicament a tragic depth by using a word – "astroso" – which recalls the firmament ("astros" is a poetic word for "stars"). He describes the worker walking along the Seine and then observes that from the "river" there "sprouts consciousness," which undeniably must be read as a reference to the politicization of the worker, whose consciousness is created by the (Marxist – though not stated) dialectic. Furthermore, later on in the poem Vallejo images oppression not in abstract terms but rather as a reversal of the natural process whereby blood produces labor and sweat, thereby eliciting the grotesque image of sweat somehow going back into the body: "¡Éste es, trabajadores, aquél / que en la labor sudaba para afuera, / que suda hoy para adentro su secreción de sangre rehusada!" (This is the one, workers, / who in labour sweated inside out, / but who now sweats outside-in his secretion of rejected blood!) (Vallejo, 2005b: 138–9). Vallejo is able to make his political point much more effectively by coining striking poetic images rather than writing straightforward poetry which attacks capitalism directly. (It is now clear, indeed, that Vallejo worked extremely hard on a number of drafts when composing his *Poemas humanos*; see Hart, 2003.) With hindsight it is clear that Vallejo was almost unique in writing sophisticated political poetry in the 1920s and early 1930s, but – when the Spanish Civil War broke out – he was joined by a number of Latin American poets who rallied to the cause of Republicanism.

Standing shoulder to shoulder with Spanish poets such Miguel Hernández, Antonio Machado, Rafael Alberti, and Emilio Prados, and English poets such as Stephen Spender and W. H. Auden, the Cuban Nicolás Guillén (1902–89) extolled the bravery of the Republican militiamen in direct verse in his *España. Poema en cuatro angustias y una esperanza* (Spain. Poem in four anguishes and one hope) (1937): "Nada importa morirse al cabo, / pues morir no es tan gran suceso; / ¡muchísimo peor que eso / es estar vivo y ser esclavo!" (It doesn't matter if you die in the end / since dying is no great shakes; / much worse than that / is being alive and being a slave!) (Guillén, 1976: 124). For Neruda, the relentless killing of innocent people in the Iberian Peninsula, which he witnessed at first hand, led him to reject the poetic manner of his former years. How could he, he asked his readers of of *España en el corazón* (Spain in the heart, 1937), carry on writing poems about flowers amid such social turmoil?: "Preguntaréis: ¿Y dónde estan las lilas? / ¿Y la metafísica cubierta de amapolas? / ¿Y la lluvia que a menudo golpeaba / sus palabras llenándolas / de agujeros y pájaros?" (You will ask: and where are the lilies? And the metaphysics covered with poppies? And the rain that often used to beat against / their words filling them / with holes and birds?) (Neruda, 1976: 44–7) Neruda's poem is predicated on the notion that the ugly events of the war have destroyed the poetic *topoi* of yesteryear; his poetry now must sound the pistol-shot so abhorred by Stendhal in an attempt to wake them up to the evils committed by the Generals Franco and Mola. Vallejo's political poetry has already been mentioned, but it is important to signal that his poetry also took on a new idiom as a result of the Spanish Civil War, though the change was not as drastic as in Neruda's case. In "España, aparta de mí este cáliz" (Spain, let this cup pass away from me) Vallejo addresses the children of the world, and advises them, if the Spanish Republic were to fall, to save "mother Spain." The poem builds up an image of Spain as a mother, as a teacher, as the earth and provider of nourishment, which leads to the notion that, if Spain were to fall, the children would become "orphans": "si no veis a nadie, si os asustan / los lápices sin punta, si la madre / España cae – digo, es un decir – / salid, niños del mundo; id a buscarla! . . ." (if you don't see anyone, if the blunted pencils scare you, if mother Spain falls – I say it for the sake of argument – go out, children of the world: go and search for her! . . .) (Caracciolo-Trejo, 1971: 331). In "Masa" (Masses) Vallejo describes the moment at which the inhabitants of the whole earth surround the dead Republican combatant and the miracle of resurrection takes place, thereby fusing Christian and Marxist strands of consciousness.

## The Cuban Revolution

The Cuban Revolution of 1959 was another decisive turning point for the Latin American lyric. In January 1959 Fidel Castro became the president of the first-ever communist Spanish-speaking country. One of the aims of the Castro government was to electrify the political world of South America and, eventually, to produce socialist republics in the whole of the Spanish-speaking southern hemisphere. Poetry – as well as cinema and theater – were to be used to bring about this aim. One of the master-minds behind the revolutionary ethos was Roberto Fernández Retamar, who published a crucial postcolonial text, *Calibán* (1971), which voiced an anti-imperialist message, and also wrote poems in which the simple, everyday values of the Revolution were extolled. His poem entitled simply "Patria" (Homeland) has the ardour of a hymn: "Eres la indignación, eres la cólera / Que nos levantan frente al enemigo. / Eres la lengua para comprendernos / Muchos hombres crecidos a tu luz. / Eres la tierra ver-dadera, el aire / Que siempre quiere el pecho respirar" (You are the indignation, you are the wrath which lifts us up before the enemy. You are the tongue with which we, the many grown in your light, understand each other. You are the true land, the air the breast always yearns to breathe) (Caracciolo-Trejo, 1971: 219). A number of poets saw to ally their art with that of the Revolution, leading to an outburst of left-wing creativity in favor of the masses. Taking their lead from Neruda's *Canto general*

(General song, 1950) – which provided a panoramic tour of Latin American culture from its prehistory right up to the various dictators of the twentieth century, such as González Videla, who were draining the lifeblood of the Latin American people, thereby offering an "alternative to already-known histories" (Rowe, 2004: 136) – a number of poets began writing "canción de protesta" (protest poetry) (see Pring-Mill, 1983; Gonzalez and Treece, 1992). The Nicaraguan poet Ernesto Cardenal (1925–) is an expert writer of barbed, satiric poems about dictators such as Anastasio Somoza García, the brutal tyrant who ruled Nicaragua with an iron fist from 1937 until 1956. "Somoza unveils the statue of Somoza in Somoza Stadium" ends with Somoza's words: "I had it raised knowing you hate it" (*Epigram XXXI*; Cardenal, 1975: 47). Though political, Cardenal's poems are always personal, such as "Propertius," a rather charming love poem written in the style of the Latin poet alluded to in the title, which ends with a political as well as personal gibe: "And she prefers me, poor, to all Somoza's millions" (Cardenal, 1975: 40). Though Somoza is not named in "For Twenty Years" we know that Cardenal is taking on the voice of the people in their hatred of the dictator: "You strove for twenty years / to get together twenty million pesos / but we'd give twenty million pesos / not to strive as you have striven" (Cardenal, 1975: 41).

Some poets took a slightly different tack. The Brazilian Harold de Campos, in "Servidão de passagem" (Transient servitude), for example, focuses on the oppression of man caused by capitalism, but does so via a clever and self-referential exploration of the phonetic fiber of language. Naming is used to point to the hunger that capitalism serves up to the workers: "poesia de dar o nome / nomear e dar o nome / nomeio o nome / nomeio o homen / no meio a fome / nomeio a fome" (poetry of giving the name / naming is giving the noun / I name the noun / I name humanity / in mid-naming is hunger / I name it hunger) (Brasil and Smith, 1983: 53). Naming, man and poetry, as a result of repetition of like-sounding words, are shown to have a necessary equivalence; their connectiveness is remotivated through wordplay. Later on in the same poem phonetic overlap is used to produce new thought processes: "e lucro a lucro / logrado / de lôgro a lôgro / lucrado / de lado a lado / lanhado / de lôdo a lôdo / largado" (from profit to profit / pinched / from pinch to pinch / profited / from pole to pole / parted / from puddle to puddle / poleaxed) ( Brasil and Smith, 1983: 54). Once more human oppression is shown to be the inevitable corollary of any investigation of language. The poem, as Harold de Campos's notes reveal, is focused on the dilemma of whether poetry should be politically committed or "pure," namely whether it should be "poesia para" (literally "poetry for") or "poesia pura" (pure poetry), that is, devoid of any social or political significance. It could be argued that de Campos's poetry manages to combine the verbal sophistication we associate with "poetry for poets" in the style of Stéphane Mallarmé with a poetry which is committed to the cause of liberation. Certainly, wordplay is used to draw attention to oppression. Similar in some respects to de Campos's fusion of politics and wordplay was Décio Pignatori's 13-word poem which attacked US imperialism by focusing on the phonetic similarity between "Coca-Cola" and "cloaca" (sewers): "beba coca cola / babe /

beba coca / babe cola caco / cao / cola / cloaca" (beba = drink; babe = slobber, cola = glue, caco = pieces) (Brasil and Smith, 1983: 139).

## Poetry and the Conversational Style

Echoing in some ways the style of *cinéma vérité*, a down-to-earth poetic style, one which had much in common with everyday speech, came to characterize much twentieth-century Latin American poetry. The Brazilian Carlos Drummond de Andrade's "Procura da poesia" (In search of poetry) is a masterfully ironic poem on the irrelevance of traditional topoi addressed to an imaginary up-and-coming poet. As the poem opens: "Não faças versos sôbre acontecimentos. / Não há criação nem morte perante a poesia" (Don't write poetry about events. There's neither creation nor death in poetry) (Caracciolo-Trejo, 1971: 82). He is ironic about the Romantic emphasis on self-expression: "Não me reveles teus sentimentos, / que se prevaleem do equívoco e tentam a longa viagem. O que pensas e sentes, isso ainda não é poesia" (And do not reveal your feelings to me / for they take advantage of misunderstandings, and try for a long trip. Whatever you think or feel, it is still not poetry) (Caracciolo-Trejo, 1971: 83). Finally the poet is reminded not to dramatize his sentiments and ideas in the classical narcissistic pose of the self-important poet: "Não dramatizes, não invoques, / não indagues. Não percas tempo en mentir" (Don't dramatize, don't invoke, / don't investigate. Don't waste your time with lies) (Caracciolo-Trejo, 1971: 83). It is the realm of words, language itself, where poetry lies, waiting to be discovered: "Penetra surdamente no reino das palavras. / Lá estão os poemas que esperam ser escritos" (Explore quietly into the realm of words. That's where the poems are waiting to be written) (Caracciolo-Trejo, 1971: 84). A similar irony about the incongruity of the poetic *topoi* of the past is evident in the poetry of Peruvian Carlos Germán Belli (1927–). In "Poema" (Poem), for example, Belli deliberately uses poetic terms such as *cierzo* (lit., the North Wind) and *austro* (lit., the South Wind) and archaisms such as *do* (modern *donde*, where) in order to contrast the glory of those words with the vulgarity of the birth of a deformed foetus: "Frunce el feto su frente / y sus cejas enarca cuando pasa / del luminoso vientre / al albergue terreno, do se truecan sin tasa / la luz en niebla, la cisterna en cieno; y abandonar le duele al fin el claustro, / en que no rugen ni cierzo ni austro, / y verse aun despeñado / desde el más alto risco, / cual un feto no amado, / por tartamudo o cojo o manco o bizco" (The foetus puckers its forehead and arches its eyebrows when it passes from luminous womb into its earthly lodging, where, without measure, light changes into mist, the cistern to slime. And at last it pains it to abandon the cloister in which neither north nor south wind howls; and it sees itself further precipitated from the highest crag, as a foetus unloved, as a stutterer, a cripple, maimed, or cross-eyed) (Caracciolo-Trejo, 1971: 344–5). Even the traditional metrical scheme used, with its rhymes such as *claustro* and *austro*, *pasa* and *tasa*, are undercut with irony by the ugliness of the poem's subject (Higgins, 1982: 46–64). Nicanor Parra (1914–), the originator of anti-poetry, combines acerbic wit with the rhythms of everyday speech (he "speaks corrosively and conversationally"; Brotherston, 1975: 182), as his "Advertencia al lector" (Warning to the reader) makes clear: "Según los doctores de la ley este libro no debiera publicarse: /La palabra arco iris no parece en él en ninguna parte, / Menos aún la palabra dolor, / La palabra torcuato. / Sillas y mesas sí que figuran a granel, / ¡ataúdes!, ¡útiles de escritorio! / Lo que me llena de orgullo / Porque, a mi modo de ver, el cielo se está cayendo a pedazos" (The doctors of the law say this book shouldn't see the light: / The word *rainbow* can't be found anywhere in it, / Much less the words *sorrow* / Or *torquate*. / Sure there's a swarm of chairs and tables, / Coffins! Desk supplies! / All of which makes with burst with pride / Because, as I see it, the sky is coming down in pieces) (Parra, 1985: 2–3). In "La montaña rusa" (The roller coaster) Parra replaces Mount Olympus where the Greek poets used to seek inspiration with the roller coaster in the modern-day fairground: "Durante medio siglo / la poesía fue / el paraíso del tonto solemne. / Hasta que vine yo / y me instalé con mi montaña rusa. / Suban, si les parece. / Claro que yo no respondo si bajan / echando sangre por boca y narices" (For half a century / poetry was / the paradise of the solemn fool. / Until I came along / and established myself with my roller coaster. / Come on – climb up if you want. / Obviously it's not my affair if you get off / spouting blood from [your] mouth and nostrils) (Caracciolo-Trejo, 1971: 151). For poets such as Drummond de Andrade, Germán Belli, and Nicanor Parra a sense of irony about humanity's trials and tribulations is complemented by a distancing from the metaphors which the poetic tradition had in the past used to describe that life.

## Gender and Ethnicity in the Poetic Canon

Latin American poetry has been traversed by new gendered and new ethnic energies in the modern era. Women's writing, notably absent from the literary establishment's radar until the beginning of the twentieth century – excluding exceptional cases such as Sor Juana Inés de la Cruz in seventeenth-century New Spain – when voices such as Delmira Agustini (1886–1914), Gabriela Mistral (1889–1957), Alfonsina Storni (1892–1938), and Juana Ibarbourou (1895–1938) began to emerge, has established itself as a significant subaltern voice in the contemporary lyric. Storni's "Hombre pequeñito" (Little man) has a suffragette combativeness about it: "Estuve en tu jaula, hombre pequeñito, / hombre pequeñito que jaula me das. / Digo pequeñito porque no me entiendes, / ni me entenderás. / Tampoco te entiendo, pero mientras tanto / ábreme la jaula, que quiero escapar; / hombre pequeñito, te amé media hora, no me pidas más (I was in your cage, little man / little man who provides my cage / I say little because you don't understand / and you never will. / Nor do I understand you , but in the meantime / open up my cage, I want to fly off / little man, I loved you for half an hour / don't ask any more of me) (Chang-Rodríguez, 1988: 353). Rosario Castellanos (1925–74) drew inspiration from this literary group and wrote simple, direct poems about the anguish of feminine identity in the modern world. As we read in "Meditación en el umbral" (Mediation on the threshold), "Debe hacer otro modo que no se llame Safo / ni Messalina ni María Egipciaca / ni Magdalena ni Clemencia Isaura. / Otro modo de ser humano y libre. / Otro modo de ser" (There must be another way of being, one that not's called Sappho / nor Meslina nor Maria Egipciaca / nor Mary Magdalen nor Clemencia Isaura) (Castellanos, 1988: 48). Castellanos was searching for a new mode of female being, one which neither went down one of the virgin/whore avenues (the biblical Mary Magdalen versus the Roman prostitute Messalina) nor down one of the traditional literary routes of women's literature (famous and lesbian, namely Sappho; or female and neglected, namely Clemencia Isaura). Some female poets were bitter about colonialism. "Tamalitos de cambray" (Little cambric tamales) by Claribel Alegría (1924–), for example, layers her political point about the conquest with a tinge of humor. The ingredients of the conquest include "dos libras de masa de mestizo" (two pounds of *mestizo* dough), "un sofrito con cascos de conquistadores" (a fry of conquistador helmets) and "tres cebollas jesuitas" (three Jesuit onions); as the poem concludes: "lo pones todo a cocer / a fuego lento / por quinientos años / y verás qué sabor" (put everything to boil / over a slow fire / for five hundred years / and you'll see what a flavor it has!) (Crow, 1988: 184). "Maldigo del alto cielo" (Cursed by heaven) by Violeta Parra (1917–67) bitterly attacks the moneyed classes because of their appropriation of heaven (Crow, 1988: 94). "Patas arriba con la vida" (Head over heels with life) by Colombian María Mercedes Carranza (1945–) reflects angrily on women's social role: " acepté el engaño: / he sido madre, ciudadana, / hija de familia, amiga, / compañera, amante./ Creí en la verdad: / dos y dos son cuatro, / María Mercedes debe nacer, / crecer, reproducirse y morir / y en ésas estoy" (I accepted the hoax: / I have been mother, citizen, / daughter, friend, / companion, lover; I believed in the truth: two and two are four, Maria Mercedes ought to be born, / ought to grow, reproduce herself and die / and that's what I'm doing) (Crow, 1988: 102–3). In her *Noches de adrenalina* (Adrenalin nights, 1981) the Peruvian Carmen Ollé focuses on the uniqueness of female experience, often via the female body: "He vuelto a despertar en Lima a ser una mujer que va / midiendo su talle en las vitrinas como muchas preocupada / por el vaivén de su culo transparente . . . Tengo 30 años (la edad del stress). / Mi vagina se llena de hongos como consecuencia del / primer parto" (I have woken up again in Lima to become a woman who / is measuring her figure in the shop windows, worried like many other women / by the toing-and-froing of her see-through arse . . . I'm thirty years old (the age of stress). / My vagina is full of mushrooms as a result of my first childbirth) (Ollé, 1992: 7). In *A las puertas del papel* (1996; At the paper gates with burning desire, 2001), Carlota Caulfield arranges a teasing collage of fragments of women's writing throughout history, ranging from Sappho to Isadora Duncan. Marita Troiano's *Extrasístole* (1999) focuses intensely on bodily sensations which are captured via intricate wordplay: "verazmente voraz el singular / afán de tu boca carnicera / cárnica cancerbera del escándalo / por recrear el celo celebérrimo" (verily voracious the singular / desire of your canivorous mouth / fleshly scandalous Cerberus / for re-creating the most renowned heat) (Troiano, 1999: 23). Modern poetry written by Latin

American women typically seeks to de-exoticize female experience and thereby authenticate its social value.

Afro-Hispanic poetry offers an intriguing test-case of the intersection between ethnicity and the lyric. The first stirrings of the Afro-Hispanic poetic consciousness in the early twentieth century often focused on the issue of race in a displaced manner, as if to address it directly would be too painful. "El dolor desconocido" (The unknown pain) by the Puerto Rican poet Luis Palés Matos (1898–1959), for example, hints at the subaltern ghosts of slavery: "Quizás las más profundas tragedias interiores, / los más graves sucesos, / pasan en estos mudos arrabales de sombra / sin que llegue a nosotros el más vago lamento (Perhaps the most profound internal tragedies, / the gravest events, / happen in those silent outskirts of shadow; / not the slightest lament reaches us) (Caracciolo-Trejo, 1971: 355). Though described as "useless" at the time it was enunciated in Palés Matos's poem, this voice would emerge later on in a variety of contexts, often in a hybrid fashion. The work of Cuban Regino Boti (1878–1958) is an intriguing half-way house of ethnic writing. Though he was of African descent, this would not be obvious from his early work written in the 1920s, which typically celebrates the whiteness of the beloved's skin: "mientras se extingue en laxitud aguda / la nieve viva de tu cuerpo blanco / sobre la nieve exámine del lecho" (sharp and relaxed the living snow / of your white body fades slowly / on the lifeless snow of the bed) (Boti, 2005: 32–3). In his later work, however, we see a movement away from the Darío-inspired whitism of *modernismo* toward the exploration of Afro-Cuban rhythms, as we find in "Babul" (1930): "Babul afrocubano, ancestro del jazz-band, / babul / babul" (Afro-Cuban babul, ancestor of the jazz band, / babul / babul") (Boti, 2005: 122–3).

Arguably the most important Hispanic poet of African ancestry is the Cuban Nicolás Guillén (1902–89). In his early work Guillén strove to reintegrate the energy of African culture and particularly its rhythms into his poetry, as in poems such as "Sóngoro Cosongo," "Canto negro" (Black song), and "Sensemayá" (Guillén, 1976: 67, 79–80, 95), but gradually his verse – and in this the Spanish Civil War was a crucial experience (see above) – became more politicized: "Látigo, / sudor y látigo. / El sol despertó temprano, / y encontró al negro descalzo, / desnudo el cuerpo llagado, / sobre el campo" (Whip, / sweat and whip. / The sun woke up early / and found the negro with no shoes, / his bare body wounded, / lying on the ground) (Guillén, 1976: 139). One important voice which pursued some of the rhythms of Guillén's poetry was the Peruvian Nicomedes Santa Cruz (1925–92), who is best known for his *décimas*, a traditional poetic form dating from the seventeenth century which he has Africanized. In "Panalivio," Santa Cruz voices the anguish of the colonized African in the New World: "Bajo el látigo español / ('¡Párate, negro mojino!') / sudando de sol a sol / cantaba mi aliento tibio. / Si fumo / paentro me como el humo. / Si aguanto paentro me trago el llanto" (Under the Spanish whip / ('Stand up, you lazy negro!') / sweating from dawn to dusk / I sing my warm breath song. If I smoke / I take the smoke down inside. / If I put up with it / I swallow my pain up inside) (Ojeda, 2003: 244). "Mujer negra" (Black woman), by the Cuban Nancy Morejón (1944–), offers a gendered angle to the story of cultural dispossession: "Todavía huelo la espuma del mar que me hicieron atravesar. / . . . Su Merced me compró en una plaza. / Bordé la casuca de Su Merced y un hijo macho le parí. / Mi hijo no tuvo nombre. Y Su Merced, murió a manos de un impecable *lord* inglés" (Still I smell the foam of the sea which they made me cross. . . . His Honour bought me in a square. / I embroidered His Honour's coat and gave birth to a son for him / My son had no name. / And His Honour, he died at the hands of an impeccable English lord) (Morejón, 2001: 226–7).

The aporia of ethnicity and the poetic canon is poetry written in the pre-Columbian languages. In 1929 the Peruvian social theorist José Carlos Mariátegui argued that genuine Indian literature would only come into being when the Indians themselves were able to create it: "Una literatura indígena, si debe venir, vendrá a su tiempo. Cuando los propios indios estén en grado de producirla" (Indigenous literature, if it must come, will come in its own time. When the Indians themselves are at the right stage to produce it) (Mariátegui, 1998: 335). Although some poets have used, for example, Quechua for their poems – notably José María Arguedas in his *Canto kechwa* (Quechua song, 1938) and *Temblar Katatay y otros poemas* (Katatay trembling and other poems, 1972) – Quechua is more likely nowadays to be the vehicle of "outspoken declarations of [Indians'] rights and proclamations of their cultural heritage" (Harrison, 1997: 694) rather than the vehicle used to create a poetic artifact. Nahuatl, though the language in which some of the most beautiful pre-Columbian poetry was written (León-Portilla, 1994), likewise does not appear to have inspired an "indigenous literature" in the sense that Mariátegui understood the term; other languages such as Maya, Aymara, and Guaraní, for example, when used as the vehicle of expression, appear to inflect the utterance overwhelmingly with a pre-Columbian nostalgia (see htpp://www.andes.org/poems.html). With the possible exception of Arguedas, the pre-Colombian languages do not appear to have had the equivalent of a writer such as Ngugi wa Thiong'o, who has championed the use of indigenous languages such as Gikuyu in Africa (Thiong'o, 1995). For this reason, perhaps, in the case of Quechua or Nahuatl poetry, we might argue that the Spivakian dictum ("the subaltern cannot speak"; Spivak, 1995) appears to apply.

## References and Further Reading

Bishop, Elizabeth, and Brasil, Emanuel (1972). "Introduction." In *An Anthology of Twentieth-Century Brazilian Poetry*, pp. xiii–xxi. Middletown, CT: Wesleyan University Press.

Boti, Regino (2005). *Kindred Spirits: Poems by Regino E. Boti*. Ed. Stephen Hart. London: Mango.

Brasil, Emanuel, and Smith, William Jay, eds (1983). *Brazilian Poetry (1950–1980)*. Middletown, CT: Wesleyan University Press.

Brotherston, Gordon (1975). *Latin American Poetry: Origins and Presence*. Cambridge: Cambridge University Press.

Caracciolo-Trejo, E., ed. (1971). *The Penguin Book of Latin American Verse*. Harmondsworth: Penguin.

Cardenal, Ernesto (1975). *Marilyn Monroe and Other Poems*. Trans. Robert Pring-Mill. London: Search Press.

Castellanos, Rosario (1988). *Meditation on the Threshold*. New York: Bilingual Press.

Caulfield, Carlota (2001). *At the Paper Gates with Burning Desire*. Trans. Angela McEwan. San Francisco: InteliBooks.

Chang-Rodríguez, Raquel (1988). *Voces de Hispanoamérica: Antología literaria*. Boston: Heinle & Heinle.

Crow, Mary, ed. (1988). *Woman Who Has Sprouted Wings: Poems by Contemporary Latin American Women Poets*. 2nd edn. Pittsburgh, PA: Latin American Literary Review Press.

Gallagher, D. P. (1973). *Modern Latin American Literature*. London: Oxford University Press.

Gonzalez, Mike, and Treece, David (1922). *The Gathering of Voices: The Twentieth Century Poets of Latin America*. London: Verso.

Guillén, Nicolás (1976). *Summa poética*. Ed. L. Iñigo Madrigal. Madrid: Gredos.

Harrison, Regina (1997). "Quechua literature." In *Encyclopedia of Latin American Literature*, pp. 693–94. Chicago: Fitzroy-Dearborn.

Hart, Stephen (1990). *Spanish, Catalan and Spanish American Poetry from "Modernismo" to the Spanish Civil War*. Lampeter: Edwin Mellen.

— (2003). "Algunos apuntes sobre los autógrafos de *Poemas humanos* y *España, aparta de mí este cáliz*." In *César Vallejo: Autógrafos olvidados: Edicion facsimilar de 52 manuscritos al cuidado de Juan Fló y Stephen Hart*, pp. 89–172. Lima: Pontificia Universidad Católica del Perú.

Higgins, James (1982). *The Poet in Peru*. Liverpool: Francis Cairns.

León-Portilla, Miguel (1994). *Quince poetas del mundo azteca*. Mexico City: Diana.

Mariátegui, José Carlos (1998). *Siete ensayos de interpretación de la realidad peruana*. Lima: Amauta.

Martí, José (1975). *Prosa escogida*. Ed. José Olivio Jiménez. Madrid: Editorial Magisterio Español.

Morejón, Nancy (2001). *Black Woman and Other Poems*. Trans. Jean Andrews. London: Mango.

Neruda, Pablo (1976). *Tercera residencia*. Buenos Aires: Losada.

Ojeda, Martha (2003). "Nicomedes Santa Cruz and the vindication of Afro-Peruvian culture." In Stephen Hart and Richard Young (eds), *Contem-porary Latin American Cultural Studies*, pp. 239–52. London: Arnold.

Ollé, Carmen (1992). *Noches de adrenalina*. 2nd edn. Lima: Lluvia.

Parra, Nicanor (1985). *Antipoems: New and Selected*. Ed. David Unger. New York: New Directions.

Paz, Octavio (1988). *The Collected Poems 1957–1987*. Ed. Eliot Weinberger. Manchester: Carcanet.

Pring-Mill, Robert (1983). "*Cantas – canto – cantemos*: Las canciones de lucha y esperanza como signos de reunión e identidad," *Romanisches Jahrbuch*, 34: 318–54.

Rowe, William (2004), "Latin American poetry." In John King (ed.), *The Cambridge Companion to Modern Latin American Culture*, pp. 136–70. Cambridge: Cambridge University Press.

Spivak, Gayatri (1995). "Can the subaltern speak?" In Bill Ashcroft, Gareth Griffiths, and Helen Tiffin (eds), *The Post-Colonial Studies Reader*, pp. 24–8. London: Routledge.

Thiong'o, Ngugi Wa (1995). "The language of African literature." In Bill Ashcroft, Gareth Griffiths, and Helen Tiffin (eds), *The Post-Colonial Studies Reader*, pp. 285–90. London: Routledge.

Troiano, Marita (1999). *Extrasístole*. Lima: Carpe Díem.

Vallejo, César (2005a). *Trilce*. Ed. and trans. Michael Smith and Valentino Gianuzzi. Exeter: Shearsman Books.

— (2005b). *Complete Later Poems*. Ed. and trans. Valentino Giannuzzi and Michael Smith. Exeter: Shearsman Books.

Watson Miller, Ingrid, ed. (1981). *Afro-Hispanic Literature: An Anthology of Hispanic Writers of African Ancestry*. Miami, FL: Ediciones Universal.

Wilson, Jason (2000). *Darío, Borges, Neruda and the Ancient Quarrel between Poets and Philosophers*. London: Institute of Latin American Studies.

— (2004). "Coda: Spanish American surrealist poetry." In Robert Havard (ed.), *A Companion to Spanish Surrealism*, pp. 253–76. London: Tamesis.

# 26

# Literature between the Wars: Macedonio Fernández, Jorge Luis Borges, and Felisberto Hernández

*Adriana J. Bergero,* translated by *Todd S. Garth*

The process of modernization in Latin America gave its stamp of approval to the state-building model anchored in a monocultural nation, industrialization, Positivist efficiency, compulsory literacy, and the control of social spaces (eugenics, xenophobia, classism, sexism, diglossia). Notwithstanding, its homogenizing cultural process was concomitant with a heteroglossic growth of old and new types of *barbarismos*, cultures resistant and asymmetrical to modernity such as the indigenous, suburban, proletarian, and middle class cultures as well as those fueled by new gender identities. This sociocultural plurality gave rise to zones of ambiguity and conflict (Cornejo Polar, 1978: 12) from which arise the modernist writing of Macedonio, Borges, and Felisberto. The imposition of modernity's sole model of economic production and cultural representation attempted to strip ethnic, economic, and gender subalternities of both their languages and their cognitive frames of reference (Schulte-Sasse, 1989: xxxvii; Horkeimer and Adorno, 1972: 154). This voluptuous heteroglossia was relegated to the obscure underside of the cultural folds, but as occurred within the confusion expressed by the Baroque, its cultural dynamics *expanded* the cultural fabric and wove it through the interactions between obverse and reverse (Deleuze, 1989: 156). This heteroglossia managed to thrive, growing out of the uneven grafting of a global culture which failed to eliminate preexisting substrates or to avoid antibodies, thus accumulating at a single point unconnected material from different cultural strains. As in the Aleph and the Borgesian Funes, "lucid spectator of an instantaneous, multifaceted world" (Borges, 1974: 490), or in the Felisbertian consciousness, "All appeared with uncontainable multiplicity" (Hernández, 1983: III, 93). The modernist mode of perception would come to be the product of at least three instances: (1) *simultaneous heterogeneity:* newspaper pages *merged* events from different fields; the *comprehension* of the city was conveyed by complex cognitive maps on the move, affected by the "incessant, interlarded style of reality" (Borges, 1974: 105); all leading to the crisis of the *observant self* (Masiello, 1989: 111) surrounded by the hyperventilation of modernity's emblematic space, for the space of the city played a fundamental role in the *visualization* of the tension and simultaneity among heterogeneous discourses, "the triumph of the popular over aspirations of exclusivity" (Monsiváis, 2000: 26); (2) *velocity and fugacity*: along with the acceleration of the rhythm of economic production, trains and cars unfolded the landscape in multi-focal sequences *in movement;* (3) *porosity and slippage of identity*: the recruitment of global culture was intersected by alternative cultural times, identities, and spaces, generating the metaphors of *filtration* and *uncontainability* expressed within the multilayered words of the literature of the Fantastic.

Modern homogenization was to be grounded on an expanded social foundation that was dramatically transforming the cultural underpinnings of the River Plate region with an unprecedented mass public and cultural industry; this cultural industry offered up newspapers of all ideological stripes, magazines of *high society*, weekly novels and translations in cheap mass publications, technical manuals, skits, columns chronicling urban life or police-related events, serials and melodramas about perdition and redemption, Anarchist and Catholic tracts, avant-garde and proletarian cultural reviews, department store catalogs. Such porous territory constituted itself in writing and literary criticism but also in an array of intractable *extra-literary* social spaces such as cafés, *tertulias*, and parliamentary as well as informal debates. Rubén Darío's iconic text "Era un aire suave" became "*debased*" in recitations by songsters, ruffians (malevos), and even "grocery clerks in greasy pizzerias" (*Martín Fierro*, 1968: 19). Borges published *Historia universal de la infamia* (*A Universal History of Infamy*) in Argentina's highest-circulation newspaper (Sarlo, 1999: 276), and not even the recalcitrant nationalism of Enrique Larreta or Hugo Wast kept them from preaching Catholicism while writing *folletines* (mass serial melodramas). Tango themes were sung on the radio and in popular theater, written in tenements and recycled by movie studios, commented on by Borges's Creole avant-garde and the literary journal *Martín Fierro*. Within these hybrid and intersecting fields of dialogical counterpoint, high culture ended up cohabiting with the "bad writing" of upstarts. How was it possible to represent the disconcerting modern scenario? With what languages? "One needs to leave literature," recommended Ricardo Piglia (1990: 124), if one wants to understand the changes in literary function. New social agents drove the redistribution of the cultural and political space and began to shape their own discursive formats; an immense ideological/ representational palimpsest (anarchism, socialism, communism, feminism, and fascism) strained the public sphere; immigrant languages newly arrived in Argentina and Uruguay mixed Creole Castilian with Genovese and Yiddish, the marginal language of the underworld of prostitutes (*lunfardo*) with the registers of new *disenfranchised* social players: proletariat, middle class, working women, *mestizos/as*, mulattos/as, *compadritos* (neighborhood bosses), and immigrants, all of them *newcomer* hybrids embedding themselves into an indecipherable modernity. Leftovers, bifocal identities, and foreignness: symbols of the laid-open *grotesque body* that discomfits social life with the *connective* nature of its communicating vessels (Mazzoleni, 1985: 19).

At the aesthetic level, this *modern scene* was represented in the confusion of genres and discourses, *intertextual* passages of flooded fields, parodying displacement, excision of the subject, perceptive-linguistic juxtapositions, auto-reflexive doubling, agoraphobia, the diluting of cultural hierarchies, and the positive valuation of deviation, randomness, and error. Macedonio, Borges, and Felisberto tackle the rich surplus of vacillation between empirical modernity – the slipping away of the grotesque city – and the control of modern rationality and aesthetics (realism), linguistic purity, expulsion of sentimentality in the degraded space of melodrama, and the *bad taste* of a semiliterate subculture: civilizing controls such as *good writing* or the urban grid imposed on the city's physical space. The tension between homogeneity and heterogeneity sums up the paradoxical modern subject torn between his subjectivity and social norms: a "self" forging itself in "its relation with objects" (Masiello, 1989: 87), for the (Cartesian) separateness of the parts merely represents passive, abstract material (Deleuze, 1989: 14). As in Baroque costume, "ample, an expansive wave, tumultuous" (Deleuze, 1989: 155), the writings of Macedonio, Borges, and Felisberto are *exuberant*: an art of abundant texture in identities, spaces, times, and causalities, like caverns to be explored gropingly; unexpected hollows and folds, labyrinthine textual palimpsests, perplexing and farcical laughter revealing the underside of culture. Is there anything more voluptuous and chaotic than the indiscernible labyrinths of authors, titles, intertextual references, and citations – fictitious, plagiarized, real, deconstructed, parodied, falsified – of Borgesian writing, multiplied in infinite volutes and mirrors, and views, seen as the puzzled Funes sees them, "in profile and face-front?"

## Macedonio Fernández (1874–1952)

"A generic version in words of the verbalization corresponding to the corner's wait never arrived," exemplifies Macedonian aesthetics in a sentence without subject or predicate: "when the Devil was busy doing things backwards; making buttonholes mismatch . . . teaching roofs to rain down and key rings to get stuck in pants pockets . . . When the Devil . . ." (*Papeles*, 96–7). Leopoldo Lugones's authorial figure was tantamount to universal harmony, a superhuman subject whose destiny was exemplary and Messianic (Viñas et al., 1989: 168); the Macedonian author, in contrast, is devilish: turning everything inside out so that *nothing works*, theatrically substituting the essential parts in the engine of meaning with adverbial clauses – *accessories* to the logical chassis – that choke off the *fullness* of meaning of the affirmative realist-rationalist discourse. That which *never arrives* parodies the instruction-title meant for foolish readers that unblinkingly consume mass quantities: "the audient open-mouthedness: No species ever before subjected itself to being lectured" (*Papeles*, 294). Macedonio is an awful and irreverent lecturer: branching all over and disconcerting, he sabotages his writing with digressions, abrupt outbursts of oral spontaneity, and all-purpose subjective marks that disregard the notion of a single canon and cultural hierarchies such as authorship, the literary character, narrative logic and semantic resolution, the circulation of culture, and the reader's submission. His aesthetic – called "The end of the reader's contentment" – is associated with the neo-Baroque by virtue of its incompleteness and dissatisfaction, its excess, the *fluorescence* of its voids as well as its narrative deceleration. "I met the mother of a friend from Rosario and came to know that . . . Not so fast, dear reader . . . they'll give us a speeding ticket. For now I'm not writing anything; get used to it" (*Papeles*, 29).

In that vein, *Adriana Buenos Aires (Ultima novela mala)* (The last bad novel, 1974) parodies sentimental literature, mass-market readers, and socio-mimetic formulas that, in the midst of the hectic modern hyperventilation, attempted to build social order over the grotesque city: troubled love, the single but decent mother, her disturbed lover, and the loyalty of another who loves her from afar mimic sentimental literature with archetypes that are condemned to a plasticized correction to their misadventures. *Museo de la Novela de la Eterna (Primera novela buena)* (The first good novel, 1968) likewise: it robs its characters of ideological consistency and robs the reader of emotional moorings to those characters. "Even the names of his characters constitute acts against the mimetic function of literature . . . 'the president of the novel' . . . the 'sweet person who died of love" resist their semantic uniqueness; they become like figures 'on a merry-go-round'" (Masiello, 1989: 202). Both novels are written simultaneously, but the wind mixes up their pages so that "I couldn't tell if a particular brilliant page belonged to the last bad novel or the first good one" (*Museo*, 267). This question of writing *well* or *badly*, Borges will tell us, is a scholarly criterion "which we should not burden ourselves with here" (*Tamaño*, 12); Macedonio's, matching bad and good novels, similarly do not burden us, since both belong to the deceptive exercise of the literary. His aesthetics (*Dudarte, Belarte*) are purely the proceedings of defamiliarization: pseudonymy, anamorphosis, trompe-l'oeil, parenthetical structures, wordplay, hyperbaton, false citations: writerly dilettantism that openly contests the productive semantic calculus of both capitalist economy and semantics. Folds in which formal Modernity – and the epistemic privilege of writing – *is shown interrupted* in its serious and lead-setting formats, an "artificial pastiche." As in the neo-Baroque: there is a tantalizing toying with the space of signs, because signs are the "symbolic pillar of society, guarantee of its functioning" (Sarduy, 1969: 209), of its communicativeness and of its preservation. Notwithstanding, the writerly squandering of this anarchist-cum-avant-gardiste is hardly a dead work: it illuminates zones of *strangeness*, *other* logics and spaces of *counter-state* (Ludmer), in which to reconstruct the nation. Ellipses and metaphors are *representative* of darkened centers that show up in order to discomfit the chosen (canon) and reveal the avoided. In this way, language necessarily becomes a desert scenario: every supplement, every whorl, refuses to enter into the dance of affirmative relations backed by bourgeois imaginaries, thus obstructing the semantic denotation (Axelrud and Calabrese, 1999: 20) so as *not to produce a legacy*. What is interrupted in Macedonio's "La desherencia" (Disinheritance), for instance, is precisely the capitalist accumulation (heritage) of culture. Opacity and strangeness interfere with the "*normal* progress of meaning" (Prieto, 2002: 43). Macedonio's *aesthetics of hollowness* questions *the normality and coherence* in *normal* meaning. When the author is "invited to eat he would enlarge the holes in the tablecloth . . . in order to find out to what dimensions the lady of the house could widen her eyes before so exasperating a spectacle. The confounded hostess-reader takes vengeance on her peculiar guest and fires the following question: Where is your grammar, my good man?" (*Papeles*, 23).

The era was saturated with anarchists, anti-statists, and *ghosts*: Macedonio attempted to be all of them; he refused to publish, sabotaged the apparatus of state consecration, of newspapers, and the cultural marketplace; he preferred to vanish behind the hybrid of multi-discursive genres and "nonexistent" characters. Letters, unfinished chapters, prologues to prologues "for entering further and further away from the novel" (*Museo*, 56), urban vignettes, coffeehouse toasts, oral articles, performances, greetings in *tertulias*: his texts capture the multi-discursiveness of the modern street with its cultural cast fully activated. His writer's den is one of the many boardinghouse rooms in which Macedonio lived, a bar, the backroom of a cultural funhouse. In fact, the boardinghouse tenant "is relieved of forms and codes, travels light and wanders freely through the city" (Piglia, 2000: 79). In other words, Macedonio recognizes culture as a zone of plurality without borders and within the confusion of the grotesque order, contrasting it with the authoritative volumetry of the lettered City: detours, levity, and illumination of heteroglossic disorder – the same itineraries as Cortázar's *Hopscotch* (1963). As Macedonio slid fluently, branching through the heterogeneity, his editors demanded, in vain, more "enclosed" texts with "a solution close by," and which "occupy one place" (*Papeles*, 73).

Like Arlt, Macedonio knows how to write *badly*: to neglect "the resolution not a little" (*Papeles*, 125), and since he keeps away from the domineering and hierarchical premises of libraries (*Museo*, 177), this trickster confesses: "I haven't read Bergson, but I write him well enough" (*Papeles*, 22), in this way foreshadowing Borgesian jabs at erudition. "I don't know much, but it doesn't matter" (III, 277), Felisberto notes. He too opens the way for the Borgesian send-up of John Wilkins's taxonomies: "fifth unclassified species E: categories of 'it is not' . . . It would be more honorable to name things according to what they don't have" (*Papeles*, 115–16). An aesthetic based on the *interruption* of language takes advantage of cinematographic discourse to slow down, dilate, and contract, giving one time to look gently and diligently over the *holes in the tablecloth*. Macedonio's "skipping reader" keeps the reading from sticking and keeps the holes *open*. What might we find in them? For starters, the understanding that knowledge is not to be found in the static of institutionalized culture but in the *authority of experience*: intellectuals don't fix on what normal people do, people who "study all aspects in . . . the practical presentation of a problem, and don't study stomach aches without having stomach aches" (*Todo y nada*, 21); knowledge is *concrete*, subjective, corporal, and arises out of the "happenstances of each moment." As a result, in Macedonio's world *all* subjects can be included in the arena of culture, foreshadowing the postcolonial vindication of the *authority* of experience and of the *knowledge* of subaltern and informal subjects. Polemicist to Sarmiento, Macedonio explains the mental poverty that "bookish scholars will suffer from, who have not had wide enjoyment of the sociability and meanderings with many companions . . . a man who has not gone to school and does not read but *who converses and interacts with many people* . . . will think for himself" (*Todo y nada*, 23, emphasis added). "Macedonio is illiterate" (*Papeles*, 39), declares "Carta abierta argentino-uruguaya" (An open Argentine–Uruguayan letter), distancing himself from the reach of grammar (*Papeles*, 109); one must not seek in grammar *universality* and the laws of *knowing how to say it well* as if such bylaws were a "disinterested culture," instead of a meta-institutional machinery devoted to disciplining "the chaotic nature of barbarism" (Ramos, 1987: 39 and passim), and to building up language-citizenship relations: of the diglossic body of the Nation.

Macedonio's defamiliarizing aesthetics can be associated with an extraliterary discursive field promoting the statist model (maximum state), "a machine of meddling, theatricality and false sentimentalism": "one gets emotional, takes pity," but it is "society, neighbors, who should understand, give aid, not the Pension . . . the Promotion, favoritism and shameful greed" (*Todo y nada,* 36). Calling civil society to action – a postcolonial urge – as a counterbalance to the falsifying and corrupt power of the bourgeois state, and playing down the "*great moment* of capitalism," is all of a piece in Macedonio's texts: "a millionaire flaunting his millions is a foolish spectacle compared to the Flavor of life of a City of Five Million proletarian and farming families, of parents and children growing old and growing up together" (55–6). This *subject of rights* pertains to the world of work and should be able to process its *own* knowledge, without accredited agents intervening to silence him or her. In Macedonio, the state *personifies* writing and calls for the armor of Leopoldo Lugones's political and cultural discourses while benefiting from the linguistic intractability of Hispanicizing scholars – *clandestine viceroys* (Borges I, 133) – such as Monner Sans, or of Ricardo Rojas. Rojas, interpreter of the grand bourgeoisie of the Centenary Generation, won a prize in 1923 for his *Historia de la literatura argentina* (A history of Argentine literature), which became a foundational text for the first national collective map, another *false* institutional mechanism of exclusion within the legitimizing knowledge of nation building, as Cornejo Polar would argue (1978: 9). Judges, capitalists, and journalists also speak-write *falsely*, but in those cases the law stands to prevent "the possibility of winning with lies, confusion and harm" (*Todo y nada*, 37). Against the (ir)responsibility of the state, Macedonio urges citizens to defend against the governmental abuse that causes them harm (*Todo y nada*, 59–60), thus forestalling the need for laws *against* the state, a crucial warning in the context of the long-lasting tradition of the state terrorism of the region.

This is not to say that Macedonio's auto-reflexive and meta-literary hybrid lives only within the literary arena or removed from daily urban life: his most noteworthy performance-text presented his candidacy for President of the Republic (1922), protesting the electoral duplicity characteristic of chaperoned democracies, following the electoral parody-protest by the feminist Julieta Lanteri Renshaw, who ardently denounced the exclusion of women's suffrage in 1920. Macedonio's alternative to the writerly recaptures the social value of orality, the communicative pragmatics of the heteroglossic, and the shifting movement of the social, removing the literary from the *serious* and taking it directly to the *street*: filling modern Buenos Aires, the arrogant, with *untenable* Dadaist objects or performed novels *(novela salida a la calle*, a novel taken to the streets): art "intermingling with 'strips of life' on sidewalks . . . homes and bars" *(Museo, 14)*. A desire for literature to replace the confined space *of literature* with the warmth of bars and homes of the performers of the grotesque city, intersecting the national identity of the bourgeois state with apprenticeships "of sociability and adventures with lots of companions."

## Jorge Luis Borges (1899–1986)

Roberto Arlt marks the end of the requisite relationship between schooling and writing, canon and erudition, as hierarchical referents. Into the cultural arena entered *upstarts* hovering on the thresholds of the institution of writing, like the readers of *El juguete rabioso (Mad Toy*, 2002), who steal from institutionalized systems – such as libraries – the opportunity to read, or like Felisberto, who takes charge of the *linguistic awkwardness of those who can't work the codes*. Borges was not a marginal author, of course, but there is much food for thought in his revulsion for libraries and in the incontinence of his erudite references, so compulsive that they overtly border on caricature. Borges detected "with sharpness the mechanisms of the system," and constitutes "the expression of its close and its transformation" (Piglia, 1990: 122). Thus the derisive parody of formal channels of culture and his passion for marginal literatures that "hold the possibility of their own, irreverent management" (Piglia, 1990: 51). For this library director, hyper-reader and arsonist of libraries, culture – the cultural arena of Modernity – goes beyond disciplines and genres; thus his profuse use of intertextuality as the Borgesian metaphor for the interconnective behavior of the spheres, the confusion of genres – and hierarchies. I believe his writings aim at vividly representing modern pluridiscursivity; hence his plagiarism and (cultural) translation as a *landscape* for the impetuous passage of referents and a sending-in of *masked performers and cultural actors*, his parody and his movements toward slippery identities, as well as the *bifocal* logic of his doubles. Borges does draw from the well of metropolitan cultural sources, but one really sees how pure the water he drinks is when he imbibes from the pools of *discard* of popular literature: Wells, Stevenson, Kipling, or Hinton and Uspenski, theosophists of esoteric sects that popularized the fourth dimension – as with Mabel M. Collins's *Light in the Path* (1936). Borges gets his hands on the British Library that the mass production of the cultural industry places "within reach of all" (Piglia, 1990: 147). Another zone of suspicion-contact comprises the foundational authors of River Plate melodrama, such as Eduardo Gutiérrez or Evaristo Carriego. In any case, what language is spoken by the Gutre family of Borges's "The Gospel According to Mark," by la Cautiva – the young and daring woman in "Story of the Warrior and the Captive Maiden" – or by the clumsy *compadritos* of the Buenos Aires ghettos? We are dealing here with Argentine *unwritten* languages, a preference that would certainly have irritated Sarmiento, that "detester and ignorer of the Creole" who "Europeanized us with his faith in those newcomers to a culture who expect miracles from her"

(*Tamaño*, 12). If not there, in the solidity of the "lettered city," where shall we look? For "The Aleph's" flamboyant Carlos *Argentino* Daneri, who speaks *with the accent* of the upstarts, has already had his taste of the National Prize for Literature.

Borges's story "The South" touches on two fundamentals of modern globalization: the port – the point of colonizing penetration through which Johannes Dahlmann enters as an agent of the national eugenic project – and the railroad, which will ensconce Juan into the latent *remains* of the nation. His maternal grandfather participates in the military campaign that smashed *barbarous* polymorphism with the genocidal sword of Julio A. Roca's New Nation and of the economic – political and cultural – assimilation of the gaucho, descendant of indigenous ethnicities and reduced to a mere labor tool of the agro-exporting latifundium. By 1939, Juan represents the *national subject* that has sealed the victory of *civilization* over barbarous heteroglossia, point of departure for modern Argentina: its first national *Frontier*. But Juan's encounter with the gauchos is not the kind that reaffirms the scene of *national consolidation* – a civilizing subject on high and a dark *barbarous* ignominy – but the assault of a crouching latency against the folds of modernizing control. A writing of liminality, "El evangelio según Marcos" ("The Gospel According to Mark") in the same way reactivates the stealthy latency of the Southern Frontier when, through an error in calculation, Espinosa abridges the distance between him and his peons, the Gutres: redheaded, Indian-featured, and excluded from Sarmiento's literacy fervor, they are vanquished descendants on the Southern Frontier, bastard sons with no patristic, disposable parts of the global economy, cut off from modern rehabilitation. Nobody expects the Gutres, sunk in the residual darkness of the nation, to open the breach that will swallow the certainties of a Modernity without a single fissure or resistance, represented in Espinosa, reader of Spencer: "They almost never spoke" and "they no longer knew how to write . . . they had forgotten English: Spanish . . . was a struggle for them." They speak a bastard or mute language, but they *speak*, like la Cautiva, once she betrays civilization and assimilates to a feral life, to "peat fires, feasts of seared meat," to the *unnamable* caresses of exogamy: she too speaks with difficulty: "it had been fifteen years since she had spoken her native language . . . a rustic English, intermingled with Araucano or Pampas dialect."

I believe that Borgesian writing acknowledges in the Gutres, la Cautiva, and the gauchos of "The South" the value of cultural hybridity; its historical agency embodies social heteroglossia as a tool for responding to modernizing oppression. The product of the hybrid is the *inappropriate other*, the inconvenient face of the double who, when he/she *speaks*, discomforts imperialist, nationalist, and even family certainties. La Cautiva *has fallen* into the deepest part of the fold of the *national arena*, challenging it in choosing her happiness with her Pampas chieftain and her children. She is in love and happy with her odd family. And it is most significant that such a woman should be the *only mother* in all of Borges's works. In the frontier literature that serves as the very foundation for modern Argentina, in the dramatic contrast between processes of *enlightenment* and shadows, this love is every bit as *monstrous* as the mother-source of national bastardism. The English Cautiva, a bifocal consciousness, makes inverse use of the frontier: instead of fleeing, she draws close. Borgesian writing also will choose: it *chooses to speak* the mute and intercultural text of the borders – the unidentifiable and unrecorded words of alternative Modernity, of alternative Argentina. Every piece of Borges's world is drafted by a *writerly double* who maneuvers his identity-places within his own writing: the entity that gives voice and textual progeny (Ludmer, 1993: 145) to la Cautiva's *crime* turns a deaf ear to the muteness to which social texts condemn her, a condemnation deposited in the discourses of the "counter-state." The narrator seeks out his true history (*his truth*), dismissing that of the barbarous male warrior, Droctulft, who embraces civilization (state narrative): "that one wasn't the *memory I was looking for.* I finally found it: it was a story I once heard from my English grandmother" (I, 558; emphasis added). The one he decides to tell is a history *without archive*: a European woman opts for the social expendability of barbarism, the discourse of love and *promiscuous* sexuality – themes that the sociability of modernity makes good use of in order to discipline the unfitting heteroglossia and subjectivities of the nation – a history the narrator tells us *betraying* the Eurocentrist, exogamic phobia of his own grandmother. There the story remains, doubly vexed by the *Englishwoman* and by that descendant of hers who chooses not to reproduce (it). La Cautiva and the narrator uncover *second lives* in the interstices of a Modernity saturated with folds, a postcolonial posture that unleashes alternative rationalities, emotionality, and sexualities: knowledge of different cultural series and subjects, repudiators of the racist foundations of modern Argentina's European civilizing venture.

Borges's bifocal writing also betrays the epistemic privilege of erudite culture to manipulate its desire, coquetry – or philanthropy (Monsiváis, 2000: 29) – with the Creole-urban populist aesthetics fed by Argentine president Hipólito Yrigoyen's (1916–22, 1928–30) integrationist imaginary, whose cultural mobilization identified with the cultural agents of the tango; Borges significantly inserts that imaginary in "Fundación mítica de Buenos Aires" (Mythical foundation of Buenos Aires): "the first little organ rescued the horizon/ with his sickly bearing, his Havana and his gringo / The warehouse wall already sure of itself argues YRIGOYEN / some piano sends out tangos by Saborido" (Borges, 1974: 81). Buenos Aires is founded with *immigrants*, Yrigoyen, and the composer of "La Morocha" (1905). In 1927, Borges officially supports the president of the middle classes who have risen from immigrants; notwithstanding, in his populist aesthetic, the tango, its *compadritos*, and languid ghettos sanitize anarchism and the smelly din of factory neighborhoods where immigrant workers barely get by: not the huddled tenement but the calming nighttime neighborhood where little houses pulsate "like lanterns in a row"; not the gauchesque – the landowning oligarchy's national model of paraphernalia and waste, not *lunfardo* – slang of the criminal caricatured in tangos and *sainetes*, not the Boca – the tragic and teeming immigrant quarter, but middle-class Balvanera or upright San Telmo, to which Rosendo (The story of Rosendo Juárez) retires from the life of a *compadrito* when he comes back a graceless gentleman.

Borges's aethetics work *sideways* with the murmur of subaltern specters, *minor* writers: "the verses of Almafuerte that Evaristo recited to us" reveal to him that language was also music, passion, and dreams (cited by Sarlo, 1999: 263). But this treason or bifocalism is *not* a *non-place*: it's the *place* of the hybrid, in this case of an intertexuality (Evaristo Carriego-Borges) that even allows a shifting of identities *without attracting notice*. Borges explains, "I decided to write about a popular, but definitively minor, poet: Evaristo Carriego. My parents pointed out that *his poetry was bad*, but I argued that he had been our neighbor and friend" (cited by Barnatán, 1999: 39; emphasis added). The argument of *neighborhood relations* allows Borges to link himself to a poet of popular districts and a writer of melodramatic tone, who even died of a proletarian illness – tuberculosis – and to whom he dedicated *Evaristo Carriego* (1930). Borges's urban Creolism emerges from the heated debate over national, popular, and oral culture, "an issue that mass democracy brings to the boil" when the distance between the elites and the masses collapses with the institution of universal suffrage and when mass culture and immigration alter the *profile* of an Argentine (Sarlo, 1999: 267). Borges gets close to modern mass culture through Evaristo's melodramas, which form the massive basis for tangos. The popular author is *innocently guilty* of the fact that "in tangos, the chippies invariably end up in the hospital and the *compadritos* dissipate under morphine" (*Tamaño*, 30). And concomitantly, he also gets closer to *bad writing*, perhaps so as better to represent "the unrealities of the outskirts," its amphibious nature between pasture and high-rise cityscape, that, like the *compadrito*, is a *double* torn between the Pampa and the city; "Carriego could portray his worlds based on this indecisive matter" (Borges, 1974: 141); such vacillation also gives room to accommodate nicely Borges's doubles, traitors, and hybrids while allowing Evaristo's cultural field to penetrate his writing: concerning the challenged authority of streetcar conductors, the speaker of *Evaristo Carriego* unexpectedly interrupts the text, to the perplexity of the classic Borgesian readers, and explains: "there was always some *compadrito* who would plant the ticket into his fly, repeating indignantly that if they wanted it all they had to do was pull it out" (1974: 108).

The identifying heart of Borges's urban Creolism, dwellers of the outlying districts with their wrath and swagger, "myths of the individual who faces down the man of the masses" (Monsiváis, 2000: 30), is ostentatiously replaced in the 1930s (Toro and Toro, 2000: 77) with his classic works replete with tigers, labyrinths, dreams, mirrors, and meta-literary deconstructive reflections *removed from the extra-textual*. But the writerly double knows how to displace the material that shoves it aside, and repeat itself inverted – and intertextual – on the underside of the fold: "Because Buenos Aires is deep and I never lost myself in its streets without getting an unexpected consolation, whether of feeling unreality or of guitars from the depths of some patio or of the brush of lives" (*Evaristo*, 112). Unreality (prime subject of the *classical Borges*), is *only one part* of the equation, because there lies more: the strum of guitars, outlying patios, and brush of lives, zones of socio-urban contact that connect *him to Carriego* and to the identity-place framed by those "impatient October nights that draw chairs and people onto the sidewalk and . . . the street was confidential and refreshing" (1974: 108). The speaker in "Carriego and the Feel of the *Arrabal*" in *El tamaño de mi esperanza* (1926; *The Extent of my Hope*, 1994) does not hide the emotion fueled by

Carriego's writing: he places him in a street "whose name I very much want to remember" (27), claims his poetic vision "is overpowering. He has filled our eyes with compassion" (30), and that "he has seen forever those things . . . that are the soul of our soul" (28). Carriego speaks *through* Borges, who still has no objection to finding it "lovely to compare his beginner's tracings . . . with the definitive, serious, and tender *celebration* in which he calls up the favorite symbols of his art: the little seamstress who made a bad move, the moon, the blind man" (29, emphasis added).

Like the tango, Carriego furnishes an identity-place in the intimate alcove of streets with languid streetlamps, able to shelter sentimentality, *our* identifying and melodramatic place capable of housing *our* soul, compassion, the overpowering tenderness of poor neighborhoods, the seamstress "who went wrong," and the blind men. The final watchword of *Tamaño de mi esperanza* notes that "I will have to return to [Carriego] some day" (31). That is to say, to write *Evaristo Carriego* (1930) but at the same time to *return to* emotion, compassion, and the tears awakened by the *celebration* of the identifying encounter with the *feminizing* and weakening nation of a poet melodramatically dead at age 29. All *watchwords* belong to a code, a sleight of hand with which the writerly double hides his emotion – particularly when he deals with the inappropriateness of kitschy affectations of Borges-Carriego. For *Evaristo Carriego,* the text, will develop antibodies and distance against a sentimentality that Borges's writing makes Carriego's when perhaps it was really Borges's own: focused on our compassion, a disenfranchised voice states, "a poetry that lives on domestic contradictions . . . strikes me as a deprivation, a suicide" (1974: 135). The flip side of Borges's literary production contains texts "banished 'forever:' as in the case of *El tamaño de mi esperanza* and *El idioma de los argentinos* (1928, *The Language of the Argentines*, 1994). The first is a text *denied* when *in Oxford* somebody asks about it: Borges "reacted immediately saying that the book didn't exist, and advised him to stop looking for it" (Kodama, 1993: 7). But the writerly double never ceases his folding; the sentimental matter that the classic Borges strives so much to attribute to Evaristo and to hide behind his allegedly universal, foreign, and dehistorizing fictions haunts the caricaturized lover in "El Aleph," who affirms, "the universe will change but I [will never stop loving her]" (1974: 617). In a rush of "desperate tenderness," he speaks of the dead woman's portrait in the style of a sentimental novella: "Beatriz, Beatriz Elena, Beatriz Elena Viterbo, Beatriz dear. Beatriz gone forever, it's me, it's Borges" (1974: 624). As in tangos and radio soap operas, the Borgesian lover expresses himself through the purest melodramatic style; lovesickness, self-flagellation, theatrical phrases fashioned for dramatic revelations (Monsiváis, 2000: 34); also intentional candor, love secrets/secret love, paradoxical self affirmation by way of loss; a *weakened* masculinity is shown off and the affectation of the tango turns on another emotional swoop of "The Threatened Man": "a woman's name denounces me. A woman hurts throughout my body" (1974: 107). No wonder that sentimentality is one of the most threatening of emotions and therefore has been rigorously regulated by modern socialization through the xenophobic, sexist, and classist preventive fright that the bourgeoisie has professed in reaction to the diluting of social borders of the grotesque city.

Before ending up appropriated by mass culture, in Carriego this "Modernity's otherness" (Huyssen, 1987) embraces the nation *discarded* by the modernizing process – its tears, evanescent figures, unspoken secrets, and *authentic* dramas. In Borges's writing, this same disturbing and unsuitable sentimentality will appear intermittent, demanding – like the female Interloper in the story of the same name – to *enter and remain* in the *great drama* of irreconcilable parts that Modernity has played with the uncomfortable utterances of Modernity's otherness. Sentimentality was doubly disqualified upon being associated with the feminine world and mass culture (Huyssen, 1987: 46), but in Borges's writings this buried sentimentality turns out to be a tempting subject for the bifocal eye of his doubles who always address their own plurality in a rather conflicted way. Or in Felisberto's words, "given another person present there is always betrayal" (III, 257). It becomes tacit that the Borgesian double speaks *two different languages – and languages historically configured* – and speaks from counterpoised identities and discursive positions: thus the violence, the duels, and the countless encounters and farewells like the one of the narrators of "Story of the Warrior and the Captive Maiden" and his grandmother.

If the lettered city expels la Cautiva from the national scene of Modernity, the Borgesian narrator reinstalls her precisely through the discourse of love and subjectivity. In addition to granting her discursive legacy, Borges ensures that the legacy of la Cautiva will remain secured in postcolonial writerly maps whose specific *foundational romance* refutes the well-formed family ("foundation of the fatherland") prescribed by Lugones in his *Historia de Roca*. Borges's writing: (a) contests the epistemic homogenization of formal Modernity; (b) conveys from the modern scene the introduction of material still without archive – the latency, multidiscursivity, and intertextuality of the multilayered alternative Modernity; a hybrid parody, sentimentality, and sexuality of identities that spark a crisis among Modernity's cultural-literary systems and their single rationality; (c) is a border writing, as are Arlt's, Macedonio's, and Felisberto's. It will seek heterogenic modernity in the interstices and breaks, from which it would trace and touch the constant circulation of the grotesque city and its stigmatized social actors. Doubles, traitors, outlaws, killers, insomniacs, and rivals act out the severe tension and displacement of the space-subject of modernity's cultural colonization. As a Frontier writing, written by two hands that do not get along very well, Borges's work will oscillate between encounters and clashes, subjects *universal* to formal Eurocentric culture, and their parody. It also underlines the folds of heterogeneous modernity denied by the universal, its asymmetrical and intersecting fields. Beyond what has been considered the classic and trans-historic Borgesian inventory, its compulsive duels, doubles, and labyrinths represent the broken home of the modern subject, a *historic* subject. The confusion of its labyrinths, the perplexity caused by its mirrors and the irresolvable nature of its doubles and traitors, also allowed Borges to anticipate the veiled connections between modernity and much of the equally historical nature of postmodern culture. Thus we find in his classic stories myriad postmodern crises: the loss of reality of the real, the advance of simulacra and hyperreality and the dematerialization of history ("Tlön, Uqbar, Orbis Tertius," "Las

Ruinas circulares" [The circular ruins], "El Simulacro" ["The Mountebank"], "Ulrica" [Ulrikke]); the oppressive and necrophiliac configuration of the systemic and the implosivity of the historic subject that Borges reads as the consequence of the Great Totalitarian State ("La Biblioteca de Babel" ["The Library of Babel"], "La Lotería en Babilonia" ["The Lottery in Babylon"]); the fallacy of Modernity's logocentrism, universal culture, and national histories as well as the self-reflexivity and self-legitimation of writing ("Tema del traidor y del héroe" ["Theme of the Traitor and the Hero"], "El Idioma analítico de John Wilkins" ["The Analytical Language of John Wilkins"], "Pierre Menard, autor del Quijote" ["Pierre Menard, Author of the *Quijote*"], "La Muerte y la brújula" ["Death and the Compass"], "Historia de la eternidad" ["History of Eternity"]); the end of history and the loss of difference ("El Inmortal" ["The Immortal"], "La Doctrina de los ciclos" ["The Doctrine of Cycles"], "La Cifra" ["The Limit"], "La Intrusa" ["The Interloper"]); the decay of transcendence and essentialism, material vertigo and mechanical reproduction ("El Aleph, "Funes el memorioso" ["Funes the Memorious"), "El Zahir"). Confronted with the loss of progressive linear time, the Borgesian world opposes – with trepidation and desire – the unyielding survival of the heterogeneous, vividly expressed in the tension of its doubles and duels clashing in "El Centinela" ("The Sentinel"), as well as in the silent monstrosity of the inappropriate other who, despite being trapped and condemned to be suppressed in the nocturnal Turdela of "There Are More Things," is rescued by Borgesian writing to leave its unyielding mark: radical difference. Asterión's worst terror is a claustrophobic one; he fears that nothing else will happen to him. Borges's fictions address immortality and the end of history with dread and panic. Curiously enough, what his words cry out for is otherness and the reinsertion of difference – and history – as a safe escape from the post-historic and systemic nullification of the subject. What makes la Cautiva so unique and truly exceptional are her opting for love and for an alternative subjectivity that fiercely defies the massive imposition of Modernity. At least one of Borges's doubles no longer is the Interloper to be eradicated to secure the eternal sameness brought about by the control of homogenizing systemic forces. On the contrary: la Cautiva turns out to be the savior of the national and subjective scene. If the lettered city expels the Cautiva from the national scene of Modernity, no wonder that the Borgesian narrator decides to reinstall her within a revised national scenario. In addition to granting her discursive legacy, Borges ensures that the discursive (and biological) legacy of la Cautiva will remain secured in postcolonial writerly maps whose specific *foundational romance* refutes the well-formed family ("foundation of the fatherland") prescribed by Lugones in his *Historia de Roca*.

## Felisberto Hernández (1902–64)

In Felisberto, the subject *is occupied* by side zones, spheres not yet *literary* that end up founding the representation of the modern subject; in *Por los tiempos de Clemente Colling* (In the time of Clement Colling), memories interrupt the narration asking for "new meanings, or creating new, fleeting tricks, or trying everything a new way" (III, 138): *leaving* literature and injecting into it resignifications, tricks and *other ways*. Uruguayan president José Batlle y Ordóñez (1893–1907) consolidated the statist model, based on a strong bureaucratic apparatus, and its middle-class clientele; upward mobility facilitated by university education, access to private property, and a lesser degree of labor dependence were the calling cards of the imaginary of the Batllistas (1902–30) and the Neobatllistas (1946–58). None of these things ever came into Felisberto's hands. Born into the first and most publicized welfare state in Latin America, his life of wandering, the loss of his family home, and his descent through "all class of hotels" until *falling* "into a shady district in the city's outskirts" (II, 154) will give Felisberto a perplexing bifocalism, unequalled in identifying modern society's asymmetries. From such perplexity, he poignantly detected the *residuals* of the Battlista bourgeoisie's "possibilism" in the opaque world of the petit bourgeoisie, excluded from the *great moment of social acknowledgement*. Because it aspires to secure its place, if at all possible, before it can be demoted, Felisbertian fiction always focuses on entering *the home* by matrimonial unions – or literary affiliation – accessible only with difficulty and hardship. In "La casa inundada" ("The Flooded House"), for example, the proprietress demands impossible contortions and juggling from the speaker-character: "you're my guest; I only ask that you row . . . and that you put up with what I have to say to you. For my part, I'll make a small contribution to your monthly savings" (1989: 255): a writer employed as rower-audience in flooded houses owned by huge, authoritarian inscrutable matrons in (with) whom any *maneuver* ends up a failure, a guest who works for small, and unilaterally imposed, salary. Contracts with *no guarantee*: elusive contracts with employers, with the state, social contracts – including those in sexuality and writing.

Felisberto follows the scent of transition: as with Carriego's dramatic little seamstresses, he traces the transition's missteps, its restless travels, and uncertain homes. One travels from the *inappropriate* identity-house to enter spaces tyrannized by "the possessor of the only possible treasure, the home" (Panesi, 1993: 12). These alienating contracts turn the character into an eternal *foreigner* always asking for admission. And until *entry* is gained, fiction will intermingle social and linguistic borders with social proximities that, although not especially desirable, are the *only real* contacts. Felisberto portrays a sweating lower middle class confronted with the wintry ideal of the grand bourgeoisie's social routines: elegant settings and composure, grandeur embraced as the utmost dream by the whole nation. The subjective and the socially correct are the reverse and obverse folds that Felisberto's narration alternates, starting from subjects *un*masked *in public* by private breakdowns: unfitness at inopportune moments; lipothymia brought on by hunger; uncontrollable narcolepsy; acute depression; implacable classist stares of reproof; stomach contractions; irresistible (and reproachable) pan-eroticism awakened by certain objects and shapes; underemployed men eroticized by the smell of money and pursuing marriages to their advantage; shameless sexist narcissism; embarrassment at arriving *too* early to events or for going to "a poor neighborhood" (III, 255) to reclaim a lent suitcase that is *badly* needed; jokes to hide the "great fear of being fired" (III, 269); the scandal of a love triangle with disturbing life-sized dolls and wives who leave, writing "you have made my life nauseating" (II, 210); a disheartening proximity to musicians who can afford to eat only bananas for lunch and who, forced to travel first class, cannot buy a second-class ticket and benefit from the difference in fare (III, 10): the *impropriety* and clumsiness of the junk heap – deviations from *national identity* – give (de)form to the asymmetrical body of Felisberto's writing, and proudly admitted inspiration for Cortázar's fictional worlds. Even rites of seduction and nights of romance – the *national* romance – are spoiled by "that food and wine brought to the table by a stumbling cripple of a boy" (III, 106). Here the grand imaginary of the Batllista bourgeoisie actually *stumbles* – like the *crippled* waiter: there is no solution but to perform *bad music*, the only kind that rescues us "from shameful misery" (III, 206). Like the *bad* music that nonetheless feeds, *bad* writing will be subject to those "who have my life in their hands" (III, 214): in other words, the employers who book the show, the audience and the literary critics.

In "Mi primer concierto en Montevideo" (My first concert in Montevideo), a pianist grows pale when required to deposit 100 pesos to be allowed to play, and upon putting on a hand-me-down smoking jacket, finds "it was very small." His rehearsed plan for entering the stage *commandingly* is discarded because "at any moment it could burst on me" and he could feel the injury to his underarms of the too-tight garment (II, 127). In "Mi primer concierto" (My first concert), while the narrator-character performs, he hears murmurs and perceives:

> a shadow making movements . . . a black cat . . . what should I do with him? . . . ridiculous to chase him around the stage . . . In the middle of the piece there were some passages where I was supposed to swat the keys . . . and it wouldn't be hard to have him too jump all over the keyboard . . . So I decided to risk it and act crazy. (III, 131)

In Felisberto, the precariousness of daily life forces him to *risk it* and *act crazy* in music as well as in writing. In "Lands of Memory," the narrator-character tells that the owner of a café "had promised us work for three years; but at the end of three months – with the season already well along – he had hired an all-girl orchestra and we were left out on the street" (III, 21). *To be left out on the street* for not performing-writing as expected: to be left out of the nation or to consider the nation *from* its zones of discard. Uruguayan critic Emir Rodríguez Monegal imperiously and severely dismissed Felisberto's writing as immature; Jaime Alazraki did likewise for its vulgar colloquialism and its spare, ungainly style. Around 1925, Uruguayan authors would seem "embarrassingly, like public employees . . . the best of them holed up in their paper refuges producing a carefully tended creation . . . They washed . . . their hands of all impurities, of all 'Phoenician' trafficking" (Rodríguez Monegal, 1966: 49). Like Arlt, Felisberto knew how to write *badly*. He did not have clean hands either: the crisis of everyday life *runs through* his narrator-characters but this same *displacement* grants them a telling centrality in fiction in the hybrid space of an aesthetics *fugitive from art's autonomous sphere*: a small-town pianist, an at-home professor, an employee of state bureaucracy, a decorated concert player, and a writer praised in Paris by Jules Super-vielle and in Montevideo by Vaz Ferreira, Felisberto interlaces his always puzzled speaker-character with *brutish* Petrona-like homemakers who scarcely read the news-paper, thus allowing his writing to be infected with *vulgar and bastardized* wit, knowl-edge, and sociality, going beyond the foundational frontiers of the lettered city's civilizing process that, from Andrés Bello onward, discards the defective languages of the rabble (González-Stephan, 1995: 29). In Felisberto, all protocol is abruptly *brought down to earth* by "beasts before delicate things" (III, 11), even taking pleasure "in tearing down and undermining the seriousness of prestigious art" (Panesi: 1993: 87). In *Por los tiempos de Clemente Colling* "higher aesthetics" are squashed by philistines who can barely hold back their spasms of open laughter so as to not to "make a scene" (I, 151): they *pretend* to submit to the formality of the *national* discipline of a single socio-corporal code that tames civil life and the excrescent body (González-Stephan, 1995: 31 passim): "What should we do with the bum?" (II, 218), snaps a spinster relative. In the case of Felisberto, *nothing*, as nobody is reeducated since his grotesque sociability, indiscriminate perception and *inconvenient* pan-eroticism are heteroglossic spaces that pretend to follow protocol, but *only* in order *to be done with it*. Besides, Felisberto's writings unmask the bourgeois imaginary that builds up a masculinity based on virility (social correctness and economic solvency), feminine vulnerability, rites of seduction, a one great love, monogamy, and the concealing of *deviant* sexuali-ties; with humor and perplexity and without dramatics, the Felisbertian male observes how little he fits the model of strong masculinity and citizenship, to what extent he lives in the backroom. Formal culture and the codes of the social contract – foundation of the bourgeois national identity – *pale* before his hybrid males: self-taught, with no fortune in either love or money, with impure languages and quick, dirty hands.

The position of the working class was uncertain enough, but that of the upstart writer, newcomer to formal culture, was even worse. Felisberto can count on Super-vielle and Vaz Ferreira, but *fears* that at some point they would feel that their support "had been cribbed. That would be anguish for me" (III, 281). *To cheat*, to be suspect – like the peripheral neighborhoods into which one *falls* – is at once the pain and the challenge of writing. If Felisberto finds himself in the severe, glaucous glare of the critical canon, it is because he *aspired to means of creating interest that were not strictly literary* (III, 194). Having emerged from the shadow of formal literature, the speaker explains: "I'm a natural critic, I don't know much, *but it doesn't matter*; I have intuition" (III, 227, my emphasis). It is for *extraliterary* reasons, above all, that his weapons are not orthodox ones. Prieto (2002: 38) associates Felisbertian eccentricity with *das Unheimlische* (the sinister juxtaposition of the familiar and the alien, a Freudian meta-phor for the self-space inhabited by others); but in Felisberto the eccentric or the strangeness of the everyday (Cortázar, 1975: 9) is too *normal*. His great contribution was to realize that the folds (errors, missteps, failures, fears, and deviations) are part of daily *normality* – its avatars, its humor: integrating them permits the interpretation of the modern subject, a lesson Cortázar acknowledges in the incontinence of the bunny rabbits in "Carta a una señorita de Paris" ("Letter to a Young Lady in Paris"). Representing "troubling things" (III, 139) and "making poetry amid this confusion" (III, 263) implies entering the fray "as if going shark fishing. Who knows what might happen!" (III, 197) The sought-for House is also another type of House: that of the *cultural field*. Felisberto's writing still occupies a space *without permission*, like being "in someone else's bed" (III, 197), "expectant and nervous like a bandit anticipating the police" (III, 249): his *bad writing* will work "without philosophical or psychological pretensions," seeing what curiosity will propose: working "the simplest and most anti-literary stuff. And working literarily – favored in whatever advantage can be found in its sparse knowledge – against literature and ready-made forms" (III, 282). With the *advantage* – postcolonialist – of empirical and *informal* knowledge, touching on "all of the parts as if it were a house for rent: here the living room, here the kitchen, the dining room" (I, 167). None of the synthesis that "does not include the rest" (I, 145), for representation arises as a problem when, hyperventilating like Funes, it sees so many things that "I would have liked to accommodate in my head . . . But it was impossible" (III, 93). In the same way, the place from which one speaks is made *into a problem*: "no, you can't look for the self in the morning. You have to wait for night, for the hour the ghosts emerge" (III, 257), for "I think my specialty is in writing about *what I don't know*" (III, 212, 138; emphasis added).

In *Tierras de la memoria* (Lands of memory) an attempt is made to dissemble "the *mush* I felt upon setting off from Montevideo. The anguish nauseated me, the sound of the railroad, the gray tones of the houses streaked by the speed . . . and the thought of what I was leaving behind in Montevideo: my wife, in the middle of a tedious wait." This *inundated* and *intertextual* mush requires representations whose "audacity would be disrespectful for whoever wasn't capable of understanding the kind of resources it used. In spite of *having preset forms*, at times *the topics* obliged me to seek *other, new forms*" (III, 29; emphasis added). In "Sobre literatura" (On literature), he defends the *exceptionality* of *his* House: "I prefer works . . . in the material in which they were born," as they would lose a great deal transposed "to a pure and literary Castilian" (III, 276); perhaps they would "lose that depth" (III, 277). Like bandits, one must choose *bad* literature and *sloppy* Spanish, "full of repetitions and imperfections of my own making," since he fears not being able to get rid of the "the ugly without getting rid of what is most natural" (III, 227), concepts that come from deeply understanding culture as fields of and in contact with the quotidian, and as well from understanding by whom and from where knowledge, discourses, and sociability are built, how *themes* and subjectivities demand *new forms* and *reauthorized* epistemic zones. He hasn't "what they call imagination. But I don't think I need it. Because it's been my lot to have a varied life" (III, 234). Battling with moralistic, classist, and straitlaced critics and public, Felisberto bet on "showing a fringe of underwear" (III, 122), *improvising* representations in the *negativity* of the fold (*Spaltung*, rip) that held as much risk as shark fishing and as much benefit as the endurance of his writing: showing what was going on backstage in Latin America while Modernity was displaying, especially in Batllismo and Neo-Batllismo, its most glittering place.

In sum, the writings of Macedonio, Borges, and Felisberto arise from historical vacillation and cultural transition: the glamour of Modernity failed to seduce any of them, for they understood that day-to-day life was incoherent when viewed from a *sole model of rationality*. They preferred instead uncatalogable registers, deforming folds, and disconcerting actors that better explained the problematic of the modern subject in the modern intersecting spaces between plural representations, accidents, deviations, divergence, fluctuations, and flaws. Their subjects, lost in labyrinths or humorously confused, personify the domestic, pedestrian lining of the grotesque and unpresentable Modernity of Gutres, Petronas, and Cautivas. They inhabit backstage regions rescued with bravura so as to question this forced Modernity. All three writings position themselves against the state; they anticipate critiques of the statist model, of formal culture, of *logos*, and of Eurocentrism; they problematize national identity and the cultural trappings of the state (national histories, grammars; modern sentimentality, sociability, and sexuality) and they propose a notion of culture as an interdisciplinary site of multiple authorships and agencies, focalizations, and cultural times. Like Arlt, Macedonio, Borges, and Felisberto comprehended in masterly fashion the density of the cultural space of Modernity, crammed with contradictions and dissent. They deciphered the *paradoxical* nature of modern implementation precisely *in* its secrets and forgetfulness, that heterogeneity and surplus that the cycles of globalization could not dilute; nothing in it would be static nor would remain in a sound location, but in the inconvenient bifocal double place of doubles, trapped in a single body (nation, modern sociability, aesthetics and sexuality). Just like Felisberto's clumsy, distracted narrator, Funes fails to *conciliate* – to represent – all that he perceives, but amply succeeds in suggesting modern disconnectedness and the exuberant register *of the other* incarnate in the figure of the double, brutally unleashed in the hyperventilated vision: that which resists being ordered. The double is unto itself, the archive of irreducible, pressure-treated covers: the juxtaposition and its heterogeneity *produce* the incoherent writing of Macedonio, Borges's pugnacity and latency and the entropic branchings of his labyrinths, as well as the vain and involuntary conduct of Felisberto's stuttering subject.

## REFERENCES AND FURTHER READING

Axelrud, Brenda Carol, and Calabrese, Laura (1999). *Macedonio Fernández: ¿Un problema crítico?* [Macedonio Fernández: a critical problem?] Serie Hipótesis, Tesis y Discusiones, 17. Buenos Aires: Facultad de Filosofía y Letras, Universidad de Buenos Aires.

Barnatán, Marcos Ricardo (1999). "Borges y la biografía" [Borges and biography]. In Alfonso de Toro and Rossana Regazzoni (eds), *El Siglo de Borges, Vol. II: Ciencia, literatura, filosofía* [The century of Borges, Vol. II: science, literature, philosophy], pp. 37–43. Madrid: Vervuet Iberoameri-cana.

Borges, Jorge Luis (1974). *Obras completas, 1923–1972* [Complete works, 1923–1972]. Vol. I. Buenos Aires: Emecé.

— (1989). *Obras completas, 1975–1985*. Vol. II. Buenos Aires: Emecé.

— (1993). *El Tamaño de mi esperanza* [The size of my hope]. Foreword by María Kodama. Buenos Aires: Espasa Calpe–Seix Barral.

— (1994). *El Idioma de los argentinos* [The language of the Argentineans]. Buenos Aires, Espasa Calpe–Seix Barral.

Cornejo Polar, Antonio (1978). "El Indigenismo y las literaturas heterogéneas: Su doble estatus socio-cultural" [Indigenism and heterogeneous literature: its double sociocultural status], *Revista de Crítica Literaria Latinoamericana*, IV (7–8): 7–21.

Cortázar, Julio (1975). "Prólogo" [Prologue]. In *La Casa inundada y otros cuentos*. Barcelona, Lumen.

Deleuze, Gilles (1989). *El Pliegue*. Barcelona, Buenos Aires, and Mexico City: Paidós.

Fernández, Macedonio (1974–87). *Obras completas*. 9 vols. Buenos Aires: Corregidor.

González Stephan, Beatriz (1995). "Las Disciplinas escriturales de la Patria: Constituciones, gramáticas y manuales," *Estudios. Revista de Investigaciones Literarias*, 3(5): 19–46.

Graziano, Frank (1997). *The Lust of Seeing: Themes of the Gaze and Sexual Rituals in the Fiction of Felisberto Hernández*. Lewisburg, VA: Bucknell University Press.

Hernández, Felisberto (1983). *Obras completas*. 3 vols. Mexico City: Siglo XXI.

Horkheimer, Max, and Adorno, Theodor W. (1972). *Dialectic of Enlightenment*. Trans. John Cumming. New York: Herder & Herder.

Huyssen, Andreas (1987). *After the Great Divide: Modernism, Mass Culture, Postmodernism*. Bloomington and Indianapolis: Indiana University Press.

Kodama, María (1993). "Inscripción." In *El Tamaño de mi esperanza*. Buenos Aires: Espasa Calpe–Seix Barral.

Ludmer, Josefina (1993). "El delito: Ficciones de exclusion y sueños de justicia," *Revista de Crítica Literaria Latinoamericana* , XIX(36): 145–53.

*Martín Fierro (1924–7)* (1968). Ed. and prologue Beatriz Sarlo. Buenos Aires: Carlos Pérez.

Masiello, Francine (1989). *Lengua e ideología: Las escuelas argentinas de vanguardia*. Buenos Aires: Hachette.

Mazzoleni, Donatella (1985). *La Cittá e l'imaginario*. Rome: Officina Edizione.

Monsiváis, Carlos (2000). *Aires de familia: Cultura y sociedad en América Latina*. Barcelona: Editorial Anagrama.

Panessi, Jorge (1993). *Felisberto Hernández*. Rosario: Beatriz Viterbo.

Piglia, Ricardo (1990). *Crítica y ficción*. Buenos Aires: Siglo XX–Universidad Nacional del Litoral.

Piglia, Ricardo, ed. (2000). *Diccionario de la novela de Macedonio Fernández*. Buenos Aires: FCE.

Prieto, Julio (2002). *Desencuadernados: Vanguardias excéntricas en el Río de la Plata. Macedonio Fernández y Felisberto Hernández*. Rosario: Beatriz Viterbo.

Ramos, Julio (1987). "Saber decir: Lengua y política." In *Desencuentros de la Modernidad en América Latina: Literatura y política en el siglo XIX*, pp. 35–49. Mexico City: Fondo de Cultura Económica.

Rodríguez Monegal, Emir (1966). *Literatura uruguaya del medio siglo*. Montevideo: Editorial Alfa.

Sarduy, Severo (1969). *Ensayos generales sobre el Barroco*. Mexico City: Fondo de Cultura Económica.

Sarlo, Beatriz (1999). "Borges: Crítica y teoría cultural." In *Jorge Luis Borges: Pensamiento y saber en el siglo XX*, ed. Alfonso de Toro and Fernando de Toro, pp. 259–71. Madrid: Vervuert/Iberoamericana.

Schulte-Sasse, Jochen (1989). "Foreword: theory of modernism versus theory of avant-garde." In Peter Burger, *Theory of the Avant Garde*, trans. Michael Shaw, pp. vii–xlvii. Minneapolis: University of Minnesota Press.

Toro, Alfonso de (2001). "La 'Literatura menor,' concepción borgesiana del Oriente' y el juego," *Iberomanía*, 53: 68–110.

Toro, Alfonso de, and Toro, Fernando de, eds (1999). *Jorge Luis Borges: Pensamiento y saber en el siglo XX*. Madrid: TKKL Vervuert/Iberoamericana.

Viñas, David et al. (1989). *Yrigoyen: Entre Borges y Arlt (1916–1930)*. Buenos Aires: Contrapunto.

# 27

# Narratives and Deep Histories: Freyre, Arguedas, Roa Bastos, Rulfo

## Adriana Michèle Campos Johnson

Peru, wrote the novelist Mario Vargas Llosa, is nothing but "an artificial gathering of men from different languages, customs and traditions whose only common denominator was having been condemned by history to live together without knowing or loving each other" (1991: 35). Despite the many projects for political and social unity, abiding fault lines still cross Peru as well as many of the other postcolonial nation-states of Latin America. Legacies of the encounter of Amerindian, European, and African peoples under 300 years of colonial rule, these fault lines take the shape of ethnic, linguistic, material, social, political, and other differences. Sometimes they can run deep enough to put into question the very viability of the project of the nation-state. Can a nation be created out of men (and women) with nothing in common but an unhappy accident of history? Can the very political structure of the nation-state substitute for missing common denominators? Or can history itself, despite accidental beginnings, forge common denominators as forces of synthesis take place over time?

What the four writers discussed here share is a common preoccupation with the internal differences of each of their respective nations. José María Arguedas and Augusto Roa Bastos grapple with an Amerindian society and worldview (or what is left with it), while Juan Rulfo addresses isolated rural spaces and Gilberto Freyre takes on the impact of African slaves and their descendants. If these differences emerge from deep histories, as the title of this chapter suggests, this is both because they are products of old and lasting structures dating back to the colonial moment and because they have not been on the surface, not immediately visible, to intellectual sectors rooted in the main urban centers in Latin America. For these intellectuals – preoccupied above all with participating in modernizing, cosmopolitan currents – the culture of the Amerindian, of the descendants of Africans, or the inhabitant of the hinterlands exist only as a relic of the past to be eliminated on the way to the future. Freyre, Arguedas, Roa Bastos, and Rulfo, on the other hand, linger precisely in those spaces that are heterogeneous to modernity and attempt, in their own ways, to rescue those spaces from the dustbins of history.

One very powerful account of the historic function of these four writers was offered by Ángel Rama in his *Transculturación narrativa en América Latina* (1982). With this book Rama popularized a hermeneutic model that has been one of the most important and widely used in Latin American literary and cultural criticism since the late 1990s. The term "transculturation" itself was not of his own making, but one that he borrowed from the Cuban anthropologist Fernando Ortiz, who had used it in his *Contrapunteo cubano del tabaco y el azúcar* (1940) to describe a particular process of cultural synthesis. Ortiz preferred the term over "acculturation" which, he said, implied simply to acquire a new culture. Transculturation, in contrast, drew attention to "the loss or uprooting of a preceding culture" as well as to "the subsequent creation of new cultural phenomena." While Ortiz underscored the loss involved in the transit from one culture to another, Ángel Rama used it instead to emphasize the agency and creativity implied in the mixing of what he termed the interior-regional (traditional rural cultures that had been sedimented in the centuries since conquest) and the external-universal (cosmopolitan modernizing cultures). The concept was meant as an antidote to viewing non-modern cultures as "merely passive or even inferior." As José María Arguedas said, in a passage partially cited by Rama (2000b: 269), "there was no reason why the route followed had to be the one imperiously demanded by the plundering conquerors, namely that the conquered nation renounce its soul and take on the soul of the conquerors, that it be, in other words, acculturated."

The Brazilian social and cultural anthropologist Gilberto Freyre (1900–87) exemplifies many of the strengths and weaknesses of models which interpret Latin American reality as syncretic. Freyre has been acclaimed most for his eulogy of racial and cultural miscegenation in his best known work, *The Masters and the Slaves* (1933), and his emphasis on the positive contributions of African slaves to Brazilian culture. Such a view was radical at a time when what predominated were discourses on racial and environmental determination which attributed Brazil's backwardness to an unhealthy tropical climate and to a weak and degenerate *mestizo* population. Paulo Prado's pessimistic *Retrado do Brasil* (1928), published only five years before Freyre's seminal work, was a classic representation of Brazil as a country of fundamentally melancholy people, exhausted by a long history of sexual excess fueled by the land, climate, and presence of the African and Amerindian.

Freyre's definition of Brazil as instead a vibrant racially and culturally mixed society was in part a consequence of his advocacy of the northeast where he was born and raised. This region had been the center of colonial Brazil, based on sugar plantations and slave labor, and became in Freyre's writings the crucible of a Brazilian national identity so that Brazil was essentially the northeast writ large. Such a project often took on the quality of a nostalgic Proustian quest for things past, since the northeast had withered into decadence with the shift of economic and political power to the south in the nineteenth century. In his writings Freyre denounced the homogenizing processes of modernization which threatened to eradicate the local way of life in the northeast. In his "Regionalist Manifesto" (1926), for example, he sharply criticized the Brazilian anxiety to copy Europe, exemplified in the fact that cafés in Recife were too embarrassed to serve local sweets and had taken to serving French pastries instead, or that Christmas was increasingly identified with Santa Claus. Instead of looking to a future in which the northeast – or Brazil more generally – would resemble ever more Europe and the United States, Freyre advocated an eye attuned to the singularities of local history and culture. This, for Freyre, meant attending to the contributions of the Amerindian and the African slave.

Freyre's claim that Brazilian society was constructed through a cultural and racial process of synthesis, in which antagonisms are ultimately reconciled or dissolved, approximates Rama's theorization of transculturation. For Freyre, the patriarchal system of colonization set up in Brazil was the result of a plastic compromise in which the colonizers had to adapt to the new environment and learn from both its indigenous inhabitants and later from the imported slave population. The result was that in Brazil the "primitive cultures" had not been "isolated into hard, dry, indigestible lumps incapable of being assimilated by the European social system" or "stratified in the form of archaisms and ethnographic curiosities" but had instead made themselves felt in their "living, useful, active" presence in Brazilian society (1933: 159) Their contribution meant that "our progress has not been purely in the direction of Europeanization" (1933: 75). While Freyre was not blind to the violence of the meeting of cultures (detailing, for example, various common tortures of slaves), it was ultimately cancelled in the harmonious final product which was Brazilian national identity.

Freyre sought out the traces of this contribution at the level of everyday life: food, vocabulary, superstitions and beliefs, children's stories, a certain juridical flexibility, the use of the hammock, and joyfulness (an African trait, according to him). One of the most privileged examples in Freyre's work of a meeting ground between private life and larger historical processes – one that caused considerable shock and discomfort when his book first came out – was that of sex. At times it almost seems to become the real motor of transculturation, as when Freyre states that "[t]he friction [between cultures] here was smoothed by the lubricating oil of a deep-going miscegenation" (1933: 159). The original scarcity of white women fueled the bewitching attraction of white Portuguese males (already predisposed to such interracial intercourse, for Freyre, by the years of Moorish presence on the Iberian peninsula) for darker women, be they Amerindian, African or, later, mulata. Such attractions did not diminish over the years, even for those established landowners with wives, who frequently kept mulata mistresses or who simply helped themselves to their slaves.

Central to Freyre's argument was the fact that such processes of racial and cultural miscegenation took place in the crucible of an economic system based on slavery, where the essential unit of power was not the Church or Crown but the family, headed by the large landowner. Thus the important relationship in Brazil was not simply that between the African or Amerindian and the white man but specifically between masters and slaves. For Freyre the unequal power dynamics forever shaped the conditions of exchange and encounter between the various social groups and continue to mark Brazilian society today. For example, he attributed the authoritarian tendencies of elites and passivity of popular classes to the sadomasochism inherent in the inter-racial relations that produced Brazilian society.

Freyre's readiness to dip into the ordinary and everyday manifests itself in his book's unorthodox form as well. *The Masters and the Slaves* is marked by a willingness to incorporate a wide variety of genres, sources, and voices. Thus its style and rhetoric range from anthropology, sociology, and history to gossip, folklore, and storytelling and draw upon an eclectic range of sources (not only medical theses, travelers' accounts, and newspapers but also family letters, archives, and oral history). His use of vocabulary includes not only erudite technical terms but also slang and words Freyre himself coined. The book's argument itself flows loosely, often following creative metonymical associations, looping back upon itself and repeating certain points. It also stops abruptly in the middle train of thought, without an identifiable ending or conclusion. In this way the very form of his writing performs a hybridization which echoes the content of his essay. Indeed, Freyre himself describes his text in terms of a mimetic project in which he attempted to produce multiple, even contradictory, perspectives so as to better perceive the multiplicity and complexity of Brazil's reality. He sought to do so by splitting himself into personalities complimentary to his own, he writes, in order to feel "not only lord but servant; not only European but non-European; or specifically Amerindian, Moor, Jewish, Negro, African and even more: woman, boy, slave, oppressed, exploited, abused, in ethos and in status, by patriarchs and masters" (2002: 702).

The strength of Freyre's vision was to propose a Brazil which would be inconceivable without these other voices he attempted to ventriloquize; a Brazil which was not only the Brazil of the masters but also that of the oppressed and exploited, not only the Brazil of great political events but of the intimate textures of everyday life. Still, as this formulation suggests, the Brazilian nation-state forms the horizon within which the African slave, the child, and the woman gain visibility. They do not exist apart from this horizon. And Freyre never doubts his ability to give them voice. Such confidence is not unique to Freyre but it does locate him within a tradition in Latin America that understood the intellectual as the voice of the voiceless, a position akin to the integrative project of the national-popular state in the twentieth century which sought to produce an ever more inclusive political community, one which would bring in all those subjects that had been previously marginalized. Intellectuals such as Freyre were considered the vehicle through which this larger political community could be first represented and consequently materialize. Although Arguedas, Roa Bastos, and Rulfo are inextricably linked to this tradition through their desire to represent the subaltern and forgotten, they also, in their own ways, question and undermine it more than Freyre ever does.

José Maria Arguedas (1911–69) also made himself the spokesman of a world threatened by modernization but, unlike Freyre, he did not see this world as the product of fusions and reconciliations. What tormented Arguedas, in fact, was living in between worlds that were profoundly divided. His mother died when he was young and his father made his living as traveling judge in Andean towns of Peru, leaving

Arguedas for long periods of time with Quechua servants. Although he was ethnically white, Arguedas was thus brought up largely in an indigenous Quechua-speaking world. When he accepted the Inca Garcilaso de La Vega Prize in Lima in October 1968, a year before his death, he described the situation of Peru's indigenous populations and his own relation to them in the following words:

> oppressed by being scorned socially, dominated politically, and exploited economically on their own soil . . . they had been transformed into a corralled nation (isolated in order to be better and more easily managed) about which only those who had walled it in spoke, while viewing it from a distance with repugnance or curiosity. But oppressively isolating walls do not extinguish the light of human reason . . . nor do they dam up the springs of love from which art flows. Inside the oppressive isolating wall, the Quechua people, rather archaized and getting along by dissembling, went on conceiving ideas, creating songs and myths. And we know very well that the walls isolating nations are never completely isolating. As for me – they tossed me over that wall for a time when I was a child. (2000b: 269)

He was to remain forever torn between these two worlds and spent his life attempting to bridge them. Fiction was one solution: "I attempted to transform into written language what I was as an individual: a strong living link, capable of being universalized, between the great, walled-in nation and the generous, humane side of the oppressors" (2000b: 269). Although he wrote anthropological texts as well as poetry in Quechua, he is best known for his narrative work in Spanish.

Unlike earlier generations of writers who were concerned with bringing attention to the plight of the indigenous population of Peru, Arguedas did not simply depict an indigenous referent in his novels but sought to transform his dual reality into "artistic language." This operation is key to Rama's specific theorization of literary transculturation. According to Rama, Arguedas did not simply transmit the legacies of interior-regional cultures using the tools and expressions of modernity; he transformed those tools in the process. Arguedas, he says, conquered "one of the best defended bastions of the culture of domination" (1987: 211) since in his hands the novel – a European bourgeois genre – is mined with Quechua linguistic and hermeneutical structures.

Arguedas's most widely read novel, *Deep Rivers* (1961), exhibits a hybridity produced by the juxtaposition of a realist narrative with the structure and characteristics of popular song, according to Rama. Thus not only is the novel peppered throughout with songs in Quechua but alternates between individual characters and choral characters (such as the marketwomen) and contains sequences governed more by questions of rhythm, repetition, or melody than "the simple logical-rational succession of realist writing" (Rama, 1987: 216). The inclusion of music and song as a structuring principle alongside that of realist narrative may explain the reason for the first chapter, since the novel's main narrative arc really begins in chapter two. This arc revolves around the story of Ernesto, the son of an itinerant country lawyer largely brought up in a Quechua-speaking world, who is placed in a Catholic boarding school at age

14 and his difficulties in living in the white, Spanish world of the school. It is a world he finds it impossible to adapt to and which he ultimately flees when a plague overtakes the town at the end. If considered the equivalent of the overture of an opera, writes Rama, the function of the first chapter becomes to introduce the themes that will appear throughout the work in abbreviated form. In effect, this first chapter recites the entrance of Ernesto and his father into Cuzco and their meeting with the Old Man, a powerful and enigmatic figure who exemplifies the oppressive social stratification of the world of the novel. The other side of the social spectrum takes the shape of an Indian who shocks Ernesto for being utterly unlike those he has lived with until then, someone so downtrodden that he bows "like a worm asking to be crushed" (1961: 14). In the same chapter, however, the relationship between the white and Indian worlds that is seemingly so hopeless in its human incarnations takes on another form in the figure of the walls of an old Inca palace upon which a colonial structure is built:

> The stones of the Inca wall . . . seemed to be bubbling up beneath the white-washed second story . . . The wall was stationary, but all its lines were seething and its surface was as changeable as that of the flooding summer rivers which have similar crests near the center, where the current flows the swiftest and is the most terrifying. (7)

The figure of the Inca wall condenses many of the complexities of the novel. On the one hand it represents a structural bridge, a meeting place, between the Quechua and white worlds, as Rama would have it. On the other hand, it is a stark reminder of the potential for conflict. It sums up the deep rivers of Indian vitality which lay just below an apparently placid surface and which could lead to an uprising like the one that effectively occurs when, amidst a shortage of salt, the market women of the town march en masse to the neighboring estates who have abundant salt and take and distribute it among the townspeople. The continued fissures and disharmony represented in the novel thus complicate Rama's argument, raising the question of the relationship between fusions in literary form and the possibilities for reconciliation in the society at large. According to the Peruvian critic Antonio Cornejo Polar, *Deep Rivers* textualizes this very question and ends up governed by a double and disarticulated rhythm: "the abolition of limits between subject and object does not coincide with the nature of the object that is represented – a fractured, conflicted universe" (1973: 156). In other words, the Inca wall can be read as both an example of transculturation in form and as a marker of the fitful, grinding shipwreck of the transculturating enterprise in the face of the abyssal fissuring of the world it attempts to represent and unite.

Cornejo Polar's comments on *Deep Rivers* hint at the important question of the role of literature in such conflicted and divided situations. Unlike Rama, he is skeptical about the extent to which internal differences like those mapped by Arguedas in Peru can be resolved within literary forms:

Transculturation would imply, in the long run, the construction of a syncretic plane that finally incorporates in a more or less unproblematical totality (in spite of the conflictive character of the process) two or more languages, two or more ethnic identities, two or more aesthetic codes and historical experiences. I add that this synthesis would be configured in the space of the hegemonic culture and literature; that at times the social asymmetry of the originating contacts would be obviated; and finally that the discourses that have not influenced the system of "enlightened" literature would be left at the margins. (2004: 117)

Cornejo Polar offers instead a concept like that of heterogeneity that would "explain sociocultural situations and discourses in which the dynamics of the multiple inter-crossings do not operate in a syncretic way, but instead emphasize conflicts and alterities" (2004: 117). The fundamental currents of Latin American literature would thus be better described, he argues, as heterogeneous literatures. These are defined as narratives that straddle dissimilar sociocultural universes and whose productive process consequently harbors disjunctions and gaps. The classic example offered by Cornejo Polar was a narrative production like that of the indigenistas that included writing, the Spanish language, European artistic conventions, and particular ideologies (such as positivism, Marxism, or nationalism) destined for reception by middle-class sectors in Lima but which sought to interpret a referent that was indigenous, agrarian, oral, frequently Aymara or Quechua-speaking, and traversed by other rationalities and social interests. The fundamental point of his argument is that form can no longer perceived as neutral terrain over which battles can be fought or lost. Neither can it be a site for the resolution of conflict. It reproduces instead the structure and history of a "divided and disintegrated reality." In this sense Cornejo Polar's theory is not only aesthetic but historical: it is not only a theory about hybrid forms, but about the social spheres within which they are produced and circulate, spheres, moreover, that are in conflict and marked by unequal power relations. Where transculturation assumes that certain contradictions have been or will be overcome through the medium of literature, in Cornejo Polar's concept of heterogeneity these contradictions run so deep that not only do they fissure the texts that try to bridge them, but they may even call into question the very existence of the nation as a meaningful category since, as he writes, "to assume that there is a non-conflictive meeting point seems to be the necessary condition to think of and imagine the nation as a more or less harmonious and coherent whole" (2004: 117).

Cornejo Polar therefore raises the thorny questions of, first, how to conceptualize the relationship between literary (or even nonliterary) representation and the referent to which it lays a claim and, second, the relationship between such literary representations and larger projects of political representation. How far can Arguedas, Freyre, Roa Bastos, and Rulfo go in their attempt to represent singular, marginal, and even disappearing worlds with tools so closely tied with a colonizing past and modernizing future such as the technology of writing, a colonial language, and aesthetic forms developed in Europe? Can they give voice to multiple perspectives, as Freyre wished? And don't the ties between the desire to produce hybrid representations and the desire to affirm the viability of a particular nation-state and its identity suggest an insurmountable limit? Even if hybrid literary forms are produced in Peru or Brazil, is such hybridity actually a representation of the differences, contacts, and fissures that constitute those countries? Is there a way to conceptualize crossings, mixtures, and fusions that are not dialectically resolved or dissolved?

Arguedas's last novel – *The Fox from Up Above and the Fox from Down Below* (1971) – can be read as an attempt to answer this last question. It is a text of extremes and one that remained impenetrable to critics for many years after Arguedas's death. It is hard to describe as a novel, properly speaking, or as a text that fits the mold of any other conventional genre since it alternates between narrative segments and Arguedas's own personal diaries. It is also an unfinished text. More precisely, it is finished with his suicide, since the last diary entry both details preparations for Arguedas's suicide and gives suggestions for how the novel could or would have ended had it been finished. In Alberto Moreiras's eloquent expression, Arguedas "signed the end of the book with two bullets" (2001: 201). Incorporating the bullets within the texture of the book, as the material inscription of a limit, Moreiras reads the *The Foxes* as the place where "the Latin American transculturating machine came to its end, in the double sense of epochal culmination and of equally epochal exhaustion" (ibid.). If Moreiras is right and *The Foxes* takes the transculturating impulse to its limits and then – I would argue – moves beyond it, this has something to do with the way it inverts the usual procedures of indigenismo: instead of using the tools and lens of modernity to represent an indigenous world, an "indigenous rationality comes to account for modernity" (Cornejo Polar, 1990: 303). Unlike the worlds depicted in Arguedas's other novels, *The Foxes* is not set in the Andes but in a coastal boomtown called Chimbote, a small fishing village propelled headlong into modernization by the fishmeal industry and transformed for some years into the world's largest fishing port only to later decline owing to overfishing. One element of the book which suggests that this rapidly changing chaotic and hybrid world – seething with prostitutes, immigrant Indian workers, corrupt managers, Peace Corps volunteers, priests, and madmen – is being processed through an indigenous rationality are the foxes that give the text its title. The foxes are godlike figures drawn from Incan legends and myths which Arguedas translated from Quechua to Spanish just before beginning this last novel under the title *Hombres y dioses de Huarochirí.* While they appear as anthropomorphic characters within the narrative of Chimbote, the foxes are also given the status of commentators on Chimbote and on the text as a whole, so that it seems at times that the closest one comes to an omniscient point of view in the narrative are the dialogues of the foxes and not Arguedas's own reflections on the process of writing. While Arguedas comments on the foxes – "why on earth did I put such difficult foxes into the novel?" (2000a: 88) – the foxes themselves comment back on Arguedas: "The individual who tried to take his own life and is writing this book was from up above; he still has *ima sapra sawing* in his bosom. Where is he from, what is he made of now?" (2000a: 54).

This question mirrors the story of some characters like Asto, who has been read as another example of the presence of a Quechua rationality organizing the text. Asto is an Indian who is seemingly transformed after he is able to pay for an encounter with an Argentine blonde prostitute. "He's steepin' firm," remarks an onlooker, "He's walking firm and whistlin' firm that Indian is." And Asto himself proclaims "Me criollo . . . from the coast, goddamnit; me from Argentina, goddamnit. Who highlander now?" (2000a: 42). In his book-length study of Arguedas, *Los universos narratives de José María Arguedas* (1973), Cornejo Polar points out that the small tale of Asto, which threatens to pass unnoticed within the novel's stormy fragments, acquires great importance and significance as a reanimation of a mythic tale recounted by the fox from up above at the end of "chapter" one. In other words, incidents in the contemporary world appear as mere incarnations of ancient Andean tales in the novel's dilated temporality. In the story a warrior, Tutaykire, is detained in a valley of the world down below by a "harlot virgin" who "stopped him to make him go to sleep and sidetrack him" (Arguedas, 2000a: 54). In his book Cornejo Polar reads the figure of Asto as a figure of extreme alienation, a sign of the fact that, like the warrior, he has been sidetracked: "Blinded by money and the blonde prostitute, the Indian Asto denies himself and annihilates himself. His new self-image is tragically grotesque and implies an extreme degree of alienation" (1973: 275). His story would also on a larger level be an allegory of the way Chimbote (or the coast) has waylaid and perverted the highlands of Peru.

Yet the story of Asto also condenses the problematic of change and transformation that traverses the text as a whole and that cannot be reduced simply to alienation. Sara Castro-Klaren argues that in translating the Huarochiri myths, what impressed Arguedas was the creative, transformative powers of the deities. The foxes, she writes, appear fundamentally in the novel as models of becomings. The Huarochirí contain many tales of "becoming, a passing from animal into human, from human into mineral, without ever performing an Ovidian metamorphosis but rather affecting a becoming in the sense that Deleuze and Guattari theorize" (Castro-Klaren, 2000: 315). The appearance of the mysterious foxlike Don Diego in chapter three, who holds a dialogue with Don Ángel, manager of a fishmeal factory – a dialogue that begins as an analysis of Chimbote but that leads to a drawing in which Don Ángel tries to map out the world and ends in a dance between the two – would be, in this view, one example of such a becoming. The story of Asto – who ends up, after all, stepping and whistling firm – could therefore be read as an example of passage and transformation in a text attempting to theorize multiple forms of becoming.

In his last article, "The Migrant Condition and Multicultural Textuality" (1998), Cornejo Polar draws a useful distinction between migration and *mestizaje* which suggests one way to understand the difference between transculturation and the transformations staged in *The Foxes*. Cornejo Polar argues that *The Foxes* proposes the migrant subject as the new historical subject, displacing the mestizo or Indian subject that had been so central to Arguedas's work until then. Migration, he writes, doesn't share the same syncretic impulse as mestizaje: "migrants stratify their experiences, neither able nor wanting to fuse them because their discontinuous nature emphasizes precisely the multiple diversity of those times and spaces" (1998: 32). There is an accumulation, but no synthesis, between the here and now and "the spaces that were left behind – which continue to disturb, angrily or tenderly" (1998: 31). If migration becomes the new center of a reflection on Andean discursivity, then the discontinuous nature of the discourse of *The Foxes* can be read as an echo of the fragmentation of its (migrant) characters who are caught up in processes of change that are so powerful they exceed degradation and alienation. In a migrant-inflected world the deep rivers that divided Ernesto's landscape do not wither away in harmonious resolution, perhaps, but neither are they permanent fissures, impermeable to transformation.

If Arguedas understood his task as the attempt to forge a bridge between the two deeply divided worlds that uneasily inhabited the space of Peru, we can phrase the project of the Paraguayan writer Augusto Roa Bastos (1917–2005) as the search for cracks in an all too easy official story of a homogeneous national identity. Like Arguedas and Freyre, Roa Bastos was born and raised far from the outward looking metropolitan centers of Latin America. Yet in his case this means that he was from the small and often overlooked country of Paraguay. He left in 1947 due to the pressures of a military regime, initiating a long exile that would end only after the fall of Alfredo Stroessner in 1989. During these years Roa Bastos lived first in Buenos Aires and later moved to France in 1976, teaching Latin American literature and Guaraní at the University of Toulouse. Paraguay has been characterized as one of the most racially and culturally homogeneous of the Americas, produced by the happy and peaceful marriage of Guaraní women with the Spanish conquistadors. Against this transculturating narrative, Roa Bastos draws attention instead to the breaches traversing its social body, suggesting ways in which it is still divided and internally colonized.

One of the signatures of Roa Bastos's attempt to rethink Paraguayan history is the theorization of negativity, of what *is not* or of what is invisible. One could say that his novel *Son of Man* (1960) explores an axis of conflict between a popular, mostly peasant, strata and the ruling order and the possibilities for resistance within structures of domination (another issue of much interest to Roa Bastos, given Paraguay's particularly deep tradition of authoritarian statehood). Yet the novel is a reflection on something for which words like resistance and conflict are inadequate. Roa Bastos once declared that Paraguay had only ever had one rebellion, the Comuneros rebellion, and that that was a false rebellion because it lacked all popular content (1997: 126). Unsurprisingly, then, *Son of Man* revolves around what does not happen (a rebellion). While all attempts at outright insurrection in the novel fail, the novel dwells on more oblique manifestations of conflict.

This relationship between power and the people in *Son of Man* is exemplified through the figure of the putative author of the "story" and sometime narrator: Miguel Vera. Sent to military school in Asunción as a young boy, Vera is uprooted from his native city of Itapé and this distance from his popular origins, this conflicted root in yet route away from an original community, marks him thereafter, as when he aids and then betrays the second attempted insurrection in the text and yet then shares in the fate of the rebels for refusing to deliver more information regarding the insurrection. With the rebels he is sent to a penal colony and then, with all the other prisoners, off to the front lines of the Chaco War. Vera's mysterious death at the end of the text punctuates his role as an unwilling traitor to the people, since he dies in what is either a suicide or an accidental shooting by the son of a veteran of the Chaco War. What is inscribed in the ambiguity of his death is both his own sense of guilt (suicide) and either divine punishment for betraying the people or revenge on their part through the accidental or not so accidental shooting by the boy. Vera is thus a figure at a crossroads. His birth in Itapé and his sympathy with the rebels point out his links to the Paraguayan popular classes. Yet his involuntary betrayal of the rebellion in a drunken stupor also suggest that, once uprooted, Vera may be inescapably part of the apparatus of power (as an officer in the army and later mayor of Itapé), and driven by a structure beyond his control to act out the logic of such an apparatus. As the 'writer' of the story his unreliability and distance from "the people" doubles the theme of the limits of writing to account for what remains outside it, despite its good intentions.

This theme recurs not only in *Son of Man*, but in Roa Bastos's best known novel *I the Supreme* (1972) and in his various essays on the status of literature in Paraguay. More often than not Roa Bastos emphasizes the fact that writing is laden with a particular history and that it cannot therefore be neutral terrain. This – rather than the attempt to make a "living link" of his writings – is one of the abiding quandaries of his work. When a narrator chooses to write in Spanish rather than Guaraní, "he/she consciously or unconsciously assumes the role and ideological position of the dominant language and culture" (1984: 16). Even more important than the relationship between languages, however, is the tension between orality and writing. "What meaning can writing have . . . when by definition it does not have the same sense as the everyday speech of ordinary people?" asks the dictator in *I the Supreme* (2000: 202). For Roa Bastos, the attempts to translate into writing the "oral tremor of the collective" (1987b: 90) which is the very stuff of Paraguay, to subvert literature through the use of oral or popular cultural forms, rarely goes beyond simple appropriation or substitution. The translation is a failure. The oral tremor is inescapably lost.

The vexed relationship between writing and orality is at the heart of *I the Supreme*. The voice of the dying nineteenth-century Paraguayan dictator José Gaspar Rodríguez de Francia occupies the center of the novel as he recounts his projects for Paraguay and justifies his actions through personal notes, a dictated "circular perpetua," interior monologues, and speeches to his assistant and scribe. His are not the only words in the text, however: in addition to the Supreme Dictator's words are the notes of the compiler supposedly publishing the texts of the Supreme, various documents and letters, and the comments of an unknown hand scribbling in the margins. More often than not these other texts gainsay the statements of the dictator. One could argue, therefore, that *I The Supreme* is about how power is not supreme. The failings of absolute power are probed through the non-coincidence between the dictator's dreams and the reality of Paraguay and the circulation of these other discourses that contradict these "statements of the state." Such a state of affairs is in part attributed to the characteristics of writing, equated with a dissemination of words that necessarily slip out of control. This point is made on the very first page, as the novel begins with a fake handwritten notice of the Supreme's death which imitates his handwriting and announces itself as a declaration of the Supreme himself. If writing is uncontrollable it is because it is equated with copying, lying, imitating, plagiarizing. The book itself literally performs this view of writing to the extent that in it Roa Bastos copies, quotes, and paraphrases entire passages of history books, accounts of travelers in Paraguay, Guaraní mythology, etc. Orality seems in this context to exert a contrary stability and truthfulness. At one point the dictator states: "you feed on the carrion of books. You have not yet destroyed oral tradition only because it is the one language that cannot be sacked, robbed, repeated, plagiarized, copied" (2000: 56). Yet this stability is a result precisely of the resistance and elusiveness of the oral world to reproduction and representation. "When a thought escapes me," says the dictator, "I would like to write it down and all I write is that it has escaped me" (2000: 415).

Roa Bastos does not eschew processes of transculturation completely. In one of his essays he holds out for the possibility that, despite its position as an apparatus of ideological hegemony, literature can be mined from within, turned into a place where popular voices can find greater and greater expression, a vehicle for democratization and politicization, or a chronicle of liberation (1984: 20). Yet he is critical of what he calls "faulty" transculturation in which the "use of popular sources . . . is generally reabsorbed in excessive fictionalization" (1987b: 89). One example of this would be magical realism, which he says is based upon a "prefabricated" mythic reality formulated according to Eurocentric models and which does not derive from Latin American popular culture. He rejects such excessive fictionalization and holds out instead for the realism of a painful mimetic pact with radically reduced claims to truth. Rather than understanding Paraguay through a concept such as "magical realism" Roa Bastos likens its reality to the delirium of a dying man. The Paraguayan lives "torn between reality as it should have been and reality as it is; between the plenitude of life that has been veiled to him by his own history and the monstrosity of this vegetative life, this no-life, imposed by causes alien to his nature and that have distorted the course of the necessity of Paraguayan history" (1987a: xxxi). The unreality in which Paraguayan life has coagulated is not simply a product of its heterogeneity with respect to universalizing European forms of knowledge and representation but a product of a history which harbors at its heart a disaster which can not be symbolized.

Roa Bastos does not suggest that this unreality can be translated into literature but instead that it produces a pressure on writers in Paraguay. If in *Son of Man* the fact that there are no open rebellions does not mean the nonexistence of resistance, similarly the fact that the oral tremor cannot be translated into literary form does not mean it lacks existence. Its relationship is one of negativity. The horizon of all writing in Paraguay is irredeemably circumscribed by the necessity to rescue a colonized, eclipsed, absent, erased, even unwritten text drawn from the oral and Guaraní coordinates of its cultural formation. This absent universe cannot be represented, it cannot make its presence felt as content, but it can wield effects on the form of representation, much like a black hole whose presence can only be deduced from the distortion of the universe around it. The Paraguay writer can't think this text, he says; it is the text that thinks the writer (1984: 15).

In a first instance this absent text can make itself felt by a profound saturation of Spanish by the Guaraní language, much like Arguedas. This does not consist in simply scattering Guaraní words throughout the text but bringing in the worldview accompanying the language so as to transform the very conception of notions such as temporality, narration, and textuality. One example of how Roa Bastos attempts to put this project into practice is the invention of words in *I the Supreme* that follow the agglutinating logic of Guaraní: air-blot-woman, ant-contraband, archive-cockroach, espiocolony. Another example is Roa Bastos's use of a "poetic of variations" which "subverts and animates 'established texts'" (1985: 3). Roa Bastos justifies it as a technique of oral narrators who change and embellish their stories so that there is never one single crystallized text but rather a palimpsest. This poetic is present in small scale within *Son of Man* in the way a single incident is told over and over from multiple perspectives. It is also present in the way fragments of *Son of Man* are carried over into other texts. One example is Roa Bastos's novel *Contravida* (1994) where the narrator poses as the writer of what is presumably *Son of Man* and explains how he fictionalized reality in his other book, now providing different endings of many of the same incidents. Rather than producing autonomous self-contained books, therefore, Roa Bastos's texts bleed into each other, forming an unstable, shifting tapestry. Although using an oral poetics of narration in written texts looks very similar to transculturation, the point to emphasize again is that Roa Bastos conceptualizes the oral, Guaraní world as a negativity, one that has neither been incorporated, as in Freyre, nor stands in open conflict with the white world as in Arguedas. It is an absence that exerts pressure on reality much like a scar or a missing book on a library shelf.

Absences such as these take shape in Juan Rulfo's (1917–86) writing as ghosts that have come back to haunt the living. Indeed, Rulfo comes perhaps closest to Roa Bastos in his attempt to think through the paradoxical presence of the dead, of the seemingly defeated and disappeared, and their relationship to the present. Such is the subject of his brief, dense and extremely beautiful novel *Pedro Páramo* (1955). Rulfo's fame is based almost exclusively on this one novel and a book of fifteen short stories titled *El Llano en llamas* (1953). He also wrote several film scripts and was an accomplished photographer, but made a living through a wide-ranging series of jobs, including several years as an immigration agent for the Secretariat of Government, working for the Goodrich-Euzkadi rubber company, a television station in Guadalajara, and a position as the director of editorial department of National Institute for Indigenous Studies. Rulfo was from a family of landowners in the province of Jalisco and it is this rural Mexico of his youth that figures in his literary works.

*Pedro Páramo* begins with the arrival of Juan Preciado to the town of Comala in search of his father Pedro Páramo according to a promise made to his mother on her deathbed. Instead of the fertile shimmering place of his mother's memory, he finds an abandoned town. His father is dead. And those he runs into in the town are, he

slowly realizes, also dead. They are lingering fragments of a past through which he –
and we – begin to piece together the past of Comala and his father. Halfway through
the novel we realize that Juan Preciado himself has died in Comala, killed off, he says,
by the murmurings of the souls crowding the town. The novel continues to pick its
way through voices from the past, but the organizing principle now seems to be a
dialogue taking place between Juan and another body sharing his grave. It ends with
the moment of his father's death. John Kraniauskas reads the novel as a story of reve-
nants that have been marginalized by the state. They live, he writes "in a continuous
but meaningless present in which the only possible remaining hope for justice and
the transcendence community is supposed to provide has been bought by the local
landowner" (1998: 142). The political system, in other words, has failed to live up to
its promise of redemption. The people of Comala have not, however, simply withered
away into nothingness and oblivion but continue to haunt the town as reminders of
this failure. The local landowner to which Kraniauskas refers, the representation of
the (failed) functioning of power in the novel, is Pedro Páramo himself. Pedro Páramo
consolidates his power by ruthlessly conquering land in the region and then uses it
to condemn the region to waste in a fit of anger when a fair takes place during the
funeral of his wife. Perhaps more damning than this last and final blow, however, is
the occasion on which Pedro Páramo literally buys the local priest's absolution for a
murder committed by his son. In consequence Father Renteria is denied absolution
by a neighboring priest and told that he cannot continue to consecrate others when
he himself is in sin. The hordes of restless souls that swarm around Comala explain
their own condition to the narrator as a result of the actions and fate of Father Renteria: they have been denied absolution and therefore linger in purgatory. Comala is
thus "filled with echoes. It's like they were trapped behind the walls, or beneath the
cobblestones" (1994: 41).

"Haunting belongs to the structure of every hegemony" (1994: 37), Derrida says,
and certainly, as Kraniauskas suggests, if these ghosts are the product of conflicting
imaginaries (or ways of death) they speak of the ways the modern Mexican nation-state
has overcoded older imaginaries. They exist as ghosts, in other words, because they
have been ushered into a Christian imaginary even if the possibilities for justice and
redemption offered by this imaginary have then been denied to them. At the same
time the novel is also populated by dead people who are testaments to the ways in
which the political system drawn up by the novel has failed to hegemonize the
meaning of death. Not only have the ghosts been captured and then abandoned by
this new sociopolitical system and its attending ideologies; there are also the dead
who were never fully absorbed by it. In this sense, Ruflo's novel, like those of Roa
Bastos, theorizes the existence of older and perhaps invisible ways of being in a land
that seems on the surface to have been completely colonized.

I am referring here to the fact that the novel displays a heterogeneity of death, a
split that is drawn with the death of the narrator, Juan Preciado. On this threshold
the novel suggests the possibility of a difference between a dead body and wandering
soul when Juan Preciado asks the person sharing his grave: "And your soul? Where
do you think it's gone?" It answers:

It's probably wandering like so many others, looking for living people to pray for it. Maybe it hates me for the way I treated it, but I don't worry about that anymore. And now I don't have to listen to its whining about remorse. Because of it, the little I ate turned bitter in my mouth; it haunted my nights with black thoughts of the damned. When I sat down to die, my soul prayed for me to get up and drag on with my life, as if it still expected some miracle to cleanse me of my sins. I didn't even try . . . I opened my mouth to let it escape. And it went. (1994: 66)

Once dead, the link between the soul and the body is cut and they live separate parallel existences. The main distinctions between the dead body and the soul are two. First, the soul is the seat of guilt and remorse – the soul has been captured by the Church, but not so the body, the novel seems to suggest by contrast. In this sense, the spirits of the first half of the novel would be the Catholic dead, whereas the dead in the second half of the novel would be dead according to a different imaginary, other ways of death, located literally underneath, submerged by the weight of a colonial and postcolonial history. The second difference is that the dead bodies we listen to in the latter half of the book know they are dead in contrast to the souls we encounter in the beginning, who act as if they were still alive and dissolve into thin air every time Juan Preciado confronts them, asking if they are alive. The bodies have no such illusion. These dead are not interested in justice or transcendence. They are, perhaps, not marginalized by the political system so much as indifferent to it, as indifferent as the body who shares the grave with Juan Preciado – Doroteo or Dorotea (it – names, gender, identity – doesn't matter, the other tells him) – seems to be to the fate of his soul.

The mark of indifference in the novel is nowhere clearer than in the figure of Susana, the second wife of Pedro Páramo. She is ex-centric to but not outside Comala. In her liminality she condenses the most obvious intractability to the apparatus of capture exemplified by Pedro Páramo and Father Renteria. Her distance from the other living inhabitants of Comala takes place through her radical indifference to both of these. If she marries Pedro Páramo it seems to be merely to spite her father. Susana's particular relationship to the body is what interferes with and interrupts her relationship to religious doctrine, so that when her first husband Florencio dies she laments precisely the absence of his body: "all You care about is souls," she says to God, "And what I want is his body" (1994: 100). Her indifference shows up most strongly in a scene at the end of her life when Father Renteria arrives to make her confess. He whispers words in her ear – "My mouth is filled with earth" – and then looks at Susana and sees that she is mouthing silent words but not those he sought to impress upon her: "My mouth is filled with you, with your mouth. Your tightly closed lips, pressed hard, biting into mine." In the original Spanish it is clear that these words echo her words when her first husband died. She answers the priest's attempt to "sow images within her" with her own insistence on the body of her dead husband, and the physical exposure of their mouths. She does not exert resistance so much as simply ignore him or appear untouched by him: "He was surprised by Susana San Juan's calm. He wished he could divine her thoughts and see her heart struggling to reject the images he was sowing within her" (1994: 114). The priest's desire to see her heart struggling to reject the images he sows suggests that he wishes for an active resistance which would acknowledge his power. Yet all he gets finally is a sleepy dismissal: "Go away, Father. Don't bother yourself over me. I am at peace and very sleepy" (1994: 115). Rulfo once wrote that "at its heart, Pedro Páramo was born of an image and was the search of an ideal that I called Susana San Juan" (1991: 725). It is an ideal one could perhaps express with words similar to the ones Giorgio Agamben uses to describe those in limbo. "God has not forgotten them," he says, "rather they have always already forgotten God; and in the face of their forgetfulness, God's forgetting is impotent . . . Their nullity, of which they are so proud, is principally a neutrality with respect to salvation (1993: 6). Like those in limbo Susana is neither elected nor damned, neither blessed nor hopeless. She is indifferent, neutral, rather than resistant to the prospect of salvation. This, says Agamben, is the most radical objection that can be levied against redemption. The unsavable life is where the Christian theological machine runs aground. If Susana is an ideal, then Rulfo's Pedro Páramo perhaps goes furthest of all in undermining the project of transculturation by speaking to us of worlds indifferent to any apparatus of capture, of particularities indifferent even to the redemption promised by writing.

## References and Further Reading

Agamben, Giorgio (1993). *The Coming Community*. Minneapolis: University of Minnesota Press.

Arguedas, José Maria (1987). *Deep Rivers*. Austin: University of Texas Press.

— (2000a [1971]). *The Fox from Up Above and the Fox from Down Below*. Pittsburgh, PA: Pittsburgh University Press.

— (2000b). "I am not an acculturated man . . . " In José Maria Arguedas, *The Fox from Up Above and the Fox from Down Below*, pp. 268–70. Pittsburgh, PA: Pittsburgh University Press.

Castro-Klaren, Sara (2000). "'Like a pig, when he's thinkin': Arguedas on affect and on becoming an animal." In José Maria Arguedas, *The Fox from Up Above and the Fox from Down Below*, pp. 307–23. Pittsburgh, PA: Pittsburgh University Press.

Cornejo Polar, Antonio (1973). *Los Universos narrativos de José María Arguedas*. Buenos Aires: Editorial Losada.

— (1990). "Un Ensayo sobre los zorros de Arguedas." In José María Arguedas, *El Zorro de arriba y el zorro de abajo*, pp. 297–306. Madrid: Archivos.

— (1998). "The migrant condition and multicultural intertextuality," *Journal of Latin American Cultural Studies*, ed. Ana Del Sarto et al., 7(1): 29–38.

— (2004). "Mestizaje, transculturation, heterogeneity." In *The Latin American Cultural Studies Reader*, pp. 116–19. Durham, NC: Duke University Press.

Derrida, Jacques (1994) *Specters of Marx: The State of the Debt, the Work of Mourning and the New International*. New York: Routledge.

Freyre, Gilberto (1969 [1933]). *The Masters and the Slaves*. New York: Alfred A. Knopf.

— (2002). "Como e porque escrevi Casa-grande & senzala." In *Casa-grande & senzala: Edição crítica*, pp. 701–21. Paris: Coleção Archivos.

Kraniauskas, John (1998). "Cronos and the political economy of vampirism: notes on a historical constellation." In Francis Barker, Peter Hulme, and Margaret Iversen (eds), *Cannibalism and the Colonial World*, pp. 142–57. Cambridge: Cambridge University Press.

Moreiras, Alberto (2001). "The end of magical realism: José Maria Arguedas's passionate signifier." In *The Exhaustion of Difference: The Politics of Latin American Cultural Studies*. Durham, NC: Duke University Press.

Ortiz, Fernando (1999). *Contrapunteo cubano del tabaco y el azúcar*. Madrid: Edito CubaEspaña.

Rama, Ángel (1987). *Transculturación narrativa en América Latina*. Mexico City: Siglo Veintiuno Editores.

Roa Bastos, Augusto (1984). "La Narrativa paraguaya en el contexto de la narrativa hispanoamericana actual," *Revista de Critica Literaria Latinoamericana*, 10(19): 7–21.

— (1985). *Hijo de hombre*. Madrid: Ediciones Alfaguara.

— (1987a). "Rafael Barrett: Descubridor de la realidad social del Paraguay (prólogo)." In Rafaell Barrett, *El Dolor paraguayo*. Caracas: Biblioteca Ayacucho.

— (1987b). "Una cultura oral," *Hispamérica*, Apr.– Aug., 16: 46–7.

— (1988 [1960]). *Son of Man*. New York: Monthly Review Press.

— (1997). "Entrevista con Augusto Roa Bastos." In Bartomeu Meliá, *El Paraguay inventado*. Asunción: Centro de Estudios Paraguayos "Antonio Guasch."

— (2000 [1972]). *I the Supreme*. Champaign, IL: Dalkey Archive Press.

Rulfo, Juan (1994 [1955]). *Pedro Páramo*. New York: Grove Press.

— (1991). "Situación actual de la novela contemporánea (1979)." In Norma Klahn (ed.), *Los Novelistas como críticos*, pp. 713–25. Hanover, NH: Ediciones del Norte.

Vargas Llosa, Mario (1991)."Questions of conquest." In *A Writer's Reality*. Boston: Houghton Mifflin.

# 28

# The "Boom" of Spanish-American Fiction and the 1960s Revolutions (1958–75)

*Gerald Martin*

This chapter is conceived as a political history of the so-called "Boom" of Spanish American fiction. The period has been much discussed (though less so recently) and occasionally theorized, but no theorization can be effective without both a critical reading of particular texts (Martin, 1989) and a history of interweaving trajectories. It is an outline version of the second of these tasks that I offer here.

## Problematic

Few literary phenomena have been as stereotyped or as misunderstood as the "Boom" – in part because the canonization of writers (though not of critics) is now *ultra vires*, and the Boom writers were canonized from the very start; and in part because literary labels get a bad press these days. So-called literary "movements" or "styles" are especially deprecated, the best-known Latin American example being the concept of "magical realism." Close behind it as a critical bugbear – and equally difficult to exorcize – is the "Boom" itself, the name neither of a movement nor a style but of a particular literary moment, the one that saw the astonishing rise of the Latin American novel to world attention in the 1960s.

One deconstructionist stereotype implies that the phenomenon was really an illusion, and that its principal protagonists were no better or more interesting than many other writers less glamorous or less able to use the new science of public relations and advertising. This seems implausible: to argue against the achievements and virtues, *in their time*, of the "big four" – Fuentes, Vargas Llosa, Cortázar, and García Márquez – is like arguing that Proust, Joyce, Woolf, Kafka, and Faulkner are just names pulled arbitrarily out of a critical hat or else canonized according to some theological agenda. This is not the assumption of the present brief history.

Another stereotype assumes that the "Boom" was either an isolated phenomenon – hence the invention of a "post-Boom" which has lasted ever since – or the beginning of something new; whereas it can be far more convincingly understood as a conclusion and even as a climax, as the end of many things. The truth is that the word itself, however irritating to many critics, was well chosen: the Boom was precisely the moment when the already remarkable Latin American novel finally "boomed," the moment when a larger number of interesting writers, both good and great, were suddenly in play, and when more readers were around to buy their books and appreciate them. Naturally the perceived message of the Boom writers, which was a message about history and identity and the role of the writer, was what turned those readers on in those now faraway days, and since then quite different messages have come to dominate our cultural panoramas.

The Boom, then, was a grand finale, the culmination of what may best be called the Spanish American New Novel, which stretched from the 1940s to the 1970s. Its origins lay in the avant-garde movements of the 1920s and particularly the works of Miguel Angel Asturias, Jorge Luis Borges, and Alejo Carpentier – all writers who wrote their first significant books in the 1920s or early 1930s yet were still writing fiction in the 1960s. The reason why critics often overlook this continuity is because they have traditionally seen the 1920s and 1930s mainly in terms of the regionalist novel – which had its own boom at that time – and not in terms of the narrators whose origins lie in the avant-garde. The 1960s Boom saw both the climax and consummation of Latin American Modernism (in the Anglo-American sense of the word) and catalyzed the inauguration of Latin American postmodern narrative (in which the Boom writers would also participate).

Most important of all, however, and this is almost always overlooked by the Boom-bashing revisionists since the mid-1960s, Latin America's literature was the only literature in the world which responded fully to the extraordinarily fertile conjuncture of the 1960s, the most interesting and exciting time, culturally and politically speaking, since the 1920s, and the last great utopian moment in Western history. The Boom confronted the problematic of Latin America's own identity with the newly emerging identity politics (not only nationality and class, but race and ethnicity and gender and sexuality) which both conjoined and separated the first (capitalist), second (Communist), and third ("developing" or "ex-colonial") worlds.

This unique conjunctural phenomenon, the Boom, stretched from Carlos Fuentes's *La región más transparente* (1958; *Where the Air is Clear*) to his *Terra nostra* (1975; *Terra Nostra*). But when most critics think about the era, they tend to concentrate, naturally enough, on the 1960s alone and the brief but intense period from Vargas Llosa's *La ciudad y los perros* (1962; *The Time of the Hero*), which received special attention by winning a major prize in Barcelona, and Fuentes's *La muerte de Artemio Cruz* (1962; *The Death of Artemio Cruz*) through Cortázar's *Rayuela* (1963; *Hopscotch*) to García Márquez's *Cien años de soledad* (1967; *One Hundred Years of Solitude*) – though, again, a minority would see José Donoso's *El obsceno pájaro de la noche* (1970; *The Obscene Bird of Night*) as marking the end of the era.

Within this perspective, the most remarkable period of the brief moment that was the Boom was the even more intense stretch of time – the eye of its hurricane – from

1963, when *Rayuela* was published, to 1967, when García Márquez's *Cien años de soledad* – the Boom novel par excellence – appeared. These were the two signature novels of the Boom. Almost everyone agreed that *Rayuela* was something like "Latin America's *Ulysses*" – appropriately enough, if one accepts that the Boom is best understood as the crystallization and culmination of Latin America's Modernist movement dating back to the 1920s. But *Cien años de soledad* changed the entire perspective, making it clear at once that something much more far-reaching had occurred for which a quite different time frame was required – because, as almost everyone again agreed, *Cien años de soledad* was something like "Latin America's *Don Quijote*." Clearly, a brief literary moment which somehow confronts a *Ulysses* with a *Quixote* is more than just a historical flash in the pan.

Nevertheless the Fuentes bookend approach mentioned above – narrating the period from *La región más transparente* in 1958 to *Terra nostra* in 1975 – is most convenient for our present purpose since it takes us from the moment just before the Cuban Revolution at the beginning of 1959 to the moment just after the Chilean coup of September 1973, two political events which undoubtedly open and close a brief era of intense socialist political optimism. And all the major writers of the Boom considered themselves "socialist" at one time or another, particularly during the period of the Boom, when their lives were so intricately and intensely intertwined, and they all worked out socialism's tensions and contradictions both in their lives and in their works.

## History

When Carlos Fuentes published *La región más transparente* in 1958, in Mexico, by then the most stable country in Latin America, the continent was on the threshold of vast changes. The era of populist politics was largely behind it and a decade of import substitution and attempts at social democracy had created a new middle class which, among other things, was prepared for a new approach to consuming culture across a wide range of manifestations. What was needed now, people felt, was a form of writing with which these new middle classes could identify. Fuentes and his peers were about to provide it. It was appropriate that Fuentes should initiate the Boom because he was undoubtedly the hinge which made the entire movement swing: he would be the leading promoter and propagandist of the new wave and the one who put all the other participants in touch with one another and, in several cases, helped them with agents, translators, and even writing facilities. He also knew all the secondary characters, like José Donoso, Juan Goytisolo, Jorge Edwards, Angel Rama, and Emir Rodríguez Monegal, as well as all the leading Cubans and all the stars of earlier generations like Pablo Neruda and Luis Buñuel. Both his person and his curriculum vitae were dazzlingly cosmopolitan and impossibly glamorous (he was even married to a film star); he was also, culturally and intellectually, unusually generous.

Like García Márquez, Fuentes had traveled to Cuba immediately after the Revolution and was a member of the first Casa de las Américas jury; already an opponent of US policy in Latin America, he led a solidarity delegation to the island in 1961, thereby provoking a long history of difficulty with the United States, which would refuse him a visa for many years. In 1962 he attended the Punta del Este conference which effectively expelled Cuba from the Organization of American States. In 1963 he traveled through Eastern Europe, trying to persuade himself that things really were improving in the Soviet bloc, and in Paris he met leading Spanish dissidents Jorge Semprún and Juan Goytisolo, as well as two of the other three Latin American Boom writers, Julio Cortázar and Mario Vargas Llosa. Before long he would meet the fourth member of the now not too distant Boom, Gabriel García Márquez.

*La región más transparente* was a long, ambitious reading of a country which hitherto, as its ironic title proposed, had been illegible not only to Mexicans themselves but to foreigners like Lawrence, Eisenstein, Breton, Greene, and Lowry. Curiously, though, Fuentes's was a reading not in the style of, say, the contemporaneous French *nouveau roman*, but that of the 1920s and 1930s European, or European-based, Modernists. Significantly, however, Fuentes's novel was achieved with an evident mastery, aggressively displayed, which suggested that, despite the achievements of Asturias, Borges, Carpentier, and Rulfo, among others (achievements which Fuentes for one never denied), the time had now come for another generation to look anew at the history of their countries, a generation whose privileged perspective would allow it to give perhaps the defining – if not definitive – readings which had hitherto been lacking. More than a mere interpretation, then, Fuentes essayed a cartography. Given that the last collective enterprise of this kind had been the chronicling of the New World conducted under the colonial gaze of the Spanish conquistadores, it is not altogether surprising that the Boom would also be so frequently and fervently attacked, both then and later.

Who knows what might have happened if Fidel Castro, Che Guevara, and companions had been defeated in Cuba's Sierra Maestra in the late 1950s. The fact is, however, that only a few months after the appearance of Fuentes's novel a revolution was proclaimed in Havana which would not only declare itself a model for Latin America as a whole but would also take a leading role in Cold War politics and challenge Latin America to consider whether it was merely a subordinate partner in the enterprise of the capitalist West or a part of what was beginning to be called the Third World. The Cuban Revolution put Latin America at the centre of world attention for the first time and gave writers and artists a choice of commitments, whether to Cuban-style revolutionary Marxism, US-style freedom and individualism, or other points in between. This echoed the equally wide range of options available to intellectuals and artists in the 1920s. There is no doubt that this temporary widening of horizons – later to be negated almost absolutely by the 1970s – created an aesthetic moment of extraordinary fertility. This openness, this choice between alternatives, is clearly visible in both the subject matter and the structures of the canonical texts of the era: *La muerte de Artemio Cruz*, *Rayuela*, *La Casa Verde*, and *Cien años de soledad*. All are about the historical formation of Latin America, the relation between that history and other mythical versions, and the contribution of both to contemporary Latin American identity: the grand themes or – as later critics would say, with pejorative intent – "master narratives" of the great *mestizo* continent.

Sociologically and historically speaking, the openness of cultural, intellectual, and political horizons mentioned above replicated an equally important freedom which the four main protagonists of the Boom themselves enjoyed: with their sudden rise to celebrity and bestseller status, all were able to conceive the prospect of living entirely from their writing, with perhaps a little part-time journalism and teaching thrown in. Such a prospect had never previously existed for Latin American writers.

In 1958 Fuentes (b. 1928) did not know the three men who would become his partners in the enterprise which public relations, and then historiography itself, would come to know as the Boom. He himself was on the progressive left and he would remain there for the rest of his career. He had both the drive and the resources to roam the planet as and when he chose, which made him not only the best traveled of an unusually well-traveled quartet but also the one with the most cosmopolitan perspective and the widest network of international contacts. Julio Cortázar (b. 1914), the oldest of the four, was a quite different case. Like many Argentinian writers and intellectuals, he had been alienated by his nation's history of dictatorship and then repelled by what he perceived as the brutality and the vulgarity of Peronism in the 1940s and 1950s. He had moved in the 1950s to Paris, where he lived a mildly bohemian existence as translator first and writer second at a time when some of the leading Surrealists were still around and Existentialism was in vogue. For him, until the early 1960s, politics came second to art and myth (not to mention jazz). Gabriel García Márquez (b. 1927), who was the same age as Fuentes but at that time much less successful, had never been a member of any political party but in a country, Colombia, where formal politics remained dominated by nineteenth-century liberal and conservative models, he had always been close to people who were members of the Communist Party, and this was also true of his periods spent in Mexico from 1961 to 1967 and Barcelona from 1967 to 1974. Moreover he had worked for Cuba's Prensa Latina press agency in Havana, Bogotá, and New York in 1960 and 1961, before Castro declared the revolution Communist, and was effectively forced out when hard-line communists took over the agency at the time of the Bay of Pigs invasion and ejected its founder director, the Argentinian Jorge Masetti. Mario Vargas Llosa (b. 1936) was both the youngest and the most individually rebellious of the four. He had been briefly involved in left-wing student politics in Lima in the early 1950s (see his *Conversación en la Catedral*, 1969) and after his arrival in Europe in the late 1950s he agonized obsessively between the different positions on *engagement* ("commitment") espoused by existentialists Jean-Paul Sartre and Albert Camus.

Cuba changed everything for all four writers. They were all wary of Soviet-style Communism (García Márquez and Fuentes had both visited Eastern Europe), and all aware that the USSR saw Latin America through a lens which, ideologically at least, was as self-serving as the United States' preaching about freedom and, eventually, human rights. But Cuba, a revolutionary socialist (or Marxist or Communist) government in Latin America itself, was a new phenomenon and a reality that had to be experienced, theorized, and worked through. This each one of them did. The results were surprising and in many ways exemplary; their correspondence during this era – the last in which celebrities ever wrote letters – is especially illuminating because the four central protagonists had exceptionally close fraternal relationships before matters Cuban finally tore them apart. Cortázar, the least politically committed in 1959, became the most fervently committed well before the end of the 1960s (the conclusion of *Rayuela*, an ideological brick wall, allowed no other outcome: the Argentinian finally had to become Latin American). Mario Vargas Llosa, the one perceived as the most "revolutionary" in the early and mid-1960s, became the most conservative by the early 1970s and would eventually take up views close to US neo-liberalism in the 1980s. García Márquez, the only one of the four who had been seriously burned by Cuban politics at the time the Boom became visible, continued to be drawn back to revolutionary Marxism like a moth to the flame, and later became the stoutest defender of Cuba and a personal friend of its leader Fidel Castro. Fuentes, undoubtedly the most lucid and widely read of the four, and also the most ideologically consistent, found himself banned, successively, by Castro's Cuba, Nixon's United States, and Franco's Spain, as well as becoming a pariah, from time to time, in his own country, Mexico. No one ever said it was easy to be a Latin American intellectual!

After *La región más transparente* the next three major novels of the Boom were all still suffused with a Liberal view of the world. Mario Vargas Llosa's *La ciudad y los perros* (1962), rewarded with a major literary prize in Spain, seemed at first sight to be not only an antimilitary but also an anti-establishment work; but the truth was that its interplay between Alberto, a petit-bourgeois protagonist with a bad conscience and Jaguar, an antihero who proved that self-reliance was really the only way in life, foreshadowed a move to the individualist right which was only four or five years away. Even Carlos Fuentes's *La muerte de Artemio Cruz* (1962), still his most popular work among left-of-centre readers, a minute and brilliant investigation of the aftermath of the Mexican Revolution, seemed to suggest, at its deepest level, and despite being signed in Havana, that everything that had happened in Mexico was inevitable and that the gulf between "ideals" and "realities" was inherently unbridgeable, then and always. Cortázar's *Rayuela* (1963) was not, as some have argued, the novel that began the Boom but it was undoubtedly the novel that confirmed, crystallized, and characterized it. A mythological work in its time and still undoubtedly one of Latin America's great representative *texts* even today, *Rayuela* seemed to imply that the meaning of life was to be searched for almost anywhere but in formal politics.

But the Cuban Revolution was having its effect on everyone. Fuentes, Vargas Llosa, and Cortázar were all invited to Cuba in the early years by Haydée Santamaría and Roberto Fernández Retamar at Casa de las Américas, though ironically García Márquez, the only one who had actually worked for Cuba, was left out in the cold. *La muerte de Artemio Cruz* (1962), a carefully, not to say obsessively, counterpointed Modernist novel, was the first to follow Miguel Angel Asturias's pathbreaking structural exploration of 1949, *Hombres de maíz*, in which personal biography and national, continental, and universal history are all arranged in concentric circles which bind the identity of the author to Latin America's own identity in a kind of anticolonialist metaphor. This is a special, "Ulyssean" version of Fredric Jameson's concept of Third World national allegory. In *Rayuela* (1963) the Latin American allegorical dimension was even more apparent, despite the book's self-evident Argentinian obsessions. A template had now emerged; and Vargas Llosa, under huge reader expectation and peer pressure, set about contributing his own version, *La Casa Verde*, which would be published in 1966 when he was only 30 and still remains, for many critics, his grandest achievement. The influence of William Faulkner on the Peruvian is unmistakable, but Vargas Llosa takes Faulkner's techniques to lengths that even Faulkner never envisaged with an audacity and a lucidity that dazzled Latin America's new readers.

Throughout this period García Márquez, whose *La hojarasca* – begun in 1950 but only published in 1955 – had been a work visibly influenced both by Faulkner and Virginia Woolf and was thus already a distant harbinger of the Boom, lived isolated in Mexico City, at once mesmerized and horrified by the progress his contemporaries were making. But he was lucky. In late 1963, after an extended period in Europe during which he met both Cortázar and Vargas Llosa, Fuentes returned to Mexico and among the first of his many activities was co-writing, with García Márquez, the film scripts of both *El gallo de oro* and *Pedro Páramo*, works by that strange writer who may well be Mexico's greatest narrator, Juan Rulfo. When did a script for a film based on the work of such a giant of literature have two such future giants of literature working on it? Fuentes would play a major role in bringing García Márquez to world attention.

It is not generally recognized that Uruguayan Emir Rodríguez Monegal, former editor of Uruguay's legendary magazine *Marcha*, borrowed most of Fuentes's ideas in his essays dating from the mid-1960s, when he identified himself with Latin America's new narrative movement and made himself its best-known critical propagandist – though unfortunately he viewed almost everything in terms of "novelties" and "anachronisms," almost as *Vogue* might have done. In 1965 Rodríguez Monegal published an article entitled "The New Novelists" in *Encounter* (1965), the internationally oriented magazine published from London, edited by Stephen Spender and financed in part, as would later be discovered, by the CIA. Rodríguez Monegal ignored Fuentes's recommendation to include García Márquez. By contrast the Chilean-American Luis Harss, author of *Los nuestros* (1966; *Into the Mainstream*, 1967), and later editor of *Review*, made a brilliant choice of writers incorporating both the most important of the older authors (Asturias, Borges, Carpentier, Guimarães Rosa, Onetti, and Rulfo) and the most promising of the new, including not only García Márquez, recommended by Fuentes, but also Vargas Llosa, recommended by Cortázar. His book became almost as much a sign of those times as *Cien años de soledad* itself, or Antonioni's film *Blowup* (1966), based on a Cortázar short story.

From 1966 Rodríguez Monegal himself directed *Mundo Nuevo*, a literary and cultural journal published in Paris. It was a sister journal to *Encounter*. Fuentes was from the start an enthusiastic collaborator – he almost always participated in cultural activities which could be construed as "progressive" – and would have a leading role in the first issue, in which he heralded the arrival of García Márquez and *Cien años de soledad*; but the Cubans began to cry foul before the magazine was even published and their allegations about CIA links made the other key writers of the Boom – Cortázar, Vargas Llosa and, eventually, García Márquez (who initially allowed Rodríguez Monegal to publish extracts of his still unfinished masterpiece) – keep well away from the journal, even though they were almost constantly mentioned within its pages.

Meanwhile Cuba was having its own dramas. Once the Revolution began, as revolutions inevitably do, to codify the relations between artists and the state, and even to begin to prescribe ways of writing and movie-making, writers and intellectuals like Guillermo Cabrera Infante, Severo Sarduy, and Carlos Franqui began to become alienated from the national status quo and think of fleeing abroad. Castro's epoch-making speech *Words to the Intellectuals* ("Inside the Revolution, everything; outside the Revolution, nothing") in 1961 had placated some writers but intimidated others, and the interpretation of its meaning has remained an essential preoccupation of Cuban artists and intellectuals down to the present time. One of the stipulations the revolutionaries began to impose on friendly writers was to have no truck with the imperialist enemy, and this included personal visits to the United States, which by then was blockading their country, even if the invitations came from such liberal organizations as universities or the international PEN Club. In the summer of 1966 the revolutionary commissars committed perhaps their single biggest error when they launched a violent verbal assault not only on Carlos Fuentes but on Pablo Neruda. Both men had recently visited New York and were accused of giving comfort to the enemy. Neruda was for many the continent's greatest poet; he was also its best-known Communist writer and a man who had risked his life, liberty, and reputation in the cause of socialist revolution well before some of his attackers were even born. He never forgave the slight and his relation with Latin America's first Communist revolution was never entirely healed. As for Fuentes, he would never overtly attack Cuba nor give comfort to its enemies (though in his correspondence he could be scathing about Cuban affairs), but equally he would never visit the island again and he would never again collaborate with its political cadres.

This gave the other Boom members plenty to think about. Though disappointed, García Márquez was not surprised; something not entirely dissimilar had happened to him. Cortázar, newly inspired with the spirit of anti-imperialist revolution, would hold on somewhat grimly to his new enthusiasm – though he would later feel much more relaxed amid the less institutionalized Sandinista revolution in Nicaragua. Vargas Llosa would meanwhile begin his long march to the right (signaled by a great monument to political skepticism, *Conversación en la Catedral*, 1969), a march which would first track and then go well beyond that of his Spanish colleague Juan Goytisolo until eventually he would be as far to the right as his fellow London resident Guillermo Cabrera Infante (self-exiled in 1965). Cortázar would make desperate attempts to keep an increasingly reluctant Vargas Llosa on board the Cuban pirate ship and to convince the Cubans that he was succeeding in doing so.

Cortázar was helped in this endeavor in 1967 when the *Mundo Nuevo* scandal finally broke and it was proved that the Cubans had been not paranoid but correct: US government funds had been secretly injected into the Congress for the Freedom of Culture, a front organization, by the CIA, and both *Encounter* and *Mundo Nuevo* were, however subtly, a clandestine part of the US's cultural propaganda mission to propagate its version of "freedom" and "human values" around the planet. García Márquez, who by now had completed *Cien años de soledad*, immediately wrote publicly to the abject Rodríguez Monegal saying that he and other well-meaning contributors had been "cuckolded" and that he would have nothing more to do with the magazine. Before long Rodríguez Monegal resigned from *Mundo Nuevo* and moved to Yale University, where he and his new department became a focus for anti-Cuban criticism in both senses of the word.

*Cien años de soledad* was finally published in May 1967 and the era of Macondo had begun. For the best part of a year beforehand extracts had been appearing in magazines all over Latin America, as well as in *Mundo Nuevo*. Carlos Fuentes had written several advance reviews declaring that García Márquez's "work-in-progress" (the implied comparison with James Joyce was unmistakable) was a masterpiece and Latin America's "Bible." And early in 1967 Mario Vargas Llosa, who must have been stupefied by the appearance of this totally unknown rival, had declared, in chivalrous fashion, that *Cien años de soledad* was another, glorious version of *Amadís* (Vargas Llosa, 1967). Had this ever happened before in the history of world literature? Had any book been considered a classic before it was even published? Had any timeless classic ever been an immediate bestseller and turned its writer overnight into a celebrity, and before very long into a rich man? Now that there was a García Márquez, there could really be a Boom; now, there could be anything. This man was magic. His book was magic, his name was magic: Gabo, as he now became known, was a Warhol-era dream and not just for 15 minutes. Yet ironically this book, which consecrated the Boom for ever, was also Latin America's first great postmodern novel and the sign that the Boom itself was historically doomed.

García Márquez and Vargas Llosa finally met in July 1967. Both attended the conference of the Instituto Internacional de Literatura Iberoamericana in Caracas, where Vargas Llosa coincidentally received the first Rómulo Gallegos Prize for fiction for *La Casa Verde*. His speech, "Literature is Fire," declared that literature was a desperately serious activity, a matter of life and death, and that it was always feared by reactionary regimes. The speech was interpreted at the time, and probably even intended, as an ideological bombardment from the Left (though the idea that literature *always* means "nonconformism and rebellion," "protest, contradiction and criticism" must have raised eyebrows in Havana). After this the two men traveled on to Bogotá and Lima together and became good friends; eventually they would even be next-door neighbors and bosom buddies in Barcelona, and in 1971 Vargas Llosa would publish a major work on García Márquez, *Historia de un decidio*, before the two men began to be estranged and eventually totally divorced after 1976, when Vargas Llosa knocked García Márquez to the ground in a Mexico City cinema, ostensibly over a "matter of skirts," as the Spaniards say, but obviously also over much more politically and ideologically significant matters as well.

In late 1967, as García Márquez left Latin America for Barcelona – where his agent Carmen Balcells was located, plus the crucial publishing house Seix Barral – he made one of his most important declarations: "the revolutionary duty of a writer is to write well." This was six years after Fidel Castro's first (and last) words on the topic, which had been somewhat different; "Words to the Intellectuals" had declared that literary form should be free but literary content rather less so; García Márquez, who would become Castro's best friend, was giving himself room to maneuver. Before long he would become an expert at this.

In October 1967 Che Guevara was killed in Bolivia and his French comrade Régis Debray was imprisoned in Camiri. Many observers interpreted this not only as the end of the Revolution's most idealistic era but also as a crisis for the Cuban model of revolutionary guerrilla warfare. Also in October Miguel Angel Asturias was awarded the Nobel Prize for Literature (as Neruda would be in his turn in 1971). Emir Rodrí-guez Monegal led the charge to prove that not only was Asturias by then a literary irrelevance (or "anachronism") but that his position as Guatemalan ambassador in Paris, at a time when the US Green Berets were rampant in the country and his own son was fighting for the Guatemalan guerrillas, made him a political and moral pariah. The fact that Asturias had for most of his adult life been well to the left of every single one of the Boom writers in no way mitigated this judgment, and his suspended sentence would be finally executed upon him when almost all shades of opinion took the side of García Márquez in an absurd spat between the two on the subject of literary "plagiarism" in mid-1971.

Neruda, Fuentes, Asturias . . . the progressive Left in Latin America could ill afford these casualties. In early 1968 Julio Cortázar could still spend two months in India with Mexican ambassador Octavio Paz, but the days of such trans-ideological friendships were numbered and much worse was to come. That year, 1968, almost everything went wrong. Liberal hopes Martin Luther King and Bobby Kennedy were assassinated in the United States. The May Revolution in Paris was snuffed out. Fuentes was present and wrote a brief memoir. Later in the year, the government of Mexico, perhaps Latin America's least repressive major country, perpetrated a massacre of students and ordinary people before the world's cameras in a desperate attempt to ensure that the October Olympic Games would take place as planned. (Both Fuentes and García Márquez were in Europe, fortunately for them.) But even before that, two Cuba-related issues began to push the contradictions between Latin American intellectuals ominously toward terminal crisis. First, Soviet troops occupied Dubček's Czechoslovakia in the summer and Fidel Castro felt constrained to justify the invasion. This caused dismay and stupefaction among the more liberal sectors of the Latin American Left: clear lines were now appearing in the shifting sands of history. Secondly, an international jury had awarded the fourth annual prize for poetry of the

National Union of Writers and Artists of Cuba (UNEAC) to the poet Heberto Padilla for his plainly dissident collection *Fuera del juego*; the army intervened and Castro effectively sequestered the jury, which included the Spanish novelist Juan Marsé, in the hope that they would change their minds. When they declined to do so the authorities insisted that the book should appear with a kind of political health warning attached. Now the cat really was among the chickens. This was the beginning of the "Padilla Affair," a drama in two acts, whose climax, in 1971, would divide Latin American artists and intellectuals for as far into the future as any of them would have wished to see. It was a drama about literature and political commitment, capitalism and socialism, and it forced all those involved to make a one-time choice, without the luxury of an escape into social democratic ambivalence.

In 1969 Cortázar would write an unforgettable literary and ideological self-presentation in *Life en Español* (one which unfortunately involved a disastrous – and shameful – polemic with Peruvian novelist José María Arguedas, whom the Boom writers deemed "provincial"); Fuentes would publish his paradigmatic *La nueva novela hispanoamericana*, somewhat inferior to the essays he had been writing earlier in the decade; the unfortunate José Donoso would finally complete his long-awaited *El obsceno pájaro de la noche*, which was to have been awarded the 1969 Biblioteca Breve Prize – until the editorial split! – and the Boom writers would unite to write an appeal for the release of Régis Debray, undoubtedly the French intellectual most closely associated with their political and literary activities during this entire period, and a figure every bit as controversial as they were.

By this time the writer most alienated from Cuba was the Spaniard Juan Goytisolo, though perhaps one might note that Cuba, where his ancestors had made a small fortune in trade, was less his business than that of the others. Up to now his literary trajectory, from a grey social realism to a linguistic and cultural deconstructionism, had been more like that of the diffident José Donoso than of the other members of the Boom. But really, if anyone was entitled to be the fifth member it was this rebellious Catalan, not the largely apolitical Donoso. Like the other four he had spent many years in exile, specifically in Paris; like them, too, he was obsessed with the identity question and cultural and ethnic miscegenation, even if in his case the culture was Spain and the miscegenation primarily Arab. And he was utterly obsessed with questions of politics, including the whole range of socialisms but also, far more than the others, with the sexuality question. Goytisolo was an anguished homosexual; and Cuba's *machista* Revolution, despite its efforts to emancipate both blacks and women, had a contemptuous and repressive attitude toward homosexuality which emanated from the very top, not excluding Castro and Guevara. This gave an extra dimension to Goytisolo's radical trajectory and an extra edge to his rapidly evolving thought. From an early social realism he had moved to *Señas de identidad* (1966), the most important novel on Spanish identity since the Generation of 1898, and was now working on *Reivindicación del conde Don Julián* (1970), a rejection not only of the time-honored but creaking Spanish literary canon but also of Spain's entire history of racial and cultural self-definition and political and religious authoritarianism. Finally *Juan sin tierra* (1973) would complete the process by cutting all ties with nationalisms of every sort and with all fixed sexual identities. Unsurprisingly, Cuba was no longer this man's cup of tea.

Goytisolo, still obsessed with the liberation of Spain from Franco's dictatorship but now also concerned that the solution should be nothing like Cuba's, became the most enthusiastic advocate of a new intellectual magazine, to be published in Paris and organized by members of the Boom group and like-minded friends and acquaintances (Goytisolo, 1990). As fate would have it, in the summer of 1970 Carlos Fuentes's play *El tuerto es rey* (*The One-Eyed Man is King*) was being premiered at the Avignon Festival, only 40 miles from Cortázar's summer home in southern France. An expedition from Barcelona was organized, with the García Márquez family, the Vargas Llosas, who had only recently moved there from London, and the Donosos, who would soon be moving out to the provinces. (Donoso was later the author of two classic chronicles of the era, his *Personal History of the "Boom"*, 1972, and his novel, *The Garden Next Door*, 1981, which casts a satirical – and envious – eye on the relationship between the already mythological literary agent Carmen Balcells, a.k.a. Núria Monclús, and her "favourite son," García Márquez, a. k a. Marcelo Chiriboga.) This was the first time that all the novelists of the Boom (plus, as it happened, Donoso and Goytisolo) had ever met up together, though unfortunately it was much closer to the end of a beautiful four-way relationship than the beginning (Cortázar, 2000: 1418).

The main topic of conversation was the proposed Paris-based magazine: whether to do it – Cortázar had been trying to dissuade Goytisolo but to no avail – and what to call it. Octavio Paz – the effects of whose epoch-making polemic from the moderate Right with his Communist rival Pablo Neruda had now lasted more than two decades – had suggested *Blanco* – "Target," but also "White" – a name perhaps not best conceived to please Afro-Caribbean Cuba. (Paz, his initiatives rebutted, went on to found his own magazine in Mexico, *Plural* – but that is another, though equally contradictory and fascinating, story.) Donoso's wife Pilar suggested *Libre*, "Free," equally naïve (or cunning), since of course this was a codeword for the US ideology of capitalist economics and liberal politics. But *Libre* the magazine became (see Goytisolo, 1990). By then the Cubans were suspicious of Goytisolo, who for some time had not been returning their calls, and their suspicions were driven from paranoia to hysteria when it emerged that the prime funder of this magazine would be the granddaughter of notorious Bolivian tin magnate Simón Patiño, who, worse, was married to a French aristocrat (though the woman herself, Albina Boisrouvray, was in fact a left-wing activist and has remained one all her life).

A week later Cortázar would write, with a perspective similar to that of his characters, and fully worthy of the author of the mysterious *Blowup*: "It was at once very nice and very strange; something outside of time, unrepeatable of course, and with some deeper meaning that escapes me." Whatever the deeper meaning, some of the ingredients were, undoubtedly, that Cortázar was already aware, more than anyone, that it was the last moment when the utopian longings enshrined in the Boom could still be partly sustained as a collective enterprise; and that this first great gathering had taken the form of a pilgrimage to his solitary dwelling, he who had always avoided crowds and false bonhomie but was now not only a member of a mafia welded together by frequent male bonding on a monumental scale but was also gravitating toward the vast collective enterprises of the socialist dream. Everyone present had a lot to lose but he, by far the oldest member of the group, had the most to lose of all of them.

That autumn Salvador Allende's Popular Unity alliance was elected to power in Chile, committed to the "democratic road to socialism," and the United States set out immediately to destabilize the new government even before its inauguration. Pablo Neruda was appointed ambassador to Paris, like Asturias before him and Fuentes after him. Chilean writer Jorge Edwards, a classic liberal from an old oligarchical family, was to have been Neruda's number two, but was sent instead as temporary representative to Havana. There he became involved in the activities and problems of dissidents like Padilla and left Cuba after only a few months in post, by which time he had spent Christmas in Mexico City with Carlos Fuentes while the rest of the Boom group spent Christmas and New Year together in Barcelona. A few weeks later Edwards, traumatized by his experiences, flew straight from Cuba to the house of Mario Vargas Llosa in Barcelona and assured him that Cuba was now effectively a police state. He would eventually record his experiences in his influential memoir *Persona Non Grata*, after returning to his duties in Paris defending Allende's government with Neruda (Edwards, 1993). Neruda himself would win the Nobel Prize in 1971 but by then was already suffering from the cancer which would take his life shortly after the 1973 Chilean coup.

Edwards's sojourn in Cuba was almost certainly instrumental in catalyzing the second and decisive phase of the Padilla affair. This time the poet was arrested and imprisoned as a spy and CIA collaborator, causing a storm of protest in the West, particularly in Paris. After three weeks he was released and made an astonishing self-criticism which involved him betraying his best friends and even his wife and thanking the Cuban secret police and Fidel Castro for the path of enlightenment on which they had set him. All ideological hell broke loose. On April 9 a letter of protest was sent to Castro from Paris which included the names of all the Boom writers and their associates, as well as Jean-Paul Sartre and Simone de Beauvoir, Italo Calvino, Marguerite Duras, Rossana Rossanda, Hans Magnus Enzensberger, Susan Sontag, and many other such left-liberal luminaries. Castro replied with unparalleled fury and ferocity, making it clear that Cuba could and would do without such petit-bourgeois lackeys of international imperialism: its doors would be closed to them. Within a few days García Márquez objected that he had never been consulted and had therefore not really signed the letter, and within a short time Cortázar also recanted and confessed that he had made a mistake; he still supported Cuba and to prove it wrote an anguished and much derided poem called "Policrítica en la hora de los chacales."

As a matter of fact Goytisolo and Vargas Llosa were the two moving forces behind the protest. Both had been looking for an opportunity to distance themselves formally from Cuba – Goytisolo more self-consciously than Vargas Llosa – and this one, supported by the whole weight of the capitalist West (as well as what would soon be known as the "Eurocommunist" Left), presented the ideal opportunity. It was, without doubt, the single most important crisis in Latin American literary politics in the twentieth century, one which split both Latin American and European intellectuals down the middle. For once writers and intellectuals had to commit themselves and take sides in this cultural equivalent of a civil war.

So this time the left-wing sheep really were separated from the liberal goats. Goytisolo and Vargas Llosa would never visit Cuba again. The Cubans, impatient of all vacillation and about to embark on a five-year process of hardline institutionalization, which some critics called Stalinization, took some time to forgive Cortázar and García Márquez, though in the end they did. In the short term, around the same time, García Márquez, who was known to be writing a not entirely unsympathetic portrait of a Latin American dictator, made things even worse by accepting an honorary degree from Columbia University, New York in June 1971 while at the same time forging links with a new Venezuelan party, MAS, now committed to the electoral road, though most of its leaders were former Communist Party guerrillas. That fall Fidel Castro made a three-week visit to Chile in November and warned Allende of the dangers of a US-backed military coup, a coup which, needless to say, Castro's own visit made much more likely. In December Vargas Llosa's *García Márquez: History of a Deicide* appeared, published in Barcelona by Seix Barral. It was undoubtedly the most remarkable act of homage ever offered by one Latin American writer to another, even if, unsurprisingly, Vargas Llosa's portrait turned García Márquez into a writer driven by the same demons and inclined to the same literary solutions as himself.

And then came the launch, in September 1971, of *Libre* (*Mundo Nuevo* had closed earlier that year), which had a rotating editorship but was managed by García Márquez's close friend and ex-socialist writer Plinio Apuleyo Mendoza. *Libre* declared itself anti-imperialist, naturally, but also, in a more coded fashion, anti-Soviet and anti-Cuban. It included not only the dissident ex-Communists of MAS from Venezuela but also Cuban exiles like Carlos Franqui and Spanish ex-Communist and now "Euro-communist" dissidents like Fernando Claudín and Jorge Semprún. García Márquez, unenthusiastically, and Vargas Llosa, passionately, remained attached but Cortázar jumped ship. The editorial board included an astonishingly representative group of the influential Hispanic "Marxisant" "New Left" over the past four decades, including those who would – briefly – be "Eurocommunist," and those who would be associated with Spain's left-liberal newspaper *El País*, together with international intellectuals of similar orientation like Calvino, Enzensberger, and Sontag. By the time the first issue appeared, at least half of these board members must have been unacceptable to the Cuban regime (Cortázar and García Márquez were really the only major figures who had refused to sign the protest letters), but the only person absolutely excluded through Cuban pressure was the most determinedly provocative Cuban exile, Guillermo Cabrera Infante. The first four issues were edited successively by Juan Goytisolo, Jorge Semprún, Teodoro Petkoff, and Mario Vargas Llosa. The failure to bring out more than four issues suggests not only a disenchantment and discouragement brought about by the political splits in the board but also, perhaps, that its promoters, above all Goytisolo, were more interested in making a political statement at a particular moment in history than in making an ongoing and sustained long-term contribution to international political debate. *Libre* was intended as a line in the sand but not a line into the future. Most of its collaborators seem to have been signaling, whether they knew it or not, that instead of the almost impossible complexities of Cold War politics, they would prefer to be the Left opposition to a single – capitalist – superpower. After 1989 they would get their way and it would be too late to change their minds.

García Márquez, who never let politics get in the way of friendship, would remain on good terms with both Fuentes and Cortázar, but Vargas Llosa would gradually be distanced from his erstwhile blood brothers until his closest literary friends in Latin America were Guillermo Cabrera Infante, Jorge Edwards, and Octavio Paz. All in all, and whether one agrees with the authors involved or not, there can be no denying that the content of all four issues of *Libre* was a direct and cumulative "provocation" against the Cuban regime, carefully calculated by Goytisolo and ingenuously tolerated by pro-Cubans such as García Márquez, Cortázar, and Salvador Garmendia. It is hardly surprising that, guilty by association (not to say participation, however reluctant), these writers were tacitly banned from the island for several years. It must have been impossible for the Cubans to believe that they were not in favor of the magazine's general editorial line.

By now, however, things were going badly for revolution all over Latin America. García Márquez and Cortázar both became members of the nongovernmental Russell Tribunal, whose main thrust was to challenge US imperialism. When Allende was overthrown in the bloody coup of September 11, 1973, García Márquez renounced narrative fiction and turned to left-wing journalism (*Alternativa*, Bogotá), declaring he would not write another novel until Pinochet fell, a promise he felt obliged to renege on in 1981. He slowly distanced himself from social democracy (though he would collaborate with ostensibly progressive politicians like González of Spain, Mitterand of France, Pérez of Venezuela, and Salinas of Mexico), in 1975 identified himself again with the Cuban Revolution, and soon afterwards became, astonishingly, Fidel Castro's only known close friend. Cortázar, whose *Libro de Manuel* (1970) had long since showed how far a political road he had traveled from *Rayuela*, remained attached to Cuba but was relieved to find new revolutionary pastures in the late 1970s with the revolutions in Central America, for which he did much selfless work. Fuentes pursued, imperturbably, his own precarious navigation between the left liberalism of social democracy and socialism *tout court*. Vargas Llosa, however, embarked on a long march to the right, inscribed perhaps in the creative ambivalence of his first, brilliant novels, later coarsened in works like *Guerra del fin del mundo* and *Historia de Mayta*, which made it clear that politics is always a road to delusion, as Vargas Llosa himself would prove, in the most extraordinary of ironies, when in 1990 he was defeated for the presidency of Peru, which he appeared certain to win, by the unknown and unscrupulous populist Fujimori.

# Postscript

Looking back, we can see that there was an explosion of interest in the Latin American novel from the early 1960s, which did indeed lead to an increased demand for the product, a demand which in its turn led to an expanded supply and a further spiral of interest. Moreover four product leaders emerged to dominate the new market: Carlos Fuentes, Julio Cortázar, Mario Vargas Llosa, and Gabriel García Márquez. Cortázar died in 1983, but the others are all still alive and remain undisputably the three leading novelists – the most prestigious literary brand names – of the continent almost forty years after the birth of their Boom. All are well known beyond the frontiers of Latin America and all are in a position to make a living from their writing. Not even Jorge Luis Borges, Alejo Carpentier, or Miguel Angel Asturias, giants from an earlier generation, could have dreamed of such favorable terms of trade when they first came to prominence in the 1940s and 1950s.

Well before the Boom, Latin American literature, represented above all by the "New Latin American Narrative" (Asturias, Borges, and Carpentier, then Onetti, Rulfo, Arguedas, Roa Bastos, and Guimarães Rosa), had certainly, at least since the 1940s, become a "world literature," but it was not recognized as such until the 1960s. Since the 1960s it has remained a "world literature" – indeed, many experts consider it one of the leading literatures, if not *the* leading literature in the world – but it has been, almost on principle, very much less confident and ambitious. It is no longer staking any claims. Yet, thanks to the Boom, Latin American literature has been "normalized" at home and "universalized" abroad. It is safe now for Latin Americans to write in minor key because the Boom writers demonstrated once and for all that the continent's literature was also capable of a major key – even if works in major key were about to go out of fashion.

It is not their fault that they arrived at the very end of one era and the very beginning of another. The truth is, however, that they all also became post-Boom, postmodern novelists. Thus in these three decades only one figure has risen to achieve the kind of impact on readers which at least two dozen writers achieved in the period 1920 to 1970; it is doubly emblematic of the era that she is a woman, Isabel Allende, and that her reception by serious critics has been infinitely less enthusiastic than her reception by the general reading public both in Latin America and (especially) abroad. Additionally, the writers who have managed, since the 1960s, to write the most convincingly "decentered" works – in contrast with the fab four's famously "finished" books – are also women: writers like the Brazilian Clarice Lispector (the greatest Latin American novelist of the 1960s outside of the Boom's boy's club) or the Chilean Diamela Eltit.

What cannot be denied, though, is that the writers of the Boom, however reluctantly and ambivalently in some cases, accepted the historic challenge to the Latin America intellectual, and took up their civic responsibility as leaders, representatives, teachers, or guides of the people. It would have been much easier, most of the time, for them to eschew these challenges and responsibilities, and on the whole they undoubtedly all lost large sums of money in terms of the opportunity cost involved in politicking instead of writing. Their efforts, gestures, and concerns, which in many ways involved a restaging of events and debates of the internationalist 1920s, are often too easily dismissed as what used to be called "petit-bourgeois" maneuvers and manipulations. In my judgment the record shows that these men lived and represented their times as best they could and that, given the unparalleled temptations to which they were subjected, their performance would compare well, both morally and politically, with that of many of the academics who have earned a comfortable living criticizing them since the mid-1970s.

## References and Further Reading

Casal, Lourdes, ed. (1972). *El Caso Padilla: Literatura y revolución en Cuba. Documentos*. Miami and New York: Nueva Atlántida.

Cortázar, Julio (2000). *Cartas*. Ed. Aurora Bernárdez. 3 vols. Buenos Aires: Alfaguara.

Donoso, J. (1977). *The Boom in Spanish American Literature: A Personal Account*. New York: Columbia University Press. (An insider's view by a man who nevertheless continued to feel like an outsider.)

Edwards, Jorge (1993). *Persona Non Grata: A Memoir of Disenchantment with the Cuban Revolution*. New York: Paragon House.

Fuentes, Carlos (1969). *La Nueva novela hispanoamericana*. Mexico: Joaquín Mortiz.

Goytisolo, Juan (1990). *Realms of Strife: Memoirs 1957–1982*. London: Quartet. (A remarkable memoir by Spain's greatest postwar novelist.)

Harss, Luis (1966). *Los Nuestros*. Buenos Aires: Sudamericana. (Historic book of interviews of the Boom writers and their leading predecessors).

*"Libre", Revista de crítica literaria (1971–1972): Edición facsimilar (números 1–4), con introducción de Plinio Apuleyo Mendoza (1992)*. Mexico City and Madrid: El Equilibrista and Ediciones Turner, Quintocentenario. (Invaluable reprint by, of all people, García Márquez's younger son.)

Martin, Gerald (1989). *Journeys through the Labyrinth: Latin American Fiction in the Twentieth Century*. London: Verso. (A general history which gives detailed attention to the Boom.)

Rama, Ángel, ed. (1981). *Más allá del boom: Literatura y mercado*. Mexico City: Marcha. (A negative presentation of the moment by an important group of leftist critics.)

Rodríguez Monegal, Emir (1965). "The new novelists," *Encounter*, London, September. (First news of what would be called the "Boom" in the English-speaking world.)

— (1972). *El Boom de la novela latinoamericana*. Caracas: Tiempo Nuevo. (A survey by the best-known academic propagandist of the "Boom.")

Vargas Llosa, Mario (1967). "*Cien años de soledad*: El Amadís en América," *Amaru*, 3, Lima, July–September. (A rave review.)

— (1971). *García Márquez: Historia de un decidio*. Barcelona: Barral. (Still the best general review of García Márquez's work up to *Cien años de soledad*.)

# 29

# João Guimarães Rosa, Antônio Callado, Clarice Lispector, and the Brazilian Difference

*Elizabeth A. Marchant*

## The Giant in the Margins

Reacting to an interview in a Brazilian newspaper in which Jorge Luís Borges suggested that censorship might be a stimulus for literary creation, Antônio Callado told an audience at Cambridge University in 1974:

> His position I think would be above any criticism if he were a writer in his beloved
> Switzerland, let us say. And he is voicing a deep yearning of certain Latin-American
> writers, who would like to get rid of a continent which gives them a bad conscience.
> Quite a few of our writers would like to devote their talent much more fully to technical
> achievement . . . I cannot help thinking that an author's responsibility as an author is
> too great for him to do only and exclusively what he pleases, in countries where people
> are far from being able to live as they please. (1974: 15)

Callado's remarks, delivered in a lecture on the challenges facing Latin American writers, address the role of the writer in societies in which large portions of the population, for a variety of reasons, are excluded from full citizenship. Over the nearly two centuries since Brazil gained political independence from Portugal, this problem has been voiced in ways that have corresponded to the nation's distinct culture and history. Callado, for example, was speaking at a time when publishing suffered government censorship and some of his fellow writers were in exile in response to repression from the authoritarian military regime that controlled Brazil from 1964 until 1985.

As one of the countries with the world's worst income distribution, Brazil presents specific challenges for the study of literature. With a population of roughly 186 million – the fifth most populous nation on Earth – it is home to tens of millions who live in poverty *and* an educated class numerous enough to sustain a national publishing industry in the Portuguese language. Since there is not a large international market for works published in Portuguese, as there is for Spanish, most of the world's readers are unfamiliar with Brazilian writing of all kinds. One consequence of such enormity/invisibility is that while Brazilian writers are quite familiar with the traditions of Western thought, the West is to a great degree ignorant of Brazilian scholarly and literary production. This imbalance is a characteristic feature of Brazil's literary production when it is considered from a global perspective.

In examining the relationship between "underdevelopment" and culture, Brazilian critic Antônio Cândido describes how his country's writers came to a "catastrophic consciousness of backwardness, corresponding to the notion of 'underdeveloped country'" (1995: 121). Though their awareness only becomes fully apparent in the 1950s, in his essay "Literature and Underdevelopment" (1969) he argues that the process began with regionalist novels of the 1930s that demystified the hyperbolic "compensatory illusion" of earlier generations of writers by pointing directly and forcefully to the country's economic and social crises. Regionalist fiction of that period "abandoned pleasantness and *curiosity*, anticipating or perceiving what had been disguised in the picturesque enchantment or ornamental chivalry with which rustic man had previously been approached" (1995: 121). By the 1950s, writers were looking more closely at the margins of Brazilian society, at difference, and at "Brazilianness," but in ways distinct from those we see in the social realist novels of earlier regionalists like Jorge Amado (1912–2001). "Discarding sentimentalism and rhetoric; nourished by non-realist elements, such as the absurd, the magic of situations, or by antinaturalist techniques, such as the interior monologue, the simultaneous vision, the synthesis, the ellipsis – the novel nevertheless explores what used to be the very substance of nativism, of exoticism, and of social documentary" (1995: 139).

The three mid-twentieth-century writers examined here – João Guimarães Rosa (1908–67), Antônio Callado (1917–97), and Clarice Lispector (1920–77) – all write in the wake of Brazilian regionalism and address the country's social and economic difficulties in different ways. They are among the very few Brazilian novelists with international reputations and works translated into English. Far from being marginal themselves, like many of their fellow writers, they sought to understand their society and their position as writers within it.

## Assimilating Difference

The prevailing drive of Brazilian culture has been to assimilate difference, a process celebrated by Brazilian Modernists through a cannibalist metaphor. Concerned with being modern without imitating European art, they referred back to the cultural practices of some of the precolonial inhabitants of Brazil and celebrated cannibalism (*antropofagismo*) as a means of reconciling their admiration of Europe's avant-garde and their need to define their unique Brazilianness. This anthropophagic paradigm shares similarities with José Vasconcelos's modernist notion of the *raza cósmica* in Mexico.

In the Brazilian case, the Other is internalized through cannibalization, its admirable qualities absorbed, and its uniqueness denied.

Interpreters of Brazilian culture, perhaps seduced by the playful qualities of Modernist writing, often understand it as hospitable and open to difference. As such, they may overlook the destruction of the Other implied by the metaphor of anthropophagy and fail to associate it with a tendency in Brazilian society to avoid differences. A counter-reading might understand cannibalism as a means of eliminating differences through assimilation rather than facing them.

Brazilian society is organized in a vertical manner – a legacy of the patriarchal master/slave hierarchy established in the colonial period. Most Brazilians find it difficult to work against the social hierarchy to establish common interests across race, class, or gender boundaries. Looking to the literary realm to understand social and cultural inequalities is complicated in Brazil. After all, Machado de Assis (1839–1908), a central figure in Brazilian letters, was of mixed race and Clarice Lispector, the Brazilian author most studied internationally, was a Jewish immigrant. The continued popularity of the anthropophagic paradigm has remained largely unchallenged, and the idea of harmonious racial and cultural mixture still informs many readings of Brazilian literature and culture. Emphasis on Brazilians' ability to harmonize differences can provide symbolic cover for widespread discrimination against Brazilian women and minorities. Thus the prevailing discourse on race and gender relations – that they are egalitarian – contradicts social practices. The Brazilian literary works briefly considered here were published in the middle decades of the twentieth century: the 1950s (*The Devil to Pay in the Backlands*), 1960s (*Quarup*), and 1970s (*The Hour of the Star*). Their respective authors – Guimarães Rosa, Callado, and Lispector – address Brazilian social reality with distinct literary techniques. The discussion that follows places these writer's best-known works in their literary and social contexts, emphasizing how they call attention to contradictions and inequalities and how these differences relate to their roles as authors.

## The *Sertão* Is Brazil

João Guimarães Rosa's *Grande Sertão: Veredas* (*The Devil to Pay in the Backlands*, 1956), is set in the *sertão* or backlands, a space often considered socially backward. Established in the Brazilian imagination a half-century earlier by Euclides da Cunha in *Os Sertões* (*Rebellion in the Backlands*, 1902) as a harsh and isolated region of climatic and social extremes, the *sertão* in Guimarães Rosa's novel serves as a removed and highly detailed setting in which he raises a series of philosophical and psychological considerations. Locating his existential drama in the *sertão* of Minas Gerais, the author emphasizes liminal spaces, watercourses, and margins in this text, just as he does in another of his best-known writings, the short story *"A Terceira margem do Rio"* (The third bank of the river, 1962). In both works, the reader is suspended in Guimarães Rosa's fictional world. In keeping with its sense of remove, events in the novel are never precisely dated, though markers in the text indicate it is set sometime during the "Old Republic" (1889–1930). During this period the Brazilian presidency alternated between the economically dominant states of São Paulo and Minas Gerais. Under a system of informal agreements called *coronelismo* or the "politics of the governors," landed oligarchies selected state governors, who in turn chose Brazil's president.

*The Devil to Pay in the Backlands* is set in the São Francisco River valley, an area where society has been shaped by sharp distinctions between the landed and the landless. The social structure of this isolated region of the interior is intensely patriarchal and is dominated by cattle barons who wield tremendous authority. They exert their control by means of violence carried out by their personal militias comprised of *jagunços* (hired gunmen). The novel unfolds within the social context of these bands of *jagunços* and of *cangaceiros* – independent groups of socially disaffected outlaws, who also use violence to gain power – and is narrated by the protagonist Riobaldo, himself a former gunman.

In this world, men adhere to a strict code requiring them to prove their manliness through acts of courage and violence. Women are men's subordinates and are routinely subjected to their aggressions. One woman plays a significant role in *The Devil to Pay in the Backlands*. The novel features a warrior maiden who, however, is only revealed to be a woman upon her death near the end of the text. Speaking as a man after listening to her companions brag about raping and abusing women, Diadorim says to Riobaldo, "Women are such poor wretches" (145). Though she differs from other warrior maidens in that she spends most of her life (and dies) in disguise, she seems more drawn from literary history than from the life of a woman of the *sertão*. (Women disguised as men are a theme in *literatura de cordel*, Brazil's popular chapbook literature.) Riobaldo's apparently homosexual attraction to Diadorim torments him and this ambiguity, together with his doubts about the existence of the Devil, provides the impulse for his narration. He questions how he can love a man and be manly himself just as he wonders how we can deny existence of the Devil without denying the existence of God.

Most critics argue that Guimarães Rosa makes heroes of his *jagunços* and *cangaceiros* and they tend to refer to his characters in epic terms. In these readings, the *sertão* is the "real" Brazil and *The Devil to Pay in the Backlands* becomes Brazil's modern epic. Antônio Callado proposes a less lofty reading in the Cambridge lectures mentioned above:

> Rosa's humanity in the backlands of Brazil, those noble warriors, those rough gentlemen living according to ancient codes, are in fact trapped in time. They are imprisoned in the middle ages that Latin-American countries still inflict on their peasants. A large part of the emotion and the awe we feel on reading *Grande Sertão* is sensing, behind the savage beauty, the sheer waste of courage and heroism. (1974: 40)

Callado's interpretation highlights the poverty and inequality of life in the *sertão*, likening the social life there to that of feudal Europe. "Guimarães Rosa, 20 years ago, could still find knights on horseback in the cattle-raising spaces of Brazil. *Grande Sertão* is too complex a book to mean only one thing. But waste of man is surely one of its lessons" (1974: 40).

Guimarães Rosa's work both draws on earlier aesthetic experiments of the Modernists and shares characteristics with more socially oriented Brazilian regionalism of the 1930s. Not easily categorized, *The Devil to Pay in the Backlands* is set apart by critics as a masterwork of mid-twentieth-century Brazilian fiction that resists classification. Guimarães Rosa was born in rural Minas Gerais and, though his medical, military, and diplomatic careers drew him away, he returned to the *sertão* repeatedly in his life and in his fiction. Drawing upon his personal experiences, the author stylizes the speech of the region, experimenting with a host of forms including neologisms, archaisms, amalgamations, onomatopoeia, Latinisms, Indianisms, and odd morphological constructions such as verbs that end in diminutives or are replaced by gerunds. The style of the narration, especially the oddity of the diction, bolsters the sense of dislocation and unreality of the text. Though *The Devil to Pay in the Backlands* was published to immediate critical acclaim, it is relatively inaccessible. The novel's language is extremely convoluted, making it a dense and difficult read in Portuguese (and it is worth noting that English translation does not approximate the linguistic innovation of the original).

Written in the voice of Riobaldo and delivered to an implied interlocutor as a monologue of more than 450 pages, Guimarães Rosa's novel also breaks with traditional narrative form. *The Devil to Pay in the Backlands* is dotted with moments of implied dialogue between Riobaldo and his listener in which Riobaldo expresses doubt about his ability to narrate: "I know that I am telling this badly, just hitting the high spots I ramble" (81). Early in the novel he asks his interlocutor: "But don't tell me that a wise and learned person like you, sir, believes in the devil! You don't? I thank you. Your opinion reassures me" (6). Moments later, however, Riobaldo reverts to his own authority: "So, the devil rules his black kingdom, in animals, in men, in women. Even in children, I say" (6). Though he claims inability to tell his story well, Riobaldo's lengthy narration, directed toward his voiceless listener, subverts the notion that writing and speech are the purview of a privileged elite since the reader does not hear the more educated man of the city speak. For Silviano Santiago, this style of narration signals a break with what he calls the "memorialist" tendency of Latin American novels: "With this, the intellectual, city-bred and master of Western culture, becomes merely a listener and a scribe, inhabiting the textual space – not with his enormous and inflated *I* – but with his silence" (2001: 87). The narrative voice here is in conflict with itself and, as Santiago emphasizes, quite distinct from the often self-assured autobiographical voice of canonical Latin American literature. Riobaldo does not speak as one who understands his life story to be *the* story of his nation. He lacks the credentials both familial (for he is a bastard), and educational (for he failed to pursue his studies) to speak with traditional authority. A traveling bandit for most of his life, he is without a legitimate profession.

In his search for meaning Riobaldo is in constant, uneasy motion, a sense carried through to the end of the novel, the last word of the text being *travessia* or "passage." As he tells his tale, he seeks reassurance from his implied interlocutor and scribe, asking repeatedly for forgiveness for his failings as a narrator: "Am I telling things badly? I'll start again" (49). Despite what Santiago calls the "silent radicalism" of the listener, *The Devil to Pay in the Backlands* is similar to other novels, including Lispector's *The Hour of the Star*, in which, he argues, "the intellectual only serves to reap the discourse of the non-city-bred individual, of that being not incorporated into the so-called cultural and Europeanized values of Brazilian society" (89). The implied exchanges with his listener suggest Riobaldo's inferiority, as does the notion that the presence of the interlocutor is what enables the Other's speech. Nonetheless, Riobaldo has much to say to his more privileged listener: "I know almost nothing – but I have my doubts about many things" (10). *The Devil to Pay in the Backlands* reveals a clash of discourses, suggesting that the narrative is formed in the intersection between the implied listener's urban perceptions and Riobaldo's rural experience. Guimarães Rosa touches upon the dilemma of the writer who records; is he inside or outside that experience? This is a question Brazilian writers and artists will take up more consistently from this point forward.

## Unthinking Idealization

When Guimarães Rosa published *The Devil to Pay in the Backlands* in 1956, Brazilians were enjoying a relatively democratic period in their political history. The "Old Republic" ended in 1930 and the subsequent political era, dominated by the "Estado Novo" regime, had come to a dramatic close with Getúlio Vargas's suicide in 1954. In the *sertão*, much remained the same and social relations continued to be characterized by sharp distinctions between landed and landless. Though the last of the cangaceiro bands had been captured and executed, romanticized versions of their way life continued to be told in literatura de cordel and in Lima Barreto's *O Cangaceiro* (released worldwide by Columbia Pictures as *The Bandit*), which won prizes in the "Adventure Film" and "Music" categories at Cannes in 1953. Six years later, yet another film that romanticized those living at the margins of Brazilian society was to achieve even greater international success. In 1959, the French-Brazilian co-production *Black Orpheus* introduced a worldwide audience to *bossa nova* (a form of *samba*) and to a carefree and sanitized version of the *favelas* (*slums*) of Rio de Janeiro. The image of the happy but poor Brazilian *favelado* depicted in this film left its mark on the international viewing public's imaginary for decades to come.

Just as *O Cangaceiro* and *Black Orpheus* were bringing idealized poor Brazilians to the world's movie screens, a new cinema of social criticism was emerging in Latin America and elsewhere in the late 1950s and 1960s. In its early phase, Brazilian *Cinema Novo* also turned its lens toward the *favela* and the *sertão* and took a closer, less idealizing view. One of the movement's main Brazilian proponents, Glauber Rocha, wrote in a critique of *Black Orpheus* titled *"Orfeu:* Metafísica da Favela" (Orpheus: metaphysics in the *favela*): "A favela is a social disaster, nothing more, nothing less; the question is not of metaphysics but of hunger" (quoted in Stam, 1977: 173). Rocha and other Cinema Novo filmmakers would go on in the 1960s to make politicized films focused on Brazilian social reality and its conflicts.

*Cinema Novo* was one feature in a constellation of new approaches to cultural production emerging in Brazil in the 1960s that also encompassed music and theater. Socially inspired art was related to global struggles against neocolonialism, to the new religious focus on poverty and injustice brought about by Vatican II (1962–5), and to other Brazilian initiatives for justice such as Paulo Freire's "Pedagogy of the Oppressed." Many artistic productions were focused on social problems and directed at large (not necessarily literate) audiences. These works helped generate a national debate on politics and aesthetics. As part of this process, the Brazilian Left attempted to use artistic expression to bring revolutionary politics to a broad audience, hoping to put art at the service of social revolution. Heloisa Buarque de Hollanda describes the relationship between literary culture and politics in the 1960s: "the themes of modernization, of democratization, of nationalism and 'faith in the people' [were] at the center of the discussions, informing and delineating the necessity of a participatory art, forging the myth of the revolutionary reach of the poetic word" (2004: 21).

## The Left and the Center

Antônio Callado's *Quarup* (1967) is the first in his series of four novels tracing the fate of the Left in the years immediately before and after the military coup in 1964. Published during a period of political upheaval, it appeared in print just prior to the 1968 implementation of the AI-5, a law which imposed severe artistic and political censorship. Callado, a novelist, playwright, and journalist, was imprisoned for his political activities once just following the coup and again in 1968 after the AI-5 was enacted. *Quarup* is his best-known novel and may be read as a literary reflection upon the social and political problems facing Brazil in the 1960s. His reflection takes the form of an exploration undertaken by a number of Brazilian writers: the quest for national self-understanding. While on an expedition to find the geographic center of the country, the novel's protagonist, Nando, asks, "Do you think any other country has had such a long history of self-discovery as ours?" The expedition's ethnologist replies, "I doubt it. We've carried on the longest sustained introspection in the history of the world" (268).

In *Quarup*, the search to know one's self and to know one's nation requires shedding the familiar and the conventional. The novel takes the form of a *Bildungsroman*, following the "diseducation" of an idealistic young priest from the northeastern state of Pernambuco. As *Quarup* begins, Father Nando's dream is to build a community based on the model of the Jesuit missions of *Sete Povos,* seventeenth-century "Indian reductions" located in what is now the border region of Brazil, Uruguay, and Argentina. Often referred to as "utopias," the reductions were attacked and largely destroyed by marauding slavers from São Paulo and later by colonial government troops.

Nando idealizes the Indians of those communities and imagines them in Edenic terms: "The Jesuits understood God's message when they organized the Guaraní Indians. With this second Adam they founded the second Roman Empire, which was destroyed by the barbarians of São Paulo" (21). His illusions about re-creating this "paradise" are destroyed when he finally comes into contact with Indians in the Amazon's Xingú River valley and discovers that they are miserable with illness, destitute, and losing their lands to unchecked illegal encroachment. A friend working at a post run by the government's Indian Protection Service warns him shortly after his arrival there: "Don't delude yourself, Father; the pure reservoir is already infected with bacteria. And even if we want to preserve the Indians as ornamental animals or specimens for the Smithsonian Institution to study, we'll have to save Brazil first. You can't keep a trickle of water pure in a gutter" (167–8). The government has promised to make a large portion of the Xingú region into a national park/reservation. The post is preparing for a visit from President Getúlio Vargas, who will attend a *quarup* (a ritual renewal of the tribe) and inaugurate the park, when they learn that he has committed suicide. Vargas's death thus delays the government action that they hope will provide increased protections and rights for the Indians.

After his first experience in the Xingú, Nando joins an expedition to the geographic center of the country. Having learned that the Indians are not a tabula rasa, he nonetheless believes that one can best understand Brazil from the inside out. Here Callado takes up a theme common to Brazilian literature and one *Quarup* shares with *The Devil to Pay in the Backlands*. Some of the expedition's members envision the center as a "temple of nationalism" and one suggests, "We should make it illegal for any foreigner to set foot anywhere near the center. That will be our hand's breadth of liberated land" (282). As a result of their journey, they hope to understand the origins and essence of their country. Their search entails an affirmation of "pure" Brazilian culture, which is to be found away from the cosmopolitan coast. These events in the novel take place at roughly the same time as the inauguration of Brasília in 1960. The shifting of the nation's capital from the coast to the interior itself may be seen as the concretization of the notion, persistent among Brazilian intellectuals since the nineteenth century, that the interior is the "real" Brazil.

The search for national authenticity through an expedition to the heart of Brazil in *Quarup* echoes the efforts of the Scientific Exploration Commission of 1859 which was joined by Romantic poet Gonçalves Dias (1823–64), who also hoped to understand Brazil in its essence by traveling to its interior. Again Callado's protagonist is stripped of his illusions. Once in the interior, the expedition can only find its way using maps made by foreigners. And having imagined that the Indians living furthest from the coast will be better off for not having been exposed to outsiders, they discover that a measles epidemic has destroyed the social structure of the Cren-acarore, the tribe living closest to the center. Once again political events on the coast penetrate the "pristine" center as news of the military coup of April 1964 reaches the expedition. Coastal "civilization" has reached the interior and corrupted indigenous culture.

To complete what might be read as a descent into hell rather than a journey to paradise, the expedition ends with the death of its leader, the militant primitivist, Fontoura, who expires after suffering an attack from the sauba ants whose enormous anthill the group finds at the geographic center of the country. The irony of discovering an anthill at the heart of the nation recalls a refrain in Mário de Andrade's *Macunaíma* (1928), "Pouca saúde e muita saúva os males do Brasil são" (poor health and too many ants are Brazil's ills), as well as the famous saying penned by French naturalist Saint-Hilaire (1779–1853), "Ou o Brasil acaba com a saúva ou a saúva acaba com o Brasil" (Either Brazil finishes off the ants or the ants will finish off Brazil). At this point in *Quarup* the crisis of national identity has come to the fore and the Indian serves as a metaphor for the dying nation. Callado depicts the indigenous culture as destined to disappear, repeating a theme of miscegenation common to Brazilian *Indianista* literature: "As they grew gaunt, withered, and pale, the Indians looked less and less like Mongolians and more and more like Brazilians. If it had not been for their nakedness they might have been a group of hungry men from Paraíba, Ceará, or Minas Gerais" (338).

Toward the end of the novel in a chapter titled "The Word," Nando is imprisoned and tortured by the military for his involvement in Pernambuco with the *Movimento de Cultura Popular*, a movement whose primary aim was to call the masses to social action through education. The MCP's literacy campaign was led by Paulo Freire (1921–77), whose pedagogical method formed its core. In *Quarup*, as in reality, the 1964 coup brings an end to this and other civil rights movements in Brazil. After his release, Nando organizes a commemorative feast in honor of a fallen comrade, Levindo. The supper mimics a *quarup* ceremony and Nando symbolically takes Levindo's name.

In *Quarup*, Callado exposes the paternalism of his intellectual protagonist whose utopian fantasies are bound to fail. Nando must find himself, leaving the priesthood and his formal education behind, before he can be of any use to his country. By the novel's end, he has had a critical awakening through his experiences with Brazilians from varying social groups. While it can be read as a critique of the intelligentsia, *Quarup* is not without hope for the future: in its final passages Nando leaves the coast to join a guerrilla movement in the *sertão*. In his next novel, *Bar Don Juan* (1971), Callado takes a far more pessimistic view, depicting egocentric revolutionaries who lack the skills to resist Brazil's right-wing government.

## Speaking without a Voice

In his analysis of film "allegories of underdevelopment" from the 1960s and 1970s, critic Ismail Xavier points to the social impact of the "conservative modernization" that took place under military rule in Brazil. "The Left – aware of the contradictions between imperialist and national interests and split between populist alliances and armed struggle – was defeated and had to face the right-wing administration, often under the military, of a model of economic growth that excluded the majority" (1997: 4). The *milagre brasileiro* or Brazilian "economic miracle" of the late 1960s and early 1970s was miraculous only for the rich. And the majority of Brazil's citizens were plunged even further into poverty with the subsequent economic downturn brought on by the worldwide oil crisis of 1973. Brazil's "democratic experiment" of the early 1960s had failed and, especially after 1968, socially committed artists and intellectuals were repressed by the military regime.

Unlike Antônio Callado, Clarice Lispector is not considered a politically "engaged" writer in the usual sense. Many of her novels and stories feature well-to-do, urban women – often mothers and housewives – who focus upon their personal sense of dislocation as they realize the inanity of their lives. Nonetheless, there is a social message in Lispector's fiction since her work may be read as an indictment of androcentrism. As Earl Fitz explains, her characters are "depicted as seeking a personally satisfying sense of psychological, political, and sexual identity within androcentric social structures" (1985: 11). Their search is conjoined with the author's constant interrogation of the relationship between language, power, and life.

Lispector's concern with the ability of the word to stunt human development and expression reaches its high mark in *The Hour of the Star*, published shortly before she died in 1977. In centering her novel on Macabéa, an impoverished and under-educated migrant from the rural northeast, Lispector calls attention to the plight of the many thousands of *nordestinos* who arrive in Brazil's crowded urban slums each year looking for, but not finding, adequate employment and shelter. Most critics consider *The Hour of the Star* to be Lispector's most socially grounded. This view is bolstered by an uncharacteristic reference she makes in its preface: "This story unfolds in a state of emergency and public calamity. It is an unfinished book because it offers no answer. An answer I hope someone somewhere in the world may be able to provide" (8). Her treatment of the problems facing a *nordestina* and the larger society links Lispector to the literary tradition of Euclides da Cunha and his *Os Sertões*, forming an unexpected connection (Fitz, 1985: 93).

Lispector was herself an immigrant. Born in Tchechelnik, Ukraine in 1920 while her Jewish family was emigrating to escape religious persecution, she arrived in Brazil as an infant two months later. A Russian emigrant who didn't feel Russian and didn't speak her parents' Yiddish language, Lispector identified herself as a Brazilian and Portuguese was her native language. Like Guimarães Rosa, she is usually described as unclassifiable in terms of her literary counterparts. Lispector's work shares with her Modernist predecessors an experimental quality, but her explorations are taken for a wholly different purpose as she is not part of a group expressly seeking to renovate Brazilian literature. Her first novel, *Perto do Coração Selvagem* (*Near to the Wild Heart*), was published in 1943 to immediate critical acclaim, despite the fact that it was radically different from the documentary realism in vogue in Brazil at the time. From this point forward, Lispector writes fiction that calls attention to the impossibility of the act of narrating reality, always alluding to what is inexpressible through the unstable medium of the written language.

The thirteen alternate titles to *The Hour of the Star*, listed vertically on the novel's title page, announce this instability and point to the multiple questions Lispector raises as she complicates the relationships between author, narrator, character, and reader:

> The Blame is Mine or The Hour of the Star or Let her Fend for Herself or The Right to Protest [followed by the author's signature in script]. As for the Future. or Singing the Blues or She Doesn't Know How to Protest or A Sense of Loss or Whistling in the Dark Wind or I Can Do Nothing or A record of Preceding Events or A Tearful Tale or A Discreet Exit by the Back Door. (9)

The semi-literate Macabéa, and her educated bourgeois narrator, Rodrigo S. M., belong to no social movements and participate in no organized struggles. Instead, the relationship between them raises questions about the ability of literature to address social differences. As he slowly works his way toward narrating Macabéa's story, Rodrigo emphasizes her social insignificance:

> There are thousands of girls like this girl from the Northeast to be found in the slums of Rio de Janeiro, living in bedsitters or toiling behind counters for all they are worth. They aren't even aware of the fact that they are superfluous and that nobody cares a damn about their existence. Few of them ever complain and as far as I know they never protest, for there is no one to listen. (14)

Lines of gender and class are in constant tension in the novel and are most evident in the implied relationship between Lispector and the novel's male narrator, and their ambivalence, in turn, toward his "creation," the immiserated Macabéa. Like most of Lispector's woman characters, Macabéa experiences intermittent flashes of self-recognition. Even as she is confused by world around her, the reader senses that she possesses a fundamental innocence and a lack of self-awareness that oddly seems to lend her strength. In not thinking about her identity, Macabéa becomes an example of a pure being, one who completely adheres to the senses and constitutes a negation of discursive reason (Rosenbaum, 2002: 59). Though she is presented in terms of the resources she lacks (money, beauty, education, food), Macabéa becomes a powerful, yet paradoxically voiceless figure in the text who mysteriously and stubbornly remains outside interpretation, despite Rodrigo's attempts to tell the "truth" about her. Rodrigo's difficulties, presented to the reader in numerous asides, echo but are a more obvious component of the text than those of Guimarães Rosa's narrator, Riobaldo. The narrator wonders how he will approach Macabéa without destroying her:

> Remember that no matter what I write, my basic material is the word. So this story will consist of words that form phrases from which there emanates a secret meaning

that exceeds both words and phrases. Like every writer, I am clearly tempted to use succulent terms: I have at my command magnificent adjectives, robust nouns, and verbs so agile that they glide through the atmosphere as they move into action. For surely words are actions? Yet I have no intention of adorning the word, for were I to touch the girl's bread, that bread would turn to gold – and the girl (she is nineteen years old) the girl would be unable to bite into it and consequently die of hunger. (14–15)

Macabéa has been excluded from cultural and economic exchange by her poverty. Like the Maccabees to whom her name alludes – Jews who resisted domination by and acculturation into Greek society in 165 BCE – she resists incorporation into urban consumerist society. At the mercy of others – the narrator Rodrigo, her bullying boyfriend Olímpico, her co-worker, Glória who steals Olímpico from her – she tends to wait for things to happen to her. When she does take action on her own behalf, the results, as this exchange with a doctor exemplifies, are both painful and absurd:

Are you dieting to lose weight, my girl?
Macabéa didn't know how to reply.
— What do you eat?
— Hot dogs.
— Is that all?
— Sometimes I eat a mortadella sandwich.
— What do you drink? Milk?
— Only coffee and soft drinks.
— What do you mean by soft drinks? — He probed, not quite knowing how to proceed.
He questioned her at random:
— Do you sometimes have fits of vomiting?
— Oh, never! – she exclaimed in a panic, for she was not a fool to go wasting food, as I've explained. (67)

The incompetent and lazy doctor, knowing full well that she is undernourished because she cannot afford adequate food, insists that Macabéa is dieting. Resentful because he must treat poor "rejects," he takes an X-ray, but makes no real effort to help her:

— You're in the early stages of pulmonary tuberculosis.
Macabéa didn't know if this was a good or a bad thing. But being ever so polite she simply said:
— Many thanks.
The doctor resisted any temptation to be compassionate. He advised her: when you can't decide what you should eat, make yourself a generous helping of Italian spaghetti. (68)

Macabéa is unable to fully communicate and therefore cannot comprehend what the doctor's prognosis means. Having suffered the effects of deprivation throughout her life, she does not allow herself hope for the future and in this way makes herself content. Only at her clearest moment of self-recognition, her "hour of the star," does she permit herself the luxury of contemplating the future. This moment occurs as she lies dying in the gutter, having been struck by a Mercedes Benz: "Today, she thought, today is the dawn of my existence" (80).

## As for the Future

This brief chapter has traced the means by which Clarice Lispector, João Guimarães Rosa, and Antônio Callado – three "stars" of twentieth-century Brazilian literature – addressed questions of identity, difference, and the place of the writer/intellectual in their best-known novels. Guimarães Rosa's *The Devil to Pay in the Backlands*, published in 1956, features an implied dialogue in which we hear the voice of the backlander and the silence of the lettered man of the city. Within this text, the voice of the *sertão* represents Brazil. In 1967, after the country has suffered a military coup, Callado's *Quarup* undoes romantic notions both about how the "truth" of the nation resides in those who live in its interior and about the ability of intellectuals to understand Brazil's people and their struggles. A decade later (with the country still under military rule), Lispector both calls attention to the "public calamity" of the urban poor and explores the limits of her narrative's ability to address an impoverished protagonist who lives at the margins of Brazilian society. Unable to fully grasp her, the author creates Macabéa out of absences: "this book is composed without words: like a mute photograph. This book is a silence and an interrogation" (17).

At the turn of the twentieth century, the poor outcast of Brazilian literature was located by Euclides da Cunha in the arid backlands and depicted as a victim of climate and geography. Today's victim of social exclusion, like Macabéa, is most likely to live in Brazil's large cities that are home to eighty percent of the country's population. In the decades since the publication of *The Hour of the Star*, the urban poor have increasingly begun to publish their own literature. *Quarto de Despejo* (*Child of the Dark*, 1960), in which Carolina de Jesús recounts her attempts to eke out a living for herself and her children by picking trash on the streets of São Paulo, may be seen as a lone early example. More recent writings by the urban poor emphasize the everyday violence and dehumanization faced by the millions who are deprived of the minimum conditions of citizenship. The world they describe echoes the machismo, violence, and lordism of Guimarães Rosa's *sertão,* but most definitely without that novel's sense of remove. Taking the publication (and film adaptation) of Paulo Lins's *Cidade de Deus* (*City of God*, 2002), as an example, we might say that the Brazilian poor have become their own cultural subjects. Perhaps they will be able to speak to Clarice Lispector's silences.

## References and Further Reading

### References

*Note:* translations of texts cited above are mine unless otherwise indicated.

Callado, Antônio (1970 [1967]). *Quarup.* Trans. Barbara Shelby. New York: Knopf.
— (1974). *Censorship and Other Problems of Latin-American Writers.* Working Paper No. 14. Cambridge: Centre of Latin American Studies, University of Cambridge.
Cândido, Antônio (1995 [1969]). "Literature and underdevelopment." Trans. Howard S. Becker. In *On Literature and Society*, pp. 119–41. Princeton: Princeton University Press.
Fitz, Earl (1985). *Clarice Lispector.* Boston: Twayne.
Hollanda, Heloisa Buarque de (2004). *Impressões de viagem: CPC, vanguarda e desbunde (1960/70).* 5th ed. Rio de Janeiro: Aeroplano.
Lispector, Clarice (1992). *The Hour of the Star.* Trans. Giovanni Pontiero. New York: New Directions.
Rosa, João Guimarães (1963). *The Devil to Pay in the Backlands: "The Devil in the Street, in the Middle of the Whirlwind."* Trans. James L. Taylor and Harried de Onís. New York: Knopf.
Rosenbaum, Yudith (2002). *Clarice Lispector.* São Paulo: Publifolha.
Santiago, Silviano (2001). "Worth its weight: Brazilian modernist fiction." Trans. Tom Burns and Ana Lúcia Gazzola. In Ana Lúcia Gazzola (ed.), *The Space In-Between: Essays on Latin American Culture*, pp. 79–92. Durham, NC: Duke University Press.
Stam, Robert (1997). *Tropical Multiculturalism: A Comparative History of Race in Brazilian Cinema and Culture.* Durham, NC: Duke University Press.
Xavier, Ismail (1997). *Allegories of Underdevelopment: Aesthetics and Politics in Modern Brazilian Cinema.* Minneapolis: University of Minnesota Press.

### Further Reading

Alonso, Cláudia Pazos, and Williams, Claire, eds. (2002). *Closer to the Wild Heart: Essays on Clarice Lispector.* Oxford: European Research Center, University of Oxford.
Barbosa, Maria José Somerlate (1997). *Clarice Lispector: Spinning the Webs of Passion.* New Orleans, LA: University Press of the South.
Fitz, Earl E. (2001). *Sexuality and Being in the Poststructuralist Universe of Clarice Lispector: The Différance of Desire.* Austin: University of Texas Press.
Hollanda, Heloisa Buarque de, and Gonçalves, Marcos A. (1975). *Cultura e participação nos anos 60.* São Paulo: Brasiliense.
Peixoto, Marta (1994). *Passionate Fictions: Gender, Narrative, and Violence in Clarice Lispector.* Minneapolis: University of Minnesota Press.
Pinto, Cristina Ferreira (1985). *A Viagem do herói no romance de Antônio Callado.* Brasilia, DF: Thesaurus.
Pontiero, Giovanni (1992). "Afterword." In Clarice Lispector, *The Hour of the Star.* Trans. Giovanni Pontiero, pp. 89–96. New York: New Directions.
Sá, Lúcia (1998). "An epic of the Brazilian Revolution: Callado's *Quarup*," *Portuguese Studies*, 14: 195–204.
Vincent, John S. (1978). *João Guimarães Rosa.* Boston: Twayne.
Zilberman, Regina, et al. (1998). *Clarice Lispector: A narração do indizível.* Porto Alegre: EDIPUC.

# 30

# Feminist Insurrections: From Queiroz and Castellanos to Morejón, Poniatowska, Valenzuela, and Eltit

*Adriana J. Bergero and Elizabeth A. Marchant*

## Introduction

Feminist engagement is understood by some Latin American intellectuals and artists as elitist and anachronistic – a remnant of the political movements of the 1960s. Though there is a lingering uneasiness around the terms "feminism" and "feminist," it is nonetheless possible to trace a strong current of counter-discourse in the writings of Latin American women. Across the region, female authors have, through written expression, called into question patriarchal constructions of the feminine in various historical and national contexts. All confront the problem of textual authority and many resist patriarchal definitions of and limits upon what womanhood means. Women often write from the margins, the uncharted regions of language where they may blur the boundaries between public and private as they articulate new spaces. Though not all necessarily call themselves feminists, the Latin American women we will discuss here undertake artistic projects that explore relationships of power and question social hierarchies.

The division of intellectual labor of modern historiography associates women with difference, the private sphere, passivity, *minor* genres, sentimentality, the body, the quotidian, and the fluidity of boundaries. Latin American women's creative expressions – be they fictions, essays, journalism, performance art, or political activism – constitute a multicentered debate and inner polemics seeking to recode women's social spaces and symbolic formations in a struggle for representation and self-representation. The goal of Victoria Ocampo (1890–1970) was to break the male-dominated literary monologue. But *how* was that monologue to be interrupted? Alicia Salomone comments on several propositions in Ocampo's personal correspondence with Gabriela Mistral (1889–1957). Ocampo seeks the endorsement of male intellectuals and relies on a Eurocentric view of culture which will cause some critics to dismiss her as elitist and out of touch with Latin American realities. Mistral's choice to highlight multicultural Latin America, children, and the dispossessed responded, as did the work of her contemporaries José Carlos Mariátegui and José Vasconcelos, to the surfacing of new social actors forged by Modernity (Salomone, 2004: 38). Ocampo and Mistral's correspondence brings into focus at least two important features of Latin American women's writing in the early twentieth century: it both debunks the notion that women writers were so exceptional that they wrote in isolation from one another and reveals marked differences between them (Marchant, 1999: 5–6). Aware of Ocampo's conflicted place as both a feminist intellectual and a powerful broker of French culture, Mistral urges Ocampo to seek her own language from her personal experience. As a writer who emphasizes her position as a migrant subject, an unsure upstart moving back and forth across the intersection of cultures in formation, Mistral explains to Ocampo that Americanness has no single definition: "There are a thousand possible directions and paths to follow, and with your subtle aim, you can choose the least expected ones" (Horan and Meyer, 2003: 30). The authors discussed below choose very different paths. Their work challenges the notion that all women's writing is similar and makes impossible a unified vision of Latin American women's writing. Rather, it bears out the assertion that gender is constituted at a crossroads overlapped by other constructions such as history, class extraction, ethnicity, ideology, sexuality, race, and community.

## Alfonsina Storni (1892–1938)

The debate as to where to address the new symbolic space written *from the woman's body* and *about life* was engaged by Alfonsina Storni (1892–1938), the first Latin American intellectual to understand the impact of mass culture and its *romance of love* as agoraphobic worlds furnished only to smooth the clashes between women's search for expression and social conventions. Storni began to seek to a readership beyond high culture, employing female-oriented mass cultural discourses such as sentimental novels, *folletín*, and autobiography (Salomone, 1994: 53). Post-boom women's writing would later seek an international readership through market-oriented use of romance literature, melodrama, *boleros*, and other popular music. But the cultural intersection between women's writing, mass culture, and a developing female audience serves, in Storni's case, to counter the hyper-dramatized and fraught image of domesticity through humor, irony and parody (54). Storni, like her Brazilian contemporary Patrícia Galvão (1910–62), called attention to the gendered effects of the negative aspects of Modernity by addressing the plight of women workers. Their social models, cast off by formal Modernity and forged within the turbulent spontaneity of the organic city, contribute to the modern debate about women's identity in plural terms.

## Rachel De Queiroz (1910–2003)

Like Storni and Galvão, Rachel de Queiroz adopted both feminist and socialist stances in her writing. Unlike Storni and Galvão, she enjoyed critical acclaim from the outset of her astonishingly long and productive career, including the distinction of being the first woman writer elected to Brazil's Academy of Letters. We will explore here some of the reasons why she achieved literary success, for her trajectory reveals important details about women's efforts to claim authority in the field of Latin American literature in the twentieth century.

Rachel de Queiroz exploded onto the literary scene in a distinctly "unfeminine" manner. The publication of her first novel, *O Quinze* (*The Year Fifteen*, 1992), in 1930 provoked disbelief that its author was a woman. In the words of Graciliano Ramos:

> *O Quinze* fell suddenly there in the middle of '30 and wounded the spirits more than José Américo's novel [*A Bagaceira*, 1928] because it was by a woman and, what was really astonishing, by a young woman. Could it really be by a woman? I didn't believe it. Having read the book and seen the picture in the newspaper, I shook my head: there is no one with this name. It's a prank. A girl like that writing a novel! It must be the pseudonym of some bearded type. (1962: 140)

With a prose style that was direct and nearly devoid of adjectives, Rachel de Queiroz, at age 20, garnered the attention and praise of Brazil's literary establishment. She is applauded by Mário de Andrade, for example, for giving Brazilians "a new way of conceiving fiction about drought" and for writing "a humane book, a real drought, without exaggeration, without sonority, a dry drought, pure, detestable, gruesome" (1976: 251–2).

Mário de Andrade's praise provides a clue as to how a young woman from Ceará achieved such early success. Brazil's literary establishment read her novel strictly as a depiction of the drought of 1915. As Ferreira-Pinto points out, they largely failed to recognize that its plot turns around a woman, Conceição, who maintains her independence by refusing to marry (2004: xi). This pattern will recur throughout her career as critics focus primarily upon the regional aspects of her novels, positioning Rachel de Queiroz as one of the foremost exponents of the *romance nordestina*, or regionalist novel, of the northeast. Through her profound identification with her homeland, she thus attains an independent position that allows her to challenge social, and particularly gender, conventions, often drawing upon a tradition of powerful northeastern matriarchs as models for independent women.

Though her novels are often read as *romances nordestinas,* Rachel de Queiroz understood her point of view as distinct from that of her male contemporaries: "José Lins do Rego's approach was that of the *menino do engenho* [plantation boy], of the master of the plantation. Mine was never that of the *sinhazinha* [master's daughter]. It is of the woman totally integrated into Northeastern life. I take this approach with all of my characters" (quoted in Hollanda, 1997: 114). In her novels, as in her many volumes of newspaper *crônicas* with which she consolidated her national renown, the author strongly identifies with her northeastern homeland, lending all of her work a touch of the autobiographical. Her blending of the autobiographical, the regional, and the unconventional is evident in *As Três Marias* (1939) (*The Three Marias*, 1963), now in its twenty-fourth edition. For Heloisa Buarque de Hollanda, this novel carries the signature of Rachel de Queiroz in its "profound identification of the feminine universe with the universe of an almost historical regional power" (1997: 114). She is the first woman writer in Brazil to achieve widespread recognition, recognition that nearly always emphasizes the regional and overlooks the feminist aspects of her work. Yet Rachel de Queiroz always expressed concern in her writing for the roles and status of women in society. In fact, today's reader may be surprised by the treatment of female sexuality in her early works which include lesbian desire, sex outside marriage, and abortion, among other unconventional literary themes.

*The Three Marias* displays well her approach to women and their place in society. The title refers to the three schoolmates it depicts, all named Maria, who live in the woman-centered world of a convent school run by nuns. In addition to its biblical references, "the Three Marias" is also the title given by Brazilians to the three stars at the center of the constellation of Orion. A nun recognizes that the three girls, like the stars in Orion, form an inseparable trio. "We ourselves took pride in it, we felt ourselves to be set apart in an aristocratic and celestial trinity, in the midst of all the other plebeians. Heavenly personages have a prestige that has always dazzled humans; and comparing us to the stars was like an intoxication newly experienced, a pretext for fantasies and whimsy" (26). Dreaming of distant places rather than the biblical Marys, the girls adopt the symbol of the three stars, drawing them in their notebooks and, in a scene with strong sexual undertones, inscribing them on their bodies:

> Hidden out behind the lavatories – our regular headquarters – sitting on the ground, with our stockings pulled down, we used the point of a scissors to make the row of three stars on our thighs. It was painful. It was done with light scraping, until the blood came. I made my cut decisively, with my teeth clenched. Glória, fainthearted and patient, made her scratches very slowly. And Maria José lost her courage on the last star, and it was necessary for Glória to come help her with her soft hand. From time to time she would make a face and groan, and Glória would raise her hand: 'Do you want me to stop?' She shook her head. She had to keep going until the end . . . Red with blood, the three stars shone on my white skin as if they had flowered from the flesh. (27–8).

The novel's protagonist, Guta, eventually leaves the convent school. As *The Three Marias* closes, she is unmarried and secretly pregnant. In the final pages, she goes to an amusement park and repeatedly gets on the most violent rides, causing herself to miscarry. At the novel's close, she moves into an uncertain, but independent, future. Guta is but one of several of Rachel de Queiroz's female protagonists who reject motherhood and family, beginning in her first novel with Conceição, who claims she was born to be an "old maid," and ending sixty-two years later with the protagonist of her final novel, *Memorial de Maria Moura* (Memorial of Maria Moura, 1992), the leader of a gang of outlaws who, in the words of the author, "is everything that I wanted to be and couldn't" (Hollanda, 1997: 113).

In her study of the uproar surrounding Rachel de Queiroz's 1977 election to the Brazilian Academy of Letters entitled "Rachel's Gown," Buarque de Hollanda signals her unusual position:

Among the several fields of observation that emerge in the enigmatic crossroads of Rachel's singular professional career and the historical obstacles raised to women's professional recognition, particularly in the first half of the century, I chose her triumph over Article 2 of the founding Statues of the Brazilian Academy of Letters, which determined that "only native Brazilians [*brasileiros natos*] can be members of the Academy." The orthodox interpretation of this sentence by members of the Academy defied even the most elementary rules of grammar when it defined the plural *brasileiros* as not including the combination of female Brazilians (*brasileiras*) and male ones (*brasileiros*). (1999: 81)

Having admitted Rachel de Queiroz, the men of the Academy must acknowledge that one of the "immortals" possesses a female body. And, as Buarque de Hollanda notes, they conduct the debate over the national consecration of a woman writer as if it were really a question of grammar (83). The ensuing discussion in the Academy and in the press centering on what the then 67-year-old author will wear to the induction ceremony – in lieu of the traditional stylized military outfit and sword – reveal the deep anxieties regarding control and authority that remained despite this woman's acceptance in to the "House of Machado de Assis" and the enormous celebration it generated.

A pillar of twentieth-century Brazilian literature who openly rejected any formal association with feminist groups, Rachel de Queiroz was nonetheless a self-styled feminist. Her work, strongly rooted in her northeastern homeland, is unconventional, unsentimental, and decidedly unmaternal. As the tattoo scene and the self-induced miscarriage of *The Three Marias* suggest, she does not employ the female body in traditional ways. Rather, she sets up a tension between tradition and transgression (Gotlib, 1991: 125) that will become more common in the work of Latin American women writers later in the twentieth century.

## Rosario Castellanos (1925–74)

Such is the case of Rosario Castellanos who, like Rachel de Queiroz, both challenges stereotypes and sets some of her best-known works in the region in which she was raised. With her early novels, *Balún-Canán* (1957) (*The Nine Guardians*, 1958) and *Oficio de Tinieblas* (1962) (*The Book of Lamentations*, 1996), Castellanos addresses the social tensions in Chiapas – the conflict between its Tzotzil Indians and its large-landholding ranchers – merging her concerns with the ideology of cultures, the status of women, and the plight of the indigenous peoples of southern Mexico. In these texts, women's bodies are the locus of subordination that mirrors the historical subordination of the indigenous (Guerra-Cunningham, 1991: 119).

*The Nine Guardians* not only subverts Modernity's triumphal narratives (Castillo, 1992: 244), but draws attention to the severing abyss of the Nation embodied by the white Western-educated child narrator and the dehumanized and semi-slave Tzeltal-speaking Indian of Chiapas. Both are captured in a bitter battle over diverse storytelling and cultural hierarchies whose genesis bypasses but includes them. A young girl, the least valued individual of the dominant class, and her indigenous nanny, the most marginalized member of the national culture, compete "for the lowest possible stakes" (250). As Castillo notes, any sense of a female collectivity in this text is deeply fragmented. The social practices of reading and writing have historically accentuated exclusions and sites of oppression while accommodating the agency of educated women of the upper and middle classes. The fact that the two speak divergent languages, one of which is public and official while the other remains oral and intermediated by cultural translation, makes it problematic, as Castillo contends, to use blanket phrases such as *women's condition* or *women's writing*. Along with Latin American women writers such as Amanda Labarca, Juana de Ibarbourou, Teresa de la Parra, Cecilia Meireles, Antonieta Rivas Mercado, Gabriela Mistral, and Alfonsina Storni, Castellanos questions universality by searching for new gendered identities beyond cultural reproduction. In doing so, she creates a new set of images and messages about women in Mexico.

Castellanos explores women's experiences throughout her writings, which span all of the literary genres. With the broad reach of her work, she serves as a role model for women writers across the Americas. She was, as Ahern asserts, ahead of her time in her approach to and critique of women's subordination: "well before the call by French feminists to write the self, decode the body, and destroy the myths inside and outside ourselves, Rosario Castellanos was practicing an *écriture feminine* in Mexico: the body as sign, puns as poems, language as oppressor, silence as meaning" (1988: xv). In her mature writings, Castellanos employs parody and pastiche to deconstruct modern femininity. And while her early texts address the situation of women and indigenous Mexicans, in her later works she employs the metaphor of domesticity to transmit subversive messages about the socially acceptable roles of wife and mother.

The apex of Castellanos's ongoing critique of Mexican culture is her posthumously published play *El Eterno Femenino: Farsa* (1975) (*The Eternal Feminine*, 1988), in which she employs the figures of female archetypes including Malinche, Sor Juana, and the Virgen of Guadalupe to explore the oppression of women. Set in the quintessentially feminine space of a beauty parlor, the play follows the experiences of Lupita, a customer, who has come to have her hair done for her wedding. A salesman has convinced the salon owner to install in a hairdryer a device meant to induce dreams appropriate to a woman, "that she is the prettiest woman in the world; that all men are falling in love with her; that all women envy her" (276). Lupita is chosen to try out the hairdryer and the ensuing scenes depict her experiences as, under the influence of the malfunctioning device, she encounters a series of women who destroy and rework the stereotyped images assigned to them by Mexican culture. Castellanos brings together in this one humorous text a set of themes that appear scattered across her other writings: domesticity as a discursive strategy, the destruction of the ideal of female self-sacrifice, women participating in their own oppression and oppressing other women. Throughout the play, women both act out stereotypes and their own collusion with them.

In the play's final act, unnamed upper-class Mexican women discuss options for confronting gender oppression. After agreeing that imitating their "blonde cousins" in North America and Europe will not solve their problems, one "lady" makes the statement that we have come to associate closely with Castellanos's artistic message: "it is not good enough to imitate the models proposed for us that are answers to circumstances other than our own. It isn't even enough to discover who we are. We have to invent ourselves" (356). Her writing may be read, then, as a series of multilayered studies of what it means, within a variety of historical and geographical contexts, to be a Mexican and a woman. Throughout her works, Castellanos stretches the limits of universal womanhood and essentialist assumptions about a unifying consensus around nation, gender, and genre.

## Nancy Morejón (1944–)

For Nancy Morejón, a black woman in post-revolutionary Cuba, to maneuver through these intersections requires unconventional resources and discursive positions. Barradas (1996) suggests that Morejón's reverse logic, pragmatism, and concreteness counter the exotic uses of Afro-Caribbean folklore promoted by masculinist *negritud*, including that of Nicolás Guillén's portrayal of the *mujer nueva* and the eroticization of her body. Morejón argues against such blithe male self-fulfillment by reinserting black women into the atrocious history of slavery and linking them to the dispossession and loss of the diasporas. Since it is impossible to trace back the slave's genealogy, Morejón claims, "[r]ace as an historical fact has marked me, more than the biological. How many relatives, how many cousins . . . have I missed?" (Cordones-Cook, 1996: 66). "That idea of dispersion has tortured me," she says, but it never confuses her compelling revision of cultural archives. Instead of the enthralling body of the *mulata*, fulfiller of male fantasies, her poem "Amo a mi amo" (Master to my master) in *Octubre imprescindible* (1982; *Essential October*, 1984) offers a distressing polysemantic loop, overcome when the female slave gradually becomes aware of her oppression and her master's cruelty. The poetic voice moves from "loving" her master every night to plotting her revenge: "I see myself knife in hand, skinning him like an innocent calf." The slave is strangled by the compulsive loop ("amo a mi amo") as much as by forced sexual intercourse.

Morejón's female model gives central stage to an historical archive of anger; compelled both by a long history of exploitation and the continuity of stereotypes fueled by gender hierarchies in pre- and post-revolutionary Cuba. Her best-known poems depict Afro-Cuban women seeking freedom both for themselves and for their communities. In these works, she links personal struggle to the collective, refusing to separate anti-racism or feminism from class struggle. She thus fuses her concerns for black Cubans, particularly women, and the aims of the Cuban Revolution. In "Mujer Negra" (Black woman) from *Parajes de una época* (Places of a time, 1979), for example, she traces the experiences of an African woman from the horrors of the middle passage through her life as a slave and her eventual participation in an armed uprising that frees her people. Morejón's women carry scars which serve as bodily reminders that "love" is made of whip's lashes, and they are committed to remembering.

Though most often read through the lens of Cuban social relations, Morejón's writing includes a Pan-Caribbean dimension that has recently drawn increased critical attention. In an interview with Elaine Fido she says: "I think it is very important in these times for us to read Caribbean literature written by women because in our tradition we have had the male view of the Caribbean and we have to recognize now that these male views have been sometimes only sexual: a view that has limited women to sex" (Morejón, 1990: 266). Morejón refers to a community of women writers in the Caribbean who present diverse literary alternatives to a narrow, sexualized view of black women.

A parallel community appears in the cultural connections she draws between Caribbean women in her poetry, in which she both emphasizes their solidarity and gives shape to their local histories. Her critical position, as Linda Howe asserts, "has implications that go far beyond her pro-revolutionary stance vis-à-vis capitalist consumer societies such as the United States" (Howe, 1999: 158). As such, critics read beyond Cuba in Morejón's work. For example, in a recent essay Lesley Feracho illustrates how Caribbean women in distinct historical, geographical, and political contexts serve as agents of resistance, survival, and regeneration in Morejón's poetry. Feracho's reading of "Escrito, Al Final del siglo, Para una Semblanza de Camila Henríquez Ureña" [Written, at the end of the century, to a portrait of Camila Henríquez Ureña] aptly traces the lines of intercultural community and agency in Morejón's poetic homage to a Dominican intellectual: "The Cuban poet, writing of the Dominican professor, highlights a coming together not only of classical Greek, Roman, and English literature but also of African, Cuban, Haitian, and Dominican culture in a communal act" (Feracho, 2005: 987). The links between these elements culminate in the poem's last stanza: "The Carbalí princesses / Bathe themselves in the waters of Artibonite / And dance a masquerade of feathers / In Quisqueya" (trans. Feracho; ibid.). The bathing dance brings together the Cuban descendants of the Caribalí of Nigeria in a river that has its source in the Dominican Republic and flows to the sea in Haiti, thus linking two of the islands of the Caribbean to each other and to Africa.

Such linking and historical movement is a common feature of Morejón's poetry. As Rosemary Geisdorfer Feal suggests, we can read in Morejón's work "a progressive or evolving" identity composed of distinct historical voices that, taken together, form a "collective constituency" (26). This constituency, though it may incorporate European elements, emphasizes multiple experiences and forms of knowledge. Morejón thus both unifies and makes distinctions between individuals who are not reducible to a narrow sameness, but whose voices transcend limits upon the meanings of blackness and womanhood in Cuba, the Caribbean, and beyond.

# Elena Poniatowska (1932–)

In her multi-discursive texts, Elena Poniatowska fiercely questions universal knowledge and poses questions about where knowledge is constructed and about its agents of production. She is one of the major political and cultural interpreters of contemporary Mexico, as is clear upon examination of her biting chronicles of the 1985 Mexican earthquake *Nada, Nadie: las Voces del Temblor* (1998) (*Nothing, Nobody: The Voices of the Mexico City Earthquake*, 1995). The versatility in her choice of discourses and genres is the result of her understanding of writing whose shape is determined by the matter involved. A recipient of Mexico's National Journalism Prize, Poniatowska has transformed formal journalism with her irreverent investigative and reporting style (Jorgensen, 1994: xv). Never bound to conventional genres, her hybrid texts examine the sociology of the quotidian and ignite debates over fiction, authorship, autobiography, and the status of the subaltern. She is an intellectual whose terms generally exceed those of the *ciudad letrada* (lettered city), and the trajectory of her writing corroborates her quest for making women's writing into the attentive inscription of the inappropriate other. The Mothers of Plaza de Mayo were the first community of women to lead the way for a political experience of extended families claiming the public sphere in order to integrate the most radical inappropriate others (the *desaparecidos*) within the nation. With her unique form of testimonial literature, Poniatowska attempts to correct the representation of Latin America provided by the limited perspective of the men and women of the *ciudad letrada*. In *¡Hasta no Verte, Jesús Mío!* (1969; *Here's to you, Jesusa!*, 2001), she transfers the authority of experience to the illiterate *mestiza* Jesusa Palancares (Josefina Bórquez), whose knowledge emerges from having navigated through the drastic evolution of capitalist, androcentric, Catholic, semifeudal modern Mexico. Jorgensen describes Jesusa as a women haunted by her solitude, displaying strength, resentment, and conformity as conflicted as the condition of poor women of mixed race in contemporary Mexico (30).

Woodrich (1995) sees Jesusa's orphanhood and nomadism as the result of her journey through Mexico's concurrent social structures as an Oaxacan peasant, soldier of the Revolution, factory worker, hospital employee, and domestic servant, among other positions, from which she learned to critically spot the backdrop of Modernity. Some critics read Jesusa as a model of feminist agency, but Jorgensen calls attention to her narrative voice based on alternating textual and ideological positions: subordinated, oppressed, confrontational, boisterous, a heavy drinker, proud of herself, violent (1994: 31). Her identity shifts (female, *mestiza*, rural peasant, urban proletarian, illiterate, elderly marginalized, widow) challenge any unifying configuration of a character identity while representing a spatial metaphor for Poniatowska's own feminism: never isolated but an intersection in motion where purity and essentialism are unthinkable. Her writing keeps otherness *opened*, prolonging its semantic instability, refusing to give closure to difference.

*La Noche de Tlatelolco* (1971; *Massacre in Mexico*, 1992) is a compelling political document in terms of redefining social laterality, or empathic sensibility, as a major component of collective contracts and social exchange. Beyond literature but within literature, it achieves a monumental task: the reconstruction of the horrors of the 1968 massacre through a wide range of sensorial registers that include but are not necessarily based on visual perception. Much of the victims' visibility was obscured and consequently, the accounts as well as the spatial reconstruction of the Plaza are carried out mainly through the senses of touch, hearing, smell, and the haptic-related systems. The blood of the wounded is recognized as such by the stunned touch of Margarita Nolasco; its density felt on the walls by the tumbling of frightened hands; its smell perceived despite the reluctance to realize what has been smelled; the trace of a daughter's blood on the floor, walked upon, provoking the mother's excruciated horror. In "The Difficulty of Imagining Other Persons," Scarry argues that there is a *circular relation* between the infliction of pain and the problem of imaging otherness:

> *the difficulty of imagining others is both the cause of and the problem displayed by, the action of injuring* . . . The action of injuring occurs precisely because you have trouble believing in the reality of other persons. At the same time, the injury itself makes visible the fact that we cannot see the reality of other persons. It displays our perceptual disability. (2000: 43; emphasis added)

Another's fate may depend on whether or not we decide to adopt or ignore their suffering. Thus the relevance of making the injury and the devastation of its violence visible through the display of public record; the other is a foreigner until we *adopt* his or her pain.

Poniatowska's rendering of the Tlatelolco massacre, forged in the direct experience of the victims, allows their bodies, comprehension, and emotions to lead the reader's body, comprehension, and emotions through a night of horror and agonizing screams. Everything worked against the possibility of understanding what was happening: the darkness of the night, the screams, the machine-gun shots coming from everywhere, the confusion and erratic waves of movement, bumping, the falls of people caught in the unprecedented brutality of the massacre. The events were understood by the testimonial subjects first through sensorial maps that compensated for the limits on rational comprehension. Every possible angle is captured in *Massacre in Mexico*: from above, from lying down, from running and yelling, and despite blurred vision caused by tears, fear, or water screens, despite the paralyzing realization of a still warm, dead body nearby. The reader is able to relive the massacre through the intersecting sensorial, cognitive, and emotional maps processed by the victims. Poniatowska's forceful text addresses crucial concepts and practices of human rights activism while bridging the distance that prevents us from imagining the other, the major achievement of legal and cultural records such as *Me llamo Rigoberta Menchú* (1983; *I, Rigoberta Menchú*, 1984). Poniatowska comprehended the groundbreaking impact of testimonial literature by understanding the heterogeneous texture of Latin American culture and how writing endeavors to be a symbolic reconciliation for ethnic, economic, and gender exclusions. As Franco asserts, "It is not that we should see these writers as contradictory . . . they . . . confront the problems of class stratification, which can no longer be overcome by simply proclaiming oneself the voice of the subaltern" (1999: 53).

## Luisa Valenzuela (1938–)

Luisa Valenzuela also combines her journalistic work with fictions "full of playfulness and a sense of humor and wit that are anything but innocent and harmless . . . [B]oth the humor and the games are bitter, perhaps even biting decoys or distractions for her deadly, though indeed subtle, attacks" (Magnarelli, 2004: 4). The narrative voice in *Cola de Lagartija* (1983; *The Lizard's Tail*, 1983) even admits in the preface to the Spanish-language text that since what is to be told is "a story awfully painful . . . Incomprehensible. Impossible to be conveyed . . . We will resort to all recourses: black humor, sarcasm, the grotesque . . . It could be dangerous. Extremely risky. Blood will be used."

At least four major fields of inquiry trigger Valenzuela's writing. On one hand, she explores censorship and amnesia as the causes and effects of the political recruitment of gendered social conventions – particularly the reinforcement of political/gendered hierarchies through violence, repression, pornography, and sadism. On the other hand, she examines the body and writing as epistemological deciphering and recoding weapons employed against the conventions of meaning and structures of interpersonal relationships. Censorship and amnesia, body and writing are battlefields for an uneven confrontation between the political and the subjective, institutions and individuals. With *other weapons*, Valenzuela fervently attempts to gain the political field for the subjective.

Valenzuela's work scrutinizes cultural archives that are foundational to the symbolic gender roles inscribed in social traditions, including religious dogma, as in "The Heretics" (1967) (*Clara: Thirteen Short Stories and a Novel*, 1976), and ritual or fairy tales, as in "If This is Life, I'm Red Riding Hood" (1993) in *Symmetries* (1998). Her writing, as Magnarelli argues, is "wrapped in an aura of sacrosanctity" that is actually sexual in its origin and is founded on a covert fear of female sexuality in particular (1998b: 29). Stone reminds us that brave male heroes prosper in the world of fairy tales, but the female characters, "if they are not witches, or sinister stepmothers, are insipid beauties for their princes" (quoted in Muñoz, 1999: 101). Unconventional females, excessive, dissolute, or lawless women such as Valenzuela's Red Riding Hood in "If this is Life, I'm Red Riding Hood," pitilessly mock fixed gender roles by exploring the value of multiplicity in recombinant options and through lightly comic, darkly comic, or grotesquely comic bodily humors (Niebylski, 2004: 50). Muñoz argues that the reading contract of the fairy tales becomes null and its structure of meanings diluted in the muddy texture of parody (1999: 85): "how many frogs do I have to kiss in order to get a hold of the prince? How many wolves, I wonder, we will get throughout our lives?" (Valenzuela, 1993: 116) In Valenzuela's fictional world, nobody waits for frogs to turn into redeemers and mirrors never return images of reassurance but rather scattered selves, dispersed by violence and culture. They touch a raw nerve instead, as in "Other Weapons," when the mirror releases for Laura a devastating, precious image: her body making love/being raped/tortured.

The narrator in Valenzuela's *Hay que sonreir* (You've got to smile, 1966) asks herself, confused: "When I was a little girl, to behave well meant to help my mother to sweep up the floors and to go to church as well. Then, to behave well was not to allow boys to kiss me in dark corners. What the hell could it mean to behave naughtily now?" (96). She defiantly questions the production and reproduction of the *socially appropriate*. The initial sentence, "I was told," in "Tango" (*Symmetries*) opens a short story that betrays the powerful visual and cultural imaginary of the perfect couple embodied in tango dancers. Much effort is dedicated by the female protagonist to the choreography, body posture, high heels, and dress, and adherence to a code of ethics rigorously required by the conventions of tango. The double name (Sonia/Sandra) allows this dancer to place herself far from the quotidian in the magical scene of the couple dancing. But Valenzuela's dancers, woman and man, refuse to engage in social reproduction and gracefully reject classical expectations of compulsive sexuality, heterosexuality, and craving for partnership as the fulfillment of both masculine and feminine identities. Both dancers manage to evaluate from their own subjectivities what part of the tango's scene they choose in degrees of implication and detachment, freeing themselves from compulsive conventions by an act of pure sincerity. Tango's images might be spellbinding, but in *this* story there is not enough money to place the dancers in its imaginary scene. In the Argentina of economic crisis, the clumsy couple belong to the grotesque city. They can manage only a roasted chicken and some wine, but the glasses are green and thus, inappropriate. At the crossroads between image and realities in *plural*, they perform another *ceremonia de rechazo*: the man goes back to his children's house where he finds shelter; the woman continues seeking the *moment*: to feel how much her body finds contentment while dancing tango.

Valenzuela's fictional world takes us from fairy tales to the concreteness of daily realities as well as to appalling tombs of suffering and pain. She moves from deceiving paradises to inescapable hells, as in "Symmetries," when the *desaparecidas* of an extermination camp – after being attended to by hairdressers and beauticians brought to their prison – are taken out to dinner in classy restaurants between torture sessions: "we take them out to supper without a blindfold on, without a hood, and without even that thread of a voice, with their eyes dim, their heads down" (1998: 157).

Magnarelli argues that in "Fourth Version" (*Other Weapons*, 1985), unlike the love story of Sleeping Beauty "who awakens to live happily ever after at the side of her Prince Charming (that is, whose sleeping inactivity is converted to walking inactivity)," Bella's awakening unveils political atrocities which lead to her death (1998b: 12). The other story told in "Fourth Version" is that of writing and censorship (186). A meta-cultural reader-writer breaks cultural codes to decipher the discursive and political texture of the violence of conventions in order to show the *other* texts; *what cannot be said*. "When I think of censorship," says Valenzuela in an interview with Magnarelli, "I always think of its multiplicity of faces: it is like a hydra with its many heads" (Magnarelli, 1998a: 204). For Valenzuela, politics assume "the role once held by eroticism" (1998: 174). The narrator of "Fourth Version" warns the reader that the love story is actually a "diversion of attention away from what is more dangerous and subversive" (1985: 10) and wonders with deceptive perplexity: "I do not understand why the crucial information has been omitted" (1985: 25). Likewise, Laura's amnesia – as well as the country's – represents a distraction of attention away from the cover up of meaning. Valenzuela seeks that other story, that other text: "what's being concealed: it isn't desire, as is usually the case" (1985: 20). Convinced that "only darkness kills shadows," she vehemently follows the inverse direction taken by the censor, thus unearthing memories that are as troubling as cadavers. Pain is voluntarily self-inflicted when we absorb the pain of others: when "your friends have been tortured and killed and when the best thing you can think of when someone has disappeared is that she is dead . . . you have to write about torture because you can not deny it" (Magnarelli, 1998a: 209). What Valenzuela's many Lauras and Bellas hauntingly show is how amnesic *desaparecidos* and corpses can have a second chance and outlive their own erasure, as Argentina's collective memory learns that the unearthing of the dead might well contain the change necessary for the country's second life, overcoming amnesia as cultural repression of Argentina's politics of oblivion.

Critics emphasize that in Valenzuela's writing, the female body is often a signifier filled with conventions, a passive surface on which cultural meaning is forcibly inscribed. Nevertheless, in "Other Weapons" the body interferes in the cultural/ political politics of amnesia, becoming a useful weapon against its oppression. As with Morejón's woman, Laura's body remembers what and when her mind cannot; what it was forced to obliterate through the scar left by the torturer's whip on her back and the chilling sensations awakened by house confinement. The oppressor's vicious surveillance fails to see the sensuous maps of her body, the untraceable feeling-thinking-remembering circuit of the sensorial registers that lead the way to the recovery of Laura's identity and the memory of the country's repressive history. Valenzuela's resourceful writing-witches look like dexterous alchemists. They have to be away from the kitchen and the erotic powers associated with it because they feel the need to track and confront their elusive predators, who are lethal sorcerers capable of inflicting unimaginable pain and torture.

The construction of a new type of heroicity celebrates women's differential epistemic resources such as intuition, spontaneity, the authority of experience, concrete thought, and experiments of many sorts. Niebylski links them to an "activity of curiosity, greed, gossip, insatiable pursuit of secret details, the reckless, inquisitive adventure of Pandora or Bluebeard's last bride. Its project is to bring us *more*, not less" (2004: 7). Valenzuela's urban *Porteño* comic skepticism finds good company in Latin American variations of local humor such as the *choteo* or Ana Lidia Vega's *guachafita*, the Mexican melodrama (*Like Water for Chocolate*), the postmodern irreverence and camp humor of the urban world of Alicia Borinsky in *All Night Movie* (2002), or Sommers's biliously gothic humor in *Rioplatenses* (Niebylski, 2004: 8). Spaces deemed socially unreliable – the quotidian, the ephemeral, the private, the subjective – are rehabilitated together with eroticism and the decolonization of women's bodies. In our judgment, this work entails far more than the substitution of gynocentrism for androcentrism.

In *Cartucho* (1931), Nellie Campobello "turns the writing of a timeless, private self of the autobiography into a shared experience of the public, grounded self" (Meyer, 2004: 53). This most poetic and violent novel of the Mexican Revolution shows the interrelatedness and dialogic texture of culture and communication in its telling of the devastating intrusions of war into normal life. It defines *normality* through an unbendable *matter of fact*. Campobello's literary mixing of what is mixed in life defies canonical separations between discourses, genres, and topics: the naïve romantic from the realist; the gothic from the epic; the autobiographical, testimonial, fictional, from history; and history from the sentimental and melodramatic, collectively personal, personally collective (54–7). Campobello's *Cartucho* performs a radical integration that defies the notion of "woman's place."

Many other Latin American women writers question women's *natural* domains and abilities as they policitize the domestic sphere and reconfigure gender roles. They often play on conventional associations of women with culinary expertise and *amatoria* and reveal varying degrees of women's self-awareness as subjects of difference. For Susan Frenk, Isabel Allende's discourse of pleasure confronts the Pinochet regime's sexual codes as "internalized self-denial, prohibited by external and self-imposed sur-veillance" (2004: 69). We believe they counter the narratives of perdition. The turn-of-the-nineteenth-century imaginary created in *Aphrodite* (1998), for example, details social punishments as warnings to women who dare to cross gendered borders and prefer desire to institutional constraints. Allende seems to declare the end of difference and a new access to equality in terms of writing opportunities for women. The self-indulgent *femme fatale* in this novel, successful in the arts of seduction and writing, rescues women in essentialist terms through enabling narratives in which hardships of all kinds are shrewdly overcome. However, Allende reshapes the feminine as the reversal of masculine narratives within a self-confining circuit that goes around the limits set by androcentric narratives and reacts only to its cultural binarism. Feminin-ity is obsessively linked to seduction and exemplary masculinity is left uncritiqued, its set of values and social hierarchies, gendered and otherwise, still in force as they are in the reverse sexual tourism endorsed in a trip to Egypt in *Aphrodite*. Allende's feminine utopia of self-indulgence – periphery turned center, female subaltern turned *consumer* – is based on the privileged social position of her cosmopolitan, globalized female heroines. They have much to celebrate: the apparent *end* of women's subalter-nity thanks to a new alliance of women writers with the institutions of power (the literary market) *and* conspicuous levels of consumption as depicted, for example, in dinners set in lavish Tuscan palaces and facilitated by the work of imperceptible servants.

Texts that create the fictional binaries present in *Aphrodite* seem to preclude gendered exploitation or the bleeding implied in difference as well as an understanding of women's writing as an expression of otherness. They disallow difference and trauma thanks to their unrevised androcentric notions of eroticism and their commitment to seduction. Mujer, the main character in Griselda Gambaro's *El Despojamiento* (The Dispossession, 1989), performs a play on stage, but what she actually performs is femininity and seduction as skills historically desirable in male systems of representation. Like Castellanos's *Eternal Feminine*, Gambaro's play dramatizes the loss/masquerade of the theatrical and oppressive performance of gender. As Magnarelli observes, much of Mujer is lost when she adjusts herself to the expectations of an invisible "spectator/director whose desire she continuously tries to anticipate . . . [She] *oversees* herself, converting herself into both seer and seen/scene as she tries to imagine how [the male spectator] would like to see her" (2004: 14). Texts are produced in relationship to the global and the market. In her essay "From Romance to Refractory Aesthetic," Jean Franco argues that as a commodity which sells well in neoliberal pluralistic regimes, Latin American women's writing became internationally known thanks to its re-encoding and re-gendering of "magical realism," romance, eroticism, and exoticism (1999: 100). One has to remember how little space Jesusa Palancares and Rigoberta Menchú give to romance, eroticism, and exoticism and how Diamela Eltit's Margarita, as we will see below, proposes a drastic revision of the notions of intimacy and eroticism, suggesting they are not universal categories. Why, then, does eroticism seem to be an indicator for the closure of women's subaltern condition?

For Franco, the seduction of romance merely reproduces the seduction of commodity culture under neoliberalism. Countries that went through the experience of dictatorship resort to traditional narratives in order to leave the *house in order*. But for the neo-avant-garde, this is a problem: "The neo-avant-garde would thus argue that to leave the 'house in order' . . . is to evade the urgent task of constituting a new aesthetic to challenge the narrative of seduction of the commodity" (1999: 101). Latin American bestsellers reassure during a change of paradigm. Neoliberal sexual politics do not punish sexually powerful women, but rather underscore two of the most successful cultural constructions of the new market: the substitution of self-sacrificing motherhood for a self-centered, high-maintenance, witty woman such as Allende's Aphrodite who fully enjoys the apparent transparency and accessibility of the textual meanings of the neoliberal city.

If female difference has turned victorious and women have achieved citizenship in the "Republic of the Letters" – if equality has been achieved in terms of legal rights and cultural production and distribution, at least for a certain demographic sector – what is there to quarrel about? To begin with, any "refractory aesthetic" would start by targeting the values of the marketplace. Franco calls upon Nelly Richard's reading of the neo-avant-garde as shifting the meaning of the *feminine* so drastically "that it is no longer associated with the limited feminist goal of equality. Rather, the feminine includes everything – transvestite performance, certain artistic practices, some by male artists – all that destabilizes the discursive structures of media-dominated societies whose discourse she describes as monumental, pluralist, and massive" (1999: 102). The *feminine* becomes striking spaces that contest the romancing of female strategies of pluralism and the massivity of the media and its obliteration of ambiguity. Refractory aesthetics within neoliberalism show the distorting mirror and the exacerbated distance of the marginal in order to reflect the monstrous image of global capitalism.

Why would pleasure and seduction seem to be the ultimate value? Pleasure as pleasure and seduction linked to a satisfying logic, tightly endorsed by the market? Pleasure defined only within a self disconnected from the social? What Franco finds transgressive in Tununa Mercado and Diamela Eltit's works is their disassociation of "affect from family romance, body from the self . . . allowing an 'eros' that is not simply tied to romantic love to emerge" (1999: 103). Thus the domestic in Mercado's work "is not an inferior compartment of existence but a tactile, sensuous relationship with things" (105). Households have never been private nor do they have kitchens or dining tables. Latin American bestsellers seem to celebrate gender reversion in a sort of essentialized utopia molded to their own self-regulated logic and designed without exchanges with other social margins.

## Diamela Eltit (1949–)

Exploring female subalternity within the neoliberal culture of equal opportunity and exposing women's writing to the semantic work forged in the contact with others at the margin allows Diamela Eltit to work against closure and stabilization of the "feminine." Eltit's neo-avant-garde critical, fictional, and performative discourse represents one of the most radical revisions of writing conventions and authorial position. It reacts to the events of daily life, unveiling the misleading pacts of impunity that laid the foundation for the Chilean social realities of the redemocratization and the *Concertación*. Her agents of resistance outlive their marginality to radiate meanings and to resignify Chile's daily life from *another place.* In her essay "Vivir, Donde" in *Emergencias* (Emergencies, 2000), Eltit argues that this is the case of the Quispe sisters whose suicide demonstrates their bodies and minds historically betrayed by the state in its many metamorphoses: "A telling suicide whose deciphering conjugates ethics, esthetics, and politics of the body and of its habitation in the interior of a landscape uprooted from the centers, from doubly and triply subaltern histories . . . They have the capacity to organize a refined and enigmatic language using . . . their impressively human bodies" (61).

Eltit's writing was triggered by Pinochet's coup. In 1973, his brutal genocide canceled social collective contracts, slashing "a cut between a moment and the next, as a shock, as a trauma, as an attack, as a pain, as an aggressive game, as a symptom" (2000: 17). As a symptom, the theatricality of Pinochet's anger in his first public appearance anticipated a sinister and yet "promising" future since the *golpista* military socio-culture facilitated the implementation of the new global order in alliance with the Catholic Church, the right, as representative of capitalism (33). During the dictatorship, Eltit began to shape her epics of the social abjection of the dispossessed who, Lorenzano contends, represent Latin America as "a lumpen in relationship to the hegemonic centers" (2004: 18). Her works portray insurrectional subjects who are insurrectional with respect to capitalism because they are unproductive (Lazarra, 2002: 31), and who resort to the anti-economical activity of tracing social memory (political, racist, and gender-repressive), a deliberately inappropriate gesture with regard to the goal-oriented swiftness of neoliberal culture. Violently unstable and distressing, *Por la patria* (For the motherland, 1986), *El Cuarto mundo* (1988; *The Fourth World*, 1995), and the *testimonio* of the homeless, *El padre mío* (My father, 1989), attempt to compensate for the claustrophiliac *truth* of fascist Chile whose dictatorial, dry, and chilly words have to compete with Eltit's linguistic excess, diasporic fragmentation, and a fluctuation of meanings that averts calming answers. As Nelly Richard explains, "Eltit's narratives turn every phrase into a multi-referential crossing where significations become multiplied and recombined due to the active (transformative) performance of the [linguistic] sign" (1996: 41). Similarly, Eltit's slippery social agents prove the ineffectiveness of the neofascist, neoliberal claims for economic, political, and military monitoring of the global world. The demented voices of her texts turn down meaning, refuse symbolic spaces of stability and closure. Marginality and difference are maintained through ambiguous dilatory suspension, the "critical subversion of the modalities of non-closure" (Richard, 1993: 38), as obdurate edges, hard to reduce.

The physical and political destruction of the bodies of the labor force under the unregulated market economy is examined in Eltit's *Mano de obra* (Manual labor, 2002). And in *Lumpérica* (1983; *E. Luminata*, 1997), "the signs that differentiate pleasure from pain have been removed" (Castro-Klarén, 1993: 101). No representation is possible considering that such defying fluidity resists Western separations between body and soul, pleasure and pain (108). The female body in Eltit's *Vaca Sagrada* (1991; *Sacred Cow*, 1995) is a radical cultural test, especially in the symbolic case of menstruation. In an interview on this subject Eltit states: "rather than deal with the subject from a biological point of view, I want . . . to see what fears it triggers, what images, what fantasies . . . I think the body is one of the most densely ideologized cultural sites, above all, it's been turned into a moral territory none of us can escape" (Labanyi, 2004: 85). Eltit tests social fears through the defying frontality of menstrual blood within the context of the executing language of the exasperated Father. Pinochet ought to feel revulsion for women's bloody incontinence: he seems to detest formlessness, abjection, residuals condemned by him to horror. The narrator in *Vaca Sagrada* says, "I ended up soaked in my own blood . . . I was suffering a kind of disintegration, I felt the whole city could explode . . . I made no attempt to halt the process because I needed to stay bound to violence to match that other violence" (quoted in and translated by Labanyi, 2004: 95). The bleeding female body is linked in this text not to fertility, as is the norm, but to disintegration and death.

The *roto* represents Chilean inappropriate otherness, as Eltit says, the "threatening and contaminated body that shows the violence of his/her human vestment-remains . . . Barefoot and defiant, picaresque and delinquent" (2000: 145). The imperfections of his/her body and accentuated racial marks uncover the extreme polarization triggered by neoliberalism. In sharp contrast, María, a character in Marcela Serrano's *Nosotras que nos queremos tanto* (We loved so much, 1991), states that "love matters more than anything else on Earth" (26). María's transformation parallels the country's: a former guerrilla member, she has left behind her "promiscuous past" and is reformed by true love, abandoning her egocentrism and thus becoming a reformed female citizen fully integrated to the social contracts of the neoliberal democracy. "This type of reading tells all women to forget their superficial differences, and to reembrace their traditional roles as they reintegrate into the new democracy" (Hines, 2002: 72). The novel's essentialism situates women as guarantors of stability and reconciliation in the new Chile: "[H]ere we are all women. We are alike; there is so much that makes us sisters. At the bottom line, we all have . . . the same story to tell" (Serrano, 1991: 11). The many open wounds of Eltit's world tell a story quite dissimilar from Serrano's celebratory feminism and nationalism. The narrator-protagonist in *Los vigilantes* says, "I write to avoid being ashamed," prompting us to reflect upon all there is to be ashamed of.

Eltit's fictional and testimonial literature, journalism, performance, and historiography are aimed at shaking social praxis with the purpose of revising interpersonal relationships. Within her "refractory aesthetic," love and social nocturnality at a psychiatric hospice are drastically revised in the literary-photographic *El Infarto del alma* (The infarct of the soul, 1994), a collaboration with Paz Errázuriz. One of the most stunning images among many in Eltit's prophetic reading of the new world order is the global militarization of the neoliberal project. In *Los Vigilantes* (1994; *Custody of the Eyes*, 2005), a complete social orphanhood signals the cancellation of collective social contracts, leaving behind victims without legal rights who are labeled as necessary sacrifices and confined to ghettos that will eventually swallow them from the surface. Borrowing the phrase from Rosalba Campra, Francine Masiello argues that *archetypes of marginality* from Latin America "continue to enjoy wide currency and override the sense of failure that has marked left-wing activism of recent years" (2001: 112). She goes on to note that "Latin American women have recently moved to the center of this narrative heroics, promising hopes for redemption of society through a narrative discourse about social change as well as a new position urgent to the necessities of literature and art" (112). Eltit's work does not function on this level and she provides no "narrative heroics." *Los Vigilantes* works squarely against this trend: "Refusing to enter the market and the fashions of marginality with which feminist theory circulates globally, Eltit's recounts the disintegration of family ties in the neoliberal age. There is no idealization of parenting, no special privilege accorded the child, no celebration of the Latin American family that satisfies the appetites of foreign readers" (Masiello, 2001: 136). The myth of the Latin American family is shattered, with its accompanying maternal image. Eltit's major accomplishment is to plainly equate neoliberalism with deadly violence. But violence and death may awaken emotional social laterality. The protagonist, Margarita, reshapes the Latin American family as a collective utopian womb, capable of keeping the outcast warm, nourished, and caressed. Despite her efforts, "the chilly temperatures will inescapably kill the homeless and destroy culture as we know it. The contaminated waters secure a guaranteed death to the dispossessed" (Masiello, 2001: 763), but at the level of the imaginary, Eltit's repoliticization of the domestic scene revises the private as a field eminently political and public. Groundbreaking social practices, such as those Margarita dares to perform despite the vigilantes, fuel the imagination of a different feminine space uncommitted to social reproduction of the neoliberal city and loyal to the renaissance of collective utopias.

When Margarita opens her house-body and turns it into a home for the dispossessed, she deconstructs social praxis central to capitalism. The single-family household has been obsessively endorsed by the bourgeoisie's culture of individualism and its socialization is based upon emotional separation. Households are linked to sexuality; their spatial-symbolic contributes to define sexuality as much as the limits of sexuality define models of social interaction. Margarita's son resents his mother's maintaining a correspondence with the father and the punishing social culture of the vigilantes; he distrusts language, political institutions, and family conventions. Placed at a pre-socializing stage of evolution, he seems to find no compelling reasons to comply with a history of social contracts that reinforces anti-humanitarian separateness. Eltit's work, as Franco asserts, reveals conflicting intentions: "to act against the authoritarian state, to take literature symbolically into the most marginal of spaces, to work against the easy readability of the commercial text, to foreground the woman's body as a site of contention, to increase or exaggerate the marginality of art, and to juxtapose literature's marginality to that of prostitutes, vagabonds, and the homeless" (1999: 52).

For the women writers discussed in this chapter, writing is an act of insurrection. From Rachel de Queiroz's quiet insistence on the independence of her female protagonists to Morejón's, Valenzuela's, or Eltit's linguistic deconstruction of the embodied female subject, their texts irrupt within the Western cultural arena. They work against literary and authorial norms, those concrete social practices that place limits on women's expressions. Qualified by the class privilege that has historically been associated with literature in Latin America, their writing shows the political implications of non-universal representations of women's specific realities and economic, gendered, ethnic, and national subjectivities that are forged within the intersecting vectors of neocolonial, postcolonial, postmodern, and migrant identities. Their unsettling margins and disquieting zones of splitting and fragmentation underline the complexity of manifold realities while struggling against the closure and stabilization of the most challenging agenda: the representation of women's conditions. If there is something their writings make us vividly aware of it is the vision of the many missing and lingering *texts* still to be found in *other* places, texts produced by the many peripheral and alternative subjects and subjectivities located beyond or even within the conventions and negotiations of the lettered city and the neoliberal city.

REFERENCES AND FURTHER READING

*References*

*Note*: Translations Of Texts Cited Above Are Ours Unless Otherwise Indicated.

Ahern, Maureen (1988). "Introduction." In *A Rosario Castellanos Reader*, pp. xiii–xix. Austin: University of Texas Press.

Andrade, Mário (1976). *Taxi e crônicas no Diário Nacional*. São Paulo: Duas Cidades.

Barradas, Efraín (1996). "Nancy Morejón o un nuevo canto para una vieja culebra," *Afro-Hispanic Review*, 15(1): 22–8.

Borinsky, Alicia (2002). *All Night Movie*. Trans. Cola Franzen. Evanston, IL: Northwestern University Press.

Castellanos, Rosario (1988). "The eternal feminine." Trans. Diane E. Marting and Betty Tyree Osiek. In Maureen Ahern (ed.), *A Rosario Castellanos Reader*, pp. 273–367. Austin: University of Texas Press.

Castillo, Debra (1992). "Rosario Castellanos: 'ashes without a face.'" In Sidonie Smith and Julia Watson (eds), *De/Colonizing the Subject: The Politics of Gender in Women's Autobiography*, pp. 242–69. Minneapolis: University of Minnesota Press.

Castro-Klaren, Sara (1993). "Escritura y cuerpo en Lumpérica." In Juan Carlos Lértola (ed.), *Una Poética de literatura menor: La narrativa de Diamela Eltit*, pp. 97–110. Santiago: Cuarto Propio.

Cordones-Cook, Juanamaría (1996). "Voz y poesía de Nancy Morejón," *Afro-Hispanic Review*, 15(1): 60–71.

Eltit, Diamela (2000). *Emergencias: Ensayos sobre literatura, arte y política*. Santiago: Planeta.

Feal, Rosemary Geisdorfer (1995). "Reflections on the obsidian mirror: the poetics of Afro-Hispanic identity and the gendered body," *Afro-Hispanic Review*, 14(1): 26–32.

Feracho, Lesley (2005). "Morejón's poetic 'persona': representations of Pan-Caribbean women," *Callaloo*, 28(4): 978–89.

Ferreira-Pinto, Cristina (2004). *Gender, Discourse, and Desire in Twentieth-Century Brazilian Literature*. West Lafayette, IN: Purdue University Press.

Franco, Jean (1999). "From romance to refractory aesthetic." In *Critical Passions*, pp. 97–108. Durham, NC: Duke University Press.

Frenk, Susan (2004). "The wandering text: situating the narratives of Isabel Allende." In Anny Brooksbank and Catherine Davies (eds), *Latin American Women's Writing. Feminist Reading in Theory and Crisis*, pp. 6–84. Oxford: Clarendon Press.

Gambaro, Griselda (1989). "El despojamiento." In *Teatro 3*, pp. 169–81. Buenos Aires: Ediciones de la Flor.

Gotlib, Nadia (1991). "Las mujeres y 'el otro': tres narradoras brasileñas," *Escritura*, 16(31–2): 123–36.

Guerra-Cunningham, Lucía (1991). "Estrategias discursivas en la narrativa de la mujer latinoamericana," *Escritura*, 16(31–2): 115–22.

Hines, Donetta (2002). "'Woman' and Chile: in transition," *Letras femeninas*, 28(2): 60–76.

Hollanda, Heloisa Buarque de (1997). "O *Éthos* Rachel," *Cadernos de Literatura Brasileira*, 4: 103–15.

— (1999). "Rachel's gown," trans. Christopher Peterson, *Estudos Feministas*, special issue, 1st sem.: 80–97.

Horan, Elizabeth, and Meyer, Doris (2003). *This America of Ours: The Letters of Gabriela Mistral and Victoria Ocampo*. Austin: University of Texas Press.

Howe, Linda S. (1999). "Nancy Morejón's womanism." In Miriam DeCosta-Willis (ed.), *Singular Like a Bird: The Art of Nancy Morejón*, pp. 153–

68. Washington, DC: Howard University Press.

Jorgensen, Beth E. (1994). *The Writing of Elena Poniatowska: Engaging Dialogues*. Austin, University of Texas Press.

Labanyi, Jo (2004). "Topologies of catastrophe: horror and abjection in Diamela Eltit's *Vaca sagrada*." In Anny Booksbank Jones and Catherine Davies (eds), *Latin American Women's Writing: Feminist Readings in Theory and Crisis*, pp. 85–103. Oxford: Oxford University Press.

Lazarra, Michael (2002) "Diamela Eltit: Conversaciones en Princeton,"*PLAS*, 5. Princeton, NJ: Program in Latin American Studies.

Lorenzano, Sandra (2004). "Vivir precariamente: En torno a la propuesta literaria de Diamela Eltit." In Diamela Eltit, *Tres novelas*, pp. 11–25. Mexico City: Fondo de Cultura Económica.

Magnarelli, Sharon (1998a). "Censorship and the female writer: an interview/dialogue with Luisa Valenzuela." In *Reflections/Refractions. Reading Luisa Valenzuela*, pp. 203–19. New York: Peter Lang.

— (1998b). *Reflections/Refractions. Reading Luisa Valenzuela*. New York, Peter Lang, 1998.

— (2004). "Acting/seeing woman: Griselda Gambaro's *El Despojamiento*." In Anny Booksbank Jones and Catherine Davies (eds), *Latin American Women's Writing: Feminist Reading in Theory and Crisis*, pp. 10–29. Oxford: Clarendon Press.

Marchant, Elizabeth (1999). *Critical Acts: Latin American Women and Cultural Criticism*. Gainesville: University of Press of Florida.

Masiello, Francine (2001). *The Art of Transition: Latin American Culture and Neoliberal Crisis*. Durham, NC: Duke University Press.

Meyer, Doris (2004). "The dialogic of testimony: autobiography as shared experience in Nellie Campobello's *Cartucho*." In Anny Brooksbank and Catherine Davies (eds), *Latin American Women's Writing: Feminist Reading in Theory and Crisis*, pp. 46–65. Oxford: Clarendon Press.

Morejón, Nancy (1979). *Parajes de una época*. Havana, Letras Cubanas.

— (1982). *Octubre imprescindible*. Havana: Casa de las Américas.

— (1990). "A womanist vision of the Caribbean. An interview: Nancy Morejón." In Carole Boyce Davies and Elaine Savory Fido (eds), *Out of the Kumbla: Caribbean Women and Literature*, pp. 265–9. Trenton, NJ: Africa World Press.

Muñoz, Willie O. (1999). *Polifonía de la marginalidad: La narrativa de escritoras latinoamericanas*. Santiago: Cuarto Propio.

Niebylski, Dianna C. (2004). *Humoring Resistance: Laughter and the Excessive Body in Contemporary Latin American Women's Fiction* Albany: State University of New York.

Queiroz, Rachel de (1963). *The Three Marias*. Trans. Fred Ellison. Austin: University of Texas Press.

Ramos, Graciliano (1962). *Linhas tortas*. São Paulo: Livraria Martins.

Richard, Nelly (1993). "Tres funciones de escritura: Deconstrucción, simulación, hibridización." In Juan Carlos Lértola (ed.), *Una Poética de literatura menor: La narrativa de Diamela Eltit*, pp. 37–51. Santiago: Cuarto Propio.

— (1996). "Feminismo, experiencia y representación," *Revista Iberoamericana*, 62(176–7): 733–44.

Salomone, Alicia N. (2004). "Mujer, ciudad subliteratura en la textualidad de Alfonsina Storni." In Alicia Salomone, Gilda Luongo, Natalia Cisterna, Darcie Doll, and Gabriela Queirolo (eds), *Modernidad en otro tono: Escritura de mujeres latinoamericanas: 1920–1950*, pp. 45–67. Santiago: Cuarto Propio.

Scarry, Elaine (2000). "The difficulty of imagining other persons." In Eugene Weiner (ed.), *The Handbook of Interethnic Coexistence*, pp. 40–62. New York: Continuum.

Serrano, Marcela (1991). *Nosotras que nos queremos tanto*. México: Alfaguara.

Valenzuela, Luisa (1966). *Hay que sonreir*. Buenos Aires: Américalee.

— (1983a). *Cola de lagartija*. México: Planeta.

— (1983b). *The Lizard's Tail*. Trans. Gregory Rabassa. New York: Farrar, Straus, & Giroux.

— (1985). *Other Weapons*. Trans. Debora Bonner. Hanover, NH: Ediciones del Norte.

—. (1993). *Simetrías*. Buenos Aires: Sudamericana.

— (1998). *Symmetries*. Trans. Margaret Jull Costa. London: High Risk Books.

Woodrich, Wendy Z. (1995). "Aspectos teóricos de la autobiografía y el testimonio femenino hispanoamericano: Las historias de vida de Jesusa Palancares y Rigoberta Menchú." In Emma Sepúlveda Pulvirenti and Joy Logan (eds), *El Testimonio femenino como escritura contestaria*, pp. 25–52. Santiago: Asterión.

*Further Reading*

Bergmann, Emilie, et al. (1990). *Women, Culture, and Politics in Latin America*. Berkeley: University of California Press.

Castillo, Debra (1992). *Talking Back: Toward a Latin American Feminist Literary Criticism*. Ithaca, NY: Cornell University Press.

Castro-Klaren, Sara, ed. (2003). *Latin American Women's Narrative: Practices and Theoretical Perspectives*. Frankfurt: Vervuert.

Castro-Klaren, Sara, Molloy, Sylvia, and Sarlo, Beatriz, eds (1991). *Women's Writing in Latin America*. Boulder, CO: Westview.

Davies, Catherine, ed. (1993). *Women Writers in Twentieth Century Spain and Spanish America*. Lampeter, Wales: Edwin Mellen.

DeCosta-Willis, Miriam, ed. (1999). *Singular Like a Bird: The Art of Nancy Morejón*. Washington, DC: Howard University Press.

Franco, Jean (1989). *Plotting Women: Gender and Representation in Mexico*. New York: Columbia University Press.

Kaminsky, Amy C. (1993). *Reading the Body Politic: Feminist Criticism and Latin American Women Writers*. Minneapolis: University of Minnesota Press.

Lindstrom, Naomi (1989). *Women's Voice in Latin American Literature*. Washington, DC: Three Continents.

Masiello, Francine (1992). *Between Civilization and Barbarism: Women, Nation, and Literary Culture in Modern Argentina*. Lincoln: University of Nebraska Press.

Norat, Gisela (2002). *Marginalities: Diamela Eltit and the Subversion of Mainstream Literature in Chile*. Newark: University of Delaware Press.

O'Connell, Joanna (1995). *Prospero's Daughter: The Prose of Rosario Castellanos*. Austin: University of Texas Press.

Quinlan, Susan (1991). *The Female Voice in Contemporary Brazilian Narrative*. New York: Peter Lang.

Rodríguez, Ileana (1994). *House/Garden/Nation: Space, Gender, and Ethnicity in Post-colonial Latin American Literatures by Women*. Durham, NC: Duke University Press.

Salvador, Álvaro (1995). "El Otro Boom de la narrativa hispanoamericana: Los relatos escritos por mujeres en la década de los Ochenta," *Revista de Crítica Literaria*, 21(4): 165–75.

# 31

# Caribbean Philosophy

## *Edouard Glissant*

### Natural Poetics, Forced Poetics

I define as a free or natural poetics any collective yearning for expression that is not opposed to itself either at the level of what it wishes to express or at the level of the language that it puts into practice.

(I call self-expression a shared attitude, in a given community, of confidence or mistrust in the language or languages it uses.)

I define forced or constrained poetics as any collective desire for expression that, when it manifests itself, is negated at the same time because of the *deficiency* that stifles it, not at the level of desire, which never ceases, but at the level of expression, which is never realized.

*Natural poetics:* Even if the destiny of a community should be a miserable one, or its existence threatened, these poetics are the direct result of activity within the social body. The most daring or the most artificial experiences, the most radical questioning of self-expression, extend, reform, clash with a given poetics. This is because there is no incompatibility here between desire and expression. The most violent challenge to an established order can emerge from a natural poetics, when there is a continuity between the challenged order and the disorder that negates it.

*Forced poetics:* The issue is not one of attempts at articulation (composite and "voluntary"), through which we test our capacity for self-expression. Forced poetics exist where a need for expression confronts an inability to achieve expression. It can happen that this confrontation is fixed in an opposition between the content to be expressed and the language suggests or imposed.

This is the case in the French Lesser Antilles where the mother tongue, Creole, and the official language, French, produce in the Caribbean mind an unsuspected source of anguish.

A French Caribbean individual who does not experience some inhibition in handling French, since our consciousness is haunted by the deep feeling of being different, would be like someone who swims motionless in the air without suspecting that he could with the same motion move in the water and perhaps discover the unknown. He must cut across one language in order to attain a form of expression that is perhaps not part of the internal logic of this language. A forced poetics is created from the awareness of the opposition between a language that one uses and a form of expression that one needs.

At the same time, Creole, which could have led to a natural poetics (because in it language and expression would correspond perfectly) is being exhausted. It is becoming more French in its daily use; it is becoming vulgarized in the transition from spoken to written. Creole has, however, always resisted this dual deformation. Forced poetics is the result of these deformations and this resistance.

Forced poetics therefore does not generally occur in a traditional culture, even if the latter is threatened. In any traditional culture, that is where the language, the means of expression, and what I call here the form of expression (the collective attitude toward the language used) coincide and reveal no deep *deficiency*, there is no need to resort to this ploy, to this counterpoetics, which I will try to analyze in relation to our Creole language and our use of the French language.

Forced poetics or counterpoetics is instituted by a community whose self-expression does not emerge spontaneously, or result from the autonomous activity of the social body. Self-expression, a casualty of this lack of autonomy, is itself marked by a kind of impotence, a sense of futility. This phenomenon is exacerbated because the communities to which I refer are always primarily oral. The transition from oral to written, until now considered in the context of Western civilization as an inevitable evolution, is still cause for concern. Creole, a not-yet-standardized language, reveals this problem in and through its traditional creativity. That is why I will try to discuss first of all the fundamental situation of Creole: that is, the basis of its orality.

## The Situation of the Spoken

1.   The written requires nonmovement: the body does not move with the flow of what is said. The body must remain still; therefore the hand wielding the pen (or using the typewriter) does not reflect the movement of the body, but is linked to (an appendage of) the page.

The oral, on the other hand, is inseparable from the movement of the body. There the spoken is inscribed not only in the posture of the body that makes it possible (squatting for a palaver for instance, or the rhythmic tapping of feet in a circle when we keep time to music), but also in the almost semaphoric signals through which the body implies or emphasizes what is said.[1] Utterance depends on posture, and perhaps is limited by it.

That which is expressed as a general hypothesis can now perhaps be reinforced by specific illustration. For instance, the alienated body of the slave, in the time of slavery, is in fact deprived, in an attempt at complete dispossession, of speech. Self-expression is not only forbidden, but impossible to envisage. Even in his reproductive function, the slave is not in control of himself. He reproduces, but it is for the master. All pleasure is silent: that is, thwarted, deformed, denied. In such a situation, expression is cautions, reticent, whispered, spun thread by thread in the dark.

When the body is freed (when day comes) it follows the explosive scream. Caribbean speech is always excited, it ignores silence, softness, sentiment. The body follows suit. It does not know pause, rest, smooth continuity. It is jerked along.

To move from the oral to the written is to immobilize the body, to take control (to possess it). The creature deprived of his body cannot attain the immobility where writing takes shape. He keeps moving; it can only scream. In this silent world, voice and body pursue desperately an impossible fulfillment.

Perhaps we will soon enter the world of the nonwritten, where the transition from oral to written, if it takes place, will no longer be seen as promotion or transcendence. For now, speech and body are shaped, in their orality, by the same obsession with past privation. The word in the Caribbean will only survive as such, in a written form, if this earlier loss finds expression.


2.   From the outset (that is, from the moment Creole is forged as a medium of communication between slave and master), the spoken imposes on the slave its particular syntax. For Caribbean man, the word is first and foremost sound. Noise is essential to speech. Din is discourse. This must be understood.

It seems that meaning and pitch went together for the uprooted individual, in the unrelenting silence of the world of slavery. It was the intensity of the sound that dictated meaning: the pitch of the sound conferred significance. Ideas were bracketed. One person could make himself understood through the subtle associations of sound, in which the master, so capable of managing "basic Creole" in other situations, got hopelessly lost. Creole spoken by the *békés* was never shouted out loud. Since speech was forbidden, slaves camouflaged the word under the provocative intensity of the scream. No one could translate the meaning of what seemed to be nothing but a shout. It was taken to be nothing but the call of a wild animal.[2] This is how the dispossessed man organized his speech by weaving it into the apparently meaningless texture of extreme noise.

There developed from that point a specialized system of significant insignificance. Creole organizes speech as a blast of sound.

I do not know if this phenomenon is common is threatened languages, dying dialects, languages that suffer from nonproductivity. But it is a constant feature of the popular use of Martinican Creole. Not only in the delivery of folktales and songs, but even and often in daily speech. A requirement is thus introduced into spoken Creole: speed. Not so much speed as a jumbled rush. Perhaps the continuous stream of language that makes speech into one impenetrable block of sound. If it is pitch that confers meaning on a word, rushed and fused sounds shape the meaning of speech. Here again, the use is specific: the *béké* masters, who know Creole even better than the mulattoes, cannot, however, manage this "unstructured" use of language.

In the pace of Creole speech, one can locate the embryonic rhythm of the drum. It is not the semantic structure of the sentence that helps to punctuate it but the breathing of the speaker that dictates the rhythm: a perfect poetic concept and practice.

So the meaning of a sentence is sometimes hidden in the accelerated nonsense created by scrambled sounds. But this nonsense does convey real meaning to which the master's ear cannot have access. Creole is originally a kind of conspiracy that concealed itself by its public and open expression. For example, even if Creole is whispered (for whispering is the shout modified to suit the dark), it is rarely murmured. The whisper is determined by external circumstances; the murmur is a *decision* by the speaker. The murmur allows access to a *confidential* meaning, not to this form of nonsense that could conceal and reveal at the same time a *hidden* meaning.

But if Creole has at its origin this kind of conspiracy to conceal meaning, it should be realized that this initiatic purpose would progressively disappear. Besides, it has to disappear so that the expression of this conspiracy should emerge as an openly accessible language. A language does not require initiation but apprenticeship: it must be accessible to all. All languages created for a secret purpose make the practice of a regular syntax irrelevant and replace it by a "substitute" syntax. So, to attain the status of a language, speech must rid itself of the secretiveness of its "substitute" syntax and open itself to the norms of an adequate stable syntax. In traditional societies this transition is a slow and measured one, from a secret code to a medium open to everyone, even the "outsider." So speech slowly becomes language. No forced poetics is involved, since this new language with its stable syntax is also a form of expression, its syntax agreed to.

The dilemma of Martinican Creole is that the stage of secret code has been passed, but language (as a new opening) has not been attained. The secretiveness of the community is no longer functional, the stage of an open community has not been reached.


3.    As in any popular oral literature, the traditional Creole text, folktale or song, is striking in the graphic nature of its images. This is what learned people refer to when they speak of concrete languages subordinate to conceptual languages. By that they mean that there should be a radical transition to the conceptual level, which should be attained once having left (gone beyond) the inherent sensuality of the image.

Now imagery, in what we call expressions of popular wisdom, is deceptive, that is, it can be seen as first and foremost the indication of a conscious strategy. All languages that depend on images (so-called concrete languages) indicate that they have implicitly conceptualized the idea and quietly refused to explain it. Imagery in a language defined as concrete is the deliberate (although collectively unconscious) residue of a certain linguistic potential at a given time. In a process as complete, complex, perfected as its conceptual origins, imaginative expression is secreted in the obscure world of the group unconscious. The original idea is reputed to have been conceived by a god or a particular spirit, in the twilight about which Hegel, for example, speaks.

But the Creole language, in addition, is marked by French – that is, the obsession with the written – as an *internal* transcendence. In the historical circumstances that gave rise to Creole, we can locate a forced poetics that is both an awareness of the restrictive presence of French as a linguistic background and the deliberate attempt to reject French, that is, a conceptual system from which expression can be derived. Thus, imagery, that is, the "concrete" and all its metaphorical associations, is not, in the Creole language, an ordinary feature. It is a deliberate ploy. It is not an implicit slyness but a deliberate craftiness. There is something pathetic in the imaginative ploys of popular Creole maxims. Like a hallmark that imposes limitation.

One could imagine – this is, moreover, a movement that is emerging almost everywhere – a kind of revenge by oral languages over written ones, in the context of a global civilization of the nonwritten. Writing seems linked to the transcendental notion of the individual, which today is threatened by and giving way to a cross-cultural process. In such a context will perhaps appear global systems using imaginative strategies, not conceptual structures, languages that dazzle or shimmer instead of simply "reflecting." Whatever we think of such an eventuality, we must examine from this point on what conditions Creole must satisfy in order to have a place in this new order.

4.   Creole was in the islands the language of the plantation system, which was responsible for the cultivation of sugar cane. The system has disappeared, but in Martinique it has not been replaced by another system of production; it degenerated into a circuit of exchange. Martinique is a land in which products manufactured elsewhere are consumed. It is therefore destined to become increasingly a land you pass through. In such a land, whose present organization ensures that nothing will be produced there again, the structure of the mother tongue, deprived of a dynamic hinterland, cannot be reinforced. Creole cannot become the language of shopping malls, nor of luxury hotels. Cane, bananas, pineapples are the last vestiges of the Creole world. With them this language will disappear, if it does not become functional in some other way.

Just as it stopped being a secret code without managing to become the norm and develop as an "open" language, the Creole language slowly stops using the ploy of imagery through which it actively functioned in the world of the plantations, without managing to evolve a more conceptual structure. That reveals a condition of stagnation that makes Creole into a profoundly threatened language.

The role of Creole in the world of the plantations was that of defiance. One could, based on this, define its new mode of structured evolution as "negative" or "reactive," different from the "natural" structural evolution of traditional languages. In this, the Creole language appears to be organically linked to the cross-cultural phenomenon worldwide. It is literally the result of contact between different cultures and did not preexist this contact, It is not a language of a single origin, it is a cross-cultural language.

As long as the system of production in the plantations, despite its unfairness to most of the population, was maintained as an "autonomous" activity, it allowed for a level of symbolic activity, as if to hold the group together, through which the *influential* group, that of the slaves, then the agricultural workers, imposed its form of expression: in their speech, belief, and custom, which are different from the writing, religion, law that are imposed by a *dominant* class.

The Creole folktale is the symbolic strategy through which, in the world of the plantations, the mass of Martinicans developed a forced poetics (which we will also call a counter-poetics) in which were manifested both an inability to liberate oneself totally and an insistence on attempting to do so.

If the plantation system had been replaced by another system of production, it is probable that the Creole language would have been "structured" at an earlier time, that it would have passed "naturally" from secret code to conventional syntax, and perhaps from the diversion of imagery to a conceptual fluency.

Instead of this, we see in Martinique, even today, that one of the extreme consequences of social irresponsibility is this form of verbal delirium that I call habitual, in order to distinguish it from pathological delirium, and which reveals that here no "natural" transition has managed to *extend* the language into a historical dimension. Verbal delirium as the outer edge of speech is one of the most frequent products of the counterpoetics practiced by Creole. Improvisations, drumbeats, acceleration, dense repetitions, slurred syllables, meaning the opposite of what is said, allegory and hidden meanings – there are in the forms of this customary verbal delirium an intense concentration of all the phases of the history of this dramatic language. We can also state, based on our observation of the destructively non-functional situation of Creole, that this language, in its day-to-day application, becomes increasingly a language of neurosis. Screamed speech becomes knotted into contorted speech, into the language of frustration. We can also ask ourselves whether the strategy of delirium has not contributed to maintaining

Creole, in spite of the conditions that do not favor its continued existence. We know that delirious speech can be a survival technique.

But it is in the folktale itself, that echo of the plantation, that we can sense the pathetic lucidity of the Creole speaker. An analysis of the folktale reveals the extent to which the *inadequacies* with which the community is afflicted (absence of a hinterland, loss of technical responsibility, isolation from the Caribbean region, etc.) are fixed in terms of popular imagery. What is remarkable is that this process is always elliptical, quick, camouflaged by derision. That is what we shall see in the folktale. The latter really emanates from a forced poetics: it is a tense discourse that, woven around the inadequacies that afflict it, is committed, in order to deny more defiantly the criteria for transcendence into writing, to constantly refusing to perfect its expression. The Creole folktale includes the ritual of participation but carefully excludes the potential for consecration. It fixes expression in the realm of the derisively aggressive.

## Creole and Landscape

1.  I do not propose to examine the Creole folktale as a signifying system, nor to isolate its component structures. Synthesis of animal symbolism (African and European), survivals of transplanted tales, keen observation of the master's world by the slave, rejection of the work, ethic cycle of fear, hunger, and misery, containing hope that is invariably unfulfilled; much work has been done on the Creole folktale. My intention is more modest in its attempt to link it to its context.

What is striking is the emphatic emptiness of the landscape in the Creole folktale; in it landscape is reduced to symbolic space and becomes a pattern of succeeding spaces through which one journeys; the forest and its darkness, the savannah and its daylight, the hill and its fatigue. Really, places you pass through. The importance of walking is amazing. "I walked so much," the tale more or less says, "that I was exhausted and I ended up heel first." The route is reversible. There is, naturally, vegetation along these routes; animals mark the way. But it is important to realize that if the place is indicated, *it is never described*. The description of the landscape is not a feature of the folktale. Neither the joy nor the pleasure of describing are evident in it. This is because the landscape of the folktale is not meant to be inhabited. A place you pass through, it is not yet a country.

2.  So this land is never possessed: it is never the subject of the most fundamental protest. There are two dominant characters in the Creole folktales: the King (symbolic of the European it has been said, or is it the *béké?*) and Brer Tiger (symbolic of the *béké* colonizer or simply the black foreman?); the latter, always ridiculed, is often outwitted by the character who is in control, Brer Rabbit (symbolic of the cleverness of the people).[3] But the right to the possession of land by the dominant figures is never questioned. The symbolism of the folktale never goes so far as to eradicate the colonial right to ownership, its moral never involves a final appeal to the suppression of this right. I do not see resignation in this, but a clear instance of the extreme strategy that I mentioned: the pathetic obsession, in these themes—in a word, the inflexible maneuver—through which the Creole folktale indicates that it has *verified* the nature of the system and its structure.

In such a context, man (the animal who symbolizes him) has with things and trees, creatures and people, nothing like a sustained relationship. The extreme "breathlessness" of the Creole folktale leaves no room for quiet rest. No time to gaze at things. The relationship with one's surroundings is always dramatic and suspicious. The tale is breathless, but it is because it has chosen not to *waste* time. Just as it does not describe, it hardly concerns itself with appreciating the world. There are no soothing shadows or moments of sweet langor. You must run without stopping, from a past order that is rejected to an absurd present. The land that has been suffered is not yet the land that is offered, made accessible. National consciousness is budding in the tale, but it does not burst into bloom.

Another recurring feature is the criterion for assessing the "benefits" that man here recognizes as his own. Where it is a matter of the pleasure of living, or the joy of possessing, the Creole tale recognizes only two conditions, absence or excess. A pathetic lucidity. The benefits are ridiculously small or excessive. Excessive in quantity, when the tale makes up its list of food, for instance; excessive in quality when the tale works out the complicated nature of what is valuable or worth possessing. A "castle" is quickly described (ostentatious, luxurious, comfortable, prestigious) then it is said in one breath, and without any warning, that it has two hundred and ten toilets. Such extravagance is absurd, for "true wealth" is absent from the closed world of the plantation. Excess and absence complement each other in accentuating the same impossible ideal. The tale thus established its decor in an unreal world, either too much or nothing, which exceeds the real country and yet is a precise indication of its structure.

We also observe that there is in the tale no reference to daily techniques of work or creation. Here, the tool is experienced as "remote." The tool, normally man's instrument for dealing with nature, is an impossible reality. Thus, equipment and machinery that are featured in the tale are always associated with an owner whose prestige—that is, who is above the rest—is implicit. It is a matter of "the truck of M. This" or the "sugar mill of M. That." The tool is the other's property; technology remains alien. Man does not (cannot) undertake the transformation of his landscape. He does not even have the luxury of celebrating its beauty, which perhaps seems to him to be a mocking one.

## Convergence

1.   Where then to locate the will to "endure"? What is the effect of such a "forced" poetics or counterpoetics, which does not spring to life from a fertile past, but, on the contrary, builds its "wall of sticks" against fated destruction, negation, confinement?

a.   This counterpoetics therefore ensures the synthesis of culturally diverse, sometimes distinct, elements.
b.   At least a part of these elements does not predate the process of synthesis, which makes their combination all the more necessary but all the more threatened.
c.   This characteristic contains all the force (energy, drama) of such a forced poetics.
d.   This forced poetics will become worn out if it does not develop into a natural, free, open, cross-cultural poetics.

The thrust behind this counterpoetics is therefore primarily locked into a defensive strategy—that is, into an unconscious body of knowledge through which the popular consciousness asserts both its rootlessness and its density. We must, however, move form this unconscious awareness to a conscious knowledge of self.

Here we need perhaps some concluding observations, relating to the link between this situation and what is called today ethnopoetics.

2.   First of all, from the perspective of the conflict between Creole and French, in which one has thus far evolved at the expense of the other, we can state that the only possible strategy is to make them *opaque* to each other. To develop everywhere, in defiance of a universalizing and reductive humanism, the theory of specifically opaque structures. In the world of cross-cultural relationship, which takes over from the homogeneity of the single culture, to accept this opaqueness—that is, the irreducible density of the other—is to truly accomplish, through diversity, a human objective. Humanity is perhaps not the "image of man" but today the evergrowing network of recognized opaque structures.

Second, poetics could not be separated from the functional nature of language. It will not be enough to struggle to write or speak Creole in order to save this language. It will be necessary to transform the conditions of production and release thereby the potential for total, technical control by the Martinican of his country, so that the language may truly develop. In other words, all ethnopoetics, at one time or another must face up to the political situation.

Finally, the previous discussion adequately demonstrates that, if certain communities, oppressed by the historical weight of dominant ideologies, aim at converting their utterance into a scream, thereby rediscovering the innocence of a primitive community, for us it will be a question of transforming a scream (which we once uttered into a speech that grows from it, thus discovering the expression, perhaps in an intellectual way, of a finally liberated poetics. I think that ethnopoetics can reconcile these very different procedures.

Counterpoetics carried out by Martinicans (in works written in France, the use of the Creole language, the refuge of verbal delirium) therefore records simultaneously both a need for collective expression and a present inability to attain true expression. This contradiction will probably disappear when the Martinican community is able to really speak for itself: that is, choose for itself. Ethnopoetics belongs to the future.

## Cross-Cultural Poetics

The epic of the Zulu Emperor Chaka, as related by Thomas Mofolo,[4] seems to me to exemplify an African poetics. Evidence of parallels with Western epic forms is not lacking: depiction of a tyrannical tendency (ambition), involvement of the Zulu community in the hero's tragedy, the rise and fall of the hero. You could not consider the magical aspect (origin of the warrior, importance of medicine men, practices and rites) as a particularly African theme. All epics that relate how peoples advance make this appeal to divine intervention. The oral form is not peculiar either; after all, Homer's poems were meant to be sung, recited, or danced.

There are two specific features that make *Chaka* particularly interesting. It is an epic that, while enacting the "universal" themes of passion and man's destiny, is not concerned with the *origin* of a people or its early history. Such an epic does not include a creation myth. On the contrary, it is related to a much more dangerous moment in the experience of the people concerned, that of its forthcoming contact with conquerors coming from the North. One is struck by the similarity between the experiences of these great, fugitive African rulers, who created from a village or tribe huge empires and all ended up in prison, exile, or dependent. (Their experience is repeated as caricature in the ambitions of these pseudo-conquerors who appeared as a postcolonial phenomenon, former subordinates or officers in colonial armies, who cause so much ridicule or indignation in the West, which created them and gave them authority.) All the great African conquerors of the eighteenth and nineteenth centuries were haunted in this way by the approach of the white man. It is to the latter that Chaka refers when he is assassinated by those close to him. It seems that his life, his actions, and his work are the ultimate barrier with which he tries to prevent their intrusion, and only he understands. African poets will also be haunted by this fate, and their poems will chronicle these experiences. We in Martinique were touched by this obsession when the King of Dahomey, Béhanzin, was deported here. The epic of these conquered heroes, which was also that of their peoples or tribes, sometimes of their beliefs, is not meant, when recounted, to reassure a community of its legitimacy in the world. They are not creation epics, great "books" about genesis, like the *Iliad* and the *Odyssey*, the Old Testament, the sagas, and the chansons de geste. They are the memories of cultural contact, which are put together collectively by a people before being dispersed by colonization. There is no evidence therefore of that "naive consciousness" that Hegel defines as the popular phase of the epic, but a strangled awareness that will remain an underlying element in the life of African peoples during the entire period of colonization.[5]

(In my reading of transcriptions of African epics [those of the Segou Empire among the Bambaras, for example, compiled and translated by African researchers and Lilyan Kesteloot], I am aware of a certain "suspension" of the narrative: as if, while composing his discourse, the poet seems *to be waiting for something* that he knows he cannot stop. The succession of kings does not give rise to [nor is it based on] a theory of legitimacy. The epic is disruptive. History comes to an abrupt end. Memory becomes secretive, it must be forced to the surface. The white man ultimately intrudes and forces it into the open. The secret fire of the communal palaver is dispersed in the wind. The foresight of the epic is to have always known that this contact with another culture *would come*. This anticipation of cultural contact has been interpreted by O. Mannoni as a dependency complex: "Wherever Europeans have founded colonies of the type we are considering, it can safely be said that their coming was unconsciously expected—even desired—by the future subject peoples."[6] Frantz Fanon denounced this interpretation—*Black Skin, White Masks*. European peoples, while being aggressive concerning the cross-cultural process, could not understand its poetics, which to them represented weakness and surrender.[7] M. Mannoni made this blindness the basis for his theory.)

The other characteristic derives from a basic feature of the epic narrative, which has disappeared almost completely from Western literature: I call it *the poetics of duration*. At no point does language in the African epic claim to delight, surprise, or dazzle. It does not harangue the listener; it appeals to him; it captivates him; it leads him through its dense accretions in which little by little its message is outlined. To my mind, the creation of distinct literary genres has facilitated the disappearance of such a poetics in Western literatures. The existence of the novel and its specific conventions has increasingly caused all exploration of time and all related techniques to be restricted to this genre. At the same time the poem became the realm of the *unsayable*: that which is dazzling is its conciseness, the brilliance of its revelations, the extreme edge of clairvoyance. A *poetics of the moment*. But to discriminate in this manner between the genres and to confine them to poetics so diametrically opposed neutralize these poetics in relation to each other, and subject them henceforth to their conventions instead of allowing the latter to be challenged.

In the poetics of the oral African text *everything can be said*. The dense mystery that surrounds the figure of Chaka does not originate in what the epic narrative hides from us but from the process of accumulation.

The poetically unsayable seems to me tied, in the West, to what one calls the dignity of the human being, in turn surpassed since the historical appearance of private property. This daring leap allows us to argue that poetic passion, insofar as it requires a self, assumes, first, that the community has abandoned its basic right to be established and has been organized around the rights of the private individual. The poetically unsayable reflects the ultimate manifestation of the economics of the right to property. Paradoxically, it is characterized by transparency and not by obscurity.

I have constantly contrasted this keen awareness of the individual with the no less intense feeling for the dignity of the group, that appears to be characteristic of many non-Western civilizations. In contrast to the progression: private property—dignity of the individual—the poetically unsayable, I placed another that seemed to me equally fundamental: indivisibility of the land—dignity of the community—the explicitness of song. Such an opposition between civilizations also helped to explain the ruptures in Caribbean culture, in which the African heritage (the feeling for the dignity of the group) came up against an impossible circumstance (the collective nonpossession of the land) and in which the explicitness of the song (the traditional oral culture) was impeded by Western education (the initiation into the poetically unsayable). We have surrendered to a fascination with poetic obscurity that it is long and painful to get rid of: Rimbaud did more than trade in Abyssinia. And I have known so many young French Caribbean poets, desperately unable to accommodate this obscurity and yet fascinated by the success of Aimé Césaire in this area, who exhausted themselves in negotiating its dazzling power, without knowing that they had the potential for creating *another way of organizing language*. Neutralized, made impotent by this dream of poetic brilliance, they paid no heed to the throbbing within them of the notion of time that had to be possessed.

But these kinds of parallel oppositions are as well founded as they are misleading. I think, for instance, that from the distinction between collective ownership of the land (in Africa) and private property (in the West), one has been able to construct the theory of African Socialism, which would appear to be more natural (and thus more "human"), whereas Western Socialism would not have been anything but a *reaction* against the received idea of private property. These theories that emphasize the natural (always more attractive than a reaction) are justifiably reassuring. We know the amazing misdeeds, ideological as well as physical, of this African Socialism, in those countries where it has become established as a principle as much as a reality.[8]

I maintain, however, that there is a profound relationship between the poetics of the moment and the belief that emphasizes the dignity of the human individual, and also the shaping influence of private property. The logic of these ideas contains implicitly the limitation of individual interests. It is difficult to separate theoretically the notion of individual dignity from the oppressive reality of private property. This makes sublimation necessary. This explains why Western philosophy and ideology all aim for a *generalizing universality*. (Even today, the part of M. Léopold Senghor's formulations most easily recognized in Western intellectual circles is that of the general idea of Universal Civilization.) A generalizing universality is ambitious enough to allow for the sublimation of individual dignity based on the reality of private property. It is also the ultimate weapon in the process of depersonalizing a vulnerable people. The first reaction against this generalizing universality is the stubborn insistence on *remaining where you are*. But for us this place is not only the land where our people were transplanted, it is also the history they shared (experiencing it as nonhistory) with other communities, with whom the link is becoming apparent today. Our place is the Caribbean.

Caribbeanness, an intellectual dream, lived at the same time in an unconscious way by our peoples, tears us free from the intolerable alternative of the need for nationalism and introduces us to the cross-cultural process that modifies but does not undermine the latter.

What is the Caribbean in fact? A multiple series of relationships. We all feel it, we express it in all kinds of hidden or twisted ways, or we fiercely deny it. But we sense that this sea exists within us with its weight of now revealed islands.

The Caribbean Sea is not an American lake. It is the estuary of the Americas.

In this context, insularity takes on another meaning. Ordinarily, insularity is treated as a form of isolation, a neurotic reaction to place. However, in the Caribbean each island embodies openness. The dialectic between inside and outside is reflected in the relationship of land and sea. It is only those who are tied to the European continent who see insularity as confining.[9] A Caribbean imagination liberates us from being smothered.

It is true that, among Caribbean cultures, we in Martinique have only been allowed access, and for historic reasons, to language. We have so many words tucked away in out throats, and so little "raw material" with which to execute our potential.

This is perhaps why I was so moved when I discovered the rhetorical power of black American speech. I remember having heard, at Tufts University, an exposé on Afro-American literature and having discovered with great surprise and feeling the spectacle of this audience that, rhythmically swaying, turned the lecturer's text into melody. I also saw the television film on Martin Luther King and discovered the doubling of the voice, the echo placed behind the speaker to repeat and amplify his speech. As in the tragic text, here repetition is not gratuitous. Therein lies a new management of language.

And just as poetic brilliance is the supreme state in exalting the self, I can also speculate that repetition in speech is a response to the group. But this group is not a form of transcendence. One can even state with justification that by its very nature it is derived from that basic symptom of the cross-cultural process that is Creolization.

If we speak of creolized cultures (like Caribbean culture, for example) it is not to define a category that will by its very nature be opposed to other categories ("pure" cultures), but in order to assert that today infinite varieties of creolization are open to human conception, both on the level of awareness and on that of intention: in theory and in reality.

Creolization as an idea is not primarily the glorification of the composite nature of a people: indeed, no people has been spared the cross-cultural process. The idea of creolization demonstrates that henceforth it is no longer valid to glorify "unique" origins that the race safeguards and prolongs. In Western tradition, genealogical descent guarantees racial exclusivity, just as Genesis legitimizes genealogy. To assert peoples are creolized, that creolization has value, is to deconstruct in this way the category of "creolized" that is considered as halfway between two "pure" extremes. It is only in those countries whose exploitation is barbaric (South Africa, for instance) that this intermediary category has been officially recognized. This is perhaps what was felt by the Caribbean poet who, in response to my thoughts on creolization in Caribbean cultures, said to me: "I understand the reality, I just do not like the word." Creolization as an idea means the negation of creolization as a category, by giving priority to the notion of natural creolization, which the human imagination has always wished to deny or disguise (in Western tradition).[10] Analyses of the phenomena of acculturation and deculturation are therefore sterile in conception. *All societies undergo acculturation.* Deculturation is able to be transformed into a new culture. Here it is important to stress not so much the mechanisms of acculturation and deculturation as the dynamic forces capable of limiting or prolonging them.

We realize that peoples who are most "manifestly" composite have minimized the idea of Genesis. The fact is that the "end" of the myth of Genesis means the beginning of this use of genealogy to persuade oneself that exclusivity has been preserved. Composite peoples, that is, those who could not deny or mask their hybrid composition, nor sublimate it in the notion of a mythical pedigree, do not "need" the idea of Genesis, because they do not need the myth of pure lineage. (The only traces of "genesis" identifiable in the Caribbean folktale are satirical and mocking. God removed the White man [pale] too soon from the oven of Creation; the Black man [burnt] too late; this version would lead us to believe that the mulatto – with whom the Caribbean would therefore wish to identify – is the only one to be properly cooked. But another version of these three baked creatures claims that the first was in fact not dark enough, the second not sufficiently cooked [mulattoes], and the third just right [blacks]. The Martinican consciousness is always tormented by contradictory possibilities. These parodies of genesis do not seriously claim, in any case, to offer an explanation for origins; they imply a satirical attitude to any notion of a transcendental Genesis.) The poetics of creolization is the same as a cross-cultural poetics: not linear and not prophetic, but woven from enduring patience and irreducible accretions.

Also a cross-cultural poetics could not constitute a science, that is, to be generalized by laws and definitions of distinct processes,. It is not known; only recognizable.

Neither the formula from Parmenides, "Being never changes," nor the related view by Heraclitus, "All is in a state of flux," through which Western metaphysics were conceived, but a transphysical poetics that could be briefly expressed as – that which is (that which exists in a total way) is open to change.

Total existence is always relative.

It is not certain that in the West materialism does not sometimes appear as the metaphysical adjunct of idealism. Since it is the same view of history, it can support the most intolerant form of transcendentalism.

Any transphysical poetics of creolization contributes to undermining this blind solidarity.

This means that creolization and history could not lead us to any belief in cultural exclusivity, nor be expressed in terms of its poetics.

Because the poetics of the cross-cultural imagination turns up in a plowing up of phenomena that acquire significance when put together, and in the domain of the unseen of which we represent the constantly shifting background.

The accumulation of the commonplace and the clarification of related obscurity, creolization is the unceasing process of transformation.

## Complementary Note Concerning a Pseudo-Encounter

This example of negative cultural contact is offered by the short story "Music for Chameleons" by Truman Capote, totally concerned with a vision of Martinique and published in the *New Yorker* of 17 September 1979. The author recounts in it his visit to an old female member of the aristocracy (*béké?*) in Fort-de-France, and the text offers a survey of many commonly held views (pertinent or false) of Martinique from the perspective of a tourist (T) and a colonialist (C).

"The whole island floats in strangeness. This very house is haunted" (C).
"Martinique is the only island in the Caribbean not cursed with mosquitoes" (T).
"My paternal grandmother was from New Orleans" (C).
"People from Martinique seem so preoccupied. Like Russians" (T).
"Martinique is *très cher*" (T).
"Martinique could not exist without subsidy from France" (C).
"The troublemakers [and] their independence" (C).
"The women. . . . Supple, suave, such beautifully haughty postures" (T).

"The men are not appealing . . . they seem . . . without character" (T).

"It belonged to Gaugin. . . . That was his black mirror" (C).

"[Your restaurants] are better than others in the Caribbean. But too expensive" (T).

". . . foreign ladies . . . wearing nothing above and very little below. Do they permit that in your country?" (C).

"Usually, I leave the island during Carnaval" (C).

"As spontaneous and vivid as an explosion in a fireworks factory" (T).

"We are not a violent people" (repeated) (C).

"Madame is toying with the same tune. A Mozartian mosaic" (T).

This noncontact results from the fact that no reader could imagine the true Martinique under this fantasy version; that this fantasy is of no value (artistic or ethnological): it is entirely superficial and verbal. In other words: that neither the thoughts nor the "substance" offered by the writer are pertinent. He is on one side; the subject of his story is on the other side.

## "The Novel of the Americas"

I will attempt to bring to light a few of the themes common to the concerns of those whom we classify here as American writers. Using my own work and my own preoccupations as points of reference, I will try to state the assumptions around which I feel the work of writers in the Americas instinctively revolves.

Certainly, one essential obsession that I characterize in these terms: a tortured sense of time.

I think that the haunting nature of the past (it is a point that has been widely raised) is one of the essential points of reference in the works produced in the Americas. What "happens," indeed, is that it is apparently a question of shedding light on a chronology that has become obscure, when it is not completely effaced for all kinds of reasons, especially colonial ones. The American novelist, whatever the cultural zone he belongs to, is not at all in search of a lost time, but finds himself struggling in the confusion of time. And, from Faulkner to Carpentier, we are faced with apparent snatches of time that have been sucked into banked up or swirling forces.

We have seen that the poetics of the American continent, which I characterize as being a search for temporal duration, is opposed in particular to European poetics, which are characterized by the inspiration or the sudden burst of a single moment. It seems that, when dealing with the anxiety of time, American writers are prey to a kind of future remembering. By that I mean that it is almost certain that we are writers in an embryonic phase and our public is yet to come. Also, that this exploded, suffered time is linked to "transferred" space. I have in mind African space as much as Breton space, the "memory" of which has become stamped on the spatial reality that we all live. To confront time is, therefore, for us to deny its linear structure. All chronology is too immediately obvious, and in the works of the American novelist we must struggle against time in order to reconstitute the past, even when it concerns those parts of the Americas where historical memory has not been obliterated. It follows that, caught in the swirl of time, the American novelist dramatizes it in order to deny it better or to reconstruct it; I will describe us, as far as this is concerned, as those who shatter the stone of time. We do not see it stretch into out past (calmly carry us into the future) but implode in us in clumps, transported in fields of oblivion where we must, with difficulty and pain, put it all back together if we wish to make contact with ourselves and express ourselves.

For us, the inescapable *shaping force* in our production of literature is what I would call the language of landscape. We can say that the European literary imagination is moulded spatially around the spring and the meadow. Ernst Robert Curtius has proposed this in *European Literature and the Latin Middle Ages*.

In European literature an intimate relationship with landscape is primarily established. From this has evolved a stylistic convention that has for a long time focused on meticulous detail, exposition "in sequence," highlighting harmony (exceptions or extensions constitute reactions to this rule). Space in the American novel, on the contrary (but not so much in the physical sense), seems to me open, explored, rent.

There is something violent in this American sense of literary space. In it the prevailing force is not that of the spring and the meadow, but rather that of the wind that blows and casts shadows like a great tree. This is why realism – that is, the logical and rational attitude toward the visible world – more than anywhere else would in out case betray the true meaning of things. As one says that a painter at work sees the light on his subject change with the movement of the sun, so it seems to me, as far as I am concerned, that my landscape changes in me; it is probable that it changes with me.

I could not say like Valéry: "Beautiful sky, true sky, look at me as I change." The landscape has its language. What is it in our world? Certainly not the immobility of Being, juxtaposed to a relative notion of what I could become, and confronted with an absolute truth that I could reach out for. The very words and letters of the American novel are entangled in the strands, in the mobile structures of one's own landscape. And the language of my landscape is primarily that of the forest, which unceasingly bursts with life. I do not practice the economy of the meadow, I do not share the serenity of the spring.

But what we have in common is *the irruption into modernity*.

We do not have a literary tradition that has slowly matured: ours was a brutal emergence that I think is an advantage and not a failing. The finished surface of a culture exasperates me if it is not based on the slow weathering of time. If the glossy surface of a culture is not the result of tradition or sustained action, it becomes empty and parochial. (That is the weakness of our intellectuals.) We do not have the time, we are everywhere driven by the daring adventure of modernity. Parochialism is reassuring to one who has not found his center in himself, and to my mind we must construct our metropoles in ourselves. The irruption into modernity, the violent departure from tradition, from literary "continuity," seems to me a specific feature of the American writer when he wishes to give meaning to the reality of his environment.

Therefore, we share the same form of expression. And I will forever oppose the notion of language to that of self-expression.[11]

I think that, beyond the language used, there is a form of expression specific to the American novel[12] that is at the same time the product of a reaction of confidence in words, of a kind of complicity with the word, of a functional conception of time (consequently, of synatactical time), and ultimately of a tortured relationship between writing and orality.

One of the effects derived from my own literary activity is concerned with precisely this interest: I am from a country in which the transition is being made from a traditional oral literature, under constraint, to a written nontraditional literature, also equally constrained. My language attempts to take shape at the edge of writing and speech; to indicate this transition – which is certainly quite difficult in any approach to literature. I am not talking about either the written or the oral in the sense that one observes a novelist reproducing everyday speech, using a style at the "zero degree of wring." I am referring to a synthesis, synthesis of written syntax and spoken rhythms, of "acquired" writing and oral "reflex," of the solitude of writing and the solidarity of the collective voice – a synthesis that I find interesting to attempt.

The fact is that we are in the midst of a struggle of peoples. Perhaps this would then be our first "axis."

The issue (experienced in the specific struggles that take place more or less everywhere along the chain of the Americas) is the appearance of a new man, whom I would define, with reference to his "realization" in literature, as a man who is able to live the relative after having suffered the absolute. When I say *relative*, I mean the Diverse, the obscure need to accept the other's difference; and when I say *absolute* I refer to the dramatic endeavor to impose a truth on the Other. I feel that the man from the Other America "merges" with this new man, who lives the relative; and that the struggles of peoples who try to survive in the American continent bear witness to this new creation.

The expression of class struggle has sometimes been "deadened" through the existence of zones of nothingness so extreme that even the perspective of a class struggle has appeared utopian or farfetched (Peruvian Indians, tribes of the Amazon). In other places, depersonalization has been so systematic that the very survival of an autochthonous culture can be questioned (Martinique). The "novel of the Americas" uses an allegorical mode that ranges from blatant symbolism (the peasant novels of South America, or, for example, *Gouverneurs de la rosée* [*Masters of the dew*] by J. Roumain) to heavy descriptive machinery (Gallegos or Asturias) to the more complex works that combine an exploration of alienation with the attempt to define an appropriate language (García Márquez). What is perhaps missing is the perspective of those zones of culture that are more threatened (by total dispossession as in the case of the Quechuas of Peru, by slow depersonalization as in the case of Martinicans), therefore more "exemplary," in which he experience of the Diverse is played out at an unknown pace that is comfortably or desperately tragic.

I am summing up what I have discussed too briefly – it is interesting to avoid sustained expositions and to try to propose points of discussion – while formulating a concept one may suspect of being designed to please. (Whom? I do not know.)

I wish to speak of the question of lived modernity, which I will not simply add to, but which I will link directly to the notion of a matured modernity. By this I am opposing, not a kind of "primitivism" to a kind of "intellectualism," but two ways of dealing with changes in contemporary reality. *Matured* here means "developed over extended historical space"; *lived* means "that which is abruptly imposed." When I witness from a little distance the very interesting work being done on a theorectical level in the West, it seems to me that two reactions are formed: I experience at the same time a feeling of the ridiculous and a feeling of the extreme importance of these ideas. For instance, on the subject of the destabilizing of the text and "its" author.

The text is destabilized (in the matured modernist theories of the West) to the extent that it is demythified, that one tries to define the system that generates it. The author is demythified to the extent that he is made into, let us say, the site where these generative systems manifest themselves, and not the autonomous creative genius he thought he was. If I say that it seems ridiculous to me, it is because (in our lived modernity) these issues have no bearing on us. We need to develop a poetics of the "subject," if only because we have been too long "objectified" or rather "objected to." And if I say that this seems important to me, it is because these queries relate to our deepest preoccupations. The text must for us (in our lived experience) be destabilized, because it must belong to a shared reality, and it is perhaps at this point that we actually relate to these ideas that have emerged elsewhere. The author must be demythified, certainly, because he must be integrated into a common resolve. The collective "We" becomes the site of the generative system, and the true subject. Our critique of the act and the idea of literary creation is not derived from a "reaction" to theories which are proposed to us, but from a burning need for *modification*.

I am suggesting that it is relevant to our discussion to try to show – if possible (and I do not think in any case that I have demonstrated it) – that "American" literature is the product of a system of modernity that is sudden and not sustained or "evolved." For instance, was not the tragedy of those American writers of the "lost generation" that they continued in literature the European (or "Bostonian") dream of Henry James? The United States thus combined two kinds of alienation in a great number of its reactions: that of wanting to continue politely a European tradition to which the United States felt itself to be the ultimate heir; and that of wanting to dominate the world savagely in the name of this ultimate legacy. Faulkner's roots in the *Deep South* free him from the dream of becoming European. This is his true modernity as opposed to Fitzgerald, for example, or Hemingway, in spite of the "modern" themes of the latter. The idea, however, is that this modernity, lived to the fullest in "new worlds," overlaps with the preoccupations of mature "modernity" in other zones of culture and thought. Therefore, I think that this problematic relationship is a strong force in our literatures. (The problematic is a larger manifestation of the "lived" reality.) And, in my capacity as an American writer, I think that any dogmatic conception of literary creation (as the highest point of an evolved system) would be opposed to this force.[13]

[. . .]

# NOTES

1   I have always been fascinated by the well-known Italian story, probably invented by the French, of the notice posted in a bus: "Do not speak to the driver. He needs his hands for driving." The motionless body in the act of writing, moreover, favors a neurotic "internalization." The orality that accompanies the "rules of writing" is that of *speaking well* (in seventeenth-century French) which is fixed in a reductive monolingualism. Stendhal says about Italy in the nineteenth century (*De l'amour*, Chapter 49) that there one speaks rarely in order to "speak well"; and also that "Venetian, Neapolitan, Genoese, Predmontese are almost toally different languages and only spoken by people for whom the printed word can exist only in a common language, the one spoken in Rome." Let us add, by contrast, that such a strategy would not be possible today for Creole. One could not simply decide, for example, to opt unanimously for the Haitian transcriptive model (probably the most elaborate one). The freedom to write is necessary for the Creole language, above and beyond the variations in dialect.

2   The Creole language will call for a noise, a disorder; thus aggravating the ambiguity.

3   We must note that this symbolism is in itself ambiguous. The King, God, the Lion. Where, in fact, is the colonizer? Where is the administrator? Rabbit is the popular ideal, but he is hard on the poor; perhaps he is "mulatto," etc. The proposed ideal is from the outset shaped by a negation of popular "values." One can only escape by ceasing to be oneself, while trying to remain so. The character of Brer Rabbit is therefore *also* the projection of this individual ingenuity that is sanctioned by a collective absence. ("Bastardizing of the race. Here is the major phenomenon. Individual solutions replace collective ones. Solutions based on craftiness replace solutions based on

force." [Aimé Césaire and René Ménil, "Introduction au folklore martiniquais," *Tropiques*, no. 4 [January 1942]: 10.)

4   Thomas Mofolo, *Chaka* (London and Nairobi: Heinemann, 1981).

5   A popular series brings back to life today these historical figures from Africa. Almost each volume insists on this encounter between the African chiefs and the inevitable colonizer, who appears as the very embodiment of their destiny. (In the series of *Les Grandes Figures Africaines*.)

6   Dommique O. Mannoni, *Prospero and Caliban: The Psychology of Colonization* (New York and London: Praeger and Methuen, 1956), p. 86.

7   The West continues to be today the most dynamic agent of cross-cultural contact, through the frightening technological capacity that enables it to control systems of communication all over the globe and to manage the wealth of the world. It is beginning, however, to realize its power, and to that extent to go further than M. Mannoni.

8   These variations on Socialism are not to be scorned, however, or rejected categorically. In his study of Indianness, the Mexican anthropologist Guillermo Bonfil Batalla ("I.a nueva presencia politica de los Indios," *Casa de las Americas*. October 1979) distinguishes four ideologies in his version of the future of South America: Restoration of the past, by excluding Western civilization; the reformist position, which adapts the existing system; Indian Socialism, which applies the model of Indian societies modified by the universal elements provided by the West; and finally, Pluralist Socialism, a revolutionary transformation of the capitalist mode of production.

9   Both on the Right and on the Left, there are those who will claim that you "vegetate" in these islands; they will seek, preferably in Paris, to improve their minds.

10 "Cross-cultural contact" has also become an argument for assimilationist propaganda. Young Martinican are told in 1980: "It is the age of cultural exchange" – which implies: "Do not isolate yourselves therefore in an outmoded and inflexible nationalism, etc."

11 "Ah ah, said the countess in Portuguese and to herself, for she spoke these two languages . . .": this passage from a story told in France fascinates me because of its meaningful ambiguity (its obscurity). There is an inner language that surpasses any acquired language (the interior monologure *cannot become external speech*. It has meaning only in obscurity: that of Benjy, at the beginning of the novel *The Sound and the Fury*).

12 I realize that I am now referring to the novel of the "Other America" (the Caribbean and South America) and not so much to that which is fixed (by word and gesture) in the urban, industrial world of the north of the United States. I also tend to relate Faulkner's work (the furthest from northern America as far as his ideas are concerned) to this group, in defiance of reality, and I need to clarify this. Such a clarification was attempted when I spoke of the *desire for history* in literature and the tragic return, which Faulkner has in common with us.

13 Western critics would certainly agree that we should remain at the level of the lived and the instinctive (we would be instinctive creators) and would sing our praises as long as they could so reserve for themselves the dimension of thought (they would be the look that organizes and appreciates). We are pushed, for instance, towards "intuitive art," which can only have meaning in the context of a civilization that has developed a tradition of "highly finished art." Congratulating M. Césaire on a speech that he gave at a conference held in Fort-de-France in 1979, a journalist from the Hersant group declared his pride in having as a compatriot this "Frenchman from the Caribbean," in being charmed by his "incantatory flourishes," by the impeccable form of his speech, after which he revealed that none of the ideas of the speaker were worth retaining, even if the latter is more Latin and Cartsian than he thinks, and no more Caribbean than a former journalist from *Le Figaro*.

*On the notion of modernity*. It is a vexed question. Is not every era "modern" in relation to the preceding one? It seems that at least one of the components of "our" modernity is the spread of the awareness we have of it. The awareness of our awareness (the double, the second degree) is our source of strength and our torment.

# PART V
# Global and Local Perspectives

# 32
# Uncertain Modernities: Amerindian Epistemologies and the Reorienting of Culture
## Elizabeth Monasterios P.

> ¿Cuándo reventará la dignidad humana?
> ¿Cuándo se sublevará la humillación?
> *Arturo Borda*

In the field of Latin American Studies, recent decades of theoretical reflection have significantly reoriented our understanding of the hegemonic modernity introduced into America by sixteenth-century European mercantilism. It became clear that since its inception, this modernity has confronted subjects, histories, cultures, and economies that have obstinately challenged its hegemony by means of collective resistances and cultural practices which refused to die or to be absorbed by the new historical force.

The empires that mobilized this first European expansion (Spain and Portugal in our case) also obstinately refused to imagine forms of social coexistence not ruled by the logic of possession, consumption, commoditization, and violence. Colonizing from its inception, this first modernity built itself upon a structure of political, economic, and theological power that claimed universal applicability, and rendered any expression of difference invisible or subaltern. Hence we should not be surprised that scholarly debates on this modernity have often been informed by postcolonial theory, given the commitment of this late twentieth-century paradigm with both the historical destinies of the colonized and the dismantling of Enlightened reason. However, as the twentieth century drew to an end, an erosion of Latin American local theorizations – which were empowered by massive radicalizations led by social, indigenous, and women's movements – have challenged the theoretical reach of postcolonial theory, creating a need to rethink the role that the Latin American corpus could or could not have in relation to this conceptual paradigm.

To start, it became evident the extent to which postcolonial primary theoretical sources (Fanon, Glissant, Said, Bhabha, Spivak, the South Asian Subaltern Studies collective), as well as Latin American responses and interventions (Beverley, Castro-Klaren, Dussel, Escobar, García Linera, Mignolo, Patzi, Quijano, Rabasa, Rodríguez, Rivera Cusicanqui, to name notable instances), operate from different historical and cognitive perspectives. In general, what the metropolitan academy promoted as "post-colonial theory" relied on the works of Said, Spivak, or Bhabha, who framed the inaugural moment of modernity in the eighteenth century, and within the limits of a South–North discussion engaged from the perspective of US-based English departments openly perceived as hegemonic centers of postcolonial master discourse. The fact that in Latin America and the Caribbean the historical experience of modernity has a colonial past of its own (which refers to the sixteenth century, when the first European expansion "turned the world upside down," in the words of Guamán Poma de Ayala) reveals a first and crucial difference between the referential frame of post-colonial theory and that of the theoretical reflection about and from Latin America. In addition, it is important to observe that while postcolonial studies "favor the mediation of knowledge via Europe and Western epistemologies" (Rodríguez, 2005: 55) and are performed by metropolitan scholars committed to what Hernán Vidal (1993: 116) once called "literary critical technocracy," the field of Latin American critical thought offers a rich tradition of decolonizing historiography in which Western mediations are conceived as problematic and indigenous and non-institutionalized thinkers (such as Guamán Poma, José Carlos Mariátegui, Fausto Reinaga, or Rivera Cusicanqui, for instance) are as relevant as academic ones.

This situation calls our attention toward a rarely mentioned but very important fact which frames the Latin American corpus in relation to postcolonial debates: as well as a criticism that produces knowledge from the needs of the metropolitan academy, there is a critical thought that is rooted directly in the Latin American context. Not to pay attention to these nuances, not to discuss them, leads to perceive decolonizing impulses as expressions of an epistemic corpus conceived and oriented only from hegemonic cultural centers. By the same token, it leaves undebated the groundbreaking critique of postcolonial episteme (but also to any reflection of decolonizing nature) posed by some skeptical cultural criticism. This critique is founded on the idea that in Latin America, owing to the hegemony of a modernity solidly identified with change, futurity, the Spanish language, and Christianity, "there has been no autochthonous sphere that could be configured and opposed overtly to the West as a strategy of containment, since cultural identity has been so inextricably bound to modernity" (Alonso, 1998: 34).

My intention in writing this chapter is to reflect on the conceptual conflict of modernity when a plurality of theoretical consciousness comes into play, and when metropolitan and highly canonical critical perspectives enter into dialogue with non-hegemonic spheres of contestation in ways Alonso's criticism – but also US hegemonic centers of postcolonial critique – do not conceive of. Theoretically, this venue remains unexplored, mainly because the metropolitan academy has not yet interrogated Latin American non-hegemonic and, in many cases, non-academic critical thought. To enter into a dialogue with those who promote such a powerful displacement of canonicality will be central to this chapter. I will begin with a discussion of the epistemological framework that made possible a Latin American postcolonial reflection. Next, I will address the different moments in which this reflection was surmounted by both the metropolitan academy, as well as by interventions produced outside the teleological frame of hegemonic modernity.

In general terms, all forms of postcolonial reflection tried to articulate a critique of epistemic Eurocentrism performed by imperial expansionisms. In the case of Latin America and the Caribbean, attention has been rooted in subjects, histories, cultures, and literatures (such as the Indigenous and African), targeted not only by imperial colonial projects but also by the Creole and *mestizo* European practices that shaped Latin American destinies long after political independence from Spain. Indigeneity and Africanism, therefore, became the critical focus of an academic critique that, in spite of its decolonizing agenda, had little to share with the *subaltern* and their rationalities, and certainly had no impact at all in the production of their daily lives. Perhaps the most solid objection to academic criticism derived from postcolonial theory resides in this difficulty to actually affect the everyday reality of their analyzed subjects. In fact, how many Aymara, Quechua, Mapuche, Maya, or Guaraní Indians, how many *palenqueros* or *zafreros* have escaped their coloniality owing to the production of expert academic knowledge? How many indigenous writers have entered as thinkers into metropolitan debates? How many indigenous-authored books have been validated in the academic market or have became part of current theoretical debates?

Yet, no one can deny that in recent decades it has been the engine of postcolonial thinking that has more radically driven the production of academic knowledge in relation to Latin American studies. In dialogue with postcolonial theory, specifically with the postcolonial historiography advanced by the South Asian subaltern collective, a branch of Latin American criticism came to realize that in Latin America the formation of culture responds to much broader and complex processes than those outlined in leading twentieth-century literary historiographies, and that notions of the "master work," the "literary canon," or even "national literature" are largely constructions coined by colonizing hegemonies. Confronted with these complexities, critics and scholars started to ask to what extent we can still validate as "national" the institutionalization of a literature produced by Westernized Creole elites detached from the multicultural, multiethnic, and multilingual societies to which they belong. Furthermore, how can we ignore that, throughout its republican life, Latin America has produced models of "national culture" that advocate homogeneity, exclusion, and civilization; precisely the very principles on which colonial logic and European hegemonic modernity were founded. In sum, by renouncing Eurocentric worldviews, postcolonial inquiries seem to have been able to produce a better understanding of Latin American cultural formations. Why is it, then, that this "epistemological shift" has rarely succeeded in escaping the colonial condition that it seeks to denounce? A possible explanation is to be found in the emergence of postcoloniality from academic metropolitan debates and its involvement with first-world cultural marketing.

Secondly, because in the conceptual and theoretical foundations of criticism inspired by postcolonial theory there has yet to be an organic incorporation of indigenous, *mestizo*, or African theoretical thought. In this sense metropolitan postcolonial criticism in the field of Latin American studies has reproduced the temporal constituency of modernity by assuming the nonexistence of theoretical reflection previous to its own. It has been commonplace among literary and cultural critics to assume that

> in the current academic situation . . . the present-day subaltern has not been able, yet, to write colonial historiography. The present-day subaltern has not been able, either, to have access to a discursive practice in the area of colonial literary studies. Those of us who promote knowledge in the field must assume the responsibility with which we are faced: to make sense of the universe of discourse of an era. (Verdesio, 2002: 3)

This statement contains the idea that the sixteenth-century collapse of the Amerindian world left the colonized subjects without the possibility of producing critical thinking. Therefore, it is the responsibility of the scholar committed to the conflict of modernity to promote a decolonized knowledge. Unwillingly trapped within the confines of the lettered city, statements like the one quoted above illustrate how hard it is to break away from patterns of thought which have ruled for more than five centuries. Even when metropolitan critique took the opposite way and pointed out the existence of a Latin American colonial historiography with which first-world theory had not yet engaged in dialogue, the authors that came up were definitely not of *subaltern* origin, nor truly representative of an "intellectual other." On the contrary, they were well-known scholars whose work, informed by European epistemologies, began to gain prestige as milestones of the Latin American canon: the Mexican Edmundo O'Gorman and the Uruguayan Ángel Rama who, according to Walter Mignolo, should be considered as representatives of decolonizing critical agendas in Latin America. In a 1993 article, when postcolonial theory strongly emerged as a new form of cultural critique, Mignolo wrote:

> The critique of what today is grouped under the label of "colonial discourse" has a long tradition in Latin America, which can be traced back to the 1950's when the writings of German philosopher Martin Heidegger began to catch the attention of Latin American intellectuals. The most spectacular example to my mind is that of Mexican historian and philosopher Edmundo O'Gorman. His *La idea del descubrimiento de América* (1952) and *La invención del América* (1958) represent the early dismantling of European colonial discourse . . . Another telling example is Uruguayan literary critic Ángel Rama's *La ciudad letrada* (1982). This magnificent little book offers a theory about the control, domination, and power exercised in the name of alphabetic writing. Poststructuralism no doubt reached Rama before he wrote the book, and the guidance of Michel Foucault is certainly visible and explicit . . . O'Gorman and Rama exemplify the perspective of social scientists and humanists located in and speaking from the Third World. They are in one sense contemporary examples of the "intellectual other," as were Inca noble

Guamán Poma and Texcocan noble Alva Ixtlilxochitl in the early seventeenth century. (Mignolo, 1993: 122–3)

This difficulty in escaping the lettered siege even when critical discourse attempts to break through, more than questioning the viability of the inquiry, may be assumed as being the difficulty of theoretical endeavors to conceive Latin America from radical decolonizing perspectives. Years after promoting O'Gorman and Rama as milestones in the formation of contemporary Latin American decolonizing thought, Mignolo shifts ground and – alongside Dussel and Quijano, but also having the experience of close contacts with the Andean academy – proposes indigenous authors such as Guamán Poma, Pachacuti Yamki, Alvarado Tezozomoc, and Chimalpain as points of departure toward a decolonizing thought with no debt to modern epistemes (Mignolo, 2005: 127–31).

Such a reorientation in the field of postcolonial reflection made it possible for the academic debate to begin thinking from the perspective of colonial histories and, therefore, away from the teleological framework of occidentalism. At the same time, it contributed to gain awareness of the limitations of postcolonial theory vis-à-vis Latin American interventions. But again, the difficulty of conceiving Latin America from radical decolonizing perspectives still challenges academic scholarship. Recovering local, subaltern thinkers and writers such as Guamán Poma de Ayala, Mariátegui, or Vallejo, and connecting them to the rhythm of current North American academic debates distorts (if not erases) the Latin American *local rhythm* of decolonizing debates. My sense is that to honor an "epistemological shift" in our thinking, metropolitan academy should strive to connect ongoing debates to the complex, yet fascinating Latin American *local rhythm* of the theoretical decolonizing process over the twentieth century. By doing so, we will enter into dialogue with texts and authors who have largely remained foreign to canonical and lettered narratives but whose cultural interventions have been crucial to the decolonizing struggles in the last century as well as to the promotion of distinct models of society.

It goes beyond the limits of this chapter to discuss this complex, disperse, and heterogeneous body of decolonizing writing. I will limit myself to the analysis of some Andean cases especially relevant to the discussion of what I call "the Latin American local rhythm of decolonizing debate." The authors I will discuss are the most radical expressions of this debate. Marginal to academia and dominant circles, they were able to build a powerful non-hegemonic critical tradition only recently acknowledged as a cultural intervention which gave birth to the emergence of a *barbaric* avant-garde independent from the one led by Mariátegui and Vallejo. Openly anti-canonical and distinct from mainstream vanguardist rituals, this insurrection can be understood as the unexpected, unthinkable outcome of an European art form – such as the twentieth-century avant-garde – expressed by means of decolonizing insurgence. The writers who enacted this provoking reorientation of culture should not be neutralized under the label of "anti-colonial intellectuals" or "indigenists" producing knowledge within the frame of the lettered city, but as cultural activists who perceived

Latin America as a still colonized space, and whose writing is consequently a demolition of hegemonic modernity.

## *Barbaric* Avant-garde: the Anti-hegemonic Critical Consciousness of an Andean Decolonizing Debate

Simultaneously with the twentieth-century avant-garde, there emerged in the Andes an anti-hegemonic, insurgent, and peripheral avant-garde which has only recently begun to attract the attention of literary studies and cultural theory. This movement shared the iconoclastic and renewing spirit emblematic to avant-garde writers but, unlike them, rooted its language and its imaginary in a radical decolonizing act that, without breaking from that other avant-garde that shocked the Andes – Mariátegui's political and Vallejo's poetic avant-garde – resisted the idea of understanding the tragedy of indigenous people through European conceptual frames (Marxism being one of them) or from interpretations derived from the *templum* of *mestizaje* (clearly the episteme of the time). Understanding Andean cultures as realities historically torn apart by the effects of conquest, colonization, and twentieth-century forms of neocolonization, the members of this insurgent avant-garde conceived the legitimization of Andean *reason*, including its myths and rituals, as an act of emancipation from Europe as well as from the Latin American republican elites. Among those who enacted this movement stand out the Peruvians Gamaliel Churata (pseudonym for Arturo Peralta, 1897–1969), Alejandro Peralta (1899–1965?), and Uriel García (1891–1965); and the Bolivians Arturo Borda (1883–1953) and Carlos Medinaceli (1898–1949). They were individuals of extraordinary charisma and creativity, whose very presence in the public sphere defied conventional norms and expectations. Churata, for instance, adopted the nickname *Calibán* half a century before Fernández Retamar's theorizations, and was known among his contemporaries as a *Barbarian* (owing in part to his leadership in the foundation of *Gesta Bárbara*, a literary group established in Potosí in 1918). Borda, on the other hand, was openly acknowledged as "el loco" (the madman). In both cases, these labels appeal to their preference for considering civilization from the position of an alterity rooted in the conflicted space between colonizing forces and decolonizing wills. Nevertheless, both writers are relatively anonymous and are largely excluded from Latin American critical thought, to the extent that Antonio Cornejo Polar, undoubtedly the scholar who has most effectively incorporated Andean cultural production into the North American academy, mentions Churata only in passing, and has no information whatsoever on Borda. And yet, it is in these authors and in their work that we find a solid decolonizing laboratory in the Andes. Deeply unconventional, anti-academic with formidable scholarly abilities, their work enacts an epistemological demolition of the Western teleological framework that steered the cultural life of their age, and resisted the passing of time with astonishing creativity and originality.

One way to approach this unique cultural intervention is by reviewing Gamaliel Churata's work after 1930, when the Orkopata Group he had created ended its activities (this group was the epicenter of a peripheral Peruvian avant-garde that operated from the city of Puno and counted among its members indigenous poets such as Inocencio Mamani and Eustaqio Aweranka) as so did the publication of the *Boletín Titikaka* (1926–30), the group's main organ of diffusion and the axle of Puno's avant-garde. Luis Alberto Sánchez once referred to this publication as "el hecho más curioso e insólito de la literatura del Perú" (the most curious and unusual of events in Peruvian literature).

During his years of cultural activism in Puno, Churata had come to understand two things that would help him to articulate his subsequent work: that Indians did not need any indigenism nor any intellectual to make themselves viable, and that the day would come in which "se afronte definitivamente el esclarecimiento de nuestro indoamericano acervo filosófico" (the enlightenment of our Indoamerican philosophical wealth must surely be confronted) (*Boletín Titikaka*, XXV: 4).

Armed with this decolonizing perception, and from a lengthy exile in Bolivia (1932–64), Churata devoted himself to finish a monumental text which he had started writing in 1927 but completed only in 1957: *El Pez de oro (Retablos del Laykhakuy)* (The golden fish (retablos of Laykhakuy)). Starting with the oddity and hybridity of its title (Miguel Angel Huamán reads it as an invitation to enter a "border writing" made up of "retablos" that give expression to Andean forms of knowledge; 1994: 49–60), this is a text deeply disruptive of the aesthetics of its time. Five hundred pages of epistemological insurrection written in a hybrid style (Spanish, Aymara, and Quechua) that conform with no established genre, and posit a protagonist who embodies the possibility of an historic *pachacuti* (a world in reverse) in the Andes.

Referring to this book, Marco Thomas Bosshard observed recently that this is "un texto que asusta" (a text that creates fear) and that the marginalization it suffered in the intellectual circles of Lima was because of the engagement of the author with Andean indigenous cultures. According to Bosshard, "the reader that Churata addresses perhaps only exists since two decades ago (it doesn't coincide with the reader of Arguedas, but certainly with a reader like Arguedas)" (Bosshard and Angeles, 2002). In the light of this provocative framework, I propose to discuss the impact of a text that, from its opening page, establishes that

> el punto de partida de toda literatura está en el idioma que la sustenta. Los americanos no tenemos literatura, filosofía, derecho de gentes, derecho público, que no sean los contenidos en los idiomas vernáculos . . . nos empeñamos en [escribir] valiéndonos de una lengua no *kuika*: la hispana. Y en ella borroneamos "como indios" aunque no en indio, que es cosa distinta. (Churata, 1957: 9–10)

> (the starting point of every literature lies in the language that sustains it. We Americans [from the Americas] don't have literature, philosophy, rights of people, public rights, that are not contained in the vernacular languages . . . [and yet] we insist on writing by means of a lingua *non kuika*: the Hispanic one. And in so doing we scribble on it "as Indians," although not in Indian, which is a different thing.)

This unsettling reflection on language enables Churata to question the authority of Garcilaso de la Vega, Inca with regard to his emancipative cultural discourse, because "él que pudo y debió [escribir] en kheswa, empleó, y con qué gracia teresiana!, el idioma de su padre, ya condenó el de su madre a una interdicción punto menos que fatal" (he, who could and should have [written] in kheswa, used instead, and with such a Theresian grace! the language of his father, condemning his mother's language to an interdiction short of being fatal) (Churata, 1957: 10).

Churata bases his critique of Garcilaso in the idea that for Andean subjects, *Kheswa* and *Aymara* play a similar role to that of Latin and Greek for Greco-Roman ones, only that they are no longer repositories of a "classical knowledge" but of a "classical sentiment of nature," of a *grammar* capable of expressing American reality by provoking thoughts that "nada tardarán en convertirse en política y estética para sus pueblos" (will take no time in becoming the politics and the aesthetics of its people) (Churata, 1957: 11). This explains why to think and write in the Andes at the fringes of an Andean cultural *grammar* showed "lo atajado que Garcilaso llevaba al indio" (how intercepted Garcilaso carried the Indian within) and the extent to which "en él contienden los gérmenes indoespañoles con evidente subalternidad de lo indio" (the struggle of his Indohispanic origin with the obvious subaltern position of his Indian identity) (Churata, 1957: 10, 14). This questioning of the colonial determinism that establishes uneven differences between cosmopolitan languages and *lenguas kuikas* (aboriginal ones) also leads Churata to question cultural *mestizaje* as a possibility for a new national identity. If Garcilaso was an icon of the biological *mestizo*, how was it going to be viable to incorporate Indians in a scheme that subalternized Andean languages? Provided with a powerful decolonizing rhetoric, Churata observes that the weakness of *Comentarios Reales* stems from the fact that when incorporated into the logic of metropolitan culture by means of *mestizaje*, the seeds of the conquered become diluted. In contrast, when preserved within the epistemological frame of the aboriginal world, their potentiality is increased, motivating creative tensions between the Andean and metropolitan cultures. In addition, he makes the unsettling observation that "un mestizo puede germinar en nueve meses y salirse toreando. Un idioma no. Los idiomas vienen de un tiempo de trino" (a *mestizo* can sprout in nine months and come out strong and healthy. Not so a language. Languages take a long time to come into being) (1957: 10). With this kind of cultural incitement, Churata concludes that "cualquier mestizaje es imposible, mas hay alguno impasable . . . es el del Hispano y las lenguas aborígenes de la América (any *mestizaje* is impossible, but some are indigestible . . . that of Spanish and the native languages of the Americas) (1957: 533).

What better introduction to a decolonizing historiography than these reflections on the subalternization of the Andean cultural grammar? Furthermore, what better argument to embark on a theoretical reflection of the colonized condition of Latin American literature? Churata himself begins this reflection when he denounces the absence of an Andean historiography in the midst of the twentieth century. In his opinion, this oblivion is not because of a nonexistence of sources (these appear, insists Churata, in Guamán Poma de Ayala's work, and the letters of Tupac Katari to brigadier Segurola during the siege of La Paz in 1872), rather it is due to a lack of any desire to assume and value the legitimacy of those sources. Emphatically, Churata maintains that

> en América [la génesis literaria] no puede venir de las patrias coloniales. La colonia española constituye la negación de la patria americana: por más que tabardillos sostengan que no sólo nos han dado naturaleza con llamarnos indios, sino que España menos conquistó América cuanto que la ha inventado.
>
> ¡No la inventó! ¡La ha borrado! Y el borrador somos nosotros, criollos y mestizos, en quienes ni España vale lo que un cuesco, y el indio menos.
>
> Nadie vio en el mugriento español de Huaman Poma o Tupac Katari la dialéctica de una estética, ningún crítico tabuló la *chaskadera,* se la dejó para los espectáculos del *tantakatu*. Quedó olvidado que la capacidad estética de la América está en el indio . . . Ese mutismo habrá de romperse un día, a juzgar por la magnitud de este mundo y de su proceso expansivo, no cabe dudas. Mas se romperá por acción del indio, que es lo único con régimen en sí mismo, con raíz y cosmos. (1957: 21, 25, 26)

> (in the Americas [literary genesis] cannot come from the colonial motherlands. The Spanish colony constitutes the negation of the American motherland: regardless of how much some gurus would say that not only they gave us definition in calling us Indians, but that Spain did not so much conquer America as invent it.
>
> It did not invent it! It has erased it! And we are the rough draft, Creoles and *mestizos*, for whom Spain is not worth a pittance, and the Indian even less.
>
> Nobody saw in the filthy Spanish of Guamán Poma or Tupac Katari the dialectic of an aesthetic, no critic tabulated the entanglement [*chaskadera*], it was left for the spectacle of the market [*tantakatu*]. It was forgotten that the aesthetic capacity of America lies with the Indians . . . Judging from the magnitude of this world and its expansive process, there is no doubt that the stillness will break one day. However, it will be broken by the action of the Indian, which is the only existence with a regimen in himself, rooted and with cosmos.)

We are certainly in the presence of a brutal emancipation of discourse regarding Western teleological frames. Bosshard is right in pointing out that Churata is writing "exactamente como lo había exigido Vallejo cuando lamentaba la inexistente 'fisonomía propia' de los escritores americanos y veía la urgencia de realizar en América un 'espíritu propio'" (exactly as Vallejo had demanded when he lamented the inexistent "unique physiognomy" of American writers and saw the urgency of attaining in America a spirit of one's own) ("Contra el secreto professional"; Bosshard, 2007).

Wasn't this reflection on the colonized condition of Latin American literature already a jump into the writing of a colonial historiography perfectly able to conceive Guamán Poma and Tupac Katari's "barbaric orthography" as the very possibility of a decolonized literature? How can we overlook the fact that in 1957 Churata was inaugurating in the Andes a decolonizing critique that, apart from proposing the unthinkable – an Andean aesthetic as a field of study – was also proposing a critical dialogue with Edmundo O'Gorman's thesis expressed in *La invención de América*

(1957)? But it was hopeless to deploy such a criticism in the 1950s, mainly because their promoters were marginal to the hegemony of an establishment that, from an indigenist perspective, considered the "Indian problem" as something already resolved, with the incorporation of Indians into the educational system, agrarian reform, universal suffrage, and the ideology of *mestizaje*. It is only in 1992, with the publication of Enrique Dussel's *1492. El Encubrimiento del Otro: Hacia el origen del mito de la modernidad*, that we can discern the innate ontological Eurocentrism in O'Gorman's thesis and, therefore, the intrinsic wit in Churata's reading. In Dussel's words:

> According to O'Gorman's completely Eurocentric thesis, the *invention* of America meant that "America was invented in the image and likeness of Europe since America could not *actualize* in itself any other form of becoming human [than the European] . . . Europe, in whose image and likeness America was invented, has its principle of individualization in its own culture. But this particular culture does not suppose a mode of being exclusive and peculiar to Europe, since it assumes that it has universal significance. (Dussel, 1995: 32, 156 n. 45)

Together with a denunciation of the colonial legacy, in *El Pez de oro* there is an extraordinary lucidity that foresees an eventual indigenous protagonism, voiced in the idea that the silence that had characterized Indians since colonial times: "habrá de romperse un día, a juzgar por la magnitud de este mundo y de su proceso expansivo, no cabe dudas. Mas se romperá por acción del indio, que es lo único con régimen en sí mismo, con raíz y cosmos" (it will be broken one day, there is no doubt of that, judging by the magnitude of this world and its expansive process. However, it will be broken by the action of the Indian, who is the only being with a regimen in himself, rooted and with cosmos) (1957: 17, 27). Obviously, for Churata, the members of the Andean avant-garde will not have a leading role in the indigenous *momentum,* but the Indians themselves. This idea is clearly expressed on the last page of *El Pez de oro*: "No columbramos qué número de siglos requiera el NUEVO NACIMIENTO, más tenemos entendido que no serán tantos que hagan cinco milenios – y así fuesen – los que permitan al americano de América expresarse, y ser, en su idioma lácteo. Esos poetas del ayllu – los orko-patas Mamani o Awaranka – son ciertamente hechos que se anticipan" (533) (We do not foresee how many centuries this NEW BIRTH will require, but we do understand that they will not be as numerous as to become five millennia – even if they were so – that will allow Americans of America to express themselves and to be in their lacteal language. Those poets of the Ayllu – the orko-patas Mamani o Awaranka – are certainly anticipated events).

With this powerful widening of perception, Churata launches a decolonizing debate that makes possible a critical theorization of concepts such as *mestizaje*, hybridity, nationality, and the condition of American subalternity in face of the Spanish metropolis. All this, accompanied by the suspicion that, as the twentieth century goes by, "las Colonias hispanas como la Metrópoli española sean ya colonias de otros países con mayor capacidad digestiva" (1957: 21) (the Spanish colonies, like the Spanish metropolis, are already colonies of other countries with a higher digestive capacity).

Churata's meticulous thinking resulted in an objectified awareness that in time, local, "Hispanic" issues will enter into constant tension with global forces.

Although Churata was not the only writer who articulated such a powerful counternarrative in his time, he is undoubtedly the referential figure for the emergence of an insurgent avant-garde in the Andes). In one way or another, he played a role in every one of its interventions: in Potosí by partaking in the foundation of the "Gesta Bárbara" literary movement; in Puno by founding the Orkopata Group and by launching the *Boletín Titikaka*; in Cuzco as an active member of the Resurgimiento Group led by Uriel Garcia; and in La Paz – where he produced 30 years of journalism – by empowering the "olímpicamente ignorada vanguardia boliviana, donde gravitaban escritores como Arturo Borda, Carlos Medinaceli y Andrés Cusicanqui" (olympically ignored Bolivian avant-garde, where writers such as Arturo Borda, Carlos Medinaceli, and Andrés Cusicanqui gravitated) (Wiethüchter and Soldán, 2002: 67). Yet today, at the dawn of the twentieth-first century, there is still a dearth of any serious engagement with the study of these interventions. There are excellent readings on Churata, Medinaceli, Borda, or the *Boletín Titikaka* (see Bosshard and Angeles, 2002; Díez de Medina, 1957; Huamán, 1994; Pantigoso, 1999, Vich, 2000, Wietüchter and Soldán, 2002; Zevallos, 2002), but until we interconnect their works, and appreciate them as the first local theorizations on the condition of coloniality to which the Andean cultures were subjected under the rule of viceroyal and republican elites, we will be wasting our best opportunity to understand a decolonizing debate proposed from within Latin America. What is most ironic is that this debate took place half a century before the emergence of postcolonial studies, when the questioning of the colonial episteme was considered to be a symptom of extravagance which stigmatized the audacious, making him or her a marginal subject, an excluded, banished from the paradise of critique.

To address this rather large gap in our understanding, it is crucial to connect the ideas put forth in *El Pez de oro* with the work of Uriel García, and with the only text we have from Borda, entitled *El Loco*, and posthumously published in 1966 in three volumes. It is not possible in this chapter to give the contributions of these authors the attention they deserve. I will limit myself to emphasizing the enriching experience of reading them as protagonists of the first decolonizing debate ever produced in Latin America. Uriel García, for example, is the author of a book essential to the measurement of the theoretical density of this debate. In a very avant-garde fashion entitled *El Nuevo indio* (The new Indian, 1930), this text gives articulation to a decolonizing thinking different to the one explored by Churata's and yet in dialogue with it.

In the first place, García insists on the idea that the continent occupied by Spain in the sixteenth century was not "una selva virgen donde Europa prolongó su historia" (an unexplored jungle where Europe prolonged its history) but rather an historically precious milieu in possession of an immense vital force (1930: 95, 99). The conquerors, García points out, took possession of that world of immense vitality, which in spite of their victory signaled them out as the defeated. The Indians, for their part, were pushed to furiously defend that force, while being converted into *emigrants* (émigrés) of the Inkario toward the new scenario created by the conquest (my emphasis). The colonial enterprise, according to this argument, is the history of that pain, of that "hervor de furia" (infuriation) which confronted the Spanish desire for possession. That "madness," that struggle between two wills, produced a new humankind that García calls "el nuevo Indio." There is no doubt that we are dealing with a concept that takes the notion of *mestizaje* to a conceptual domain other than that imagined by Vasconcelos. Here *mestizaje* is no longer conceived from racial perspectives, but from the comprehension of a tragedy, that reformulated history as well as the fate of its protagonists (Indians and conquerors). Understood as a "history-forging" category, García's notion of *mestizaje* emerges as the possibility of the colonized to enter with dignity into a different and irreversible historic reality:

> La colonia es el proceso de aproximación o alejamiento tanto del español como del indio en relación a los Andes "mestizos". El indio que se aleja es el alma muerta, el mitayo, el yanacona, el siervo de encomienda. Es el ayllu que se vuelve a encaramar a su montaña . . . Mas el indio que asoma con audacia a la dolorosa realidad y la afronta serenamente es el que vuelve a domar la piedra de las catedrales, el que acepta la nueva Idea y la expresa con su emoción, el que reconquista la tierra con voluntad directiva. Son Garcilaso, Lunarejo, Tupak Amaru . . . Así, el amestizamiento de América que genera un nuevo espíritu que avanza hacia el porvenir, trae consigo a su vez el grave problema de infundir en el indio esa alma juvenil y hacerle un *nuevo indio* total. Y en el caso singular de nuestra sierra surperuana, vasta zona de la indianidad, el problema de la cultura arrastra también el problema social de la *redención del indio*, problema que como bien dice José Carlos Mariátegui, afecta principalmente a las generaciones jóvenes de la sierra, pues es la cuestión *regionalista* por excelencia. Sólo que este regionalismo tiene que ser forzosamente . . . lucha no sólo contra el gamonal sino también contra el centralismo que opera desde Lima tanto como un gamonal. (1930: 109, 120). (The colony is the process of proximity or distancing of both the Spaniard and the Indian with regard to the Andes "*mestizos*." The Indian who moves away is the dead soul, the *Mitayo*, the *Yanacona*, the servant of the Encomienda. He is the Ayllu reverted back to its mountain . . . But the Indian who audaciously looks at painful reality and serenely faces it is the one who retakes the cathedral stones, the one who accepts the new Idea and expresses it with his own emotion, the one who reconquers the land with his ruling will. They are Garcilaso, Lunarejo, Tupak Amaru . . . Thus, the *amestizamiento* of America that creates a new spirit going forward to the future embraces the serious issue of infusing in the Indian that youthful soul, making of him a complete new Indian. In the specific case of our South Peruvian highland, a vast zone of Indianness, the issue of culture drags along the social problem of the redemption of the Indian, a problem that, as José Carlos Mariátegui points out, affects mainly the young generations of the highlands, since it is the *regionalist* issue par excellence. Only this regionalism necessarily has to be . . . a struggle not only against the *gamonal* [large-landowner] but also against the centralism that, from the capital city of Lima, operates as a *gamonal*.)]

Proposing *mestizaje* as a "history-forging" category as well as the possibility of the colonized "para ingresar con dignidad en una realidad histórica distinta e irreversible" (to enter with dignity into a historical reality that is both distinct and irreversible) opened up unsuspected horizons of cultural reflection and anticipated theorizations such as those put forward by Néstor García Canclini (1992), which would not be heard until the last decades of the twentieth century. However, the "cost" of this rethinking of *mestizaje*, clearly formulated within a liberal ideological framework which legitimates the modern utopia of progress and the project of "educating" and "redeeming" the Indian, remains implicit in García's work.

Churata, as already noted, refuses to pay the cost demanded by the process of making the "templum mestizo" a viable option (1930: 18). Despite his closeness to García, he violently disagrees with his friend, stressing that the "posibilidad Garcilaso" (Garcilaso possibility) does not make viable a decolonized literature. Churata insists that in Garcilaso the seeds of the conquered become diluted and, therefore, the only possible motherland is offered by the Spanish language and its cultural logic. He prefers to bet on the "posibilidad Huamán Poma"(Guamán Poma possibility), where the strength of the conquered is empowered, thus making possible the articulation of "plebes emancipadas" (emancipated plebs) from mental meridians originating in the Old World. It is at this point of his reflection when he fiercely attacks the modern utopia of progress and the Hegelian thesis of American infantilism:

América antes que fruto debe ser raíz. Antes que al Porvenir su deber es mirar al Pasado; pulsarse a sí misma; sin que le acochinen gollerías como ésa de su infantilidad. No hay universos infantiles . . . en fenomenismo cósmico no hay juventud ni vejez en nada ni en nadie. Necesariamente, el hombre de hoy es el de ayer. Acá, en nosotros, debe hablar El. No obstante las animosas diligencias de Ameghino y de otros paleontólogos, se llega a la conclusión de que El no se ha dado en suelo americano. Nosotros, también, somos hijos de la "grosura" de la mar: *Wirakhochas*. (1930: 26)

(The Americas, before flowering, must find its roots. Before gazing towards the Future, it must look at the Past; to take its own pulse without being candy-coated with stupidities such as that of its infantilism. There are no infantile universes . . . in cosmic phenomenology there is no youth nor old age in anything nor in anybody. By necessity, today's human being is the same as yesterday's. Here, in us, he must speak. In spite of the enthusiastic attempts of Ameghino and other paleontologists, the conclusion is that He was not from American soil. We, too, are children of the "vastness" of the sea: *Wirakhochas*.)

To this "He" – which does not necessarily imply a gender exclusion – expelled from the philosophy of history, Churata dedicates all of his work. "He," the *Pez de Oro*, should, then, be understood as an effort from within literature to preserve the Andean *reason*, even though Churata suspects that the Iberoamerican nations (including those in which an Amerindian sensibility still exists) no longer understand their "deberes arcaicos" (archaic duties) once they become affected by the transfusion of the West, represented by migratory avalanches and the submissiveness to its civilizing process (1930: 33). It is truly moving to read Churata when he addresses the *Khori-Challwa* (*Pez de oro*) in poetic mode:

Khori-Challwa: ¿Eres el Chullpa-tullu a que mis huesos se saben enfeudados? Relámpago de mi carne, tú la iluminas en El, y El eres con todos los caudales del Universo. Bien sé que en ti hay sólo un hombrecito del Titikaka . . . Sé bien que El Pez eres, aquél que en mi sangre latía cuando esperaba, y esperaba en los barros del álveo, y ni el Sol era Lupi, ni se había animado dios alguno en las profundidades del átomo. Eres mi existente porque eres mi habitante. Y, cuanto amo, y beso, y lloro, es más que manera de ser en Ti, sentimiento y espasmo de mi hueso. Tú eres naya! Tú eres naya! Tú eres naya! Tú eres naya! Tú eres naya! (1930: 36).

(Khori-Challwa: Are you the Chullpa-tullu to which my bones are known to be indebted? Lightning of my flesh, which you illuminate in him, and He you are with all the riches of the universe. Well I know that in you there's only a little man from Titikaka . . . I know well that you are The Fish, the one which pulsed in my blood when I waited and waited in the mud of the river beds, nor was the Sun Lupi, nor had any god been animated within the depths of the atom. You are my existent because you are my inhabitant. And, all that I love, and kiss, and weep, is more than a way to be in You, emotion and tremor of my bones. You are naya! You are naya! You are naya!)

What can possibly be said in the presence of such an overflowing consciousness? To be confronted by so much poetry, so much lucidity, and so much pain is almost paralyzing. One thing remains clear, however: even if Churata – as some critics observe – can still be considered as a "modern provincial intellectual" writing on the borders of the lettered city without really penetrating Andean rationality (Zevallos, 2002: 120, 127), his work succeeds in challenging the reproduction of hegemonic modernity and rethinking the way in which a writer functions in the public sphere.

In spite of the fact that when *El Pez de oro* was published, no literary critic was able to perceive the decolonizing avant-garde generated in the region, there were those who felt the disturbing and demolishing force that animated Churata's discourse. Fernando Díez de Medina, the then Bolivian Minister of Education, openly admitted that "Nadie, en la América de hoy, ni en la anterior, fue tan lejos – y tan hondo – en punto a hibridación idiomática. Si críticos y artistas se deleitarán en esta obra, para filósofos y hablistas ¡qué revelación! . . . En *El Pez de Oro* vibra un soplo de metafísica aymará" (Nobody in the Americas, nor in the former one, went so far – and so deep – with regard to linguistic hybridity. If critics and artists will be delighted with this work, what a revelation for philosophers and good speakers! . . . In *El Pez de oro* a breath of Aymara metaphysics resonates) (*El Diario*, June 1957).

Almost a decade later, in 1966, the Honorable Alcaldía Municipal de La Paz published posthumously the last work of this decolonizing saga: Arturo Borda's *El Loco* (The madman). As in the case of Churata, this is also a text that creates fear. Complex, witty, and irreverent with its times, unclassifiable according to conventional parameters (it is not a novel, nor a diary, nor poetry, nor drama, nor ritual, nor essay, nor testimony, but exhibits the features of all these literary genres); multilingual, fragmented, without any pretension of trying to be a finished work, or even "literature," *El Loco* challenged everything that had been previously written in Bolivia. By questioning the colonial episteme in an epoch still coopted by the Hispanic civilizing impulse, *El Loco* was immediately categorized as a bastardized literary expression. To this, one should add Borda's own unsettling personality, which loudly accused his contemporaries of lending themselves to a "pongueaje intelectual" (intellectual servility) that canceled out any possibility of social and historic dignity in America. Also loudly, he resisted being labeled with the adjectives "intellectual" or "bohemian" that so often served to domesticate disobedience expressed by means of artistic creation. Defiant of any form of domesticated language, Borda claimed for himself the status of a "*lari*," an Aymara expression that alludes to "gente que no conoce autoridad" (people who recognize no authority), *sauvage* existences openly opposed to hegemonic modernity. For this "*lari*," the only way to reorient conventional and colonized relations between art, history, and literature was the experience of writing an "unacceptable" book. Something that, still a book, is also a ritual, a performance, an act of insurrection accomplished by civilization's barbarous other.

With few exceptions (among them Carlos Medinaceli, one of the founders of *Gesta Bárbara*), this *lari's* work received no critical attention nor was it included in any literary history or anthology. It was simply perceived as an unacceptable piece of work. How could the lettered culture accept the protagonist of *El Loco*, a character that lacks a proper name – we only know him by the appellative of Loco – and perceives himself as a *multitude-person*, as a symptom of the social experience of collective indignity? This *madman*, besides rejecting modern Bolivian history, seeks its demolition, to build upon its ruins a society other than that imagined by the Creole elites who founded and led the nation toward cultural and social alienation. To do so, he constructs himself as a "demolisher of modernity" and from that epistemological standpoint, raises true cultural insubordination:

> Tengo fe en mi destino: sé que seré en algo, no sé en qué, el primero y el único; pero la angustia me mata, porque no logro saber dónde está mi fuerza, no puedo calcular en la actividad de qué facultades está mi triunfo. Esto me enloquece, y no obstante al fondo de mi existencia reposa la serena fe de la victoria (Borda, 1966, I: 37) (I have faith in my destiny: I know that I can make something out of myself. In something, I don't know what, I'll be the first and the only one; but my anguish is killing me, because I have no means of finding out where my strength lies, I cannot guess in what activity or which faculty my triumph will be found. This is driving me crazy, and yet in the very depths of my existence the serene faith of victory is waiting.)

Borda was not mistaken. That fictionalized *madman* was indeed "el primero y el único" (the first and the only person) to conceive a decolonized writing in Bolivia's first half of the twentieth century. However, unlike Churata, who had always known that his strength came from the Andean world and epistemologies, Borda lived tormented by not knowing exactly where to pinpoint the source of his strength. Perhaps it came from that decolonizing project that inspired his work? Perhaps it arose from an aesthetic project that led him to imagine new territories along the artistic horizon? Or perhaps it derived from that extraordinary charge of indignation and fury with which he wanted to demolish everything, including the literary canon and the "mentira social" (social lie)? We can go as far as to think that Borda conceived what we can now properly call the last -ism of the avant-garde: *demolitionism*. What makes this Andean -ism so powerful and charged of theoretical validity even today, is that besides the demolition of a colonized culture and society, it proposes the demolition of the perverse "mansedumbre de los subalternos" (subservient will of the subaltern). In Borda's own words: "Lo que en esto hay de insoportable es la vil mansedumbre de los subalternos que se hacen sobajear como a perros muertos de hambre. Cuándo reventará la dignidad humana? Cuándo se sublevará la humillación? (1966, I: 79) (What's unbearable in all this is the vile subservience of the subalterns that allow themselves to be denigrated like hungry dogs. When will human dignity burst? When will humiliation rebel?)

The Andean lettered elites were largely unable to or incapable of dismantling the symbolic force irradiated by Churata and Borda's work. Although a veil of silence was drawn over their work, there was nothing to stop their proposals from breaking the weak discursive and ideological arena of lettered culture. In a cultural process that spans the second half of the twentieth century, the decolonizing horizons opened up by this insurgent avant-garde gradually destabilized the colonial rituals of dominant culture. Other languages, other histories, and other protagonists began to populate the Andean cultural imaginary, producing an aesthetic legitimation of territories so far perceived as degraded: a "yatiri" (Aymara wise man), an Aymara ritual, an Andean textile, a handful of coca leaves. In the Andes, this *momentum* of cultural legitimization was channeled in various ways. On occasions, it kept itself within the discursive limits of culture, creating situations in which modernity was symbolically and intellectually demolished by the action of insurgent writers (Churata being the best example). In other cases, however, it was surpassed by a more radical *momentum* of insurgence led by emancipated indigenous plebs. Insurgence, in this sense, resulted in social movements and mass rebellions such as those recently witnessed in Bolivia, when thousands of Aymara and Quechua Indians – who had since the 1970s been politicizing their ancestral cultures and producing their own narratives of insurgence – gave expression to the most important social movement of the last twenty years of Andean political history. Literally "reventada la dignidad humana, sublevada la humillación" (human dignity burst, humiliation rebelled) on January 22, 2006, almost half a century after the immolation of the Inca Atahuallpa in Cajamarca, an Indian took command of an Andean nation. At the presidential induction ceremony of Evo Morales, the first Indian president in the Americas, nobody remembered Churata, Borda, or their *barbaric* avant-garde. There was no need to, since the "mutismo del subalterno" (the silence of the subaltern) was not broken through the mediation of intellectuals committed to the indigenous conflict but, as Churata once warned, by the action of the Indians themselves.

The insurgent nature of this indigenous intervention proved its ability to produce material political action that can potentially transform coloniality and ethnic domination in the Andes. By the same token, it has been a powerful call to appreciate how limited academic reflection can be when assuming that in Latin America any expression of cultural resistance "resides in a space created by the text within and against itself rather than in a collectively acknowledged social sphere of contestation" (Alonso, 1998: 35–6).

If *demolitionism* demanded a *time* of dignity, that time seems to be the present, and it has not be reached through the linear progression of Western modernity – which can only conceive futurity in terms of going forward in the myth of progress – but throughout the *time* of insurgence, which heads to the future by embracing the past. Whether this *time* of insurgence, deeply contextualized in the Andean indigenous cultures, will be able to interrupt the reproduction of Western philosophy of power by the enactment of a more inclusive, sovereign, and equalitarian society, is at the core of reflections on Amerindian epistemologies and the reorienting of culture.

## References and Further Reading

Alonso, Carlos (1998). *The Burden of Modernity: The Rhetoric of Cultural Discourse in Spanish America*. New York: Oxford University Press.

Beverley, John (2004). *Subalternidad y representación: Debates en teoría cultural*. Madrid: Iberoamericana.

Bhabha, Homi K. (1986). "The other question: difference, discrimination and the discourse of colonialism." In Francis Barker, Peter Hulme, and Margaret Iversen (eds), *Literature, Politics and Theory: Papers from the Essex Conference 1976–1984*, pp. 148–72. London: Methuen.

— (1994). *The Location of Culture*. New York: Routledge.

*Boletín Titikaka* (2004 [1926–30]). Reproduced in facsimile by Dante Callo Cuno. Arequipa: Universidad Nacional de San Augustín.

Borda, Arturo (1966). *El Loco*. 3 vols. La Paz: Biblioteca Paceña, Honorable Alcaldía Municipal de La Paz.

Bosshard, Marco Thomas (2007). "Mito y mónada: La cosmovisión andina como base de la estética vanguardista de Gamaliel Churata," *Revista Iberoamericana*, 220: 515–39.

Bosshard, Marco Thomas, and César Angeles, L. (2002). Entrevista a Marco Thomas Bosshard en torno a su libro *Hacia una estética de la vanguardia andina: Gamaliel Churata entre el indigenismo y el surrealismo*, http://www.andes.missouri.edu/andes/Cronicas/CAL_Bosshard.html

Castro-Klaren, Sara (2002). "Writing with his thumb in the air: coloniality, past and present." In Álvaro Félix Bolaños and Gustavo Verdesio (eds), *Colonialism Past and Present: Reading and Writing about Colonial Latin America Today*, pp. 261–87. New York: SUNY Press.

Chakrabarty, Dipesh (2000). "Subaltern studies and postcolonial historiography," *Nepantla: Views from the South* 1.1, http://muse.jhu.edu/journals/nepantla/toc/nep1.1.html

Churata, Gamaliel (1957). *El Pez de oro (retablos del Laykhakuy)*. La Paz: Editorial Canata.

Cornejo Polar, Antonio (1994). *Escribir en el aire: Ensayo sobre la heterogeneidad socio-cultural en las literaturas andinas*. Lima: Editorial Horizonte.

Díez de Medina, Fernando (1957). "Gamaliel Churata y *El Pez de Oro*," *El Diario*, La Paz, June.

Dussel, Enrique (1995 [1992]). *The Invention of the Americas: Eclipse of "the Other" and the Myth of Modernity*. Trans. Michael D. Barber. New York: Continuum.

— 2000. "Europa, modernidad y eurocentrismo." In Eduardo Lander (ed.), *La Colonialidad del saber: Eurocentrismo y ciencias sociales, perspectivas latinoamericanas*, pp. 41–53. Buenos Aires: CLACSO.

Escobar, Arturo (1995). *Encountering Development*. Princeton, NJ: Princeton University Press.

Fanon, Frantz (1961). *Les Damnés de la terre*. Paris: Maspéro.

García Canclini, Néstor (1992). *Culturas híbridas: Estrategias para entrar y salir de la modernidad*. Buenos Aires: Paidós.

García Linera, Álvaro (2000). *El Retorno de la Bolivia plebeya*. La Paz: Muela del Diablo.

— (2001). *Tiempos de rebelión*. La Paz: Muela del Diablo.

— (2002). *Democratizaciones plebeyas*. La Paz: Muela del Diablo.

García, Uriel (1973 [1930]). *El Nuevo indio*. Lima: Editorial Universo.

Glissant, Édouard (1981). *Le Discours antillais*. Paris: Seuil.

Grupo de Estudios Subalternos Latinoamericanos (1995). "Founding statement." In John Beverley, José Oviedo, and Michael Arona (eds), *The Postmodernist Debate in Latin America*, pp. 110–21. Durham, NC: Duke University Press.

Guha, Ranajit, ed. (1982–9). *Subaltern Studies: Writings on South Asian History and Society*. Vols. 1–7. Delhi: Oxford University Press.

Huamán, Miguel Angel (1994). *Fronteras de la escritura: Discurso y utopía en Churata*. Lima: Editorial Horizonte.

Mariátegui, José Carlos (1975 [1928]). *Siete ensayos de interpretación de la realidad peruana*. La Habana: Casa de las Américas.

Mignolo, Walter (1993). "Colonial and postcolonial discourse: cultural critique or academic colonialism?," *Latin American Research Review*, 28(3): 120–34.

— (2000). "Human understanding and (Latin) American interests: the politics and sensibilities of geohistorical locations." In Henry Schwarz and Sangeeta Ray (eds), *A Companion to Postcolonial Studies*, pp. 180–201. Oxford: Blackwell.

— (2005). "Un Paradigma otro: Colonialidad global, pensamiento fronterizo y cosmopolitanismo crítico," *Dispositio*, 52: 127–46.

Monasterios, Elizabeth (2007). "Poéticas del conflicto andino," *Revista Iberoamericana,* 220: 541–61.

O'Gorman, Edmundo (1957). *La Invención de América*. Mexico City: FCE.

Pantigoso, Manuel (1999). *El Ultraorbicismo en el pensamiento de Gamaliel Churata*. Lima: Universidad Ricardo Palma.

Patzi Paco, Félix (2004). *Sistema comunal: Una propuesta alternativa al sistema liberal*. La Paz: CEA.

Quijano, Aníbal (2000). "Coloniality of power and Eurocentrism in Latin America," *International Sociology*, 15(2): 215–32.

Rabasa, José, and Sanjinés, Javier (1996 [1994]). "Introduction: the politics of subaltern studies," *Dispositio/N*, 19(46): v–xi.

Reinaga, Fausto (1978). *Indianidad*. La Paz: Imprentas Unidas.

Rivera Cusicanqui, Silvia (1991). Pachakuti: *Los Aymara de Bolivia frente a medio milenio de colonialismo*. Chukiyawu: Taller de Historia Oral Andina.

Rivera Cusicanqui, Silvia, and Barragán, Rossana, ed. 1997. *Debates post coloniales: Una introducción a los estudios de la subalternidad*. La Paz: Sierpe Publicaciones.

Rodríguez, Ileana (2005). "Is there a need for subaltern studies?," *Dispositio/N*, 52: 43–62.

Said, Edward (1978). *Orientalism*. New York: Pantheon.

Spivak, Gayatri (1988). "Can the subaltern speak?" In Cary Nelson and Lawrence Grossberg (eds), *Marxism and the Interpretation of Culture*, pp. 217–313. Urbana: University of Illinois Press.

Spivak, Gayatri, and Guha, Ranajit (1988). *Selected Subaltern Studies*. New York: Oxford University Press.

Vallejo, César (1927). "Contra el secreto profesional: acerca de Pablo Abril de Vivero," *Variedades*, 1001. Reprinted in Jorge Schwartz, *Las Vanguardias latinoamericanas: Textos programáticos y críticos,* Buenos Aires: Fondo de Cultura Económica, 2002, pp. 513–16.

Verdesio, Gustavo (2002) "Colonialism now and then: colonial Latin American studies in the light of the predicament of Latin Americanism." In Álvaro Félix Bolaños and Gustavo Verdesio (eds), *Colonialism Past and Present: Reading and Writing about Colonial Latin America Today*, pp. 1–17. New York: SUNY Press.

Vich, Cynthia (2000). *Indigenismo de vanguardia en el Perú: Un estudio sobre el Boletín Titikaka*. Lima: Pontificia Universidad Católica del Perú.

Vidal, Hernán (1993). "The concept of colonial and postcolonial discourse: a perspective from literary criticism," *Latin American Research Review*, 28(3): 113–19.

Wiethüchter, Blanca, and Soldán, Alba María Paz (2002). *Hacia una historia crítica de la literatura en Bolivia*. 2 vols. La Paz: PIEB.

Zevallos Aguilar, Ulises Juan. 2002. *Indigenismo y nación: Los retos a la representación de la subalternidad aymara y quechua en el Boletín Titikaka (1926–1930)*. Lima: IFEA and BCRP.

# 33
# *Testimonio*, Subalternity, and Narrative Authority
## *John Beverley*

In a justly famous essay, Richard Rorty (1985) distinguished between what he called the "desire for solidarity" and the "desire for objectivity" as cognitive modes:

> There are two principal ways in which reflective human beings try, by placing their lives in a larger context, to give sense to those lives. The first is by telling the story of their contribution to a community. This community may be the actual historical one in which they live, or another actual one, distant in time or place, or a quite imaginary one, consisting perhaps of a dozen heroes and heroines selected from history or fiction or both. The second way is to describe themselves as standing in an immediate relation to a non-human reality. This relation is immediate in the sense that it does not derive from a relation between such a reality and their tribe, or their nation, or their imagined band of comrades. I shall say that stories of the former kind exemplify the desire for solidarity, and that stories of the latter kind exemplify the desire for objectivity. (3)[1]

The question of *testimonio* – testimonial narrative – intertwines the "desire for objectivity" and "the desire for solidarity" in its very situation of production, circulation, and reception.

*Testimonio* is by nature a demotic and heterogeneous form, so any formal definition of it is bound to be too limiting.[2] But the following might serve provisionally: A *testimonio* is a novel or novella-length narrative, produced in the form of a printed text, told in the first person by a narrator who is also the real protagonist or witness of the events she or he recounts. Its unit of narration is usually a "life" or a significant life experience. Because in many cases the direct narrator is someone who is either functionally illiterate or, if literate, not a professional writer, the production of a *testimonio* generally involves the tape-recording and then the transcription and editing of an oral account by an interlocutor who is a journalist, ethnographer, or literary author.

Although one of the antecedents of *testimonio* is undoubtedly the ethnographic life history of the *Children of Sánchez* sort, *testimonio* is not exactly the same thing as a life history (or oral history). In the life history it is the intention of the interlocutor-recorder (an ethnographer or journalist) that is paramount; in *testimonio*, by contrast, it is the intention of the direct narrator, who *uses* (in a pragmatic sense) the possibility the interlocutor offers to bring his or her situation to the attention of an audience – the public sphere – to which he or she would normally not have access because of the very conditions of subalternity to which the *testimonio* bears witness.[3] *Testimonio* is not intended, in other words, as a reenactment of the anthropological function of the native informant. In René Jara's (1986: 3) phrase, it is rather a "narración de urgencia" – an "emergency" narrative – involving a problem of repression, poverty, marginality, exploitation, or simply survival in the act of narration itself.

The predominant formal aspect of the *testimonio* is the voice that speaks to the reader through the text in the form of an "I" that demands to be recognized, that wants or needs to stake a claim on our attention. Eliana Rivero (1984–5) notes that "the act of speaking faithfully recorded on the tape, transcribed and then 'written' remains in the *testimonio* punctuated by a repeated series of interlocutive and conversational markers . . . which constantly put the reader on the alert, so to speak: True? Are you following me? OK? So?" (220–1). The result, she argues, is a "snaillike" discourse (*discurso encaracolado*) that keeps turning in on itself, in the process invoking the complicity of the reader through the medium of his or her counterpart in the text, the direct interlocutor.

This presence of the voice, which the reader is meant to experience as the voice of a *real* rather than fictional person, is the mark of a desire not to be silenced or defeated, to impose oneself on an institution of power and privilege from the position of the excluded, the marginal, the subaltern. Hence the insistence on the importance of personal name or identity often evident in titles of *testimonios*: *I, Rigoberta Menchú* (even more strongly in the Spanish: *Me llamo Rigoberta Menchú, y así me nació la conciencia*), *I'm a Juvenile Delinquent* (*Soy un delincuente*), or *Let Me Speak* (*Si me permiten hablar*).

This insistence suggests an affinity between testimony and autobiography (and related forms, such as the autobiographical *bildungsroman*, the memoir, and the diary). Like autobiography, *testimonio* is an affirmation of the authority of personal experience, but, unlike autobiography, it cannot affirm a self-identity that is separate from the subaltern group or class situation that it narrates. *Testimonio* involves an erasure of the function and thus also of the textual presence of the "author" that is so powerfully present in all major forms of Western literary and academic writing.[4] By contrast, in autobiography or the autobiographical *bildungsroman*, the very possibility of "writing one's life" implies necessarily that the narrator is no longer in the situation of marginality and subalternity that his or her narrative describes, but has now attained the cultural status of an author (and, generally speaking, middle or upper class economic status). Put another way, the transition from storyteller to author implies a parallel transition from *gemeinschaft* to *gesellschaft*, from a culture of primary and secondary orality to writing, from a traditional group identity to the privatized, modern identity that forms the subject of liberal political and economic theory.

The metonymic character of testimonial discourse – the sense that the voice that is addressing us is a part that stands for a larger whole – is a crucial aspect of what literary critics would call the *convention* of the form: the narrative contract with the reader it establishes. Because it does not require or establish a hierarchy of narrative authority, *testimonio* is a fundamentally democratic and egalitarian narrative form. It implies that *any* life so narrated can have symbolic and cognitive value. Each individual *testimonio* evokes an absent polyphony of other voices, other possible lives and experiences (one common formal variation on the first-person singular *testimonio* is the polyphonic *testimonio* made up of accounts by different participants in the same event).

If the novel is a closed form, in the sense that both the story and the characters in it involve end with the end of the text, in *testimonio*, by contrast, the distinctions between text and history, representation and real life, public and private spheres, objectivity and solidarity (to recall Rorty's alternatives) are blurred. It is, to borrow Umberto Eco's expression, an "open work." The narrator in *testimonio* is an actual person who continues living and acting in an actual social space and time, which also continue. *Testimonio* can never create the illusion – fundamental to formalist methods of textual analysis – of the text as autonomous, set against and above the practical domain of everyday life and struggle. The proliferation of *testimonios* in recent years means that there are experiences in the world today (there always have been) that cannot be expressed adequately in the dominant forms of historical, ethnographic, or literary representation, that would be betrayed or misrepresented by these forms.

Because of its reliance on voice, *testimonio* implies in particular a challenge to the loss of the authority of orality in the context of processes of cultural modernization that privilege literacy and literature as a norm of expression. The inequalities and contradictions of gender, class, race, ethnicity, nationality, and cultural authority that determine the "urgent" situation of the testimonial narrator may also reproduce themselves in the relation of the narrator to the interlocutor, especially when (as is generally the case) that narrator requires to produce the *testimonio* a "lettered" interlocutor from a different ethnic and/or class background in order first to elicit and record the narrative, and then to transform it into a printed text and see to its publication and circulation. But it is equally important to understand that the testimonial narrator is not the subaltern as such either; rather, she or he functions as an organic intellectual (in Antonio Gramsci's sense of this term) of the subaltern, who speaks to the hegemony by means of a metonymy of self in the name and in the place of the subaltern.

By the same token, the presence of subaltern voice in the *testimonio* is in part a literary effect – something akin to what the Russian formalists called *skaz*: the textual simulacrum of direct oral expression. We are dealing here, in other words, not with reality itself but with what semioticians call a "reality effect" that has been produced by both the testimonial narrator – using popular speech and the devices of oral storytelling – and the interlocutor-compiler, who transcribes, edits, and makes a story out of the narrator's discourse. Elzbieta Sklodowska (1982) cautions in this regard that

> it would be naïve to assume a direct homology between text and history [in testimonio]. The discourse of a witness cannot be a reflection of his or her experience, but rather a refraction determined by the vicissitudes of memory, intention, ideology. The intention and the ideology of the author editor further superimposes the original text, creating more ambiguities, silences, and absences in the process of selecting and editing the material in a way consonant with norms of literary form. Thus, although the testimonio uses a series of devices to gain a sense of veracity and authenticity – among them the point of view of the first-person witness-narrator – the play between fiction and history reappears inexorably as a problem. (379, my translation: see also Sklodowska, 1996)

The point is well-taken, but perhaps overstated. Like the identification of *testimonio* with life history (which Sklodowska shares), it concedes agency to the interlocutor-editor of the testimonial text rather than to its direct narrator. It would be better to say that what is at stake in *testimonio* is the *particular* nature of the reality effect it produces. Because of its character as a narrative told in the first person to an actual interlocutor, *testimonio* interpellates the reader in a way that literary fiction or third person journalism or ethnographic writing does not. The word *testimonio* carries the connotation in Spanish of the act of testifying or bearing witness in a legal or religious sense. Conversely, the situation of the reader of *testimonio* is akin to that of a jury member in a courtroom. *Something* is asked of us by *testimonio*, in other words. In this sense, *testimonio* might be seen as a kind of speech act that sets up special ethical and epistemological demands. (When we are addressed directly by an actual person, in such a way as to make a demand on our attention and capacity for judgment, we are under an obligation to respond in some way or other: we can act or not on that obligation, but we cannot ignore it.)

What *testimonio* asks of its readers is in effect what Rorty means by solidarity – that is, the capacity to identity their own selves, expectations, and values with those of another. To understand how this happens is to understand how *testimonio works* ideologically as discourse, rather that what it *is*.

In one of the most powerful sections of her famous *testimonio I, Rigoberta Menchú* (1984), Menchú describes the torture and execution of her brother Petrocinio by elements of the Guatemalan army in the plaza of a small highland town called Chajul, which is the site of an annual pilgrimage by worshipers of the local saint. Here is part of that account:

After he'd finished talking the officer ordered the squad to take away those who'd been "punished," naked and swollen as they were. They dragged them along, they could no longer walk. Dragged them to this place, where they lined them up all together within sight of everyone. The officer called to the worst of the criminals – the *Kaibiles*, who wear different clothes from other soldiers. They're the ones with the most training, the most power. Well, he called the *Kaibiles* and they poured petrol over each of the tortured. The captain said, "This isn't the last of their punishments, there's another one yet. This is what we've done with all the subversives we catch, because they have to die by violence. And if this doesn't teach you a lesson, this is what'll happen to you too. The problem is that the Indians let themselves be led by the communists. Since no-one's told the Indians anything, they go along with the communists." He was trying to convince the people but at the same time he was insulting them by what he said. Anyway, they [the soldiers] lined up the tortured and poured petrol on them; and then the soldiers set fire to each one of them. Many of them begged for mercy. Some of them screamed, many of them leapt but uttered no sound – of course, that was because their breathing was cut off. But – and to me this was incredible – many of the people had weapons with them, the ones who'd been on their way to work had machetes, others had nothing in their hands, but when they saw the army setting fire to the victims, everyone wanted to strike back, to risk their lives doing it, despite all the soldiers' arms. . . . Faced with its own cowardice, the army itself realized that the whole people were prepared to fight. You could see that even the children were enraged, but they didn't know how to express their rage. (178–9)

This passage is undoubtedly compelling and powerful. It invites the reader into the situation it describes through the medium of the eyewitness narrator, and it is the sharing of the experience through Menchú's account that constitutes the possibility of solidarity. But "What if much of Rigoberta's story is not true?" the anthropologist David Stoll (1999: viii) asks. On the basis of interviews in the area where the massacre was supposed to have occurred, Stoll concluded that the killing of Menchú's brother did not happen in exactly this way, that Menchú could not have been a direct witness to the event as her account suggests, and that therefore this account, along with other details of her *testimonio*, amounted to, in Stoll's words, a "mythic inflation" (232).

It would be more accurate to say that what Stoll was able to show in his polemic against Menchú, which itself became an issue in the so-called "culture wars" in the United States, is that *some* rather than "much" of Menchú's story is not true. He does not contest the fact of the murder of Menchú's brother by the army, and he stipulates that "There is no doubt about the most important points [in her story]: that a dictatorship massacred thousands of indigenous peasants, that the victims included half of Rigoberta's immediate family, that she fled to Mexico to save her life, and that she joined a revolutionary movement to liberate her country" (viii). But he does argue that the inaccuracies or omissions in her narrative make her less than a reliable spokesperson for the interests and beliefs of the people for whom she claims to speak. In response to Stoll, Menchú herself publicly conceded that she grafted elements of other people's experiences and stories onto her own account. In particular, she admitted that she was not herself present at the massacre of her brother and his companions in Chajul, and that the account of the event quoted in part above came instead from her mother, who (Menchú claimed) was there. She says that this and similar interpolations were a way of making her story a collective one, rather than a personal autobiography. But the point remains: If the epistemological and ethical authority of testimonial narratives depends on the assumption that they are based on personal experience and direct witness, then it might appear that, as Stoll put it, "*I, Rigoberta Menchú* does not belong in the genre of which it is the most famous example, because it is not the eyewitness account it purports to be" (242).

In a way, however, the argument between Menchú and Stoll was not so much about what really happened as it is about who has the authority to narrate. (Stoll's quarrel with Menchú and *testimonio* is a *political* quarrel that masquerades as an epistemological one.) And that question, rather than the question of "what really happened," is crucial to an understanding of *testimonio*. What seems to bother Stoll above all is that Menchú *has* an agenda. He wants her to be in effect a native informant who will lend herself to *his* purposes (of ethnographic information gathering and evaluation), but she is instead functioning in her narrative as an organic intellectual, concerned with producing a text of local history — that is, with elaborating hegemony.

The basic idea of Gayatri Spivak's essay "Can the Subaltern Speak?" (1998) might be reformulated in this way: if the subaltern could speak — that is, speak in a way that really *matters* to us, that we would feel compelled to listen to — then it would not be subaltern. Spivak is trying to show that behind the gesture of the ethnographer or solidarity activist committed to the cause of the subaltern in allowing or enabling the subaltern to speak is the trace of the construction of another who is available to speak to us (with whom we *can* speak or with whom we would feel comfortable speaking), neutralizing thus the force of the reality of difference and antagonism to which our own relatively privileged position in the global system might give rise. She is saying that one of the things being subaltern means is not mattering, not being worth listening to, or not being understood when one is "heard."

By contrast, Stoll's argument with Menchú is precisely with how her *testimonio* comes to matter. He is bothered by the way it was used by academics and solidarity activists to mobilize international support for the Guatemalan armed struggle in the 1980s, long after (in Stoll's view) that movement had lost whatever support it may have initially enjoyed among the indigenous peasants for whom Menchú claims to speak. That issue — "how outsiders were using Rigoberta's story to justify continuing a war at the expense of peasants who did not support it" (Stoll: 241) — is the main problem for Stoll, rather than the inaccuracies or omissions themselves. From Stoll's viewpoint, by making Menchú's story seem (in her own words) "the story of all poor

Guatemalans" – that is, by its participating in the very metonymic logic of *testimonio* – *I, Rigoberta Menchú* misrepresents a more complex and ideologically contradictory situation among the indigenous peasants. It reflects back to the reader not the subaltern as such, but a narcissistic, "politically correct" image of what the subaltern *should be*.

In one sense, of course, there is a coincidence between Spivak's concern with the production in metropolitan ethnographic and literary discourse of what she calls a "domesticated Other" and Stoll's concern with the conversion of Menchú into an icon of academic political correctness. But Stoll's argument is also explicitly *with* Spivak, as a representative of the very kind of "postmodern scholarship" that would privilege a text like *I, Rigoberta Menchú*.

Stoll states, for example:

> Following the thinking of literary theorists such as Edward Said and Gayatri Spivak, authropologists have become very interested in problems of narrative, voice, and representation, especially the problem of how we misrepresent voices other than our own. In reaction, some anthropologists argue that the resulting fascination with texts threatens the claim of anthropology to be a science, by replacing hypothesis, evidence, and generalization with stylish forms of introspection. (247)

Or: "Under the influence of postmodernism (which has undermined confidence in a single set of facts) and identity polities (which demands acceptance of claims to victimhood), scholars are increasingly hesitant to challenge certain kinds of rhetoric" (244). Or: "With postmodern critiques of representation and authority, many scholars are tempted to abandon the task of verification, especially when they construe the narrator as a victim worthy of their support" (274).

Where Spivak is concerned with the way in which hegemonic literary or scientific representation effaces the effective presence and agency of the subaltern, Stoll's case against Menchú is precisely that: a way of, so to speak, *resubalternizing* a narrative that aspired to (and to some extent achieved) cultural authority. For in the process of constructing her narrative and articulating herself as a political icon around its circulation. Menchú is becoming not-subaltern, in the sense that she is functioning as a subject of history. Her *testimonio* is a *performative* rather than simply descriptive or denotative discourse. Her narrative choices, including her silences and evasions, entail that there are versions of "what really happened" that she does not or cannot represent without relativizing the authority of her own account.

It goes without saying that in any social situation, indeed even within a given class or group identity, it is always possible to find a variety of points of view or ways of telling that reflect contradictory, or simply differing, agendas and interests. "Obviously," Stoll observes, "Rigoberta is a legitimate Mayan voice. So are all the young Mayas who want to move to Los Angeles or Houston. So is the man with a large family who owns three worn out acres and wants me to buy him a chain saw so he can cut down the last forest more quickly. Any of these people can be picked to make misleading generalizations about Mayas" (247). The presence of these other voices makes Guatemalan indigenous communities – indeed even Menchú's own immediate family – seem irremediably driven by internal rivalries, contradictions, and disagreements.

But to insist on this is, in a way, to deny the possibility of subaltern agency as such, because a hegemonic project by definition points to a possibility of collective will and action that depends precisely on the transformation of the conditions of cultural and political disenfranchisement, alienation, and oppression that underlie these rivalries and contradictions. The appeal to diversity ("any of these people") leaves intact the authority of the outside observer (the ethnographer or social scientist) who is alone in the position of being able to both hear and sort through all the various conflicting accounts.

The concern about the connection between *testimonio* and identity politics that Stoll evinces is predicated on the fact that multicultural rights claims carry with them what Canadian philosopher Charles Taylor (1994) has called a "presumption of equal worth" (*I, Rigoberta Menchú* is, among other things, a strong argument for seeing the nature of American societies as irrevocably multicultural and ethnically heterogeneous). That presumption in turn implies an epistemological relativism that coincides with the postmodernist critique of the Enlightenment paradigm of scientific objectivity. If there is no one universal standard for truth, then claims about truth are contextual: They have to do with how people construct different understandings of the world and historical memory from the same sets of facts in situations of gender, ethnic, and class inequality, exploitation, and repression. The truth claims for a testimonial narrative like *I, Rigoberta Menchú* depend on conferring on the form a special kind of epistemological authority as embodying subaltern voice and experience. Against the authority of that voice – and, in particular, against the assumption that it can represent adequately a collective subject ("all poor Guatemalans") – Stoll wants to affirm the authority of the fact-gathering and -testing procedures of anthropology and journalism, in which accounts like Menchú's will be treated simply as ethnographic data that must be processed by more objective techniques of assessment, which are not available to the direct narrator. "[B]ooks like *I, Rigoberta Menchú* will be exalted because they tell academics what they want to hear," Stoll concludes (247). But, in the final analysis, what Stoll is able to present as evidence against the validity of Menchú's account are, precisely, *other testimonios*: other voices, narratives, points of view, in which, it will come as no surprise, he can find something *he* wants to hear.

We know something about the nature of this problem. There is not, outside the realm of human discourse itself, a level of facticity that can guarantee the truth of this or that representation, given that society itself is not an essence prior to representation, but rather the consequence of struggles to represent and over representation. That is the deeper meaning of Walter Benjamin's aphorism "Even the dead are not safe": Even the historical memory of the past is conjunctural, relative, perishable. *Testimonio* is both an art and a strategy of subaltern memory.

We would create yet another version of the native informant if we were to grant testimonial narrators like Rigoberta Menchú only the possibility of being witnesses, and not the power to create their own narrative authority and negotiate its conditions of truth and representativity. This would amount to saying that the subaltern can of course speak, but only through *us*, through our institutionally sanctioned authority and pretended objectivity as intellectuals, which give us the power to decide what counts in the narrator's raw material. But it is precisely that institutionally sanctioned authority and objectivity that, in less benevolent forms, but still claiming to speak from the place of truth, the subaltern must confront every day as war, economic exploitation, development schemes, obligatory acculturation, police and military repression, destruction of habitat, forced sterilization, and the like.

There is a question of agency here. What *testimonio* obliges us to confront is not only the subaltern as a (self-) represented victim, but also as the agent — in that very act of representation — of a transformative project that aspires to become hegemonic in its own right. In terms of this project, which is not our own in any immediate sense and which may in fact imply structurally a contradiction with our position of relative privilege and authority in the global system, the testimonial text is a *means* rather than an end in itself. Menchú and the persons who collaborated with her in the creation of *I, Rigoberta Menchú* were certainly aware that the text would be an important tool in human rights and solidarity work that might have a positive effect on the genocidal conditions the text itself describes. But *her* interest in the text is not to have it become an object for us, our means of getting the "whole truth" – "toda la realidad" – of her experience. It is rather to act tactically in a way she hopes and expects will advance the interests of the community and social groups and classes her *testimonio* represents: "poor" (in her own description) Guatemalans. That is as it should be, however, because it is not only *our* desires and purposes that should count in relation to *testimonio*.

This seems obvious enough, but it is a hard lesson to absorb fully, because it forces us to, in Spivak's phrase, "unlearn privilege." And unlearning privilege means recognizing that it is not the intention of subaltern cultural practice simply to signify its subalternity to us. If that is what *testimonio* does, then critics like Sklodowska are right in seeing it as a form of the status quo, a kind of postmodernist *costumbrismo*.

The force of a *testimonio* such as *I, Rigoberta Menchú* is to displace the centrality of intellectuals and what they recognize as culture – including history, literature, journalism, and ethnographic writing. Like any testimonial narrator (like anybody), Menchú is of course also an intellectual, but in a sense she is clearly different from what Gramsci meant by a traditional intellectual – that is, someone who meets the standards and carries the authority of humanistic and/or scientific high culture. The concern with the question of subaltern agency and authority in *testimonio* depends, rather, on the suspicion that intellectuals and writing practices are themselves complicit in maintaining relations of domination and subalternity.

The question is relevant to the claim made by Dinesh D'Souza (1991) in the debate over the Stanford Western Culture undergraduate requirement (which centered on the adoption of *I, Rigoberta Menchú* as a text in one of the course sections) that *I, Rigoberta Menchú* is not good or great literature. D'Souza wrote, to be precise: "To celebrate the works of the oppressed, apart from the standard of merit by which other art and history and literature is judged, is to romanticize their suffering, to pretend that it is naturally creative, and to give it an aesthetic status that is not shared or appreciated by those who actually endure the oppression" (87). It could be argued that *I, Rigoberta Menchú* is one of the most powerful works of *literature* produced in Latin America in the past several decades; but there is also some point in seeing it as a provocation in the academy, as D'Souza feels it to be. Beatriz Sarlo has argued against the "giro subjetive" represented by *testimonio*, championing, like Stoll, the procedures of the academic social sciences. But the subaltern, by definition, is a social position that is not, and cannot be, adequately represented in the human sciences or the university, if only because the human sciences and the university are among the institutional constellations of power/knowledge that create and sustain subalternity.

This is not, however, to draw a line between the world of the academy and the subaltern, because the point of *testimonio* is to intervene in that world – that is, in a place where the subaltern is not. In its very situation of enunciation, which juxtaposes radically the subject positions of the narrator and interlocutor, *testimonio* is involved in and constructed out of the opposing terms of a master/slave dialectic: metropolis/periphery, nation/region, European/indigenous, creole/mestizo, elite/popular, urban/rural, intellectual/manual, male/female, "lettered"/illiterate or semi-literate. *Testimonio* is no more capable of transcending these oppositions than are more purely literary or scientific forms of writing or narrative; that would require something like a cultural revolution that would abolish or invert the conditions that produce relations of subordination, exploitation, and inequality in the first place. But *testimonio* does involve a new way of articulating these oppositions and a new, collaborative model for the relationship between the intelligentsia and the popular classes.

To return to Rorty's point about the "desire for solidarity," a good part of the appeal of *testimonio* must lie in the fact that it both represents symbolically and enacts in its production and reception a relation of solidarity between ourselves – as members of the professional middle class and practitioners of the human sciences – and subaltern social subjects like Menchú. *Testimonio* gives voice to a previously anonymous and voiceless popular-democratic subject, but in such a way that the intellectual or professional is interpellated, in his or her function as interlocutor/reader of the testimonial account, as being in alliance with (and to some extent dependent on) this subject, without at the same time losing his or her identity as an intellectual.

If first-generation *testimonios* such as *I, Rigoberta Menchú* effaced textually in the manner of the ethnographic life story (except in their introductory presentations) the presence of the interlocutor, it is becoming increasingly common in what is sometimes called the "new ethnography" to put the interlocutor into the account, to make the dynamic of interaction and negotiation between interlocutor and narrator part of what *testimonio* testifies to. Ruth Behar's *Translated Woman: Crossing the Border with Esperanza's Story* (1993), for example, is often mentioned as a model for the sort of ethnographic text in which the authority (and identity) of the ethnographer is counterpointed against the voice and authority of the subject whose life history the ethnographer is concerned with eliciting. In a similar vein, Philippe Bourgois's innovative ethnography of Puerto Rican crack dealers in East Harlem, *In Search of Respect* (1995), often puts the values of the investigator – Bourgois – against those of the dealers he befriends and whose stories and conversations he transcribes and reproduces in his text. In *Event, Metaphor, Memory: Chauri Chaura, 1922–1992* (1995), the subaltern studies historian Shahid Amin is concerned with retrieving the "local memory" of an uprising in 1922 in a small town in northern India in the course of which peasants surrounded and burned down a police station, leading to the deaths of 23 policemen. But he is also concerned with finding ways to incorporate formally the narratives that embody that memory into his own history of the event, abandoning thus the usual stance of the historian as omniscient narrator and making the heterogeneous voices of the community itself the historian(s).

These ways of constructing testimonial material (obviously, the examples could be multiplied many times over) make visible that what happens in *testimonio* is not only the textual staging of a "domesticated Other," to recall Spivak's telling objection, but the confrontation through the text of one person (the reader and or immediate interlocutor) with another (the direct narrator or narrators) at the level of a *possible* solidarity. In this sense, *testimonio* also embodies a possibility of political agency. But that possibility is necessarily built on the recognition of and respect for the radical incommensurability of the situation of the parties involved. More than empathic liberal guilt or political correctness, what *testimonio* seeks to elicit is *alliance*. As Doris Sommer (1996) puts it succinctly, *testimonio* "is an invitation to a tête-à-tête, not to a heart to heart" (143).

## NOTES

An earlier version of this chapter appeared in Norman Denzin and Yvonna Lincoln (eds), *The Sage Handbook of Qualitative Research*, Thousand Oaks, CA: Sage, 2005.

1 Rorty's (1985) distinction may recall for some readers Marvin Harris's well-known distinction between *emic* and *etic* accounts (where the former are personal or collective "stories" and the latter are representations given by a supposedly objective observer based on empirical evidence).

2 Widely different sorts of narrative texts could in given circumstances function as *testimonios*: confession, court testimony, oral history, memory, autobiography, autobiographical novel, chronicle, confession, life story, *novela testimonio*, "nonfiction novel" (Truman Capote), or "literature of fact" (Roque Dalton).

3    Mary Louise Pratt (1986) describes the *testimonio*
     usefully in this respect as "autoethnography."
4    In Miguel Barnet's (1986) phrase, the author
     has been replaced in *testimonio* by the function

of a "compiler" (*compilador*) or "activator" (*gestante*), somewhat on the model of the film producer.

# REFERENCES

Amin, S. (1995). *Event, Metaphor, Memory: Chauri Chaura 1922–1992*. Berkeley: University of California Press.

Barnet, M. (1986). La novela *testimonio*: Socioliteratura. In *Testimonio y literatura*, R. Jara ed. and H. Vidal Minneapolis: University of Minnesota, Institute for the Study of Ideologies and Literatures.

Behar, R. (1993). *Translated Woman: Crossing the Border with Esperanza's Story*. Boston: Beacon.

Benjamin, W. (1969). *Illuminations*. Trans. H. Zohn. New York: Schocken.

Beverley, J., and H. Achúgar (eds.) (2002). *La voz del otro: Testimonio, subalternidad, y verdad narrativa*. Second edition. Guatemala: Universidad Rafael Landivar.

Bourgois, P. (1995) *In Search of Respect*. Cambridge: Cambridge University Press.

Carcy Webb, A., and S. Benz (eds.). (1996). *Teaching and testimony*. Albany: State University of New York Press.

Clifford, L., and G. E. Marcos (eds.). (1986). *Writing Culture: The Poetics and Politics of Ethnography*. Berkeley: University of California Press.

D'Souza, D. (1991). *Illiberal Education*. New York: Free Press.

Gugelberger, G. M. (ed.). (1996). *The Real Thing: Testimonial Discourse and Latin America*. Durham, NC: Duke University Press.

Gugelberger, G. M., and M. Kearney (eds.). (1991). [Special issue]. *Latin American Perspectives*. 18–19.

Guha, R. (ed.). (1997). *A Subaltern Studies Reader*. Minneapolis: University of Minnesota Press.

Guha, R., and G. C. Spivak (eds.). (1988). *Selected Subaltern Studies.*, New York: Oxford University Press.

Jara, R. (1986). "Prólogo." In *Testimonio y literatura*, ed. R. Jara and H. Vidal, pp. 1–3. Minneapolis: University of Minnesota, Institute for the Study of Ideologies and Literatures.

Jara, R., and H. Vidal (eds.). (1986). *Testimonio y literatura*. Minneapolis: University of Minnesota, Institute for the Study of Ideologies and Literatures.

Menchú, R. (1984). *I, Rigoberta Menchú: An Indian Woman in Guatemala*. Ed. E. Burgos-Debray, Trans. A. Wright. London: Verso.

Pratt, M. L. (1986). "Fieldwork in common places." In *Writing Culture: The Poetics and Politics of Ethnography*, ed. I. Clifford and G. F. Marcos. Berkeley: University of California Press.

Rabasa, J., J. Sanjinés, and R. Carr (eds.). (1996). *Subaltern studies in the Americas* [Special issue]. *disposition*. 19(46).

Randall, M. (1985). *Testimonios: A Guide to Oral History*. Toronto: Participately Research Group.

Rivero, E. (1984–5). "*Testimonio y* conversaciones como discurse literario: Cuba y Nicaragua," *Literature and Contemporary Revolutionary Culture*, 1.

Rorty, R. (1985). "Solidarity or objectivity?" In *Post analytic philosophy*, ed. J. Rachman and C. West. pp. 3–19. New York: Columbia University Press.

Sarlo, Beatriz (2005). *Tiempo pasado: cultura de la memoria y giro subjetivo*. Buenos Aires: Siglo XXI.

Sklodowska, E. (1982). "La forma testimonial y la novelistica de Miguel Baret," *Revista/Review Interamericana* 12: 368–80.

— (1996). "Spanish American testimonial novel: some afterthoughts." In *The Real Thing: Testimonial Discourse and Latin America*. ed. G. M. Gugelberger, pp. 84–100. Durham, NC: Duke University Press.

Sommer, D. (1996). "No secrets." In *The Real Thing Testimonial Discourse and Latin America*. ed. G. M. Gogelberger pp. 130–60. Durham, NC: Duke University Press.

Spivak, G. C. (1988). "Can the subaltern speak:" In *Marxism and the Interpretation of Culture*, ed. C. Nelson and I. Grossberg, pp. 280–316. Urban University of Illinois Press.

Stoll, D. (1999). *Rigoberta Menchú and the Story of All Poor Guatemalans*. Boulder. CO: Westview.

Taylor, C. (1994). "The politics of recognition." In *Multiculturalism: Examining the Politics of Recognition*. C. Tavlor, K. A. Appiah. J. Habermas, S. C. Rockefeller, M. Walzer, and S. Wolf. Ed. A. Gutmann. Princeton. MI: Princeton University Press.

# 34
# Affectivity beyond "Bare Life": On the Non-Tragic Return of Violence in Latin American Film
## Hermann Herlinghaus

In his essay *Critique of Violence*, written in 1921 when the aftermaths of both World War I and the October Revolution in Russia were strongly resonating among intellectuals in Germany's Weimar Republic, Walter Benjamin made a far-reaching statement: "The proposition that existence [*Dasein*] stands higher than a just existence is false and ignominious, if existence is to mean nothing other than *mere life*" (Benjamin, 1996: 251; emphasis added). The remark, focused on what would better be translated as "bare life," stands out for its complexity, especially when discussed in relation to global modernity. On the one hand, it contrasts with the ethical exhaustion of today's "public consciousness," within which these questions seem to have been turned into outmoded issues, allegedly having been overwritten by "reality." Widely prevalent, sometimes unconscious cynicism has it that many humans – as well as "discourses" – endure as best as they can, irrespective of higher values or historical projections. On the other hand, however, several philosophers have been advancing new critical projects in relation to the concept of life, rather than conforming to the out-of-jointness of the world.

The purpose of this chapter is to explore relationships between current debates on violence and ethics, and cinematic imagination as it helps to articulate dimensions of conflict in Latin America. With his singular study *Homo Sacer*, and reinterpreting Benjamin's almost forgotten remarks on "blosses Leben" ("bare life"), Giorgio Agamben has contributed to an uncommon rethinking of the relationships between religiosity and power. Regarding the notion of the "sacred," that author has neither followed the precepts of Christian morality, nor of a "scientific mythologeme" based on the French school of sociology and anthropology (see Agamben, 1998: 75, 76). However, if the notion of "bare life" has been resituated deeply *within* modernity by thinkers such as Arendt, Foucault, Negri, and decisively Agamben, the biopolitical critique of oppressive capitalism's having become normal and all-pervasive has just begun. Today's reproduction *and* dispensation of labor, matter, and life – with both tendencies being fundamentally violent – have become increasingly functional, but not only because unity and abstraction operate as exclusive mechanisms of a worldwide economic and political domination. Major global strategies and networks of rule – which Negri and Hardt have placed under the rubric of "Empire" – have succeeded in subduing and outsourcing heterogeneity. At the same time, the imperial mechanisms of scaling and control are haunted by movements and images of reterritorialization, since they have become susceptible to vampirization by heterogeneous interests. Culturally speaking, at issue are, once again, modernity's borders and peripheries. However, for Arendt and Foucault, and even for Agamben, the reterritorializing force of peripheral knowledges and cultures within a dominant global design has remained secondary, if not irrelevant.

Filmic imagination in Latin America can be perceived to have generated affective territories in its own right. As "global localizations" (Bové, 1998: 372) intervening in the worldwide realm of expression and circulation, a remarkable number of films that are produced today in Mexico, Colombia, Argentina, and Brazil, as well as in other countries, call for conceptual discussion. In order to approach vital problems through film, the present study focuses on phenomenological and philosophical questions. Film engages experience and thought by virtue of "affective configurations," as well as energies. As one of the crucial domains of contemporary culture, it can be understood as a realm of "second nature," acting through presence and immanence, breaking down modern abstractions and elusions of identity. In addition, film is susceptible to establishing a peculiar relationship to "bare life," contained in its epistemological propensity. For example, have not the surfaces of innumerable fiction films in the past century provided a "pure form" of the potentiality of violence? Have they not created a ubiquitous forum for making violence and terror visible, omnipresent, and even "possessive" in modern life? Has not film contributed to an imagination and thus to the existence of a non-Heideggerian, "non-authentic," that is to say "violent," dimension of *Dasein* (being-in-the-world)?

Let me start by demarcating film as symbolic formation(s) constituting a wide, i.e., multilayered realm through which experience is translated into features and figures of immanence. At the same time, film calls for a shift regarding our take on immanence: an "anthropological materialism" (Benjamin) becomes necessary, one that looks at life and history through the lenses of image-making. The concept of immanence points toward experience without transcendence, faith without doxa, for example, when immanent ethical differences take the lead over absolute moral dispositions (see Smith, 1998: 252). We are thus returning to Benjamin. An *immanent ethical difference* can be perceived by consciously addressing the tension between "mere existence" and "just existence." Yet the difficulty lies in the absence of "just existence" from the plane of conclusive historical categories. Discussing ethical difference requires an exploration of the surfaces of the visible and palpable world – the ways of aesthetic and cultural expression and understanding, in short, the dimensions of that which is dealt with in terms of recognition rather than cognition and logical construction. My study converses with, among others, Deleuze's reflections on cinema. However, it advances the hypothesis that cinematic culture in Latin America is giving prominence to ethics over abstract ontology. A series of questions arises from this. What are the zones in which the Western transcendental apparatus becomes shallow, even as it remains redundantly prone to a dominant concept of reason? How can "bare life" be meaningfully approached beyond either nihilistic perspectives or traditional Christian morals? What are the conceptually and ethically compelling spaces in today's world where "bare life" – despite an omnipresent domination – avoids representing the "lowest" level of existence, i.e., where there is investment in energies directed against tolerating "much suffering and hold[ing] on to life [*zoē*] as if it were a kind of serenity [*euemēria*, 'beautiful day'] and a natural sweetness" (cited in Agamben, 1998: 2)?

How can contemporary films coming from Mexico, Brazil, Colombia, and Argentina contribute to mapping out, or understanding, these "timely" yet drastically "unworldly" spaces, in which life itself is at stake, having become immanently political? Placing Benjamin in this context makes his insights more suggestive than he himself could have foreseen. This refers, in the first place, to his critique of the "dogma" of the "sacredness of life." Benjamin wrote:

> Man cannot, at any price, be said to coincide with the mere life in him, any more than he [my correction] can be said to coincide with any other of his conditions and qualities, including even the uniqueness of his bodily person. However sacred man is (or however sacred that life in him which is identically present in earthly life, death, and afterlife), there is no sacredness in his condition, in his bodily life vulnerable to injury by his fellow men. (Benjamin, 1996: 251).

These words call for strategies of translation that help address the historicity of the present by wresting experience away from collapse, or from its leveling by the deceitful powers of blindness, consumption, and exhaustion. In other words, we are concerned with that order of immanence which is related to the aesthetic presence of the image through film. As much as the "affect" seems to have contributed to the numbness that violence in and through film has widely generated, this very notion will now help cut a path through the pervasiveness of violent images and montage.

The topic of the "non-tragic" return of violence in Latin American film is situated within a shift in the perception of reality. Discussions during past decades have made evident that, once the field of experience is addressed beyond or beneath the marks of representation and explanation, interpretive notions are needed that are "impure" and non-deterministic. Concepts are required which are not already part of the answers that analysis is striving for. Existence conceived of as "bare life," "power," "affectivity," "drama," "melodrama," "event," "montage," "figurality," or "repertoire" are examples of such indeterminate notions which can help advance the epistemological and aesthetic discussion. Viewed in relation to the global periphery, Latin America, with its incorporation in strategic neoliberal assets and its conversion into wastelands at the same time (Harvey, 2005: 214), "bare life" acquires a new urgency. Its problematization can lead us into more particular, and less abstract, ethical questions than those put forward by Agamben in his vision of a "global" state of exception. Filmic creation in Latin America has been addressing the "worldliness" of the periphery from local histories of "post-authoritarian" pacification and neoliberal reterritorialization in particularly intense, sometimes existentialist, yet not unreflective ways. New tendencies in cinema in the Southern Cone, Mexico, the Andean countries, and Brazil have depicted and reimagined "bare life," and death, by contrasting them with the geopolitical project of purification.

The Argentine film *Un Oso Rojo* (2002), directed by Adrián Caetano, is made up of elements of montage which seem conventional, together with an argument that appears to be ordinary at first glance. Yet, common typological takes are of little use once we accept "sensuous elaboration" (Sontag, 1969: 212) as a quality in its own right. The narration starts on the day on which *el Oso* ("the Bear"), a taciturn man in his late thirties, is released from a Buenos Aires jail into which armed robbery and homicide had propelled him seven years earlier. The robbery had occurred on the first birthday of his daughter, Alicia, a coincidence that discredited the man in the eyes of his pretty wife, Natalia, who struggles to make a precarious living in a suburban, lower middle-class neighborhood. Upon the day of *el Oso*'s return, Natalia is living with another man, and 8-year-old Alicia is being raised with the knowledge that her father is a criminal. However, *el Oso* does not accept being treated as an unwelcome intruder; he instead strives to regain his authority as father, and to provide the family (including Natalia's new partner) with the financial support he thinks he owes them. His economic condition is as precarious as it was before, so his project cannot be carried out without violent means that lead him, once again, into the arena of delinquency. *El Oso*, who now works as a driver, becomes involved in retaliation and murder (*el Turco*, who still owes him big money, is killed for betraying him again), but he manages to get away with it and to provide the family with an impressive sum. Natalia and Alicia's stepfather can thus pay their debts. After that, *el Oso* walks away and into the dark, following the principle: "A veces, para hacerle bien a la gente que uno quiere, lo mejor es estar lejos" ("At times, in order to do right by the people you love, you have to be far away").

Caetano is one of the main protagonists of the so-called *nuevo cine argentino*, a movement that has evolved since the second half of the 1990s, originating in independent film and short film productions, and carried forward by a generation of well-schooled filmmakers who came from television or advertising (see Oubiña, 2003: 29). In Argentina, a controversial recovery of the "submerged universe of marginalized people" by contemporary filmmakers came to bear later than in other countries like, for example, Mexico and Colombia. Caetano's film should be judged against the grain of an interpretive tradition in Argentina which still favors the adherence to "Adornian" high cultural values. Hence, one criterion for evaluating the status of violence lies in the "possibility" (or the deconstruction of the idea of) of tragedy. Oubiña, in his analysis of the film, asserts that the construction of the hero misses the point: "the figure lacks transcendence" and does not display the traits of a "modern", i.e., properly tragic, hero (ibid., 32). From the balance between lacking "*grandeza*" (greatness) and "*densidad*" (density), it is only a small step to dismissing the legitimacy of Caetano's protagonist: *el Oso* is qualified as being a "simply violent" creature – "*es un lumpen*" ("he's *lumpen"*) (ibid.). This approach becomes still more problematic when *el Oso* is denied the status of a "popular hero": popular agency would be recognized only if it offered a matrix that fits the "educated" sentiment – it would have to become sublime by striving for absolute values of good or evil; otherwise it remains inauthentic.

To mourn the lack of transcendence in the marginal subject has become a most inadequate, although not uncommon argument in ethical discussions. "Tragedy" still marks a powerful watershed that has, for a long time, been in the service of either an aesthetic "purification" of violence or a sublimation of political and social conflicts. As believed by the above-cited critic, *el Oso* fails to be authentically tragic because his crisis is not a catastrophe translatable into an individual's drama that could claim for genuine "truth." *El Oso's* condition is not tragically significant in that he does not deserve "true pity." To say it with Hegelian criteria, his actions (and failures) cannot be measured by the "eternal and inviolable" values that a tragic subject would summon up against itself (Hegel, 1998: 452). Hegel wanted to be overtly clear: "Beggars and rascals cannot inspire us with pity of this kind" (ibid.). In that vein, *el Oso's* is, rather, a "sad story," "a misfortune as such. Such miseries may befall a man . . . merely as a result of the conjuncture of external accidents" (ibid.), not of deeper *necessities*. Hence, "sad" collisions and "tragic" conflicts are separated by the famous essentializing partition. My study questions "tragedy" as a hegemonic aesthetic category by which the "entirety" of a subject is to be defended under circumstances of violence and death.

Contemporary Latin American films have generated a narrative and visual repertoire with which a "normative concept" of tragedy (Eagleton, 2003: 8) has been widely challenged, although it was sometimes affirmed. Melodramatic narrative and affective strategies, in particular, question a sublime pathos that refers back to God, the law, or other transcendental insignias. Melodrama has subverted good taste and established rules by staging the most incredible and absurd stories whose only promise consists of limitless love, heartbreak, and quotidian negotiations between these two. Film melodrama has engaged an obsessive imagination nurturing the fury and the day-to-day desires of those whose lives have been emptied of the images and hopes for superior justice (see Herlinghaus, 2002: 14). However, to approach cinematic imagination in these present times may require different conceptual frameworks. Films like *Un Oso Rojo*, together with numerous others such as *La Ciénaga* (Argentina, 2001), *Amores Perros* (Mexico, 2000), and *La Vendedora de Rosas* (Colombia, 1998), to name only a few, introduce a sobriety of experience that also seems to suspend melodramatic empowerment. This tendency was pioneered by the Colombian film *Rodrigo D. No futuro* by Victor Gaviria (1988). From this moment onward, the appraisal of the affective strategies of these films can enable a specific involvement in the current discussions on ethics and violence, and especially on the problematics of "bare life."

The role of the hero in *Un Oso Rojo* is disconcerting. Let us look at two scenes in the film and thus address the affective traits of the visual language. In both scenes, the status of exception with regard to the meaning of life is at issue. Shortly after being released from prison, *el Oso* overhears in a street conversation that a young, elegant, business type has received a salary advance. *El Oso* approaches him to ask for ten *pesos*, to which the haughty character answers: "andá a trabajar" ("get a job"). El Oso violently drags the fellow into his luxurious car to steal all his money. Intensity arises from the emotional abyss between the two men. Whereas *el Oso's* posture, behind his aggressive act, is entirely passionless, the rich man bursts into inconsolable weeping. This leads *ad absurdum* any possibility of individual tragic distinction in the Hegelian sense. The sharp, affective contrast is grounded on common knowledge shared by both men. For the social outsider and the businessman, sheer life is at stake, although from opposite angles. That is to say, they share a strange sense of a contemporary "state of exception" which is pervasive, yet not directly dependent on the positive power of the law, nor on a sovereign decision known as the Schmittian paradigm. This scene points instead toward what looks like an "existentialist" situation, one that reaches beyond the assumptions of the juridical theory of the state. In Argentina's post-dictatorship, the political state of exception has passed, since "democracy" implies a normalized society. However, this normalized existence in market society has become anachronistic, now that it is contaminated by *situations of exception in the spaces of daily life*. Another still more significant scene constructs an encounter between *el Oso* and his daughter Alicia, leading to a traumatic revelation. The father has taken the 8-year-old girl to a suburban fairground where she climbs on a merry-go-round. The camera is mounted on it, so that every time it goes around, when Alicia travels past the man, she sees him up close, then moving out of angle until he disappears from sight, before circling back, and so forth. *El Oso* watches his daughter on the carousel from behind a fence. Alicia notices two policemen approaching her father from behind. The girl grows anxious while she is stuck on the moving platform. The father looks toward her in a state of emotional attachment until he "awakens" at the moment when the policemen, from behind, push him against the fence to search him for weapons or drugs. The girl's stupor is heightened – the carousel keeps moving so she can only turn her head as far to the left or right as possible in order to keep her father in sight. It is there – in the silent relationship between the face of the daughter and that of the father marked by successive reencounter and separation – that the film produces its "argument" by virtue of the "affection-image."

According to Deleuze, film has reshaped the problematics of affection, especially with visual figurations related to the use of the close-up. The filmic construction of the face (Deleuze, 1996: 96) has made affect apprehensible through visual ecstasies that surpass the immediate coordinates of space and time (see ibid.). Deleuze addresses particular powers of "abstraction" and intensification in their relationship to the film image. Much earlier, Benjamin had already spoken of the "dialectical image." This experimental notion has served as an indicator as to how the material surfaces of expression can be approached beyond their empirical, i.e., contextual immediacies. That is to say, how can the complexity of experience and even reflection be explored when they are related, not to transcendence but to "immanence"? How does filmic expression help us to conceive the cultural and epistemological sphere that lies between empiricism and transcendentalism? It comes as a necessary surprise that, through film, affect can be made "specifically" independent of the coordinates of a concrete place. Montage is able to create unique relationships between visual isolations and contextual environments: affect becomes an "entity" by means of image construction. The relationship between *el Oso* and Alicia can thus be addressed in terms of intensity and empathy, or of "proposition" (ibid., 97). "Proposition" discloses a virtuality that is "not a sensation, a feeling or idea, but the quality of a possible sensation, feeling or idea." Deleuze describes the "affection-image" as distinct from the "action-image": "it is quality or power, it is potentiality considered for itself as expressed" (ibid., 98). Regarding the scene described above, the traumatic "encounter" of father and daughter is, on the one hand, due to the specific circumstances of the situation. At the same time, the particular *affect* created by the silent communication between the two faces, both depicted as alternating close-ups, is "distinct from every individuated state of things" (ibid.) – it is like a new experience, powerful and transgressive in itself.

The mutual mirroring of the two faces (as close-ups) expresses the "compound affect" of longing for intimate proximity, and of a sudden bewilderment working against the longing. The *affection-image* gives shape to a double abandonment as proposition: Alicia is abandoned by her father, who is "taken away" from her by the unlimited power that the police force can exert on the man even in a moment of togetherness with his daughter. Secondly, *el Oso* is abandoned by the existing law. This abandonment rests on the assumption that interventions of the police often go beyond "law-preserving" violence with practices of "law-making" violence (see Benjamin, 1996: 242, 243). The fact that the policemen walk away after searching the man does not diminish the affective state of affairs that, on the contrary, is pushed toward a perception of the virtual omnipresence of the police. An abandonment of the daughter is caused by the exposedness of the father – his being susceptible to discipline by "superior" coercive violence at any time. To use Agamben's expression, the father in *Un Oso Rojo* has become a "sacred" person. This is the moment in which the "immanent" guilt of *el Oso* is crystallized by an image of strong affection. The man had not been doing anything wrong – his mere existence, together with his "suspicious" appearance, sufficed to expose him to reprehension. At last, the affection-image gives shape to a double exposedness: in his abandonment to the all-pervasive, ghostly presence of the police, the father is exposed to the eyes of his daughter, which is worse than his being in prison. While *el Oso* watches his daughter watching him, he is forced to recognize himself as a criminal-in-advance – a kind of "wandering delinquent." In that sense, both father and daughter are taken away from each other, since the father cannot overcome the immanent *sacredness* that characterizes his condition after having left prison.

Viewed from the standpoint of multiple abandonments, the next step toward *el Oso's* relapse into criminal action does not make an essential difference: if he is only a "revenant" to life – not being able to assume a normal existence after jail – his transgressing the existing rules constitutes his only "freedom." Oubiña, the critic referred to earlier, is not interested in the affective situation *created* by the film when he asserts: "In a country where taking justice into one's own hands has so frequently been the clearest indication of fascism, at very least a heroic character like *el Oso* should be in doubt" (Oubiña, 2003: 32). The atavism of Caetano's movie points in a different direction, in that it is a historical phenomenon – as is fascism – yet it is subjectified by those who have been biopolitically dispensed by authoritarianism and by "democratic" neoliberalism alike. In the film, the "loss" of the melodramatic option still enables a strategy of empowerment. Once *el Oso* realizes that his longing for love and harmony has broken down owing to his "immanent criminality," he decides that he can still help Alicia, Natalia, and her new partner get out of destitution and indebtedness. He does so by participating in a robbery and settling scores with old companions, finally being able to contribute big money to Alicia's new family. The final scene shows the compact body of *el Oso*, seen from behind, framed in a medium-shot, as he walks away from the camera into the darkness of urban nocturnal space. Now it is no longer the face that constitutes the site of the affection-image. Instead, it is the body of the protagonist which has become "pure affect." The nocturnal, empty streets are depicted in such a way that they loose their specificity and become "any space whatever" (see Deleuze, 1986: 97). The affection-image reveals its magic to "abstract" from spatio-temporal coordinates; moreover, it can even abstract from a face or a body. In that sense, the man's body expresses a de-individualized experience, a posture of life at its limit revealing a strange power and affective consistency.

Realistically, *el Oso* would be dead after the shootouts that he, alone, had with many other men. Yet the film places the man in a virtual space "beyond death," since society has abandoned creatures like him. In conventional terms, two possible solutions would have sufficed. On the one hand, death could have occurred in a way that enabled the tragic distinction of the person, a situation arising, for example, from Alicia's losing her beloved father so dramatically. On the other hand, violent death could have sealed the destiny of a person who did not deserve otherwise. Caetano's film avoids these schemata, both of which are inherent in a long-traditioned, morally and politically affirmative middle-class imagination. Within this tradition, violence and death have represented the abject side of modern life. In other words: violence has occupied its legitimate place within a modern "means–ends dialectics" that has always seemed to be ultimately secured by enlightened law, normative universalism, or regulative Christian morality. When cinematic ethics, however, engage "bare life" as a normalized condition, the problem is not violence as an ultimate, remote possibility, or as a "means" that under certain conditions serves either the attainment or the preservation of the "higher end," nor as a sad occurrence suddenly irrupting into someone's destiny. At issue is *existence qua experience* under the conditions of life's having been sacrificed to an omnipresent, "virtual" non-existence of the *"human condition."* Seen from this perspective, an atavistic philosophy resonates in the final scene, as well as within the affective makeup, of the whole film. This posture has corrosive implications for the ways in which modern life has been conceived and dreamt of. Violence is suddenly made visible outside the means–ends dialectics: it has become the central feature of immanence in the life of figures such as Caetano's hero, *el Oso Rojo*.

The affective arguments set forth by a series of recent films from different Latin American countries can be placed within a similar framework, an observation that allows us to historicize the perception of ethical survival in times of advanced global capitalism and imperial rule. Speaking in narratological terms, at issue is the conscious decision of the outsider-protagonist to move "beyond death" by using the means at his disposal, not for a higher end but for the sake of sheer existence. This is neither a simple question of counter-violence, nor of terrorism, although it could be viewed as an affirmation of nihilist identities (see Žižek, 2002: 40). It has to do with the heroes' active inhabiting of a space of abandonment created by society at the point where no other alternatives can be seized, yet where the creation of "violent events" serves as an act of solidarity – the support of loved ones or family members who still have a chance to outlive the exception. In the case of these antiheroes, violence does not serve personal enrichment or the creation of corrupted power networks. For example, at the end of the Mexican film *Amores Perros* (2000), the eccentric protagonist, *el Chivo* – a former *guerrillero* who eventually started working as a contract killer – walks "out of the picture" and into a "space beyond death" – a semi-dark, desolate countryside, his stature becoming one with the mass of dry, broken earth extending toward the horizon. Is it accidental that *el Chivo's* adoring love as well as supportive attitude, as was *el Oso's*, is focused on his only daughter who – living on the side of "full citizenry" – has become inaccessible to him? If, from the father's perspective, the sentiments toward the daughter become more essential than his own life, then existence appears as an active stance that contests the supposed impotence and "guiltiness" of "bare life."

Among Latin American films of the beginning of the twenty-first century, the Mexican production *Amores Perros*, directed by Alejandro González Iñarritu, has probably earned the most spectacular attention, along with an impressive array of festival awards. Sharply condensing a world of urban squalor that belongs to Mexico City, the film deals with a range of topics that are all linked to contemporary cinematic conventions. Its characters are grouped around the idea of a vertical slice through society where meanness and poverty are seen contrasting, and suddenly colliding, with wealth and frivolity. There are marginal youths engaged in underground dog-fighting, robbery, and a violent search for romance; there is a top model, together with her wealthy lover, who is crippled in an accident that destroys her precious body; furthermore, there is a mythic street character – an old vagrant– who was once a guerrilla rebel, spent 20 years in prison, and then became destitute, surviving by occasionally hiring himself out as a hit-man. In addition, there are car races, dog fights, scenes of street violence and obsessive passion, jealousy, hate, and revenge – offensive gestures and belligerent acts looming everywhere. The onlooker can recognize features of the supergenre *telenovela* which are synthesized in a well-made action drama. At the same time, familiar dramaturgical ingredients come as a matter of "generational" schooling – Alejandro G. Iñarritu has not hesitated to borrow stylistic and narrative elements from Tarantino's *Pulp Fiction* and *Reservoir Dogs*.

But something that is compelling in a different manner makes the movie significant beyond these parameters of success. The title "Amores perros" reveals a twofold
meaning. The persons involved in the three love-and-repugnance relationships that
together constitute the narrative grid of the film are all attached to dogs. Secondly,
the obsessive presence of dogs within all three constellations marks the centrality of
(dog-)life – and death – as the catalyst of a visceral force. It is a compulsion that
accompanies and even enables human life the way it is shown to pervade an end-of-
the-twentieth-century Mexico City. The film starts with brutal, smash-cut images of
a fleeing car driven by two young fellows, and a bleeding, mortally wounded dog in
the backseat of the car. Later, dogs are present in different settings of human interaction, either behaving aggressively or being vulnerable and victimized by other dogs.
González Iñarritu thus creates a powerful allegory of "bare life." These dogs do not
"symbolize" the affection that humans can devote to animals in situations of personal
loneliness. They lend "bare life" an ongoing physical presence. Their role is attached
to both aggressiveness and the extreme vulnerability of the body, constituting a parallel that unites humans and animals under the circumstances of what appears as a
shared "state of exception."

Humans and animals sharing a common "state of exception" is one of the aspects
that lends the film particular strength and a great deal of the dismay that it has generated among critics. However, it is necessary to understand this archaic component
as a conceptual factor. At issue is a "politicization" of life as it unfolds in a realm
spanning the highly operative capitalist dynamics of power, palpable as an omnipresent drive toward commodification, and an exhaustion of the spaces of daily existence
in Mexico's capital. When discussing *El Oso Rojo*, I alluded to democratic society's
susceptibility to daily situations of exception (see also Herlinghaus, 2006: 49–50).
*Amores Perros* shows, in an even more accentuated way, zones of exception irrupting
from beneath the surfaces of democratically normativized life. Within these peripheral
territories, democracy, which is supposed to define the space that separates "full citizens" from "homo sacer," is neither self-understood, nor is it guaranteed to the people
through the unity of "law-preserving" structures and the role of the state itself. This
is one of the substantial subjects addressed by the works discussed here. Scenarios like
those created by González Iñarritu can be viewed as "global localizations" suggesting
that, for example, countries like Mexico and Argentina have come close to each other,
not in terms of homogeneous developments, but from the standpoint of perturbing
experiences inscribed in urban neoliberal modernity and thus, historical
heterogeneity.

Illustrious metaphors circumscribing Mexico's stake in modernity seem to display
a genealogy of decline. There is Paz's *Labyrinth of Solitude*, Bartra's *The Cave of Melancholy*, or Monsiváis' *Rituals of Chaos*. The director of *Amores Perros* abandons them all
and creates another one: *rituals of violence*. Has modernity, beyond all premonitions,
generated huge "public" territories in which a growing number of people survive by
ritualistic incursions into violence? This question is not a deterministic one, and it

should not be seen as just dependent on the specific conditions that threaten Latin American civil societies. At issue in these films is not a violent Latin America, but violence in global, and still "modern" terms. To put it differently – what distinguishes González Iñarritu's perspective from the playfully unhistorical, cynical, yet entertaining blood-spilling violence in several of Tarantino's films? Are the protagonists of *Amores Perros* like Octavio and Ramiro, and El Chivo, "natural born killers," to paraphrase Oliver Stone? It would be difficult to imagine that a film like *Amores Perros* could incite teenagers to follow the examples of these protagonists in real life. There is an ethical difference, tiny though it may be, that prevents affective montage from being absorbed into certain Hollywood-based economies of terror.

Let us look into how the three juxtaposed narratives in *Amores Perros* form a conceptual grid. First, there is the story of "*Octavio and Susana*," set in a poor, working-class neighborhood where numerous youngsters live together within a small housing space, facing all kinds of trouble. Cofi is the name of a stout Rottweiler that Octavio uses to raise money from dog fights, as he dreams of running off with his young sister-in-law, Susana. Ramiro, Susana's aggressive husband, works in a grocery store and applies his respective know-how to robbing other stores at night. Things go wrong and Octavio, threatened by the chief of the local dog-fighting scene, has to resort to a wild car flight, producing the accident that entwines the three different story-spaces of the film. All these are ingredients of common action plots. Yet the film's dramatic gift lies in the surprises it creates. The handsome, almost sweet, Octavio, who pursues Susana against all odds, turns the Rottweiler into a sacred animal: to assume Agamben's definition somewhat drastically, Cofi can "naturally" be sacrificed in the dog fights, but Octavio is inconsolably shocked when the owner of some pit-bulls shoots his dog. On the other hand, Octavio hires three men and "sacrifices" his brother Ramiro to a terrible beating, with the condition that he not be killed. Octavio is then severely injured himself in the car crash.

The implications for the structuring of affective space are telling. Octavio is presented by "action images" that relate to physically and socially defined environments. Close-ups of his face are notably missing, except for the frantic initial scene of Octavio's driving the pursued car, in which his grimace appears as part of hyperkinetic cross-cuts showing his terror, the bleeding dog on the back seat, and glimpses of street environs. According to a phenomenology of the *action-image*, character and milieu are "organically" tied together: "The milieu and its forces . . . act on the character, throw him a challenge, and constitute a situation in which he is caught. The character reacts in his turn (action properly speaking) so as to respond to the situation" (Deleuze, 1986: 141). Now, the purpose of the protagonist's "realistic" construction through action and reaction lies in situating the "affection-image" elsewhere. What acquire affective intensity in their own right are the depictions of Cofi the Rottweiler, as well as of the other fighting dogs. Canines crashing into each other cause a sensation of pure combustive energy, of bodies in their immediate crossing of the threshold between life and death. The director's editing logic is explicit in forcing abject sensations: repeatedly, a cut interrupts the scene of fighting dogs at the moment at which the canines attack each other, so that the deadly spectacle is deferred, that is to say transferred into a different realm – that of human relationships. Affection-images, in this context, are not centered on the body, or the look of a particular dog; they are the result of a de-individuating motion that makes affect "pure" and "all-embracing." The viewer is thus haunted with the sheer potentiality of blood-soaked, ripped-apart bodies to surface everywhere and at any turn of the film. The movie induces experiences of fear as aesthetic sensations. However, shock-like effects are not produced wholesale but require thinking.

In the second story, *"Daniel and Valeria,"* the ritual constellation is different. Although the director is said to have borrowed several shots from Kieslowski's film *Red* (see Kipp, 2001: 2), a sacrificial constellation lends his subplot an atmosphere of its own. The relationship between Valeria and her boyfriend Daniel, a married businessman, becomes crucial at the point at which the supermodel is injured in the car crash caused by Octavio. Put in the moralizing terms of the intimidated citizen, Octavio has been ruthlessly endangering, and potentially sacrificing the lives of innocent people around him. Innocent people? Indeed, the laceration and eventual destruction of Valeria's right leg equals the suspension of her career. This is one of the few experiences prone to generating tragic sentiment, since it is the future of a young and sophisticated woman that is at stake. Visual contours of tragic sensation are framed in a match-cut, a sort of establishing shot in terms of intensity, moving from a gigantic street poster that shows a supermodel towering over the heads of passersby, to Valeria's stupefied face depicted in close-up. It is the model who now sits in a wheelchair, staring out of the window of her new apartment at her commodified, timeless self-image displayed on the street, and unable to make sense of her situation. At this point, the director invents a doubling of sacrifice that will turn out to be devastating to the tragic momentum. While Valeria is paralyzed physically and mentally, her puppy Richi falls into a parallel drama: the little dog disappears beneath the floorboards of the apartment, and the vision that takes hold of the woman is her pet's being devoured by rats. Daniel, the lover is drowned in helpless stupidity, being unable to understand how Valeria relives, through the disappearance of Richi, her own laceration, only to end up in melancholic hysteria revealing that the exclusive center of her love was the perfect icon of her female body. The body of the model loses its sacredness – its existence as a superior, religiously adored fetish object – when it is physically shattered: sacrifice as collateral damage among the rich.

The film contributes a remarkable hero to present-time imagination, and he belongs to the third story: *"El Chivo and Maru."* It is Martín who bears the nickname of *"el Chivo,"* referring to the popular metaphor given to a "trimmed" gun or, more satirically, to the man's being a strange apostate. *El Chivo's* attire is that of a long-haired and bearded Methuselah in tunic-like rags and tatters. As a phantom figure, he inhabits an abandoned storage-shack, frequently roaming through the streets with a horde of dogs surrounding the wheelbarrow in which he gathers trash and recyclables. People tell each other that this urban nomad had started out, decades ago, as a university professor, but left his job and family – his daughter Maru was then 2 years old – to join a guerrilla movement. On his return he was convicted to 20 years in prison for kidnapping a wealthy businessman and committing other crimes. After his release he occasionally carries out contract killings in order to survive; at the same time, he arrives at a point where his only desire is to reintroduce himself as a human to his daughter who doesn't know that he is alive. Apart from the somewhat tendentious storyline, *el Chivo*'s role as the crucial figure is due to his religious appearance, combining myth with iconic corporality.

*El Chivo* has already been lurking throughout the previous stories, establishing an uncanny authority. In a scene of the first story, the man is seen in front of a garbage pile, standing up with a raised machete in his right hand, as a threatening statue, to symbolically shelter his dogs from a pit-bull that is about to attack them. In the central scene of the car crash, pertaining to story two, Martín, who was walking along the sidewalk, takes action immediately. Helping the injured Octavio out of the car, he makes sure to "rescue" the money that was earned by the youngsters in the dog fights for him. He then rescues the wounded Cofi, Octavio's brutish Rottweiler, from the shattered car in order to heal it. These acts function as skillfully edited counterpoints to Martín's pursuit of a young rich fellow he's been hired to kill by the man's business partner. Everything has been prepared for the assignment to be carried out, but when the moment arrives, Martín cannot use his gun because a group of children gets in the way. On another day, returning to his shelter, Martín has to endure a terrible picture: his stray dogs have all been bitten to death by Cofi, who has recovered from his wounds. Inconsolable and with tears streaming down his face, *el Chivo* gets ready to punish the Rottweiler with a shot in the head, but in the final moment decides to let the animal live. All these scenes suggest a peculiar stake that Martín has in the issue of power over life and death. A most disconcerting aspect is Martín's role as a marginal person who is equal to someone who self-consciously decides about the killing, or not killing, of other beings. Both humans and animals are exposed to "bare life"; the rich business people are destined for a good and protected life, but Martín shows a strong sense for the exception. This sense is displayed in one of the final scenes in which *el Chivo*, instead of carrying out an execution, kidnaps the client together with his victim, and then confronts both businessmen with each other as they are lying, tied up, on the floor. *El Chivo* places a revolver at an equal distance between them, and leaves them to a destiny in which each will try to get the advantage that will allow him to kill his partner. In other words, to view *el Chivo* as a brutalized individual or as an ideological fanatic would miss the point that the film is offering to critical readings.

It has been observed that *el Chivo* is constructed as a conservative parody of the image of Karl Marx. Sánchez-Prado suggests an interpretation according to which the director fell prey to a prejudice that conceives of the urban criminal "terrorist" as a natural outcome of the political rebel. In that vein, the film could be read as a tribute to the fears of a conservative Mexican middle class during a time of the decay of the symbolically and legally protective nation state (see Sánchez-Prado, 2006). However, the film is more complex. What if *el Chivo* functioned, in a diffuse yet compelling realm of "postnational" imagination, as a revenant, embodying deep-rooted religious-political myths and masculine moral fantasies? Martín unites in his personal history representative patterns of identity: the educator, the family father, and the political rebel. What we see is his having become a phantom figure roaming through present-day urban life. Like the *Moses* of Sigmund Freud, Martín has been "repressed" by the community; his contours are those of a martyr or of a prophet presenting an image of cursed and sometimes violent saintliness. When he shuffles down the city's side-walks at a steady pace, pushing his wheelbarrow in a majestic manner, exhibiting an immutable, charismatic appearance, surrounded by his dogs and avoided by the pass-ersby, he inhabits a world "beyond." However, his penetrating look behind his appar-ent detachment shows that he is more from "this world" than many others. Martín is not constructed as an exotic person; he is uncomfortable and unpredictable. His is the posture of the forgotten prophet, a post-traumatic hero, still an overbearing presence in his ghostliness, disavowed by his own daughter, and banned from the space inhab-ited by a citizenship that has become corrupted, amnesic, and mindless. His only community is the pack of dogs and, in a sense, youngsters like Octavio and Ramiro who have become violent in their struggle against destitution and aborted hope.

Somewhat theatrically construed as a prophet without doctrine, *el Chivo* confers an image of authority – an archaic father who is relegated to the margins, but claims an occasional right to violence which is ambiguous in that it belongs both to the *pater* and to the marginal at the same time. This father, unlike Freud's *Moses*, takes action in order to be restored in the consciousness of his former family, secretly introducing his picture to the photo altar in the house of his daughter and his former wife. If that which resonates in *el Chivo* is the fantasy of a fallen original father, a masculine super-ego in search of a community, this character stands out as a political postscript to the crisis of secularization. Several associations regarding the relationship between reli-gion, politics, and national trauma could be drawn from here. What makes the hero special is his opposition to a Freudian psychopathology. The repressed figure is neither restored to a public (or family) consciousness by virtue of collective guilt, nor can he sustain a symbolic order as a metaphor of (lost) morals and law. Yet nor is the impos-sibility for the prophet to rise again by virtue of a collective neurosis converted into tragedy. On the other hand, a melodramatic turning point might have conferred a proper aesthetic place for an unrecognized father. *Amores Perros* shows how far a direc-tor can go, using a conventional dramaturgy and still undermining influential aes-thetic styles. He succeeds in thoroughly enacting negatively heightened passions without bending his knee to either tragedy or melodrama. It is, of course, a question of "values" that goes with these dispositifs, since modern incursions into the possibil-ity of either melodrama or tragedy are "exercises in cultural diagnostics" (Sontag, 1969: 138).

After the adopted fighting dog has slaughtered *el Chivo's* animal community, the man experiences sensations of torment which lead him to a point of conversion. He decides to abandon his legendary appearance and to take on an external façade that seems, at first glance, absurd. A closer look reveals the parodist touch of what appears to be the formal outfit of a weary professor, his fierce eyes veiled behind a pair of very old, broken glasses. It is this image of his that he now takes a picture of, and which he secretly mounts among the photo collection of his former family by breaking into their house in their absence. He also leaves a bundle of banknotes under his daughter's pillow, a fetish that middle-class families tend to equate with a father's traditional responsibility. Martín then chooses to go away, based on his experience that there is no choice to make. One might paraphrase Deleuze at this point – his thoughts on the immanent links between a knowledge of "missing choice" and "pure potential" (see Deleuze, 1986: 114, 115) – but it is necessary to surpass the ontological frame. In *el Chivo's* case, the "pure potentiality" of assuming a space "beyond despair" is negatively defined. He departs from the role of the urban nomad whose "reterritorializing" *habitus* could rely on occasional acts of violence. He moves from his previous sphere of abandonment into an open space, a "plain" space where such distinctions as the ones between "nomad" and "migrant," vagrant and prophet are becoming blurred.

*El Chivo* is the only figure in the film whose appearance is framed by "action-images" and "affection-images" alike; yet at the end, his presence mutates entirely into an "affection-image," erasing any tie between character and milieu. The man's final walking away from the camera, depicting both his and the dog's bodies from behind as they move into an inscrutable void, evokes the affective metaphor of "any-space-whatever" (see Deleuze, 1986: 120, 122). His stature is gradually absorbed by the somber grey earth that potentializes the void as an "expressionist" darkness. There is nothing left except "bare life." Yet the subject of "bare life" is not the marginal vagrant. It is the conscious individual who is excluded from all meanings, that is to say from the "constituent powers" of society's public space. The fact that *el Chivo* "chooses" to (re)enter this affective space, not as a prophet, nor as a marginal figure, but as a ghostly intellectual, makes González Iñarritu's film an extraordinary statement on the situation of today's world.

A Brazilian film acquires significance as an adjacent yet strongly contrasting case: *Carandiru* (2003), directed by Héctor Babenco. "Carandiru," once located in São Paulo, was Brazil's largest penitentiary and existed until October, 1992, when police squads stormed the complex, putting an end to a prisoners' revolt by carrying out an atrocious massacre. The slaughter by the state forces caused a wave of nationwide indignation, which led to the closure of the facility and the relocation of remaining detainees. On the basis of *Estação Carandiru* (*Carandiru Station*, 2000), an eyewitness account written by Drauzio Varella who had worked for several years in the penitentiary as a physician, Babenco, together with Fernando Bonassi and Victor Navas, produced the script of the film.

Babenco has been well known since *Pixote* (Brazil, 1980) and his adaptation of Manuel Puig's novel *El beso de la mujer araña* (*The Kiss of the Spider Woman*, 1985). His recent work is not a prison movie of Foucaultian style. How does he address the "exception" which comes related either to prison reality or to a possibly wider context of state intervention? Babenco decided to mould his central hero based on the original prison doctor, Drauzio Varella, the author of the testimony. The book, *Carandiru Station*, evokes the trope of the *medicus* as ethnographer: Varella appears as an attentive and thus committed chronicler, that is to say, as the author gathering the tales of patients who desired to tell their stories "back to the world." The narrative design of the film corresponds to this model, in that it is constructed around the actions and the perspective of the "Doctor." This physician, about 40 years old, is a model care-taker, calm and attentive, professional, with infinitely gentle eyes – a man of goodness and confidence. He offers basic treatment to all inmates, irrespective of their chances of being cured. His infirmary becomes a unique meeting place where patients tell their stories, and from where – through retrospective montage – a panorama of human histories unfolds: some anecdotes, others parables, and still others dramas with epic and tragic peripeties. There are the gorgeous transvestite "Lady Di" and her dwarfish lover; the mulato Ebony ("*Nego Preto*"), the highest authority of the prison population; "*Majestade*," an ebullient black man who is courted and cursed – during visiting hours – by his two "wives" who are also the mothers of his several children; there is also "*Deusdete*," an adolescent who was detained for killing his sister's rapist, and his pal "*Zico*," who now kills his young friend when acting in a drug frenzy.

The epidemic reality of AIDS and venereal diseases is addressed as the doctor regu-larly performs blood tests. However, these are rather symbolic examinations: the tests give the doctor access to the men's stories, i.e., to a reality that can still be appropri-ated anecdotally (or epically), and thus escapes an abyss that is life-destroying. AIDS is a medical issue, or a narratological device, but it is not an immanent experience that involves patients as much as it could directly affect the doctor. Probably for that reason, prisoners are depicted mainly through action-images, conveying the narrative memory of their past. The doctor is the only person who is occasionally absorbed into affection-images like his astonished or melancholic face, which transcend the immedi-ate environment. There is another, very different "transcending" image at the end of the film. It shows the remnants after the massacre that has put down the prisoners' rebellion, in which over a hundred inmates were brutally slaughtered. When the camera slowly moves through ghostly corridors filled with naked bodies that are spat-tered with blood, one might have the sensation that the images belong to a different film. The doctor had finished his humanitarian assignment a while ago. He will return to the place once more, only to see cleaned-up, dark and empty spaces. A laconic subtext, expressing his inner voice, says: "The only ones who know what really hap-pened are God, the police, and the inmates."

A peculiar evolution from melodrama to tragedy has taken place. During extensive parts of the film, one could be reminded of Peter Brook's thesis: in a world deprived of traditional religious beliefs in the existence of higher justice, melodramatic imagi-nation can generate a "moral occult," illuminating and sustaining life under the most profane circumstances. Romantic personal memory and entanglement kept the prison-ers alive – their marginality was emotionally defined, and their heightened expressive behavior often transgressed "sane" language but always held tight to the meaning of existence as happiness, thus resisting "bare life." The film's overall ethical posture was thus defined by the presence and attitude of the doctor-narrator, combining charity and human compassion. At the end, when images of impersonal state violence replace the narrative perspective based on the presence of the eyewitness, the ensuing void is tragically defined. Yet at the same time it dissipates the ethical alertness the film is striving for. An excess of violence may have accounted for the brutal intervention of the state as a higher force. Affective involvement is remade into a distancing aesthetic strategy, seconded by the above-cited subtext. If there is suffering, it either works "in representation" or from a distance that is kept intact. And probably, a glimmer of a Hegelian transcendental spirit emerges, according to which "true tragic sympathy" is inspired by our "fear of the power of the . . . order" that has been violated (see Hegel, 1998: 452). In other words, the *Doctor* in *Carandiru*, and *el Chivo* in *Amores Perros* can be viewed as opposing figures regarding the subject-oriented experiences of violence, sovereignty, and life. They both represent critical affective postures whose strange synchronicity forms part of contemporary struggles.

The notion of "bare life," in its social, existential, and imaginary relationships to violence, has been emerging as a force field that concerns the status of aesthetic and ethical experience today. Along the lines that our study has been developing, a larger number of Latin American films in times of global modernity could be discussed – being, as they are, genuine contributions to the historicality of present-day ethics. To recall Walter Benjamin, his pointing toward the difference between "bare life" and "fair life" did not only imply a wager for ethical alertness during one of modernity's most dramatic crises. It also expressed the urgency to take "bare life" into the considerations of critical thinking. As became evident, this was not a category that modernity had rendered obsolete, pointing rather toward the intricate closeness of modernity and terror, and reason, violence, and sovereignty. In other words, "bare life" was not an irrecoverable "other," or the uncanny remainder of the dynamics of "progress," nor was it an unhistorical, religiously conditioned "quality" that existed for itself. It could reveal, first and foremost, the relationships between violence and life beyond – or beneath – the Western normative means–ends dialectics. "Bare life," as category, could point toward violent existence as normalized existence, that is to say, to a life world that must be addressed in its conditions of abandonment to the daily, immanently political forces of alienation and destruction.

REFERENCES AND FURTHER READING

Agamben, Giorgio (1998). *Homo Sacer. Sovereign Power and Bare Life*. Trans. Daniel Heller-Roazen. Stanford, CA: Stanford University Press.

Benjamin, Walter (1996). "Critique of violence." In *Selected Writings. Volume 1: 1913–1926*. Cambridge, MA and London: The Belknap Press of Harvard University Press.

Bové, Paul (1998). "Afterword." In Fredric Jameson and Masao Miyoshi (eds), *The Cultures of Globalization*. Durham, NC: Duke University Press.

Brooks, Peter (1995). *The Melodramatic Imagination: Balzac, Henry James, Melodrama, and the Mode of Excess*. New Haven, CT and London: Yale University Press.

Deleuze, Gilles (1986). *Cinema 1: The Movement-Image*, Minneapolis: University of Minnesota Press.

Eagleton, Terry (2003). *Sweet Violence: The Idea of the Tragic*. Malden, MA and Oxford: Blackwell.

Hardt, Michael, and Negri, Antonio (2000). *Empire*. Cambridge, MA and London: Harvard University Press.

Harvey, David (2005). *The New Imperialism*. Oxford: Oxford University Press.

Hegel, Georg Friedrich Wilhelm (1998). "Tragedy, comedy and drama" (*Aesthetics*). In Stephen Houlgate (ed.), *The Hegel Reader*. Oxford: Blackwell.

Herlinghaus, Hermann (2002). "La imaginación melodramática." In Hermann Herlinghaus (ed.), *Narraciones anacrónicas de la modernidad: Melodrama e intermedialidad en América Latina*. Santiago de Chile: Editorial Cuarto Propio.

— (2006). "En contra del dogma de la mera vida," *Revista de Crítica Cultural*, 34. Santiago de Chile.

Kipp, Jeremiah, "Amores Perros, " filmcritic.com, 2001, http://filmcritic.com/misc/emporium.nsf

Oubiña, David (2003). "El Espectáculo y sus márgenes: Sobre Adrián Caetano y el nuevo cine argentino," *Punto de Vista. Revista de Cultura* (Buenos Aires), 26(76).

Sánchez-Prado, Ignacio (2006). "*Amores Perros*: exotic violence and neoliberal fear," *Journal of Latin American Cultural Studies*, 15(1): 39–57.

Smith, Daniel W. (1998). "The place of ethics in Deleuze's philosophy: three questions of immanence." In Eleanor Kaufman and Kevin John Heller (eds), *Deleuze and Guattari: New Mappings in Politics, Philosophy, and Culture*, pp. 251–69. Minneapolis and London: University of Minnesota Press.

Sontag, Susan (1969). *Against Interpretation and Other Essays*. New York: Dell.

Varella, Drauzio (2000). *Estação Carandiru*. São Paulo: Companhia das Letras.

Žižek, Slavoj (2002). *Welcome to the Desert of the Real: Five Essays on September 11 and Related Dates*. London and New York: Verso.

# 35

# Postmodern Theory
# and Cultural Criticism
# in Spanish America and Brazil

*Ileana Rodríguez*

The debates on postmodernism and cultural studies in Latin America are inextricably intertwined. A review of the anthologies on the subject reveals that the same scholars that are invited to write about the former appear on the lists of those invited to write for the latter.[1] All of them are presented as constituting a turning point in the domain of Latin American studies, a scission that marks a move away from "the political" and the strictly literary to "the theoretical" and the politics of democracy and consumption. This is a group of scholars that has undertaken the task of rethinking the continent at the moment neoliberal politics become dominant and leftist utopian projects dwindle. Most of them were contemporaries of the debates on "liberation" and "leftist utopias" and actively participated in them, but reconsidered their position as a result of the events that were hitting all of us hard in the face. In this regard, the postmodernism debate in Latin America is also a post-left utopian debate, the debate on disenchantment (Norbert Lechner). This is a moment where thinking about human agency and labor as possibilities for transforming the referent is foreclosed and the criticism of commodity production disarticulated. Actually, postmodernism is what is left after culture has totally encroached upon nature and the sphere of commodity production (manifested as ubiquitous consumption) has left no residual zones of nature and of being where culture can still be critical and exert pressure over nature (Fredric Jameson). This new face of capitalism also brings an opacity to the national as a political space that manifests itself in a profound refurbishing of the nature and function of the state and the transformations of the meaning of dependency (Jesús Martín Barbero).

What brings all these intellectuals together is the necessity to critically reassess the particularities of the Latin American modern (and hence the "postmodern") and, by extension, of modernist and modernizing impulses. Their work denotes urgency and in some cases zest in reexamining all the artifacts and technologies that constitute the new popular and populist cultural regimes as they drift away from letters and literacy and move closer to the visual in cinema and television, as well as to the new politics of democracy, consensus, and consumption. This is a serious probing and critical examination of the set of structures, articulations, and themes that the project of modernization brings to the constitution of all kinds of continental narratives, an examination that produces a series of adjectives that qualify the term modern and mark its difference with and adjustments to the model. Peripheral, deficit-ridden, alternative, were terms that pointed to the drastic modifications and differentiation of the cultural ontologies of Latin America with respect to European or North American cultures of the modern. This was done at the moment neoliberalism and the new technologies of mass media made this examination and adjustment imperative. The unabated drift toward consumption gave them cogency. Many were the angles covered and there is no way of doing justice in this short chapter to the wealth of knowledge this discussion brought to the Latin American domain. Therefore I will limit myself to a review of the main trends and proposals and a critical assessment of them. With that purpose in mind I offer a bird's-eye review of the subject and concentrate on three categories of analysis: hybridity, heterogeneity, and the popular. I also touch on the discussion of the transition from high to mass culture, from letters and literacy to the televisual, and from the city of letters to the city of signs, which I believe summarizes the main points of the postmodernism debate in Latin America.

Let me start with the obvious, the claim that postmodernism is primarily European and North American, a concept fabricated in well-developed capitalist societies to indicate a reflection on knowledge production and the effects of technology on it (Jean-François Lyotard); an interest in a historical and theoretical evaluation of the production of culture under high capitalism (Jameson), and/or the examination of the stylistics of "postmodern texts" (Linda Hutcheon).[2] The prefix "post" indicates both the saturation and intensification in the reorganization or disorganization of the modern. In theoretical terms, it refers to the waning of use value and the saturation of the world with value, an unprecedented acculturation of nature (Walter Benjamin's aesthetization of reality; Raymond Williams's new sensibility structure) that alters the functions of knowledge, narrative, and the subject; to the collapse of the cultural and the economic into itself and the erasure of the former distinction of base/superstructure, which implies that in the current stage of capitalism, capitalism itself generates its own superstructures and compels us to speak of culture in business terms if not in those of political economy (Jameson, Lyotard). The development of these ideas constitutes the discourse of the postmodern.[3]

When the aforementioned are taken as general statements on the development of capitalism and its logic there is no contention or divide, there is no disagreement between Western and Latin American scholars. Norbert Lechner, for instance, tells us that "we could not interpret the national reality without recurring to the explicative categories of capitalism" (Herlinghaus and Walter, 1994: 197), because Latin American internal dynamism is conditioned by the capitalist logic, although we must recognize the *sui generis* character of its reality. So, it is acknowledged that we all live in a capitalist world, inside it, but that we all occupy dissimilar positions and the difference resides in the disparities these positions create. Consequently, the postmodernism debate in Latin America will take on the analysis of the specificities of this "post" in the continent, always considering it axiomatic that:

> [I]n all fields of culture . . . the important modern cultural syntheses are first produced in the North and descend later to us, via a process in which they are "received" and appropriated according to local codes of reception. This is how it has happened with sociology, pop art, rock music, film, data processing, models of the university, neoliberalism, the most recent medicines, armaments, and, in the long run, with our very incorporation of modernity (José Joaquín Brunner) and postmodernity. (Beverley et al., 1995: 52)

This double condition as "receivers" and "appropriators" constitutes the fulcrum of difference, the spot from whence Latin American scholars will establish the conditions of possibility of difference and their knowledge regimes, and where they will propose the categories of the hybrid, the heterogeneous, and the popular as pertinent clarifications, contributions, and adjustments. This is also the site where discrepancies as to whether Latin American scholars stand in a relation of dependence, subordination, and subalternity with respect to scholars situated at the center will be played out.

The Latin American modern is specifically diverse and consequently the postmodern is as well. Thus, if the term "post" were to have any validity, it could solely be as a reflection on the proper conditions of possibility of the "post," a fact that explains that theoretically, postmodernism presents a variety of analyses and tendencies.[4] In one of its many definitions "post" is the uncomfortable and disoriented sense that comes along the epochal changes marked by the dissemination and contamination of meaning (Nelly Richard), a way of taking the temperature of the age without proper instruments and in a situation of insecurity in which there is even doubt as to whether there is an "age," "vision," "system," or postmodern condition (Jameson). In conclusion, postmodernism is basically historical, decisively contradictory, and unavoidably political (Hutcheon). It is an internally conflicted concept and, for Jameson, it goes beyond the dialectics of essence and appearance, the Freudian model of the latent and manifest, the existential model of the authenticity and inauthenticity that are closely related to alienation and disalienation, the opposition between signifier and signified. For Richard, the concept signals a fracture at the heart of the ideas and ideologies that regulated Western modernity and the heterogeneization of all its signs, senses, and sensibilities that respond to the sacralization of univocal meanings. It is the shift from the macro- to the micro-social, the abandonment of certainties, and the instatement of the politics of doubt within. It is also the disembodying of the social-real that is transformed into a mass media artifice through the image, and the loss of historical density. Reviewing the literature on the subject, one has the uncanny impression that the saturation of the system spreads throughout the whole universe of meaning and geographies and that it is multiply faceted depending on the borders it reaches when.

The point of departure for Latin American scholars is first and foremost a reflection on the nature and character of the modern; second on the contents and nature of the post; and third on the new technologies of cultural production focusing on the power and reach of mass media. Brunner explains it clearly:

> At this time when a confusing fog of "posts" . . . hovers over modernity, it becomes necessary to recover the specific character of modernization in Latin America. Here . . . the malaise in culture does not, could not, spring from the exhaustion of modernity . . . It arises from exasperation with modernity, with its infinitely ambiguous effects, with its inevitable intentionalism, with its distortions, and with the problems that it bequeaths for the future of the region. (Beverley et al., 1995: 53)

For Hermann Herlinghaus and Monica Walter,

> the new thinking about modernity . . . erupts within the foundation of a theory established by the impact of difference. It is about a movement of reflection and cultural analysis with obvious affinities to postmodern thought . . . "[P]eripheral modernity" is an open notion; it implies methodologies of research that are located by means of a new transdisciplinarity of "nomad sciences," in the strategic spaces that are open in between the sociology of culture, the studies of communication, the new anthropology, a "cultural politology" and a field of literary studies that have stopped conceiving culture from the canon of literature itself. (1994: 15; my translation)

The rich reflections on the merging of knowledge and technologies and its effects is left untouched, as is the relationship between knowledge and power that impinges upon the privileges of the states to the point of driving a wedge between economic power and politics that so much concerned Lyotard. An allusion to how computerized knowledge is operative and tailored to fit the new channels, how it travels through the same conduits as money, and gradually assumes the form of commodity exchange with the result of radically modifying the nature of the institutions of learning, is likewise absent in this discussion.

Judging by the material included in the volumes dealing with the postmodern debate in (and from) Latin America and taking postmodernism to be a new stage in the development of capitalism, we can distinguish two discussions: one on cultural production – Nestor García Canclini, Jesús Martín Barbero, Beatriz Sarlo, Nelly Richard, Roberto Schwartz, Silviano Santiago, Renato Ortíz, and Raul Antelo are some of its representatives; another on democracy, consensus, and the new social movements – José Joaquín Bruner, Norberto Lechner, Martin Hopenhaym, Silvia Rivera Cusicanqui, Luis Tapia, Xavier Albó, Aníbal Quijano, Fernando Calderón, Stuart Hall, and Ralph Premdas are some of the scholars working on this aspect of the debate. The discussion on cultural production focuses on the nature of culture and examines the move toward populist aesthetics, and the point at which the dividing line between high, popular, mass, and industrial culture blurs. The most productive concept here is hybridity. The discussion on democracy, consensus, and the new social movements focuses on the nature of Latin American citizenry, their ways of life, and nature of governance. The central and most generative concept here is that of heterogeneity. Both, hybridity and heterogeneity are closely intertwined with the popular and up to a certain point, predicated on it.

For cultural critics, the point of departure is the notion of high culture they debunk by moving from letters and literacy to the visual cultures of simulacra. The work produced by the Brazilian school demarcates these positions with accuracy. Their line of argumentation takes the prefix "post" to stand either for an examination of the "ideas out of place" (Schwartz); for a shift from the culture of politics to the cultures of multiculturalism and consumption (Santiago); or for the understanding of *mundialización* (Ortiz). In the rest of the continent, "post" means a synthesis (Canclini), a saturation that demands a reflection (Richard, Sarlo); a radical veering from letters to images and from the politics of representation to the politics of recognition (Barbero, Monsiváis); a post-labor and disenchanted society (López, Lechner) "Post" also seems to create a space to debate how disciplines perceived themselves and the gaze that organized their protocols, and how institutions promoted ideas of culture and identity, which were copied verbatim from other realities. The floating categories of the "residual," or of conversion and adaptation are, also, some of the central notions that always present in the debate of the "post" in the Latin American domain.

What is, then, the nature of the Latin American modern? It is marked by a series of adjectives that underpin its specificity as a deviation from the model, as true deprivations or lacks. Thus Latin American modernity is deemed incomplete, unfinished, alternative, peripheral, deficit-ridden, a modernity that does not measure up, is not the same as the model, and the model is Western European and North American (Bruner, Calderón). Nonetheless, like all of its synonyms, periphery

> is nothing but a notion of search, given that it signals the departure as much from the geographical descriptive reference as from the functional notion within the frame of dependency. It means that "periphery" is loaded with complex meaning; it is the experimental metaphor of a perspective from which a specific and heterogeneous modernity and hardly classifiable is experienced and problematized . . . We experience in it virtual denotative inexactitude, that is in its terminological provisional character nothing short of a strategic resource that helps question the academicist prejudices and to reorganize the whole field of interrogations over a transdisciplinary base.[5] (Herlinghaus and Walter, 1994: 23; my translation)

The general theoretical strategy of the social scientists (primarily the Chilean school) is thus to reposition the continent in reference to (a) a model of which Latin America is an infelicitous copy and to which it will never measure up; (b) the lacks, which are many; and (c) the nature of Latin American modernity – and, by assumption, of Latin America historical identity – through the concept of heterogeneity. The general theoretical strategy of cultural critics is to (a) acknowledge the limitations of the culture of letters and (b) analyze the conditions imposed by the culture of the televisual. Hybridity is the term used to capture the "essence" of this new cultural production.

"Post" is not, then, a concept that travels easily; it is rather a somewhat perturbing concept because it reveals two obstacles: (a) that we do not know how to think modernity within modernity; and (b) that we do not believe for a single moment that we have gone beyond modernity. The central idea of a ruptural "beyond" is transformed in Latin America into the question of adjustments, adaptations or translations and modifications of the original.

In this regard we must acknowledge a difference. The postmodernist debate in Latin America does not partake in the feeling of the end of history, or the end of all times and ideologies that characterizes the debate at the center. It is rather a pretext for revisiting the history of continental ideas and institutions to understand how totalities have constructed an image, vision, or identity of the continent that is not quite in tune with its realities. It is a proposal for looking at Latin American for what it is. In this sense, postmodernism in Latin America drives a wedge between present and past ideological imaginaries of the modern and becomes a critical approach to the history of ideas, a mise en abyme of the great local narratives. The best articulated position in this regard is Martin Hopehhayn, who posits that postmodernism is a discourse that presents itself as

> a sane antidote to the excessively ethnocentric, rationalist, and mechanist tendencies of modern society. If that is the case, postmodernism could be thought of as an internal movement of modernity itself, a critique that modernity puts into effect in order to exorcise its entropy. But, in fact, postmodernism frequently acquires very different pretensions and functions: In effect, it transforms itself into an ideology, disguising its normative judgments as descriptions, and ends up seeing what it wants to see. The ideologization of postmodern discourse may be glimpsed when one focuses on the service that it lends to the political-cultural offensive of the market economy. (Beverley et al., 1995: 98)

We would be quite remiss to ignore that the market economy is the master narrative underlying the postmodern debate on both sides of the divide. Yet peripheries experience quite a different relation to that domain. The effects of this market economy on Latin America constitute the context of the debate, as does also the transition from revolutionary to new social movements and "democracy," all of which are new elements that establish a radical distinction between the postmodern in the center and in the periphery. Both Fernando Calderón and Aníbal Quijano, for instance, point out this divergence when establishing the rift between the colonial elites and the people. Calderón considers that the most genuine Latin American contribution to the modernist impulse "was the intellectual elaboration of revolutionary nationalism and of national popular, or populist movements," and cites Victor Raúl Haya de la Torre and Lombardo Toledano as two of his paradigmatic examples (Beverley et al., 1995: 57). This naturally does not take us back to Lyotard, but to discussions on particulars and universals undertaken by postcolonial and subaltern studies – also part and parcel of the postmodern debate? From these perspectives, postmodernism has a liberating effect in the re-formation of disciplines, and for stating continental ideas anew. This would account for the perceived cathartic effect in the social sciences, and the celebratory tone in the work of cultural critics.

Two of the main concepts that frame the postmodernist discussion in Latin America are hybridity and heterogeneity. Hybridity organizes the cultural field and heterogeneity the field of social sciences. Other interesting themes that I will not address in this chapter are the post-political and post-work societies (Beatriz Sarlo, María Milagros López). The post-political speaks about politics as virtual simulation or simulacra that representation that simulates an object whose original has never existed. Post-work refers to the organization of societies in post-Taylorist, post-Fordist environments and addresses the changes in the nature of labor. Here I will limit myself first to the concept of hybridity and will follow with a discussion of heterogeneity.

The concept of hybridity relates to a discussion on how a change in economic policies, coupled with and supported by a change of technologies (the new industrial revolution), deeply affect the production of knowledge and bring liberal ideologies to the edge – individualism, emancipation, expansion, innovation. Nestor García Canclini, the scholar responsible for coining the term, analyzed two fields of knowledge, anthropology and sociology, to pinpoint their limitations. Anthropology's limitation was to solely take notice of the micro-communal and to defend the 'traditional'; sociology's was to take notice solely of the macro-social and defend the modern. Traditional and modern became two of the large signatures that organized the new discussion on the regimes of knowledge in Latin America that, in turn brought about the central discussion on the modern – modernism, modernist, modernization.

These reflections were not called postmodern. There was a severe reticence to use that rubric, for it was considered unfit for the Latin American domain. The favorite term used to refer to these new debates on culture was cultural criticism or cultural analysis. However, the truth is that if hybrid – the new concept Canclini proposed to organize the understanding of the cultural regimes throughout the continent – was to become hegemonic – as in fact it did – the articulation of local and foreign knowledges and debates was unavoidably part of it. As so it was later reiterated in the works resulting from both the social sciences and the humanities. Clearly, Lyotard had already spoken about the consequential changes in the condition of knowledge production and their effects on the social and coined the term postmodern, and Jameson was to use the same rubric to speak about the direct impact of the "new era" on artistic production. Canclini's reflections on these changes were simply a way of partaking of a discussion on knowledge production, articulation, and circulation under the present conditions in Latin America – postmodern or not. Many papers have been written on and debated on the concept of hybridity and have related it to the concept of heterogeneity and *mestizaje*. I have offered many answers addressing the misunderstandings of the term. My purpose is not rehash this concept in detail, but rather to use it as a hinge to document a shift in the perception of culture, society, and subjects.[6]

Hybrid is Canclini's synthetic concept of speaking about the effects of the new technologies in the production of culture in Latin America. I see in this concept three very productive moments: (1) the benefits it draws from the crossover connotations with all kinds of experimentation with products in the hard sciences, particularly in biology, where hybrid stands for a new and often better product – Canclini's defense of Antonio Cornejo Polar's criticism of hybridity for considering it unproductive, like a mule, to which Cornejo counterposes his own concept of heterogeneity runs along these lines; (2) the relation it maintains with the concept of *mestizaje*, which serves it as a mistaken referent for in fact, hybrid is a concept of a different kind – in truth, hybrid renders *mestizaje* obsolete by taking the analogy of mixtures away from the biological into the cultural-social, disengaging it from their adherence to the racial (traditional), and relocating into the ethnic (cultural); and (3) the overlap with other types of use of the hybrid that circulate in postcolonial studies, thus engaging Canclini with a larger cultural polemic worldwide.

Actually, contrary to the ideas that hybrid is a liminal condition, beyond knowledge and representation because it is always on the edge, always flipping over from one component to the other and oscillating in the in-betweenness it stands for (after Homi Bhabha), "a material whose existence exhibits the dual affirmation of a substance and its lack of identity, that which is in the interstices, which profiles itself in a zone of shadow, which escapes . . . repetition" (Beverley et al., 1995: 77), Canclini believes "the hybrid is almost never indeterminate" (ibid.: 79). It is, on the contrary, a way of stabilizing a cultural condition. Hybridity is precisely a construct to negotiate that cultural condition, an identity, if you will. Hybrid is neither traditional, nor modern entirely – but "post." Invoking the concept of hybrid for cultures as the effect of cultural crossings, Canclini however comes to the conclusion that (a) these crossings have been intensified and attributes their speed to paradigm shifts, and the multiplicity of meanings; and (b) accepts that a progressive intensification of hybridity could potentially disorganize the field of culture and of knowledge and make the defense of this position untenable.

In the United States it is inevitable after Homi Bhabha to read the hybrid as that condition of in-betweenness, a positionality that is always affirming and escaping its otherness. This is not so for Canclini, for whom hybrid is a theoretical wager to negotiate an identity, a condition which is either/and, and in this sense, becomes related to heterogeneity. It posits a neither/nor that becomes something, as in neither modern nor postmodern in Latin America. What is most important is the double move to stabilize and destabilize a condition of culture simultaneously as a way not so much of escaping Western norms as much as of trying to grasp what is particular and unique to a locality. This double articulation bears a relation with the unbearable, a notion relevant to our discussion for two reasons, (1) because it is in dialogue with the discussions on globalization and (2) because it can also be related to studies developed within the lacanian psychoanalytical paradigm – much in fashion today. Samir Amin considers the processes of globalization to be unbearable in that the reorganization of labor results in intolerable duress to people and turns the politics of organization into politics of resentment, leading to chaos and terrorism. And in psychoanalytic theory, unbearable relates to the notion of "limitless consumption" and choice. The sense of a limitless world places the subject in a situation similar to psychosis, for like in psychosis, criteria disappears in limitless consumption, rendering choice not only the organizing principle of postmodern or globalized societies but also that of the formation of a psychotic personality (Renata Salecl).[7]

Nonetheless, hybridity is a historical bet. Canclini believes it obeys historical logics such as in the combination of pre-Columbian and colonial traditions, of modern and postmodern epistemes, of lettered and visual cultures. Social institutions, museums, politics bear out the validity and credibility of this concept and legitimize these processes of cross-cultural communication and understanding that freeze meaning in time. Furthermore, hybridity carries a theory of the subject and its agency, given that it is the local subject who reorganizes cultural objects in different fields and it is the convergence of personal rituals and objective social systems what cements the category of the hybrid in time. Therefore, "we don't understand the hybrid if we only look at it as complete dissemination, rather than as something that is also ordered, that is experienced as classified or as in need of classification in order to contain the dissolution of the signifieds" (Beverley et al., 1995: 81).

Thus far I have spoken about Canclini's relevant position in the debate on the transition that, for the sake of this chapter, I have called from the modern to the postmodern – a somewhat passé discussion, already displaced by the debate on globalization, a much more accepted rubric worldwide. Now, a brief comment on "the political" is in order. Indeed, the most shocking aspect of *Hybrid Cultures* was precisely its scission with politics, as we knew it, a scission that became symptomatic of the new cultural horizon. In a field that had been so deeply politicized, Canclini located the analysis of culture in the post-political or neopolitical, "post" not in the sense of politics as simulacra, after Sarlo, but in the sense that the political had to be redefined, relegated, or bracketed. This was a much bigger challenge, one that still stands. It seemed that cultural criticism like theory could actually do without politics. But given that Canclini's *Hybrid Cultures* was produced right at the moment of the implementation of the neoliberal policies in Latin America, his direct disregard of politics was symptomatic of the new age. The unraveling of "the political" was a task that the social scientists had to address.

Hybridity is a concept that moves in between the disciplines of sociology, anthropology, and culture; heterogeneity is a concept that criss-crosses the domains of sociology and politics. If hybridity represents a consensus over the new televisual, populist cultures, then heterogeneity rests on the system of a differential and segmented participation produced by the market. Heterogeneity, according to Brunner, originates in a radical revision of the concept of culture put forward by CEPAL (the Economic Commission for Latin America), a concept predicated on development. CEPAL's notion of culture is eclectic and overemphasizes development and adaptation. It allows for tracing the distinction between formal and substantive rationality, although the rationality it espouses "makes implicit a comprehensive concept of efficiency in the administration of resources and opportunities" (Beverley et al., 1995: 37). For CEPAL, modernization is the "internalization of rational norms" (ibid.). The centerpiece of this model is individual or social creative modernization, that is, "the stylization of a political process of the search for social efficiency" (ibid.), one that presupposes a modern type of creativity.

Brunner analyzes CEPAL's document to expose two fallacies, rationalism and adaptation. Rationalism, because there is more than one type of rationality – developmental, political, technocratic, bureaucratic, and market rationalities – and these rationalities are acquired through teaching, transference, and experience. "In culture, these rationalities imprint cognitive styles, define values, introduce habits, and stimulate varied personality structures. Therefore, there are no 'rational norms' that can be so outside of their context" (Beverley et al., 1995: 38). Adaptation is a fallacy in that these learning situations are diverse. In Latin America it is impossible to "'adapt' models of behavior, an aspirations capable of shaping demands from the most advanced capitalist centers, and, at the same time, to do this 'creatively' according to our 'specific histories, indigenous resources and possibilities'." Furthermore, Brunner pinpoints an aporia: since Latin America is not culturally autonomous, how could it be creatively so? What differentiates Latin America is a cultural heterogeneity that overturns CEPAL's paradigm for the social sciences, a paradigm entirely modern, developmentalist, and predicated on homogeneity.

Having said that, the question for us now is, how is heterogeneity defined? Heterogeneity is neither a superimposition of historical and cultural identities nor sedimentation, but a situation that has not reached a complete synthesis.

> Cultural heterogeneity . . . refers to a double phenomenon: (1) of segmentation and segmented participation in this global market of messages and symbols whose underlying grammar is North American hegemony over the imaginary of a great part of humanity . . . (2) of differential participation according to local codes of reception, group and individual, in the incessant movement of the circuits of transmission that extend from advertising to pedagogy. (Beverley et al., 1995: 41)

After this definition, Brunner turns towards consensus. Consensus is related on the one hand to heterogeneity and on the other to secularization. Heterogeneity defines difference, gradation and degradation, unequal access, and therefore visions that are regulated according to degrees of consumption. How, in view of this difference, can the social reach consensus? Secularization points to a sequential and progressive disengagement with tradition, normativity, and legitimation. Markets play a great role in this process of dissolution because they organize ideas, desires, seductions and, ultimately, the process of secularization. Carlos Monsiváis and Jesús Martín Barbero study the formation of the popular-public-abject as the powerful effect of the cultural market on the masses. Based on the heterogeneous nature that characterizes the identity of Latin America we must conclude that the principles of social integration are so scarce that "it would appear no system of society should be able to function" (Beverley et al., 1995: 47) in Latin America. The result is authoritarian forms of governing – be they considered from the viewpoint of "the political" or "the economic." Here we are directly confronted with the force and power of the model. Modernity, coupled with the heterogeneity it produces, presents itself as a terminal condition for Latin America, and although not all schools of thought are of this nature, other more hopeful perspectives are rendered inoperative and unviable under the present conditions of globalized capitalism. For instance, in the works of Xavier Albó and Silvia Rivera Cusicanqui, the Bolivian school presents alternative and more hopeful models of heterogeneity grounded on indigenous perspectives and the proposal of incorporating indigenous epistemes into the analytical models, but these models are also foreclosed.

The cancellation of more optimistic grounds includes, also, Norbert Lechner's faith in democracy and secularization, although his work is argued within the modern epistemes. Lechner is of the opinion that secularization could benefit democracy by producing a climate of civil tolerance and liberating the social from its commitments to ethical, political, and religious absolutes:

> there is a criticism of the idea of complete subjects, an abandonment of the "master narratives," a conversion of time into a continuous present, a reduction of politics to an exchange of material and symbolic goods . . . The "disenchantment" of and with power in Latin America . . . passes through a dis-dramatization of power: a reduction of its symbolic-expressive aspects and an increase in the instrumental capacities of its gestation; loss of ideological aura in favor of the practical interests of actors, which are lost and found in the political market. (Beverley et al., 1995: 48)

For Lechner, then, postmodernism has a liberating effect in the organization of politics in Latin America. Consensus, democracy, governability, and the market are the variables social scientist juggle to discuss "the political." Cultural critics, in the meantime, examine the power of images and the extrapolation of aesthetics and entertainment as the cultural that has become, also, the site of "the political."

It is noteworthy how the reorganization of the social, understood as governability and administration, coupled with the new concepts of populist cultures and the agency put forth by new social movements, replace the idea of modernity as development as well as the concepts of the state and nation by highlighting the reconfiguration of the social networks of authority and power. Society is reorganized around a different type of productivity, or rather, around dominant forms of consumption. Heterogeneity thus names the reorganization of domination around the market rather than around the state and constitutes a proposal for reformatting all the social institutions and their functions.

Brunner also takes issue with the organization of culture put forth by Latin American letters and argues the transition from the city of letters to the city of signs – from Macondoamerica to Tamaramerica. This transition shifts the attention from books to signs; from elites to markets; and from utopian ideas to competitive pragmatism. It seems evident that the pragmatic turn is supported by libidinal economies of all kinds, from melancholia to euphoria, accepted as the new structures of sensibility brought about by the disruptive forces of consumption. The wager now is to consider if the culture of consumption produces democracy in debilitating racist and elitist traditions; if this also implies the tacit acceptance of the curtailing of state action and its repressive agency implicit in the weakening of elite power. Do we find here implicit the idea that the neoliberal state is better than the welfare state because it accelerates modernization and democratization?

Brunner's critical approach to culture is harsh and, to a certain point, unfounded. He is of the opinion that Latin American cultures have not expressed an order – neither of nation, nor of class, religion, or of any other type; that they reflect contradictory and heterogeneous processes in the constitution of a belated modernity, constructed under the accelerated conditions of the internationalization of symbolic markets globally. Actually, Latin American cultural production has always expressed an order in terms of class, gender, and ethnicity, an order that can and does serve Brunner to ground his own concept of heterogeneity. All the critical examinations of the histories of literature and high culture have amply demonstrated this fact that is perhaps not so self-evident to an affiliate of a different discipline.

There is no point, however, in denying that what is always in question in Latin American high culture is the tension between difference and normativity and a certain willfulness about thinking modernization as a question of ideas – at least this is so when examined from the vantage point of the social sciences. All this conceded, Brunner's purpose in criticizing high culture is to take the discussion to the arena of markets, and it is in this point that the social and cultural sciences become conversant. Brunner argues that to think culture solely as a symbolic product is a fallacy, for "La cultura es un universo de sentidos que no se comunica ni existe independientemente de su modo de producción, de circulación de recepción, consumo o reconocimiento" (Culture is a universe of meaning that does not communicate nor exists independently of its mode of production, circulation of reception, consumption or recognition) (Herlinghaus and Walter, 1994: 53). The corollary is a proposal: the reformatting of all cultural institutions – mass media, training schools, universities – to the end of being market competitive, to follow the logic of supply and demand. It is axiomatic that modern culture cannot do without markets. Hence the idea of competitiveness, pragmatism, and creativity: cultural institutions must work in tandem with the political, administrative, and economic system; they must collaborate in this enterprise rather than being centers of intellectual criticism. How felicitous it is, then, that political pragmatism is turning Latin American populations puritanical by the force of needs and of competing markets. So the old cultural paradigm, elitist and indifferent to the societal, is substituted for a "new" paradigm that becomes a very close relative to CEPAL's.

True, empirically considered, Latin America cultural contexts are underdeveloped, illiterate, suffer from infrastructural deficits, manifest a disparity between the cultivated and the oral that produces alienation, and, in the area of books and letters, are characterized by the scarcity of publics. Nonetheless, to think the possibilities of creating integrated spaces and communication networks around common themes, styles, semantic structures, and perceptions of value is chimerical in view of Brunner's own definition of Latin America as heterogeneous, a condition that curtails all promises of consensus. There is hope that the new culture will dissolve the "great intellectuals" and become a vehicle for the integration of the masses, with their shared experiences within a common matrix provided by schooling, communication, television, consumption, and the necessity to live connected to the city of signs, sharing the same experiences and the same signfieds whose value continues to be diverse.

It is evident that the assessment of the Latin American modern is not only a reflection on the epistemes of modernity but also a reflection on the politics of modernity (neo- or post) that I will examine further through the concept of the popular. It is, also, a critical probing of neoliberalism and a demonstration of the difficulties of shifting paradigms. The propensity to think the future as a mental product, as an ideological utopia has been foreclosed. Postmodernist new utopias are once more obsessed with and traumatized by the model; it is, again, developmentalist and market-oriented.

The third important concept of the postmodern debate concerns the urban popular public. We can understand this concept via a reformulation of heterogeneity. In fact, heterogeneity brings the social and literary sciences together in one crucial point, the place of subordination. Actually, the flipside of the transition from elite to mass culture is an increasing concern with the popular–subaltern. In literary-cultural criticism, Antonio Cornejo Polar has already used the term heterogeneity to organize the disparity between oral and written cultures that besieges the entire Peruvian literary regimes. For Brunner, we understand, heterogeneity is the catchword to pinpoint, in CEPAL's concept of culture, the discrepancy between instrumental and formal reason, and communicative or substantive reason. But what are the contents of the heterogeneous and how can cultural institutions and their productivity relate to this concept and work in tandem with other social institutions? Carlos Monsiváis and Jesús Martín Barbero can provide answers to this question in their elaboration of the popular and public in relation to the state and the institutions of culture. The popular-public is for me the place of the heterogeneous.

Monsiváis thematizes the popular by defining its articulations with the public, urban, and mass cultures. Popular is conceived as that which is constituted by exclusion, configured thanks to the sedimentation of traditions, and marked by a subordinated relation with authority. The popular is that which is a copy of the dominant classes, something made of fragments, stitched together through mediations of all types, and defined as fetid, ragged, ugly, and abject.

The definition of the popular as a position of subordination and psychological subjection and reduction betrays the uncertain relation of the popular to the state and translates in the popular a sense of impotence or insignificance, a historical or personal experience dominated by the sense of destiny or fatality. The feeling of the urban popular is of subalternity, anachronism, and stasis. Although the popular is constituted via migration from the rural to the urban, there is a persistence of rural cultural and regional traditional elements in its constitution. Examples of these residues are a nonlinear vision of order and progress, the maintenance and reproduction of oral cultural and traditional medical knowledge and technical assimilation. The popular subject is presented as a victim of mass media, male chauvinistic and sexually repressive; s/he is a limited subject that becomes an easy prey to the hierarchical and authoritarian function of knowledge, and blindly obeys authority and its excesses. Popular culture is the culture of necessity, woven through repression and corruption and pointing toward a more ample and radical type of urbanity than that which is recognized as public.

After this drastic definition of the popular, Monsiváis offers abundant examples of the heterogeneous, contradictory, and often aporetic contents of the popular in Mexican culture. He does so by examining the urban popular from the moment of independence through its multiple metamorphosis to the present, when indigenous influences wane and the popular is transformed into a tourist incitation, a national style that celebrates and mystifies slums to commercialize them.

Once the people are in the streets, the popular becomes public and is the object of close scrutiny and repression because their demographic impulse becomes the place of horror and the abject. Meanwhile, the popular tries to survive and to constitute a space for itself, a space generated by the operative modes of the city-capital in response to subjection. This is the type of agency Monsiváis classifies as the popular. In this space, the popular, urban, and mass cultures measure the irrationality and voracity of capitalism.

As an addendum to the notion of the popular, Monsiváis offers an examination of the influence and power of the mass media over it. For Monsiváis and Martín Barbero, the experience of the nation passes through the media circuit and is articulated by it. The services it renders to the nation are doubly articulated and are often contradictory. For instance, the media designs the same national sensibility that it later destroys; reproduces and obliterates the traditional simultaneously by always aligning itself with the commercialization of values and the repressive uses of modernity; builds a type of national class-consciousness that evaporates easily or is exchanged for a consumer avidity, a fabric of dreams, that modernizes and unifies speech, introduces themes and modes of representation corresponding to North American models, and proposes virtuality as a healthy alternative to "the political." Thus, mass media is stylistically committed to the ratification of styles of life, maintains a relationship to traditions, and sustains old technologies that reinforce respect of the family, private property, and the state. The urban poor do not have access to a critical vision of national identity and thus its ambition is to become a body of consumers instead of proletarians.

Stylistically, the media proceeds through lines of least resistance and what it says becomes public faith. Emotionally, it constitutes itself as the ideological and sentimental national school for the popular, interpellates it, produces fantasies, and becomes the ultimate or unique alternative for them. For instance, the perception of women and the feminine is provided by television, photography, and radio soap operas where women are portrayed as absolute victims in submission.

The real shortcoming of the media is that it covers the sense of national unity for the poor with an ideology transmitted visually and verbally, enhancing and broadening a hegemonic function that rationalizes direct repression to manage the threat they represent as degrading hordes, or popular stain. Moreover, mass media accepts modernity without its risks and privileges, validates markets and cultural industries, deforms the beliefs and ideologies it divulges, broadcasts neutralized news, breaks parochial schemes, and destroys traditions. Mass culture becomes real, making people experience their lives in accordance with industrial models, and covers all spaces with the industries of "free time." Mass-media culture feeds the anti-intellectualism of the popular and promotes a defensive attitude and limitation that encourages an a-critical devotion to all forms of real or assumed knowledge in this sector, feeds lay devotions to sports, and nourishes hidden passions in the treatment of horror and crime. These mediations constitute a sense of community in which individuals feel solidarity through an elemental catharsis provided by the aesthetic of shock and the morbid.

Jesús Martín Barbero, alongside Fernando Calderón, discusses the popular via Latin American populism of the 1930s and considers that populist regimes organize power through the articulation of the masses and the state. The state responds to the visibility of the masses nationalizing them and constituting a national social subject with them (Herlinghaus and Walter, 1994: 87). In the case of populist regimes in Latin America, the popular is a dense space of interactions and reappropriations, the site of the movement of *mestizaje* enacted in films like *El Chacotero sentimental*. The popular constitutes a pressured space, crossed over by the processes and logics of an economic and symbolic market in which the standardization of production and the uniformation of gestures demands a constant struggle against entropy; a periodic renovation of the differentiation patterns.

In conclusion, after reading the critiques of modernism and mass media as parts of the debate on postmodernity in Latin America one is left with the following certainties. The large majority of Latin American scholars analyze Latin America from the perspective of its lacks. Latin America suffers from a terminal condition that consists in never reaching up to the "real" modern and is therefore always being defined at best by its mixtures. This is the effect of its colonial and postcolonial condition. Here is where the postmodern and postcolonial debates criss-cross each other, the difference between them being that the postcolonial debate truly wants to find alternative modes of thinking and of being. However, since postcolonial models and impulses are provided by indigenous cultures, their arguments, élan, and desires are imperiled by the same global-capitalist factors that besiege those cultures and traditions. In addition to which, very few critics of the modern will accept the existence of "the indigenous" as different and distinct from the hybrid and the heterogeneous.

The paradox of postmodern analysis lies in the recognition that if there is an agency, a local idiosyncrasy, an identity properly speaking, it is constantly positioned and repositioned in the mixtures – hybrid or heterogeneous – which could be also the self-same place of the popular – public or abject. This is at least the way I read Brunner's prognosis that he works in analogy with Macondo, a rain that falls on Latin American heterogeneous popular-public: The poverty that is trained in the evening schools; the expectations that become separated from experience; the slow degradation of autochthonous cultures of indigenous basis; drugs that configure the new map where the center of production is the south and of consumption the north; utopian violence that runs through its last luminous path; the televisual melodrama inviting us to its games of recognition; signs that dance without stopping while identities make and remake themselves, comprising us as the changing subjects of Latin American modernity (Herlinghaus and Walter, 1994).

As stated above, the direction of this logic is the problematization of consensus, creativity, and writing. Consensus because the heterogeneous condition of the social is intercepted by several gradations of information and access to goods and therefore agreement on any issue becomes problematic. This leads in the direction of dictatorships whose project is a forced concurrence. Creativity, because the questions have already been posed elsewhere and the answers must fit the resultant model. Latin American intellectuals are thus always checkmated: their creativity always predicated on what has already been created. This underscores a fill-in-the-blank condition, since the pressing theoretical questions have already been formulated elsewhere. Creativity is thus reduced to quantitative analysis, of providing the numerical figures that serve as funereal evidence of their peripheral in-deficit domains. Numbers perpetually underscore lacks, and scholar's projects and projections are always a priori flawed. They never measure up. And, last but not least, writing because the republic of letters has proposed a telluric concept of culture in which the mysterious and intangible is what constitutes the main traits of Latin with regard to their own data and projections, social scientists are in the same position of literati, right in the middle of the crack between ideas and social contexts, both always out of step.

## NOTES

1   To mention the most conspicuous: Hermann Herlinghaus and Monica Walter, eds, *Postmodernidad en la periferia: Enfoques latinoamericanos de la nueva teoría cultura* (Berlin: Langer Verlag, 1994); John Beverley, José Miguel Oviedo, and Michael Aronna, eds, *The Postmodernism Debate in Latin America* (Durham, NC: Duke University Press, 1995); Mabel Moraña, ed., *Nuevas perspectivas desde/sobre América Latina: El desafío de los estudios culturales* (Santiago de Chile: Editorial Cuarto Propio, Instituto Internacional de Literatura Iberoamericana, 2000); Ana del Sarto, Abril Trigo, and Alicia Ríos, eds, *The Latin American Cultural Studies Reader* (Durham NC, London: Duke University Press, 2004); Claudia Ferman, *The Postmodern in Latin and Latino American Cultural Narratives: Collected Essays and Interviews Claudia Ferman* (New York: Garland, 1996); Claudia Ferman, *Política y posmodernidad: Hacia una lectura de la anti-*modernidad en Latinoamérica (Buenos Aires: Almagesto, 1994).

2   Jean-François Lyotard, in *The Postmodern Condition: A Report on Knowledge* (Minneapolis: University of Minnesota Press, 1984); Linda Hutcheon, *A Poetics of Postmodernism: History, Theory, Fiction* (New York and London: Routledge, 1988); Fredric Jameson, *Postmodernism: Or the Cultural Logic of Late Capitalism* (Durham, NC: Duke University Press).

3   One of the key players in the postmodernism debate is Jean-François Lyotard, because he refers to the momentous changes in the system of knowledge production that, in my view, constitutes an indirect substratum for the discussion of culture. Another is Fredric Jameson, because he outlines several of the conditions for properly thinking the postmodern. And last but not least Linda Hutcheon, because she refers directly to artistic production. In each of

these three writers, the point of departure is the modern era they see as either having come to an end or having undergone a logical metamorphosis that radically alters its features to the point of making it unknowable or unrepresentable by ordinary means – hence, horror. This result is shocking not simply because it appears unmanageable, but also because it implies an intensification of the logic of late capitalism. Lyotard examines this intensification in the terrain of knowledge, narrative, and subjective production; Jameson in the nature/culture divide; and Hutcheon in the parodial nature of artistic production. They all roughly coincide with a definition of the postmodern, but I privilege Jameson's analysis because it brings history to bear on the question. For them, in the postmodern era, narratives, great heroes, dangers, and events lose their function, and doubt, pessimism, and lack of hope set in. The system's logic is optimal performance and the only real and true narratives are efficiency, effectiveness, and profitability. With regard to subjects, they are interpellated by a gamut of non-dialogical, highly unstable, and relative narratives, marked by their imaginary character. The new subject lives in the intersection of language particles and their games, in a total relativity and heterogeneity, within "clouds of sociability" managed by the decision-making powers according to input/output matrixes. The economic discourse is thus the master narrative that organizes the system and its meaning. The ideological task of postmodernism is the coordination of new forms of practices and social and mental habits with the new forms of economic production and organization; and the production of people capable of functioning in a logic of optimal performance, in a world that would give us more than mere postmodernist theory. With respect to reaching consensus on meaning, justice, and truth, technology is of no use, however much postmodern knowledge refines our sensibility to difference and reinforces our ability to tolerate the incommensurable. Thus for Lyotard, "post" is the moment in which the discourse on modernity, predicated on the hegemony of scientific discourse and the prestige of the great metanarratives of legitimation, breaks. The effect is a drastic change in the conditions of

knowledge, narrative, and subject production and consumption.

For Hutcheon modernity is marked by the hegemony of the scientific discourse, with its faith in positivist empiricism and objectivism, a faith in knowledge and its possibilities. Modernity believed in progress and entrusted technology with the production of a better world for all. Developmental utopias were essentially democratic in character. Art, the highest expression of the spirit and illustrated reason, was to contribute to the triumph over chaos and unreason. In contrast, postmodernism is usually associated with a negative rhetoric, expressed as discontinuity, disruption, dislocation, decentering, indeterminacy, anti-totalization. Nonetheless, postmodernism is a contradictory phenomenon that uses and abuses, installs and then subverts the very concepts it challenges. Actually it is a historical parody in that it rethinks modernism and marks the site of the struggle for the emergence of something new. Its properties are the mixtures of genres, times, voices, styles, the promotion of heterogeneity, and the rethinking of and reworking the forms and contents of the past. Postmodernism could also be considered as anti-modern in that it is unstable, provisional, characterized by the absence of universals, and its positioning against the eternal, empiric, rationalist, and humanist. In this regard, it challenges humanism when it interrogates the notion of consensus by acknowledging difference. Consensus becomes an illusion or the inner logic of homogeneity. Yet the question for Hutcheon is if it is really possible to think that by contradicting and dramatizing, postmodernism can provoke change from within, or rethink and question the bases of Western modes of thinking such as liberal humanism. Is postmodernism a writing – as-experience-of-limits? Postmodernism challenges the institutions, from the media to the university, from museums to theater; raises the questions of boundaries and margins of social and artistic conventions; and asserts that borders have become fluid. It forces a reconsideration of the idea of origin or originality and hence the loss of the modernist unique. The three main registers of discourse – the literary-historical, the theological-philosophical; the popular-cultural – are all challenged, as so are the concepts of subjective consciousness and continuity. The perceiving subject is no longer assumed to be a coherent, meaning-generating entity.

4 Renata Salecl, "Worries in a limitless world," *Cardozo Law Review*, 26:3 (2005): 101–19.

5 no deja de ser noción de búsqueda, y que señala la despedida tanto de la referencia geográfica descriptiva, como de la noción funcional en el marco de la dependencia. Quiere decir que "periferia" se ha cargado de sentidos complejos; es la metáfora experimental de una perspectiva desde la cual se experimenta y se problematiza una modernidad específicamente heterogénea y difícilmente clasificable... Vemos en su virtual "inexactitud" denotativa, es decir, su provisoriedad terminológica, nada menos que un recurso estratégico que ayuda a cuestionar prejuicios academicistas y a reorganizar todo un campo de interrogaciones sobre una base trasdisciplinaria. (Herlinghaus and Walter, 1994: 23)

(it does not stop being a kind of search, which signifies the leaving behind of the descriptive geographic reference, as much as the functional notion within the framework of dependency. It means that the term "periphery" has been loaded with complex meanings; it is the experimental metaphor of a perspective from which a specifically heterogeneous and hard-to-classify modernity is experienced and problematized ... We see in its virtual denotative "inaccuracy," that is to say, its terminal provisionality, nothing more than a strategic resource that helps us question academic prejudices and to reorganize a complete raft of interrogations on a transdisciplinary basis.)

6 Just to offer a sample, see for instance, John Kraniauskas, "Hybridity and reterritorialization," in *Travesía*, 1 (1992): 143–51; Ileana Rodríguez, "Geografías físicas, historias locales, culturas globales," in Moraña, *Nuevas perspectivas desde/sobre América Latina*, pp. 475–88; Alberto Moreiras, "A storm blowing from paradise: negative globality and critical regionalism," in Ileana Rodríguez, *The Latin America Subaltern Studies Reader* (Durham, NC: Duke University Press, 2002), pp. 81–107; Alberto Moreiras, "Hybridity and double consciousness," *Cultural Studies*, 13(3) (1999): 373–407; Rosaleen Howard, "Translating hybridity: a case from the Peruvian Andes," in Stephen Hart and William Rowe (eds), *Studies in Latin American Literature and Culture in Honour of James Higgins*, pp. 159–72 (Liverpool: Liverpool University Press, 2005).

7 Salecl, "Worries in a limitless world," pp. 1139–58.

# 36
# Post-Utopian Imaginaries: Narrating Uncertainty
*Silvia G. Kurlat Ares*

During the early 1980s, most Latin American countries were slowly returning to democracy after years of brutal military regimes. Whereas the most distinctive trend of the 1960s and 1970s was the uprising of a wide variety of guerrilla movements and a series of violent military coups (from Peru in 1968 to Argentina and Ecuador in 1976), the main characteristic of the 1980s was a "newly minted faith in democratic values" (Sarlo, 1984) that could bring justice, social peace, and individual rights to states whose public spheres had completely collapsed and whose economies were in a shambles. In 1984, during his successful presidential campaign, Raúl Alfonsín (Argentina, 1927–) summarized this feeling in the slogan: "With democracy, one lives, one eats, one educates, one works." Despite its naïveté, the statement illustrated how democracy seemed to offer a political alternative that would bring transparency to the political process, and allow for economic projects based on a certain level of social consensus.

The return to democracy was a complicated puzzle for the intellectual classes of Latin American countries which longed for a sociopolitical agenda fit for the brave new world of *realpolitiks*. After so much violence, thinkers questioned how to reconnect intellectual praxis with social and political programs as described by the Sartrean model prevalent since the 1950s. Debates in Mexico, Argentina, and Chile pointed to the unclear outcome of the processes of ideological revision taking place throughout the continent. For intellectuals who fashioned themselves as the heirs of the nineteenth-century founders of the national state, the lack of a clear-cut sociopolitical role was nothing less than a tragedy: what Ángel Rama described as the "lettered city" was coming to an end. This situation was also perceived as a gap between those who produced most of their intellectual projects from the mid-1950s, and those who entered the cultural field in the late 1980s. Although the rift was not as wide as the debates led one to believe back then, this was a sign of the human toll the military regimes had taken upon intellectual groups.

In the 1980s, Latin American literary production showed signs of a paradoxical situation: a large number of novels reviewed historical narratives in an attempt to explain the roots of violence and the failures of the 1960s revolutionary aspirations. Novels dissected and rewrote historical events, re-created or replaced social subjects, and attempted to give voice to those forgotten by history. Examples of this trend range from the historical novels focused on nineteenth-century Argentina written by Andrés Rivera (Argentina, 1928–), to Napoleón Baccino Ponce de León's (Uruguay, 1947–) *Maluco, la novela de los descubridores* (1988; *Five Black Ships: A Novel of Discoverers*, 1994) and Elena Poniatowska's (México, 1932–) *La piel del cielo* (2001; *The Skin of the Sky*, 2004). Novels that dealt with issues of memory, identity, and violence, and their relationship to history further emphasize this tendency. Although few novels could be labeled as testimonial, social criticism and political denunciation were still the signature-writing mode in Latin America.

Simultaneously, a second current was taking form both as an answer to and as a movement against such trends. As early as 1981, novels attempting to break with established ways of narrating the Latin American experience were published by up-and-coming writers who were in their twenties at the time. Many of these young authors worked for newspapers that hired them in order to revamp the structures of their cultural sections by generating fresh ways to approach culture and literature. The concurrence of an increasing number of publications along with the visibility of their authors in the media came into view as the explosion of a new narrative. This narrative was mostly urban, generally dealing with issues related to the daily lives of young people, and exploring in very graphic ways topics ranging from sex and drugs, to the cultural market and the relationship between literature and other media. The apparent lack of a common aesthetic trend drove early criticism to emphasize the generational aspect as a way to label what was called a "narrative of cruelty." But many "young" intellectuals rejected any tag, preferring to underline how their narratives approached the urban experience across the Spanish-speaking world, clear of regional and/or generational barriers. The nature of the writing projects became the more relevant characteristic cited when novelists were asked to recognize their peers in interviews. Hence, very young Argentine writers recognized as peers much older authors like Alberto Laiseca (Argentina, 1941–) or Copi (Argentina, 1939–France, 1987). And Bolivian writers emphasized the existence of a transnational cultural field whose epicenter was in the presses of Barcelona, Spain, rather than in any particular Latin American city. The term "new writers" simply became an artificial way to explain a "new sensibility," encased by the marketing effect of the publication of novels written by an undefined under-30 crowd. Nevertheless, writers fitting this category were by no means members of a generation.

Criticism also labeled these writers "postmodern" even though Latin American intellectuals pondered over the applicability of that theoretical framework in the region, and resisted using it. As debates took sway, postmodernism helped in the analysis of the new sociopolitical atmosphere, and lent an easy, ready-made casing to intellectuals who did not appear to fit the traditional politicized, engaged model and whose narratives did not seem to establish a direct dialogue with Latin American history. From a political point of view, writers entering the cultural field in the late 1980s felt alienated from what they perceived as the failure of the revolutionary dreams of the previous twenty years. And, from an aesthetical point of view, they wanted to utterly distance themselves from the grand historical narratives that accompanied those political projects. As early as 1989, Argentine writer Martín Caparrós (1957–) proclaimed in the magazine *Babel* that from now on, literature would be a minor product when compared with mass media since literature had lost its social function. For Caparrós, that was cause for celebration since it liberated writers from the slavery of ideology, and restored freedom to the creative process. Eventually, this freedom would allow for the incorporation of materials coming from what was called "minor genres" (science fiction, police novels, erotic literature), as well as the adoption of languages from different spaces of the cultural field (codes of rock and roll, comics), and a renewed dialogue with other media (video clips, movies).

To summarize: during the late 1970s and early 1980s, the political revision carried out by the intellectual groups that held the political hegemony of the Latin American cultural field showed that core ideological assumptions of the canon were unable to provide answers to the changing environment. As a result, this process made the cultural fields' organizational rules more lax, and allowed for the unrestrained circulation of materials and aesthetics, giving visibility to narrative operations that until then had been confined to the margins of the cultural field or were considered experimental. The case of (Rodolfo Enrique) Fogwill (Argentina, 1941–) illustrates this contradictory situation. Because of his crass, violent depictions and unconventional narrative, critics considered him a marginal writer of exceptional talent, especially because he went against the grain of the politicized model prevalent in the 1970s. Upon closer examination, however, his narrative foreshadows what would happen in the late 1980s, when literature would change its way of perceiving reality by deconstructing basic ideological assumptions within hegemonic narratives. His novel *Los pichiciegos* (1994; *Malvinas Requiem*, 2007) brings to light the nationalistic discourse that underlines most political projects within the Argentinean cultural field. A similar assessment can be made regarding many writers of Colombia's "lost generation" (including writers such as R. H. Moreno, 1946– and Fernando Vallejo, 1942–), whose violent, urban narratives predate the aesthetic searches of the late 1980s and 1990s.

Before continuing, I would like to convey two more relevant traits of the period. First, although the "young" writers abhorred the generational tag, they also used it to their advantage in order to promote their own individual literary agendas and, by doing so, to establish themselves as legitimate (and sometimes hegemonic) agents within their national cultural fields. Even when the label was just a mask, it became a useful operational tool by creating the ghost of an identity that could be marketed and utilized so writers could recognize each other, not as a group or as a generation, but as rightful cultural agents, regardless of the fact that they were not following established political and/or intellectual models. Writers turn out to be very conscientious of their place both in the cultural field *and* in the cultural market. Moreover, they have a very clear understanding of the mechanisms by which they can enter and secure a place in the first by following the rules of the later. This is what sociologist Pierre Bourdieu has described as positional operations undertaken by writers attempting to enter a cultural field. I do not imply that these operations were a ploy to promote second-rate literature. On the contrary, I would like to highlight the level of professionalism that in many respects changed how the literary was to be perceived in years to come. So, the three movements that I chose to study in this chapter (Shangai, McOndo, and crack) are the most successful and representative of cultural operations carried out since the mid-1980s throughout Latin America by many writers, young or otherwise. The manifestos of these networks of writers (since we cannot recognize them as unified groups) provide the main aesthetic and ideological materials of the most important current of Latin American narrative since at least the mid-1980s. However, here manifestos are, in Bourdieusian terms, a position stance vis-à-vis the cultural field writers are about to enter, much more than aesthetic programs in a traditional sense.

The above paragraph brings us to the second characteristic I mentioned. It is important to make a distinction between the aforementioned operations and the actual narratives writers developed at the time they entered local and regional cultural fields. As the previous examples illustrate, the "new" narrative had roots with a long and complex genealogy in Latin American culture. It is important to emphasize this difference, because later criticism had confused these position stances and the common aesthetic tendencies as constitutive parts of a cohesive program and/or movement, which is a misrepresentation of the events. Writers were not always aware that the literary/aesthetic operations they carried out in the name of loose or explicit manifestos (or even press groupings of doubtful critical weight) were already present within their cultural fields, albeit sometimes relegated to decentralized or marginalized areas. However, they wrote ferociously against what they perceived as a frozen political and cultural status quo, assuming the role of the critical outsider. Echoing Caparrós, Efraim Medina (Colombia, 1969–) would eventually say: "Only an idiot will take literature as matter of life or death" (Osorio and Linares, 2002). Yet, one cannot confuse the squeals of the *enfants terribles* with their actual production. The fact that literature was not to be taken seriously provided room to experiment with literary materials in a more playful way, without the pressure to answer or to fit within a sociopolitical mold. It should be noted that such initial detachment from the political debates of the 1970s did not imply an apolitical perspective or a lack of ideological markers, no matter how much critics (or writers) insisted on this point at the time. What we called post-utopian narratives is, above all, a process by which the aforementioned operations became visible and shifted the hegemonic models of the regional cultural field. Rodrigo Fresán's (Argentina, 1963–) first book, *Historia Argentina* (Argentinean history, 1991), is a prime example of such practice, in which a highly politicized narrative attempts to distance itself from the ideological failures and literary choices of its predecessors by renouncing realism and consequently, by denouncing the force of myth within literature. Although not fully successful, in the book history is the only thing that stories attempt to forego. Texts are built around what grand narratives obliterate: the individual experiences and tragedies of everyday life, the randomness of individual fears, pettiness, and yes, sometimes grandeur. However, the characters of *Historia Argentina* reflect on the political experiences of their parents or older siblings and try to reach distinct evaluations for the collective projects and the individual efforts. No matter how misguided they think the former might have been, one can sense a level of critical admiration, even in the face of tragedy. But history as a grand project in itself is no more within the individual perception: in doing so, Fresán unexpectedly returns to the aesthetic operations of writers like Manuel Mujica Láinez (Argentina, 1910–84), whose politics and theatrics were detested by more politicized intellectuals. In Mujica Láinez the absence of history (therefore criticized as an apolitical dictum) allows for time to flow freely, with no more direction that the one the individual can impose on its development. History is, therefore, a consequence of individual choices and not a fixed project. Even if "new" writers did not always share Mujica Láinez's sense of despair, they shared his view of a demythologized narrative and his interest in looking at reality in a more sensual, immediate way.

Although Caparrós and Medina seemed to be in celebratory mood, the other side of their position revealed a level of disenchantment that carried a keener and more cynical take on literature both as a practice and as an ideological tool. Most "new" writers tried to avoid the tradition of social criticism fashioned in the 1960s and 1970s. But this tradition came back with a vengeance. That is the case of *Mala Onda* (1991; *Bad Vibes*, 1997) by Alberto Fuguet (Chile, 1964–), a crude depiction of the lives of middle- and upper-class youngsters under the Pinochet regime in the early 1980s. In the novel, the alienation from the public sphere, which the characters feel as an expulsion from the adult world, is a relief. This is a *Bildungsroman* turned upside down, since the learning experience only shows the disintegration of the family structure, the hypocrisy of society, the utter irrelevance of values (political, religious, etc.), and the loneliness and futility of the individual experience. Criticism has emphasized that the characters' lives, devoid of purpose, are filled with consumerism, casual sex, recreational drugs, and the transnational tribalisms of diverse rock music groups. However, the existential malaise of the novel, the emptiness that characters try to fight, is transformed by the unexpected social alliances that those tribalisms supply, and by the meaning and answers provided by rock-music poetics and movie aesthetics.

Fresán and Fuguet's novels share a dispassionate approach to their materials despite being extremely different in style. Characters are not judged and there are no morals to the story, as history has lost direction and finality. Both novels also share some of the crudest depictions of youth culture since the Mexican *Onda* of the late 1960s. As in the case of the so-called *Onda*, writers that entered the cultural field in the mid-1980s shared something akin to "family resemblances" rather than the cohesiveness of a formal movement. The post-utopian novels I analyze in this chapter and the *Onda*'s depictions of youth life narrate a level of immediacy between the everyday experience and the stories themselves. Romanticized elegies of historical or personal pasts were absent from the discourse, for there was no set past . . . or fixed future: everything could be condensated in the complexity of an ever-changing, mobile present. In a description of the *Onda* that could very well fit a portrayal of post-utopian narratives, José Agustín (México, 1944–) said in 2004 that there was no such thing as the *Onda*, given that the name was a label that allowed critics to analyze a literature that approached culture with a more democratic, universal aim. For Agustín, as for the "new" writers, literature was the place to experiment with new materials, to break barriers between high and low culture, and to be free from the conventions of set ideological goals and/or the authoritarianism of conventional wisdom.

But unlike the *Onda*, post-utopian narratives are not localized or marginalized cultural phenomena. Novels exploring the relationship between literature, youth culture, rebellion, and the mass media have been published all over the continent. And although these texts do not ascribe to an organized aesthetic program, at least three documents scattered throughout Latin America provided readers and critics with clues on how to approach these "new" writings.

## Where *Shangai* Meets McOndinos and *Cracks*

Let us return for a moment to Martín Caparrós and his *Babel* article of 1989. The piece was a manifesto of sorts for the *Shangai* group, an informal gathering of writers that started to meet in Buenos Aires around 1987, and which included Caparrós himself, Sergio Chejfec (1956–), Luis Chitarrone (1958–), Daniel Guebel (1956–), and Alan Pauls (1959–). Although the group did not have any particular agenda, they described themselves as sharing the same distrust of politics and a general disengagement with literary programs as narratives of "the real," because

> many among us work for mass media, for those who actually shape the possibility of a reading different than the real; a reading that shapes the real. Television or radio programs, newspapers, magazines, even movies: our desire for a mass audience – should we have it – is solved in those less prestigious places that are the great newspaper serials of the twentieth century. (Caparrós, 1989; my translation)

At these early stages, criticism was only able to see this combative distrust of the ideological agency of literature as a rejection of all possible political programs, which were in turn replaced by a celebration of mass media. Critical articles defined the new postmodern mood by talking about the disintegration of the classical subject, alienation, cynicism, commercialization of literature, disengagement from reality, and apathy. As a matter of fact, many writers cultivated this image in carefully constructed, theatrical operations that played all angles of possible perception of high and popular culture. For example, book presentations at the prestigious Instituto de Cooperación Iberoamericana (ICI) in Buenos Aires were staged as boring happenings with the ubiquitous rock star as a presenter, thus underlining that literature was just one product among others in the market of cultural goods. Or, as an extreme counter-example, writers collaborated in avant-garde movie projects so codified that it was almost impossible for the neophyte viewer to even follow a plot (e.g., *Lo que vendrá* – Argentina, 1988), transforming mass media into a cultural expression completely alien to the common consumer.

When Alberto Fuguet (Chile, 1964–) and Sergio Gómez (Chile, 1962–) presented their book, *McOndo* (1996), they built upon this imagery, establishing a new level of rupture both with preceding generations of Latin American writers and with academic constructions of Latin American culture. Hence, the obvious title "McOndo" was an ironic take on Gabriel García Márquez's Macondo, complete with Eva eating the trademark Macintosh apple on the cover. The book is a small map of an international-ized cultural field, with its citizens coming everywhere from Bolivia to Costa Rica, Chile and Spain. Not since the Hispanista movement from the early twentieth century and with the brief romantic pause of the Spanish Civil War in the 1930s had Spain been included as close literary kin anywhere in Latin America. Debates over the utter difference and uniqueness of Latin American culture had been prevalent among writers and academicians alike since the end of World War II. The inclusion of Spain as an integral part of McOndo speaks clearly of a cultural agenda that has already tran-scended the local towards a globalized view of culture as something that reaches further than the artificial borders of national states. The authors stated that "Spain, meanwhile, is present because we feel very close to some writers, movies, and to an aesthetic that goes further than a peninsula that is now European, but that is no longer the Motherland. The Spanish texts do not have bulls, or switchblades, or civil war" (1996: 19; my translation). This point of view is also reflected on their comments about how representations of Latin America needed to change not only within the region, but also in other areas of the world. Fuguet and Gómez complain that

> The most orthodox [academicians] believe that the Latin American essence is the indig-enous, the folkloric, the Left. Our cultural icons should be people that dress in ponchos and flip-flops. Mercedes Sosa [a folk singer] is Latin American, but Pimpinela [a pop duo] is not. And what about the bastard, the hybrid? . . . To be afraid of a bastard culture is to deny our own *mestizaje*. (1996: 17; my translation)

The authors aimed to abolish local color and to underline the complexity of a multi-leveled culture; to make culture their hybrid, universal country in the same way that Jorge Luis Borges talked about an (inter)national tradition that did not need to resort to the trickery of clichés to be authentic. The presentation of McOndo is an ideologi-cal operation intended to create a reading effect untainted by the marketing upshots of the 1960s boom or the reductionism of magical realism created by European and North American attempts to exoticize Latin America as the ultimate Other. Instead of trying to grasp a particularized essence of Latin American reality, the *McOndo* authors turned away from mythical, foundational spaces, toward personal narratives that better reflected on the everyday life of the continent since it did not make any sense "to sell a rural continent when it is truly urban" (1996: 18; my translation). Or better yet, the political sense it might have in the 1960s did not comply with the political and social realities of the 1990s and/or the aesthetic focus of writers who needed to deal with the aftermath of oppressive political regimes.

The introduction to *McOndo* starts with the education of both the writers and their global, would-be audience at the International Writer's Workshop of the University of Iowa. Notice that the cultural Mecca for writers is no longer Paris, but a small, specialized writing program in the US Midwest: the key word here is professionaliza-tion. Several of the writers included in the index took the workshop, and most of them have Ph.D. degrees or equivalent qualifications, although not all are academi-cians. Writing is no longer a call or a duty, but rather a highly competitive career. This process started in Latin America as a desideratum of the Modernista intelligentsia and it slowly built up throughout the twentieth century. Although this tendency coalesced during the 1920s, only by the end of the century did it become a fully factual reality, when culture became an industry with a market whose agents were meant to produce cultural goods and money instead of ideological programs. The opening scene of *McOndo* brings up several issues simultaneously: it is a description of the interaction between market and culture, it is an anecdote about the relationship between writers, public, and cultural constructs, and finally it is also a marker of the level of technical expertise required from writers who needed to attend workshops to further specialize in their craft, to network, and to develop marketing strategies. *McOndo* does not try to avoid this last facet; on the contrary, the book operates as a calling card. By the mid-1990s, this tendency had coalesced so much that novels such as *Frivolidad* (1995) by Juan Forn (Argentina, 1959–) and *Esperanto* (1995) by Rodrigo Fresán (Argentina, 1964–) showed not only this transformation but also its impact in both writers and society. Even writers like Vlady Kociancich (Argentina, 1941–) would explore the subject in a novel like *Los bajos del temor* (The low stabs of fear, 1992). These novels narrate how cultural agency flows from newspapers, cultural magazines, and marketing agencies, etc., how writing careers are forged by new modes of cultural production and organization, and how, in the end, these changes erase the rigid limits between elite and popular genres, between high and low culture. All the above-mentioned writers initially met and associated through newspapers such as *El Mercurio* in Chile and cultural magazines like *Babel* in Argentina or *Descritura* in Mexico. In that sense, Caparrós's manifesto is less about the lack of the social function of literature, and more about its complex role in a diversified cultural market, as described much later by Beatriz Sarlo in *Escenas de la vida posmoderna* (1994; *Scenes from Postmodern Life*, 2001).

By 1996, in Mexico, another group of writers had taken the same road. This group called itself "crack" (as in the written word that comics use to describe the sound of a breaking object) and included among its members Jorge Volpi (1968–), Ignacio Padilla (1968–), Ricardo Chavez Castañeda (1961–), Pedro Angel Palou (1966–), Eloy Urroz (1967–), and Vicente Herrasti (1967–). Like the writers selected in the *McOndo* anthology, the *crack* writers attempted to break away from the exotic view of Latin

America that crystallized in the North American and European readings of magical realism. As they explored genres such as science fiction or hyperrealism, their novels departed from the "for export" narratives, and sought a language, a style, and a narrative mode that could better describe the Latin American urban experience, the nuances of its social fabric, and the common threads of life in a globalized world. Years later, Jorge Volpi summarized this search as follows:

> Writers born since the sixties . . . face the challenges whose most extreme consequence will be the probable disappearance . . . of an *object* which critics such as Berry call "Latin American literature" . . . However, it does not mean that Latin American literature has disappeared. It simply means that it has become transformed, taking elements from other traditions and modifying its nature with unusual speed. Nostalgic feelings are childish: preservation is for museums. (Volpi, 2004: 41; my translation)

If *McOndo* made a clear-cut case for the end of folk-like localism, for experimentation, and for professionalism in literature; the *crack* made the case for the end of artificial identity issues attached to outdated ideological constructions, and for an erasure of artificial barriers that set a rigid compartmentalization of spaces within a culture in permanent state of flux. For these writers, any given label or category (ideological, generational, literary) became an absurd imposition on a culture's ability to renew itself. Literature as it was understood in Latin America had reached a fulcrum and was about to undergo a profound transformation.

## Farewell to the Arms

Even though the 1960s and 1970s were imprinted with revolutionary dreams of social equality and economic justice, literature showed signs that the utopian impulse was not as solid as everyday politics led to believe and that doubts both in the means and in the men involved in the fight formed an unspoken current. Novels such as *Libro de Manuel* (1973; *A Manual for Manuel*, 1978) by Julio Cortázar (Argentina, 1914–84) and *Historia de Mayta* (1984; *The Real Life of Alejandro Mayta*, 1998) by Mario Vargas Llosa (Peru, 1936–) signal the range of those reservations. Although extremely different in their views of the policies of armed movements, the novels narrate the force and the weakness of revolutionary movements throughout Latin America. In the first case, Cortázar focuses on the idealism and sacrifices necessary for the triumph of the revolution. In the second, Vargas Llosa centers his attention on the individual frustrations and on the constant bickering and betrayals of several leftist groups. A careful examination reveals that, in spite of themselves, both novels conceal their criticism behind events (rape, homosexuality, thieving, disorganization) that are inconsistent with the high expectations of the revolutionary models at work in the texts. The narrative is blind to the ideological contradictions portrayed as moral stands. And, in both texts, the quixotic will seems to obliterate the personal and social cost for those involved and those directly touched by armed revolutions either in their preparatory stages or in fully-fledged guerrilla warfare. By the early 1990s it was very clear that armed movements in Latin American countries had failed to achieve their goals. A book like *Unarmed Utopia. The Future of the Left in Latin America* (1993) by Mexican historian Jorge Castañeda remains a revealing account of the inner workings and connections of the different armed movements, an accurate analysis of the political consequences of the 1960–80 era, and a sad narration of the human cost of violence.

Although many writers turned to history to find the roots of this failure, history did not seem to hold the same allure for the writers who started publishing during the early 1980s. For them, history did not hold a prescribed mandate on politics or on ideology. Novels that dealt directly with politics were rather critical of the revolutionary mode of the previous decades, as in the cases of *Ansay o los infortunios de la gloria* (Ansay or the misfortunes of glory, 1984) by Martín Caparrós, *El Dock* (1993) by Matilde Sánchez (Argentina, 1958–), *Los detectives salvajes* (1998, *The Savage Detectives*, 2007) by Roberto Bolaño (Chile, 1953–2003), and *El fin de la locura* (*An End to Madness*, 2003) by Jorge Volpi, among others. Here, narratives made plain what was hidden in the above-mentioned examples: the inner contradictions and ideological problems of the revolutionary agendas of the previous decades.

The case of *Ansay o los infortunios de la gloria* is remarkable because it follows the path taken by other writers: it attempts to explain the roots of present-day violence by going back to history. But here, the fictional narrative is often replaced by original historical sources. By avoiding second-hand readings, the quotes have a devastating effect on the narration, which turns against itself and makes all utopian projects explode. *Ansay* is amongst the first to successfully criticize the ideological constructions of utopian literature without falling into its traps. As a result, the text is permeated by a bitterness that is absent in other texts. The novel is a fictional biography of the real Commander Faustino Ansay who was in charge of the Mendoza fort in 1810. The narration focuses on the relationship between his perceptions of the May Revolution, his prison experiences, and the *Operations Plan* of the Lautaro Logia (the ideological organization of the revolutionary movement) believed to have been penned by Mariano Moreno (1778–1811), whose articles in the *Gazeta* newspaper are also quoted. The three-way dialogue confronts the heroics of Ansay's childhood daydreaming with the realities of a dull life in a frontier garrison, as well as the idealism and desires of possible revolutions with the realities of an increasingly violent revolutionary movement. Moreno's Jacobinist discourse destroys both the idealism of the adventure-seeking Ansay and the purity of the revolutionary movement. In the novel, all forms of utopia end up in tragedy and betrayal, since only the state can actually prevail with ideological constructs of any kind. Hence, the novel renounces historical teleology, and searches unsuccessfully for a grasp on a present not tainted by the delusions of history. But, in *Ansay*, grand narratives are relegated to the mechanisms of treason and impossibility, and therefore only revolutions that betray themselves, work.

Treachery also permeates other novels. Bitterness gives way to irony, since narrations point out the inbuilt system for failure within the revolutionary discourse. In the case of *El Dock* the end of the revolutionary paradigm opens history to freedom of choice. The narration is really a search for an unattainable meaning within the

revolutionary impulse. The novel opens with the agonizing televised death of a guerrilla fighter, whose son will be adopted by one of her friends and her boyfriend. This
odd family will try to explain how and why that guerrillera came to the conclusion
that she needed to die, that there was no possible alternative to history:

> Poli reflected on her destiny. Each night, before sleeping, she told herself that the day
> had run away without her finding her destiny. She was really obsessed with acquiring
> beforehand the direction of her destiny, but she made no effort to build it. She believed
> in it as a birthright, something that simply you have or you have not. (Sánchez, *El Dock*,
> p. 176; my translation)

In the end, her obsession with fate and her death will be impossible to explain for
the other characters, particularly for her son, who will reach the conclusion that his
mother's choices were chained to the logic of madness.

Collective madness is the definition that Jorge Volpi uses for his acidic description
of the intellectual world of the 1960s and 1970s. The novel is both an individual and
a collective intellectual biography that deeply explores the history of ideas in Latin
America. The narrator explores the influence of French thinkers such as Jacques Lacan,
Michel Foucault, Roland Barthes, Regis Débray, Gilles Deleuze, and Louis Althusser,
each of whom is thoroughly analyzed. The main character participates in all the key
events of the revolutionary mythology: Paris in 1968, Castrist Cuba, Allende's Chile,
and, in the late 1970s and early 1980s, the cultural and political magazines that led
the ideological debates of Latin America from Mexico by portraying in detail the
different political lines that marked the debates of the Left. The novel takes issue with
the way European leftists see Latin America: as the locus of adventure, as the land of
homogenized exploited peoples who need to be educated on their rights by *illuminati*
revolutionaries from the Parisian upper classes. What emerges from the text is the
lack of connection between revolutionary projects and reality, and the contradictions
between grandiose discourses about the future and the immediate necessities of real
individuals and communities. The narrator asks himself about the possibility of being
an engaged intellectual in Mexico given its social and historical status, and about his
ability to remain loyal to himself in spite of political pressures. He fails miserably.
Eventually, he will give in to the pressure; he will become as corrupt as those he
criticized, he will, in sum, become his own caricature.

In the above-mentioned novels, revolutionary and intellectual projects equating
history with fate finish when those projects disintegrate. They annihilate those involved
in carrying on such revolutionary projects. *Los detectives salvajes* follows this line, going
as far as disintegrating language itself, in a way reminiscent of the last part of the
poem *Altazor* (1931) by Vicente Huidobro (Chile, 1893–1948): meaning is forever
lost. As in the case of Volpi's novel, Bolaño makes the search for historical truth an
intellectual adventure, where the word adventure seems to have more weight than
anything else. After years of looking for the iconic figure of Cesárea Tinarejo, the
mythical founding figure of the Mexican avant-garde, the characters would accept the

impossibility of reconciling ideals and reality, and the notion that for either one to prevail, the other one must die. The characters call themselves "real visceralistas," the ones who choose to see the guts of reality even at the cost of breaking the law or renouncing origins or allegiances of any kind. Myths, Bolaño seems to tell us, are there to be destroyed, otherwise they would destroy us: true freedom resides in the ability to exorcize the mermaid songs of the unfeasible and to accept the immediacy of experience. Mountains would never again be something more than immense green steppes.

## Virtual Realism Takes Over

One of the most brilliant and bitterly humorous novels to appear in the mid-1990s was *La literatura nazi en América* (1996; *Nazi literature in the Americas*, 2008) by Roberto Bolaño. The novel is a parody that follows the collapse of the hegemony of the intellectual right in Latin America during the twentieth century, and a study of how a literary movement becomes conservative by losing its ability to understand (and adapt to) a changing reality. At times organized as a biographical dictionary, at times as an academic research book, it covers all the key literary topics of the century: nationalism, communitarian life, gender issues, extreme political movements, literary experimentation, the function of magazines, etc. In doing so, the book is able to catalog the ongoing debates of conservative sectors of the cultural field, but it also makes evident that the Left has shared many of those issues. Parody allows the self-effacing narrator to point out the caducity not only of those debates but also of the topics themselves. To make sure the reader does not lose the point, at the very end, within the long list of apocryphal bibliography that in many ways quotes Borges, the narrator says:

> It was only necessary to change certain names: Mussolini instead of Stalin, Stalin in lieu of Trotsky. Slightly readjusting the adjectives and changing some nouns, any person could by now re-create an ideal model for the pamphlet-poem that they publicly commended by necessary historical hygiene but never enthroned. (Bolaño, *La literatura nazi en América*, p. 215; my translation)

So, if in fact it was impossible to return to the political agendas of the 1960s and 1970s, if it was truly absurd to return to the narratives of historical grand narratives, if even aesthetic projects could be reduced to a farce, then what?

The first answer came in the form of a dialogue of sorts between literature and the always changing aesthetics of rock and roll. *El país de la dama eléctrica* (The country of the Electric Ladyland, 1984 [a wordplay on Jimi Hendrix's album of that name]) by Marcelo Cohen (Argentina, 1951–) is a small, complex novel where the same story is narrated from multiple points of view and takes. The main character is alternatively living in a hippie commune somewhere on a Mediterranean island, and in his mother's house in a Buenos Aires neighborhood under the dictatorship. His parents are divorced, and both versions of the mother made her a contradiction in terms, sometimes a free spirit, and sometimes an orderly housewife. The character also oscillates between these images, at times a fierce figure, a hardcore rock-and-roll musician whose cynical view of the world collides with his mother's utopian views; at times a naïve teenager trying to build his perception of reality in opposition to his mother's almost crass domesticity. As he searches for a girlfriend who has stolen some money from him, the two versions also offer two possible explanations for what has happened to the girl and to the money. But the most important aspect of the novel, even more than this multiple take on reality that follows the kaleidoscopic narrative of a video clip, is the way in which reality is perceived. For reality can only be understood through the quotation system of the lyrics of rock and roll, which underline how characters read events in an almost nonliterary way. It is as if the book has a soundtrack that brings music into the pages of the novel when language fails the narrator. Rock and roll conveys poetics from all places and times, replacing narrative when necessary, and requiring a very informed reader who is able to decode not only what is disguised in these poetics, but also the social codes implied in the quotations, so narrative language becomes extremely concise and economic, and it conjures up a different kind of sociability:

> I love him; it is a pity that he does not understand me. Neither he nor anybody else will know that I am not alone. Morrison and his mattress-like mouth, Sid Vicious, Janis, Elvis, even Billie Holiday get together behind me. Black Jimi carries his guitar across his back and he is like the emaciated shadow of a cross. Tonight he is so black that he looks blue. In the sky there is a crescent moon that looks like a tin button: it poorly illuminates the country, which is a brownish sugar puddle. And the hairs of my dear spirits twinkle froufrou. Rimbaud and Verlaine come with muskets. (Cohen, *El país de la dama eléctrica,* p. 168; my translation)

Even in the loneliness of the individual experience, even when friends and family do not comprehend the character, he belongs to a circle that transcends time and geography, since his understanding of the social is made through aesthetic choices and collective ties that underline a certain affinity of discontented feelings.

This uncomfortable relationship with everything that is set, organized, solid, and reliable emphasizes the absence of institutional allegiances (political parties, organized religion, a structured family) since they had been replaced by a free-floating search for an identity that is also always changing. Rodrigo Fresán puts it succinctly in *Vidas de Santos* (1993; *The Lives of Saints*, 2006) when he argues that God is a virus, a cell, or maybe just another great character. If there is no room for grand narratives, nor is there room for any form of monologic discourse. Perception becomes multiple and its diversity allows for narrative to go beyond language or, better yet, for texts to bring to the sacred space of literature, nonliterary languages. Again, Fresán summarizes this matter when Esperanto, the main character of his homonymous novel of 1995, loses his ability to speak, to sing, and to be understood. Notice that the main character's name is also the given name of an artificial language invented at the beginning of the twentieth century by utopian thinkers and meant to become a universal lingua franca that would abolish national, local languages in order to foster universal communication.

In the particular case of *Esperanto*, the novel defines identity and perception through the impact of technological changes and mass culture. Esperanto tells his brother:

> When I was young, television was black and white and it was not very difficult to think that not *everything* happened there. Because TV was a meager imitation of reality. It did not seek to replace reality and I swear to you there even were advertisements for older people who did not have to just be grandparents. Television was fun, but it was also grey and it was better, I tell you, to play guessing games about the colors of cartoons. The real colors were somewhere else. *Outside.* (Fresán, *Esperanto*, p. 62; original emphasis, my translation)

Even when they understand that there is no turning point, Fresán's characters still long for that already fleeting, forever lost past. However, a writer like César Aira (Argentina, 1949–) simply immerses his characters into the mass-media reality created by television in his novel *La mendiga* (The beggar, 1998). In Aira's novel the real gets tangled within the narrative of a soap opera, because the memories of the main character are distorted by the language and structure of the newspaper serial. The reader is left with a puzzle about the nature of experience and memory, as well as queries about the very nature of perception.

The same operation appears in novels like *Por favor, rebobinar* (Please rewind, 1998) and *Las películas de mi vida* (2003; *The Movies of my Life*, 2003) by Alberto Fuguet. In both cases the lives of the characters are narrated as scenes of a movie or through the memory of a movie and its impact on the characters' perception of their environments. The basic unit of the movie, the shot, allows the narrative to move forward even when actions are delayed. The sum of these multiple images makes up a continuous narration, and only in retrospect and through a very cerebral operation can a story actually be restored to the novel. All scenes within a particular section of the text are connected through the eyes of a character that guides the reader through the maze of useless information that only later can be linked as a whole. The second novel in particular underlines how the relationship with mass media modifies the perception of reality and the consciousness of the individual person. In a way, what Manuel Puig (Argentina, 1932–90) did for radio and soap operas, Fuguet would do for movies by appropriating its language and symbolic icons. But here selectiveness is everything. The novels establish a dialogue with specific genres and aesthetics rather than choosing arcane artistic films, although some are mentioned here and there. For example, when opting for science-fiction movies the selection includes *Blade Runner* (1982), *Logan's Run* (1976), and *Close Encounters of the Third Kind* (1977). The first two movies evoke a post-apocalyptic universe where the notions of humanity and social institutions are questioned and where all forms of teleological searches are fatal. The third movie addresses issues of knowledge and public information as perceived by the "common man." A combined reading of the three movies by the main character of the novel brings forward not only the difficult dialogue between sciences and humanities, but more importantly an analysis of how individuals read and decode information, how memories and knowledge are constructed within the individual psyche and as collective experience. Although in many cases critics have emphasized that Fuguet's novels seem to be the capricious lament of the privileged young, to focus on that aspect of the novels alone is to miss the point entirely. New forms of communication, new forms of sociability that permeate all classes and all social sectors replace what is lost. The novels are, above all, about how those forms translate into (and transform) language, into perception, and into memory. True, it is the middle class of Latin America speaking, but is a middle class that has recovered its voice in order to look inward . . . from a cruelly critical perspective.

As the above paragraphs have shown, political and social criticism did not disappear from the emergent aesthetics. As a matter of fact, the main topics of debate within the cultural field were not completely abandoned and some remained almost unchanged. However, literary production lost its sense of transcendence since it was unnecessary to link it to major political and ideological projects in order to think about the nature of reality or about social issues. Literature was now free to reflect upon its own operations and free to test its own ideological materials without the pressures of a given political agenda. Literary experimentation became a way to test social and political models. Thus, science fiction was a natural choice for many writers, since it provided some generic rules that allowed for creating imaginary social spaces as if narrators were playing a Syms game. However, it would be wrong to assume that science fiction as a genre was fixed. Although the classic moment of futuristic narratives that developed in other places between the 1920s and 1950s never took root in Latin American countries, its local expressions were completely intertwined with the development of fantastic literature. Therefore, and to loosely quote Samuel Delany, by the time science fiction started to flourish, it already was a very fluid, complex, almost indefinable way to *read* literature.

Criticism has shown either a resistance to read science-fiction novels as such or to admit the plasticity of the genre by confining novels to minor-genre status. These attitudes reflect a lack of understanding of the literary process that started in the 1980s as whole. The loose appropriation of the language and aesthetics of science fiction by Latin American writers since the 1980s intends to renew the way ideological programs are tested, and to establish a serious dialog with areas of knowledge that until then was simply not there. Marcelo Cohen's *Insomnio* (Insomnia, 1985) and *Los acuáticos* (The water people, 2001) bring forward post-apocalyptic societies where all social and political projects are reviewed in order to re-create the intellectual subject not as an engaged political figure, but rather as a critical voice that questions projects from within; they analyze them, deconstruct, and dissect them. And in the light of the evident internal contradictions and intimate betrayals, the utopian impulse is denounced as a form of mysticism. The same case can be made for most of Angélica Gordischer's (Argentina, 1928–) novels, particularly for *Kalpa Imperial* (1983; *Kalpa Imperial: The Greatest Empire That Never Was*, 2003). *Kalpa Imperial*'s short stories reorganize the relationship between literature and the real by skipping the ubiquitous mediation of history, particularly nineteenth-century history, which forces narrative to constantly re-create myths of origin. *Kalpa Imperial* provides a myth that imitates the ideological inner working of the utopian impulse of any revolutionary process. The stories are in themselves myths with their own circular narratives, perpetually in search of themselves, and in the end, they provide a mirror, monstrous image of the realist narrative of the 1960s and 1970s.

For its part, Volpi's novel *En busca de Klingsor* (1999; *In Search of Klingsor*, 2003) constitutes one of the most serious attempts to establish a dialog with science since Borges. The main character of the novel is called Francis Bacon (as the seventeenth-century philosopher who set the pillars of contemporary scientific method), who is looking for one of Hitler's scientific advisors. As the search progresses, the novel reflects on the history of science since the publication of Einstein's seminal paper of 1905, the confrontation between applied science and the theories of relativity and quantum physics and mechanics, as well as the hunt for a link between these two theories. The novel also explores how the political uses of scientific discoveries have real social and moral consequences that affect our perception of reality, and transform our political and ideological views. However, here, as in many science-fiction novels of the period, the genre is merely the background for a critical reflection upon any form of utopian project. Klingsor, whose name comes from the Arthurian traditions of the Holy Grail, is never found. And the search ends in a long list of failures. Realism, or the realism that accompanied the discourse of the Nation–State projects, even in its most radicalized forms, was unable to answer for the collapse of the utopia. The literary could no longer claim the virtues of its transformative power. And literature became just another way to test the possible, either by looking at the guts of reality as Bolaño's "real visceralistas" wanted, or as an almost cold, rational exercise about social and political practices. If literature was to be free from the constraints of a manifest destiny, language would abandon its previous entanglement with historic discourse and refurbish itself by retrieving from within the cultural field the aesthetics of the margins in order to renew its operations and vocabulary. In the end, virtual realism allowed for a renovation of literary codes and reality was, from now on, to be perceived through the unfixed eyes of uncertainty.

## REFERENCES AND FURTHER READING

Beverley, John, Aronna, Michael, and Oviedo, José, eds (1995). *The Postmodern Debate in Latin America*. Durham, NC: Duke University Press.

Ferman, Claudia (1996). *The Postmodern in Latin and Latino American Cultural Narratives: Collected Essays and Interviews*. New York: Garland.

Fuguet, Alberto, ed. (1993). *Cuentos con Walkman*. Santiago: Planeta.

Fuguet, Alberto, and Paz Soldán, Edmundo (2000). *Se habla español: Voces latinas en U.S.A.* Miami, FL: Santillana.

Sarlo, Beatriz (1994). *Escenas de la vida posmoderna: Intelectuales, arte y videocultura en la Argentina*. Buenos Aires: Ariel.

— (2001). *Scenes from Postmodern Life*. Minneapolis: University of Minnesota Press.

Williams, Raymond L. (1995). *The Postmodern Novel in Latin America: Politics, Culture, and the Crisis of Truth*. New York: St. Martin's Press.

# 37

# Cultural Modalities and Cross-Cultural Connections: Rock across Class and Ethnic Identities

*Gustavo Verdesio*

It is not easy to write about rock because that word has been used, in different historical moments, to refer to a wide variety of musical genres that may have little to do with each other. For example, MTV (the most successful music channel in history) and *Rolling Stone* (the legendary rock music magazine) play or comment on, indistinctly, the music made by artists who play heavy metal, new wave, hip-hop, classic rock, punk rock, and the most unapologetic pop. All these styles and many more find room under the umbrella of the music industry, comprising music channels, specialist magazines, radio stations, and record stores, among others.

Another problem one faces when one talks about rock is that rock is not just a musical genre or a series of musical styles, but it is also a concept. This concept is a fluctuating notion and it has changed throughout the several decades (more than five now) rock has been with us. This situation is complicated, also, by the fact that, as Carlos Polimeni rightly points out, rock is not only a concept but also a *mise en scène*, or a staging (2001: 63). That is to say, rock cannot be understood or even conceived of without taking into account the attitude(s) of the musicians, their distinctive looks, the spectacle they offer, and the public(s) they create. Rock is today (as it probably was from its beginnings) as much a kind of music as an attitude, and a concept as well as how it is received. In other words, rock is a complex social, cultural, and economic (and some would say political) phenomenon as well as an aesthetic one that does not lend itself to easy interpretations or understandings of it.

Yet, there is agreement about one thing: the vast umbrella we call rock music started its life as a hybrid between several preexisting music genres. It is the result of two centuries of musical styles that originated in different cultures. There is the Chicago-based blues, which transformed the original, acoustic Delta blues, into bands who went electric – bands (two guitars, drums, string bass, piano, and a harmonica or harp) that would become the model for many rock bands of the classic period and beyond (Friedlander, 1996: 17). Even today bands as legendary as the Rolling Stones pay homage in their concerts and records to the blues greats – they were known for their after-show surprise visits to the clubs were the Chicago blues greats played. Gospel and Rhythm and Blues (R&B) are also important as influences with roots in African-American culture – Elvis, for one, was a great fan of gospel and sung songs from the genre until the end of his life. Of these two genres, the one that most decisively influenced rock was R&B, at least in two aspects: one, because its feeling was more upbeat than that of the Blues, and second, because of the band format, which barely transformed the basic electric (Chicago-style) combo with the important addition of a saxophone (Friedlander, 1996: 18). Two other important influences were Folk and Country music, with Hank Williams as the latter's most popular hero – even Chuck Berry, so reluctant to admit any influences to his musical production, acknowledges he was inspired by the giant of country music.

This hybrid product did not crystallize, at least for the masses, until 1955, when it became a popular phenomenon with vast economic and social repercussions. It was in that year that the movie *Blackboard Jungle* became the vehicle for the first contact of rock and roll music with a public mostly comprising young people. Bill Haley and the Comets' "Rock Around the Clock" served as the background music for the opening credits and it made such an impression on its young audience that it soon became the first mega-hit in rock history when it sold twelve million copies of the single. From that moment on, the doors opened for the new genre and a myriad of great artists reached the new, young audience: Chuck Berry, Little Richard, Fats Domino, Jerry Lee Lewis, and many others. Yet the genre did not reach the heights of truly massive appeal until a young man from the South hit the charts. It was Elvis Presley who, in 1956, after appearing live on several TV shows, took rock and roll to hitherto unheard-of levels of popularity and himself to a new form of royalty: he became simply The King.

Elvis (as everybody calls him) was a transgressor in the eyes of the parents of the young listeners who were crazy about rock and roll. His delivery, his looks (especially his sideburns and his flashy clothes), his body language (sensual movements and gestures that included his snug smile and, above all, his famous pelvis shake, which earned him the nickname "Elvis the pelvis"), and the lyrics of his songs (which were an invitation to talk about, and to practice, romance or sex) were a little too much for Eisenhower-era America. This historical time, with its political and social conservatism and its defense of the status quo that depended on, among other things, the respect for a hierarchical organization of society, could not see Elvis in particular and rock and roll in general with sympathy. But if things are viewed from the perspective of some of the victims of that conservatism (American youth), the situation was ripe for some kind of rebellious behavior. Here's when rock music enters the scene.

However, the system (that is, the political and socioeconomic status quo or, if you prefer, the powers that be) managed to do some damage control and in a little more than two years coopted the King himself: he volunteered to go to Korea and fight for his country. After his return, he was never the same: he dedicated most of his energy to sweet ballads and to acting and singing in several movies that pleased the parents of his former audience. Now a patriot and a successful actor, Elvis stopped being dangerous to his former detractors and became part of the star system.

Yet, rock and roll was (t)here to stay. It became, in spite of cooptation and all, the music of a new public: youth. For the first time in Western history, the youth of the planet became an identifiable group that extended beyond national boundaries. One could be Chilean, French, American, or Nigerian, but one was, above all, young. This new awareness of being part of an age-based group did not go unnoticed to the forces behind that complex machinery we call capitalism: the market began to consider this new collective subject as another legitimate target. From the late 1950s on, a series of new products coming from different industries – clothing, films, and especially music – were directed exclusively to the young ones. The young ones, no matter how rebellious they appeared to their parents' eyes, were now a significant source of revenue for more than one industry. Therefore, youth's needs or desires were not only satisfied but also fostered by a music industry that found and created new audiences around the world.

This is where the history of what is called today *rock en español* begins. It is at this point, when rock had already become an international phenomenon and a source of wealth for the great capitalist companies, that the first bands that sang rock in Spanish appeared. In 1962, a young Mexican called Enrique Guzmán ("the Mexican Elvis") started to sing covers of the great (pre-Beatles) rock and roll hits in Spanish. He and his band, the Teen Tops, flooded the charts with songs whose lyrics could be understood by audiences that did not speak English. His significant success started a new fashion that soon became an industry: to sing in Spanish the greatest hits or the top forty songs of the English-speaking countries' charts. Soon after Guzmán's success, other Spanish-speaking rockers entered the scene: Sandro in Argentina (called, predictably, and with more reason than in Guzman's case, "the Argentinean Elvis," whose first album was released in 1963), Roberto Carlos in Brazil, Miguel Ríos in Spain, and many others. This trend was not limited to Latin America and Spain, however. It flourished also in France and in Italy, where singers like Johnny Hallyday and Bobby Solo (again predictably, also known as "the Italian Elvis") topped the charts with French and Italian covers of songs originally released in English.

Unfortunately, all these artists (with the exception, perhaps, of Guzmán), like (the original) Elvis, were rapidly coopted by the music industry and became singers of sweet ballads that reached an increasingly older, more mature audience – that is, they started to sing to wider segments of the public and, therefore, to make more money for themselves and for their record labels. They ended up sounding and looking like the imperfect predecessors of *rock en español*: the made-for-TV Argentinean collective of solo artists known as *El club del clan*, a show which ran from 1958 to 1963. They became, so to speak, appropriate for general audiences – in Spanish, and according to Polimeni (2001), *aptos para todo público*. These singers were shaped after what in Europe was called "the new wave" (*la nueva ola*), which was a complex musical phenomenon that comprised both interesting and occasionally very creative artists as well as mere seekers of commercial success. It is very difficult to separate, sometimes, the artistic from the commercial, in the works of a single artist. For example, how can one distinguish between what's creative and what's mere muzak in the *oeuvre* of people like Charles Aznavour, Lucio Dalla, Serge Gainsbourg, Françoise Hardy, Jane Birkin, Domenico Modugno, Mina, and many others? And yet, all of them are respected composers, interpreters, or singer-songwriters today.

Ironically, it is not until the appearance of a band that sung and composed their original songs in English that the seeds of what will be later called *rock en español* were sown. In 1964, four young Uruguayan men formed a band, Los Shakers, who would change the history of popular music in Spanish. They started as a band strongly influenced by the Beatles, to the point that they sounded almost exactly like the British group. And yet they dared to add, little by little, their own musical ideas to the ones of their model. In their farewell album, *La conferencia secreta del Toto's Bar*, they included a song whose importance has yet to be thoroughly evaluated by music historians and cultural critics alike. I am referring to "Candombe," which is a tune that incorporates an Afro-Uruguayan rhythm (*candombe*) to the rock-song structure popularized by the Beatles. This is the first time a Latin American or Spanish-speaking rock band added local musical elements to the rock song format in a successful way. The importance of this move will be fully appreciated only from the present state of *rock en español*, as we will see later. Los Shakers thus became, as Polimeni suggests, the missing link between the clones who sang the English-speaking world hits in Spanish and the Latin American rock that chose a less mimetic path (2001: 48).

In Uruguay, too, another band appeared, Los Mockers, who made music that sounded more like the Rolling Stones than like the Beatles. Unlike Los Shakers, they did not last long enough to move to a different creative level and remained a very good but mostly mimetic band. It was only when another band with an English name, Los Beatniks, made their entrance on the rock scene that *rock en español* began to earn its name. This was because despite their foreign name, they sang their own songs in Spanish. In hindsight, it does not matter that they only sold 200 copies of their single in 1966. What really matters is the effect they had on other Argentinean musicians who, encouraged by the brave behavior of Los Beatniks, started to compose and sing their own songs in Spanish. This is a more daring move than it may seem, because at that time, and for many years to come, the predominant belief among record industry owners and directors was that to sing in Spanish was *mersa* and *grasa*: that is to say, vulgar or in bad taste.

At this point, it may be opportune to point out that *rock en español* emerged as a phenomenon either in big countries (Mexico, Argentina) or in societies with a strong middle class (Argentina, Uruguay). Both size and a strong middle class are elements that create the conditions for the development of a decent market for mass-produced artifacts. The former's importance goes without saying: the bigger the population, the higher the chances to sell more products. The latter's importance is also clear: the middle and upper-middle classes are social sectors with higher levels of education and a thirst for information and cultural artifacts coming from the central societies of capitalism – the United States and Europe – which has its foundation in a desire to emulate the models – a desire to be à la mode, to be in the know, and to show it. Another element that contributes to make the middle and upper classes so important for the diffusion of rock and other products is their comparatively affluent status, which allows them to acquire goods in significant quantities.

In both Argentina and Uruguay rock was mostly an urban phenomenon.[1] In Uruguay in particular, there was a big difference between the bands that came from the upper and upper-middle classes and those who were from the middle class. The former were able to buy more imported records (and therefore to be more in touch with what was happening in the great centers of rock music) and to buy better instruments, while the latter had more difficulty in accessing the music produced by English and US bands and an even more difficulty in acquiring musical instruments and equipment.[2] Yet the majority of rock consumers were mostly members of the upper-middle and middle classes. That this was the situation in Latin America should not surprise anyone, because it is not only a natural consequence of the logic of capitalism, but also a replication of what happened in the United States at the beginnings of rock and roll, where it was a musical and social phenomenon consumed mostly by young, middle-class Americans (Friedlander, 1996: 21).

But let us go back to the new wave of Argentinean bands who decided, against all odds, to sing rock in Spanish. This new trend coincides with the progressive awareness of the musicians from the periphery that the lyrics of the English-speaking rock whose music they liked so much were, at best, funny and/or sensual, and at worst, plain stupid. In any case, the lyrics of these models were, in general – and despite their expression of desire and their glorification of human instincts such as the sex drive (two revolutionary traits for the historical moment) – very simplistic. This means that the lyrics penned by the rock-and-roll heroes of the classic era were not a good source of inspiration for musicians who were interested in expressing themselves in a personal way. If they wanted to say something of artistic or social import, they had to write a different kind of lyrics. It is in this historical moment, at this conjuncture that the work of Bob Dylan, a folk musician-gone-rocker (but most of all, the epitome of the singer-songwriter), appears as the preferred model to those who wanted to produce a more complex artistic message.

Yet, the essentialist opinion predominant then was that to sing rock in Spanish was like singing tango in Japanese – that is to say, it was considered something ridiculous. Of course, this kind of essentialism is, among other things, profoundly racist and chauvinistic: tango, salsa, rock, and other musical genres are being (and have been for a while) sung today not only in Japanese but also in Russian, and other languages, in an artistically successful manner. So the situation at that time (the mid-1960s) in Argentina presents us with a confrontation between, on the one hand, the record industry moguls and the most conservative and reactionary segment of the audience, and on the other, the rock musicians who wanted to compose and sing in Spanish.

The conflict was solved in favor of the Argentinean rockers when a song interpreted by one of their bands, Los Gatos, topped the charts. It was "La balsa," the song that sold 250,000 copies in 1967, that changed the fate of the genre in Spanish. This song is important not only because it achieved a significant commercial success, but also because it synthesized the aspirations and feelings of a generation of Argentineans – and the interpellating power of this song is a unique phenomenon, perhaps the first of its kind, in the history of Argentinean popular music.[3] It conveyed a feeling of rebelliousness different from that transmitted by the original English language rock songs: it was based on the idea that life should be understood as a constant exploration, as an adventure (Polimeni, 2001: 68). However, and in spite of what a relatively recent movie suggests (*Tango feroz*, 1995), the paths of rock and political activism did not coincide. The culture of rock fostered rebellious behavior, but one different from the dissent promoted by left-wing political parties, student organizations (their unions, which are very different from – and much more politicized than – US-based student unions), and guerrilla groups.[4]

The fragmentary, spotty knowledge Argentinean rockers had of English and American rock contributed to the originality of the former's product, because the very same imperfect access to, and grasp of, the cultural phenomenon they were trying to emulate or build upon forced them to be more creative in their interpretations of it. This lack of information made room for the flourishing of many a talented artist with a strong personality. It is after this change took place that Argentinean rock, and what later will be called *rock en español*, became what they are today. The history of Argentinean rock required a first period or era of experimentation with the possibilities of adapting the Spanish language to the needs and requirements of the rock song.[5] This history is very long now and cannot be told in its entirety here. Suffice it to say that it is filled by names such as Luis Alberto Spinetta, Charly García, Gustavo Cerati, Andrés Calamaro, and Fito Páez, just to name the most famous, who built consistent and creative careers over the years.[6] They have, at different times, influenced rock musicians from all over the Spanish-speaking world, including Spain – whose rock history is, by the way, poorer than Latin America's, due in good part to the Franco years.

Yet, in spite of the considerable variety and creativity that characterized Argentinean rock for many years, it was only after the Falklands/Malvinas war (in 1982) that the genre took off commercially and became a dominant cultural phenomenon. Thanks to the ridiculous decree passed by the Argentinean military junta, which prohibited the airing of songs in English on the radio, AM and FM stations, faced with the challenge of filling hours and hours of programming with music in Spanish, decided to take recourse in the music made by local rockers. After 1982, the number of bands multiplied and in the 1990s myriad styles of rock and pop developed in Argentina alone.[7] What is important, however, is not the number of bands and the variety of their styles, but the local touch that most of those bands and solo artists gave to an already international genre. This attitude produced a hybrid artifact that, in turn, produced other grafts by experimenting with genres and styles from different parts of Latin America.

In this respect, the pioneering work of Los Shakers, with the incorporation of *candombe* into their songs, deserves a special mention. Another Uruguayan band, El Kinto (a.k.a. El Kinto conjunto), led by the musical vision and talent of Eduardo Mateo, made, from 1967 on, a more consistent and seminal use of *candombe* in their compositions, as well as an incorporation of bossa nova rhythms and arrangements to their tunes. But it was Gustavo Santaolalla's band, Arco Iris, that started the trend that is now predominant in Latin America. He began to experiment with cross-pollinations between rock and Latin America's very diverse folkloric genres – a process that reached its peak with the release of the record *Sudamérica* in 1972, which was followed by another South American folklore-inflected album, *Inti Raymi*, in 1973. This latter, like some of his music, was inspired by his visit to Cuzco, which had both a mystical and political impact on his life and music: he was touched by the spirituality of the place and modern-day Amerindians, as well as by their musical traditions.

The musical ideas he got and the spiritual changes he underwent after his travels and the release of those two records made him – in order to spread the new musical gospel he had discovered – go beyond his own career as composer and performer and to venture into a new territory: that of the production of other musicians' records. An important moment in his career as a producer is Leon Gieco's groundbreaking album, *De Ushuaia a la Quiaca*, a record that registers an itinerary, a voyage across both the territory and musical landscape of Argentina.

Santaolalla's musical program and artistic vision are very important because they ended up being the predominant ones in the current production of most of the *rock en español* landscape. This happened in part owing to market conditions (a renewed interest in things Latin American), but also because of Santaolalla's growing influence on the music business as a producer. In order to get an idea of how successful his career has been, suffice it so say that he produced several albums by some of the most popular and talented bands and solo artists in the world of *rock en español*: Café Tacuba, Divididos, Bersuit Vergarabat, Peyote Asesino, Molotov, La Vela Puerca, Juanes, and many others. Some of the artists he has produced and promoted have gone on to win several Grammies in the "Latin Music" category, and one of the most recent of those awards was for the tango and hip-hop album by the collective Bajofondo Tango Club, which successfully mixes tango, rock, electronica, and hip-hop. Thanks to all these hits and awards, not only did he get credit (and deservedly so) for supporting creative artists, but also for helping record labels to sell large numbers of copies. Yet, not satisfied with this new role as *arbiter elegantiarum* or *rock en español* mogul, Santaolalla set out to produce film soundtracks. In this he has also been extremely successful: he produced soundtracks, which included songs by some of the bands mentioned above and other Latin American musicians, for films as successful as *Amores Perros* and *The Motorcycle Diaries* – one of the songs from the latter ("Al otro lado del río"), penned and performed by Uruguayan singer-songwriter Jorge Drexler, won the 2005 Oscar for best song.

Arguably, Santaolalla is today, together with his peer and rival Emilio Estefan, one of the two most influential producers of Latin-inflected music. There are at least two main differences between the modus operandi and the musical preferences of these two. The first one has to do with quality or creativity: Santaolalla has preferred to work, in general (although not always), with musicians who are trying to achieve artistic goals, while Estefan is more interested in producing acts that are treated as commercial projects whose only aim is to make money. This is just my interpretation of Estefan's goals. It is also possible that he really likes the artistically poor records he produces. The second difference rests in the combinations of musical traditions they favor: while Estefan promotes, above all, musicians that draw mostly from rhythms and styles from the Caribbean, Santaolalla is interested in producing music that finds inspiration in all the l.atin American genres and traditions.

These pop/rock moguls could not have risen to the prominent places they occupy today without the creation, in 1993, of a vehicle that would change the future of *rock en español*: MTV Latino. The real internationalization of what the bands and solo artists were doing starts to take place only after that moment. Since then, bands in Colombia are more aware of what other bands are doing in Mexico or Argentina, and vice versa. MTV Latino, then, and the ideas advanced by producers Santaolalla and Estefan, have an effect that could be called "the Latin-Americanization" of *rock en español* in general and Argentinean rock (the pioneer in Spanish) in particular. What I mean by this is the incorporation of Latin American traditional rhythms and styles into the by now multiple musical formats of international (English-speaking) rock. A good example of this transformation is the evolution of a band like Los Fabulosos Cadillacs, from Argentina, who started as a ska band who followed in the footsteps of the British band Madness, who in turn were inspired by Jamaican bands and rhythms. They were, arguably, a copy of a copy. With the internationalization created by MTV Latino and the predominant production strategies of the two most important trendsetters in the Latin American music business, Los Cadillacs started to incorporate not only stylistic elements from Argentinean folklore, but traditional music from other Latin American countries as well. Another form of Latin Americanization Santaolalla-style is to allude to revolutions of the past, to left-wing icons of yesteryear, and to present-day leftist writers like Uruguayan Eduardo Galeano in the bands' lyrics – see, for example, *Rey Azúcar* (whose title is based on one of the stories told by Galeano in *The Open Veins of Latin America*), one of the Cadillacs' albums that registers the change I am referring to. Another case in point is the power trio from Argentina, Divididos, who continued to incorporate traditional rhythms – they had done it before, in *Acariciando lo áspero*, where they offered, among other examples, a punk/hard rock version of the Mexican traditional tune "Cielito lindo" – and leftist themes in their album *La era de la boludez*, produced by Santaolalla.

These changes in the themes and styles of *rock en español* have made it possible for its bands to enter, albeit timidly, the US market. Nowadays it is not unusual – and it has not been for a while – to find reviews of Latin American bands' records in mainstream US music magazines such as *Rolling Stone* and *Spin*. Yet it is a different kind of musical trend that has really made it in the United States and Europe: *pop latino*. This category includes artists as diverse as Ricky Martin, Jennifer Lopez, Shakira, and others, some of whom are from Latin America and others from the Latino population of the United States – or, in the case of Ricky Martin, from a Latin American country (Puerto Rico) with strong cultural, economic, and political ties to the

United States. These acts have all released albums produced in the United States, sang in English, and with the American audiences and their thirst for things Latin American in mind.

American audiences are now more receptive than ever to Latino cultures. The demographics since the late 1980s show a steady growth of the Latino population in the country and an increasingly powerful presence in the most diverse social activities and professions. Yet mainstream American audiences' tendency to consume more and more Latino products cannot be explained by demographics and social mobility alone. This phenomenon also necessitates some psychological explanation. According to John Beverley, some of the success of Latin American "literary" genres such as testimonio can be explained by the yearning of American audiences for what they lost by becoming modern.[8] It is not unlikely that today we could be witnessing a manifestation of that yearning in the musical arena. It suffices to remember, in support of this hypothesis, the trend that dominated the mid-1980s in both the United States and England: that of famous artists (Sting, Paul Simon, David Byrne, Peter Gabriel, and others) looking for third-world rhythms and styles for a desperately needed inspiration.

This entrance to the US market has been facilitated, also, by the fact that MTV Latino is located in Miami, which makes two important goals possible: first, to be based in the United States itself, and to prevent any struggle between Latin American nations who could aspire to be the capital of *rock en español* or *pop latino* production and distribution – Argentina and Mexico are the first potential competitors that come to mind. This centralization of the production and strategizing of MTV Latino helps, also, to achieve something capitalism deems very important: the homogenization not only of the products but also of the audiences for which they are destined. Together with these trends that are effects of the penetration of things Latino in the United States and the international musical world, there is another important one, according to Santaolalla: the Latinicization of the world undertaken, perhaps inadvertently, by the United States.[9] As part of US culture, Spanish and artifacts produced in that language are now marketed as one of the ways in which the cultural diversity of that powerful country manifests itself. This favors, undoubtedly, the careers of bands and solo artists that have the chance to tour, and produce their albums in, the United States.

Unfortunately, the most creative bands and solo acts from Latin America are yet to be marketed massively in the international arena. Neither Charly García nor Luis Alberto Spinetta, arguably the two greatest rockers in the history of the genre in Spanish – and two major poets in their own right – have made even a small dent in the world of MTV Latino or that of the mainstream music magazines. Other great artists, like Gustavo Cerati or Andrés Calamaro, are still waiting for a promoter or a producer who could make them sell more records in the US market. Too bad for them that, for the standards created by MTV Latino and the most current trends in production and distribution of Latin American music, they are not Latino enough: samba, salsa, *corridos*, *cumbia*, and other regional and traditional rhythms appear only sporadically in their songs. Too bad, indeed.

The musical creativity and the artistic innovation of the products promoted by the big media as Latino or Latin American are low – perhaps with the exception of Shakira, a talented pop artist with a strong rocker personality – and the messages they send are, in general, innocuous or merely silly. Thus, as always, as in its beginnings, rock is today controlled by international capitalism. However, it cannot be denied that, as Michel Foucault suggested many years ago, where there is power there is also resistance. This dictum is confirmed by some musicians and producers who try, amid the constraints imposed on them by the industry, to create spaces for messages of resistance and dissent even when their songs have to go through the filters and controls exerted by MTV Latino – which are based on rules that, like those of its US parent, MTV, severely limit artists' freedom of expression by banning certain kinds of lyrics and body language. Let us hope their crusade ends up succeeding despite the superior forces they are confronting and despite the temptations that the industry always has in store for the rebellious ones. Let us hope, then, that not all our best musicians and poets are coopted like Elvis, the King.

## NOTES

1  For the Argentinean case see Grinberg (1993); for the Uruguayan, see Peláez (2002, 2004).

2  For a detailed description of the differences between bands from different social backgrounds see Peláez (2002).

3  According to Polimeni (2001), this is a first in the history of any genre of music in Spanish.

4  For an analysis of the differences between the rebellious attitude of rockers and leftist activists see Grinberg (1993: 8–9).

5  This first period of Argentinean rock is described by Grinberg as one in which musicians dedicated themselves to dominate (or create) the art of singing rock in their native language: Spanish (1993: 9 and passim). See also Verdesio (1997) on this topic.

6  For a history of Argentinean rock see Fernández Bitar (1993); Romay (2001); Polimeni (2001), and Grinberg (1993). For an overview of Charly García's life and career see Marchi (1997). For Andrés Calamaro's ideas and opinions on music and life in general, see his book of conversations with Alejandro Rozitchner (2000).

7  For a detailed discussion of this period of Argentinean rock see Guerrero (1994).

8  For a full development of this argument see Beverley (1999).

9  See Santaolalla's opinions in Polimeni (2001: 174).

## REFERENCES AND FURTHER READING

Beverley, John (1999). *Subalternity and Representation: Arguments in Cultural Theory*. Durham, NC: Duke University Press.

*Blackboard Jungle* (1955). Dir. Richard Brooks. Perf. Glenn Ford, Sidney Poitier, Anne Francis, Vic Morrow. MGM.

Calamaro, Andrés, and Rozitchner, Alejandro (2000). *Tirados en el pasto*. Buenos Aires: Editorial Sudamericana.

Fernández Bitar, Marcelo (1993). *Historia del rock en la Argentina*. Buenos Aires: Distal.

Friedlander, Paul (1996). *Rock and Roll: A Social History*. Boulder, CO: Westview.

Grinberg, Miguel (1993). *Cómo vino la mano: Orígenes del rock argentino*. Buenos Aires: Distal.

Guerrero, Gloria (1994). *La Historia del palo: Diario del rock argentino 1981–1994*. Buenos Aires: Ediciones de la urraca.

Marchi, Sergio (1997). *No digas nada: Una vida de Charly García*. Buenos Aires: Editorial Sudamericana.

Peláez, Fernando (2002). *De las Cuevas al Solís. Cronología del rock en el Uruguay: 1965–1975. Vol. 1*. Montevideo: Perro Andaluz.

— (2004). *De las Cuevas al Solís. Cronología del rock en el Uruguay: 1965–1975. Vol. 2*. Montevideo: Perro Andaluz.

Polimeni, Carlos (2001). *Bailando sobre los escombros: Historia crítica del rock latinoamericano*. Buenos Aires: Editorial Biblos.

Romay, Héctor (2001). *Historia del rock nacional*. Buenos Aires: Bureau Editor.

*Tango Feroz: La Leyenda de Tanguito* (1993). Dir. Marcelo Piñeyro. Perf. Fernán Mirás, Cecilia Dopazo. Mandala Films SA/Kuranda Films SA.

Verdesio, Gustavo (1997). "Pop latino y espejitos de colores," *Posdata*, Montevideo.

# 38
# Film, Indigenous Video, and the Lettered City's Visual Economy
*Freya Schiwy*

Audiovisual media are becoming increasingly pervasive in contemporary Latin America. Television antennas dot the urban landscape while satellite and cable are reaching ever more remote rural areas. While much of what is shown on small and large screens is still made in the United States, Latin American cinema, video, and television production has been experiencing a boom. Two major tendencies characterize contemporary film and video production. On the one hand, young filmmakers, particularly from Mexico, Argentina, Chile, and Brazil, are taking advantage of the global currency of multiculturalism, manifested since the early 1990s through increasing opportunities for corporate funding and international co-productions. Established directors such as Walter Salles and Hector Babenco are returning to their home countries after working for Hollywood during the 1980s and early 1990s. Together with the export of Latin American *telenovelas*, this audiovisual production has been projecting Latin American lives to an increasingly global audience. Latin American film has become popular not only with critics, but with national audiences who, for a long time, preferred Hollywood spectacles to local productions made with limited financial and technological resources and few distribution outlets. Film and television has turned into a privileged medium for reaching vast audiences, producing a sense of regional coherence while enacting multicultural diversity in the global marketplace. Commercially successful Latin American cinema thereby contributes to the importance of audiovisual media as a practice that creates meaning and shapes the perception of reality.

On the other hand, in almost all of Latin America there is a proliferation of low-budget documentary and fiction videos produced by indigenous-movement organizations such as CONAIE (the National Indigenous Council of Ecuador), CAIB (the Organization of Indigenous Communicators of Bolivia), CSUTCB (the Union Confederation of Peasant Workers of Bolivia), CIDOB (the Confederation of Indigenous Peoples of Bolivia), CRIC (the Regional Indigenous Council of the Cauca, Colombia), Ojo de Agua Comunicaciones (based in Oaxaca, Mexico), the Chiapas Media Project,

Video in the Villages (Brazil), and so on. While some native cinema from North America and New Zealand (e.g., *Smoke Signals*, 1998; *Atanarjuat, The Fast Runner*, 2001; and *Whale Rider*, 2002) has achieved surprising box-office success in Europe and North America, indigenous video from Latin America is primarily distributed and viewed at international indigenous film and video festivals and through independent communication networks in rural communities. Indigenous media in Latin America has largely bypassed commercial cinema and television stations as well as the co-funding of the film industry. Yet indigenous communicators in Bolivia, Ecuador, Chile, Brazil, and Mexico (like aboriginal and native filmmakers in Canada, Australia, and New Zealand) respond at once to audiences' desire for entertainment and narrative suspense and to a cultural politics of decolonization. Reynaldo Yujra (Aymara), Juan José García (Zapotec), Dante Cerano (P'urhépecha), Marcelina Cárdenas (Quechua), Julia Mosúa (Moxeña), and many others use audiovisual technology to revive indigenous cultures. They see film as a means of challenging Western representations of Indians and as counteracting the colonization of the soul, that is, the self-denigrating effects that colonialism and its aftermath have had on the perceptions and self-perceptions of indigenous communities. What does this surge in media production mean for relations of power and representation in Latin America?

Literacy and literature have long been perceived as the hegemonic form of representing and enacting social power. The Uruguayan literary critic Ángel Rama coined the concept "lettered city" as a metaphor for this entrenched power relation. Rama's study suggests that with the conquest literacy became an auratic practice, sustaining a class of *letrados* (lettered men) who, at the service of the state, have since controlled the symbolic and discursive production of reality (Rama, 1996). For some cultural theorists the omnipresence of television and film is ushering in "the decline and fall of the lettered city" (Franco, 2002). Unlike the sphere of letters and literacy, mass media seem to open up a space where the people's ideas and desires find expression and where democracy can be enacted through consumer choice (Martín-Barbero, 1993; García Canclini, 2001). The audiovisual medium, however, is not a new technology. Rather, cinematic representation builds on a long tradition of visualizing Otherness. Like the lettered city, audiovisual media are bound up with a colonial history as well as with capitalist market interests and production (Miller et al., 2005). Given the way cinema has been entangled with the exercise of power, celebrating mass media and audiovisual technology as a democratization is therefore problematic. In effect, the role of film and video in Latin America calls attention to the lettered city's visual economy, that is, it mitigates the importance placed on literature and literacy as a privileged means of creating meaning and power relations. At the same time the lettered city's visual economy indicates a certain instability in the opposition between literate and oral cultures. The production and usages of film and video today shed light on different strategies of negotiating the realm of power and knowledge dominated by late capitalism and the global desire for multicultural images.

## Film and the Coloniality of Power

Although Rama emphasizes that in the sixteenth century the power of the *letrados* lay not only in their management of written documents and the law, but also in their creation of symbols and graphic diagrams (even the creation of architectural space), the lettered city has come to signal a binary opposition: literacy versus orality. The colonial beginnings of modern power/knowledge seem routed in literacy as the technology of the intellect. The *letrados* constructed a sense of inalterable signs in opposition to an apparently ephemeral orality. In other words, the power of alphabetic writing entailed the creation of orality as an idea. The notion has survived tenaciously, yet the binary of "literacy" and "orality" abstracts from the plethora of visual representations and performative enactments of power that accompanied the exercise of administrative and literary writing. The notion of orality disregards the complex visual and performative forms of transmitting knowledge across different indigenous cultures, such as codices and glyphs, Andean kipus and weavings, as well as dances, rituals, and the inscription of meanings into the landscape (e.g., Mignolo, 1995).

If visual representation and performance (including the performance of writing itself) enacted power as much as alphabetic representation, documentary and fiction film can be seen as extending a colonial gaze inaugurated with colonial engravings. Films have contributed on a global scale to the construction of racial otherness by establishing a gaze that is both masculine and imperial (Kaplan, 1997: 79; Shohat and Stam, 1994, especially chapter 3). Cinema was part of the colonial enterprise, documenting and controlling "the 'primitive' cultures that missionaries, administrators and the military encountered" (Kaplan, 1997: 61). It became an important tool for visualizing the tropes and metaphors of conquest and colonization put forth by popular fictions and exhibitions. In the twentieth century cinema thus helped to spread the enthusiasm for the imperial projects beyond the lettered elites and into the popular strata (Shohat and Stam, 1994: 100). Crucially, cinema pretended to see objectively as it projected images of colonial power relations, fraught with the anxiety of having the gaze returned, both on screen as well as by parts of the audience. It was an at once colonial and male gaze that visualized otherness (Kaplan, 1997). Brian Winston argues that even the development of dyeing processes in color film responded to racist ideas about skin color and privileged the mimetic rendering of whiteness over blackness. Color technologies that would have actually recorded the structure of color and been able to realistically represent hues of white and black were neglected. As Winston summarizes, "essentially, the research agenda for colour film (and more latterly colour television) was dominated by the need to reproduce Caucasian skin tones" (1996: 39). Film can thus be seen to participate in the reproduction of what has been termed the "coloniality of power" (Mignolo, 2000), that is, the construction of particular imaginaries of subjectivity where notions of race and gender have been called into being to legitimize social and geopolitical systems of economic exploitation and epistemic privilege.

Cinema is a colonial as well as capitalist technology that rapidly became an industrial complex in its own right, representing and producing US interests worldwide (King, 1990; Miller et al., 2005). During the twentieth century, after having displaced European productions from France and Italy by 1916, up to ninety percent of the films seen by audiences in Latin America were US-made. The cost of filmmaking and technological innovation and the distribution difficulties in the face of Hollywood's aggressive global media policies, often supported by US government interests, held national film production in Latin America in check. Only around five percent of the films shown in commercial theaters were national productions (King, 1990: 10, 19, 32–6; Miller et al., 2005: 13, 20–1, 67). Like the literary and essayistic imaginaries conjured up by the lettered city, film was a powerful technology of representation caught up in the global geopolitics of knowledge. As an important means of entertainment and education, it has complemented and reinforced scientific and literary imaginaries about colonial others and national selves.

As John King recounts, Mexican viewers were exposed to representations of themselves as racial others:

[The US film industry] created a vision of the Revolution and of an "other" – the Mexican people. The United States was seen as a repository of democratic values with a "Manifest Destiny" to democratize other childlike or incapable nations. The imaginary construct of Mexico could then be plotted in terms of geography and the people . . . The indigenous inhabitants of this landscape were depicted in the stereotype of the "greaser": the Mexican was innately violent, irresponsible, treacherous and possessed of an uncontrollable sexual appetite . . . The women were viewed differently, and put in the category of "beautiful señorita", a mixture of docility and sensuality; exotic, but with creole or Spanish rather than *mestizo* looks and clothes. (1990: 16–17)

With time Hollywood made its films meant for export more palatable to audiences abroad, but the number of Latin American-made films, even in those countries with a relatively sustainable film industry, remained minuscule in comparison with Hollywood's market dominance. Nevertheless, industrial as well as art-house film production has always existed alongside US and European films, flourishing at times when global market relations and US government interests favored Latin American production, such as during World War II and the Roosevelt administration's Good Neighbor policy (King, 1990: 31–2; Miller et al., 2005: 62).

Although many studies of Latin American cinema construct national histories, cinema has always been part of an intricate global web of production and commerce, contributing to and contesting existing constellations of power and knowledge. Perhaps because most of the cinematic footage has been lost or destroyed, there are few studies dedicated to the role and importance of early audiovisual technology in Latin America (López, 2000: 50). Film historians have, however, reconstructed the presence of film in Latin America through bits and pieces of found film, the memories of those still alive, newspaper reports, and changing legislations. The advent of moving pictures in Latin America dates back to 1896 when the first film was exhibited in Buenos Aires. By the beginning of the twentieth century, shorts and feature films were being produced in Mexico, Brazil, Argentina, and Cuba (Gumucio Dagrón, 1982: 28). Already at the beginning of the twentieth century government officials in La Paz, Santiago, Buenos Aires, Lima, Rio de Janeiro, and other cities debated over whether cinema was to be considered a curiosity, an acceptable art form, or a morally questionable entertainment for the masses. They also recognized film as a medium for educating the nation and promoting patriotic feelings (Gumucio Dagrón, 1982: 31–68). Military parades and footage of trains projected through the new cinematic technology created a sense of participating in Western modernity and affirmed the power of local authorities. Both cinema enthusiasts and the ruling powers sought to maintain a hold on cinematic technologies of representation in the face of the US-based film industry's rapidly increasing dominance. Indeed, local production was not always strictly opposed to Hollywood's colonial gaze (cf. López, 2000). The following examples are certainly not exhaustive of the extremely diverse experiences with early film across Latin America, but they give a brief impression of how film, like photography, was implicated in the process of dealing with ethnic diversity and colonial legacies.

Along with scenes of urban life, warfare and silent melodrama were some of the preferred genres of the time, even in remote places such as the Bolivian Andes. Historical themes such as the French film *Cristophe Colomb* (1904) exhibited in Bolivia in 1905 (Gumucio Dagrón, 1982: 36) already contributed to the framing of Indian otherness, complementing US-made dramas such as *Cowboys and Indians* (1904). Alongside internationally distributed French and Italian silent dramas and documentaries, film served to create a visual archive of local culture (Gumucio Dagrón 1982: 39–43). Even though cinema was increasingly considered a lowbrow pastime, it was a powerful propaganda tool, used to promote public health and patriotic feelings. *Las Ruinas de Tiahuanacu* (1912) and *La vestal del Sol Inca* (1920), partially filmed in Cuzco, Peru, celebrated the Inca past. The films paralleled similar framings in photography (see Poole, 1997) and extrapolated from the Andean indianista literary tradition that had flourished in the nineteenth century. Bolivia's first feature-length drama *Corazón Aymara* (1925) denounced abuses against Aymara Indians; *La Gloria de la Raza* (1926), which included dramatized acting by the Uru, and the silent "superproduction" *Wara Wara* (1929) further testify to the effort to create visual contributions to the *indigenista* debates of the twentieth century. Working in Bolivia before 1929 and in Peru afterward until his death in 1936, the Italian-born documentary filmmaker Pedro Sambarino filmed patriotic and *indigenista* shorts such as *Por mi Patria* (1924) and *Inca Cuzco* (1934). After the revolution of 1952, the cinematographer Jorge Ruíz, working for the state-funded Instituto Cinematográfico Boliviano (ICB), became an official representative of Bolivia's *indigenista* politics. Ruiz's documentary *Vuelve Sebastiana* (1953) includes a Chipaya community's enactment of social life on screen and is today considered one of Bolivia's most important films. His fictionalized documentaries such as *La Vertiente* (1958) and *Las Montañas no cambian* (1962) frame visions of modernization and progress in the hands of benevolent and aspiring patriarchs working against rural backwardness, embodied by Quechua and Aymara populations.

While film attests to the elite's pressing need to come to grips with the past and present of Quechua and Aymara populations, it became an increasingly contested technology of knowledge and power. Since the 1960s Jorge Sanjinés, Oscar Sorias, and others in the Ukamau Group have contributed very different images of the colonial contradictions of race and class. From a sociopolitical perspective akin to José Carlos Mariátegui, the Ukamau Group has denounced racist class exploitation of the highland native populations in films such as *Revolución* (1963), *Ukamau* (1969), *Blood of the Condor* (1969), *The Courage of the People* (1971), and *Secret Nation* (1989), to mention just a few of the Group's outstanding films. Similarly Antonio Eguino's first feature films, *Pueblo Chico* (1974) and *Chuquiago* (1977), grappled with race and class conflicts in the Andes.

In Mexico, film was early on recognized as a medium for creating national identification and enthusiasm for the Revolution. Although support for the medium again was not consistent – José Vasconcelos, for example, eschewed film in favor of literature and painting – Pancho Villa fashioned himself as a star of the revolution by taking advantage of cinema's possibilities (King, 1990: 17–19). The national film industry in Mexico charted not only popular urban culture but also explored the integration of indigenous populations into the new revolutionary *mestizo* identity. In the melodrama *Maria Candelaria*, for example, Dolores del Río performed a whitening and romanticization of indigenous subjectivity for the national imaginary. Cinematographer Gabriel Figueroa and the star actors Dolores del Río and Pedro Armendáriz contributed to the film's audience success. As a popular form of entertainment cinema was not usually embraced by intellectual elites and vanguard movements (King, 1990: 19, 23), yet it was an important means, parallel to that of the novel and more accessible to a broad audience, for imagining the nation and its coherence.

Many of the locally produced films focused on popular culture (comedy, musicals, and melodrama). The audiovisual construction of a national self-image and its exportation to other regions, as in the case of films with Carlos Gardel in Argentina or Mexico's *comedia ranchera*, is complex, but in many instances it meant dealing with race, gender, and class. Robert Stam writes that even in the case of Brazil where actual indigenous populations were very small, "one is struck by the frequent, almost obsessive adaptation of indianist novels such as *O Guaraní* (four versions in the silent period), *Iracema* (three versions) and *Ubirajara* (one version)" (1997: 66), thus avoiding the depiction of Afro-Brazilian themes in favor of an idealized concept of miscegenation (ibid.).

Similar to literature, film has been a contested medium that has continued to reproduce colonial relations of power, knowledge, and representation in nominally independent nation-states. Like literacy, audiovisual technology has been sought after by those desiring to reshape pervasive images and ideas. Filmmakers in the 1950s and 1960s, such as those associated with the Bolivian Ukamau Group, regarded the globally dominant Hollywood cinema as a tool of US imperialism. Inspired by Mariátegui, dependency theory, and by the Cuban revolution and its potential for creating a more egalitarian society, "third cinema" filmmakers across the continent saw their struggle against US neocolonialism allied with anticolonial struggles in Africa and Asia. The camera became a weapon of the revolution, "the projector a gun that can shoot at 24 frames per second," as the filmmakers Fernando Solanas and Octavio Getino once put it (Martin, 1997: 50). Access to film technology, however, was limited to those with cultural and economic capital, in other words, to those who inhabited the lettered city built upon the subalternization of indigenous populations and the descendants of African slaves. The ability to deploy film's indexical effects (the notion that what we see on screen, particularly if it is in documentary format, is somehow more "real" than a description, literary or otherwise) has thus been limited. Yet it is important to note that the participation of indigenous actors early on exposed some indigenous and rural populations to audiovisual technology. When indigenous populations were employed in the filming process, they enacted their roles and, at times, returned the gaze of those viewing the ethnographic spectacle (Rony, 1996: 13).

It is worth looking in a little more detail at third cinema since it is an important precursor of new Latin American film and indigenous video. Although film scholars have continuously emphasized that the so-called "New Latin American Cinema" was not a unified movement with a coherent film politics and aesthetics, they have also insisted that there was a common ground and connection among filmmakers such as Tomás Gutiérrez Alea, Julio García Espinosa, Glauber Rocha, Nelson Pereira Dos Santos, Octavio Getino and Fernando Solanas, Fernando Birri, Arturo Ripstein, Paul Leduc, Jorge Sanjinés, Miguel Littin, and many others. Frequently educated at the Italian Centro Sperimentale, influenced by Italian neorealism and anticolonial strug-gle, these filmmakers sought a third kind of cinema that was neither commercially oriented Hollywood film nor European art cinema. They tried to combat profound social injustice, which they perceived as a result of US imperialism and its extension through internal colonialism, that is, the collaboration of national elites with foreign monetary interests for their own benefits and to the detriment of the majority of the population. Cinema was seen as a tool for denouncing racism and class exploitation and rousing the people to revolutionary action. As a medium it could avoid at least part of the fundamental heterogeneity at the heart of literature, where those repre-sented in the narrative are of a different social and ethnic class than those writing, producing, and reading the books. If the practice of literature thus replicated a social structure that the narratives denounced, audiovisual media reach audiences regardless of their level of literacy. Filmmakers in Cuba carried electric generators and reels to rural villages, exposing these populations to audiovisual media even before the advent of television. Getino and Solanas in Argentina organized filmmaking according to the logic of guerrilla struggle where all members of the film crew should be potentially replaceable and thus trained in all aspects of filmmaking, from camerawork, to light-ing and editing. They screened their films at community and labor union centers. Jorge Sanjinés and the Ukamau Group in the Andes similarly distributed their films in Quechua and Aymara communities in the countryside, irrespective of the existence of electricity. They consciously moved from a cinema for the people to a cinema with the people, where indigenous and Quechua- and Aymara-speaking mining communities were increasingly integrated into the planning and production of film itself, even though the Ukamau Group never fully relinquished directorial control. As actors or subjects of documentary films, cinema, though expensive, could incorporate the people it represented into the production process (see the filmmakers' manifestos collected in Martin, 1997).

"Imperfect Cinema," "Cinema with the People," "Cinema Novo," though not in a unified way, experimented with different forms of breaking Hollywood aesthetics, turning the dearth of financial resources in Latin America into a creative reservoir. Most commonly the limits between fiction and documentary filmmaking were blurred and melodramatic plots rejected. Most radically, Jorge Sanjinés and the Ukamau Group came to eschew close-ups in favor of long and medium shots and minimal cutting, thus favoring a collective protagonist and a critical distance on the part of the audience in contrast to industrial cinema's emotional seduction and numbing of the mind. The result often made for very difficult films to watch, even at a time when spectators were not yet used to television and MTV's proliferation of close-ups and rapid cuts. Often the audiences these films sought were not only elusive because of lack of national political support for the distribution of these films (let alone for distribution across national boundaries), but also because viewers preferred the narratives of suspense, melodrama, and comic entertainment that Hollywood brought to cinemas worldwide. As recent research has shown, alongside the US productions audiences favored the locally produced B- and C-movies that coincided with Hollywood genres and strategies for entertainment, shock, and other forms of emotional release (e.g., various essays in Dennison, Nágib, and Shaw, 2003; and recent publications in the *Journal for Latin American Cultural Studies*).

## Marketing Diversity and the "New International Cultural Division of Labor"

Third cinema, not only in Latin America, started changing in the 1970s. Dictatorship, the onset of disillusionment with the Cuban Revolution, and the realization that nominal independence in postcolonial countries was giving way to new, more subtle forms of international rule over former colonized territories (such as the growing importance of the IMF and the World Bank, for instance), went hand in hand with a decrease in state sponsorship. Film production in the 1980s reached a crisis while television began to expand and form regional monopolies. The multicultural image became a commodity that started to replace the deeply problematic ideal of a modern nation built upon the common interests of a homogenous population. Literature as a form of high culture has gone into crisis, along with the idea of the modern intellectual as purveyor of consciousness. Contemporary filmmakers and indigenous communicators reject the paternalistic role assumed by the revolutionary filmmakers of the

1960s who sought to energize the people into anticolonial resistance. Indigenous videomakers have stayed with the theme of colonialism but are redefining what decolonization means. Filmmakers not allied with indigenous movements, such as the Chilean director Gonzalo Justiniano, for example, reject the Marxist analysis and solution as unviable. Young filmmakers no longer conceive of themselves as imbued with revolutionary consciousness; the enthusiasm characterizing anticolonial and revolutionary filmmaking in the 1960s has given way to a different kind of global consciousness. Latin Americans have been configured into the global multicultural market and most are suffering the adverse effects of neoliberal policies endorsed or enforced by international moneylending institutions. Filmmakers show what they see, and what they see is no longer a clear class or race contradiction that social revolutions could solve. Both, indigenous videomakers (who promote a cultural politics of decolonization) and young filmmakers (who seek commercial success and are not tied to indigenous social movements) have also discarded the often radical aesthetic politics that had put Latin American third cinema onto the global map of experimental and socially committed films.

As audiovisual technology becomes more accessible and filmmakers express a more humble or less ambitious attitude toward the possibilities of film ushering in social change, audiovisual cultural production is seen to be becoming more democratic, both internally and globally. Filmmakers such as Alejandro Gónzalez Iñarritu, Walter Salles, Hector Babenco, Gonzalo Justiniano, or Daniel Burman, like Latin American actors, welcome opportunities to work in international co-production or even for the film corporations associated with Hollywood. Internationally marketed and successful films from Latin America are paving the way for filmmakers to get their visions out. As Daniel Burman put it in an interview with Walter Salles, "*Amores Perros* [2000] and *Y Tu mamá también* [2001] showed the Anglophone world that films like these could make it beyond press reviews and film festivals. They got their foot in the door to the market, a door that is much more difficult to open than it is to gain critical acclaim" (in Dennison, Nágib, and Shaw, 2003: 68). In light of the transnationalization of film production and the unprecedented visibility of films from places like Latin America in the US market, it may seem more difficult to speak of a continuing global dominance of Hollywood film. Yet upon closer inspection one finds that filmmaking has become outsourced, creating a New International Cultural Division of Labor (NICL, or NICDL). Hollywood can be seen as a continual mode of doing film business, a capitalist and now neoliberal economic mode, based on profit maximization, that has permeated film production worldwide. Latin American filmmakers are courted by international production companies, proving that Brazil does not only sell in Brazil but also to a global audience. Many Latin American films are now commercially supported by the large Hollywood production companies. This transnationalization allows for new and diverse ways of negotiating the co-opting power of global markets primarily at a textual level. Yet content is constrained by profit principles and limited production budgets that are still in the hands of few. The creation of cinematic imaginaries is harnessed ever tighter to the demands of the market, whether in the United

States, Latin America, or elsewhere. Revenues of the immaterial labor of cultural production are still primarily filtered back to few primary shareholders (Miller et al., 2005: 52, 65). One can also argue, therefore, that the boom of commercially successful film from Latin America does not fundamentally break with the lettered elite's monopoly on power and representation. Current international co-productions and the travel of actors, directors, and film crews amplify earlier transnational flows of cinema industry employees. Audiovisual representation is not becoming automatically more democratic with the advent of newer and cheaper technologies. The message supported by global capital is no longer enunciated only from its highly sophisticated centers of film technology, and cinema does coexist with cheaper, digital video recording. Critical video and filmmaking that challenges established meanings, knowledge politics, and socioeconomic relations, however, is the result of organized efforts.

## Indigenous Video and the Decolonization of Film

Indigenous media share with recent commercial Latin American cinema a desire to please their audience. In contrast with the anticolonial cinema of the 1960s (where filmmakers experimented with neorealist aesthetics, the blurring of boundaries between documentary and fiction, and the invention of new cinematic genres), digital indigenous video frequently uses a conventional documentary format (exposition, alternating talking heads) and the low-budget fiction shorts make ample use of Hollywood codes, such as the cinematic horror genre, the melodrama, and extreme close-ups. Nevertheless, unlike their better trained and financially better supported, commercially oriented peers, indigenous communicators are not primarily producing for the general market and their film production is not guided by the principal of profit maximization. They continue but also reinvent the tradition of anticolonial filmmaking.

The most important centers for indigenous media are in Mexico, Brazil, and Bolivia. In Mexico, the internationally sponsored Chiapas Media Project/Promedios has supported indigenous video production, primarily in documentary format, but indigenous media in Mexico has also been strong in Oaxaca and among the P'urhépecha in Michoacan. Video production here has become independent of an originally state-initiated effort at providing indigenous and peasant populations with video technology (Wortham, 2004). Mexican indigenous media (video and community television) document local traditions but also transmit news and information about the struggles of indigenous communities in a context of often violent oppression by the Mexican state. Another important initiative of indigenous video production is Brazil, where the indigenous identified population is small, constituting only 0.2 percent of the national population, unlike Mexico, where currently about thirty percent of the population identify as indigenous. Xavante and Waiãpi videomakers affiliated with Video in the Villages, like the young men making video in Kayapó communities, have used the technology to document rituals but also as a sociopolitical tool to enable remote villages to communicate with each other. The Kayapo have also drawn international attention to their struggle through a conscious, media-savvy politics of framing the exotic – such as in the apparent clash produced by painted bodies wielding camcorders. The most acclaimed films at international indigenous film festivals come from Bolivia, where CEFREC (the Center for Training in Cinematography) and CAIB (the multiethnic Organization of Indigenous Audiovisual Communicators of Bolivia) have maintained an extensive and growing communication network through video since 1996. In Bolivia the majority of the population identifies as indigenous, and diverse and strong political indigenous movements shape culture and politics. CEFREC–CAIB are not the only indigenous video producers there, but their "Indigenous National Plan for the Audiovisual Communication of the Indigenous Peoples" has, from the beginning, been independent of the state and a most influential force.

Like third cinema, indigenous media treat the issue of decolonization. The problem, however, is no longer that of ousting an external colonizing force. A central theme in indigenous fiction and docudrama shorts is the self-denigrating effect of colonialism. Linked to the "decolonization of the soul" is the effort to reverse the project of the lettered city, that is, the disciplining of apparently oral cultures into a Western modernity dominated by racial and economic elites and a patriarchal worldview. If the colonial experience creates a division between the West and the many and diverse indigenous cultures, indigenous audiovisual communication affirms this difference and converts it into a resource for thinking. The "colonial difference" (Mignolo, 2000: 14) thus produces a border space where pan-indigenous identity is constructed and vindicated as an alternative modern ethos. At stake is not so much the relationship between indigenous populations and nation-states but the design of development programs and role of the global capitalist system, where, as some have argued, an outside has become impossible to conceive.

A genealogy that traces indigenous video back to anticolonial Latin American cinema risks losing sight of one of indigenous media's most important precursors. As the videomakers themselves have emphasized (e.g., on CEFREC's website) they consider audiovisual communication an extension of community radio (www.videoindigena.bolnet.bo). Instead of seeing access to digital technology as a Western gesture of giving the camera to the natives, indigenous mediamakers insist on their own agency. At film festivals and during interviews videomakers such as Julia Mosúa, Marcelino Pinto, and Alfredo Copa have explained that when video presented itself as a possibility to the communities, they took advantage of the technology. The communities selected interested persons or those already involved in radio communication to be trained in the use of video in order to continue a process of ethnic vindication and anticolonial resistance that had already been in process at least since the beginning of the 1970s.

For George Yudice culture and economy, even the performance of indigenous politics, have become reciprocally permeated, "not just as a commodity – which would be the equivalent of instrumentality – but as a mode of cognition, social organization, and even attempts at social emancipation, seem to feed back into the system they resist or oppose" (Yudice, 2003: 28). Yet fiction shorts such as *Qulqui Chaliku/The Silver Vest* (1998), *Qati Qati/Whispers of Death* (1999), *El Oro Malidito/Cursed Gold* (1999), *El Espíritu de la Selva/Forest Spirit* (1998), *Llanthupi Munakuy/Loving Each Other in the Shadows* (2001), etc., extend a long-lived strategy of incorporating and transforming what is useful of Western culture into a continuously evolving indigenous culture. Instead of wholesale rejecting the codes of commercially successful cinema, like the anticolonial cinematographers from the 1960s, indigenous videomakers adapt established cinematic genres that have themselves functioned to promote sales by the film industry. They become part of traditional formats and themes of storytelling, such as the Andean tales of the walking dead. Melodramatic elements are linked to those of the comedy, creating an image of indigenous culture that is diametrically opposed to the melancholic and suffering subject prone to irrational violence projected by indigenista literature and film. Through *mise en scène*, editing choices, and the soundtrack the videomakers recontextualize film conventions (Schiwy, 2003). In other words, indigenous videos document and enact cultural traditions of transmitting social memory as they seek to turn subalternized knowledge into sustainable knowledge. The process points to a subtle, multifaceted indianization of film.

Cinema and video are social practices as well as representations in a more conventional sense. What we see on screen is the result of bodily performances and social relations just as much as the result of scripts, editing, lighting, and framing decisions. Indigenous videomakers have sought to transform the medium in all its dimensions into an expression of the vitality of indigenous cultures. Within the long colonial horizon indigenous media find their place among an array of survival strategies. Video builds on the transmission of knowledge and social memory through diverse bodily practices (celebrations, dances, dress, and food), storytelling, a complex visual production – for example in textiles, weaving, ceramic design, and the "reading" of an animate landscape.

Distribution is a topic of debate as indigenous video-makers seek to take advantage of the cultural currency of indigenous video without becoming fully integrated into the neoliberal market place where culture is reduced to a commodity. For example, video makers and their communities reject the liberal ideal of free access to all knowledge, just as much as the neoliberal notion of knowledge as commodity (freely available to those who can afford to pay). Instead, knowledge is conceived as subjective; it is produced, diffused, and sold according to particular interests. The distribution and creation of knowledge and images through indigenous video is meant to conform to the ethical and political needs of indigenous communities. In other words, indigenous communicators adapt audiovisual technology to a pan-indigenous economic order that video making itself enacts as viable while simultaneously securing intellectual and image property rights within the global legal/market system.

Instead of seeking their incorporation into the global media business, many indigenous video makers are challenging the economic and epistemic configurations of power that mass media continue to enact. Building on the distribution techniques developed by third cinema and taking advantage of cheaper and more portable technologies, video makers have set up networks that bypass literacy and transform the rules of the multicultural market for goods and ideas, including the one formed by academic consumption. Some, such as the videomakers associated with the Chiapas Media Project/Promedios, take advantage of the marketability of their films in order to promote a thinking process that challenges the place of indigenous communities within the global economy. The Chiapas Media Project maintains a website and distribution center and proactively engages in university visits and screenings in the United States (www.promedios.org). Its films are easily available. Access to *Ojo de Agua* productions or P'urhépecha EXE indigenous video is more difficult, although both organizations are not opposed to circulating their films commercially. Films by Xavante videomakers working with Video in the Villages were distributed through the US-based LavaVideo website. Kayapó footage has circulated through films such as *Taking Aim* (1993). While video documents and enacts indigenous culture, it also serves as a means of provoking consideration of how the global economy itself might be reshaped under ethical principles that, for instance, would privilege social equity and conserve the environment. Film is also a means of drawing attention and international support to the political and cultural struggle of organizations such as the EZLN (Zapatista National Liberation Army). Others, such as CONAIE in Ecuador, have assumed a flexible pricing policy for their films (indigenous communities pay significantly less than US academics) without, however, making their films accessible through international distribution outlets or websites. CEFREC-CAIB productions are primarily distributed through noncommercial means, that is, through the network of indigenous communication, free of charge. For universities prices have varied according to the resources of those interested in purchasing copies of films. In 2006 the communities and regional organizations supporting the Indigenous National Plan agreed to halt all sales. Films like *Qati Qati* and *Llanthupi Munakuy* are hence couched in an alternative economy, an alternative market space based on reciprocity and mutual obligations. At times, those interested in purchasing films are asked to reciprocate with other services they might be able to provide, such as translation and other forms of assistance. At the same time, the uneven sale of indigenous video reflects debates and concerns over intellectual property rights (Schiwy, 2003). The limited distribution also points to a conviction that had already characterized Ukamau's distribution policy: the notion that reception can be controlled or at least influenced favorably through the viewing context. That is, screening an indigenous video in a peasant village accompanied by a facilitator who guides a discussion afterward creates a different result from showing the same film in a university classroom, which again, is different from a commercial or television release without organized discussion. Indigenous media in Bolivia form part of an economic borderland where a reciprocal economy has coexisted with capitalism since the conquest.

Indigenous-made fictions, documentaries, docudramas, and community television are bringing together ever broader indigenous and peasant audiences across ethnic and linguistic differences. They circulate unevenly in the global marketplace. These low-budget production and distribution networks are unconnected with the national film schools and commercial production centers. Funding comes from various sources. In Bolivia, for example, the Basque NGO, Mugarik Gabe, as well as AECI (the Spanish state agency for international economic cooperation) and even SEPHIS (a Dutch organization that also supports academic publishing) have contributed to indigenous video production. Throughout Latin America CLACPI (the Latin American Cinema and Video Council of the Indigenous and First Nation Peoples) has offered logistical and technical support since it was founded by visual anthropologists and independent filmmakers in 1985. The non-profit organization is moving increasingly into indigenous hands. CLACPI's current director is the Zapotec Juan José García. Some independent filmmakers (for example, Iván Sanjinés, Vincent Carelli, Guillermo Monteforte, and Alexandra Halkin) continue to collaborate with the indigenous communicators on a local as well as continental scale. The major financial and logistical responsibilities, however, are shouldered by the communities and their audiovisual communicators who provide labor and time.

The Bolivian video makers' negotiation of the star system, a staple of the film industry, sheds further light on the indianization of film. In CEFREC/CAIB's fiction short *Llanthupi Munakuy*, for instance, Aidée Álvarez is again, as in the short *El Oro Maldito*, cast as the young object of male desire. Her face and body are framed in close-ups and she figures on the production still announcing the film in 2001 on the CEFREC website. The advertisements on this site use the female image to attract potential viewers in the communities through a process of complex identification based on sexual desire just as much as on ethnic recognition. While some see the need to promote talented actors as actors, others want to maintain the collective and deprofessionalized distribution of roles and tasks in the filming process. This debate forms part of the pan-indigenous self-reflection that seeks possibilities of incorporating Western elements of filmmaking into an indigenous order instead of being incorporated into that of the West, as Iván Sanjinés (director of CEFREC) explained in 2003 during the New Latin American Film Festival in Providence, Rhode Island.

The director figure presents a similar issue. Marcelino Pinto, from the coca leaf-growing Chapare region of Bolivia, for instance, is "responsible" for the script and directing of *El Oro Maldito*. Some technical ideas, such as using an improvised traveling shot during the climax of the film in order to heighten suspense, are his. Nevertheless, Pinto insists that the film is the result of a collective production, a collaboration between CEFREC, CAIB, and the community that participated in the filming. During the international indigenous film festival in New York in 2000, Reynaldo Yujra insisted that the idea for the script of *Qati Qati* is based on a legendary story that does not assume an individual author but a long history of oral narrators. But Yujra has also inscribed his responsibility for the film on screen. In *Qati Qati*, a profile of his face is twice shown briefly and in close-up during the establishing shots, illuminated by a blue moonlight that introduces the mysterious ambient of this horror tale. In the documentary *K'anchariy* (2002), Yujra enacts the Aymara director-documentary filmmaker who travels to learn about medicinal practices among the Quechua-speaking Kallawaya. His role constitutes the director as an alternative filmmaker figure, distinct from the anthropologist and situated on the same side of the colonial difference as the community that he visits. The information obtained, at the same time, becomes part of the indigenous intercultural exchange instead of being integrated into the anthropological archive. Yujra's construction of the director figure is thus an example of indigenous intercultural communication that has been intensifying through the production and distribution of indigenous video. At the same time it points to the coexistence of concepts of the individual and the collective – linked through processes of reciprocity and responsibility – that some indigenista writers and filmmakers (e.g., José Carlos Mariátegui, Jorge Sanjinés) used to comprehend as proto-socialist collectivities.

In Bolivia the videos are a product of reciprocal relations and the communicators' responsibility toward their communities, who participate, together with a multiethnic indigenous production crew and non-indigenous technological advisors, in the filming. Indigenous videomakers patiently repeat that the process of audiovisual communication is collective. The different roles are shared, decisions about scripts, editing, soundtrack, cinematic style, etc., are discussed by the production group consisting of indigenous communicators from diverse cultures and language groups, members of CEFREC – some of whom identify as indigenous while others do not – and of the communities where the filming takes place. The videomakers see a need to take individual responsibility for the final version of the film. Thus, Marcelina Cárdenas is responsible for *Llanthupi Munakuy*, Faustino Peña for *El Espíritu de la Selva*, Reynaldo Yujra for *Qati Qati*, etc. CEFREC/CAIB prefers using the term "responsable" to that of "director" in order to mark the difference from the western director-star. Unlike the case of filmmakers such as Alejandro González Iñárritu, Pablo Trapero, or María Luisa Bemberg, however, indigenous communicators reject the romantic and marketable notion of the auteur and artist-creator who expresses his or her personality through the medium in favor of a conceptualization that is more adequate to the "proceso integral" that constitutes indigenous video-making in Bolivia (Himpele, 2004: 358).

As the decentralized indigenous networks expand and link up with community and satellite television, indigenous audiovisual communication is creating a new imaginary for considerable audiences in Latin America. Indigenous peoples here are no longer folkloric, marginal, or objects of literary imaginings or ethnographic film. Rather they are protagonists of an alternative modernity. Although video is certainly not a medium at the reach of everyone – it is firmly linked to the political goals of indigenous social movement organizations – it has become an expression of a cultural, political, and epistemic vision that seeks alternatives instead of integration. Without substituting one technology of knowledge for another, perhaps the indianization of film does indicate the beginning of the lettered city's downfall. It is certainly a challenge to its visual economy.

# Media and Cultural Studies

Film critics have largely ignored the field of indigenous media, not only because of difficulties accessing these films. However, selections of the vast indigenous film and video productions have been screened at international indigenous film and video festivals in Latin America. Indigenous films have also been shown in Europe (e.g., Expo 2000), in Canada (Montreal and Toronto) and the United States (in New York and elsewhere). The limited attention given to indigenous films and videos results perhaps rather from a traditional disciplinary division of labor where whatever is associated with the indigenous is considered proper to the field of anthropology, opposed to or distinct from artistic creativity in experimental or commercial cinema.

For anthropologists indigenous video also creates difficulties, given ethnographic film's complicity with colonial history. The ones wielding the camera here have been the anthropologists, not the indigenous communities shown on screen. Audiovisual technology, moreover, is often considered paradigmatic of the society of the spectacle. Some even argue that its use can only turn supposedly non-mediatic societies into Western ones. The anthropological focus on non-Western cultures has masked the construction of indigeneity as an instance of the pre-modern. Researchers for many years concentrated on the most authentic and apparently endangered cultures, eliminating the hybrid and transculturated life of most indigenous peoples from their reports. One of the most famous ethnographic films is the above-mentioned docudrama *Nanook of the North* (1922) directed by Robert Flaherty, where the protagonists enact a lifestyle on screen that no longer corresponds to life in actuality (Ginsburg, 2002: 39). The notion that audiovisual technology is something completely new for indigenous cultures is "in part the product of the deliberate erasure of indigenous ethnographic subjects as actual or potential participants in their own screen representations" (40). Considering the intimate connection between the ethnographic gaze and the construction of a patriarchal and colonial gaze in Hollywood fiction films (Kaplan, 1997) on one hand, and the participation of indigenous peoples not only as "actors" in front of the lens, but actively returning the gaze (as Fatimah Rony has argued), it is difficult to sustain the argument that audiovisual media are exclusively Western phenomena.

Indeed, the notion of an opposition between audiovisual technology and indigenous cultures has been challenged from within the field of anthropology. Anthropology's self-reflective questioning of its colonial roots in the 1970s and 1980s coincided with the resurgence of indigenous movements in Latin America and elsewhere. Many anthropologists agree with the indigenous social movements that indigenous cultures are not outside of history but rather part of a globalization that began with the conquest of the Americas. Just like the West and the East, these populations have been living changes and adaptations. Faye Ginsburg, Terence Turner

(1991), and others have redefined the field of visual anthropology. They study changes in the construction of identity brought on by aboriginal and indigenous media-makers' creative use of video, and they work toward developing a transnational media theory that would help to account for the presence and diffusion of diverse forms of media among indigenous communities (Ginsburg, Abu-Lughod, and Larkin, 2002: 14).

Latin American film criticism has also experienced a change of perspective. Until recently, critics have been primarily interested in third cinema, *cinema novo*, or imperfect cinema, that is, in the aesthetic and practical strategies for creating a revolutionary, anti-imperialist cinema in Latin America. Now many focus on the possibilities of critically studying commercial film, film industries, even B-movies. The production and consumption of film is increasingly regarded as equally important to textual analysis. On the other hand, the question of national cinema as a form of resistance against the cultural imperialism of Hollywood has also become more complicated in light of transnational co-productions, both in the present and the past. At the same time, technological boundaries (cinema vs. video) and what has survived of the distinction between elite culture and mass media is collapsing with the sheer proliferation of low-cost digital camcorders and editing suites. Social movements, young filmmakers, but also, increasingly, established directors employ digital video. They pave the way for a critical, interdisciplinary engagement with audiovisual media in light of concerns over power and representation.

## REFERENCES AND FURTHER READING

*References*

Franco, Jean (2002). *The Decline and Fall of the Lettered City: Latin America in the Cold War*. Cambridge, MA and London: Harvard University Press.

Ginsburg, Faye, Abu-Loghud, Lila, and Larkin, Brian, eds (2002). *Media Worlds: Anthropology on New Terrain*. Berkeley, Los Angeles, and London: University of California Press.

Himpele, Jeff, ed. (2004). "Gaining ground: indigenous video in Bolivia, Mexico, and beyond. Dossier of three articles/interviews," *American Anthropologist*, 106(2): 353–73.

Kaplan, E. Ann (1997). *Looking for the Other: Feminism, Film, and the Imperial Gaze*. New York: Routledge.

King, John (1990). *Magical Reels: A History of Cinema in Latin America*. New York: Verso.

López, Anna M. (2000). "Early cinema and modernity in Latin America," *Cinema Journal*, 40(1): 48–78.

Martin, Michael T., ed. (1997). *New Latin American Cinema*. 2 vols. Detroit, MI: Wayne State University Press.

Mignolo, Walter D. (1995). *The Darker Side of the Renaissance: Literacy, Territoriality and Colonization*. Ann Arbor: Michigan University Press.

— (2000). *Local Histories/Global Designs: Coloniality, Subaltern Knowledges and Border Thinking*. Princeton. NJ: Princeton University Press.

Rama, Ángel (1996). *The Lettered City*. Ed. and trans. John Charles Chasteen. Durham, NC and London: Duke University Press.

Shohat, Ella, and Stam, Robert (1994). *Unthinking Eurocentrism: Multiculturalism and the Media*. London and New York: Routledge.

## Further Reading

Beverley, John (1993). *Against Literature*. Minneapolis: University of Minnesota Press.

Dennison, Stephanie, Nagib, Lúcia, and Shaw, Lisa, eds (2003). "Latin American film and media," special issue of *Framework. The Journal of Cinema and Media*, 44(1).

Flores, Daniel (2001/2). "Bolivian links. Indigenous media: interview with Julia Mosúa, Alfredo Copa and Marcelino Pinto," transcribed by Freya Schiwy, trans. Susan Briante, *Bomb*, 78: 30–5.

García Canclini, Néstor (2001). *Consumers and Citizens: Globalization and Multicultural Conflicts*. Trans. and intro. George Yúdice. Minneapolis: University of Minnesota Press.

Ginsburg, Faye D. (2002). "Screen memories. Resignifying the traditional in indigenous media." In Faye Ginsburg, Lila Abu-Lughod, and Brian Larkin (eds), *Media Worlds: Anthropology on New Terrain*, pp. 39–57. Berkeley: University of California Press.

Gumucio Dagrón, Alfonso (1982). *Historia del cine en Bolivia*. La Paz: Editorial Los Amigos del Libro.

Martín-Barbero, Jesús (1993). *Communication, Culture and Hegemony: From the Media to Mediations*. Trans. Elizabeth Fox and Robert A. White; intro. Philip Schlesinger. London and Newbury Park, CA: Sage.

Miller, Toby, Govil, Nitin, McMurria, John, Maxwell, Richard, and Wang, Ting (2005). *Global Hollywood 2*. London: British Film Institute.

Poole, Deborah (1997). *Vision, Race, and Modernity: A Visual Economy of the Andean Image World*. Princeton, NJ: Princeton University Press.

Rony, Fatimah Tobing (1996). *The Third Eye: Race, Cinema, and Ethnographic Spectacle*. Durham, NC: Duke University Press.

Schiwy, Freya (2003). "Decolonizing the frame: indigenous video in the Andes," *Framework*, 44(1): 116–32.

Stam, Robert (1997). *Tropical Multiculturalism: A Comparative History of Race in Brazilian Cinema and Culture*. Durham, NC and London: Duke University Press.

Taylor, Diana (2003). *The Archive and the Repertoire: Performing Cultural Memory in the Americas*. Durham, NC: Duke University Press.

Turner, Terence (1991). "The social dynamics of video media in an indigenous society: the cultural meaning and the personal politics of videomaking in Kayapo communities," *Visual Anthropology Review*, 17(2): 68–76.

Winston, Brian (1996). *Technologies of Seeing: Photography, Cinematography, and Television*. London: BFI.

Wortham, Erica Cusi (2004). "Between the state and indigenous autonomy: unpacking video indígena in Mexico," *American Anthropologist*, 106(2): 363–8.

Yúdice, George (2003). *The Expediency of Culture: Uses of Culture in the Global Era*. Durham: Duke University Press.

# Index